THE BIOGRAPHICAL DIRECTORY OF NATIVE AMERICAN PAINTERS

Patrick D. Lester

SIR PUBLICATIONS • TULSA • OKLAHOMA

THE BIOGRAPHICAL DIRECTORY OF NATIVE AMERICAN PAINTERS

Patrick D. Lester

 First edition 1995
Printed in the United States of America

99 98 97 96 95 5 4 3 2 1

Published by SIR Publications
P.O. Box 700156
Tulsa, Oklahoma 74170

Distributed by University of Oklahoma Press
Norman & London

Designed by Carl Brune

Library of Congress Catalog Card Number: 95-069012

ISBN 0-8061-9936-9 (regular edition)

ISBN 0-9640706-3-4 (limited edition)

To my wife, Patti, who has loved me all these years,
and to our Lord and Savior, Jesus Christ, through whose
love and grace this book was made possible.

Contents

Foreword

Interest in Indian painting has continued on an upswing. The field of Indian painting attracts more artists annually, and there are more competitions, exhibitions, and markets in which they may participate and from which collectors may purchase new acquisitions. Artists now produce a wide spectrum of styles and techniques and use more media than ever before. Keeping all this in mind, it is obvious this update of my original directory is needed.

One of the most frustrating aspects of any compilation such as this one, is the inability to locate vital statistics on some artists. Along with Patrick Lester, I ask the reader to put him in touch with those artists or their families if the information is incorrect or incomplete.

This volume does not list exhibitions in commercial galleries located in the United States, but it does list numerous Canadian galleries since the ones cited are, for the most part, governmental museums.

For a better understanding of this volume, the reader is urged to see the Explanatory Notes section and the appendix of abbreviations, which hold the keys to the codes used throughout. It should also be said that in addition to painters, this volume lists graphic artists; a large number of Inuit/Canadian are in the latter group. In most instances the use of the term "prints," as used in this volume, generally encompasses original pulled works as well as mass produced images. Further clarification becomes awkward when the process cannot be examined.

I continued to collect new data on artists after my directory was published in 1968 and as a result, those data were accessed for this volume. However, my files served only as a springboard for Dr. Lester and his assistant, Ginger Kingman. This landmark volume lists more Indian artists than does any other reference. Mrs. Kingman's devotion to the grind of obtaining, sorting, and entering the mass of data could be done only by one who is concerned with the smallest detail and who also loves Indian art. Dr. Lester's willingness to undertake and stay with this lengthy and expensive project puts him in the "hero" category. It was a delight to be associated with this team. They did an outstanding job.

Jeanne O. Snodgrass
(Mrs. M. E. King)
January 1995

Preface

The genesis of this project was mostly circumstantial. It had been a quarter century since Jeanne Snodgrass-King compiled her comprehensive biography of Native American painters (*American Indian Painters: A Biographical Directory*, 1968). As a collector who had grown fond of this reference book and its compiler, I nevertheless discovered that there were artists who had progressed significantly in their careers and others who apparently had ceased painting (or died). It was also apparent that many fine American Indian artists had come on the scene. An updated volume was obviously needed.

Although I had experience in research and writing, this was limited principally to scientific and medical subjects. When approached by Linda Greever, a gallery owner in Tulsa, and Jeanne Snodgrass-King, to consider writing a similar volume, I was understandably hesitant to accept the challenge. To update and expand the cataloging of Native American painters seemed worthwhile, but the task was monumental (and had I been less naive, I would have known *how* monumental!). I do not consider myself an historian, but with my love for Native American painting and the encouragement of friends, I proceeded fearlessly upon "the road less traveled." Limited to Native American painters of the continental United States and Canada, this is not a book on the history of Indian painting, but is an historical journey through the lives of those who have pictorially recorded their customs and history for us all to enjoy.

As the research progressed, I saw what a debt of gratitude we all owe Snodgrass-King for having compiled that first comprehensive directory. That she was able to collect and organize the data prior to the advent of the personal computer is a tribute to her tenacity, organizational skills, and extensive knowledge of the art of the American Indian. In four years, 1963 through 1966, she manually filed data on nearly twelve hundred Indian painters, surveying the published literature (of which there was little), interviewing artists, and reviewing exhibition catalogs, museum collections, and the records of artists. Admitting her data were incomplete, she pleaded for readers to supply missing or incomplete data. Little response was received.

Although our team has updated information on hundreds of those listed in 1968, and has researched hundreds of additional sources to expand the list to over three thousand artists, I recognize the limitation of our data. We provided biographical survey forms for painters or their families to complete if we were able to get in touch with them. While we did have an excellent response to our requests, many did not comply. This may have been because they did not receive the requests due to an address change, were not inclined to respond to any request for personal information, or simply procrastinated doing something that was not a high priority. If an artist is not included but wants to be in subsequent editions of this directory, I hope that its success will encourage the artist to send adequate biographical data to our editorial office.

This directory is organized similar to Snodgrass-King's compilation but with some notable exceptions. I have deleted references to private collections because the world has changed over the last twenty-five years, and it is doubtful that many collectors would want their names published. Also, private collections are less stable than public collections and, with a few exceptions, are not as significant to an artist's biography. I deleted references to specific biographical publications and private galleries to avoid commercial promotion. Also, some biographical categories have been added, deleted, or altered. For example, I have excluded the artist's spouse and children unless they also are artists. Some abbreviations have been altered to reflect my preference or logic, and all abbreviations have been combined into one appendix.

My original intent was to include only "significant Indian painters." Determination of "significant," however, proved problematic. Initially I decided that only recipients of higher awards at juried art shows would be included, but it was obvious this would exclude many fine artists: several well-known artists do not enter juried shows, and others in their early careers have not yet matured enough to achieve high award status. Finally I was persuaded by some members of our Editorial Advisory Board that we should be as inclusive as possible, allowing those artists who are yet young in their careers to be represented. Therefore, the only criteria for inclusion in this directory are that the artist consider himself or herself to be Native American and be actively seeking a career as a painter. The latter is usually indicated by the artist's selling paintings and participating in exhibitions and markets as well as being active in the Indian art world. Having another vocation does not exclude an artist.

Although the question of "Indian-ness" could be an issue, it is not my responsibility to define "Indian," nor do I intend to become embroiled in the Indian Arts and Crafts Act of 1990 definition of "Indian-ness." It is sufficient that there are generally accepted genealogical proofs of ancestry. I have, therefore, accepted each artist's attestation as to his or her Indian heritage, whether or not he or she is on a particular tribal roll. To the best of my knowledge, all included artists are legitimate Native Americans. If not, I will make corrections in the next edition.

Because the original directory is no longer in print, all artists in Snodgrass-King's book are included. Some of those in her directory were students at the time and may not have painted since. Future editions will include only artists who do or did devote a significant amount of their time to painting. Occasional artists will be deleted unless information is received that they continue to paint as a vocation or an avocation. For artists painting today, this directory should reflect their accomplishments. As to whether or not a particular artist is "significant," we leave to the reader's judgment. For the artist younger in his career, I hope that inclusion in this text will be a stimulus to achieve greater heights.

The enormity of this research was eased by the availability of modern communications and computer technology. Even so, we have spent more than five years collecting data, compiling records, and researching the available literature. For four of these years I have been blessed to have the tireless assistance of Ginger Kingman, my editorial assistant, to whom the credit belongs for the majority of the research, which included communications with artists, museums, and Indian art authorities. In addition she was responsible for organizing and compiling most of the data. For her, as well as me, this has been a labor of love, and her love for Indian art kept her going even when I was busy with my medical practice and unable to devote immediate time to her questions and efforts.

Patrick D. Lester
February 1995

ACKNOWLEDGMENTS

A book of this scope could not be done without the work of those who came before. The length of the bibliography is an indication of the magnitude of this debt. There are some whose works have been of such inestimable value that they deserve special recognition.

The first and most obvious debt is owed to Jeanne Snodgrass-King, not only for her pioneer effort, which is the foundation on which this directory was built, but also for her constant guidance and encouragement. In addition to her wise counsel she made available her extensive library and lifetime collection of information on Native American painters. Going well beyond what was expected of a member of the Editorial Board, she proofed and edited the entire manuscript. Her valuable insights and experience could not have been provided by any other individual.

In addition, works by Clara Lee Tanner, Tryntje Seymour, Christina Johannsen and John Ferguson, Jamake Highwater, Peggy and Harold Samuels, and Mary Southcott have been not only a tremendous help but an inspiration.

Although it is impossible to list all the people who made this book possible, there are those whose contributions were so generous that they deserve special recognition. In grateful appreciation we acknowledge our debt:

To the painters whose talent and tireless work are the reason for this directory, especially to those who filled out and returned forms and those who so patiently answered multitudes of questions, a profound thanks. For sharing addresses, artist lists, and information obtainable nowhere else, special thanks go to Benjamin Harjo Jr., Kay WalkingStick, and G. Peter Jemison.

To the Editorial Board for their assistance and support, Nadema Agard, Margaret Archuleta, Jeanne Snodgrass-King, Father Peter J. Powell, Charles Banks Wilson, who were always available with advice and encouragement. Special thanks go to the board members: Frederick J. Dockstader, for sharing his vast experience in the field of Native American art and his extensive knowledge in the publishing world, allowing us to use data he has gathered for an upcoming book of his own, endless hours of excellent proofing and editing, helping establish guidelines from the project's inception, matchless advice and constructive criticism, and for encouragement throughout the years of research; Brother C. M. Simon for sharing his own vast files and those of the Red Cloud art shows, educating us on the tribes of the Northern Plains, and for invaluable advice and constant encouragement; John Anson Warner whose unparalleled knowledge of Canadian native art and its artists was essential and invaluable; Ruthe Blalock Jones and Joan Hill, whose advice in the early stages helped establish necessary guidelines.

To the private collectors whose interest and encouragement were an inspiration. Especially to Maxine and Jack Zarrow and Robert N. Sears whose financial support was a tangible expression of their support of Native American art and the directory. To Sue and Bill Hensler, who not only made their artist files and extensive library available but also contacted artists and found answers to a multitude of questions. To Charles DeWitt who contacted artists in Florida and Catherine Baker Stetson who shared her corporate collection files.

To gallery owners and managers who were a valuable source of information. Especially to Linda Greever of the Art Market, Tulsa, Oklahoma, who was the original instigator of updating the Snodgrass directory and who, in addition to being a source of information and encouragement, spent many hours helping get the research started. To Joyce Huldermann, The House of the Six Directions, Scottsdale, Arizona, who not only offered support and shared her artist files, but also provided information from the files of her late husband, Paul, on the Scottsdale National Indian Art Exhibition. To Doris Littrell, Oklahoma Indian Art Gallery, Oklahoma City, Oklahoma, who collected biographical information for us from the artists she represents and, no matter how busy, took time to answer questions. To Shirley Wells, Indian Territory Gallery, Sapulpa, Oklahoma, for furnishing information on artists she represented, and for her advice and encouragement. To the late Lovina Ohl, Scottsdale, Arizona, who graciously offered guidance and information on many important painters. To Glenn Leighton, Notah Dineh, Cortez, Colorado, for his generous help getting data on the many talented painters in his area. To Nancy Gautsche, Ufundi Gallery, Ottawa, Ontario, Canada, who provided difficult-to-obtain information on Canadian Native painters.

To the directors, librarians, and curators of many museums and associations who provided lists of artists in their collections, made their files available, and answered innumerable questions. Very special thanks to Mario Klimiades, Librarian/Archivist, and his staff at The Heard Museum Library, which proved to be a gold mine of information, and to Peggy Fairchild, Guild volunteer who provided lists of artists and their addresses from their annual show. Special thanks also to Larry Linford, Director, The Inter-Tribal Indian Ceremonial Association who made available more than twenty years of records of this most important event. To Lynne Williamson, American Indian Archaeological Institute, Washington, Connecticut; Mora Dianne O'Neill, Art Gallery of Nova Scotia, Halifax, Nova Scotia, Canada; Peter L. Macnair, Campbell River Museum, Campbell, British Columbia, Canada; Tom Moody, Cherokee National Museum, Tahlequah, Oklahoma; Vicki Copenhaver and Robert Tucker, Eiteljorg Museum, Indianapolis, Indiana; Lola Shropshire, Five Civilized Tribes Museum, Muskogee, Oklahoma; Lisa Christensen, Glenbow Museum, Calgary, Alberta, Canada; Penelope M. Smith and Marsha V. Gallagher, Joslyn Art Museum, Omaha, Nebraska; JoAnn Sage Track, Millicent Rogers Museum, Taos, New Mexico; Marie T. Marek, Nez Percé National Historical Park, Spalding, Idaho; Tom Young, Philbrook Museum of Art, Tulsa, Oklahoma; Ann Morand and Sarah Erwin, The Thomas Gilcrease Museum of American History and Art, Tulsa, Oklahoma; Alan L. Hoover and John Veillette, Royal British Columbia Museum, Victoria, British Columbia, Canada; Steve Rogers, Wheelwright Museum of the American Indian, Santa Fe, New Mexico. Thanks for all the vital information and advice.

To governmental entities and employees, who are often perceived as uncaring but proved to be the opposite. Special thanks go to Robert G. Hart, Indian Arts and Crafts Board, United States Department of the Interior, Washington, D.C., who never failed to respond and generously provided hard-to-obtain books and pamphlets as well as advice. To the remarkable people who staff the Southern Plains Indian Museum, Anadarko, Oklahoma; the Plains Indian Museum, Browning, Montana; the Sioux Indian Museum, Rapid City, South Dakota. Thanks for the excellent exhibition brochures and catalogs. They have been a wonderful source of information on many painters. To Valerie Decontee, Indian and Northern Affairs Canada, Ottawa, Ontario, who did the research and sent not only extremely valuable information on Canadian Native painters but their addresses as well. To Ingo Hessell, Inuit Art Section, Indian and Northern Affairs Canada, Ottawa, Ontario, whose help made it possible to include these very important artists.

To other individuals who have made very important contributions: To Martin Link co-owner of The Indian Trader, who not only provided back issues when possible, but made available bound volumes of his newspaper and access to a copy machine. His uniqu publication was a valuable source of information on Native American painters. To Vincent Rickard, Pacific Editions Limited, Vancouver, British Columbia, Canada, a special thanks for information and advice concerning Northwest Coast painters and graphic artists. To Deidre A. Simmons, Winnipeg, Manitoba, Canada, for valuable information about early Canadian Native painters. To Scott Tipton, Mesa Verde Pottery, Cortez, Colorado, for help in getting information from some of the Navajo and Ute painters who work for him. To Pat Ellis and her daughter Patty, Blackwater Trading Post, Arizona, for advice and information about Indian painters from that area. To Isabel MacIntosh, a very special thanks for so very capably accessing information from The Heard Museum Library and compiling it. She was responsible for updating most of the original directory. To Carl Brune, who provided artistic direction for this volume, including the cover design, and Andra Whitworth for publishing assistance. To Nancy Mashburn, who initially provided the secretarial skills involved in organizing surveys and corresponding with the artists, scholars, and museums and who later helped keep the computers functioning. Her cheerful assistance and efficiency did much to smooth the way.

Finally, to the Servant Education and Research Foundation and its Board of Directors, Pat and Patti Lester, Paul Taylor, and A. C. Johnson, for providing the funds for this project. Their support and encouragement were crucial to its completion.

Patrick D. Lester, editor
and Ginger E. Kingman

EXPLANATORY NOTES

The following is provided to explain the composition and contents of this directory, and is arranged for the reader's convenience by the various headings. To the extent possible, the information in this directory came directly from that submitted by the artist or his/her family. We have avoided any assumption regarding heritage, family ties, deaths, etc., relying on this direct information as well as published data.

ARTIST NAME: The principal listing of the artist is the name by which he/she is most commonly known in the art world. Some artists have one (or more) Native American names, as well as a European name. These auxiliary names are referenced to the most common name. If the artist has a known Indian name, it is provided immediately below the principal listing, and is italicized.

Because the spelling of Indian names is phonetic, variations of spelling have occurred, especially among the Inuit. In the 1970s, various Inuit communities approved specific name spellings, which we have used, when known. We have listed the variant spellings and names as a.k.a., and cross-referenced these in the directory.

We have included all the artists from Snodgrass' book, recognized by the use of Snodgrass (1968) under the PUBLISHED heading.

TRIBE: Generally, Indian artists in the United States prefer to be designated "Native American" while those in Canada prefer "Native" or "of Native heritage." Tribal affiliations listed are those provided by the artist, or determined by published data. We have used the official tribal preference for the spelling of names (e.g., Otoe, rather than Oto) even though artists vary in their spelling. In recent years, some tribes have changed their names from the European given name to a native one. Prominent changes include:

PRIOR EUROPEAN NAME	CURRENT OFFICIAL NAME
Papago	Tohono O'odham
Kwakiutl	Kwakwaka'wakw
Nootka	Nuu-chah-nulth
Canadian Eskimo	Inuit

Some tribes are known by different names in the United States and in Canada. These distinctions are maintained throughout the Directory.

UNITED STATES	CANADA
Blackfeet	Blackfoot
Eskimo	Inuit
Chippewa	Ojibway
Piegan	Peigan

Occasionally an artist listed an unofficial name for his tribe (e.g., Diné instead of Navajo), but we used only the official name.

Some artists further classify themselves by a particular reservation or regional division, especially the Sioux and Apache (e.g., Pine Ridge Sioux, White Mountain Apache, Southern Cheyenne, etc.). We have respected their preference of subclassification.

"Pueblo" or "Plains" were used only where a specific tribal designation was not available.

Some painters in Snodgrass' directory had an unknown tribal affiliation designated by "?," although it was apparently recognized, at the time, that they were Native Americans. We have included these artists with a similar designation, but have excluded subsequent artists without a known tribal affiliation, except in those cases in which the painter has been accepted by a Native guild.

In the Tribal Index of this book, painters are listed under each of their tribal affiliations, with the exception of Mexican tribes.

STATISTICS: Statistical data, such as birth date, were not always available. Except for those artists already specified in Snodgrass' book, no attempt has been made to estimate birth or death dates. We have included the fact of death, if published, even if the specific date is not known. Dates are in the international style (day/month/year). When known, parents, grandparents and relatives who are significant historically, or as artists, are included in this paragraph.

NARRATIVE: We have continued the tradition established by Snodgrass by including narrative or human interest paragraphs. Where these have been drawn from Snodgrass' directory with little or no change, they are included in quotation marks followed by *Snodgrass 1968.* Others are gleaned from various references, personal observations, and the artists themselves (e.g., artist, p.c., 19**)

RESIDENCE: This is the artist's last known location, stated in the past tense if the painter is deceased. If in the present tense, we have assumed the artist is still living; however, he/she may not be at this location currently.

EDUCATION: Formal and informal education is listed, including other artists under whom the artist studied. Where another artist is referenced under any heading, the notation (q.v.) is used. This, as well as (qq.v.) for more than one artist, indicates that these artists are also in the directory.

OCCUPATION: All known occupations, not just most recent positions and jobs, are included.

MEDIA: All known media are included, even if the painter is principally known for work in some other technique, such as sculpting.

PUBLISHED: Books are listed by author and year. Following this, periodicals are listed by name and date, with volume and number if appropriate. Biographical publications that are periodically updated are considered periodicals. "Who's Who" type biographical directories are not specifically listed here or in the Bibliography since many of these are commercial. Listed books and periodicals are those that contain information on the artist or actual reproductions of the artist's work.

BOOKS ILLUSTRATED: This category lists only books in which all or a significant portion of the art work was done by the artist. If it is only authored by the artist, or if it contains works by other painters, it is listed under PUBLISHED.

COMMISSIONS: This includes all known public and corporate commissions, but is limited by the scarcity of information available.

PUBLIC COLLECTIONS: All known public collections are included as well as many corporate collections.

EXHIBITS (including SOLO EXHIBITS): Most known exhibits have been listed. I have exercised editorial prerogatives to abbreviate lengthy lists of exhibits to the more significant shows. Exhibits in commercial galleries have not been listed individually since this would result in a much more extensive volume, private galleries are not necessarily stable and the incompleteness of such listing could result in commercial advantage or disadvantage. Commercial galleries are, therefore, indicated by states such as "galleries in AZ, OK, and NM." An exception is made for Canadian galleries. In that country, a museum is frequently called a gallery (e.g., Winnipeg Art Gallery) and commercial galleries may function in a quasi-official role with government support in promoting Native painting.

Artists may have reported exhibitions that do not reflect the true name of the sponsor. If we were unable to verify that two exhibitions with similar names were the same, both were listed as separate exhibitions.

AWARDS: We have listed known awards, but only indicated the year — when known — if less than first place was received. First place and greater awards (e.g., Grand Award) and named awards are specifically listed. Code "MA" used for the Lawrence Indian Art Show is equivalent to a first-place award.

In the Snodgrass book, award specifics were not noted; therefore, any artist receiving awards prior to 1968 may not have them identified as to award level.

HONORS: We have included all special recognitions that we have discovered in our research as well as awards and recognitions that the artist considers meritorious.

TRIBAL INDEX *(see Tribe)*

ABBREVIATIONS: Codes were created in order to conserve space and are listed after the Tribal Index. All codes are combined in one appendix rather than establishing a separate appendix for each heading. We developed codes that most closely represented each named exhibit or institution, while avoiding confusion of codes (exception may be "BC" which represents Bacone College as well as the Canadian province, British Columbia. This distinction should be self-evident). C/. . . is used to indicate that the subsequent code is for Canada. Schools, especially Indian schools, are partially spelled out (e.g., Santa Fe, Inter-Mt., Phoenix, etc.) rather than designating them with separate codes.

BIBLIOGRAPHY: The Bibliography is extensive yet includes only books and catalogs. Periodicals are excluded since a list including each article or publication would be unwieldy.

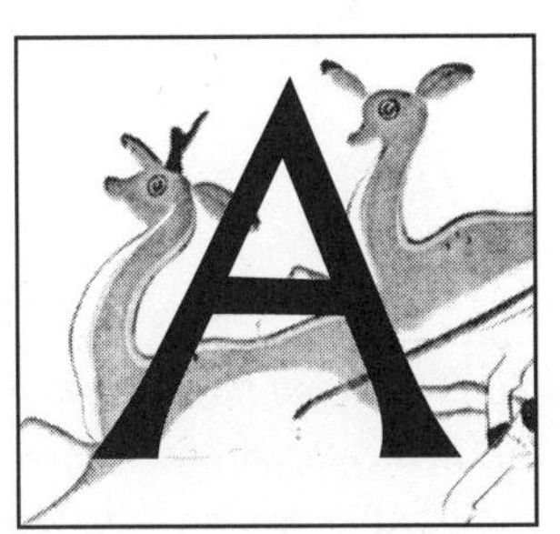

AANOTE (see Tohausen)

ABBEY, TED *Alabama/Coushatta*

EXHIBITS: HM/G, SN

ABEITA, EMERSON *Navajo*

Born 1957 in Crownpoint, NM; brother of Jim Abeita (q.v.)

RESIDENCE: Gallup, NM

EDUCATION: AAA; Evanston (IL) Art Center

OCCUPATION: Full-time painter

MEDIA: Oil

PUBLISHED: *The Indian Trader* (June 1987)

EXHIBITS: ITIC, NMSF, NTF

AWARDS: ITIC, NMSF, NTF

ABEITA, JIM *Navajo*

A.K.A. James Abeita; James Abeyta

Born 1947 in Crownpoint, NM; son of Mary and Howard Abeita

RESIDENCE: Crownpoint, NM

EDUCATION: Gallup (NM) High School, 1966; AAA

OCCUPATION: Artist

MEDIA: Oil, watercolor, pen and ink, pastel, charcoal, and scratch board

PUBLISHED: Tanner (1973); Samuels (1982). *New Mexico, Dandick Travel Tips*, cover; *Rick Tanner Publications* (1974), cover; Navajo Tribal Fair (1974), program cover; *Arizona Highways* (Aug 1974, cover; Oct 1974; Dec 1974, inside cover; July 1976; Sept 1978); *Southwest Art* (July 1974); *Artists Of The Rockies* (fall 1974); *Arizona Living* (29 Jan 1976, cover; 1 Mar 1982); *The Indian Trader* (Dec 1980; Aug 1982); *New Mexico Magazine* (Sept 1983)

COMMISSIONS: *Portraits:* Johnny Cash's family; Tanner's Annual Invitational, Scottsdale, AZ, group portraits of winners, 1974-1978

PUBLIC COLLECTIONS: MNA

EXHIBITS: HM/G; ITIC; NMSF; NT; PBS ('89); SN; SWAIA

AWARDS: HM/G ('71, 1st, Best of Show); ITIC ('72, 1st, Best in Class, Woodard Award; '76, 1st, Best in Class; '79, 2-1st; '85, 1st, Mullarky Award; '86, 1st; '87, 1st, Best in Category, Best in Class, Mullarky Award; '88; '91, 1st); NMSF ('73, Grand Prize); SN ('74, Grand Award); SWAIA ('75, 1st)

JIM ABEITA

A request for Johnny Cash to sign a portrait of the singer that Abeita had done led not only to a commission to do portraits of Cash's family but to a friendship. An artist since a teenage uncle taught him to draw when he was a child, Abeita is well known for his realistic portraits and landscapes of the Navajo people and their world.

New Mexico Magazine
Sept 1983

ABEYTA, ANTONIO (see Abeyta, Tony)

ABEYTA, AUGUSTINE *Tesuque*

Born 1917 at Tesuque Pueblo; son of Julio Abeyta, silversmith and former governor of his pueblo; brother of Crucita, potter

PUBLISHED: Snodgrass (1968)

EXHIBITS: AIEC

ABEYTA, CECIL (see Abeyta, Narciso Platero)

ABEYTA, EMILIANO *San Juan*

Sa Pa

PUBLISHED: Snodgrass (1968)

PUBLIC COLLECTIONS: MAI, OU/MA

EXHIBITS: OU/ET

ABEYTA, JAMES (see Abeita, Jim)

DETAIL: Narciso Abeyta, *Navajo Deer Hunt*, 1946. Philbrook Museum of Art, Tulsa, Oklahoma

Narciso Platero Abeyta

"It is recorded that Abeyta drew his first creations on canyon walls. Approximately 32 years later, in 1961, his work was published in Art In America. *An excellent painter with a unique style, his production has suffered because of shellshock in WWII."*

Snodgrass 1968

Abeyta, Narciso Platero *Navajo*

Hoskiel Ha So Deh, Fiercely Ascending

A.K.A. Cecil; Cisso. Signatures: Ha So Deh; Ha So De

Born 15 Dec 1918 in Cañoncito, NM; son of Pablita and Narciso Abeyta

RESIDENCE: Gallup, NM

MILITARY: U.S. Army, WWII, four years

EDUCATION: Santa Fe, NM, 1939; Sumerset Art Institute, Williamsburg, PA, scholarship, 1940; B.F.A., U of NM, 1953; studied under Raymond Jonson

OCCUPATION: Silversmith, boxer, job placement interviewer and field recruiter, personnel and vocational counselor, interpreter, and painter

MEDIA: Tempera

PUBLISHED: Jacobson and d'Ucel (1950); Tanner (1957, 1968, 1973); Dunn (1968), cover; Snodgrass (1968); Brody (1971); Stuart and Ashton (1977); Silberman (1978); Highwater (1980); Broder (1981); Hoffman, et al. (1984); Samuels (1982); Archuleta and Strickland (1991). *Art In America* (no. 3, 1961); *American Indian Art* (summer 1976); *Plateau* (Vol. 54, no. 1, 1982); *Navajo Times* (7 Apr 1982); *The Indian Trader* (Aug 1982; Mar 1988; Jan 1990; Apr 1994; May 1994); *Southwest Art* (June 1983); *Arizona Highways* (July 1956; May 1986)

BOOKS ILLUSTRATED: Birney (1935)

COMMISSIONS: *Murals*: Santa Fe, NM, social science classroom, 1934; Maisel's Indian Trading Post, Albuquerque, NM, 1939

PUBLIC COLLECTIONS: ASM, MAI, MNM, MNA, OU/MA, PAC, WOM, WWM

EXHIBITS: AIEC; AIW; BAA; CAI; CNM; FAG/S; HM; HM/G; IGAM; IK; ITIC; JGS; MAI; MFA/O; MNM; NGA; NJSM; NMSF; OMA; OU/ET; OU/MA; PAC; RE; SFWF; SI; SMM; SN; SV; SWAIA; WWM; in Europe

SOLO/SPECIAL EXHIBITS: NTM, WWM (dual show with son, Tony)

AWARDS: ITIC ('75, 1st, Grand Award; '79; '82; '87); MNM; NMSF ('47, 1st); PAC; SDFAG; SFWF (poster contest); SN ('63, 1st, Chamber of Commerce Award)

HONORS: Santa Fe (NM) Indian School, awarded Bronze Medal inscribed "most consistent, conscientious, and willing worker"; ITIC, poster artist, 1938; SFWF, demonstrated painting, 1938; Stanford University, scholarship (unable to accept due to service in WWII); Golden Gloves (boxing) Competition, Chicago, IL, semi-finalist, 1953

Tony Abeyta

Tony Abeyta is the son of Narciso Abeyta (Hoskiel Ha So Deh) who was one of the trail blazers for today's Indian painters. Narciso encouraged Tony to "pursue a professional career." However, Tony enjoyed working with clay and stone as a child and, at that time, decided to become an artist. He said, "Once I make a decision and set a goal, I go for it."

artist, p.c. 1992

Abeyta, Tony *Navajo*

Ha So De, Fierce Ascension

A.K.A. Antonio Abeyta

Born 6 Nov 1965 in Gallup, NM; son of Sylvia Shipley and Narciso Abeyta (q.v.); brother of Elizabeth Abeyta, ceramist

RESIDENCE: Santa Fe, NM

EDUCATION: Gallup (NM) High School; A.A., IAIA, 1986 (Honors); B.A., MI, 1988 (included study in Lacoste, France, and Florence, Italy); Santa Fe (NM) Institute of Fine Arts; CAI

MEDIA: Oil, acrylic, mixed media, and prints

PUBLISHED: Tryk (1993); Campbell, ed. (1993). *Phoenix Gazette* (5 Jan 1988); *Santa Fe Reporter* (16 Aug 1989); *The Indian Trader* (Jan 1990; Apr 1994); *Arizona Highways* (Nov 1992); *The Santa Fean Magazine* (Aug 1994)

EXHIBITS: ABQM; AC/SD; ACS/PG; AICH; IAIA/M; ITIC; SWAIA; Gibbs Museum of Art, NC; Pembroke (NC) State University; Crow Canyon Exhibition, Washington, D.C., 1994

SOLO/SPECIAL EXHIBITS: WWM (dual show with father, Narciso); École de Beaux Arts, Lacoste, France

AWARDS: ITIC ('88, 1st; '93, 1st, Best in Category); SWAIA ('88, 1st, Best of Division; '89, 1st, Best of Class, Best of Division; '90, 1st, Best of Division; '91, 1st)

HONORS: *Scholarships and Fellowships:* Navajo Tribal Scholarships, eight from 1984-1989; Association of American Indian Affairs, New York, NY; Maryland Institute, College of Arts; Ford Foundation Minority Scholarship. *Other:* SWAIA, poster artist, 1992

A BIRD (see Herrera, Justino)

ABLE TO STAND UP AGAIN (see Eckiwaudah, Tennyson)

ABOVE (see New Bear)

ABRAMS-LITTON, G. M. *Kwakwaka'wakw (Kwakiutl)*

RESIDENCE: Lytton, BC, Canada

MEDIA: Watercolor

PUBLIC COLLECTIONS: HM

ACENEMAH (see Zotigh, Barbara Tallamonts)

ACHEFF, WILLIAM *Athabaskan*

Born 1947 in Anchorage, AK

RESIDENCE: Taos, NM

EDUCATION: Apprenticed to Roberto Lupetti, San Francisco, CA

OCCUPATION: Barber and artist

MEDIA: Oil

PUBLISHED: Samuels (1982). *Taos Arts* (11 Sept 1980); *Southwest Art* (Feb 1981); *Artists Of The Rockies And The Golden West* (summer 1984); *Art-Talk* (Dec 1988)

EXHIBITS: ABQM; CFD; GM; HSM/D; NAWA; NCHF; Great American West Show, Tucson, AZ; galleries in AZ, NM, and NY

WILLIAM ACHEFF

Acheff is classified as a realistic painter and works in a kind of realism known as trompe l'oeil, *"to fool the eye." His Southwestern still-life paintings appear to be three dimensional. He is quoted in* Taos Arts *(11 Sept 1980) as saying, "I'm interested in capturing the essence of the object painted. I try to show its inner spirit by giving it the illusion of depth."*

ACOSTA, RAUL *Apache*

Born 6 Feb 1978

OCCUPATION: Sculptor and painter

EXHIBITS: AIE

AWARDS: AIE ('87, 1st)

ACQUE, PHILBERT *Zuni*

RESIDENCE: Zuni Pueblo, NM

EXHIBITS: MNM, 1965

PUBLISHED: Snodgrass (1968)

ADAIR, MARY HORSECHIEF *Cherokee*

A.K.A. Mary Adair HorseChief; Mary Adair

Born 2 July 1936 in Sequoyah County, OK; daughter of Velma and Corrigan Adair; P/GP: Mary Catherine Rider and Oscar F. Adair; M/GP: Ida Hart and Elmer Warwick; Artist is a descendant of Nanye-hi (Nancy Ward).

RESIDENCE: Muskogee, OK

EDUCATION: Sallisaw (OK) High School, 1953; BC, 1955; B.A., NSU, 1957; B.F.A., TU, 1967; M.E., NSU, 1983

OCCUPATION: Art teacher; professional artist since 1967

MEDIA: Acrylic, watercolor, pen and ink, pencil, and prints

PUBLISHED: Campbell, ed. (1993). *Art-Talk* (June/July 1985); *Oklahoma Today* (July/Aug 1985); *Women Of Power* (No. 15, 1989)

EXHIBITS: AIE; BC/McG; CNM; DE; FCTM; HM/G; OAC; PAC; RC; TM/NE; Choctaw Fair, AL; Bacone College (HorseChief family exhibit); NSU, Indian Heritage Art Show, 1981; see also Awards

MARY HORSECHIEF ADAIR

Adair's paintings usually depict Indian people doing everyday things, or taking part in traditional ceremonies. She especially enjoys painting children. Although her married name is HorseChief the artist uses her maiden name to avoid being confused with her daughter Mary Catherine HorseChief (q.v.) who is also a painter.

artist, p.c. 1992

SOLO/SPECIAL EXHIBITS: FCTM; Stovall Museum, Ardmore, OK; Milwaukee (WI) Public Library; Muskogee (OK) Civic Center (dual show)

AWARDS: AIE ('74, Grand Award); CNM ('85, 1st; '89, 1st); FCTM ('69, 1st; '73, IH; '74, 1st; '75, 1st; '77, IH; '82; '87, 1st, Grand Award, IH; '89, IH); MCI ('85, 1st); PAC ('67; '70); Pawnee Bill Indian Show, Pawnee, OK ('70); Muskogee (OK) State Fair (2-1st); Muskogee (OK) Public Library ('74, Purchase Award)

ADAKAI, PAT *Navajo*

Born 7 Aug 1946 in Blackrock, NM

RESIDENCE: Blackrock, NM

EDUCATION: Gallup (NM) High School, 1966

PUBLISHED: Snodgrass (1968)

EXHIBITS: NACG; Gallup (NM) Public Schools

AWARDS: NACG ('64)

ADAMS, ANNA MARIA *Winnebago*

Born 4 Apr 1961 in Washington, D.C.

EDUCATION: A.F.A., IAIA, 1981; B.F.A., U of OK, 1984; OSU, 1981-1982

OCCUPATION: Osage County (OK) Republican delegate, studio owner, and artist

PUBLISHED: *Directory of Indian Artists*, U.S. Department of Interior

EXHIBITS: See Awards

AWARDS: Bartlesville Art Show; Ponca Art Show (1st)

HONORS: IAIA, Miss IAIA Powwow Princess

ADAMS, ELLIOTT *Hopi*

Tyma

Born 20 May 1920

RESIDENCE: Keams Canyon, AZ

MILITARY: U.S. Army

OCCUPATION: Heavy equipment operator, carver, and painter

KEITH ADAMS

The artist's goal is to reach the highest form of self-discipline possible so that each painting will truly reflect his feelings toward the subject. He wishes to use God's gift in a way that will honor Him. In addition, he wants his work to help preserve Indian heritage by drawing parts of the past into the present.

artist, p.c. 1991

ADAMS, KEITH *Blackfeet*

Born 7 Dec 1938

RESIDENCE: Dalton, IL

EDUCATION: Blue Island High School, IL; Chicago (IL) Vocational School; AAA; Art Instruction School, Minneapolis, MN

EXHIBITS: C/CS; GPWAS; RC; WH; Kalispell (MT) Art Show

AWARDS: Listing includes: RC ('84)

ADAMS, LEO *Yakama*

RESIDENCE: Yakima, WA

EXHIBITS: ADIA

AWARDS: ADIA ('67, 1st)

ADIEUX, ADA (see Eyeeteetowak, Ada)

ADLOOAT, WARREN (see Sowle, Warren Adlooat)

ADOL BEAK KA (see Rowell, Charles Emery)

ADULA (see Audla, Alassie)

NADEMA AGARD-SMITH

In addition to being a painter, Agard-Smith is a Native American art studies educator specializing in Native American women in the arts. Over the past twenty years she has lectured extensively across the country.

AGARD-SMITH, NADEMA *Cherokee/Lakota/ Powhatan*

Birth date unknown; daughter of Frieda and James Agard; P/GP: Lillian and Moses Agard; M/GP: Margarette and William Phillips

RESIDENCE: Bemidji, MN

EDUCATION: High School of Music and Art, New York, NY; New York University;

Columbia University, Teacher's College, New York, NY

OCCUPATION: Art Educator

PUBLISHED: *Bulletin,* Council for Interracial Books for Children (Vol. 11, no. 5, 1980); *The New York Daily News* (28 Feb 1982); *The Santa Fe Reporter* (25 Aug 1982); *The Daily News Miner*, Fairbanks, AK (18 July 1985)

BOOKS ILLUSTRATED: Sneve (1975); *United Black Christians*, Commission for Racial Justice, NY, NY, 1980

COMMISSIONS: *Logo Designs:* Museum of the American Indian, Heye Foundation, New York, NY; New York Multicultural Forum, New York, NY

PUBLIC COLLECTIONS: U of WI

EXHIBITS: AICH; NACLA; MAI; NYU; KCPA; NARF; CWPC; Marymont Manhattan College, NY; and galleries

HONORS: *Scholarships amd Fellowships*: NEA, NYU, SI, Phelps Stokes Institute Scholar. *Other*: New York Foundation for the Arts, artist-in-residence; Native American Heritage Committee, calendar coordinator; *Biographical Directory of Native American Painters*, Editorial Board

AGUILAR, ALFRED *San Ildefonso*

Sa Wa Pin

Born 1 July 1933 at San Ildefonso Pueblo, NM; son of Rosalie and José A. Aguilar, potters; P/GF: Ignacio Aguilar; M/GM: Suzanna Aguilar

RESIDENCE: Santa Fe, NM

MILITARY: U.S. Air Force, Korea

EDUCATION: Pojoaque (NM) High School, 1962; U of NM

OCCUPATION: Teacher's aide, classroom instructor, jeweler, sculptor, potter, and painter

MEDIA: Watercolor, pen and ink, pastel, silver, gemstone, and clay

PUBLISHED: Snodgrass (1968)

BOOKS ILLUSTRATED: Monthan and Monthan (1979); *Source Directory,* USDI

PUBLIC COLLECTIONS: MNM, SI

EXHIBITS: AC/ENP; HM/G; ITIC; MNM; PAC; IPCC; SN; SWAIA; Tulsa (OK) Art Fair; see also Awards

AWARDS: HM/G ('81); SWAIA ('73); New Jersey Indian Art Fair (Best of Show)

ALFRED AGUILAR

"Aguilar is recognized not only for his painting but for his pottery, especially his pottery buffalo and Pueblo-style nativity sets. His paintings are, at times, executed on a sandlike surface using natural earth materials."

Snodgrass 1968

AGUILAR, DUGAN *Maidu/Pit River/Paiute*

EXHIBITS: RC

AGUILAR, FRANCIS *San Ildefonso*

EXHIBITS: SWAIA

AWARDS: SWAIA ('78, Richard Hurff Student Award)

AGUILAR, FRED *San Ildefonso*

EXHIBITS: SWAIA

AWARDS: SWAIA ('77)

AGUILAR, HENRY *Santo Domingo*

PUBLIC COLLECTIONS: MNA

AGUILAR, JOSÉ ANGELA *San Ildefonso*

Birth date unknown

OCCUPATION: Pottery decorator and painter

PUBLISHED: Snodgrass (1968); Seymour (1988)

PUBLIC COLLECTIONS: DAM, MAI, U of CA/LMA

EXHIBITS: JGS

JOSÉ ANGELA AGUILAR

"The artist has been actively engaged in art and related subjects since 1944. In 1949, he began his painting experiments in new directions."

Snodgrass 1968

In 1987 the artist was working in the California aerospace industry doing technical drawings and only an occasional painting for friends. He says, when inspired, he will also do a "regular" landscape painting.

Seymour 1988

AGUILAR, JOSÉ VINCENTE *San Ildefonso/Picurís*

Sua Peen, Warm Mountain

A.K.A. Suwa

Born 8 Jan 1924 at San Ildefonso Pueblo, NM; son of Rosalie Simbola, potter, and José Angela Aguilar (q.v.)

RESIDENCE: Buena Park, CA

MILITARY: U.S. Army, WWII

EDUCATION: Hollywood (CA) High School, 1944; Otis, 1947-1949; U of NM; Hill, 1949-1950; Los Angeles (CA) Trade Technical Junior College, 1951; LACAI, 1954; LAACS, 1959

OCCUPATION: Commercial and technical artist, and painter

MEDIA: Tempera

PUBLISHED: Dunn (1968); Snodgrass (1968); Brody (1971); Tanner (1973); Broder (1981); Golder (1984); Seymour (1988). *Southwest Art* (June 1983)

PUBLIC COLLECTIONS: AC/RM, DAM, IACB/DC, MAI, MNM, PAC, SFRR

EXHIBITS: DAM, FAIEAIP, FWG, HH, HM, HM/G, ITIC, LGAM, MAI, MNM, PAC, WRTD

SOLO EXHIBITS: San Gabriel (CA) Women's Club, 1952

AWARDS: DAM (Watrous Award); MNM (Stewart Award); PAC; ITIC ('52, Grand Award)

HONORS: Indian Arts Fund Award, 1962

AGUILAR, MARTIN WAYNE *San Ildefonso*

RESIDENCE: Santa Fe, NM

PUBLIC COLLECTIONS: HCC

EXHIBITS: HM/G, RC, SWAIA

AWARDS: HM/G ('80, 1st); RC ('77, 1st, Woodard Award), SWAIA ('73)

AGUILAR, TONY *Santo Domingo*

RESIDENCE: Santo Domingo Pueblo, NM

MILITARY: U.S. Army, WWII

OCCUPATION: Jeweler and painter

MEDIA: Watercolor, silver, and gemstone

EXHIBITS: SFFA, SWAIA

AGUINO, JUAN B. *San Juan*

RESIDENCE: San Juan Pueblo, NM

OCCUPATION: Electronic technician at Los Alamos (NM) National Laboratory, painter, and woodcarver

PUBLISHED: *The Indian Trader* (May 1982)

COMMISSIONS: Los Alamos (NM) National Laboratory, painting used for recruitment poster; San Juan Pueblo, NM, seal and flag design

HONORS: Governor of San Juan Pueblo, NM, 1973, 1977

AGUSTA, TODD M. *Oglala Sioux*

RESIDENCE: Oglala, SD

EXHIBITS: LIAS ('90)

AHASTEEN, JACK *Navajo*

Birth date unknown; born on the Navajo Reservation, AZ

OCCUPATION: Illustrator, political cartoonist, and artist

PUBLISHED: Mayes and Lacy (1989). *Scottsdale Arizona Progress* (4 June 1990)

AHDUNKO, DON *Caddo/Delaware*

OCCUPATION: Sculptor and painter

EXHIBITS: AIE

AWARDS: AIE ('71, 1st; '78; '85)

AHGUPUK, GEORGE ADEN *Eskimo*

Twok, Man

Born 8 Oct 1911 in Shishmaref, AK, on the Bering Sea coast of Seward Peninsula; son of Mary and John Ahgupuk ("missionaries named them")

RESIDENCE: Anchorage, AK

EDUCATION: Ahgupuk attended school through 4th grade, when he quit due to his father's illness.

OCCUPATION: Railroad "gandy dancer," roofer, commercial fisherman, hunter, maintenance man, and full-time painter

MEDIA: Oil stain, watercolor, pen and ink, animal skins, and prints

PUBLISHED: Snodgrass (1968); Ray (1969); Yorba (1990); Archuleta and Strickland (1991). *The New York Times* (11 Jan 1937); *Time* (25 Jan 1937); *The Alaska Sportsman* (Dec 1958); *The Alaska Journal* (fall 1972; summer 1975); *Alaska Geographic* (Vol. 12, no. 3, 1985)

BOOKS ILLUSTRATED: Keithahn (1945), Ahgupuk (1953), Green and Abbott (1959), Adams (1959)

PUBLIC COLLECTIONS: ASM/AK; CAS; IACB; MAI; MFA/AH; U of AK/M; The Seattle (WA) Museum of History and Industry

EXHIBITS: ITIC; MFA/AH; PAC; SV; USDS; Seattle, WA; St. Paul, MN; San José, CA; in Alaska, Holland, Germany, and Sweden

AWARDS: ITIC ('50, Grand Prize)

HONORS: The American Artists Group, New York, NY, full membership, 1937

GEORGE ADEN AHGUPUK

"In 1934 the artist began to draw while in the Alaska Native Service Hospital in Kotzebue recovering from several operations on his leg which was badly broken while hunting. His first drawings were on toilet paper done with burned matches. Ahgupuk's favorite medium is ink and he generally sketched on reindeer, caribou, moose, and seal hides or paper. He prepared his own hides which required hours of careful scraping and days of drying and bleaching. Some of his drawings are tinted with paint or colored ballpoint laundry markers."

Snodgrass 1968

In recent years Ahgupuk suffered two strokes which caused problems with his drawing arm. His last completed drawing was in 1980.

artist, p.c. 1992

AHENAKEW, WILLARD *Plains Cree*

MEDIA: Mixed-media

EXHIBITS: C/ROM

AHHAJUMBA (see Anderson, Jimmy)

AHMEHATE (see Goodbear, Paul J.)

AHMOO (see Angeconeb, Allen)

AHOSTA (see Johnson, Tracy)

AH QUADE (see Alberty, Dewey)

AH SAY (see Blue Eagle, Acee)

AHSEY SUTUTUT (see Jake, Albin Roy)

AHSIT *Southern Cheyenne*

Ahsit, White Man

A.K.A. White Man; Whiteman

Born 1853; died 1931

EDUCATION: Hampton

MEDIA: Pigment, wood, cotton, and silk

PUBLISHED: Snodgrass (1968); Maurer (1992)

PUBLIC COLLECTIONS: HI, MNH/A, YU/BRBML

EXHIBITS: BPG, VP

AHSIT

"The artist was among the 72 Plains Indians taken as prisoners from Fort Sill, OK, to Fort Marion, St. Augustine, FL, in 1875. After prison and government schooling, he returned to Oklahoma in 1880."

Snodgrass 1968

While in prison and in school, Ahsit earned money by executing pictographic drawings on fans.

AHTONE, DEBORAH *Kiowa*

RESIDENCE: Mountain View, OK

Born 2 July 1947 in Carnegie, OK; daughter of Evelyn Tahome and Jacob Ahtone; P/GP: Tahdo and Sam Ahtone; M/GP: Meta Jane and Stephen Tahome; sister to Sharron Ahtone Harjo and Virginia Stroud (q.q.v)

EDUCATION: Billings (MT) West High School, 1965; BC, 1965-1967; B.A., RMC, 1970; U of OK, 1970-1971

OCCUPATION: Teacher of adult education and Indian studies, Indian studies coordinator, public information officer, newspaper editor, journalist, photographer, and painter

PUBLISHED: *The New Mexican* (13 Oct 1978); *Association News*, SPIM (Oct 1993)

PUBLIC COLLECTIONS: SPIM, KTM

EXHIBITS: AIE, ACS/RSC, BC/McG, IAIA, LIAS, RE, SPIM

SOLO EXHIBITS: SPIM

AWARDS: AIE ('76, 1st); ACS/RSC ('81); RE ('94)

AHVALAKIAK (see Avaalaqiaq, Irene)

AHVALAQLAQ (see Avaalaqiaq, Irene)

AHVALAQUAQ (see Avaalaqiaq, Irene)

AIKENS, WADE *Crow/Creek/Sioux*

EDUCATION: Chamberlain (SD) High School

OCCUPATION: Started painting in 1987

MEDIA: Oil

EXHIBITS: RC

WADE AIKENS

Because of his concern with what is happening in the world today, Aikens uses his paintings to try to promote a sense of balance and harmony, to make people aware of the simpler things in life, the way it used to be in the past and the way it should be in the future.

AJAGUTAINA (see Tukala, Isah Ajagutaina)

AKEE, BENNY *Navajo*

PUBLIC COLLECTIONS: MNA

AKERS, NORMAN *Osage/Pawnee*

Born 25 Oct 1958 in Fairfax, OK; son of Judy Harris and Victor Akers; P/GP: Elenor Little Star and Maxwell Akers; M/GP: Alta and D. E. Harris

RESIDENCE: Fairfax, OK

EDUCATION: Skiatook (OK) High School, 1977; U of IL; B.F.A., KCAI, 1982; internship, MNM, 1983; certificate, IAIA, 1984

OCCUPATION: Ranch worker, maintenance man, press operator, and artist

PUBLISHED: Coe (1986). *The New Mexican, Pasatiempo Magazine* (20 Apr 1984); *Art-Talk* (Aug/Sept 1985); *The Indian Trader* (Nov 1986); *The Tulsa World* (9 Jan 1994)

PUBLIC COLLECTIONS: IAIA; SPIM; USDI; Drover's Bank, Chicago, IL; White Hair Memorial Resource Center, Hominy, OK

EXHIBITS: AA; IAIA; AW/HH; HM; LAF; MSM; NARF; NMSC; OAW; OIO; OSC; OTO; PMSU; PSMA; RC; SJCC; SNAICF; SWAIA; U of NM; Lubbock (TX) Arts Festival, 1986; San Juan College, Farmington, NM; Pembroke (NC) State University, 1985

SOLO EXHIBITS: IAIA; SPIM; Living Arts Space, Tulsa, OK

AWARDS: SNAICF ('87, 1st); SWAIA ('84, 1st; '87; '88)

AKILAK, HATTIE (see Hagpi, Hattie)

AKIMA, CALVIN *Hopi*

PUBLISHED: Snodgrass (1968)

PUBLIC COLLECTIONS: SM

AKOONGISS (see DesJarlait, Robert)

AKOURAK *Inuit (Eskimo)*

RESIDENCE: Holman Island, NWT, Canada
PUBLISHED: *Courier,* UNESCO (Jan 1976)
PUBLIC COLLECTIONS: C/TDB
EXHIBITS: C/EACTDB

AKOVAK, PATRICK *Inuit (Eskimo)*

Born 1944; died 1976
RESIDENCE: Lived in Holman Island, NWT, Canada
PUBLIC COLLECTIONS: C/TDB
EXHIBITS: C/EACTDB, C/HEC

AKULUKJUK, JEETALOO *Inuit (Eskimo)*

A.K.A. Akulukuk
RESIDENCE: Pangnirtung, NWT, Canada
Born 1939
OCCUPATION: Graphic artist (1969-1970); stopped drawing in 1977
MEDIA: Felt tip pen and crayon
PUBLISHED: Goetz, et al. (1977)
EXHIBITS: C/TIP

AKULUKJUK, MALAYA *Inuit (Eskimo)*

Born 1915
RESIDENCE: Pangnirtung, NWT, Canada
OCCUPATION: Graphic artist
MEDIA: Pencil and colored felt tip pens
PUBLISHED: Goetz, et al. (1977); Collinson (1978)
PUBLIC COLLECTIONS: C/U of AB, DAM
EXHIBITS: C/CG, C/TIP

MALAYA AKULUKJUK

Akulukjuk is a prolific artist whose drawings are usually of birds and the camp scenes of her early life. She has a well-defined color sense.

Goetz, et al. 1977

AKULUKUK (see Akulukjuk, Jeetaloo)

ALAGOO, ADAMIE *Inuit (Eskimo)*

RESIDENCE: Povungnituk, PQ, Canada
PUBLIC COLLECTIONS: C/TDB
EXHIBITS: C/EACTDB

ALBANY, GAIL *Mohawk*

Born 15 Nov 1949
RESIDENCE: Caughnawaga, PQ, Canada
OCCUPATION: Craftswoman and painter
MEDIA: Acrylic, canvas board, leather, bone, beads, wood, and stone
PUBLISHED: Johannsen and Ferguson, eds. (1983)

ALBERT, CEDRIC *Hopi*

Dawa Gui Va, Beauty of the Sunrise
A.K.A. Dawavendewa
Born 1960 in Moencopi, AZ
RESIDENCE: Tuba City, AZ
MILITARY: U.S. Marine Corps
OCCUPATION: Aircraft mechanic, silversmith, potter, and painter
MEDIA: Acrylic, watercolor, clay, silver, and gemstone

EXHIBITS: ACS/ENP, RC, SJBIM, SWAIA
AWARDS: ACS/ENP; SKBIM (1st); SWAIA

ALBERT, RAMON, JR. *Hopi/Navajo*
PUBLIC COLLECTIONS: MNA
EXHIBITS: HM/G
AWARDS: HM/G ('70, 1st)

ALBERT, ROBERT STEPHEN *Hopi*
Sakhomenewa
Born 27 Mar 1964 in Ganado, AZ
EDUCATION: A.F.A., IAIA, 1968
OCCUPATION: *Katsina* carver and painter
MEDIA: Watercolor
EXHIBITS: HM, MNA, SM
AWARDS: MNA ('91)
HONORS: T. C. Cannon nominee, 1986; Council for Tribal Employment Rights, Artist of the Year, 1988

ALBERTY, DEWEY *Cherokee*
Ah Quade, Limping
Born 17 Mar 1926 in Sand Springs, OK
RESIDENCE: Tulsa, OK
MILITARY: U.S. Navy, WWII and Korea
EDUCATION: Graduated Chilocco, 1946; BC, 1949; U of OK, 1953
OCCUPATION: American Airlines employee; paints intermittently
PUBLISHED: Snodgrass (1968)

ALBRO, JANICE *Sioux*
RESIDENCE: Bartlesville, OK
PUBLIC COLLECTIONS: HCC
EXHIBITS: IS, NPTA, RE

ALCOTT, MICHAEL *Navajo*
Born 6 Dec 1954
RESIDENCE: Mobridge, SD
EDUCATION: Coconino High School, Flagstaff, AZ; Maricopa Technical Community College, Phoenix, AZ; studied under R. Brownell McGrew
EXHIBITS: C/U of SK, RC

ALEEKUK, AGNES *Inuit (Eskimo)*
RESIDENCE: Canada
PUBLISHED: Napran (1984)
EXHIBITS: C/VRS

ALEXANDER, DENNIS *Chickasaw*
EXHIBITS: RC
AWARDS: RC ('78)

ALEXANDER, NIKKI MARGUERITE *Wyandot*
Born 24 Jan 1954
RESIDENCE: Idyllwild, CA
EDUCATION: Lincoln High School, San Francisco, CA; Fitch High School, Groton, CT; Instituto de San Miguel Allende, Guanajuato, Mexico
EXHIBITS: RC; Idyllwild (CA) Art Association Exhibits; galleries in Idyllwild, CA

ALEXEE, FREDERICK *Tsimshian/Iroquois*

Wiksomnen, Great Deer Woman

A.K.A. Alexis; Allxcee; Alexix; Alexcie; Alexei; Alexie

Born ca. 1853 in Port Simpson, BC, Canada; died ca. 1944

RESIDENCE: Lived in Port Simpson, BC, Canada

OCCUPATION: Carver and painter

MEDIA: Oil, watercolor, wood, and glass lantern slides

PUBLISHED: Harper (1970). *Canadian Review of Music and Art* (Vol. 3, nos. 11 & 12, 1945); *The Beaver* (summer 1945); *The Journal of Canadian Art History* (July 1982)

PUBLIC COLLECTIONS: C/CMC; C/AG/O; C/MMMN; C/VCM; C/U of BC/MA; Wellcome Institute, London, England; Thomas Burke Memorial, Washington State Museum

EXHIBITS: C/NGCA

FREDERICK ALEXEE

Alexee was the son of a Tsimshian woman from the Gilndzano tribe on the Skeena River and an Iroquois father who came to Port Simpson with the Hudson's Bay Company. "[He was] converted to Christianity in his youth. Selected in his youth by the tribe to specialize in wood carving and sculpturing of monsters for Tsimsyan secret society rites. [He] painted native Skeena River and Port Simpson landscapes. . . ."

Harper 1970

Alexee's paintings, done in the folk-art genre, were of historical events and the people and scenes he saw around Port Simpson.

ALFONSO (see Roybal, Alfonso)

ALFRED, BRUCE *Kwakwaka'wakw (Kwagiulth)*

Born 1950 in Alert Bay, BC, Canada

RESIDENCE: Alert Bay, BC, Canada

EDUCATION: Studied with his cousin, Richard Hunt, and Doug Cranmer (qq.v.)

OCCUPATION: Commercial fisherman, carver, printmaker, and painter

PUBLIC COLLECTIONS: HCC

EXHIBITS: AC/NC, AUG, NSU/SD, SDSMT, U of SD

ALFRED, WAYNE *Kwakwaka'wakw (Kwakiutl)*

Born 1958 in Alert Bay, BC, Canada

RESIDENCE: Canada

OCCUPATION: Graphic artist, painter; carver since 1975

PUBLIC COLLECTIONS: HCC

EXHIBITS: HCC, SDSMT

ALIKATUKTUK, ANANAISEE *Inuit (Eskimo)*

A.K.A. Ananaisie Alikatuktuk

Born 1944

RESIDENCE: Pangnirtung, NWT, Canada

OCCUPATION: Graphic artist

MEDIA: Black and colored pencil

PUBLISHED: Goetz, et al. (1977)

EXHIBITS: C/TIP

ALIKATUKTUK, THOMASEE *Inuit (Eskimo)*

Born 1953

RESIDENCE: Pangnirtung, NWT, Canada

OCCUPATION: Printmaker and graphic artist

PUBLISHED: Collinson (1978)

PUBLIC COLLECTIONS: C/U of AB

EXHIBITS: C/CT

ALIKNAK (see Aliknak, Peter)

ALIKNAK, PETER *Inuit (Eskimo)*

A.K.A. Aliknak; Aliknok

Born 1928

RESIDENCE: Holman Island, NWT, Canada
OCCUPATION: Sculptor; graphic artist after 1970
PUBLISHED: Goetz, et al. (1977); Blodgett (1978a); Collinson (1978); Napran (1984)
PUBLIC COLLECTIONS: C/HEC, C/U of AB, DAM
EXHIBITS: C/CG, C/TIP, C/VRS

ALIKNOK (see Aliknak, Peter)

ALLEN, GARY *Cherokee/Navajo*
RESIDENCE: Tahlequah, OK
OCCUPATION: Sculptor and painter
MEDIA: Oil, pencil, and wood
EXHIBITS: CNM, FCTM
AWARDS: FCTM ('92, 1st)

ALLEN, LARRY *Cherokee*
RESIDENCE: Ardmore, OK
EXHIBITS: CNM
AWARDS: CNM ('87, 1st)

ALLEN, MARY *Navajo*
EDUCATION: Santa Fe, ca. 1938
PUBLISHED: Snodgrass (1968)
EXHIBITS: AIW

ALL RUNNER, CLARENCE *Chickasaw*
EXHIBITS: AIE
AWARDS: AIE ('72; '73; '74, 1st)

ALLUKPUK, JOHN *Inuit (Eskimo)*
A.K.A. Allukpik
Born 1935
RESIDENCE: Coppermine, NWT, Canada
OCCUPATION: Hunter and painter
MEDIA: Oil on plywood
PUBLISHED: *The Beaver* (autumn 1976)

JOHN ALLUKPUK

The artist has suffered from tuberculosis since he was a boy and has repeatedly spent time in the hospital.

ALLXCEE, FREDERICK (see Alexee, Frederick)

AL QUA KOU (see Toppah, Herman)

ALUH HOCHI (see Toledo, José Rey)

ALVANNA, DAVID *Eskimo*
Born 1944 on King Island, AK
RESIDENCE: Nome, AK
EDUCATION: DCTP, 1964-1965; U of AK/C, 1966-1968
PUBLISHED: Ray (1969)

AMAROOK, MICHAEL *Inuit (Eskimo)*
A.K.A. Amarook; Amaruq
Born 1941
RESIDENCE: Baker Lake, NWT, Canada
PUBLISHED: Goetz, et al. (1977)
EXHIBITS: C/TIP

AMARUQ (see Amarook, Michael)

AMASON, ALVIN ELI *Aleut*

Born 6 Apr 1948 on Kodiak Island, AK

RESIDENCE: Vashon Island, WA

EDUCATION: Kodiak High School, Kodiak Island, AK; B.A. and M.A., CWU; M.F.A., ASU, 1976

OCCUPATION: Art organizer, teacher, lecturer, and artist

MEDIA: Oil and prints

PUBLISHED: Highwater (1980); Gentry, et al. (1990). *American Indian Art* (summer 1978); *The Alaska Journal* (summer 1978; summer 1979); *Native Arts/West* (Aug 1980); *Arizona Arts and Lifestyle* (autumn 1981); The *Scottsdale Daily Progress* (27 Nov 1981); *The Arizona Republic* (8 Mar 1983); *Alaska Geographic* (Vol. 12, no. 3, 1985)

COMMISSIONS: U.S. Federal Art in Architecture Program, United States Federal Courthouse Building, Anchorage, AK, 1978, 1979; Lower Kuskokwim School District, Bethel, AK

PUBLIC COLLECTIONS: AB; ASM/AK; IACB; MFA/AH; SI; U of AK/F; Baranof Museum, Kodiak, AK; Nordjyllands Kunstmuseum, Aalborg, Denmark

EXHIBITS: ASU/M; CWU; EM; HM; JM; MFA/AH; NACLA; NU/BC; PAC; SC; SCA; SI; U of AK/A; Historical and Fine Arts Museum, AL; Nordjyllands Kuntsmuseum, Denmark; see also Awards

AWARDS: SCA; WSC ('73, 1st, Graphics Award, Purchase Award; '74, Graphics Award); Pacific Northwest Arts and Crafts Fair, Belview, WA ('72, Juror's Award); Four Corners State Biennial, Phoenix, AZ ('75, Juror's Award)

HONORS: Alaska State Council on the Arts, Individual Artist Assistance Grant, 1979; Alaska State Council on the Arts, member, 1979; Board of the Institute of Alaskan Native Arts, member, 1979.

ALVIN ELI AMASON

Amason says that, although he is from Alaska and paints animals, he is not an Alaskan wildlife painter. In addition, he says that, although he is Aleut, he is not an Indian artist. He is not trying to carry on an ethnic tradition, his work simply reflects who and what he is.

AMERICAN HORSE *Oglala Sioux*

Wasechun Tashunka; Manishee, Cannot Walk (name as a young man)

Born 1840 in the Black Hills; died 1908 at Pine Ridge, SD; son of Sitting Bear; nephew of another American Horse killed at Slim Buttes, Dakota Territory, 1875

PUBLISHED: Ewers (1939); Jacobson and d'Ucel (1950); Dunn (1968); Snodgrass (1968); Dockstader (1977). *4th Annual Report,* BAE (1882-1883)

PUBLIC COLLECTIONS: GM; MNH/A; SI/OAA; OU/SM (A buffalo robe illustrating the artist's personal combats during the period ca. 1870-1880; This work is variously attributed to the elder American Horse and his nephew.)

AMERICAN HORSE

"American Horse asserted that the Oglala Winter Count in his possession was started by his grandfather and continued by his father and himself. It contained 104 pictographic drawings and covered the period from 1775 to 1879. Cloud Shield (q.v.) made copies of this Count."

Snodgrass 1968

American Horse was an orator and a skilled diplomat, and on several occasions, served as a tribal representative in Washington, D.C. Because of his concern for the survival of his people, he was an advocate for peace with the Whites.

Dockstader 1977

AMERMAN, MARCUS *Choctaw*

Born 10 Sept 1959 in Phoenix, AZ; son of Harriet and Dale Amerman; P/GP: Francis and Dale Amerman

RESIDENCE: Santa Fe, NM

EDUCATION: Pendleton (OR) High School; B.A., Whitman College, Walla Walla, WA, 1981; CSF/SF, 1982; IAIA, 1983; Anthropology Film Center, Santa Fe, NM, 1984

OCCUPATION: Painter and beadwork artist

MEDIA: Acrylic, glass beads, and mixed-media

PUBLISHED: Coe (1986); Hill (1992). *New Mexico Today* (26 Dec 1984); *Playboy* (Apr 1985); *The Daily News Record* (23 Feb 1987); *Antiques and Fine Art* (Nov 1988); *American Indian Art* (winter 1989); *Phoenix Magazine* (Nov 1989); *Elle* (Jan 1990); *Native Peoples* (1994), cover

PUBLIC COLLECTIONS: IAIA, SPIM, OCSA, USDI

EXHIBITS: ACS/ENP, AICA/SF, HM, IAIA, NARF, NMSC, OWE, RE, SPIN

SOLO EXHIBITS: IAIA, SPIN, SWAIA

MARCUS AMERMAN

Amerman creates his paintings in a unique combination of acrylic paint and glass beads on canvas thus combining his Anglo and Indian heritage, the old and the new in Native art.

Arthur Douglas Amiotte

"With his mother and stepfather, George A. Erring, Amiotte moved to Custer, SD, in 1946. While a sophomore at Northern State, he became acquainted with Oscar Howe, who introduced him to Indian art. Initially he painted in what is now called the traditional style using water based paints, however he soon diversified and began experimenting not only in style and subject matter, but in materials. As a result he has developed his own highly individualistic style."

Snodgrass 1968

Amiotte said, "Being an Indian, I believe from the time I was very young I was taught by my grandparents who reared me to be sensitive to things as well as to sounds and colors . . . growing up with this sensitivity you eventually learn to see and hear only as an Indian."

Libhart 1970

Amiotte is a member of the Dream Catchers Artists Guild, Ltd. (q.v.).

AWARDS: ACS/EMP ('84, Most Creative New Design); RE; SWAIA ('84, 1st, Innovative Use of Traditional Techniques; '90, 1st, Best Out of Area)

AMGALGAK (see Kailukiak, John)

AMIOTTE, ARTHUR DOUGLAS *Oglala Sioux*

Warpa Tanka Kuciyela, Low Black Bird (given 1942); *Wanbli Ta Hocoka Waste*, Good Eagle Center (given 1972)

Born 25 Mar 1942 at Pine Ridge, SD; son of Olive Louise Mesteth and Walter Douglas Amiotte; M/GF: George Mesteth; great grandson of Standing Bear (q.v.)

RESIDENCE: Custer, SD

EDUCATION: Custer (SD) High School, 1960; U of OK; IAIA; B.S., NSTC/SD, 1964; M.S., PSU, 1969; M.S., U of MT, 1983; workshops under Oscar Howe (q.v.), U of SD

OCCUPATION: Craftsman, art teacher, curriculum specialist, college professor, college department head, consultant, author, lecturer, and artist

MEDIA: Oil, acrylic, watercolor, fiber, fabric, glass beads, mixed media, and prints

PUBLISHED: Snodgrass (1968); Libhart (1970); Brody (1971); Gridley (1947); Silberman (1978); Amiotte (1988); Dooling and Smith, eds. (1989); Huseboe, ed. (1989); Maurer (1992). *Missoulian* (25 July 1981); *American Indian Art* (spring 1985); *Christian Science Monitor* (11 Aug 1987); *The Rapid City Journal* (20 Jan 1987; 4 Aug 1988; 3 Dec 1989); *South Dakota Art Museum News* (spring 1989); *The Argus Leader* (10 Sept 1989); *Inside the Black Hills* (fall 1990), cover

BOOKS ILLUSTRATED: DeMallie and Parks, eds. (1987)

COMMISSIONS: *Murals:* Little Eagle (MT) Day School. *Logos:* Fort Peck Community College, Poplar, MT; Yellowquill College, Portage La Prairie, MB; Brandon University, Brandon, MB; Society for the Advancement of Native Studies, Brandon, MB. *Paintings:* National Park Service, 1981; Sisters of Notre Dame, Porcupine, SD, 1987; South Dakota Foundation for the Arts, four paintings, 1989. *Other:* Parabola Books, New York, NY, book covers; Justin Publishing, Brandon, MB, book covers; Mitchell (SD) Chamber of Commerce, Mitchell Corn Palace, proscenium design, 1980

PUBLIC COLLECTIONS: BIA/AOK; CPS; HCC; HPTU; IACB; MIA; NSTC/SD; SDAM; SJIS; TM/NE; WTF; W. H. Over Museum, Vermillion, SD; Office of former Senator George McGovern, Washington, D.C.

EXHIBITS: AICA/SF; AICH; ANC; BIA/A; BM/B; BNIAS; CAS; CS; FAC/D; FNAIC; GM; HCC; HS/N; KCPA; LAC; LSS; NACLA; NARF; NDM; NPTA; NSTC/SD; NU/BC; OM; OMA; PAC; PIA; RC; SDMM; SI; SIM; SNMA; TRP; U of SD; USDI; VH; VP; VT; Northern Virginia Fine Arts Association, Arlington, VA; South Dakota Memorial Art Center, Brookings, SD; Creighton University Galleries, Omaha, NE; Eastern Montana College, Billings, MT; Centennial Art Exhibition, Pierre, SD; Plains Art Exposition, Sioux Falls, SD; High Plains Heritage Center, Spearfish, SD; see also Awards

SOLO EXHIBITS: BIA/A; C/AC/BA; FAC/CS; ISU; NSU/SD; SDAM; U of NE; U of MT; U of SD/OHG; Waterloo (IA) Municipal Galleries; Civic Fine Arts Center, Sioux Falls, SD; Augustana College, Sioux Falls, SD; Aberdeen (SD) Civic Auditorium; Fort Collins (CO) Fine Arts Center; Huron (SD) Fine Arts Center

AWARDS: NPTA ('88, 1st; '89; '90; '91; '92, Governor's Award); RC ('73; '75, Best of Show, Begay Award; '76; '77; '86, Pepion Family Award; '90, Barkley Art Center Award, Begay Award); UTAE ('92); Sioux City (IA) Art Center ('65, MA); Foundation of North American Indian Culture Exhibition, GA ('64, Grand Award)

HONORS: *Scholarships and Fellowships:* South Dakota Indian Scholarship, 4 years; BIA Scholarship Grant, 4 years; C. A. Schwartz Art Education Scholarship; O.A.S. Fellowship to Ecuador; Bush Leadership Fellowship, 1980-1983; Phelps Stokes Foundation Fellowship, 1979-1981. *Other:* Membership in four honor fraternities;

IAIA, member Council of Regents; State of South Dakota Indian Education Association, "Outstanding Contribution to Indian Education" Award, 1976; State of South Dakota, Governor's Biennial Award for Outstanding Creative Achievement in the Arts, 1980; Indian Arts and Crafts Board, appointed Commissioner, 1988; Northern State College, Aberdeen, SD, Distinguished Alumni Award, 1988; Oglala Lakota College, Honorary Doctorate, 1988; South Dakota Art Museum, Board of Trustees, Brookings, SD, Annual Artistic Achievement Citation, 1989; Augustana College, Sioux Falls, SD, National Board of Directors, 1990; Foundation for the Arts in South Dakota, Rapid City, SD, Board of Directors

AMIOTTE, LOUIS D. *Oglala Sioux*

Born 2 Mar 1951 in Newcastle, WY

RESIDENCE: Pauma Valley, CA

EDUCATION: Maryvale High School, Phoenix, AZ; RVSA; SFAI, 1977

EXHIBITS: U of IL/CCC, SFAI, SIM

AMIT, DAVIDIALU ALASUA (see Davidialuk)

AMITOOK (see Awp, Syollie)

AMITTU (see Awp, Syollie)

AMITTU, DAVIDIALUK ALASUA (see Davidialuk)

AMITUK, SYOLLIE (see Awp, Syollie)

AMMITU (see Awp, Syollie)

AMMITU, SYOLLIE ARPATUK (see Awp, Syollie)

AMOS, PATRICK *Nuu-Chah-Nulth (Nootka)*

Kakawin

Born 1957 in Friendly Cove, Nootka Island, BC, Canada

EDUCATION: Christie Residential School; Provincial Museum of British Columbia, Victoria, BC

OCCUPATION: Artist

MEDIA: Acrylic, watercolor, latex, and pen and ink

PUBLISHED: Hall, Blackman, and Rickard, eds. (1981). *Four Winds* (1980)

COMMISSIONS: *Murals:* Victoria Native Friendship Centre, Victoria, BC

PUBLIC COLLECTIONS: HCC

EXHIBITS: AUG, C/RBCM, NSU/SD

AMYLEE *Iroquois*

She-Who-Catches-The-Rainbow

Born 1952 in Ohio; daughter of Yehoweh and Bear Bow

RESIDENCE: Tippecanoe, OH

EDUCATION: Kent (OH) State University; SUNY

OCCUPATION: Lecturer and artist

MEDIA: Oil, acrylic, watercolor, pencil, pen and ink, pastel, metal, and firepainting on leather

PUBLIC COLLECTIONS: Native American Resource Center

EXHIBITS: CIM; MCI; RC; Museum of Roanoke, VA; Michigan Women's Music Festival; West Coast Women's Culture Festival; a traveling exhibit of her lineage, featuring her work; regional exhibits and fairs

SOLO EXHIBITS: Kent (OH) State University (1983)

AWARDS: Local fairs

ANASTEEN *Navajo*

PUBLISHED: Snodgrass (1968)

PUBLIC COLLECTIONS: MAI

ANERGA (see Oshuitoq, Anirnik)

ANERNGNA (see Oshuitoq, Anirnik)

ANERNIK (see Oshuitoq, Anirnik)

ANDERSON, CARMEN *Rosebud Sioux*

A.K.A. Carmen Atkinson Anderson

Born 5 Dec 1938 in Rosebud, SD; daughter of Violet Atkinson and Chester Lambert; P/GF: Guy Lambert; M/GP: Annie Jackson and John Atkinson

RESIDENCE: Greenwood, MS

EDUCATION: Sisseton (SD) High School; Memphis (TN) State University

OCCUPATION: Gallery owner and painter

PUBLISHED: *The New York Review* (1990); biographical publications

EXHIBITS: CNM, RC

HONORS: Television appearance, *Professional Women of Mississippi*

ANDERSON, JIMMY *Creek*

Ahhajumba, Sweet Potato

Born 14 Aug 1932 in Kansas City, MO

EDUCATION: Haskell; BC; CSC/OK; U of OK

OCCUPATION: Singer and recording artist,Christian religious worker, and artist

PUBLISHED: Snodgrass (1968); Brody (1971)

PUBLIC COLLECTIONS: PAC

EXHIBITS: AIE, FCTM, ITIC, JGS, PAC, SN

AWARDS: AIE; FCTM ('67; '71, IH; '72); ITIC ('68); PAC ('68); SN ('68)

ANDERSON, RON *Choctaw*

A.K.A. Ronald Wayne Anderson

Born 1 Sept 1938 in Talihina, OK

RESIDENCE: Bull Head City, AZ

EDUCATION: Haskell, 1957; B.F.A., U of OK, 1977; U of NM

OCCUPATION: Teacher, sculptor, and painter

PUBLISHED: *The Scottsdale Progress* (3 July 1987)

PUBLIC COLLECTIONS: HM

EXHIBITS: ABQM; AIE; CAI/KC; CNM; HM; NMSF; see also Awards

AWARDS: AIE ('73); NMSF ('77, 1st; '79, 1st); Hughes County (OK) Art Show ('49); Friends of the Navajo Library, Window Rock, AZ ('76, Purchase Award); Rendezvous, Anadarko, OK ('86)

ANDERSON, TROY *Cherokee*

Born 23 Sept 1948 in Siloam Springs, AR

RESIDENCE: Siloam Springs, AR

EDUCATION: Connors State College, Warner, OK, 1967; West Texas State University, Canyon, TX, 1970

OCCUPATION: Teacher, coach, full-time sculptor and painter since 1979

MEDIA: Oil, acrylic, watercolor, pencil, pastel, bronze, and prints

PUBLISHED: Samuels (1982). *Southwest Art* (Feb 1990); *Arizona Living* (16 Feb 1979); *Southwest Art Contemporary Western Artists* (1982); *The Muskogee Phoenix* (25 Mar 1984); *The Santa Fe Reporter* (Aug 1988); *Twin Territories* (Year of the Indian Edition 1992); *The Muskogee Daily Phoenix* (4 Oct 1993)

TROY ANDERSON

Anderson paints Indian history, myths, and legends, especially of the Cherokee. He is perhaps best known for his paintings depicting the "Trail of Tears," the removal of the Cherokee from North Carolina to Oklahoma. He has classified his work as being contemporary realistic. Not content to do the same thing over and over, Anderson continues to experiment and explore new techniques. In 1982 he took up sculpture and more recently he has added a sculptural effect to his paintings. Using a special technique he adds contours to his canvas and then paints over it.

BOOKS ILLUSTRATED: Illustrated and authored *The Origin of Corn* (1980)

COMMISSIONS: Cherokee Trail of Tears Sesquicentennial Commemorative Medallion

PUBLIC COLLECTIONS: BIA, TTSP

EXHIBITS: ACAI, AICA, CNM, FAIE, FCTM, FCTM/M, HM, ITIC, LIAS, MCI, MNH/AN, OAC, PAC, PF, RE, SWAIA, TIAF, TTSP

SOLO EXHIBITS: CNM, FCTM

AWARDS: ACAI ('93); AICA (Gold Medal Award, six consecutive years); CNM ('82, 1st; '83, 1st; '84, Tiger Award; '85, 1st; '86, 1st; '89, Grand Award; '90, 1st; '92; '93, 1st); FCTM ('77; '78, IH; '79, 1st; '80, 1st, IH); FCTM/M ('81, 1st; '82, Grand Award; '83, Grand Award; '84, Grand Award; '85, 1st; '86; '87, Best of Show; '88, IH; '90, 1st; '91, Best of Show; '92, Best of Show; '93, 1st; '94, Spirit of Oklahoma Award); HM/G ('79, 1st; '80, 1st); ITIC ('87; '89, 3-1st; '90, 2-1st; '91, 1st); LIAS ('89, 3 Merit Awards); MCI (1st, Grand Award); PAC ('79); RE ('87; '88; '89; '92, 1st, Best of Division); SWAIA (1st); TIAF ('93)

HONORS: 75th Arkansas General Assembly, Resolution of Commendation; AICA, President; FCTM, designated a Master Artist, 1980

ANDERSON, WILLIAM T. *Cherokee*

Born 1936 in Minneapolis, MN

EDUCATION: B.A./M.A. CSU/LA

OCCUPATION: Art professor and painter

MEDIA: Paint, mixed-media, plexiglass, high gloss plastic inks, and prints

EXHIBITS: NACLA

ANDREW, LEO *Hopi*

Born 1906 in Shungopovi, Second Mesa, AZ; brother of Alice Talayaonema, wife of Fred Kabotie (q.v.)

EDUCATION: Phoenix, AZ

OCCUPATION: Fred Harvey Company, employee (Grand Canyon, AZ), grocer, farmer, *katsina* carver, and painter

MEDIA: Watercolor and cottonwood root

PUBLISHED: Seymour (1988)

PUBLIC COLLECTIONS: IACB/DC

EXHIBITS: ITIC, WRTD

AWARDS: ITIC ('49, 1st)

ANDREWS, WILLIAM A. *Navajo*

RESIDENCE: Mesilla, NM

PUBLISHED: Snodgrass (1968)

EXHIBITS: MNM

AWARDS: MNM

ANERGNA (see Anirnik)

ANERNIK (see Anirnik)

ANGECONEB, ALLEN *Ojibwa*

Ahmoo, The Bee

A.K.A. Signature: Ahmoo

Born 19 Apr 1955 at Sioux Lookout, ON, Canada, on the Lac Seul Reserve

RESIDENCE: Thunder Bay, ON, Canada

EDUCATION: Graduated high school with honors, Beaver Brae Secondary School, ON, 1975; C/YU; Humber College, Toronto, ON; B.F.A., Lakehead University; additional studies in Malaysia, France, Spain, and Morocco

ALLEN ANGECONEB

An intellectual painter who is widely traveled, Angeconeb has at various times in his career been influenced by the works of: Kenneth Noland, Johannes Itten, Andy Warhol, and Pablo Picasso. In addition, his work shows the influence of Woodland Indian art.

Southcott 1984

MEDIA: Acrylic, pen and ink, birch bark, wax, dye, and fabric

PUBLISHED: Southcott (1984); Menitove, ed. (1986b); Menitove and Danford, ed. (1989); Podedworny (1989). *Arts Atlantic* 30 (winter 1988); *Site Sound* (Sept/Oct 1991)

BOOKS ILLUSTRATED: Kenny (1978)

COMMISSIONS: *Murals:* Inuvik General Hospital, 1975; Pelican Lake Residential School, Sioux Lookout, ON; Baie St. Paul, PQ

PUBLIC COLLECTIONS: C/AG/NS; C/AG/TB; C/CGCQ; C/CMC; C/INAC; C/ROM; Art Centre Group, London, England; National Health and Welfare, Inuvik, NWT; Sioux Lookout (ON) Public Library; Ontario Ministry of the Environment, Toronto, ON

EXHIBITS: C/AG/NS; C/AG/TB; C/CA; C/MSVU; C/NCC; C/WCAA; C/WICEC; Ukrainian Canadian Art Foundation, Toronto, ON; Nova Scotia School of Architecture, Halifax, NS; Kenora (ON) Fellowship Centre; Discovery Centre, Fort Lauderdale, FL

SOLO EXHIBITS: C/AG/TB; C/CGCQ; C/MSVU; C/U of BC/MA; C/YU; IAIA; SCG; Lakewood Secondary School, Kenora, ON; Centre d'Art, Baie St. Paul, PQ; Mount Allison University, Sackville, NB; galleries in Canada

HONORS: Canada Council Grant, 1992

ANGELO, JOHN *Navajo*

EXHIBITS: SN

AWARDS: SN ('68)

ANGHIK, ABRAHAM *Inuit (Eskimo)*

Born 1951 in Paulatuk, Canada, 250 miles north of the Arctic Circle

RESIDENCE: Saltspring Island, BC, Canada

EDUCATION: High school in Inuvik, NWT; U of AK/F

OCCUPATION: Painter and sculptor

EXHIBITS: Eleven group exhibits

ANGLUSOI, RUTH ANN *Inuit (Eskimo)*

RESIDENCE: Canada

OCCUPATION: Graphic artist

MEDIA: Crayon

PUBLISHED: *Artscanada* (Vol. 30, nos. 5 & 6, 1973-1974)

ANGOKWAZHUK *Eskimo*

A.K.A. Happy Jack

Born ca. 1870 near Ayasayuk, Cape Nome, AK; died 1918 in Nome, AK, of influenza

OCCUPATION: Carver and engraver

MEDIA: Ivory

PUBLISHED: Ray (1961; 1969)

ANGOKWAZHUK

Happy Jack was one of the major Eskimo artists during the turn of the century. He was outgoing and gregarious as well as an innovator and teacher.

Ray 1969

ANGOSAGLO (see Anguhadluq, Luke)

ANGOTIGALOOK *Inuit (Eskimo)*

RESIDENCE: Cape Dorset, NWT, Canada

PUBLISHED: Houston (1967a)

PUBLIC COLLECTIONS: C/TDB

EXHIBITS: C/CD, C/EACTDB

ANGOTIGULU *Inuit (Eskimo)*

RESIDENCE: Canada

PUBLISHED: Houston (1967); Larmour (1967)

ANGRNA'NAAG, RUBY *Inuit (Eskimo)*

A.K.A. Ruby Arngna'naaq

Born 1947

RESIDENCE: Baker Lake, NWT, Canada

PUBLISHED: *North* (Mar/Apr 1974)

EXHIBITS: Robertson Galleries, Ottawa, ON

ANGUHADLUQ *(see Tuu'luq, Marion)*

ANGUHADLUQ, LUKE *Inuit (Eskimo)*

A.K.A. Angosaglo; Anguhalluq

Born ca. 1895; died 1982; husband of Marion Tuu'luq (q.v.)

RESIDENCE: Lived at Baker Lake, NWT, Canada

OCCUPATION: Hunter, fisherman, camp leader, and graphic artist

MEDIA: Colored and black pencil, ball point pen, felt tip pen, and prints

PUBLISHED: Vallee (1967); Burland (1973); Blodgett (1976; 1978a; 1978b; 1979; n.d.); Goetz, et al. (1977); Routledge (1979); Latocki, ed. (1983); Jackson and Nasby (1987); McMasters, et al. (1993). *Artscanada* (Vol. 30, nos. 5 & 6, 1973-1974)

PUBLIC COLLECTIONS: C/AC/MS, C/AG/WP

EXHIBITS: C/AC/MS; C/AG/WP; C/CID; C/CMC; C/BLPD; C/IA7C/LS; C/MAD; C/NGCA; C/TIP; Musikhuset Aarhus, Denmark

LUKE ANGUHADLUQ

Anguhadluq's artistic career started about 1968 when he was more than 70 years old. The majority of his drawings represented animals, people, events, and activities from his life on the land. Sitting on the floor with the paper between his outstretched legs, he drew things as they had been before the old lifestyle ended.

Blodgett 1976

ANGUHALLUQ (see Anguhadluq, Luke)

ANIRNIK *Inuit (Eskimo)*

A.K.A. Anergna; Anernik

Born 1909

RESIDENCE: Cape Dorset, NWT, Canada

OCCUPATION: Graphic artist since the 1960s

MEDIA: Colored pencil

PUBLISHED: Goetz, et al. (1977); Blodgett (1978a). *The Beaver* (spring 1975)

PUBLIC COLLECTIONS: C/WBEC

EXHIBITS: C/AG/WP, C/TIP

ANKO *Kiowa*

Ankopaaingyadete, In The Middle Of Many Tracks

A.K.A. Aunko

Birth date unknown; died early in the 20th century

PUBLISHED: LaFarge (1956); Mayhall (1962); Snodgrass (1968). *17th Annual Report*, BAE (1895-1896)

PUBLIC COLLECTIONS: USNM/OA (?)

ANKO

"Anko kept a Kiowa pictographic calendar, originally on brown wrapping paper and representing the years from 1863-1864 to 1884-1885. One copy was made for Gen. Hugh L. Scott before 1900 and is recorded as being at the Smithsonian Institution, although it cannot be located. Another calendar for the same years, executed in black pencil and kept in a notebook, is attributed to the artist. A copy was reportedly made on buckskin in the 1890s for James Mooney, and Charles E. Rowell has also reproduced it."

Snodgrass 1968

As a young child Mrs. R. Hall watched her grandfather, Anko, work on the canvas calendar now in her possession.

ANKOPAAINGYADETE (see Anko)

ANNA *Inuit (Eskimo)*

RESIDENCE: Cape Dorset, NWT, Canada.

OCCUPATION: Graphic artist

PUBLISHED: *The Beaver* (spring 1975)

ANNANOORUK (see Immana, Annie Weokluk)

ANNAQTUSII (see Annaqtuusi, Ruth)

RUTH ANNAQTUUSI

Ruth Annaqtuusi's drawings are brightly colored and interestingly textured. She began drawing about 1971.

Jackson and Nasby 1987

BOB ANNESLEY

Annesley won his first painting award when he was fourteen and had his first solo show when he was eighteen. He became a full-time artist in 1973. Many of Annesley's works are in unusual media. His goldpoint and silverpoint drawings involve the use of pure silver and 24 karat gold. The encaustic mixed-media technique is an exacting process involving the use of beeswax which is interspersed with the painting media to set the colors. The final step requires that the work be baked in an oven. All three of these media require a great deal of time and effort and he does not produce very many in a year.

artist, p.c. 1990

ANNAQTUUSI, RUTH *Inuit (Eskimo)*

A.K.A. Annaqtusii; Annuktoshe; Ruth Annaqtuusi Tulurialik

Born 1934 in the Kazan River area; raised at Baker Lake, NWT, Canada; adopted by an aunt and uncle

RESIDENCE: Baker Lake, NWT, Canada

OCCUPATION: Mother, homemaker, seamstress; has drawn since 1971

MEDIA: Colored pencil, crayon, graphite, and prints

PUBLISHED: Goetz, et al. (1977); Blodgett (1978a, 1978b); Routledge (1979); Woodhouse, ed. (1980); Latocki, ed. (1983); Jackson and Pelly (1986); Jackson and Nasby (1987)

PUBLIC COLLECTIONS: C/AC/MS; C/AG/; C/AG/WP; C/SC; Sanavik Fine Art Cooperative

EXHIBITS: C/AG/W, C/AG/WP, C/AG/O, C/CID, C/BLPD, C/IA7, C/SS

ANNEE (see Oshuitoq, Anirnik)

ANNESLEY, BOB *Cherokee*

A.K.A. Robert Annesley

Born 11 Feb 1943 in Norman, OK; son of Zeta E. and Sylvester C. Annesley

RESIDENCE: Houston, TX

EDUCATION: Norman (OK) High School, 1961; U of OK; OCU

OCCUPATION: Poet, Indian historian, graphic artist, sculptor, and painter

MEDIA: Oil, acrylic, watercolor, pencil, pen and ink, pastel, goldpoint, silverpoint, bronze, terra-cotta, and encaustic mixed-media

PUBLISHED: Boyd, et al. (1983); Samuels (1982); Highwater (1976; 1980). *The Indian Trader* (Apr 1976); *Oklahoma Art Gallery* (spring 1980); *Art Voice/South* (Sept 1980); *Native Arts/West* (July 1980); *Southwest Art* (June 1981); *Twin Territories* (Year of the Indian Edition 1992); *The Muskogee Daily Phoenix* (4 Oct 1993)

BOOKS ILLUSTRATED: Vogel (1990), cover; Worchester (1992), cover

COMMISSIONS: Franklin Mint, designed one side of the Texas Bicentennial coin

PUBLIC COLLECTIONS: CNM; FCTM; IACB; SPIM; TTSP; U of OK/MA; The Royal Academy of Fine Arts, London, England

EXHIBITS: ACAI, AICA/SD, CHAS, CNM, CTWA, FCTM, FCTM/M, HM, ITIC, KCPA, LAAA, LC, NACLA, OAIS, PAC, RE, SDCC, SFFA, SN, TTSP, TWIA, WIB, WWM

SOLO EXHIBITS: CNM, SPIM

AWARDS: ACAI ('92, 1st; '93, 1st); AUCA/SD ('84, Gold Medal); CHAS ('90, 1st); CNM ('80; '81, Best of Class; '83, 1st, Tiger Award; '84, SM, Tiger Award; '85, 1st; '86, 2-1st; '88, SM; '89, 1st; '91, 1st; '92, 1st; '93); CTWA ('89, 1st), FCTM ('77, 1st, Grand Award, Grand Heritage Award; '83, 1st; '84); FCTM/M ('88; '89, 1st; '90, Best of Show; '91, 1st; '92, 1st; '93, 1st); FMBC ('75 winner TX division); HM/G ('74; '75; '78, 1st); ITIC ('79, 1st; '80, 1st, SM; '84, 1st; '85); LAAA ('76, Best of Class Painting); LC ('89, Grand Prize); OAIS ('76, Best of Show); PAC ('74, Painting Award; '75, Graphics Award; '76, 1st; '78; '79); RE ('89; '88; '90, 1st); SN (1st); TWIA (1st, Special Award); Chisholm Trail Western Art Show ('89, 1st)

HONORS: National Scholastic Award, High School; Oklahoma City (OK) University, State of Oklahoma, Distinguished Native American Award, 1981; Santa Fe, NM, made an Honorary Citizen and given the Key to City, 1983; Color of Hope, Muskogee, OK, poster artist; FCTM, designated a Master Artist, 1986

ANNICK (see Oshuitoq, Anirnik)

ANNNANOORUK (see Immana, Annie Weokluk)

ANNOHE (see Anoee, Eric)

ANNUKTOSHE (see Annaqtuusi, Ruth)

ANOEE, ERIC *Inuit (Eskimo)*

A.K.A. Annohe

Born 1925 near Baker Lake, NWT, Canada

RESIDENCE: Eskimo Point, NWT, Canada

OCCUPATION: Sculptor, author, graphic artist, and painter

PUBLISHED: Anoee (1982). *Inuttituut* (winter 1977)

PUBLIC COLLECTIONS: C/AG/WP

EXHIBITS: C/AG/WP, C/IGV

HONORS: The Order of Canada, appointed a member, 1981; Canada Council Grant, to compile a book of Inuit songs and biographies, 1984

ANQUOE, DELILAH CONNER (see Conner, Delilah Dianne)

ANQUOE, JACKIE *Kiowa*

EXHIBITS: OIAP

ANTELOPE, LOUIS *Flathead*

PUBLISHED: Snodgrass (1968)

PUBLIC COLLECTIONS: CCHM

ANTELOPE, VERLYS *Sioux*

PUBLIC COLLECTIONS: HCC

ANTELOPE, WILLIAM *Cheyenne*

PUBLISHED: Snodgrass (1968)

PUBLIC COLLECTIONS: ACM

ANTOINE, ELVIS *Sioux*

Birth date unknown; born on the Sioux Valley Reserve, MB, Canada

RESIDENCE: Brandon, MB, Canada

OCCUPATION: Artist

MEDIA: Watercolor

PUBLISHED: *American Indian Art* (spring 1990)

ANTOINE, MURIEL *Rosebud Sioux*

EXHIBITS: AICA/SF

APACHE MAN (see Williams, David Emmett)

APIE BEGAY (see Begay, Apie)

APOMONU *San Ildefonso*

PUBLISHED: Snodgrass (1968)

PUBLIC COLLECTIONS: SM

APOWMUCKCON (see Racine, Albert Batiste)

APPIE BE GAY (see Begay, Apie)

APPLE, CECIL *Oglala Lakota*

PUBLIC COLLECTIONS: HCC

EXHIBITS: TM/NE, RC, WTF

AQUASU (see McMurtry, Robert)

AQUINO, FRANK *San Juan*
RESIDENCE: Albuquerque, NM
EDUCATION: Albuquerque, 1962-1963
PUBLISHED: Snodgrass (1968)
EXHIBITS: School-sponsored exhibits and local Indian functions

AQUINO, JUAN B. *San Juan*
RESIDENCE: San Juan Pueblo, NM
EDUCATION: BC
PUBLISHED: Snodgrass (1968)
PUBLIC COLLECTIONS: CGPS, MNM
EXHIBITS: LGAM, MNM, PAC
AWARDS: PAC

AQUINO, ROBERT *San Juan*
RESIDENCE: San Juan Pueblo, NM
EDUCATION: Santa Fe, ca. 1960
PUBLISHED: Snodgrass (1968)
PUBLIC COLLECTIONS: MNM
EXHIBITS: MNM, PAC

ARAGON, ARNOLD *Crow/Pueblo*
Born 9 July 1953 at Crow Agency, MT
EDUCATION: A.F.A., IAIA, 1979; U of NV, 1980-1984
OCCUPATION: Sculptor and painter
MEDIA: Watercolor, pencil, and pastel

ARAGON, RALPH *Zia*
Born 1944 in Algodones, NM
RESIDENCE: San Ysidro, NM
EDUCATION: IAIA, 1965-1966
OCCUPATION: Craftsman, beadworker, and painter
PUBLISHED: Snodgrass (1968)
PUBLIC COLLECTIONS: IAIA
EXHIBITS: ACS/ENP, HM, IAIA, NMSF, OWE, SAIEAIP, YAIA
AWARDS: NMSF (1st); ACS/ENP

ARCHAMBAULT, ALDEN DEAN, JR. *Hunkpapa Sioux*
RESIDENCE: Billings, MT
EDUCATION: EMC
OCCUPATION: Graphic artist and painter
MEDIA: Watercolor and pencil
EXHIBITS: CIAE/MT; GFNAAS; NAVAM; Miller Foundation for the Arts, Billings, MT
AWARDS: GFNAAS ('85, Best of Show)

ARCHAMBAULT, JOALLYN *Sioux/Creek*
Born 13 Feb 1942 in Claremore, OK
RESIDENCE: Oakland, CA
EDUCATION: St. Vincent Ferrar High School, Vallejo, CA, 1960; U of CA/B
OCCUPATION: Educator, craftswoman, and painter
PUBLISHED: *The Indian Trader* (Aug 1980)
COMMISSIONS: Navajo Tribal Museum, painted a winter count on a buffalo robe

PUBLIC COLLECTIONS: HCC
EXHIBITS: BM, HM/G, PAC, RC, SN
SOLO EXHIBITS: SIM
AWARDS: HM/G, RC ('78; '79, 1st, Woodard Award)
HONORS: *Scholarships and Fellowships:* National Merit Scholarship; Ford Foundation Fellowship; U of CA, Regents Fellowship

ARCHER, DRUE R. *Chickasaw*
Born 9 Mar 1950 in Okay, OK; daughter of Betty Ann Steber and Fred A. Ridley Jr.; P/GP: Uldean Garrett and Fred A. Ridley Sr.
RESIDENCE: Morris, OK
EDUCATION: Harding High School, 1968; Centenary College, Hackettstown, NJ; OCU
OCCUPATION: Teacher and painter
MEDIA: Acrylic, watercolor, and mixed media
EXHIBITS: OIAC; see also Awards
AWARDS: OIAC ('94, New Artist Award); Okmulgee (OK) Art Guild Show ('91, 1st)

ARCHER, LAURIE *Cherokee*
EXHIBITS: SFFA

ARCHIE, ED *Coast Salish*
EXHIBITS: AICH

ARCHILTA, CLARA *Kiowa/Apache/Tonkawa*
Born 26 Sept 1912 in Tonkawa, OK; daughter of Helen Sunrise and David Williams
RESIDENCE: Ogallala, NE
EDUCATION: Boone School, Apache, OK; Chilocco; schooling through 8th grade
OCCUPATION: Part-time guide at Indian City U.S.A. (Anadarko, OK), and painter
PUBLISHED: Snodgrass (1968); Brody (1971). Oklahoma Health and Welfare Administration (1959), program cover
PUBLIC COLLECTIONS: BIA/D (Department of Welfare); Department of Public Welfare, Anadarko, OK
EXHIBITS: AIE, CSPIP, PAC
AWARDS: AIE ('61; '67; '73)

CLARA ARCHILTA

"Although handicapped by a severely injured arm, Archilta began to paint in 1957 and was selling her work shortly afterward. She has had no formal art training but received encouragement from Susie Peters and Catherine Cochran, Indian Welfare Service workers."

Snodgrass 1968

ARCHULETA, ANTONIO *Taos*
A.K.A. Tony Archuleta
Birth date unknown; death date unknown
PUBLISHED: Snodgrass (1968); Tanner (1973)
PUBLIC COLLECTIONS: MNM, SAR

ANTONIO ARCHULETA

Very little is known of this artist. The paintings included in the School of American Research Collection were done in a European-influenced style and appear to be of Plains Indian life. They were given to the collection by Mary Austin in 1933.

Sam E. Watson, p.c. 1994

ARCHULETA, BETTY KEENER *Cherokee*
Qued
Born 22 May 1928 in Pawhuska, OK
RESIDENCE: Woodward, OK
EDUCATION: Dord Fitz School of Art, Woodward, OK
OCCUPATION: Housewife and artist; active in local art club
PUBLISHED: Snodgrass (1968)
EXHIBITS: ITIC, MNM; Lil-Red School, Shattuck, OK; Enid, OK; Spearman, TX; Amarillo, TX; Liberal, KS; New York, NY; see also Awards
AWARDS: Woodward (OK) County Fair, eight ribbons, 1962-1963

BETTY KEENER ARCHULETA

"Although Archuleta first showed an interest in drawing at the age of five, she did not start painting until 1961."

Snodgrass 1968

ARCHULETA, MANUEL *Picurís*

Pian Whe Le Ne, Mountain Bow
RESIDENCE: Picurís Pueblo, NM
EDUCATION: IAIA
OCCUPATION: Artist
EXHIBITS: ACS/ENP; SWAIA; Southwest Indian Art Collectibles Exhibition, Carefree, AZ

ARCHULETA, TRINIDAD *Taos*

PUBLISHED: Snodgrass (1968)
PUBLIC COLLECTIONS: MNM, RAM

ARCOREN, EUGENE, SR. *Rosebud Sioux*

RESIDENCE: Mission, SD
EDUCATION: G.E.D.; Sinte Gleska Art Institute, Mission, SD
EXHIBITS: RC, SIM

ARIPA, LAWRENCE D. *Coeur d'Alene*

Born 1926 in Plummer, ID
RESIDENCE: Plummer, ID
EDUCATION: Plummer (ID) High School
OCCUPATION: Illustrator and artist
MEDIA: Oil, watercolor, pen and ink, charcoal, pencil, and terra cotta
EXHIBITS: CIA; Kyi-Yo Indian Youth Conference, Missoula, MT; see also Awards
AWARDS: La Grande (OR) Indian Festival of Arts ('71, 1st)

BENJAMIN ARKEKETA

"Inspired by Brummett Echohawk and Acee Blue Eagle (qq.v.), the artist has received several award ribbons. His paintings often reflect his strong interest in Indian archaeology and ethnology, and in Christian philosophy."
Snodgrass 1968

In 1993 Arkeketa retired from his job as an X-ray technologist at Hissom Memorial Center. In recent years he has done very little painting, but hopes he will have more time for it now.
artist, p.c. 1993

ARKEKETA, BENJAMIN *Otoe/Missouri*

Ark Kaketa, Waiting Up
Born 27 Feb 1928 in Red Rock, OK; son of Edna Jones and George B. Arkeketa; P/GF: Benjamin Arkeketa
RESIDENCE: Sand Springs, OK
MILITARY: U.S. Marine Corps, Korea
EDUCATION: Oklahoma public schools; X-ray Technician Certificate, St. John Hospital, Tulsa, OK, 1954
OCCUPATION: X-ray technologist and painter
PUBLISHED: Snodgrass (1968)
EXHIBITS: PAC, SN; Ponca Indian Free Fair, Ponca City, OK; Public Library, Clinton, OK
AWARDS: PAC ('71)

ARK KAKETA (see Arkeketa, Benjamin)

TIRADOR ARMSTRONG

"Encouraged, as many Plains Indian artists were, by Susie Peters, Armstrong has been interested in art since elementary school."
Snodgrass 1968

ARMSTRONG, TIRADOR *Cheyenne/Caddo*

Born 8 May 1935 in Clinton, OK
RESIDENCE: Clinton, OK
MILITARY: U.S. Marine Corps, WWII
EDUCATION: Concho
PUBLISHED: Snodgrass (1968); Dupree (1979)
PUBLIC COLLECTIONS: DAM, HSM/OK
EXHIBITS: AAIE; HSM/OK; PAC; Baltimore, MD
AWARDS: Honorable mentions

ARNAKTAUYOK, GERMAINE *Inuit (Eskimo)*

Born 26 Sept 1946 near Igloolik, NWT, Canada; daughter of Therese Natsiq Tulugatjuk and Isidore Iytok, carvers

RESIDENCE: Frobisher Bay, NWT, Canada

EDUCATION: Schools in Chesterfield, NWT; Churchill and Winnipeg, MB; C/U of MB; commercial art in Ottawa, ON

OCCUPATION: Illustrator, arts and crafts supervisor, publications editor, free-lance artist, designer, and painter

MEDIA: Pen and ink

PUBLISHED: Kappi (1977). *Star Weekly* (Sept 12, 1970); *The Ottawa Citizen* (5 Nov 1970); *The Montréal Star* (30 June 1973); *Northern Peoples* (1976)

BOOKS ILLUSTRATED: Markoosie (1970), Hodgson (1976); Alivatuk, et al. (1976); textbooks and children's books

COMMISSIONS: El Al airline, illustrations for promotional posters, 1973; Dominion Glass, Ltd., drawings for glassware, 1976; National Film Board, stage set

EXHIBITS: C/GNAF; Surry Art Gallery, 1981; Royal Bank, Montréal, PQ; Paris, France

ARNGNA'NEEQ, RUBY (see Angrna'naag, Ruby)

ARNIRNIK (see Oshuitoq, Anirnik)

ARPATU (see Awp, Syollie)

ARQUERO, AVELINO *Cochití*

EDUCATION: Santa Fe, ca. 1938

PUBLISHED: Dunn (1968); Snodgrass (1968)

EXHIBITS: AIW

ARQUERO, DOMINIC *Cochití*

PUBLIC COLLECTIONS: HCC

ARQUERO, SAM *Cochití*

PUBLISHED: Tanner (1973)

ARQUERO, TONITA (see Peña, Tonita)

ARQUETTE, MARY FRANCIS *Mohawk*

Tewahiarita

Born 25 Mar 1962; daughter of Marlene and Francis Arquette; P/GP: Margaret and James Arquette; M/GP: Elizabeth and Mitchell Jacobs

RESIDENCE: Rochester, NY

EDUCATION: Salmon River Central High School, Fort Covington, NY, 1980; Syracuse (NY) University, 1984

OCCUPATION: Student and artist

MEDIA: Oil, acrylic, watercolor, pencil, and pastel

EXHIBITS: AICH; AOSOS; C/WICEC; TFAG

ARROW, FRED, SR. *Yankton Sioux*

RESIDENCE: Wood, SD

EDUCATION: Andes Central High School

PUBLIC COLLECTIONS: Sinte Gleska College, Rosebud, SD

EXHIBITS: RC

ARROW, RAYMOND *Sioux*

Born 1 Jan 1930 at Fort Thompson, SD, on the Crow Creek Reservation

RESIDENCE: Sioux Falls, SD

EDUCATION: Stephan's Indian Mission, Fort Thompson, SD

OCCUPATION: Painter since 1966

MEDIA: Oil
EXHIBITS: SN, SIM
SOLO EXHIBITS: SIM

ARTIST HOPID

"Our group is basically involved with values. We are trying to educate the non-Indian as to what the Hopi is through visual arts. . . . "
Michael Kabotie

Artist Hopid

LOCATION: Second Mesa, Hopi Reservation, AZ

Artist Hopid is a subsidiary of the Hopi ArtsCrafts Cooperative Guild. It was founded May 18, 1973, by Doochsiwukioma (Delbridge Honanie), Dawakema (Milland Lomakema), Lomawyewesa (Michael Kabotie), Honvantewa (Terrance Talaswaima) and Neil David (qq.v.) who had resided on the Hopi mesas most of their lives. Artist Hopid organized numerous exhibits and tours of their work throughout the United States. In addition, they were also available for lectures, poetry readings, and singing at cultural events.

The stated objectives of the organization were to:

1) utilize the artistic talents of the Hopi to instill pride and identity;
2) educate the Hopi, non-Hopi, and the non-Indians to the aesthetic and cultural values of the Hopi;
3) experiment and test new ideas and techniques in art, using traditional Hopi designs and concepts;
4) control their artistic talents and market;
5) research and document Hopi history and events through the visual arts for posterity.

By the 1990s the artists were no longer working as a group.

Arviso, Thomas *Navajo*

A.K.A. Tomás Arviso
EXHIBITS: HM/G, SN

Arviso, Wilber Paul *Navajo*

Born 13 Nov 1964
RESIDENCE: Phoenix, AZ
EDUCATION: Chinle (AZ) High School; CAC/AZ; Maricopa Technical Community College, Phoenix, AZ; ASU
OCCUPATION: Artist
MEDIA: Watercolor
EXHIBITS: ITIC, NTF, SNAICF
AWARDS: ITIC ('86; '87, 1st; '88; '89; '93, 1st); SNAICF ('88, 1st; '87)

SPENCER ASAH

"Asah grew up in an atmosphere of tribal legends and rituals, the influence of which is evident in his paintings. Asah is one of the original Five Kiowas (q.v)."
Snodgrass 1968

Asah, Spencer *Kiowa*

Lallo, Little Boy

Born ca. 1905-1910 near Carnegie, OK; died 1954 in Norman, OK; son of a Buffalo Medicine Man

EDUCATION: St. Patrick's; non-credit classes, U of OK, 1926-1927
OCCUPATION: Farmer, dancer, and painter
MEDIA: Tempera
PUBLISHED: Jacobson (1929); Sloan and LaFarge (1931); Jacobson and d'Ucel (1950); Blue Eagle (1959); Dunn (1968); Snodgrass (1968); Brody (1971); Dockstader (1977); Highwater (1976); Silberman (1978); Boyd et al. (1981); King (1981); Fawcett and Callander (1982); Hoffman, et al. (1984); Samuels (1985); Williams, ed. (1990); Archuleta and Strickland (1991). *Introduction To American Indian Art* (1931); *American Magazine of Art* (Aug 1932); *American Art and Antiques* (Jan/Feb 1979)
COMMISSIONS: *Murals:* Fort Sill; OHSM; U of OK; Riverside; St. Patrick's; Anadarko (OK) Federal Building

PUBLIC COLLECTIONS: ACM, DAM, GM, HM, IACB, IACB/DC, MAI, MKMcNAI, MNA/KHC, MNA, MNM, OSAH/GC, OU/MA, PAC, SPL, WOM
EXHIBITS: AC/A, AIE, AIEC, CSPIP, EITA, HM, IK, MAI, MKMcNAI, NAP, OMA, OU/MA, OU/MA/T, PAC, SMA/TX, SPIM, SV

ASAUTE (see Keahbone, George Campbell)

ASAWOYA (see Davis, Jesse Edwin, II)

ASCENCIO, HARRIET *Acoma*
EXHIBITS: HM/G

ASCENDING (see Abeyta, Narciso Platero)

ASENAP, HOLLIS, JR. *Comanche*
Gray Foot
Born 1947 in Frederick, OK
EDUCATION: Walters (OK) High School; OSU/O; BC; NSU
OCCUPATION: Teacher and artist
COMMISSIONS: Oklahoma road maps, illustrations; *Oklahoma Today*, art work
EXHIBITS: PAC
AWARDS: PAC ('78)

ASH, SAMUEL *Ojibwa*
Born 1951 in Sioux Lookout, ON, Canada; raised by foster parents
EDUCATION: Ontario School for the Deaf, Belleville, ON, 1970
OCCUPATION: Painter since 1974
MEDIA: Acrylic and prints
PUBLISHED: Warner (1975, 1979); Highwater (1980); Menitove, ed. (1986b). *The Beaver* (spring 1977); *The Indian Trader* (July 1978); *Masterkey* (winter 1984)
PUBLIC COLLECTIONS: C/AG/TB; C/CMC; C/INAC; C/MCC; HCC; Government of Ontario
EXHIBITS: C/AG/TB; C/CNAC; RC; Canada House Gallery, London, England; galleries throughout Canada
AWARDS: RC ('78)

SAMUEL ASH

Samuel Ash has overcome many handicaps in order to be an artist. He was born deaf and mute and his mother died when he was born. In spite of this he has learned to read and write in order to communicate. Ash is one of the Algonquin Legend Painters and, as John Anson Warner stated, "His most notable characteristics are an absolutely sure sense of line along with a phenomenal understanding of color."

The Beaver, *spring 1977*

ASHEVAK, KENOJUAK UDLURIAQ AMARO SIAJA (see Kenojuak)

ASHKEWE, DEL H. *Ojibwa*
Born 26 Nov 1947 on Cape Croker Reserve, ON, Canada
RESIDENCE: Canada
EDUCATION: Ryerson Public School, Toronto, ON; Central Technical School, Toronto, ON
OCCUPATION: Commercial artist, teacher, and painter
MEDIA: Tempera
PUBLISHED: Southcott (1984); McMasters, et al. (1993)
BOOKS ILLUSTRATED: Johnson (1978)
PUBLIC COLLECTIONS: C/INAC, C/ROM
EXHIBITS: C/NCCT, C/ROM, C/WICEC, NACLA

DEL H. ASHKEWE

Ashkewe paints the legends and symbols of the Ojibway. His paintings are done in a stylized, geometric style. He considers himself to be a designer more than a painter.

Southcott 1984

ASHKIE, LARRY *Navajo*
Born 9 June 1947; parents and grandparents were Navajo
RESIDENCE: Phoenix, AZ
EDUCATION: Holbrook (AZ) High School, 1967; Grand Canyon College, Phoenix, AZ, 1974; ASU
OCCUPATION: Artist

PUBLIC COLLECTIONS: HCC; Grand Canyon College, Phoenix, AZ

EXHIBITS: CNM; CPS; HM/G; ITIC; LIAS; RC; SNAICF; TM/NE; WTF; South Mountain Festival of Arts, Phoenix, AZ; Sunburst, Scottsdale, AZ; see also Awards

AWARDS: ITIC ('87, 1st); RC ('89, 1st; '94, White Buffalo Award, Rostkowski Award); SNAICF (Buck Sanders Memorial Award); RC ('84, 1st, Begay Award, Aplan Award; '85, 1st; '87; '89, 1st; '90, 1st; '91, 1st, Decker Award, Rostkowski Award); Cave Creek (AZ) Arts and Music Festival

ASHOONA, PITSEOLAK (see Pitseolak)

ASSIGALOOK, JOHN *Inuit (Eskimo)*

Born 1912

RESIDENCE: Povungnituk, PQ, Canada

OCCUPATION: Graphic artist

MEDIA: Pencil

PUBLISHED: Blodgett (n.d.)

PUBLIC COLLECTIONS: C/AG/WP

EXHIBITS: C/LS

ASSINIBOINE, CYRIL *Saulteaux/Ojibwa*

RESIDENCE: Long Plain Reserve, MB, Canada

MEDIA: Acrylic

PUBLISHED: *American Indian Art* (spring 1990)

CYRIL ASSINIBOINE

According to John Anson Warner, Assiniboine is a realist/representational painter whose subjects, in the main, focus upon Plains Indian warriors. Indian dancers are another of his favorite subjects. In some ways his style is reminiscent of American Indian paintings of the Southern Plains.

American Indian Art
spring 1990

ATCHEALAK, DAVIE *Inuit (Eskimo)*

Born 1947

RESIDENCE: Igaluit (Frobisher Bay), NWT, Canada

OCCUPATION: Carver and graphic artist

MEDIA: Pen and ink and soapstone

ATCHISON, CANDACE MARIE *Cowlitz/Salish*

A.K.A. Candy

Born 2 Nov 1946; daughter of Evelyn May Cloque and Robert N. Thompson

RESIDENCE: Union, WA

EDUCATION: Marcus Whitman High School, 1966; Olympic College, Bremerton, WA; art seminars

OCCUPATION: Seamstress and painter

EXHIBITS: RC; Poulsbo (WA) Artfest; North Kitsap Art Show, Leavenworth, WA; see also Awards

AWARDS: Celebration of Western Art, Olympia, WA ('94, Diamond Award); Omak (WA) Stampede Art Show ('94, Artist's Choice Award)

ATEITOQ, SIASI *Inuit (Eskimo)*

A.K.A. Atitu; Siasi Attitu; Siassi Attitu

Born ca. 1896

RESIDENCE: Povungnituk, PQ, Canada

OCCUPATION: Graphic artist

PUBLISHED: Goetz, et al. (1977); Myers, ed. (1980)

EXHIBITS: C/TIP, C/TMBI

ATENCIO, GILBERT BENJAMIN *San Ildefonso*

Wah Peen

Born 1930 in Greeley, CO; died Apr 1995; son of Isabel M. Montoya; nephew of María Martínez

RESIDENCE: Lived in Santa Fe, NM
MILITARY: U.S. Marine Corps
EDUCATION: San Ildefonso, NM; graduated Santa Fe, 1947
OCCUPATION: Medical and technical illustrator, ceramist, and painter
MEDIA: Watercolor and clay
PUBLISHED: Jacobson and d'Ucel (1950); Tanner (1957; 1968; 1973); Carlson (1964); Dunn (1968); Snodgrass (1968); Brody (1971); Silberman (1978); Mahey, et al. (1980); Broder (1981); Fawcett and Callander (1982); Golder (1984); Hoffman, et al. (1984); Seymour (1988); Archuleta and Strickland (1991); Williams (1991); Tryk (1993). *Arizona Highways* (Aug 1952); *Smoke Signals*, IACB (No. 42, 1964); *Southwest Indian Arts II*, CPLH (1965); *Four Winds* (spring 1982)
PUBLIC COLLECTIONS: AF, BIA, DAM, GM, HM, IAIA, IACB/DC, LNBTC, MAI, MHDYMM, MNA, MNM, NPC, PAC, RMC/AZ, SAR, SM
EXHIBITS: AC/HC, ASM, CPLH, FAIEAIP, FWG, HH, HM, IK, ITIC, JGS, LGAM, MFA/A, MFA/O, MKMcNAI, NAP, NGA, OMA, OU/ET, OWE, PAC, PAC/T, PM, RMC/AZ, SFFA, SN, SV, U of OK, USDI, USDS, WRTD
AWARDS: Partial listing includes: HM/G ('72; '73); ITIC (Grand Award); MNM ('62, Rogers Award); NMSF; PAC (Grand Award); SN ('62, 1st; '63, 1st)
HONORS: Governor of San Ildefonso Pueblo, NM, 1966

ATENCIO, JOHN *San Juan*
A.K.A. Juan Atencio
PUBLISHED: Snodgrass (1968)
EXHIBITS: YAIA

ATENCIO, LORENCITA *San Juan*
To Pove
EDUCATION: Santa Fe, NM; studied under Dorothy Dunn
OCCUPATION: Crafts instructor and painter
PUBLISHED: LaFarge (1960); Dunn (1968); Snodgrass (1968); Brody (1971)
PUBLIC COLLECTIONS: WWM
EXHIBITS: AIW, MFA/O, NGA, OU/ET

ATENCIO, PAT *San Ildefonso*
Koo Peen, Mountain Rock
Born 22 Jan 1932; son of Isabel M. Montoya; brother of Gilbert and Tony Atencio (qq.v.)
EDUCATION: Santa Fe, NM
PUBLISHED: Snodgrass (1968)
PUBLIC COLLECTIONS: MAI, MNM, MRFM

ATENCIO, TONY *San Ildefonso*
Su Ta, Painted Arrow
Born 25 Jan 1928; son of Isabel M. Montoya; brother of Gilbert and Pat Atencio (qq.v.)
RESIDENCE: Santa Fe, NM
MILITARY: U.S. Navy
EDUCATION: Through 11th grade, Santa Fe, ca. 1945
PUBLISHED: Snodgrass (1968); Golder (1985)
PUBLIC COLLECTIONS: MIA
EXHIBITS: HH, ITIC, MNM, NMSF

ATITU (see Ateitoq, Siasi)

GILBERT BENJAMIN ATENCIO

"Atencio's strong sense of family and tribal responsibility has resulted in his seldom venturing from his native pueblo. He experimented with adaptations of his flat style paintings."

Snodgrass 1968

The artist believes in the traditional Indian ways and his favorite subjects were ceremonies, ceremonial figures, and scenes from Pueblo life. Much of his inspiration came from stories his aunts told him about their lives. His style varied from the traditional flat style done early in his career, to abstract or semi-abstract paintings done in the 1980s.

LORENCITA ATENCIO

"Until 1950, Atencio was an active artist. Since she has become the mother of several children, she has seldom painted."

Snodgrass 1968

PAT ATENCIO

"Atencio has painted infrequently in recent years. He lives at the pueblo with his six children."

Snodgrass 1968

TONY ATENCIO

"Atencio painted only animals while he was in school. Since then, he has painted very little. Most of his adult life has been spent in the Navy. . . ."

Snodgrass 1968

JAMES AUCHIAH

"Although not officially one of the Five Kiowas, Auchiah joined the group in their special classes at the University of Oklahoma in the fall of 1927."

Snodgrass 1968

"As an elementary student, the artist was once caught drawing and painting, which was not allowed in the Indian schools at that time. As punishment he was required to finish his painting after school and thus, miss supper. Auchiah said he was glad to do so, 'because I would rather paint than eat.'"

Dockstader 1977

ATTAIKI, KEYA *Navajo*

PUBLIC COLLECTIONS: MNA

ATTITU, SIASI (see Ateitoq, Siasi)

AUCHIAH, JAMES *Kiowa*

Born 1906 near where Medicine Park, OK, now stands; died 28 Dec 1974 in Carnegie, OK; son of Mark Auchiah; grandson of Chief Satanta and Red Tipi, medicine man and tribal artist

MILITARY: U.S. Coast Guard, WWII

EDUCATION: St. Patrick's; special non-credit art classes at U of OK

OCCUPATION: Teacher, USDI illustrator, museum curator, and painter

MEDIA: Watercolor

PUBLISHED: Jacobson (1929); Jacobson and d'Ucel (1950); Dunn (1968); Snodgrass (1968); Brody (1971); Highwater (1976); Dockstader (1977); Silberman (1978); Boyd, et al. (1981); King (1981); Fawcett and Callander (1982); Williams (1990); Archuleta and Strickland (1991). *The Art Digest* (1 Sept 1931); *The American Magazine of Art* (Aug 1932); *American Indian Exposition and Congress*, Tulsa (OK) Chamber of Commerce (1937), program cover; *American Indian Art* (spring 1995)

COMMISSIONS: *Murals:* HSM/OK, 1984; Anadarko (OK) Federal Building; St. Patrick's; USDI, 1938

PUBLIC COLLECTIONS: ACM; FSM; GM; HSM/OK; IACB; IACB/DC; MAI; MKMcNAI; MNM; OSAF/GC; OU/MA; PAC; SI; Castillo de San Marcos National Monument, St. Augustine, FL

EXHIBITS: AC/A; AI; ASM; CSPIP; H;, HSM/OK; EITA; MKMcNAI; OMA; OU/ET; OU/MA/T; PAC; PAC/T; SMA/TX; SPIM; SV; throughout the U. S. and abroad

AWARDS: ITIC; Southwest States Indian Art Show, Santa Fe, NM, 1930

HONORS: IACB, Certificate of Appreciation, 1966

AUDLA, ALASSIE *Inuit (Eskimo)*

A.K.A. Alisi Audla; Alassie Audlak; Audla

Born 1935

RESIDENCE: Povungnituk, PQ, Canada

OCCUPATION: Graphic artist

PUBLISHED: Larmour (1967); Goetz, et al. (1977); Myers, ed. (1980)

PUBLIC COLLECTIONS: C/TDB

EXHIBITS: C/TDB, C/TIP, C/TMBI

AUDLAK, ALASSIE (see Audla, Alassie)

AUDRIA (see Loreen-Wulf, Audrea)

AUGER, DALE *(?)*

Born 1958 at Lesser Slave Lake, AB, Canada

RESIDENCE: Calgary, AB, Canada

EDUCATION: Grant MacEwan Community College; C/ACA; C/U of C

OCCUPATION: Painter

MEDIA: Acrylic

PUBLISHED: Cardinal-Shubert (1992)

PUBLIC COLLECTIONS: C/U of C

EXHIBITS: C/OWAO, C/TFD

AUGUSTINE, JIMMIE *Navajo*

PUBLISHED: Snodgrass (1968)

EXHIBITS: SN

AWARDS: SN

AUKEMAH (see García, María; Terasaz, Marian)

AULD, VICTOR S. *Blackfeet*

Born 1943 in Browning, MT; died 1967 in an automobile accident

RESIDENCE: Browning, MT

EDUCATION: Browning (MT) High School

PUBLIC COLLECTIONS: *The Great Falls (MT) Tribune*; First National Bank, Great Falls, MT

EXHIBITS: CIA

AUNKO (see Anko)

AUN SO BEA (see Creepingbear, Mirac)

AUN SO TE (see Belindo, Dennis)

AUPALUKTUK, NANCY PUKINGRNAK (see Pukingnak, Nancy)

AUSTIN, FRANK *Navajo*

Bahah Zhonie, Happy Boy

Born 10 Apr 1938 in Tsegi Canyon, near Tonalea, AZ; son of Martha and Buck Austin

RESIDENCE: Santa Fe, NM

EDUCATION: Phoenix, AZ, 1958; ASU; U of AZ, "Southwestern Indian Art Project," scholarship, four summers

OCCUPATION: Silk screen designer, textile painter, fabric manufacturer and store owner, and painter

MEDIA: Watercolor and prints

PUBLISHED: Snodgrass (1968); Brody (1971); Tanner (1973). *The Denver Post* (4 Feb 1972)

PUBLIC COLLECTIONS: IACB, MAI

EXHIBITS: AIAE/WSU; ASF; ITIC; LGAM; PAC; SN; regional galleries and fairs

AWARDS: Listing includes: SN (Grand Award)

HONORS: American Institute of Interior Designers, International Design Award, 1962

FRANK AUSTIN

"Although he has been interested in art for as long as he can recall, it was in 1954 that Austin, encouraged by Lloyd H. New, began to express himself as a creative artist."

Snodgrass 1968

AUSTIN, SAMUEL *Navajo*

EXHIBITS: HM/G

AWARDS: HM/G ('70)

AUTAUBO, DELORES *Delaware*

EXHIBITS: AIE

AWARDS: AIE ('74; '76; '78, 1st)

AU TUP TA (see Hood, Rance)

AVAALAQIAQ, IRENE *Inuit (Eskimo)*

A.K.A. Avalakiak; Ahvalakiak; Ahvalaquaq; Ahvalaqlaq; Irene Tiktaalaaq Avaalaqiaq; Irene Tiktalaq Avaalaqiaq

Born 1941 at Warton Lake, NWT, Canada

RESIDENCE: Baker Lake, NWT, Canada

OCCUPATION: Craftswoman, sculptor, and graphic artist.

MEDIA: Graphite, colored pencil, fabric, wool yarn, stone, and prints

PUBLISHED: Goetz, et al. (1977); Routledge (1979); Latocki, ed. (1983); Jackson and Nasby (1987). *The Sunday Oklahoman* (24 Oct 1993)

PUBLIC COLLECTIONS: C/AC/MS, C/AG/WP, DAM.

EXHIBITS: C/AC/MS; C/AG/WP; C/CID; C/CMC; C/IA7; C/TIP; Dallas (TX) Museum of Natural History, 1993

AVALAKIAK (see Avaalaqiaq, Irene)

AVRETT, MARTY *Coushatta/Choctaw/Cherokee*

A.K.A. Martin Avrett

Born 26 June 1942 in Dallas, TX

RESIDENCE: Stillwater, OK

EDUCATION: Irving (TX) High School, 1960; U of TX, Arlington; B.F.A./M.F.A., SFAI, 1966/1968.

OCCUPATION: Associate Professor of Art and professional artist

MEDIA: Oil

PUBLISHED: Ward, ed. (1990); Zurko, ed. (1992). *Art Voices South* (Sept/Oct 1980); two publications produced in Lancaster, England

PUBLIC COLLECTIONS: OU/MA; SFAI; *Art in Public Places*, Washington State Arts Commission, Olympia, WA

EXHIBITS: AICA; CWAM; HM; MMA/WA; OCSA; OLO; OS;, SCG; WHB; Norick Art Center, Oklahoma City, OK; Palace of Nations, United Nations, Geneva, Switzerland

SOLO EXHIBITS: CNGM; OAC; OSU/G; Galería San Miguel II, San Miguel de Allende, Guanajuato, Mexico

HONORS: University of Lancaster, England, artist-in-residence, 1973-1974

AWA TSIREH *San Ildefonso*

Awa Tsireh, Cattail Bird

A.K.A. Alfonso Roybal. Signatures: Awatsireh; AwaTsireh; Alfonso Roybal San Ildefonso NM

Born 1 Feb 1898; died May 1955 at San Ildefonso, NM; son of Alfonsita Martínez, potter, and Juan Estebán Roybal; nephew of Crescencio Martínez (q.v.)

EDUCATION: San Ildefonso

OCCUPATION: Farmer, pottery painter, museum employee, painter, and silversmith

MEDIA: Watercolor, transparent colored ink, pencil, silver, and gemstone

PUBLISHED: Sloan and LaFarge (1931); Alexander (1932); Underhill (1944); Jacobson and d'Ucel (1950); Josephy (1961); Dunn (1968); Snodgrass (1968); Tanner (1968; 1973); Brody (1971; 1992); Highwater (1976); Dockstader (1977); Silberman (1978); King (1981); Fawcett and Callander (1982); Hoffman, et al. (1984); Golder (1985); Seymour (1988); Archuleta and Strickland (1991). *International Studio* (Mar 1922; Feb 1930); *American Magazine Of Art* (Sept 1928; Aug 1932); *Travel* (1931); *Exposition of InterTribal Arts, Inc.* (Dec 1921), cover; *Theatre Arts Monthly* (Aug 1983); *Cincinnati Art Museum, Bulletin* (Jan 1938); *Arizona Highways* (Aug 1952); *El Palacio* (1956); *Paintings by American Indians*, CPLH (1962); *Southwestern Art* (Vol. 2, no. 1, 1967); *Southwest Art* (June 1983); *Art-Talk* (Mar 1986)

COMMISSIONS: *Murals:* Maisel's Indian Trading Post, Albuquerque, NM, 1939

PUBLIC COLLECTIONS: AF, BM, BA/AZ, CAM/OH, CGA, CGFA, CIS, CMA, DAM, DCC, IACB/DC, JAM, MAI, MAM, MFA/A, MIM, MMA, MNA/KHC, MNH/A, MNM, MNM/SAR, MRFM, OU/MA, PAC, RM, SAR, SHSW, SI, SM, WOM, WWM

AWA TSIREH

"By 1917, Alice Corbin Henderson had commissioned the artist to execute paintings for her. Later, Awa Tsireh painted daily with Fred Kabotie and Velino Shije Herrera (qq.v.) at the School of American Research. 'Awa Tsireh's drawings are, in their own field, as precise and sophisticated as a Persian miniature. The technique that has produced pottery designs as perfect as those of an Etruscan vase has gone into his training The New York Times, 6 Sept 1925).'

The St. Louis Post Dispatch *of November 5, 1933, quoting John Sloan, said: '. . . when Awa Tsireh sits down to paint a leaping deer he remembers not only the way a deer looks when leaping over a log but he feels himself leaping in the dance, with antlers swaying on his forehead and two sticks braced in his hands for forelegs.'*

*Later, he turned, for a time, to silversmithing and various jobs unrelated to art. 'Because of his poor eyesight, shaky hands, and other personal reasons, this famous artist abandoned painting almost completely, although there continued to be a demand for his work (*El Palacio, *Aug 1950).'"*

Snodgrass 1968

Awa Tsireh painted in three different styles; a simple realism, a combination of symbolism and realism, and a completely non-realistic style.

Samuels 1985

EXHIBITS: AC/A; ACC; ASM; EITA; FAC/CS; HH; HM; IK; JAM; JGS; LGAM; MAM; MFA/O; NAP; NGA; OMA; OU/ET; PAC; PM; SI; SV; WRTD; WWM; Newberry Library, Chicago, IL, 1925; Society of Independent Artists, New York, NY, ca. 1918, entered by John Sloan

SOLO EXHIBITS: National Museum, Hall of Ethnology, Memorial Exhibition, 1955

AWARDS: AIW; EITA ('31, 1st, publication cover); SWAIA

HONORS: French Government, Palmes d'Académiques, 1954

AWP, SYOLLIE *Inuit (Eskimo)*

A.K.A. Arpatu; Sajuili Arpatu; Syollie Arpatu; Syollie Arpatuk; Syollie Amituk, Syollie Arpatuk Ammitu; Amitook; Ammitu; Amittu

Born 1936; died 1986

RESIDENCE: Lived in Povungnituk, PQ, Canada

OCCUPATION: Graphic artist

MEDIA: Draws on stone

PUBLISHED: Goetz, et al. (1977); Myers, ed. (1980). *Arts West* (Vol. 3, no. 5, 1978)

EXHIBITS: C/TIP, C/TMBI

A WUSH (see Bird, JoAnne)

AYAC, ALOYSIUS *Eskimo*

Born ca. 1927 on King Island, AK; died 1969 in Seattle, WA

RESIDENCE: Lived in Alaska

OCCUPATION: Employee of Leonard F. Porter, Inc., Seattle, WA

PUBLISHED: Ray (1969)

AYAWAT, WILLIAM *Comanche*

PUBLISHED: Snodgrass (1968)

PUBLIC COLLECTIONS: Castillo de San Marcos National Monument, St. Augustine, FL

EXHIBITS: BPG

WILLIAM AYAWAT

"The artist was among the 72 Plains Indians taken as prisoners from Fort Sill, OK, to Fort Marion, FL, in 1875."

Snodgrass 1968

AYEK, SYLVESTER *Eskimo*

Born ca. 1940 on King Island, AK

RESIDENCE: Anchorage, AK

EDUCATION: U of AK; Alaska Methodist University

OCCUPATION: Sculptor, dancer, mask maker, teacher, and printmaker

MEDIA: Wood, mixed-media, stone, ivory, and prints

PUBLISHED: New (1981); Larsen and Dickey (1982); Steinbright (1986). *Alaskan Journal* (fall 1971); *The Tundra Time* (18 Sept 1978); *Sunset Magazine* (Mar 1981); *Journal of Alaska Native Arts* (Mar/Apr 1988)

PUBLIC COLLECTIONS: AFNA, IACB, U of AK

EXHIBITS: AFNA; AICA/SF; MFA/AH; NACLA; U of AK/M; Institute of Alaska Native Arts, Fairbanks, AK; All-Alaska Juried Show, Anchorage, AK

SOLO EXHIBITS: MFA/AH

HONORS: Arctic Winter Games, guest artist, 1974; Visual Arts Center of Alaska, Sculptor-in-Residence, 1974

AYRES, SONJA KAYE *Cherokee*

RESIDENCE: Muldrow, OK

Born 26 May 1946 at Fort Smith, AR; daughter of Roxi Edna Vaughn and Leonard Alfred Jennings; P/GP: Lorena and John O. Jennings; M/GP: Roxi Lena and Alfred Lee Vaughn

EDUCATION: McFarland (CA) High School, 1965; Bakersfield (CA) Junior College

OCCUPATION: Artist

MEDIA: Pastel, pencil, and clay

PUBLIC COLLECTIONS: Partial listing of more than 15 coporate and public collections includes: HCC; Contel Telephone Company, Boron, CA; Muldrow (OK) City Hall; St. Jude's Hospital, Memphis, TN; Sparks Regional Medical Center, Fort Smith, AR; and in AR, CA, OK, SD, and TN

EXHIBITS: CHASC; CNM; FCTM; KCPA; RC; SI; WTF; Old Fort River Festival, Fort Smith, AR; see also Awards

SOLO EXHIBITS: Partial listing includes: FCTM; Fort Smith (AR) Art Center; Fort Smith (AR) Library;

AWARDS: CHASC ('93, 1st); CNM ('84, 1st; '88, 1st; '94, 1st); FCTM ('86; '88, IH; '92; '93); RC ('90, Woodard Award); Carl Albert Junior College, Shawnee, OK ('87); Crawford County Art Association Art Festival ('85, 1st); Ozark Native Art Show, Winslow, AR ('84, Best Exhibit)

AZITTAUNA (see Olanna, Melvin)

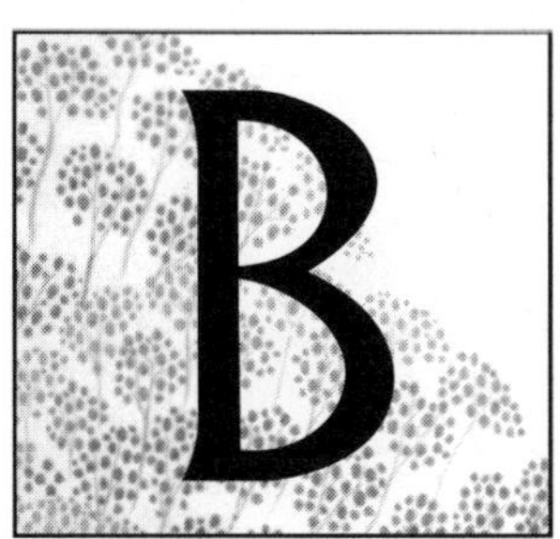

Baatasoslanii (see Joe, Eugene)

Baby (see Collins, Adele)

Baca, Henry *Santa Clara*

Oku-Wa-Tsa

a.k.a. Joe Tafoya; Oku-Wa-Tsa

Birth date unknown; death date unknown

published: Snodgrass (1968)

public collections: MNA

exhibits: MNA, MNM (dated 1936)

Baca, Lorenzo *Isleta/Mescalero Apache*

a.k.a. Lorenzo

Born 9 Sept 1947 in Morenci, AZ

residence: Sonora, CA

education: San Pedro (CA) High School, 1966; Harbor Junior College, Wilmington, CA, 1969; B.A., CSU/LB, 1972; CSU/T, 1974: NCC, 1974 (silversmithing)

occupation: Teacher, counselor, consultant, actor, poet, sculptor, photographer, illustrator, silversmith, and painter

media: Oil, acrylic, watercolor, pen and ink, silver, gemstone, and prints

public collections: HM; Tuolumne County Library, Sonora, CA

exhibits: CNM; CVCP; HM/G; IAIA; MNH/LA; MNH/LA; NACLA; NU/BC; RC; Scottsdale (AZ) Community College

awards: HM/G ('79, Judge's Choice)

honors: *Fellowships and Grants:* California State University, Stanislaus, CA, Graduate Fellowship; UCLA, American Indian Studies Graduate Fellowship; UCLA, Institute of American Cultures Grant; NEA, Folk Arts Division Grant. *Other:* California Arts Council, artist-in-residence

Backford, Alexandra *Aleut*

Birth date unknown; born in Alaska

education: IAIA, ca. 1954

published: Snodgrass (1968)

public collections: IACB

exhibits: FAIEAIP, MNM

awards: MNM

Back Track (see Geionety, George)

Bad Hand Boy (see Claymore, Thomas William)

Bad Heart Buffalo (see Bad Heart Bull, Amos)

Bad Heart Bull, Amos *Oglala Sioux*

Tatanka Cante Sice, Bad Heart Buffalo

a.k.a. Eagle Lance; Amos Bad Heart Buffalo Bull

Born ca. 1869; died 1913; son of Tatanka Cante Sice (Bad Heart Buffalo), Oglala warrior and participant in the Battle of Little Big Horn; nephew of He Dog, Sioux chief

occupation: Cowboy, Indian policeman, tribal historian, and artist

media: Graphite pencil and colored pencil

published: Alexander (1938); Jacobson and d'Ucel (1950); Josephy (1961a); Sandoz (1961); Dunn (1968); Snodgrass (1968); Brody (1971); Irvine, ed. (1974); Dockstader (1977); Highwater (1978b)

Amos Bad Heart Bull

"From the stories told him by his father and uncle, the artist filled three army ledgers with detailed pictographic drawings of the Battle of the Little Big Horn (at the time of the battle, he was seven). Alexander (1938) wrote that this artist was the 'most notable northern Indian artist whose work is known.'"

Snodgrass 1968

From 1890-1913 Bad Heart Bull drew over 400 pictures and wrote thousands of words of captions in his role as tribal historian. It was his duty to compile a narrative of important events in tribal activity; in addition, he recorded everyday events.

Dockstader 1977

detail: Harrison Begay, *Washing Hair*, 1949. Philbrook Museum of Art, Tulsa, Oklahoma

BOOKS ILLUSTRATED: *A Pictographic History of the Oglala Sioux* (1967)
PUBLIC COLLECTIONS: The University of Nebraska Press, Lincoln, NE

BAD HEART BULL, VINCENT *Oglala Sioux*
Hoshila Waste, Good Boy
Born 1926 in Oglala, SD, on the Pine Ridge Reservation; descendant of Amos Bad Heart Bull (q.v.), creator of an Oglala pictographic history
MEDIA: Oil
PUBLISHED: Libhart (1970)
BOOKS ILLUSTRATED: Blish (1967)
PUBLIC COLLECTIONS: IACB, HCC
EXHIBITS: CPS, SIM

BADONIE, THOMAS *Navajo*
EDUCATION: U of AZ, "Southwestern Indian Art Project," scholarship, summer 1961
PUBLISHED: Snodgrass (1968)

BAGSHAW-TINDEL, MARGARETE *Coushatta/Choctaw/Cherokee*
Birth date unknown; born in Albuquerque, NM
EDUCATION: U of NM
OCCUPATION: Artist
MEDIA: Mixed-media
PUBLISHED: Zurko, ed. (1992)
EXHIBITS: CWAM, NMFA, NMSF, IPCC, WHB

BAHA ZHONIE (see Austin, Frank)

BAHE, STANLEY K. *Navajo*
Born ca. 1935
EDUCATION: Phoenix
PUBLISHED: Snodgrass (1968); Brody (1971). *Arizona Highways* (July 1956)
EXHIBITS: ASF, PAC
AWARDS: ASF ('53, 1st)

BAHEE, KEE, JR. *Navajo*
Born 6 Sept 1962; son of Moretta Keams and Kee Bahee Sr.
RESIDENCE: Flagstaff, AZ
EDUCATION: L. D. Bell High School, Flagstaff, AZ, 1982; IAIA, 1983; NEC, 1990; Scottsdale (AZ) Artists' School
OCCUPATION: Sculptor and painter
MEDIA: All media including stone and bronze
PUBLISHED: *Art-Talk* (Mar 1991)
EXHIBITS: ITIC, MNA, SNAICF
AWARDS: Partial listing of more than 17 includes: SNAICF ('88, 2-1st, Woodard Award); Best of Shows
HONORS: National Honor Society, three scholarships

BAHNIMPTEWA, CLIFF *Hopi*
Born ca. 1937 in Old Oraibi, Third Mesa, AZ; died 26 Nov 1984
RESIDENCE: Lived at Old Oraibi, AZ
EDUCATION: Phoenix
OCCUPATION: Plasterer, sheet-metal worker, builder, *katsina* carver, and painter
MEDIA: Watercolor, tempera, and cottonwood root

CLIFF BAHNIMPTEWA

At the suggestion of Don Hoel, an Oak Creek Indian trader, and with his encouragement, the artist in 1968 started painting the katsinas *catalogued by Dr. Harold S. Colton in* Hopi Kachina Dolls. *Bahnimptewa's grandfather was chief of the Hopi village of Old Oraibi and his mother was chief in 1971, and thus he brought to his work a strong background in the Hopi religion. By 1971, he had produced 300 separate* katsina *portraits. Don Hoel introduced Dr. and Mrs. Dean Nichols to the Bahnimptewa* Katsinas, *and they purchased each painting as it was completed.*

PUBLISHED: Tanner (1973; 1987). *The Phoenix Gazette* (11 Jan 1971); *The Indian Trader* (May 1985); *Heard Museum Newsletter* (Jan/Feb 1991)

BOOKS ILLUSTRATED: Bahnimptewa (1971); Wright (1983); Forty-eight paintings of *katsinas* included in *Dancing Kachinas,* The Heard Museum (1971)

COMMISSIONS: Dr. and Mrs. Dean Nichols, series of three hundred *katsina* portraits, completed in 1970

PUBLIC COLLECTIONS: BA/AZ, CGPS, HCC, HM

EXHIBITS: CGPS, HM

BAILEY, SHARON K. *Cherokee*

Born 5 Sept 1938; daughter of La Vonne and James Redman; P/GF: Clarence Redman; M/GF: Adam Rehm

RESIDENCE: Clark, MA

EDUCATION: Alden (IA) High School, 1956

OCCUPATION: Artist

MEDIA: Oil and prints

PUBLIC COLLECTIONS: OTM

EXHIBITS: CNM

BAIRD, REBECCA *Métis/Cree*

A.K.A. Rebecca Gloria Jean Baird

Born Oct 1954 in Edmonton, AB, Canada

RESIDENCE: Canada

OCCUPATION: Installation artist and film producer

MEDIA: Mixed-media

PUBLISHED: Greenfield (1984); Menitove, ed. (1986). *Vanguard* (Sept 1983)

PUBLIC COLLECTIONS: C/AG/TB; galleries in Toronto, ON

EXHIBITS: C/ACA, C/AG/TB, HM

SOLO EXHIBITS: Eight in galleries in Toronto, ON

HONORS: *Grants:* Canada Council, three, 1983, 1984, 1986; Ontario Arts Council, 1983

REBECCA BAIRD

Baird's Cree heritage and the American Southwest are sources of inspiration for her art work.

BAJE (see Whitethorne, Baje, Sr.)

BAKER, GARY KEITH *Cherokee*

RESIDENCE: Tallahassee, FL

EDUCATION: North Brantford (CT) High School; B.A., U of CT; Southern Connecticut State College, New Haven, CT; Florida State University, Tallahassee

OCCUPATION: Educator and artist

EXHIBITS: RC; Creative Arts Workshop Show, New Haven, CT; Faculty Art Show, Bridgeport, CT; Southern Connecticut University Traveling Show, 1973; Southern Center for Contemporary Art, Winston-Salem, NC

BAKER, JOE *Delaware*

Born 14 Jan 1946 in Bartlesville, OK; son of J. R. Baker; P/GF: James Harland Baker: M/GP; Stella and Roy Wright; M/GGM: Lillie Whiteturkey

RESIDENCE: Phoenix, AZ

MILITARY: U.S. Air Force, Vietnam

EDUCATION: Dewey (OK) High School, 1964; OSU; U of KS; U of AR/LR; B.F.A./M.F.A., U of Tulsa, 1968/1978

OCCUPATION: Illustrator, artist-in-residence, commercial artist, museum staff artist, graphic designer, lecturer, art instructor, art professor, poet, and painter

MEDIA: Oil, mixed-media, and prints

JOE BAKER

Although Baker's earliest paintings were photorealistic, in the 1980s he turned to Abstract Expressionism. He says that at this point he discovered he could "paint for me." His paintings are of dogs, cats, horses, and people, done with humor, satire, and social commentary. They are colorful interpretations of contemporary western life.

Arizona Arts and Lifestyle *winter 1982*

PUBLISHED: Britton (1981); Hoffman, et al. (1984). *The Arizona Republic* (11 Feb 1981; 18 Mar 1982); *Arizona Arts and Lifestyle* (autumn 1981; winter 1982); Art Voices (Sept/Oct 1981); *The Scottsdale Daily Progress* (27 Nov 1981; 9 Apr 1982); *Art News* (Dec 1981); *Artspace* (fall 1983); *The Phoenix Gazette* (Oct 1983); *The Santa Fean* (Dec 1984); *Art-Talk* (Aug/Sept 1985; Jan 1987); *The Tulsa World* (23 Jan 1994)

PUBLIC COLLECTIONS: ABQM; ARC; CMB; FAC/CS; HM; MMA/NY; MNM; PAM/AZ; SI; U of Tulsa; U of WI/G; VNB; Chase Manhattan Bank, New York, NY; Goddard Museum; Indianapolis (IN) Museum of Art

EXHIBITS: Partial listing of more than sixty includes: ABQM; AC/Y; BM/B; CGA; FAC/CS; IK; LAICAF; MFA/O; PAC; S; SCA; SFMA; SM; SWSE; TMA/AZ; U of TULSA; Cayuga Museum, Auburn, NY; Long Beach (CA) Museum of Art; Centro de Arte Moderno de Guadalajara, Mexico; galleries throughout the U.S. and Europe

SOLO EXHIBITS: Partial listing of 26 includes: FAC/CS; HM; Mt. Holyoke Museum, South Hadley, MA; East Central University, Ada, OK; Louisiana State University, Shreveport, LA; galleries in AZ, CO, ID, MA, MN, NY, and Berlin, Germany

BALDWIN, ELVA *Cherokee*

RESIDENCE: Meridian, ID

EDUCATION: Franklin (ID) High School

EXHIBITS: FCTM, RC

BALES, JEAN *Iowa*

A.K.A. Jean Myers Bales; Jean Elaine Myers Bales

Born 25 Dec 1946 in Pawnee, OK; daughter of Lydia and T. S. Myers; P/GP: Grace and Espy Myers; M/GP: Kate and Jack Lincoln

RESIDENCE: Tahlequah, OK

EDUCATION: Chickasha (OK) High School, 1965; B.A., OCLA, 1969; Institute de San Miguel Allende, Guanajuato, Mexico

OCCUPATION: Teacher, lecturer, research consultant, poet, ceramist, sculptor; professional artist since 1970

MEDIA: Acrylic, pastel, bronze, clay, and prints

PUBLISHED: Samuels (1982). *Arizona Art and Lifestyle* (spring 1980); *Southwest Art* (Apr 1981); *The Indian Trader* (July 1978, Dec 1984); *Oklahoma Today* (July-Aug 1985); *High Plains Literary Review* (spring/fall 1988); *Lefthander Magazine* (Sept/Oct 1988); *Indian Market* (1991); *The Tahlequah Daily Press* (8 May 1991)

COMMISSIONS: Robert Comstock (Boise, ID), clothing designer, textile designs, 1990

PUBLIC COLLECTIONS: HM; HCC; HSM/OK; ITIC; MNH/D; MNA; OAC; OCSA; USDI; The Vatican, Rome, Italy; The World Bank; Museum of the Western Prarie, university and college collections in AZ, CA, and OK

EXHIBITS: CAI/KC; CNM; CW; DE; HM; HSM/OK; IAF; ITIC; MCC/CA; MFA/AK; MIF; MM/NJ; MNH/D; OAC; OCSA; OHT; PAC; RC; RE; SDCC; SDMM; SFFA; SN; SPIM; SWAIA; TIAF; WWM; Hunter Museum, Chattanooga, TN; Museum of the Western Prairie, Altus, OK; Nicholausen Art Museum, Casper, WY; United States Senate and House of Representatives, Washington, D.C.; galleries in AK, AZ, CO, OK, and NM; see also Awards

SOLO EXHIBITS: SPIM, 1974

AWARDS: Partial listing of more than one hundred includes: ACS/ENP ('75, 2-1st, '77, 2-1st, Best of Show; '79, 1st); AIE('73, 1st; '74, 1st); CNM ('80; '82; '83, 1st; '84, Best of Category, Tiger Award; '85, 1st; '86, 1st; '87, 1st; '88, 1st; '89, 1st;

JEAN BALES

The artist's paintings depict the culture and the everyday life of the Plains Indian. The life, religion, and culture of these people are important to her. Bales is one of only 243 Iowa Indians left on the tribal roles. Her mother is one of only 24 that are full-blood.

'91); CIM ('86, Best of Category; '87); IACA ('84, Artist of the Year); HM/G ('77, 1st; '78; '79, 1st); ITIC ('76, 1st; '79); OT ('83, 1st; '84, 1st, Best of Class; '85, 1st; '86; '87, 1st; '88, 2-1st; '89, 2-1st); PAC ('74); RE ('87, 1st); TIAF ('88; '89, 1st); RC ('75; '76, Begay Award; '89); RE ('87, 1st); SN ('74); SHM; SWAIA ('78, 1st; '79, 1st, Best of Division, Best of Class; '80, 2-1st; '83, 1st; '84; '85; '87; '88; '89, 1st; '91; '94, Helen Hardin Award); Comanche Cultural Center Indian Art Exhibition ('77, 2-1st)

HONORS: Oklahoma Governor's Cup for Outstanding Indian Artist of the Year, 1973; Oklahoma Diamond Jubilee, Outstanding Woman of the Southern Plains, 1982; Indian Arts and Crafts Association, Artist of the Year, 1984; Citation from the State of Oklahoma House of Representatives for exceptional abilities and bringing recognition to State of Oklahoma, 1984

BALES, JEAN MYERS (see Bales, Jean E.)

BALL, LOIS HARJO *Creek*

Birth date unknown; born in Okmulgee, OK; GF: Menawa, Creek chief and warrior; maternally related to the Paddy Carr family, an historic Creek family;

EDUCATION: Okmulgee (OK) High School, 1926; OCU; A.A., Stephens College, Columbia, MO; private study under Minta B. Walker

PUBLISHED: Snodgrass (1968)

PUBLIC COLLECTIONS: CCHM

BALLARD, LOUIS WAYNE *Quapaw/Cherokee*

Honganoshe (or *Honganozhe*), Grand Eagle

Born 8 July 1931 in Quapaw, OK; son of Leona Quapaw and Charles G. Ballard; M/GM: Newakis Quapaw, interpreter for the Quapaw Indian Agency; raised by Newakis Quapaw

RESIDENCE: Santa Fe, NM

EDUCATION: BC, 1949; A.A., NSU, 1951; U of OK, 1950; B.A. and B. Mus. Ed., 1954, M.M., 1962, U of Tulsa; Darius Milhaud School of Music, Aspen, CO, 1963

OCCUPATION: Music teacher, composer, draftsman, illustrator, educator, and artist

PUBLISHED: Snodgrass (1968). *Twin Territories* (Year of the Indian Edition 1992)

PUBLIC COLLECTIONS: EOC, KM, PAC, U of OK

EXHIBITS: AIE, BC, NAMC, PAC

HONORS: F. B. Parriott Graduate Fellowship, 1961; United States Department of State and Jelmoli, Inc., lecture tour of Switzerland, 1964

LOUIS WAYNE BALLARD

"Although active in the visual arts early in his career, Ballard's primary interest now is confined to music."

Snodgrass 1968

BALLOUE, JOHN *Cherokee*

Born 19 Apr 1948 in Richmond, CA; son of Judy and Mayburn Leo Balloue; P/GP: Maggie Dawning and James Balloue

RESIDENCE: Hayward, CA

MILITARY: Vietnam

EDUCATION: John F. Kennedy High School, Fremont, CA, 1966; Ohlone College, Fremont, CA; Chabot College, Hayward, CA; B.F.A., CSU/H, 1975

OCCUPATION: Musician, waiter, and artist

MEDIA: Oil, watercolor, pencil, pen and ink, and prints

PUBLISHED: *The Indian Trader* (Nov 1991); biographical publications

PUBLIC COLLECTIONS: SPIM; USDI; Indian Centers in San Jose, Oakland, and Livermore, CA

EXHIBITS: Partial listing of more than forty includes: CID; CNM; IACA; ITIC; KCPA; PAC; RC; SJBIM; Triton Museum, Santa Clara, CA; Lodi (CA) Art Fair; Hayward (CA) Festival of the Arts; see also Awards

SOLO EXHIBITS: Redwood City (CA) Law Library

JOHN BALLOUE

According to the artist, "I have worked with many different media and styles over the years in an attempt to evolve as an artist. As my life changes so goes my art." He describes his art in this way, "I try to capture the spirit of ceremonies and individuals, and feel I am helping to sustain the lively traditions of Native Americans."

artist, p.c. 1990

AWARDS: CID (1st); CNM ('83, 1st); IACA ('93); ITIC ('86); SJBIM (3-1st, Best of Show); Fremont HUB Show ('76, 1st); San Luis Obispo (CA) Native American Art Exhibition (1991, Best of Show)

HONORS: IACA, Artist of the Year, 1992

BAÑAGAS, SAMUEL S. *Luiseño/Cahuilla*

A.K.A. Samuel Salgado Bañagas

Born 13 May 1953 in Downey, CA; son of Consuelo and Brijido M. Bañagas

RESIDENCE: Whittier, CA

EDUCATION: Excelsior High School, Norwalk, CA, 1971; CSU/F

OCCUPATION: Petroleum production inspector and painter

MEDIA: Watercolor, charcoal, pencil, and prints

PUBLIC COLLECTIONS: MNA; SNM; BIA Health Center, Wewoka, OK

EXHIBITS: CIM; CNM; GPWAS; HM/G; ITIC; RE; SDMM; SJBIM; TFA; Fall Roundup of Western Art, Tustin, CA; see also Awards

AWARDS: CIM; SJBIM ('87, 1st; '88, 1st; '89, 1st); Western Impression, Indio, CA ('88)

BANKS, KEN *Diegueño*

EDUCATION: M.A., U of C/B

OCCUPATION: Painter

MEDIA: Paint on ceramics

PUBLISHED: *Native Vision* (Nov/Dec 1985); *Phoenix Magazine* (Sept 1989)

EXHIBITS: AC/T; AICA/SF; FSMCIAF; Pacific States Crafts Fair, San Francisco, CA

BANTISTA, RUDY *Kiowa*

RESIDENCE: Anadarko, OK

EXHIBITS: AIE

AWARDS: AIE ('77, 1st; '78; '88)

BAPTISTE, RAY *Saulteaux*

RESIDENCE: Long Plain Reserve, MB, Canada

OCCUPATION: Graphic artist and painter

MEDIA: Watercolor

PUBLISHED: *American Indian Art* (spring 1990)

RAY BAPTISTE

Refusing to be limited to one style, Baptiste uses eight different styles or approaches in doing his paintings.

BARBOUR, JEANNIE *Chickasaw*

RESIDENCE: Wilson, OK

EXHIBITS: BB, LIAS, RE

AWARDS: RE ('91, '94)

BARK DYE (see Moses, James Kivetoruk)

BARNES, MARJORIE *Mohawk*

Born 7 Jan 1957

RESIDENCE: Hogansburg, NY

EDUCATION: Salmon River Central School; City College of New York, NY, 1975-1977; St. Lawrence University, Canton, NY, 1977-1979

OCCUPATION: Teacher, ceramist, sculptor, photographer, and painter

MEDIA: Acrylic, pen and ink, pencil, and clay

PUBLISHED: Johannsen and Ferguson, eds. (1983)

BOOKS ILLUSTRATED: Publications for: North American Indian Traveling College, Cornwall, ON, Canada; Upward Bound Program, Operation Ka Nenka Haka, The Native American Organization, and The Black Student Union, all at St. Lawrence University, Canton, NY

MARJORIE BARNES

Using Iroquois symbols or drawing from traditional Iroquois stories to execute her somewhat abstract paintings, Barnes concentrates on clean sharp lines and blocks of color.

Johannsen and Ferguson, eds. 1983

EXHIBITS: Cazenovia (NY) College; St. Lawrence University, Canton, NY

BARNEY, NATHANIEL C. *Shoshoni*

Born 1951 in Lander, WY

RESIDENCE: Fort Washakie, WY

MEDIA: Oil, watercolor, pastel, pen and ink, and pencil

EXHIBITS: CIA; MPI; local exhibits

BARNOSKIE, CHEBON *Creek/Seminole/Cherokee*

Born 9 May 1967 in Tahlequah, OK; son of Shirley Anne Lena and Hayden Lee Barnoskie; P/GP: Lou Anne and Barney Barnoskie; M/GP: Stella and Walter Lena

RESIDENCE: Tahlequah, OK

EDUCATION: Muskogee (OK) High School, 1985; A.A., BC, 1987; studied under Dick West (q.v.) at Bacone

MEDIA: Oil, pencil, and prints

EXHIBITS: CNM; FCTM; see also Awards

AWARDS: CNM ('89, 1st); Bacone (OK) College Spring Art Show ('87, 1st, Best of Show)

BARRY, C. H. (see Horsechief, Barry)

BARTON, BURTON *Navajo*

PUBLIC COLLECTIONS: MNA

BARTOW, R. E. *Yurok*

A.K.A. Rick Bartow

Born 16 Dec 1946 in Newport, OR; son of Richard Bartow; P/GF: John Bartow

RESIDENCE: South Beach, OR

MILITARY: U.S. Army, Vietnam

EDUCATION: B.S., Western State College, Monmouth, OR, 1969; Graduate Study, 1971

OCCUPATION: Teacher and artist

MEDIA: Acrylic, pastel, graphite, and mixed-media

PUBLISHED: Adams, Hass, and Lopez (1979); Banks (1986); Longfish, et al. (1987); Archuleta and Strickland (1991); Roberts, ed. (1992). *Fedora* (1980-1982); *Native Vision* (Nov/Dec 1985; May/June 1986; Sept/Oct 1986; Jan/Feb 1987); *Oregon Magazine* (Feb/Mar 1987; Mar/Apr 1988); *Shaman's Drum* (summer 1988); *North Dakota Quarterly* (1985); *America West* (July 1990); *The Indian Trader* (Dec 1992)

PUBLIC COLLECTIONS: PAM, WSAC

EXHIBITS: AICA/SF; AICH; CNGM; HM; MMA/WA; MMM; MPM/CA; NCGM; NDN; OCV; OGC; PAM; PNCA; SAM; SCG; SI; SMA/OR; SS/CW; SV; TPAS; TYAC; Craft and Folk Art Museum, San Francisco, CA; Oregon Artist's Show, Portland, OR; Seattle (WA) Center House; see also Awards

SOLO/SPECIAL EXHIBITS: AICA; ESC (dual show); SCG; Sun Valley (ID) Center for Arts and Humanities; Seattle (WA) Arts Festival; galleries in NY, OR, and WA

AWARDS: SI; National Geographic Society, Washington, D.C.; Newport (OR) Jazz and Art Festival; Oregon Coast Council for the Arts; Washington State Arts Commission

HONORS: *Fellowships:* Brandywine Visiting Artist, Philadelphia PA; Oregon Arts Commission, Portland, OR. *Other:* Washington State Arts Commission, Art in Public Places, painting selected, 1985; Seattle Art Museum, PONCHO, Betty Bowen Special Recognition Award, 1990

R. E. BARTOW

Although Bartow was interested in art when he was six, he began his transformation into an artist in 1979. He drew furiously in an effort to draw out and exorcise the demons of Vietnam and alcohol. He spent several years drawing heavy black graphite images on old newsprint. As he healed, his work began to include color. Although his images are often troubling, communication is Bartow's goal, not shock.

Shaman's Drum, *summer 1988*

BARTOW, RICK (see Bartow, R.E.)

BATES, SARA P. *Cherokee*

Born 10 Dec 1944 in Muskogee, OK

EDUCATION: B.A., California State University, Bakersfield, 1986; M.F.A., U of CA/SB, 1989

HONORS: *Scholarships:* California State University, Bakersfield, Dorian Scholarship, 1986; Regent's Scholarship, 1987. *Other:* Cherokee Nation, Tahlequah, OK, artist-in-residence, 1988-1990; California State University, Bakersfield, Dorian Society member

BATISTE, FRANCIS *Métis*

Sis-Hu-Lk

A.K.A. Signatures: F. Batiste; Sis-Hu-Lk

Born 6 Dec 1920

RESIDENCE: British Columbia, Canada

EDUCATION: Inkameep Residential School, near Oliver, BC; Santa Fe

OCCUPATION: Printmaker and painter

MEDIA: Watercolor

PUBLISHED: *Who's Who in Northwest Art* (1941); *European Review of Native American Studies* (Vol. 5, no. 1)

BOOKS ILLUSTRATED: Anonymous (1941); *The Tale of the Nativity* (1945)

COMMISSIONS: Union Library, Kelowna, BC, frieze

PUBLIC COLLECTIONS: C/RBCM, British Columbia Provincial Archives; League of Red Cross Societies, Paris, France

EXHIBITS: Guildhall, London, England, 1936-1939; Cizek Studio, Vienna, 1937; Junior Red Cross Headquarters, Paris, France, 1937 and Prague, Czechoslovkia, 1938; National Gallery, Ottawa, 1937; U of AB, 1939; Glasgow Empire Fair, Glasgow, Scotland; see also Awards

AWARDS: Royal Drawing Society, London, England (1936-38, first class honors, Silver Star, two Bronze Stars)

HONORS: Royal Drawing Society, London, England, painting selected for an exhibit

FRANCIS BATISTE

When Batiste attended Inkameep, the British Columbia Society for the Furtherance of Indian Arts and Crafts was active in reintroducing the children in the residential schools to their Indian heritage and he was encouraged to paint Native subjects. For some unexplained reason, even before he attended Santa Fe, his early paintings reflected the contemporary style of the American Southwest.

Deidre Simmons, p.c. 1992

BATTESE, STANLEY *Navajo*

Kehdoyah, Follower

Born 29 Jan 1936 at Fort Defiance, AZ; son of Gee Eh Bah and Charlie Smith; adoptive parents, Josephine Bruner and Anthony Battese

RESIDENCE: Gallup, NM

EDUCATION: St. Michaels (AZ) Catholic High School, 1956; B.A., ASU, 1961; studied under Martha Kenney, Gallup, NM

OCCUPATION: Arts and crafts teacher, warehouse employee, carpenter, welder, Navajo Tribal Utilities Authority employee, and painter

MEDIA: Watercolor

PUBLISHED: Tanner (1957; 1973); Carlson (1964); Snodgrass(1968); Brody (1971); Samuels (1985). *Arizona Highways* (July 1956)

COMMISSIONS: *Murals:* ASU, Hayden Hall and TKE Fraternity House

PUBLIC COLLECTIONS: RMC/AZ

EXHIBITS: GCIC; ITIC; MNM/T; RMC/AZ; LGAM; NTF; PAC; VNB; Concord (MA) Art Association; Daughters of the American Revolution Exhibit, Greenwich, CT; Riverside (CA) Art Center; National High School Art Exhibit, Carnegie Institute, Pittsburgh, PA

AWARDS: Nineteen awards, 1952-1957

STANLEY BATTESE

"Battese began painting at an early age and made remarkable progress during his school years. Since his university graduation, however, he appears to have lost interest in painting and exhibiting."

Snodgrass 1968

BATTIEST, LARRY DEAN *Choctaw*

Born 7 Oct 1953 in Antlers, OK; son of Catherine Williams and Abner Battiest Jr.; P/GP: Lena Simpson and Abner Battiest Sr.; M/GP: Annie Cusher and Raphey Williams

RESIDENCE: Bernalillo, NM

MILITARY: U.S. Army, Vietnam

EDUCATION: Hugo (OK) High School, 1972; BC

OCCUPATION: Artist

MEDIA: Acrylic and prints

EXHIBITS: FCTM, TIAF, PAC

AWARDS: FCTM ('77, 1st)

BATTLES, ASA *Choctaw*

A.K.A. Asa Louis Battles

Born 12 Aug 1923 in Buckeye, AZ; son of Ada and Ira Battles

RESIDENCE: Littleton, CO

MILITARY: U.S. Army, WWII

EDUCATION: Buckeye (AZ) High School, 1941

OCCUPATION: Ranch-hand and artist

MEDIA: Oil, acrylic, watercolor, pencil, pen and ink, and scratchboard

PUBLISHED: Highwater (1980). *Colorado Art Show News* (Jan1976); *Diverson Magazine* (June 1977); *Western Heritage Art Fair Directory* (1977); *The Independent* (May 30, 1978); *Cricket Magazine* (Jan 1979; Feb 1979; Mar 1979; Apr 1979); *Americas* (Aug 1981); *Rocky Mountain Visual Arts Directory*(1981); *Colorado Art Index* (1982-1984); biographical publications

BOOKS ILLUSTRATED: Highwater (1975; 1977; 1978a; 1978b; 1980)

COMMISSIONS: *Paintings:* National Parks Service, two paintings for traveling exhibit

PUBLIC COLLECTIONS: HCC; SIM; Denver (CO) Public Library; U of WI Indian Museum; Pratt (KS) Community College

EXHIBITS: Partial listing of more than sixty includes: BM/CO; CNM; FHG; FCTM; GPWAS; GWWAS; HCAI; LSS; MNAC; MNH/D; PAC; PPW; RC; SIM; TC, WH; WT; WTF; Medicine Lodge (KS) Professional Western Art Show; White Horse Indian Market, Boulder, CO; see also Awards

SOLO EXHIBITS: SIM

AWARDS: CNM ('82); BM/CO ('78; '79, 3-1st); FCTM ('82); FHG ('76, 1st, Best of Show); GPWAS ('76, Silver Medal); HCAI ('77, 1st); PAC ('78, 1st); WH ('79, Bronze Medal); WT ('77, Gold Medal); Mayor's Bicentennial Exhibition ('76, Best of Category, Best of Show)

HONORS: Colville Confederated Tribes, honorary membership; Nez Percé, Chief Joseph Band, honorary Chieftainship

ASA BATTLES

Although he works in many media, Battles is best known for his scratchboard drawings. In a scratchboard drawing, India ink is used to coat a sheet of scratchboard. Various instruments are then used to "scratch" or etch the drawings. Creating a picture this way is an exacting, painstaking, time-consuming process. Asa has been widely recognized for the authenticity and accuracy of his art.

artist, p.c. 1992

BAXTER, TERRY LEE *Omaha*

Born 21 Apr 1963

RESIDENCE: Macy, NE

EDUCATION: Macy (NE) High School

MEDIA: Oil

EXHIBITS: CIM; RC; Wayne State Exhibition, Detroit, MI; see also Awards

AWARDS: CIM; Pender Art Exhibition

BEACH, DIANA (see Hudgens-Beach, Diana)

BEAM, CARL EDWARD *Ojibwa*

Born 1943 in West Bay, Manitoulin Island, ON, Canada; son of Barbara and Edward Cooper

RESIDENCE: Peterborough, ON, Canada

EDUCATION: Kootenay School of Art; B.F.A., University ofVictoria, BC, 1975; graduate studies, C/U of AB

OCCUPATION: Construction worker, millwright assistant, logger, ironworker, high-rise construction, sawmill worker, artist-in-residence, printmaker, ceramist; full-time artist since 1976

MEDIA: Acrylic, watercolor, pen and ink, mixed-media, clay, and prints

PUBLISHED: Amerson, ed. (1981); McLuhan (1984); Southcott (1984); Menitove, ed.(1986b); McMasters, et al. (1993). *Native Perspective* (Vol. 3, no. 2, 1978); *The Kitchener-Waterloo Record* (May 13, 1981); *Artlines* (Jan 1982); *The Chronicle Journal* (16 Oct 1984); *Santa Fe New Mexican* (10 June 1984); *Masterkey* (winter 1984); *Artpost* (Aug/Sept 1985), *Parchute* (Nov 1985); *Canadian Art* (winter 1985; winter 1986); *The Globe and Mail* (5 June 1986); *Windspeaker* (12 Dec 1986); *Ottawa Citizen* (10 Feb 1990; 20 Sept 1991); *Artscraft* (summer 1990); *C Magazine* (fall 1991); *American Indian Art* (autumn 1992)

COMMISSIONS: Thunder Bay National Exhibition Center and Center for Indian Art, Thunder Bay, multimedia construction

PUBLIC COLLECTIONS: C/AG/H; C/AG/TB; C/CMC; C/I; C/INAC; C/GOAC; C/LUM; C/MCC; C/NGCA; C/OCF; C/WICEC; CTC; HM; City of Buffalo; City of Rovelstoke, BC; City of Sudbury, ON; Wilfred Laurier University, Waterloo, ON; New College, University of Toronto (ON); more than 38 corporate collections

EXHIBITS: Partial listing of more than seventy includes: AICH; C/AC/AE; C/ACCCNA; C/AG/TB, C/AG/TT; C/AG/V; C/CIIA; C/CMC; C/ECC; C/I; C/NGCA; C/NNEC; C/OCF; C/U of R/MG; C/WICEC; CTC; HM; IAIA; NACLA; SM; U of NM; United Nations Building, New York, NY; University of Toronto (ON)

SOLO EXHIBITIONS: Partial listing includes: C/AC/AE; C/AG/LUM; C/AG/TB; C/MCA; C/MCC; C/WICCI; U of NM/MM; De Meervaart Cultural Centre, Amsterdam, Netherlands

HONORS: Canada Council, Artist's Grand Award, 1984; Artspace, Peterborough, ON, artist-in-residence, 1988

BEAR (see Robinson, John)

BEAR, J. MICHAEL (see Byrnes, James Michael)

BEAR, JAMES (see Byrnes, James Michael)

BEAR, JOBIE (see Byrnes, James Michael)

BEAR, SHIRLEY *Maliseet*

Birth date unknown; born on the Tobique Reserve, NB, Canada

RESIDENCE: Perth, NB, Canada

EDUCATION: Art classes, Whistler House Gallery and Boston Museum

OCCUPATION: Activist for Native women's rights, political lobbyist, artist in residence, exhibits curator, and painter

MEDIA: Oil, acrylic, conté, and prints

PUBLISHED: *Arts Atlantic* (winter 1989)

PUBLIC COLLECTIONS: C/CMC, C/NAC, C/NBAB

EXHIBITS: Gallery Principal, Altos De Chavon, Dominican Republic, 1988; Regent Gallery, Fredericton, NB, 1989; Saw Gallery, ON, 1989

SHIRLEY BEAR

Because of a dedicated concern for Native Women's rights, Bear's art has taken second place to her work as an activist and feminist. Her paintings are intentionally feminine because she believes that it is important "to tell the women's story." They often superimpose Maliseet stories and myths against petroglyphs found in the New Brunswick region.

exhibition catalog C/AG/MSVU, 1990

SOLO EXHIBITS: C/AG/MSVU; galleries in Ottawa and New Brunswick, ON

HONORS: Ford Foundation Scholarship, 1969; Canada Council Grant, 1983

BEAR, SHONA *Creek*

RESIDENCE: Santa Fe, NM

EDUCATION: OSU/O; IAIA; Studied under Will Sampson (q.v.) and Roy Archikado

OCCUPATION: Clothing designer, poet, silversmith, sculptor, and painter

EXHIBITS: TWF

BEAR CLAW (see Byrnes, James Michael)

BEARCLOUD (see Berry, Rod Bearcloud)

BEARD, LORENZO *Cheyenne/Arapaho*

HORSE CHIEF

Born 1914

RESIDENCE: Watonga, OK

EDUCATION: Concho; graduated Santa Fe

PUBLISHED: LaFarge (1956); Dunn (1968); Snodgrass (1968). *The Bulletin of The Cleveland Museum of Art* (Jan 1982)

PUBLIC COLLECTIONS: CMA, IACB/DC, OU/MA, SM

EXHIBITS: AIEC, CMA, NGA, OU/ET, OU/MA/T

BEARDEN, MATTHEW *Potawatomi/Blackfeet*

RESIDENCE: Hominy, OK

Born 9 June 1969 in Hominy, OK; son of Mary Bruno and Burt Bearden; P/GP: Vida and Con Bearden; M/GP: Irene and John Bruno

EDUCATION: Hominy (OK) High School, 1987; B.A., NSU, 1992; IAIA, 1993

OCCUPATION: Oil field supply company employee and painter

MEDIA: Acrylic, pencil, and pen and ink

COMMISSIONS: Granny's Attic, Tahlequah, OK, logo; Charlie Mitchell Restaurants, Broken Arrow and Tulsa, OK, menu covers

EXHIBITS: CNM; TIAF; Mohawk Park Powwow, Tulsa, OK

BEARDY, JACKSON *Cree/Saulteaux/Ojibwa*

Born 24 July 1944 on Garden Hill Reserve, Island Lake, MB, Canada; died 1984 in Winnipeg, MB, Canada

RESIDENCE: Lived at Island Lake, MB, Canada

EDUCATION: Technical Vocational School, Winnipeg, MB, 1963-1964; C/U of MB, 1966

OCCUPATION: Commercial artist, laborer, band councilor, teacher, writer, photographer, college lecturer, museum field researcher, and painter

MEDIA: Oil, acrylic, tempera, and prints

PUBLISHED: Dickason (1972); Johnston (1976), cover; Hughes (1979); Highwater (1980); Menitove and Danford, ed. (1989); Podedworny (1989); McMasters, et al. (1993). *Indian News* (Apr 1968; June 1977); *The Beaver (Vol. 300, 1969); Mosaic* (spring 1970)*; Artscanada* (autumn 1972)*; The Native Perspective* (Vol. 1, no. 1, 1975; Vol. 3, no. 2, 1978); *Artsmagazine* (Oct/Nov 1977); *Arts Manitoba* (Vol. 1, no. 1, 1977); *Winnipeg Free Press* (23 May 1978; 12 Dec 1984); *American Indian Art* (Vol. 3, no. 3, 1978; spring 1990); *Canadian Dimensions* (Vol. 12, no. 6, 1979); *Native Arts/West* (Sept 1980); *Arts West* (Sept 1982); *The Canadian Journal of Native Studies* (Vol. 4, no. 1, 1983), cover; *Ottawa Citizen* (11 Dec 1984); *Masterkey* (winter 1984); *Canadian Encyclopedia* (1988)

BOOKS ILLUSTRATED: Morgan (1974)

JACKSON BEARDY

Beardy was considered one of the leaders of the Algonquin Legend Painting School (also called the Woodlands School of Art) which was founded by Norval Morrisseau in the 1960s. His vibrant acrylic paintings were highly stylized with an emphasis on design. The subject matter came from Cree legends and stories, many of which were related to him by his grandmother. He painted actively from 1970 to 1984.

American Indian Art
spring 1990

COMMISSIONS: *Murals:* C/MMMN; C/INAC; St. John's College, U of MB. *Paintings:* Province of Manitoba, for presentation to Queen Elizabeth II; City of Winnipeg, for presentation to the Governor General Edward Schreyer; International Association for the History of Religion, for presentation to the Crown Prince of Japan. *Other:* Winnipeg Women's O.R.T; City of Winnipeg, coin design; C/INAC, book illustrations of Northern Manitoba legends

PUBLIC COLLECTIONS: C/CCAB; C/CMC; C/GM; C/INAC; C/MCC; C/MMMN; C/ROM; C/SCC; C/SFG; Crown Prince of Japan; Mother Theresa's Hospital, Calcutta, India; Supreme Court of Canada, Ottawa, ON; Windsor Castle, London, England

EXHIBITS: C/AC/P; C/AG/WP; C/AG/TB; C/CIARH; C/CIIA; C/CNAC; C/GM; C/LTAT; C/NAC; C/ROM; C/TU; C/U of R/MG; C/WCAA; C/WICEC; Expo '67, Montréal, PQ; Manitou Citizens' Bursary Fund for Native Peoples Show, Winnipeg, MB; galleries in Canada, England, Germany, and Holland

SOLO EXHIBITS: Partial listing of more than 17 includes: C/NAC; C/RBC; C/U of W; Gallery Antropos, London, England; Merritt College, Oakland, CA; United College, Winnipeg, MB

HONORS: Canadian Centennial Award, 1967; Young Achiever's Award, 1974; Canada Council Grant, 1982; Outstanding Young Manitoban Award, 1982; elected a member of his Band Council; Board of Directors of Manitoba Arts Council

BEAR FEATHERS (see Bushyhead, Allan)

BEAR ROBE *Cheyenne*

A.K.A. Signature: Thomas B. Robe

MILITARY: U.S. Army

EDUCATION: Carlisle

OCCUPATION: Scout and painter

PUBLISHED: *American Indian Art* (winter 1992)

PUBLIC COLLECTIONS: SI/OAA

BEAR ROBE

Bear Robe was one of fifty Cheyenne and twenty Arapaho men who were recruited to serve as scouts at Fort Reno, Indian Territory, in 1985. Their duties were to police the reservation and to support the military and agency staff in peacekeeping.

American Indian Art *winter 1992*

BEAR RUNNER, HAROLD *Oglala Sioux*

RESIDENCE: Porcupine, SD

EDUCATION: Tucson (AZ) Indian School; Mankato (MN) Senior High; BHSU; RVSA

MEDIA: Oil, acrylic, watercolor, tempera, crayon, pastel, and charcoal

EXHIBITS: RC, RVSA

AWARDS: RC, RVSA

BEAR'S ARM, MARTIN *Mandan*

Loc-pitz-he-á-lish, Bear's Arm

PUBLISHED: Snodgrass (1968); Maurer (1992)

PUBLIC COLLECTIONS: HS/ND

EXHIBITS: VP

MARTIN BEAR'S ARM

"Bear's Arm, considered a tribal historian, executed a picto-graphic chart on heavy canvas long before the late 1890s. The drawings represent the Like-a-Fish-Hook Village on the Fort Berthold Reservation in central North Dakota."

Snodgrass 1968

BEAR'S HEART, JAMES *Cheyenne*

Nockkoist

A.K.A. Nah-Koh-Hist

Born 1851; died 25 Jan 1882 in Darlington, Indian Territory

EDUCATION: Hampton

OCCUPATION: Warrior, carpenter, wagon driver, farmer, and artist

PUBLISHED: Dunn (1968); Snodgrass (1968); Supree (1977); Dockstader (1977); Fawcett and Callander (1982); Hoffman, et al. (1984); Highwater (1986).

JAMES BEAR'S HEART

"The artist was among the 72 Plains Indians taken as prisoners from Fort Sill, OK, to Fort Marion, St. Augustine, FL in 1875."

Snodgrass 1968

National Museum of Canada, Bulletin No. 163 (Ottawa); *Tamaqua* (winter/spring 1991); *Native Peoples* (summer 1993)

PUBLIC COLLECTIONS: HI, HS/MA, IK, MAI, USNM/OA, YU/BRBML

EXHIBITS: BPG, WWM

BEAR SHIELD (see Russell, Harvey)

BEATIEN YAZZ *Navajo*

Beatien Yazz, Little No Shirt

A.K.A. Jimmy Toddy

Born 5 Mar 1928 near Wide Ruins, AZ; son of Desbah and Joe Toddy

RESIDENCE: Wide Ruins, AZ

MILITARY: U.S. Marine Corps, Code Talker, WWII

EDUCATION: Santa Fe; Fort Wingate; Mills, 1949, under Yasuo Kuniyoshi; CAI

OCCUPATION: Navajo Police Dept. (Fort Defiance, AZ), Carson Indian School art teacher, illustrator, and professional painter

MEDIA: Oil, acrylic, casein, tempera, pencil, pen and ink, pastel, and prints

PUBLISHED: Hannum (1945; 1958); Jacobson and d'Ucel (1950); Tanner (1957; 1968; 1973); Carlson, et al. (1964); Snodgrass (1968); Brody (1971); Highwater (1978b); Silberman (1978); Broder (1981); King (1981); Fawcett and Callander (1982); Wagner and Brody (1983); Samuels (1985); Seymour (1988); Archuleta and Strickland (1991); *Tryk* (1993). *The Gallup Independent* (May 14, 1953); *Arizona Highways* (July 1956; Dec 1958; July 1959); *New Mexico* (1960); *Amerindian* (May/June 1961); *Plateau* (Vol. 54, no. 1, 1982); *The Indian Trader* (Sept 1985; Mar 1990; July 1990); *The Arizona Republic* (Sept 6, 1991; Aug 1993)

BOOKS ILLUSTRATED: Hannum (1945; 1958); Steiner (1961)

COMMISSIONS: *Murals:* Navajo Tribal Court Room, Navajo Police Headquarters Building, Fort Defiance, AZ. *Other:* Gila Pottery Designs, tile designs; Tumble-weed Prints, fabric designs; several designs reproduced on greeting cards

PUBLIC COLLECTIONS: BM; DAM; GM; HCC; IACB/DC; ITIC; LMA/BC; MAI; MNA/KHC; PAC; RMC/AZ; SAR; SDMM; SMNAI; SM; WOM; WWM; Bern Museum, Switzerland; Southeast Museum (FL)

EXHIBITS: AAIE; AC/A; AC/HC; AC/RM; AIAE/WSU; ASM; BG; CAI; DAM; EM; FAIEAIP; FWG; HM; ITIC; JGS; LGAM; MAI; MNM; MFA/O, MFA/D; MHDYMM; MIF; MNH/CI; NGA; OMA; PAC; PAC/T; PM; RC; RMC/AZ; SAIEAIP; SN; SV; WRTD; WTF; WWM; Riverside (CA) Museum of Art; Cleveland Museum of Art, Cleveland, OH; Santa Barbara (CA) Museum of Art; Illinois State Museum, Springfield, IL

SOLO EXHIBITS: BG; HM; SM; La Jolla (CA) Gallery of Art

AWARDS: HM/G ('78, 1st); ITIC ('68; '70, 1st; '72; '76; '79; '82, 1st, Elkus Award; 85; '86; '87); PAC ('69; '71; '72); RC ('76, 1st, Woodard Award)

HONORS: Mills College, Oakland, CA, scholarship; named a "Living Legend" by Ralph Oliver, 1990

BEAUDRY, HENRY *Plains Cree*

Born 1921 west of North Battleford, SK, Canada, on Poundmaker's Reserve; GGF: Poundmaker, Plains Cree Chief

RESIDENCE: Canada

MILITARY: Armed Forces of Canada, WWII, prisoner of war

EDUCATION: Indian Residential School, Delmas, SK, Canada

OCCUPATION: Railroad worker; painter after 1958

MEDIA: Acrylic

PUBLISHED: *The Indian Trader* (Apr 1979)

BEATIEN YAZZ

The artist was drawing with crayons at eight years of age. Sallie and Bill Lippincott, operators of the Wide Ruins Trading Post, influenced him most by recognizing and encouraging his talents. While still a student, he sometimes worked in oils from a model. Today, Beatien Yazz prefers to paint 'animals and people, not landscapes' in the casein medium.

Snodgrass 1968

Beatien Yazz stated that he had been, "Painting since 8, a long career in art that spanned over a 50 year period. I established myself nationally and internationally. In addition to my three oldest sons, Irving, Marvin, and Calvin (qq.v.), I have three other children entering in the field of art: my daughter, Frances Toddy (q.v.), who has been painting since she was ten, Jimmy Jr., and Orland Toddy. They are 11 thru 22 years of age."

artist, p.c. 1991

In recent years the artist's eyesight has deteriorated and he has only peripheral vision. According to his long-time friend, Sallie Lippincott Wagner, he has glaucoma and it has progressed too far to be treatable. He continues to paint but only in a limited way.

Wagner, p.c. 1991

PUBLIC COLLECTIONS: HCC

EXHIBITS: C/AG/TB; C/TU; C/U of T; RC; Assiniboin Gallery Limited, Regina, SK

SOLO EXHIBITS: Royal Canadian Mounted Police Museum

BEAUTIFUL *(see Susunkewa, Manfred)*

BEAUVAIS, JOSEPH *Mohawk*

Kanawarenton

Born 6 Apr 1922 ; death date unknown

OCCUPATION: Construction worker and artist

MEDIA: Oil, acrylic, and wood

PUBLISHED: Johannsen and Ferguson, eds. (1983)

EXHIBITS: Benefit for Retarded Children, Stuart Hall, Point Claire, PQ

BEAVER *(see Hawk, Jonny)*

BEAVER, AMOS *Cheyenne*

Born 16 June 1952 in Clinton, OK; son of Pauline Whiteturtle and Amos Malcom Beaver

RESIDENCE: Clinton, OK

EDUCATION: Pryor (OK) High School

OCCUPATION: Mechanic, roofer, laborer, free-lance artist, and painter

MEDIA: Oil, watercolor, pencil, pastel, pen and ink, and mixed-media

EXHIBITS: RE; galleries in Oklahoma

BEAVER, FRED *Creek*

Eka La Nee, Brown Head

Born 2 July 1911 in Eufaula, OK; died 18 Aug 1980 in Muskogee, OK; son of Annie Johnson and Willie Beaver; GF: Itshaus Micco, subchief of Okfuskee town group in Alabama, who moved his people to what is now Eufaula, OK

MILITARY: U.S. Air Force, WWII in Italy

EDUCATION: Eufaula (OK) High School, 1931; BC, 1931; Haskell, 1935; private instruction in art and voice, Italy, 1944

OCCUPATION: Clerk, interpreter, B.I.A. Indian Field Service; full-time artist after 1960

MEDIA: Gouache and prints

PUBLISHED: Snodgrass (1968); Milton, ed. (1969); Broder (1981); Dunn (1968); Highwater (1976); Pierson and Davidson (1960); Seabourn (1976); Highwater (1978b); Silberman (1978); Mahey, et al. (1980); King (1981); Fawcett and Calander (1982), Hoffman, et al. (1984); Samuels (1985); Archuleta and Strickland (1991); Ballantine and Ballantine (1993). *Newsweek* (4 Sept 1950); *American Indian Exposition Program Booklet* (1956); *Museum News* (June 1962); *The Sunday Oklahoman, Orbit Magazine* (10 May 1964; 23 Jan 1966); *The Record-Register* (7 Oct 1965); *The Daily Ardmoreite* (7 Sept 1969; 6 Sept 1970); Algoma (WI) *Record-Herald* (22 Aug 1973); *The Indian Trader* (Sept 1974; July 1978); *The Tulsa World* (20 Aug 1980; 22 Feb 1981); *Lake Eufaula World* (27 Nov 1980); *Twin Territories* (Year of the Indian Edition 1992)

BOOKS ILLUSTRATED: Gregory and Strickland (1971)

COMMISSIONS: *Murals:* Thunderbird Restaurant and Motel, Oklahoma City, OK; Seminole Arts and Crafts Center, West Hollywood, FL; restored Acee Blue Eagle mural, Coalgate (OK) Post Office, 1965. *Paintings:* State of Oklahoma, painting for Governor's Art Gallery; Oklahoma Republican Committee, gift to President Eisenhower. *Other:* Franklin Mint, three medallions for Bicentennial Celebration, 1976

HENRY BEAUDRY

During World War II Beaudry was captured by German troops in Italy and held as a prisoner of war in Germany. His suffering during this period led to chronic bronchitis. After the war he went to work for the Canadian National Railways but had to retire due to his health problems. He began to paint about the time of his retirement in 1958, initially as a hobby. Beaudry's paintings are usually simple and straight-forward. One of the founders of the narrative tradition in Canadian Native art, his subject matter is the historical culture of the Cree in the nineteenth century, and religious themes.

The Indian Trader, *Apr 1979*

JOSEPH BEAUVAIS

The artist was a construction worker who began painting about 10 years before his death. Beauvais was in an accident which left him completely paralyzed. In spite of the fact that his injuries were so severe that he spent 18 years in a hospital, he taught himself to paint. He painted detailed landscapes, sea scenes, and still-lifes.

Johannsen and Ferguson, eds. 1983

PUBLIC COLLECTIONS: AC/RM; BIA; CGPS; DAM; EM; FCTM; GM; HCC; IACB; KM; MAI; MNA; NPS; OSAC; PAC; WOM; Hotel Lawtonka, Ardmore, OK; Carnegie Library, Ardmore, OK; Ardmore (OK) Sanitarium; Stephen A. Foster Memorial, White Springs, FL

EXHIBITS: Partial listing includes: AAID, AC/A, AC/HC, AIE, ASM, BC/McG, BNIAS, CIAI, DAM, FAIEAIP, HM, HSM/OK, HPTU, IK, ITIC, JAM, KCAHM, LGAM, MFA/O, MHDYMM, MKMcNAI, MNM, NAP, OMA, PABAS, PAC, PAC/T, PBS, PM, SN, SPIM, SV, SWAIA, USDS, U of WV, WTF; Kewaunee (WI) County Museum; every major Indian art competition; group shows in Europe and the Americas

SOLO/SPECIAL EXHIBITS: Partial listing of more than 19 includes: DAM; FCTM; GM (dual show); JAM; PAC; SPIM

AWARDS: Partial listing includes: AAID ('68); ITIC ('68, 1st); FCTM ('67, 1st; '68, IH; '70; '72, 1st, Grand Award; '73, IH); FCTM/M ('78, IH); HM/G ('69; '71); PAC ('69; '70; '71; '72; '73, Painting Award; '79, Wolf Robe Hunt Award); SWAIA ('70, 1st; '73, 1st; '78); and from every major Indian art competition

HONORS: FCTM, Designated a Master Artist, 1973; Outstanding Oklahoman of the year (1976); Outstanding Indian of the Year (1979); McIntosh County (OK)) Historical Society honored him, 1980; McIntosh County (OK) Distinguished Citizen Award, 1980; PAC, Waite Phillips Trophy Award; FTCM dedicated its third Master's Exhibition in his memory

BEAVER, RICK *Ojibwa*

Born 1948 at Rice Lake, ON, Canada, on the Alderville Indian Reserve

RESIDENCE: Victoria, BC, Canada

EDUCATION: B.S., U of G, 1973; M.S., U of AB, 1980

OCCUPATION: Wildlife biologist, writer, photographer; full-time painter since 1981

MEDIA: Acrylic, gouache, and prints

PUBLISHED: *The Edmonton Journal* (10 Aug 1979; 13 Aug 1979; 4 May 1985); *Dimensions Magazine* (Vol. 9, no. 2, 1981); *Canada Journal* (Sept 1983); *The Peterborough Examiner* (1 Apr 1986; 9 Jan 1987); *Villagers* (Dec 1986; Nov 1987); *The Calgary Herald* (25 Feb 1987; 23 Jan 1988); *The Port Hope Evening Guide* (21 Aug 1987)

COMMISSIONS: *Paintings:* Village Aid, painting for poster; Public Service Commission, painting for calendar. *Other:* Shadow Puppet Theatre, Edmonton, AB, 1980

PUBLIC COLLECTIONS: Partial listing of more than 35 corporate and public collections includes: C/CCC/CL; C/CMC; C/HBCC; C/INAC; U of T; U of WON; Alderville First Nation, Alderville Indian Band, ON; Department of Tourism and Renewable Resources, Regina, SK; Edmonton (AB) Symphony Orchestra; Northern Canada Power Commission, Edmonton, AB; Public Service Commission of Canada, Toronto, ON; Western Canada Wilderness Committee, Victoria, BC; Wildlife Game Branch (M.O.E), Victoria, BC; World University Services of Canada, Toronto, ON

EXHIBITS: Partial listing of more than 14 includes: C/ACCCNA; C/AG/W; C/INAC; C/OCA; C/NCCT; C/NLNA; C/U of G; C/WICEC; SM; Blue Heron Art Festival, Hastings, ON; Buckhorn (ON) Wildlife Art Festival; Corbyville (ON) Art Festival; N'Amerind Art Fair, London, ON; Rideau Valley Art Festival, Westport, ON

SOLO EXHIBITS: More than 14 in galleries in AB, ON, and SK

BEAVON, DAPHNE ODJIG (see Odjig, Daphne)

BEBAMINOJMAT (see Bell, Leland)

FRED BEAVER

"At first interested in music and athletics, Beaver began to paint as a hobby in 1945. Since then, he has achieved a distinguished record."

Snodgrass 1968

Although employed full time with the Bureau of Indian Affairs, by painting at night Beaver was able to enter and receive awards in every major Indian art competition. In 1960 he retired from the Indian Field Service to devote full time to his art. Of Creek descent, Beaver is best known for his paintings of Seminole life. When asked why he painted the Seminoles he said that he wanted to be different.

exhibition catalog, GM, Mar 1981

RICK BEAVER

Rick Beaver's paintings reflect the influence of two wildlife biology degrees and his concern for the environment. His work is known for its brilliant colors and abstract flowing shapes.

BECENTI, ROBERT *Navajo*

Born 13 Jan 1949 in Rohoboth, NM

RESIDENCE: Crownpoint, NM

EDUCATION: Gallup (NM) High School, 1969; CAI

MEDIA: Oil and casein

PUBLISHED: Jacka and Jacka (1994)

EXHIBITIONS: ACS/SW, HM/G, ITIC, NMSF, OT, SFFA, SWAIA; see also Awards

AWARDS: ACS/SW ('73; '74, 1st; '75, 1st, Grand Award); ITIC ('74; '75; '76, 1st; '79, 1st; '89, 1st; '93, 1st); MNSF ('73; '74, 1st; '74, Best of Show; '76, 1st); SWAIA ('76; '78, 1st); Rio Grande Arts and Craft Show, Albuquerque, NM ('76, 1st)

BECK, CLIFFORD *Navajo*

A.K.A. Clifford Beck Jr.

Born 11 Jan 1946 in Keams Canyon, AZ; son of Esther Yellowhair, weaver, and Clifford Beck, tribal councilman for more than twenty years

RESIDENCE: Flagstaff, AZ

EDUCATION: Flagstaff (AZ) High School, 1963; B.F.A., CCAC, 1968; U of N AZ, 1974-1975

OCCUPATION: Illustrator, photographer, educator, high school art department director; full-time artist since 1979

MEDIA: Oil and pastel

PUBLISHED: Jacka and Jacka (1988; 1994); Tanner (1973); Snodgrass (1968). *Navajo Times* (9 Sept 1965); *Exxon Magazine* (Mar 1975); *Four Winds* (autumn 1980); *Oklahoma Art Gallery* (summer 1981); *Arizona Arts and Travel Magazine* (Aug 1981); *Arizona Arts and Lifestyles* (autumn 1981); *Showcase USA* (fall 1982); *Plateau* (Vol. 54, no. 1, 1982); *Southwest Art* (Mar 1984; Nov 1994); *Art-Talk* (Mar 1985); *Southwest Profile* (Mar/Apr 1986; May/June 1990); *The Indian Trader* (July 1986; June 1989; June 1990); *American Indian Art* (winter 1987); *Southwest Profile* (May/June 1990)

BOOKS ILLUSTRATED: Hoffman (1974a)

PUBLIC COLLECTIONS: HCC, MNA

EXHIBITS: AC/K; AIAF; CIM; FAC/CS; FSMCIAF; HM; HM/G; HM/VA; HS/AI; ITIC; KF; MNA; NACG; NCC; NM Highlands U; NMSF; NTF; OIO; PSA; PSA/T; RC; SCA; SDMM; SFFA; SI; SM; SN; SWAIA; TM; U of NM; United Bay Area Art Festival, Oakland, CA; The Finnish Film Institute, Helsinki, Finland

SOLO/SPECIAL EXHIBITS: AC/K; CG; NCC; NM Highlands U; NMSU; NTM; Berkeley, CA, 1965 (dual show); galleries in AZ, CA, CO, FL, and NJ

AWARDS: HM/G ('70, 1st; '72, 1st; '73, 1st; '74, 1st, Best of Show, Avery Award, Woodard Award; '79, 2-1st, Judge's Choice; '80, 1st); ITIC ('76; '79, 2-1st); NMSF ('80, 1st); OIO ('79, 1st, Best of Show); MNA ('89, 1st); NTF (6 Awards); RC ('77; '79, 1st, Begay Award); SN ('70; '71; '75, 2-1st); SWAIA ('80; '83, 1st; '92, Best of Division; '93, 1st)

HONORS: Navajo Tribe Scholarship, four years, 1964-1968; U of N AZ, Dean's List, 1975

BECK, CLIFFORD, JR. (see Beck, Clifford)

BECKMAN, MARY THOMPSON *Onondaga*

Jostwi

A.K.A. Mary Thompson Bowers Beckman

Born 18 Feb 1917 in Onondaga Nation, NY; daughter of Alice and Howard Beckman; P/GP: Mallisa and John Beckman; M/GP: Charlotte Laffort and Mr. Johnson

RESIDENCE: Nedrow, NY

EDUCATION: Roosevelt School, Syracuse, NY, 1956; Cayuga Museum, 1956; studied painting under Professor Long at Cayuga Museum

OCCUPATION: Seamstress, crafts instructor, consultant, and artist; has painted very little since 1969

MEDIA: Oil, acrylic, watercolor, pencil, pen and ink, charcoal, pastel, beads, porcupine quill, leather, felt, and polished stone

PUBLISHED: Johannsen and Ferguson, eds. (1983). *Syracuse Post Standard*

PUBLIC COLLECTIONS: Everson Museum, Syracuse, NY; Tyller Hall, Oswego State University; Syracuse University

EXHIBITS: ACS/EM; CAOR; Roberson Center for the Arts and Sciences, Binghamton, NY; Everson Museum, Syracuse, NY

MARY THOMPSON BECKMAN

Beckman is a multi-talented artist. In addition to her success as a painter she has received recognition for her writing and musical compositions.

artist, p.c. 1992

BEDAH, TIMOTHY *Navajo*

Born 4 Oct 1945 in Tohatchi, NM

RESIDENCE: Tohatchi, NM

EDUCATION: Gallup (NM) High School, 1965

PUBLISHED: Snodgrass (1968). *The Indian Trader* (Sept 1982)

EXHIBITS: ITIC; Gallup (NM) Community Indian Center

AWARDS: ITIC

TIMOTHY BEDAH

"Listed as a promising student by Duane O. Berg, his art instructor, Bedah has been painting since 1960."

Snodgrass 1968

BEDONIE, GILBERT *Navajo*

RESIDENCE: Shonto, AZ

EDUCATION: Richfield High School

EXHIBITS: RC

BEDONNI QUID (see Maulson, Gerald)

BEE'DIT'LO (see King, James B.)

BEELER, JOE *Cherokee*

Born 25 Dec 1931 in Joplin, MO; son of Lena Setser and Jack Beeler

RESIDENCE: Sedona, AZ

MILITARY: U.S. Army, Korea

EDUCATION: Joplin (MO) High School; LAACS; U of Tulsa; B.F.A., KSC; Art Center School, Los Angeles, CA, one year; studied under Alexandre Hogue

OCCUPATION: Writer, illustrator, sculptor, and painter

MEDIA: Oil, watercolor, pencil, charcoal, clay, bronze, and prints

PUBLISHED: Snodgrass (1968); Samuels (1982; 1985); Hedgpeth (1983). *The Cattleman* (1959); *Montana Magazine of Western History* (summer 1961; Apr 1964); *Western Horseman* (Sept 1961), cover; *Mankind* (Vol. 3, no. 4, 1971), cover; *The Tulsa Tribune* (8 Sept 1977); *Artists of the Rockies And The Golden West* (winter 1984); *Art-Talk* (Apr/May 1986; Dec 1993); *Modern Maturity* (Aug/Sept 1992)

BOOKS ILLUSTRATED: Beeler (1967; 1974); University of Oklahoma Press, ca. 15 books; Grosset and Dunlap, ca. six books

COMMISSIONS: Justin Boot Company, painting; Spring River Indian Baptist Church, Quapaw, OK, baptistry

PUBLIC COLLECTIONS: BA/AZ; GM; HSM/MT; MNA; NCHF; OWM; VNB; Cowboy Artists of America Museum, Kerrville, TX

EXHIBITS: BBHC; CMRM; GM; GPWAS; NCHF; SIRU; Albuquerque (NM) Public Library, 1959; Cowboy Artists of America Museum, Kerrville, TX; Phippen Museum of Western Art, Prescott, AZ, 1993

SOLO EXHIBITS: BG; CMRM; FCTM; GM; HM; HSM/MT; NCHF; Missouri Southern College, Joplin, MO, 1967

JOE BEELER

"'I am goin' (sic) full steam ahead now with sculpturing and casting bronzes, and the paintings I do are done on commission only,' said the artist in 1965. Beeler's early paintings were inspired by the 'old Devil's Promenade Powwow at Quapaw, OK.' Today he paints the West as a westerner sees it."

Snodgrass 1968

Beeler is one of the four founding members of the Cowboy Artists of America, an organization that has been a major factor in the growing popularity of western art.

AWARDS: CAA/AZ ('67, Best of Show; '69, Silver Medal; '70, Silver Medal; '74, 2-Silver Medals, '93, Best of Show, Gold Medal); Higgins Ink Award, 1949; Franklin Mint ('74, Gold Medal)

HONORS: NCHF, first contemporary artist solo show

BEER, R. SHANE *Navajo/Laguna*

Born 25 June 1953 in Albuquerque, NM; son of Donna Mae Gatewood, artist, and Ronald Beer; M/GP: Emma Sousea and Henry D. Gatewood; M/Uncle: Clarence Sousa, silversmith

RESIDENCE: Austin, TX

EDUCATION: Valley High School, Albuquerque, NM, 1971

OCCUPATION: Construction company manager, silversmith, cartoonist, and artist

MEDIA: Silver, turquoise, pencil on embossed paper, and prints

PUBLISHED: *Southwest Art* (Feb 1992)

EXHIBITS: ACS/ENP; AIAF; AIAFM; ITIC; HM/G; A.I.T.G. Indian Art Expo, Austin, Texas

SOLO EXHIBITS: ITIC ('75, 1st; '77)

BEESON, MYRON *Navajo/Hopi*

Born 1963 on Second Mesa, AZ; son of Harold Beeson

EDUCATION: Winslow (AZ) High School; BC

MEDIA: Oil and acrylic

PUBLISHED: *Qua'toqti* (16 Dec 1982)

EXHIBITS: BC/McG; Octoberfest, Muskogee, OK

BEGAY, AMBROSE *Navajo*

Born 26 Sept 1962

RESIDENCE: Thoreau, NM

EDUCATION: Tuba City (AZ) High School; Haskell

MEDIA: Watercolor and pencil

EXHIBITS: ITIC

BEGAY, AMOS *Navajo*

PUBLIC COLLECTIONS: MNA

BEGAY, APIE *Navajo*

Begay Apie, Son of Milk

A.K.A. Appie Be Gay

Birth date unknown; died "many years before 1936."

MEDIA: Watercolor

PUBLISHED: Dunn (1968); Snodgrass (1968); Tanner (1973); Samuels (1985); Seymour (1988). *El Palacio* (Dec 1948); *Arizona Highways* (July 1956)

PUBLIC COLLECTIONS: MNM

EXHIBITS: HM

APIE BEGAY

"In 1902, Dr. Kenneth Chapman found the artist sitting on the floor of his hogan attempting to reproduce sand painting designs in the only two colors he had: red and black. When Dr. Chapman gave Begay a full box of crayons, he immediately set out to execute detailed replicas of sand paintings. Three of these first crayon drawings are now in the Indian Arts Fund Collection at the Museum of New Mexico, Santa Fe, NM."

Snodgrass 1968

BEGAY, ARTHUR C., SR. *Navajo*

Born 15 Dec 1932 in Newcomb, NM

RESIDENCE: Shiprock, NM

EDUCATION: Phoenix (AZ) High School; Famous Artist's School, Westport, CT

OCCUPATION: Electrician and artist

PUBLISHED: Snodgrass (1968); Brody (1971)

PUBLIC COLLECTIONS: HCC, AF

EXHIBITS: ITIC, LIAS, NTF, PAC

SOLO EXHIBITS: Numerous at Farmington (NM) Civic Center
AWARDS: ITIC ('86; '87; '88, 1st; '89, 2-1st); LIAS ('90, MA)

BEGAY, CHARLIE *Navajo*
PUBLIC COLLECTIONS: HCC
EXHIBITS: PAC ('77)

BEGAY, CHESTER B. *Navajo*
Birth date unknown; born in Shiprock, NM
RESIDENCE: Tahlequah, OK
EXHIBITS: CNM ('82)

BEGAY, ELLA MAE *Navajo*
EXHIBITS: SWAIA
AWARDS: SWAIA

BEGAY, EMERSON *Navajo*
RESIDENCE: Farmington, NM
OCCUPATION: Art teacher, sculptor, and painter
PUBLISHED: *The Farmington Daily Times* (12 June 1987; 16 June 1993)
COMMISSIONS: *Murals:* Farmington (NM) Mall, 1987, 1993
EXHIBITS: TF

BEGAY, ERVIN *Navajo*
PUBLIC COLLECTIONS: MNA

BEGAY, FRANK *Navajo*
PUBLISHED: Tanner (1973)

BEGAY, FRED *Navajo*
PUBLISHED: Snodgrass (1968)
EXHIBITS: AIAE/WSU, ABQM

BEGAY, HARRISON *Navajo*
Haskay Yah Ne Yah, Warrior Who Walked Up To His Enemy
Born 15 Nov 1917 in White Cone, AZ; son of Zonie Tachinie and Black-Rock Begay; stepson of Katherine Begay
RESIDENCE: Albuquerque, NM
MILITARY: U.S. Army, WWII
EDUCATION: Santa Fe, 1939; Black Mt., 1940-1941; Phoenix J. C., 1941; studied briefly with Gerard Curtis Delano
OCCUPATION: Co-founder of Tewa Enterprises (silkscreening) and painter
MEDIA: Tempera, watercolor with an acrylic base, and prints
PUBLISHED: Jacobson and d'Ucel (1950); Tanner (1957; 1968; 1973); LaFarge (1956; 1960); Dockstader (1961); Bahti (1964); Carlson (1964); Dunn (1968); Snodgrass (1968); Brody (1971); Highwater (1976); Silberman (1978); King (1981); Broder (1981); Hoffman, et al. (1984); Samuels (1985); Wade (1986); Jacka and Jacka (1988; 1994); Seymour (1988); Williams, ed. (1990); Archuleta and Strickland (1991); Schiffer (1991); Ballantine and Ballantine (1993); Tryk (1993). *Arizona Highways* (Feb 1950; July 1956; Dec 1958; Aug 1968, cover); *New Mexico Magazine* (July 1957); *Plateau* (Vol. 54, no. 1, 1982); *Southwest Art* (June 1983); *The Indian Trader* (Feb 1990; Mar 1990); *The Arizona Republic* (Mar 1990); *Tamaqua* (winter/spring 1991)
BOOKS ILLUSTRATED: Clark (1957); Wyman (1967)
COMMISSIONS: *Murals:* Maisel's Indian Trading Post, Albuquerque, NM, 1939

HARRISON BEGAY

"Begay's paintings have exerted greater influence on Navajo artists than any other person. His work is internationally known."

Snodgrass 1968

The artist says he decided in his teens that he wanted to be a painter. When he attended the Indian school in Santa Fe he received his first formal training in art. After he returned from service in the Army Signal Corps during World War II he began to paint full time. From that time on he has made his living from his art.

PUBLIC COLLECTIONS: AF, ASM, BA/AZ, BIA, CGPS, DAM, EM, GM, HCC, HM, IACB, IACB/DC, JAM, MAI, MAM, MKMcNAI, MNA/KHC, MNM, MRFM, OU/MA, PAC, RMC/AZ, SAR, SM, SMNAI, WOM, WWM

EXHIBITS: AC/A; AC/HC; AIAE/WSU; AIHA; AIW; ASF; CGPS; CPLH; DAM; FAIEAIP; FNAIC; FWG; HM; HM/G; IK; ITIC; JGS; LGAM; MAM; MFA/A; MFA/O; MKMcNAI; MNM; NAP; NGA; NJSM; OMA; OU/ET; PAC; PAC/T; PM; RC; RMC/AZ; SAIEAIP; SI; SN; SV; WRTD; Montclair (NY) Art Museum

SOLO EXHIBITS: Gumna, Japan, 1989

AWARDS: ITIC (2 Grand Awards before 1968; '68, 1st, SA; '70, 1st; '72; '85, 1st; '86; '92, 1st); PAC; SN ('67); state and tribal fairs

HONORS: High School Salutatorian; Palmes d'Académiques, 1945; named a "Living Legend" by Ralph Oliver in 1990

BEGAY, HARRY B. *Navajo*

EDUCATION: Santa Fe, ca. 1959

PUBLISHED: Snodgrass (1968)

EXHIBITS: MNM

AWARDS: MNM

BEGAY, JAMES (see Begay, Jimmy)

BEGAY, JEROME *Navajo*

Born 1953

EDUCATION: U of AZ, Southwestern Indian Art Project," scholarship, summers 1960, 1961 (sculpture major)

PUBLISHED: Snodgrass(1968)

BEGAY, JIMMY *Navajo*

A.K.A. James Begay

EDUCATION: U of AZ, "Southwestern Indian Art Project," scholarship, summer 1961 (textile major)

PUBLISHED: Snodgrass (1968)

PUBLIC COLLECTIONS: MNA

BEGAY, KEATS *Navajo*

Born ca. 1920 near Chinle, AZ

RESIDENCE: Chinle, AZ

EDUCATION: Santa Fe

PUBLISHED: Dunn (1968); Snodgrass (1968); Tanner (1973); Seymour (1988)

PUBLIC COLLECTIONS: IACB/DC, MNA, MNM, MNA/KHC, SM

EXHIBITS: AIW, ASU, NGA, WRTD

HONORS: State Champion long distance runner

KEATS BEGAY

"The artist did most of his painting in the late 1930's, mainly while he was at Santa Fe and shortly thereafter. His paintings were stylized; a distinguishing feature was the unreal way he depicted the cliffs and buttes of his homeland."

Snodgrass 1968

BEGAY, KEE BAHE *Navajo*

PUBLIC COLLECTIONS: MNA

BEGAY, MARCUS *Navajo*

RESIDENCE: St. Francis, SD

PUBLIC COLLECTIONS: HCC

EXHIBITS: HPTU, RC

AWARDS: RC ('92)

HONORS: RC, Thunderbird Foundation Scholarship, 1992

BEGAY, NELSON *Navajo*

Birth date unknown; born at Low Mountain in northeastern Arizona; son of Hosteen Begay, medicine man; cousin of Tony Begay (q.v.)

RESIDENCE: Tucson, AZ

EDUCATION: B.A., U of AZ, 1978

OCCUPATION: Teacher, dancer, silversmith, and painter

MEDIA: Acrylic, tempera, silver, gemstone, and prints

PUBLISHED: *The Indian Trader* (July 1978; Sept 1980)

SOLO EXHIBITS: Pima Community College, Tucson, AZ; galleries in Arizona

BEGAY, PAUL LEE *Navajo*

PUBLISHED: Snodgrass (1968)

PUBLIC COLLECTIONS: JAM

BEGAY, RAYMOND *Navajo*

Born 9 Dec 1945 in Crownpoint, NM

EDUCATION: Gallup (NM) High School, 1964

PUBLISHED: Snodgrass (1968)

EXHIBITS: ITIC, NACG

AWARDS: Four awards received, 1963-1964

RAYMOND BEGAY

"The artist began painting in 1959. Duane O. Berg, his art instructor, listed him as a promising student."

Snodgrass 1968

BEGAY, RICHARD *Navajo*

RESIDENCE: Flagstaff, AZ

EDUCATION: Fort Sill

OCCUPATION: Silversmith and painter

MEDIA: Acrylic, silver and gemstone

PUBLISHED: Snodgrass (1968); Hill (1992). *Arizona Highways* (July 1956)

PUBLIC COLLECTIONS: IAIA

EXHIBITS: IAIA, IACA, HM/G, PAC, SWAIA, WWM; Hozo Center, Sedona, AZ

AWARDS: SWAIA ('89, 1st)

BEGAY, RONALD S. *Navajo*

EDUCATION: IAIA

EXHIBITS: AC/SD

BEGAY, SHONTO W. *Navajo*

A.K.A. Wilson Shonto; Wilson Begay

Born 7 Feb 1954 in Shonto, AZ; son of Faye and Mailboy Begay; P/GF: Hosteen haa'l tsoos Na'ye'be'; M/GP: Bessie and John Smith

RESIDENCE: Kayenta, AZ

EDUCATION: IAIA High School, 1973; A.A., IAIA, 1976; CSF/SF, 1975-1976; B.F.A., CCAC, 1980

OCCUPATION: Art consultant, illustrator, lecturer, park ranger, naturalist, associate professor, and painter

MEDIA: Oil, acrylic,watercolor, pencil, pen and ink, mixed-media, and prints

PUBLISHED: Anonymous (1982a); Tryk (1993); Jacka and Jacka (1994). *Navajo Times Today* (8 Jan 1986); *The Eagle Free Press* (May 1987); *The Indian Trader* (July 1987)

BOOKS ILLUSTRATED: Cohen (1988), Begay (1992), Casler (1994); authored and illustrated brochures for schools, universities, and the National Park Service

COMMISSIONS: *Murals:* Indian Health Service, Albuquerque, NM, 1976; Indian Health Service, Kayenta, AZ, 1977; Inter-Tribal Friendship House, Oakland, CA, 1977; Santa Fe Multi-Cultural Mural Association, 1981; Inscription House, Kayenta, AZ, 1983. *Other:* Children's books

PUBLIC COLLECTIONS: FAC/CS, IAIA, WWM

EXHIBITS: AICA/SF; CCAC; CSF/SF; FNAA; HM/G; IAIA; ITIC; NACLA; NICCAS; NTF; SNAICF; SWAIA; WWM; Gallup (NM) Public Library, 1987; LaPeña Cultural Center, Berkeley, CA; Oakland (CA) Art Festival, 1979

SOLO EXHIBITS: CNGM, IAIA, U of CA/D, WWM (two)

AWARDS: HM/G ('92, Best of Division); ITIC ('87, 1st; Best of Show); NACLA; NTF; SNAICF ('87; '88, 1st; '90); SWAIA ('93, 1st; '94, 1st)

HONORS: Ford Foundation Grant; National Park Service, Special Achievement Award, 1978; one of top 15 illustrators for children's book art, 1989; Shika-Sha Co. Ltd., Tokyo, Japan, "Owl Award" nominee, 1989; AAA, poster artist, 1990; FNAA, poster artist, 1991

BEGAY, TIMOTHY *Navajo*

Birth date unknown; Chinle, AZ

MILITARY: WW II

EDUCATION: Santa Fe, 1942

PUBLISHED: Snodgrass (1968)

PUBLIC COLLECTIONS: WOM

EXHIBITS: ITIC; MNM; PAC; Los Angeles (CA) Public School Exhibit

BEGAY, TONY *Navajo*

Born 30 May 1941 in Ganado, AZ; died 1 Aug 1973 in an accident; son of Lucy Tanesini and Seth Begay

RESIDENCE: Lived in Chinle, AZ

MILITARY: U.S. Marine Corps, 1962-1966

EDUCATION: St. Michaels (AZ) High School, 1959; American School of Commercial Art, Dallas, TX; NCC

OCCUPATION: Dishwasher, NCC staff artist; full-time painter after 1970

MEDIA: Oil, acrylic, watercolor, pen and ink, and pastel

PUBLISHED: Tanner (1973); Williams (1990); Schiffer (1991). *Arizona Highways* (Mar 1974); *Plateau* (Vol. 54, no. 1, 1982)

COMMISSIONS: *Murals:* Camp Horno and Camp Pendleton, officer's clubs, CA

PUBLIC COLLECTIONS: HCC, EM, MKMcNAI, MNA, NCM, NTF

EXHIBITS: ASF, CPS, HM, HPTU, ITIC, MNA, NCC, NMSF, NTF, PAC, SN, RC

SOLO EXHIBITS: HM

AWARDS: Partial listing of fifty includes: AAID (Grand Award); ASF; HM/G ('70; '71); ITIC ('68; '69, 1st; '70, 1st; '72, 1st); NTF ('68; '69, 1st; '70, 1st; '71, 3-1st); PAC ('71; '72, 1st); SN ('70; '71, 1st, Read Mullen Award); RC ('71, 1st, Best of Show; '73, 1st)

TONY BEGAY

Clara Lee Tanner said, " Tony Begay was proficient in all of the styles in which he painted. His brushwork is clean, his colors rich; in graphics he proved equally capable, whether handling pen and ink or charcoal."

"Begay was not only respected for his art work but he was popular with his peers. After his funeral, members of several different tribes gathered art works to sell in order to establish a fund in his honor and for his children. Unbelievable are the numbers of individuals from additional tribes who have joined in this tribute to a beloved Indian artist."

Tanner 1973

BEGAY, WALLACE N. *Navajo*

RESIDENCE: Window Rock, AZ

EDUCATION: B.A., ASU

MEDIA: Watercolor

EXHIBITS: HM; ITIC; Maricopa (AZ) Fine Art Show

AWARDS: ITIC ('86, 1st; '91); Phoenix (AZ) Indian Art Show ('82, Best of Show)

BEGAY, WILSON (see Beagy, Shonto)

BEGAYE, ALVIN E. *NAVAJO*

EXHIBITS: ITIC

AWARDS: ITIC ('76; '86, 2-1st)

BEGAYE, PHIL T. *Navajo*

EXHIBITS: ITIC

AWARDS: ITIC ('89, 1st)

BEGAYE, REX AL *Navajo*

Born 13 Jan 1953 in Tuba City, AZ; son of Juanita Johnson Begay Yazzie and Allen Begaye; P/GM: Evelyn Yazzie; M/GP; Grace Johnson and Frank Bilagodi Johnson

RESIDENCE: Flagstaff, AZ

EDUCATION: Poway (CA) High School; Molar Barber School, Cleveland, OH

OCCUPATION: Hairdresser; full-time painter since 1987

MEDIA: Acrylic, pencil, pen and ink, and prints

EXHIBITS: CIM, ITAE/M, LIAS, MNA

BEGAYE, SHERWOOD *Navajo*

Born 27 July 1953 in Fingerpoint, AZ on the Navajo Reservation; son of Mary Johns and Harry N. Begay

RESIDENCE: Sanders, AZ

EDUCATION: Fort Wingate (NM) High School, 1974; IAIA, 1981; studied art under Ernest Franklin (q.v.)

OCCUPATION: Artist

MEDIA: Acrylic, watercolor, pen and ink, sandstone, and mixed-media

PUBLISHED: *Spawning The Medicine River* (1981), cover

PUBLIC COLLECTIONS: HCC; IAIA; NTM; Save The Children Foundation

EXHIBITS: CNM, HPTU, IAIA, ITIC, MNA, NAA, NTF, NTM, OT, RC, SNAICF, WIEAS

AWARDS: CNM ('91); ITIC ('86; '87, Woodard Award; '90; '91; '93, 1st; '94, 1st); MNA ('82; '84; '86, 1st; '90; '91); NTF; OT ('86); RC ('86; '87, Woodard Award; '88; '90; '94); SNAICF ('91); WIEAS ('79; '82; '85, 1st)

BEGAYE, WALLACE N. *Navajo*

PUBLISHED: Jacka and Jacka (1994)

MEDIA: Acrylic, mixed-media and prints

EXHIBITS: MNA; see also Awards

AWARDS: MNA ('93, 1st)

BEIKOIGEI (see Geionety, George)

BELANGER, LANCE *Maliseet*

Born 1956 on Tobique Reserve, NB, Canada

RESIDENCE: Ottawa, ON, Canada

EDUCATION: Manitou Community College, Lamacaza, PQ, 1976; C/U of R, 1977-1979

OCCUPATION: Full-time artist since 1982

PUBLISHED: Fortin (1988); Fry and Maracle (1988); McMasters, et al. (1993). *Artspeak Gallery Review* (Vol. 6, no. 8, 1984); *Artscraft* (Vol. 1, no. 1, 1988); *American Indian Art* (autumn 1992)

PUBLIC COLLECTIONS: C/AAF; C/INAC; Woodland Cultural Institute

EXHIBITS: Partial listing includes: AICH; C/I; C/WICEC; Le Grand Palais, Paris, France; International Multimedia Centre, Salerno, Italy; Museo d'Arte Contemporanea di Villa Croce, Genova, Italy; The Museum of Modern Art, Tampere, Finland; The Andrea Demdtshuis, Sint-Baafs-Vijve, Belgium; National Museum of Fine Arts, Havana, Cuba

SOLO EXHIBITS: Ottawa (ON) City Hall (2); Saskatchewan Cultural Exchange Society, Regina, SK

HONORS: C/BSFA, artist-in-residence

DENNIS BELINDO

The four major influences on Belindo's art were Stephen Mopope, Dick West, Oscar Howe (qq.v.) and Pablo Picasso. He says that Oscar Howe and Picasso simplified form to basic planes, which is what he does. He continues the traditions of Kiowa art which he says are decorative, patterned and two-dimensionally based. Because of teaching and community activities, Belindo did not paint between 1969 and 1978. He resumed painting in 1979.

artist, p.c. 1992

LELAND BELL

According to Southcott (1984), Bell's style is distinguished by its large flat shapes, although it continues to change as he experiments with new concepts. The artist states that his paintings contain a spiritual meaning and he often uses prayer as a subject.

BELINDO, DENNIS *Kiowa/Navajo*

Aun So Te, Foot

Born 12 Dec 1938 in Phoenix (AZ) Indian School Hospital; son of Ruby Goomda and Damon Jarrack Belindo (Be-Lin-Hilje, His Spotted Horse); father of Jon Belindo (q.v.); M/GF: Wind Goomda, who devoted his life to being Keeper of the Taime (Sun Dance God); P/GF: Red Whiskers, Navajo medicine man; descendant of Red Cloud (Sioux) and Lone Wolf (Kiowa). Belindo's Kiowa ancestry may have originated when the Sioux captured a Kiowa woman.

RESIDENCE: Oklahoma City, OK

EDUCATION: Mountain View (OK) High School; graduated, BC High School, 1956; BC, 1956-1958; NSC/OK, 1959-1960; B.F.A., U of OK, 1962; OCU (law school), 1968-1969; M.B.A., U of NM, 1973-1974

OCCUPATION: Educator, curriculum consultant, legislative analyst, research and development analyst, national Indian affairs activist, and painter

MEDIA: Acrylic, watercolor, and casein

PUBLISHED: Snodgrass (1968); Brody (1971); Irvine, ed. (1974); Ellison (1972); Boyd, et al. (1981); King (1981); New (1981). *Southwest Art* (June 1981); biographical publications

COMMISSIONS: Central High School, Oklahoma City, OK; State of Oklahoma, painted tipi for presentation to Government of Kyoto, Japan, 1987

PUBLIC COLLECTIONS: HSM/OK, ITIC

EXHIBITS: AC/A; AIE; BC/McG; CAI/KC; CNM; CSPIP; FAIE; HM; HSM/OK; IK; ITIC; KCPA; MNM; MIF; MPI; MRFM; NACLA; OAC; PAC; RE; SAIEAIP; SI; SPIM; Abilene (TX) Fine Arts Museum; Texas Technical University, Lubbock, TX

SOLO EXHIBITS: CNM, HM, SPIM, U of OK

AWARDS: AIE ('67, 1st); CNM ('85, 1st); ITIC ('76; '79; '90); KCPA; PAC ('57; '60, 1st; '61); RE ('89)

HONORS: Delta Tau Delta Honorary Art Fraternity; ITIC, poster artist, 1965

BELINDO, JON *Kiowa/Navajo/Pawnee/Choctaw*

A.K.A. Jon Edwin Belindo

Born 4 Aug 1963 in Oklahoma City, OK; son of Julia Bayhylle and Dennis Belindo (q.v.); P/GP: Ruby Goomda and Damon Jerrick Belindo; M/GP: Elsie and Edwin Bayhylle

RESIDENCE: Stratford, OK

EDUCATION: Anadarko (OK) High School, 1981; ECSC/OK, 1986

OCCUPATION: Teacher and painter

MEDIA: Acrylic, watercolor, pencil, pen and ink, colored pencil, and prints

EXHIBITS: CNM

SOLO EXHIBITS: ECSC/OK, 1986

AWARDS: CNM ('85, 1st); ECSC/OK ('86, Fine Arts Award)

HONORS: Susan Peters Award, art scholarship; *Norman Transcript,* selected as one of top 10 second-generation Indian artists; Oklahoma State Honor Scholar (high school), 1971; *Ada News,* listed as one of top buys in Indian art, 1986

BELL, BEBAMINOJMAT L. (SEE BELL, LELAND)

BELL, LELAND *Ojibwa*

Bebaminojmat, The Kindly Person Who Tells Stories

Signature: Bebaminojmat L. Bell (since 1982)

Born 1953 in Wikwemikong, ON, Canada

EDUCATION: C/LUM, 1980

OCCUPATION: Comedian, storyteller, musician, teacher, and painter
MEDIA: Acrylic
PUBLISHED: Southcott (1984)
EXHIBITS: C/AG/TT, C/AMK, C/OCF

BELLEGARDE, ROBERT *Plains Cree*
RESIDENCE: Little Black Reserve, SK, Canada
MEDIA: Pastel, pen and ink, and charcoal
PUBLISHED: *The Indian Trader* (Apr 1979)

ROBERT BELLEGARDE

Bellegarde is best known for his portraits of historical Indian leaders.

BELLROCK, BUSTER *Crow*
PUBLISHED: Snodgrass (1968)
PUBLIC COLLECTIONS: GM

BELMORE, BECKY (see Belmore, Rebecca)

BELMORE, REBECCA *Ojibwa*
A.K.A. Becky Belmore
Born 1960 in Upsala, ON, Canada
RESIDENCE: Thunder Bay, ON, Canada
EDUCATION: C/OCA
OCCUPATION: Artist
MEDIA: Pastels, pencil, and mixed-media
PUBLISHED: Menitove, ed. (1986b)
PUBLIC COLLECTIONS: C/AG/TB
EXHIBITS: C/AG/TB, C/WI, HM
AWARDS: C/AC/TB ('84, Special Juror's Award); C/WI (Special Juror's Award)
HONORS: *Grants:* Ontario Arts Council, Special Project Assistance Grant; Ontario Arts Council, Creative Artists in the Schools Grant; Ontario Arts Council, Individual Project Grant

BELONE, PHILLIP *Navajo*
RESIDENCE: Tuba City, AZ
EDUCATION: Gallup (NM) High School; U of N AZ
OCCUPATION: Musician, silversmith, sculptor, and painter
PUBLIC COLLECTIONS: HCC
EXHIBITS: HM/G, ITIC, NMSU, RC, SNAICF
AWARDS: HM/G (1st); ITIC (4-1st); NTM (1st); SNAICF; RC (Begay Award)

BENALLY, ANDERSON LEE *Navajo*
Born 9 Nov 1954
RESIDENCE: Baker, OR
EDUCATION: Rough Rock (AZ) Demonstration School; IAIA, 1969-1973; B.A., Eastern Oregon State University, Le Grande, OR, 1984; Rutgers University, New Brunswick, NJ
OCCUPATION: National Forest Service employee, and artist
MEDIA: Acrylic and watercolor
PUBLISHED: *The Indian Trader* (May 1990); *Inter-Tribal America* (1990), cover
PUBLIC COLLECTIONS: HCC, IAIA, ITIC
EXHIBITS: CNM; CPS; DAM; GFNAAS; HM/G; HPTU; IAIA; ITIC; MNAC; NTM; PAC; RC; SIM; U of WV; WTF; Native American Expo '88; Diamond Jubilee, Vancouver, BC; see also Awards
AWARDS: Partial listing includes: ITIC ('86; '87; '88, 1st; '89; '94); RC ('83, 1st; '84; '86, 2-1st, Begay Award; '87, Begay Award; '89; '90, 1st); Le Grande County

ANDERSON LEE BENALLY

Although his style is distinctively his own, Benally credits the paintings of Blackbear Bosin and Tony Sandoval (qq.v.) with having influenced his artistic development. He paints the legends, myths, and stories his grandfather told him. Benally describes his paintings as "Visionary Art." It is his intention to promote a positive view of Indians through his work.

Inter-Tribal America, *1990*

Fair, Le Grande, OR; Yavapai Junior College Art Show, Prescott, AZ; more than 24 first-place awards, 2 purchase awards, and 3 special awards

HONORS: RC, Thunderbird Foundation Scholarships, 1983, 1985, 1986, 1989; ITIC, poster artist, 1990

BENALLY, CHEE B. *Navajo*

Born 6 June 1947 in Blackrock, NM

EDUCATION: Gallup (NM) High School, 1966; Engineering Drafting School, Denver, CO; B.A., Nebraska Wesleyan University, Lincoln, NE

OCCUPATION: Illustrator and painter

MEDIA: Oil, acrylic, watercolor, pastel, and charcoal

PUBLISHED: Snodgrass (1968); Tanner (1973)

PUBLIC COLLECTIONS: HCC, ITIC

EXHIBITS: ITIC, NACG, RC, SN, WTF; see also Awards

AWARDS: ITIC ('71); RC; SN ('68); White Buffalo Council, Denver, CO (1st)

CHEE B. BENALLY

According to Tanner (1973), Benally most frequently painted both traditional and nontraditional subjects in a semi-European or almost traditional style, although at times his approach was abstract.

BENALLY, DANIEL *Navajo*

RESIDENCE: Keams Canyon, AZ

EXHIBITS: ITIC

AWARDS: ITIC ('89, 1st)

BENALLY, DARRELL *Navajo*

Born 1973; son of Arlene and Sam Benally, silversmiths

RESIDENCE: Kayenta, AZ

MEDIA: Prismacolor and pen and ink

EXHIBITS: ITIC, TWF

AWARDS: ITIC ('93, 1st)

BENALLY, ERIC *Navajo*

RESIDENCE: Farmington, NM

OCCUPATION: Artist

EXHIBITS: ACS/MV, CHAS, ITIC, RE

AWARDS: CHAS

BENALLY, LARRY *Navajo*

RESIDENCE: Rough Rock, AZ

EXHIBITS: ITIC

AWARDS: ITIC ('86, 1st, Best In Category)

BENALLY, TIMOTHY *Navajo*

Born 10 July 1956

RESIDENCE: Shiprock, NM

EDUCATION: IAIA

OCCUPATION: Artist

MEDIA: Oil, acrylic, watercolor, pen and ink, pencil, pastel, and charcoal

PUBLIC COLLECTIONS: HCC

EXHIBITS: CNM; HMC; HM; HM/G; ITIC; PAC; RC; NMSF; SNAICF; WTF; San Juan County Fair, Farmington, NM

AWARDS: HM/G ('73, 1st); ITIC ('85, 1st; '87; '91; '93, 1st; '94, 1st); RC ('78; '84, Powers Award)

BENALLY, VERTNAIEL *Navajo*

PUBLIC COLLECTIONS: WWM

BENHAM, JAY *Kiowa*
Birth date unknown; nephew of Al Momaday (q.v.)
RESIDENCE: Springdale, AR
MEDIA: Oil and acrylic
EXHIBITS: CNM ('83)

BENNETT, ELLSON *Navajo*
Born 1969 on the Navajo Reservation, AZ
RESIDENCE: Tulsa, OK
EDUCATION: Graduated High School, 1989
EXHIBITS: IS; TIAF; TWF; Powwow of Champions, Tulsa, OK
AWARDS: First and Best of Show in High School competitions

BENNETT, JOE *Navajo*
PUBLIC COLLECTIONS: MNA

BERNAL, ELOISA *Taos*
PUBLISHED: Snodgrass (1968)
EXHIBITS: AIEC, MFA/O

BERO, JAMES *Mohawk*
PUBLIC COLLECTIONS: SMII

BERO, MIKE *Mohawk*
Born 2 Aug 1921
RESIDENCE: St. Regis, PQ, Canada
OCCUPATION: Painting instructor, sculptor, and artist
MEDIA: Acrylics, oil, pencil, charcoal, pastel, and clay
PUBLISHED: Johannsen and Ferguson, eds. (1983)
PUBLIC COLLECTIONS: ALCC, C/WICEC
EXHIBITS: INAAT

MIKE BERO

Bero paints realistic portraits, animal scenes, and the everyday life of the early Iroquois.

Johannsen and Ferguson, eds. 1983

BERRY, ROD BEARCLOUD *Osage*
Bearcloud
Born 1950 in Amarillo, TX
RESIDENCE: Columbia, CA
EDUCATION: Amarillo (TX) College; Texas State Institute; University of Maryland, England
PUBLIC COLLECTIONS: Corporate Collections in California
EXHIBITS: CAINS
HONORS: CAINS, poster artist, 1994

BESJEARS, MAX *Ponca*
RESIDENCE: Muskogee, OK
EXHIBITS: CNM

BETONI, JOHNNY W., JR. *Navajo*
RESIDENCE: Nageezi, NM
EXHIBITS: RC, SN

BETTELYOUN, BUCK *Oglala Sioux*
Born 17 Aug 1925 in Wanblee, SD
EDUCATION: Bennett County High School, Martin, SD, 1942; Valley State College, Burbank, CA

OCCUPATION: U.S. Post Service employee, lecturer, set designer, art teacher, Oglala Sioux Tribal Tax Department supervisor, and artist

EXHIBITS: RC, SIM

SOLO EXHIBITS: SIM

BETTIS, MACK *Cherokee/Narragansett*

Born 15 Mar 1934; son of Iva Belle Perrin and Richard Watt Bettis; P/GP: Martha Louise Underwood and James Monroe Bettis; M/GP: Mary Baker and Carl Perrin

RESIDENCE: Tulsa, OK

EDUCATION: Spiro (OK) High School, 1952; NSC/OK; BC; U of Tulsa, 1955-1967

OCCUPATION: Attorney, Tulsa (OK) Deputy County Assessor, sculptor, and painter

MEDIA: Oil, acrylic, watercolor, and flint

EXHIBITS: CNM

AWARDS: CNM

BEYALE, WAYNE NEZ *Navajo*

WAYNE NEZ BEYALE

Beyale uses multiple lines to create the impression of movement. He says his work was directly influenced by watching his father make ceremonial sand paintings. The artist is well known for his paintings of dancing figures especially the Navajo Yeibichai.

artist, p.c. 1990

Born 1953 in the area of Pueblo Pintado, NM, in a wagon when returning home from an aunt's hogan; son of Ruth, weaver, and John Nez Beyale, medicine man

RESIDENCE: Englewood, CO

EDUCATION: Arapahoe High School, Littleton, CO, 1973; U of NM (2 years)

OCCUPATION: Carpenter and painter

MEDIA: Oil, acrylic, watercolor, pencil, pastel, pen and ink, and prints

PUBLISHED: Jacka and Jacka (1994). *The Denver Post* (17 July 1988); *Southwest Art* (Nov 1994)

PUBLIC COLLECTIONS: GAWHM, HCC, RC

EXHIBITS: ACS/ENP; ACS/PG; AIM/W; CIM; CNM; FNAA; GAWHM; GPWAS; ITAE; ITIC; LIAS; MNA; OT; RC; RE; SNAICF; SWAIA; TIAF; WH; WMNAAF; Colorado Indian Holiday Festival, Flagstaff, AZ, 1990; Dallas (TX) Indian Market, 1990; Endangered Species Show, Denver, CO, 1990; Festival of the Pines, Flagstaff, AZ, 1990; M.A.M.A. Fall Festival, Tempe, AZ, 1990; Peoples' Fair, Denver, CO, 1990; see also Awards

AWARDS: ACS/ENP ('89, 1st; '90; '91, 1st); CIM (1st); GAWHM ('90, Best of Show); ITAE ('88, 1st; '90, 2-1st; '91); ITIC ('90, 1st; '90, 2-1st; '92, 3-1st, Elkus Award; '93; '94); MNA ('89); OT ('90); RC ('84); SNAICF ('90); SWAIA ('90; '93, 1st); TIAF ('90, 1st, SM); Beaver Creek Art Festival, Beaver, CO ('89, Best of Show); Emerald City Classic Contemporary Show, Wichita, KS ('86); Western Art Rendezvous, Denver, CO ('86, 1st, Best Original Drawing, Theme Award; American Artists Award)

HONORS: ITAE, poster artist, 1992

BIA, FRED *Navajo*

Born 10 June 1949

RESIDENCE: Rough Rock, AZ

EDUCATION: IAIA; workshops in CA, NM, and TX

OCCUPATION: Educator, photographer, and painter

MEDIA: Oil, watercolor, pencil, pen and ink, charcoal, and pastel

BOOKS ILLUSTRATED: Wallace, Lynch, and Yellowhair (1984)

PUBLIC COLLECTIONS: HCC

EXHIBITS: HM, ITIC, NMSF, NTF, RC, SWAIA, TAAII

AWARDS: ITIC ('78, 1st; '79, 1st; '83; '84, 1st; '85; '86, 1st, Best in Category;

'89, 1st; '90; '91, 1st); NMSF ('76, 1st, Purchase Award; '79, 1st; '80; '83; '84; '85, 1st); NTF ('87; '90); SWAIA ('79); TAAII ('75; '76)

BICHITTY, NELSON *Navajo*

Birth date unknown; born near Indian Wells, AZ

PUBLISHED: Tanner (1973)

EXHIBITS: SN

AWARDS: SN

NELSON BICHITTY

While in a hospital in Tucson in 1965, Bichitty was encouraged to paint and entered a painting in the Scottsdale National which received a second prize.

Tanner 1973

BIES, JANET *Brûlé Sioux*

Wahca Ska

Born 3 Mar 1949 in Pierre, SD

RESIDENCE: Piedmont, SD

EDUCATION: Central High School, Rapid City, SD; SDSMT; Black Hills State College, Spearfish, SD

OCCUPATION: Plumber, religion educator, and artist

MEDIA: Oil, tempera, mixed-media, and pastel

PUBLISHED: *The Indian Trader* (May 1984)

EXHIBITS: CNM; CSF/SD; MBC; RC; SIM; Boy's Club Western Art Auction, Rapid City, SD; South Dakota State Fair

SOLO/SPECIAL EXHIBITS: SIM (dual show)

AWARDS: MBC (Best of Show); CSF/SD (Purchase Award)

BIG BACK *Cheyenne*

Birth date unknown; death date unknown

PUBLISHED: Dodge (1883); Hamilton (1950); Snodgrass (1968)

BIG BACK

"Richard Irving Dodge's Our Wild Indians *(1883) has 'reproduced in exact facsimile from the original drawings, expressly for this work, drawings done with colored pencil by Big Back.'"*

Snodgrass 1968

BIG BEAR, FRANK, JR. *Chippewa*

Born 8 July 1953 on the White Earth Reservation, MN

EDUCATION: U of MN/TC; studied with George Morrison (q.v.)

OCCUPATION: Artist

MEDIA: Prismacolor

PUBLISHED: Highwater (1976)

PUBLIC COLLECTIONS: MIA; NDM; PIM; Northwestern National Life Insurance, Co. Minneapolis, MN; St. Paul Companies, St. Paul, MN

EXHIBITS: HM, MCAD, NDM, PMA, TI

SOLO EXHIBITS: Partial listing of ten includes: NDM; Art in the Mayor's Office Program, Minneapolis, MN, 1986; galleries in Minneapolis and St. Paul, MN, and New York, NY

HONORS: Heart of the Earth School, Minneapolis, MN, artist-in-residence, 1973; Bush Foundation Fellowship, 1986; Jerome Foundation, winner, 1982

BIGBEAR, GARY *Winnebago*

EXHIBITIONS: NPTA

AWARDS: NPTA ('93; '94, 1st)

BIG BLACK (see Hollowbreast, Donald)

BIG BOW, CHIEF (see Big Bow)

BIG BOW *Kiowa*

Zepko Ettee, Big Bow Man; *Zipkiyah*

A.K.A. Bow Big Man; Chief Big Bow

Born ca. 1845; died 1901 in Hobart, OK; brother of White Horse (q.v.)

MILITARY: U.S. Army

BIG BOW

"As a warrior, Big Bow was active with Kicking Bird and Satanta (q.v.) in Texas and Oklahoma raids during the mid-1800s. He later served in the U.S. Army, under Lt. Richard H. Pratt and Gen. Hugh L. Scott, as a sergeant in charge of a detachment of Kiowa scouts stationed on Sweetwater Creek. He was honorably discharged a few years before his death."

Snodgrass 1968

OCCUPATION: Chief, warrior, U.S. Army scout, and artist
PUBLISHED: Snodgrass (1968); Dockstader (1977)
PUBLIC COLLECTIONS: MAI

BIG BOW, ABEL *Kiowa*

PUBLISHED: Snodgrass (1968)
PUBLIC COLLECTIONS: GM (pictographic style on paper)

BIG BOW, HARDING *Kiowa*

Born 17 Aug 1921 in Carnegie, OK; descendent of Chief Big Bow (q.v.), Kiowa leader and War Chief
RESIDENCE: Mountain View, OK
EDUCATION: Carnegie (OK) High School, 1938
OCCUPATION: Indian school employee, craftsman, and artist
MEDIA: Acrylic
PUBLISHED: *Oklahoma Today* (July/Aug 1989)
EXHIBITS: AIE, SPIM
SOLO EXHIBITS: SPIM
AWARDS: AIE ('74, 1st)
HONORS: National Advisory Board to the U.S. Senate, Oklahoma representative, 1977; Native American Church of Oklahoma, President, 1989

HARDING BIG BOW

Big Bow said, "... When I was 10 years old, I saw Monroe Tsatoke in a room in a house at Rainy Mountain, looking in a mirror and painting a self-portrait of himself dressed in a big hat and beaded vest. I was so impressed, he was my inspiration to become an artist."

"I believe in what I paint, it's old, it's original. I believe in the traditional style of painting. I use the stories of my grandparents. I believe in the old ways, this is what I want to show. My primary interest is to show the people what I believe in as a Kiowa.... I like to do things honestly and right if there is any way possible to do so...."

brochure, SPIM, 1990

BIG BOW, WOODROW WILSON (see Big Bow, Woody)

BIG BOW, WOODY *Kiowa*

Tse Ko Yate, Big Bow
A.K.A. Woodrow Wilson Big Bow
Born 29 Jan 1914 in Carnegie, OK; died July 1988; grandson of Chief Big Bow (q.v.)
RESIDENCE: Lived in Yukon, OK
EDUCATION: U of OK, 1939
OCCUPATION: Set painter for western movies, contractor, builder, and painter
PUBLISHED: Jacobson and d'Ucel (1950); Snodgrass (1968); Brody (1971); King (1981); Boyd, et al. (1983); Samuels (1985). *The Wichita Eagle and Beacon* (28 July 1974)
COMMISSIONS: *Murals:* RCA Building, New York, NY; Southwest Museum, Los Angeles, CA
PUBLIC COLLECTIONS: GM; HCC; HSM/OK; KM; MAI; OAC; OU/L; OU/MA/T; PAC; SM; WAM; YMCA, Tulsa, OK; Abilene (TX) Public Library
EXHIBITS: AC/A; CSPIP; LGAM; PAC; PSC; SMA/TX; WAM; Tulsa County Libraries, Tulsa, OK
SOLO EXHIBITS: JH

WOODY BIG BOW

"Big Bow designed the red and yellow thunderbird insignia of the Oklahoma 45th Infantry Division."

Snodgrass 1968

Big Bow did not like to paint feet, and often painted a bunch of grass or a bush where feet should be.

Snodgrass, p.c. 1992

The artist so admired the work of other Southern Plains artists that he was well known for copying their style.

BIG BOW MAN (see Big Bow)

BIG FOOT (see Creepingbear, Mirac)

BIG CLOUD *Cheyenne*

MEDIA: Graphite and colored pencil
PUBLISHED: Maurer (1992)
PUBLIC COLLECTIONS: MIA (attributed to)
EXHIBITS: VP

BIGCRANE, JOANNE *Salish/Kootenai*

Born 1946 in St. Ignatius, MT

MARRS BIGGOOSE

The Native American Church has greatly influenced Biggoose's art and he often depicts its spiritual aspect. His work has been described as poetic in color and form — free flowing spiritual art.

artist, p.c. 1990

RESIDENCE: Ravalli, MT
EDUCATION: Dixon (MT) High School; IAIA, 1983-1984
OCCUPATION: Beadworker, fashion designer, sculptor, and painter
MEDIA: Oil, acrylic, watercolor, pen and ink, gouache, polyform, clay, and beads
EXHIBITS: IAIA; NAVAM; Ronan (MT) Art Show; Kyi-Yo Indian Youth Conference, Missoula, MT

BIG FIREWEED (see Vickers, Roy Henry)

BIGGOOSE, MARCELLUS (see Biggoose, Marrs)

BIGGOOSE, MARRS *Ponca*

A.K.A. Marcellus Biggoose
Birth date unknown; born in Pawnee, OK
RESIDENCE: Tulsa, OK
EDUCATION: Pawnee Indian School; Haskell; BC; IAIA, 1963
OCCUPATION: Tailor; full-time artist since 1970
MEDIA: Acrylic, tempera, and gouache
BOOKS ILLUSTRATED: Mathews (1988), cover
COMMISSIONS: Ability Resources, Tulsa, OK, brochure cover, 1992
EXHIBITS: BC/McG; CC/OK; CNM; IAF; ITIC; LIAS; PAC; RC; Western Heritage Show, Tulsa, OK; Muskogee (OK) Public Library; Ponca City (OK) Art Association
AWARDS: CNM ('85, 1st; '91); ITIC ('90, 1st; '91, 1st; '94); PAC ('72; '75)

BIG HEART (see Ziegler, Alfred Y.)

BIG HORSE, HUBBLE *Cheyenne*

A.K.A. Signature: H. B. Horse
MILITARY: U.S. Army
EDUCATION: Carlisle
OCCUPATION: Scout and illustrator
PUBLISHED: *American Indian Art* (winter 1992)
PUBLIC COLLECTIONS: SI/OAA

BIG LEFTHANDED *Navajo*

Klah Tso, Lefthanded Big
A.K.A. Old Hostin Claw; (see also Choh)
Birth date unknown
RESIDENCE: Lived near either Indian Wells or near Tuba City, AZ, probably the former.
PUBLISHED: Wyman (1965); Snodgrass (1968); Brody (1971)
PUBLIC COLLECTIONS: MNA/KHC, SI (five secular paintings)

BIG LITTLE (see Kahn, Chester)

BIG MAN, MAX *Crow*

Birth date unknown; born at Crow Agency, MT; death date unknown
PUBLISHED: Snodgrass (1968)
HONORS: Made an honorary chief by Chief Plenty Coups; Commercial Club, Medal of Service, Rapid City, SD

BIGMAN, VERNON *Navajo*

EXHIBITS: AICH

HUBBLE BIG HORSE

Big Horse was one of forty Cheyenne men who were recruited by the U.S. Army to serve as scouts at Fort Supply in 1885. Their duties were to police the reservation and to support the military and agency staff in peacekeeping. Between 1901 and 1904, Big Horse worked as an illustrator for James Mooney, ethnologist, who was doing research on the Cheyenne. Unlike most Plains Indian artists of his time, Big Heart frequently put his name and the date on his drawings.

American Indian Art
winter 1992

BIG LEFTHANDED

"The artist 'made paintings between 1905 and 1912 . . . on dark tan-colored cotton cloth. The pigments employed were native pigments in some native adhesive, opaque commercial watercolors, and some commercial oils. One painting (SI) of galloping horses and the dust thrown up by their flying hooves, and the attitudes of the riders, make this one of the loveliest known early American Indian paintings (Wyman 1965).'"

Snodgrass 1968

MAX BIG MAN

"Painting was Big Man's hobby. He was active in tribal functions, promoted the Custer Battlefield Association, and conducted an educational program about Indians for CBS radio and New York schools. His paintings reflect his own activities and tribal life."

Snodgrass 1968

BIG MISSOURI

"Big Missouri is known to have executed a Dakota Winter Count for the years 1796 to 1926 (see Bulletin 173, *BAE, 1960)."*

Snodgrass 1968

ISAAC BIGNELL

In the early 1970s, Wahsa Gallery produced photo-mechanical prints of Bignell's paintings that caught the attention of the public. His early art was realistic; however, his more recent works reflect the influence of Chee Chee (q.v.).

American Indian Art *spring 1990*

BIG TREE

As a warrior and chief, Big Tree led raids into Texas. He was captured and sent to prison at Huntsville, TX, and later paroled. He settled on his reservation allotment near Redstone, OK, and was living in Mountain View, OK, at the time of his death. In 1922, Big Tree permitted Susie Peters, a Field matron to the Kiowas, to copy his calendar and to record the meaning of the symbols. The years 1850 through 1879 are reproduced in Boyd.

Boyd, et al. 1983

BIG MISSOURI *Teton Sioux*

PUBLISHED: Snodgrass (1968). *Bulletin 173,* BAE (1960)

BIGNELL, ISAAC *Cree*

Birth date unknown; born on Pas Reserve, MB
RESIDENCE: Winnipeg, MB
PUBLISHED: *American Indian Art* (spring 1990)
PUBLIC COLLECTIONS: HCC
EXHIBITS: C/WICEC, HCC

BIG ROAD *Sioux*

A.K.A. Chief Big Road
PUBLISHED: Snodgrass (1968). *4th Annual Report,* BAE (1882-1883)
PUBLIC COLLECTIONS: SI/OAA

BIG SPRINGS, WILLIAM, SR. *Blackfeet*

Born 1919 in East Glacier Park, MT
RESIDENCE: East Glacier Park, MT
EDUCATION: Browning (MT) High School
OCCUPATION: Rancher and painter
MEDIA: Oil and pastel
PUBLISHED: Snodgrass (1968)
EXHIBITS: BNIAS, CIA, FAIEAIP, USDI
HONORS: First Annual Western Art Show, Glacier Park, MT, Chairman; Indian Arts and Crafts Board, U.S. Dept. of the Interior, Commissioner

BIG TREE *Kiowa*

A.K.A. A'do-ette
Born 1850; died 1927 at Mountain View, OK
PUBLISHED: Boyd, et al. (1983)

BILLEDEAUX, DONALD *Blackfeet*

A.K.A. Napi; Signature: Napi
Born 23 May 1917 in Kalispell, MT
RESIDENCE: Portland, OR
EDUCATION: Browning (MT) High School
OCCUPATION: Carpenter; full-time sculptor and painter since 1971
MEDIA: Acrylic, oil, watercolor, tempera, metal, wood, and terra cotta
EXHIBITS: CIA, MPI
SOLO EXHIBITS: MPI

BILLEDEAUX, DWIGHT *Blackfeet*

Born 1947 in Dillon, MT
EDUCATION: U of MT, 1971-1973; Western Montana College, Dillon, MT, 1970-1971; Academy of Arts, San Francisco, CA, 1965-1966
PUBLISHED: Roberts, ed. (1992)
EXHIBITS: AICH, CMAC, FSMCFA, MMA/MT, SS/CW, SWAIA
AWARDS: SWAIA
HONORS: Governor of Montana Distinguished Art Award, nominee, 1985

BILLIE, PAUL *Seminole*

PUBLISHED: Fawcett and Callander (1982)
PUBLIC COLLECTIONS: MAI

BILL NIX (see Red Corn)

BILLY, MARK *Navajo*

EDUCATION: IAIA

EXHIBITS: AC/SD

BILOKILA (see Luján, Lorenzo A.)

A BIRD (see Herrera, Justino)

BIRD CHIEF (see Piapot, Algie)

BIRD, GREG *Ojibwa*

Born 1953 in Fort Francis, ON, Canada; GF: Gert Yerxa, Fe-Na-She

RESIDENCE: Brandon, MB, Canada

EDUCATION: Graduated High School, 1972

OCCUPATION: Architectural drafting; started painting in 1976

MEDIA: Acrylic and India ink

EXHIBITS: C/BU; C/WICEC; Allied Art Centre; Townsite Gallery; Wahsa Gallery

BIRD, JIM DALE *Cherokee*

EXHIBITS: FCTM

AWARDS: FCTM

BIRD, JOANNE *Sisseton Sioux*

A Wush, Earth

Born 7 Mar 1945 in Oakland, CA; daughter of Rena White and Simon Maestas; P/GM: Benita Maestas; M/GP: Ella and Charles White

RESIDENCE: Brookings, SD

EDUCATION: Flandreau (SD) Indian School, 1964; Dakota State College, Madison, SD; Macalaster College, St. Paul, MN; IAIA

OCCUPATION: Sculptor and painter

MEDIA: Oil, acrylic, watercolor, bronze, and prints

PUBLISHED: *Newsletter*, IACA (Mar/Apr 1993)

COMMISSIONS: *Sculptures:* Shakopee Mdewakanton Sioux Tribe, Shakopee, MN; Minnesota State Capitol, St. Paul, MN; Three Affiliated Tribes, Newtown, ND; Minnesota Historical Society, St. Paul, MN; Town of Sleepy Eye, MN; Karl Mayspiele, Bad Segeberg, West Germany

PUBLIC COLLECTIONS: HCC, SJIS

EXHIBITS: AIAF, AIAFM, CIM, IS, ITAE/M, LIAS/M, NPTA, TIAF, UTAE, WIAME, WTF; see also Awards

SOLO EXHIBITS: Brookings (SD) Cultural Center; Oscar Howe Art Center, Vermillion, SD

AWARDS: IS ('92); NPTA ('88, 1st; '90; '92, '93, 1st); CIM ('85; '89, 1st); TIAF ('90); UTAE ('91); WIAME ('94, HM); Minnesota State Arts Show ('90, Best of Show)

HONORS: South Dakota Hall of Fame, Artist of the Year, 1992

JOANNE BIRD

Although Bird's paintings most often have Native American themes, they are very impressionistic. She says, "The themes of my paintings are influenced by the rich culture of our ancestors and the beauty of nature. My painting technique is the result of my many years of experience and creations of art work in many media."

artist, p.c. 1991

BIRD, LARRY *Santo Domingo/Laguna*

A.K.A. Larry Little Bird

Born 1941

RESIDENCE: Santo Domingo, NM

EDUCATION: IAIA

OCCUPATION: Museum employee and painter

PUBLISHED: Snodgrass (1968). *Southwest Profile* (Aug/Sept/Oct 1992)

EXHIBITS: FAIEAIP, IAIA/M, MNM, SN, YAIA

AWARDS: *Interior Design* magazine, award for painting

BITER (see Zotom)

BITSUIE, MARIE *Navajo*

EXHIBITS: ITIC

AWARDS: ITIC ('93, 1st)

BISS, EARL, JR. *Crow/Chippewa*

Meadow Lark Boy (as a child); Spotted Horse (as an adult)

Born 29 Sept 1947 in Renton, WA; GGF: White Man Runs Him, scout for General George Custer

RESIDENCE: San Francisco, CA

EDUCATION: Mount Si High School, Snoqualmie, WA; Wapato (WA) High School; IAIA, 1966; B.A., SFAI, 1971; studied and painted in Europe

OCCUPATION: Artist

MEDIA: Oil and watercolor

PUBLISHED: Snodgrass (1968); New (1974); Highwater (1976); Hoffman, et al. (1984); Wade, ed. (1986); Hill (1992); Campbell, ed. (1993); Tryk (1993). *Southwestern Art* (winter 1977-1978); *Southwest Art* (Aug 1978); *The Santa Fean* (Aug 1978); *Art Voices South* (Sept/Oct 1979); *Arizona Arts and Lifestyle* (autumn 1981); *Santa Fe Profile* (Aug 1982); *Southwest Profile* (Aug/Sept/Oct 1992); *Rocky Mountain News* (7 Feb 1993)

PUBLIC COLLECTIONS: HM, IAIA, WWM

EXHIBITS: AC/K; AC/SD; ACE; ACMWA; BBHC; EIAF; HM; HS/NA; IAIA/M; IK; MFA/O; MNM; ND; NU/BC; OWE; PBS; RMA; SFAI; SI; SJSC; SN; SWAIA; TRP; USDI; WSC ; WWM; YAIA; Cuyahoga Valley Art Center, Cuyahoga Falls, OH; Institute of Contemporary Indian Art, Washington, D.C.; San Jose (CA) Museum of Fine Art; Berlin Festival, West Berlin, Germany; World's Fair, Osaka, Japan; galleries in AZ, CA, CO, and NM

SOLO EXHIBITS: Partial listing of more than twenty includes: IAIA/M; MAAIC; MPI; Yakima (WA) Regional Library

AWARDS: HM/G, MNM

HONORS: SFAI, scholarship

EARL BISS JR.

According to Biss, he was drawing by the time he was three and never stopped. When he was eleven years of age, he was stricken with rheumatic fever, an illness that forced him to spend a year in bed, and his art work became even more important. When he eventually returned to school, he was unable to participate in sports because of the effects of the illness, and as a result he channeled his energy into painting. He says he became the high school artist, which was a source of recognition from his peers. In 1977, Biss, when comparing his work to that of Fritz Scholder, his former teacher, said, "Fritz and I do not view life from the same frame of reference . . . I am a dreamer — a non-realist. My paintings say, 'If I had my way, this is the way the world would be — beautiful, alluring, idyllic, simple, poetic and heroic.'"

Horne 1977

BIXBY, LYN ROSS *Northern Cheyenne*

Born 1955 at Crow Agency, MT

RESIDENCE: Busby, MT

EDUCATION: High School, Denver, CO

MEDIA: Acrylic, pastel, and charcoal

EXHIBITS: NAVAM; Bureau of Indian Affairs, Lame Deer, MT; St. Labré Indian School, Ashland, MT

LYN ROSS BIXBY

An accident in 1984 damaged the nerves in the artist's right arm. Rather than give up his art, he learned to paint with his left hand.

BLACK (see Sweezy, Carl)

BLACK, KEITH *Cherokee*

RESIDENCE: Prairie Grove, AR

EXHIBITS: CNM

BLACK BEAR *Miniconjou Sioux*

Mato Sapo, Bear Black

Birth date unknown

RESIDENCE: Lived near Fort Sully, Dakota Territory, on the Cheyenne Agency Reservation from 1868-1869

PUBLISHED: Snodgrass (1968). *4th Annual Report*, BAE (1882-1883)

BLACK BEAR

"The artist executed a Winter Count chart (1800-1801 to 1868-1869), referred to as a 'History of the Miniconjous,' which covers almost the same period as that recorded by The Flame, The Swan, and Lone Dog"

Snodgrass 1968

BLACKBEAR (see Bosin, Blackbear)

BLACKBEAR, LEVI *Plains*

PUBLISHED: Snodgrass (1968)

PUBLIC COLLECTIONS: MAI

BLACK CLOUD (see Levings, Martin)

BLACK CROW *Sioux*

PUBLISHED: Snodgrass (1968). *4th Annual Report,* BAE (1882-1883); *10th Annual Report,* BAE (1888-1889)

BLACK EAGLE *Shoshoni/Yokut*

Born 13 Aug 1954 in Elko, NV; son of Helen Mose and Ernest Christman; M/GP: Maggie and Brownie Mose

RESIDENCE: Carmel Valley, CA

EDUCATION: Porterville (CA) Union High School, 1973

OCCUPATION: Craftsman and painter

MEDIA: Watercolor, pencil, charcoal, pen and ink, mixed-media, animal skin, beads, bone, and wood

PUBLISHED: *Southwest Art* (Feb 1994)

EXHIBITS: ACAI, AIAFM, EM, HM/G, ITAE, ITIC, OT, TIAF, RE, SM

AWARDS: ACAI ('93, 1st, Best of Class); AIAFM ('92, 1st, Best of Class, Best of Division, People's Choice; '93, 2-1st); EM ('93, 2-1st, Best of Class); HM/G ('93, Best of Division; '94, Best of Class, Best of Division); ITIC ('92, 1st; '93, 3-1st, Best of Category); ITAE ('93, 4-1st); OT ('92, Best of Class, Best of Category; '93, 3-1st, Best of Class); RE ('94, Best of Division); TIAF ('92, 1st); Hunter Mountain (NY) Eagle Indian Festival ('93, 1st)

BLACKHAIR (see Warner, Boyd, Jr.)

BLACK HEART *Oglala Sioux*

PUBLISHED: Snodgrass (1968)

PUBLIC COLLECTIONS: MAI

BLACK HORSE *Sioux*

Shunka Sapa, Black Horse

PUBLISHED: Snodgrass (1968)

PUBLIC COLLECTIONS: MNH/A

BLACK HORSE (see Tointigh, Jackie D., Jr.)

BLACK HORSE, FRANK *Oglala Sioux*

A.K.A. James Black Horse

Born 1891 in Wood, SD; died Oct 1967

OCCUPATION: Artist

COMMISSIONS: *Murals:* WPA

BLACK HORSE, JAMES (see Black Horse, Frank)

BLACK LANCE, LORENZO *Rosebud Sioux*

A-Nuk-A Sun Wam-bli, Golden Eagle

A.K.A. Lorenzo Ivan Black Lance

Born 13 Sept 1956 in Wagner, SD

RESIDENCE: Lower Brûlé, SD

EDUCATION: Todd County High School, Mission, SD, 1974; SGC

BLACK CROW

"Black Crow, chief of the Milk River Band, painted a buffalo hide record of exploits occurring in the 1870s."

Snodgrass 1968

BLACK EAGLE

Black Eagle lived the first two years of his life on the Te-Moak Reservation in Lee, NV. The next eighteen years were spent on the Tule River Reservation in Central California where the forests of the Sierras provided him with solitude and the opportunity to learn about himself and his place in nature. Inspired by the spirits of his grandmother and ancestors and his own experiences, Black Eagle strives to express his belief in the full circle of life in his art. It is his hope that his creations will inspire other Indian artists to also reach within themselves and revive native tribal arts before they are lost.

artist brochure 1994

BLACK HEART

"At the Pine Ridge Agency, SD, 12 men drew their autographs in a book. Among them is the signature of Black Heart — a figure with a triangular black heart."

Snodgrass 1968

BLACK HORSE

"One of the five artists whose works, now referred to as the Cronau Album (see Sinte), were commissioned and collected by Rudolf Cronau during 1880-1883."

Snodgrass 1968

OCCUPATION: Instructor, arts and crafts store manager, artist-in-residence, and artist

MEDIA: Acrylic, oil, watercolor, pencil, pastel, charcoal and mixed-media

PUBLISHED: *Buckskin Tokens*, cover

COMMISSIONS: *Murals:* Todd County High School, Mission SD. *Other:* Native American Heritage Foundation, Rapid City, SD, special edition prints, 1994

EXHIBITS: BHAA; RC; SIM; SPAC; Center for Western Studies Art Show, Rapid City and Sioux Falls, SD; South Dakota Memorial Art Center Traveling Art Exhibit, 1974; see also Awards

SOLO EXHIBITS: SIM

AWARDS: BHAA ('74); SPAC ('75, Award of Excellence); Siouxland Art Club Show, Mission, SD ('75, Best in Show)

LORENZO BLACK LANCE

"In my painting I try to depict the true life of the Lakota people. I also try to bring out the natural beauty of the Rosebud countryside and the animals that are so important to us. My point of view varies, sometimes traditional and sometimes contemporary. I try to make the people proud of what and who they are without romanticizing."

brochure, SIM, 1977

BLACK MOON (see Riddles, Leonard)

BLACKMORE, BILL *Athabascan*

Nazia, Great Hunter

A.K.A. William Arvin Blackmore

Born 3 Aug 1940 in Whitehorse, Yukon Territory; son of Bessie Johnson and Mickey Alvin Blackmore

RESIDENCE: Salmon Arm, BC, Canada

MILITARY: Canadian Armed Forces

EDUCATION: High school, Celista, BC, Canada; High school, Salmon Arm, BC, Canada; IAIA

OCCUPATION: Construction worker, hunting guide, and artist

PUBLISHED: Snodgrass (1968)

EXHIBITS: MNM; BC; Juneau, AK

BILL BLACKMORE

"Interested more in textile and fashion design than in painting, the artist received encouragement from Lloyd H. New and Carl Heinmiller."

Snodgrass 1968

BLACKMORE, WILLIAM ARVIN (see Blackmore, Bill)

BLACK MULE *Plains*

MEDIA: Pencil and crayon

PUBLIC COLLECTIONS: JAM (pictographic map, ca. 1880)

EXHIBITS: JAM

BLACKOWL, ARCHIE *Cheyenne*

Mis Ta Moo To Va, Flying Hawk

Born 23 Nov 1911 in Weatherford, OK; died Sept 1992 in Oklahoma; M/GGF: Crow Necklace, Cheyenne chief; descendant of Roman Nose, Cheyenne chief

RESIDENCE: Lived in Cushing, OK

EDUCATION: Fort Sill; Haskell; U of KS; CAI; studied painting under Olaf Nordmark

OCCUPATION: Teacher, government muralist, civil service employee, Walt Disney Studios employee, industrial painter for the aircraft industry, and artist

MEDIA: Tempera and prints

PUBLISHED: Jacobson and d'Ucel (1950); Petersen (1968); Dunn (1968); Snodgrass (1968); Jacobson (1964); Brody (1971); Highwater (1976); Silberman (1978); Broder (1981), Hoffman, et al. (1984); Samuels (1985). *Southwest Art* (Dec 1974); *Plateau* (V. 54, no. 1, 1982); *The Norman Transcript* (17 Oct 1980); *Oklahoma Art Gallery* (fall 1980); *Art Gallery* (Mar/Apr 1983; *Muskogee Phoenix* (4 Mar 1984); *The Indian Trader* (Mar 1990); *The Anadarko Daily News* (16 May 1992)

COMMISSIONS: *Murals:* PAC; The Palmer House, Chicago, IL; Fort Sill (OK) Officer's Club, cafeteria and gymnasium; Riverside Indian School; Kiowa Hospital, Lawton, OK

ARCHIE BLACKOWL

"Blackowl became aware of art at the age of six when he saw old Red Tooth painting a skin tipi. Encouraged by Woodrow Wilson Crumbo (q.v.), he began to paint seriously in the early 1930s." During his many years as an artist he maintained his traditional style, portraying accurately the Cheyenne traditions and culture that he experienced in his life. In his art as in his life he remained faithful to his heritage.

Snodgrass 1968, p.c. 1992

PUBLIC COLLECTIONS: ACM, GM, HCC, HSM/OK, IACB, KM, MAI, MNA/KHC, MRFM, OSAC, OU/SM, PAC, SPIM, LGAM

EXHIBITS: AC/A, AIAE/WSU, CNM, CPS, CSPIP, GM, HSM/OK, IK, ITIC, LGAM, MNM, MFA/O, MIF, MPABAS, NACLA, OAC, OMA, OU/MA/T, PAC, PAC/T, SPIM, USDS, WWM, VV

AWARDS: AIAE/WSU; ITIC ('80); PAC; state and tribal fairs

HONORS: Phillips 66 Foundation, grant study at U of OK; named a "Living Legend" by Ralph Oliver, 1990

BLACKRIDER, RADFORD (?)

Sings About Everything

Born 1962 in Bassano, AB, Canada

RESIDENCE: Bassano, AB, Canada

EDUCATION: Wheatland county schools

OCCUPATION: Grass Dancer, singer, and artist

MEDIA: Acrylic, watercolor, and mixed-media

PUBLISHED: Cardinal-Schubert (1992)

PUBLIC COLLECTIONS: C/AAF

EXHIBITS: C/AAF; C/TFD; C/TGVA; Master's Gallery, Calgary, AB

BLACKSHEEP, BEVERLY *Navajo*

Geneha

A.K.A. Beverly Blacksheep Geneha

RESIDENCE: Salina Springs, AZ, on the Navajo Reservation

EDUCATION: U of N AZ

OCCUPATION: Interior designer, illustrator, and painter

MEDIA: Gouache and technical ink

PUBLISHED: Jacka and Jacka (1994)

EXHIBITS: ITIC, NTF, SWAIA

AWARDS: ITIC ('87; '89, 1st; '91, 1st; '93, 1st, Best in Category; '94); NTF

HONORS: ITIC, poster artist, 1994

BEVERLY BLACKSHEEP

Blacksheep's paintings have been described as "Traditional Contemporary." She says, "My paintings are my connection with a way of life, simple, yet rich in tradition and history. Thorugh my art I have come to realize a deep appreciation of my heritage and the importance of preserving that heritage for generations to come."

artist brochure 1992

BLACK THUNDER *Teton Sioux*

PUBLISHED: Snodgrass (1968). *Bulletin 61,* BAE (1918)

BLACK WEASEL, WILBUR *Blackfeet*

Born 3 Nov 1956 in Browning, MT

RESIDENCE: Blackfeet Indian Reservation, MT

EDUCATION: Browning (MT) High School, 1975; U of MT, 1976-1977; Flathead Valley Community College, Kalispell, MT

OCCUPATION: Museum of the Plains Indian employee, and painter

EXHIBITS: MSF; Blackfeet Winter Expo, Browning, MT

SOLO EXHIBITS: MPI

AWARDS: MSF ('70, 1st)

WILBUR BLACK WEASEL

Black Weasel sold his first painting when he was in the 6th grade. He devotes his paintings to the subject he loves and knows best, ranching and rodeo.

brochure, MPI, 1978

BLACKWOOD, SUSAN *Cherokee*

Birth date unknown; daughter of Betty Vance and Dave Swartwout; P/GP: Bernadet and Rudy Swartwout; M/GP: Inez and Sanford Vance

RESIDENCE: Fort Collins, CO

EDUCATION: Niles East High School, Skokie, IL, 1966; Northern Illinois U, 1970; AAA

OCCUPATION: Sculptor and painter

MEDIA: Watercolor, pencil, pen and ink, bronze, and prints

PUBLISHED: *Woolgrower's Magazine* (Oct 1981); *Outdoor America* (winter 1989); *Art Links* (Nov/Dec 1989)
EXHIBITS: CLW, KWS/FS, NWCA, WAW
SOLO EXHIBITS: Statewide Woolgrower's Convention, Vail, CO
AWARDS: CLW, KWS/FS, NWCA, WAW

BLAINE, TERRY *Yankton Sioux*
Born 30 Oct 1955
RESIDENCE: Mitchell, SD
EDUCATION: G.E.D., Marty Indian Educational Program; Mitchell (SD) Vocational Technical School
OCCUPATION: Auto mechanic and artist
EXHIBITS: RC

BLAIR, BILL G. *Cherokee/Creek*
Born 13 Dec 1956
RESIDENCE: Fort Gibson, OK
EDUCATION: Fort Gibson (OK) High School
EXHIBITS: FCTM, RC
AWARDS: FCTM ('74, 1st; '75, Best in Show)
HONORS: Fort Gibson (OK) High School, honor roll, 4 years; All District, football and basketball; Boy's State Delegate

BLAKE, GEORGE *Hupa/Yurok*
RESIDENCE: Hoopa, CA
EXHIBITS: AICA/SF, CAM/S, RC, WWM
SOLO EXHIBITS: MPI

THE BLAZE (see The Flame)

BLAZE, RANDALL *Oglala Sioux*
RESIDENCE: Aloha, OR
OCCUPATION: Sculptor and painter
MEDIA: Mixed-media
PUBLIC COLLECTIONS: HCC
EXHIBITS: ACAI, NPTA, RC, TM/NE
AWARDS: NPTA ('91, 1st)

BLINDMAN, NATHAN *Oglala Sioux*
Born 3 Sept 1956
RESIDENCE: Chadron, NE
EDUCATION: Oglala Community High School, Pine Ridge, SD; Blackfoot (ID) High School; IAIA
COMMISSIONS: Shoshoni/Bannock Festival, logos, 1982
PUBLIC COLLECTIONS: HCC
EXHIBITS: RC; RE; TM/NE; Southern Idaho State Fair, Blackfoot, ID; Shoshoni/Bannock Festival Art Show, Fort Hall, ID

BLOODY KNIFE *Sioux*
PUBLISHED: Snodgrass (1968)
PUBLIC COLLECTIONS: SI/OAA (photographs of a pictographic robe)

BLUE, KAREN SAVAGE (see Savage-Blue, Karen)

BLUE ARM, NORMAN *Cheyenne River Sioux*
EXHIBITS: RC

BLUE BIRD (see Herrera, Joe Hilario)

BLUE EAGLE, ACEE *Creek/Pawnee*

Che Bon Ah Bu La (or *Chebona Bula*), Laughing Boy; *Lumhee Holatee*

A.K.A. Ah Say; Alex C. McIntosh

Born 17 Aug 1909 north of Anadarko, OK, on the Wichita Reservation; died 18 June 1959 in Muskogee, OK; son of Mattie Odom and Solomon McIntosh; P/GF: William McIntosh, Creek chief; P/GGF: Roley McIntosh, chief of the Creeks for 31 years

MILITARY: U.S. Air Force, WWII

EDUCATION: Chilocco, 1928; Oxford University, Oxford, England, non-credit classes, 1935; BC; U of OK; OSU/O, commercial art classes, 1951-1952

OCCUPATION: Craftsman, writer, illustrator, lecturer, teacher, college art department director, museum staff member, Indian flute player, dancer, and painter

PUBLISHED: Jacobson and d'Ucel (1950); Dunn (1968); Snodgrass (1968); Pierson and Davidson (1960); Jacobson (1964); Brody (1971); Highwater (1976); Dockstader (1977); Silberman (1978); Mahey, et al. (1980); Broder (1981); King (1981); Hoffman, et al. (1984); Samuels (1985); Wade, ed. (1986); Williams, ed. (1990); Archuleta and Strickland (1991). *4th Pawnee Indian Homecoming Program,* 1949; *Dancing Moccasins* (1957), program cover; *Blue Eagle – A Retrospective Exhibition,* PAC (1969); *Indians of Oklahoma,* BIA (1966); *The Sunday Oklahoman, Orbit Magazine* (23 Jan 1966; 27 Feb 1972); *The Muskogee Phoenix* (17 Aug 1960); *National Geographic* (n.d.); *American Indian Art* (spring 1985); *Twin Territories* (Special Edition 1991); biographical publications

BOOKS ILLUSTRATED: Blue Eagle (1959; 1971)

COMMISSIONS: *Murals:* Edmond (OK) Teacher's College; Oklahoma College for Women, Chickasha (OK); Muskogee (OK) Public Library; Veteran's Administration Hospital, Muskogee, OK; Colgate (OK), Federal Building; Seminole (OK), Federal Building; Black Hawk Club, Oklahoma City, OK; *U.S.S. Oklahoma* (the mural was lost at Pearl Harbor); Works of Art Project, murals throughout Oklahoma, 1934; Lions Clubs of Oklahoma, paintings for presentation to the *U.S.S. Oklahoma*, 1934

PUBLIC COLLECTIONS: BC; BIA; CCHM; DAM; GM; HSM/OK; IAIA; ITIC; KM; MNM; MNA; MRFM; OU/MA; OU/SM; PAC; SPL; WOM; National Art Museum of Ethiopia

EXHIBITS: AAIE, AC/A, AIE, AIEC, AIW, BC/McG, CCP, CSIPIP, CWC/I, DAM, EITA, FANEA, FCTM, GM, HM, HSM/OK, IAESS, IK, JGS, LGAM, MIF, MKMcNAI, MPABAS, OMA, OU/MA/T, OWE, PAC, PAC/T, USDS, SV

SOLO EXHIBITS: PAC; Muskogee (OK) Garden Club; Muskogee (OK) Public Library; PAC, Retrospective; GM, Memorial

AWARDS: Partial listing of more than forty includes: AIE; DAM; IAESS; ITIC; PAC; fairs and Indian ceremonials

HONORS: Represented Oklahoma Boy Scouts on European tour, 1929; International Education Conference, Oxford University, England, invited to lecture on Indian art, 1935; *American Magazine*, one of nine "colorful personalities" and "foremost living Indian Artists," 1937; named "Outstanding Indian in the United States," Anadarko, OK, 1958; National Art Museum of Ethiopia, medal presented by Haile Selassie for eight paintings; memorial biography, *Indian Life*; State of Oklahoma Legislature, honored post-humoously by Resolution for service to the state, 1959; Haskell Indian Junior College, Lawrence, KS, building named in his honor

ACEE BLUE EAGLE

"Although he never used it professionally, the artist's given name was Alex C. McIntosh; rather, he adopted the name Blue Eagle from his paternal grandfather. Blue Eagle was gregarious and outgoing, a showman who sold himself and Indian art to the world. Charles Banks Wilson, Oklahoma artist and muralist, who knew him well, is quoted as saying, 'Acee was the Dale Carnegie of Indian Art. If Oklahoma has a foundation in Indian Art, it is with Acee Blue Eagle.'"

Snodgrass 1968

Blue Eagle established the Art Department at Bacone College and was its first Director.

BLUE FLOWER (see Pop Chalee)

BLUE HORSE (see Keith, C. Hobart)

BLUEHORSE, GEORGE *Navajo*
EDUCATION: Albuquerque, 1960
PUBLISHED: Snodgrass (1968)
EXHIBITS: MNM

BLUE JAY (see De Groat, Jay)

BLUE SPRUCE *Tewa*
Standing Deer
Born 21 Jan 1946; son of Frances and Joe Suazo
RESIDENCE: Taos, NM
EDUCATION: Graduated high school, 1965
OCCUPATION: Painter
MEDIA: Acrylic
EXHIBITS: MRFM

BLUE THUNDER *Yanktonai Sioux*
PUBLISHED: Maurer (1992)
PUBLIC COLLECTIONS: HS/ND
EXHIBITS: VP

BLYTHE, BILL *Cherokee*
RESIDENCE: Checotah, OK
EXHIBITS: CNM, FCTM
AWARDS: FCTM ('87, 1st)

BO (see Bocock, Lee)

BOB, DEMPSEY *Tlingit*
Born 1948 at Telegraph Creek on the Stikine River, BC, Canada
EDUCATION: Prince Rupert, BC; Prince George, BC; C/KSNCIA, 1972, 1974
OCCUPATION: Teacher, carver, jeweler, and graphic artist
MEDIA: Wood, silver, gold, and prints
PUBLISHED: Macnair, Hoover, and Neary (1980)
PUBLIC COLLECTIONS: C/CMC; C/U of BC/MA; SI; Ethnology Museum, Hamburg, Germany; National Museum, Osaka, Japan
EXHIBITS: C/CMC, C/RBCM, PAC

DEMPSEY BOB

In addition to doing silkscreen prints, Bob is known for his bowls, masks, helmets, large totem poles and button blanket designs. He also works in silver and gold, but his favorite medium is wood.

Macnair, Hoover, and Neary 1980

BOBB, HENRIETTA *Navajo*
RESIDENCE: Reno, NV
EDUCATION: U of AZ, "Southwest Indian Art Project," scholarship, summer 1962
PUBLISHED: Snodgrass (1968)

BOCOCK, LEE *Choctaw/Cherokee*
A.K.A. Bo
RESIDENCE: Oklahoma City, OK
PUBLISHED: *Preview* (June 1992), cover
EXHIBITS: ITIC, FAIE; see also Awards
AWARDS: ITIC ('88); El Reno (OK) Art Show, 1982

BOHANAN, TERRY *Choctaw*
EXHIBITS: CNM, FCTM
AWARDS: FCTM ('78, 1st, IH; '80)

BOIDE (see The Flame)

BOLIN, FLOYD *Cherokee*

EDUCATION: IAIA, 1965-1966
PUBLISHED: Snodgrass (1968)
EXHIBITS: YAIA

BOLLER, LEWIS, JR. *Shoshoni*

Born 1928 in Fort Collins, CO
RESIDENCE: Lander, WY
OCCUPATION: Rancher, rodeo contestant, store manager, sculptor, and painter
MEDIA: Oil, watercolor, pen and ink, pencil, and bronze
EXHIBITS: CIA, SN
AWARDS: SN

BOMBERRY, ALEX *Cayuga*

Born 9 Feb 1953
RESIDENCE: Caledonia, ON, Canada
EDUCATION: Manitou Arts Foundation at Manitoulin Island (ON), summers 1971, 1973; Opportunities for Youth Project, Sheridan College, Oakville, NY, 1972
OCCUPATION: Artist
MEDIA: Acrylic, watercolor, pen and ink, and pencil
PUBLISHED: Johannsen and Ferguson, eds. (1983)
EXHIBITS: C/MAF; NACLA; C/WICEC; Canadian National Exhibition, Toronto, ON; Education Centre of the Toronto (ON) Board of Education

ALEX BOMBERRY

Bomberry is best known for his stylized portraits of Native Americans. He would like people viewing his portraits to look at them as though they were photographs.

Johannsen and Ferguson, eds. 1983

BOMBERRY, LARRY *Mohawk*

Born 1948 on the Six Nations Reserve, ON, Canada
RESIDENCE: Canada
EXHIBITS: C/WICEC

BOMBERRY, VINCE *Mohawk*

A.K.A. Vincent Bomberry
Born 1958 on the Six Nations Reserve, ON, Canada
RESIDENCE: Canada
EXHIBITS: C/AC/MS; C/WICEC; NACLA; galleries in Ontario

BONAPARTE, ARAWARATHE (see Bonaparte, Brad)

BONAPARTE, BRAD *Mohawk*

A.K.A. Bradford Bonaparte; Arawarathe Bonaparte
Born 1969 in Syracuse, NY
RESIDENCE: Bombay, NY
EDUCATION: Humber School of Applied Arts and Technology, Toronto, ON; Toronto (ON) School of Fine Arts
PUBLISHED: *Albuquerque Journal* (7 June 1992)
EXHIBITS: OLO; Steinman Festival of the Arts, St. Lawrence University, Canton, NY; Akwesasne Museum Community Show, Hogansburg, NY; Akwesasne Library and Museum

BONE SHIRT, WALTER *Sioux*

MEDIA: Colored pencil and pen and ink
PUBLISHED: Maurer (1992)
EXHIBITS: VP

Boney, Kenneth *Chippewa*

Born 18 Sept 1941

RESIDENCE: Orr, MN

EDUCATION: Orr (MN) High School; IAIA, one year

EXHIBITS: RC; throughout MN

Boni, Delmar *Apache*

Delmar Boni

"Boni believes the 'Pop' approach to painting affords the most direct route for artistic commentary on the anomalies and inconsistencies that he has observed in the position of the American Indian in today's society. 'The longer I live the more I come full circle to the values of my elders.'"

New 1981

Born 1948 on the San Carlos Apache Indian Reservation, AZ

RESIDENCE: Sacaton, AZ

EDUCATION: Fort Thomas (AZ) High School; Eastern Arizona College, Thatcher, and Central Arizona College, Coolidge; A.F.A., IAIA; B.A., College of Santa Fe, NM, 1977; M.A., ASU, 1982

OCCUPATION: Art director, art instructor, teacher, director of youth programs, craftsman, and painter

MEDIA: Oil, acrylic, and mixed-media

PUBLISHED: Highwater (1976, 1980); New (1979; 1981); Hill (1992). *Native Arts/West* (Jan 1981); *Santa Fean Magazine* (June 1992)

COMMISSIONS: American Junior College Board, Washington, D.C., painting, 1975

PUBLIC COLLECTIONS: IAIA, PAC

EXHIBITS: HM; IAIA; NACLA; NICCAS; PAC; PAIC; SFFA; SN; The Scottsdale (AZ) Artist League Show; Santa Fe (NM) Armory Show

AWARDS: PAC ('75, 1st)

HONORS: SWAIA, Board of Directors

Bonita, Peña *Apache*

RESIDENCE: New York, NY

PUBLISHED: *America West* (July 1990)

EXHIBITS: AICA/SF

Booka, Connie *Zuni*

A.K.A. Connie Cooka

EDUCATION: Santa Fe, 1946

PUBLIC COLLECTIONS: PAC

EXHIBITS: PAC

AWARDS: PAC

Bordeaux, Gregory P., Sr. *Rosebud Sioux*

Gregory P. Bordeaux Sr.

The artist explains, "I do my art and keep some and sell some for exposure."

p.c. 1991

Born 2 Apr 1947; son of Mary Louise and Cleveland Bordeaux; P/GP: Cecilia and William Bordeaux; M/GP: Clementine and Felix LaRoche

RESIDENCE: Gluek, MA

EDUCATION: St. Francis Indian School, 1965; SGC, 1989

OCCUPATION: Skilled carpenter and painter

MEDIA: Oil, acrylic, watercolor, pencil, and pen and ink

Bosin, Blackbear *Kiowa/Comanche*

Tsate Kongia, Blackbear

A.K.A. Francis Blackbear Bosin

Born 5 June 1921 near Anadarko, OK; died 9 Aug 1980 in Wichita, KS; son of Ada Tivis, beadworker, and Frank Blackbear Bosin; P/GF: Mahnkee; M/GM: Kahchatscha, Comanche Awl Band medicine woman

RESIDENCE: Lived in Wichita, KS

MILITARY: U.S. Marine Corps, WWII

EDUCATION: Cyril (OK) High School, 1940

OCCUPATION: Color separator and platemaker, illustrator, commercial artist, gallery owner, sculptor, and painter

MEDIA: Gouache, casein, and steel

PUBLISHED: Sterling (1955); LaFarge (1956; 1960); Carlson (1964); Petersen (1968); Dunn (1968); Snodgrass (1968); Pierson and Davidson (1960); Dockstader (1961); Brody (1971); Ellison (1972); Irvine, ed. (1974); Highwater (1976); Silberman (1978); Mahen, et al. (1980); Boyd (1981); Broder (1981); Boyd, et al. (1981; 1983); Hoffman, et al. (1984); Samuels (1985); Wade, ed. (1986); Archuleta and Strickland (1991); Maurer (1992); Ballantine and Ballantine (1993). *National Geographic Magazine* (Mar 1955); *Oklahoma Today* (summer 1958; winter 1965; Dec 1990); *Life International* (16 Mar 1959); *American Indian Paintings From the Collection of Philbrook Art Center* (1964), cover; *Sunday Bonanza, San Francisco Chronicle* (22 Aug 1965); *The Western Review* (Paris, France); *Pictorial History of the American Indian; The Journal of the American Medical Association; The Wichita Eagle-Beacon* (17 Sept 1972; 28 July 1974; 21 Feb 1982); *The Indian Trader* (Nov 1972); *The Wichita Beacon* (20 July 1973; 25 June 1974); *Southwest Art* (Dec 1974; June 1981); *The Sunday Oklahoman, Orbit Magazine* (8 Aug 1976), cover; *The Wichita Eagle* (12 Aug 1980); *The Tulsa Tribune* (20 Aug 1980); *The Wichitan* (July 1984); biographical publications

BOOKS ILLUSTRATED: Martin (1963)

COMMISSIONS: *Murals:* McConnell Air Force Base, Wichita, KS; North High School, Wichita, KS; Broadview Hotel, Wichita, KS; Farm Credit Banks of Wichita (KS). *Other:* Indian Arts and Crafts Board, Department of the Interior, Washington, D.C., painting series; City of Wichita (KS), *Keeper of the Plains*, sculpture, 1974

PUBLIC COLLECTIONS: BIA, DAM, EM, GM, HM, IACB, PAC, RMC/AZ, WAAG, WAM

EXHIBITS: AAID; AIHA; CAI; CPLH; CSPIP; DAM; IK; JGS; KCPI; LACM; LGAM; MFA/A; MFA/O; MKMcNAI; MPABAS; MPI; NAP; NGA; OMA; OU/MA/T; PAC; PAC/T; RMC/AZ; SI; SPIM; SV; TAI; UMA; VP; WAM; Abilene (TX) Fine Arts Museum; Miami Beach (FL) Art Center; White House Festival of the Arts, Washington, D.C.

SOLO EXHIBITS: AHNHG, HM, PAC, SPIM, WAAG, WMWA

AWARDS: Partial listing of more than 33 includes: AAID; CPLH; DAM; ITIC; MNM; PAC; SN; four grand awards

HONORS: U.S. Chamber of Commerce, Civil Servant Award, 1959; Wichita (KS) Art Guild, Board of Directors; IACB, Certificate of Appreciation, 1966; International Arts and Letters, Kreuzlingen, Switzerland, made a fellow; PAC, Waite Phillips Trophy for Outstanding Contributions to American Indian Art, 1967

Blackbear Bosin

"The artist was the eldest of four children. At 17, he helped maintain the family farm, painting in spare moments. Although unable to accept two university art scholarships because of family obligations, he achieved success with little formal training and became the only American Indian artist to be represented in the 1965 White House Festival of the Arts."

Snodgrass 1968

According to Jeanne Snodgrass-King, a close friend of Bosin's, his later works were so innovative and distinctive that they became a model for a younger generation of Indian artists.

p.c. 1993

BOSIN, FRANCIS BLACKBEAR (see Bosin, Blackbear)

BOSWELL, HELEN *Cherokee/Chippewa*

Born 1906 in Chicago, IL

RESIDENCE: Birmingham, AL

PUBLISHED: Snodgrass (1968); Brody (1971)

EXHIBITS: BMA, FAIEAIP, ITIC, JGS, PAC

SOLO/SPECIAL EXHIBITS: HM, PAC (dual show)

BOTELLA, EMMETT *Mescalero Apache*

RESIDENCE: Mescalero, NM

PUBLISHED: Snodgrass (1968)

EXHIBITS: MNM

BOUDETAH (see Smoky, Lois)

BOUGETA (see Smoky, Lois)

BOUGETAH (see Smoky, Lois)

BOWANNIE, FILBERT (see Bowannie, Philbert)

BOWANNIE, PHILBERT *Zuni*

A.K.A. Filbert Bowannie
RESIDENCE: Zuni, NM
EXHIBITS: ITIC
AWARDS: ITIC ('89)

BOW-ARROW (see Waano-Gano, Joe T.N.)

BOW BIGMAN (see Big Bow)

BOWEKATY, MARK *Zuni*

EXHIBITS: HM/G, SN

BOWERS, NIKKI *Cherokee*

Born 29 Nov 1939
EXHIBITS: QACM

BOWKER, R. G. *Minnecoujou Sioux*

A.K.A. Burke
Born 14 Dec 1938 on the Cheyenne River Sioux Reservation, SD
RESIDENCE: Azle, TX
EDUCATION: Cheyenne River (SD) Boarding School, 1957; Aberdeen (SD) School of Commerce, 1958; Northern State College, Aberdeen, SD, 1958-1960
OCCUPATION: Sculptor and painter
MEDIA: Oil, clay, wax, and bronze
PUBLISHED: *The Indian Trader* (Oct 1982)
PUBLIC COLLECTIONS: HCC, Capitol Building, Pierre, SD
EXHIBITS: AICA/SF; HM/G; NPTA; PAC; RC; SIM; Cheyenne River Tribal Fair, Eagle Butte, SD; galleries in Texas
SOLO EXHIBITS: SIM
AWARDS: RC ('76, 1st; '78; '80; '91, 1st, Hensler Award; '92,)

R. G. BOWKER

"As an artist, I want to put before the people a sense of pride through my art. Pride in being Indian and pride in things Indian. I want people who view my art to say, 'Hey, an Indian did that!' As for my media, sculpture and oil paintings are great art forms for preserving the dignity and spirit of the American Indian for future generations. I find a lot of satisfaction for myself in creating a moment in history. . ."

brochure, SIM, 1982

Bowker is a member of the Dream Catchers Artist Guild, Ltd. (q.v.).

BOXLEY, DAVID *Tsimshian*

Born 1952 in Ketchikan, AK; raised by his grandparents in Metlakatla, AK
RESIDENCE: Metlakatla, AK
EDUCATION: B.A., Seattle (WA) Pacific University; studied under Jack Hudson and Duane Pasco (qq.v.)
OCCUPATION: Teacher, coach, carver, printmaker, and painter
PUBLISHED: Gerber and Bruggmann (1989)

BOY (see Gorman, Alfred Kee)

BOY OF THE WOODS (see Des Jarlait, Patrick Robert)

BOYD, GEORGE A., JR. *Sioux/Assiniboin*

Born 20 Jan 1910 in Blair, MT
RESIDENCE: Brockton, MT
EDUCATION: Brockton (MT) Public Schools
OCCUPATION: Rancher, Sioux Tribal Credit Program Committee Board Member, and painter

GEORGE A. BOYD JR.

"Boyd has worked with livestock nearly all his life, an interest reflected in his representational paintings."

Snodgrass 1968

PUBLISHED: Snodgrass (1968)

EXHIBITS: CIA; MSF; National Indian conference, Bismarck, ND; local exhibits

AWARDS: MSF ('34, 1st)

BOYER, BOB *Métis*

Born 1948 in Prince Albert, SK, Canada

RESIDENCE: Canada

EDUCATION: B.Ed., C/U of SK, 1971

OCCUPATION: Art and drama teacher, community program officer, assistant professor, consultant, college department head, lecturer, traditional dancer, and painter

MEDIA: Oil, acrylic, watercolor, pastel, charcoal, and cotton fabric

PUBLISHED: Menitove (1986b); McMasters, et al. (1993). *New Breed* (Sept 1980, Sept 1982); *Arts West* (Vol. 6, no. 10, 1981; Nov 1982), *Indian News* (Oct 1981); *The Saskatchewan Indian* (Aug 1982); *Great Plains Quarterly* (summer 1982); *Arts Canada* (Dec 1982); *Vanguard* (Nov 1984; Jan 1986); *American Indian Art* (spring 1985; autumn 1992); *Indian Art Sketchbook* (spring 1985); *Windspeaker* (12 Dec 1986; Feb 1987); *Artscraft Quarterly* (1989); *Fuse Magazine* (Aug 1989; fall 1990); *Artscraft* (summer 1990; fall 1990)

COMMISSIONS: *Murals:* C/MNH/SK, 1990; Odeon Cineplex, Regina, SK, 1988. *Other:* NAIC, 1984; Government of Canada, Department of Supply and Services, reproductions for use at two national exhibits; Regina Public Library Board, art work

PUBLIC COLLECTIONS: Partial listing includes: C/AG/M; C/AG/TB; C/AG/WP; C/CCAB; C/CMC; C/ESSOC; C/GM; C/INAC; C/MCC; C/MNH/SK; C/NCCT; C/NGCA; C/NHFC; C/RPL; C/SAB; C/U of R/MG; SM; Ben Gurion University, Israel; Canadian Broadcasting Corporation, Regina, SK; City of Regina, SK; Federation of Saskatchewan Indian Nations, Regina, SK; Interprovincial Pipe and Steel Corporation, Regina, SK; Native Heritage Foundation, Regina, SK; Sheraton Hotels Corporation, Toronto, ON

EXHIBITS: Partial listing of more than seventy (since 1971) includes: C/AC/AE; C/AC/M; C/ACA; C/AG/TB; C/CAC; C/ACCCNA; C/AG/E; C/AG/M; C/AG/NS; C/AG/O; C/AG/TB; C/AG/V; C/CIIA; C/CR; C/GM; C/ISS; C/LUM; C/NAC; C/NGCA; C/NCCT; C/NWNG; C/O; C/OM; C/OS; C/RPL; C/TI; C/U of BC/MA; C/U of R/MG; C/U of SK; Beau Art Galerie, Paris, France; Government of Saskatchewan Legislative Building, Regina, SK; Museo Contempráneo de Monterrey, Mexico; Saskatchewan Library, Saskatoon, SK

SOLO EXHIBITS: C/AG/E, C/UG, C/U of BC/MA, C/U of SK

HONORS: Society of Canadian Artists of Native Ancestry, chairperson

BOB BOYER

Boyer's art is concerned with global and Native issues, and personal experiences. Although it incorporates traditional Plains Indian designs, his art also uses modern art concepts in a highly personal style. His paintings can be appreciated for their color relationships, for the meaning imparted by the Plains symbolism and spirituality, and for the interplay between the paintings and their titles. His unique use of flannel blankets as a painting surface came from his knowledge of Plains Indian paraphernalia; specifically, tipi liners.

Museum Note No. 23
C/Uof BC/MA, *1988*

BOY HERO (see Silverhorn, George)

BOYIDDLE, PARKER, JR. *Kiowa/Wichita/Delaware/Chicksaw*

Born 21 July 1947 in Chickasha, OK; son of Thamar and Parker Boyiddle; P/GP: Nettie and Adeli Boyiddle; M/GP: George and Noka May

RESIDENCE: Westcliff, CO

MILITARY: U.S. Air Force, 1967-1971

EDUCATION: Classen High School, Oklahoma City, OK; IAIA, 1964-1966, Pima Community College, Tucson, AZ, 1972-1973

OCCUPATION: Sculptor; painter since 1977

MEDIA: Oil, acrylic, watercolor, pencil, pastel, bronze, clay, plastic, and prints

PUBLISHED: Snodgrass (1968); New (1979); Samuels (1985). *Tulsa Tribune* (28 Apr 1978); *The Indian Trader* (July 1978; Jan 1979; Sept 1980; June 1982); *Southwest Art* (July 1987); *Oklahoma Today* (May/June 1994)

PARKER BOYIDDLE JR.

The artist studied under renowned Indian artist/educators, Allan Houser and Fritz Scholder (qq.v.) while at The Institute. They were significant influences on his artistic development. According to Boyiddle, "What I am trying to do is reflect my environment and transcend a cultural gap. People can only idealize their (continued)

Parker Boyiddle Jr.

(continued) ancestral past. My ancestors were Plains Indians — Kiowa on my father's side and Delaware on my mother's, both hunted buffalo and were nomads. Today there is no way I could live that life, but I can exercise some of the customs, morals, and religion of my people and still function in this twentieth century life."

brochure, SPIM, 1979

David Bradley

The artist stated, "I do like to have fun with my art and I like to find humor. In some paintings I try to put humor in, but there are also some very grave, serious symbols there, too. I'll put symbols in my paintings that might suggest the state of the world today. Even though it's a scene from the Old West, all of a sudden it will relate to what's going on today."

Samuels 1982

COMMISSIONS: *Murals:* Kiowa Tribal Complex, Carnegie, OK [with Mirac Creepingbear and Sherman Chaddlesone (qq.v.)]

PUBLIC COLLECTIONS: SPIM; The Kiowa Tribal Museum, Carnegie, OK

EXHIBITS: ACAI; AICA; AIE; CIM; CMN; GPWAS; ITIC; MMO; PAC; PAIC; SDMM; SN; SPIM; TCBA; YAIA; Galerie Pierre Cardin, Paris, France

SOLO EXHIBITS: SPIM

AWARDS: AICA ('79, Gold Award); AIE ('77, Grand Award); CIM ('86, Best of Class); CNM ('77, Class II Award; '84, Grand Award; '91; '92); GPWAS; ITIC ('86); PAC ('78, Grand Award); RE ('87, 1st); SN ('68, 1st; '76)

HONORS: Oklahoma Science and Art Foundation, Oklahoma City, OK, art scholarship

Brabant, Gene *Cree*

Born 1946 in Victoria, BC, Canada

EDUCATION: Apprenticeship with Tony Hunt and John Livingston (q.v.)

PUBLISHED: *Colonist* (1976)

PUBLIC COLLECTIONS: C/INAC

Bradley, David *Chippewa/Sioux*

A.K.A. David Paul Bradley; David P. Bradley

Born 1954 in Eureka, CA

RESIDENCE: Santa Fe, NM

EDUCATION: College of St. Thomas, St. Paul, MN; A.F.A., IAIA, 1977-1979; U of AZ, 1979; CSF/SF, 1980; Peace Corps, Guatemala, two years

OCCUPATION: Peace Corp volunteer, educator, printmaker, ceramist, sculptor, and painter

MEDIA: Oil, acrylic, stone, clay, and bronze

PUBLISHED: Amerson, ed. (1981); New (1981); Samuels (1982); Hoffman, et al. (1984); Wade, ed. (1986); Gentry, et al. (1990); Williams, ed. (1990); Hill (1992); Tryk (1993); *Artspace* (1981, 1987); *The New York Post* (17 Apr 1981); *Santa Fean Magazine* (Aug 1981; Jan 1982; Aug 1989; Aug 1994); *Santa Fe Reporter* (20 Aug 1981; 15 Aug 1984); *The Indian Trader* (Oct 1981); *The Arizona Republic* (12 Nov 1982); *The New York Times* (19 Nov 1982); *The Scottsdale Progress* (29 Oct 1982); *Southwest Art* (Dec 1983); *The New Mexican* (14 Aug 1986); *The Albuquerque Journal* (13 Aug 1991); *Indian Market,* SWAIA (1991); *Southwest Profile* (Aug/Sept/Oct 1992)

BOOKS ILLUSTRATED: Bruchae (1993)

PUBLIC COLLECTIONS: ABQM; BBHC; C/U of R/MB; DAM; HM; IACB; IAIA; JAM; MAI; MNM; NMAA; Atlantic Richfield Corp., Tucson, AZ; Bruce Museum, Greenwich, CT; Maytag Foundation; Museum of Mankind, Vienna, Austria; Northern Illinois University, DeKalb, IL; Stamford (CT) Museum; U.S. Embassy, Oslo, Norway

EXHIBITS: AA; ABQM; AC/SD; AICH; BBHC; BSU; C/ACA; CNGM; CTC; EM; HM; HM/G; HMA; IAIA/M; IK; ITIC; JAM; KCPA; MAI; MFA/O; MIA; MIC; MKMcNAI; MNM; MRFM; NACLA; NMSC; NMSF; OAE; OWE; RC; SFFA; SI; SWAIA; TI; TRP; U of CA/D; U of MN/B; U of MN/TC; U of MN/AM; U of ND; WIB; WWM; Amerika Haus, Stuttgart, Germany; Armory for the Arts, Santa Fe, NM; National Museum Institute, Lima, Peru, 1981

SOLO EXHIBITS: BSU; IAIA; PIM; Plains Art Museum, Fargo, ND

AWARDS: HM/G ('79, Pierce-Avery Award; '80, Purchase Award); IAIA; ITIC ('78; '79); MIC; NMSF; OAE; RC ('79); SWAIA ('80, Hinds Award)

HONORS: IAIA Valedictorian 1979; Minnesota Chippewa Tribe, Award of Merit in Art, 1979; SWAIA Fellowship, 1980; *Santa Fean Magazine,* Artist of the Year, 1982; SWAIA, Board of Directors, 1991

BRADLEY, ROBERTA C. (see Weckeah)

BRANDED CORN (see Sánchez, Ramos)

BRANDO, STEPHEN *Chippewa/Ottawa*

Born 27 July 1949; son of Marian and Vincent Brando
RESIDENCE: Mountain Top, PA
EDUCATION: Crestwood (PA) High School
PUBLISHED: Snodgrass (1968)
EXHIBITS: Local shows and exhibits

STEPHEN BRANDO

"This young artist is interested in many art forms and has received considerable local recognition."

Snodgrass 1968

BRANT, DOUGLAS, JR. *Mohawk*

Born 1949 on the Thayendanegea Reserve, ON, Canada
RESIDENCE: Brantford, ON, Canada
MEDIA: Pen and ink
PUBLISHED: *Indian News* (Mar 1974); *The Expositor* (28 July 1984); *Universal Engineer* (Oct 1984); *The Hamilton Spectator* (Aug 1986); *The Manitoulin Recorder* (Oct 1986); *The Burlington Post* (Nov 1986)
PUBLIC COLLECTIONS: SMII
EXHIBITS: C/NIACC; C/NWPCAL; C/WICEC; London (ON) Arts and Crafts Show, 1980-1982; Rainbow Fine Art Show, Niagara Falls, NY, 1982; Canadian National Exhibition, Toronto, ON, 1984; Indian fairs, arts and crafts shows, and powwows; see also Awards
SOLO EXHIBITS: Joseph Brant Museum, Burlington, ON, 1986
AWARDS: Seneca Indian Fall Fair, Brant, NY ('82, 1st)

BRANT, LYNDA HAYFIELD *Mohawk*

Born 17 Aug 1954
RESIDENCE: Kingston, ON, Canada
EDUCATION: Moira Secondary School, Belleville, ON; Ontario College of Arts
OCCUPATION: Volunteer art teacher and artist
MEDIA: Oil, watercolor, pastel, pencil, and pen and ink
PUBLISHED: Johannsen and Ferguson, eds. (1983)
EXHIBITS: Mohawk Fall Fair

BRASCOUPÉ, CLAYTON *Mohawk/Algonquin*

EXHIBITS: NACLA

BRASCOUPÉ, SIMON *Mohawk/Algonquin*

Born 1948 on the Tuscarora Indian Reservation, NY
RESIDENCE: Sanborn, NY
EDUCATION: Algonquin College, Ottawa, ON; M.A., SUNY/B; Ph.D. Candidate, SUNY/B
OCCUPATION: Marketing and advertising consultant, art director, editor, special projects manager, arts organization director, professor, beadworker, and artist
MEDIA: Acrylic, pen and ink, beads, fabric, and prints
PUBLISHED: Chevalier (1982). *Turtle Quarterly* (Vol. 2, no. 4, 1980; Vol. 3, no. 3, 1981); *The Brantford Expositor* (9 Aug 1980); *The Ottawa Citizen* (2 July 1981); *The Indian Leader* (spring 1986); *Northeast Indian Quarterly Journal* (1991; 1992), cover
COMMISSIONS: *Murals:* NACLA, 1984. *Other:* Heart Institute, Civic Hospital, painting, 1989; Department of Health and Welfare, poster; Canadian Council for Native Business, prints, 1990, 1991
PUBLIC COLLECTIONS: C/CMC; SMII; MAI; SI; SM; Sichuan Management, Chengdu, Sichuan, China

EXHIBITS: Partial listing of more than ninety includes: AICA/SF; AICH; C/AC; C/AG/TB; C/AG/W; C/FCIA; C/CIIA; C/CMC; C/MCAF; C/MNH; C/NCCT; C/NIACC; C/WICEC; CNAIA; HM; MIA; NACLA; NU/BC; QM; RCAS; SI; SU/NY; SWAIA; TRP; WASG; Winterlude Festival, Ottawa, ON; Trenton (NJ) State College; Ottawa (ON) School of Art; Peking, China; Brest and Bordeaux, France

SOLO EXHIBITS: C/AG/W, SM

BRAVE BULL *Sioux*

PUBLISHED: Snodgrass (1968)

PUBLIC COLLECTIONS: MPM (pictograph on paper)

BRAVE, FRANKLIN P. *Osage/Cherokee*

Wa Shun Keh, Thorn (or Sand Burr)

Born 21 Dec 1932 in Pawhuska, OK

MILITARY: U.S. Army

EDUCATION: Haskell; KCAI/MO

OCCUPATION: Advertising artist and painter

PUBLISHED: Snodgrass (1968)

EXHIBITS: PAC

BRAVEHEART, GENE *Rosebud Sioux*

EXHIBITS: NPTA

AWARDS: NPTA ('91, 1st)

BREAD, JACKIE LARSON (see Larson, Jackie)

BREWER, BARBARA *Chippewa*

RESIDENCE: Quenemo, KS

EXHIBITS: LIAS

BREWER, DEANNA M. *Oglala Sioux/Potawatomi*

RESIDENCE: Edwardsville, KS

MEDIA: Pastel

EXHIBITS: AIE, LIAS

AWARDS: AIE

BREWER, DONALD A. *Cheyenne River Sioux*

Wakpa

RESIDENCE: Denver, CO

PUBLIC COLLECTIONS: HCC

EXHIBITS: ITAE/M, NPTA, PBS, RC, UTAE

AWARDS: RC ('89, Aplan Award); UTAE ('92)

BRIAN, BENNETT *Chippewa*

EXHIBITS: HM/G

AWARDS: HM/G ('78, 1st)

BRIGHT WING (see Fox, Guy)

BRIM, MARY *Cherokee*

PUBLISHED: Snodgrass (1968)

EXHIBITS: AAIE

BRINGS PLENTY, STUART *Oglala Sioux*

Born 17 June 1953

RESIDENCE: Sioux Falls, SD

EDUCATION: RC; Oglala Community School, SD; Chadron (NE) State College; National College of Business; Highline Community College, Midway, WA
EXHIBITS: AIE, RC
AWARDS: AIE (1st)

BRODIGAN, N'DE *Oglala Sioux*

Born 14 Feb 1947
EDUCATION: High school; night school in Ohio
EXHIBITS: RC; county and state fairs and regional exhibits throughout Ohio
AWARDS: More than twenty, including eight first places

BROER, ROGER L. *Oglala/Lakota Sioux*

Born 9 Nov 1945 in Omaha, NE; son of Evelyn Carney; adopted by Frieda and Ludwig Broer
RESIDENCE: Kent, WA
MILITARY: U.S. Air Force
EDUCATION: Randolph (NE) High School, 1964; B.A., EMC, 1974; M.A., Central Washington University, 1975
OCCUPATION: Teacher, lecturer, consultant, sculptor, ceramist, and painter
MEDIA: Oil, watercolor, pencil, pen and ink, pastel, mixed-media, stone, clay, and prints
PUBLISHED: Samuels (1982). *The Puget Sound Group of Northwest Painters First Fifty Years* (1978); *Lutheran Brotherhood Bond* (1980); *The Indian Trader* (Aug 1983); *Nebraskaland Magazine* (1984); biographical publications
COMMISSIONS: *Murals:* DIA, 1993. *Other:* American Telephone and Telegraph Corp., 1991
PUBLIC COLLECTIONS: BIA; EMC; ESC; HCC; MNAC; RC; SIM; SJIS; USDI; Pierre Cardin, Paris, France; Nebraska State Art Museum, Kearney, NE; ATKA Lakota Museum, Chamberlain, SD; SAFECO Insurance Co. of America, Seattle, WA; Seafirst Bank, Seattle, WA; and Washington Arts Commission, Olympia, WA
EXHIBITS: Partial listing of more than fifty includes: AC/DS; AC/Y; AICA; CIAE; CIM; CNM; CPS; FAM; HCC; HPTU; MNAC; LAC; NPTA; NWASA; PAC; RC; RCBC; RVW; SDCC; SWAIA; TM/NE; WTF; Ball State University, Muncie, IN; Frank Tenney Johnson Memorial, Palm Springs, CA, 1979; Yakima Valley Annual, WA, 1978
SOLO EXHIBITIONS: Partial listing of 26 includes: BIA; CC/WA; MNAC; MPI; USDI
AWARDS: Partial listing includes: AICA ('79; '81; '82, Best of Show); AC/Y; CIM; CNM ('83, 1st); MNAC; NPTA ('88; '91; '92; '93, 1st; '94, 1st); NWASA ('79, Jurors Award); RC ('83, 1st; '84, 1st; '87, 1st; '89, 1st); RCBC ('81, Best of Show; '82, Best of Show); RVW (Gold Award); YAC ('78, Best of Show)
HONORS: Washington State Arts Commission, artist-in-residence, 1986-1990; Indian Nations Rendezvous and Trade Fair, Denver, CO, Media Awards, 1991; Great Falls (MT) Native American Art Show, guest artist, 1988; NPTA, poster artist, 1993

ROGER L. BROER

Artist's statement: "I perceive my major strength as a 'no holds barred' approach to painting. How a painting is accomplished is of little value when in retrospect one observes the sense of spiritualism in the finished product." His style has been described as realism laced with both post-impressionism and surrealism. He is a member of the Dream Catchers Artists Guild, Ltd. (q.v.).

p.c. 1992

BROKEN LEG (see Cohoe, William)

BROKEN ROPE, GODFREY *Brûlé Sioux*

Tohanni Ku Sni, Never Returns
Born 1908 in Okreek, SD, on the Rosebud Reservation
EDUCATION: Flandreau (SD) Indian School, 1928
OCCUPATION: Minister and artist
MEDIA: Latex paint

GODFREY BROKEN ROPE

A self-taught minister of the Christian gospel, the artist has traveled throughout the West. His paintings, which are exclusively landscapes, are painted with latex house paints and reflect early 20th century life on the Rosebud Reservation.

PUBLISHED: Libhart (1970)
PUBLIC COLLECTIONS: IACB, HCC
EXHIBITS: CIA, CSP, SIM

BROKESHOULDER, NICK *Hopi*

Birth date unknown; GF: Guy Maktima, *katsina* carver
RESIDENCE: Flagstaff, AZ
MILITARY: U.S. Army
OCCUPATION: Career military, *katsina* carver, and painter
PUBLIC COLLECTIONS: Germany, Scotland, and England

BRONTIE (see Edwards, Bronson, Wilbur)

BROOKE-FISK, SUSAN *Cherokee*

Born 8 Oct 1942 in California
EDUCATION: Idaho Falls (ID) High School, 1960; U of NM; Idaho State University, Pocatello, ID
OCCUPATION: Professional artist since 1967
MEDIA: Watercolor, casein, pencil, and clay
PUBLIC COLLECTIONS: MNAC
EXHIBITS: ABQM; CMRM; NMSF; state fairs and arts and crafts shows in AZ, CO, MO, NM, NV, and NY

BROOKS, DAVID J. *Micmac*

Born 12 Aug 1950 in Turo, NS, Canada, on the Indian Brook Reserve
RESIDENCE: Indian Brook Reserve, NS, Canada
OCCUPATION: Chemical addiction counselor and painter
MEDIA: Oil and acrylic
COMMISSIONS: Public Service Commission, painting for calendar; Native Capital Consultants, painting for census poster
PUBLIC COLLECTIONS: C/INAC; Canadian High Commissioner's Office; Canadian Federation of Labor; Canadian Embassy, Washington, D.C.
EXHIBITS: C/AFIA; galleries in Nova Scotia; see also Awards
AWARDS: Atlantic Region Indian Art Exhibition ('85, Purchase Award)

BROWN, EDSEL *(?)*

EXHIBITS: ITIC, RC
AWARDS: ITIC ('91, 1st)

BROWN, JOAN *Cherokee*

A.K.A. Joann Brown
RESIDENCE: Muskogee, OK
EDUCATION: BC
OCCUPATION: Director of Murrow Indian Children's Home and artist
MEDIA: Watercolor, gouache, and pencil
PUBLISHED: *Oklahoma Today* (July/Aug 1985); *The Indian Trader* (Feb 1987); *Southern Living* (Oct 1988); *Twin Territories* (Special Edition 1991; Year of the Indian Edition 1992); *Muskogee Daily Phoenix* (4 Oct 1993)
COMMISSIONS: FCTM, *Pow Wow Chow*, cover
EXHIBITS: CNM, BC/McG, DE, FCTM, FCTM/M, HM, ITIC, RE, RC
SOLO EXHIBITS: FCTM
AWARDS: CNM ('83, 1st; '85, 1st); FCTM ('72; '73, IH; '78; '83, IH; '85); FCTM/M ('92; '93, 1st); ITIC ('85; '88); RE ('89)
HONORS: FCTM, designated a Master Artist, 1986; City of Muskogee (OK), Joan Brown Day, 1988

JOAN BROWN

Brown paints household scenes filled with women, children, and older people. Her paintings are often filled with gentle humor and warm family relationships.

BROWN, JOANN (see Brown, Joan)

BROWN, KATHRYN *Creek*

EXHIBITIONS: FCTM

AWARDS: FCTM ('77, 1st)

BROWN, LEWIS *Navajo*

Born 12 Nov 1945

RESIDENCE: Tohatchi, NM

EDUCATION: Sherman

MEDIA: Watercolor

EXHIBITS: ITIC, NTF

HONORS: Santa Fe Railroad Award

BROWN, MARY TIGER *Creek*

Born 23 Aug 1943; died 20 Jan 1992; daughter of Muriel Henry and Amos Tiger

RESIDENCE: Lived in Tahlequah, OK

EDUCATION: B.A./M.A., NSU

OCCUPATION: Junior high school art teacher and painter

EXHIBITS: CNM, FCTM

AWARDS: FCTM ('90; '91; '92)

BROWN, MELVIN J., JR. *Shoshoni/Paiute*

EDUCATION: IAIA

PUBLIC COLLECTIONS: IAIA

EXHIBITS: NACLA

BROWN, MICHAEL *Kiowa*

Born 11 Feb 1961 in Lawton, OK; son of Alice Ramona Satoe and Clyde William Brown Jr.; P/GP: Daisy Walker and Clyde W. Brown Sr.; M/GP: Toigope Dautobi and Fred Satoe; descendent of Gotebo

RESIDENCE: Skiatook, OK

EDUCATION: Ross Case High School, Fairfax, OK, 1979; A.F.A, AIAI, 1989; B.F.A, SFAI, 1991

OCCUPATION: Artist

MEDIA: Oil, acrylic, watercolor, pencil, pen and ink, pastel, mixed-media and prints

PUBLISHED: Antoine and Bates (1991); Zurko, ed. (1992)

EXHIBITS: AICA/SF, AICH, CNM, CSF/SF, CWAM, IAIA/M, OTM, SFAI, SFSC, SM, WHB

SOLO EXHIBITS: IAIA

AWARDS: CNM ('88, 1st); IAIA ('89, TC Cannon Award, Two-Dimensional Award); OTI ('87, Best of Show)

HONORS: *Scholarships and Fellowships:* Harry S. Truman Scholarship, nominee, 1989; SAIF, merit scholarship, 1990; Yale University, Ellen Bartell Stoeckel Fellowship, nominee, 1990; SFAI, Honors Studio Program, 1991

MICHAEL BROWN

The artist states, "The dialogue between a work and myself is a continual battle. By learning to trust my intuition through the physical act of painting, I have discovered a world apart from the influences of modern culture. The challenging element of this process has been to accept and learn from this inner world and to continually disregard the influences of the outer world."

p.c. 1992

BROWN, SHERRY LYNN *Cherokee/Creek*

Ha Tlv We Da, Where Have You Been

Born 16 June 1953 in Dallas, TX; daughter of Wanda Lee Cox Vinson and John Henry Brown; P/GP: Pearl Smart Bratcher and John Henry Brown; M/GP: Ethel Norman Laffoon and Lee Roy Cox Vinson

RESIDENCE: Parsons, KS

EDUCATION: G.E.D., Columbus, KS; School of Interior Design, Wurzburg, West Germany, 1976; Labette Community College, Parsons, KS, 1992

OCCUPATION: Student and artist
MEDIA: Oil, acrylic, pencil, and pen and ink
EXHIBITS: CNM; FCTM; American Indian Center, Dallas, TX; Labette (KS) Community College Art Show; see also Awards
AWARDS: Dallas-Fort Worth Indian Exposition ('83, 1st); Southeast Kansas Community College Art Show ('91; '92)
HONORS: Labette (KS) Community College, President's List, 1991, 1992

BROWN HAT (see Good, Baptiste)

BROWN HEAD (see Beaver, Fred)

BRUNETTE, J. M. *(?)*
PUBLISHED: Snodgrass (1968)
PUBLIC COLLECTIONS: ASM

BRUGUIER-WICHNER, SHARON *Yankton Sioux*
EXHIBITS: NPTA
AWARDS: NPTA ('94)

BRUNO, PAULINE BONVILLAIN *Oglala Sioux*
Born 3 Feb 1952 at Ellsworth Air Force Base, SD
RESIDENCE: Destrehan, LA
EDUCATION: Schools in Louisiana
OCCUPATION: Artist
MEDIA: Watercolor pencil, pastel and composite materials
EXHIBITS: CAC/NO, ITM, NAC, PNAS; see also Awards
AWARDS: St. Charles Art Guild, Luling, LA; Old South Art Guild, LaPlace, LA

PAULINE BONVILLAIN BRUNO

In 1981, Bruno was concentrating her efforts on a synthesis of expressionist and symbolist elements to form visual equivalents for a death theme. She said " I consider the style of work I do as symbolic of the ideas I have about dying. The basis of my ideas come from a variety of sources, including Sioux legends. I started working on this theme sometime in 1976-1977, and I felt that it was so important that I destroyed nearly all of the work I had done previously. . . ."

brochure, SIM, 1981

BRYCELEA, CLIFFORD *Navajo*
Born 26 Sept 1953 in Shiprock, NM, on the Navajo Reservation; nephew of Harry Walters, artist, educator, and museum director
RESIDENCE: Santa Fe, NM
EDUCATION: Fort Wingate (NM) High School: B.A., Fort Lewis College, Durango, CO, 1975
OCCUPATION: Professional painter since 1975
MEDIA: Acrylic, watercolor, pencil, pen and ink, pastel, and prints
PUBLISHED: Jacka and Jacka (1988; 1994); Tryk (1993). *Plateau* (Vol. 54, no. 1, 1982); *The Indian Trader* (July 1978; July 1981; Nov 1986); *Southwest Art* (June 1992)
BOOKS ILLUSTRATED: Williams (1985); L'Amour (1988), cover; "An Indian Christmas," *American Way Magazine* (1977)
PUBLIC COLLECTIONS: HCC, NTM
EXHIBITS: ACAI, AICA, CNM, IACA, ITIC, NMSF, NNTF, PBS, PF, RC, RE, SWAIA
AWARDS: ITIC ('85, 1st; '86, 2-1st, Woodard Award; '87; '88, 1st; '90, 1st); AICA (4 Gold Medals); NNTF (1st); RC ('85, 1st; '86); SWAIA ('86, '91)
HONORS: IACA, Artist of the Year, 1987; City of Santa Fe (NM), Mayor's Poster Contest, 1991

CLIFFORD BRYCELEA

Louis L'Amour, author, was an early collector of Brycelea's work and became a good friend and mentor. The artist is known for his spiritual paintings and landscapes. He has said of his art, "I approach my work with a cultural feeling. I endeavor to present my land and my understanding of it in a way that the viewer can feel the wonder of my creation . . . symbolically and spiritually . . . a message for everyone through my paint brush."

The Indian Trader, *July 1978*

BUCHOLZ, MADONNA *Oglala Sioux*
Born 10 Nov 1956
RESIDENCE: Rapid City, SD
EDUCATION: Central High School, Rapid City, SD
EXHIBITS: RC

BUCKTOOTH, LES *Onondaga*

Born 14 Sept 1957

RESIDENCE: Nedrow, NY

OCCUPATION: Janitor, park aide, and artist

MEDIA: Acrylic, pen and ink, pencil, chalk, and prints

PUBLISHED: Johannsen and Ferguson, eds. (1983). North American Bowling Tournament (1979),program cover

EXHIBITS: NYSF, OIS

AWARDS: NYSF (various ribbons)

HONORS: MONY Scholastics Competition, Gold Key Award

BUELL, JOY DAI *Susquehanna*

Born 12 Dec 1941

RESIDENCE: Gloucester, MA

EDUCATION: School of the Museum of Fine Arts, Boston, MA, 1964; B.S., Tufts University, 1964; Academy of Fine Arts, Vienna, Austria, 1967; B.F.A./M.F.A., Yale U, 1969/1971

OCCUPATION: Teacher, ceramist, jeweler, gallery manager, and artist

MEDIA: Pencil, pen and ink, mixed-media, clay, gold, silver, gemstone, and prints

PUBLISHED: *The Gloucester Daily Times* (25 Aug 1983); *Phoenix Magazine* (Sept 1989)

PUBLIC COLLECTIONS: MFA/B; Tufts University, Medford, MA

EXHIBITS: AC/T; MFA/B; Bayview Resource Center, Gloucester, MA, 1979; Copely Society, Boston, MA, 1963; Garland Junior College, Boston, MA, 1972, 1974; National Print Show, Silvermine, CT, 1970; Old Town Hall, Salem, MA, 1982; Prudential Center, Winterfest, Boston, MA, 1967

HONORS: MFA/B, fellowship, 1965-1969; Yale University, scholarship, 1970-1971

BUFFALO, BENJAMIN, SR. (see Buffalo, Bennie)

BUFFALO, BENNIE *Cheyenne*

Going South

A.K.A. Benjamin Buffalo Sr.

Born 30 Jan 1948 in Clinton, OK; died 5 Nov 1994 of accidental injuries

RESIDENCE: Lived in Irving, NY

MILITARY: U.S. Army, Vietnam

EDUCATION: Seiling, OK, public schools; IAIA, 1963-1967; SFAI, 1970-1972; SWOSU, 1972-1973; U of OK, 1975-1976

OCCUPATION: Artist

MEDIA: Oil, acrylic, pencil, pen and ink, and prints

PUBLISHED: New (1974; 1979); Highwater (1976; 1980); Wade and Strickland (1981); Hoffman, et al. (1984). *Oklahoma Art Gallery* (winter 1980)

EXHIBITS: ACAI, ACMWA, ADIA, AIE, CMN, CSPIP, DAM, IK, MFA/O, NACLA, ND, OIO, OSC, OWE, PAC, PAIC, RE, SI, SN, SNAICF, SPIM, WWM, VV

SOLO EXHIBITS: SPIM

AWARDS: ADIA ('67, 1st); AIE ('71, 1st; '74); CNM ('86, 1st); PAC ('74, Painting Award; '75); RE ('89, 1st; '90, President's Award; '91, 1st); NAICF; OIO; SN ('67)

BENNIE BUFFALO

In his almost photographic portraits of Native Americans, Buffalo tried to capture the personality of the person he painted. In many of his paintings he used a great deal of red and blue which reflects the influence of the Native American Church. When speaking of his paintings Buffalo said, "I wanted to get away from the traditional, two-dimensional type of work. I'm trying to express the realism of our American Indians by photographic exactness. . . ."

brochure, SPIM, 1980

BUFFALO, JUDITH K. *Winnebago*

Born 31 Oct 1943

RESIDENCE: Logsden, OR

EDUCATION: John Edwards High School, Port Edwards, WI; Layton School of Art, Milwaukee, WI

EXHIBITS: RC; Eugene and Le Grande, OR

BUFFALO MEAT *Southern Cheyenne*

Oewotoh, Buffalo Meat

Born 1847; died 1917

MEDIA: Pencil, pen and ink, colored pencil, and crayon

PUBLISHED: Dunn (1968); Snodgrass (1968); Highwater (1976; 1983); Silberman (1978); Wade, ed. (1986); Maurer (1992). *Tamaqua* (winter/spring 1991)

PUBLIC COLLECTIONS: ACMWA, HS/MA, HS/OK ("Apache" drawings thought to be the artist's), OMA, SI/OAA, YU/BRBML

EXHIBITS: BPG, VP

BUFFALO MEAT

"The artist was among the 72 Plains Indians taken as prisoners from Fort Sill, OK, to Fort Marion, St Augustine, FL, in 1875."

Snodgrass 1968

Buffalo Meat was arrested 3 April 1875, and did not return to the reservation until 1878.

BULL CHILD, GEORGE *Blackfeet*

Born 1891; death date unknown

MEDIA: Paint, ink, muslin, and hide

PUBLISHED: Maurer (1992)

PUBLIC COLLECTIONS: DAM

EXHIBITS: VP

GEORGE BULL CHILD

With the coming of the railroad a market for Indian crafts developed. Bull Child was one of the most active Blackfeet painters in Montana between 1920 and 1950. He painted hides and muslins for trade or sale.

Maurer 1992

BUNIYUK (see Smart, Clara Mary)

BURDEAU, GEORGE HENRY *Blackfeet/Winnebago*

Born 16 Nov 1944 in Great Falls, MT; son of Ada C. Burbridge and George Burdeau

RESIDENCE: Spokane, WA

MILITARY: U.S. Army

EDUCATION: Wasatch Academy, Mount Pleasant, UT; U of AZ, "Southwest Indian Art Project," scholarship, summers 1961, 1962; IAIA, ca. 1963; Anthropology Film Center, Albuquerque, NM

OCCUPATION: Gallery assistant, creative film maker, educator, and artist

MEDIA: Acrylic, watercolor, and pen and ink

PUBLISHED: Snodgrass (1968). *Smoke Signals* (autumn 1965)

EXHIBITS: ASM; BNIAS; CIA; FAIEAIP; SN; SWAIA; YAIA; National Scholastic Art Contest; see also Awards

AWARDS: BNIAS; SN ('70, 1st); SWAIA ('77); Utah State High School Exhibition (1st, Best Painting of Show, gold medallion for sculpture)

BURGESS, F. JAN *Choctaw*

Born 27 July 1936

RESIDENCE: Tulsa, OK

EDUCATION: Crowder (OK) High School, 1954; OSU, 1959

OCCUPATION: Artist

MEDIA: Oil and pastel

EXHIBITS: CNM; see also Awards

AWARDS: Henryetta (OK) Art Show

BURGESS, JIM *Creek*

EXHIBITS: FCTM

AWARDS: FCTM ('90, IH; '93, Best of Show)

BURGESS, KEN R. *Creek/Cherokee*

Born 2 Feb 1939; son of Willia Garfton and Jewell Overturf Burgess; P/GP: Tyler and Norm Perryman Burgess; M/GP: Georgia Chadwick and James Overturf

RESIDENCE: Tulsa, OK
EDUCATION: G.E.D
OCCUPATION: Artist
MEDIA: Oil, acrylic, watercolor, pencil, pen and ink, pastel, stone, gold, silver, gemstone, and beads
EXHIBITS: CNM; TIAF; TWF; RE; Pryor (OK) Art Show; see also Awards
AWARDS: Oklahoma Indian Market, Okmulgee, OK

BURKE (see Bowker, R.G.)

BURLISON, BOB *Choctaw/Chickasaw*
EXHIBITS: FCTM
AWARDS: FCTM ('77, IH; '78)

BURNS, CHARLIE *Yurok*
A.K.A. Charley E. Burns
Born 1960 in Eureka, CA
RESIDENCE: Arcata, CA
EDUCATION: B.A., Humboldt State U, Arcata, CA, 1984
OCCUPATION: Dancer, craftsman, photographer, videographer, and painter
MEDIA: Watercolor
PUBLISHED: Banks (1986)
PUBLIC COLLECTIONS: HSU
EXHIBITS: AICA/SF; HSU; Carnegie Museum for Cultural Arts, Oxnard, CA; ISURI United Indian Health Show, Trinidad, CA; galleries in California
SOLO EXHIBITS: Humboldt State U, Arcata, CA

BURNS, KAYLA *Pima*
EXHIBITS: HM/G
AWARDS: HM/G ('72)

BURR, RYAN *Mandan/Hidatsa*
Born 19 Aug 1956 in Watford City, ND; son of Inez Rush and Newton Burr; P/GP: Mary and Oscar Burr; M/GP: Laura and Robert Rush
RESIDENCE: Fort Worth, TX
EDUCATION: Diamond Hill High School, Fort Worth, TX, 1974
OCCUPATION: Commercial artist and painter
MEDIA: Acrylic, pencil, colored pencil, pen and ink, and prints
EXHIBITS: CHAS, CIM, ITAE, NPTA, RE, SDCC, SWAIA, TAIAF, TCIM, TIAF, TWF, UTAE; see also Awards
AWARDS: CHAS; CIM ('89, 1st); ITAE ('91); NHAIA ('86, Best of Show); NPTA ('89; '91; '94); SWAIA ('89); TCIM ('91, 1st); TIAF ('92; '93,1st); UTAE ('90, 1st); Celebration of American Indian Art, Las Colinas, TX ('90, Best of Texas Award); City of Fort Worth (TX) Employees Art Show ('87, 1st, People's Choice Award; '88)
HONORS: UTAE, poster artist, 1993

BURRUS, S. S. *Cherokee*
Nannehi Tolese Siam, Going About Grasshopper
A.K.A. Sammye S. Burrus
Born 9 Feb 1947 in Pryor, OK; daughter of Cherokee Baker and G. A. Pat Sampsel; P/GP: Ethelyne Parks and George Arv Sampsel; M/GP: Nannie McNair and John O. Baker
RESIDENCE: Pryor, OK

EDUCATION: Pryor (OK) High School, 1965; CSU/OK, 1968
OCCUPATION: Artist
MEDIA: Oil, acrylic, watercolor, pencil, pen, gouache, gourd, and prints
PUBLISHED: Campbell, ed. (1993). *The Tulsa World* (9 Dec 1989)
PUBLIC COLLECTIONS: TTSP
EXHIBITS: ACAI; CNM; FCTM; ITAE/M; ITIC; LIAS; TIAF; TTSP; RC; Log Cabin Craftique, Germantown, TN; see also Awards
AWARDS: FCTM ('89; '90, 1st); Trail of Tears Museum, Jackson, MO (Purchase Award)
HONORS: Dallas Mural Project, selected as winner over five hundred entries, mural is displayed on exterior wall of El Central Community College, Dallas, TX, 1989

JIMALEE BURTON

"Shortly after her husband's death, Mrs. Burton moved from Tulsa to Florida and began to concentrate on writing and painting Indian legends. In her extensive research in the field of Indian lore, she traveled throughout the Western Hemisphere."

Snodgrass 1968

Burton was the first Indian woman exhibitor at PAC. A woman of many talents, she edited The Native Voice in Vancouver, BC, and in the 1930s produced a radio program.

Dockstader, p.c. 1994

BURTON, JIMALEE *Creek/Cherokee*

Ho Chee Nee, Leader
Born 23 Jan 1906 in El Reno, Indian Territory; death date unknown; daughter of Mary Beck and James A. Chitwood
EDUCATION: Indian schools in Colony, Geary, and Weatherford, OK; Southwestern Teachers College; U of Tulsa; studied sculpture under H. Q. Edwards at U of Tulsa, 1938, and painting under Carlos Mérida, U of Mexico, Mexico City, DF
OCCUPATION: Radio program supervisor; songwriter, poet, associate editor, and artist
PUBLISHED: Dunn (1968); Snodgrass (1968); Brody (1971); Burton (1974)
PUBLIC COLLECTIONS: GM, PAC
EXHIBITS: C/GM; DAM; FAIEAIP; FCTM; MHDYMM; OAC; PAC; RM; Brown University, Ringling Museum, Providence, RI; Galveston (TX) Art Center
SOLO EXHIBITS: U of FL; U of GA; gallery in Florida
AWARDS: PAC ('47, Purchase Award)

BUSH

"This artist was known to have executed a Dakota Winter Count for the Years 1800-1801 to 1869-1870 (see Bulletin 173, *BAE, 1960)."*

Snodgrass 1968

BUSH *Sioux*

PUBLISHED: Snodgrass (1968). *Bulletin 173,* BAE (1960)

GEORGE BUSHOTTER

*"The artist's stepfather belonged to the Society of Those Who Have Revelations From The Buffalo, whose mysteries the artist often illustrated. His collection (known as the Bushotter Collection) was described as 'the most extensive that had been gained from among the tribes of the Siouan family, and it is the first contribution by an Indian (*8th Annual Report, *BAE, 1886-1887).'"*

Snodgrass 1968

BUSHOTTER, GEORGE *Teton Sioux*

Born 24 Dec 1860 at the forks of Owl Creek, Dakota Territory (now Butte County, SD); died 2 Feb 1892 at Hedgesville, WV; son of Gray Good Road and Amos
EDUCATION: HI; Virginia Theological Seminary
OCCUPATION: Teacher, BAE Dakota dialect specialist, and painter
PUBLISHED: Snodgrass (1968). *8th Annual Report,* BAE (1886-1887)
PUBLIC COLLECTIONS: SI/OAA

BUSHYHEAD, ALLAN *Cheyenne/Arapaho*

Nakowhoadoniulzi, Bear Feathers
Born 1917; raised in OK
MILITARY: U.S. Army, WWII
EDUCATION: Santa Fe
PUBLISHED: Jacobson and d'Ucel (1950); LaFarge (1960); Dunn (1968); Snodgrass (1968)
PUBLIC COLLECTIONS: MNM, MNA, OU/MA, PAC
EXHIBITS: AIEC, AIW, MFA/O, OU/ET

BUSHYHEAD, JEROME *Cheyenne/Arapaho*

Coyote Walks By
A.K.A. Jerome Gilbert Bushyhead
Born 1929 in Calumet, OK

RESIDENCE: El Reno, OK

EDUCATION: El Reno (OK) High School, 1948; Centenary College, Shreveport, LA, 1949-1951

OCCUPATION: Indian spokesman, lecturer, radio and TV personality, Oklahoma State Fair and Indian Dance Program Director, gallery owner; professional artist since 1970

MEDIA: Acrylic and prints

PUBLISHED: *The Anadarko Daily News* (12 Aug 1973); *The Chronicles of Oklahoma* (summer 1974), cover

BOOKS ILLUSTRATED: *The Chronicles of Oklahoma* (1974), cover

COMMISSIONS: Picello Press, Yukon, OK, illustrations

PUBLIC COLLECTIONS: HCC

EXHIBITS: CSPIP, ITAE, OSA, PIPM, TIAF

AWARDS: ITAE

BUTLER-WHITEHEAD, ROBERTA ANN *Cheyenne*

RESIDENCE: San Antonio, TX

EXHIBITS: AIE, CNM

AWARDS: AIE, CNM

BUTTERFLY *Mandan*

PUBLISHED: Howard (1960); Snodgrass (1968)

BUTTERFLY (see Paraclita, Sister Mary)

BUTTERFLY, VIOLET *Blackfeet*

Born 1934 in Browning, MT

RESIDENCE: Browning, MT

EDUCATION: Browning (MT) High School

OCCUPATION: Volunteers In Service to America (VISTA) Program Director and artist

EXHIBITS: CIA

BUUM, J. W. *Eskimo*

A.K.A. Ponto Buum

Born 1949 at Fort Randall, SD, on the Yankton Sioux Reservation

RESIDENCE: Molokai, HI

EDUCATION: Lake Andes and Aberdeen, SD, 1955-1967; Northern State College, Aberdeen, SD, 1968-1971; U of SD/S, 1978-1980; U of SD, 1980-1982

COMMISSIONS: *Murals:* U of SD/S, Student Union, 1980; Kilohana School, Molokai, HI, 1984, 1991. *Other:* Hawaiian Sovereign Nation, banner design, 1991

PUBLIC COLLECTIONS: Damien Museum, Waikiki, Oahu, HI

EXHIBITS: RC; Damien Museum, Waikiki, Oahu, HI; Libraries Tour; *Floral Exhibits* tour of the Hawaiian islands

HONORS: U of SD, Magna Cum Laude, 1980; Maui (HI) Artist of the year, 1985

BUUM, PONTO (see Buum, J. W.)

BUZZARD *Cheyenne*

Born 1855; died ca. 1881 (believed to have been executed while a prisoner at Fort Marion)

PUBLISHED: Snodgrass (1968); Deupree (1978)

PUBLIC COLLECTIONS: HSM/OK, YU/BRBML

EXHIBITS: HSM/OK

JEROME BUSHYHEAD

After completing a painting in which he discovered an unplanned image, Bushyhead said, "As an artist you try to create and paint your vision as it comes to you in various images. Sometimes one is really not aware of the painting as it evolves. You paint what you feel and sometimes things happen within the painting that cannot be explained until you see it. I always feel this is a blessing from the Great Spirit."

The artist was co-founder of the Oklahoma Indian Art League, Inc. and, in 1972, founded the Cheyenne Nation Arts and Crafts Show and Inter-Tribal Powwow in El Reno, OK.

BUTTERFLY

"The artist executed a Winter Count covering the period 1833-1876."

Snodgrass 1968

BUZZARD, DUCEE BLUE *Creek*

A.K.A. Howard Rufus Collins

Born 8 July 1894 in Checotah, Indian Territory; son of Aurora and Henry R. Collins; related to William F. McIntosh and W. E. McIntosh, Creek chiefs

RESIDENCE: Muskogee, OK

EDUCATION: Oktaha (OK) High School, 1909; St. Joseph College, Muskogee, OK, 1910-1912

OCCUPATION: Commercial artist and painter

PUBLISHED: Snodgrass (1968)

EXHIBITS: FCTM; MNM; local shows and exhibits

AWARDS: FCTM ('67)

BYRNES, JAMES MICHAEL *Acoma/Laguna/Sioux*

Kyash Petrach; *Hofyee*; *Hotyee*

A.K.A. J. Bear; J. Michael Bear; James Bear; Bear Claw; James Byrne; Jobie Bear; Standing Bear; Sunrise

Born 1938 in New Mexico

EDUCATION: Graduated Albuquerque, ca. 1956

OCCUPATION: Hospital orderly and painter

MEDIA: Watercolor, pen and ink, and prints

PUBLISHED: Snodgrass (1968); Brody (1971); Fawcett and Callander (1982)

COMMISSIONS: *Murals:* Barelos Community Center, with Charles Vicenti and Dixon Shebola (qq.v.)

PUBLIC COLLECTIONS: MAI, MNM

EXHIBITS: PAC, HM/G, ITIC, MNM, NMSF

SOLO EXHIBITS: ASU, HM

AWARDS: HM/G, ITIC ('76)

C. D. T. *Zuni*

A.K.A. Last name possibly Tullma
PUBLISHED: Snodgrass (1968)
PUBLIC COLLECTIONS: DAM (dated 1905)
EXHIBITS: DAM

CABANISS, DONNIE *Kiowa/Apache*

To-Bo-Hown-Tha
EXHIBITS: BB

CACHINI, RONNIE D. *Zuni*

Born 13 Nov 1965
RESIDENCE: Zuni Pueblo, NM
EDUCATION: Through 11th grade
OCCUPATION: Artist
MEDIA: Acrylic and watercolor
EXHIBITS: ITIC, MNA
AWARDS: ITIC ('87, 1st, Best of Category); MNA (1st)

CADZI CODY *Shoshoni*

Codsiogo
Born 1865; died 1912
MEDIA: Paint, ink, and hide
PUBLISHED: Alexander (1916); Maurer (1992)
EXHIBITS: VP

CAIBAIOSAI, LLOYD *Ojibwa*

Birth date unknown; died 1975 in Alberta, Canada, in an automobile accident
RESIDENCE: Lived in Spanish River, ON, Canada
OCCUPATION: Painter and printmaker
MEDIA: Enamel on canvas and prints
EXHIBITS: C/ROM

CAIN, EDGAR *Hopi*

PUBLIC COLLECTIONS: HCC

CAJE, RICHARD *Apache*

Born 1941
RESIDENCE: Mescalero, NM
EDUCATION: Albuquerque, 1958-1960; U of AZ, "Southwest Indian Art Project," scholarship
PUBLISHED: Snodgrass (1968)
EXHIBITS: ITIC, MNM
AWARDS: ITIC, MNM

CALABAZA, DIANE *San Ildefonso*

Born 1954
PUBLIC COLLECTIONS: ABQM, WWM

CALACHAW (see Wa Wa Chaw)

CALDWELL JACKSON, ANITA SUE *Cherokee*

A.K.A. Anita Sue Jackson
Born 9 July 1951 in McAlester, OK; daughter of Fairel and Clifford Caldwell; P/GP: Mae and Virgil Caldwell; M/GP: Lula and Thomas Ivey

CADZI CODY

In 1900, Codsiogo had his name changed to Cadzi Cody in the tribal rolls. He is said to have produced more hide paintings in this time period than any other Plains Indian artist. With the advent of the railroad a market for traditional Indian arts developed and Cadzi Cody was able to earn a living as well as make a cultural statement with his paintings.

Maurer 1992

LLOYD CAIBAIOSAI

Caibaiosai traveled and worked throughout North America. Legendary myths were the main subject matter for his paintings.

ANITA SUE CALDWELL JACKSON

Caldwell Jackson's great aunt by marriage, Winnie Gibson, was included in Charles Banks Wilson's book, Search for the Truebloods. In addition, she reports that her great-great-grandfather, whose name was Adam Gibson, was shot and left for dead on the Trail of Tears walk. After recovering, he settled north of McAlester, Oklahoma. It is believed he may have gone on record as a Choctaw because of where he lived; however, no record has been found to verify this.

artist, p.c. 1991

DETAIL: Woodrow Wilson Crumbo, *Burning of Cedar*, n.d. Philbrook Museum of Art, Tulsa, Oklahoma

RESIDENCE: Kiowa, OK
EDUCATION: Kiowa High School, 1969; SOSU, 1973
OCCUPATION: Teacher, counselor, and artist
MEDIA: Acrylic, watercolor, pen and ink, mixed-media, and Prismacolor
PUBLIC COLLECTIONS: HCC, RC
EXHIBITS: CHAS, CHASC, CNM, CPS, FAIE, FCTM, MCI, LIAS, RC, WTF
AWARDS: CHAS; CHASC ('93, 1st); CNM ('86, 1st; '87, 1st; '90; '91; '92, 1st; '94); FCTM ('86, 1st; '87; '88, 1st; '89, 1st; '91, Best of Show; '92; '93, Southeastern Wildlife Award); MCI ('91 , Best of Show); LIAS ('89, MA); RC ('87, 1st, Pepion Award, Aplan Award; '89, 1st, Erickson Award; '90)

CALF TAIL, ALICE *Blackfeet*
Born 1924 in Heart Butte, Blackfeet Reservation, MT
RESIDENCE: Browning, MT
EDUCATION: Heart Butte (MT) public school and Cut Bank (MT) Boarding School, Browning, MT
MEDIA: Oil and beads
EXHIBITS: CIA

CALLING LAST, PATTI JO *Blackfeet*
RESIDENCE: Browning, MT
MEDIA: Oil and charcoal
EXHIBITS: GFNAAS; MPI; area shows

CALNIMPTEWA, E. *Hopi*
PUBLIC COLLECTIONS: MNA

CALNIMPTEWA, VERNON *Hopi*
PUBLIC COLLECTIONS: MNA

CALVERT, JOHN *San Juan*
EDUCATION: Santa Fe, ca. 1958
PUBLISHED: Snodgrass (1968)
EXHIBITS: MNM

CAMEL, KENNETH LLOYD *Salish/Pend d'Orelle/Kootenai*
Warhoop Kamel
Born 2 Aug 1956
RESIDENCE: Polson, MI
EDUCATION: Roan Senior High, 1974; Salish Kootenai Tribal College, 1991; U of MT
OCCUPATION: Professional firefighter and painter
MEDIA: Oil, acrylic, pencil, pen and ink, clay, and fabric
COMMISSIONS: *Murals:* Salish Kootenai College, Media Center
PUBLIC COLLECTIONS: Roan Museum, Polson, MT
HONORS: Roan Senior High, *Dove Tail*, illustrator

KENNETH LLOYD CAMEL

Camel has said, "Most of my work deals with an inner spiritual nature, which I live in my physical life. My work expresses a struggle that allows me freedom of expression, to cool the fire that my soul contains. . . ."

p.c. 1990

CAMPBELL, DONALD *Assiniboin/Gros Ventre*
Birth date unknown; born on Fort Belknap Reservation
MEDIA: Oil, pen and ink, and pencil
EXHIBITS: GFNAAS

CAMPBELL, JAMES *Salish/Kootenai*
Born 10 Apr 1943 in Oregon City, OR
RESIDENCE: Missoula, MT

EDUCATION: High School, Seattle, WA; IAIA; U of WA; SFAI; B.F.A., U of MT
OCCUPATION: Painter
MEDIA: Acrylic and mixed-media
PUBLISHED: Biographical publications
PUBLIC COLLECTIONS: IAIA
EXHIBITS: AC/DS, CAS, CW, GFNAAS, HM, IAIA, NARF, NMSC, SCG, SWAIA, U of MT
SOLO EXHIBITS: AC/DS; MPI; SCG; Governor's Invitational, New Mexico State Capitol, Santa Fe, NM
HONORS: Montana Indian Artist Project, Board of Directors

CANNON, T. C. *Caddo/Kiowa/Choctaw*

Pai-Doung-U-Day, One Who Stands In The Sun
A.K.A. Tommy Wayne Cannon
Born 24 Sept 1946 in Lawton, OK; died 8 May 1978 near Santa Fe, NM, in an automobile accident; son of Walter Cannon
MILITARY: U.S. Army, 101st Air Cavalry, Vietnam
EDUCATION: Gracemont (OK) High School; IAIA, 1965-1966; SFAI, 1966; College of Santa Fe, NM, 1969-1970; B.A., CSU/OK, 1972; studied under Fritz Scholder
OCCUPATION: Musician, composer, writer, and artist
MEDIA: Oil, acrylic, watercolor, casein, pen and ink, mixed-media, and prints
PUBLISHED: Snodgrass (1968); New (1974); Broder (1981); Highwater (1976, 1980); Hoffman, et al. (1984); Wade (1986); Wallo and Pickard (1990); Archuleta and Strickland (1991); Hill (1992); Campbell, ed. (1993). *Native American Arts 2* (1968); *American Indian Art* (May 1977); *The Indian Trader* (July 1978); *Southwest Art* (June 1981; Sept 1990); *Americas* (Aug 1981); *Anadarko Daily News* (19 Aug 1988); *The Santa Fean* (Aug 1989); *Tamaqua* (winter/spring 1991); *Southwest Profile* (Aug/Sept/Oct 1992)
COMMISSIONS: *Murals:* United Indians of All Tribes Foundation, Seattle, WA; Day Break Star Indian Cultural Center, Seattle, WA, 1977. *Other:* Santa Fe Opera Guild, program, 1978
PUBLIC COLLECTIONS: EM, HM, IAIA, OSAC, PAC, WWM.
EXHIBITS: AC/K; AC/SD; ACMWA; AIE; BIA; BM/B; CSPIP; CSU/OK; DC; EIAF; FAC/CS; HM; HMA; IAIA/M; IK; MNM; NACLA; ND; OAC; OU/MA; OWE; RM; SAIEAIP; SAM; SN; SPIM; SU; SV; USDI; WIB; WWM; Amerika Haus, Berlin, Germany; Art Ankara, Turkey; Cultural Olympics, Mexico City, Mexico
SOLO/SPECIAL EXHIBITS: BBHC; HM; NMAA (dual show); SPIM; TCC; WWM; Central State U, Edmond, OK.
AWARDS: AIE ('64); SN ('66, Governor's Trophy)
HONORS: *Artist-in-Residence:* Dartmouth College; Colorado State U; National Park Service. *Other:* National Hall of Fame for Famous American Indians, first artist inducted, 1988

T. C. CANNON

Cannon took his art very seriously and was in the forefront of what has been called the "New Wave" of Native American art. The "New Wave" is made up of young Indian artists who reject traditional Indian art and strive to find a means of expressing their experiences and feelings about being Indian in an Anglo dominated world. Cannon wrote that he wanted not to be just another Indian painter, but to be a painter judged by the merits of his art alone.

CANNON, TOMMY WAYNE (see Cannon, T. C.)

CANTE WANI CA (see No Heart)

CARDINAL-SCHUBERT, JOANE *Peigan*

Born 22 Aug 1942 in Red Deer, AB, Canada; daughter of Frances Marguerite Rach and Joseph Treffle Cardinal; M/GGM: Peigan holy woman
RESIDENCE: Calgary, AB, Canada
EDUCATION: Lindsay Thurber Composite High School, Red Deer, AB, 1961;

diploma, C/ACA, 1968; B.F.A., C/U of C, 1968; certificate, C/BCA; additional courses and workshops

OCCUPATION: Ward aide, window decorator, curatorial assistant, assistant curator, artist in residence, lecturer, poet, writer, sculptor, and painter

MEDIA: Oil, acrylic, crayon, pencil, conte, wood, fabric, and mixed-media

PUBLISHED: Preston (1985); Cardinal-Schubert (1992). Partial listing of more than sixty journal publications includes: *The Alberta Report* (Nov 5, 1984); *Visual Arts Newsletter* (Oct 1985); *AMMSA* (25 Oct 1985); *Ottawa Citizen* (1 Nov 1985); *The Toronto Star* (1 July 1986); *Windspeaker* (12 Dec 1986); *Matriart* (Vol. 2, no. 1, 1991); *Muse* (fall 1991); *The Edmonton Journal* (8 Nov 1991); *American Indian Art* (autumn 1992)

PUBLIC COLLECTIONS: Partial listing of more than 33 corporate and public collections includes: C/AAF; C/AC/TB; C/AG/U of L; C/INAC; C/CMC; C/ESSOC; Chevron Canada Resources, Calgary, AB; Petro Mark; Nelson Small Legs Family Trust; Nickle Family Foundation; Leighton Foundation; Alberta Historical Resources Foundation, Calgary, AB; Gulf Canada Resources, Calgary, AB; Board of Education, Regina, SK; Collection of Queen Elizabeth II, London, England; embassies in New York, NY, and Stockholm, Sweden

EXHIBITS: Partial listing of more than forty includes: ASMG; C/AC/AE; C/ACCCNA; C/AG/E; C/AG/TB; C/AG/U of L; C/AG/;, C/C; C/CMC; C/GM; C/I; C/NGCA; C/TGVA; C/U of AB; C/U of C/G; C/UG; C/WDY; SM; Gleichen (AB) Art Park, International Art Exposition, Stockholm, Sweden; Alberta House, London, England; Beaux Arts Galerie, Paris, France

SOLO EXHIBITS: Partial listing of 23 throughout the U.S. and Canada includes: C/AC/TB; C/RDM; C/U of C; C/UG; Ottawa (ON) School of Art Gallery; Gulf Canada Gallery, Calgary, AB

HONORS: *Scholarships and Grants:* Queen Elizabeth II Scholarship, 1967; Alberta Culture Assistance Award, 1974-1976; C/BCA, 1983; Canadian Museums Associations Bursary, 1983; Alberta Culture Travel Grant, 1984. *Other:* C/U of C, elected to Alumni Board, 1984; Royal Canadian Academy of Arts, elected, 1986

CARIZ, SANTIAGO *Pueblo (?)*

PUBLISHED: Snodgrass (1968)

PUBLIC COLLECTIONS: RM

CARLO, MARGARET E. *Choctaw*

Kaa Am

Born 9 Mar 1945

RESIDENCE: Pueblo, CO

EDUCATION: South High School, Pueblo, CO; G.E.D., 1982; U of Southern Colorado, Pueblo, CO, 1986

OCCUPATION: Free-lance writer, calligrapher, and painter

MEDIA: Watercolor, pencil, and pen and ink

EXHIBITS: CNM, LIAS

AWARDS: CNM ('85, 1st)

MARGARET E. CARLO

"I'm active only on commission at this time. I am deaf — I'm not proud of it or ashamed of it, it's just how I am. I have many talents and abilities but I just can't hear."

artist, p.c. 1990

CARNEY, DORRIS *Cherokee*

EXHIBITS: HM/G

CARRAHER, RONALD G. *Colville*

Born 1935 in Omak, WA, on the Colville Reservation

RESIDENCE: Ellensburg, WA

EDUCATION: U of WA, 1956; SJSC, 1961; studied photography under Ansel Adams, 1962

OCCUPATION: Gallery assistant, adult education teacher, art instructor, assistant professor, and artist

MEDIA: Watercolor

PUBLISHED: Snodgrass (1968)

COMMISSIONS: *Educational Films:* National Defense Education Title VII Project, SJSC, graphic artist-photographer, 1959-1961; *Print With a Brayer*; *Mosaics for Schools*

PUBLIC COLLECTIONS: IACB

EXHIBITS: PAC; SFAI; SAM; WASF; Kingsley Art Annual, Crocker Gallery, Sacramento, CA; Palace of the Legion of Honor, Winter Invitational, San Francisco, CA; Pacific Arts Associations Invitational; San Jose (CA) Art Center Invitational; San Jose (CA) City College Arts Festival Invitational; 20th American Drawing Annual, Norfolk, VA; Western Association of Art Museums Traveling Exhibit; represented in an exchange exhibit with Fukuoka, Japan; see also Awards

SOLO EXHIBITS: Central Washington State College

AWARDS: PAC (Grand Award); WASF (2 purchase awards); Pacific Northwest Arts and Crafts National Fair, Bellevue, WA; San Jose (CA) Spring Arts Festival

CARRIER, JAY *Onondaga*

PUBLISHED: *Opening Up* (1989), exhibition brochure

EDUCATION: IAIA

EXHIBITS: IAIA; AIAI, 1989

JAY CARRIER

The artist uses Iroquois stories and images in his paintings to express his concern with issues that are important to all native people — concern and love for the natural world, native and non-native conflicts, and traditional spiritual values.

Lynne Williamson 1989

CARRIVEAU, KIM *Ottawa/Sioux*

Born 17 Nov 1951

RESIDENCE: Oconomowoc, WI

EDUCATION: Oconomowoc (WI) Senior High

PUBLISHED: *The Waukesha Freeman*; *The Oconomowoc Enterprise*

EXHIBITS: RC

CARRYS THE COLORS (see Stewart, Kathryn)

CARTER, BRUCE P. *Nez Percé*

Born 1917 in Webb, ID; died 1955; son of Mary Amera and Caleb Carter

RESIDENCE: Lived in Spalding, ID

OCCUPATION: Musician and painter

MEDIA: Oil and watercolor

PUBLISHED: Minthorn (1991)

PUBLIC COLLECTIONS: Nez Percé Tribal Office; Nez Percé National Historical Park

EXHIBITS: SAP

BRUCE P. CARTER

Because of tuberculosis, Carter spent much of his early life in government hospitals. It was during this time that he started painting. Much of his work was lost in a fire in the mid-1970s. Portraits of many noted tribal members and prominent figures of other tribes have survived.

Minthorn 1991

CARTER, JAY *Osage*

Born 1964

EDUCATION: OSU/O

OCCUPATION: Sign painter, T-shirt designer, and painter

PUBLISHED: *The Tulsa World* (2 May 1993)

COMMISSIONS: *Murals:* Building exteriors in downtown Pawhuska, OK

CASIAS, JOHNNY G. *Navajo/San Juan*

Cea Shoe Pin, Pine Mountain

Born 26 Dec 1934 in San Juan Pueblo, NM; son of Aurelia H. Casias and Miguel L. Casias

RESIDENCE: San Juan Pueblo, NM
MILITARY: U.S. Navy, 1956-1960; New Mexico National Guard
EDUCATION: Espanola (NM) High School
OCCUPATION: Storekeeper, editor, art instructor, and painter
PUBLISHED: Snodgrass (1968). Española (NM) High School, *Tah-Weh* (1956), yearbook cover; *USS Hopper-Wespac*, U.S. Navy publiction (1960), cover; *Crossroads*, cover
EXHIBITS: BNIAS; Española (NM) High School

CASIQUITO, LUCY *Jémez*

EDUCATION: Jémez, 1961
PUBLISHED: Snodgrass (1968)
EXHIBITS: MNM

CASIQUITO, VIDAL, JR. *Jémez*

Birth date unknown; born in Jémez Pueblo, NM
RESIDENCE: Jémez Pueblo, NM
EDUCATION: Jémez, ca. 1954
OCCUPATION: United Pueblo Agency (Albuquerque, NM) education department employee, and painter
PUBLIC COLLECTIONS: MNM
EXHIBITS: MNM, PAC
AWARDS: National Cartoonists Society and the Savings Bond Division of the U.S. Treasury Department, one of 12 poster contest winners

VIDAL CASIQUITO JR.

"At age 14, while attending Jémez Day School under Al Momaday (q.v.), Casiquito was one of 12 winners in a national poster contest sponsored by the National Cartoonists' Society and the Savings Bond Division of the U.S. Treasury Dept. His poster, based on 'the dream you save for,' received national recognition, and he was granted a personal interview with President Harry S. Truman."

Snodgrass 1968

CASON-COCHE, JEANNE *Cherokee*

PUBLIC COLLECTIONS: HCC
EXHIBITS: CNM, FCTM, LIAS, RC
AWARDS: FCTM ('87)

CASS, FRANK *Choctaw*

RESIDENCE: Oklahoma City, OK
EXHIBITS: PAC ('74)

CASSADY, ANN VIRGINIA *Cherokee*

Dhealdh Yazzie Bitsi, Little Mustache's Daughter
Born 12 July 1909 in Durango, CO
RESIDENCE: Vallejo, CA
EDUCATION: Reno (NV) public schools; Carson City (NV) public schools; Vallejo (CA) public schools; San Francisco (CA) public schools; Tulsa (OK) public schools
OCCUPATION: Commercial artist and professional painter
PUBLISHED: Snodgrass (1968)
EXHIBITS: FAIEAIP, PAC; extensively in Nevada and California
SOLO EXHIBITS: Three
AWARDS: Seven for pottery, mosaic, watercolor, and collage
HONORS: Nevada Art Gallery, *Indian Heritage '62*, exhibit coordinator, 1962; National League of American Penwomen, Art, Design, and Mosaic ratings

ANN VIRGINIA CASSADY

"Her parents left Oklahoma for the Navajo Reservation, where they operated a trading post at Red Rock, NM."

Snodgrass 1968

CASTRO, DALBERT S. *Maidu*

Born 1934 in Holacku, Auburn, CA; M/GF: Jim Dick, Maidu chief
RESIDENCE: Auburn, CA
OCCUPATION: Artist
MEDIA: Oil, acrylic, and watercolor

DALBERT S. CASTRO

The artist has said of his work, "Each time I do a painting I feel as if I am looking through the elders' eyes and that makes me feel proud of my Maidu culture."

catalog, CAM/S, 1985

EXHIBITS: CAM/S; CNM; HM/G; Loomis (CA) Public Library; Gold County Fair, Auburn, CA

AWARDS: HM/G ('80, 1st)

CATON, NARDA *Cherokee/Iroquois*

Narda

Born 28 Mar 1936 in Oklahoma City, OK; daughter of Eva Pugh and John Wilcox; P/GP: Mary and John Wilcox; M/GP: Florence and Silas Pugh

RESIDENCE: Tulsa, OK

EDUCATION: Enid (OK) High School, 1954; Northwestern State University, OK

OCCUPATION: Journalist, poet, fashion illustrator, art instructor, gallery owner, lecturer, and painter

MEDIA: Oil, acrylic, watercolor, pencil, porcelain, and prints

PUBLISHED: *Miniatures and Monochromes,* co-author; *Colorado Indian Market,* program cover; *Independence Sunday Reporter* (10 June 1984); *The Stillwater News Press* (3 Mar 1985); *The Decorator* (Jan 1985), cover; *Sunshine Artists* (June 1985); *Porcelain Artist* (Aug 1985); *Decorative Arts Digest* (Dec 1986); *The Bartlesville Examiner-Enterprise* (21 Nov 1986; 18 Dec 1988); *Creative Products News* (Jan 1989), *The Caney Chronicle* (21 Mar 1990; 17 July 1991; 4 Dec 1991); *The Stitchery* (summer 1989), cover

COMMISSIONS: Central Telephone Directory Company, regional phone book cover, 1991, 1992

PUBLIC COLLECTIONS: Porcelain Artists Hall of Fame

EXHIBITS: CNM; IS; TIAF; Mayfest, Caney, OK; Oklahoma Arts and Crafts Festival, Tulsa, OK; galleries in AR, OK, and FL

SOLO EXHIBITS: PIPM; Bartlesville (OK) Community Center; The Independence (KS) Museum

HONORS: Profesional Picture Framers Association, New Orleans Framing Competition, print selected for competition

CATTAIL BIRD (see Awa Tsireh)

CAWASTUMA *Laguna*

PUBLISHED: Snodgrass (1968)

EXHIBITS: AIEC

CA WATE WA (see Trujillo, Andrew)

CEA SHOE PIN (see Casias, Johnny G.)

CEHU'PA (see Jaw)

CE KOMO PYN (see Naranjo, José Dolores)

CEPANE (see Diacon, Johnnie Lee)

CE'TAN'GI (see Yellowhawk, James Mark)

CETANIYATAKE (?) (see Sitting Hawk)

CETAN LUTA (see Red Hawk)

CHADDLESONE, SHERMAN *Kiowa*

Born 2 June 1947 in Lawton, OK; son of John Chaddlesone; Artist is a descendant of Satanta (White Bear) q.v., Kiowa war chief.

RESIDENCE: Anadarko, OK

MILITARY: U.S. Army, Vietnam

EDUCATION: IAIA, High School, 1967; IAIA, post graduate work; CSU/OK, 1972-1973

SHERMAN CHADDLESONE

Chaddlesone's early training in art was received at home from his father who provided basic instruction in anatomy, portraiture, and pencil sketching. John Chaddlesone also taught his son the art of serigraphy.

brochure, SPIM, 1981

OCCUPATION: Teacher, workshop director, administrative manager for Kalispel (WA) Indian Reservation; full-time sculptor and painter after Oct 1982

MEDIA: Acrylic, watercolor, pastel, stone, bronze, mixed-media, and prints

PUBLISHED: New (1974; 1979); Boyd, et al. (1983); Gentry, et al. (1990); Hill (1992). *The Indian Trader* (Nov 1982); *Southwest Art* (July 1987); *Jules of Oklahoma* (Aug 1988); *Association News* ,SPIM (June 1992); *The Anadarko Daily News* (16-17 Aug 1986; 19 Aug 1988); *The Anadarko Daily News, Visitors Guide* (16 May 1992); *Oklahoma Today* (May/June 1994)

COMMISSIONS: *Murals:* Kiowa Tribal Complex, Carnegie, OK, 1984 (with Parker Boyiddle and Mirac Creepingbear). *Other:* NHFFAI, busts of T. C. Cannon and Satanta (White Bear)

PUBLIC COLLECTIONS: BIA, IAIA, SPIM

EXHIBITS: ACMWA; AIE; CNM; EM; IAIA; MFA/O; MMO; MNM; ND; NU/BC; RE; OAC; OIO; PAIC; RC; RE; SI; SNAICF; SPIM; TIAF; Lawton (OK) Junior Chamber of Commerce Art Show; Bank of California, San Francisco, CA; galleries in CA, OK, NM, WA, and Washington, D.C.

SOLO EXHIBITS: SPIM

AWARDS: AIE ('83; '85; '92); CNM ('84, 1st; '85, 1st); OIO ('82, Best of Show); RE ('87); SN('67)

HONORS: Eitlejorg Museum, Indianapolis, IN, artist-in-residence

CHALFANT, DAVID *Oglala Sioux*

RESIDENCE: Hill City, KS

EXHIBITS: PAC ('77)

CHAMON, JOHN A. *Jémez*

A.K.A. Juan Chamon

PUBLISHED: Snodgrass (1968)

EXHIBITS: MNM

CHAMON, JUAN (see Chamon, John A.)

CHAPITA, DEMPSEY *Zuni*

Born 1922 in Zuni Pueblo, NM

MILITARY: Discharged 1945

OCCUPATION: Laborer

PUBLISHED: Jacobson and d'Ucel (1950); Snodgrass (1968)

PUBLIC COLLECTIONS: IACB/DC

DEMPSEY CHAPITA

"During his schooling, the artist painted for pleasure. He has not painted since he left school, ca. 1939."

Snodgrass 1969

CHAPITO, ANTONIO (see Chapito, Tony)

CHAPITO, TONY *Zuni*

A.K.A. Antonio Chapito

EDUCATION: Santa Fe, 1937

PUBLISHED: Snodgrass (1968)

EXHIBITS: AIEC

CHAPMAN, CHARLES W. *Pawnee*

Birth date unknown; Pawnee, OK; son of Henry Chapman

RESIDENCE: Pawnee, OK

MILITARY: U.S. Air Force, Vietnam

OCCUPATION: Drapery installer, interior decorator, carpenter, race horse breeder, gold buyer, and artist

MEDIA: Oil and watercolor

PUBLISHED: *The Tulsa World* (25 July 1989); *The Tulsa Tribune* (Mar 1990)

CHARLES W. CHAPMAN

Chapman credits former Pawnee Police Chief, Carl Roberts, with encouraging his interest in art. In his childhood, the artist often visited Roberts at his place of business and heard him tell everyone that "one of these days, this boy's going to be a famous artist." Henry Chapman, the artist's father who died when his son was ten, helped document his tribe's history and worked on the first Pawnee dictionary. One of Chapman's goals is to preserve his father's legacy by documenting Pawnee tribal rituals and famous historical figures on canvas.

EXHIBITS: CIM; CNM; LIAS; TIAF; Native American Renaissance Show, Anadarko, OK; galleries in Arkansas and Oklahoma; see also Awards

AWARDS: CIM ('88); CNM ('86, 1st); TIAF ('88, 1st; '89, 1st); Western Art Show, Cimmarron, NM (Best of Show)

HONORS: TIAF, poster artist, 1990

CHAPMAN, JEFF *Chippewa*

A.K.A. Jeffrey Chapman

Born 14 Sept 1958 in Minneapolis, MN

RESIDENCE: Minneapolis, MN

EDUCATION: Minneapolis (MN) South High School, 1976; Minneapolis (MN) Community College, 1977-1978; B.F.A., MCAD, 1984

OCCUPATION: Artist

MEDIA: Watercolor and pencil

PUBLISHED: Ward, ed. (1990); Zurko, ed. (1992). *Public Cable Access* (Nov 1986); *The Minneapolis Star and Tribune, Sunday Magazine* (8 Mar 1987); *The St. Paul Pioneer and Dispatch* (Nov 1989); *Winds of Change Magazine* (summer 1989); *Hurricane Alice* (spring 1994).

BOOKS ILLUSTRATED: Anonymous (1984)

COMMISSIONS: *Logos*: Mankato State University; Florida HoneyWell, Indian Education Program; Minneapolis Community College, Indian Studies Program. *Other:* SMOM, poster and T-shirt image, 1984

PUBLIC COLLECTIONS: BBHC; BF; NDM; SMOM; SPIM; Bemis Group, Minneapolis, MN; Minnesota Chippewa tribe, Fond du Lac Indian Reservation

EXHIBITS: BBHC; CIM; CWAM; HM; HU/VA; HWU; MIC; MMA/MT; NDM; OAE; OLO; SCG; SMOM; SPIM; TE; TI; U of MN/B; WHB; Montana Indian Contemporary Artists, Bozeman, MT, 1990; galleries in Minnesota and Washington

SOLO EXHIBITS: BF, MN, SPIM

AWARDS: OAE, BBHC

JEFF CHAPMAN

Chapman grew up in Minneapolis and his art reflects his experiences there. He combines contemporary symbols with traditional Chippewa symbols in dealing with complex current issues. In doing so, his almost surrealistic paintings make a statement about the Native American in today's world.

5th Biennial catalog, HM, 1992

CHARGES STRONG *Crow*

PUBLISHED: Snodgrass (1968). *Anthropological Papers*, AMNA, (Vol. 21, pt. 4, autobiographical pictographic style painting on a buffalo robe)

CHARGING BEAR (see Grass, John)

CHARGING MAN (see Whitehorse, Roland N.)

CHARLES, MICHAEL *Eskimo*

RESIDENCE: Bethel, AK

EXHIBITS: PAC

AWARDS: PAC

CHARLETTE, OVIDE *Cree*

Wapusk, White Bear

EDUCATION: Quit school sometime before age 13

PUBLISHED: *American Indian Art* (spring 1990)

OVIDE CHARLETTE

When he was fourteen, Charlette set out to find his identity while living a nomadic life. His rebellious nature led him into conflict with the law and, in 1990 he was in prison in Canada. While incarcerated he is studying the Cree Culture and the anthropology of Native Americans as a whole, especially the Sioux, Ojibway, and Assiniboine. He is also working on his painting.

American Indian Art *spring 1990*

CHARLEY, JOHNSON *Navajo*

Born 27 Aug 1949

RESIDENCE: Cuba, NM

EDUCATION: Inter-Mt.

OCCUPATION: Artist

MEDIA: Oil and pen and ink

PUBLISHED: Jacka and Jacka (1994)
EXHIBITS: ITIC, NMSF
AWARDS: ITIC ('86, 1st, Best in Category, Elkus Award; '87, 1st; '90; '93 1st)

CHARLEY, NELSON *Navajo*
PUBLIC COLLECTIONS: MNA

CHARLEY, WELTON *Navajo/Hualapai*
Born 1962
RESIDENCE: The Teec Nos Pos, AZ, area of the Navajo Reservation
EDUCATION: IAIA, two years, ca. 1980
MEDIA: Oil, acrylic, pastel, and pencil
PUBLISHED: Schiffer (1991)
COMMISSIONS: Four Winds Trading Company, Denver, CO, catalog cover, 1993
EXHIBITS: Galleries in AZ, NM, and CO

WELTON CHARLEY

The artist started drawing at the age of three or four. This versatile artist works successfully in media as diverse as pencil and oil. His subject matter, painted in a realistic, European style, is most commonly concerned with his Navajo heritage, especially the people.

catalog, Four Winds Trading Company, 1993

CHARLIE, FRANK (see Frank, Charlie)

CHARLIE BOY *Zuni*
PUBLISHED: Snodgrass (1968)

CHATIE, PATONE (see Cheyatie, Patone)

CHA' TULLIS (see Tullis, Cha)

CHAUNCEY, FLORENCE NUPOK *Eskimo*
Nupok, Upright Post
A.K.A. Florence Nupok; Florence Malewotkuk; Florence Nupok Chauncey Malewotkuk
Born 4 Mar 1906 in Gambell, St. Lawrence Island, AK; died 1971
RESIDENCE: Lived on St. Lawrence Island, AK
EDUCATION: DCTP, 1964-1965
OCCUPATION: Artist
MEDIA: Watercolor, pen and India ink, pencil, crayon, seal skin, and poster board
PUBLISHED: Geist and Rainey (1936); Snodgrass (1968); Ray (1969); Yorba (1990), Archuleta and Strickland (1991). *Alaskan Journal* (summer 1979); *Alaska Geographic* (Vol. 12, no. 3, 1985)
BOOKS ILLUSTRATED: Silook (1976)
PUBLIC COLLECTIONS: CAS, MAI, PAC, SI, U of AK
EXHIBITS: MFA/AH, MNM, PAC, PAC/T, U of AK/F, PSC, SV
SOLO EXHIBITS: U of AK, 1971

FLORENCE NUPOK CHAUNCEY

Chauncey was known as the "Grandma Moses of the Bering Sea." Her first drawings were done when she was eight years old; she drew on any paper she could find. In 1955, she was discovered by artist Kay Roberts who commissioned a series of paintings. She stopped producing art for a while and when she started again in 1964, she used the name Florence Malewotkuk. She was the only woman in the Designer-Craftsman Training Project held in Nome, AK, in 1964-1965. With the completion of this training she set out to design Christmas cards, note paper, and plastic placemats.

Yorba 1990

CHAVARRIA, ELMER *Santa Clara*
RESIDENCE: Española, NM
EDUCATION: U of AZ, "Southwest Indian Art Project," scholarship, summer 1962
PUBLISHED: Snodgrass (1968)
PUBLIC COLLECTIONS: ASM
EXHIBITS: SN
AWARDS: SN ('68)

CHÁVEZ, ALPHONSO *Zuni/Laguna*
Born 28 May 1962
EDUCATION: Zuni Pueblo (NM) High School, 1982
MEDIA: Acrylic, watercolor, and pen and ink
PUBLISHED: *The Eagle's Cry* (11 Mar 1982)
COMMISSIONS: *Murals:* Zuni Pueblo (NM) High School

EXHIBITS: HM; ITIC; Gallup (NM) Library; First Annual Earth Week, Washington, D.C.

AWARDS: HM ('91); ITIC ('89)

HONORS: National Foundation for the Advancement in the Arts, Arts Recognition and Talent Search, semi-finalist

CHÁVEZ, BOB (see Chávez, Manuel)

CHÁVEZ, CALVIN FENLEY *San Felipe/Laguna*

Born 27 Dec 1924 in Winslow, AZ; son of Amy Bell and Lazaro B. Chávez

RESIDENCE: Cubero, NM

EDUCATION: Winslow (AZ) High School, 1947; U of N AZ; Art Instruction, Inc., Minneapolis, MN, 1948-1950; studied with John R. Salter at U of N AZ

OCCUPATION: Sign painter, commercial artist; currently a full-time artist

MEDIA: Oil and tempera

PUBLISHED: Snodgrass (1968); Tanner (1973)

COMMISSIONS: *Murals:* Chamber of Commerce, Flagstaff, AZ. *Portraits:* J. Howard Pyle, Governor of Arizona, 1954

EXHIBITS: ASF, ITIC, MNM, PAC, SWAIA

SOLO EXHIBITS: MNM, MNA, PAC, U of N AZ

AWARDS: ASF, ITIC

CALVIN FENLEY CHÁVEZ

"The artist often exhibited his oil portraits at the Annual Indian Market, Santa Fe, NM. He is also known as a carver of plaques with katsina *motifs. In 1964, he underwent brain surgery which, for a time, threatened his career in art."*

Snodgrass 1968

Many of Chávez's paintings show a European influence in the use of background, modeling of the figures, and the use of muted colors.

Tanner 1973

CHÁVEZ, MANUEL *Cochití*

Owu Tewa, Echo of a Song

A.K.A. Bob Chávez; Signature: Owa Tewa

Born 1915, Cochití Pueblo, NM

RESIDENCE: Santa Fe, NM

MILITARY: U.S. Army, WWII, prisoner of war

EDUCATION: Graduated St. Catherine's

OCCUPATION: Fabric designer, stained glass worker, leather worker, printer, statuary carver, New Mexico State Highway Department employee, volunteer teacher, and painter

PUBLISHED: Snodgrass (1968); Brody (1971); Tanner (1973); Seymour (1988); Williams, ed. (1990). *La Turista* (7 June 1957)

COMMISSIONS: *Murals:* IPCC

PUBLIC COLLECTIONS: IACB/DC; ITIC; MKMcNAI; OSU; SM; WOM; Cornwall Hights, Philadelphia, PA

EXHIBITS: HM; HM/G; MKMcNAI; PAC; SAIEAIP; SWAIA; WRTD; galleries in Scottsdale, AZ

SOLO EXHIBITS: WWM

HONORS: State of New Mexico, Exceptional Service Award

MANUEL CHÁVEZ

Stationed in the Philippines at the start of World War II, Chávez was captured April 9, 1942, and was a survivor of the Batáán Death March. His four years in a prison camp affected his health and it was ten years before he began to paint again. In gratitude for surviving his imprisonment, he founded an art department at St. Catherine's and became its volunteer teacher. Chávez paints every night in the studio at St. Catherine's. His subject matter is life in Cochití Pueblo, its dances and its people.

Seymour 1988

CHÁVEZ, RAY *Jémez*

A.K.A. Raymond Chávez

EDUCATION: Jémez; studied under Al Momaday (q.v.)

PUBLISHED: Tanner (1973)

PUBLIC COLLECTIONS: MNA

CHÁVEZ, SUZETTE *Zuni*

EXHIBITS: SWAIA

AWARDS: SWAIA ('78, 1st)

CHÁVEZ, TONITA (see Peña, Tonita)

CHAW, WA WA (see Wa Wa Chaw)

CHEA SE QUAH (see Hill, Joan)

CHEBON (see Dacon, Chebon)

CHE BON AH BU LA (see Blue Eagle, Acee)

CHE CHILLY TSOSIE (see Mitchell, Stanley C.)

CHEE, G. *Navajo*

PUBLIC COLLECTIONS: HCC

CHEE, AL *Navajo*

RESIDENCE: Phoenix, AZ

EDUCATION: IAIA; Columbus (OH) College of Art and Design

MEDIA: Watercolor

EXHIBITS: Partial listing of more than fifty includes: HM/G; ITIC

AWARDS: ITIC ('86; '87)

CHEE, CARLIS M. *Navajo*

Birth date unknown; brother of Norris Chee (q.v.)

RESIDENCE: Fort Worth, TX

EXHIBITS: ITAE/M, ITIC, TIAF, RE

AWARDS: RE ('94, 1st)

CHEE, JASON D. *Navajo*

Hashké Naalwod, Warrior Descended Running

A.K.A. Signature: Jason D. Chee, Kenyaaani (clan name); recently Jason D. Chee, Hashké Naalwod

Born 15 Feb 1939 in Lake Valley, NM; son of Da Tez Bah Nola Chee; M/GM: Ol Dez Bah

RESIDENCE: Farmington, NM

EDUCATION: Inter-Mt., 1958; Commercial Art, Westport, CT, 1967

OCCUPATION: Art director, curriculum development, commercial artist, technical illustrator; involved in fine arts since 1980, full-time painter since 1988

MEDIA: Oil, watercolor, pencil, pen and ink, and pastel

PUBLISHED: Mayes and Lacy (1989)

PUBLIC COLLECTIONS: HCC

EXHIBITS: ACS/MV; ACS/PG; HM/G; ITIC; NTF; RC; TF; TM/NE; Mesa Verde (CO) Art Show; galleries in AZ, NM, SD, and UT

AWARDS: ACS/MV ('93, 1st)

CHEE, NORRIS M. *Navajo*

Born 2 Feb 1960 in Mexican Hat, UT; son of Alice Edwards and Morris Chee; brother of Carlis Chee (q.v.); P/GF: Dan Chee; M/GP: Dorothy and Okee Maloney; cousin of Larry Yazzie, sculptor

RESIDENCE: Lexington, NE

EDUCATION: Tuba City (AZ) High School

OCCUPATION: Machine operator and painter

MEDIA: Acrylic, pencil, pen and ink, and prints

PUBLIC COLLECTIONS: HCC; Cozad (NE) Library

EXHIBITS: AICH; GWWAS; HCC; LIAS; LSS; MNA; OWM; RC; SM/NE; TAS; TM/NE; Grand National Art Show, Denver, CO; Robert Henri Museum, Cozad, NE; Jacob Javits Show, NY; Paul VI Institute for the Arts, Washington, D.C.; House of Representatives, Washington, D.C.

AWARDS: TAS ('89); GWWAS ('89; '90, Best of Show); RE ('93); Jacob Javits Show, NY ('92, Award of Distinction)

BENJAMIN CHEE CHEE

Chee Chee's father died when he was two months old and his mother left him with friends and went to the city to find work as a cleaning woman. By his seventh birthday he had lost contact with her. He was passed

CHEE, ROBERT *Navajo*

Hashke-Yil-E-Cale

Born 1938; died 1972

RESIDENCE: Lived in St. Michaels, AZ

MILITARY: 1958-1961

EDUCATION: Inter-Mt.; studied with Allan Houser (q.v.)

OCCUPATION: Full-time artist

MEDIA: Watercolor

PUBLISHED: Snodgrass (1968); Tanner (1968); Broder (1981); King (1981); Hoffman, et al. (1984); Schiffer (1991). *New Mexico Magazine* (Dec 1960); *Inter-Tribal Indian Ceremonial Annual Magazine* (1961; 1962); *The Arizona Republic* (7 Aug 1966; 17 Sept 1972); *Plateau* (Vol. 54, no. 1, 1982)

BOOKS ILLUSTRATED: Chee (1975)

COMMISSIONS: *Murals:* Army Buildings, Germany

PUBLIC COLLECTIONS: AC/RM, ASM, BIA, HCC, IACB, JAM, KM, MAI, MNA, MNM, PAC, SM, SMNAI, WOM, WWM

EXHIBITS: AC/A, AIAE/WSU, ASM, FAIEAIP, JAM, HM, IK, LGAM, MNA, MNM, NAP, PAC, PAC/T, SN, PSC, SN

AWARDS: AIAE/WSU, ITIC, FAM, NM, PAC, SN

CHEE CHEE, BENJAMIN *Ojibwa*

Born 1944 on Bear Island, ON, Canada, on the Temagami Reserve; died 1977

RESIDENCE: Canada

OCCUPATION: Painter

MEDIA: Acrylic, pencil, pen and ink, and prints

PUBLISHED: Southcott (1984); Menitove, ed. (1986b); Cardinal-Schubert (1992); McMasters, et al. (1993). *Native Perspective* (Vol. 3, no. 2, 1978); *Indian News* (Aug 1981); *Masterkey* (winter 1984)

PUBLIC COLLECTIONS: C/AG/TB; C/CMC; C/GM; C/INAC; C/MCC; C/ROM; C/WICEC; corporate collections in the U.S. and Canada

EXHIBITS: C/AG/TB; C/CIARH; C/CMC; C/LTAT; C/ROM; C/TFD; C/U of O; C/WICEC; Outerversa, Hamburg, Germany, 1979; galleries throughout Canada

SOLO EXHIBITS: C/AG/TB; C/U of O; Glebe Community Centre, Ottawa, ON; galleries in Ottawa and Waterloo, ON, and Vancouver, BC

BENJAMIN CHEE CHEE

(continued) from home to home and by the time he was twelve he was in trouble and spent his teen years in a series of training schools. In his twenties he was introduced to painting by Mrs. Robin Watt, the wife of a Montréal portrait painter. Chee Chee's favorite subjects were the small animals of Bear Island where he spent his childhood. Working mostly in black and white he simplified the figures into bold flowing lines. According to the Thunder Bay Art Gallery, "Chee Chee has been widely praised as an innovator who stripped Indian Art of its 'legend painting' trappings and returned to it the rigours of strong design and structural minimalism."

Menitove 1986b

In March 1977, the artist hung himself while in an Ottawa jail cell after a drunken brawl in a restaurant.

Southcott 1984

CHEECHOO, SHIRLEY *Cree*

A.K.A. Shirley Cheechoo Debassige

Born 1952 in Eastmain, PQ, Canada

RESIDENCE: Canada

EDUCATION: Lakeview Secondary School, Sault Ste. Marie, ON; Oakwood Collegiate Institute, Toronto, ON, Canada; Schreiber Island Art Project, 1970-1971; C/U of T; OCLA

OCCUPATION: Musician, actress, playwright, music teacher, writer, and painter

MEDIA: Acrylic, mixed-media, stained glass, and prints

PUBLISHED: Southcott (1984). *Masterkey* (winter 1984); *Matriart* (Vol. 2, no. 1, 1991)

COMMISSIONS: *Illustrations:* The Royal Ontario Museum, *The Tales The Elders Told;* additional illustrations for Christmas cards and calendars. *Other:* The Ontario Native Woman's Association, 37 acrylic works on paper

PUBLIC COLLECTIONS: C/INAC; C/MCC; C/ROM; Woman Teacher's Federation, Toronto, ON; Hospital for Sick Children Foundation, Toronto, ON; Laurentian Museum and Art Center, Sudbury, ON; Air Canada Collection, Toronto, ON

SHIRLEY CHEECHOO

Already a writer and actress, Cheechoo became interested in painting watching her husband, Blake Debassige (q.v.), paint. She believes her artistic talent comes from her mother but admits that she learned her technical painting skills from her husband. Her art style is simple, clear, and precise.

Southcott 1984

EXHIBITS: C/AG/TT; C/AG/TB; C/CIIA; C/MCC; C/ROM; C/WICEC; Buckhorn (ON) Wildlife Festival; Aviva Art Auction, Toronto, ON; Holy Blossom Temple, Toronto, ON; Clearly Auditorium, Windsor, ON; Nippissing College, North Bay, ON; Hart House Gallery, University of Toronto, ON; galleries in Ontario

HONORS: Canadian Native Princess, 1975

CHEEK, JOHN *Cherokee*

A.K.A. John David Cheek

RESIDENCE: Russellville, AR

EDUCATION: SWOSU

OCCUPATION: Commercial artist, and painter

EXHIBITS: CAI/KC, CNM, RE, RSC, TIAF

SOLO EXHIBITS: SWOSU

JOHN CHEEK

The artist states: "...When viewing my art, try to realize that the Native American lives in contradiction with the values of his forefathers. Even his position in modern-day society is at best a paradox. My work enables me to come to terms with myself as a Native American artist living in and between two societies."

p.c. 1990

CHEEK, RONALD *Cherokee*

Born 6 Dec 1942 in Greenville, SC

RESIDENCE: Sarasota, FL

EDUCATION: Ringling School of Art, Sarasota, FL; ASL; BFA, New School for Social Research, New York, NY, 1971; Texas A & I, Kingsville, TX

OCCUPATION: Art teacher, and painter

MEDIA: Oil, charcoal, pastel, and pencil

EXHIBITS: SAA; juried exhibits in Florida and South Carolina since 1969; see also Awards

SOLO EXHIBITS: AC/OHC; JRAM; MFA/G; SIM; TCM; Manatee County Central Library, Brandenton, FL

AWARDS: SAA; Venice (FL) Area Art League Exhibition

RONALD CHEEK

Cheek says, "In my drawings I depict people in a natural way. I concentrate on the facts of life. I believe these are common to all people of the earth. Although the facts may be the same for all people, we may differ in our attitudes and behavior toward them. Some facts we cannot escape and we must reconcile ourselves to them; others we do not wish to escape, on the contrary, we wish they would last forever...."

brochure, SIM, 1983

CHENENAETE (see Shave Head)

CHE-NOGIE (see Moran, Rose Azure)

CHESBRO, ROBERT F., JR. *Creek*

Born 5 Nov 1953 in Danville, IL; son of Floriene and Robert Chesbro

RESIDENCE: Pawhuska, OK

MILITARY: U.S. Public Health Service

EDUCATION: Hulbert (OK) High School, 1972; NSU, 1976; M.D., Dartmouth College, Hanover, NH, 1980

OCCUPATION: Physician and artist

MEDIA: Acrylic

EXHIBITS: FCTM

AWARDS: FCTM ('71)

CHESTER, EDDIE *Navajo*

EDUCATION: Albuquerque, 1959

PUBLISHED: Snodgrass (1968)

EXHIBITS: MNM

CHESTER, RICHARD *Apache*

A.K.A. R. E. Chester

PUBLISHED: Snodgrass (1968)

PUBLIC COLLECTIONS: MNA

EXHIBITS: ITIC

AWARDS: ITIC

CHETHLAHE (see Paladin, David)

CHET-TOINT, CHARLES (see Ohet Toint)

CHEVARILLO, DARIO *San Felipe*

PUBLISHED: Snodgrass (1968)

PUBLIC COLLECTIONS: MNM (dated 1926)

CHEW, BILLY (see Chew, Wilford)

CHEW, WILFORD *Tuscarora*

A.K.A. Billy Chew; Wilford Leone Chew

Born 1938 in Niagara Falls, NY

RESIDENCE: Lewiston, NY

EDUCATION: SUNY/B; Frank Art School, Tampa, FL

OCCUPATION: Assembly line worker, museum staff artist; full-time sculptor and artist since the mid-1970s

MEDIA: Oil, watercolor, and stone

PUBLISHED: *The Buffalo Courier-Express* (23 Sept 1973)

PUBLIC COLLECTIONS: SMII

EXHIBITS: C/WICEC, NU/BC, TRP

HONORS: Artpark, Lewiston, NY, artist-in-residence, 1978-1980

WILFORD CHEW

Chew feels that the Indians of the Eastern seaboard have been overlooked and neglected by authors, artists, and the media. He, through extensive research, attempts to portray the Woodland Indians in all their finery. He paints in a realistic style.

CHEYATI, PATONE (see Cheyatie, Patone)

CHEYATIE, PATONE *Zuni*

A.K.A. Patone Cheyati; Patone Chatie

PUBLISHED: Snodgrass (1968)

PUBLIC COLLECTIONS: IACB/DC, MNA, MNM (dated 1928)

CHIAGO, MICHAEL M. *Tohono O'odham (Papago)/Maricopa/Pima*

Born 6 Apr 1946 in Kohate Village, AZ, on the Tohono O'odham Reservation; son of Amy M., basket maker, and Philip F. Chiago

RESIDENCE: Sells, AZ

MILITARY: U.S. Marine Corps, Vietnam

EDUCATION: St. John's Indian School, Laveen, AZ, 1964; Maricopa (AZ) Community College, 1972

OCCUPATION: Barber, commercial artist, dancer; full-time painter since 1970

MEDIA: Acrylic, watercolor, and prints

PUBLISHED: Axford (1980). *Arizona Highways* (May 1980); *The Mesa Tribune, The Tempe Tribune, The Chandler Tribune* (1 Mar 1990); *The Phoenix Gazette* (2 Mar 1990; 31 May 1990); *Earthsong* (summer 1993); biographical publications

BOOKS ILLUSTRATED: Underhill (1979); Bahti (n.d.)

COMMISSIONS: *Murals:* Phoenix (AZ) Arts Commission, Sky Harbor International Airport Terminal; Sacaton (AZ) Memorial Hospital; public schools throughout AZ. *Other:* HM; Arizona Governor, inaugural poster, 1991.

PUBLIC COLLECTIONS: HM; Gila River Arts and Crafts Center, Sacaton, AZ; Hoo-Hoogam Ki Museum, Scottsdale, AZ

EXHIBITS: HM; HM/G; OT; West Fest Art Exhibition, Houston, TX; Historical Society Museum, NY; Sells (AZ) All-Indian Rodeo and Fair; galleries in Arizona and California

AWARDS: Partial listing includes: HM/G ('90, Featured artist; '91, Best of Division); OT ('1st); SNAICF ('87); eleven Best of Shows

HONORS: O'odham Tash, Casa Grande, AZ, poster artist; HM, poster artist, 1990

CHIEF BULL (see Sanderville, Richard)

CHIEF CHARGING SKUNK (see Newton, Ranzy Alison)

CHIEF KILLER *Southern Cheyenne*

Born ca. 1849; died 1922

OCCUPATION: Warrior, police officer, butcher, teamster, and graphic artist

MEDIA: Watercolor, pencil, colored pencil, crayon, and pen and ink

PUBLISHED: Snodgrass (1968); Peterson (1971). *American Indian Art* (spring 1994)

PUBLIC COLLECTIONS: YU/BRBML; John Hay Library, Brown University, Providence, RI

EXHIBITS: BPG

CHIEF KILLER

"The artist was among the 72 Plains Indians taken as prisoners from Fort Sill, OK, to Fort Marion, St. Augustine, FL, in 1875."

Snodgrass 1968

CHIEF OF HUMOR (see Wagoshe, Russell William)

CHIEF NAKAPENKUM (see Martin, Mungo)

CHINANA, CHRISTINA *Jémez*

EDUCATION: Jémez, 1962

PUBLISHED: Snodgrass (1968)

EXHIBITS: MNM, SN

AWARDS: MNM

CHINANA, FELIPE *Jémez*

Born 1944

EDUCATION: Jémez

PUBLISHED: Snodgrass (1968)

COLLECTIONS: CGPS

EXHIBITS: AAIE, AIE, CGPS, MNM, PAC

AWARDS: AIE

CHINANA, LARRY, JR. *Jémez*

A.K.A. Lawrence Chinana Jr.

PUBLISHED: Snodgrass (1968); Brody (1971); Tanner (1973)

EXHIBITS: MNA, MNM, SN

AWARDS: SN ('67)

CHINANA, MARÍA *Jémez*

EDUCATION: Jémez; studied under Al Momaday (q.v.)

MEDIA: Watercolor

PUBLISHED: Tanner (1973)

EXHIBITS: MNM, SN

CHINANA, PAUL *Jémez*

Born 1946

EDUCATION: Jémez, 1958

PUBLISHED: Snodgrass (1968)

PUBLIC COLLECTIONS: MAI, MNM

EXHIBITS: AAIE, MNM

AWARDS: MNM

CHINANA, RICHARD *Jémez*

A.K.A. Ricky Chinana

EDUCATION: Jémez, 1962

PUBLISHED: Snodgrass (1968)

EXHIBITS: MNM, SN

AWARDS: MNM

CHINANA, RICKY (see Chinana, Richard)

CHINO, CHARMAINE *Acoma*

EXHIBITS: SWAIA

AWARDS: SWAIA

CHINO, C. MAURUS *Acoma*

Káiámiastiwa

A.K.A. Signature: C. Maurus Chino

Born 28 Jan 1954 in Albuquerque, NM; son of Myrna Antonio and Elmer Chino; P/GF: Joe Chino; M/GM: Mamie Torivio

RESIDENCE: Corrales, NM

EDUCATION: Grants (NM) High School, 1971; B.F.A., New Mexico State University, Las Cruces, 1980

OCCUPATION: Forest firefighter, teacher, miner, illustrator, art consultant, potter; full-time painter since 1992

MEDIA: Oil, pastel, and pen and ink

EXHIBITS: CIM, ITIC, MPM/CA, NSF, RE, SWAIA

AWARDS: RE ('94)

CHINO, JOSEPH A. *Laguna/Acoma*

RESIDENCE: Laguna, NM

EXHIBITS: LAIS/M

CHINOSA (see Lone Dog)

CHIPPEWA, THOMAS GOODWIND, JR. *Chippewa/Cree*

Goodwind

A.K.A. Thomas Goodwind

Born 16 Dec 1954; son of Thomas Goodwind Chippewa Sr.

RESIDENCE: Buena Vista, CO

OCCUPATION: Artist

MEDIA: Oil, acrylic, watercolor, pencil, pen and ink, pastel, and prints

PUBLIC COLLECTIONS: HCC; State of Colorado

EXHIBITS: CNM, LCIAS, LIAS, LSS, RC, WTF; Chaffee (CO) County Council On the Arts Open Show

SOLO EXHIBITS: Collegiate Peaks Bank, CO

AWARDS: RC ('92)

CHISHOLM, CALVIN *Cherokee/Shawnee*

Born 1924 in Sperry, OK

PUBLISHED: Snodgrass (1968)

EXHIBITS: AIEC

CHIU TAH (see Mirabel, Vicente)

CHOH (see Big Lefthanded)

CHOH *Navajo*

Born ca. 1856; death date unknown; nephew of Mariano, Navajo chief

RESIDENCE: Lived in Fort Wingate, NM

PUBLISHED: Shufeldt (1889), Tanner (1950, 1973); Dunn (1968); Snodgrass (1968). *Smithsonian Institution Annual Report* (1886); *American Indian Art* (summer 1981)

CHOH

In 1886, Dr. Robert W. Shufeldt, while stationed at Fort Wingate, New Mexico, observed Choh in the trader's store making drawings on wrapping paper. Shufeldt thought Choh's drawings of animals and people were superior to those of the average Indian artist, but he was the most impressed with his drawings from memory of a railway locomotive. He had the artist draw him two other locomotives. One of these he used to illustrate an article he wrote for the Smithsonian Institution's Annual Report. "... Choh became the first named Indian artist in the Southwest to have one of his works both identified and published."

Ewers 1981

CHOPITO, DEMPSEY *Navajo*

PUBLIC COLLECTIONS: IACB/DC

CHRISTMAS, ARLENE *Maliseet*

Dozay, Little Girl

Birth date unknown; born in Tobique, NB, Canada

RESIDENCE: Sydney, NS, Canada

EDUCATION: High School in U.S.; C/NSCAD

OCCUPATION: Museum trainee, gallery owner, and painter.

MEDIA: Acrylic, conté, and pencil

COMMISSIONS: Illustrations for Native schools

EXHIBITS: C/AFIA; C/AG/NS; C/MIE; C/OCF/OT; Moncton Railroad Days, Moncton Coliseum, NB; Medical Arts Centre, Sydney, NS; International Gift Show, Toronto, ON; galleries in the U.S. and Canada

HONORS: Assembly of First Nations, painting chosen for national report on aboriginal languages; C/AFIA, painting chosen for the theme and as a logo for the festival

ARLENE CHRISTMAS

In her surrealistic style, Dozay combines abstract forms with wildlife, trees, landscapes, and beautiful faces. Many of her works reflect her traditional Maliseet family and home values. It is her intention to express the beauty and simplicity of her people's centuries-old culture.

artist, p.c. 1992

CHRISTY, LUCITA WOODIS *Navajo*

RESIDENCE: San Ysidro, NM

EXHIBITS: CNM, HMA, ITIC

AWARDS: CNM ('87, 1st); ITIC ('91)

CHU-LUN-DIT (see Jones, Ruthe Blalock)

CHUNA *Eskimo*

Birth date unknown; born in Eek, AK

EDUCATION: High school, Bethel, AK, and Hartford, VT; U of AK/F; Sonoma (CA) State University

OCCUPATION: Emergency medical technician, dancer, actor, Head Start cultural coordinator, and painter

EXHIBITS: RC

CHUNESTUDEY, DON *Cherokee*

A.K.A. Donald Chunestudey

Born 16 July 1948 in Fairfield, CA

RESIDENCE: Santa Fe, NM

MILITARY: U.S. Army, 1969-1971

EDUCATION: Benicia (CA) High School, 1966; IAIA, 1968; A.A., Solano Community College, Fairfield, CA, 1975; apprenticed to Allan Houser (q.v.) 1977-1980

OCCUPATION: Painter and sculptor

MEDIA: Oil, acrylic, watercolor, clay, and stone

PUBLISHED: Highwater (1980). *Arizona Highways* (Jan 1972); *The Santa Fean* (Sept 1979; Aug 1987)

EXHIBITS: AIAI; FAIEAIP; HM; MFA/O; NACLA; OWE; PAC; SFFA; SIAS; St. John's College, Santa Fe, NM, see also Awards

AWARDS: HM ('68); PAC ('68, 1st); Fairfield-Suisun Fine Arts Show, Fairfield, CA ('74, MA)

HONORS: Bank of America, Achievement Award in the Field of Art, 1966

CHARLIE CHUYATE

Chuyate was a Zuni historian and religious leader who painted a series of small murals on the walls of the church and rectory of St. Anthony's at Zuni Pueblo in the early 1930s.

Native Peoples, *winter 1992*

CHUYATE, CHARLIE *Zuni*

Birth date unknown; death date unknown; father of Alex Seowtewa (q.v.)

COMMISSIONS: *Murals:* St. Anthony's Mission, Zuni, NM

CHUN SHA SHA (see Trimble, Charles)

CIA, MANUEL LÓPEZ *Navajo*

Born 4 Jan 1937 in Las Cruces, NM; son of Merced Rivera and Anastacio López; P/GP: Felicita Zaiz-Cea and Hipolito López; M/GP: Valentina and Pedro Rivera

RESIDENCE: Albuquerque, NM

MILITARY: U.S. Air Force

EDUCATION: G.E.D., United States Air Force, 1956; AAA; SFAI; Los Angeles (CA) Trade Technical School

OCCUPATION: Billboard painter, commercial artist, technical illustrator, and artist

MEDIA: Oil, watercolor, pastel, mixed-media, and prints

PUBLISHED: Samuels (1982); Cia (1991). *Artists of the Rockies* (fall 1981); *Southwest Art* (Aug 1983); *The Single Scene* (Apr 1983); *The Santa Fean* (Aug 1989); *El Hispano* (Feb 1986); *Albuquerque Magazine* (Jan 1989)

BOOKS ILLUSTRATED: Shumard (1973); *Southwestern Old Times Newspaper*

COMMISSIONS: *Paintings (reproduced):* Coca-Cola U.S.A.; Hispano Chamber of Commerce (national conference); Mariachi Spectacular; Public Service of New Mexico; SAGA, painting reproduction; US West Telephone Company. *Other:* Saudargas, Baker Classical Guitar Record, jacket cover; Channel 5 KNME, *TV Guide*, cover; Youth Development Inc., *Annual Report*, cover; Starline Corporation, *Annual Report*, cover

PUBLIC COLLECTIONS: GPWAS

EXHIBITS: ABQM; U of NM; Albuquerque (NM) Convention Center; Fiesta de Santa Fe, NM; French Art Society, Paris, France; Hispanic Arts and the Quincentennial, Albuquerque, NM; New Mexico State Fair Gallery, New Mexico Tapestry, Albuquerque; Phoenix (AZ) Civic Plaza; Sedona (AZ) Spring Group Show; Superbull Western Art Exhibit, Del Rio, TX; Tegucigalpa, Honduras; galleries in AZ, CA, CO, IL, NM, and NV

HONORS: City of Albuquerque (NM), street named in his honor; Youth Development, Inc., Albuquerque, NM, Outstanding Individual Award

MANUEL LÓPEZ CIA

Cia has synthesized and refined many techniques and aesthetic areas of creativity to arrive at his current style. He says that his complex expressionism has come from a combination of amorphous and geometric abstractionism with realism and impressionism. He describes complex expressionism as "an artistic quest for the unified theory of art."

artist, p.c. 1992

CISNEROS, DOMINGO *Métis*

Born 1942 in Monterrey, Mexico

RESIDENCE: Canada

EDUCATION: National Autonomous University of Mexico

OCCUPATION: Teacher and artist

MEDIA: Mixed-media

PUBLISHED: Lippard (1990). *L'Information du Nord* (July 1990; Feb 1991); *The Massachusetts Review* (spring/summer 1990); *Wytt Om Navn,* Lillehammer, Norway (1991); *American Indian Art* (autumn 1992)

PUBLIC COLLECTIONS: C/AG/TB, C/INAC

EXHIBITS: C/AG/V, C/CMC, C/D, C/NGCA, C/NWNG, C/O, C/U of R/MG, C/ZS, OG; Casa de la Cultura, Havana, Cuba; Centro Internacional Multimedia, Weilsbeke, Belgium; International Art Festival, Lucznica, Warsaw, Poland; International Multimedia Centre, Salerno, Italy; Museum of Modern Art, Tampere, Finland; Washington State University, Pullman, WA

SOLO EXHIBITS: Windham College, Putney, VT, 1975; Emily Carr College of Art, Vancouver, BC, 1981; Saidye Bronfman Centre, Montréal, PQ, 1983; *Laurentian Bestiary,* six venue tour, 1988

HONORS: Aide Aux Artistes, Minister of Cultural Affairs, PQ, 1978; Soutien a la Creation, Minister of Cultural Affairs, PQ, 1987; Soutien a la Pratique, Minister of Cultural Affairs, PQ, 1988

CLAH, ALFRED *Navajo*

Born 1945 in Ganado, AZ

EDUCATION: Inter-Mt.; IAIA, 1962-1964

PUBLISHED: Snodgrass (1968); Tanner (1973)

PUBLIC COLLECTIONS: BIA

EXHIBITS: PAC, SN, SWAIA, YAIA

AWARDS: SN, SWAIA

CLAIRMONT, CORWIN *Salish/Kootenai*

Born 1947

RESIDENCE: Pablo, MT

MILITARY: B.A., MSU; M.F.A., CSU/LA

OCCUPATION: College administrator and painter

MEDIA: Mixed-media

PUBLISHED: Ward, ed. (1990)

EXHIBITS: CCDLR, CWY, CWAM, FSMCFA, I, MMA/MT, OLO

CLARK, BILL *Cherokee*

EXHIBITS: FCTM (4)

CLARK, DAN B., JR. *Ute*

Born 4 Jan 1956

RESIDENCE: Fort Duchesne, UT

EDUCATION: Albuquerque; Utah Technical College, Provo, UT

EXHIBITS: PAC; RC; Bottle Hollow Indian Art Show, Fort Duchesne, UT; Utah Technical College Art Show, Provo, UT; see also Awards

AWARDS: PAC; Alva (OK) Art Show (1st)

CLARK, DON *Navajo*

Born 22 Mar 1955; brother of Bill Dixon Jr. (q.v.) and Carl Clark, jeweler

RESIDENCE: Tuba City, AZ

EDUCATION: Winslow (AZ) High School, 1974; U of N AZ, 1980

OCCUPATION: Artist

MEDIA: Oil, pastel, charcoal, and prints

PUBLISHED: Jacka and Jacka (1994). *The Navajo-Hopi Observer* (3 Feb 1988); *Yellow Front Register* (Special Edition 1987); *The Navajo Times* (20 Aug 1987)

PUBLIC COLLECTIONS: HM, MNA, NTM

EXHIBITS: CIM, FSMCIAF, HM/G, IACA, ITIC, MNA, NTF, RE, SNAICF, SWAIA, TAIAF, TF; see also Awards

AWARDS: CIM; HM/G ('92); ITIC ('93, 1st); MNA; NTF; SNAICF; SWAIA ('91); TAIAF ('94); TF ('93, 1st, Best of Show); Palm Springs (CA) Indian Art Show

HONORS: ITIC, poster artist, 1993

DON CLARK

In describing one of his Blanket Series paintings which depicts a child wrapped in a blanket, Clark says, "Each of the elements you see in the painting has a certain meaning for me. For instance, the background will always be black, meaning darkness and uncertainty. When I was a child, I was afraid of the dark, and I know most children are. Therefore, the blanket means protection and security. With an overall meaning of, though I live in a conflicting, troubled world, I live with confidence and hope. The blanket is a symbol of all that trust and all that is good."

p.c. 1990

CLARK, LARI *Cherokee*

MEDIA: Watercolor, pencil, and mixed-media

EXHIBITS: CNM, FCTM

AWARDS: FCTM ('94)

CLARK, RAYMOND JACK, SR. *Navajo*

Born 9 Jan 1950 in Flagstaff, AZ; son of Marie G. and Jack Clark; P/GP: Mary Westley and Bitahnii Tsosie; M/GP: Atzaa Yazzie and John Nez Begaye

RESIDENCE: Many Farms, AZ

RAYMOND JACK CLARK SR.

Clark was born with health problems. When he was about eight years old he broke his hip which prevented him from lifting heavy objects. Because his poor health prevented him from completing his art studies, he is largely self-taught. He feels prayers have guided him in his artistic efforts.

artist, p.c. 1992

EDUCATION: Holbrook (AZ) High School, 1970; NCC; IAIA
OCCUPATION: Museum employee; full-time artist since 1992
MEDIA: Oil, acrylic, pencil, pastel, and scratchboard
COMMISSIONS: *Murals:* NCC
PUBLIC COLLECTIONS: NCC
EXHIBITS: ITIC, NTF, MNA; see also Awards
AWARDS: ITIC; NTF; Holbrook (AZ) County Fair

CLARKE, JOHN *Blackfeet*

Cutapuis, Man Who Talks Not
A.K.A. John Louis Clarke
Born 10 May 1881 in Highwood, MT; died 1971
RESIDENCE: Lived in East Glacier Park, MT
EDUCATION: North Dakota School for the Deaf, Devil's Lake, ND; Montana School for the Deaf and Blind, Boulder, MT; St. John's School for the Deaf, Milwaukee, WI
OCCUPATION: Artist
MEDIA: Oil, watercolor, pen and ink, and wood
PUBLISHED: Snodgrass (1968); Ray (1972); Ewers (1986); biographical publications
COMMISSIONS: Carved panels for public buildings, 1930's; Museum of the Plains Indians, Browning, MT, panels, 1940
PUBLIC COLLECTIONS: GM; HSM/MT; MPI; MSU, Museum of the Rockies, Bozeman, MT; Charles M. Russell Gallery, Great Falls, MT
EXHIBITS: CAI; Pennsylvania Academy of Fine Arts, Philadelphia, PA
SOLO EXHIBITS: MPI ('70)
AWARDS: Philadelphia Academy of Fine Arts ('19, Gold Medal); Spokane Art Association ('28, Silver Medal)

JOHN CLARKE

"Scarlet fever in childhood left the artist unable to hear or speak. Well-known as a painter and sculptor, he became blind in his later years."

Snodgrass 1968

CLASHIN, TIMOTHY *Navajo*

EXHIBITS: HM/G
AWARDS: HM/G

CLAUS, LESLIE *Mohawk*

Born 21 Oct 1909 on the Tyendinaga Reserve, ON, Canada
RESIDENCE: Deseronto, ON, Canada
EDUCATION: Schneider School of Fine Arts, Actinolite, ON; Art supervisor certificate, Ontario College of Arts; Cameron School of Water Colour Artists; All-media certificate, Loyalist College, Belleville, ON
OCCUPATION: Educator, Indian liaison officer, and painter
MEDIA: Oil, watercolor, oil pastel, dry pastel, pencil, pen and ink, charcoal, clay, and wood
PUBLISHED: Johannsen and Ferguson, eds. (1983)
EXHIBITS: C/WICEC; Bellevile (ON) Art Association Exhibitions
HONORS: C/WICEC, Board of Governors; Association for the Advancement of Native North American Arts and Crafts, Advisory Board, 1979

LESLIE CLAUS

For over 50 years Claus has been a school teacher, an active participant in the affairs of the Tyendinaga Reserve and an ardent painter. His paintings are often of local scenes of Tyendinaga or of the Six Nations Reserve. Some scenes he sketches from life while others he recreates from photographs.

Johannsen and Ferguson, eds. 1983

CLAUS, MARY *Mohawk*

Born 1945 on Tyendinaga Reserve, ON, Canada
RESIDENCE: ON, Canada
EDUCATION: B.A., C/U of WON; B.Ed., C/U of SK; studied with Carl Shaffer, Schneider Art School
EXHIBITS: C/WICEC, LIAS
AWARDS: LIAS ('93, MA)

CLAY, CYNTHIA *Comanche*

RESIDENCE: Lawton, OK

EXHIBITS: CNM

CLAY, HARRY *Navajo*

PUBLIC COLLECTIONS: HCC

CLAYMORE, THOMAS WILLIAM *Sioux*

Nape Sica Hoksila, Bad Hand Boy

Born 30 Mar 1909; Cheyenne River Reservation, SD; son of Katherine Carter and John Claymore

RESIDENCE: Los Angeles, CA

EDUCATION: Haskell, 1929-1932; BC, 1936-1938; U of Redlands, 1938-1939; Northern, 1949-1951, 1963; B.F.A., U of ND, 1965; U of CA/LA, 1966; studied oil painting under William Dietz (q.v.) at Haskell, 1929

OCCUPATION: Art instructor, university department head; full-time painter since the early 1960s

MEDIA: Acrylic

PUBLISHED: Snodgrass (1968); Libhart (1970); Brody (1971)

PUBLIC COLLECTIONS: BIA, IACB

EXHIBITS: CSP; Bismarck, ND; Aberdeen, SD; Charlotte, NC; Washington, D.C.; Phoenix, AZ; Rapid City, SD; see also Awards

SOLO EXHIBITS: SIM

AWARDS: Territorial Art Show, Range Days; Wahpiya Luta Club Art Show, Rapid City, SD

THOMAS WILLIAM CLAYMORE

Claymore started painting in the early 1960s while recuperating from a series of strokes. He has concentrated on contemporary styles and media. According to the artist, "Though I am an Indian I have studiously avoided traditional Indian art partly because of a lack of knowledge of the lore, but mostly to keep myself in a 'reach out' experimental position to evolve a modern style. Over the past year and a half (1970), I have worked out the media which I will hence employ. I consider myself a 'now man"'- a colorist with expertise in this media; I will subtly include the Indianess of me in my work, I know."

Libhart 1970

CLAYTON, LORENZO *Navajo*

Chorti, Shortest Distance From Mind To Hand

Born 29 Apr 1952 at Cañoncito, NM, on the Navajo Reservation; son of Virginia Clayton and John Chorti

RESIDENCE: Edgewater, NJ

MILITARY: U.S. Army Special Forces

EDUCATION: St. Michael's High School, Santa Fe, NM, 1969; CCAC, 1972-1974; B.F.A., Cooper Union, New York, NY, 1977

OCCUPATION: Lithography instructor, display artist, printmaker, and painter

MEDIA: Oil, acrylic, and prints

PUBLISHED: *The Philadelphia Inquirer* (14 Dec 1982); *Artspeak* (17 Feb 1983); *Village Voice* (27 Dec 1983); *The New York Times* (30 Nov 1984; 3 Apr 1988; 30 Oct 1988)

COMMISSIONS: Jane Voorhees Zimmerli Art Museum, Rutgers University, NJ, print, 1984

PUBLIC COLLECTIONS: HM; MM/NJ; NM; Jane Voorhees Zimmerli Art Museum, Rutgers University, NJ

EXHIBITS: Partial listing of more than thirty includes: AC/SWA; AICH; C/AG/Q; CSU/CAR; HM; MAI; MR; OSU/G; PDN; PIG; SCG; Philadelphia Art Alliance, 1982; Jane Voorhees Zimmerli Art Museum, Rutgers University, NJ, 1985; Jersey City (NJ) Museum, 1988; galleries in NJ, NM, and NY

HONORS: MAI, visiting artist, 1982; New Jersey State Arts Council Grant, 1983; Pollock-Krasner Foundation Award, 1986

LORENZO CLAYTON

Clayton's family left the reservation when he was five. After his graduation from Cooper Union in 1977, he decided to cut his artistic ties with the past and be an "American" painter and printmaker. More recently he has gone back to visit New Mexico and has come to realize that "the gift of ancestors is not to be taken lightly but rather to be cherished and used in new creations."

artist, p.c. 1992

CLEPPER, MARGARET DEWOLF *Oglala Sioux*

Born 7 July 1924 in Gordon, NE; daughter of Harry DeWolf

RESIDENCE: Pharr, TX

EDUCATION: Gordon (NE) High School, 1943; Kirkwood College, Cedar Rapids, IA, 1975; art seminars

OCCUPATION: Retired Dental Lab Technician, teacher, and artist

MEDIA: Oil, watercolor, pencil, pen, pastel, and feather

PUBLIC COLLECTIONS: HCC

EXHIBITS: RC; TM/NE; Rio Grande Winter Art Shows; Edinburg (TX) Library; Pharr (TX) Chamber of Commerce; City Savings Bank Gallery, McAllen, TX; local art shows in TX, IA, and SD

CLEVELAND, FRED *Navajo*

A.K.A. Frederick Cleveland

EDUCATION: Albuquerque

PUBLISHED: Snodgrass (1968)

PUBLIC COLLECTIONS: HCC

EXHIBITS: HM/G, HPTU, ITIC, MNM

AWARDS: HM/G ('71); ITIC ('79)

CLEVELAND, FREDERICK (see Cleveland, Fred)

CLINCHER, RONALD *Oglala Sioux*

Born 1951 in Pine Ridge, SD

EDUCATION: IAIA; studied with Bob Watts, Wolf Point, MT

MEDIA: Oil and pencil

EXHIBITS: IAIA/M; NAVAM; Cultural Center and Museum, Poplar, MT; Annual Hi-Line Show, Plentywood, MT

CLOUD EAGLE *Nambé/San Juan*

OCCUPATION: Sculptor and painter

MEDIA: Acrylic, stone, and bronze

PUBLISHED: Tryka (1993)

EXHIBITS: SWAIA

CLOUD NORTH, WOESHA *Chippewa/Winnebago*

Born 7 Sept 1918 in Wichita, KS

RESIDENCE: Lincoln, NE

EDUCATION: B.A., Vassar College, Poughkeepsie, NY; M.F.A., SU; M.F.A., Ohio University, Athens, OH; Ph.D., U of NE

OCCUPATION: Educator and artist

MEDIA: Oil

EXHIBITS: SIM; U of NE; American Indian Artist's Association, San Francisco, CA; Governor Brown's Minorities/Native American Exhibition, Sacramento, CA (1975)

CLOUD SHIELD *Oglala Sioux*

Birth date unknown

RESIDENCE: From the Pine Ridge Agency area, SD

PUBLISHED: Snodgrass (1968). *45th Annual Report,* BAE (1927-1928)

PUBLIC COLLECTIONS: SI/OAA [a 34-page book containing 102 sketches copied by Cloud Shield from the original Winter Count of 1777-1879 in his possession; 104 sketches copied by Cloud Shield from the original Winter Count of 1775-1879 in the possession of American Horse, (q.v.)]

CLUTESI (see Clutesi, George Charles)

CLUTESI, GEORGE CHARLES *Nuu-Chah-Nulth (Nootka)*

Clutesi, Whale Hunter

Born 1 Jan 1905 in Alberni, BC, Canada; died 27 Feb 1988

RESIDENCE: Lived in Alberni Valley, BC, Canada

EDUCATION: Alberni Boarding School through 8th grade; art work influenced by Emily Carr

OCCUPATION: Packinghouse worker, pile driver, bridge and dock worker, author, storyteller, ethnographer, teacher, lecturer, dancer, actor, poet, and painter

MEDIA: Oil and watercolor

PUBLISHED: Street (1963); Snodgrass (1968); McMasters, et al. (1993). *Colonist* (22 Mar 1966); *The Indian News* (Oct 1969); *Native Perspective* (Vol. 3, no. 2, 1978); *Masterkey* (winter 1984); *European Review of Native American Studies* (Vol. 5, no. 1, 1991)

BOOKS ILLUSTRATED: Street (1963); Clutesi (1967, 1969)

COMMISSIONS: *Murals:* Indian Pavilion, Expo '67, Montréal, PQ, 1967

PUBLIC COLLECTIONS: C/AC/PA, C/CMC, C/GM, C/INAC; C/U of BC; Provincial Archives of British Columbia, Victoria, BC

EXHIBITS: Expo '67, Montréal, PQ, and Seattle World's Fair; addditional exhibits throughout Canada and the U.S.

SOLO EXHIBITS: C/AC/PA; C/MAM; Victoria, BC; Ogema, SK; Edmonton, AB; Toronto, ON; Seattle, WA

AWARDS: Actra Award for Best Actor, 1978

HONORS: Canadian Council Grant, 1961-1962; Named "One of the Indians of North America," 1961; Canadian Centennial Medal, 1967; University of Victoria, LLD Honoris Causa, 1971; City of Victoria, Honorary Citizen, 1973; Order of Canada (by Queen Elizabeth II), 1973; ACTRA Award for Best Actor, 1978

GEORGE CHARLES CLUTESI

Clutesi started painting in the 1930s. In 1943, he had a serious accident while working as a pile driver and it was seven and one-half years before he could work again. His physical incapacity did not prevent his reaching his goals. His drawings enhanced the stories he wrote to preserve the culture he feared was being lost. Warner (Masterkey 1984) calls him, "one of the two Deans of Native American painting in Canada." He was encouraged and sponsored by the broadcaster and critic, Ira Dilworth, and artists Emily Carr and Lawren Harris.

"The artist has said it is his desire to depict on canvas the 'past culture of my own race on the west coast of Vancouver Island, BC, Canada.'"

Snodgrass 1968

COBINESS, EDWARD *Ojibwa*

A.K.A. Eddy Cobiness

Born 1933 in Warroad, MN; grew up on the Buffalo Point Reserve, MB, Canada

RESIDENCE: Buffalo Point Reserve, MB, Canada

MEDIA: Oil, acrylic, watercolor, pen and ink, and colored pencil

PUBLISHED: Cardinal-Schubert (1992); McMasters, et al. (1993). *The Kitchener-Waterloo Record* (21 Feb 1977); *The Windsor Star* (28 Mar 1977); *Native Perspective* (Vol. 3, no. 2, 1978); *The Winnipeg Tribune* (8 May 1978); *The Edmonton Sun* (11 May 1979); *The Edmonton Journal* (23 July 1980); *Windspeaker* (12 Dec 1986); *American Indian Art* (spring 1990)

COMMISSIONS: *Murals:* Government Building, Churchill, MB

PUBLIC COLLECTIONS: C/CMC; C/INAC; C/MCC; C/ROM; C/WICEC; Children's Hospital, Winnipeg, MB; Her Majesty Queen Elizabeth II, England; Province of Manitoba Offices, Winnipeg, MB; Winnipeg (MB) City Hall

EXHIBITS: Partial listing from Canada, the U.S., and Europe includes: C/AG/TB; C/ACCCNA; C/ROM; C/TFD; C/WICEC; SM; Folklorama '74, Winnipeg, MB; Manitoba Indian Days, Winnipeg; Terrasses de la Chaudiére, Hull, PQ; galleries in AB, ON, and MB

SOLO EXHIBITS: Partial listing of 23 includes: C/ROM; C/U of MB; U of MN/TC

EDWARD COBINESS

Cobiness is one of the best known of Canada's Native painters. His paintings have gone through several stages. His earliest work was of realistic village scenes. The next stage was more abstract. His more recent works are largely of Manitoba's wildlife and reflect the influence of Benjamin Chee Chee.

American Indian Art
spring 1990

COCHE, JEANNE (see Cason-Coche, Jeanne)

COCHRAN, BENJAMIN *Cherokee*

RESIDENCE: Kansas, OK

OCCUPATION: Sculptor and painter

MEDIA: Acrylic and wood

EXHIBITS: CNM, FCTM
AWARDS: FCTM ('92)

COCHRAN, GEORGE *Cherokee*

Man Alone
A.K.A. George McKee Cochran
Born 5 Oct 1908 in Stilwell, OK; died Dec 1989; son of Ada Redbird and Oscar Cochran; GF: Redbird, signer of the Oklahoma Constitution at statehood
RESIDENCE: Lived in Tahlequah, OK
EDUCATION: Hominy (OK) High School; Haskell, 1927
OCCUPATION: Rancher, jockey, author, cartoonist, lecturer, and artist
MEDIA: Oil, watercolor, and pen and ink
PUBLISHED: Snodgrass (1968); Brody (1971). *The Indian Trader* (Nov 1974); biographical publications
BOOKS ILLUSTRATED: Cochran (1939); *ABC Book* (1947); *The Celilob Indians (1949); Who Did It First* (1959); *Indian Portraits of the Pacific Northwest*
COMMISSIONS: Warm Springs Tribal Council, 45 drawings and paintings, 1965
PUBLIC COLLECTIONS: BIA; MNA; Haskell Institute; Truman Library, Independence, MO; Seattle (WA) Public Library; The Oregonian, Portland, OR; Warm Springs Tribal Council, OR
EXHIBITS: AAID; CNM; IFA; KCPA; OAC; SI; TIAF; U of AZ; U of OR; U of SD; U of UT; American Indian Festival of Arts, La Grande, OR; galleries in AZ, CA, and NM, see also Awards
AWARDS: AAID ('61, Grand Award); IFA ('69, Grand Award); Oregon State Fair
HONORS: A.D.A.M.S. Theater, charcoal drawing hung to honor C. W. Bryant, 22 Aug 1991; American Indian Council, Chicago, IL, American Eagle Feather Award, 1960; Seattle Public Library, *Indian Portraits of the Pacific Northwest,* chosen for permanent display; *Indian Portraits of the Pacific Northwest,* adopted for northwest Native American Studies curricula

GEORGE COCHRAN

"After WWII, the artist traveled around the country sketching various tribes. He later organized the Northwest Cartoonists' and Gagwriters' Association."

Snodgrass 1968

COCHRAN, J. WOODY *Cherokee*

A.K.A. James Woodrow Cochran
Born 28 Sept 1919 in Tahlequah, OK; died Mar 1975; son of George W. Cochran and Nellie Ann Ballard
RESIDENCE: Lived in Tulsa, OK
MILITARY: U.S. Air Force, WWII
EDUCATION: OSU, 1937-1941; CAI, 1946-1947; U of Tulsa, B.A. 1950, M.A. 1956
OCCUPATION: Associate professor of art, and painter
PUBLISHED: Snodgrass (1968); Brody (1971)
PUBLIC COLLECTIONS: MFA/D
EXHIBITS: BM/B; CAI; MFA/A; MFA/D; NYWF; OAC; PAC; SAM/S; SN; TAI; WAM; WWM; Mid-America Exhibition; Invitational Print Show, Philadelphia (PA) Art Alliance; 18th Annual International Exhibition, The National Serigraph Society, 1957
SOLO EXHIBITS: PAC; NSU; U of Tulsa; East Branch Library, Tulsa, OK
AWARDS: MFA/D, OAC, PAC, SN

CODSIOGO (see Cadzi Cody)

CODY, CADZI (see Cadzi Cody)

CODY, JAMES *Sioux*

RESIDENCE: Winslow, AZ
MEDIA: Oil

EXHIBITS: HM/G, ITIC, MCC/CA
AWARDS: HM/G ('71); ITIC ('76, 1st; '86)

COFFEE *Cheyenne (?)*

The artist Coffee is possibly the same Coffee who was once Southern Cheyenne, but who later lived with the Northern Cheyenne and acted as a helper to the chief medicine man of the tribal medicine lodge.

PUBLISHED: Alexander (1938); Snodgrass (1968)
PUBLIC COLLECTIONS: Lowe Art Gallery, University of Miami, Coral Gables, FL

COFFEE

"With the aid of an old man, Coffee painted a war record of mounted men on deerskin. The skin was heavily damaged when a torrential rain flooded a portion of the Lowe Gallery."

Snodgrass 1968

COFFEE, ALEX *Cherokee*

RESIDENCE: Kansas City, MO
EXHIBITS: CNM, FCTM

COFFEY, E. J. *Creek*

EXHIBITS: FCTM
AWARDS: FCTM ('67)

COFFIN, TOM *Potawatomi*

EDUCATION: IAIA
PUBLISHED: Hill (1992)
COMMISSIONS: *Murals:* IAIA, 1976-1977

COHO, VERNON *Navajo*

RESIDENCE: Dallas, TX
EDUCATION: Riverside, ca. 1961; U of AZ, "Southwest Indian Art Project," scholarship, summer 1962
PUBLISHED: Snodgrass (1968)
EXHIBITS: PAC

COHOE, BILL *Navajo*

A.K.A. Bill Tillman Cohoe

Born 8 Feb 1962 in Pine Hill, NM; son of Esther and Billy Cohoe

RESIDENCE: San Carlos, NM
EDUCATION: Pine Hill (NM) High School, 1980; IAIA, 1984; U of NM
OCCUPATION: Cowboy, saddlemaker, sculptor, and painter
MEDIA: Oil, acrylic, watercolor, pencil, pastel, stone, and clay
PUBLISHED: *Art of the West* (1989); *New Mexico Quarter Horse Magazine* (1989); biographical publications
PUBLIC COLLECTIONS: WWM; Pine Hill (NM) Schools; Ramah Navajo Chapter, Mountain View, NM; First State Bank of Santa Fe, NM
EXHIBITS: IAIA, ITIC, MNA, NMSC, NMSF, NTF, WWM
SOLO EXHIBITS: WWM
AWARDS: ITIC ('88, 1st; '89); NMSF (1st); NTF (1st)

GREY COHOE

Tanner (1973) considered Cohoe's work to be transitional between the tradition-bound Indian painting and a new style that was on the fringe of the fine arts. Although his subject matter was Indian-dominated, his media and styles were far removed from the traditional.

COHOE, GREY *Navajo*

Shiprock

Born 1944 in Tocito, NM, on the Navajo Reservation; died Nov 1991; son of Georgia Ann, weaver, and Woodrow Cohoe, medicine man; brother of Jerry Cohoe (q.v.)

RESIDENCE: Lived in Santa Fe, NM
EDUCATION: IAIA; College of Santa Fe, NM; Fort Lewis College, Durango, CO; Haystack Mountain School of Crafts, Deer Isle, ME; B.F.A., M.F.A, U of AZ, 1971, 1974
OCCUPATION: Educator, printmaker, writer, poet, and artist

MEDIA: Oil, acrylic, watercolor, and prints

PUBLISHED: Tanner (1973); Highwater (1976); New (1974; 1979); Hoffman, et al. (1984); Wade, ed. (1986). *Four Winds* (spring 1982); *American Indian Art* (spring 1985); *Southwest Profile* (Aug/Sept/Oct 1992)

PUBLIC COLLECTIONS: IAIA, PAC

EXHIBITS: ADIA, ASM, HM/G, HS/OH, IAIA/M, IK, MFA/O, NACLA, ND, OWE, PAC, PAIC, SI, SN

SOLO EXHIBITS: ASM; Farmington, NM, 1969

AWARDS: ADIA ('67); HM/G; SN ('67, Buehler Award)

COHOE, JERRY *Navajo*

Born 20 Dec 1957 in Cortez, CO; son of Georgia Ann, weaver, and Woodrow Cohoe, medicine man; brother of Grey Cohoe (q.v.)

RESIDENCE: Cortez, CO

EDUCATION: Aztec (NM) High School, 1976; A.A., Fort Lewis College, Durango, CO

OCCUPATION: Environmental employee and painter

MEDIA: Oil, pencil, and prints

PUBLISHED: *The Montezuma Valley Journal* (29 July 1993)

EXHIBITS: ACS/MV, ITIC, TF

SOLO EXHIBITS: Colorado University Center, Cortez, CO

AWARDS: ASC/MV ('93, Best of Show); ITIC ('90, Judges Choice Award)

COHOE, WILLIAM T. *Southern Cheyenne*

Mohe, Elk; *Mapera Mohe,* Water Elk; *Nohnicas,* Lame Man

A.K.A. Broken Leg; Cojo; Cripple; Nibbs

Born ca. 1854 in Colorado; died 18 Mar 1924 near Bickford, OK; son of Plain Looking and Sleeping Bear; Cohoe's father was killed in the massacre of Black Kettle's camp, 1864.

MILITARY: U.S. Army, scout at Fort Supply, 1887-1888

EDUCATION: After imprisonment, one of the first Indian students admitted to Hampton, Apr 1878; among the first students enrolled at Carlisle, 1879

OCCUPATION: Warrior, scout, laborer, millhand, teamster, farmer, baker, butcher, clerk, and artist

PUBLISHED: Cohoe (1964); Snodgrass (1968); Dockstader (1977). *American Indian Art* (winter 1992)

PUBLIC COLLECTIONS: HS/MA, YU/BRBML

EXHIBITS: BPG

HONORS: Head Chief of the Onihanotria (War Dancers Society) in his last years

COJO (see Cohoe, William)

COLBERT, FRANK OVERTON *Chickasaw*

Red Feather

A.K.A. Chief F. Overton Colbert

Born 6 Aug 1895 in Riverside, Indian Territory; died 20 Mar 1935, Fort Lyon, CO; son of Holmes Colbert, drafter of the 1856 Chickasaw Nation constitution (with Sampson Folsom)

MILITARY: U.S. Navy, WWI

EDUCATION: Calera (OK) High School; Murray State Agricultural College, Tishomingo, OK; art classes in New York, NY, and Paris, France, 1918-1925

OCCUPATION: Artist

PUBLISHED: Snodgrass (1968)

JERRY COHOE

Cohoe's father, Woodrow, was a member of the Salt People Clan and a medicine man. His mother, who is a weaver, is a member of the Leaf Clan. From these two important people he learned the Navajo language and its traditions. He grew up watching his mother create intricate designs in her rugs and his father create complex ritualistic sand paintings. Jerry says of his art, "I want to express the tradition of my culture, preserving the past and the present."

p.c. 1993

WILLIAM T. COHOE

"Cohoe was one of 72 Plains Indians taken as prisoners from Fort Sill, OK, to Fort Marion, St. Augustine, FL, in 1875. During his three years there, he drew pictures of his relatives and of the events in his life. He apparently drew little, if at all, after leaving prison."

Snodgrass 1968

FRANK OVERTON COLBERT

"The artist is descended from a long line of distinguished and prosperous Chickasaws (see Oklahoma Almanac, *1959). He lived in Paris from 1923 to 1926 and in Greenwich Village, New York City, after WWI. A member of the Whitney Club, he was a well-known 'Village' personality in the 1920s. He later moved to Santa Fe, NM, traveled extensively, and studied the arts and crafts of many Indian tribes."*

Snodgrass 1968

PUBLIC COLLECTIONS: HSM/OK

EXHIBITS: Architectural League, New York, NY; The Independents, Groupe de Parnasse, Paris; exhibit with sculptress Renée Prahar

SOLO EXHIBITS: Montrose Gallery, New York, NY; Galerie Paula Insel, New York, NY, retrospective show of one hundred paintings and drawings, 1963

COLBERT, GARY L. *Creek*

Birth date unknown; born in Tahlequah, OK

RESIDENCE: Muskogee, OK

EDUCATION: B.A., NSU, 1974

OCCUPATION: Educator, Bacone College Art Department director, secondary school art teacher, and artist

EXHIBITS: BC, CNM, FCTM

AWARDS: FCTM

GARY L. COLBERT

The artist describes his art as contemporary, using elements of design, surrealism, abstraction and realism.

COLEMAN, GARY *Choctaw*

EXHIBITS: FCTM

AWARDS: FCTM ('93, IH)

COLEMAN, GWEN *Choctaw*

A.K.A. Gwendolyn A. Coleman

Born 13 Oct 1956 in Claremore, OK; daughter of Lucille Tims and Jimmie Coleman; P/GF: Jimmie Coleman; M/GF: Calvin P. Tims

RESIDENCE: Norman, OK

EDUCATION: Claremore (OK) High School, 1974; OSU/O, 1980; B.A., SWOSU, 1984

OCCUPATION: Computer graphic artist and painter

MEDIA: Oil, acrylic, watercolor, colored pencil, and prints

EXHIBITS: BB, CAI/KC, CNM, OIAC, RE, SWFA; see also Awards

AWARDS: IOAC ('93); SWFA ('84, 1st); Festival of the Arts, Oklahoma City, OK ('91); Women's Arts Festival, Norman, OK ('89, 1st); Canterbury Art Festival, Edmond, OK ('87); Clinton (OK) Arts Festival ('84)

COLFAX, LEROY *Yakama*

Tush-wik

Born 22 Oct 1942

RESIDENCE: Wapato, WA

EDUCATION: White Swan High School, WA; Yakima Valley Community College, Yakima, WA; Edison Technical College

OCCUPATION: Illustrator for Yakama Tribe and painter

COMMISSIONS: *Murals:* Lloyd Pinkhorn, Wapato. *Other:* Toppenish Community Center, Yakama Nation, signs; Wapato Long House Park and Charles Pend Park, designs; Yakama Nation Canneries, design; Yakama Nation, gymnasium floor design

PUBLIC COLLECTIONS: HCC

EXHIBITS: ASM/SM, IFA, RC; see also Awards

AWARDS: ACS/SM (2-1st); IFA (2-1st); RC ('79; '84); All-Indian Arts Invitational, Toppenish, WA (1st); Granger (WA) Cherry Festival (People's Choice); Northwest Indian Artist Association Show (2-1st); Yakima County Fair, WA (1st)

COLLINS, ADELE *Chickasaw*

Pucunubbi, Baby

A.K.A. Martha Adele Collins

Born 14 Jan 1908 in Blanchard, OK; daughter of Lee Desmond and Emmett L. Victor; P/GM: Lucy Moncrief, half sister of Douglas Johnston, governor of the Chickasaws

RESIDENCE: Oklahoma City, OK

EDUCATION: Mount St. Mary's Academy, Oklahoma City, OK, ca. 1913-1926; St. Elizabeth's Indian School, Purcell, OK, ca. 1927; private art instruction under Emalita Newton Terry; Art League short courses, 8 years

OCCUPATION: Housewife, active in community art affairs, teacher, and painter

MEDIA: Oil, acrylic, casein, watercolor, egg tempera, and mixed-media

PUBLISHED: Klein and Icolari (1967); Snodgrass (1968). *American Indian Art* (Feb 1985); biographical publications

PUBLIC COLLECTIONS: IACB; HM; MNM; Gonzaga University Indian Center, Spokane, WA; Southern Nevada University, Las Vegas, NV

EXHIBITS: AAID; BB; FCTM; GM; HM/G; IACB; IFA; ITIC; MNM; NLAP;, OAC; OSC; PAC; SAIEAIP; SI; SN; U of SD; USDI USDS; Art Fair, Community Fair, National Art Roundup, Las Vegas, NV; Art League Exhibition, Las Vegas, NV; Center of Art in America, Washington, D.C.; Junior League Art Show, Lawton, OK; see also Awards

SOLO/SPECIAL EXHIBITS: HM; Riviera Hotel, Las Vegas, NV; TAMBA (sponsor), Las Vegas, NV (dual show); J. Phillips Oil Company, Ponca City, OK (dual show)

AWARDS: FCTM ('67, 1st; '68, 1st, IH; '71; '73, 1st); ITIC (18 awards); MNM; NLAPW; SN ('68; '70); GM; Sierra Vista Ranchos Exhibition; two trophies; Jaycee's County Fair, Las Vegas, NV; Henderson (NV) Industrial Days; Art Guild Exhibit, Duncan, OK; exhibits in Las Vegas, NV

COLLINS, HOWARD RUFUS (see Ducee Blue Buzzard)

COLLINS, MARTHA ADELE (see Collins, Adele)

COLOQUE, MARY NANCY *Jémez*

EDUCATION: Jémez, 1960

PUBLISHED: Snodgrass (1968)

PUBLIC COLLECTIONS: MRFM

EXHIBITS: MNM, MRFM

AWARDS: MNM

COLVILLE, CLYDE *Navajo*

PUBLISHED: Snodgrass (1968)

PUBLIC COLLECTIONS: U of PA/M

COMANCHE ENEMY (see Geionety, George)

COMA PESVA (see Lomayesva, Louis)

COMPELUBE, JOHN E. *Choctaw*

EXHIBITS: FCTM

AWARDS: FCTM

CONCHA, JOHN *Taos*

Born ca. 1873; died ca. 1973

PUBLISHED: Snodgrass (1968)

PUBLIC COLLECTIONS: CGPS, MNM

EXHIBITS: CGPS, SV

JOHN CONCHA

"The artist was still painting in 1950, although his work was not readily available to the general public."

Snodgrass 1968

CONKLIN, DON *Seneca*

Born 14 May 1957

RESIDENCE: Irving, NY

EDUCATION: Silver Creek Central High School; SUNY/F
OCCUPATION: Student and artist
MEDIA: Acrylics, pen and ink, and prints
PUBLISHED: Johannsen and Ferguson, eds. (1983). Silver Creek Central High School Class Night (1976), program cover
EXHIBITS: IBIIB

CONNER, CELESTE (see Conner, Lynn Celeste)

CONNER, DELILAH DIANNE *Quapaw/Seneca/Cayuga*
A.K.A. Delilah; Delilah Conner Anquoe
Born 8 Mar 1954; daughter of Glenna McQuire and William L. Conner; P/GP: Oulia and William Conner; M/GM: Alta and Omar McQuire
RESIDENCE: Claremore, OK
EDUCATION: Miami (OK) High School, 1972; OSU/O, 1978
OCCUPATION: Artist
MEDIA: Acrylic, watercolor, and pencil
PUBLIC COLLECTIONS: Dobson Memorial Museum
EXHIBITS: CNM, TIAF, RC
AWARDS: TIAF

CONNER, LYNN CELESTE *Chiricahua Apache*
A.K.A. L. Celeste Conner
Born 1 Feb 1954
RESIDENCE: Berkeley, CA
EDUCATION: Galileo High School, CA; A.F.A, IAIA; SFSC; CSF/SF; CCAC
OCCUPATION: Multi-media artist
EXHIBITS: CCAC; HM; LIAS; MPI; RC; San Francisco (CA) Festival for the Arts
SOLO EXHIBITS: IAIA
AWARDS: LIAS ('91, MA)

CONNERY, STANLEY *(?)*
RESIDENCE: Denver, CO
PUBLISHED: Snodgrass (1968)
EXHIBITS: MNM
AWARDS: MNM

CONNYWERDY, KEVIN QUASSICKER *Kiowa/Comanche*
O'Boy Yahn
RESIDENCE: Norman, OK
EDUCATION: Lawton (OK) High School; BC; U of OK
OCCUPATION: Artist-in-residence, teacher, curator, fancy dancer, beadworker, sculptor, and painter
MEDIA: Oil and acrylic
EXHIBITS: AIE; BC/McG; CNM; HM; JH; Oklahoma State Capital, Oklahoma City; UNITY Shows
AWARDS: AIE ('77, 1st; '78; '80; '83; '87, 1st, Best of Category; '90)
HONORS: RC, Thunderbird Foundation Scholarship, 1994

CONSTANT, ALVIN *(?)*
Wandering Spirit
Born 1946; James Smith Reserve, SK, Canada
RESIDENCE: Calgary, AB, Canada

EDUCATION: C/U of R, 1977-1978; C/ACA, 1985-1988
OCCUPATION: Free-lance artist and painter
MEDIA: Mixed-media
PUBLIC COLLECTIONS: Melfort (SK) Clinic; Kinistino, SK
EXHIBITS: C/ACA

CONTE FERI (see Hard Heart)

COOCHSIWUKIOMA (see Honanie, Delbridge)

COOCHWATEWA, VICTOR H. *Hopi*
PUBLISHED: Snodgrass (1968)
PUBLIC COLLECTIONS: MAI

COODAY, JESSE *Tlingit*
Born 18 Feb 1954 in Ketchikan, AK
RESIDENCE: New York, NY
EDUCATION: SVA, 1979-1981
OCCUPATION: Photographer and artist
MEDIA: Paint, film, and computer graphics
PUBLISHED: Lippard (1990); Roberts, ed. (1992); Zurko, ed. (1992). *America West* (July 1990)
EXHIBITS: AICA/SF; AICH; HM; PDN; PU; SC; SS/CW; WHB; The Native American Film and Video Festival, Lincoln Center, New York, NY

COOKA, CONNIE (see Booka, Connie)

COOKE, CONNIE *Hopi*
PUBLISHED: Snodgrass (1968)
EXHIBITS: PAC (possibly the same as "Booka/Cooka")

COOPER, DARRAN G. *Cherokee/Choctaw*
Jumping Rock
Born 15 Nov 1962 in Poteau, OK; son of Betsy and Jim Hill; P/GP: Pearl and Rob Cooper; M/GP: Mildred and Perry Babb
RESIDENCE: Poteau, OK
EDUCATION: Poteau (OK) High School, 1981; OSU/O
OCCUPATION: Gallery manager and painter
MEDIA: Acrylic, watercolor, colored pencil, graphite, pastel, modeling paste, earth mask, and prints
EXHIBITS: CNM; FAIE; FCTM; LAIS; OHT; RE; Oklahoma State Capitol Exhibit, Oklahoma City, OK, 1989; see also Awards
AWARDS: CNM ('88, 1st; '89, 1st, '90, 1st; '91; '92; '93; '94, 1st); FCTM ('88; '91, 1st; '92, Best of Show; '93); MCI (Cherokee Heritage Award); RE ('94, 1st); Butterfield Art Show, Poteau, OK, ('84, Best of Show; '89, Best of Show)

DARRAN G. COOPER

"Through my art, I try to share the unique beauty of the Native American spirit, their reverent bond with nature and their ceremonial approach to life and the Creator."

artist, p.c. 1990

COOPER, WAYNE *Yuchi*
Born 7 May 1942; son of Mary and Orval Cooper; P/GF: John Cooper
RESIDENCE: Hebron, IN
EDUCATION: Depew (OK) High School, 1960; Valparaiso (IN) University; Famous Artist School, CT; American Atelier, New York, NY
OCCUPATION: Artist
MEDIA: Oil, acrylic, watercolor, pencil, pastel, and prints
PUBLISHED: *Art of the West* (Jan/Feb 1994); biographical publications
COMMISSIONS: Will Rogers Heritage Trust, Bartlesville, OK, painting, 1990

WAYNE COOPER

A car accident which cost Cooper the use of his right hand and arm, as well as temporarly blinding him, almost ended his painting career. A year of hard work and persistence enabled him to regain full use of his hand and arm and resume painting.

Art of the West, *Jan/Feb 1994*

PUBLIC COLLECTIONS: NCHF, WRM
EXHIBITS: CNM; FAIE; GM, MIF; galleries in CA, IL, LA, MA, MO, NY, NJ, OR, PA, and TX
SOLO EXHIBITS: U of KY
AWARDS: CNM ('84, 1st, Jerome Tiger Award; '85, 1st); GM ('76, Best of Show)

COOYAMA, HOMER *Hopi*

A.K.A. Coyama; Homer S. Cooyama
EDUCATION: Sherman; KCAI/MO; School of Applied Arts, Bear Creek, MI
OCCUPATION: Cabinetmaker, sign-painter, and painter
PUBLISHED: Snodgrass (1968); Brody (1971); Tanner (1973)
PUBLIC COLLECTIONS: AF, MNA
EXHIBITS: FWG, HM

HOMER COOYAMA

"The artist began his art career at 12. He has painted church fonts throughout the United States. In 1927, he executed a painting on a curtain for the stage of the Western Navajo Indian School. He operated a painting shop in Flagstaff for several years."

Snodgrass 1968

Cooyama painted in both oil and watercolor. His oil paintings were done in the European style although he painted traditional Hopi subjects. In the 1970s he was also painting landscapes. He entered very few exhibitions because most of his work was done on commission.

COPPER THUNDERBIRD (see Morrisseau, Norval)

CORDOVA, LOUIS *Santa Clara*

A.K.A. Luis Cordova
EDUCATION: Santa Fe
PUBLISHED: Snodgrass (1968); Golder (1985)
PUBLIC COLLECTIONS: MAI, MNA
EXHIBITS: AC/A

CORDOVA, LUIS (see Cordova, Louis)

CORIZ, NAT *Tesuque*

PUBLISHED: Snodgrass (1968)
PUBLIC COLLECTIONS: U of C/LMA

CORLETTE, JUDY *Nez Percé*

EDUCATION: MCAD
MEDIA: Acrylic
PUBLISHED: *Art In America* (July/Aug 1972)
EXHIBITS: BM/B

CORNELIUS, RAY P. *Oneida*

Born 19 Apr 1955
RESIDENCE: Southwold, ON, Canada
EDUCATION: Laurier Secondary School, London, ON, Canada
OCCUPATION: Shipping company employee, sculptor, and graphic artist
MEDIA: Pen and ink, pencil, and stone
COMMISSIONS: Oneida Girls' Ball Team, emblem design; Oneida Junior Men's Hockey Team, emblem design; Oneida Men's Hockey Team, emblem design
EXHIBITS: Oneida Fall Fair
AWARDS: Oneida Fall Fair ('74-'77, 1st)

CORNINE, BARBARA *Cherokee*

EDUCATION: BC
PUBLISHED: Snodgrass (1968); Brody (1971)
EXHIBITS: PAC
AWARDS: PAC

CORNPLANTER, CARRIE *Seneca*

PUBLISHED: Snodgrass (1968)
PUBLIC COLLECTIONS: MAI

Cornplanter, Jesse *Seneca*

A.K.A. Jesse J. Cornplanter

Born 1889; Cattaraugus Reservation, NY; died 1957; last direct descendant of the well-known Cornplanter of the Revolutionary era

MILITARY: WWI

OCCUPATION: Instructor, master carver, author, singer, and painter

MEDIA: Watercolor, wood, and pencil

PUBLISHED: Starr (1903); Parker (1913); Snodgrass (1968); Brody (1971); Fenton (1978); Trigger (1978); Fawcett and Callander (1982); Wade, ed. (1986); McMasters, et al. (1993)

BOOKS ILLUSTRATED: Cornplanter (ca. 1903; 1938); Starr (1903); Parker (1910; 1913; 1923); Hamilton (1950)

COMMISSIONS: State of New York, executed sketches of life among the Long House people, completed ca. 1898 at age nine

PUBLIC COLLECTIONS: MAI; RMAS; New York State Library

Jesse Cornplanter

Cornplanter received no formal training but was well known for his lively, accurate drawings that depicted scenes of everyday Seneca life. He also did reconstructions of earlier days and illustrations of myths.

Wade, ed. 1986

"The artist held many distinguished tribal positions, including: ritual chief of the Long House; chief of New Town, the Indian village of the Snipe Clan; singer for the Great Feather Dance; head singer for many tribal ceremonies."

Snodgrass 1968

Cornshucker, Mel *Cherokee*

A.K.A. Melvin Cornshucker

EXHIBITS: LIAS

AWARDS: LIAS

Coronado, Norberto *Yaqui*

Born 15 Oct 1942

RESIDENCE: Mesa, AZ

EDUCATION: Maricopa Technical Community College, Phoenix, AZ, 1979

OCCUPATION: Electronic technician, carver, and painter

MEDIA: Oil, watercolor, batik, and wood

EXHIBITS: ACS/PG; CNM; HM/G; KCPA; PAC; SI; SM; SNAICF; Arizona Folk Fair, Tempe, AZ; Native American Recognition Week, Phoenix, AZ; local exhibits and markets; see also Awards

AWARDS: SNAICF; KIFN Southwest Art Show (AZ)

HONORS: Painting taken to Hanover, Germany, as an exchange gift representing the artistic culture of the Southwest, 1978

Cosen, Gilbert *Apache*

Born 23 Aug 1941 in Canyon Day, AZ

RESIDENCE: Whiteriver, AZ

EDUCATION: BC, 1960-1967; U of AZ, "Southwest Indian Art Project," scholarship, summer 1962; studied under Dick West (q.v.)

OCCUPATION: BIA Forestry Department employee and painter

MEDIA: Tempera

PUBLISHED: Snodgrass (1968); Brody (1971); Seymour (1993)

PUBLIC COLLECTIONS: MN

EXHIBITS: PAC

Gilbert Cosen

Cosen was interested in painting at an early age, however, once his education was completed and he went to work for the Bureau of Indian Affairs, his job and family responsibilities severely limited his time for artistic endeavors. His painting is now limited to an occasional one done for family or friends.

Seymour 1993

Cosen, Lydia M. *Apache*

Born 1935

RESIDENCE: Whiteriver, AZ

EDUCATION: U of AZ, "Southwest Indian Art Project," scholarship

PUBLISHED: Snodgrass (1968)

Coser, Pete G. *Creek*

EDUCATION: TJC; B.S.ED. and M.B.S., SOSU

OCCUPATION: Teacher, assistant director of a collegiate Native American studies program, and painter
PUBLIC COLLECTIONS: CNM
EXHIBITS: CC/OK, FCTM; see also Awards
AWARDS: FCTM ('75, IH; '76, Tiger Award; '80, IH; '87, IH); Ardmore (OK) All-Indian Fair (seven awards)

COSGROVE, EULA (see Paraclita, Sister Mary)

COSGROVE, KENNETH R. *Shoshoni/Bannock*

Crazy Horse
Born 1919; Fort Hall Reservation, ID
RESIDENCE: Blackfoot, ID
OCCUPATION: Rancher and artist
MEDIA: Oil, acrylic, house paint, and mixed-media
EXHIBITS: CIA

KENNETH R. COSGROVE

This self-taught artist is best known for his paintings of scenes of contemporary rodeo competitions. However, he also paints more traditional Indian subjects.

Ray, ed. 1972

COSTILOW, EUNICE *Cherokee*

RESIDENCE: Jay, OK
PUBLISHED: Snodgrass (1968)
EXHIBITS: FCTM, PAC

COUCHIE, WAYNE *Ojibwa*

Birth date unknown; North Bay, ON, Canada
RESIDENCE: Red Rock, ON, Canada
EDUCATION: B.Ed., Nipissing University, North Bay, ON; M.Ed., C/CU; B.F.A., C/NSCAD; Communication Arts Diploma, Canadore College, North Bay; C/TU
OCCUPATION: Art teacher and painter
MEDIA: Acrylic and graphite
EXHIBITS: C/AG/TB; North Bay (ON) Indian Friendship Centre; La Galeruche Gallery, Timmins, ON

COUP MARKS

LOCATION: Ronan, MT

Coup Marks is an inter-tribal organization of Native American artists and craftsmen living on the Flathead Indian Reservation in Montana. Assisted by Jaune Quick-to-See Smith, the organization was formed in December of 1982. The founding members were Larraine Big Crane, Michael Big Crane, Dwight Billedeaux (q.v.), J. E. Matt, Sylvia Matt, and Ruth Silverthorne.

The objectives of the cooperative include providing marketing possibilities to reservation artists and craftsmen, encouraging the production of traditional arts and crafts, and preserving cultural traditions. A long-range goal was the development of an art center and museum on the Flathead Indian Reservation. The cooperative has organized and coordinated exhibitions and sales throughout the United States.

COUTNOYER, FRANK *Yankton Sioux*

RESIDENCE: Wagner, SD
MILITARY: U.S. Army
EDUCATION: G.E.D. while in U.S. Army
EXHIBITS: RC; and in San Francisco and Long Beach, CA; Steamboat Springs, CO; Rapid City, Sioux Falls, and Chamberlain, SD; see also Awards
AWARDS: Center For Western Studies, Sioux Falls, SD

COX, ALGIN L. *Assiniboin*

EXHIBITS: HSM/KS, RC

COX, SAM *Cherokee*

EXHIBITS: FCTM

AWARDS: FCTM ('77, 1st)

COYAMA (see Cooyama, Homer)

COYOTE, MAC *Ute Mountain Ute/Navajo*

A.K.A. MacDougal Coyote Jr.

Born 26 Oct 1954 in Cortez, CO; son of Betty Ann Harrison and MacDougal Coyote; husband of Cecelia Coyote (q.v.)

RESIDENCE: Cortez, CO

EDUCATION: G.E.D., 1974; Fort Lewis College, Durango, CO, three years

OCCUPATION: Ceramic designer and painter

MEDIA: Oil, acrylic, watercolor, pencil, pastel, stone, mixed-media, and scraffito on pottery

PUBLISHED: *The Cortez Sentinel* (13 June 1992)

EXHIBITS: ACS/PG; FNAA; IACA; ITIC; LIAS; Native American Invitational Show, Sedona, AZ; New York (NY) Exposition

SOLO EXHIBITS: Colorado University Center, Cortez, CO, 1992

AWARDS: ITIC ('90; '91, 1st; '94, 2-1st); LIAS ('92, MA)

COYOTE, CECELIA *Navajo*

Born 15 Mar 1958; daughter of Harry and Daisy Bylillie Kee; wife of Mac Coyote (q.v.)

RESIDENCE: Cortez, CO

EXHIBITS: ITIC ('94); Indian Arts and Crafts Fair, Cortez, CO

AWARDS: ITIC ('94)

COYOTE, MACDOUGAL, JR. (see Coyote, Mac)

COYOTE WALKS BY (see Bushyhead, Jerome Gilbert)

CRAKER, RICHARD JOSEPH *Cherokee/Quapaw*

Nawtlunsi Galagina, Star Buck

Born 29 July 1940; son of Inez Price and Fred E. Craker; F/GP: Nellie Bradley and Charles Craker; M/GP: Lena Lane and William Price

RESIDENCE: Monett, MO

EDUCATION: Monett (MO) High School; B.S., Southwest Missouri State University, Springfield, MO, 1973

OCCUPATION: Welder, teacher, powwow dancer, and artist

MEDIA: Acrylic, watercolor, pen and ink, and prints

PUBLISHED: Burkhart (1976). *Art and Craft News* (Aug 1988); *Show Time News* (May 1972)

BOOKS ILLUSTRATED: *Favorite Indian Recipes* (1979); *Restoration Witness* (1977), *Old Way - Today* (1976)

COMMISSIONS: Oklahoma and Missouri powwows, 57 drawings and program covers

EXHIBITS: AIPSN; CNM; LIAS; PAC; RC; TIAF; WAM; American Association of University Women Show, Miami, OK; Cotty College, Nevada, MO; 19th Annual Brush and Pallette Show, Grove, OK; Metro Art Guild, Joplin, MO; art galleries in IL, KS, MO, NY and OK; see also Awards

SOLO/SPECIAL EXHIBITS: Monett (MO) Public Library; Cotty College, Nevada, MO (dual show)

AWARDS: CNM ('88, 1st); Ozark Writer and Artist Guild

RICHARD JOSEPH CRAKER

The artist has been a powwow dancer since the early 1960s and is active in local Indian organizations. He says "My main theme is based on the traditions of the Quapaw and Cherokee tribal backgrounds. I try to symbolically tell the old stories and histories. I also do some non-Indian themes, mainly seascapes and trains and an occasional abstract."

p.c. 1990

Cranmer, Doug *Kwakwaka'wakw (Kwakiutl)*

Born 1927 in Alert Bay, BC, Canada

RESIDENCE: Deep Cove, BC, Canada

EDUCATION: Studied with Mungo Martin and Bill Reid (qq.v.)

OCCUPATION: Gallery manager, teacher, carver, and painter

MEDIA: Acrylic, mixed-media, and wood

PUBLISHED: Macnair, Hoover and Neary (1980); Hall, Blackman, and Rickard (1981); Wade and Strickland (1981); McMasters, et al. (1993)

COMMISSIONS: C/U of BC, seven carvings with Bill Reid, 1962

PUBLIC COLLECTIONS: C/GM; C/RBCM; C/TL; Campbell River (BC) Museum

Cranmer, Kevin *Kwakwaka'wakw (Kwakiutl)*

Birth date unknown; Alert Bay, BC, Canada

EDUCATION: Arts of the Raven Workshop

OCCUPATION: Teacher, dancer, carver, printmaker, and painter

COMMISSIONS: C/RBCM, 1988

Cravatt, Kristy *Chickasaw*

EXHIBITS: FCTM

AWARDS: FCTM ('77)

Crazy Horse (see Cosgrove, Kenneth R.)

Crazy Horse (see Narcomey, Jackson)

Cree *Crow*

Birth date unknown; born at Fort Benton, MT

PUBLISHED: Snodgrass (1968)

PUBLIC COLLECTIONS: MAI

Creepingbear, Mirac *Kiowa/Pawnee/Arapaho*

Aun-So-Bea, Big Foot

Born 8 Sept 1947 in Lawton, OK; died 28 Oct 1990; son of Rita Little Chief and Ted Creepingbear; P/GP: Fannie Eaves and Stone Hammer Creepingbear; M/GP: Anne Tofpi and John Little Chief

RESIDENCE: Lived in Carnegie, OK

EDUCATION: Carnegie (OK) High School; South Community College, Oklahoma City, OK; OSU/O

OCCUPATION: Electric company employee; full-time sculptor and painter after 1974

MEDIA: Oil, acrylic, watercolor, tempera, pencil, pen and ink, pastel, soapstone, and prints

PUBLISHED: King, (1981). *The Indian Trader* (Nov 1980); *Oklahoma Today* (Dec 1990, Sept/Dec 1991; May/June 1993); *Southwest Art* (Sept 1992)

COMMISSIONS: *Murals:* The Kiowa Tribal Museum, Carnegie, OK [with Parker Boyiddle and Sherman Chaddlesone (qq.v.)]

PUBLIC COLLECTIONS: HCC, IAIA, KTM

EXHIBITS: AC/A; AIE; CNM; IAIA; ITIC; KCPA; MFA/O; NACLA; OIO; PAC; RE; Kiowa Five Show at IAIA

SOLO EXHIBITS: CAI/KC; JH; SPIN; galleries in Texas

AWARDS: AIE ('82; '85, 1st); CNM ('82; '84, 1st); ITIC ('79, '80, 1st, Special Award); PAC ('79); RE ('89)

Crews, Faren Sanders *Cherokee*

Se-Dah-Ni

Cree

"A medallion of strouding outlined with a band of black and white beads, quilled horizontal strips, and painted drawings of horses and men, was given by the artist to W. M. Cary. In 1861, this gift was acquired by M. H. Schiefflin and is now in the MAI collection."

Snodgrass 1968

Mirac Creepingbear

The story is told that at his birth Creepingbear's mother was inspired to name him Miracle but when she filled out the form she ran the letters over into the middle name squares. The clerk recorded his name into Mirac Lee.

The artist grew up in two Indian communities, Carnegie and Pawnee, OK, and he maintained close ties with both sides of his family. He was nurtured by the traditional values of sharing, community, and spirituality. As he said, ". . . In my work I try to show the strength and character of our people, how we live now. The feeling comes from the heart and my work reflects my feelings of pride for my people. I feel that I am recording history, one person's view about who we are, the positive as well as the negative aspects of Indian culture. . . . "

SPIM, Mar 1981

Tragically, Creepingbear, an undiagnosed diabetic who had been dieting, went into a coma and died in October, 1990, at the age of 43.

Born 30 Sept 1950 in Tahlequah, OK; son of Catherine Blythe and Soldier E. Sanders; P/GP: Lydia Buzzard and William (Tim) Sanders; M/GP: Mary Catherine Dormire and James Blythe; M/uncle: Jerrett Blythe, Chief

RESIDENCE: Jesup, GA

EDUCATION: Swain High School, 1968; Gardner Webb Junior College, 1968-1969; Western Carolina University, Cullowhee, NC, 1969-1972; B.A., University of Georgia, Athens, GA, 1973

OCCUPATION: Contractor and painter

MEDIA: Acrylic, watercolor, pencil, pen and ink, pastel, and prints

BOOKS ILLUSTRATED: Gardner (1990)

EXHIBITS: K; MCI; RC; Augusta (GA) Futurity; Atlanta (GA) Western Art Show; Coastal Center for the Arts, St. Simons Island, GA

SOLO EXHIBITS: Wayne County Library, Jesup, GA.

AWARDS: K ('91, 1st); MCI ('89, Special Theme Award; '90, 1st; '91)

CRIPPLE (see Cohoe, Willam)

CRISPIN, SANTIAGO *Santo Domingo*

EDUCATION: Santa Fe, 1924

PUBLISHED: Snodgrass (1968)

PUBLIC COLLECTIONS: MNM (dated 1924)

CRISPIN, SUTERO *Santo Domingo*

EDUCATION: Santa Fe, 1958; Albuquerque, 1959

PUBLISHED: Snodgrass (1968)

EXHIBITS: MNM

CROUSE, BILL *Seneca*

Gahatageyat

Born 4 Mar 1963

RESIDENCE: Salamanca, NY

EDUCATION: Salamanca (NY) Central High School

OCCUPATION: Illustrator sculptor, and painter

MEDIA: Oil, acrylic, watercolor, pencil, pen and ink, charcoal, pastel, and wood

PUBLISHED: Johannsen and Ferguson, eds. (1983)

EXHIBITS: Cattaraugus County Fair, Little Valley, NY, regional fairs and festivals

HONORS: Seneca School, award for outstanding achievement in art

CROW, THE *Navajo*

Kanribeloka, The Crow

A.K.A. Chief The Crow

PUBLISHED: Dunn (1968); Snodgrass (1968)

EXHIBITS: MNH/A

CROW INDIAN (see Yellow Nose)

CROW NOSE (see Roman Nose)

CRUMBO, MINISA (see Halsey, Minisa Crumbo)

CRUMBO, WOODROW WILSON *Potawatomi*

A.K.A. Woody Crumbo

Born 21 Jan 1912 in Lexington, OK; died 4 Apr 1989 at Cimarron, NM; son of Mary and Alex Crumbo; father of Minisa Crumbo Halsey (q.v.); Artist's father died when he was four, and his mother when he was seven.

RESIDENCE: Lived in Cimarron, NM, and Checotah, OK

THE CROW

"One of five artists whose works, commisioned and collected by Rudolf Cronau, 1880-1883, are now referred to as the Cronau Album (see Sinte)."

Snodgrass 1968

WOODROW WILSON CRUMBO

"At the end of the 3rd grade, Crumbo's schooling was interrupted for nearly ten years. During this period he, and other young Indian boys of Anadarko, OK, were encouraged by Susie Peters, who worked with them, finding them materials with which to paint and a market for their work. 'Some of us were so small,' Crumbo said, 'that we sat on gallon buckets and used the backs of chairs for easels.' The artist returned to school at 17 to study art, anthropology, and history and to pursue his many talents. In 1952, he said, 'Half of my life passed in striving to complete the pictorial record of (continued)

EDUCATION: Chilocco; AII, 1931-1933; U of Wichita, 1933-1936; U of OK, 1936-1938; studied murals under Olaf Nordmark, watercolor under Clayton Henri Staples, and painting and drawing under O. B. Jacobson

OCCUPATION: Musician, singer, dancer, writer, educator, museum director, prospector, sculptor, painter, originator and innovator of marketing and promotion of American Indian art

MEDIA: Oil, watercolor, egg tempera, bronze, wood, and prints

PUBLISHED: LaFarge (1956); Snodgrass (1968); Dunn (1968); Highwater (1976); Silberman (1978); Broder (1981); Fawcett and Callander (1982); Boyd, et al. (1981; 1983); Hoffman, ed. (1984); Samuels (1985); Wade, ed. (1986); Williams (1990), Archuleta and Strickland (1991); Ballantine and Ballantine (1993). *3rd Annual American Indian Week Brochure*, Tulsa, OK (18-22 Oct 1938); *The Tulsa World, Sunday Magazine* (7 Dec 1952); *Sooner Magazine* (Nov 1954); *Oklahoma Today* (summer 1958); *Life International* (16 Mar 1959); *The Arizona Republic* (17 Mar 1968), *The Wichita Eagle and Beacon* (28 July 1974); *The Bulletin of the Cleveland Museum of Art* (Jan 1982); *The Indian Trader* (May 1989); *American Artist* (Oct 1992); *American Indian Art* (spring 1995)

COMMISSIONS: *Murals:* PAC; U of OK; USDI; Fort Sill Indian School; Nowata Federal Building; home of Sequoyah, Sallisaw, OK; home of G. A. Hoult, Wichita, KS. *Other:* BC, Rose Chapel, stained-glass window (destroyed in 1991 when the chapel caught fire)

PUBLIC COLLECTIONS: BIA; CCHM; CGPS; CMA; EM; GM; IACB; IACB/DC; JAM; KM; MAI; MIA; MNA/KHC; MNA/NY; OU/L; OU/SM; PAC; SI; SIM; SFMA; SM; SMNAI; WAM; Pottawatomi Tribal Museum

EXHIBITS: Partial listing of more than two hundred includes: AAU;, AIEC; AIW; ASM; BC/McG; CGA; CMA; DAR; FWG; HM; HNSM; IK; ITIC; JAM; KM; LGAM; MKMcNAI; MNH/A; MNH/D; MNM; MIF; NARF; OAC; OMA; PAC; PAC/T; SFMA; SN; SV; TIAF; U of OK; WAM; WWM; YALE U; Bartlesville (OK) City Library; Enid (OK) Art Show; Fayetteville (AR) City Library; Junior League of Tulsa (OK) Building; throughout Europe, North America, and South America

SOLO/SPECIAL EXHIBITS: Partial listing of several hundred includes: CCHM (dual show); LIAS; MNH/A; OAC; PAC; U of OK; USDI; WAM

AWARDS: Sixteen from 1938-1960, including: ITIC

HONORS: *Scholarships and Fellowships:* American Indian Institute, Wichita, KS, scholarship, 1931-1933; Julius Rosenwald Fellowship, 1945-1946. *Other:* American Indian Institute, Wichita, KS, valedictorian; Delta Phi Delta, National Collegiate Art Fraternity; National dance contest winner, 1935; Oklahoma Hall of Fame, inducted 1978; Oklahoma State Arts Council, 1978-1984; Oklahoma Ambassador of Good Will, 1982; AIRF, Artist of the Year, 1987; AICA, Artist of the West, 1987; NARF, featured artist, 1987

WOODROW WILSON CRUMBO

(continued) Indian history, religion, rituals, customs, way of life, and philosophies. It is now accomplished — a graphic record that a million words could not begin to tell.' In 1939, Philbrook Art Center was given the first Indian painting in its collection, Crumbo's Deer and Birds.*"*

Snodgrass 1968

The artist was the second director of the Art Department at Bacone Indian College, Muskogee, OK, following Acee Blue Eagle (q.v.). He spent many years as a close friend and advisor to Thomas Gilcrease, founder of The Thomas Gilcrease Museum, as he assembled his art collection. He was one of the three Indian artists who were closest to Mr. Gilcrease, the other two being Acee Blue Eagle and Willard Stone (qq.v.).

CRUMBO, WOODY (see Crumbo, Woodrow Wilson)

CRUZ, RAMONCITA *San Juan*

EDUCATION: Santa Fe, 1938

PUBLISHED: Snodgrass (1968)

EXHIBITS: AIW

CRYING WIND (see Doonkeen, Eulamae Narcomey)

CURLEY *Crow*

Birth date unknown; brother of White Swan (q.v.)

MEDIA: Watercolor, pencil, and crayon

PUBLISHED: Maurer (1992)

CURLEY

An Indian scout for the Seventh Cavalry, Curley fought in the Battle of the Little Big Horn and was one of the few survivors on his side of the engagement.

Maurer 1992

PUBLIC COLLECTIONS: HS/MT
EXHIBITS: VP

CURRAN, VICTOR *Quechan*

Born 1 Nov 1945 in Winterhaven, Fort Yuma Quechan Reservation, CA
RESIDENCE: Yuma, AZ
EDUCATION: St. John's High School, Laveen, AZ, 1965; Phoenix (AZ) City College; American River College, Sacramento, CA; Antelope Valley College, Lancaster, CA; A.A., AWC, 1974; ASU, 1977-79
OCCUPATION: Commercial artist, illustrator, museum consultant, ceramist and painter
MEDIA: Acrylic and clay
PUBLISHED: Anonymous (1982a); Stewart (1988)
COMMISSIONS: *Murals:* Federal Credit Union, Yuma, AZ, 1975; AWC, three murals, 1973
PUBLIC COLLECTIONS: AWC, TYAC; Yuma (AZ) Civic and Convention Center; Yuma (AZ) Regional Medical Center
EXHIBITS: AICA/SF; AWC; HM/G; NICCAS; SCA; SCG; TYAC; Scottsdale (AZ) Community College
SOLO EXHIBITS: TYAC, AW
AWARDS: HM/G
HONORS: Arizona Commission on the Arts Grant, 1973

CURTIS, GEORGE *Southern Cheyenne*

Hé-Hein, Blackbird
A.K.A. Ameil George Curtis Jr.; A. G. Curtis; Ameil Curtis
Born 30 Aug 1932 in Geary, OK; son of Margaret Amelia Riggs and Amiel George Curtis Sr. Artist is a descendant of Stacey Lonewolf Riggs, Cheyenne chief.
RESIDENCE: Clinton, OK
MILITARY: U.S. Marine Corps, Korea, 1951-1955
EDUCATION: Clinton (OK) High School; SWOSU, 1964-1979
MEDIA: Watercolor, pencil, pen and ink, and pastel
PUBLIC COLLECTIONS: HCC
EXHIBITS: AIE, NTF, OIO, RC, U of WV
AWARDS: RC
HONORS: OIO, Board of Directors

CUSICK, DAVID *Tuscarora*

Birth date unknown; died 1840; son of Nicholas Cusick, interpreter and Tuscarora chief; brother of Dennis Cusick (q.v.)
RESIDENCE: Believed to have lived near Lewiston, NY
OCCUPATION: Physician, historian, author, and painter
MEDIA: Watercolor, pen and ink, and prints
PUBLISHED: Snodgrass (1968). *American Indian Art* (spring 1995)
BOOKS ILLUSTRATED: Cusick (1828; 1848; 1961)
PUBLIC COLLECTIONS: SI/OAA (watercolor and ink sketches credited to Cusick); National Library of Canada

DAVID CUSICK

"Although his education was not extensive, the artist was 'thought to be a good doctor by both Whites and Indians.'"

Snodgrass 1968

Cusick attempted to record Iroquoian mythology and history using paintings, drawings, and woodcuts in addition to written accounts. Starting in 1827 he published several editions of David Cusick's Sketches of Ancient History of the Six Nations.

American Indian Art *spring 1995*

CUSICK, DENNIS *Tuscarora*

Born 1799; died early 1920s; son of Nicholas Cusick, interpreter and Tuscarora chief; brother of David Cusick (q.v.)
RESIDENCE: Believed to have lived near Lewiston, NY

EDUCATION: Seneca School House, Buffalo Creek Reservation; studied with James Young, United Foreign Mission Society teacher

MEDIA: Watercolor

PUBLISHED: *American Indian Art* (spring 1995)

PUBLIC COLLECTIONS: Museum of American Folk Art, New York, NY

EXHIBITS: Museum of American Folk Art, New York, NY

CUTAPUIS (see Clarke, John)

CUT EAR *Apache*

PUBLISHED: Snodgrass (1968)

PUBLIC COLLECTIONS: HSM/OK

EXHIBITS: BPG

CUT EAR

"The artist was one of the 72 prisoners taken from Fort Sill, OK, to Fort Marion, St. Augustine, FL, in 1875."

Snodgrass 1968

CUTHAND, RUTH *Plains Cree*

A.K.A. S. Ruth Cuthand

Born 1954 in Prince Albert, SK, Canada

RESIDENCE: Saskatoon, SK, Canada

EDUCATION: B.F.A., C/U of SK, 1983; U of MT; M.F.A., C/U of SK, 1992

OCCUPATION: Painter

MEDIA: Acrylic and graphite pencil

PUBLISHED: Zepp (1985); Podedworny (1987)

COMMISSIONS: C/CCAB, 1992

PUBLIC COLLECTIONS: C/AG/M; C/AG/TB; C/CCAB; C/INAC; C/LUM; C/U of R/MG; C/U of SK; Saskatchewan Arts Board, Regina, SK

EXHIBITS: C/AG/M; C/AG/TB; C/C; C/LUM; C/U of R/MG; C/U of SK; HM; Peace Hill Trust Company Annual Art Competition, Edmonton, AB, 1983; Indian Affairs Regional Art Show and Sale, 1984; Amerika Haus, Hamburg, Germany, 1986

SOLO EXHIBITS: C/AG/M, C/U of SK, C/U of R/MG

AWARDS: Canada Art Council, 1992

RUTH CUTHAND

Best known for her large acrylic paintings of shirts, Cuthand is now exploring drawing. An abstractionist, she draws on reality-based objects for aesthetic inspiration.

5th Biennial catalog, HM, 1992

CUTNOSE, JOHN PAUL *Sioux/Cheyenne/Arapaho*

EXHIBITS: AICH

CUTSCHALL, COLLEEN *Oglala and Rosebud Sioux*

A.K.A. Colleen Larvie; Colleen Cutshall-Larvie

Born 3 Aug 1951 in Pine Ridge, SD; daughter of Geraldine Mae Sherman and Calvin Thomas Cutschall; P/GP: Mary Dillon and Antoine Cutschall; M/GM: Victoria Standing Bear and William Sherman

RESIDENCE: Brandon, MB, Canada

EDUCATION: St. Paul's High School, Marty, SD, 1969; B.F.A., Barat College of the Sacred Heart, Lake Forest, IL, 1973; Black Hills State College, Spearfish, SD, 1976; studied under Oscar Howe and Arthur Amiotte (qq.v.)

OCCUPATION: Bilingual bicultural education training specialist, teacher orientation assistant, coordinator and Assistant Professor of Fine Arts, and artist

MEDIA: Acrylic, watercolor, pencil, pen and ink, and prints

PUBLISHED: Ballantine and Ballantine (1993). *Canadian Journal of Native Studies* (Vol., no. 2, 1987), cover; *Brandon University Student Handbook* (1988); *Argus Leader* (13 Sept 1991); *Newsletter, NASAC/ACEAA* (winter 1991)

BOOKS ILLUSTRATED: Sioux History and Culture textbooks, Center of Indian Studies, BHSU, 1977; Teacher's Manual and Student Activity Cards, Government Printing Office, WA; Northwest Regional Educational Laboratory, Northwest Indian Reading Program, Portland, OR, 1980

COMMISSIONS: *Logos:* C/BU, Women's Conference; C/BU, *Native Studies History Report*, 1988

PUBLIC COLLECTIONS: C/INAC, HCC, SIM

EXHIBITS: AICH; BBHC; CAS; C/AG/SM; C/SIFC; CU/NE; FAC/D; HCC; HPTU; LAC; MLAS; NDM; NPTA; OLC; OSU/OR; PIE; RC; SIAA; SI; SIM; U of MT/WRC; U of SD/OHG; galleries in CO, ND, NM, NY, OR, SD; Washington, D.C.

SOLO EXHIBITS: SIM; Barkley Art Center, Custer, SD; South Dakota Archaeological Research Center, Fort Meade, SD

AWARDS: BBHC; MLAS ('65, Best of Show; '66); PIE ('78, 1st, Best of Show); RC; SIAA

HONORS: Brandon University Research Grant; Winnipeg Art Gallery, Native artist-in-residence, 1992

CUTS THE ROPE, CLARENCE B. *Gros Ventre*

Born 12 Apr 1935 in Hays, MT, on the Fort Belknap Reservation; son of Matilda and Frank Cuts The Rope

RESIDENCE: Hays, MT

MILITARY: U. S. Army Airborne

EDUCATION: St. Paul's Mission High School, 1954; A.A., Haskell, 1956

OCCUPATION: Painter and sculptor

MEDIA: Oil, watercolor, acrylic, and pen and ink

PUBLISHED: *Grit* (6 July 1980)

COMMISSIONS: *Murals:* United States Army Corps of Engineers, Garrison Dam, ND. *Other:* Pacific Northwest Indian Center, Christmas cards; dust jackets

PUBLIC COLLECTIONS: HCC

EXHIBITS: CMRM; MPI; GFNAAS; WTF; galleries in the U.S., Canada, Spain, and West Germany

SOLO EXHIBITS: MPI

HONORS: GFNAAS, featured artist 1984, 1986

CYRETTE, DORIS *Ojibwa*

Birth date unknown; born at Thunder Bay, ON, Canada, on the Fort William Indian Reserve

EXHIBITS: International Woman's Year Exposition, Northwestern Ontario

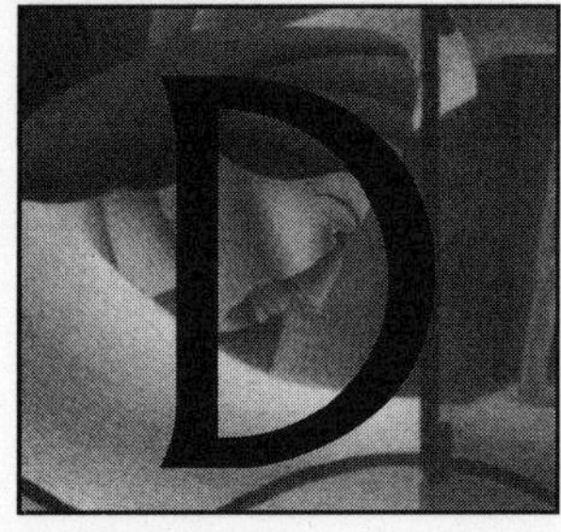

Popovi Da

The artist legally changed his name from Tony Martínez to Popovi Da. He is the son of María Martínez, the internationally known potter.

"Like his father who painted the designs on Maria's pots, the artist did his best work with symbolic designs and geometric figures. After his father's death in 1943, he did little painting; instead he assisted his mother in the decoration of her clay forms and developed a two-color firing process that produced the unique black-on-black pottery María is famous for."

Snodgrass 1968

"His special skill was in beautifully balanced geometrical and symbolic designs."

Dockstader 1977

Tony Da

Da began using casein in the late 1950s and until the late 1960s he was recognized for his outstanding paintings. In about 1966, he moved into his grandmother's home and began making pottery. After 1972, he did very little painting. The artist was injured in a serious motorcycle accident and is now disabled. According to his mother he still paints occasionally but no longer works in pottery.

Anita Montoya, p.c. 1990

DETAIL: Patrick DesJarlait, *Maple Sugar Time,* 1946. Philbrook Museum of Art, Tulsa, Oklahoma

Da, Popovi *San Ildefonso*

Popovi Da, Red Fox

A.K.A. Tony Martínez; Popovi-Da Martínez; Popovi Da Martínez; Popovi; Popovida

Born 10 Apr 1923; died 17 Oct 1971 in Santa Fe, NM; son of Maria Montoya and Julian Martínez (q.v.)

RESIDENCE: Lived in San Ildefonso Pueblo, NM

MILITARY: U.S. Army, WWII

EDUCATION: Santa Fe, 1939

OCCUPATION: Arts and crafts shop owner, Governor of San Ildefonso Pueblo, NM, ceramics painter and designer, silversmith, and painter

MEDIA: Watercolor

PUBLISHED: Dunn (1968); Snodgrass (1968); Tanner (1973); Dockstader (1977); New (1981); Houlihan (1981); Trimble, S. (1987); Seymour (1988); Williams, ed. (1990). *El Palacio* (Mar 1972)

COMMISSIONS: *Murals:* Maisel's Indian Trading Post, Albuquerque, NM

PUBLIC COLLECTIONS: EM, GM, IACB, IACB/DC, ITIC, MAI, MNA, MR, MRFM

EXHIBITS: HM, IAIA, LGAM, MFA/O, MKMcNAI, NACLA, NGA, OWE, SV, WRTD

HONORS: San Ildefonso Pueblo, NM, elected Governor, 1952; All-Indian Pueblo Council, elected Chairman; Representative at national and international conferences on Pueblo Art

Da, Tony *San Ildefonso*

A.K.A. Anthony Da

Born 1 Apr 1940 at San Ildefonso Pueblo, NM; son of Anita Montoya and Popovi Da (q.v.); P/GP: María, potter, and Julian Martínez (q.v.); M/GM: Virginia Montoya

RESIDENCE: Santa Fe, NM

MILITARY: U.S. Navy

EDUCATION: High School

OCCUPATION: Ceramist and painter

MEDIA: Casein, pencil, pen and ink, and clay

PUBLISHED: Dunn (1968); Snodgrass (1968); Tanner (1968; 1973); Brody (1971); Monthan and Monthan (1975); Highwater (1976); Silberman (1978); Houlihan (1981); Medina (1981); New (1981); Trimble, S. (1981); Fawcett and Callander (1982); Hoffman, et al. (1984); Coe (1986); Wade, ed. (1986); Seymour (1988). *The Arizona Republic* (17 Mar 1968)

PUBLIC COLLECTIONS: HM; MAI; MIM; MNM; MRFM; Laboratory of Anthropology, Santa Fe, NM

EXHIBITS: ADIA, ASM, CAIA, HM, IK, ITIC, LGAM, MKMcNAI, MNM, MFA/O, MIM, NACLA, OMA, PAC, SI, SN, SWAIA, USDI, WWM

AWARDS: All State High School Art Award, (ca. '38, age 15); ADIA ('67); ITIC ('67, 2-1st; '68, special awards; '72, Woodard Award); MNM; PAC ('67, 1st; '72); HM; SN ('67); SWAIA ('76, 1st)

Dacon, Chebon *Creek*

A.K.A. Chebon

Born 11 Nov 1946 in Oklahoma City, OK; son of Christine and Sandy Dacon; P/GF: Sardy Dacon; M/GM: Ida Berger

RESIDENCE: Allenspark, CO

EDUCATION: Capitol Hill High School, Oklahoma City, OK, 1965; U of OK, 1969

OCCUPATION: Dancer and artist

MEDIA: Watercolor, pencil, and prints
BOOKS ILLUSTRATED: *Thlopthlocco Tribal Town* (1976)
PUBLIC COLLECTIONS: GM
EXHIBITS: AC/Y; ACAI; CIM; FAIE; FM; IACA; IMA; ITIC; MIF; NARF; PAC; RE; SWAIA; WIAME; U.S. Department of Commerce - Australia; Westfest, Copper Mountain, CO; galleries in CA, CO, IN, OK, WY, and Washington, D.C.
SOLO EXHIBITS: IMA; FM; galleries in Washington, D.C., Jackson Hole, WY, Palm Springs, CA, and Hobart, IN
AWARDS: Partial listing of more than thirty includes: PAC ('71; '76)

DAGADAHGA (see Dick, Cecil)

DAGE, LYNN *Choctaw*
RESIDENCE: Las Cruces, NM
PUBLISHED: Snodgrass (1968)
EXHIBITS: MNM
AWARDS: MNM

DAHADID, POSEY *Navajo*
PUBLISHED: Snodgrass (1968)
PUBLIC COLLECTIONS: MNM

DAILEY, JAMES ROMAN *Osage*
EXHIBITS: HM/G
AWARDS: HM/G

DALLAS, LOGAN *Hopi*
MEDIA: Oil
PUBLISHED: Tanner (1973)
PUBLIC COLLECTIONS: MNA
EXHIBITS: MNA
AWARDS: MNA

DALTON, GUS *Navajo*
EXHIBITS: SN
AWARDS: SN

DALY, JIM *Osage/Cherokee*
Born 1940 in Holdenville, OK
MILITARY: U.S. Army
EDUCATION: LAACS
OCCUPATION: Illustrator and artist
PUBLISHED: Samuels (1982). *Southwest Art* (Oct 1975)

DAMRON, JANET *Osage/Cherokee*
EXHIBITS: CNM, FCTM

DANAY, RIC (see Danay, Richard Glazer)

DANAY, RICHARD GLAZER *Mohawk*
A.K.A. Ric Danay; Richard Glazer; Richard Alan Glazer; Ric Glazer-Danay
Born 12 Aug 1942 in Coney Island, NY; son of Charlotte Maliniak and Frank Danay; P/GP: Margaret Stacey and Francis Xavier Danay; M/GM: Liggy Maliniak
RESIDENCE: Corona, CA
MILITARY: U.S. Army Reserves

CHEBON DACON

Dacon spent his earlier years as an outstanding athlete, then toured the country bareback riding on the rodeo circuit and participating in competitive Indian dancing.

LOGAN DALLAS

Dallas consistently painted in oil and his subject matter was predominantly katsinas *and village scenes. According to Barton Wright he was still actively painting in the 1970s.*

Tanner 1973

RICHARD GLAZER DANAY

Danay's art works have been signed in several ways. He was born Richard Danay. His parents divorced when he was young and he stayed with his mother. She remarried and his name became Richard Glazer. When he first started exhibiting he signed his work, Richard Glazer. He says that changed when some of his uncles on his father's side attended one of his exhibitions and wanted to know if he was ashamed of being a Danay. He now signs his work Richard Glazer Danay.

artist, p.c. 1992

Danay and his work often display a unique sense of humor. He has been quoted as saying "One should not take this business of art all too seriously. I often wonder why humorous art is not accorded the legitimacy that so-called 'high art' is." Although at times making some very serious statements with his art, Danay has a good time doing it.

EDUCATION: Reseda (CA) High School, 1960; B.F.A., CSU/N; M.A., CSU/C, 1971; M.F.A., U of CA/D, 1978

OCCUPATION: Iron worker/high-rise construction worker, educator, consultant, acting museum director, American Indian studies director, and artist

MEDIA: Oil, acrylic, watercolor, pencil, pen and ink, enamel, and mixed-media

PUBLISHED: Anonymous (1976); Castellon (1978); Highwater (1980); Krantz (1985); Amerson, ed. (1981); Wade and Strickland (1981); Hoffman, et al. (1983); Lippard (1990); Wade, ed. (1986); Stewart (1988); Archuleta and Strickland (1991); Abbott (1994). *Arizona Arts and Lifestyles* (autumn 1981); *The Tulsa World* (12 June 1982); *American Indian Art* (winter 1987); *The Indian Trader* (Aug 1989); *American West* (July 1990); *The Metro Downtowner* (3 June 1991); *Southwest Art* (Mar 1992)

PUBLIC COLLECTIONS: HM; NACLA; PAC; SDMM; SINM; SM; USDI; WSAC; The British Museum, London, England; Museum für Völkerkunde, Vienna, Austria; University of Lethbridge, AB

EXHIBITS: AC/Y; AICA/SF; AICH; C/U of L; CNGM; CTC; FWMA; HM; HS/OH; IK; MM/NJ; NACLA; MPM; NU/BC; OSU/G; PAC; PDN; RC; SCG; SDMM; SFFA; SFMA; SIU/M; SM; SPIM; SW; SV; TPAS; U of UT/FAM; U of ND/AG; U of WI; WNAA; The British Museum, London, England (three exhibits); The Museum für Völkerkunde, Vienna, Austria; Utrecht, Holland; Musee de l'Homme, Musée National d'Historie, Paris, France; Bologna, Italy; Cologne, West Germany

SOLO/SPECIAL EXHIBITS: AICA/SF; CNGM (dual show); SPIM; Atwood Gallery, St. Cloud State University, Saint Cloud, MN (dual show)

HONORS: Indian Arts and Crafts Board, U.S. Department of the Interior, Commissioner, 1991; U of CA/R, Rupert Costo Chair of American Indian History, 1991-1993

DANIELS, JERRY *(?)*

Born 1953 at Swan Lake, MB, Canada

RESIDENCE: Gleichen, AB, Canada

OCCUPATION: Carpenter and painter

MEDIA: Watercolor and pen and ink

EXHIBITS: C/OWAO; Royal Canadian Mounted Police stations and hospitals throughout Alberta

JERRY DANIELS

Always interested in drawing and sketching, it was not until a back injury in the 1980s that Daniels started painting seriously. His family and friends were very supportive and encouraged him to become a full-time artist. He uses Native symbols and legends to create paintings that tell a story.

DARBY, RAY *Kiowa*

Thayhaiya; Hunting Horse

A.K.A. Raymond Lee Darby

Born 1 Aug 1938 in Carnegie, OK; son of Ethelene Darby

RESIDENCE: Lawton, OK

EDUCATION: Cache Elementary and High Schools; Cameron Junior College, Lawton, OK

OCCUPATION: Night club entertainer and artist

PUBLISHED: Snodgrass (1968)

EXHIBITS: LGAM

DARK MOUNTAIN, DAWN (see Dunkleberger, Dawn)

DARLING, MARCELL J. *Potawatomi*

Wasconadie, Prairie Flower

Born 1911 in Mayetta, KS; died 18 Dec 1976 in Tulsa, OK

RESIDENCE: Lived in Tulsa, OK

EDUCATION: Haskell

OCCUPATION: House painter and artist

PUBLISHED: Snodgrass (1968); Brody (1971)
EXHIBITS: AIE, PAC
AWARDS: AIE ('71)

DAVENPORT, JULIA CHISHOLM *Chickasaw/Cherokee*
EXHIBITS: PAC

DAVID, GEORGE *Nuu-Chah-Nulth (Nootka)*
EXHIBITS: LGAM

DAVID, JOE *Nuu-Chah-Nulth (Nootka)*
Born 1946 in Opitsaht village, Clayoquot Sound, Vancouver Island, BC, Canada; son of Hyacinth David
RESIDENCE: Vancouver, BC, Canada
EDUCATION: Commercial Art Training; studied under Bill Holm; apprenticed to Duane Pasco, Frank Charlie (qq.v.), and Russell Spatz
OCCUPATION: Commercial artist, teacher, dancer, jeweler, carver, printmaker, and painter
MEDIA: Oil, bronze, wood, mixed-media, and prints
PUBLISHED: Stewart (1979); Macnair, Hoover, and Neary (1980); Hall, Blackman, and Rickard (1981); Gerber and Katz (1989); McMasters, et al. (1993). *Vancouver Sun* (2 Aug 1974); *Museum Notes* (1978); *Four Winds* (1980); *American Indian Art* (autumn 1989); *Newsletter,* NADAC/ACEAA (winter 1991)
COMMISSIONS: State of Washington, Governor's Arts Awards Serigraphs, 1974; Expo '74, 25-foot totem pole presented to the City of Spokane, WA, 1974
PUBLIC COLLECTIONS: C/CRM; C/INAC; C/McMBC; C/NMC; C/RBCM; C/RF; C/U of BC/AM; C/VCM; HCC; Washington State Capitol Museum, Olympia, WA; Alberni Valley Museum, Port Alberni, BC; City of Seattle, WA; City of Vancouver, BC
EXHIBITS: AUG; BHSU; C/AMO; C/CM; C/IGV; C/U of BC/MA; C/RBCM; C/TL; HM; MNH/F; NSU/SD; SDSMT; Museum of Ethnology, University of Zürich, Switzerland, 1989; National Museum of Greece, Athens; Northwest Coast Indian Artist's Guild
SOLO EXHIBITS: C/U of BC/MA

JOE DAVID

David's father was an accomplished speaker, singer and dancer, who passed on his extensive knowledge of West Coast Indian traditions and culture to his son. After his family moved to Seattle in the 1960s, the artist spent as much time as possible in museums studying and photographing old carvings and paintings of all the Northwest Coast tribes, but especially those of his own area. His concern for the preservation of nature and the spiritual elements of his culture are reflected in his work.

DAVID, JOE T. *Mohawk*
A.K.A. Joseph Tehawehron David
Born 1957 in Kanehsatake Mohawk Territory, PQ, Canada
EDUCATION: C/CU
OCCUPATION: Native land rights activist, carver, sculptor, installation artist, and painter
MEDIA: Various paints, mixed-media, wood, and stone
COMMISSIONS: Federal School, Kanesahsatake, PQ, sculpture, 1987; Public Service of Canada, works of art, 1989
PUBLIC COLLECTIONS: C/INAC
EXHIBITS: C/CMC; C/FC; C/I; C/LPC; 4th Havana Biennial, Cuba, 1991

DAVID, JOHN RANDOLPH *Hopi*
Born 23 Feb 1970 at Keams Canyon, AZ; son of Dealva Tewaguna and Neil David Sr. (q.v.); P/GP: Sun Beam and Randolph David; M/GP: Marjorie and Smiley Tewaguna
EDUCATION: Hopi High School
OCCUPATION: *Katsina* carver and graphic artist
MEDIA: Acrylic, pen and ink, Prismacolor, and cottonwood root

EXHIBITS: ACS/SC, CIM; Oakton, IL
AWARDS: CIM (1st, Best of Show)

DAVID, JOSEPH TEHAWEHRON (see David, Joe T.)

DAVID, NEIL (see David, Neil, Sr.)

DAVID, NEIL, SR. *Hopi*

A.K.A. Neil Randall David, Sr; Neil David

Born June, 1944 at Hano, AZ, on First Mesa; son of Sun Beam and Randolph David, painter and carver; father of John Randolph David (q.v.); P/GP: Irma and David Kochhonowah (White Bear), weaver; M/GP: Lena, potter, and Victor Charlie

RESIDENCE: Polacca, AZ

MILITARY: U.S. Army, 1965-1968

EDUCATION: Phoenix, 1962; studied art under Fred Kabotie (q.v.) in 8th grade

OCCUPATION: *Katsina* carver; painter since 1970

MEDIA: Oil, acrylic, watercolor, pen and ink, Prismacolor, cottonwood root, bronze, and prints

PUBLISHED: Snodgrass (1968); Tanner (1973); Broder (1978, 1981); Silberman (1978); New (1979); Jacka and Jacka (1988); Bassman (1991); Teiwes (1991). *The Arizona Republic* (17 Mar 1968); *Encanto Magazine* (Apr/May 1972); *Wassaja* (20 Sept 1975); *Southwest Art* (June 1982); *American Indian Art* (spring 1984); *Arizona Highways* (May 1986)

BOOKS ILLUSTRATED: Dockstader (1994)

COMMISSIONS: *Murals:* Hopi Cultural Center Museum

PUBLIC COLLECTIONS: AC/RM, HCC, HM, MAI, MNA, WWM

EXHIBITS: AC/RMl ACS/ENP; ACS/SC; ACS/PG; CIM; FAC/CS; HCCM; HM; HM/G; HT; IPCC; ITIC; MAAIC; MCC/CA; MNA; MNH/A; MNH/CA; MNH/D; NACLA; NICCAS; OT; PAIC; PM; RMAS; SDMM; SFFA; SM; SPIM; SWAIA; TIAF; U of N AZ; U of WV; WCCA; WWM; Arizona State Capitol Building, Phoenix, AZ; Cochise College, Douglas, AZ; Hillsborough County Museum, Tampa, Fl; Riverside (CA) Community College; Texas A & M, College Station, TX; Texas Tech University, Lubbock, TX; Tucson (AZ) Art Center; West Texas Museum, Lubbock, TX; galleries in AZ, CA, CO, IL, NY, and Washington, D.C.; see also Awards

AWARDS: CIM (1st); HM/G ('75, 1st); ITIC ('70; '88, 1st); MNA (Best of Class, Curator's Award); NMSF; SN ('71); SWAIA ('90); TIAF ('94, 2-1st); Navajo County Fair, Holbrook, AZ ('79, 1st, Best of Show; '80, 1st)

NEIL DAVID SR.

David is one of four Hopi artists who founded Artist Hopid (q.v.). His father, Randolph, was from the Hopi village of Walpi and his mother, Sun Beam, came from Tewa ancestry that settled among the Hopi after the great Pueblo Rebellion against the Spanish in 1680. He is a member of the Katsina/Parrot Clan in Hano. His earliest art instruction was from his father, who would make a drawing and have him copy it. His father died when he was not quite six years old.

artist, p.c. 1993

Once recognized for his paintings, David is now best known for his katsina *carvings.*

DAVID, NEIL RANDALL, SR. (see David, Neil, Sr.)

DAVIDEALUK (see Davidialuk)

DAVIDI (see Davidialuk)

DAVIDIALU (see Davidialuk)

DAVIDIALUK *Inuit (Eskimo)*

A.K.A. Davidi; Taviti; Davidealuk; Davidialu; Davidialu Alasua Amittu; Davidialuk Ammitu Alasuaq; Taavitialuk Alaasuaq

Born ca. 1910 at Nunagiirniraq Island in Hudson's Bay; died 1 Aug 1976

RESIDENCE: Lived in Povungnituk, PQ, Canada

OCCUPATION: Hunter, trapper, carver, printmaker, and painter

MEDIA: Pen and ink, felt pen, ballpoint pen, crayon, colored pencil, graphite, prints

PUBLISHED: Driscoll (1974); Goetz, et al. (1977); Blodgett (1978a); Routledge (1979); Myers, ed. (1980); Woodhouse, ed. (1980); Latocki, ed. (1982); Jackson and Nasby (1987); McMasters, et al. (1993). *North* (Mar/Apr 1974); *Art West* (Vol. III, no. 5, 1978)

DAVIDIALUK

Born in poverty and poor in his youth, Davidialuk is described as being "a man rich in the creative powers of his own imagination, a man aware of the cultural heritage that was his birthright and also his gift to share." He began to draw in the early 1960s and he became one of the most prolific artists in Arctic Québec. His abilities at carving, printmaking and drawing led to some prosperity thus he was able to own dogs and eventually even a skidoo.

Driscoll 1982

PUBLIC COLLECTIONS: C/AC/MS, C/LFCNQ, C/AC/MS, C/TDB

EXHIBITS: C/AC/MS; C/AG/W; C/AG/WP; C/CID; C/CMC; C/EACTDB; C/IA7; C/TIP; C/TMBI; DAM; Robertson Galleries, Ottawa, ON

DAVIDSON, REG *Haida*

Born 1954 at Old Masset, Queen Charlotte Island, BC, Canada; son of Claude Davidson, carver; brother of Robert Davidson (q.v.); P/GF: Robert Davidson Sr., carver

EDUCATION: Apprenticed to older brother Robert Davidson (q.v.)

OCCUPATION: Graphic artist, jeweler, and sculptor

MEDIA: Prints, silver, gold, wood, and stone

PUBLISHED: Macnair, Hoover and Neary (1980); Hall, Blackman, and Rickard (1981)

COMMISSIONS: Tamagawa University, Japan, 30 foot totem pole, 1980; Province of British Columbia, 8 foot totem pole, 1988

PUBLIC COLLECTIONS: C/CMC; C/GM; C/MNBC; C/RBCM; Queen Charlotte Islands Museum, Skidegate, BC

EXHIBITS: C/GM; C/IGV; C/RBCM; C/TL; Craft Alliance Education Centre and Gallery, St. Louis, MO; galleries in British Columbia

SOLO EXHIBITS: MHDYMM; galleries in British Columbia

DAVIDSON, ROBERT *Haida*

A.K.A. Bob Davidson

Born 1946 in Old Masset, Queen Charlotte Island, BC, Canada; son of Claude Davidson, carver; P/GF: Robert Davidson Sr., carver

RESIDENCE: Queen Charlotte Island, BC, Canada

EDUCATION: High School, Vancouver, BC; C/VSA; apprenticed to Bill Reid (q.v.)

OCCUPATION: Teacher, silversmith, graphic artist, sculptor, and painter

MEDIA: Argillite, wood, silver, and prints

PUBLISHED: Dickason (1972); Stewart (1979); Macnair, Hoover, and Neary, eds. (1980); Hall, Blackman, and Rickard, eds. (1981), Cardinal-Schubert (1992); McMasters, et al. (1993). *Artscanada* (Vol. 30, nos. 5 & 6, 1973-1974); *Masterkey* (winter 1984); *C Magazine* (summer 1991)

COMMISSIONS: National Historic Sites, monument to Charles Edenshaw, 1977; Pepsico, Kendall Park, NY, bronze, 1984; additional sculptures, feast dishes, doors, panels, and silver and gold jewelry

PUBLIC COLLECTIONS: C/AG/TB, C/INAC

EXHIBITS: C/AG/TB, C/CIARH, C/CIIA, C/GM, C/RBCM, C/ROM, C/TFD, C/TL, C/VCM

SOLO EXHIBITS: C/IGV; C/TAG; C/VCM; Whatcom Museum, WA

HONORS: British Columbia Cultural Fund, grant to carve a 40-foot totem pole, Masset, BC, 1969; World Council of Craftsmen Conference, Dublin, Ireland, delegate, 1970; University of Victoria, BC, honorary degree, 1991

ROBERT DAVIDSON

Davidson was already an accomplished carver in 1968 when he decided to try serigraphs. He is still best known for his carvings, but his silkscreen prints are in great demand. His work has been described as exhibiting a high degree of craftsmanship and a thorough understanding of traditional Haida sculpture and design. In addition, his work is often highly innovative.

Macnair, Hoover, and Neary, eds. 1980

DAVIS, ALEX *Seneca/Cayuga*

RESIDENCE: Miami, OK

EXHIBITS: CNM, LIAS

AWARDS: CNM

DAVIS, CHERYL *Cherokee/Choctaw/Delaware*

A.K.A. Cheryl Marie Wilson Davis

Born 24 Nov 1956; daughter of Sara Wright and David Wilson; P/GP: Bessie Willison and David Wilson; M/GP: Icy and Nathan Wright

RESIDENCE: Norman, OK

CHERYL DAVIS

The artist says, "I have always found great pleasure in creating my art. The response to my work is very important, and each time someone loves my *(continued)*

CHERYL DAVIS

(continued) work enough to want to have it become a permanent part of their lives, it's a thrill and honor beyond description." Davis feels she is defined by her Native American heritage and seeks to reveal her love of that heritage in the art she creates.

p.c. 1992

EDUCATION: U of OK; TJC; Missouri Southern State College, Joplin, MO
OCCUPATION: Artist
MEDIA: Acrylic, watercolor, and colored pencil
PUBLISHED: *Indian Gaming* (Aug 1993)
EXHIBITS: BB; FAIE; JH; OIAC; RE; SNF; TIMSS; WWM; Celebration of American Indian Art, Las Colinas, TX; Festival of the Singing River: Native Americans, Florence, AL; Kansas City Indian Market, Overland Park, KS; Native American Intertribal Society of Germany Tour, 1993; Poldi Hirsch Memorial National Invitational Art Exhibition, Havre de Grace, MD; Red River (NM) Booster Club Western Artist's Showcase; Salmagundi Club Gallery, Non-member National Juried Art Exhibition, NY; Women's Arts Festival, Norman, OK; Stuttgart, Germany; see also Awards
AWARDS: OIAC ('94, Grand Award); RE ('92); Colman Studios National Juried Fine Arts Invitational Exhibition, Santa Barbara, CA; May Fair Arts Festival, Norman, OK (1st); Oklahoma Art Guild (1st)

DAVIS, DARNELLA *Creek*

Birth date unknown; born in Beggs, OK
EDUCATION: B.F.A, U of MI, 1976; M.F.A., Massachusetts College of Art, Boston, MA, 1986
OCCUPATION: Educator and artist
MEDIA: Watercolor
PUBLISHED: Zurko, ed. (1992)
EXHIBITS: WHB; Massachusetts College of Art, Boston, MA, 1988; Mid-Atlantic Regional Watercolor Exhibit, Baltimore, MD, 1989; Maryland College of Art and Design, Silver Springs, MD, 1991; Martin Luther King Library, Washington, D.C., 1991

DAVIS, JESSE EDWIN, II *Comanche*

JESSE EDWIN DAVIS II

"The artist was never a prolific painter, and each year he painted less as he become more active in photography and music. At the peak of his painting career, about 1957, he showed promise of becoming one of the outstanding Plains Indian painters."

Snodgrass 1968

Asawoya, Running Wolf
Born 9 July 1921 in Anadarko, OK; died 1976; son of Richenda E. Merrick and William G. Davis; P/GF: Jesse Edwin Davis; M/GP: Mary Inkanish and Eustace Merrick
RESIDENCE: Lived in Oklahoma City, OK
MILITARY: U.S. Navy, WWII
EDUCATION: B.F.A, U of OK, 1949
OCCUPATION: Production planner at Tinker Air Force Base, Oklahoma City, OK
MEDIA: Watercolor
PUBLISHED: Jacobson and d'Ucel (1950); Dunn (1968); Snodgrass (1968); Brody (1971); Mahey, et al. (1980). *Oklahoma Today* (winter 1961-1962; spring 1962); *Hughes News* (12 Mar 1965)
PUBLIC COLLECTIONS: MNA, PAC
EXHIBITS: AAID; AIE; BNIAS; MNM; MNM/T; MPI; OU/MA; PAC; Frontier City, U.S.A.
SOLO EXHIBITS: PAC
AWARDS: PAC ('57, Grand Award; 5 additional awards); AAID ('57, Best in Show)

DAVIS, RALPH U. *Navajo*

PUBLISHED: Snodgrass (1968)
PUBLIC COLLECTIONS: IACB (silk screened cards)

DAVIS, RAY C. *Blackfeet*

EXHIBITS: ITIC, SN
AWARDS: ITIC, SN ('68)

DAVIS, RICHARD A. (see Thunder Cloud)

DAVIS, ROY *Blackfeet*

PUBLIC COLLECTIONS: HCC

DAVIS, TRUMAN *Navajo*

EDUCATION: Santa Fe
PUBLISHED: Snodgrass (1968)
EXHIBITS: FWG

DAV-LAW-T'SINE (see Tsoodle, Darwin Cabaniss)

DAWA GUI VA (see Dawavendewa, Cedric)

DAWAHOYA, BERNARD *Hopi*

EXHIBITS: SWAIA
AWARDS: SWAIA ('71, 1st)

DAWAKEMKA (see Lomakema, Milland, Sr.)

DAWANGYUMPTEWA, DAVID *Hopi/Navajo*

A.K.A. Signature: Jack Smith
Born 17 Oct 1957
RESIDENCE: Flagstaff, AZ
EDUCATION: A.F.A., IAIA, 1976; Haskell, 1979-1980; A.F.A., U of N AZ, 1983; B.F.A., U of N AZ, 1986; Northern Arizona Institute of Technology, 1989-1990
OCCUPATION: Counselor, consultant, National Park Service seasonal technician, coordinator of FNAA, and painter
MEDIA: Watercolor, tempera, casein, gouache, and prints
PUBLISHED: Jacka and Jacka (1988); Williams, ed. (1990). *The Santa Fe Reporter* (15 Aug 1984); *The Indian Trader* (Aug 1989)
PUBLIC COLLECTIONS: Haskell, HM, IACB, IAIA, MNA, U of KS, WWM
EXHIBITS: ACAI; CIM; FNAA; FSMCIAF; HM/G; IAIA; IACA; KCPA; MCC/CA; MKMcNAI; MNA; MNM; OWE; RISD; SDMM; SM; SPIM; SWAIA; TYAC; U of N AZ; WWM; Arizona State Capitol Building, Phoenix, AZ, 1992; Zeitgenossische Indianische Kunst, Germany, 1986, 1989
SOLO EXHIBITS: WWM
AWARDS: ACAI ('93); CIM; IACA ('94, Best of Category); MNA ('79-'90, 1st); SWAIA ('81, 1st; '82, 1st; '83, 1st, Hinds Award; '84, 1st)
HONORS: FNAA, poster artist, 1982, 1983; American Indian Heritage Foundation, Falls Church, VA, poster artist, 1985; CIM, poster artist, 1988; HM/G, poster artist, 1991

DAVID DAWANGYUMPTEWA

The artist says that he would like to be thought of as a painter of mythical or spiritual subjects. Dawangyumptewa is a member of the Water Clan and often uses water as a theme. His paintings are distinguished by his use of jewel-like color and Hopi symbolism.

DAWAVENDEWA, CEDRIC *Hopi*

Dawa Gui Va, Beauty Of The Sunrise; Sun's Trail In The Sky
A.K.A. Cedric Albert; Dawavendewa
Born 4 Dec 1960 in Moencopi, AZ
RESIDENCE: Acoma Pueblo, NM
MILITARY: U.S. Marine Corps
EDUCATION: IAIA
OCCUPATION: Aircraft mechanic, silversmith, ceramist, and painter
MEDIA: Oil, acrylic, watercolor, and pen and ink
EXHIBITS: ACS/ENP, ACS/PG, IAIA, MNA, RC, SJBIM, SWAIA
AWARDS: MNA ('90; '91, 2-1st, Best of Contemporary)

RICHARD DAWAVENDEWA

A self-taught painter, Lomahinma started painting as a child. He says of his talent, "I acknowledge that I was given a gift, but in accepting this, I have the responsibility to properly treat my ideas as a living entity. I believe if I do not, then my ideas will no longer come to be with me." He further states, "When I paint I put my heart and spirit into it, so that I may give life to a painting."

p.c. 1993

FRANK DAY

Day was taught the language and traditions of his tribe by his father Twoboe who was a headman and historian for the Concow Maidu. After the death of his father in 1922, Day became something of a vagabond, traveling and working at a variety of jobs. Involved in a serious automobile accident in 1960, he began to paint seriously during his convalescence. With the encouragement of anthropologist Donald P. Jewell, he used his paintings to record Maidu tribal lore and legends. The artist said of his paintings, "I talk my paintings, say them, sing them and then paint them."

brochure, MPI, 1977

DAWAVENDEWA, RICHARD *Hopi*

Lomahinma, Handsome Sun In The Sky

A.K.A. Richard Lomahinma Dawavendewa. Signature: Includes a cornstalk surrounded by rain clouds

Birth date unknown; brother of Cedric Dawavendewa (q.v.)

RESIDENCE: Tuba City, AZ

EDUCATION: U of N AZ

EXHIBITS: ACS/ENP, HT, MNA

AWARDS: ACS/ENP ('88; '89; '90; '91; '92); HT ('92, 1st, Best In Category); MNA ('92)

DAWES, ERMALEEN *Cheyenne*

PUBLISHED: Snodgrass (1968)

EXHIBITS: PAC

DAWES, MIKE *Cherokee*

RESIDENCE: Stilwell, OK

EXHIBITS: CNM, FCTM

DAWN WALKER (see Pushetonequa, Charles)

DAWSON, SHIRLEY *Cherokee*

RESIDENCE: Oklahoma City, OK

EXHIBITS: CNM ('87)

DAY, EVANGELINE LOPE *Navajo*

A.K.A. Vangi Day

Born 25 Feb 1954; daughter of Hazel and Andrew Lope; P/GF: Monty Lope Sr.; M/GF: David Brewster

RESIDENCE: Umatilla, OR

EDUCATION: Shiprock (NM) High School, 1972; Eastern Oregon State College, La Grande, OR, 1988-1989

OCCUPATION: Store owner, archaeological survey and census employee, and artist

MEDIA: Oil and acrylic

EXHIBITS: RC, RE, TM/NE

AWARDS: First and second-place ribbons in local art shows and fairs

DAY, FRANK *Maidu*

Ly-Dam Lilly, Fading Morning Star

Born 24 Feb 1902 in Berry Creek, CA; died 13 Aug 1976 in Sacramento, CA; son of Twoboe; GF: Big Bill Day

RESIDENCE: Lived in Sacramento, CA

EDUCATION: Berry Creek (CA) Public Schools; Greenville Indian School; BC

OCCUPATION: Laborer, sign painter, preacher, ranch worker, singer, cultural historian, linguist, lecturer, author, and painter

MEDIA: Oil on canvas

PUBLISHED: Anonymous (1967); New (1981); Archuleta and Strickland (1991). *The Indian Trader* (Aug 1981); *Southwest Art* (Mar 1992)

PUBLIC COLLECTIONS: BIA, CSU/S, IACB, U of CA/D

EXHIBITS: CAM/S; HM; HS/AI; MPI; NACLA; SV; U of CA/D; Governor Edmund G. Brown Jr.'s office, Sacramento, CA

SOLO/SPECIAL EXHIBITS: CAM/S; CNGM; HM (dual show); HS/AI; MPI; Sacramento (CA) History Center

HONORS: California Indian Days Art Exhibit, Frank Day Memorial Award established in his honor

Day, Vangie (see Day, Evangeline Lope)

Day After Day (see Kabotie, Fred)

Daychild, William *Chippewa/Cree/Assiniboin*

Born 3 May 1933 on the Rocky Boy Reservation, MT

EDUCATION: Flandreau (SD) Indian School; Dallas (TX) Independent School; U of MT, 1970-1972; American School of Commercial Art, Dallas, TX

OCCUPATION: Artist apprentice, lithography stripper, staff artist, and painter

MEDIA: Oil and watercolor

BOOKS ILLUSTRATED: Textbooks, bibliographies, and calendars

SOLO EXHIBITS: MPI

HONORS: BIA, Education Grant, 1970-1972

Daylight, Larry Clayton *Shawnee/Delaware/Quapaw*

Wa-se-be-Wes-ska-ka, Best Feather

Born 20 Jan 1950 in Tulsa, OK

RESIDENCE: Cushing, OK

EDUCATION: McLain High School, Tulsa, OK, 1968; B.F.A., U of Tulsa, 1972; U of Tulsa, 1972-1973

OCCUPATION: Commercial artist, teacher, race car driver, lecturer, entertainer, and painter

COMMISSIONS: Tulsa (OK) Little Theater and The American Indian Theater Company of Oklahoma, Tulsa, OK, program covers, posters, and set designs

PUBLIC COLLECTIONS: GM

EXHIBITS: PAC, PBOIA

SOLO EXHIBITS: SPIM

AWARDS: PAC ('66, 1st; '67, 1st; '72; '73, Painting Award); PBOIA ('71, 1st)

HONORS: U.S. Department of Commerce, appointed Goodwill Ambassador to Ireland and Israel, 1967; World Champion Fancy War Dancer, 1977; Annual Tulsa Indian Club Powwow, 1st in senior division; Annual Quapaw Powwow, 1st

Larry Clayton Daylight

Daylight said of himself as an artist, "... The outlook I have as an 'artist' is aesthetically an attitude of mind. I'm not what one would consider an Indian artist, but an artist who is an Indian. Music and dance play an important part in my life, not just one kind of music or dance, but of various cultures. Just like art, they constitute elements of a complex entity — each making its own statement...."

brochure, SPIM, 1977

Dayzie, Tom *Navajo*

PUBLIC COLLECTIONS: MNA

Deadman, Patricia *Tuscarora*

Born 24 Apr 1961 in Ohsweken, ON, Canada

RESIDENCE: Woodstock, ON, Canada

EDUCATION: Diploma, Fanshawe College, London, ON 1986; B.F.A., C/U of W/ON, 1988; C/BSFA, 1991

PUBLIC COLLECTIONS: C/AG/TB, C/INAC

EXHIBITS: C/AG/D, C/AG/G, C/AG/H, C/AG/TB, C/BCC, C/NIIPA/G, C/ROM, C/WICEC, HM; see also Awards

SOLO EXHIBITS: C/AB/TB; C/NIIPA/G; The Photo Club, Philadelphia, PA

AWARDS: Look '89, Sarnia, ON ('89, Juror's Award); Oxford County Annual Art Show, Woodstock, ON ('91, Juror's Award)

HONORS: Chevron Canada Resources Scholarship; Mackie Cryderman Award, 1985; Jill Dynan-Perry Memorial Bursary, 1988; Ontario Arts Council, exhibition assistance grant, 1989; Barbara Spohr Endowment Fund, 1991

Deale, Roger, Jr. *Navajo*

Born 6 Nov 1968; son of Angeline and Leroy Deale Jr.; P/GP: Virginia and Leroy Deale; M/GP: Helen and John Harrison

RESIDENCE: Shiprock, NM

Roger Deale Jr.

The artist considers Oscar Howe, Harrison Begay, and Benjamin Harjo Jr. (qq.v.) his greatest artistic influences.

p.c. 1991

EDUCATION: Shiprock (NM) High School; CAI
OCCUPATION: Full-time artist
MEDIA: Watercolor, pen and ink, gouache, and mixed-media
EXHIBITS: ITIC, SWAIA
AWARDS: ITIC
HONORS: U.S. Congressional Arts Caucus Award, representing the State of New Mexico

DEBASSIGE, BLAKE R. *Ojibwa*

Born 22 June 1956 in Mindemoya, Manitoulin Island, ON, Canada; husband of Shirley CheeChoo (q.v.)

RESIDENCE: West Bay, Manitoulin Island, ON, Canada

EDUCATION: Manitoulin Secondary School, West Bay Reserve, ON; Manitou Arts Foundation, Schreiber Island, ON; Laurentian University, Sudbury, Ontario; Ojibwa Cultural Foundation Workshops

OCCUPATION: Teacher, poet, design consultant, set designer, carver, and painter

MEDIA: Acrylic, watercolor, wood, and prints

PUBLISHED: Southcott (1984); Menitove, ed. (1986b); Menitove and Danford, eds. (1989); Podedworny (1989); McMasters, et al. (1993). *The Toronto Daily Star* (1 Aug 1974); *Glove and Mail* (22 Mar 1976); *The Manitoulin Expositor* (4 Aug 1982; winter 1982); *The Sudbury Star* (6 Aug 1982; 19 May 1983); *Masterkey* (winter 1984); *Windspeaker* (12 Dec 1986).

COMMISSIONS: *Illustrations:* British Museum and Indigenous Survival International of Canada, London, England, 1988; The New Internationalist, Toronto, ON, 1988. *Logos:* Anishnawbe Spiritual Centre, Espanola, ON, 1991; Focus Program, West Bay First Nation, Manitoulin Island, ON, 1991. *Murals:* West Bay (ON) Sports Centre, 1973; Mississauga (ON) R.C. Church, 1980; Anderson Lake Faith and Justice Centre, Espanola, ON, 1982; Mohawks of the Bay of Quinte Band, Deseronto, ON, 1984; Province of Ontario, Sudbury Office Building, 1991; Niagara Child Development Centre, Welland, ON 1990; Ojibwa Cultural Foundation, West Bay, NB, 1975. *Paintings:* Martyrs' Shrine, Midland, ON, 1983; Ontario Police Academy, Aylmer, ON, 1979. *Posters:* Debajehmujig Theater Group, 1985, 1991; Heritage Canada, Ottawa, ON, 1992. *Other:* Chinguacousy Centennial Park, Bramlea, ON, eight bas-reliefs, 1975; Debajehmujig Theater Group, Manitoulin Island, ON, set design, 1986, 1988 (3); Pas-Arts Exchange, Toronto, ON, costume design, 1991

PUBLIC COLLECTIONS: C/AG/G; C/AG/LR; C/AG/TB; C/AG/TT; C/AG/W; C/CMC; C/INAC; C/LUM; C/MCC; C/OCF; C/ROM; C/U of T; CIL Corporate Collection; Hospital for Sick Children, Toronto, ON; National Indian Brotherhood, Ottawa, ON; Petro Canada Collection, Calgary, AB; Statens Etnografiska Museet, Stockholm, Sweden

EXHIBITS: C/ACCCNA; C/AG/O; C/AG/TB; C/AG/TT; C/AG/W; C/CIIA; C/CMC; C/CNAC; C/LUM; C/MCC; C/NCCT; C/ROM; C/U of R/MG; C/WCAA; C/WICECl C/YUl HM; NACLA; SM; Ontario Institute for Studies in Education, Toronto, ON, 1973; Chinguacousy Public Library and Art Gallery, 1973; see also Awards

SOLO EXHIBITS: C/AG/TB; Canada House, London, England; Ontario Institute for Studies in Education, Toronto, ON; galleries in Toronto, ON

AWARDS: Aviva Art Show ('78); Young Canadians Excelling in the Arts and Sciences Award, 1977

HONORS: *Grants:* INAC, Cultural Grant, 1972; Canada Council Short-Term Grant in Visual Arts, 1983; Ontario Arts Council Grant, 1984, 1988; Canada Council Travel Grant, 1985. *Other:* Queen's Silver Jubilee Commemorative Medal of Achievement, 1977

DEBASSIGE, SHIRLEY CHEECHOO (see CheeChoo, Shirley)

DE CINQ-MARS, TAHEAWIN ROSEBUD JOSEPHINE MARIE LOUISE (see Tahcawin)

DECKER, VERNON EDWARD *Shoshoni*

Little Bear

Born 1943 in Schurz, NV; son of Evlyne Pete Decker

RESIDENCE: Chico, CA

EDUCATION: Graduated Stewart; IAIA, 1963

PUBLISHED: Snodgrass (1968)

EXHIBITS: IAIA, SAIEAIP

DE CORA, ANGEL (see Dietz, Angel Decora)

DECORY, JACK *Rosebud Sioux*

Wambli Hota

Born 30 June 1933 in Rosebud, SD, on the Rosebud Reservation

RESIDENCE: Rapid City, SD

MILITARY: South Dakota National Guard, 1950-1955

EDUCATION: Rapid City (SD) High School; Famous Artist's Studio of New England, 1969

OCCUPATION: Construction worker and artist

MEDIA: Acrylic

EXHIBITS: ANCAIC, PIE, SIM; see also Awards

SOLO EXHIBITS: SIM

AWARDS: Community Action Program Convention, Rapid City, SD

JACK DECORY

The artist said of his career, "As one who believes that rational knowledge and ultimate wisdom exists in the abstract, my pursuits have been pointed in that direction, primarily in the complexities of music; and now after years of procrastination, my attempt is to fulfill another life-long dream — to interpret my philosophy through a more serious pursuit of painting and writing."

brochure, SIM, 1980

DECOTEAU, LARRY *Chippewa*

EXHIBITS: RE

DEER, ANDY *Onondaga*

Born 31 Oct 1951

RESIDENCE: Nedrow, NY

OCCUPATION: Guitar player, composer, and painter

MEDIA: Watercolor and cloth dyes

PUBLISHED: Johannsen and Ferguson, eds. (1983)

DEERE, NOAH *Creek*

Born 23 Aug 1929 in Eufaula, OK

MILITARY: U.S. Army

EDUCATION: BC; Benedictine

OCCUPATION: Commercial artist, illustrator, and painter

PUBLISHED: Sterling (1955); Dunn (1968); Snodgrass (1968); Brody (1971). *National Geographic* (Mar 1955)

PUBLIC COLLECTIONS: MHDYMM, PAC

EXHIBITS: JGS, NGA, PAC, PAC/T, SFWF

AWARDS: PAC

DEERNOSE, KITTY BELLE *Crow*

Born 1958 at Crow Agency, MT

RESIDENCE: Wyola, MT

EDUCATION: A.A., IAIA, 1983-1985

OCCUPATION: Museum intern, teacher, lecturer, sales clerk, museum employee, writer, photographer, ceramist, silversmith, and painter

EXHIBITS: IAIA; NAVAM; INMED Art Show and Auction, Grand Forks, ND; Custer Battlefield Trading Post, Crow Agency, MT

Ed Defender

Defender's paintings are of historical and contemporary situations involving Plains Indians. He often uses clever, witty titles for his humorous, sometimes satirical works. Although he uses other media, Defender prefers watercolor because of its spontaneity and challenge.

The Indian Trader, *Nov 1993*

Defender, Ed *Standing Rock Sioux*

Born 15 Mar 1953 in Poplar, MT
RESIDENCE: Albuquerque, NM
MILITARY: U.S. Navy
EDUCATION: Flandreau (SD) Indian School; Eastern Montana College, Billings, MT; IAIA
OCCUPATION: Full-time painter since 1989
MEDIA: Acrylic and watercolor
PUBLISHED: *The Indian Trader* (Nov 1993)
COMMISSIONS: Pfizer Pharmaceutical Co., New York, NY, paintings, 1993
PUBLIC COLLECTIONS: HCC
EXHIBITS: ACAI; NPTA; TAIAF; TCIM; UTAE; galleries in NM, VA, and Sweden
SOLO EXHIBITS: SIM
AWARDS: NPTA ('91, 1st, '93; '94); TCIM ('91, '92); UTAE ('90; '91, 1st; '92, 1st)

De-Ga-Ya-Wela-Ge (see Two-Arrows, Tom)

De Groat, Jay *Navajo*

Joogii, Blue Jay
Born 16 May 1947
EDUCATION: Gallup (NM) High School, 1965; NM Highlands U
PUBLISHED: Snodgrass (1968); Tanner (1973); King (1981)
PUBLIC COLLECTIONS: MNA
EXHIBITS: AC/A; ITIC; SN; Window Rock, AZ; Crownpoint, NM; Gallup, NM
AWARDS: ITIC ('69; '72); three, 1962-1963

Del Baugh, Trisha *Cherokee/Otoe/Shawnee/Creek*

RESIDENCE: Norman, OK
EXHIBITS: CNM, FCTM
AWARDS: CNM ('89, 1st); FCTM ('88)

Delena, Sam *Zuni*

PUBLISHED: Snodgrass (1968)
PUBLIC COLLECTIONS: MNM

Delilah (see Conner, Delilah Dianne)

De Mott, Helen *Seneca*

Born 1923 in New York, NY
RESIDENCE: Long Island City, NY
EDUCATION: National Academy of Design; ASL
PUBLISHED: Snodgrass (1968)
EXHIBITS: RM; Queens College, New York, NY; Research Institute, Maitland, FL

Denaljosie, Hokie (see Denetsosie, Hoke)

Denetdale, Myron *Navajo*

PUBLISHED: Snodgrass (1968); Tanner (1973)
PUBLIC COLLECTIONS: ITIC
EXHIBITS: HM, ITIC

Hoke Denetsosie

"Toward the end of his studies at Phoenix Indian School, Denetsosie met Lloyd H. New, then art director, whose encouragement was his major influence during this period. The artist's most productive years were between 1930 and 1940."

Snodgrass 1968

Denetsosie, Hoke *Navajo*

Kiya Ahnii, Slim Navajo
A.K.A. Hoke Denaljosie

Born ca. 1919 near Cameron, AZ, on the Navajo Reservation
RESIDENCE: Tuba City, AZ
EDUCATION: Schools in Leupp and Tuba City, AZ; graduated Phoenix
OCCUPATION: Visual aid employee, logger, commercial artist, and painter
PUBLISHED: Jacobson and d'Ucel (1950); Snodgrass (1968); Tanner (1968; 1973); Brody (1971)
BOOKS ILLUSTRATED: Clark (1939); Hoffman (1974a; 1974b); Beck, Walters, and Francisco (1990)
COMMISSIONS: *Murals:* Arizona Craftsmen Building, Scottsdale, AZ, ten panels
PUBLIC COLLECTIONS: MNA, MNM
EXHIBITS: FWG, HM

DENNIS, D. M. (see Dennis, Danny)

DENNIS, DANNY *Tsimshian*
A.K.A. D. M. Dennis
Born 6 Apr 1951 in Kitwanga, BC, Canada
RESIDENCE: Santa Fe, NM
OCCUPATION: Jeweler, carver, graphic artist; painter since 1978
MEDIA: Oil, watercolor, pen and ink, pencil, gold, silver, ivory, mixed-media, and prints
PUBLIC COLLECTIONS: C/RBCM, HCC
EXHIBITS: AUG, BHSU, NSU/SD, SDSMT, U of WV, WTF

DANNY DENNIS

Dennis began studying and producing art in February of 1978. Although self-taught, he credits Francis Williams, Robert Davidson and Bill Reid (qq.v.) with inspiring him.

DENNY, EUGENE *Micmac*
RESIDENCE: Eskusoni, NS, Canada
OCCUPATION: Aboriginal fish hatchery worker and painter

EUGENE DENNY

The artist works in a realistic style.

DENNY, MILTON *Navajo*
RESIDENCE: Morris, OK
EXHIBITS: PAC ('75; 76)

DENTON, COYE ELIZABETH *Cherokee*
Born 14 Oct 1914 in Romulus, OK; daughter of Izetta Robins and Lester Jerome Hathcock
RESIDENCE: Ada, OK
EDUCATION: Ada (OK) High School, 1933; B.S., ECSC/OK, 1946
OCCUPATION: Housewife, arts and crafts teacher, and painter
PUBLISHED: Snodgrass (1968)
EXHIBITS: FAIEAIP; ITIC; PAC; Oklahoma Federated Women's Clubs; East Central State College, Ada, OK; Linschield Gallery, Ada, OK; Ada (OK) Public Library
AWARDS: Four awards received from 1947-1948
HONORS: Salvation Army Advisory Board, member

COYE ELIZABETH DENTON

"Denton is a nontraditionalist. She is a charter member of the Ada Artists' Association and was instrumental in establishing an art center in Ada, OK. From 1950 to 1964, she toured numerous countries to study art."

Snodgrass 1968

DEO, STEVEN THOMAS *Creek/Yuchi*
A.K.A. Steven Deo
Born 30 Sept 1956; son of Martha Brown and Thomas Deo; P/GP: Ada and Amos Deo; M/GP: Alice and John Brown
RESIDENCE: Tulsa, OK
EDUCATION: Webster High School, Tulsa, OK, 1974; NSU; IAIA
OCCUPATION: Student and artist
MEDIA: Oil, acrylic, pencil, pastel, and tempera
EXHIBITS: CNM, FCTM, PAS, TSF

STEVEN THOMAS DEO

Deo says that the major influences on his art have been the works of T. C. Cannon and Jerome Tiger (qq.v.).

p.c. 1990

SOLO EXHIBITS: PIPM

AWARDS: PAS ('89); TSF ('91, 2-1st)

DE POE, PATRICIA BELGARDE *Turtle Mountain Chippewa*

EXHIBITS: NPTA, TCIM

AWARDS: NPTA ('91); TCIM ('91)

DESAUTEL, ERNIE *Colville*

Born 14 Mar 1944

RESIDENCE: Elmer City, WA

EDUCATION: Santa Fe

PUBLISHED: Snodgrass (1968)

EXHIBITS: MNM, PAC

AWARDS: MNM

DESJARLAIS, LARRY J., JR. *Chippewa*

Born 24 July 1945 in Belcourt, ND, on the Turtle Mountain Indian Reservation

RESIDENCE: Santa Fe, NM

EDUCATION: IAIA, 1966; NM Highlands U, 1966-1968; Anchorage (AK) Community College; Belcourt (ND) Community College; IAIA; U of NM; B.A. 1987

OCCUPATION: Commercial artist, educator, sculptor, and painter

MEDIA: Acrylic and clay

PUBLISHED: *The Indian Trader* (July 1978)

EXHIBITS: AAE; ACS/ENP; IAIA; NARF; NEA; SFFA; SPIM; SWAIA; WWM; galleries in AK, AZ, NM, and Washington, D.C.

SOLO EXHIBITS: MAAIC, 1978; SPIM, 1989

AWARDS: ACS/ENP ('87, 1st); SWAIA (awards in sculpture)

HONORS: New Mexico Governor's Conference on Youth, Certificate of Appreciation from the Governor, 1981

LARRY J. DESJARLAIS JR.

DesJarlais' first formal exhibit was in 1975 in Anchorage, AK.

DESJARLAIT, PATRICK R. *Chippewa*

Magawbo, Boy Of The Woods

A.K.A. Patrick Robert DesJarlait

Born 1 Mar 1921 at Red Lake, MN; died 1973; son of Elizabeth Blake and Solomon DesJarlait; father of Robert DesJarlait (q.v.)

RESIDENCE: Lived in Red Lake, MN

MILITARY: U.S. Navy, WWII

EDUCATION: Red Lake (MN) High, 1939; Phoenix (AZ) Junior College, 1940-1941

OCCUPATION: Commercial artist, and painter

PUBLISHED: Dunn (1968); Snodgrass (1968); Silberman (1978); Broder (1981); Hoffman, et al. (1984); Wade, ed. (1986); Williams, ed. (1990); Archuleta and Strickland (1991). *The Arizona Republic* (17 Sept 1972); *Southwest Art* (Mar 1992)

PUBLIC COLLECTIONS: PAC

EXHIBITS: AAID; HM; IK; ITIC; MKMcNAI; NAP; OMA; PAC; PAC/T; SN; SV; Central America

SOLO EXHIBITS: San Diego (CA) Fine Arts Gallery

AWARDS: AAID ('68, Silver Cup, Special Award); PAC ('69, 1st); SN ('68, Adler Award, Grand Award)

PATRICK R. DESJARLAIT

"Before WWII, the artist organized an art department in an Arizona War Relocation Center. Although he was interested in both painting and music, he chose art as a more satisfying means of self-expression."

Snodgrass 1968

DesJarlait, Robert *Red Lake Chippewa*

Akoongiss, Between Two Worlds

Born 18 Nov 1946 at Red Lake, MN; son of Ramona and Patrick Robert DesJarlait (q.v.); P/GP: Elizabeth Blake and Solomon DesJarlait; M/GP: Belle and John Needham

RESIDENCE: Crystal, MN

EDUCATION: Robbinsdale/Cooper High School, Minneapolis, MN, 1963; IAIA; B.F.A., MCAD; Bemidji State University, Bemidji, MN

OCCUPATION: Educator, illustrator, commercial artist, author, art and cultural consultant, lecturer, traditional dancer, and painter

MEDIA: Acrylic, watercolor, pencil, pen and ink, and prints

PUBLISHED: Partial listing of journal and periodical publications inlcudes: *The Minneapolis Star and Tribune* (9 May 1986); biographical publications

BOOKS ILLUSTRATED: Partial listing includes: *DesJarlait* (1986; 1989; 1990; 1990a); Anoka-Hennepin Indian Education Press, six books, 1987-1989

COMMISSIONS: *Illustrations:* American Indian AIDS Program, 1989; American Indian Outreach Program, 1989; BIHA Women In Action, 1987; Hennepin County Heart of the Earth Survival School, 1986; Hennepin County Indian Foster Care Program, 1986; Ikwe Education Project, 1988; Minnesota Indian Women's Resource Center, Minneapolis, MN, 1986, 1987, 1988,, 1990; New Visions Program, 1987; Red Lake School District, 1988; Red Lake Social Services Program, 1989; Robbinsdale American Indian Education Program, 1992; United Way, 1990; White Earth Land Project, 1989; Women's Dance Health Project, 1985. *Murals:* Red Lake High School, 1988; Minnesota Indian Women's Resource Center, 1991

PUBLIC COLLECTIONS: NDM; Meridel LeSueur Library, Augsburg College, Minneapolis, MN; Minneapolis (MN) Indian Health Board; Minnesota Indian Women's Resource Center; Red Lake (MN) High School

EXHIBITS: AICH; CNM; MIC; NACLA; NARF; NDM; NDSU/G; OAE RC; SMOM; TM; U of KS, U of MN/B; Anoka-Ramsey Community College, 1990; Bemidji (MN) Community Arts Center, 1987; First Universalist Church, MN, 1988, 1989; Red Lake Ojibwa Art Exposition, 1987; galleries in MA, MN, and WI; see also Awards

SOLO EXHIBITS: Minneapolis (MN) Indian Women's Resource Center, 1991

AWARDS: OAE ('84, '85, '87, '88); Ni Mi Win Ojibwa Invitational ('84 ; '85)

HONORS: Minneapolis (MN) School System, 13 paintings reproduced in a Minnesota Indian artists portfolio; Arts Midwest Advisory Panel, member, 1986

Robert DesJarlait

DesJarlait's themes are visual images of Ojibwa cosmology, traditions, and spiritual beliefs. "In the language of art, I've created a representational, figurative imagery which gives expression to the tribal spirit of the past and to the tribal spirit of the present. In essence, my art is a celebration of the life of this tribal spirit — the tribal spirit of the Ojibwa people."

artist, p.c. 1992

De Pojoaque, Stefan (see Watson, Stephen)

DesRosier-Grant, Anne *Blackfeet/Gros Ventre*

A.K.A. Anne DesRosier Grant; Anne DesRosier

Born 16 Feb 1961 in Cutbank, MT; daughter of Ramona Croff and Fred DesRosier; P/GP: Freda and LeRoy DesRosier; M/GP: Katie and Edward Croff; G/uncle: Chief Bull (Richard Sandoval)

RESIDENCE: East Glacier, MT

EDUCATION: Browning (MT) High School, 1979; A.A., CIA/CO, 1981

OCCUPATION: Printing and graphics supervisor, commercial artist, advertising designer, photographer, and painter

MEDIA: Oil, acrylic, pencil, pen and ink, and film

PUBLIC COLLECTIONS: MPI; Indian Health Care Facility, Blackfeet Indian Reservation, MT; Redlands (CA) Community Hospital

Anne DesRosier-Grant

". . . I am fortunate to be surrounded by such beauty that is so rich in history. I find interpreting the ever-changing scenery, whether past or present, the most rewarding and constant experimentation — always a challenge. In retrospect, there cannot be existence without reflection."

brochure, MPI, 1989

EXHIBITS: CCAC/MT; CIAE/MT; CMRM; GFNAAS; MPI; MR; NAAS; NAVAM; Custer County Art Center, Miles City, MT; Hockaday Center for the Arts, Kalispell, MT; Governor's Residence, Helena, MT; see also Awards

SOLO EXHIBITS: MPI

AWARDS: GFNAAS; NAAS; NAVAM; Electrum XIV Fine Art Show, Helena, MT (Award of Merit); 1st Annual Native American Art Show, Helena, MT (Best of Show)

HONORS: Forrest Little Dog Memorial Art Scholarship; *100 years of Montana Women Artists* (exhibit), one of 12 emerging artists included; Native American Visual Arts in Montana Project, painting selected for inclusion; *Montana on Film*, Kalispell, MT, work featured

DEVATEA, TED *Hopi*

PUBLIC COLLECTIONS: HCC

DEWA, DON *Zuni*

PUBLISHED: Tanner (1973)

EXHIBITS: ITIC

DEWA, R.B. *Zuni*

PUBLISHED: Snodgrass (1968)

PUBLIC COLLECTIONS: OU/SM

DEWAYESVA (see Talahytewa, Gibson)

DEWEY, WILSON *San Carlos Apache*

Sundust

Born 25 June 1915 on the San Carlos Reservation, AZ; died Jan 1969

RESIDENCE: Lived in Santa Fe, NM

MILITARY: U.S. Army, WWII

EDUCATION: San Carlos, ca. 1923, 1927, 1931-1933; St. John's, Komatke, AZ, 1928; Santa Fe, 1935-1938; graduated Albuquerque, 1939

OCCUPATION: Football and basketball player, rodeo contestant, and painter

MEDIA: Tempera

PUBLISHED: Jacobson and d'Ucel (1950); Dunn (1968); Snodgrass (1968); Tanner (1973); Seymour (1988; 1993). *Paintings By American Indians,* CPLH (1962)

COMMISSIONS: *Murals:* Maisel's Indian Trading Post, Albuquerque, NM, 1939

PUBLIC COLLECTIONS: IACB/DC, ITIC, GM, MNA, MNM, MRFM, PAC

EXHIBITS: AIW; CPLH; FWG; HM; MNM; OU/ET; PAC; PAC/T; WRTD; Paul Elder Co., San Francisco, CA

WILSON DEWEY

Dewey wrote, "... I am a natural born artist — I guess that's what you would say. What I like to paint best are animals and Apache Crown dancers. I am a full-blooded Apache Indian from San Carlos — I am very proud of my tribe and to be one of them."

Seymour 1988

DHEALDH YAZZIE BITSI (see Cassady, Ann Virginia)

DIACON, JOHNNIE LEE *Creek*

Cepane

Born 8 Jan 1963; son of Margaret Harjochee and Cecil Iron; M/GP: Jennie and Adam Harjochee; adopted by Helen and Delmer Diacon; adoptive P/GP: Mike and Julia Diacon; adoptive M/GP: Pete and Minnie Amds

RESIDENCE: Springdale, AR

EDUCATION: Springdale (AR) Senior High School, 1981; BC, 1990

OCCUPATION: Sculptor and painter

MEDIA: Acrylic, watercolor, pencil, pen, pastel, mixed-media, bronze, and silver

PUBLIC COLLECTIONS: HCC, BC

EXHIBITS: BC, CNM, FCTM, GFNAAS, ITIC, LIAS, OIAC, RC, SNAICF, TIAF, TM/NE; see also Awards

JOHNNIE LEE DIACON

In the artist's words, "I feel comfortable with both traditional and contemporary styles. In my contemporary works I usually have a traditional theme."

p.c. 1990

SOLO EXHIBITS: BIA, Federal Building, Muskogee, OK

AWARDS: BC ('89, 1st; '90, 2-1st); CNM ('94); FCTM ('86; '93); ITIC ('91); OIAC ('93); Willard Stone Memorial Show, Locust Grove, OK ('88); Phi Theta Kappa Regional Convention, Arkansas/Oklahoma Art Competition ('89, 1st)

HONORS: RC, Thunderbird Foundation Scholarship, 1990; OIAC Scholarship Award, 1995

DICK, BEAU *Kwakwaka'Wakw (Kwakiutl)*

Born 1955 at Kingcome Inlet, Alert Bay, BC, Canada

RESIDENCE: Vancouver, BC, Canada

EDUCATION: Studied under his father, grandfather, and Doug Cranmer (q.v.); apprenticed to Henry Hunt (q.v.)

OCCUPATION: Carver, dancer, printmaker, and painter

MEDIA: Oil, wood, and prints

PUBLISHED: Stewart (1979); Macnair, Hoover, and Neary (1980); Hall, Blackman, and Rickard (1981)

PUBLIC COLLECTIONS: C/CMC; C/CRM; C/INAC; C/RBCM; C/U of BC/MA; HCC; HM; TBMM; U'Mista Cultural Society Museum, Alert Bay, BC

EXHIBITS: C/IGV; C/RBCM; C/TL; EIAF; HM; RC; SDSMT; Expo '86, Vancouver, BC, 1986

BEAU DICK

Dick's early paintings are done in a naturalistic style and depict Southern Kwakiutl mythological figures and ceremonial dancers. He is also well known for his carved masks and silkscreen prints. His silkscreens incorporate Kwakiutl and Northern design styles, but the overall effect is Kwakiutl.

Hall, Blackman, and Rickard 1981

DICK, BEN *Kwakwaka'wakw (Kwakiutl)*

RESIDENCE: Alert Bay, BC, Canada

MEDIA: Watercolor and pencil

PUBLISHED: Hawthorn (1988)

PUBLIC COLLECTIONS: C/RBCM

DICK, CECIL *Cherokee*

Da'-Ga-Dah'-Ga, Standing Alone

Born 16 Sept 1915 near Rose Prairie, OK; died 25 Apr 1992 in Tahlequah, OK; son of Rachel and Andy Dick, U.S. Marshall to Indian Territory

RESIDENCE: Lived in Tahlequah, OK

EDUCATION: Bagley High School, Tahlequah, OK; BC; Santa Fe

OCCUPATION: Art instructor, illustrator, draftsman, tool designer, sign painter, and artist

PUBLISHED: Jacobson and d'Ucel (1950); Snodgrass (1968); Dunn (1968); Brody (1971); Highwater (1976); Broder (1981); Strickland (1984); Archuleta and Strickland (1991). *Oklahoma Today* (summer 1958); *Live International* (16 Mar 1959); *San Francisco Chronicle, Sunday Bonanza* (22 Aug 1965); *Southwest Art* (June 1983); *The Tulsa World* (4 Sept 1983); *American Indian Art* (spring 1985); *The Tulsa Tribune* (2 Sept 1991); *The Metro Downtowner* (3 June 1991); *Twin Territories* (Special Edition 1991; Year of the Indian Edition 1992)

COMMISSIONS: *Murals:* Bagley High School; Sequoyah; Rocky Ford Indian Day School, Jay, OK; Chilocco; U.S. Indian Hospital, Claremore, OK; Oak Hill School, Valliant, OK

PUBLIC COLLECTIONS: FCTM, GM, HM, MAI, PAC, SI

EXHIBITS: AIEC, AIW, BC/McG, CNM, MFA/O, NGA, PAC, PAC/T, RE, SV

SOLO EXHIBITS: CNM (50 year retrospective, 1983); FCTM

AWARDS: FCTM ('72, IH), PAC

HONORS: Cherokee Nation of Oklahoma, Sequoyah Medal, 1983; Five Civilized Tribes Museum, received Master of Heritage Award, 1988; Red Earth Festival, Oklahoma City, named the "Honored One," June 1991; Five Civilized Tribes Museum, Cecil Dick Master of Heritage Award established in his honor for the Annual Competitive Art Show, 1992

CECIL DICK

As a small child Dick spoke only Cherokee. "Orphaned at 12 and reared in Indian boarding schools, the artist became an authority on Cherokee mythology and the Cherokee written language."

Snodgrass 1968

While at The Studio in Santa Fe, the artist was the only student who painted in the Woodlands style, an individualist who didn't conform, so he was left to paint in his own way.

artist, p.c. 1991

DICK, CLARENCE *Coast Salish*

RESIDENCE: Victoria, BC, Canada

EDUCATION: Camosun College, Victoria, BC; Vancouver (BC) School of Art; studied with Tony Hunt

OCCUPATION: Teacher, counselor, and artist

PUBLIC COLLECTIONS: HCC

EXHIBITS: AUG, NSU/SD, SDSMT

DICK, FRAN (see Dick, Frances)

DICK, FRANCES *Kwakwaka'wakw (Kwagiulth)*

A.K.A. Fran Dick

Born 1959 at Kingcome Inlet, BC, Canada

EDUCATION: B.A., C/U of V

OCCUPATION: Carver, jeweler, printmaker, and painter

PUBLIC COLLECTIONS: HCC

EXHIBITS: AUG, NSU/SD, SDSMT

DICKSON, LARRY *Zuni*

EDUCATION: Albuquerque, 1962-1963

PUBLISHED: Snodgrass (1968)

EXHIBITS: MNM

DICKSON, ROGER *Apache*

RESIDENCE: San Carlos, AZ

MEDIA: Gouache

PUBLISHED: Seymour (1993)

PUBLIC COLLECTIONS: MNA, MNM/DD

DIESING, FREDA *Haida*

Born 1925 in Prince Rupert, BC, Canada

RESIDENCE: Victoria, BC, Canada

EDUCATION: C/VSA; C/KSNCIA; studied under Robert Davidson, Bill Holm, Tony Hunt, Henry Hunt, Duane Pasco (qq.v.)

OCCUPATION: Instructor, sculptor, graphic artist, and painter

PUBLISHED: Stewart (1979); Macnair, Hoover, and Neary (1980); Hall, Blackman, and Rickard (1981); Gerber and Bruggmann (1989); Cardinal-Schubert (1992)

PUBLIC COLLECTIONS: C/CMC, C/INAC, C/ROM

EXHIBITS: C/C; C/CIIA; C/IGV; C/CMC; C/INAC; C/TFD; C/TL; C/U of BC/MA; C/WICEC; MFA/AH; Edinburgh, Scotland, 1980; Australia and Japan

FREDA DIESING

Diesing is one of several Canadian Southwest Coast women who have broken into what was once an exclusively male domain.

DIETZ, ANGEL DECORA *Winnebago*

Hinookmahiwi-kilinaka, Fleecy Cloud Floating Into Place; The Word Carrier

A.K.A. Angel DeCora

Born 3 May 1871 on the Winnebago Reservation, NE; died 6 Feb 1919 in an influenza epidemic; daughter of LaMére (?)and David DeCora (Hagasilikaw), a descendant of the Dakaury family

EDUCATION: Santee Reservation School, NE; Hampton, 1891; Smith College; Drexel Institute; Boston Museum of Fine Arts; studied under Dwight Tryon and Howard Pyle

OCCUPATION: Illustrator, teacher, art department head, lecturer, and painter

PUBLISHED: La Flesche (1900); Snodgrass (1968); Dockstader (1977)

BOOKS ILLUSTRATED: Books by Gertrude Bonnin

ANGEL DECORA DIETZ

Dietz was the first head of the art department and a teacher at Carlisle where she introduced the then-new philosophy of using Indian designs. While at Carlisle she met William Dietz (q.v.), a Sioux teacher who became her husband. They became very involved with Indian affairs and activities. Dietz also spent many years working with Gertrude Bonnin to improve Indian conditions.

Dockstader 1977

DIETZ, WILLIAM *Sioux*

Wicahpi Isnala, Lone Star

Birth date unknown; death date unknown; married to Angel DeCora, 1908-1918

OCCUPATION: Art teacher, Indian rights activist, and painter

DILLARD, W.M. (see Dillard, Wanda Marcel)

DILLARD, WANDA MARCEL *Cherokee*

Tsi-Sga-Tsi Da-Lo-Ni Di-Gado-Li, Sees With Eyes Of The Weasel

A.K.A. W. M. Dillard

Born 4 Jan 1953 in Hamilton, Bermuda; daughter of Ruby Irene Panter and William Irvine Dillard; P/GP: Della Jane Poe and James Claude Dillard; M/GP: Gayla Magness and Robert Panter

RESIDENCE: Houston, TX

EDUCATION: Charleston (TN) High School, 1971; Tennessee Technological University, Cookeville, TN; Coastal Carolina Community College, Jacksonville, NC

OCCUPATION: Author, lecturer, and artist

MEDIA: Oil, acrylic, watercolor, pencil, pen and ink, pastel, Prismacolor, and prints

PUBLISHED: *USO Today* (1987-1989), covers

EXHIBITS: Throughout Louisiana and Texas

DINEH LIGAAI (see Mitchell, George Charlie)

DISHTA, DUANE *Zuni*

Birth date unknown; death ca. 1992; nephew of Virgil Dishta Jr. (q.v.)

RESIDENCE: Zuni Pueblo, NM

EDUCATION: Through 9th grade

PUBLISHED: Snodgrass (1968); Tanner (1973). *The Indian Trader* (Sept 1982)

BOOKS ILLUSTRATED: Wright (1985)

EXHIBITS: AAIEAE, HM/G, ITIC, SDMM, SN, SWAIA

AWARDS: HM/G ('91, Best of Division); ITIC ('79; '86; '88; '89; '91; '94)

DISHTA, VIRGIL, JR. *Zuni*

Birth date unknown; uncle of Duane Dishta (q.v.)

RESIDENCE: Zuni Pueblo, NM

PUBLISHED: Snodgrass (1968)

EXHIBITS: MNM

AWARDS: MNM ('65, Special Award)

DITTBENNER, CAROL *Mescalero Apache/Aztec*

A.K.A. Paz

RESIDENCE: Roy, WA

EDUCATION: St. Catherine's, 1966; Evergreen State College, Olympia, WA, 1987

OCCUPATION: Program Manager for Title V Indian Education, and artist

EXHIBITS: SN; Bethel High School Display; Fort Steilacoom Community College, Tacoma, WA; Tacoma (WA) Historical Society

DIXON, BILL, JR. *Navajo*

A.K.A. William Dixon Jr.

Born 6 May 1950 in Winslow, AZ; son of Modesta E. Clark and William Dixon Sr.; brother of Don Clark (q.v.) and Carl Clark, jeweler

RESIDENCE: Winslow, AZ

EDUCATION: G.E.D., 1970; diploma, drafting school, 1970

BILL DIXON JR.

Dixon has been painting since the early 1960s. According to his brother, his paintings, which are large and done in bold vivid colors, are in great demand.

Don Clark, p.c. 1993

OCCUPATION: Art instructor and painter
MEDIA: Oil and acrylic
PUBLISHED: Jacka and Jacka (1994)
EXHIBITS: RE; Arizona State Capitol Building, Phoenix, AZ; Sedona, AZ; galleries in AZ, ID, NM, and Nurenburg, West Germany

DOANMOE, ETAHDLEUH(see Etahdleuh)

DOCKSTADER, JOHN *Oneida*

Hi-You-Os
A.K.A. John Dockstadter
RESIDENCE: Six Nations Reserve, ON, Canada
EDUCATION: Swedish Institute, Stockholm
OCCUPATION: Commercial artist, teacher, researcher, writer, ceramist, sculptor, printmaker, and painter
PUBLISHED: McMasters, et al. (1993)

DODGE, ADEE *Navajo*

A.K.A. Aydee Dodge; Bittany Adee Dodge; Adolph Bitanny Dodge
Born ca. 1911 in Wheatfield, AZ.; died 4 Jan 1992 in Albuquerque, NM; P/GF: Henry Chee Dodge, the first Navajo Tribal Chairman
RESIDENCE: Lived in Albuquerque, NM
MILITARY: U.S. Army, WWII, Navajo Code Talker
EDUCATION: B.A., U of NM, 1933; M.A. and law degree, Columbia University, New York, NY, 1935, 1945
OCCUPATION: Interpreter and artist; began to paint actively in 1954
MEDIA: Casein
PUBLISHED: Brody (1971); Tanner (1973); Seymour (1988). *Arizona Highways* (Dec 1958; July 1959; Aug 1965); *The Arizona Republic* (19 Apr 1961); *The Indian Trader* (Feb 1992)
COMMISSIONS: *Murals:* ASU Administration Building, Tempe, AZ
PUBLIC COLLECTIONS: ASU; HCC; IACB/DC; RMC/AZ; VNB, Sedona, AZ
EXHIBITS: ASM; HM; ITIC; PM; RMC/AZ; WRTD; Hastings (NE) College Art Center

ADEE DODGE

Dodge was born Adolph Bitanny Dodge but was given the name Adee by his teachers at Bacone Junior College. In his introduction to The American Indians of Abeita, His People *(1976), Joseph Stacey said, "...There have been some great names in the roll of Navajo artists... Adee Dodge, one of the most prolific Navajo artists, is collected for his spirit horses and fastidiously drawn interpretations of Navajo myths and legends."*

DODGE, ADOLPH BITANNY (see Dodge, Adee)

DODGE, AYDEE (see Dodge, Adee)

DODGE, BITTANY ADEE (see Dodge, Adee)

DOHA (see Tohausen)

DOHASAN (see Tohausen)

DOHATE (see Tohausen)

DOHAUSEN (see Tohausen)

DOLWIFTEMA (see Nahsohnhoya, Thomas Dolwiftema)

DONA (see Flood, Donna Colleen Jones)

DONATIONS (see Paukei, George)

DON'T BRAID HIS HAIR *Sioux*

PUBLISHED: Snodgrass (1968)
PUBLIC COLLECTIONS: MAI (pictographic painting on paper)

DONVIRAK (see Smith, Johnny)

DOONKEEN, EULAMAE NARCOMEY *Seminole*

Hah Gay Kee Hooduh Lee, Crying Wind

Born 12 Dec 1931 in Oklahoma City, OK; daughter of Maggie Coker and John Osceola Narcomey; M/GP: Jennie Lasley, descendant of Hitchiti and Cheyaha, and Dave Coker; P/GGGF: Narkome, killed in the Civil War while serving in the Confederate Home Brigade under General Stand Watie; M/GGGF: Landon Coker, lighthorseman; M/GGGU: Isparhecher, circuit judge at Okmulgee, OK, chief of the Creeks during the Green Peach War and a Confederate officer during the Civil War

RESIDENCE: Oklahoma City, OK

MILITARY: Continental Air Command, WAF, 1951-1954

EDUCATION: BC, 1950; Hills Business University, 1955-1956; B.F.A., CSU/OK, 1965

OCCUPATION: Stenographer, model, commercial artist, and painter

MEDIA: Acrylic, textiles, silver, and beads

PUBLISHED: Snodgrass (1968); Brody (1971)

EXHIBITS: BB; CNM; FCTM; SI; RE; Conservative Artists' Sidewalk Show, Oklahoma City, OK, 1961; see also Awards

AWARDS: AIE ('67); FCTM ('77; '78); Duncan (OK) Arts and Crafts Show (1st); Oklahoma Artist Association Show; Oklahoma Federation of Indian Women Show ('84, 1st)

HONORS: Princess of the Seminole tribe of Oklahoma, 1946-1956; Oklahoma Collegiate Novice State Fencing Champion, 1965; Kappa Pi Honorary Art Fraternity; Seminole Nation, first woman elected to the General Council and Vice-Chief; Oklahoma Federation of Indian Women, past president

EULAMAE NARCOMEY DOONKEEN

Doonkeen has spent a lifetime portraying Seminole lives and heritage. Out of respect for other tribes, she paints only Seminole subjects.

artist, p.c. 1993

DO-RHA-AH (see Hill, Tom)

DORSEY, TOM (see Two-Arrows, Tom)

DORSEY, TOM, JR. *Onondaga*

Born 1943; son of Tom Two-Arrows (q.v.)

PUBLISHED: Snodgrass (1968)

EXHIBITS: PAC

DOUBLE RUNNER *Blackfeet*

PUBLISHED: Snodgrass (1968)

DOUBLE RUNNER

"The artist assisted in the execution of a 61-year count (see Elk Horn)."

Snodgrass 1968

DOUBLE SHIELDS (see Pepion, Victor)

DOUGI, THOMAS *Navajo*

EXHIBITS: SN

AWARDS: SN ('67, 1st)

DOXTADOR, ALTA *Cayuga*

Born 3 Mar 1909; daughter of Jim Beaver, one of the first Iroquois painters in Canada

RESIDENCE: Caledonia, ON, Canada

EDUCATION: Kholer Night School

OCCUPATION: Farmer's wife and painter

MEDIA: Oil

PUBLISHED: Johannsen and Ferguson, eds. (1983)

EXHIBITS: See Awards

AWARDS: Caledonia (NY) Fair ('61)

DOYCE, CLARENCE *Jémez*

EDUCATION: Jémez, 1961

PUBLISHED: Snodgrass (1968)

EXHIBITS: MNM

DOYETO, CLIFF *Kiowa*

RESIDENCE: Tahlequah, OK

EXHIBITS: CNM, PAC

AWARDS: PAC ('79)

DOYLE, ROBERT D., SR. *Crow*

Born 5 May 1936 in Crow Agency, MT; son of Florence Yarlott and John T. Doyle; P/GP: Margaret Shane and Thomas Doyle; M/GP: Ollie Horton and Frank Yarlott

RESIDENCE: Crow Agency, MT

EDUCATION: Hardin (MT) High School; SFAI, 1966

OCCUPATION: Heavy equipment operator and painter

MEDIA: Oil, acrylic, watercolor, pencil, and pastel

EXHIBITS: AC/Y; HM; NAVAM; RC; Ashland (MT) Indian Museum; BIA Office, Billings, MT; College of St. Teresa, Winona, MN; Cheyenne Museum, Ashland, MT; Federal Building, Billings, MT; San Francisco (CA) Film Festival; galleries in Montana and Wyoming

SOLO EXHIBITS: AC/Y

AWARDS: RC ('77; '78)

DOZAY (see Christmas, Arlene)

DRAPER, ROBERT D. *Navajo*

Born 20 Nov 1938 in Chinle, AZ; son of Janet Descheeny and Frank Martin

RESIDENCE: Chinle, AZ

MILITARY: U.S. Marine Corps

EDUCATION: Chinle, 1947-1951; Inter-Mt., 1951-1956; IAIA

OCCUPATION: Art instructor, instructional aid, and artist

MEDIA: Oil, acrylic, watercolor, and pastel

PUBLISHED: Snodgrass (1968); Brody (1971); Tanner (1973); Median (1981); Jacka and Jacka (1994). *Plateau* (Vol. 54, no. 1, 1982); *Arizona Republic* (17 Sept 1972)

PUBLIC COLLECTIONS: HCC, MNA, WWM

EXHIBITS: AIAE/WSU, AICA, ASM, HM, HM/G, ITIC, MNA, NTF, PAC, RC, SAIEAIP, SN, WTF

SOLO EXHIBITS: NTF; galleries in Denver, CO, and Scottsdale, AZ

AWARDS: AICA ('79, Gold Medal); HM/G ('71, '73, '74); ITIC ('66, 1st; '67, 1st; '68, 2-1st, Best in Class, SA; '70, 1st; '76; '79; '85; '86;); NMSF ('70; '78, 1st); NTF ('88); PAC ('69); RC ('72, 1st, Best of Show); SN ('71, Q.V. Distributing Special Award)

ROBERT D. DRAPER

From the age of two the artist, who was born Robert Martin, was raised by his grandparents whose name was Draper. When he was eight years old and sent to the Chinle Boarding School, the school changed his name to Robert Draper. Draper is well known for his realistic landscapes of the Navajo Reservation.

DRAPER, TED, JR. *Navajo*

A.K.A. Teddy Draper Jr.

Born 3 Oct 1949 in Ganado, AZ; son of Teddy Draper Sr. (q.v.); P/GP: Margaret and Elsitty Draper

RESIDENCE: Chinle, AZ

EDUCATION: Chinle (AZ) High School; AAA; NCC

OCCUPATION: Illustrator, rodeo contestant, and painter

MEDIA: Oil, acrylic, watercolor, pen and ink, pastel, and prints

TED DRAPER JR.

Draper reports that he had a 16-year hiatus from his art work due to alcoholism. In January of 1983 he took his last drink. He believes that this period of turmoil profoundly affected his art and led to his present style. Draper describes his work as realism in the surrealism realm, with his bright colored clouds and skies created as if the color was "slammed" onto the work.

The Indian Trader, *Dec 1994*

PUBLISHED: Jacka and Jacka (1940). *The Indian Trader* (Jan 1985; Dec 1994); *NCC Spirit* (Nov 1985)

COMMISSIONS: *Murals:* Ned A. Hatathli Museum, Tsaile, AZ, financed by Metropolitan Life Foundation

EXHIBITS: AIAF, ITIC, NMSF, NTF, SWAIA, U of NM; see also Awards

AWARDS: ITIC ('86, 1st, Best in Category; '87, 1st; '90, 1st; '91, 1st; '92, 1st; '93; '94, 1st); NMSF ('88, 1st); NTF ('87, 2-1st; '86, 3-1st; '87, 1st; '88, 2-1st); SWAIA ('86; '88, 1st); Gallup Area Arts Council Art Fair ('84, 2-1st; '85, 1st)

DRAPER, TEDDY, SR. *Navajo*

Keeti Bahi

Born 2 Apr 1923 in Chinle, AZ; son of Margaret and Elsitty Draper; father of Ted Draper Jr. (q.v.)

RESIDENCE: Chinle, AZ

MILITARY: U.S. Marine Corps, WWII, Navajo Code Talker

EDUCATION: Box High School, Brigham City, UT; USU; U of AZ, 1962

OCCUPATION: Supervisory instructional aide, child guidance counselor, and painter

PUBLISHED: Snodgrass (1968). *The Indian Trader* (Jan 1985); *Smithsonian* (Aug 1993)

PUBLIC COLLECTIONS: Inter-Mt.

EXHIBITS: HM

DREADFULWATER, FRANKY *Cherokee*

RESIDENCE: Tahlequah, OK

MEDIA: Acrylic and charcoal

EXHIBITS: CNM, FCTM, PAC

AWARDS: FCTM ('80; '90; '92, 1st)

DREAM CATCHERS ARTISTS GUILD, LTD.

LOCATION: Aberdeen, SD

The Dream Catchers Artists Guild, Ltd., Aberdeen, SD, founded in 1983, was organized by Sioux Indian artists who wanted to set standards, open markets, and help educate artists, educators, and students about Sioux art.

The idea for the guild came from an 1983 exhibition of tribal and contemporary art in Taos, New Mexico, that was organized by a Deadwood, South Dakota, gallery owner. The original idea was for a tribal arts group, but the tribal and contemporary artists were unable to agree on goals for the organization. At this point, the contemporary artists decided to form their own group and the Dream Catchers Artists Guild was born. In addition to the three original organizers, Richard Red Owl, Don Ruleaux, and Vic Runnels (qq.v.), guild members are: Arthur Amiotte, R. G. Bowker, Roger Broer, Robert Freeman, Donald Montileaux, Robert Penn (qq.v.). They are painters, printmakers, and sculptors who live throughout the United States while producing art related to the Lakota culture.

The Guild members attempt to fulfill their purposes and goals by organizing group shows, and conducting workshops for students and teachers around the United States.

DRYWATER, MICHAEL *Cherokee*

A.K.A. Mike Drywater

EXHIBITS: FCTM

DUKEPOO, ANTHONY *Hopi*

A.K.A. Anthony Duahkapoo

RESIDENCE: Shungopovi, AZ

PUBLISHED: Snodgrass (1968)
PUBLIC COLLECTIONS: MNM

DuBois, Betty Jean Nilchee *Navajo*

Ka-Has-Ba, Peacemaker – Went Out To Make Friends

Born 15 Oct 1944 in Tohatchi, NM; daughter of Amelia Edsitty and Warren Nilchee; P/GP: Barbara Betsi, weaver, and Hosteen Nilchee, sand painter and medicine man; M/GP: Nellie, weaver, and Henry Edsitty, silversmith

RESIDENCE: Elmer, NJ

EDUCATION: Sandia High School, Albuquerque, NM, 1962; College of Arts and Crafts, Berkeley, CA; IAIA, 1962-1963; B.A., Glassboro (NJ) State College, 1972

OCCUPATION: Art teacher, jeweler, and artist

MEDIA: Oil, acrylic, watercolor, silver, gold, and turquoise

PUBLISHED: Snodgrass (1968)

EXHIBITS: AICH; IAIA; MNM; galleries in AZ, FL, NJ, NM, NY, and OK

AWARDS: MNM; awards and prizes throughout the Southwest

Betty Jean Nilchee DuBois

Ka-has-ba specializes in primitive Indian scenes in watercolors and oils. She has been recognized and rewarded by her tribe with scholarships and awards for her renditions of their life and culture. She paints from memory and has never painted two scenes alike.

artist, p.c. 1992

Ducee Blue Buzzard (see Buzzard, Ducee Blue)

Ducharme, Noel *Ojibwa*

Born 1922 in Fort William, ON, Canada; died 24 Feb 1988 in Calgary, AB, Canada, of pneumonia; son of Josephine Ducharme

RESIDENCE: Lived in Thunder Bay, ON, Canada

OCCUPATION: Seaman and painter

PUBLISHED: Southcott (1984); Menitove, ed. (1986b). *The Toronto Daily Star* (24 Aug 1973); *The Indian Trader* (May 1988)

COMMISSIONS: Indian and Northern Affairs Canada, painting for Queen Elizabeth II, 1973

PUBLIC COLLECTIONS: C/AG/TB; C/NGCA; Queen Elizabeth II Collection, London, England

EXHIBITS: C/AG/TB; C/CS; C/NGCA; Ottawa (ON) Center for Indian Art; Canadian National Exhibition, Toronto, ON; throughout the U.S. and England

Noel Ducharme

While working on a freighter in 1967, Ducharme broke his back and hip in an accident. Because of this accident he turned to art for diversion and therapy. When he returned to the reserve to recover, he started painting seriously. He is quoted as saying, "I am a lucky man. You see my work is also my greatest pleasure."

Ducharme's paintings are outlined with a broad black outline and use ovoid holes to create an X-ray-like style. The X-ray effect is purely decorative and does not refer to anatomical features. He includes a suggestion of landscape in his work.

Southcott 1984

Ducharme was educated in a sanatorium where, as a teenager, he was treated for tuberculosis.

Dukepoo, Anthony (see Duahkapoo, Anthony)

Duncan, Clifford *Northern Ute*

RESIDENCE: White Rocks, UT

PUBLISHED: Snodgrass (1968)

EXHIBITS: MNM, Senior High/College Division, 1962; PAC, 1959

Duncan, Dallas *Sauk-Fox*

Born 19 June 1944

EDUCATION: IAIA

PUBLISHED: Snodgrass (1968)

PUBLIC COLLECTIONS: IAIA

EXHIBITS: IAIA, PAC, SN

Duncan, Marcellus *Sauk-Fox*

Born 1904

EDUCATION: Chilocco; Haskell

PUBLISHED: Snodgrass (1968)

EXHIBITS: AIEC

Dunkleberger, Dawn *Oneida*

Dark Mountain

A.K.A. Dawn Dark Mountain

Born 18 June 1955 in Milwaukee, WI; daughter of Patricia Kelly and Eugene Silas; P/GP: Gertrude Jordan and Dewey Silas

RESIDENCE: Monona, WI

EDUCATION: Riverside High School, Milwaukee, WI, 1973; B.F.A., U of AZ, 1982; U of WI

OCCUPATION: Teacher; painter since 1989

MEDIA: Watercolor, pencil, pen and ink, and prints

COMMISSIONS: Curtis Wilson Co., Tucson, AZ, logo; Wintercount Card Co., Glenwood Springs, CO, greeting cards, 1991

EXHIBITS: CNM; IACA; RC; Madison (WI) Area Technical College; regional art fairs, powwows, and galleries in Wisconsin

SOLO EXHIBITS: St. Benedict's Center, Middleton, WI

AWARDS: Indian Summer Poster Contest ('91, 1st)

HONORS: Art Fair Off the Square, featured artist, 1991

DAWN DUNKLEBERGER

Dunkleberger works strictly in transparent watercolor and her soft brush work is often mistaken for airbrush. Applying this style to a heavily symbolic Native American subject matter results in a mystical quality. Her heritage is an important part of her work. For an example, the use of a turtle (she is a member of the Turtle Clan) is either prominent or hidden in all of her paintings.

artist, p.c. 1992

DUPREE, WILLIAM *Sioux*

PUBLISHED: Snodgrass (1968)

EXHIBITS: NGA

DURÁN, GEORGE *Picurís*

Birth date unknown; son of Roland Durán (q.v.); P/GP: Lucía Martínez and Julián Antonio Durán

EDUCATION: Santa Fe, 1946-1947

PUBLISHED: Snodgrass (1968); Tanner (1973)

PUBLIC COLLECTIONS: MAI

EXHIBITS: MAI

GEORGE DURÁN

Durán's paintings of traditional Pueblo subjects exhibited a Navajo influence in its subjects and details. He stopped painting about 1950.

Tanner 1973

DURÁN, JOE EVAN *Tesuque*

Pove Peen

A.K.A. Joseph Durán

EDUCATION: Hiler; Hill

PUBLISHED: Dunn (1968); Snodgrass (1968); Brody (1971); Tanner (1973); Seymour (1988)

COMMISSIONS: *Murals:* DAM; SFWF [with Charles Loloma, and Ignacio Moquino (qq.v.)]

PUBLIC COLLECTIONS: DAM, MNA, OU/MA, SM

EXHIBITS: OU/ET, SFWF

DURÁN, ROLAND *Picurís*

To-Le-Ne, Sun

A.K.A. Roland Durand; Signature: Tolene

Born 29 July 1897; died 1 Apr 1959 in Holbrook, AZ, in an automobile accident; son of Lucía Martínez and Julián Antonio Durán

MILITARY: U.S. Army

EDUCATION: Through 8th grade, Santa Fe, 1917; NM Highlands U., 1926

OCCUPATION: Store clerk, bookkeeper, teacher, interpreter, skilled laborer, and painter

PUBLISHED: Snodgrass (1968); Tanner (1973)

PUBLIC COLLECTIONS: MNM

EXHIBITS: ITIC

AWARDS: ITIC ca. 1930s

ROLAND DURÁN

According to his wife, in about 1929, Durán saw some paintings somewhere and decided he could paint. He bought some oil paint and started painting. Because of his teaching job he mostly painted on weekends. His favorite subjects were the traditional dances of the Pueblo. His wife says that she does not remember his having sold paintings but, instead he gave them to his friends for their birthdays or Christmas. After about 10 years he quit painting to write poetry and stories about historic events at the Pueblo.

El Palacio, *winter 1981-1982*

HONORS: Picurís Pueblo, NM, Lieutenant Governor (2 years) and Governor, 1947, 1950; All-Indian Pueblo Council, Vice-Chairman, 1950-1953; Taos County Welfare and Youth Organization, appointed representative of Southern Taos County; Picurís Pueblo Council, secretary, 1951-1953

DURAND, ROLAND (see Durán, Roland)

DURANT, RON *Choctaw*

A.K.A. Signature: Four crossed arrows and a tepee (Durant family seal)

Born 4 June 1950 in Poteau, OK; son of Rachel Gibson and Johnny G. Durant; P/GP: Cleo and Walter Durant; M/GP: Evie and "Papaw" Gibson

RESIDENCE: Tulsa, OK

MILITARY: Air National Guard

EDUCATION: Central High School, Tulsa, OK, 1969; Oklahoma Junior College, Tulsa, OK; studied under Don Moore

OCCUPATION: Welder, leatherworker; full-time artist since 1990

MEDIA: Pen and ink, leather, and scratchboard

EXHIBITS: TIAF; local shows and markets

RON DURANT

Initially, economics led Durant away from a career as an artist. Just out of high school he had to choose between a job at a newspaper doing fashion drawing or a welding job. The welding job paid a dollar more an hour and since he was newly married and needed the additional income, he became a welder. Twenty-three years later health problelms ended his welding career and enabled him to return to his first love, art.

artist, p.c. 1994

DURHAM, JIMMIE *Cherokee*

PUBLISHED: *Southwest Art* (Oct 1991); *Newsletter*, NASAC/ACEAA (winter 1991); *Art News* (Feb 1992)

EXHIBITS: C/CMC, CSU/OK

DUVAYESTEWA (see Polelonema, Tyler)

DUWENIE, DICK *Hopi*

EDUCATION: Hopi

PUBLISHED: Snodgrass (1968)

EXHIBITS: ITIC

AWARDS: ITIC (student exhibit), 1959

DUWENIE, PRESTON *Hopi*

Loma-I'-Quil-Va-A, Carried In Beauty

Birth date unknown; born at Hotevilla, Third Mesa, AZ; son of Edith Kuyiyesva and Lorenzo Hubbell Duwyenie; P/GP: Sarah and Andrew Duwyenie; M/GP: Belle and Thomas Kuyiyesva

RESIDENCE: Santa Fe, NM

EDUCATION: A.A., IAIA, 1982; B.A., CSU/CO, 1985; M.A. CSU/CO

OCCUPATION: Phoenix (AZ) City employee, educator, lecturer, silversmith, ceramist, and painter. He is best known for jewelry and ceramics.

MEDIA: Acrylic, watercolor, pencil, pen and ink, and prints

PUBLISHED: *Focus/Santa Fe* (Apr/May 1993)

PUBLIC COLLECTIONS: HM; IAIA; DAM; MRFM; Cummings Petroleum Co. Art Collection, Oklahoma City, OK

EXHIBITS: ACS/ENP; ACS/PG; AIAF; CIM; FAC/CS; FNAA; HM/G; MNA; MFA/O; NARF; RE; SM; SWAIA; Lincoln Center for the Arts, New York; National Center for Atmospheric Research, Boulder, CO

AWARDS: Partial listing of 26 (1991-1992) includes: ACS/ENP, HM/G, MNA, SWAIA; Best of Division and Grand Awards in jewelry and ceramics

HONORS: *Scholarships and Fellowships:* Sequoyah Fellowship; Hopi Tribe Scholarship; T. C. Cannon Memorial Scholarship; Harry S. Truman Scholarship, candidate. *Other:* IAIA, President's Honor List

EAGLE, FRED *Pueblo*
PUBLIC COLLECTIONS: DAM

EAGLE, THOMAS, JR. *Arikara*
RESIDENCE: Emmet, ND
PUBLISHED: Snodgrass (1968)
EXHIBITS: BNIAS

EAGLE, WAYNE *Cherokee*
EXHIBITS: FCTM
AWARDS: FCTM ('67; '71)

EAGLE CROW *Sioux*
PUBLISHED: Snodgrass (1968)
PUBLIC COLLECTIONS: MPM

EAGLE ELK (see Red Elk, Herman)

EAGLE FEATHER, ELI (see Eagle Feather, Elijah)

EAGLE FEATHER, ELIJAH *Sioux*
Hehon Womblee, Owl Eagle
A.K.A. Eli Eagle Feather
Born 15 June 1926 in Hamill, SD; P/GF: Owl Eagle; M/GF: Felix Crazy Bull, tribal officer and advisor
MILITARY: U.S. Army, WWII
OCCUPATION: Farm laborer and artist
PUBLISHED: Snodgrass (1968)
EXHIBITS: BNIAS, PAC

EAGLEHAWK, CHRIS *Oglala Sioux*
EDUCATION: IAIA
EXHIBITS: IAIA, NACLA

EAGLE LANCE (see Bad Heart Bull, Amos)

EAGLE SHIELD *Teton Sioux*
OCCUPATION: Medicine man
PUBLISHED: Snodgrass (1968). *Bulletin 61,* BAE (1918), pictographic style

EAGLE'S TAIL (see Tsabetsaye, Roger)

EAH HA WA (see Mirabel, Eva)

EBERSOLE, BARBARA TATE *Cherokee*
RESIDENCE: Oklahoma
Born 1956
MEDIA: Gouache
EXHIBITS: CNM, FCTM, HM

ECHOHAWK, BRUMMETT *Pawnee*
Born 3 Mar 1922 in Pawnee, OK; father was a member of Pawnee Bill's Wild West Show; GF: a U.S. calvary scout under Major Frank North
RESIDENCE: Tulsa, OK
MILITARY: U.S. Army, WWII
EDUCATION: School of Arts and Crafts, Detroit, MI; CAI; U of Tulsa, OK
OCCUPATION: Newspaper staff artist, public speaker, writer, actor, consultant for films, and painter

BRUMMETT ECHOHAWK

Echohawk is a commercial artist and illustrator whose work is generally available through special commission and contract. His comic strip, Little Chief, *appeared in the* Tulsa World *and was familiar to many Oklahomans.*

Snodgrass 1968

Echohawk served in WWII with the Oklahoma 45th Division as a sketch artist, and his war sketches were reproduced in 88 syndicated newspapers across the United States.

DETAIL: Bronson Edwards, *Hunting Party,* 1966. Philbrook Museum of Art, Tulsa, Oklahoma

MEDIA: Oil and watercolor

PUBLISHED: Snodgrass (1968); Brody (1971); Samuels (1985). *Oklahoma Today* (spring 1965); *Oklahoma Home and Garden* (Oct 1985); *Tulsa World* (28 July 1983; 23 Jan 1994)

COMMISSIONS: *Murals:* Truman Memorial Library, Independence, MO (worked with Thomas Hart Benton); Aluminum Co. of America; U.S. Navy, *U.S.S. Anzio* (missile cruiser)

PUBLIC COLLECTIONS: CGPS; GM; MHDYMM; Imperial War Museum, London, England; Bad Segeberg, Hamburg, Germany; American Embassy, Pakistan

EXHIBITS: ACMWA; GM; HM/G; MHDYMM; PBOIA; SI; SN; Imperial War Museum, London, England; Germany, Pakistan, and India

AWARDS: PBOIA ('71)

HONORS: Unknown Indian Award, Committee for the Preservation of the Unknown Indian, North Platte, NE, 1983; Chairman of the Board, American Indian Artists Guild of Tulsa, OK, and Hollywood, CA

ECKER, GLADYS LEE *Oglala Sioux*

RESIDENCE: Pierre, SD

EDUCATION: Lead (SD) High School; BHSU, two years; Northern State College, Aberdeen, SD, two years

OCCUPATION: Teacher and painter

PUBLIC COLLECTIONS: HCC

EXHIBITS: RC; WTF; South Dakota State Fair, Huron, SD; Black Hills Art Association Shows; local shows and markets

AWARDS: RC ('80; '82)

ECKIWAUDAH, TENNYSON *Comanche*

Yutsuwuna, Able To Stand Up Again

Born 26 Sept 1912 in Cyril, OK; son of Bernice Looking Glass; M/GF: Big Looking Glass, chief of the Comanches during the early settlement of Oklahoma

RESIDENCE: Cyril, OK

EDUCATION: Tower Town Studios, Chicago, IL, 1935

OCCUPATION: Sign painter and artist

MEDIA: Oil

PUBLISHED: Snodgrass (1968); Brody (1971); King (1981)

COMMISSIONS: Ute Mountain Ute Tribe, Towaoc, CO, designed and produced ritual paraphernalia and paintings, 1965

PUBLIC COLLECTIONS: Cyril (OK) State Bank

EXHIBITS: AAID, AIE, CSPIP, DAM, PAC, SPIM, VV

AWARDS: AIE ('61; '62; '67, 1st)

TENNYSON ECKIWAUDAH

"Although the artist has been painting since 1935, he has not exhibited with any frequency. His greatest encouragement came from Susie Peters and James Auchiah (q.v.)."

Snodgrass 1968

EDAAKIE, ANTHONY PAUL *Zuni*

Eedeeahkai

A.K.A. Tony Edaakie; A. E. Tomahawk

Born 6 June 1927; died 25 Dec 1989

RESIDENCE: Lived in Zuni, NM

OCCUPATION: Silversmith and painter

MEDIA: Oil, acrylic, watercolor, pastel, silver, and gemstone

PUBLISHED: Snodgrass (1968); Tanner (1973)

PUBLIC COLLECTIONS: IACB/DC, MAI, MNA/KHC

EXHIBITS: AAIE, ITIC

AWARDS: ITIC ('72)

EDAAKIE, PAUL *Zuni*

PUBLISHED: Tanner (1973)
EXHIBITS: ITIC
AWARDS: ITIC ('66)

EDAAKIE, THEODORE *Zuni*

PUBLISHED: Tanner (1973)
PUBLIC COLLECTIONS: MAI, MNA

EDAAKIE, TONY (see Edaakie, Anthony P.)

EDENSAW, CHARLES *Haida*

Takayren, Noise in the House (as a baby); *Edensaw,* Glacier; *Itinsa,* Waterfall
A.K.A. Charles Edenshaw
Born 1839; died 12 Sept 1924 in Masset, BC, Canada; nephew of Albert Edward Edensaw (Gwaigu-unithin)
OCCUPATION: Village chief, cultural historian, carver, silversmith, and painter; best known for his carvings
MEDIA: Pencil, crayon, argillite, wood, and silver
PUBLISHED: Dockstader (1977)
EXHIBITS: C/RBCM

EDER, EARL *Yanktonai Sioux*

Tancan Hanska, Longchase
Born 17 Nov 1944 in Poplar, MT
RESIDENCE: Santa Fe, NM
EDUCATION: IAIA, 1962-1965; B.F.A, SFAI, 1967-1971; U of MT, 1971-1972
OCCUPATION: Plasterer, construction worker, maintenance man, jeweler, sculptor, and painter; current artistic endeavors primarily focused on sculpture
MEDIA: Oil, acrylic, pastel, pencil, charcoal, wood, stone, and metal
PUBLISHED: Snodgrass (1968); Libhart (1970); Ray, ed. (1972); New (1974; 1979); Median (1981). *Smoke Signals,* IACB (autumn, 1965); *Southwestern Art* (Vol. 2, no. 1, 1967); *Life Magazine* (1968); *Native American Arts 2* (1968); *The San Francisco Chronicle* (1968); *Art In America* (July/Aug 1971; July/Aug 1982); *The Santa Fean* (Apr 1982; Jan/Feb 1983; June 1992); biographical publications
PUBLIC COLLECTIONS: BIA, IACB, IAIA
EXHIBITS: AC/SD, ACE, ACS/ENP, ACMWA, BEAIAC, BM, BM/B, CPS, EAIF, FAIEAIP, HM/G, HS/AI, IAIA, IACA, MPI, NACLA, ND, PAC, PAIC, RM, SAIEAIP, SWAIA, U of SF, YAIA
AWARDS: BEAIAC ('67, 1st); HM/G ("70, 1st; '72); IACA ('80, Best of Class; ITIC ('78, 1st); ACS/ENP ('80; '90, 1st); SM ('70); SWAIA ('79)
HONORS: SFAI, scholarship

EDJYVUDLUK (see Eegyvudluk)

EDSITTY (see Edsitty, Jay W., Sr.)

EDSITTY, JAY W., SR. *Navajo*

Edsitty, Silversmith
Born 1 Sept 1932 in Rehoboth, NM; son of Lasanda and Wilson Edsitty
RESIDENCE: Newcomb, NM
MILITARY: U.S. Army, Korea
EDUCATION: Phoenix, 1955
OCCUPATION: School liaison officer and painter
MEDIA: Oil, acrylic, and watercolor
EXHIBITS: ITIC

CHARLES EDENSAW

The best known of the Haida artists of his generation, Edensaw's knowledge of the iconography of the Haida made him a greatly sought after figure by collectors, visitors, anthropologists, and art collectors. He was especially famed for his carvings which were collected by museums and art patrons. In the late 1800s he made drawings and crayon sketches for Franz Boas, which have been used as a key to the meanings of much of the visual symbology of Northwest Coast art.

Dockstader 1977

EARL EDER

Eder says, "After many art changes since childhood, I'm still changing. Being more aware of my tradition and ethnic background, I use ideas and designs to incorporate my own experiences through painting. . . . When I paint I become a spirit. You have to give every painting living magic so that it affects people when they read into it."

Ray, ed. 1972

Bronson Wilbur Edwards

"Edwards was interested in art as a child but did not begin to paint seriously until 1947. His work is similar to the European gouache style, but, on close examination, it contains a degree of the flat technique so common to Indian painting...."

Snodgrass 1968

Edwards, Bronson Wilbur *Ottawa*

A.K.A. Brontie

Born 22 May 1913 in Miami, OK; died 9 Nov 1973; son of Elizabeth Jones and Marvin E. Edwards; M/GP: Skash and Mon Ton Kee, Ottawa chief, 1880-1888 and veteran of the Union Army; GGF: Ottawa Chief, John W. Early, Wask-Kos

RESIDENCE: Lived in Miami, OK

EDUCATION: Miami (OK) High School, 1932; correspondence course in commercial art, Art Instruction, Inc., Minneapolis, MN

OCCUPATION: Sign painter, commercial artist, free-lance artist, and painter

MEDIA: Oil and watercolor

PUBLISHED: Snodgrass (1968); Brody (1971). *Indian Tribal Series* (No. 34, 1962), cover; a biographical publication

COMMISSIONS: *Murals:* Burtrum Motor Company, Miami, OK; National Boy Scout Jamboree, Colorado Springs, CO; St. James Hotel, Miami, OK, 1947

PUBLIC COLLECTIONS: GM; MAI; Assembly of God Church, Miami, OK; Seneca Indian School, Wyandotte, MI

EXHIBITS: AAID; AIEC; AIW; BNIAS; DAM; FAIEAIP; HM/G; ITIC; LAIC; LGAM; MHDYMM; MNM; PAC; SAIEAIP; SN; SPIM; Greenville (SC) Arts Festival; Miami County (OK) Historical Society; Northeastern Oklahoma A & M, Miami, OK; Ottawa County (OK) Fair

SOLO EXHIBITS: HM, SPIM

AWARDS: Partial listing of more than 29 includes: PAC; ITIC; county fairs

Ken Edwards

The artist's favorite subjects are medicine people and spirits. He finds he can best express his ideas and feelings using a surrealistic approach.

artist, p.c. 1990

Edwards, Ken *Colville*

Rainbow Cougar

A.K.A. Kenneth L. Edwards

Born 8 Feb 1956 in Greenville, SC

RESIDENCE: Omak, WA

EDUCATION: IAIA High School, 1974; Haskell, 1974-1975; A.F.A, IAIA, 1977; U of AK/A, 1977

OCCUPATION: Storyteller, oral historian, speaker, and artist

MEDIA: Oil, acrylic, watercolor, pen and ink, and prints

BOOKS ILLUSTRATED: *How the Animals Got Their Names; How Food Was Given; Neekna and Chemai; Turtle and The Eagle*

COMMISSIONS: Wintercount Card Co., Glenwood Springs, CO, greeting cards

PUBLIC COLLECTIONS: HCC

EXHIBITS: ACAI; AIAFM; ASC/SM; CCT; CNM; HCC; HIF; LIAS; LIAS/M; RC; SWAIA; TCIM; U of WV; WTF; First National Indian Art Show, Washington, D.C., 1986; International Friendship House, Moscow, U.S.S.R, 1987; see also Awards

AWARDS: ACAI ('94); AIAFM ('94, 1st, Best in Division); ASC/SM ('85, 1st); HIF ('88, 1st); TCIM ('91); Colville Confederated Tribes Indian Art Show; Hunter Net Indian Festival, Hunter, NY ('94, 1st)

HONORS: Galena, Alaska, artist-in-residence, 1981; Miss Indian USA Pageant, poster, 1985; Indian Summer Festival, Milwaukee, WI, poster artist, 1993

Eedeeahkai (see Edaakie, Anthony P.)

Eegivadlook (see Eegyvudluk)

Eegivudluk (see Eegyvudluk)

Eegyvudluk *Inuit (Eskimo)*

A.K.A. Egivadlook; Eegivudluk; Edjyvudluk; Egevadluq Ragee

Born Oct 1920; died 1983

RESIDENCE: Lived in Cape Dorset, NWT, Canada
OCCUPATION: Graphic artist
MEDIA: Pencil
PUBLISHED: Houston (1967; 1967a); Larmour (1967); Goetz, et al. (1977); Blodgett (1978b); Woodhouse, ed. (1980). *North* (Mar/Apr 1974)
PUBLIC COLLECTIONS: C/TDB
EXHIBITS: C/AC/MS; C/AG/WP; C/EACTDB; C/MCC; C/TIP; Robertson Galleries, Ottawa, ON

EESEEMAILEE, ATOOMOWYAK *Inuit (Eskimo)*
Born 1923
RESIDENCE: Pangnirtung, PQ, Canada
OCCUPATION: Graphic artist
MEDIA: Felt tip pen and pencil
PUBLISHED: Goetz, et al. (1977)
EXHIBITS: C/TIP, DAM

EEBALOOKJUK (see Evaluardjuk, Henry)

EETS-PAHP-AWAG-UH'KA (see Tailfeathers, Gerald)

EEVIK, TOMMY *Inuit (Eskimo)*
A.K.A. Tommy Evvik
Born 23 Feb 1951
RESIDENCE: Pangnirtung, PQ, Canada
OCCUPATION: Sculptor and graphic artist
PUBLISHED: Collinson (1978)
PUBLIC COLLECTIONS: C/V of AB
EXHIBITS: C/CG

EEYEETEETOWAK, ADA *Inuit (Eskimo)*
A.K.A. Eeyeetowak; Eeyeetowak; Eyeetowak; Adieux; Ada Adieux; Ada Eyetoaq
Born 1934
RESIDENCE: Baker Lake, NWT, Canada
OCCUPATION: Carver, textile designer, and graphic artist
MEDIA: Pencil, colored pencil, textiles, and stone
PUBLISHED: Goetz, et al. (1977); Collinson (1978)
PUBLIC COLLECTIONS: C/U of AB
EXHIBITS: C/AG/WP, C/CG, C/TIP

EEYEETOWAK (see Eeyeeteetowak, Ada)

EILEOHI, ANTONIO *Zuni*
PUBLISHED: Snodgrass (1968)
EXHIBITS: FWG

EKAK, THOMAS *Eskimo*
Born 1934 in Wainwright, AK
RESIDENCE: Seattle, WA
OCCUPATION: Graphic artist and employee of Leonard F. Porter, Inc., Seattle, WA
PUBLISHED: Ray (1969)

EKA LA NEE (see Beaver, Fred)

EKOOTAK (see Ektootak, Victor)

EEGYVUDLUK

Eegyvudluk spent most of her early years on the southern tip of Baffin Island. Her career as a graphic artist was already established in 1967 when she and her second husband, Sakkiassie, moved to Cape Dorset to give their children the opportunity for an education.

EKTOOTAK, VICTOR *Inuit (Eskimo)*
A.K.A. Ekootak
Born 1916
RESIDENCE: Holman Island, NWT, Canada
OCCUPATION: Graphic artist
MEDIA: Pencil
PUBLISHED: Larmour (1967); Goetz, et al. (1977)
PUBLIC COLLECTIONS: C/TDB
EXHIBITS: C/EACTDB, C/TIP

ELEESHUSHE *Inuit (Eskimo)*
A.K.A. Elishushi; Iisusi; Eleeshushe Parr
Born ca. 1886; died 1975; wife of Parr (q.v.)
RESIDENCE: Lived in Cape Dorset, NWT, Canada
PUBLISHED: Blodgett (n.d.); Houston (1967); Goetz, et al. (1977). *The Beaver* (spring 1975)
PUBLIC COLLECTIONS: C/AG/WP
EXHIBITS: C/AC/MS, C/LS, C/TIP

ELEESHUSHE

Eleeshushe was famous for her clever designs and fine sewing. The mother of Kovinatilliak (q.v.) and Nuna, well-known artists, she was also Peter Pitseolak's (q.v.) half-sister.

Houston 1967

ELI, ERMALINDA *Zuni*
Born 19 May 1962
EDUCATION: Fort Sill
EXHIBITS: HM/G; RC; high school art shows; see also Awards
AWARDS: HM/G

ELISHUSHI (see Eleeshushe)

ELIZONDO, VICKI *Oneida*
RESIDENCE: Chicago, IL
PUBLIC COLLECTIONS: HCC
EXHIBITS: RC, TM/NE

ELK (see Cohoe, William)

ELK (see Tyndall, Calvin T.)

ELK HEAD *Gros Ventre*
MEDIA: Pencil
PUBLISHED: Powell (1981); Maurer (1992)
PUBLIC COLLECTIONS: HS/MT
EXHIBITS: VP

ELK HEAD

Ca. 1883-1885, Elk Head turned to drawing to occupy his time while incarcerated for murder in the territorial prison at Deer Lodge, MT.

Maurer 1992

ELK HORN *Piegan*
Born 1845; died 1901
PUBLISHED: Snodgrass (1968)

ELK HORN

"Along with Big Brave and Double Runner (qq.v), the artist executed a 61-year count (see Wissler 1911)."

Snodgrass 1968

ELK WOMAN (see Whitman, Kathy)

ELLEN, MARY *Navajo*
EDUCATION: Santa Fe, NM
MEDIA: Watercolor
PUBLISHED: Dunn (1968); Snodgrass (1968); Seymour (1988)
PUBLIC COLLECTIONS: IACB/DC, OU/MA, MNM, MNA, SM
EXHIBITS: AIEC, NGA, OU/ET, WRTD

MARY ELLEN

According to Seymour (1988), little is known about Ellen. She was at the Santa Fe Indian School at the same time as Gerónima Montoya and Joe Herrera (qq.v.). She apparently only painted while she was there.

ELLIOTT, CHARLES *Coast Salish*

Birth date unknown; born on the Tsartlip Reserve, BC, Canada

EDUCATION: Grades 1-6, Tsartlip Indian Day School; grades 7-12, Victoria, BC; St. Louis College, Victoria, BC

OCCUPATION: Graphic artist, carver, and painter

COMMISSIONS: St. Andrew's Cathedral, eight altar panels, 1988

PUBLIC COLLECTIONS: HCC; C/RBCM; St. Andrew's Cathedral

EXHIBITS: AC/NC, BHSU, C/RBCM, RC, SDSMT, U of SD

ELLIOTT, LAVERNE *Cherokee*

Born 8 June 1932 in Carlsbad, NM; GGM: full-blood Cherokee, married a Scotch-Irishman

RESIDENCE: Clovis, NM

EDUCATION: Carlsbad (NM) High School, 1950; Carrizo Art School, Ruidosa, NM, 1975-1985

OCCUPATION: Sculptor and painter

MEDIA: Oil, acrylic, watercolor, pen and ink, pencil, pastel, clay, and prints

PUBLISHED: *Side Saddle* (1988)

COMMISSIONS: *Paintings:* Wagon Train Museum, Texas Sesquicentennial

PUBLIC COLLECTIONS: Marbridge Foundation Collection, Austin, TX

EXHIBITS: Texas Indian Market and Southwest Showcase, Arlington, TX; galleries in AZ, CA, CO, NM, OK, TN, and TX; see also Awards

AWARDS: Diné Bi Keyah Museum, Page, AZ (1st)

ELLIS, MARSHALL *Oneida*

Born 9 Feb 1959

RESIDENCE: Oneida, WI

EDUCATION: IAIA, 1975-1977; MCAD, 1978

OCCUPATION: Teacher, illustrator, and artist

MEDIA: Oil, acrylic, sterling silver, and clay

PUBLISHED: Johannsen and Ferguson, eds. (1983)

EXHIBITS: IAIA, MRNAC, SNAICF

AWARDS: IAIA ('76, American Legion Certificate; '77, Award of Merit)

ELSWA, JOHNNY KIT *Haida*

Birth date unknown; born in the Klue district of Moresby Island, BC, Canada; death date unknown

OCCUPATION: Jeweler, wood carver, and illustrator

MEDIA: Pen and ink, silver, and wood

PUBLISHED: *The West Shore* (Aug 1884); *American Indian Art* (summer 1981)

PUBLIC COLLECTIONS: SI

JOHNNY KIT ELSWA

James Gilchrist Swan, while collecting for the Smithsonian Institution during the summer and fall of 1883, employed Elswa to serve as cook and interpreter on an extended trip to the Haida villages. Swan discovered that Elswa was an artist and had him draw series of mythological sketches. Five of these India ink sketches were used to illustrate a short article which appeared in the August 1884 issue of The West Shore.

American Indian Art
summer 1981

EMARTHLE, ALLEN D. *Seminole/Choctaw*

RESIDENCE: Kiowa, OK

MEDIA: Pencil

EXHIBITS: CNM, FCTM

AWARDS: FCTM ('88, IH; '89, IH; '90, 1st; '91; '92)

EMBER OF FIRE (see Saul, C. Terry)

EMERAK (see Emerak, Mark)

EMERAK, MARK *Inuit (Eskimo)*

A.K.A. Emerak; Imerak; Imigak

Born 1901 near Cambridge Bay on Victoria Island, NWT, Canada; died 1983

RESIDENCE: Lived on Holman Island, NWT, Canada

OCCUPATION: Sculptor; graphic artist since 1968

MEDIA: Pencil and stone

PUBLISHED: Goetz, et al. (1977); Napran (1984); Driscoll (1987); Jackson and Nasby (1987); McMasters, et al. (1993)

PUBLIC COLLECTIONS: C/HEC, C/U of AB, DAM

EXHIBITS: C/CG, C/CID, C/NGCA, C/TIP, C/VRS

MARK EMERAK

In 1966, Father Henri Tardy, O.M.I., encouraged Emerak to draw. He became one of the most prolific artists from Holman Island in the 1970s.

Jackson and Nasby 1987

EMERSON, ANTHONY CHEE *Navajo*

Born 1 May 1963 in California; son of Betty and Albert Emerson; M/GP: Lydia and Clyde Begay

RESIDENCE: Farmington, NM

EDUCATION: Rehoboth Christian School, 1980; U of NM

OCCUPATION: Teacher, commercial and residential painting business owner, and artist

MEDIA: Oil, acrylic, watercolor, pencil, and prints

PUBLISHED: *Art-Talk* (Mar 1984)

EXHIBITS: ITIC, NTF, SWAIA, TF; see also Awards

AWARDS: ITIC ('84; '85; '86; '92; '93, 1st; '94); NTF ('94, 1st); SWAIA ('86); TF ('93; '94); Gallup (NM) Art Council Show ('82, 1st; '83, 1st)

EMERSON, LARRY W. *Navajo*

Born 19 Apr 1947 in Rehoboth, NM

RESIDENCE: Albuquerque, NM

EDUCATION: Fort Lewis College, Durango, CO, 1967; NCC, 1972; B.A., U of NM, 1975

OCCUPATION: Educator and painter

MEDIA: Oil

EXHIBITS: AC/T, AICH, C/U of R/MG, CHM, FSMCIAF, GDC, HM, NACLA, NU/BC, OSU/G, IPCC, SCG, SFFA, SI, WWM

SOLO EXHIBITS: SCG, 1982; Lovelace-Bataan Hospital Art Gallery, Albuquerque, NM, 1975

LARRY W. EMERSON

Emerson began to paint seriously around 1974. He was one of the original members of the Grey Canyon Artist's group from Albuquerque, NM.

EMERSON, LAWAUNNA *Choctaw/Chickasaw/Cherokee*

Birth date unknown; daughter of Ola and Lewis Stephens; P/GF: Saul Stephens; M/GF: C. H. Harris

RESIDENCE: Chickasha, OK

EDUCATION: NSU, 1972

OCCUPATION: Teacher and artist

MEDIA: Oil, acrylic, watercolor, pencil, pastel, and clay

EXHIBITS: CNM, FCTM

AWARDS: FCTM

LAWAUNNA EMERSON

According to the artist, "Art is my means of expressing my feelings. It is sometimes my mirror, sometimes my window to the past, sometimes my window to the future, but always my most enjoyable hobby and pleasurable pastime."

p.c. 1990

EMERSON, MICHELLE Y. *Kiowa/Comanche*

EXHIBITS: HM/G, RC

AWARDS: HM/G ('76, 1st)

EMERSON, ROBERTA JOAN BOYD *Sioux/Assiniboin*

Born 18 June 1931 in Brockton, MT; daughter of Helen Roberta Sparks and George A. Boyd

EDUCATION: High school, 1951; Montana State College, Bozeman, MT

PUBLISHED: Snodgrass (1968)

EXHIBITS: See Awards
AWARDS: Local school shows (1st)
HONORS: Outstanding Young Indian Artist Award (high school)

EMHEE (see Redbird, Robert, Jr.)

ENEMY BOY, LEVI *Assiniboin*

Born 1941 on the Fort Belknap Reservation, MT; nephew of William Standing (q.v.)
RESIDENCE: Harlem, MT
EDUCATION: Pine Hills School, Miles City, MT; Flandreau (SD) Indian School
MEDIA: Oil and pen and ink
PUBLIC COLLECTIONS: HCC
EXHIBITS: CIA; RC; TM/NE; St. Labré Indian Mission Museum, Ashland, MT; throughout western Montana
SOLO EXHIBITS: MPI

ENGLISH, JANELLE *Shawnee*

Kindiwa Mi Tamsa, Young Eagle Woman
Born 15 Nov 1937
RESIDENCE: Bat Cave, NC
EDUCATION: Spartanburg (SC) High School, 1956; U of SC/S, 1974-1976
OCCUPATION: Gift shop owner, craftswoman, and artist
MEDIA: Acrylic, pencil, pen and ink, pastel, and gourds
COMMISSIONS: *Murals:* Spirit Animal Wall for Native American Media Center, SC
EXHIBITS: RC; regional shows and powwows

ENGLISH, RONALD R. *Chippewa/Cree*

Green Feather
Brother of Sam English, Sr. (q.v.)
RESIDENCE: Anadarko, OK
OCCUPATION: Sculptor and painter
EXHIBITS: AIE, LIAS/M, RC, RE, TWF
AWARDS: AIE ('89, 1st; '90, 1st; '91, 1st); TWF ('93)

ENGLISH, SAM, JR. *Chippewa*

Born 12 Apr 1965; son of Sam English, Sr. (q.v.); P/GP: Blanche M. Delorme and Samuel E. English
RESIDENCE: Albuquerque, NM
OCCUPATION: Gallery manager and painter
MEDIA: Watercolor
PUBLISHED: *White Earth* (June 1991)
EXHIBITS: BSIM; galleries in AZ, CA, CO, IL, NM, and NY
AWARDS: BSIM ('93, 1st)

ENGLISH, SAM, SR. *Chippewa*

Born 2 June 1942 in Phoenix, AZ; son of Blanche M. Delorme and Samuel E. English; P/GP: Mary and Samuel English; M/GP: Margaret and Francis Delorme
RESIDENCE: Albuquerque, NM
EDUCATION: Ignacio (CO) High School, 1960; BC; U of SF
OCCUPATION: Gallery owner and painter
MEDIA: Oil, acrylic, watercolor, pencil, pen, pastel, and prints
PUBLISHED: *America West Airlines* (Aug 1986); *Southwest Art* (Dec 1989); *U.S. Art* (Nov 1991)

LEVI ENEMY BOY

In addition to excelling in art in high school, Enemy Boy was an athlete and participated in very successful basketball and wrestling programs. The artist says, "I draw what should be recorded so that others who never knew the Old Ones or heard stories about their lives would know what it was like then. In my drawings and paintings, I try to put it down as it really was."

Ray, ed. 1972

JANELLE ENGLISH

The artist says that she lives simply with many of the traditions from her culture. She devotes much of her time teaching other people to use their artistic abilities. English earns most of her income from her arts and crafts. She works almost entirely on commissions, making primarily Spirit Catcher gourds, medicine gourds, cheese boxes, and medicine bags.

p.c. 1990

SAM ENGLISH SR.

The artist grew up in Arizona, New Mexico, and Colorado and was a member of the North American Indian Artist Group in California during the 1960s. He became a full-time artist in 1981. He is very involved with Indian issues and considers himself a role model. In the early 1970s he was a director of the National Indian Youth Council, which is now located in Albuquerque, NM.

artist, p.c. 1990

EXHIBITS: AICH; NMSF; NPTA; TCIM; TWF; UTAE; galleries in AZ, CA, CO, IL, NM, and NY

AWARDS: NMSF ('81, 1st); NPTA (''89; '91, 1st; '92); TCIM ('91, 1st); TWF ('93, 1st); RE ('94, Best of Division); UTAE ('92)

ENJADY, ERROL *Mescalero Apache*

EDUCATION: Albuquerque, NM, 1962-1963

PUBLISHED: Snodgrass (1968)

EXHIBITS: MNM

ENJADY, OLIVER *Mescalero Apache*

RESIDENCE: Mescalero, NM

EXHIBITS: HM/G, PAC

SOLO EXHIBITS: WWM

ENOOESWEETOK *Inuit (Eskimo)*

A.K.A. Nungusuituq; Noogooshoweetok

Born ca. 1890; died ca. 1950

RESIDENCE: Lived in Cape Dorset, NWT, Canada

OCCUPATION: Guide and graphic artist

PUBLISHED: Jackson and Nasby (1987). *Artscanada* (Vol. 28, no. 6, 1971-1972)

BOOKS ILLUSTRATED: Carpenter (1968)

PUBLIC COLLECTIONS: C/ROM

EXHIBITS: C/AC/MS, C/CID

> **ENOOESWEETOK**
>
> *1913-1914 Enooesweetok acted as a guide to Robert Flaherty, pioneering documentary filmmaker, on one of his trips with Sir William MacKenzie to the Arctic. At Flaherty's urging Enooesweetok made drawings of the Inuit life. These drawings were among the earliest pencil drawings made by North American Inuit.*
>
> Arts Canada
> *Vol. 28, no. 6, 1971-1972*

ENOS, TERRY A. *Pima/Tohono O'odham (Papago)*

Born 4 Aug 1952 on San Xavier Indian Reservation, AZ

RESIDENCE: Española, NM

EDUCATION: Tucson (AZ) High School; A.F.A (two-dimensional design), IAIA, 1982; A.F.A (three-dimensional design), IAIA, 1984; B.F.A., CSF, 1985

OCCUPATION: Illustrator and artist

EXHIBITS: ACS/ENP; CSF; IAIA; MPI; RC; SWAIA; Bond House Museum, Española, NM, 1986

SOLO EXHIBITS: MPI

ENSE, DON *Ojibwa*

Born 1953 at Mindemoya on Manitoulin Island, ON, Canada; brother of Bernard Ense, painter

EDUCATION: West Bay, ON; London, ON; Sudbury, ON; Toronto,ON; Ojibwa Cultural Foundation Summer Art Program, 1975; C/CC/NB; Laurentian University, Sudbury, ON; BYU

OCCUPATION: Musician and painter

PUBLISHED: Southcott (1984). *Native Perspective* (Vol. 3, no. 2, 1978)

COMMISSIONS: Canadian Council of Christians and Jews, paintings for a calendar, 1979; Ojibwa Cultural Foundation, paintings for calendars

EXHIBITS: C/WICEC; Bernhardt's Centre, 1977; Manitoulin painter's group

> **DON ENSE**
>
> *Ense started painting in 1974 after encouragement from several friends as therapy for failing health due to drugs and alcohol. Painting resulted in his discovery of his heritage which led to self-confidence, self-respect, and a change in life-style. In addition to legend paintings done in the Anishnabe style, Ense paints views of daily life rendered in a simplified realism.*
>
> *Southcott 1984*

ESA, MARJORIE *Inuit (Eskimo)*

A.K.A. Marjorie Iisa; Margery Eso; Iisa; Isa

Born 1934 in Iglulik, NWT, Canada; adopted by Louis Tapatai

RESIDENCE: Baker Lake, NWT, Canada

OCCUPATION: Sculptor, textile artist, and graphic artist

MEDIA: Colored pencil, graphite pencil, stone, and textile

> **MARJORIE ESA**
>
> *Adopted as an infant by Louis Tapatai who worked as a native assistant for traders and others in the Baker Lake Area, Esa grew up in contact with other cultures. Her drawings, which she began doing in 1970, show a special interest in depicting the characteristics of different kinds of birds and fish.*
>
> *Jackson and Nasby 1987*

PUBLISHED: Goetz, et al. (1977); Latocki, ed. (1983); Jackson and Nasby (1987). *Artscanada* (Vol. 28, no. 6, 1971-1972)
PUBLIC COLLECTIONS: C/AG/WP
EXHIBITS: C/AG/WP, C/BLPD, C/CID, C/TIP

ESH-BA'-E-LOUA-IT-CHAY (see Stewart, Susan)

ESKEY, DAVID *Navajo*
AWARDS: MNA (3)

ESO, MARGERY (see Esa, Marjorie)

ESTE SONGAH (see Wolfe, Edmond Richard)

ETAHDLEUH *Kiowa*
A.K.A. Edwin Etahdleuh; Etahdleuh Doanmoe; E'talyi-donnmo
Born 1856; died 1888
EDUCATION: Hampton
OCCUPATION: Warrior, Indian School employee, cultural and language informant, and painter
MEDIA: Watercolor, pencil, and crayon
PUBLISHED: Dunn (1968); Snodgrass (1968); Highwater (1976); Hoffman, et al. (1984); Maurer (1992)
PUBLIC COLLECTIONS: HI, HS/MA, SI/OAA, YU
EXHIBITS: BPG, IK, VP

ETAHDLEUH

"The artist was among the 72 Plains Indians taken as prisoners from Fort Sill, OK, to Fort Marion, St. Augustine, FL, in 1875."

Snodgrass 1968

Jamake Highwater (1976) describes Etahdleuh's style as vivid and somewhat reminiscent of Middle Eastern court painting.

ETAHDLEUH, EDWIN (see Etahdleuh)

E'TALYI-DONNMO (see Etahdleuh)

ETEDLOOIE (see Etidlooie, Etidlooie)

ETEEYAN, WARREN HARDY *Potawatomi*
Born 9 Oct 1950 in Claremore, OK; son of Elizabeth Eteeyan
RESIDENCE: Mayetta, KS
OCCUPATION: Heavy equipment operator and painter
MEDIA: Oil, acrylic, and pencil
PUBLIC COLLECTIONS: Potawatomi Tribal Office

WARREN HARDY ETEEYAN

Eteeyan has painted more than 300 paintings and sells them to people who come to the reservation to buy them. He does not exhibit publicly.

artist, p.c. 1992

ETIDLOIE (see Etidlooie, Etidlooie)

ETIDLOIE, KINGMEATA (see Etidlooie, Kingmeata)

ETIDLOOIE, ETIDLOOIE *Inuit (Eskimo)*
A.K.A. Etidlui; Etedlooie; Etidloie
Born 5 Jan 1911 in Aqatalaulavik, South Baffin Island, NWT, Canada; died 2 Nov 1981; husband of Kingmeata (q.v.), artist; father of Omalluk Oshutsiaq, artist
RESIDENCE: Lived in Cape Dorset, NWT, Canada
OCCUPATION: Hunter, graphic artist, sculptor, and painter
MEDIA: Acrylic, watercolor, pen and ink, felt pen, crayon, and stone
PUBLISHED: Swinton (1972); Routledge (1979); Blodgett (1984); Jackson and Nasby (1987). *The Ottawa Citizen* (13 Jan 1989)
PUBLIC COLLECTIONS: C/AC/MS, C/AG/WP, C/CCAB, C/CGCQ, C/CMC, C/INAC, C/WBEC
EXHIBITS: C/AC/MS; C/AG/U of L; C/AG/WP; C/AV; C/CDG; C/CID; C/CGCQ; C/IA7; SUNY/BH; galleries in the U.S. and Canada
SOLO EXHIBITS: The Inuit Gallery of Eskimo Art, Toronto, ON; London (ON) Regional Art Gallery; galleries in the U.S.

ETIDLOOIE ETIDLOOIE

Encouraged by Terry Ryan in 1964, Etidlooie began to draw in mid-life. With an intuitive sense for color and formal rhythms, he attempted to show to the White people in southern Canada the way the Inuit used to live. He was also fascinated with the modern technology (skimobiles, airplanes, etc.) from southern Canada and his paintings often included objects from outside his traditional culture.

Jackson and Nasby 1987

KINGMEATA ETIDLOOIE

Kingmeata Etidlooie's subjects range from birds, people, and animals to a wide variety of composite and transformed creatures. Her paintings are not as complex as those of her second husband, Etidlooie (q.v.). She explained that she intentionally kept her compositions simple because of her poor eyesight and to make it easier to print. She enjoyed painting with acrylics more than drawing since she found it easier and liked its appearance. She and her husband sometimes drew or painted together; however, shortness of breath due to a heart problem forced her to work at home instead of at the Co-op acrylic studio.

INAC, Inuit Art Section, 1991

TIVA ETOOK

Violent confrontations are a common subject for Etook's drawings.

Goetz, et al. 1977

ETIDLOOIE, KINGMEATA *Inuit (Eskimo)*

A.K.A. Etidlui; Etidloie; Kingmeata; Kingmeattar; Kingmeeatta

Born 25 Dec 1915 at Itinik, a small camp near Lake Harbour, NWT, Canada; died 22 Feb 1989

RESIDENCE: Lived in Cape Dorset, NWT, Canada

OCCUPATION: Sculptor, graphic artist, and painter

MEDIA: Acrylic, watercolor, graphite pencil, crayon, pen and ink, felt pens, and stone

PUBLISHED: Routledge (1979); Blodgett (1983); Jackson and Nasby (1987). *The Beaver* (spring 1975); *City and Country Home* (Apr 1979); *Tableau* (Vol. 1, no. 5, 1988)

PUBLIC COLLECTIONS: C/AC/MS; C/AG/O; C/AG/TT; C/AG/U of L; C/AG/WP; C/CCAB; C/CGCQ; C/CMC; C/DEA; C/LUM; C/MAG; C/MBAM; C/NGAC; C/PWNAHC; C/SFG; NMC; Woodstock (ON) Public Art Gallery

EXHIBITS: C/AC/MS; C/AG/U of L; C/AG/WP; C/AG/M; C/AGO/U of G; C/CDG; C/CEL; C/CID; C/CGCQ; C/GTPW; C/IA7; C/IGV; C/LS; GM; JAHM; QM; galleries in the U.S. and Canada

SOLO/SPECIAL EXHIBITS: C/HNG (dual show); The Inuit Gallery of Eskimo Art, Toronto, ON; Waddington Galleries, Montréal, PQ

ETIDLUI (see Etidlooie, Etidlooie)

ETIDLUI, KINGMEATA (see Etidlooie, Kingmeata

ETOOK, TIVA *Inuit (Eskimo)*

A.K.A. Tiui Etook

Born 1929

RESIDENCE: George River, NWT, Canada

OCCUPATION: Graphic artist

MEDIA: Pencil

PUBLISHED: Goetz, et al. (1977); Myers, ed. (1980). *North* (Mar/Apr 1974)

PUBLIC COLLECTIONS: DAM

EXHIBITS: C/TIP; C/TMBI; Robertson Galleries, Ottawa, ON

HONORS: Print used for poster, 1978

ETOOLOOKUTNA (see Ittulukatnak, Martha)

EUSTACE, LEBECK *Zuni*

PUBLISHED: Snodgrass (1968)

EXHIBITS: MNM

EVALUARDJUK, HENRY *Inuit (Eskimo)*

A.K.A. Evaloardjuk; Evaluakjuak; Evaluarjuk; Evalurarjuk; Ivaluardjuk; Eevalookjuk

Born 1923 in Igloolik, NWT, Canada

RESIDENCE: Frobisher Bay, NWT, Canada

OCCUPATION: Hunter, sculptor, and painter

MEDIA: Graphite pencil, colored pencil, stone, and prints

PUBLISHED: Swinton (1972)

PUBLIC COLLECTIONS: C/AG/LR; C/AG/WP; C/ICI; C/CMC; C/EM; C/GM; C/MBAM; C/N; C/NGCA; C/PWNHC; Northwestern Michigan College, Traverse City, MI; Nunatta Sunaqutangit Museum, Iqaluit, NWT

EXHIBITS: C/AG/IGEA; C/AG/S; C/AV; C/CIIA; C/CMC; C/IGV; C/INAC;

C/LFCNQ; C/MA; C/MCC; C/NGCA; SUNY/BH; Baffin Regional School Exhibition, Iqaluit, NWT; galleries in AB, CA, MA, MB, NY, ON, PQ, and VA

SOLO EXHIBITS: C/RBC, 1969; Waddington Galleries, Toronto, ON, 1978

AWARDS: Frobisher Bay Carving Competition

HONORS: Sculpture presented to President and Mrs. Ronald Reagan during their official visit to Canada.

EVALOARDJUK (see Evaluardjuk, Henry)

EVALUAKJUAK (see Evaluardjuk, Henry)

EVALUARJUK (see Evaluardjuk, Henry)

EVALURARJUK (see Evaluardjuk, Henry)

EVANS, LESLIE D. *Potawatomi/Laguna*

Born 29 Dec 1936

RESIDENCE: Lawrence, KS

EDUCATION: St. Gregory's High School; B.F.A., OSU; Western Kentucky University, Bowling Green, KY; U of KS

EXHIBITS: LIAS, SWAIA

AWARDS: LIAS

EVARTS, MARK *Pawnee*

PUBLISHED: Snodgrass (1968)

PUBLIC COLLECTIONS: Castillo de San Marcos National Monument, St. Augustine, FL

EXHIBITS: BPG

EVENING SNOW COMES (see Suazo, David Gary)

EVVIK, TOMMY (see Eevik, Tommy)

EYA (see Johnson, Alfred)

EYEETOWAK (see Eeyeeteetowak, Ada)

EYETOAQ, ADA (see Eeyeeteetowak, Ada)

LESLIE D. EVANS

"A diverse experiential edge exists along which being Indian and the events of acculturation interact, transforming cultural identity in spite of tradition and tribe. The character of the transformation process and the results it has produced are uniquely Indian though relatively unexplored. With my art I like to speculate on how this transformation has impacted cultural identity."

artist 1990

MARK EVARTS

"The artist was among the 72 Plains Indians taken as prisoners from Fort Sill, OK, to Fort Marion, St. Augustine, FL, in 1875."

Snodgrass 1968

JOHN FADDEN

Fadden's paintings have been greatly influenced by the paintings of two early Iroquois painters, Ernest Smith (q.v.) and Sanford Plummer. Incorporating what he learned from their paintings he has moved in a slightly different direction. His work has become filled with dynamic symbolism and deals with the meanings and core values of Iroquois cosmology.

Johannsen and Ferguson 1983

DETAIL: Franklin Fireshaker, *The Papoose,* 1941. Philbrook Museum of Art, Tulsa, Oklahoma

FADDEN, ELIZABETH *Mohawk*

Karonhesake

Born 1945 in Akwesasne, ON, Canada

RESIDENCE: Canada

PUBLIC COLLECTIONS: AKM, SMII, SNIM

EXHIBITS: AICH, ALCC, AM, SMII

FADDEN, JOHN *Mohawk*

Kahionhes, Long River

Born 26 Dec 1938 in Massena, NY; son of Christine and Ray Fadden; P/GP: Matilda and Carroll Fadden; M/GP: Louise and Mitchell Chubb

RESIDENCE: Onchiota, NY

EDUCATION: Massena (NY) High School, 1957; B.F.A., Rochester (NY) Institute of Technology, 1961; SUNY/P; St. Lawrence University, Canton, NY

OCCUPATION: Educator, illustrator, sculptor, and painter

MEDIA: Acrylic, pen and ink, pastel, soapstone, and wood

PUBLISHED: Johannsen and Ferguson (1983). Partial listing of journal publications includes: *Akwesasne Notes* (1975-1978); *Mohawk Nation at Akwesasne, Contact II*; The *Beloit Poetry Journal* (1980); *The Rezz* (1980)

BOOKS ILLUSTRATED: Partial listing of more than thirty includes books authored by: Bernard Assiniwi, Joseph Brucac, Tehanetorens, Mary Tall Mountain; cover art for 15 publications

COMMISSIONS: *Illustrations:* National Film Board of Canada, Montréal, PQ, *Who Were the Ones,* film illustration; three additional films and 15 periodicals

PUBLIC COLLECTIONS: SMII, SNIM, C/WICEC

EXHIBITS: AICH; AKM; AM; AOSOS; C/AC/S; C/AG/MS; C/WICEC; SMII; LPCA; NYSF; PSM; RCAS; SMII; SNIM; Erie County Savings Bank, Buffalo, NY; Herbert F. Johnson Museum of Art, Ithaca, NY, 1984; North Country Community College, Saranac Lake, NY; Museum Voor Land-en Bolkenkunde, Rotterdam, Holland, 1979; New York State Fair, Syracuse, NY, 1977; Potsdam (NY) Public Museum, 1983; Remington Art Museum, Ogdensburg, NY, 1983

SOLO EXHIBITS: PSM, 1962; North Country Community College, Saranac Lake, NY, 1980

AWARDS: NYSF (1st)

HONORS: United Teachers Journalism Award; Iroquois Festival II, Cobleskill, NY, featured artist, 1983

FAIRBANKS, FLORIAN KERMIT *Chippewa*

A.K.A. Slats Fairbanks

Born 4 Aug 1948; son of Alice Spears and Ruben A. Fairbanks; P/GP: Catherine McKinze and Robert Fairbanks; M/GF: William Spears

RESIDENCE: Minneapolis, MN

EDUCATION: Brainerd (MN) Senior High School, 1967; U of MN/D, 1971; MCAD, 1967; U of MT, Missoula, MT, 1972-1974

OCCUPATION: Art teacher and artist

MEDIA: Oil, acrylic, watercolor, pencil, pen and ink, pastel, and prints

EXHIBITS: AC/D; OAE; MAI; MPI; TCIM; School of Communication Arts, Minneapolis, MN

SOLO EXHIBITS: MRNAC ('80); Vermillion Community College, Ely, MN

AWARDS: OAE ('82, 2-1st; '83, Grand Prize, Best of Show; '84; '85; '86; '87, 1st; '88); TCIM ('91; '92)

FAIRBANKS, SLATS (see Fairbanks, Florian Kermit)

FALLING WHITE SNOW (see Honanie, Delbridge)

FARMER, ERNEST *Shoshoni/Bannock*

A.K.A. Ernie Farmer
Born 1932; died 1970 in an automobile accident
EDUCATION: BC, 1953
OCCUPATION: Firefighter and artist
MEDIA: Casein
PUBLISHED: Snodgrass (1968)
PUBLIC COLLECTIONS: MNA
PUBLISHED: Johannsen and Fergusen, eds. (1983)
EXHIBITS: CIA, PAC, MPI
HONORS: President of the Sho-Ban Firefighters

FARMER, MITCH *Onondaga*

Born 28 Mar 1957; death date unknown
OCCUPATION: Graphics and layout artist for *Akwesasne Notes*, T-shirt designer, carver, and painter
MEDIA: Paints, catlinite, and wood
EXHIBITS: Onondaga Indian School

FARRAR, BURTON *Blackfeet*

PUBLIC COLLECTIONS: HCC
EXHIBITS: WWM

FAST DEER *Sioux*

Hechaka Lucahan, Fast Deer
PUBLISHED: Snodgrass (1968)
PUBLIC COLLECTIONS: MNH/A

FAST DEER

"One of five artists whose works, commissioned and collected from 1880 to 1883 by Rudolf Cronau, are now referred to as the Cronau Album (see Sinte)."

Snodgrass 1968

FAST EAGLE *Oglala Sioux*

Wanble Orko
Birth date unknown; One of 13 autographs (see Black Heart)
RESIDENCE: From Pine Ridge Agency, SD
PUBLISHED: Snodgrass (1968)
PUBLIC COLLECTIONS: MAI

FAST HORSE, DOUGLAS *Oglala Sioux*

Born 27 Sept 1943 in Manderson, SD, on the Pine Ridge Reservation
RESIDENCE: Rapid City, SD
EDUCATION: Central High School, Rapid City, SD; MCAD, 1975-1978
OCCUPATION: Craftsman and artist
MEDIA: Oil, pen and ink, and prints
PUBLIC COLLECTIONS: Minnesota Historical Society, Minneapolis, MN; Bloomington Historical Society, Minneapolis, MN
EXHIBITS: RC; SN; Images of the Old West, Minneapolis, MN, 1978; Rapid City (SD) Arts and Crafts Exposition, 1978
SOLO EXHIBITS: SIM

BUDDY FEATHER

One of Feather's teachers told him, "Learn as much as you can from the white man's way of painting, but never lose your identity as an Indian." He says that is what he is trying to do.

brochure, SIM, 1973

FEATHER, BUDDY *Yankton Sioux*

Born 23 Feb 1920 at Greenwood, SD, on the Yankton Reservation
RESIDENCE: Tucson, AZ
MILITARY: U.S. Navy
EDUCATION: Haskell, 1938; SU, 1940; Huron (SD) College, 1946-1947; CAI, 1948-1949; CCAC, 1951-1952

OCCUPATION: Welder, policeman, boxer; full-time artist since 1972
PUBLISHED: Snodgrass (1968)
EXHIBITS: FWG
SOLO EXHIBITS: SIM ('73)

FEATHER, RALPH A., JR. *Cherokee*
RESIDENCE: Jay, OK
EXHIBITS: CNM

FEATHERHAT, HOWARD *Navajo/Paiute*
RESIDENCE: Fredonia, AZ
OCCUPATION: Mechanic and painter
EXHIBITS: RC

FEATHERS, GERALD T. (see Tailfeathers, Gerald)

FEATHERS, KIRBY *Ponca/Sioux*
EDUCATION: IAIA, 1965-1966
PUBLISHED: Snodgrass (1968)
EXHIBITS: IAIA, YAIA

FEATHERS, MARK *Sioux (?)*
RESIDENCE: Kansas City, KS
EXHIBITS: CNM ('83)

FEDDERSEN, JOE *Colville/Okanagan*
Born 1953 in Omak, WA
RESIDENCE: Olympia, WA
EDUCATION: A.A., Wenatchee Valley College, Went, WA, 1979; B.F.A., U of WA, 1983; M.F.A., U of WI, 1989
OCCUPATION: Teacher; professional artist since 1982
MEDIA: Oil, mixed-media, and prints
PUBLISHED: Brokschmidt (1982); Hartje (1984); Banks (1986); Longfish, et al. (1986); Lippard (1990); Roberts (1992); Zurko, ed. (1992). *The Seattle Times* (1983); *The New York Times* (26 Apr 1984); *The New York Daily News* (22 Apr 1983); *North Dakota Quarterly* (1985); *America West* (July 1990)
PUBLIC COLLECTIONS: USDI; WSAC; King's County Arts Commission, Seattle, WA; University of Hawaii, Hilo, HI
EXHIBITS: AICA/SF; AICH; CCDLR; CNGM; CWAM; HM; IK; MCCG; MMA/WA; MSU; NCGM; NDN; OLO; OSU/G; PDN; PIG; SCG; SPIN/PO; SS/CW; TPAS; U of N AZ/G; WHB; Galerie Akmak, Berlin, Germany, 1982; Willamette University, Salem, OR, 1984; University Art Gallery, California State University, Carson, CA, 1985
SOLO EXHIBITS: SCG
HONORS: Colorado College, Colorado Springs, CO, artist-in-residence, summer 1984

FENTON, LELA MARIE *Osage*
Born 10 Feb 1934
RESIDENCE: Milwaukee, WI
EDUCATION: Mother of Sorrows High School; B.A., MMC; M.A., Cardinal Stritch College, Milwaukee, WI
EXHIBITS: RC

FERGUSON, CARL *Cherokee*
EXHIBITS: FCTM

FERNANDO, GILBERT *Navajo/Laguna*

EXHIBITS: HM/G

FERRIS, ALBERT *Chippewa*

Born 17 June 1939 in Belcourt, ND, on the Turtle Mountain Reservation; died 7 Aug 1986; son of Dora Sullivan and Samuel Ferris; P/GP: Vera and Albert Ferris; M/GM: Charette Sullivan

RESIDENCE: Lived in Rolla, ND

MILITARY: U.S. Army

EDUCATION: Rolla (ND) High School; U of ND, 1956-1958; CAI, 1959

OCCUPATION: Illustrator, commercial artist, sculptor, and painter

MEDIA: Acrylic, pencil, pen and ink, clay, bronze, and prints

PUBLISHED: *The Indian Trader* (Mar 1982); *Art West Magazine* (1984)

PUBLIC COLLECTIONS: SI; The Pentagon, Washington, D.C.

EXHIBITS: CNM; KCPA; galleries in MN, NM, NY, OK, SD, and TX

SOLO EXHIBIT: SPIM

AWARDS: North Dakota State Bicentennial Medallion Design contest, 1975; Centennial Medallion Design contests, Fargo, ND and Moorhead, MN

ALBERT FERRIS

Ferris used an almost photographic realism in his paintings, and he put a great deal of emphasis on detail. He said, "I am illustrating the past as it was lived and told to me. I paint fact, not fiction. I paint life, not pretty pictures. . . ."

brochure, SPIM, 1982

FETTER, KENT JOHN *Mohawk*

Born 28 Sept 1963

RESIDENCE: Norwood, NY

EDUCATION: Norwood-Norfolk (NY) Central High School; Potsdam College of Arts and Science

EXHIBITS: RC

FIDDLER, RINGO *Ojibwa*

Birth date unknown, in Kenora, ON, Canada

RESIDENCE: Sandy Lake, ON, Canada

EDUCATION: Studied under Wally Kakekapetum

OCCUPATION: Teacher and painter

EXHIBITS: C/M

FIDDLER, ROCKY *Ojibwa*

Born 14 Feb 1959 on the Sandy Lake Reserve, ON, Canada

RESIDENCE: Thunder Bay, ON, Canada

EDUCATION: Lakehead University, Thunder Bay, ON

OCCUPATION: Teacher and painter

MEDIA: Acrylic

PUBLIC COLLECTIONS: C/AG/TB, HCC

EXHIBITS: C/AG/TB; C/M; HCC; Chateau Laurier, Ottawa, ON, 1988

HONORS: Ontario All Chiefs Conference, achievement award for his depiction of traditional Native values, 1980

ROCKY FIDDLER

Although Ojibwa by birth, the artist was adopted and raised as a Cree. When Fiddler was about seventeen he began to paint, although his activities were restricted because of severe arthritis. His art has been strongly influenced by Carl Ray, who was his mentor, and Cree traditions and legends. The relationship between the animal and spirit worlds in the sacred legends, and the conflict between traditional and contemporary lifestyles are the subject matter of Fiddler's paintings.

FIFE, JIMMIE CAROL (see Fife-Stewart, Jimmie Carol)

FIFE, PHYLLIS (see Fife-Patrick, Phyllis)

FIFE-PATRICK, PHYLLIS *Creek*

A.K.A. Phyllis Fife

Born 22 June 1948 in Dustin, OK; daughter of Carmen Griffin and James Fife; P/GP: Louisa Lowe and Sunday Fife; M/GP: Fannie Watson and William C. Griffin; sister of Jimmie Carol Fife-Stewart (q.v.)

RESIDENCE: Tahlequah, OK

EDUCATION: IAIA, 1963-1966; U of C/SB, 1966-1967; NSU, 1969; B.F.A., U of OK, 1973

OCCUPATION: Bilingual/multicultural education curriculum specialist, art consultant, teacher, museologist, graphic artist, fashion designer, and painter

MEDIA: Acrylic and prints

PUBLISHED: Snodgrass (1968); Highwater (1976; 1980); New (1974; 1979; 1981); Wade and Strickland (1981); Hill (1992)

PUBLIC COLLECTIONS: CCHM, HM, IAIA, FCTM, OU/MA, MNM, NACLA

EXHIBITS: CAIA; CIAI; CCHM; C/U of R/MG; CNM; HM; HM/G; IAIA; NACLA; ND; OAC; OIAP; PAC; PAIC; SFFA; SN; SPIM; U of OR; YAIA; Pawnee Bill Museum, Pawnee, OK; Scottsdale (AZ) Museum

AWARDS: CIAI ('75, 1st, Purchase Award); FCTM ('70, IH; '71, Grand Award; '77); HM/G ('72); PAC ('70)

FIFE-STEWART, JIMMIE CAROLE *Creek*

A.K.A. Jimmie Carole Fife

Born 23 Dec 1940 in Dustin, OK; daughter of Carmen Griffin and James Fife; sister of Phyllis Fife-Patrick (q.v.); P/GP: Louisa Lowe and Sunday Fife; M/GP: Fannie Watson and William C. Griffin

RESIDENCE: Tahlequah, OK

EDUCATION: Chilocco, 1954-1958; OSU/O; U of AZ, "Southwest Indian Art Project," scholarship, summers 1960, 1961; B.F.A., OSU, 1963

OCCUPATION: Teacher, secretary, illustrator, fashion designer, and painter

PUBLISHED: Brody (1971); New (1979)

COMMISSIONS: *Murals:* Daybreak Star Indian Cultural Center, Seattle, WA

PUBLIC COLLECTIONS: MNA, PAC

EXHIBITS: CIAI, CNM, FCTM, OIAP, PAC, PAIC, RC

AWARDS: CNM ('88, 1st); FCTM ('67; '68; '69, 1st; '70, IH; '71, 1st; '72; '74, 1st, IH; '75, 1st, Grand Award; '76, 1st; '77, 1st; '78; '83, 1st, IH; '85, 1st); HM/G ('71); PAC ('68)

FIFE-WILSON, SANDY *Creek*

EXHIBITS: CNM, FCTM

AWARDS: FCTM ('81; '85)

FINNEY, BRUCE FALCON *Chickasaw*

Born 27 May 1951 in Denver, CO; son of Asta I. Kerr and Richard F. Finney; M/GM: Rita Kerr, on the Dawes Commission Rolls; M/GGM: Ida Irene Kerr, on the Dawes Commission Rolls

RESIDENCE: Santa Fe, NM

EDUCATION: Denver (CO) High School, 1969; U of CO, 1976

OCCUPATION: Silversmith and painter

MEDIA: Watercolor, silver, and prints

PUBLIC COLLECTIONS: National Bank of Alaska, Anchorage, AK; Alaska Federal Credit Union

EXHIBITS: Longmont (CO) Artist's Guild Show; All-Alaska Juried Watercolor Exhibition, Anchorage, AK; Fur Rendezvous

SOLO EXHIBITS: Alaska Mutual Bank, 1984

BRUCE FALCON FINNEY

Finney's great grandmother, Ida Irene Kerr, who founded the Paul's Valley (OK) Art League and taught art classes in Oklahoma, receives credit for inspiring him to be an artist. Although he considers himself a self-taught artist, Finney says that his father, who earned a degree in art, taught him the basics. He was also influenced by formal training he received in Chinese calligraphy and brush painting while he lived in China.

artist, p.c. 1992

FIRE BEAR (see Standing, William)

FIRESHAKER, FRANKLIN *Ponca*

Ti Ookeah Bahze

Born 12 Aug 1918 in Grayhorse, OK; son of Anna Black Cloud and Joseph Firey Eyes

FRANKLIN FIRESHAKER

At the age of 11, after his mother's death, Fireshaker was adopted by McKinley Horse Chief Eagle and reared by his aunt, Mrs. Albert Four Eyes Roy. "Fireshaker is a dedicated student of Ponca history and

RESIDENCE: Ojai, CA
EDUCATION: Chilocco; BC
OCCUPATION: House painter and artist
MEDIA: Acrylic and watercolor
PUBLISHED: Snodgrass (1968); Brody (1971). *The Indian Trader* (July 1978); *American Indian Crafts and Culture* (Nov 1972); biographical publications
PUBLIC COLLECTIONS: GM, PAC
EXHIBITS: AC/K; GM; HM; ITIC; MPI; PAC; SPIM; VV; Tulsa County Libraries, Tulsa, OK; Art Guild, Kauai, Hawaii
AWARDS: AIE, ITIC, PAC

FIRESHAKER, QUANNAH EAGLE *Ponca/Creek*

Born 1956; daughter of Jerry Ann Marshall and Franklin Fireshaker (q.v.)
RESIDENCE: Muskogee, OK
PUBLISHED: Snodgrass (1968)
EXHIBITS: ITIC, SWAIA
AWARDS: ITIC (student classification), 1964

FIRETHUNDER, DUANE *Oglala Sioux*

Born 2 Feb 1944 at Custer, SD
RESIDENCE: Rapid City, SD
EDUCATION: Lincoln High School, Plankinton, SD
MEDIA: Oil and pencil
EXHIBITS: RC
SOLO EXHIBITS: SIM

FISH (see Vann, Charles Leo)

FISHER, GELINEAU *(?)*

Born 1951 in Longlac, ON, Canada
RESIDENCE: Longlac, ON, Canada
OCCUPATION: Painter
MEDIA: Acrylic
PUBLISHED: Menitove (1986b)
PUBLIC COLLECTIONS: C/AG/TB
EXHIBITS: C/AG/TB; galleries in Geraldton and Thunder Bay, ON

FISHER, SANFORD *Plains Cree*

Born 1927 on Gordon's Reserve; died ca. 1988
RESIDENCE: Regina, SK, Canada
EDUCATION: Anglican boarding school, Gordon's Reserve
OCCUPATION: Painter
MEDIA: Oil
PUBLISHED: *The Indian Trader* (Apr 1979)
PUBLIC COLLECTIONS: C/NHFC, HCC
EXHIBITS: C/AG/TB; C/NHFC; HCC; RC; galleries throughout Canada, primarily the prairie provinces
HONORS: Painting presented as a gift from Canada to the people of China, 1973

FITE, FRANCES M. *Cherokee*

Birth date unknown; daughter of Dr. and Mrs. Pat Fite; P/GF: Dr. Francis B. Fite, first surgeon in Indian Territory and Mayor of Muskogee, OK
RESIDENCE: Muskogee, OK

FRANKLIN FIRESHAKER

(continued) customs. He and his family have traveled 'throughout the world and have learned to speak several languages.' The artist is an authority on Indian dances and is a frequent judge at tribal dance contests. His paintings and murals are done as special commissions."

Snodgrass 1968

Fireshaker's paintings depict the traditions, legends, and rituals of the Ponca tribe.

GELINEAU FISHER

A self-taught artist, Fisher's work has been described as "legend painting with a certain amount of surrealism."

Menitove 1986b

SANFORD FISHER

A train accident in 1972 caused Fisher's left arm to be amputated below the elbow. Because his left hand was his painting hand, it appeared his painting career was over. However, he learned to paint with his right hand with equal success. In fact, in the words of John Anson Warner, "He possesses one of the surest techniques of any of the modern Cree painters." His painting style was that of realism with a distinctive use of color.

John Anson Warner
Sanford Fisher: Realist Painter of the Canadian Plains *(manuscript)*

OCCUPATION: Artist

MEDIA: Oil, acrylic, watercolor, tempera, and pencil

PUBLISHED: *Twin Territories* (Year of the Indian Edition, 1992)

EXHIBITS: CNM, FCTM

AWARDS: CNM ('91); FCTM ('80, 1st; '84; '85; '86, Grand Award; '87; '89; '90; '92, 1st)

Five Kiowas

"In 1926, at Anadarko, Oklahoma, the late Susie C. Peters, then a government field matron, organized a 'Fine Arts Club' for Indian girls and boys who showed talent in drawing and painting pictures, beadwork, and other native work. Mrs. Willie Baze Lane gave them a few lessons and great encouragement.

In 1936, Mrs. Peters recalled, 'about this time I sent some of the fifteen or more boys' and girls' work to Ralph Mores, artist and dealer of Taos, NM. He bought some of the drawings and asked for more to be sent to him. He wrote that these boys had something fine to give to the world. So we were encouraged. Mrs. Lane told me that if I could interest O. B. Jacobson at the University he could make them famous.'

Edith Mahier, member of the teaching staff at the art school of the University of Oklahoma, said, 'Mrs. Peters brought Asah and Hokeah (qq.v.) to Norman one Sunday afternoon. Dr. Jacobson was out of town. She brought the boys' paintings of Indian dancers done on brown paper bags and the covers of shoe boxes. They looked like Leon Bakst, and I felt that I was seeing for the first time an Oklahoma art expression, true and fresh, and deserving of interest from educators.'

In the fall of 1926, Asah, Hokeah, Mopope, and Tsatoke (qq.v.) were taken to the University for an interview. In 1965, Dr. Jacobson recalled, 'the boys had none of the necessary entrance requirements to be enrolled as students in the University and it was just as well, since I did not wish for them to attend regular art classes and absorb the usual things deemed essential in White art.'

Jacobson, then head of the University art school, enlisted the understanding of Miss Mahier, whose office was used as a studio for the boys since 'at no time did they attend regular University art classes.' Mahier did 'a splendid job, giving them instruction in technique, criticisms at the proper time and steady encouragement.' And, as Asah said, 'she understands us.'

Dr. Jacobson assumed the responsibility of more-or-less supporting the students financially during the first four or five months they remained at Norman in 1926-1927. He did so by persuading friends and the University to purchase the boys' paintings. He lectured to clubs and eventually arranged for the group to give programs as a further means of providing interest and income for them. 'Tsatoke was the singer and drummer, Hokeah and Mopope performed the Eagle Dance. Asah, too, was a dancer . . . rhythmic, methodical, ritualistic. Martha, Tsatoke's wife, sang a lullaby.' Miss Mahier also recalls, 'It was never necessary to discuss design and composition or drawing or colors with these boys because they were dancers, singers, and drummers and rhythm was a natural living thing for them.'

There were several prominent people who did not look with favor on Jacobson's work with the Indians. They 'growled at [his] bringing troupes of Indians to give dances in Oklahoma, Texas, and at the noted National Folk Festival in St. Louis, where the performers received further acclaim. They claimed that [he] was wasting valuable time on something that "we must get away from."'

In January, 1927, Lois Smoky joined the four boys at the University, and in the late spring, the boys 'returned to the reservation to plant their crops. In the fall of 1927, the five returned with Auchiah. Lois later became the first to drop from the office-studio classes.'

The group required more financial aid than Dr. Jacobson or the programs could provide if they were to remain at the University. Dr. Jacobson said: 'With the help of Lewis Ware, a Caddo-Kiowa member of the Oklahoma Legislature, we turned to Lew H. Wentz, an oil multimillionaire at Ponca City, Oklahoma. Mr. Wentz was agreeable to help, provided I gave my word that it was a worthwhile project. I gave my word of honor that if he assisted, I would make the boys famous in a few years. Quite an order; one I fear he didn't believe. His support, while far from lavish, was enough to make it possible for the group to devote full-time to painting, with less financial worries. When the Kiowas were ready for shows, I began to secure them a national hearing. I was able to book shows of their works at leading museums and universities throughout the country.' At the First International Art Exposition, held in Prague, Czechoslovakia, in 1928 they created a sensation. The outcome of this exhibit was *Kiowa Indian Art*, published in France in 1929, and later in 1950, *American Indian Painters*. Then after the world had acclaimed it, Oklahoma finally discovered Indian art as a living phenomenon, giving considerable attention to it in the press after such magazines as *American Magazine of Art*, *International Studio*, *Creative Arts*, *Western Arts*, *Connoisseur of London*, had acclaimed it much earlier.

'During the great depression of the 1930s, I was a supervisor of artists on relief in Oklahoma. Among others, I placed all my competent Indian artists to work decorating public, state and federal buildings with murals. When two of the Kiowas were selected to execute murals at the Department of Interior Building in Washington, D.C., I sent a newspaper clipping and a note to Mr. Wentz saying, 'I hereby redeem my promise to you that I'd make these Indians famous,' said Jacobson.

Mrs. Peters had recognized the Kiowa's ability when they were ten years old, and 'gave them watercolors and encouraged them to paint what they knew.' In 1936, however, she said that it was 'through Mr. Jacobson that the small group of Kiowas gained fame.'

'All of our Indian artists, by remaining Indian, have made a magnificent contribution to American culture,' said Jacobson, and continued, 'I am happy to have had a small part in encouraging and coaxing many towards this goal. I fear that I am even guilty of "Indianizing" some who had lost their heritage. . . .'"
Snodgrass 1968

FLAME, THE *Teton Sioux*

Boide

A.K.A. The Blaze

PUBLISHED: Snodgrass (1968). *4th Annual Report*, BAE (1882-1883)

PUBLIC COLLECTIONS: SI/OAA

THE FLAME

"In 1877, the artist lived at Peoria Bottom, 18 miles south of Fort Sully, Dakota Territory. He generally lived with the Sans Arcs, although by birth he was of the Two Kettle group. His Winter Count chart covered a longer period than that of Lone Dog and The Swan (qq.v.)."

Snodgrass 1968

FLETT, GEORGE *Spokane*

Born 20 Oct 1946 in Wellpinit, WA; son of Nancy Brown and Charles Flett

RESIDENCE: Wellpinit, WA

MILITARY: U.S. Army

EDUCATION: Wellpinit (WA) High School, 1964; IAIA, 1966; U of CO

OCCUPATION: Museum curator, museum director, rodeo contestant, silversmith, sculptor, and painter

MEDIA: Oil, acrylic, watercolor, pencil, silver, gold, bronze, stone, and prints

PUBLISHED: *The Indian Trader* (May 1980)

COMMISSIONS: *Buckle designs:* National Finals Rodeo; Washington Rodeo Association; Northwest Junior Rodeo Association; White Swan Treaty Days All-Indian Rodeo. *Medal designs:* Museum of Native American Cultures, Spokane, WA, medal design; Spokane Tribe, medal design

PUBLIC COLLECTIONS: HM; IAIA; MNAC; PAC; St. Joseph (MO) Museum

EXHIBITS: ACS/SM, CIM, CNM, DAM, GFNAAS, HM/G, MPI, MNAC, OWE, PAC, RC, RE, SN, SWAIA, U of WA, UTAE

AWARDS: ACS/SM (1st); GFNAAS; CNM ('87); PAC ('74, Painting Award); SWAIA ('90); UTAE ('92)

FLOOD, DONNA COLLEEN JONES *Shawnee/Ponca*

A.K.A. Signature: Dona

Born 31 May 1937; daughter of Velma Louise Pensoneau and Lee Otis Jones; P/GP: Nancy Bellzona Collins and Joseph Herbert Jones; M/GP: Elizabeth Little Cook Pensoneau-Hernández and Narcisse Pensoneau

RESIDENCE: Ponca City, OK

EDUCATION: Chilocco, 1955; Northern Oklahoma College, Tonkawa, OK; 30 years of private art instruction

OCCUPATION: Art instructor and artist

MEDIA: Oil, acrylic, watercolor, pencil, pen and ink, pastel, and prints

EXHIBITS: KCPA; in TX, OK, and KS

FLORES, FABIAN *Pima*

EXHIBITS: HM/G

AWARDS: HM/G ('70)

FLORES, WILLIAM VANN *Cherokee/Tohono O'odham (Papago)*

Laughing Bull

Born 2 Oct 1927 in Appleton, WI; son of Jesse E. Vann and Alonzo Flores

RESIDENCE: Bethany, OK

MILITARY: U.S. Army, Korean War

EDUCATION: Chilocco, 1947; KCAI/MO, 1950-1952; Los Angeles, 1956-1957; OCU

OCCUPATION: Printer, medical illustrator, cartoonist, lecturer, and artist

PUBLISHED: Snodgrass (1968); Brody (1971). *FAA Horizons* (July 1963); *The Oklahoma Journal* (29 Feb 1965)

PUBLIC COLLECTIONS: HM

EXHIBITS: AAIE; BNIAS; CNM; FAIEAIP; FCTM; HM/G; PAC; SN; galleries in CA, MO, NY, OK, and Washington, D.C.

SOLO EXHIBITS: U of AR

AWARDS: FCTM ('67)

WILLIAM VANN FLORES

Flores is well known for the series of humorous cartoons which he has published over the years.

Dockstader, p.c. 1994

FOLSOM, GORDON L. *Choctaw*

EXHIBITS: CNM, FCTM

AWARDS: FCTM ('80; '82, IH; '83, IH)

FOLSOM, GORDON L., JR. *Choctaw*

RESIDENCE: Tulsa, OK

EXHIBITS: CNM, FCTM, PAC

AWARDS: FCTM ('83, IH); PAC ('79)

FONSECA, HARRY *Maidu*

Born 5 Jan 1946 in Sacramento, CA

RESIDENCE: Sacramento, CA

MILITARY: U.S. Navy

EDUCATION: Sacramento (CA) City College; CSU/S

OCCUPATION: Janitor, business manager, teacher, dancer, printmaker, gallery owner, jeweler, sculptor, and artist

MEDIA: Oil, acrylic, pen and ink, clay, wood, and prints

HARRY FONSECA

In the words of the artist, "My work is of the old, transformed into a contemporary vision." An example of this is Fonseca's Coyote series. In that series he transformed the traditional

PUBLISHED: Anonymous (1976); New (1979); Highwater (1980); Amerson, ed. (1981); Hoffman, et al. (1984); Wade, ed. (1986); Antoine and Bates (1991); Archuleta and Strickland (1991); Zurko, ed. (1992). *Christian Science Monitor* (2 Mar 1988), *The Native American AIDS Prevention Center Resource Catalog*, cover; *The Santa Fe Reporter* (14 Aug 1980); *Arizona Arts and Lifestyle* (autumn 1981); *Four Winds* (winter 1981); *The Albuquerque Journal* (14 Feb 1982); *The Indian Trader* (Aug 1981; June 1989); *New Mexico Craft* (Vol. 3, no. 4, 1981); *The Santa Fean* (Aug 1984); *The Arizona Republic* (21 Sept 1980); *California State Indian Museum* (folder cover); *Albuquerque Journal Magazine* (18 Feb 1986); *Native Vision* (Sept/Oct 1986), cover; *Artists of the Sun*, SWAIA program (1981); *The New Mexican* (18 Aug 1982); *The Fresno Bee* (21 Feb 1988); *Art Week* (14 Dec 1989); *American West* (July 1990); *Native Peoples* (winter 1991); *Tamaqua* (winter/spring 1991); *American Indian Art* (winter 1993).

PUBLIC COLLECTIONS: HM, JAM, USDI, WSAC

EXHIBITS: AICA/SF; AICH; C/U of R/MG; CAM/S; C/U of R/MG; CSU/S; CTC; CWAM; HM; HS/OH; HS/NV; IK; JAM; KCPA; MCC/CA; MFA/O; MM/NJ; MNA/WA; MPI; NACLA; NCHF; NMSF; NU/BC; OAC; OLO; OSU/G; PAC; PAM; PAIC; SFFA; SI; SM; SV; SW; TPAS; U of AZ/G; WNAA; WHB; WWM; International Invitational Exhibit, Hamburg, Germany; Lock Haven Art Center, Orlando, FL, 1985; Northern Illinois University, De Kalb, IL; University of Hawaii, Hilo, HI; see also Awards

SOLO EXHIBITS: AICA/SF, MPI, CNGM, MRFM, MNH/LA, SCG, SM, SWAIA, WWM

AWARDS: NMSF ('79, 1st); SWAIA ('79, 1st; '80, 2-1st, Best of Division); WWM ('78, Best of Show); Auburn Art Festival ('78, Purchase Award); *Indian Art Now*, Santa Fe, NM (Best of Show)

HONORS: *Grants:* California Arts Council, a grant to depict the Maidu story of creation, 1976; California Arts Council, Artist-in-Schools and Community Grant, 1977. *Other:* SWAIA, fellowship, 1980; SWAIA, poster artist, 1982

FOOT (see Belindo, Dennis)

FORD, HENRY *Inuit (Eskimo)*

Born 1925 at Baker Lake, NWT, Canada

RESIDENCE: Baker Lake, NWT, Canada

OCCUPATION: Sculptor and painter

MEDIA: Watercolor and stone

EXHIBITS: C/WICEC; C/YU; Brock University, St. Catherine's, ON, 1979; Niagara College, Welland, ON, 1982; galleries in Niagara-on-the Lake and St. Catherine's, ON

FORD, JACKSON *Kwakwaka'wakw (Kwakiutl)*

PUBLIC COLLECTIONS: DAM

FOSTER, ERIC *Creek*

Born ca. 1958

RESIDENCE: Benbrook, TX

OCCUPATION: Technical designer, illustrator, draftsman, and painter

MEDIA: Pastel, Prismacolor, pencil, pen and ink, and chalk

EXHIBITS: RE

FOSTER, LANCE M. *Iowa*

RESIDENCE: Helena, MT

EXHIBITS: LIAS

HARRY FONSECA

(continued) Indian image of the coyote, the trickster, into that of a survivor who knows how to have a good time in the modern world. In addition to these satirical paintings, Fonseca's earlier series were of the Maidu Sacred Dances and the Maidu Story of Creation. A more recent series is titled Stone Poems. *He has explained, "... the* Stone Poems *are giving me a chance to confront myself in a new world. It is a world where the blacks and whites are slowly, very slowly, turning into grays — with all their shades of uncertainty, fear, growth, and wonder."*

Four Bears

"Prince Maximilian's collection contains examples of paintings by Four Bears, collected during the winter sojourn of Karl Bodmer and the Prince at Fort Clark, 1833-1934 (see Yellow Feather). It is quite possible that Four Bear's interest in painting was spurred by sitting for portraits for Bodmer and George Catlin, the latter having said, 'There is no man amongst the Mandans so generally loved.'"

Snodgrass 1968

Four Horns

In 1870, Four Horns made copies of autobiographical drawings made by Sitting Bull and his adopted son, Jumping Bull. These copies were later sold to Assistant Surgeon James Kimball at Fort Buford, Dakota Territory.

Maurer 1992

Guy Fox

"Fox is a self-taught non-traditionalist painter, who has been active since 1948. His hobby, hunting, is often reflected in his paintings."

Snodgrass 1968

Four Bears *Mandan*

Mato Tope; Mah To Toh Pa

Born ca. 1800; died 30 July 1837 near Fort Clark, ND, in a smallpox epidemic

OCCUPATION: Second chief and the most prominent warrior of the tribe

MEDIA: Watercolor, pencil, pigment, and hide

PUBLISHED: Catlin (1841); Ewers (1939; 1965); Jacobson and d'Ucel (1950); Petersen (1968); Snodgrass (1968); Dockstader (1977); Maurer (1992). *American Indian Art* (summer 1981); *Smithsonian* (Nov 1992)

PUBLIC COLLECTIONS: BM; JAM; MNH/A; NNGCC; Bern (Switzerland) Historical Museum

EXHIBITS: JAM; MIA; VP; St. Louis (MO) Art Museum

Four Horns *Hunkpapa Sioux*

MEDIA: Watercolor and ink

PUBLISHED: Maurer (1992)

PUBLIC COLLECTIONS: SI

EXHIBITS: VP

Fox, Elaine *Arikara/Sioux*

RESIDENCE: Emmet, ND

PUBLISHED: Snodgrass (1968)

EXHIBITS: BNIAS

Fox, Guy *Hidatsa/Sioux*

Bright Wing

Born 4 Mar 1902 on the Fort Berthold Reservation, SD

RESIDENCE: New Town, ND

EDUCATION: Through 7th grade, Pipestone (MN) Indian School

PUBLISHED: Snodgrass (1968)

EXHIBITS: BNIAS

Fox, John *Potawatomi*

A.K.A. Johnny Fox

EDUCATION: IAIA

PUBLISHED: Hill (1992)

PUBLIC COLLECTIONS: IAIA

EXHIBITS: IAIA

Fragua, Augustine *Jémez*

Born 1945

EDUCATION: Jémez; graduated Albuquerque

PUBLISHED: Snodgrass (1968)

EXHIBITS: MNM, PAC

Fragua, Cliff *Jémez*

EXHIBITS: ABQM, SFFA

Fragua, Laura *Jémez/Pecos*

Wa-Pa-Wa-Gie

A.K.A. Laura J. Fragua

EDUCATION: IAIA, 1984

PUBLISHED: *Art-Talk* (Feb 1995)

EXHIBITS: AC/SD, CNM, MFA/O, RC, SWAIA, WWM

AWARDS: CNM ('88, 1st); RC ('83, Aplan Award)

HONORS: RC, Thunderbird Foundation Scholarship, 1983, 1984; IAIA, student body president, 1983-1984

FRANCE, GARY *Seminole*

Born 20 Dec 1939 in Pawnee, OK; son of Vera Franklin and Jim Andrews; P/GP: Fannie Renton and Jim Andrews Sr.; M/GP: Nelly and Moses Perrymon; adopted by his aunt, Thelma Franklin, and Jim France

RESIDENCE: Edmond, OK

EDUCATION: Edwards County High School, 1958; B.A., Roosevelt University, Chicago, IL, 1967; M.S., Illinois State University, 1969, 1972; Ph.D., OSU, 1974

OCCUPATION: Clinical psychologist, author, and painter

MEDIA: Acrylic and prints

PUBLISHED: Biographical publications

PUBLIC COLLECTIONS: FCTM, Seminole Nation Museum, Wewoka, OK

EXHIBITS: CNM; FCTM; HM/G; ITIC; OAC; RC; Canterbury Art Show, Edmond, OK; Edmond (OK) Association of Mental Health Art Show; Edmond (OK) Art Association Gallery

AWARDS: FCTM ('81, IH; '82; '83, 1st, IH; '84, IH; '85, IH); HM/G ('83)

HONORS: NEA Fellowship, 1968-1969

GARY FRANCE

The artist says that the major influence on his art has been the art of Woody Crumbo and Blackbear Bosin (qq.v.). He further credits artists such as: Joan Hill, Enoch Kelly Haney (qq.v), Grace Medicine Flower and the Kiowa Five (q.v.) with inspiring him. According to France, "Al and Scott Momaday [qq.v.] manifest my motto 'Be all you can be.' My major interest in art technique is the use of color and design to convey Indian culture."

artist, p.c. 1992

FRANCIS, JOHN *(?)*

Born 22 June 1950

RESIDENCE: Colville, WA

EDUCATION: Northport (WA) High School, 1968; B.A., Fairhaven College, Bellingham, WA, 1968-1974; Eastern Washington State College, Cheney, WA, summers

COMMISSIONS: *Murals:* Western Washington State College, 1972

EXHIBITS: RC; Drawing and Small Sculpture Show, Ball State University, Muncie, IN; see also Awards

AWARDS: Columbia Basin College Annual Exhibition, Pasco, WA; Drawings '74, Spokane, WA

FRANCIS, PETE *Navajo*

PUBLIC COLLECTIONS: MNA

FRANCISCUS, AUBREY *Navajo*

PUBLIC COLLECTIONS: MNA

FRANCO, D. *Tohono O'odham (Papago)*

PUBLISHED: Snodgrass (1968)

EXHIBITS: AF

FRANCO, MANUEL S. *Apache*

Born 19 Feb 1946; son of Soledad and Eleuterio Franco Jr.; P/GP: Micaela and Eleuterio Franco Sr.; M/GP: Anita and Andrés Juárez

RESIDENCE: Dumas, TX

EDUCATION: Escuela Preparatoria, Mexico (1969); University of Chihuahua, Mexico, 1974; Moore County Art Center, TX

OCCUPATION: Artist

MEDIA: Oil, watercolor, pencil, pen and ink, bronze, and prints

EXHIBITS: SWAIA; Art Expo, Los Angeles, CA; Rotary Club Show, Amarillo, TX; Annual High Plains Epilepsy Association Art Show, Amarillo, TX; National Western Stock Show, Denver, CO; galleries in CA, CO, NM, and TX; see also Awards

AWARDS: Top of Texas Art Fest, Pampa, TX (Best of Show); Cimarron County Art Show, TX (Best of Show)

FRANK, CHARLIE *Nuu-Chah-Nulth (Nootka)*

Kwya Tseeck Tchuss Miyuh

Born 1953 in Port Renfrew, near Tofino Inlet, BC, Canada

EDUCATION: Studied with Joe David and Ron Hamilton (qq.v.)

OCCUPATION: Carver and graphic artist

MEDIA: Pen and ink

PUBLISHED: Stewart (1979)

PUBLIC COLLECTIONS: C/RBCM, HCC

EXHIBITS: SDSMT

FRANKLIN, CARMEN MEEDEN *Washoe/Paiute/Quechan*

RESIDENCE: Converse, TX

EXHIBITS: CNM ('87)

FRANKLIN, ERNEST, SR. *Navajo*

Born 1942

RESIDENCE: Gallup, NM

EDUCATION: Albuquerque, 1960; U of AZ, "Southwest Indian Art Project," scholarship

MEDIA: Watercolor

PUBLISHED: Snodgrass (1968); Jacka and Jacka (1994)

EXHIBITS: HM/G, ITIC, MNM, SN

AWARDS: ITIC ('76; '86, 1st; '87; '89, 1st; '90; '91; '92, 2-1st; '93, 2-1st, Best in Category; '94, 3-1st, Best In Category, Mullarky Award); MNM ('60)

FRANKLIN, HERMAN *Sauk-Fox*

Born 1912

EDUCATION: Chilocco; Haskell

PUBLISHED: Snodgrass (1968). *The Oklahoma Indian School Magazine* (Nov 1932)

EXHIBITS: AIEC

FRANKLIN, WILLIAM B. *Navajo*

A.K.A. Bill Franklin; W. B. Franklin

Born 17 May 1947 at Ganado, AZ; son of Amy and Scott Franklin; M/GF: Hosteen Roan Horse

RESIDENCE: Flagstaff, AZ

EDUCATION: Galileo High School, San Francisco, CA, 1971; U of N AZ

OCCUPATION: Sociologist, energy planner, silversmith; full-time painter since 1986

MEDIA: Oil, acrylic, watercolor, pencil, pen and ink, pastel, stone, silver, gemstone, and prints

PUBLISHED: Jacka and Jacka (1988; 1994). *Plateau* (Vol. 54, no. 1, 1982); *Arizona Highways* (May 1986); *Phoenix Home and Garden* (Jan 1988); *The Indian Trader* (Aug 1989; Nov 1989); *Santa Fe Reporter* (Aug 1994)

COMMISSIONS: Sacred Lands Project, Washington, D.C., *Cry The Sacred Ground*, illustrations, 1986

EXHIBITS: HM/G; ITIC; MCC/CA; MNA; SDMM; SWAIA; Tokyo Book Fair, Tokyo, Japan (1990); Native Americans for Community Action-Benefit Art Show, Flagstaff, AZ; Verde Valley Art Association Show, Jerome, AZ

WILLIAM B. FRANKLIN

Franklin's earliest artistic efforts were as a silversmith. In 1977, he switched his emphasis to paints and canvas.

artist, p.c. 1990

SOLO EXHIBITS: WWM, 1994

AWARDS: ITIC ('94); MNA ('74, 1st; '81, 1st, Special Division Award; '84, 1st; '85, 1st; '86, 1st); SWAIA ('80; '81, 1st; '84, 1st, Hines Award; '85, 1st, Best of Division, Best of Class; '86, Hardin Award; '89)

HONORS: SSWAIA Fellowship; Northland Press, Inc., trip to Tokyo Book Fair, Tokyo, Japan, 1990; SWAIA, poster artist, 1994

FRANKS, RHONDA *Cree/Ojibwa*

Tora Qua Tay, Shines Like The Moon

Born 1959 near Bala, ON, Canada, close to the Mohawk reservation on Gibson River

OCCUPATION: Artist

PUBLIC COLLECTIONS: C/CMC; throughout the U.S. and Canada

EXHIBITS: C/WICEC

RHONDA FRANKS

The subjects of Franks' paintings are the result of her close observation of nature and interpretations of Native legends.

gallery brochure

FRASER-KING, MARILYN *Blackfoot*

Born 1954 in Ponoka, AB, Canada

RESIDENCE: Calgary, AB, Canada

EDUCATION: C/ACA; 1984-1987; C/U of C, 1988; C/ACA, 1987-1990; C/U of C, 1990

MEDIA: Acrylic

PUBLISHED: Cardinal-Schubert (1992)

COMMISSIONS: *Illustrations: Kainai News*, Cardston, AB, Christmas scenes, 1980; Blood Tribe Education Board video production, 1990. *Other:* Viscount Bennett High School, yearbook cover design and school crest, 1972

PUBLIC COLLECTIONS: C/AIAC; C/IAA; C/NCC/AB; Alberta Native Secretariat; Blood Tribe Administration, Standoff, AB; Kainai News, Cardston, AB; Ninastako Culture; Universiade Collection, Edmonton, AB

EXHIBITS: C/AM; C/TFD; C/TGVA; Esso Plaza, Calgary, AB

AWARDS: C/AM ('87, Second Runner-up Award, $500 bursary; '88; '90); *Blood Tribe Irrigation Summary* Cover Design Contest (1st)

FRAZIER, CAROL LEE *Paiute*

RESIDENCE: Nixon, NV

EDUCATION: IAIA, 1965-1966

PUBLISHED: Snodgrass (1968)

EXHIBITS: HM/G, PAC, SN, YAIA

AWARDS: PAC ('75), SN ('69)

FREDENBERG, DENISE *Menomini*

EXHIBITS: HM/G

AWARDS: HM/G ('70)

FREDERICKS, OSWALD (see White Bear)

FREDERICKS, TERRA COONS *Cherokee*

EXHIBITS: CNM, LIAS

FREE, JOHN D. *Osage/Cherokee*

Born 1929 in Pawhuska, OK

OCCUPATION: Cowboy, rancher, sculptor, and painter

MEDIA: Oil, pastel, pencil, and bronze

PUBLISHED: Samuels (1982; 1985)

PUBLIC COLLECTIONS: CAA, NAWA, NCHF

JOHN D. FREE

Even though of Indian heritage, Free is primarily considered a "Western" artist, as indicated by his membership in NAWA and CAA. His works are based on his experiences growing up on a ranch.

Samuels 1982

EXHIBITS: NAWA
SOLO EXHIBITS: NCHF (1971)
AWARDS: NAWA ('79, Silver Medal)
HONORS: CAA, membership; NAWA, membership

FREEMAN, ROBERT LEE *Luiseño/Sioux*

Born 14 Jan 1939 at Valley Center, CA on the Rincón Indian Reservation; son of Pauline Pratt and Herman Freeman; artist is a descendant of Bone Necklace, Sub-chief of the Santee Sioux

RESIDENCE: Murreta, CA
MILITARY: U.S. Army, Korea, 1957-1960
EDUCATION: Escondido (CA) High School, 1957; Mira Costa Junior College, Oceanside, CA; Palomar College, San Marcos, CA, 1976
OCCUPATION: Teacher, author, lecturer, gallery owner, sculptor, and painter
MEDIA: Oil, acrylic, watercolor, pencil, pen and ink, mixed-media, wood, metal, and prints
PUBLISHED: Snodgrass (1968); Libhart (1970); Brody (1971); Medina (1981); Samuels (1982); Kilman (1984). *Western Horseman; Ford Times; Gene Magazine; Southwest Art Scene; Indian Voices; The Indian Trader* (Aug 1989); biographical publications
BOOKS ILLUSTRATED: Freeman (1971; 1981)
COMMISSIONS: *Murals:* Los Angeles County Library, San Gabriel, CA, 1984; State Museum, Lake Perris, CA, 1986
PUBLIC COLLECTIONS: HCC; HM; IAC; SIM; Gonzaga University, Spokane, WA
EXHIBITS: AAID; AICA; CPS; CSP; HCC; HM; HM/G; HPTU; IACB; ITIC; LAC; LGAM; LSS; MCC/CA; RC; SAIEAIP; SIM; SDMM; SN; TM/NE; U of WV; WTF; San Diego (CA) County Fair; galleries in AZ, CO, MO, OK, SD
SOLO EXHIBITS: SIM, 1972; Oceanside, CA, 1962
AWARDS: Partial listing of more than 150 includes: AAID ('70; '72, 1st); AICA ('78, Gold Award); HM/G ('71; '72, 1st; '74, 1st; 76, 1st; '77); ITIC ('72, Elkus Award; '79, 1st); OT; RC ('73, 1st; '74, 2-1st; '76, 1st; '77, 1st; '78, 1st, Begay Award; '79, 1st; '80; '83, Woodard Award, Pepion Family Award; '85, Woodard Award; '89; '90, Decker Award; '91, Barkley Art Center Award; '92, Barkley Art Center Award, Rostkowski Award; '93, 1st); SN ('64, 1st; '65; '67; '68; '69, 1st, *Phoenix Gazette* Award; '70, 1st; '71; '72, 1st)

ROBERT LEE FREEMAN

Freeman began to paint in 1961 and, since 1980, the majority of his work has been done in the etching medium. His favorite subject has always been the everyday world of today's Indian people, both the good and the bad.

artist, p.c. 1990

The artist is a member of The Dream Catchers Artists Guild, Ltd. (q.v.).

FREEMONT, NAOMI *Santee Sioux*

Born 36 Dec 1934
EDUCATION: Haskell; MMC
EXHIBITS: RC; see also Awards
AWARDS: MMC Art Show (1st)

FREIMARK, ROBERT M. *Chippewa*

RESIDENCE: Toledo, OH
PUBLISHED: Snodgrass (1968)
EXHIBITS: PAC

FROMAN, ROBERT *Peoria/Miami*

EDUCATION: BC
PUBLISHED: Snodgrass (1968)
EXHIBITS: PAC

FRONEBERGER, PHIL *(?)*

Born in Forth Worth, TX

MEDIA: Oil, pencil, and pen and ink

EXHIBITS: TIAF; see also Awards

AWARDS: TIAF ('92); Chickasha (OK) Art Guild ('87, Best of Show); Great Southern Plains Indian Rendezvous, Anadarko, OK ('87, 1st); Festival of Lights, Oklahoma City, OK ('87, Gold Medal)

FULLER, BRYON *Navajo*

PUBLIC COLLECTIONS: MNA

FULLER, CAROL *Cherokee/Choctaw*

RESIDENCE: Pryor, OK

EXHIBITS: CNM, FCTM

AWARDS: CNM ('87, Special Merit Award); FCTM ('88)

Gabriel, Ellen *Mohawk*

RESIDENCE: Canada

PUBLISHED: *Newsletter,* NASAC/ACEAA (winter 1991)

EXHIBITS: C/AMO

Gachupín, Juan *Jémez*

PUBLISHED: Snodgrass (1968)

PUBLIC COLLECTIONS: MIA, MNA, MNM, SM

Gachupín, Manuelino *Jémez*

Born 1934

PUBLISHED: Snodgrass (1968)

PUBLIC COLLECTIONS: MNM

Gachupín, Mary *Jémez*

EDUCATION: Jémez; studied art under Al Momaday (q.v.)

PUBLISHED: Tanner (1973)

PUBLIC COLLECTIONS: MNA

Gachupín, Maxine *Jémez*

Born 1948

RESIDENCE: Jémez Pueblo, NM

EDUCATION: Jémez; St. Catherine's; IAIA

PUBLISHED: Snodgrass (1968); Fawcett and Callander (1982)

PUBLIC COLLECTIONS: MIA, MNA

EXHIBITS: AAIE, AC/SD, MNM, NACLA, PAC, SFFA, SN

AWARDS: MNM, PAC, SN

Maxine Gachupín

When Gachupín was a child, she exhibited in the Annual Indian Art Exhibition (PAC) in the student classification. Her art was submitted by her teacher, Al Momaday (q.v.). Snodgrass purchased a painting and later sold it to the Museum of the American Indian. It was subsequently reproduced on note cards.

Snodgrass, p.c. 1992

Gachupín, Paul *Jémez*

Born 1947

EDUCATION: Jémez

PUBLISHED: Tanner (1973)

EXHIBITS: AAIE, ITIC

AWARDS: ITIC ('58, student division)

Gachupín, Rose M. *Jémez*

EDUCATION: Jémez

PUBLISHED: Snodgrass (1968)

PUBLIC COLLECTIONS: MNM, MNA

EXHIBITS: MNM, SN

AWARDS: MNM

Gachupín, Waldo *Zia*

PUBLISHED: Snodgrass (1968)

PUBLIC COLLECTIONS: SM

Gaco, Philip *Laguna*

RESIDENCE: Paguate Pueblo, NM

EDUCATION: St. Catherine's, 1965

PUBLISHED: Snodgrass (1968)

EXHIBITS: MNM, PAC

Gad-Hi-Ya (see Joachim, Lola Kathryn)

Gahatageyat (see Crouse, Bill)

DETAIL: Agnes Gough, *Eskimo Ceremonial Dancers,* 1952. Philbrook Museum of Art, Tulsa, Oklahoma

GA HEA KA (see Two-Arrows, Tom)

GAHGAHGEH (see Thomas, Roy)

GAHN (see Johnson, Garrison)

GALLOWAY, LENET *Bannock/Shoshoni*

Born 24 May 1955; daughter of Althea Stone Keating and Roderick Galloway; P/GP: Lillian Dixie and Charles Galloway; M/GP: Ramona Kutch and Charles Stone

RESIDENCE: San Diego, CA

EDUCATION: Mission Bay High School, San Diego, CA, 1973; Mesa (AZ) Community College; SDSU

OCCUPATION: Laboratory computer operator, jeweler, sculptor, and painter

MEDIA: Acrylic, watercolor, pencil, pen and ink, precious metals and gemstone

EXHIBITS: CNM; see also Awards

AWARDS: Del Mar Exposition ('87; '88, 1st); Rose Society National Rose Show ('86, 1st); Shoshoni-Bannock Festival ('90)

GALVÁN, ANDRÉS *Zia*

Henate, Cloud

A.K.A. Signature: Henate

Born early 1900s

PUBLISHED: Snodgrass (1968); Seymour (1988)

PUBLIC COLLECTIONS: DAM, IACB/DC

EXHIBITS: NGA, WRTD

ANDRÉS GALVÁN

Many of Galván's paintings were collected by Amelia Elizabeth White of Santa Fe, an important early supporter of Indian Art. According to José Rey Toledo (q.v.), "... He drew very many authentic designs for her. She collected a lot of his paintings."

Seymour 1988

GAMBLE, THOMAS J. *Navajo*

EDUCATION: Albuquerque, 1961

PUBLISHED: Snodgrass (1968)

EXHIBITS: MNM

GAMEL, GERALDINE *Cherokee*

A.K.A. Jerry G. Gamel

Born 6 Mar 1927; daughter of Lora and Hobart Smith; P/GF: W. T. Smith; M/GP: Elbie and Tom Cloud

RESIDENCE: Shawnee, OK

EDUCATION: Central High School, Oklahoma City, 1945; Seminole (OK) Junior College; St. Gregory College, Shawnee, OK

OCCUPATION: Teacher and artist

MEDIA: Oil, pencil, pastel, charcoal, and prints

PUBLIC COLLECTIONS: St. Gregory College, Shawnee, OK; Rock Creek Church

EXHIBITS: CNM; OSC; VIP Cafeteria, Baptist Hospital; galleries in FL, MS, and OK

GAMEL, JERRY G. (see Gamel, Geraldine)

GA NE SHEKA (see Supernaw, Kugee)

GAON YAH (see Smith, Ernest)

GARBUTT, YVONNE *Ojibwa*

Born 1964 in Peterborough, ON, Canada

EDUCATION: B.A., C/U of G, 1967

OCCUPATION: Painter

PUBLIC COLLECTIONS: C/INAC

EXHIBITS: C/AG/W, C/QU, C/U of G, C/WICEC

GARCÍA, ALEXANDER *San Juan*

Birth date unknown; born in New Mexico
EDUCATION: IAIA
PUBLISHED: Snodgrass (1968)
EXHIBITS: FAIEAIP, YAIA

GARCÍA, CARLOS *San Juan*

Nanatside
Birth date unknown
RESIDENCE: Once lived in Chamita, NM
PUBLISHED: Snodgrass (1968)
EXHIBITS: AIEC

GARCÍA, ERNEST P. *Isleta*

Oysla
Born 25 Jan 1944 in Los Angeles, CA; son of Ignacita B. Cordova and Climoca D. García
EDUCATION: Sierra High School, Whittier, CA, 1962; Río Hondo Junior College, Whittler, CA; Cerritos Junior College, Norwalk, CA
OCCUPATION: Commercial screen painter and artist
PUBLISHED: Snodgrass (1968)
EXHIBITS: FAIEAIP, PAC

GARCÍA, FRANK *Hopi*

PUBLIC COLLECTIONS: MNA

GARCÍA, JOSÉ J. *Santo Domingo*

Born 8 Aug 1914 at Santo Domingo Pueblo, NM
RESIDENCE: Peña Blanca, NM
EDUCATION: Santa Fe, ca. 1937
OCCUPATION: Painter; silversmith since 1942
MEDIA: Tempera
PUBLISHED: Dunn (1968); Snodgrass (1968); Seymour (1988)
PUBLIC COLLECTIONS: IACB/DC, MNA, SM
EXHIBITS: AIEC, HM, WRTD

GARCÍA, LORENZO *Santo Domingo*

RESIDENCE: Peña Blanca, NM
MILITARY: WWII
EDUCATION: Santa Fe; studied under Dorothy Dunn
PUBLISHED: Dunn (1968); Snodgrass (1968)
PUBLIC COLLECTIONS: GM
EXHIBITS: AIW, NGA

GARCÍA, MARCELINO *San Juan*

Born 1932
PUBLISHED: Snodgrass (1968)
PUBLIC COLLECTIONS: MNM

GARCÍA, MARÍA *(?)*

Aukemah
EDUCATION: Studied under Acee Blue Eagle (q.v.)
PUBLISHED: Snodgrass (1968)
PUBLIC COLLECTIONS: MAI

EXHIBITS: PAC

GARCÍA, PETER *Acoma*

RESIDENCE: San Juan Pueblo, NM
EDUCATION: Santa Fe
PUBLISHED: Snodgrass (1968)
PUBLIC COLLECTIONS: HCC, SPL
EXHIBITS: Throughout New Mexico

GARCÍA, RUTH BUSSEY *Cherokee*

Born 25 Aug 1916 in Claremore, OK; M/GP: Eliza Downing and Willie Vann, who arrived in Oklahoma on the "Trail of Tears"
RESIDENCE: Albuquerque, NM
EDUCATION: Hominy (OK) Public Schools; Oaks Indian Mission, OK
OCCUPATION: Art instructor, occupational therapist, arts and crafts instructor; portrait artist
PUBLISHED: Snodgrass (1968)
EXHIBITS: NMSF; YWCA; New Mexico Health Building, Albuquerque, NM; Bacas Restaurant, Albuquerque, NM; Cedars Supper Club, Cedar Crest, NM

GARDNER, DARRELL A. *Ute*

Born 30 Dec 1934
RESIDENCE: Whiterocks, UT
EDUCATION: Through 8th grade
EXHIBITS: ITIC; RC; U of UT; Utah State Capitol Building, Salt Lake City, UT; Utah State Fair
AWARDS: Several 1sts

GARRIOTT, DOROTHY *Cherokee*

Born 17 Aug 1929; daughter of Bonnie Moore and Troy Edgar Wall; P/GP: Jemima Combest and Newton DeCalb Wall; M/GP: Inez Isabelle Pitts and Coleman Harvell Moore
RESIDENCE: Oklahoma City, OK
EDUCATION: Capital Hill High School, Oklahoma City, OK, 1947; South Community Junior College, Oklahoma City, OK
OCCUPATION: Artist
MEDIA: Oil, pencil, and pastel
EXHIBITS: BB; CNM; State Capital Cafeteria, Oklahoma City, OK; Baptist Hospital, Oklahoma City, OK; see also Awards
AWARDS: Central Oklahoma Art Association Exhibition (Judge's Choice, Member's Choice); El Reno (OK) Art Festival; Eufaula (OK) Art Guild Show; Hobart (OK) Art Festival; Crossroads Mall Art Show, Oklahoma City, OK; Penn Square Art Show, Oklahoma City, OK

GARZA, MARIO *Mescalero Apache*

RESIDENCE: Austin, TX
EXHIBITS: LIAS

GASDIA, TERRY *Hopi*

RESIDENCE: Tuba City, AZ
EXHIBITS: LIAS

GASEOMA, LEE ROY *Hopi*

PUBLISHED: Snodgrass (1968)
PUBLIC COLLECTIONS: MAI

GASEOMA, LOREN *Hopi*

PUBLIC COLLECTIONS: MNA

GASHWYTEWA, IVAN S. *Hopi*

OCCUPATION: Carver and painter

PUBLISHED: Snodgrass (1968)

PUBLIC COLLECTIONS: MNM (painting)

IVAN S. GASHWYTEWA

"In addition to his paintings, the artist is considered an outstanding carver of katsina *dolls."*

Snodgrass 1968

GASPAR, PETER *Zuni*

RESIDENCE: Zuni Pueblo, NM

EDUCATION: Santa Fe, 1958

PUBLISHED: Snodgrass (1968); Brody (1971)

PUBLIC COLLECTIONS: MNM, SMNAI

EXHIBITS: AAIE, ITIC, MNM

AWARDS: ITIC, MNM

GASPÉ, GASTON *Mohawk*

Born 12 Dec 1933

RESIDENCE: Oka, PQ, Canada

EDUCATION: Montréal (PQ) College, 1947-1953; B.G.A., Pédagogie Artistique degree, Fine Arts School of Montréal, PQ, 1963, 1966

OCCUPATION: Teacher, photographer, graphic artist, and painter

MEDIA: Watercolor, pen and ink, charcoal, and film

PUBLISHED: Johannsen and Ferguson, eds. (1983)

EXHIBITS: Indian Handicraft Exhibit, Winnipeg, MB; local and regional exhibits

GAUTHIER, ANTHONY *Menomini/Winnebago*

Born 13 Nov 1942 on the Menomini Reservation, WI

RESIDENCE: Baraboo, WI

MILITARY: 101st Airborne Division

EDUCATION: Shawano (WI) High School; IAIA, 1975-1978; A.F.A., NM Highlands U, 1979

OCCUPATION: Tribal employee, sculptor, and painter

MEDIA: Pastel and mixed-media

PUBLISHED: New (1981); Hill (1992). *Southwest Art* (June 1992)

COMMISSIONS: *Murals:* Menomini Tribe of Wisconsin, high school and clinic

PUBLIC COLLECTIONS: IAIA

EXHIBITS: IAIA; NACLA; SIM; RC; U of WI/G; Highland University Library, Las Vegas, NM, 1979

GAUTHIER, JOHN *Menomini/Winnebago*

Born 14 July 1946

RESIDENCE: Keshena, WI

MILITARY: U.S. Marine Corps

EDUCATION: Shawano (WI) High School; B.S., U of WI, 1976; IAIA; B.A., U of WI/M

OCCUPATION: Teacher, bead and feather work instructor, gallery owner, and artist

MEDIA: Acrylic, pencil, beads, and feathers

COMMISSIONS: *Murals:* Partial listing includes: Menomini School District; Menomini Medical Center; Menomini Tribe of Wisconsin

EXHIBITS: SIM; regional exhibits

HONORS: Wisconsin Arts Board, Individual Artist Grant, 1984

GAWBOY, CARL *Chippewa*

Born 21 May 1943 in Cloquet on the Fond du Lac Reservation, MN; son of Helmi Jarvinen and Robert Gawboy; P/GF: Martha and James Gawboy; M/GP: Alexandra and Isaac Jarvinen

RESIDENCE: Bennett, WI

EDUCATION: Ely (MN) High School, 1960; B.A., U of MN, 1965; M.A., U of MT, 1972

OCCUPATION: High school art teacher, assistant professor, bilingual curriculum specialist, consultant, lecturer, gallery owner, and painter

MEDIA: Oil, acrylic, watercolor, pen and ink, pencil, and prints

PUBLISHED: Snodgrass (1968); Highwater (1980); Katz (1980); New (1981). *Minneapolis/St. Paul Magazine* (July 1981); *The Indian Trader* (Nov 1985); biographical publications

BOOKS ILLUSTRATED: Martinson (1977)

COMMISSIONS: *Murals:* HS/MN, 1973; BSU, 1977; Nett Lake (MN) Government Center, 1979; Ely (MN) Miner's Museum, 1983

PUBLIC COLLECTIONS: BSU; HS/MN; IACB; MIM; SIM; Agar, Juring, and Whitman Associates, Duluth, MN; Augsburg College, Minneapolis, MN; City of Petrozavodsk, USSR; Ely-Bloomington (MN) Community Hospital; Ely-Winton (MN) Historical Society; Federal Reserve Bank, MN; First Bank, Duluth, MN; Minnesota Chippewa Tribe, Cass Lake, MN; Northwestern Bank of Commerce, Duluth, MN

EXHIBITS: CNM; HN; MIA; NACLA; NCC; OAE; PAC; PBS; SIM; SN; TE; Mille Lacs Indian Museum, MN, 1981; Minnesota Zoological Gardens, Shakopee, MN, 1983; see also Awards

SOLO EXHIBITS: Partial listing of more than 14 includes: HS/MN; MRNAC; U of MN/TC; U of WI/EC; U of WI/M; WSU; Augsburg College, Minneapolis, MN, 1978

AWARDS: NCC; OAE ('90, 1st; '95, 1st; 16 additional awards); SN ('73); Wisconsin Indian Art Festival

HONORS: BSU, artist-in-residence; Grand Marais Art Colony, artist-in-residence; National Association of Indian Artists, 1986; Lake Superior Watercolor Society, 1988

CARL GAWBOY

The artist considers himself to be a "Regional Realist," a style that developed independent of the Southwest influence, but not in reaction to it. His main themes are the land and the Ojibwa people of northern Minnesota where he grew up.

Highwater 1980

GAYTON, KATHERINE *Sioux*

Born 21 Mar 1947 in Berlin, WI; daughter of Evelyn and James Gayton; P/GP: Ann and Charles Gayton; M/GP: Elizabeth and Steve Wermes

RESIDENCE: Wildrose, WI

EDUCATION: Riverside High School, Milwaukee, WI; certificate in art advertising, Minneapolis, MN

MEDIA: Oil, pen and ink, pencil, and prints

PUBLISHED: *The Indian Trader* (Nov 1984)

PUBLIC COLLECTIONS: HCC

EXHIBITS: CNM; HCC; LIAS; SIM; SNAICF; RC; Mondak Heritage Center, Sidney, MT; see also Awards

SOLO EXHIBITS: SIM

AWARDS: Rural Rembrandt Art Show, Wautoma, WI ('74); Waupaca (WI) Art Show ('89)

KATHERINE GAYTON

The artist says, "The Native American culture and people are fascinating, and my goal is to portray the lifestyle and culture of the people so that the public may be educated and have a better understanding of the Native American people."

p.c. 1990

GEDI (see Joachim, Lola Kathryn)

GEIONETY, GEORGE *Kiowa/Comanche*

Beikoigei, Water Bag to Travel; *Geionety*, Comanche Enemy; *Oyebi*, Side Of A Mountain

GEORGE GEIONETY

Geionety says that his inspiration to "really paint" came in the 1930s when he saw a picture on buckskin at Fort Sill that had been painted by Haungooah (Silverhorn) (q.v.), a well-known early Kiowa painter. Geionety's grandfather, Haubaht, and Silverhorn were very close friends, and when Haubaht died Silverhorn raised his daughter (Geionety's mother). The artist credits Mrs. Templeton, wife of the pastor at Mt. Scott Methodist Church, with being the one who encouraged him to paint.

artist, p.c. 1982

According to his son, Geionety had stopped painting by 1992.

Born 23 Oct 1913 in a tipi on a campground surrounding the old Red Store, north of the Indian Hospital in Cache, OK; father of Ron Geionety (q.v.); P/GF: Haubaht; M/GF: Stumblingbear, Kiowa chief and a signer of the Medicine Lodge (KS) treaty, 1876

RESIDENCE: Apache, OK

EDUCATION: Lakeview (OK) Public School, west of Lake Lawtonka, 1922-1923; Fort Sill, OK, 1924-1928

MEDIA: Tempera

PUBLISHED: Snodgrass (1968); Boyd, et al. (1983)

PUBLIC COLLECTIONS: CGPS, MNA, USDI

EXHIBITS: CGPS, CSPIP, GM, PAC, SPIM, VV

GEIONETY, R. W. *Kiowa*

A.K.A. Ron Geionety

Born 17 July 1950; son of George Geionety (q.v.); GGF: Stumblingbear, Kiowa chief and a signer of the peace treaty at Medicine Lodge (KS), 1876

RESIDENCE: Anadarko, OK

MILITARY: U.S. Marine Corps, 1967-1971

EDUCATION: Custer High School, 1968; Lawton (OK) Police Academy

OCCUPATION: Police officer, refrigeration technician, business owner; full-time painter since 1992

MEDIA: Watercolor, pencil, and prints

COMMISSIONS: U.S. Marine Corps, division logo

EXHIBITS: ACAI; EM; LIAS; RE; TIAF; TWF; WIAME; Tribal Reflections Festival of Art, Houston, TX

AWARDS: TIAF ('95, 1st); RE ('94)

GENE, JACK TOBÁÁHE *Navajo*

Tobááhe, Navajo Clan

A.K.A. Signature: Jackie Gene Tobááhe

Born 14 Sept 1953 in Winslow, AZ

RESIDENCE: Winslow, AZ

EDUCATION: Holbrook (AZ) High School, 1972; CAC/AZ; North American College of Data Processing; Scottsdale (AZ) Artists' School, 1984-1988

OCCUPATION: Lecturer, actor, and painter

MEDIA: Acrylic, watercolor, and mixed-media

PUBLISHED: *The Winslow Mail* (July 1980; Apr 1985); *The Arizona Republic* (4 May 1983); *The Navajo Times* (1984); *The Indian Trader* (Jan 1985); *The Scottsdale Progress* (1 Apr 1988); *The Navajo-Hopi Observer* (7 Feb 1990); *Art-Talk* (Feb 1991; Mar 1991); *The Albuquerque Journal* (13 Aug 1991)

PUBLIC COLLECTIONS: NTM; Alta Home Management; Chinle (AZ) Indian Hospital; Leasing Corporations of America; Products Incorporated

EXHIBITS: ACS/ENP; CNM; FNAA; HM/G; ITIC; MNA; NCC; NICCAS; NTF; NTM; SM; SNAICF; SWAIA; TAAII; WIEAS; WWM; Fountain Hills (AZ) Art Show; Mountain Oyster Club, Western Art Show, Tucson, AZ; Scottsdale (AZ) Artist's School

SOLO EXHIBITS: NTM

AWARDS: ACS/ENP ('87; '88); HM/G ('92, Best of Class, Best of Division; '93, Best of Show); ITIC ('76); MNA ('91, 1st); NICCAS; NTF; SM; SNAICF ('88, Best of Show; '89, Saunders Award); SWAIA ('89, 1st, Best of Division, Hinds Memorial Award; '90, 1st); TAAII; WIEAS ('80; '81, 1st, Best of Show)

HONORS: SWAIA Fellowship, 1991; SNAICF, poster artist, 1989

JACK TOBÁÁHE GENE

The artist says, "I describe myself as a 'cultural painter' from the Navajo community, depicting the diversity of Native peoples in a contemporary society. My pastels reflect my life experiences as taught to me by my grandfather, a medicine man, and my grandmother, a herbalist. . . . I paint Native peoples as they are today, integrating contemporary icons with traditional ways of life. In my compositions, I am striving to balance realistic images that are supported by abstract shapes and forms."

p.c. 1992

GENEHA (see Blacksheep, Beverly)

GENERAL, DAVID M. *Oneida*

Tawit, David

Born 1950 on the Six Nations Reserve, ON, Canada

RESIDENCE: Six Nations Reserve, ON, Canada

EDUCATION: Graduated, Hagersville, ON; B.A., Wilfred Laurier University, Waterloo, ON; Hamilton (ON) Teachers College.

OCCUPATION: Ironworker/high-rise construction, teacher, sculptor, and painter. Initially a painter, the artist is now best known for his sculpture.

PUBLISHED: *The Indian Trader* (July 1978); *Native Perspective* (Vol. 3, no. 2, 1978); *The Kitchener-Waterloo Record* (12 Mar 1980); *The Brantford Expositor* (14 May 1982; 3 Oct 1982; 19 Sept 1983)

COMMISSIONS: Wayne Gretzky Charity Tennis Classic, trophy design, 1982

PUBLIC COLLECTIONS: C/CMC, C/INAC, C/NAITC, C/SCC, C/WICEC

EXHIBITS: C/AC/TB; C/LTAT; C/NCCT; C/NNEC; C/WICEC; Inukshuk Gallery, Waterloo, ON; McDonald Gallery, Government of Ontario, Toronto, ON; Ontario Crafts Council, Toronto, ON; Seneca College, Toronto, ON; Sir Wilfred Laurier University, Waterloo, ON; The Buckhorn (ON) Wild Life Festival

SOLO EXHIBITS: C/AC/TB, C/WICEC

HONORS: *Grants:* Department of Indian and Northern Affairs, Ottawa, ON; Ontario Arts Council

GENESKELOS *Haida*

Birth date unknown; died ca. 1876 of smallpox

OCCUPATION: Tattoo artist and carver

MEDIA: Tattoo

PUBLISHED: *American Indian Art* (summer 1981)

PUBLIC COLLECTIONS: SI

EXHIBITS: SI

GENESKELOS

Geneskelos was the brother of Kitkun, the principal chief of a Haida village, and was a carver and tattooer of renown. In the spring of 1873, James Gilcrist Swan, while collecting for the Smithsonian Institution in the Northwest Coast area, copied tattoos off of the breasts, backs, arms and legs of a group of Haida Indians. He was able to identify two of these as having been done by Geneskelos. He later engaged Geneskelos and another Haida artist to paint a canoe that he had purchased for the Smithsonian. According to John C. Ewers (1981), these are the earliest known Haida graphic designs that are identified as having been done by a specific artist.

American Indian Art
summer 1981

GEORGE, DAVID L. *Shawnee/Delaware*

RESIDENCE: Tulsa, OK

EXHIBITS: CNM, PAC

GERARD-MITCHELL, BARBARA *Blackfeet*

Born 15 Sept 1952 in Cut Bank, MT; daughter of Marjorie Brown and James Gerard; P/GP: Rose Douglas and Fredrick Gerard; M/GP: Rose Connolly and James Brown

RESIDENCE: Roundup, MT

EDUCATION: Cut Bank (MT) High School, 1971; Eastern Montana College, Billings, MT

OCCUPATION: Artist

PUBLIC COLLECTIONS: HCC, MPI

MEDIA: Oil, pencil, pen and ink, ballpoint pen, and colored pencil

EXHIBITS: AIAFM; AICA/SF; BSIM; LCAA; GFNAAS; RC; LCAA; MPI; NPTA; TM/NE; U of WV; WTF; Conrad (MT) Fall Art Show; Shelby (MT) Fall Art Show; Shriner's Benefit Art Auction, Billings, MT; Custer County (MT) Art League (traveling exhibit, 1992); local and regional exhibits; see also Awards

SOLO EXHIBITS: MPI

AWARDS: LCAA ('86, 1st); NPTA ('91); RC ('90, Aplan Award, Erickson Award; '91); Tri-County Fair, Roundup, MT ('88 2-1st; '89 2-1st)

GESHICK, JOE *Chippewa*

Sundance

RESIDENCE: St. Paul, MN

EXHIBITS: ITAE/M, TCIM

AWARDS: TCIM ('92, 1st)

GET MAD EASY (see Oxford, Eva Mae)

GHAHATT, BARTON *Zuni*

RESIDENCE: Zuni Pueblo, NM

EDUCATION: Fort Lewis College, Durango, CO; U of AZ, "Southwest Indian Art Project," scholarship, summer 1962

PUBLISHED: Snodgrass (1968)

GHERE, JESSIE *Choctaw*

Born 29 Apr 1939 in Abilene, TX; daughter of Grace Hill Minter and The Reverend Edward Sifford; P/GP: Lodie Foster and Rev. Starling Alexander Sifford; M/GF: Milton F. Hill, naturalist and artist

RESIDENCE: Sapulpa, OK

EDUCATION: Keys (OK) High School, 1957; B.A., OSU, 1961

OCCUPATION: Carver, scrimshander, and painter

MEDIA: Oil, Prismacolor, pencil, pen and ink, bone, horn, antler, and ivory

EXHIBITS: CIM; IS; NAF; NARF; SWFA; TIAF; TIMSS; Children's Medical Center Arts and Craft Show, Tulsa, OK; shows and markets in CO, LA, MS, OK, and TX; see also Awards

AWARDS: Partial listing of more than one hundred includes: SWFA (Best of Show); Nescatunga Arts Festival, Alva, OK; Oklahoma City (OK) Community College Show; Oklahoma Wild Life Festival, Tulsa, OK; Ponca City (OK) Arts Festival

GHOST BEAR, THEODORE *Sioux*

PUBLISHED: Snodgrass (1968)

PUBLIC COLLECTIONS: MFA/A

GIBSON, DIANE STAR (see Starr, Diane)

GIBSON, GORDON PHILIP, JR. *Paiute/Shoshoni*

Sn'ks, Snickers

Born 15 Apr 1954 in Reno, NV; son of Theora W. and Gordon Gibson; P/GP: Mamie Wiley and Stanley Gibson; M/GP: Edna Wasson and Elliot Wadsworth

RESIDENCE: Reno, NV

EDUCATION: Phoenix, 1973; Maricopa Technical Community College, Phoenix, AZ

OCCUPATION: Artist

MEDIA: Acrylic, watercolor, pencil, pen and ink, pastel, and prints

PUBLIC COLLECTIONS: BA/AZ; Sparks Indian Colony Clinic, Reno, NV; Reno (NV) Courthouse, Judge's Chamber

EXHIBITS: HM/G

HONORS: Gold Key Award, Phoenix, 1973

GIBSON, JACK *Seminole*

RESIDENCE: Edgewood, NM

EXHIBITS: FCTM, ITIC

AWARDS: FCTM ('76, 1st); ITIC ('87)

GIBSON, JOHN L. *Mohawk*

Born 24 Sept 1962

RESIDENCE: Hagersville, ON, Canada

EDUCATION: Dundas Valley School of Art; Mohawk College, Brantford, ON; Art Gallery of Brantford (ON), 1976

OCCUPATION: Artist

MEDIA: Oil, acrylic, watercolor, pastel, and pen and ink

PUBLISHED: Johannsen and Ferguson, eds. (1983)

EXHIBITS: C/WICEC; Royal Sheridan Hotel, Toronto, ON

GIFTS (see Paukei, George)

GILLENWATER, RALPH *Cherokee*

Birth date unknown; born in Arkansas

RESIDENCE: Muskogee, OK

OCCUPATION: Museum display artist and painter

MEDIA: Acrylic

EXHIBITS: CNM, FCTM, SI

GILLEY, JANELLE DAE *Eastern Shawnee/Wyandot/Chippewa*

A.K.A. Janelle Dae Nichols Gilley

Born 9 Oct 1953 in Pasco, WA; daughter of Marjorie Merriam Merry and William Mason Nichols; P/GP: Ella Jane Mason and Levi A. Nichols; M/GP: Olietta Laura Marie Wold and Walter Early Merry

RESIDENCE: Pasco, WA

EDUCATION: Columbia High School, Richland, WA; Moscow (ID) High School, 1971; Columbia Basin College, Tri-Cities, WA

OCCUPATION: Full-time artist

MEDIA: Oil, acrylic, watercolor pencil, pen and ink, pastel, Prismacolor, and prints

PUBLISHED: *Tri-City Herald* (26 May 1991)

PUBLIC COLLECTIONS: Yakama Cultural Center, Toppenish, WA; Eastern Shawnee Tribal Office, Seneca, MO

EXHIBITS: PAS/OR; TAS; Tiinowit International Powwow and Fine Arts Invitational Show, Yakima, WA; Trails West Art Show; Lake Chelan Fine Arts Invitational Show; see also Awards

SOLO EXHIBITS: MPI

AWARDS: PAS/OR ('91); TAS ('90, 1st); Latah County (ID) Fair

JANELLE DAE GILLEY

Gilley has the collagen disease, Lupus, which has damaged her heart, lungs, and joints. In 1989, bedridden with constant pain, she went to the University of Washington Pain Center. They suggested painting as therapy which has helped her learn to deal with her pain. She credits her unshakable religious beliefs and the support of her family and friends with making her art possible.

artist, p.c. 1992

GILMORE, CONNIE CARPENTER *Cherokee*

EXHIBITS: FCTM

AWARDS: FCTM ('79, IH)

GLAD, TERRY HOLT *Juaneño*

Born 2 Dec 1957 in Santa Monica, CA; daughter of Marie Manriquez and Tim Holt; M/GP: Dorothy Ruiz and Enick Manriquez

RESIDENCE: Santa Monica, CA

EDUCATION: Venice (CA) High School, 1975; studied under Robert Freeman (q.v.) and Deni Herckt

OCCUPATION: Artist

MEDIA: Oil, acrylic, pencil, and pen and ink

EXHIBITS: Escondido (CA) Public Library; Autumn Fine Arts Show and Exhibit, Ramona, CA; see also Awards

AWARDS: Escondido (CA) Arts Association ('92)

GLAZER, RICHARD (see Danay, Richard Glazer)

GLAZER-DANAY, RIC (see Danay, Richard Glazer)

GOBIN, HENRY *Tulalip*

Born 19 May 1941 on Tulalip Indian Reservation, Washington

RESIDENCE: Santa Fe, NM

EDUCATION: Santa Fe, 1960-1961; IAIA, 1965; B.F.A., SFAI, 1970; M.F.A., Sacramento (CA) State College, 1971

OCCUPATION: Park Service firefighter, educator, art director, poet, actor, ceramist, and painter

MEDIA: Oil, watercolor, and prints

PUBLISHED: Snodgrass (1968); New (1974; 1979); Highwater (1980); Hill (1990). *The Taos News* (11 Dec 1980); *Southwest Art* (July 1982); *The Santa Fean* (Apr 1984)

PUBLIC COLLECTIONS: BIA; IAIA; MNM; PAC; American Embassies in Spain and Kenya

EXHIBITS: AICA/SF; CIAE; EIAF; FAIEAIP; HM; HM/G; HS/AI; IAIA; IPCC; KCPA; MAI; MNM; NACLA; ND; NU/BC; PAC; PAIC; RC; RM; SFFA; SI; SN; TRP; U of SF/G; YAIA; Berlin Festival, West Germany; Lincoln Center, Group Exhibition, New York, NY; San Francisco (CA) Civic Center Square Arts Festival, 1969; see also Awards

SOLO/SPECIAL EXHIBITS: IAIA, 1973 (dual show)

AWARDS: HM/G ('77); MNM; SN; Annual Contemporary Indian Art Exhibition, Washington State('74)

HENRY GOBIN

Gobin has stated that his Northwest Pacific Coast will always be reflected in his art. Color is important to him, and his palette includes the vivid greens, blues, oranges, reds, and purples of the coastal area. He says, "I strongly identify with the masks and blankets, songs and dances, legends, art, and lifestyle of my own people." He tells of returning to his reservation after a long absence and finding in the ancient Long House of his people what he had long sought, a sense of everything coming together, a oneness.

Southwest Art, *July 1982*

GOING SOUTH (see Buffalo, Bennie)

GOLDEN DAWN (see Velarde, Pablita)

GOLSH, LARRY *Pala/Cherokee*

Born 31 Jan 1942 in Phoenix, AZ

RESIDENCE: Phoenix, AZ

EDUCATION: North Phoenix (AZ) High School; El Camino Junior College, Gardena, CA; ASU

OCCUPATION: Cosanti Foundation Project staff member, Kiva Craft Center employee, sculptor, jeweler, and painter

PUBLISHED: Monthan and Monthan (1975). *Arts In America* (July/Aug 1972)

EXHIBITS: HM; HM/G; PAM/AZ; SN; Arizona Commission on the Arts and Humanities Exhibition; Southwestern Invitational, Yuma, AZ

AWARDS: HM/G ('72); SN ('74, 1st)

HONORS: Arizona Commission on the Arts and Humanities, Artist-in-Residence Grant, 1973-1974

LARRY GOLSH

Initially a painter and then a sculptor, Golsh is now best known for his jewelry.

GONE MAN (see Wolfe, Edmond Richard)

GONNIE, RICHARD *Navajo*

EXHIBITS: HM/G

AWARDS: HM/G ('70)

GONYEA, RAYMÓN *Onondaga*

Born 1941 in Syracuse, NY

RESIDENCE: Santa Fe, NM

EDUCATION: Marion (IL) College; Seattle (WA) Pacific University; USDI, Personnel Management Training

OCCUPATION: Curator, research assistant, exhibit consultant and organizer, museum assistant, museum technician, writer, illustrator, and artist

MEDIA: Oil and acrylic
EXHIBITS: NACLA, NU/BC, TFAG
HONORS: President Carter's Inaugural Committee, Coordinator for Native American Activities

GONYEA, STEPHEN *Onondaga*

Born 10 Apr 1946 on the Onondaga Indian Reservation, NY
RESIDENCE: Alexandria, VA
EDUCATION: IAIA, 1964-1966; CSAW, 1966-1968; B.F.A., ACCD, 1972
OCCUPATION: Illustrator and painter
MEDIA: Acrylic, pen and ink, and pencil
PUBLISHED: Johannsen and Ferguson, eds. (1983). *American Artist Magazine* (1969); *Air Force Magazine* (1974)
EXHIBITS: AAID; ACS/EM; HM/G; NACLA; SFFA; SN; USDI; Everson Museum, Syracuse, NY
AWARDS: AAID ('72, 1st)

GONZALES, CAVAN *San Ildefonso*

PUBLIC COLLECTIONS: WWM
EXHIBITS: WWM

GONZALES, LOUIS *San Ildefonso*

Wo Peen, Medicine Mountain
A.K.A. Luis Gonzales
Born 10 Sept 1907; died ca. 1990; son of Juan Gonzales
RESIDENCE: Santa Fe, NM
EDUCATION: Santa Fe
OCCUPATION: Model for sculptor Philip S. Sears, pottery demonstrator, traditional singer and dancer, and painter
MEDIA: Oil and tempera
PUBLISHED: Alexander (1932); Jacobson and d'Ucel (1950); Dunn (1968); Snodgrass (1968); Tanner (1973); Fawcett and Callander (1982). *The Art Digest* (1 Sept 1931); *American Indian Art 1920-1972,* Peabody Museum (1973)
COMMISSIONS: *Murals:* YMCA's Lodge of Seven Fires, Springfield, MA (seven murals)
PUBLIC COLLECTIONS: DAM, EM, KM, MAI, MNA/KHC, MNM, MRFM, PAC, U of CA/LMA, U of OK, WOM
EXHIBITS: AIEC; ASM; BAC; CCP; EITA; ITIC; JGS; LGAM; MNM; NGA; PM; U of CA; WWM; Exposition of Indian Tribal Arts, New York, NY; Hastings (NE) College
HONORS: Governor of San Ildefonso Pueblo, NM, 1944-1945

LOUIS GONZALES

"Known as a pioneer Pueblo muralist, Wo Peen painted actively in the early 1920s. A hunting accident caused the loss of his right hand; however, he still paints occasionally."

Snodgrass 1968

Wo Peen is considered one of the early artists that made up the "San Ildefonso School." According to Tanner (1973), in the mid to late 1950s he painted powerful, dramatic horses. By the late 1960s he was no longer painting.

GONZALES, LUIS (see Gonzales, Louis)

GOOD, BAPTISTE *Brûlé Sioux*

Wapostangi; Brown Hat; High Hawk
A.K.A. John Good (*see also* High Hawk)
Born ca. 1822; died 1894; son of Afraid of Horse
RESIDENCE: Lived at Rosebud Agency, Dakota, 1879-1880
PUBLISHED: Dunn (1968); Snodgrass (1968). *4th Annual Report,* BAE (1882-1883); *10th Annual Report,* BAE (1888-1889)
PUBLIC COLLECTIONS: DAM; SI/OAA (copy of Winter Count); SIM (original Winter Count)
HONORS: Tribal sub-chief after 1865

BAPTISTE GOOD

"Good's son, Joseph Good, continued his father's Winter Count and added the years 1894-1922 (see 10th Annual Report, *BAE, 1888-1889)."*

Snodgrass 1968

Good's Winter Count was the only one among the Sioux that recorded events prior to 1775 (see Hyde 1961).

GOOD, JOHN (see Good, Baptiste)

GOOD, JOHN *Sioux*

Birth date unknown; possibly the son of Baptiste Good (q.v.), also named John

PUBLISHED: Snodgrass (1968)

PUBLIC COLLECTIONS: MNM

GOODBEAR, PAUL J. *Cheyenne*

Ahmehate, Flying Eagle

Born 1913 on the Cheyenne Reservation, MT; death date unknown; GF: Chief Turkey Legs

MILITARY: U.S. Army, WWII

EDUCATION: Santa Fe, 1936; U of Wichita; U of NM; CAI

OCCUPATION: Dancer, singer, teacher, professional boxer, department store clerk, and painter

PUBLISHED: Dunn (1968); Snodgrass (1968); Brody (1971); Silberman (1978)

COMMISSIONS: *Murals:* Coronado Monument, Bernalillo, NM; Frankfurt, Germany; hotels and restaurants throughout the U.S.

PUBLIC COLLECTIONS: GM, MNA/KHC, MNA, MNM, SAR, U of OK

EXHIBITS: ASM, GM, ITIC, MMA/NY, NAP, OMA, OU/MA/T

AWARDS: ITIC (4-1st)

PAUL J. GOODBEAR

"Goodbear spent his childhood in Oklahoma where he attended public elementary and high schools. Many of his illustrations and paintings have been reproduced in school books."

Snodgrass 1968

His paintings were described by J. J. Brody (1971) as having "overtones of Futurism and a refinement of the Kiowa style." At one time he worked for the School of American Research and the Museum of New Mexico in Santa Fe.

GOODLUCK, BARBARA *Navajo*

EDUCATION: IAIA

BOOKS ILLUSTRATED: Bataille (1984)

GOOD RAIN *Taos*

PUBLISHED: Snodgrass (1968)

EXHIBITS: FWG

GOODRIDER, VALERIE *Blackfoot*

Born 1946, in Brockett, AB, Canada, on the Peigan Reserve

RESIDENCE: Lethbridge, AB, Canada

EDUCATION: M.Ed., C/U of L, 1989

OCCUPATION: Artist

MEDIA: Acrylic

PUBLISHED: Cardinal-Schubert (1992)

PUBLIC COLLECTIONS: C/AGM, C/LCC

EXHIBITS: C/AGM; C/IFNA; C/LCC; C/TFD; Martha Cohen Theatre, Calgary, AB; Peigan Reserve, Standoff, AB; Pincher Creek (AB) Film Festival

VALERIE GOODRIDER

Goodrider paints two different subjects or types of paintings. One, which she considers a fun style, depicts dancers and the other, a deeply spiritual style, depicts dreams and legends.

Cardinal-Schubert 1992

GOODSHOT, IMOGENE *Oglala Sioux*

PUBLIC COLLECTIONS: HCC

EXHIBITS: HM/G, RC

AWARDS: HM/G ('70); RC ('71, 1st)

GOOD WALKER (see Wooden Leg)

GOODWIN, MARIAN *Cherokee*

Born 3 Oct 1929 in Sallisaw, OK; daughter of Elsie and Bate Reed; P/GP: Ida B. and George Reed; M/GP: Margaret Foreman and Sam Ussrey

RESIDENCE: Cherokee, OK

EDUCATION: Sallisaw (OK) High School; Connors State College, Warner, OK; Northwestern Oklahoma State, Alva, OK; A.A., Northern Oklahoma College, Tonkawa, OK

MARIAN GOODWIN

"Born in Sallisaw, Oklahoma, near the heart of the Cherokee Nation, of mixed Scotch and Cherokee Indian heritage, I started exhibiting in 1986. I specialize in contemporary Southwest and Indian art suggestive of the Indian's efforts to preserve their culture."

artist, p.c. 1990

OCCUPATION: Funeral director and painter
MEDIA: Oil, acrylic, pen and ink, pencil, pastel, and prints
PUBLIC COLLECTIONS: PIPM; Kimberly-Clark, Conference Room, Jenks, OK
EXHIBITS: CHAS; CNM; FCTM; LC; LIAS; PIPM; TIAF; RE; Nescatunga Art Show, Alva, OK; Harvest of the Arts, Wichita, KS; see also Awards
AWARDS: CNM ('93); FCTM ('91, 1st); PIPM ('89, 1st; '90, 1st); TIAF ('89; '91, 1st; '93); RE ('92, 1st); Alva (OK) Centennial Art Show ('89, 1st); Enid (OK) Art Show ('89, 1st); Fairview (OK) Art Show ('90, 1st); Nescatunga Art Show, Alva, OK ('89, 1st; '90, 1st); Northern Oklahoma College ('89, Harvest Award, Best in Painting)
HONORS: PIPM, featured artist, Dec 1991

GOODWIND, THOMAS (see Chippewa, Thomas Goodwind, Jr.)

GOPHER, ROBERT W. *Chippewa/Cree*
Born 1951 in Fort Belknap, MT
RESIDENCE: Rocky Boy, MT
EDUCATION: U of WI; B.A., EMC
OCCUPATION: Educator and painter
MEDIA: Oil, acrylic, and multi-media
PUBLISHED: Ward, ed. (1990)
EXHIBITS: CWY, I, MIA/MT, OLO
SOLO EXHIBITS: EMC

GORDON, DAVID A. *Seneca*
Born 9 Mar 1948
RESIDENCE: Irving, NY
EDUCATION: IAIA, 1967-1969; United South Eastern Tribes Indian Center, silversmith classes
OCCUPATION: Teacher and artist
PUBLISHED: Johannsen and Ferguson, eds. (1983)
EXHIBITS: IAIA

GORDON, HARLEY *Seneca*
Born 15 Jan 1922
RESIDENCE: Basom, NY
OCCUPATION: Housing construction and artist
MEDIA: Pencil, pen and ink, charcoal, crayon, and wood
PUBLISHED: Johannsen and Ferguson, eds. (1983)
PUBLIC COLLECTIONS: SMII
HONORS: Sub-chief of the Tonawanda Chief's Council

GORMAN, ALFRED KEE *Navajo*
Kee, Boy
Born 12 Apr 1957 in Encino, CA; died Apr 1966; son of Mary Excie Wilson and Carl Nelson Gorman (q.v.); half brother of R. C. Gorman (q.v.)
EDUCATION: Window Rock (AZ) Public School
PUBLISHED: Snodgrass (1968)
PUBLIC COLLECTIONS: MNM
EXHIBITS: AC/K, ITIC, MNM, NTF
AWARDS: ITIC ('64, 1st, special award)

DAVID A. GORDON

"The subject matter of all of his pieces is Indian, but since his return from the west [IAIA], he is using more Iroquois traditional themes."
Johannsen and Ferguson, eds. 1983

ALFRED KEE GORMAN

Alfred Kee Gorman was only nine years old when he was killed in an automobile accident. As young as he was he was already an accomplished artist. In addition to having won many important awards, his work had been exhibited in a Taos, NM, art gallery and one of his paintings was acquired by the Museum of New Mexico.

In 1967, the Scottsdale National Indian Arts Exhibition established the Alfred Kee Gorman Memorial Award which was to be given to the most promising artist of his age group (5 to 14). In announcing the award they said, "Kee . . . was the youngest and most mature painter that had ever traveled the road to art in his own or any other tribe. Thus, Kee has endowed youngsters of all ages with a wonderful heritage. Its lesson: Strive and do not become discouraged when failure seems to strike; allow the world to share your gifts because the world wants to share with you."
program, SN, 1967

GORMAN, CARL NELSON *Navajo*

Kinyeonny Beyeh, Son Of The Towering House People

Born 5 Oct 1907 in Chinle, AZ; son of Alice Peshlakai and Nelson Gorman, founders of the Presbyterian Mission at Chinle, AZ; M/GF: Beshlagai Ithline, silversmith and leader in the Crystal area of the Navajo reservation

RESIDENCE: Window Rock, AZ

MILITARY: U.S. Marine Corps, Navajo Code Talker, WWII

EDUCATION: Albuquerque, 1928; Otis, 1951; studied under Norman Rockwell, Joseph Magnaini, and Nicolai Fechin

OCCUPATION: Clerk, timekeeper, range rider, technical illustrator, business owner, store manager, director and administrator of tribal organizations, and artist

MEDIA: Oil, acrylic, watercolor, casein, encaustic, silver, textiles, and prints

PUBLISHED: Snodgrass (1968); Brody (1971); Tanner (1973); Greenberg and Greenberg (1984). *Westways Magazine* (Aug 1956; Aug 1962, cover); *The Sacramento Bee* (17 May 1970); *The Press-Enterprise* (26 May 1971); *The Gallup (NM) Independent* (17 Sept 1983; 31 Dec 1983; 10 Nov 1984; 20 Aug 1988); *Indian Historian* (winter 1973); *The Indian Trader* (July 1984; May 1990; Nov 1990; Dec 1990); *The Taos News* (29 Nov 1984); *The Albuquerque Tribune* (7 Dec 1984); biographical publications

COMMISSIONS: Los Angeles Indian Center and Los Angeles Navajo Club, ceremonial designs

PUBLIC COLLECTIONS: BIA/DC, MNA, NTM, SM, U of CA/D

EXHIBITS: AC/G; AC/SD; ASF; ASU/M; BIA; FAIEAIP; HM; HS/AI; ITIC; LGAM; MHDYMM; MNA; MNM; NCGM; NMSF; NTF; NTM; PAC; SN; U of CA/D; American Friends Service Committee Indian Art Exhibit, Seattle, WA; Gallup (NM) Chamber of Commerce; Management and Procedures Office, Navajo Tribe, Window Rock, AZ; Riverside (CA) Art Association; University of the Pacific, Stockton, CA; festivals, galleries, and shows in AZ, CA, NM, and WA; see also Awards

SOLO EXHIBITS: HM; MNA; PAC; U of CA/D; Gallup (NM) Public Library; United Nations Delegation Dinner, Window Rock, AZ; Los Angeles YMCA and Women's University Club, Los Angeles, CA; University of the Pacific, Stockton, CA

AWARDS: AC/SD; ITIC; NMSF; NTF; SN; Hobby Recreation Show, Los Angeles, CA; Indian Center Art Show; Douglas Aircraft Annual Art Show, Santa Monica, CA; Compton Gem and Mineral Club Show, Long Beach, CA

HONORS: State of Arizona, The Arizona Indian Living Treasure Award, 1989; U of NM, Honorary Doctorate, 1990; television appearances in AZ, CA, and GA; U of CA/D, Carl N. Gorman Museum named in his honor

CARL NELSON GORMAN

"As a boy, Gorman liked to draw horses, but his stockman father warned him there was 'no money in that kind of horses.' Despite the passing years and the extensive military action he saw at Guadalcanal, Tarawa, and Saipan, he never relinquished his desire to become an artist. The GI Bill made possible his dream of a formal education. He believes 'not only in the traditional but in the adaptation of the traditional to the modern, whether in painting, silver, or music.' He, with his good friend, the late Ralph Roanhorse (q.v.), was one of the first to lead Navajo artists in art directions other than the traditional."

Snodgrass 1968

GORMAN, R. C. *Navajo*

A.K.A. Rudolph Carl Gorman

Born 26 July 1932 in Chinle, AZ; son of Adella Katherine Brown and Carl Nelson Gorman (q.v.)

RESIDENCE: Taos, NM

MILITARY: U.S. Navy

EDUCATION: Ganado (AZ) High School; Guam Territorial College, Marianas Islands; Mexico C.C.; SFSC; U of N AZ

OCCUPATION: Gallery owner and artist

MEDIA: Oil, acrylic, watercolor, pencil, pen and ink, bronze, and prints

PUBLISHED: Bahti (1966); Klein and Icolari (1967); Snodgrass (1968); Brody (1971); Findley (1972); Dockstader (1973); Morrill (1973); Tanner (1968; 1973); Monthan (1975; 1978; 1988; 1990); Stuart and Ashton (1977); Highwater (1976; 1980); Katz (1980); Hurst (1980); Silberman (1980); Broder (1981); Dooley, ed.

R. C. GORMAN

"Although Gorman majored in literature at the University of Northern Arizona and is a gifted writer, he has chosen painting, his first love, as a career. The artist has said: 'The reservation is my source of inspiration for what I paint; yet I never come to realize this until I find myself in some far-flung

(1981; 1989); Samuels (1982); Parks (1983); Green (1983); Hoffman, et al. (1984); Adams and Newlin (1987); Archuleta and Strickland (1991); Gorman (1992); Campbell, ed. (1993). *Western Review* (winter 1965); *Southwestern Art* (Vol.2, no. 1, 1967); *Nimrod* (spring/summer 1972); *Southwest Art* (Sept 1972; May 1974; June 1974; June 1978; June 1988); *Arizona Highways* (Aug 1976); *The Indian Trader* (July 1978; Feb 1982; Oct 1982; June 1989; Mar 1990; June 1991; Nov 1993); *American Indian Art* (summer 1978; spring 1985); *People* (18 Dec 1978); *Taos Magazine* (Sept/Oct 1979; Aug 1987; May/June 1988; Aug 1988; Aug 1990); *Phoenix Home and Garden* (Mar 1989); *New Mexico Magazine* (spring 1971; Mar 1980; Apr 1990); *The Santa Fean* (Aug 1976; Aug 1980; Jan/Feb 1991); *Four Winds* (summer/autumn 1981); *Southwest Profile* (July 1988; May/June/July 1991); *Fine Art Collector* (Aug 1991); *Native People* (winter 1990; winter 1992); *U.S. Art* (Apr 1992); *The* (Aug 1994)

BOOKS ILLUSTRATED: Rosen, ed. (1974; 1975); Gorman (1992)

PUBLIC COLLECTIONS: BIA; HCC; HM; HS/AI; IACB; IMA; MAI; MMA/NY; MNA; MNM; MRFM; PAC; PNIC; SDMM; SI; U of N AZ; USDI; WWM; Mexico City College; Ganado (AZ) High School; Grover, Stetson and Williams, Albuquerque, NM; Gonzaga University Museum, Spokane, WA

EXHIBITS: ABQM; AIAE/WSU; BM; CPS; FAIEAIP; HM; HMA; HNSM; HPTU; IK; IMA; ITIC; KF; LGAM; MNA; MNM; MFA/O; MMA/NY; MNCA; MRFM; NACG; NCHF; NAP; OMA; PAC; PBS; SAIEAIP; SCG; SDMM; SFFA; SI; SN; SV; U of N AZ; USDI; USDS; WTF; WWM; Musée Municipal, St. Paul de Vence, France; Tubac (AZ) Center for the Arts; galleries world wide; see also Awards

SOLO/SPECIAL EXHIBITS: Partial listing of more than one hundred includes: AC/SW, ACA, BU, KSU, MAI, MRFM, NCC, U of N AZ, U of CA/B, WWM. *Father/Son Exhibitions:* CNGM, HM, HS/AI, NTM, PAC

AWARDS: AAID ('68, 1st, Special Award); AIAE/WSU; HM/G ('69, Motorola Award); ITIC ('68); KF ('66, Grand Award); NCHF; NTF; PAC ('68, 1st); SN ('67; '68, 1st; '69, 1st; '70; '71); Center of Arts for Indian Americans, Washington, D.C.

HONORS: *Honorary degrees:* College of Ganado, Ganado, AZ, Honorary Doctorate of Fine Arts, 1978; Eastern New Mexico University, Portales, NM, Honorary Doctorate of Humane Letters, 1980; U of N AZ, Honorary Doctorate of Humane Letters, 1990. *Other:* Navajo Tribe, first scholarship for study outside the U.S., given to a student of outstanding merit; American Indian Artists, San Francisco, CA, Painting Committee Chairman; Metropolitan Museum of Art, New York, NY, first living Indian artist to be included in permanent collection; *Today Show*, television appearance, referred to as the "Indian Picasso," 1978; New Mexico Governor's Award for the Visual Arts, 1989; Harvard University Humanities Award; San Francisco (CA) and the State of New Mexico, "R.C. Gorman Day"; El Paso (TX), San Antonio (TX), Houston (TX), and Scottsdale (AZ), given Keys to the Cities; named a "Living Legend" by Ralph Oliver, 1990

GORMAN, RICHARD *Navajo*

EXHIBITS: ITIC

AWARDS: ITIC ('90)

GORMAN, RUDOLPH CARL (see Gorman, R. C.)

GOROSPE, JOSEPHINE *Laguna*

EDUCATION: St. Catherine's, 1965

PUBLISHED: Snodgrass (1968)

EXHIBITS: MNM, PAC

AWARDS: MNM

R. C. GORMAN

(continued) place like the tip of Yucatán or where-have-you. Perhaps when I stay on the reservation I take too much for granted. While there, it is my inspiration and I paint very little, and off the reservation it is my realization.'

In addition to the encouragement he has received from his father, the artist says that Miss Jenny Louis Lind, his high school art teacher, 'made art important' to him and that too often art teachers neglect to do so."

Snodgrass 1968

According to Dr. Frederick J. Dockstader, "Gorman has been experimental and uninhibited with his art and was one of the earliest to break out of the old-style Indian School art shell and to create a bridge between the traditional and the avant-garde."

GOSHORN, SHAN *Cherokee*

U Do Dalona Gei, Yellow Moon

A.K.A. D. Shan Goshorn

Born 3 July 1957 in Baltimore, MD; daughter of Edna Savnooke Goshorn and John Calvin Goshorn Jr.; P/GP: Elizabeth Swan and Calvin Goshorn; M/GP: Stacey Powell and Anderson Savnooke

RESIDENCE: Tulsa, OK

EDUCATION: Bel Air Senior High, 1975; Cleveland (OH) Institute of Art; B.F.A., Atlanta (GA) College of Art, 1980

OCCUPATION: Lecturer, exhibit technician, teacher, storyteller, artist-in-residence, photographer, and painter

MEDIA: Oil, acrylic, pencil, pastel, mixed-media, film, and prints

PUBLISHED: Starr (1988); Perrone, Stockel, and Krueger (1990); Abbott (1994). *Turtle Quarterly* (spring 1989); *Tamaqua* (winter/spring 1991); *The Broken Arrow Scout* (15 Jan 1992)

BOOKS ILLUSTRATED: Perrone, et al. (1990). *Women of Power Magazine* (spring/fall 1988; winter 1989)

COMMISSIONS: *Illustrations:* IACB, basket book, 27 illustrations; Arts and Humanities Council of Tulsa, OK, four illustrations for *Nimrod. Other:* State Arts Council/Center for the American Indian, Oklahoma City, OK, poster and art for cassette tape

PUBLIC COLLECTIONS: HCC; IACB; IAIA; MCI; SI; Deaconess Hospital, Oklahoma City, OK; John Blair Publishing Company, Winston-Salem, NC; Pelican Sound, Fort Lauderdale, FL; Blue Cross and Blue Shield, Tulsa, OK; City of Tulsa (OK); Prudential Insurance Company, Tulsa, OK; Santa Fe Pacific Pipeline, Tulsa, OK; Shadow Mountain Institute, Tulsa, OK; Tulsa (OK) Cancer Clinic

EXHIBITS: AICA/SF; AICH; CSU/OK; CNGM; CNM; FAIE; FCTM; IAIA; K; LIAS; MCI; OAC; OCU; RC; SCG; SPIM; TIAF; TM/NE; RC; RE; U of Tulsa; The Cleveland (OH) Institute of Art; Towson (MD) State University, Annual Show; Atlanta (GA) Memorial Arts Center; Oklahoma City (OK) University; East Gallery, Oklahoma State Capitol; galleries in CA, NY, and OK

SOLO/SPECIAL EXHIBITS: C/NIIPA/G; CHMG; HG; MCI; PIPM; QACM; SPIM; Memorial Art Center, High Museum, Atlanta, GA, 1980; Theater Tulsa, OK, 1982; Native Indian/Inuit Photography Association Gallery, ON; International Photography Hall of Fame, Oklahoma City, OK, 1988; Ursuline College, Pepper Pike, OH, 1992

AWARDS: FCTM ('84, 1st); K ('91); LIAS ('91, MA); MCI ('90, 1st); RE ('87)

HONORS: SCG, poster artist, 1988

GOUGE, RANDY *Creek*

Born 19 July 1958

RESIDENCE: Oklahoma City, OK

EDUCATION: Capitol Hill High School, Oklahoma City, OK; A.A., RSC; U of OK

EXHIBITS: CNM; FCTM; RC; Kiamichi Owa-Chito Art Show

AWARDS: FCTM ('82)

HONORS: M.V.P. trophy, baseball; State A.A.U. Junior Olympics competitor award

GOUGH, AGNES *Cherokee*

PUBLISHED: Snodgrass (1968)

PUBLIC COLLECTIONS: DAM, PAC

EXHIBITS: DAM, PAC, PAC/T

AWARDS: PAC

GOULD, JAY *Navajo*

PUBLISHED: Snodgrass (1968)

PUBLIC COLLECTIONS: MNM

GOYA, ROBERT *Hopi*

Avach'hoya Katsina, Spotted Corn

Born 1937; died 1952

OCCUPATION: Painter

MEDIA: Tempera

PUBLISHED: Seymour (1988)

PUBLIC COLLECTIONS: IACB/DC

EXHIBITS: WRTD

GRANADOS, BERNIE, JR. *Apache/Inca/Zacatec*

Born 1 May 1948 in East Los Angeles, CA; son of Lucila Carrasco and Bernie Granados Sr.; P/GP: Amalia and Francisco Granados; M/GP: Guadalupe and Rafael Carrasco; M/uncle: Jorge Carrasco, artist

RESIDENCE: Glendale, CA

EDUCATION: Pioneer High School, Whittier, CA, 1966; Río Hondo College, Whittier, CA; Miracosta College, Oceanside, CA; paramedic training, USC School of Medicine, Los Angeles, CA

OCCUPATION: Paramedic, missionary, teacher, sculptor and painter

MEDIA: Acrylic, watercolor, pencil, Prismacolor, bronze, and prints

PUBLISHED: *Native Peoples* (spring 1991)

COMMISSIONS: *Murals:* Los Angeles (CA) Olympic Organizing Committee, 1984. *Other:* Sherman Indian High School, poster; El Tecolote Restaurant, built and installed *Magical Oak Tree*; painting, sculpture, mural, and craft projects for films and television

EXHIBITS: SM; galleries in California

SOLO EXHIBITS: Partial listing of 14 (1968-1992) includes: Pacificulture Center, Pasadena CA; Goetz Institute of Murals and Fine Arts, Los Angeles, CA

HONORS: CSU/LA, Los Angeles County High School, School for the Arts, federal grant to teach painting; County of Los Angeles, CA, one of the first eighty paramedics to be certified

GRAND EAGLE (see Ballard, Louis Wayne)

GRANT, ANNE DESROSIER (see DesRosier-Grant, Anne)

GRANT, JOHN A. *Yakama/Nez Percé*

Born 5 Sept 1931 at Ahtanum, WA; paternally descended from Chief Kamiakin; maternally descended from Chief Joseph

RESIDENCE: Nespelem, WA

MILITARY: U.S. Army, Korea

EDUCATION: Chemawa Indian School, Salem, OR

OCCUPATION: Logger, cartographer, official Colville tribal artist; painter since 1977

MEDIA: Watercolor, pen and ink, and scratchboard

PUBLISHED: Minthorn (1991)

EXHIBITS: ACS/SM, RC, SAP, SN; see also Awards

AWARDS: ACS/SM (1st, three consecutive years); RC ('81, 1st); SN; Omak Indian Art Show ('79, Best of Show); Seattle (WA) American Indian Art Show ('80)

HONORS: Colville Tribal Artist, 1976

BERNIE GRANADOS JR.

Granados can trace his Apache heritage to all four of his grandparents. In the 1970s he began to explore his heritage and all his previous artistic explorations began to converge into Native American art. His basic belief is simple, "I believe in human and animal rights and the responsibility we have to protect them and our planet (Mother Earth)."

artist, p.c. 1992

JOHN A. GRANT

Following an injury to his back while working in the logging industry, Grant took a job with a cartographer. He later studied art and printmaking under Russell Bradley, who was hired by the Colville tribe. With his art, Grant wants "to show, describe, promote and preserve the old Indian way of life. To show our people as they really were, as opposed to non-Indian concepts. To bring our people out of the cowboy-and-Indian stages into real life, with respect and dignity."

According to his wife, Marie, he is strictly a traditional person and his art work reflects his background, personality, and the way he lives his life.

artist resumé, 1983

GRANT, PAUL WAR CLOUD *Sisseton Sioux*

A.K.A. Paul War Cloud

Born 18 June 1930 on the Sisseton-Wahpeton Sioux Reservation near She-Cha Hollow, SD

RESIDENCE: Sisseton, SD

MILITARY: U.S. Army and Air Force, 12 years, including Korea

OCCUPATION: Author, lecturer, art teacher, substance abuse counselor, and painter

MEDIA: Oil

PUBLISHED: *American Indian Crafts and Culture* (Feb 1972); *The Indian Trader* (Apr 1974; Apr 1975)

COMMISSIONS: *Murals:* State Governor's Conference Room, South Dakota, 1972

PUBLIC COLLECTIONS: Pohlen Indian Cultural Center, Sisseton, SD

EXHIBITS: AAID

SOLO EXHIBITS: Chicago, IL; Columbus, GA; South Dakota

AWARDS: AAID ('73)

GRASS (see Grass, John)

GRASS, JOHN *Blackfeet (?)/Hunkpapa Sioux*

Pezi, Grass; *Mato Wantakpe*, Charging Bear; *Wahacanka Yapi*, Used As A Shield

A.K.A. Jumping Bear; Chief John Grass

OCCUPATION: Army scout, presiding judge on the Standing Rock Reservation, (SD) Court of Indian Offenses (for more than thirty years), and painter

PUBLISHED: Snodgrass (1968)

PUBLIC COLLECTIONS: MAI (autograph sketch; see Black Heart)

JOHN GRASS

"Chief Grass was one of four Sioux chiefs who relinquished all claims to the Black Hills and Powder River country to the government at Standing Rock Agency, ca. 1883 (see Bulletin 61, *BAE, 1918; Hyde 1956; Vestal 1933)."*

Snodgrass 1968

GRASS, JOHN, JR. *Hunkpapa/Teton Sioux*

Birth date unknown; son of John Grass (q.v.)

RESIDENCE: Lived on the Standing Rock Reservation, SD, during 1902

PUBLISHED: Snodgrass (1968). *News Letter,* CIS (Nov 1945)

PUBLIC COLLECTIONS: CIS

GRAVES, SHAROL *Shawnee/Chippewa*

Born 31 May 1953

RESIDENCE: San Francisco, CA

EDUCATION: IAIA, 1970; B.A., Mills College, Oakland, CA, 1977

OCCUPATION: Artist

PUBLISHED: Antoine and Bates (1991)

PUBLIC COLLECTIONS: IAIA

EXHIBITS: AICA/SF; AICH; CNGM; IAIA; LIAS; RC; SM; College of Arts and Crafts, Oakland, CA, 1987; San Jose (CA) Indian Center, 1984; Southwestern University, Georgetown, TX, 1987; Southwest Museum of Science and Technology, Dallas, TX, 1986; University of the Pacific, Stockton, CA, 1986

AWARDS: IAIA, awards for printmaking, dance, and drama

GRAY, CLANCY *Osage*

RESIDENCE: Tulsa, OK

EDUCATION: B.A., M.A.Ed., CSU/OK

OCCUPATION: Teacher, silversmith, sculptor, ceramist, and painter

MEDIA: Acrylic, watercolor, silver, gemstone, metal, and clay

PUBLISHED: *Tulsa World* (15 Feb 1995)

EXHIBITS: TIAF, TWF

GRAY, FLOYD *Ojibwa*

Birth date unknown; born in Osnaburgh House, ON, Canada

RESIDENCE: Thunder Bay, ON, Canada

MEDIA: Graphite and felt markers

EXHIBITS: C/AG/TB

GRAY, GINA *Osage*

Pah-Pu-Son-Tse

Born 21 July 1954 in Pawhuska, OK; daughter of Margaret and Andrew Gray; P/GF: Clerence Gray; GGF: Henry Roan Horse; related to Jim Redcorn, Loren Pahsetopah, and Paul Pahsetopah (qq.v.); cousin of Clancy Gray (q.v.)

RESIDENCE: Tulsa, OK

EDUCATION: IAIA, 1972; California Institute of the Arts, Valencia, CA

OCCUPATION: Actress, singer, dancer, commercial artist, and painter

MEDIA: Oil, watercolor, pencil, pastel, and prints

PUBLISHED: *Southwest Art* (May 1989); *Newspaper Personnel Relations Association* (June 1989), cover; *The Santa Fe New Mexican, Pasatiempo* (17-23 Aug 1990); *The Santa Fe New Mexican, Indian Market Edition* (15 Aug 1991); *New Mexico Magazine* (Aug 1991); *The Tulsa World* (14 Feb 1992); *Indian Territories* (Vol. 3, no. 1, 1993); *The Tulsa World* (3 Dec 1993); *Tulsa People* (Feb 1994)

COMMISSIONS: Tulsa County Medical Society, directory cover, 1994; Smithsonian Institution, first work by a Native American painter used for catalog cover, 1993

PUBLIC COLLECTIONS: HCC

EXHIBITS: ACAI; AIAF; AIWSAF; BB; CIM; CNM; HM; IAIA; ITIC; MMO; NMSC; PAC; RC; RE; SWAIA; TAIAF; TCIM; TWF; WWM; Daybreak Star Museum, Seattle, WA; Texas Indian Market and Southwest Showcase; El Farol Indian Market Show, Santa Fe, NM; galleries in CA, HI, KS, NM, NY, and OK

SOLO EXHIBITS: WWM

AWARDS: ACAI ('92); ACS/ENP ('91); IS ('92, 1st); ITIC ('91, 1st; '92, 1st); NNACAF ('90, 2-1st); OIAC ('94, 1st); PAC ('76, Painting Award); RC (Purchase Award); RE ('91, 1st; '93, Best of Division; '94, 1st); SWAIA ('90; '93, 1st; '94, 1st); TCIM ('91); TIAF ('91, 1st; '91; '92; '93, 2-1st; 94, 1st; '95, 1st); TWF ('92, 1st, '93)

HONORS: SWAIA Fellowship, 1991; TIAF, featured artist, 1993; TWF, poster artist, 1993

GRAY FOOT (see Asenap, Hollis, Jr.)

GRAYSON, WEBSTER *Cherokee*

RESIDENCE: Tahlequah, OK

PUBLISHED: *The Columns* (fall 1993)

PUBLIC COLLECTIONS: CGPS, CNM

EXHIBITS: CC/OK; CGPS; CNM; FCTM; PAC; RC; Muskogee (OK) Library; U of NE

SOLO EXHIBITS: CNM

AWARDS: CNM ('85, Special Award); FCTM ('84, Traditional Indian Art Award; '85)

GREATEST, THE (see Speck, Henry)

GREAT HUNTER (see Blackmore, Bill)

GREBB, ALVIN *Navajo*

PUBLIC COLLECTIONS: MNA

FLOYD GRAY

The artist does very detailed drawings that are closely related to the formal principles of the Woodland School of Legend painting. His first exhibition was The New Traditionalists which was held at the Thunder Bay Art Gallery in 1988.

GINA GRAY

Primarily working in oils and monotypes, Gray combines traditional Native American subjects with abstract designs. An early interest in art led to an apprenticeship to an artist when she was ten. Her first recognition was achieved at the age of thirteen when she won a purchase award at the Red Cloud Indian Arts Show in Pine Ridge, SD. Gray says, "Motherhood and the Arts have always been the most important priorities of my life. I have always drawn from my Osage traditions, incorporating those traditions into my own contemporary lifestyle; particularly with my paintings. . . ."

p.c. 1991

GREEN, HOMER *Peoria/Cherokee*

Born 1938 at Fort Defiance, AZ

PUBLISHED: Snodgrass (1968)

EXHIBITS: AAIE, FAIEAIP, PAC, USDS

GREEN CORN (see Mirabel, Eva)

GREENE, GARY E. *Nez Percé*

Born 1950 Lewiston, ID

RESIDENCE: Seattle, WA

EDUCATION: Lapwai (ID) High School; A.A., Lewis Clark State College, Lewiston, ID, 1983; IAIA, 1983-1986; U of WA

OCCUPATION: Advertising designer, sculptor, jeweler, and painter

MEDIA: Acrylic, metal, and stone

PUBLISHED: Minthorn (1991)

PUBLIC COLLECTIONS: IAIA

EXHIBITS: IAIA, SAP

GREENE, STAN *Coast Salish*

Born 1953 in Semiahmoo, BC, Canada

RESIDENCE: Chilliwack, BC, Canada

EDUCATION: C/KSNCIA; studied with Vernon Stephens, Ken Mowatt (qq.v.) and Murphy Green

OCCUPATION: Full-time painter and carver since 1976

MEDIA: Watercolor, wood, and prints

PUBLISHED: Hall, Blackman, and Rickard (1981); Gerber and Bruggmann (1989). *The Chilliwack Progress* (31 Aug 1983)

COMMISSIONS: *Carvings*: 86 houseposts for Expo '86

PUBLIC COLLECTIONS: C/INAC, HCC

EXHIBITS: BHSU, SDSMT

GREENE, WANDA ANNETTE *Yuchi/Creek*

A.K.A. W. A. Standridge; W. A. Greene

Born 3 Sept 1949 in Claremore, OK; daughter of Pauline Hay and Fimmie Greene; P/GP: Lochar Techarna and John Greene; M/GP: Eliza Bigpond and Deshalecoweney "Joe" Greene

RESIDENCE: Bixby, OK

EDUCATION: Bixby (OK) High School, 1967; OSU/O, 1970; A.A., IAIA, 1986; B.F.A., U of OK, 1993

OCCUPATION: Museum exhibits preparator and curator, and painter

MEDIA: Acrylic and prints

PUBLISHED: *Plateau* (Vol. 60, no. 1, 1988)

PUBLIC COLLECTIONS: IAIA

EXHIBITS: IAIA/M; JH; MMO; OU/MA; Los Illonas Exhibit, Santa Fe, NM; Murray State College, Tishomingo, OK; Pennsylvania State University, University Park, PA

SOLO EXHIBITS: The Muscogee (Creek) Nation, Okmulgee, OK

GREEN FEATHER (see English, Ronald R.)

GREEN RAINBOW (see Mofsie, Louis Billingsly)

GREGG, WILKIE *White Mountain Apache*

Born 1942

EDUCATION: U of AZ, "Southwest Indian Art Project," scholarship, summer 1960
PUBLISHED: Snodgrass (1968)

GREY BOY (see Draper, Teddy, Sr.)

GREY CANYON ARTISTS

A.K.A. Grey Canyon Group; Grey Canyon Artists Group
LOCATION: Albuquerque, NM

In December 1977, Jaune Quick-To-See Smith (q.v.) was instrumental in the formation of a cooperative of Native American painters that became known as the Grey Canyon Artists. The purpose of the cooperative was to preserve their identity as Indian artists and to promote their art and maintain control over it. They exhibited extensively throughout the United States in the late 1970s and the 1980s. Other members of the group were Loïs Sonkiss Brill, Karita Coffee, Larry Emerson, Conrad House, Emmi Whitehorse, and Paul Willeto (qq.v.).

GREY CANYON ARTISTS

"All of us are trying to make things that truly come from us. They must be aesthetic and they must maintain our identity. There is a great risk of losing that, especially in the city."

Jaune Quick-To-See Smith

GREY SQUIRREL (see Hinds, Patrick Swazo)

GREY WIND, KENNETH *Sioux*

Born 26 July 1954 at Devil's Lake, ND
EDUCATION: Devil's Lake (ND) High School; IAIA, 1978: U of ND
MEDIA: Oil, acrylic, tempera, watercolor, pastel, and prints
EXHIBITS: SIM; see also Awards
SOLO EXHIBITS: SIM
AWARDS: Ramsey County Fair, Devil's Lake, ND ('73, 1st); First Annual Indian Cultural Art Show, Bismarck, ND ('80, 1st)

GRIFFIN, T. A. *Catawba*

A.K.A. T. A. Griffith
EXHIBITS: HM/G
AWARDS: HM/G ('79)

GRIFFITH, BRUNETTA BERNARD *Choctaw/Chickasaw*

RESIDENCE: Rush Springs, OK
EDUCATION: OCLA, studied under Derald Swineford
OCCUPATION: Lecturer and artist
PUBLISHED: *Oklahoma Today* (Will Rogers Centennial Souvenir Series 1979); *Twin Territories* (Vol. 2, no. 1, 1991); *The Muskogee Daily Phoenix* (16 Oct 1992)
COMMISSIONS: *Murals:* Black Kettle Museum, Cheyenne, OK. *Other:* Oklahoma Educational Department, textbook illustrations
EXHIBITS: OCSA; OSC; TIAF ('87); Pioneer Woman Museum, Ponca City, OK; Thomas-Foreman Historical Home, Muskogee, OK
HONORS: Official Oklahoma Bicentennial History, painting included; Security National Bank of Duncan, Duncan, OK, scholarship to Bacone College given in her name; Oklahoma Historical Society, Board of Directors; received Oklahoma's Diamond Jubilee Award; Oklahoma Historical Society, Outstanding Artist

GRIFFITH, KATHY *Oglala Sioux*

Born 20 Jan 1956
RESIDENCE: Littleton, CO
EDUCATION: Red Cloud Indian School, Pine Ridge, SD; Oglala Sioux Community College, Pine Ridge, SD; CIA/CO
OCCUPATION: Commercial artist and painter
EXHIBITS: RC

GRIFFITH, T. A. (see Griffin, T. A.)

GRIGG, CAROL *Cherokee*

PUBLISHED: *The Santa Fean* (Aug 1991)

GRIMM, MARION *Cherokee*

RESIDENCE: McCloud, OK

EXHIBITS: FCTM

GRITTS, FRANKLIN *Cherokee/Potawatomi*

Oau Nah Jusah, They Have Returned; *Oon Nah Susah,* They Have Gone Back

Born 8 Aug 1914 in Vian, OK

RESIDENCE: St. Louis, MO

MILITARY: U.S. Navy, WWII

EDUCATION: Haskell; B.F.A., U of OK, ca. 1939; studied mural technique under Olaf Nordmark, painting under Acee Blue Eagle (q.v.); summer classes in anthropology, U of NM

OCCUPATION: Art instructor and artist

PUBLISHED: Jacobson and d'Ucel (1950); Snodgrass (1968); Brody (1971); Silberman (1980)

COMMISSIONS: *Murals:* Haskell; Fort Sill Indian School. *Other:* Progressive Education Convention, Chicago, IL, assisted in preparing a series of exhibits, 1940

PUBLIC COLLECTIONS: GM, JAM, MNA/KHC, OU/MA, PAC

EXHIBITS: AIW, DAM, ITIC, OMA, PAC, PAC/T; Palmer House, Chicago, IL; Mandel Brothers, St. Louis, MO

AWARDS: ITIC

GRITTS, JOHN *Cherokee*

Born 31 Oct 1947

RESIDENCE: Spearfish, SD

EDUCATION: Joplin (MO) Senior High School; IAIA; Sioux Falls (SD) College

PUBLISHED: Biographical publications

PUBLIC COLLECTIONS: HCC

EXHIBITS: HM/G, PAC, RC, SN, U of ND

AWARDS: RC ('91), SN ('76)

GROS VENTRE, CYRUS *Crow*

Born 1948 at Crow Agency, MT

RESIDENCE: Santa Fe, NM

EDUCATION: IAIA, 1965-1968; post graduate-graphics, IAIA, 1971-1973

OCCUPATION: Musician, songwriter and artist

COMMISSIONS: *Murals:* Eagle's Building, Bozeman, MT

PUBLIC COLLECTIONS: IAIA, SI

EXHIBITS: AAID, IAIA, MPI, NAVAM; galleries in AZ, MT, and WY

GROWING PLANT (see Hunt, Wolf Robe)

GRUBER, RAY *Navajo*

A.K.A. Raymond Gruber

RESIDENCE: Crownpoint, NM

PUBLISHED: Snodgrass (1968)

PUBLIC COLLECTIONS: CGPS, MNA

EXHIBITS: CGPS, ITIC, MNA

AWARDS: ITIC ('86; '89)

GRUMMER, BRENDA KENNEDY *Potawatomi*

Birth date unknown; born in El Reno, OK

RESIDENCE: Yukon, OK

EDUCATION: Calumet (OK) High School; B.A., SWOSU; independent study

OCCUPATION: Public relations, free-lance writer; full-time artist after 1978

MEDIA: Oil, acrylic, watercolor, pencil, Prismacolor, charcoal, pastel, pen and ink, alklyd, mixed-media, and prints

PUBLISHED: Mahey, et al. (1980). *American Artists* (1990); *Southwest Art* (Sept 1988; Feb 1989); *Oklahoma Today* (Dec 1990); *The Broken Arrow Scout* (15 Jan 1992)

BOOKS ILLUSTRATED: Sapulpa (OK) Area Telephone Directory, 1990/1991, cover

COMMISSIONS: Muskogee (OK) Centennial, medallion design, 1972; Fort Gibson (OK) 150th Birthday Party, medallion design, 1974

PUBLIC COLLECTIONS: PAC; SPIM; Potawatomi Cultural Center; Oklahoma Governor's Mansion

EXHIBITS: AC/K, AICA, BB, CNM, FAIE, KCPA, MIF, OAC, OSC, PAC, RE, SDMM, SFFA, SI, SM, SPIM; see also Awards

SOLO EXHIBITS: SPIM

AWARDS: CNM ('80; '81; '82; '84, Painting Award; '86; '87; '88, Miniature Award; '94); ITIC ('91, 1st); PAC ('75, Painting and Graphics Awards; '77, 1st; '78; '79, Grand Award); RE ('89; '92, Best of Division; '93); Fort Smith (AR) Art Center, Six State Exhibition ('74, Grand Award); Indian Summer Festival, Muskogee, OK ('74, Grand Award); Spiva Art Center, Joplin, MO ('73, Purchase Award); First Annual Potawatomi National Art Exhibition, Shawnee, OK ('80); Oklahoma Art Gallery Magazine's First Annual State Art Competition ('80); Western Colorado Center for the Arts Biennial, Grand Junction, CO ('75, Delta Products Award, Graphics Award)

HONORS: SWOSU, graduated Magna Cum Laude; Governor's Gallery, State Capitol Building, Oklahoma City, OK, featured artist, 1979; Oklahoma State Capitol, East Gallery, Oklahoma City, OK, *Year of the Indian Exhibition*, one of eight Indian artists exhibited, 1992

BRENDA KENNEDY GRUMMER

A popular artist, Grummer's favorite subjects are women, children, and scenes from contemporary Indian life. Successfully uniting color and light, her realistic paintings exhibit an impressionistic style that softens the sometimes harsh reality of that life and creates an aura of serenity.

GUATOGUE, LEO *Zuni*

PUBLISHED: Snodgrass (1968)

EXHIBITS: EITA

GU HAU DE (see Wohaw)

GUTATOGUE, LEO (see Guatogue, Leo)

GUTÉRIEZ, CHRISTINE *Santa Clara*

PUBLIC COLLECTIONS: HCC

GUTIÉRREZ, CLARENCE *Santa Clara*

EDUCATION: Santa Fe, ca. 1937

PUBLISHED: Snodgrass (1968)

EXHIBITS: AIEC

GUTIÉRREZ, GERALDINE *Santa Clara/San Ildefonso*

Birth date unknown; daughter of Helen Atencio and Frankie Gutiérrez, potter; niece of Gilbert Atencio (q.v.)

RESIDENCE: Santa Clara Pueblo, NM

OCCUPATION: Potter and painter

MEDIA: Watercolor and clay

EXHIBITS: SWAIA; area and regional shows and markets

GUTIÉRREZ, J. B. (see Gutiérrez, Juan B.)

GUTIÉRREZ, JOSÉ LA CRUZ *Santa Clara*

Birth date unknown; brother of José Leandro Gutiérrez (q.v.)

EDUCATION: Santa Fe, mid-1930s

OCCUPATION: Employed at U.S. Naval Station, Salt Lake City, Utah, 1963

PUBLISHED: Snodgrass (1968); Seymour (1988)

PUBLIC COLLECTIONS: IACB/DC, MNA, SM

EXHIBITS: HM, WRTD

GUTIÉRREZ, JOSÉ LEANDRO *Santa Clara*

Kgoo Ya

A.K.A. José Leandro

Born 1918 in Santa Clara Pueblo, NM; died ca. 1977; brother of José La Cruz Gutiérrez (q.v.)

MILITARY: Military service, branch unknown

EDUCATION: Santa Fe

MEDIA: Watercolor

PUBLISHED: Dunn (1968); Snodgrass (1968); Seymour (1988)

PUBLIC COLLECTIONS: IACB/DC, U of OK

EXHIBITS: OU/ET, WRTD

GUTIÉRREZ, JUAN B. *Santa Clara*

A.K.A. Signature: J. B. Gutiérrez

RESIDENCE: Santa Fe, NM

EDUCATION: Santa Fe, ca. 1937

MEDIA: Watercolor

PUBLISHED: Snodgrass (1968). *The Bulletin of the Cleveland Museum of Art* (Jan 1982)

PUBLIC COLLECTIONS: CAM, OU/SM

EXHIBITS: AIEC, CAM

HAARALA, LLOYD *Ojibwa*

Ke-Sha-Ona-Quat

Born 27 Aug 1940 in Port Arthur, ON

HA A TEE (see Quintana, Ben)

HACHIVI (see Heap of Birds, Edgar)

HADACÜTSE (see Red Corn)

HADLEY, WADE *Navajo*

To'dachine

MILITARY: U.S. Army, WWII

EDUCATION: Santa Fe, 1936-1937

OCCUPATION: Trading post clerk and painter

MEDIA: Watercolor, pen and ink, hide, and prints

PUBLISHED: Dunn (1968); Snodgrass (1968); Tanner (1973). Arizona Highways (July 1956)

EXHIBITS: FWG, NGA

HAGAN, MELODY *Tsimshian*

RESIDENCE: Paul's Valley, OK

EXHIBITS: RC

HAGPI, HATTIE *Inuit (Eskimo)*

A.K.A. Hattie Akilak

Born 1938

RESIDENCE: Baker Lake, NWT

PUBLISHED: Collinson (1978)

PUBLIC COLLECTIONS: C/U of AB

EXHIBITS: C/CG, C/SC

HAH GAY KEE HOODUH LEE (see Doonkeen, Eulamae Narcomey)

HALE, ROGER D. *Cherokee*

Born 29 Sept 1952 in Vinita, OK; son of Faye Corner and P. George Hale, knife maker; P/GP: Georgia and Phelan Hale

RESIDENCE: Bartlesville, OK

MILITARY: U.S. Army

EDUCATION: Caney Valley High School, Ramona, OK, 1970; OSU/O, 1972

OCCUPATION: Computer graphics analyst and painter

MEDIA: Oil and acrylic

EXHIBITS: Sunfest, Bartlesville, OK; IICOT Powwow, Tulsa, OK; Bartlesville (OK) Indian Women's Club Exhibition; Tulsa (OK) Gun Show

HALL, RONALD *Okanagan/Thompson*

Born 1962

RESIDENCE: British Columbia

OCCUPATION: Artist

MEDIA: Oil, acrylic, wood, rawhide, and buckskin

COMMISSIONS: Inter-Tribal Forestry Association of British Columbia

PUBLIC COLLECTIONS: C/INAC

EXHIBITS: Indian Arts and Crafts Society of British Columbia; Summerland, Kelowna, and Penticton Art Galleries

DETAIL: Rance Hood, *Untamed Hearts*, 1970. Philbrook Museum of Art, Tulsa, Oklahoma

HALSEY, MINISA CRUMBO *Creek/Potawatomi*

A.K.A. Minisa Crumbo

Born Sept 1942 in Tulsa, OK; daughter of Lillian Hogue and Woodrow "Woody" Crumbo (q.v.); P/GP: Mary and Alexander Crumbo; M/GP: Harriett and William Hogue

RESIDENCE: Nashville, TN

EDUCATION: Wasatch Academy, Mt. Pleasant, UT, 1961; U of TX/EP; Taos (NM) Academy of Fine Art, 1972-1974; Contemporary School of Visual Arts, New York, NY, 1974-1975

OCCUPATION: Teacher, manager of art collections, art gallery owner/manager, and painter

MEDIA: Oil, watercolor, pencil, charcoal, pen and ink, pastel, and prints

PUBLISHED: Biographical publications

COMMISSIONS: *Murals:* State of New Mexico, mural series in public buildings

PUBLIC COLLECTIONS: GM; HM; HSM/KS; PAC; U of Tulsa; Puskin Museum of Art, Moscow, USSSR

EXHIBITS: GM; MIF; PAC; U of NV/LV/M; U of OR; Three City Tour of USSR, 1978-1979; Tennessee State Museum, 1988; Museum of Ethnology, Hungary, 1987; Museum of Ethnology, Zagreb, Yugoslavia, 1987; Museum of National Literature, Prague, Czechoslovakia, 1987

SOLO EXHIBITS: GM; PACC; TSU; Oklahoma Governor's Special Showing, Oklahoma City, OK; Traveling Exhibition in USSR; Museum of Ethnology, Budapest, Hungary, 1988

AWARDS: PAC ('74, Graphics Award, Painting Award)

HONORS: New Mexico Arts Commission; Wasatch Academy, Mt. Plesant, UT, Distinguished Alumni Award; Baker University, Baldwin City, KS, Distinguished Service Award, 1982

HALWOOD, BENSON *Navajo*

Born 1963 in Keams Canyon, AZ; son of Annie T. and Ben Wilson Halwood Sr., Presbyterian minister and artist; P/GP: Pauline and Wilson Halwood Sr.; M/GM: Mae Yazzie

RESIDENCE: Arizona

EDUCATION: Chinle (AZ) High School, 1982; Albuquerque (NM) Technical Vocational School, 1986

OCCUPATION: Lesson aide for the boarding schools at Chinle and Many Farms, AZ, and artist

MEDIA: Acrylic, watercolor, and pastel

EXHIBITS: AC/ENP, FNAA, HM/G, ITIC, MNA, IPCC, SNAICF

AWARDS: ITIC ('91); MNA; IPCC ('88, 1st); SNAICF ('88, 1st)

HONORS: Bien Mur Market, Albuquerque, NM, poster artist, 1988

BENSON HALWOOD

A lecture by Justin Tso (q.v.), Navajo artist, to Halwood's high school senior class was an early influence on his art. Additional important influences have been David John, Dan Namingha and especially, Robert Draper (qq.v.) who is a relative as well as a friend.

artist, p.c. 1992

HAMILTON, RAY *Miwok*

A.K.A. Raymond Hamilton

MEDIA: Oil

PUBLISHED: Hill (1992)

PUBLIC COLLECTIONS: HCC, IAIA

EXHIBITS: IAIA

HAMILTON, RON *Nuu-Chah-Nulth (Nootka)*

Hupquatchew

Born 1948 Barkley Sound, Vancouver Island, BC, Canada, on Ahaswinis Reserve; nephew of George Clutesi (q.v.)

RESIDENCE: Ahaswinis, BC, Canada

EDUCATION: Apprenticed to Henry Hunt (q.v.), 1971

OCCUPATION: Fisherman, carver, graphic artist, and painter

MEDIA: Watercolor, wood, silver, gold, argillite, and ivory

PUBLISHED: Stewart (1979); Macnair, Hoover, and Neary (1980); Hall, Blackman, and Rickard (1981); McMasters, et al. (1993). *Canadian Indian Artcraft* (Vol. 1, no. 2, 1972); *The Native Voice* (Jan 1972); *Artscanada* (Jan/Dec 1973); *The Daily Colonist* (30 Aug 1970; 27 June 1974; 25 Aug 1974); *Four Winds* (1980); *Indian Artist* (spring 1995)

BOOKS ILLUSTRATED: *When The Morning Stars Sang Together*, by John S. Morgan

PUBLIC COLLECTIONS: C/RBCM

EXHIBITS: C/RBCM, C/TL

SOLO EXHIBITS: C/RBCM; C/U of BC/MA; British Columbia Archives, Victoria, BC, 1974; National Museum of Ethnology, Osaka, Japan, 1974; Port Alberni Museum, 1971

HAMVAS, TOBY *Yankton Sioux*

Born 4 Sept 1962 in Yankton, SD; son of Rosemary Fiddler and Duaine Rouse; adopted son of Louis and Carol Hamvas

RESIDENCE: Independence, MO

EDUCATION: Yankton (SD) High School, 1981

OCCUPATION: Computer clerk, roofer; full-time painter since 1990

MEDIA: Acrylic, watercolor, and prints

EXHIBITS: LIAS; TIAF; TWF; WIAME; Blue Valley Home Tour and Art Show, Overland Park, KS; Blue Ridge Fine Art Fair, Kansas City, MO; Kansas River Valley Art Fair, Topeka, KS; Topeka (KS) Art Fair; Powwow of Champions, Tulsa, OK, 1993

HANEMI DA (see Whitehorse, Roland N.)

HANEY, ENOCH KELLY *Seminole/Creek*

Born 12 Nov 1940 in Seminole, OK; son of Hattie and Woodrow Haney, flute maker and craftsman; P/GF: Willie Haney, contributor to Smithsonian Institution oral history project

RESIDENCE: Seminole, OK

MILITARY: Oklahoma National Guard

EDUCATION: Prairie Valley High School, Earlsboro, OK, 1959; A.A., BC, 1962; U of AZ, "Southwest Indian Art Project," scholarship, summer 1962; CSU/OK; B.A./M.A., OCU, 1965

OCCUPATION: Counselor, television show host, art director, business consultant, gallery owner, tribal official, editor, politician, legislator, and painter

MEDIA: Oil, acrylic, watercolor, pastel, and prints

PUBLISHED: Snodgrass (1968); Seabourn (1976); New (1981). *The Tulsa Tribune* (19 Oct 1977); *Southwest Art* (Sept 1979); *The Indian Trader* (Apr 1980); *Oklahoma Art Gallery* (spring 1980); *Inter-Tribal Voice* (Vol. 1, no. 6, 1983); *The Tulsa World* (15 Jan 1984; 18 Jan 1986); *Southern Living* (Oct 1988); *Oklahoma Today* (Dec 1990); *Country Treasures Gazette* (Mar 1991); *The Spirit* (Feb 1992)

COMMISSIONS: Westoaks Restaurant, Oklahoma City, OK, 24 paintings; private commissions

PUBLIC COLLECTIONS: FCTM, GM, HCC

EXHIBITS: AICA; BC/McG; CNM; FAIE; FAIEAIP; FCTM; FCTM/M; IAF; ITIC; MNA/D; NACLA; PAC; RE; SN; SWAIA; TIAF; TWF; USDI; UTAE; WIAME; Singapore, Malaysia; Switzerland; South Korea

ENOCH KELLY HANEY

In addition to being an artist and a gallery owner, in 1981 Haney was elected to the Oklahoma House of Representatives and has since been elected to the State Senate. He finds time to paint at night after he leaves the Capital, often painting until 1:00 am.

artist, p.c. 1992

SOLO EXHIBITS: FCTM; SPIM; U.S. Capitol Building, sponsored by Speaker of the House, Carl Albert, 1976; Oklahoma State Capitol Building, Blue Room, Oklahoma City, OK, 1984; Center Gallery, Bartlesville (OK) Community Center, 1994

AWARDS: AICA ('78, Gold Award); CNM ('86); ITIC ('76, Special Award); FCTM ('69, 1st, IH, Tiger Award; '70, IH; '71, 1st, IH, Tiger Award; '72, 1st, IH; '73, Needle Point Guild Award, Tiger Award; '74, 1st, Grand Award); FCTM/M ('83; '85, IH; '92); SWAIA ('77, 1st; '78, 2-1st, Best of Division); TIAF ('92; '94, Best of Show, Peoples Choice); PAC ('71, 1st; '72; '73; '76; '77; '78); UTAE ('92, 1st); WIAME ('94, 1st)

HONORS: Named one of the Outstanding Young Men of America, 1972; FCTM, designated a Master Artist, 1976; State of Oklahoma, Governor's Art Award, 1978; Bacone (OK) College Board of Trustees; Oklahoma City (OK) University, Distinguished Alumni Award, 1982; Seminole (OK) Chamber of Commerce, Community Service Award, 1984; Inducted into Bacone (OK) College Hall of Fame, 1986; National Black Caucus of State Legislators, Statesman's Award for Excellence, 1987; Norman (OK) Chamber of Commerce, Legislator of the Year, 1989; State of Oklahoma, Oklahoma Distinguished Service Award, 1991

HANK, CARL *Eskimo*

RESIDENCE: Kotzebue, AK

Born 1910 at Point Hope, AK

EDUCATION: DCTP, 1964-1965

PUBLISHED: Ray (1969)

HANNA, R.W. *Kiowa*

PUBLISHED: Snodgrass (1968)

PUBLIC COLLECTIONS: AF

HANNAH, MATTIE *Cherokee*

OCCUPATION: Carver, jeweler, and painter

MEDIA: Oil, watercolor, silver, leather, and wood

EXHIBITS: CNM, HM

HANSEN, MONICA JO *Cherokee*

Born 11 Nov 1964 in Muskogee, OK; daughter of Theodora Gale Griffith and Kenneth Lloyd Hansen; P/GP: Frances Schnieder and Hans Lloyd Hansen; M/GP: Nonnie and Theodore Griffith

RESIDENCE: Tulsa, OK

EDUCATION: Bishop Kelley High School, Tulsa, OK, 1983; U of Tulsa, 1987

OCCUPATION: Artist

MEDIA: Gouache and prints

BOOKS ILLUSTRATED: Kershen (1993)

EXHIBITS: CNM, FCTM, ITIC, OIAC, RC, TIAF, TWF

AWARDS: FCTM ('93); OIAC ('95)

HONORS: RC, Thunderbird Foundation Scholarship, 1992

HANSON, JOAN STONE *Cherokee*

Born 1945 in New Orleans, LA

RESIDENCE: Muskogee, OK

PUBLISHED: Snodgrass (1968)

EXHIBITS: FCTM, FAIEAIP, PAC

AWARDS: FCTM ('67)

HANUSE, ROY JAMES *Kwakwaka'wakw (Kwakiutl)*

Born 15 Oct 1943 in Bella Bella, BC, Canada

RESIDENCE: Canada

EDUCATION: Schools in Alert Bay, BC; studied under Doug Cranmer (q.v.)

MEDIA: Watercolor, pencil and prints

PUBLISHED: Hall, Blackman, and Rickard (1981)

PUBLIC COLLECTIONS: C/RBCM, C/U of BC/MA

EXHIBITS: Expo '67

ROY JAMES HANUSE

Hanuse became interested in silk screening in 1974. His style is characterized by expert draftsmanship, innovations in design elements, and tight compositional control. An important theme in his work is the killer whale.

brochure, Indian Artists Guild, 1978

HAOZOUS (see Houser, Allan)

HAPAHA, L. *Navajo*

PUBLISHED: Snodgrass (1968)

EXHIBITS: EITA

HA-PAH-SHU-TSE (see Red Corn, Jim)

HAPPY BOY (see Austin, Frank)

HAPPY FACES (see Smith, O.J.)

HAPPY JACK (see Angokwazhuk)

HARD HEAD (see Oxford, Eva Mae)

HARD HEART *Oglala Sioux*

Conte Feri

Birth date unknown

RESIDENCE: Lived in the vicinity of the Pine Ridge Agency, SD

PUBLISHED: Snodgrass (1968)

PUBLIC COLLECTIONS: MAI

HARDIN, HELEN *Santa Clara*

Tsa Sah Wee Eh, Little Standing Spruce

A.K.A. Signature: Tsa-Sha-Wee-Eh with H.H. and spruce symbol

Born 28 May 1943 in Albuquerque, NM; died 9 June 1984 in Albuquerque, NM, of cancer; daughter of Pablita Velarde (q.v.) and Herbert O. Hardin; M/GF: Herman Velarde

RESIDENCE: Lived in Española, NM

EDUCATION: Pius X High School, Albuquerque, NM; U of NM; U of AZ, "Southwest Indian Art Project," scholarship, summer 1960

MEDIA: Oil, acrylic, watercolor, pen and ink, casein, and prints

PUBLISHED: Snodgrass (1968); Brody (1971); Tanner (1968; 1973); Stuart and Ashton (1977); Silberman (1978); Katz (1980); Broder (1981; 1984); Medina (1981); Samuels (1982); Jacka and Jacka (1988); Seymour (1988); Scott (1989); Williams, ed. (1990); Gully, ed. (1994). *Seventeen* (June 1959); *The Denver Post* (25 May 1973); *Artists of the Rockies and the Golden West* (spring 1977); *American Indian Art* (summer 1979); *Southwest Art* (Aug 1978; Apr 1981; June 1985; June 1994); *Voices South* (Sept/Oct 1980); *Portfolio* (July/Aug 1981); *The Toronto Globe and Mail* (21 Aug 1982); *The Indian Trader* (Nov 1984); *Art of the West* (Nov/Dec 1991); *Native People* (winter 1992)

COMMISSIONS: *Murals:* IPCC

PUBLIC COLLECTIONS: HM; IACB; MNM; MRFM; OU/MA; SM; U of CA/LB; WWM; Loyola Marymount College of Law, Los Angeles, CA

EXHIBITS: AAID, AIAE/WSU, AICH, AIWSAF, ASM, HM, HM/G, ITIC, IK, KCPA, LGAM, MCC/CA, MCC, MKMcNAI, MNM, NAP, NU/BC, OMA, OU/MA, PAC, PBS, WSCS, SFFA, SI, SN, SV, SWAIA, WWM

HELEN HARDIN

Hardin sold her first painting when she was six and entered her first painting at the Inter-Tribal Indian Ceremonial exhibition when she was nine. She admitted that after a while she took time out for "being just a kid" but began serious painting about 1967. Of her painting she said, "I don't want to be rich and famous, I want to be the best."

Samuels 1982

In 1991 a painting by Hardin sold for $45,000, a record price for a painting by a female Native American.

SOLO EXHIBITS: HM; KSU; USIS (Colombia and Guatemala); Coronado State Monument, NM

AWARDS: AAID ('68); HM/G ('75, 1st, Avery Award); ITIC ('68, 1st; '70; '77, Best of Class; '79); MNM; PAC ('68; '69; '77, 1st); SN ('68, 1st; '69; '72, Best of Show, Special Award); SWAIA ('71, 1st; '72, 1st; '73, 1st; '74, 1st, Hinds Award)

HONORS: Public Broadcasting System documentary, *American Indian Artists I*, only female featured, 1974; SWAIA and WWM, member of the Board of Directors

HARDIN, KATHY *Cherokee*

EXHIBITS: FCTM

AWARDS: FCTM ('71)

HARING, MARGUERITE LEE *Seneca*

Born 22 June 1944

RESIDENCE: Irving, NY

EDUCATION: A.A., BC, 1965; OCLA, 1966; B.S., Rose Hill College, Buffalo, NY, 1970; M.A., SUNY/B

OCCUPATION: Instructor, consultant, and artist

MEDIA: Oil, acrylic, watercolor, charcoal, pastel, and prints

PUBLISHED: Snodgrass (1968); Johannsen and Ferguson, eds. (1983)

EXHIBITS: ACS/EM, ECFE, INAAT, NYSF; Erie County Savings Bank, Buffalo, NY; Indian Falls Festival, Cattaraugus, NY

HARJO, ALBERT *Creek*

RESIDENCE: Okemah, OK

EXHIBITS: FCTM, PAC, RE; see also Awards

SOLO EXHIBITS: CCHM

AWARDS: FCTM ('78); American Red Cross of Tulsa (OK), Native American Bone Marrow Recruitment Poster Contest ('93, 1st)

HARJO, BENJAMIN, JR. *Seminole/Shawnee*

A.K.A. Ben Harjo

Born 19 Sept 1945 in Clovis, NM; son of Viola and Benjamin Harjo Sr.; P/GP: Jimmy and Ruth Harjo; Cousin of Randy Wood (q.v.)

RESIDENCE: Oklahoma City, OK

MILITARY: U.S. Army, Vietnam, 1969-1971

EDUCATION: Byng (OK) High School, 1964; IAIA, 1966; B.F.A., OSU, 1974; U of Tulsa

OCCUPATION: Cultural recreational coordinator, teacher; professional artist since 1976

MEDIA: Oil, acrylic, watercolor, gouache, conté, pencil, pen and ink, pastel, clay, stone, and prints

PUBLISHED: King (1981). *Art Voices* (1981); *American Indian Art* (spring 1985); *Contemporary Southeastern Indian Artists* (1988); *Southwest Art* (Mar 1988; Aug 1988); *Southern Living* (Oct 1988); *The Tulsa World* (6 June, 1988; 2 June 1992; 9 Jan 1994); *Santa Fe Indian Market Catalog* (1989); *The Anadarko Daily News* (22 Aug 1990); *Intertribal* (Oct 1990); *Oklahoma Today* (Dec 1990; May/June 1994); *Oklahoma Rural News* (May 1991); USA *Today* (3 June 1993); *The Muskogee Daily Phoenix* (4 Oct 1993)

COMMISSIONS: Tulsa (OK) Indian Actors' Workshop, design stage sets, 1994

PUBLIC COLLECTIONS: GM; Museum of Art, Shawnee, OK; U.S. Embassy, Mogadishu, Somalia

EXHIBITS: AC/A; AC/K; ACAI; AIAFM; AICA; BB; CANA; CNM; GM; HM;

BENJAMIN HARJO JR.

According to the artist, "Art is a continual learning process for me. It is a lifelong process, one in which I am constantly changing, and my ideas are constantly changing and fresh."

Art Voices, *May 1981*

Much of Harjo's work displays his lively sense of humor and the fun he has working with line and color. A brillant colorist, his current direction is the geometric depiction of Indian subjects, although his earlier works were more realistic.

FAIE; FCTM; MFA/O; MIF; MNH/AN; MNH/LA; MPABAS; NACLA; OAC; OIAP; OSAC; PAC; RE; RM; SDMM; SFFA; SN; SPIM; SWAIA; TIAF; TWF; VL; WIAME; World Exposition of Historical Cities, Kyoto, Japan (1987); see also Awards

SOLO/SPECIAL EXHIBITS: CAI/KC (dual show), SPIM, WIAME, WWM

AWARDS: ACAI ('93, 1st, Best of Waterbase Painting, Best of Class); AICA ('86, Gold Medal, '91, Gold Medal and Native American Heritage Award; '93, Bronze Medal); CIM ('87); CANA ('79, Award of Merit); CNM ('80, Painting Award; '81, Trail of Tears Award; '82; '83, 1st; '84; '85, Best of Category; '86, 1st; '94); FCTM ('80, 1st; '82, 1st); FCTM/M ('88, 1st; '88, 1st; '90; '91, '93, 1st); OCSA ('78, 1st; '79); RE ('87; '88, 1st, Grand Award; '89; '90; '92, People's Favorite Artist Award); SWAIA ('83, 1st, Best of Division; '84, 1st; '85; '86, 1st, Best of Class, Best of Division; '87, 2-1st; '88, 2-1st, Grand Award, '89, 2-1st, Best of Division; '90, 3-1st, Woody Crumbo Award; '94, 1st, Best of Division); TWF ('92); WIAME ('94 Grand Award); Cultures and Arts of Native Americans, U of OK ('79)

HONORS: Red Earth, appointed Arts Coordinator, 1987; IEEPF, Easter egg design, 1988; FCTM, designated a Master Artist, 1988; HM/G, poster artist, 1992; Absolut Vodka Commission, selected to represent Oklahoma, (International advertising of artist and work), 1992; IACA, poster artist, 1994

HARJO, L. P. *Creek*

EXHIBITS: FCTM

AWARDS: FCTM ('88)

HARJO, MARCELLE SHARRON (see Harjo, Sharron Ahtone)

HARJO, MASON *Creek*

EXHIBITS: FCTM

AWARDS: FCTM ('82)

HARJO, SHARRON AHTONE *Kiowa*

Sain-Tah-Oodie, Killed With a Blunted Arrow

A.K.A. Marcelle Sharron Harjo

Born 6 Jan 1945 in Carnegie, OK; daughter of Evelyn Tahome and Jacob Ahtone, Kiowa Tribal Chairman, 1978-1980; P/GP: Tahdo and Sam Ahtone; M/GP: A. Jane Goombi and Stephen Poolant (Tahome)

RESIDENCE: Oklahoma City, OK

EDUCATION: Billings (MT) West High School, 1963; A.A., BC, 1965; B.A., NSU, 1968

OCCUPATION: Art instructor, basket maker, and painter

MEDIA: Oil, acrylic, watercolor, pencil, and gouache

PUBLISHED: Boyd, et al. (1981; 1983). *Art-Talk* (June/July 1985); *Oklahoma Today* (July/Aug 1985; Dec 1990); *The Eagle* (June/July 1988); *The Broken Arrow Scout* (15 Jan 1992)

PUBLIC COLLECTIONS: CAI/KC; CGPS; SPIM; Haffenreffer Museum of Anthropology, Brown University, Providence, RI; Oklahoma State Historical Society, Oklahoma City, OK

EXHIBITS: ABQM, ACAI, AIE, BB, BC/McG, CNM, CSPIP, DE, HMA, JH, LIAS, OAC, OIAP, OSC, PAC, RC, RE, SPIM

SOLO EXHIBITS: CAI/KC; SPIM; BIA; Federal Building, Billings, MT

AWARDS: ACAI ('92, 1st); AIE ('70; '71; '72; '73, 1st, Grand Award; '74; '75, 2-1st; '76, 1st; '77, 1st; '78, 2-1st; '79, 1st; '80; '81); PAC ('71)

HONORS: Miss Indian America, 1966; AAID, scholarship, 1976; SPIM, Board of Directors; Oklahoma Federation of Indian Women, Outstanding Indian Woman of Oklahoma Award; Oklahoma State Capitol Building, East Gallery, *Year of the Indian Exhibition*, one of eight Oklahoma Indian artists exhibited

HARNEY, CECIL *Apache*

EXHIBITS: HM/G

AWARDS: HM/G ('70; '72)

HARRIS, ED *Paiute*

PUBLISHED: Snodgrass (1968)

PUBLIC COLLECTIONS: SM

HARRIS, SAM L., JR. *Choctaw*

Born 18 June 1952

RESIDENCE: Tohatchi, NM

EDUCATION: Poteau (OK) High School; SOSU

OCCUPATION: Teacher and painter

EXHIBITS: HM/G; RC; Green Country Art Association, Dogwood Festival; and local and county shows

AWARDS: First, second, and third-place awards from local and county shows

HARRIS, WALT *Otoe/Missouri*

Born 2 Dec 1923 on the Otoe reservation near Red Rock, OK; died 14 July 1986 in Tulsa, OK

RESIDENCE: Lived in Ponca City, OK

MILITARY: U.S. Army, 101st Airborne, WWII

EDUCATION: Ponca City (OK) High School, 1942; Northern Oklahoma Junior College, Tonkawa, OK; U of OK

OCCUPATION: Professional baseball player, illustrator, cartoonist, rural mail carrier, and artist

MEDIA: Oil, watercolor, and prints

PUBLISHED: McMasters, et al. (1993). *The Southwest Times Record* (3 Oct 1975); *The Indian Trader* (July 1978); *Oklahoma Art Gallery* (spring 1980); *Art Gallery* (Aug/Sept 1984); *The Tulsa Tribune* (14 July 1986)

COMMISSIONS: *Portraits:* Portrait of General Morris which hangs in the Pentagon, Washington, D.C.; Scioto Historical Society of Ohio, portrait of Tecumseh. *Other:* Mountain Eagle Indian Festival, Hunter Mountain, NY, poster; Ponca City (OK) Bicentennial film, *Bride of Morning Star,* thirty paintings

PUBLIC COLLECTIONS: OAC; SGC/OK; Ponca City (OK) Cultural Center and Indian Museum

EXHIBITS: CNM, KCPA, OAC, OIAP

SOLO EXHIBITS: SPIM

AWARDS: First-place and Best of Shows in Oklahoma and Arizona

HONORS: French Market Show, Oklahoma City, OK, Outstanding Indian Artist, 1975; Governor of Oklahoma, Artist of the Month, 1978; Mrs. Walter Mondale selected one of his paintings to hang in the White House.

WALT HARRIS

An outstanding athlete, the artist attended college on athletic scholarships and was a professional baseball player until he was disabled by an injury. He is best known for his portrait work. Of his art Harris was quoted as saying "... It's my way of preserving our way of life. Some of us have certain ways of leaving something of our culture behind and this is the only way I have to preserve our heritage. I do it so it'll live on after I'm gone. I portray the Indian as a happy, home-loving person. I try to relay the happy way of life...."

brochure, SPIM, 1979

He was known as "the Happy Indian Artist."

HARRIS, WALTER *Tsimshian*

Born 1931 in Kispiox, BC, Canada

RESIDENCE: Canada

EDUCATION: C/KSNCIA, 1969

OCCUPATION: Teacher, carver, jeweler, graphic artist, muralist, and painter

PUBLISHED: Steltzer (1976); Macnair, Hoover, and Neary (1980); Hall, Blackman, and Rickard (1981). *Gazette* (Vol. 6, nos. 5 & 6, 1973); *Sunset Magazine* (May 1973); *Artscanada* (Dec/Jan 1973); *The Indian News* (Vol. 19, no. 4, 1978); *The*

Native Perspective (Vol. 3, no. 2, 1978); *Western Living* (Oct 1980)

COMMISSIONS: *Murals:* Canadian Embassy, Paris, France; Royal Centre, Vancouver, BC. *Other:* House of Commons, Parliament Building, Ottawa, ON, stone relief sculpture

PUBLIC COLLECTIONS: C/RBCM, C/CMC, C/INAC

EXHIBITS: C/TL, EIAF

HARRISON, LOUISE *Southern Cheyenne/Arapaho*

Red Turtle

Born 14 Jan 1949 in Watonga, OK; daughter of Rose and Adam Harrison

RESIDENCE: Lapwai, ID

EDUCATION: Chilocco, 1968; A.A., IAIA, 1971

OCCUPATION: Beadworker and painter

MEDIA: Acrylic and glass beads

EXHIBITS: LCIAS; PAF; RE; Valley Art Center, Clarkston, WA

AWARDS: RE ('93)

HARRISON, THOMAS W. *Navajo*

EXHIBITS: HM/G

AWARDS: HM/G ('71)

HARRY HAND (see Sitting Eagle)

HART, ELIZABETH K. *Cherokee*

EXHIBITS: CNM, PAC

AWARDS: CNM ('84, 1st)

HARVEY, ANDERSON *Navajo*

Born 13 Mar 1962; son of Nellie and Andrew Harvey; P/GP: Betty and John Harvey; M/GP: Yacasbah and Hosteen Y. Begay

RESIDENCE: Chinle, AZ

EDUCATION: Chinle (AZ) High School and Hellgate High School, Missoula, MT, 1981; BC, 1982; IAIA, 1985

OCCUPATION: Navajo Tribal Ranger and artist

MEDIA: Oil, acrylic, watercolor, pencil, and pen and ink

COMMISSIONS: *Murals:* Ned A. Hatathli Museum, NCC, Tsaile, AZ, funded by Metropolitan Life Foundation

PUBLIC COLLECTIONS: IAIA; Museum für Völderkunde, Vienna, Austria

EXHIBITS: BC, HM/G, IAIA, MNA, RC

AWARDS: BC ('82, Best of Show); HM/G ('79, Best of Student Graphics); MNA, RC ('83)

HONORS: RC, Thunderbird Foundation Scholarship, 1984; Certified Law Enforcement Officer, 1986; Ranger of the Year, 1989; accepted to the Federal Law Enforcement Training Center, Marana, AZ, 1989

HARVEY, DOUG *Northwest Coast*

EXHIBITS: ITIC

AWARDS: ITIC ('90, 1st)

HARVEY, PETE, JR. *Navajo*

EDUCATION: Fort Sill

PUBLISHED: Snodgrass (1968)

EXHIBITS: PAC

HARVIER, MICHAEL *Taos*

Quameomah

Birth date unknown; son of Tonita Harvier, who lives and works in Taos, NM

EDUCATION: BC

OCCUPATION: USDI employee, BIA artist, and painter

PUBLISHED: Snodgrass (1968)

PUBLIC COLLECTIONS: MNM

EXHIBITS: DAM, FWG, MNM, PAC

HARWOOD, RAYMOND, JR. *Sioux/Blackfeet*

Born 25 Apr 1958 in Sisseton, SD

RESIDENCE: Babb, MT

EDUCATION: Browning (MT) High School

OCCUPATION: Rancher, rodeo contestant, construction worker, sculptor and painter

MEDIA: Oil, watercolor, charcoal, wax, and bronze

EXHIBITS: GFNAAS; Invitational Show, Sun Valley, ID; Jay Contway and Friends Show of Western Art, Great Falls, MT

SOLO EXHIBITS: MPI

HASHKE NAALWOD (see Chee, Jason D.)

HASHKE-YIL-E-CALE (see Chee, Robert)

HASHKAY-HA-NAH (see Shirley, Nelson Dodge)

HASKAY YAH NE YAH (see Begay, Harrison)

HASKEW, LULA M. *Potawatomi*

Born 7 Feb 1921 in Hydra, OK; daughter of Bertha Murry and Martin Richard Self; mother of Denny Haskew, sculptor; P/GP: Carolyn Roof and Martin Self; M/GP: Isabelle Pettifer and Charlie Shallus

RESIDENCE: Loveland, CO

EDUCATION: Thomas High School, 1939; SWOSU, 1942; Scottsdale (AZ) Art School and Loveland (CO) Art Center

OCCUPATION: Teacher and artist

MEDIA: Oil, watercolor, and pen and ink

EXHIBITS: Poudre Valley Art Show, CO; Western Heritage Museum Show, Cheyenne, WY; see also Awards

AWARDS: Thompson Valley Regional Art Show (1989, 2-1st; 1990, 2-1st)

HAS NO HORSES, SIDNEY *Oglala Sioux*

RESIDENCE: Batesland, SD

EXHIBITS: NPTA, RC

HA SO DE (see Abeyta, Tony)

HA SO DE (see Abeyta, Narciso Platero)

HA SO DEH (see Abeyta, Narciso Platero)

HASTINGS, CAIN *Navajo*

Born ca. 1923

RESIDENCE: Whiteriver, AZ

EDUCATION: Fort Apache Boarding School

OCCUPATION: Civilian Conservation Corps, copper miner, BIA employee, carver and painter

MEDIA: Oil, acrylic, watercolor, and wood
PUBLISHED: Snodgrass (1968)
EXHIBITS: ITIC, NICCAS

HATAU, DENNIS *(?)*
EXHIBITS: ITIC
AWARDS: ITIC ('91, 1st, Best in Category)

HATCH, GLEN *Ute*
PUBLISHED: Snodgrass (1968)
EXHIBITS: SMNAI

HATCH, WILLIAM *Navajo*
Born 2 Nov 1955
RESIDENCE: Fruitland, NM
EDUCATION: Kirtland (NM) Central High School; U of NM; NMSU; B.F.A., BYU, 1982
OCCUPATION: Artist
EXHIBITS: ITIC, NMSF, RC
AWARDS: NMSF (1st)
HONORS: RC, Thunderbird Foundation Scholarship, 1983

HA TLV WE DA (see Brown, Sherry Lynn)

HATTEN, DUANE *Northern Cheyenne*
RESIDENCE: Lame Deer, MT
EXHIBITS: RC ('86)

HAUKAAS, LINDA *Rosebud Sioux*
EXHIBITS: NPTA
AWARDS: NPTA ('93)

HAUKAAS, TOM *Sioux*
EXHIBITS: SWAIA
AWARDS: SWAIA ('94, 1st)

HAUNGOOAH (see Silverhorn)

HAUNGOOAH, ARTHUR GERALD *Kiowa*
A.K.A. Cody Haungooah
Born 25 Apr 1943 in Lawton, OK; M/GF: Haungooah (Silverhorn, q.v.), Army scout and Kiowa artist
RESIDENCE: Española, NM
MILITARY: U.S. Army
EDUCATION: Fort Sill; Cameron College, Lawton, OK; U of NM; A.A., IAIA
OCCUPATION: Potter, sculptor, and graphic artist
MEDIA: Pen and ink, stone, bronze, and clay
EXHIBITS: HM/G, SIAF
SOLO EXHIBITS: SPIM
AWARDS: HM/G ('72, 1st; '76, 1st; '79, Best of Show, Best of Sculpture); SIAF ('73, 1st); SN ('74, 1st)

ARTHUR GERALD HAUNGOOAH

The artist is best known for his sculpture and the pottery he creates with his wife, Martha.

HAUNGOOAH (see Silverhorn)

HAUNGOOAH, CODY (see Haungooah, Arthur Gerald)

HAUNGOONPAU (see Silverhorn)

HAUSMAN, JUANITA PAHDOPONY *Comanche*

RESIDENCE: Lawton, OK

EXHIBITS: CNM, PAC

HAVARD, JAMES *Chippewa/Choctaw*

JAMES HAVARD

Havard paints in a style he calls "abstract illusionism." He achieves a three-dimension effect by the use of shadows and flotation.

Wade, ed. 1986

Born 1937 in Galveston, TX

RESIDENCE: Philadelphia, PA

EDUCATION: B.S., Sam Houston State College, Huntsville, TX, 1959; Atelier Chapman Kelly, Dallas, TX, 1960; Pennsylvania Academy of Fine Arts, Philadelphia, PA, 1965

OCCUPATION: Artist

MEDIA: Oil and acrylic

PUBLISHED: Highwater (1980; 1983); Amerson, ed. (1981); Wade and Strickland (1981); Hoffman, et al. (1984); Wade, ed. (1986). *Art News* (summer 1977); *Arts Magazine* (May 1977)

PUBLIC COLLECTIONS: GM/NY; HM; LACM; MMA/NY; NYU; OAC; PMA; SI; W; WWM; Byers Museum of Arts, Evanston, IL; Pennsylvania Academy of Fine Arts; Temple University, Philadelphia, PA; corporate collections in IL, NJ, NY, PA, and Sweden

EXHIBITS: AI; BAM; CTC; CWPC; DAM; GM/NY; HM; IK; IMA; MFA/H; MFA/O; MHDYMM; OAC; PAC; PAM/AZ; PMA; SAM; SI; TMA; U of CA/D; Albright Knox Museum, Buffalo, NY; Baltimore (MD) Museum of Art; Butler Institution of American Art, Youngstown, OH; Cooper-Hewitt Museum of Art, NYC; Danforth Museum, Framingham, MA; Edwin Ulrich Museum, Wichita, KS; Fine Arts Museum, Los Angeles, CA; High Museum of Art, Atlanta, GA; Paul Mellon Art Center, Wallingford, CT; Taft Museum, Cincinnati, OH

SOLO EXHIBITS: Temple University, Philadelphia; galleries in the U.S., Canada, and Europe

HAWELANA (see Herrera, Marcelina)

HAWGONE (see Silverhorn)

HAWK *Gros Ventre*

PUBLISHED: Snodgrass (1968)

PUBLIC COLLECTIONS: HS/PA (three sheets, 1858-1860)

HAWK (see Pratt, Charles)

HAWK, JONNY *Creek/Seminole*

A.K.A. Johnson Lee Scott, Johnny Hawk

RESIDENCE: Oklahoma City, OK

EDUCATION: Sequoyah High School, 1955; OSU/O

OCCUPATION: Artist

MEDIA: Acrylic, watercolor, and prints

PUBLISHED: Snodgrass (1968)

EXHIBITS: FAIE, FCTM, HM, ITIC, OAC, PAC, TWF; see also Awards

AWARDS: CNM (1st, Grand Award); FCTM ('67; '70; '73; '78); ITIC ('77, 1st); Five State Regional National Watercolor Show, Oakland, CA ('78, Best of Show)

HAWK MAN *Sioux*

HAWK MAN

"Hawk Man is thought to have been among the Indian Police from the Fort when the 1890 skirmish at Sittings Bull's camp took place and the chief was killed (see Vestal 1933)."

Snodgrass 1968

Birth date unknown; death ca. 1890

RESIDENCE: Lived on the Standing Rock Reservation, Dakota Territory

OCCUPATION: Indian policeman and artist

PUBLISHED: Snodgrass (1968)

PUBLIC COLLECTIONS: MAI (dated ca. 1884)

HAW VAHTE *Kiowa*

Haw Vahte was the keeper of a Winter Count (calendar) that bears his name. At his death Jimmy Quoetone and Charles Emery Rowell (qq.v.) assumed the responsibility for recording subsequent tribal history.

HAWZIPTA, GUS D. *Kiowa*

RESIDENCE: Park Hill, OK
EXHIBITS: LIAS/M, PAC, RE, TWF
AWARDS: PAC ('73)

HAYDAH, WILLIAM D. *Hopi*

PUBLISHED: Snodgrass (1968)
PUBLIC COLLECTIONS: MNM

HAYOKAH (see Mana)

HEAP OF BIRDS, EDGAR *Cheyenne/Arapaho*

Hachivi
A.K.A. Hachivi Edgar Heap of Birds
Born 22 Nov 1954 in Wichita, KS
RESIDENCE: Geary, OK
EDUCATION: East High School, Wichita, KS, 1972; Haskell, 1974; B.F.A., U of KS, 1976; Royal College of Art, London, England, 1976-1977; M.F.A., Temple University, Philadelphia, PA, 1979
OCCUPATION: Educator and artist
PUBLISHED: Amerson, ed. (1981); Abbott (1994). *Native Arts/West* (Apr 1981); *Arizona Arts and Lifestyle* (autumn 1981); *The Indian* (May 1982; Apr 1990); *C Magazine* (summer 1991); *The Tulsa World* (9 June 1991); *Front* (Nov/Dec 1991); *Art News* (Feb 1992)
COMMISSIONS: Walker Art Center, Minneapolis, MN, Building Minnesota
PUBLIC COLLECTIONS: JAM, WSAC
EXHIBITS: AC/S; AICA/SF; AICH; C/AG/V; CNGM; CSU/OK; CTC; FWMA; HSM/OK; JAM; MFA/A; MNH/KS; NACLA; OSU/G; TPAS; U of KS; U of MA; U of TULSA/AC; W; New Museum of Contemporary Art, New York, NY; Hunter College, New York, NY; Museum of Modern Art, New York, NY; Institute of Contemporary Art, Boston, MA
SOLO EXHIBITS: SPIM; The Balch Institute for Ethnic Studies, Philadelphia, PA; San Jose (CA) Museum of Art, 1991
AWARDS: U of KS ('75 & '76, Ward Lockwood Competitive Painting Award)
HONORS: Public Art Fund of New York and Spectacolor, *Messages to the Public*, one of twelve artists selected, 1982

EDGAR HEAP OF BIRDS

Influenced by East Coast American art, Heap of Birds is a perceptual artist who creates through the interplay of visual and mental images. Working with painted images as well as word images and associations, Heap of Birds provides an environment in which the viewer is free to make his or her own mental images -thus creating an entirely new and often uniquely individual aesthetic experience.

brochure, SPIM, 1982

HEAVY SHIELD, FAYE *Blackfoot*

Birth date unknown; born in Alberta, Canada, on the Blood Reserve
RESIDENCE: Canada
EDUCATION: C/U of C; C/ACA
PUBLIC COLLECTIONS: HM; Alberta Indian Arts and Crafts Society, Edmonton, AB; Indian Art Center, Ottawa, ON
EXHIBITS: C/AM; C/C; C/TGVA; DC; HM; U of MA; galleries in Calgary and Edmonton, AB
AWARDS: C/AM
HONORS: *Scholarships:* Heinz-Jordan Memorial Scholarship, 1984; Ben Calf Robe Memorial Scholarship, 1985

Anna Sue Hebert-Wilcox

The artist began painting in 1964, when she was nine years old and was living in Tucson, AZ; she was tremendously influenced by the art and culture of the Southwest. Since that time she has lived throughout the western and southern United States and in Europe. In 1975, she started painting privately commissioned portraits.

artist, p.c. 1992

Hebert-Wilcox, Anna Sue *Cherokee/Choctaw*

A.K.A. Anna Sue Wilcox

Born 30 Aug 1955 in Fresno, CA; daughter of Anna Sue Garrett and Robert James Link; P/GP: Clara and Hubert Link; M/GP: Julia and W. B. Garrett

RESIDENCE: Van Buren, AR

EDUCATION: Tucson (AZ) High School, 1973; University of Maryland Extension, West Germany; private art instruction, John Bell Jr.

OCCUPATION: Artist

MEDIA: Oil

COMMISSIONS: *Murals:* Cedarville (AR) Elementary School, AR; *Other:* IBM, Northwest Arkansas Offices, logos

PUBLIC COLLECTIONS: FSAC; Bayou Country Art Association, Sulphur Springs, LA

EXHIBITS: CNM; Pima County Fair, Tucson, AZ; annual exhibits in Arkansas and Louisiana; see also Awards

AWARDS: Bayou Country Heritage Art Association Exhibition; Beauregard Parish Fair; Louisiana State Fair

Hechaka, Lucahan (see Fast Deer)

Hehaka Wamabdi (see Red Elk, Herman)

Hehon Womblee (see Eagle Feather, Elijah)

Hehúwésse (see Yellow Nose)

Helele (see Ladd, Edmund J.)

Helin, William Herbert *Tsimshian*

A.K.A. Bill Herbert

Birth date unknown; born in Prince Rupert, BC, Canada

RESIDENCE: Vancouver Island, BC, Canada

EDUCATION: C/KSNCIA

OCCUPATION: Carver, printmaker, and painter

Helper, Marvin *Oglala Sioux*

RESIDENCE: Oglala, SD

PUBLIC COLLECTIONS: HCC

EXHIBITS: RC

Henate (see Galván, Andrés)

K. Henderson

Although she paints a variety of subjects, Henderson is perhaps best known for her paintings of Native Americans. Using whichever medium fits the subject and frequently working from photographs she has taken, she paints the contemporary Native American. She gives special attention to faces and a great deal of effort goes into developing the individual personality of the subject. "I like to portray the American Indians as they are today. So many artists show only the past, I like to remind people that the traditions and culture are still alive and well."

p.c. 1992

Henderson, K. *Cherokee*

A.K.A. Kathy Henderson

Born 1 Dec 1954; daughter of Betty Copeland and Bert J. Henderson; P/GP: Janie O'Connor and A. J. Henderson; M/GP: Jessie Glenn and Leslie Copeland

RESIDENCE: Muskogee, OK

EDUCATION: Nathan Hale High School, Tulsa, OK, 1973; De Anza College, Cupertino, CA; Art Students Academy, Tulsa, OK; Bob Gerbracht's Studio, San Jose, CA

OCCUPATION: Costume designer, seamstress, graphic artist, and painter

MEDIA: Oil, watercolor, pencil, pastel, colored pencil, and prints

PUBLISHED: *Twin Territories* (Vol. 3, no. 1, 1993)

BOOKS ILLUSTRATED: Thomas, et al. (1983)

PUBLIC COLLECTIONS: HCC; SNM; Chatam Corporation, Chicago, IL; First National Bank, Tahlequah, OK; Ozark Guidance Center, Springdale, AR; Women in Safe Homes, Muskogee, OK; Muskogee (OK) Little Theater; Muskogee (OK) Performing Arts; Seminole Nation Museum, Wewoka, OK

EXHIBITS: BB; CHASC; CNM; CMRM; CPS; FAC/ETG; FCTM; LC; LIAS; MCI; PSA; RC; RE; TIAF; U of WV; WTF; American Academy of Equine Art; Mountain Oyster Club, Tucson, AZ; Pastel Society of America; Pastel Society of the Southwest, Prairie Home Carriage Classic Art Competition; St. Hubert's Giralda, Animal Imagery; see also Awards

SOLO EXHIBITS: CNM, FCTM, SNM

AWARDS: CHASC ('93); CNM ('88; '89; '90; '92; '93; '94); FCTM ('87; '88, Indian Heritage Grand Award; '89, 1st; '90; '91; '92, SW Award; '93, 1st); FAC/ETG ('84, Certificate of Merit; '89, Best of Show, Best of Pastel); LIAS ('89, MA; '90, MA); LC ('89, 1st); MCI ('88, 1st, People's Choice Award; '89, 1st; '92, 1st; '93, 2-1st); RC ('89); RE ('90; '91, 1st; '92; '93, 1st); TIAF ('90, 1st; '92, 1st; '93, 1st; '94; '95, Best of Show, People's Choice Award); Cherokee History Art Show, Tahlequah, OK ('93); Fine Arts Center En Toas (NM) Galleries ('84, Certificate of Merit; '85, Best of Show, Best of Pastel); Kansas Pastel Society Exhibit ('86); Mid-West Pastel Society ('88); Oklahoma Arts Workshop ('85, Best of Show; '87, Douglas Warren Memorial); Springfield (MO) Realistic Fine Art Society Show ('86)

HENDERSON, MARK *Kwakwaka'wakw (Kwakiutl)*

Born 1953 at Campbell River, BC, Canada; son of Sam Henderson

RESIDENCE: Canada

OCCUPATION: Fisherman, painter, and graphic artist

MEDIA: Watercolor, graphite, pen and ink, and prints

PUBLISHED: Hall, Blackman, and Rickard (1981)

PUBLIC COLLECTIONS: C/CRM, C/RBCM, HCC

EXHIBITS: AUG, BHSU, NSU/SD, SDSMT, U of WV

HENRY, FRED *Hopi*

RESIDENCE: From Shungopovi, Second Mesa, AZ

PUBLISHED: Snodgrass (1968)

PUBLIC COLLECTIONS: MAI

HENRY, GARY *(?)*

EDUCATION: Phoenix, 1964

PUBLISHED: Snodgrass (1968)

EXHIBITS: FAIEAIP

HENRY, WOODWORTH V. *Snohomish*

Born 8 May 1931

RESIDENCE: Tacoma, WA

MILITARY: U. S. Air Force

EDUCATION: Burnley School of Art and Design, Seattle, WA

OCCUPATION: Cartoonist, commercial artist, and painter

PUBLISHED: Snodgrass (1968)

EXHIBITS: FAIEAIP; PAC; College of Puget Sound Annual Exhibition; Lakewood Artists Annual

AWARDS: FAIEAIP, PAC

HENSLEY, ROBERT *Chickasaw*

EXHIBITS: FCTM

AWARDS: FCTM ('82, 1st, IH; '83; '87, IH; '88, IH)

HENSON, BROOKS *Cherokee*

A.K.A. Kevin Brooks Henson

Born 20 June 1960 ; son of Ada and Jim Henson; P/GP: Olusta and Jess Henson; M/GP: Nannie and Jack Sac

RESIDENCE: Locust Grove, OK

EDUCATION: Locust Grove (OK) High School, 1978

OCCUPATION: Welder; full-time painter since 1993

MEDIA: Oil, acrylic, pencil, pastel, and Prismacolor

PUBLISHED: *Tulsa People* (4 Mar 1993)

COMMISSIONS: Murrow Indian Children's Home, Muskogee, OK, cards

EXHIBITS: BB, CNM, FCTM, LIAS, OIAC, RE/M, TIAF, TWF; see also Awards

SOLO EXHIBITS: CNM; FCTM; American Indian Heritage Center, Tulsa, OK

AWARDS: CNM ('88, 1st; '90, 1st; '93); FCTM ('92; '93); ITIC ('91); TWF ('93, Best of Show); American Indian Images Show (Best of Show); Northeast Oklahoma Art Show

HENSON, KEVIN (see Henson, Brooks)

HE NUPA WANICA (see No Two Horns)

HERMAN, JAKE *Oglala Sioux*

Igla-Ka-Terila, Loves To Move Camp

Born 1892 at the Pine Ridge Agency, SD; died 1969 in Rapid City, SD

RESIDENCE: Lived in Kyle, SD

EDUCATION: Carlisle, 1914-1916

OCCUPATION: Wild west show and rodeo clown, tribal council member (19 years), tribal executive board member (6 years), author, and artist

MEDIA: Oil

PUBLISHED: Snodgrass (1968); Libhart (1970)

PUBLIC COLLECTIONS: HCC, IACB, SM

EXHIBITS: CPS, PAC

JAKE HERMAN

The artist wrote a column, Wa Ho Si, for the Shannon County News, in Pine Ridge, SD. In addition, he wrote Oglala legends, folktales and historic sketches as well as autobiographical articles, which he illustrated and published by Ditto and Mimeograph. He was one of the first of the Pine Ridge painters and was completely self-taught.

Libhart 1970

HERNÁNDEZ, PAUL *Kiowa*

A.K.A. Paul Clarence Hernández

Born 30 Dec 1961

RESIDENCE: Anadarko, OK

EDUCATION: OSU/O

OCCUPATION: Law enforcement and painter

EXHIBITS: AIE

AWARDS: AIE ('88, 1st; '92)

PAUL HERNÁNDEZ

Hernández credits Tim Saupitty (q.v.) with influencing and inspiring him.

artist, p.c. 1992

HERNE, SUE ELLEN *Mohawk*

Kwa Ne Ra Ta Ieni

Born 28 Nov 1960

RESIDENCE: Hogansburg, NY

EDUCATION: IAIA, 1977-1978; B.F.A., RISD

OCCUPATION: Artist

MEDIA: Oil

PUBLISHED: Johannsen and Ferguson, eds. (1983). *Turtle Quarterly* (fall 1987); *Newsletter*, NASAC/ACEAA (winter 1991)

EXHIBITS: AIAI; C/AMO; IAIA; NYSF; TFAG; Warren Memorial Library Exhibit, Massena, NY

AWARDS: NYSF ('76, 1st)

SUE ELLEN HERNE

Herne has said, "Where we are in history is really important to us as artists, no matter what style of art we do — traditional, narrative or contemporary. We're all concerned with issues like preserving culture. That's what I want to do through my art, but still keeping it in a personal way."

Turtle Quarterly, *fall 1987*

HERRERA, CALVIN *Zuni*

PUBLIC COLLECTIONS: WWM

HERRERA, DELPHINO *Cochití*

EDUCATION: Albuquerque

PUBLISHED: Snodgrass (1968)

EXHIBITS: MNM

HERRERA, DIEGO *Tesuque*

O-Ge-Id

RESIDENCE: Tesuque Pueblo, NM

PUBLISHED: Snodgrass (1968)

PUBLIC COLLECTIONS: MNA, OU/MA, U of CA/LMA

EXHIBITS: AIW, FWG

HERRERA, ELROY *Tesuque*

PUBLISHED: Snodgrass (1968)

PUBLIC COLLECTIONS: MNM

HERRERA, ERNEST *Tesuque*

RESIDENCE: Tesuque Pueblo, NM

EDUCATION: Tesuque, ca. 1959

PUBLISHED: Snodgrass (1968)

EXHIBITS: MNM

AWARDS: MNM

HERRERA, JOE HILARIO *Cochití*

See Ru, Blue Bird

Born 17 May 1923 at Cochití Pueblo, NM; son of Tonita Peña (q.v.) and Felipe Herrera

RESIDENCE: Santa Fe, NM

MILITARY: U.S. Army Air Corps, WWII

EDUCATION: Santa Fe, 1940; B.A., U of NM, 1953; M.A., Ed., U of NM, 1962; U of Puerto Rico; studied briefly under Raymond Jonson in Puerto Rico

OCCUPATION: Educator, retired Director of Indian Education, New Mexico State Department of Education, and artist

MEDIA: Oil, acrylic, watercolor, pencil, pen and ink, pastel, and casein

PUBLISHED: Jacobson and d'Ucel (1950); Tanner (1957; 1973); Highwater (1976); Dunn (1968); Snodgrass (1968); Brody (1971); New (1979); Broder (1981); Fawcett and Callander (1982); Hoffman, et al. (1985); Samuels (1985); Wade, ed. (1986); Seymour (1988); Archuleta and Strickland (1991); Ballantine and Ballantine (1993). *The Desert Magazine* (Aug 1949); *Arizona Highways* (Feb 1950); *El Palacio* (Aug 1950; Dec 1952); *New Mexico Magazine* (Jan 1960); *The Rocky Mountain News* (24 Sept 1964; 25 Sept 1964); *America Illustrated*, USDS, Office of Internal Information (No. 33); *American Indian Art* (spring 1985); *Southwest Art* (June 1983; Aug 1993); *Native Peoples* (fall 1991)

BOOKS ILLUSTRATED: Grammer (1991)

COMMISSIONS: *Murals:* Santa Fe (NM) Indian School; Maisel's Indian Trading Post, Albuquerque, NM, 1939

PUBLIC COLLECTIONS: AF, CGPS, DAM, FAC/CS, IACB, IACB/DC, MAI, MNA/KHC, MRFM, OU/MA, PAC, SDMM, SM, TM

EXHIBITS: AIEC; AIW; ASM; CGPS; DAM; FWG; HM; IK; IAIA; ITIC; LGAM; MFA/O; MNA; MNM; MNM/T; NAP; OU/ET; PAC; PAC/T; PAIC; PM; SV; SWAIA; WRTD; Europe, China, Japan, South America

JOE HILARIO HERRERA

"Herrera is closely associated with tribal and state affairs. In 1968, he conducted a radio program from Santa Fe that served as an information center to the Pueblos. In recent years his many-faceted interests unfortunately took him away from painting his well-known symbolic expressions."

Snodgrass 1968

Herrera admits he is something of a rebel. He was one of the first of the Indian artists to move away from traditional representational art into the more abstract forms of self-expression. Although Herrera started working actively as a painter again after his retirement, serious eye problems that worsened in 1994 have curtailed his work production.

SOLO EXHIBITS: IAIA

AWARDS: Partial listing includes: AC/RM (Grand Award); ITIC (Grand Award); MRFM; SWAIA; American Youth Forum Contest (when he was very young)

HONORS: French Government, Palmes d'Académiques, 1954; All-Pueblo Council, executive secretary; Save the Children Federation, Inc., area consultant; Annual Governors Inter-State Indian Council, chairman, 1964-1965

HERRERA, JUSTINO *Cochití*

Stimone, A Bird

Born 1920

MILITARY: U.S. Army, WWII

EDUCATION: Santa Fe, ca. 1937-1940

OCCUPATION: Farmer and artist

PUBLISHED: Snodgrass (1968); Brody (1971); Tanner (1973); Williams, ed. (1990)

PUBLIC COLLECTIONS: CAMSL, GM, HCC, MAI, MNM, MRFM, PAC, WWM

EXHIBITS: MKMcNAI, MNM, PAC, SWAIA

AWARDS: SWAIA

JUSTINO HERRERA

In the 1940s the artist wrote: 'I figured a plan to do while I was in the army when I come home. I'd marry my sweetheart and have our own home on my farm, raise stock and I could keep painting, too. Well, it happened. We got married and we had a little girl. Couple months later my wife took sick. ... It took her strong and she left me and my little baby daughter to raise. I am employed as a farmer here at St. Michael's Indian School.'"

Snodgrass 1968

HERRERA, MARCELINA *Zia*

Haweleana

RESIDENCE: San Juan Pueblo, NM

EDUCATION: Santa Fe; U of NM; studied under Dorothy Dunn

PUBLISHED: Dunn (1968); Snodgrass (1968)

EXHIBITS: NGA

HERRERA, MARTÍN *Cochití*

PUBLISHED: Snodgrass (1968)

PUBLIC COLLECTIONS: SM

HERRERA, SENEFORE (see Herrera, Senofre)

HERRERA, SENOFRE *Cochití*

Oye Gi

A.K.A. Senefore Herrera

EDUCATION: Santa Fe

PUBLISHED: Snodgrass (1968)

PUBLIC COLLECTIONS: U of CA/LMA

EXHIBITS: AIE, FWG

HERRERA, VAL *Cochití*

PUBLIC COLLECTIONS: WWM

HERRERA, VELINO SHIJE *Zia*

Ma Pe Wi

A.K.A. Signatures: Velino Shije Herrera; *Ma Pe We* (by 1928)

Born 22 Oct 1902 at Zia Pueblo, NM; died 30 Jan 1973 in Santa Fe, NM; son of Reyes Ancero and Pedro Herrera; cousin of José Ray Toledo (q.v.)

RESIDENCE: Lived in Santa Fe, NM

EDUCATION: Santa Fe

OCCUPATION: Educator, rancher, and painter (painted briefly for School of American Research)

MEDIA: Oil, watercolor, and tempera

PUBLISHED: Spinden (1931); Alexander (1932); Jacobson and d'Ucel (1950);

VELINO SHIJE HERRERA

"Herrera began painting ca. 1917. He adopted his childhood nickname Ma Pe Wi as a nom-de-plume. The name has a punning significance, meaning either 'oriole' or 'bad egg.' He has credited Dr. Edgar L. Hewett for getting him started in the field of art. When the state of New Mexico adopted the sun symbol of the Pueblo Indians as its official insignia, he was accused by his own people of betraying them by giving the design to the Whites.

LaFarge (1956; 1960); Pierson and Davidson (1960); Dockstader (1961); Dunn (1968); Snodgrass (1968); Brody (1971; 1992); Tanner (1973); Highwater (1976); Silberman (1978); Broder (1981); Hoffman, et al. (1984); Samuels (1985); Seymour (1988); Williams, ed. (1990). *School Arts Magazine* (Mar 1931); *American Magazine of Art* (Sept 1928; Aug 1932); *El Palacio* (Oct 1930; Apr 1950); *The New York Times* (29 Nov 1931); *Compton's Picture Encyclopedia* (1957); *Arizona Highways* (Feb 1950); *Arts Focus* (1981); *American Indian Art* (spring 1985; spring 1995); *Art-Talk* (Apr/May 1988)

BOOKS ILLUSTRATED: Clark (1941; 1943); Underhill (1939; 1941; 1945; 1946; 1951)

COMMISSIONS: *Murals:* KM; USDI; Albuquerque (NM) Indian School; Rancho San Ignacio, Sapello, NM; Tecoleteños Ranch, near Las Vegas, NM; reproduced (in fresco) the kiva drawings at Kuaua, near Bernalillo, NM

PUBLIC COLLECTIONS: ACMWA, CAM/OH, CAMSL, CGA, CGFA, CMA, DAC, DAM, GM, HM, IACB, IACB/DC, KM, MAI, MAM, MKMcNAI, MNA/KHC, MNH/A, MNM, MNM/SAR, MRFM, PAC, RMC/AZ, SAR, SDMM, SM, U of PA/M, WOM, WWM

EXHIBITS: AIEC; AIW; ASM; EITA; FAC/CS; HM; HSM/OK; IK; ITIC; JGS; LGAM; MAM; MFA/O; MKMcNAI; MNM; MRFM; OMA; OU/ET; PAC; PAC/T; PM; RMC/AZ; SM; SWAIA; WRTD; WWM; Corona Mundi International Center, New York, NY, 1927

AWARDS: ITIC ('48, Grand Award); PAC; SWAIA

HONORS: French Government, Palmes d'Académiques, 1954

VELINO SHIJE HERRERA

(continued) José Rey Toledo (q.v.) describes Herrera as a 'singing artist' — one would know which ceremony he was painting by the song he sang at the drawing board. A tragic auto accident in 1958 killed his wife Mary and injured him for life. As of 1968 he no longer painted."

Snodgrass 1968

Herrera was considered one of the members of the "San Ildefonso movement."

HERRERA, VICTOR *Cochití*

EDUCATION: Santa Fe

PUBLISHED: Snodgrass (1968)

PUBLIC COLLECTIONS: MAI

HE'SHE, FLOWER *San Ildefonso*

EXHIBITS: SWAIA

AWARDS: SWAIA ('77, 1st, Division Award)

HESSING, VALJEAN MCCARTY *Choctaw*

Born 30 Aug 1934 in Tulsa, OK; daughter of Madelyn Helen Beck and Vernon Clay McCarty; P/GP: Etta Regina Davis and Carl McCarty; M/GP: Sada Lewis and F. L. Beck; sister of Jane McCarty Mauldin (q.v.)

RESIDENCE: Onarga, IL

EDUCATION: Central High School, Tulsa, OK, 1952; Mary Hardin-Baylor College, Belton, TX, 1952-1954; U of Tulsa, 1954-1955

OCCUPATION: Commercial artist, housewife and mother, and painter

MEDIA: Acrylic, watercolor, pencil, pen and ink, clay, and prints

PUBLISHED: Snodgrass (1968); Seabourn (1976); Broder (1981); Fitzpatrick (1982); Rubenstein (1982); Archuleta and Strickland (1991); Ballantine and Ballantine (1993); Gully, ed. (1994). *Arizona Living; American Airlines; The Chicago Tribune* (23 Mar 1979); *The Washington Post; Aura* (Nov/Dec 1980); *American Indian Journal* (1981), cover; *The Muskogee Phoenix* (26 Sept 1982); *Oklahoma Today* (winter 1981; July/Aug 1985); *Southwest Art* (Jan 1987); biographical publications

COMMISSIONS: Triangle Blueprint and Supply Co., Tulsa, OK, advertisement which appeared in *Today's Art* (Apr 1956)

PUBLIC COLLECTIONS: HM; FCTM; IACB; MIM; MRFM; PAC; SPIM; WWM; Southeast Missouri State University Museum, Cape Girardeau, MO; Gallery of American Indian Art, Washington, D.C.

VALJEAN MCCARTY HESSING

"The artist's interest in painting began in grade school. After high school, and until 1964, she had devoted most of her time to rearing a family. Now she is painting again and giving more time to exhibiting regularly."

Snodgrass 1968

Hessing's paintings are done in a flat style and often display her delightful sense of humor. In recent years she has extended her artistic endeavors to include miniature figures done in clay.

EXHIBITS: AAID; ACS/RSC; AICH; CAI/KC; DAM; DE; FCTM; GM; HM; HM/G; HMA; ITIC; KCPA; MNH/AN; PAC; RC; RE; SI; SAIEAIP; SFFA; SN; SV; SWAIA; TAAII; TIAF; USDI; Art Unlimited Exhibitions; Tulsa (OK) Council of Indians Art Show, 1965

SOLO/SPECIAL EXHIBITS: HM (dual show with her sister, Jane Mauldin); PAC; Iroquois Historical Society, Watseka, IL (1991); galleries in AR, AZ, CO, FL, GA, IL, NE, NM, OK, TX, WI, and Washington, D.C.

AWARDS: Partial listing of more than ninety includes: AAID ('68); CNM ('83, Grand Award; '84, Grand Award; '86, 1st; '87, 1st; '88, 1st; '89, 1st; '90; '91; '92; '93, 1st; '94); FCTM ('67, 1st; '68; '69, IH; '70, 1st; '71, 1st, IH; '72, 1st, IH; '74, 1st, Indian Heritage Grand Award); FCTM/M ('79; '81; '82, 1st); HM/G ('68; '72, 1st; '73, 1st, Wynn Award; '74; '75, 1st, Best of Cherokee; '76, 1st, Begay Award; '78, 2-1st, Pierce-Avery Award, Popovi Da Award; '80, Pierce-Avery Award, Outstanding Watercolor); NCHF ('66); ITIC ('76, 1st); PAC ('68; '70; '71; '72; '73, 1st; '74, 1st; '77); RC ('93, Powers Award); RE ('93, Best of Division); SN ('68, 1st; '69, 1st, Buehler Award; '70, program cover artist; '71, Buehler Award); SWAIA ('83, 1st)

HONORS: *Scholarships:* PAC art classes, 1945; Mary Hardin-Baylor College, Belton, TX, 1952. *Other:* Central High School, Tulsa, OK, yearbook artist, 1949-1952; Mary Hardin-Baylor College, Belton, TX, yearbook art editor, cover artist for journalism magazine, and student union staff artist; FCTM, designated a Master Artist, 1976

HEVOVITASTAMIUTSTS (see Whirlwind)

HICKS, BOBBY *Navajo*

Born 1934 in Arizona

EDUCATION: U of N AZ; U of AZ, "Southwest Indian Art Project," scholarship

OCCUPATION: Art instructor and painter

PUBLISHED: Dunn (1968); Snodgrass (1968); Tanner (1973); Monthan and Monthan (1975); Samuels (1985)

PUBLIC COLLECTIONS: MNA, RM

EXHIBITS: ITIC, MNM, PAC, SN, WWM

AWARDS: Four in 1958, including: ITIC, PAC

HICKS, LOUINDA *Paiute/Shoshoni*

EDUCATION: Schurz (NV) High School; IAIA

PUBLISHED: *The Indian Trader* (July 1978)

EXHIBITS: See Awards

AWARDS: Schurz (NV) Art Show, (Grand Prize)

HIDE AWAY (see Watchetaker, George Smith)

HIGDON, NINA (see Vaughn, Nina)

HIGH DOG *Sioux*

RESIDENCE: From the Standing Rock Reservation, Dakota Territory

PUBLISHED: Snodgrass (1968)

PUBLIC COLLECTIONS: HS/ND

HIGH DOG

"High Dog's Winter Count on unbleached muslin covers 114 years (at HS/ND)."

Snodgrass 1968

HIGH HAWK *Teton Sioux*

PUBLISHED: Curtis (1907-1930), Winter Count illustrating 221 events; Snodgrass (1968)

HIGH HAWK

"Baptiste Good (q.v.) was also called High Hawk and executed a Winter Count. These names apparently refer to the same man."

Snodgrass 1968

HIGH HAWK (see Good, Baptiste)

HILL, BOBBY *Kiowa*

White Buffalo

A.K.A. Whitebuffalo

Born 24 Mar 1933 in Lawton, OK; died 7 June 1984

RESIDENCE: Anadarko, OK

MILITARY: U.S. Air Force, Korea

EDUCATION: Anadarko (OK) High School, 1953; USAF, trained as a draftsman

OCCUPATION: Technical illustrator, commercial artist, promotional director for manufacturing companies, scenic artist and set designer, free-lance artist, and painter

MEDIA: Watercolor

PUBLISHED: Snodgrass (1968); Blackboy, et al. (1973); Libhart and Ellison (1973); Medina (1981); Boyd, et al. (1981; 1983)

COMMISSIONS: SPIM, exhibit projects (including a Ghost Dance shirt), 1967; Oklahoma Indian Arts and Crafts Cooperative, Anadarko, OK, two southern Plains Indian tipis, 1974

PUBLIC COLLECTIONS: IACB; MNA; Carnegie (OK) High School

EXHIBITS: AIE; CSPIP; PAC; SPIM; Peabody Museum of Salem, MA (signed Whitebuffalo)

SOLO EXHIBITS: SPIM

AWARDS: AIE ('67, 1st; '68, Grand Award; '69)

HILL, DONALD *Cayuga/Tuscarora/Mohawk*

Born 10 Aug 1959

RESIDENCE: Lewiston, NY

EDUCATION: SUNY/B

OCCUPATION: Student and artist

MEDIA: Acrylic, pen and ink, steatite, and clay

PUBLISHED: Johannsen and Ferguson (1983)

PUBLIC COLLECTIONS: C/WICEC

EXHIBITS: C/WICEC

DONALD HILL

Most of Hill's subject matter concerns the Iroquois prior to White contact. He also explores the relationship among humans, birds, and animals. Next to his art, lacrosse is important to Hill, and he was on the Niagara Wheatfield lacrosse team in 1977.

Johannsen and Ferguson 1983

HILL, JOAN *Creek/Cherokee*

Chea-Se-Quah, Red Bird

Birth date unknown; born in Muskogee, OK; daughter of Winnie Davis Harris and William McKinley Hill; P/GF: Lucy Grayson and George Washington Hill, chief of the Creek Nation, 1922-1928

RESIDENCE: Muskogee, OK

EDUCATION: Central High School, Muskogee, OK, 1948; BC; A.A. Muskogee, 1950; B.A., NSU, 1952; studied under Dick West at BC, and with other well-known artists

OCCUPATION: Art instructor; full-time professional artist after 1956

MEDIA: Oil, acrylic, tempera, watercolor, polymers, pen and ink, pencil, pastel, conté, and mixed-media

PUBLISHED: Work reproduced in more than sixty publications and nine film documentaries including: Hamm and Inglish (1960), cover; Gregory and Strickland (1967); Snodgrass (1968); Brody (1971); Seabourn (1976); Highwater (1976, 1980); Silberman (1978); Humphrey and King (1980); Mahey, et al. (1980); Broder (1981); Turner, et al. (1989); Gentry, et al. (1990); Archuleta and Strickland (1991); Campbell, ed. (1993); Baron and Byrne (1994); Gully, ed. (1994). *The Sunday Oklahoman, Orbit Magazine* (21 July 1963); *The Arizona Republic* (14 Feb 1965; 17 Mar 1968; 17 Sept 1972); *Southwest Review* (summer 1966); *Southwestern Art* (Vol. 2, no. 1, 1967); *The Tulsa World* (27 June 1968);

JOAN HILL

"In 1956, Hill decided to become a full-time artist. She has remained dedicated to her career, rightly earning national recognition."

Snodgrass 1968

In the 1980s Joan's parents became ill, and she temporarily ceased painting to assist them. She recently returned to painting and (as she has declared) is "making a comeback." Hill works in a number of different styles, including, Representational Realism, Subjective Expressionism, Abstract Symbolism, Abstract Expressionism, and Non-Objective.

artist, p.c. 1991

Her paintings of Native American subjects are frequently done in a flat, two-dimensional technique using her favorite rich, earthy colors, especially yellow and orange.

Nimrod (spring/summer 1972), cover; *The Pen Woman* (Nov 1976); *Oklahoma Art Gallery* (spring 1980); *The Muskogee Phoenix* (26 Sept 1982; 17 Oct 1982; 4 Oct 1993); *Centerboard* (spring 1984); *The Creative Woman* (fall 1987), cover; *Twin Territories* (Vol. 1, no. 9, 1991; *Year of the Indian*, 1992); *U.S. Art* (Nov 1991); *The Broken Arrow Scout* (15 Jan 1992); *Indian Territories* (Vol. 3, no. 1, 1993); *Southwest Art* (Mar 1995); biographcal publications

BOOKS ILLUSTRATED: Posey (1969); Gregory and Strickland (1967); Strickland (1982); cover art for ten publications

COMMISSIONS: *Murals:* Day Break Star Indian Cultural Center, Seattle, WA. *Paintings:* Hardin Nelson, eleven famous Cherokees; FCTM, eight of the Five Tribes Chiefs; Smithsonian U.S. Center of Military History, painting for the celebration of the U.S. Bicentennial; Central State College, Edmond, OK; Cherokee Nation, Tahlequah, OK, 1990; Oklahoma Institute of Indian Heritage, Norman, OK, 1991. *Other:* FCTM brochure, 1957; Cosmetic Specialties Co., trademark, 1959; Corning Glass Works, *In the Sooner State*, cover and thirty illustrations, 1960

PUBLIC COLLECTIONS: BC/McG; CSU/OK; FCTM; HCC; HM; IACB; MAI; MNA; MNM; PAC; SI; SPIM; USDI; Western Hills Lodge, Sequoyah State Park, Oklahoma; Performing Arts Center, Tulsa, OK

EXHIBITS: Partial listing of more than three hundred includes: AAID; AIE; BC; CHASC; CIAI; CNM; EM; FAIEAIP; FCTM; FCTM/M; HM; HM/G; IACB; ITIC; KCPA; LIAS; MFA/O; MIF; MNH/AN; MNM; MNM/T; MTF; NAP; NARF; OAC; OIAC; OIAP; OMA; OSC; OWE; PAC; PBOIA; PU; RC; SI; SN; SV; USDI; Hastings (NE) College Art Center, 1973

SOLO EXHIBITS: Partial listing of 16 includes: HM, NSU, PAC, SPIM

AWARDS: Partial listing of more than 260 includes: AAID ('68, 1st; '70, 2-1st; '73); CHASC ('93); CNM ('80, 1st; '91); FCTM ('67; '68, 1st, IH); FCTM/M ('76, IH; '79, Grand Award; '81, Grand Award; '85, 1st; '90; '91, IH; '93, 1st; '94, Spirit of Oklahoma Award); HM/G ('70; '71, Purchase Award, Committee's Choice; '73); OIAC ('93, 1st; '94, Best of Show); PAC ('68, 1st; '69; '71, 1st; '73, 2-1st, Waite Phillips Award; '75, 1st); PBOIA ('70, 1st; '71); RC ('70, 1st; '71); SN ('67; '68, 1st, Grand Award, Buehler Award; '69; '70, 1st; '71, 1st); seventy-eight from Tulsa and Muskogee, OK, state fairs

HONORS: Muskogee (OK) Junior College, Phi Theta Kappa, Honorary Scholastic Fraternity, 1952; Fashion Industry of New York, honored as one of the ten outstanding Indians in the United States, 1972; PAC, Waite Phillips Indian Artists' Trophy, 1973; FCTM, first woman to be designated a Master Artist, 1974; one of 24 American artists invited to visit China and meet with the Professors of the Central Art Academy of Peking, 1978; USDI, appointed to the Review Panel of American Indian Art and Culture, 1980; National League of Pen Women, Inc, Atlanta, GA, Distinguished Pen Women Award, 1982; State of Oklahoma, Oklahoma Diamond Jubilee Arts Festival, selected to exhibit, 1982; Academia Italia, Cremona, Italy, Oscar D'Italia Award, 1985; SI, honored as one of the *People of the Century*; State of Oklahoma's Governor's Commission on the Status of Women, Commissioner, 1990; University of Central Oklahoma, Edmond, OK, painting, 1990; The Bacone College Hall of Fame, Bacone, OK, inducted, 1991; Great Britain, received a commemorative medal; Oklahoma State Capitol Building, East Gallery, Oklahoma City, OK, *Year of the Indian Exhibition*, one of eight American Indian artists exhibited, 1992; *Biographical Directory of Native American Painters*, Editorial Board

HILL, MICHAEL FARRELL *Kiowa*

EXHIBITS: AIE

AWARDS: AIE ('69; '71, 1st; '72, 1st; '74)

HILL, RICHARD (see Hill, Rick)

HILL, RICK *Tuscarora*

A.K.A. Richard Hill

Born 1950 in Buffalo, NY; son of Stanley Hill

RESIDENCE: Santa Fe, NM

EDUCATION: CAI, 1968-1970; M.A., SUNY/B, 1980; CAI

OCCUPATION: Ironworker/high-rise construction, educator, research assistant, museum director, writer, photographer, and artist

MEDIA: Watercolor and prints

PUBLISHED: New (1979); Abbott (1994); Hill and Hill (1994). *Four Winds* (1980); *Indian Market*, SWAIA (1991); *Art News* (Feb 1992); *Native Peoples* (Special Edition 1994); *Indian Artist* (spring 1995); biographical publications

COMMISSIONS: IACB, 1980; Museum of Man, Ottawa, ON, 1982

PUBLIC COLLECTIONS: C/CMC, C/INAC, C/WICEC, CMA, IACB, NACLA, PAC, SINM, SMII, SPIM

EXHIBITS: AM; C/WICEC; CNGM; DAM; EM/NY; KCPA; MAI; MNH/CL; NA/BC; NACLA; OAG; PAC; PAIC; QM; SPIM; TFAG; TRP; WASG; Carleton University, Ottawa, ON, 1982; Niagara Community College, Sanborn, NY, 1983; Canoe Festival, Ottawa, ON, 1984; Siena College, Loudonville, NY, 1982; University Museum, Philadelphia, PA, 1976

SOLO EXHIBITS: C/AG/TB; MAI; Buffalo (NY) Museum of Science, 1973; Museum of the Hudson Highlands, Hudson, NY, 1975; Siena College, Loudonville, NY, 1982

AWARDS: PAC ('77)

HONORS: *Fellowships:* America the Beautiful Fund, 1973; Creative Artists Public Service, 1967. *Other:* North American Indian Museums Association, director, 1980

HILL, SHEILA *Taos*

RESIDENCE: Santa Fe, NM

EDUCATION: B.A., U of NM

OCCUPATION: Commercial artist, museum exhibit designer, and painter

MEDIA: Pastel and prints

PUBLISHED: New (1981)

EXHIBITS: AIWSAF; NACLA; SWAIA; Santa Monica (CA) Indian Art Show; Art Fest, Phoenix, AZ; galleries in CA, CO, NM, and OK

AWARDS: SWAIA ('78)

SHEILA HILL

The artist has said, "I am intrigued with the beauty and quietness of Indian women. There is an air of innocence about them, a thoughtfulness, that I wish to portray.... My drawings are not portraits of real people, but rather portraits of feelings. Using simplicity and softness I try to capture the essence of my Indian heritage."

gallery brochure 1983

HILL, TOM *Seneca*

Do-Rha-Ah

Born 9 May 1943

RESIDENCE: Ohsweken, ON, Canada

EDUCATION: C/OCA, 1963-1967; C/NGCA, 1967

OCCUPATION: Promoter and economic developer of Indian arts and crafts, consultant, author, editor, and artist

MEDIA: Oil, acrylic, pen and ink, plastic, and wood products

PUBLISHED: Hill (1983); Johannsen and Ferguson, eds. (1983); Hill and Hill (1994). *Native Peoples* (Special Edition 1994)

COMMISSIONS: *Murals:* Expo '69, Indian Pavilion, *Tree of Peace*

EXHIBITS: C/AG/G, C/IAF, C/NAF, C/SNAC

HONORS: National Gallery, museology scholarship, 1967; Six Nations Arts Council, president, four years

Patrick Swazo Hinds

"Not long after he was adopted by Professor Hinds, the artist moved to California where, except for the years he was away at school, he resided until his death. He usually spent his summer vacations at Tesuque Pueblo. He was active in the Society of Western Artists, the Oakland Art Association, the Berkeley Arts and Crafts Cooperative, and American Indian Artists."

Snodgrass 1968

Swazo used a variety of techniques, including palette knife, oil on paper, drybrush, soft brush with spatter, and mixed-media

Tanner 1973

Hinds, Patrick Swazo *Tesuque*

Grey Squirrel

A.K.A. José Patrico Swazo

Born 25 Mar 1929 at Tesuque Pueblo, NM; died 30 Mar 1974; adopted son of Dr. Norman A. E. Hinds, honorary member of Tesuque Pueblo and Professor of Geology at the University of California for 45 years

RESIDENCE: Lived in Berkeley, CA

MILITARY: U.S. Marine Corps, Korea

EDUCATION: St. Mary's College High School, Berkeley, CA, 1941-1946; Hill, 1948; B.A., CCAC, 1952; Mexico CC, 1952; CAI, 1953-1955

OCCUPATION: Teacher, lecturer, silk screen processor; full-time painter after 1968

MEDIA: Oil, acrylic, watercolor, and prints

PUBLISHED: Snodgrass (1968); Brody (1971); Tanner (1973), dust jacket; Monthan and Monthan (1975); Hoffman, et al. (1984); *The Taos News* (23 Sept 1972); *The Quarterly,* SWAIA (summer 1974); biographical publications

PUBLIC COLLECTIONS: BIA/DC; HM; HS/AI; MNA; MRFM; OAM; SN; CCAC Alumni Collection

EXHIBITS: AAID; ASM; CAI; CCAC; CPLH; HM; HM/G; IK; ITIC; KF; MNM; OAM; PAC; SFMA; SN; SWAIA; U of OR, WWM; Oakland (CA) Art Museum; University of California Medical Center, San Francisco, CA; Hastings (NE) College; Oregon State University, Corvallis, OR; regional exhibits and galleries in California; see also Awards

SOLO EXHIBITS: HM; HS/AI; SWAIA; U of CA/B; Pacific School of Religion, Berkeley, CA; galleries in California

AWARDS: AAID ('68, Special Award); HM/G ('69; '70, Holiday Award; '71); ITIC ('69, 1st); NCHF ('67); PAC ('67; '69, 1st; '71; '69, 1st); SN ('66, 1st, Grand Award; '67, 1st; '68; '70, 1st; '71, 1st, *Phoenix Gazette* Special Award); SWAIA ('69, 1st; '70, 1st; '73, 1st); Center for Indian Art in Washington, D.C. ('68, 1st)

Hinhan Wicahca (see Two Bulls, Edward E.)

Hinsley, Tanis *Tlingit*

Born 1941 in Sasquana, NY

EDUCATION: USU, 1970-1980; B.F.A., U of AK/F, 1987

PUBLISHED: Stewart (1988)

EXHIBITS: AICA/SF, U of AK/F; The Keeping Room, Delta Junction, Alaska

AWARDS: U of AK/F ('84, Best in Drawing; '85, Best in Drawing, Best in Printmaking; '86, Best of Show)

HONORS: U of AK/F, Art Student of the Year, 1987

Hinookmahiwi-kilinaka (see Dietz, Angel Decora)

His Battle (see Jaw)

His Crazy Horse *Sioux*

PUBLISHED: Snodgrass (1968)

PUBLIC COLLECTIONS: MPM (pictographic style)

His Fight *Hunkpapa Sioux*

RESIDENCE: Lived near Fort Buford, MT, 1868

PUBLISHED: Smith (1943); Snodgrass (1968)

PUBLIC COLLECTIONS: MAI (line drawing executed in ink)

Histito, Alonzo *Zuni*

PUBLISHED: Snodgrass (1968)

PUBLIC COLLECTIONS: MNM

HITCHCOCK, SHARON *Haida*

RESIDENCE: Canada

MEDIA: Acrylic

PUBLISHED: Stewart (1979)

PUBLIC COLLECTIONS: C/RBCM

HIUWA TUNI *(?)*

PUBLISHED: Snodgrass (1968)

PUBLIC COLLECTIONS: DAC

HI-YOU-OS (see Dockstader, John)

HKOVAK, PATRICK *Inuit (Eskimo)*

Born 1944; died 1976

RESIDENCE: Lived on Holman Island, NWT, Canada

PUBLIC COLLECTIONS: C/HEC

EXHIBITS: C/HEC

HOBAH *Comanche*

PUBLISHED: Snodgrass (1968)

PUBLIC COLLECTIONS: FSM (painting on deerskin in native colors, before 1922)

HO CHEE NEE (see Burton, Jimalee)

HOFFMAN, DELORES *(?)*

PUBLISHED: Snodgrass (1968)

EXHIBITS: SWAIA

HOFYEE (see Byrnes, James Michael)

HOGAN LUTA (see Red Fish)

HOGOON (see Silverhorn)

HO HAW *Kiowa*

PUBLISHED: Snodgrass (1968). *Bulletin of the Missouri Historical Society* (Oct 1950); *The St. Louis Post Dispatch* (13 Aug 1950)

PUBLIC COLLECTIONS: HS/MO, SI/OAA

EXHIBITS: BPG

HOHNANIE, RAMSON (see Honahniein, Ramson R.)

HOKEAH, JACK *Kiowa*

Born 1902 in western Oklahoma; died 14 Dec 1969 at Fort Cobb, OK; grandson of the warrior White Horse

EDUCATION: Santa Fe; U of OK, special classes

OCCUPATION: Actor, BIA employee, and artist

MEDIA: Tempera and prints

PUBLISHED: Jacobson (1929; 1964); Jacobson and d'Ucel (1950); Dunn (1968); Snodgrass (1968); Brody (1971); Highwater (1976); Dockstader (1977); Silberman (1978); Broder (1981); Boyd, et al. (1981), Fawcett and Callander (1982); Hoffman, et al. (1984); Samuels (1985); Archuleta and Strickland (1991). *American Magazine of Art* (Aug 1933); *The American Scene*, Gilcrease Museum (Vol. 6, no. 3)

COMMISSIONS: *Murals:* Santa Fe (NM) Indian School; St. Patrick's Mission, Anadarko, OK, 1927

PUBLIC COLLECTIONS: ACM, CMA, DAM, GM, IACB, IACB/DC, JAM, MAI, MKMcNAI, MNA/KHC, MNM, MRFM, PAC, SPL

HO HAW

"The artist was among the 72 Plains Indians taken as prisoners from Fort Sill, OK, to Fort Marion, St. Augustine, FL, in 1875."

Snodgrass 1968

JACK HOKEAH

"Orphaned while still a young boy, he was reared by his grandmother. Although Hokeah was one of the Five Kiowas (q.v.), he did not contribute to the art world in his later years."

Snodgrass 1968

Hokeah was an exceptional dancer and this interfered with his painting time.

Dockstader, p.c. 1994

EXHIBITS: AIE/T; EITA; HM; IK; JAM; MIF; MKMcNAI; NAP; OMA; OU/MA/T; PAC; SMA/TX; SPIM; SV
HONORS: IACB Certificate of Appreciation, 1966

HOLDEN, BRENDA *Miwok*
EXHIBITS: SN
AWARDS: SN ('68)

HOLGATE, EUGENE, JR. *Navajo*
Born 1938 in Utah
EDUCATION: Phoenix, AZ
OCCUPATION: Jeweler and painter
MEDIA: Watercolor, silver, and gemstone
PUBLISHED: Snodgrass (1968); Tanner (1973). *The Taos News* (11 May 1978)
PUBLIC COLLECTIONS: BIA, HCC, IACB, MNA
EXHIBITS: ASF, HM/G, NMSF, PAC, SN, USDS
AWARDS: ASF, NMSF, SN

EUGENE HOLGATE JR.

Holgate's favorite subjects are the animals of the Navajo Reservation with red rocks and hazy blue mountains in the background. He has done traditional, three-dimensional, and abstract paintings.

Tanner 1973

HOLGATE, J. *(?)*
PUBLISHED: Snodgrass (1968)
PUBLIC COLLECTIONS: MAI

HOLLOWBREAST, DONALD *Cheyenne*
Maxhebaho
Born 17 May 1917 in Birney, MT, on the Northern Cheyenne Reservation
RESIDENCE: Lame Deer, MT
EDUCATION: Ashland (MT) Public School
OCCUPATION: Adult educator, editor, columnist, writer, video projects, and artist
MEDIA: Oil, watercolor, pen and ink, pastel, pencil, and charcoal
PUBLISHED: Snodgrass (1968); Brody (1981). *Montana* (autumn 1964)
COMMISSIONS: Westmark Production, Santa Monica, CA, Northern Cheyenne Sign Language Project, video
PUBLIC COLLECTIONS: MPI
EXHIBITS: Partial listing of more than 13 includes: AAID; AIE; BNIAS; CIA; DAM; ITIC; GFNAAS; HSM/MT; NAVAM; PAC; RC; Northern Cheyenne Indian Fair, Lame Deer, MT; Richest Hill of Earth Art Show, Butte, MT; see also Awards
SOLO/SPECIAL EXHIBITS: MPI (dual shows); Dull Knife Memorial College, Lame Deer, MT
AWARDS: Midland Empire Fair, Billings, MT ('32); Rosebud County Fair, Forsyth, MT ('52, 1st); local fairs
HONORS: St. Labré Indian School, Ashland, MT, Elder of the Month

DONALD HOLLOWBREAST

"The artist was interested in painting even as a child. He began to paint with oils in 1950. Since then he has experimented with other media."

Snodgrass 1968

HOLM, ADRIAN L. *Colville*
Seamuc
Born 3 Dec 1943 in Tonasket, WA; daughter of Modesta Adolph and George Fry; P/GP: Florence and Robert Fry; M/GP: Dora and John Adolph; cousin of Mary Francis Nelson, artist and art instructor
RESIDENCE: Inchelium, WA, on the Colville Reservation
EDUCATION: Inchelium (WA) High School, 1964; Spokane Falls Community College, Spokane, WA; Wenatchchee Valley College, Wenatchchee, WA; Northwest Indian College
OCCUPATION: Teacher's aide, tutor, and artist

MEDIA: Oil, pencil, pen and ink, and fabric
EXHIBITS: Regional shows

HOLMES, GORDON *Hopi*
PUBLISHED: Snodgrass (1968)
PUBLIC COLLECTIONS: MAI

HOLMES, RODERICK *Hopi*
RESIDENCE: Tuba City, AZ
EDUCATION: Santa Fe
OCCUPATION: Carver and painter
MEDIA: Watercolor and cottonwood root
PUBLISHED: Snodgrass (1968)
PUBLIC COLLECTIONS: MNM
EXHIBITS: JGS

HOLMS, ART (see Lomayaktewa, V.)

HOLTON, ANNE TENNYSON *Cherokee*
Born 1 Feb 1921 in McNairy County, TN; daughter of Mattie Lucille Jernigan and H. Frank Tennyson; M/GP: Delia and Joseph Ingle; P/GGP: Sally Ann Vaughters and Hiram Olney Tennison
RESIDENCE: Okmulgee, OK
EDUCATION: Central High School, Bolivar, TN; Memphis (TN) School of Commerce
OCCUPATION: Clerk, cosmetics sales representative, poet, and artist
PUBLISHED: Holden (1964); Snodgrass (1968); a biographical publication
EXHIBITS: CCHM; FANAIAE; PAC; Okmulgee (OK) Art Exhibit and Library Art Exhibit; Fort Gibson (OK) Arts and Crafts Exhibit; Tahlequah (OK) Arts and Crafts Exhibit; American Association of University Women Art Exhibit and Book Fair, Bartlesville, OK; see also Awards
AWARDS: Several from Okmulgee (OK) County Annual Art Exhibit

HOLY BUFFALO (see Levings, Martin)

HOLY STANDING BUFFALO *Sioux*
PUBLISHED: Snodgrass (1968)
PUBLIC COLLECTIONS: HM, MPM (pictographic style on paper)

HOME OF THE ELK (see Martínez, Crescencio)

HOMER, BERNARD *Zuni*
RESIDENCE: Zuni, NM
PUBLISHED: Snodgrass (1968)
EXHIBITS: MNM

HONAHNI, AL *Hopi*
PUBLISHED: Snodgrass (1968)
PUBLIC COLLECTIONS: MNA/KHC (dated ca. 1952)

HONAHNIE, ANTHONY E. *Hopi*
Mun De Ma
A.K.A. Antonio Elmer Honahnie
Born 23 May 1947; son of Kathe Lomatewama and Roland Honahnie; P/GP: Anita and Fred Honahnie; M/GP: May and Mike Lomatewama
RESIDENCE: Santa Fe, NM
MILITARY: U.S. Army, Vietnam

EDUCATION: Tuba City (AZ) High School, 1967; Scottsdale (AZ) Community College, 1975; Arizona School of Art, Phoenix, AZ, 1970; ASU
OCCUPATION: Graphics designer, technical illustrator, and studio artist
MEDIA: Oil, acrylic, watercolor, pencil, pen, pastel, and prints
PUBLIC COLLECTIONS: HCC, MNA
EXHIBITS: ACS/ENP; FNAA; HM/G; HPTU; MNA; NMSF; NTF; SM; SN; SNAICF; SWAIA; Festival of Native American Arts, Sedona, AZ; see also Awards
AWARDS: ASC/ENP ('90, Best of Traditional Painting); FNAA; HM/G ('71); MNA; NTF ('81, Grand Prize); SN ('67); SNAICF; SWAIA ('76; '77, 1st; '78; '79, Best of Division); Tucson (AZ) Indian Arts and Crafts Show ('78, Best of Show); South Mountain Festival of Arts, Phoenix, AZ ('79, Ruffin Award)
HONORS: Intel Corporation, Achievement Award and Divisional Recognition Award, 1988

HONAHNIE, ANTONIO ELMER (see Honahnie, Anthony E.)

HONAHNIE, RAMSON (see Honahniein, Ramson R.)

HONAHNIEIN, RAMSON R. *Hopi*

Suhonva
A.K.A. Ramson Honahnie; Ramson Hohnanie; Ramson Honanie
Born ca. 1928 in Moenkopi, AZ
PUBLISHED: Snodgrass (1968); Tanner (1973)
PUBLIC COLLECTIONS: MNM

HONANIE, DELBRIDGE *Hopi*

Coochsiwukioma, Falling White Snow
Born 7 Jan 1946 in Winslow, AZ; son of George and Geneva Honanie
RESIDENCE: Flagstaff, AZ
EDUCATION: Phoenix, 1968; A.A., IAIA, 1970
OCCUPATION: Teacher, *katsina* carver, jeweler, and painter
MEDIA: Oil, acrylic, watercolor, wood, clay, stone, and silver
PUBLISHED: Tanner (1973); Broder (1978; 1981; 1984); New (1979); Peiper-Riegraf (1986); Seymour (1987); Jacka and Jacka (1988). *Wassaja* (20 Sept 1975); *Arizona Living* (Feb 1982); *Southwest Art* (June 1982); *The Scottsdale Daily Progress* (4 Feb 1983); *Arizona Highways* (May 1986)
COMMISSIONS: *Murals:* Two at the Hopi Cultural Center Museum, Second Mesa, AZ; IAIA, Academic Building; ASU, Dean's Building; Indian Museum, USDI building, six murals
PUBLIC COLLECTIONS: AC/SD; AC/RM; ASM; CGPS; HCC; HM; IAIA; EM; MNA; MRFM; Phoenix (AZ) Indian School
EXHIBITS: ACS/ENP; ACS/PG; ASM; CGPS; FAC/CS ; HCCM; HM; HM/G; IAIA ; ITIC; MAI; MFA/O; MNA; NACLA; OWE; PAC; PAIC; RE; SDMM; SFFA; SM; SN ; SNAICF; SPIM; SWAIA; WCCA; WWM; Riverside (CA) Community College; Hillsborough County Museum, Tampa, FL; Arizona State Capitol Building, West Wing Annex, Phoenix, AZ
AWARDS: HM/G ('68; '69; '70; '75, Swazo Award; '91, Best of Division); MNA; ITIC ACS/ENP; PAC ('75, 1st); SN ('68, 1st); SNAICF; SWAIA ('83, Best of Show; '83; '89, 1st; '90); WWM ('82, Most Promising Sculptor/Carver Award); Discover America Poster Contest ('69, 1st)

DELBRIDGE HONANIE

Honanie is one of the original members of Artist Hopid (q.v.). He is a member of the Bear Clan, spiritual leaders of the Hopi. Honanie's sculptures represent a transition in Hopi carving from the traditional katsina *carvings to three-dimensional, abstracted sculptures.*

artist, p.c. 1992

HONANIE, RAMSON R. (see Honahniein, Ramson R.)

HONANISTTO (see Howling Wolf)

HONE-SA, S. B. *Choctaw*
EXHIBITS: CNM

HONEWYTEWA, LOUIS CALVIN F. *Hopi*
Quayesva, Sitting Eagle
A.K.A. Queyesva
Born 30 June 1930 in Keams Canyon, AZ
RESIDENCE: Second Mesa, AZ
EDUCATION: Hopi
PUBLISHED: Snodgrass (1968)
PUBLIC COLLECTIONS: PAC

HONGANOSHE (see Ballard, Louis Wayne)

HONGANOZHE (see Ballard, Louis Wayne)

HONHONGEVA, MARTIN *Hopi*
PUBLIC COLLECTIONS: MNA

HONIE, LEWIS *Hopi*
EXHIBITS: HM/G
AWARDS: HM/G ('70).

HONVANTEWA (see Talaswaima, Terrance, Jr.)

HOOD, GARY ALLEN *Choctaw*
RESIDENCE: Wichita, KS
EXHIBITS: FCTM, PAC
AWARDS: PAC ('75, 1st)

HOOD, LARRY *Comanche*
Thu-Yine-Hootsuu, Bird Killer
A.K.A. Paul Larry Hood. Signature: L Hood and a buffalo skull
Born 28 Jan 1950 in Lawton, OK; son of June Pahcoddy Tenequer and Tom Hood; brother of Rance Hood (q.v.); P/GP: Macil and John Hood; M/GP: Agnes and Oscar Tenequer, spiritual leader
RESIDENCE: Lawton, OK
MILITARY: U.S. Marine Corps
EDUCATION: Through 10th grade
OCCUPATION: Full-time painter
MEDIA: Acrylic, watercolor, pencil, bone, and prints
PUBLISHED: *Southwest Art* (June 1985; Oct 1986)
PUBLIC COLLECTIONS: SPIM; Comanche Tribal Complex, Lawton, OK; Apache Tribal Complex, Anadarko, OK
EXHIBITS: AIE; OAC; PAC; National Congress of American Indian Artist Show, Washington, D.C., 1980; see also Awards
AWARDS: AIE ('75; '76; '77); Rendezvous Art Show, Indian City U.S.A., Anadarko, OK ('87)

HOOD, PAUL LARRY (see Hood, Larry)

HOOD, RANCE *Comanche*
Au Tup Ta, Yellow Hair
Born 3 Feb 1941 near Lawton, OK; son of June Pahcoddy Tenequer and Tommy Hood; brother of Larry Hood (q.v.); M/GP: Agnes and Oscar Tenequer, spiritual leader; raised by M/GP

RESIDENCE: Oklahoma City, OK

EDUCATION: Cache (OK) High School

OCCUPATION: Miscellaneous jobs, mill worker, oil field work, designer, sculptor, and painter

MEDIA: Acrylic, watercolor, tempera, mixed-media, stone, bronze, and prints

PUBLISHED: Snodgrass (1968); Highwater (1976; 1978b; 1980; 1983; 1984); Silberman (1978); Wade and Strickland (1981); Hoffman, et al. (1984); King (1984). *The Indian Trader* (July 1981); *Americas* (Aug 1981); *Art Gallery* (Mar/Apr 1983); *The Sunday Oklahoman* (22 Dec 1985); *Southwest Art* (Dec 1974; Nov 1985); *The Miami Herald* (12 Dec 1986); *Art of the West* (July/Aug 1991); *U.S. Art* (Nov 1991)

COMMISSIONS: Turbo West Aircraft Co., exterior design for Cheyenne III jet; Comanche Nation, commemorative emblem, medallion; Comanche County, OK, directory cover

PUBLIC COLLECTIONS: EM; GM; MAI; OSAC; PAC; SI; SPIM; New Britain (CT) Museum of American Art

EXHIBITS: AC/A; AIE; CSPIP; FAIE; FAIEAIP; HM/G; IK; OCSA; OMA; PAC; SDMM; SI; SN; SPIM; VV; USDI; European touring exhibit, 1988; New Britain (CT) Museum of American Art; Easter At the White House, Washington, D.C.; see also Awards

SOLO EXHIBITS: SPIM

AWARDS: AIE ('67, 1st, Grand Award; '69, 1st; '70; '71, Grand Award; '72, 1st); PAC ('68; '69; '70, 1st); Western Writers of America ('85, Best Western Cover Art); American Indian Film Festival (Annual Award, sculpture); American Artists Lithograph Competition (Best Poster Art)

HOPKINS, MERINA LUJÁN (see Pop Chalee)

HORN, DENVER *Northern Cheyenne*

Born 1930 in Lame Deer, MT

RESIDENCE: Lame Deer, MT

EDUCATION: Busby (MT) Indian School

MEDIA: Oil

PUBLIC COLLECTIONS: St. Labré Indian Mission Museum, Ashland, MT

EXHIBITS: CIA

HORN, MYLES S. *Arikara*

White Crow

Born 1894 on the Fort Berthold Reservation, ND; GGGF: Chief One Star; nephew of Red Star, a scout enlisted in the Seventh Calvary under General George Custer

RESIDENCE: Miles City, MT

MILITARY: WWI; WWII

EDUCATION: OTIS

OCCUPATION: Musician, professional baseball player, cowboy, range rider, actor, and painter

PUBLISHED: Snodgrass (1968); Brody (1971)

PUBLIC COLLECTIONS: BIA/B

EXHIBITS: AAID; BNIAS; MPI; throughout the U.S.

AWARDS: Listing includes: AAID ('68)

MYLES S. HORN

"The artist was encouraged to paint by Charles Russell and was a popular artist in the Upper Great Plains area for many years."

Snodgrass 1968

Horn was seriously wounded and partially disabled by a land mine in World War II.

HORNE, PAULA *Sioux*

RESIDENCE: Marshall, MN

EXHIBITS: RC

HORSE, PERRY *Kiowa*

PUBLISHED: Snodgrass (1968)
EXHIBITS: AAIEAE, USDS

HORSE, THURMAN *Oglala Sioux*

RESIDENCE: Porcupine, SD
PUBLIC COLLECTIONS: HCC

HORSE CHIEF (see Beard, Lorenzo)

HORSECHIEF, BARRY *Pawnee*

A.K.A. Signature: C. H. Barry
Born 13 Oct 1947 in Pawnee, OK
RESIDENCE: Tulsa, OK
MILITARY: U.S. Army, Vietnam
EDUCATION: McLain High School, Tulsa, OK; IAIA, 1977-1978; TJC
OCCUPATION: Silkscreen printer and stencil cutter; painter
MEDIA: Acrylic
EXHIBITS: CNM, SPIM

HORSECHIEF, DAN *Pawnee/Cherokee*

A.K.A. Daniel Milton HorseChief
Born 3 Jan 1969 in Muskogee, OK; son of Mary Adair (q.v.) and Samuel HorseChief Sr.; P/GP: Sophie Butler and Hugh HorseChief; M/GP: Velma and Carrigan Adair; brother of Mary Catherine and Sam HorseChief (qq.v.)
RESIDENCE: Sallisaw, OK
MILITARY: U.S. Navy Reserves
EDUCATION: Muskogee (OK) High School, 1987; BC; IAIA
OCCUPATION: Pest control employee, sculptor, and painter
MEDIA: Acrylic, watercolor, pencil, pen and ink, and prints
COMMISSIONS: *Murals:* Roland, OK. *Other:* Cherokee Nation Clinic, Sallisaw, OK, painting, 1992
PUBLIC COLLECTIONS: BC
EXHIBITS: BC, CHASC, CNM, FCTM, RC
AWARDS: BC (Student '88, 1st, '89, 1st); CHASC ('93, Grand Award); CNM ('92; '93); FCTM (Student '86, 1st; '87, 1st); RC ('92)
HONORS: FCTM, Frances Roser Brown Award (Bacone College Art Scholarship), 1987

HORSECHIEF, MARY ADAIR (see Adair, Mary HorseChief)

HORSECHIEF, MARY CATHERINE *Pawnee/Cherokee*

Born 18 Sept 1961 in Dallas, TX; daughter of Mary Adair (q.v.) and Samuel HorseChief Sr.; P/GP: Sophie Butler and Hugh HorseChief; M/GP: Velma and Carrigan Adair; sister of Daniel and Sam HorseChief (qq.v.)
RESIDENCE: Tahlequah, OK
EDUCATION: Muskogee (OK) High School, 1979; U of OK; BC; NSU
PUBLIC COLLECTIONS: HCC, PAC
EXHIBITS: AIE; BC/McG; CNM; FCTM; OIO; PAC; RC; SWAIA; TM/NE; Creek Nation Art Show; Oklahoma State Fair; see also Awards
AWARDS: AIE ('80, 1st); FCTM ('77; '78; '78, Brown IH Award); OIO; PAC; Muskogee (OK) High School Art Award (senior year); Bacone College Art Show (Best of Show)
HONORS: BC Art Scholarship; Indian Club Princess, Bacone College, 1981

SAM HORSECHIEF

An outstanding athlete in high school and college, winning many medals and trophies, HorseChief also excelled in art. As a student he won many awards and his work was included in a traveling exhibition of Indian children's art work that was organized by the Smithsonian Institution in 1973.

Muskogee Phoenix, *n.d.*

HORSECHIEF, SAM *Pawnee/Cherokee*

Ussa Hud'it, Little Pony

A.K.A. Samuel HorseChief Jr.

Born 30 Aug 1959 in Dallas, TX; son of Mary Adair (q.v.) and Samuel HorseChief Sr.; P/GP: Sophie Butler and Hugh HorseChief; M/GP: Velma and Carrigan Adair; brother of Daniel and Mary Catherine HorseChief (qq.v.)

RESIDENCE: Muskogee, OK

EDUCATION: Muskogee (OK) High School; A.A., Haskell; B.A., CSU/OK, 1982

MEDIA: Oil, pen and ink, and pencil

COMMISSIONS: *Murals:* Muskogee (OK) High School

EXHIBITS: CNM; FCTM; PAC; RC; SI; Creek Nation Art Show; Capitol Rotunda, Oklahoma City, OK; see also Awards

AWARDS: FCTM ('74, 1st; '84); Unity Show, Oklahoma City, OK ('83, 1st); Oklahoma Indian Youth Art Festival (Best of Festival Award)

HONORS: Smithsonian Institution traveling exhibit of Indian children's art works, painting used for publicity, 1973

HORSECHIEF, SAMUEL, JR. (see HorseChief, Sam)

HORSE TAIL *Crow*

PUBLISHED: Snodgrass (1968)

PUBLIC COLLECTIONS: DAM

ARDEN HOSETOSAVIT

Originally a painter, the artist is now better known for his sculpture.

HOSETOSAVIT, ARDEN *Mescalero Apache*

Born 21 May 1945 at Mescalero, NM

RESIDENCE: Ruidoso, NM

EDUCATION: Santa Fe, ca. 1962; IAIA, 1965-1966

OCCUPATION: Painter and sculptor

MEDIA: Watercolor and stone

PUBLISHED: Snodgrass (1968). *Art of The West* (Mar/Apr 1992)

PUBLIC COLLECTIONS: BIA, IACB

EXHIBITS: MNM, PAC, SAIEAIP, SIRU, SN, USDI, USDS

AWARDS: *Interior Design Magazine* award, 1964

HOSHILA WASTE (see Bad Heart Bull, Amos)

HOSKIE, LARRY *Navajo*

RESIDENCE: Lived in St. Michaels, AZ

PUBLISHED: Snodgrass (1968)

COMMISSIONS: *Murals:* ASF/Coliseum, 1965 (with four other Navajo artists)

HOSKIEL (see Abeyta, Narciso Platero)

HOSKIEL HA SO DA (see Abeyta, Narciso Platero)

HOTYEE (see Byrnes, James Michael)

ROBERT HOULE

Houle grew up, one of a family of fifteen, on the Sandy Bay Indian Reserve in southern Manitoba and speaks the Saulteaux-Ojibwa language

HOULE, ROBERT *Saulteaux/Ojibwa*

Born 1948 in St. Boniface, MB, Canada

RESIDENCE: Toronto, ON, Canada

EDUCATION: B.A., McGill University, Montréal, PQ 1975; Academy of Beaux-Arts, Salzburg, Austria, summer 1972; B.A., C/U of MB, 1972

OCCUPATION: Educator, museum curator, exhibition curator, art consultant, constructionist, installation artist, and painter

MEDIA: Acrylic and mixed-media

PUBLISHED: Menitove, ed. (1986b); Roberts, ed. (1992). *Native Perspective* (Vol. 2, no. 10, 1978); *Artswest* (Vol. 6, no. 10, 1981); *Artscanada* (no. 248/249, 1982); *American Indian Art* (spring 1985, winter 1987); *Canadian Art* (Vol. 2, no. 4, 1985); *Windspeaker* (12 Dec 1986); *The Globe and Mail* (19 Apr 1989); *Winnipeg Freepress* (17 Jan 1989); *The Ottawa Citizen* (June 1989); *C Magazine* (summer 1991; fall 1991)

PUBLIC COLLECTIONS: Partial listing of more than 27 includes: C/AG/H; C/AG/TB; C/AG/WP; C/CMC; C/INAC; C/IOC; C/MCC; C/NCCT; C/NGCA; C/ROM; HM; Council Art Bank, Ottawa, ON; Sandy Bay Education Board, Marius, MB

EXHIBITS: C/ACCCNA; C/AG/H; C/AG/TB; C/AG/V; C/AG/WP; C/CR; C/LUM; C/NGCA; C/NWNG; C/ROM; C/UG; C/U of R/MG; HM; OSU/G; PDN; PIG; SM; SS/CW; Concordia University, Montréal, PQ, 1978; De Meervart, Amsterdam, Netherlands, 1985; Gettysburg (PA) College, 1990

SOLO EXHIBITS: Partial listing of more than twenty includes: C/AG/TB; C/AG/WP; C/CMC; C/GM; C/UG; C/U of BC/MG; C/U of TC/WM; Hood College, Frederick, MD, 1991; galleries in Ottawa and Toronto, ON, and Montréal, PQ

HONORS: *Scholarships and Grants:* Canadian Guild of Crafts Scholarship, Montréal, PQ, 1973; Canada Council Short Term Grant, 1985; Canada Council Art Grant, Ottawa, ON, 1992. *Other:* Indian and Northern Affairs Cultural Award, Winnipeg, MB, 1967; C/AG/WP, first Native artist-in-residence, 1989; C/MCC, artist-in-residence, 1989

ROBERT HOULE

(continued) fluently. He found the Canadian residential school system to be a traumatic experience that led to a feeling of dispossession. These early school experiences have resulted in a concern for cultural issues which are reflected in his art. His first serious art training at McGill University gave him a means of exploring his emotions and expressing who he was. Houle considers his work to be a declaration of independence.

HOUSE, CONRAD *Navajo/Oneida*

Born 29 Nov 1956 in Rehoboth, NM

RESIDENCE: Thoreau, NM

EDUCATION: Thoreau (NM) High School, 1974; Fulton-Montgomery Community College, Johnstown, NY; SUNY, Johnstown, NY; B.F.A., U of NM, 1980; graduate studies, U of OR, 1980

OCCUPATION: Artist

MEDIA: Oil, acrylic, watercolor, pencil, pen and ink, pastel, Swiss crayon, clay, and mixed-media

PUBLISHED: Wade, ed. (1986); Jacka and Jacka (1988; 1994); Stewart (1988); Ward, ed. (1990); Krantz (1990); Roberts, ed. (1992). *The Arizona Tribune* (Feb 1981); *The Albuquerque Tribune* (24 May 1981); *Artnews* (Dec 1981); *Arizona Arts and Lifestyle* (autumn 1981); *Artspace* (fall 1981); *The Seattle Times* (Oct 1984); *Native Peoples* (Special Edition 1994); *Art-Talk* (Feb 1995)

PUBLIC COLLECTIONS: AICA/SF, HM, IACB, MPI, SFNB/WA, SPIM, U of NM/MM, USDI

EXHIBITS: AC/T; ACA; ACAI; AICA/SF; AICH; CNCM; ESC; FNAA; FSMCIAF; FWMA; HM; MMA/WA; NDM; OLO; PAC; PAM; PDN; SCG; SFFA; SS/CW; SWAIA; U of NM; WIB; WNAA; WWM; Bellevue (WA) Art Museum; Fort Wayne (IN) Museum of Art; throughout CA, NY, OR, WA, and the southwestern U.S.

SOLO EXHIBITS: AICA/SF, MPI, SCG

AWARDS: ITIC ('87); SWAIA ('90, Best in Class, Best in Category, 1st); U of NM ('83, Purchase Award)

HONORS: *Scholarships and Fellowships:* Philchurch Glass School Scholarship; SWAIA Fellowship Award, 1990. *Other:* FNAA poster artist; U of NM, Office of International Studies Grant, 1979

CONRAD HOUSE

House was a member of the Grey Canyon Artists Group which included Emmi Whitehorse, Larry Emerson, Paul Willeto, and Juane Quick-To-See Smith (qq.v.) and exhibited extensively in the late 1970s and the 1980s.

Laurie Jay Houseman-Whitehawk

"I try to capture the mystical feelings that are such an important part of Native American rituals and lifestyles. These are spiritual powers, magical feelings, which cannot always be spoken, but only seen and experienced by the viewer. I hope to bring the American Indian culture, both past and present, together for others to be able to relate to, not just exclusively for the American Indian, but for everyone. This is a spiritual message. I hope to dispel a lot of misunderstanding, and I feel like an image will speak louder than words."

artist, p.c. 1992

Allan C. Houser

Originally a painter, Houser became the premier Native American sculptor whose works are in demand throughout the world. In 1993 he expressed a desire to return to his painting roots.

The first large sculpture that Houser did was for the Haskell Institute in 1948. Using only a few hand tools and a plumbbob he sculpted an eight foot tall, four and a half-ton piece of marble. He said that once the

Houseman-Whitehawk, Laurie Jay *Winnebago/Santee Sioux*

Wakan'-Je-Pe-Wein-Gah

Born 17 Nov 1952 in Omaha, NE; daughter of Jesse Cora White Steward; M/GP: Mary Whitehawk and Charles C. White

RESIDENCE: Lawrence, KS

EDUCATION: Shawnee Mission West High School, Overland Park, KS, 1971; Johnson County Community College, Shawnee Mission, KS; KSTC; KSU; IAIA; KCAI/MO; Haskell

OCCUPATION: Professional painter

MEDIA: Gouache

PUBLISHED: *The Indian Trader* (Vol. 21, no. 6, 1990)

COMMISSIONS: *Portraits:* Willie Nelson; Hank Williams Jr.

PUBLIC COLLECTIONS: CGPS; SPIM; Nebraska State Museum of History, Lincoln, NE

EXHIBITS: AIE; BHIAE; CNM; HSM/KS; KIAA; LC; LIAS; NPTA; RC; RE; SPIM; Kaw Valley Art Fair, Topeka, KS, 1983; St. Paul (MN) Science Museum (1986); Smoky Hill Museum, Salina, KS; see also Awards

SOLO EXHIBITS: IAIA; Riley County Historical Museum, Manhattan, KS; Lawrence (KS) Public Library; Lawrence (KS) Arts Center

AWARDS: BHIAE ('88, 1st); CNM ('84, 1st; '85, 1st); GPIAE ('88, Best of Show); KIAA ('84); LIAS ('91, MA); NPTA ('91, '93, 1st, Best of Fine Arts; '94); Kansas Artists Postcard Series XII and XIV ('89; '90)

HONORS: LIAS, poster artist, 1990; One woman show, requested by Congressman Jim Slattery, Topeka, KS; invited to lecture and conduct workshops in schools and universities throughout Kansas

Houser, Allan C. *Chiricahua Apache*

Haozous, The Sound of Pulling Roots

A.K.A. Allan Haozous

Born 30 June 1915 at Apache, OK; died 22 Sept 1994 in Santa Fe, NM; son of Blossom and Sam Haozous; father of Bob Haozous, sculptor; G/uncle: Geronimo, Chiricahua warrior in Oklahoma Territory

RESIDENCE: Lived in Santa Fe, NM

EDUCATION: Chilocco; Haskell; Santa Fe; studied under Dorothy Dunn, mural instruction under Olaf Nordmark

OCCUPATION: Pipe fitter, boxer, educator, public speaker, painter; full-time sculptor after 1975

MEDIA: Oil, acrylic, watercolor, egg tempera, charcoal, pastel, wood, stone, and bronze

PUBLISHED: Jacobson and d'Ucel (1950); Carter (1954); Pierson and Davidson (1960); Arnold (1960), dust jacket; Dockstader (1961); Carlson (1964); Jacobson (1964); Dunn (1968); Snodgrass (1968); Brody (1971); Tanner (1973); Monthan and Monthan (1975); Highwater (1976); Silberman (1978); New (1979); Kratz (1980); Mahey, et al. (1980); Broder (1981); King (1981); Samuels (1982; 1985); Hoffman, et al. (1984); Coe (1986); Seymour (1988); Perlman (1991); Archuleta and Strickland (1991). *Arizona Highways* (Feb 1950; Nov 1962); *The Indian Trader* (Aug 1984; Sept 1984; Sept 1994); *Compton's Picture Encyclopedia* (Vol. 7, 1947); *Oklahoma Today* (summer 1948; Dec 1990); *Sunday Bonanza, The San Francisco Chronicle* (22 Aug 1965); *Indians From Oklahoma*, BIA (1966); *Southwestern Art* (Vol. 2, no. 1, 1967); *The Anadarko Daily News* (15 Aug 1969); *Artists of the Rockies and the Golden West* (spring 1979); *Southwest Art* (June 1981; June 1983; Aug 1991; Dec 1992; Sept 1993; Dec 1994); *Americas* (Aug 1981); *The Santa Fean* (Oct 1982); *International Fine Art Collector* (May 1991), cover;

The Santa Fe New Mexican, Indian Market Edition (15 Aug 1991); *Native Peoples* (fall 1991; Special Edition 1994; Jan/Feb/Mar 1995); *The Tulsa World* (22 July 1992; 24 Aug 1994); *Art-Talk* (Oct 1994); *Persimmon Hill* (summer 1994; autumn 1994); *American Indian Art* (spring 1995); biographical publications

COMMISSIONS: *Murals:* Fort Sill; Riverside; Jicarilla; Inter-Mt.; SPIM; USDI (1939, 1940); New York World's Fair, 1936. *Portraits:* USDI, Official portrait of U.S. Secretary of the Interior, Stewart Udall; State of Arizona, Capitol Building, Phoenix, portrait of Geronimo. *Sculptures:* Haskell Institute, Lawrence, KS, *Comrades in Mourning*, 1948; *Of Sacred Rain*, commemorating Indian people who served in the military and died in WWII (first public monument in U.S. done by a Native American); State of Oklahoma, Capitol Building grounds, Oklahoma City, *As Long As the Waters Flow*; BBHC, *Drama on the High Plains*, 1993. *Other:* SPIM, diorama; The Society of Medalists, 59th medal issued, May 1959

PUBLIC COLLECTIONS: AF; BA/AZ; BIA; DAM; FSM; GM; HCC; HM; IACB; IACB/DC; JAM; MAM; MNM; MNA/KHC; OU/MA; OU/SM; PAC; PAIC; RMC/AZ; SDMM; SM; USDI; WWM; Arizona State Capitol Building, Phoenix; British Royal Collection, London, England; Dahlem Museum, West Berlin, Germany; Linden Museum, Stuttgart, Germany; Metropolitan Museum of Art, New York, NY; United States Mission to the United Nations

EXHIBITS: AAIE; ABQM; AC/A; AC/SD; AHALA; AIEC; AIW; BBHC; CAI; CGA; CPS; CSPIP; DAM; DC; EITA; HM; HSM/D; IAIA/M; IK; ITIC; JGS; LGAM; MAM; MFA/O; MNM; NACLA; NAP; NAWA; NGA; OMA; OU/MA; PAC; PAC/T; PAIC; RMC/AZ; SDMM; SFFA; SFWF; SI; SN; SPIM; SV; SWAIA; WIB; WRTD; WTF; WWM; National Exhibition of American Art, New York, NY (only Indian represented), 1937; New York World's Fair, 1939; Blair House, Washington, D.C., 1964; New Mexico State Capital Building, Governor's Gallery, Santa Fe, NM, 1976; Salon d'Automne, Grand Palais, Paris, France, 1981; Artists of America, Gala Sale and Exhibition, Denver, CO, 1989; Kunstler Haus, Vienna, Austria

SOLO/SPECIAL EXHIBITS: CAI; DAM; EM; GM; Haskell; MNM; OU/MA; PAC; PSDM; U of OK; WWM (dual show)

AWARDS: DAM; HM (Gold Medal); ITIC ('76); NAWA ('93, Prix de West, Purchase Award); PAC ('68, Grand Award); SN; 3 Grand Awards, 1978

HONORS: Santa Fe Indian School, trophy for Outstanding Work in Indian Art, senior year; John Simon Guggenheim Scholarship for Sculpture and Painting, 1948; French Government, Palmes d'Académiques, 1954; IACB, Certificate of Appreciation, 1967; PAC, Waite Phillips Trophy, 1969; Heard Museum, National Advisory Board, 1980; State of New Mexico, Governor's Award for the Visual Arts, 1980, 1983, 1984; Oklahoma Cultural Ambassador, 1984; Oklahoma Hall of Fame, inducted, 1985; University of Maine, Honorary Doctorate of Fine Arts, 1987; American Indian Resources Institute, Washington, D.C., American Indian Distinguished Achievement Award and Lifetime Achievement Award, 1989; National Council on the Arts and President of the United States, National Medal of Arts (first Native American recipient), 1992; U.S. Mission to the United Nations, New York, NY, sculpture placed on permanent exhibit; Ellis Island Medal of Honor, May 1993; National Academy of Western Art, inducted, 1993; NMAI, Art and Cultural Achievement Award, 1994

HOUSE STANDING UPRIGHT (see Denetsosie, Hoke)

HOWE, OSCAR *Yankton Sioux*

Mazuha Hokshina, Trader Boy

Born 15 May 1915 at Joe Creek, SD, on the Crow Creek Indian Reservation; died 7 Oct 1983; son of Ella Not Afraid of Bear and George T. Howe; M/GF: Not Afraid of Bear, Yanktonai chief

ALLAN C. HOUSER

(continued) sculpture was in place, he went to see it for one last time, and an admiring spectator asked him, "How would you like to do something like that?"

Houser advised others to search for what satisfies them, and then to strive to improve what they are doing. Of his work he said, "I first please myself. If I don't please myself, no one else will be pleased."

Houser Lecture notes, Oklahoma City Fine Arts Museum

OSCAR HOWE

"While a child in government boarding school, the artist developed a serious skin disease and trachoma. He was sent home and given little chance to escape blindness and disfiguration, but he vowed to get well and 'be the best.' He returned to school and completed his education."

Snodgrass 1968

RESIDENCE: Lived in Vermillion, SD

MILITARY: U.S. Army, WWII

EDUCATION: Santa Fe, 1938; B.A., Dakota Wesleyan University, Mitchell, SD, 1952; M.F.A., U of OK, 1953; studied mural techniques under Olaf Nordmark, at Indian Arts Center, Fort Sill, OK

OCCUPATION: Art instructor, artist-in-residence, art professor, and painter

PUBLISHED: Douglas and D'Harnoncourt (1941); LaFarge (1956); Pierson and Davidson (1960); Pennington (1961); Dunn (1968); Petersen (1968); Brody (1968); Snodgrass (1968); Soladay (1968); Milton, ed. (1969); Libhart (1970); Highwater (1976; 1980; 1983); New (1979); Mahey, et al. (1981); Silberman (1980); Broder (1981); Hoffman, et al. (1984); Samuals (1985b); Wade, ed. (1986); Archuleta and Strickland (1991); Maurer (1992). Partial listing of more than one hundred journal articles includes: *Oklahoma Today* (summer 1958); *Museum News* (June 1962); *Smoke Signals*, IACB (autumn 1965); *South Dakota Review* (Vol. 7, no. 2, 1969); *The Indian Trader* (Apr 1976; July 1978); *The Argus-Leader* (1 Feb 1979); *The Daily Republic* (14 June 1980; 3 Aug 1982); *Americas* (Vol. 32, no. 8, 1981); *The Christian Science Monitor* (June 30, 1981); *The Daily Oklahoman* (30 Aug 1981); *The Providence Sunday Journal* (9 Aug 1981); *Four Winds* (autumn 1982); *Southwest Art* (June 1983; Mar 1992); *The Tulsa World* (9 Oct 1983); *America West* (July 1990); *Native Peoples* (Vol. 5, no. 1, fall 1991)

BOOKS ILLUSTRATED: Raabe (1942); Clark (1943a); Jacobson (1952); Hassrick (1964); *Legend of the Mighty Sioux,* South Dakota Writers' Project, (1941)

COMMISSIONS: *Murals:* Carnegie Library and Corn Palace, Mitchell, SD; City Auditorium, Mobridge, SD; Park Building, Nebraska City, NE; Proviso High School, Hinsdale, IL; Steinhart Park, Steinhart Lodge, Nebraska City, NE

PUBLIC COLLECTIONS: AC/OH; BIA; CGPS; DAM; FAC/D; HCC; HM; IACB; IACB/DC; JAM; MAI; MAM; MFA/A; MNA; MNM; OU/MA; OU/SM; PAC; SCAC; SIM; SM; U of SD; Civic Fine Arts Center, Sioux Falls, SD; Eisenhower Library, Abilene, KS; Evansville (IN) Museum; Robinson Museum, Pierre, SD; South Dakota Memorial Art Center, Brookings, SD

EXHIBITS: BNIAS; CAI; CSP; DAM; GM; HM; HMA; HPTU; HS/OH; IK; ISU; JAM; LGAM; MAM; MCC/CA; MNM; MMA; NAP; NGA; OMA; OU/ET; OU/MA; OU/MA/T; PAC; PAC/T; PAIC; PM; SAIEAIP; SCAC; SIM; SM; SU; SV; U of KS; USDI; USDS; VP; U.S. embassies in Europe; see also Awards

SOLO EXHIBITS: Partial listing of more than 47 includes: AIW; DAM; GM; HM; JAM; MNM; NPTA; PAC; SIM; U of ND; U of SD; U of WI; USDI; Sioux City (IA) Art Center

AWARDS: Partial listing of more than 28 includes: DAM ('52, Field Award; '53, Purchase Prize; '54, Santa Fe Railroad Award); MNM ('56, Purchase Prize; '58, Benjamin Award); PAC ('47, Grand Award; '49; '50; '51, 1st; '52; '53; '54, Grand Award; '56; '59, Grand Award; '60; '65, 1st); National Indian Art Exhibition, Bismarck, ND ('63, 1st)

HONORS: *Honorary degrees:* South Dakota State University, Brookings, SD, Doctor of Humanities, 1968; Dakota Wesleyan University, Mitchell, SD, Doctor of Humanities, 1972; Hamline University, St. Paul, MN, Doctor of Humanities, 1973. *Other:* High School Salutatorian; Dakota Wesleyan University, Mitchell, SD, Harvey Dunn Medal In Art, 1952; Artist Laureate of South Dakota, 1960; International Institute of Arts and Letters, Geneva, Switzerland, elected a Fellow, 1960; IACB, Certificate of Appreciation, 1962; The Foundation for North American Indian Culture, Bismarck, ND, Award of Recognition, 1964; PAC, Waite Phillips Outstanding Indian Artist Trophy, 1966; USDS, appointed lecturer to the Far East and South Asia, 1971; State of South Dakota, First Annual Governor's Award for Outstanding Creative Achievement in the Arts, 1973; U of OK, Golden Bear Award, 1979; South Dakota Cowboy and Western Heritage Hall of Fame, inducted, 1979; U of SD, appointed Professor Emeritus of the Department of Art; South Dakota Memorial Art Center, Brookings, SD, Artistic Achievement Citation; Governor of South Dakota, proclamed Oscar Howe Day, 19 Sept 1981

HOWLING WOLF *Southern Cheyenne*

Honanisto, Howling Wolf

Born ca. 1850; died 1927 in Waurika, OK, in an automobile accident; son of Minimic Eagle Head, war leader and principal chief of the Cheyenne

MEDIA: Crayon, pencil, and pen and ink

PUBLISHED: Dunn (1968); Peterson (1968); Snodgrass (1968); Szabo (1983; 1994); Maurer (1992). *Allen Memorial Art Museum Bulletin* (No. 46, 1992); *Native Peoples* (summer 1993)

PUBLIC COLLECTIONS: HI, JAM, MAI, MNH/F, YU/BRBML

EXHIBITS: BPG, VP

HOWLING WOLF

"The artist was among the 72 Plains Indians taken as prisoners from Fort Sill, OK, to Fort Marion, St. Augustine, FL, in 1875. By 1880, he had returned to the area of the Darlington (OK) Cheyenne Agency. . . ."

Snodgrass 1968

Several years after Howling Wolf returned to the reservation a sketch book of his drawings was collected by anthropologist and writer, Captain John G. Bourke.

Peterson 1968

HUAN TOA (see Momaday, Al)

HUDGENS, HUGH *Choctaw*

Born 20 Mar 1945

RESIDENCE: Rogers, AR

EDUCATION: U of AR

OCCUPATION: Full-time sculptor and painter since 1988

MEDIA: Pencil, stone, and mixed-media

EXHIBITS: CNM, FCTM, RC; see also Awards

AWARDS: CNM ('88, 1st); FCTM ('91; '92); RC ('92); Indian Images Show, Joplin, MO ('88); Oklahoma Centennial Land Run Art Show, Guthrie, OK ('89, 1st); Springtime On the Mall Art Show, Blytheville, AR ('89)

HUDGENS-BEACH, DIANA *Cherokee/Shawnee/Delaware*

RESIDENCE: Meers, OK

EDUCATION: North Texas State University, Denton, TX

OCCUPATION: Artist

MEDIA: Oil, acrylic, watercolor, gouache, pencil, clay, wood, and prints.

PUBLISHED: Campbell, ed. (1993). *Cherokee Heritage*, cover; *Journal of Cherokee Studies*, cover

COMMISSIONS: Cooper Communities Inc., painting, 1987

PUBLIC COLLECTIONS: CNM; HCC; Tyson Foods Corporation, Springdale, AR

EXHIBITS: ACAI; CAI/KC; CHMG; CIM; CNM; FCTM; HCC; ITIC; LC; LIAS; MCI; RC; RE; SIM; TIAF; WTF; Anderson County Museum, Anderson, SC; El Cajón Museum, San Diego, CA; see also Awards

AWARDS: CHMG ('84, 1st, '85, 2-1st; '86, 1st, Grand Award, Peoples Choice Award; '87, 1st, People's Choice Award); CNM ('86, 1st; '89, 1st; '92, Grand Award); FCTM ('85, 2-1st; '86, 1st; '87, Grand Award; '89, 1st); HCC ('89, 1st); ITIC ('89); LC ('89, Oklahoma Land Run Award; '90); LIAS ('89, Grand Award); RC ('87); TIAF ('90); Las Colinas (CA) Indian Arts Competition (1st); Sequoyah Birthplace Museum, Vonore, TN ('87, Grand Prize); Smoky Mountain Heritage Show, Cherokee, NC ('87, People's Choice Award; '88, 1st, Best of Show, People's Choice Award)

HONORS: Remington Park Red Earth Race, Oklahoma City, OK, *Our Tears Flowed Like Rivers* chosen for presentation trophies, 1991

HUDSON, JACK *Tsimshian*

RESIDENCE: Metlakatla, AK

Born 17 July 1936 in Metlakatla, AK; father of John Hudson (q.v.)

OCCUPATION: Teacher, carver, printmaker, and painter

HUDSON, JOHN *Tsimshian*

Born 1967 in Seattle, WA; son of Jack Hudson (q.v.), carver and professor of Tsimshian art and culture

RESIDENCE: Seattle, WA

EDUCATION: Studied with his father

OCCUPATION: Fisherman, carver, graphic artist, and painter

HUFF, TOM *Seneca/Cayuga*

RESIDENCE: Versailles, NY

EXHIBITS: AICH

HUGH, VICTOR C. *Hopi*

OCCUPATION: Carver and painter

MEDIA: Watercolor and cottonwood root

PUBLISHED: Snodgrass (1968)

PUBLIC COLLECTIONS: AF

EXHIBITS: FHMAG, 1987

HUGHTE, PHILBERT *Zuni*

A.K.A. Phil Hughte

Born 27 Apr 1954 at Zuni Pueblo, NM; son of Mary Lou and Joe Quampehone

RESIDENCE: Zuni Pueblo, NM

EDUCATION: Zuni (NM) High School, 1973; B.F.A., U of N AZ, 1977

OCCUPATION: Art instructor, cartoonist, and painter

MEDIA: Oil, acrylic, watercolor, pencil, and prints

PUBLISHED: Panda (1993)

COMMISSIONS: *Murals:* IPCC

EXHIBITS: ITIC; MNA; IPCC; SWAIA; U of N AZ; U of NM/MM; A:Shiwi A:Wan Museum and Heritage Center, Zuni Pueblo, NM; galleries in Gallup, NM, and Hobart, IN

AWARDS: ITIC ('90, 1st; '91, 1st); MNA ('91, Best of Show); SWAIA ('85, 1st; '87, 1st); ITIC, juvenile division

HONORS: Zuni Tribe, scholarship; Chicago Art Institute, addmittance; Rhode Island School of Design, admittance

PHILBERT HUGHTE

Hughte has been painting since the age of seven. He enjoys painting scenes as he remembers them from his childhood. Consulting with the Pueblo elders, he accurately reflects the strong cultural ties and beautiful surroundings of Zuni Pueblo.

artist, p.c. 1992

HUHNOHUHCOAH (see White Bear)

HULSE, LOIS *Cherokee*

RESIDENCE: Fort Smith, AR

OCCUPATION: Art teacher and painter

EXHIBITS: CNM

AWARDS: CNM ('87, 1st; '88, 1st; '93)

HUMETEWA (see Humetewa, James Russell, Jr.)

HUMETEWA, EDWARD R. *Hopi*

EXHIBITS: PM

HUMETEWA, ERIC *Hopi*

Birth date unknown; born near Tuba City, AZ; uncle of James Russell Humetewa Jr. (q.v.)

RESIDENCE: Tuba City, AZ

MEDIA: Watercolor

PUBLISHED: Snodgrass (1968); Brody (1971); Tanner (1973)

PUBLIC COLLECTIONS: MNA

ERIC HUMETEWA

The colors that Humetewa used in his paintings were not as dynamic as those of most Hopi artists but his attention to detail was typical. He was no longer painting in 1970.

Tanner 1973

HUMETEWA, JAMES RUSSELL, JR. *Hopi*

Humetewa, Shelling Corn; *Soowoea,* Morning Star

A.K.A. Russell, James, Jr.

Born 28 May 1926 near Tuba City, AZ; nephew of Eric Humetewa (q.v.)

RESIDENCE: Bernalillo, NM

EDUCATION: Santa Fe, 1945

OCCUPATION: Museum of New Mexico employee and painter

MEDIA: Casein

PUBLISHED: Jacobson and d'Ucel (1950); Tanner (1957; 1973); Snodgrass (1968); Brody (1971); Broder (1981); Seymour (1988)

PUBLIC COLLECTIONS: FM, HCC, IACB/DC, MAI, MNM, PAC

EXHIBITS: FWG, ITIC, MNA, MNM, NMSF, PAC, PAC/T, SFWF; galleries in Santa Fe, NM

SOLO EXHIBITS: MNM

JAMES RUSSELL HUMETEWA JR.

"Records at the Museum of New Mexico disclose that the artist has exhibited extensively in New Mexico and Arizona. In 1950, he was reportedly the most prolific of the younger Hopi artists."

Snodgrass 1968

HUMMINGBIRD, JEROME *Kiowa*

Born 1930 in Lawton, OK

RESIDENCE: Cache, OK

EDUCATION: Riverside

PUBLISHED: Snodgrass (1968)

EXHIBITS: PAC

HUMMINGBIRD, JESSE T. *Cherokee*

A.K.A. Jesse Travis Hummingbird

Born 12 Feb 1952 in Tahlequah, OK; son of Margaret Brackett and Jess T. Hummingbird; P/GP: Nancy Ragsdale and Jesse Hummingbird; M/GP: Jane A. Batt and Migel Brackett

RESIDENCE: Tucson, AZ

OCCUPATION: Painter

MEDIA: Acrylic, pen and ink, mixed-media, and prints

PUBLIC COLLECTIONS: HCC, TTSP

EXHIBITS: CNM, FCTM, IACA, LIAS, RC, SWAIA, TTSP, WTF

AWARDS: FCTM ('84; '86, Grand Heritage Award; '87, 1st); ITIC ('91, 1st; '94)

HONORS: ITIC, poster artist, 1991

JESSE T. HUMMINGBIRD

Hummingbird says, "I am a traditionalist — both in spirit and art. The subject matter of each piece is based on Cherokee or Native American heritage, as I know it. I'm influenced by the nature that's around me, its colors, sounds, and creatures. No matter how difficult, I want people to know I'm proud of my culture and traditions. I want to preserve what we have left as I create the new."

p.c. 1990

HUMPED WOLF *Crow*

RESIDENCE: Montana

OCCUPATION: Warrior and painter

PUBLISHED: *American Indian Art* (spring 1993)

PUBLIC COLLECTIONS: MIA

EXHIBITS: MIA; JAM; St Louis (MO) Art Museum

HUNT, CALVIN *Kwakwaka 'wakw (Kwakiutl)/Nuu-Chah-Nulth (Nootka)*

Born 1956 in Alert Bay, BC, Canada; son of Emma and Chief Thomas Hunt; brother of Eugene and Ross Hunt (qq.v.)

RESIDENCE: Fort Rupert, BC, Canada

EDUCATION: Apprenticed to Henry Hunt, Tony Hunt, and Doug Cranmer (qq.v.)

OCCUPATION: Carver, jeweler, printmaker, and painter

PUBLISHED: Stewart (1979); Macnair, Hoover, and Neary (1980); Hall, Blackman, and Rickard (1981)

COMMISSIONS: Partial listing of 15 includes: Canadian Museum of Civilization, carved dish

PUBLIC COLLECTIONS: C/INAC, C/RBCM

EXHIBITS: C/HFH; C/TL; EIAF; HMA/WG; MHDYMM; U of SD; Expo '86; Kleinburg (ON) Museum

HUNT, EUGENE *Kwakwaka'wakw (Kwakiutl)/Nuu-Chah-Nulth (Nootka)*

Born 1946 in Alert Bay, BC, Canada; son of Emma and Chief Thomas Hunt; brother of Calvin and Ross Hunt (qq.v.)

RESIDENCE: Victoria, BC, Canada

EDUCATION: Studied under Mungo Martin, Henry Hunt, and Tony Hunt (qq.v)

OCCUPATION: Commercial fisherman, carver, printmaker, and painter

PUBLIC COLLECTIONS: HCC

HUNT, GEORGE, JR. *Kwakwaka'wakw (Kwakiutl)*

PUBLIC COLLECTIONS: HCC

EXHIBITS: HCC, ITIC, RC

AWARDS: ITIC ('87, 1st)

HUNT, HENRY *Kwakwaka'wakw (Kwakiutl)*

Born 16 Oct 1923 at Fort Rupert, B.C., Canada; died 1985; son of Jonathan Hunt; P/GF: George Hunt; father of Richard and Tony Hunt (qq.v.)

EDUCATION: Trained by Mungo Martin (q.v.)

OCCUPATION: Carver, painter, and printmaker

MEDIA: Felt pen, pencil, and wood

PUBLISHED: Macnair, Hoover, and Neary (1980); Hall, Blackman, and Rickard (1981)

PUBLIC COLLECTIONS: C/GM, C/RBCM, HCC

EXHIBITS: C/TL, SDSMT

HENRY HUNT

Hunt was senior carver at the British Columbia Provincial Museum from 1954 to 1975. While there he reproduced many of the old and historic totem poles of the Northwest Coast. In the 1960s he trained many of the younger artists including his sons Richard, Tony, and Stanley.

Hall, Blackman, and Rickard 1981

HUNT, RICHARD *Kwakwaka'wakw (Kwakiutl)*

Born 1951 in Alert Bay, BC, Canada; son of Henry Hunt (q.v.); brother of Tony Hunt (q.v.) P/GF: Jonathan Hunt; M/GF: Mungo Martin (q.v.); P/GGF: George Hunt

RESIDENCE: Victoria, BC, Canada

EDUCATION: Victoria (BC) High School, 1971; trained at the British Columbia Provincial Museum, Vancouver, BC; apprenticed to Henry Hunt and Tony Hunt (qq.v.)

OCCUPATION: Carver, dancer, silver engraver, printmaker, and painter

PUBLISHED: Steltzer (1976); Stewart (1979); Macnair, Hoover, and Neary (1980); Hall, Blackman, and Rickard (1981); Gerber and Bruggmann (1989). *Westworld* (Jan/Feb 1973); *Four Winds* (1980)

COMMISSIONS: Partial listing of 21 includes: C/RBCM; Canadian Cultural Centre, Paris, France; City of Arts Centre, Edinburgh, Scotland; Museum of Ethnology, Osaka, Japan; City of Liverpool, England; Expo '86, Vancouver, BC

PUBLIC COLLECTIONS: C/INAC, C/RBCM, HCC, MNH/A.

EXHIBITS: C/TL, BHSU, HCC, SDSMT

SOLO EXHIBITS: Vancouver, BC, 1990

HONORS: Mask presented to Queen Elizabeth II, 1983; received the Order of British Columbia, 1991

HUNT, ROSS *Kwakwaka'wakw (Kwakiutl)/ Nuu-Chah-Nulth (Nootka)*

Born 1948 in Alert Bay, BC, Canada; son of Emma and Chief Thomas Hunt; brother of Calvin and Eugene Hunt (qq.v.)

RESIDENCE: Fort Rupert, BC, CAnada

EDUCATION: Apprenticed with Henry Hunt, Tony Hunt (qq.v.), John Livingston, and Calvin Hunt (q.v.)

PUBLIC COLLECTIONS: HCC

EXHIBITS: BHSU, HCC, SDSMT

HUNT, TOM *Kwakwaka'wakw (Kwakiutl)*

Born 1964 in Victoria, BC, Canada

EDUCATION: Apprenticed to his uncle, Calvin Hunt (q.v.)

OCCUPATION: Carver, painter, and printmaker

HUNT, TONY, JR. *Kwakwaka'wakw (Kwakiutl)*

Born 1942 at Fort Rupert, North Vancouver Island, BC, Canada; son of Henry Hunt (q.v.); brother of Richard Hunt (q.v.); M/GF: Mungo Martin (q.v.)

EDUCATION: Apprenticed to Mungo Martin (q.v.)

OCCUPATION: Consultant, gallery owner, carver, jeweler, printmaker, and painter

MEDIA: Acrylic, watercolor, pencil, wood, and silver

PUBLISHED: Stewart (1979); Macnair, Hoover, and Neary (1980); Hall, Blackman, and Rickard (1981); Gerber and Bruggmann (1989); McMasters, et al. (1993). *The Craftsman* (Vol. 6, no. 2, 1973); *West World* (Vol. 1, no. 1, 1975); *Art Canada* (Special Issue, 1977); *The Malahat Review* (Vol. 1, no. 50, 1979); *Masterkey* (winter 1984); *Windspeaker* (12 Dec 1986); *Canadian Art* (spring 1988); *Artswest* (May/June 1989)

COMMISSIONS: Partial listing of more than fifty includes: FM, two Kwakiutl houses; C/RBCM, 12 totem poles

PUBLIC COLLECTIONS: Partial listing of 16 includes: C/CCCAC; C/CMC; C/INAC; C/RBCM; C/ROM; C/U of BC/MA; HM; HMA/WG; MNH/F; Canadian Embassy, Mexico City, Mexico; Government House, Victoria, BC; National Museum of Japan, Osaka, Japan

EXHIBITS: Partial listing of more than thirty includes: AICA/SF; ASM/AH; C/ACCCNA; C/AG/TB; C/CMC; C/HFH; C/INAC; C/MGC; C/ROM; C/TL; C/VCM; DAM; HM; HMA/WG; MNH/F; MHDYMM; U of CA/LMA; U of PA/M; Expo '70, Osaka, Japan; International Trade Shows in Frankfurt, Germany and Tokyo, Japan

SOLO EXHIBITS: Five including: C/AG/V; MNH/F; Lowie Museum, Berkeley, CA

HONORS: Guest of Honor and presentation to Her Majesty Queen Elizabeth, Ottawa, ON, 1978; C/U of BC, Alumni Association, Honorary Life Membership

TONY HUNT JR.

Tony Hunt was one of the first contemporary Northwest Coast artists to produce silkscreen prints. In conjunction with the Women's Committee of the Victoria Art Gallery he published four or five prints.

Hall, Blackman, and Rickard 1981

HUNT, WAYNE HENRY (see Hunt, Wolf Robe)

HUNT, WOLF ROBE *Acoma*

Kewa, Growing Plant

A.K.A. Wayne Henry Hunt

Born 14 Oct 1905 at Acoma Pueblo, NM; died 10 Dec 1977 in Tulsa, OK; son of Morning Star, potter and weaver, and Edward Hunt, Chief of the Delight Makers and medicine man

RESIDENCE: Lived in Tulsa, OK

EDUCATION: Albuquerque (NM) High School; studied privately under Carl Redin in Albuquerque, NM, and Frank Von Der Laucken in Tulsa, OK

OCCUPATION: Lecturer, author, dancer, dance group organizer, instructor, motel owner and operator, interpreter, Indian trader, silversmith, and painter

MEDIA: Oil, casein, silver, and gemstone

PUBLISHED: Snodgrass (1968); Brody (1971); Tanner (1973); Schmid and Houlihan (1979); Mahey, et al. (1980). *The Arizona Republic* (8 May 1966); *Tulsa* (5 May 1977); *The Tulsa World* (10 Dec 1977)

BOOKS ILLUSTRATED: Rushmore and Hunt (1963)

PUBLIC COLLECTIONS: BIA, IACB, MNA, MRFM, PAC

EXHIBITS: AIE; FANAIAE; HM; HM/G; ITIC; JAM; LGAM; MIF; MNM; NAP; PAC; PM; SAIEAIP; SN; USDS; United States Food Exhibition, Hamburg, Germany; Spain and France

SOLO EXHIBITS: HM, PAC ('67, Grand Award)

AWARDS: FANAIAE, MNM, PAC

HONORS: U of Chicago, Department of Anthropology, scholarship; U.S. Department of Agriculture, selected to represent American Indians at a food exhibition, Hamburg, Germany, 1964; Council of American Indians, Oklahoma Indian of the Year, 1973; PAC, Waite Phillips Trophy, 1974

HUNTER, ELWOOD *Navajo*

PUBLISHED: Snodgrass (1968)

EXHIBITS: FWG, HM

HUNTER, KEITH *Cherokee*

RESIDENCE: Inola, OK

OCCUPATION: Craftsman, jeweler, and graphic artist

EXHIBITS: TWF

HUNTING HORSE (see Darby, Raymond Lee)

HUNTING HORSE (see Tsatoke, Lee Monette)

HUNTING HORSE (see Tsatoke, Monroe)

HUNTING WOLF *Apache*

MEDIA: Graphite and colored pencil

PUBLISHED: Snodgrass (1968)

PUBLIC COLLECTIONS: HSM/OK

EXHIBITS: BPG

HUNTING WOLF

"Hunting Wolf was among the 72 Plains Indian prisoners taken from Fort Sill, OK, to Fort Marion, St. Augustine, FL, in 1875; while there, he executed paintings and drawings on writing paper."

Snodgrass 1968

HUNTLEY, STEPHEN *Creek*

EXHIBITS: CNM

HUPQUATCHEW (see Hamilton, Ron)

HUSER, YVONNE *Choctaw*

Princess Pale Moon, Leader of Women

A.K.A. P. Pale Moon

Born 17 Dec 1925 in Poteau, OK; daughter of Dora May McClure and Tom Lyons; P/GP: Viola L and C. B. Lyons; M/GP: Ida Wall and P. J. McClure

RESIDENCE: Holdenville, OK

EDUCATION: L.L.B, Cumberland, Williamsburg, KY; SU; studied art under John Metcalf and R. V. Goetz

OCCUPATION: Manager, art teacher, and artist

MEDIA: Oil, charcoal, and clay

EXHIBITS: CNM; FCTM; Pittsburgh County Historical Society, Wewoka, OK; area art exhibits

AWARDS: Holdenville (OK) Society of Painters and Sculptors (20-1sts, 8 Best of Shows)

HONORS: Holdenville, OK, voted Outstanding Citizen, 1986; Choctaw Tribe, named a Princess, 1940; Creek Nation Tribal Council, Honorary Member

HUSHKA YELHAYAH (see Lee, Charlie)

HUSKETT, JOHN *Navajo*

MILITARY: U.S. Navy, WWII

EDUCATION: Commercial art course, Chilocco, after WWII

PUBLISHED: Snodgrass (1968)

EXHIBITS: PAC; Midwest Rural Conference, OSU

HUTCHINSON, BRYAN *Chippewa/Crow*

Born 1964 in Glendale, CA

RESIDENCE: Pryor, MT

EDUCATION: Marty Indian School, Yankton Sioux Indian Reservation, SD, 1981; IAIA, 1986

MEDIA: Acrylic

EXHIBITS: AAID; IAIA; RC; Coyote Indian Art Show, Missoula, MT

BRYAN HUTCHINSON

Hutchinson says, "My paintings are contemporary Indian art . . . not of any specific tribe. They are my conception of Indians. I use very bright colors, such as pinks, yellows, and purples. I want people to look at my paintings and to remember them."

artist, p.c. 1988

HYDE, DOUG *Nez Percé/Assiniboin/Chippewa*

Born 1946 in Hermiston, OR

MILITARY: U.S. Army, Vietnam

EDUCATION: IAIA, 1965-1966; SFAI; apprenticed to a monument maker, 1969-1971; studied under Allan Houser (q.v.) at IAIA

OCCUPATION: Memorial carver, educator, painter, and sculptor

MEDIA: Acrylic, stone, bronze, and mixed-media

PUBLISHED: Snodgrass (1968); Monthan and Monthan (1975); Highwater (1980); New (1980); Broder (1981); Samuels (1982); Wade et al.(1986); Minthorn (1991). *Artists of the Rockies and the Golden West* (spring 1975); *Arizona Highways* (May 1986); *Southwest Profile* (Aug/Sept/Oct 1992); *Art-Talk* (Jan 1995)

COMMISSIONS: *Sculptures:* American Indian Society, Washington, D.C., bust of Apache leader Taza, 1973; Palm Springs Public Art Commission, Agua Caliente Women, bronze, 1994. *Other:* Created Josiah Redwolf memorial tombstone for Nez Percé Tribe, 1971

EXHIBITS: ACE; ACMWA; ABQM; AC/K; BBHC; BIA/DC; CIA; EIAF; HM; HSM/D; IAIA; IAIA/M; KCPA; MCC; MCC/CA; MPI; NACLA; PAC; SAIEAIP; SAP; SDAM; SFFA; SN; SWAIA; USDI; WWM; Berlin Festival, West Germany, 1966; Olympics, Mexico, 1968; Nez Percé Community, Lapwai, ID, 1971; throughout Idaho and Washington

SOLO EXHIBITS: IAIA, MPI

AWARDS: Partial listing includes: HM (Gold Medal); PAC ('65); SN ('66, 1st; '76, Best in Stone, Best in Sculpture, Best in Show)

HONORS: San Francisco (CA) Art Institute, scholarship, 1966

DOUG HYDE

Although Hyde painted at the beginning of his career, he is now best known for his sculpture. His paintings, to which he often added yarn and beads, were a reflection of his Plains Indian heritage.

HYEOMA, LUCILLE *Hopi*

EDUCATION: IAIA, 1965-1966

PUBLISHED: Snodgrass (1968)

EXHIBITS: YAIA

Igla-Ka-Terila (see Herman, Jake)

Ihunter (see Orr, Howell Sonny)

Iisusi (see Eleeshushe)

Iisa (see Esa, Marjorie)

Iisa, Marjorie (see Esa, Marjorie)

Ikayukta *Inuit (Eskimo)*

Born 1911

RESIDENCE: Cape Dorset, NWT, Canada

OCCUPATION: Graphic artist

MEDIA: Felt tip pen, pencil, and prints

PUBLISHED: Goetz, et al. (1977); Blodgett (1978a). *The Beaver* (spring 1975)

PUBLIC COLLECTIONS: C/CAP

EXHIBITS: C/AG/WP, C/TIP

Ikseetrkyuk (see Iksiktaayuk, Luke)

Iksiktaayuk, Luke *Inuit (Eskimo)*

A.K.A. Iksikuaaryuk/Kanak; Ikseetarkyuk

Born 1909; died 1977

RESIDENCE: Lived at Baker Lake, NWT, Canada

OCCUPATION: Hunter, carver; graphic artist after 1969

MEDIA: Colored pencil

PUBLISHED: Goetz, et al. (1977); Woodhouse, ed. (1980); Latocki, ed. (1983); Collinson (1978). *North* (Mar/Apr 1974)

PUBLIC COLLECTIONS: C/AG/WP, C/U of AB

EXHIBITS: C/AG/WP; C/CG; C/TIP; Robertson Galleries, Ottawa, ON

Iksikuaaryuk/Kanak (see Iksiktaayuk, Luke)

Illiana (see Ingram, Veronica Marie Orr

Imerak (see Emerak, Mark)

Imigak (see Emerak, Mark)

Immana, Annie Weokluk *Eskimo*

Annnanooruk

Born 1903 at Big Diomede, Siberia, Russia

RESIDENCE: Nome, AK

PUBLISHED: Snodgrass (1968)

EXHIBITS: Nome (AK) Skin Sewers; Poliet's Store, Nome, AK

Ingram, Jerry *Choctaw/Cherokee*

A.K.A. Jerry Cleman Ingram

Born 13 Dec 1941 in Battiest, OK; Son of Jincy Cobb and Charley Ingram

RESIDENCE: Ilfeld, NM

EDUCATION: Battiest (OK) High School, 1958; Chilocco, 1963; IAIA, 1964; B.A., OSU/O, 1966

OCCUPATION: Free-lance designer, advertising and commercial artist, sculptor, bead worker, and painter

MEDIA: Oil, watercolor, acrylic, mixed-media, leather, beads, bronze, and prints

PUBLISHED: Snodgrass (1968); Brody (1971); Monthan and Monthan (1975);

Annie Weokluk Immana

"The artist's travels along the coast of Siberia in a skin boat have provided her with the subject matter for her paintings."

Snodgrass 1968

Jerry Ingram

"I'm trying to bring back images of what it was like in the old days. I've always been fascinated by the Northern Plains Indians, although I'm not of that tribal group. In truth, I don't know a lot about those cultures on a firsthand, personal basis, but I try anyway to capture the mystique, the colorfulness, the essence." Ingram's concern with authenticity leads him to do careful research on his subjects.

artist, p.c. 1991

DETAIL: Jerry Ingram, *Sign of Strength*, 1981. Philbrook Museum of Art, Tulsa, Oklahoma

Broder (1981); Hoffman, et al. (1984). *The Arizona Republic* (17 Mar 1968); *Art Voices South* (Sept/Oct 1979); biographical publications

BOOKS ILLUSTRATED: Byrd (1974)

COMMISSIONS: *Murals:* OSU/O, Oklahoma Room. *Other:* New World Records, New York, NY, album cover, 1993

PUBLIC COLLECTIONS: CNM, GM, HM, MNA, MRFM, PAC

EXHIBITS: AICA/SF; CCHM; DAM; FCTM; HM/G; HNSM; HS/OH; IAIA/M; IK; ITIC; MFA/AH; MFA/O; MMA/MT; MNH/D; NACLA; NMSF; PAC; RE; SFFA; SN; SWAIA; TAAII, TRP; WIB; WWM; Charles W. Bowers Museum, Santa Ana, CA; Hunter Museum, Chattanooga, TN, 1981; Loveland (CO) Art Museum, 1980; Nicolaysen Art Museum, Casper, WY, 1980; OSU Art Show; Pecos (NM) Arts and Crafts Show; Santo Domingo Pueblo (NM) Arts and Crafts Show, 1992; galleries in New Mexico; see also Awards

SOLO/SPECIAL EXHIBITS: CNGM (dual show); HM; SPIM

AWARDS: FCTM ('73, IH); HM/G ('71; '72; '76, 1st; '78, 1st; '79, 1st, Best of Watercolors); ITIC ('72, 1st); NMSF ('70, 1st); PAC ('77, Hunt Award; '78); SN ('71); RE ('90, 1st); SWAIA ('77; '91); WWM; Dallas (TX) Indian Market ('90, 1st); Okmulgee County Art Show, Okmulgee, OK, 1965

HONORS: American Indian Lore Association, Catlin Peace Pipe Award, 1974; HM, design chosen for The Heard Museum Prize medal, 1972; United Artists, Hollywood, CA, beaded outfit used, 1984

INGRAM, VERONICA MARIE ORR *Colville*

Suctwa Quinkum

A.K.A. Veronica Orr; Illiana

Born 12 Jan 1945 in Omak, WA; daughter of Caroline Nelson and Samuel A. Orr; sister of Caroline Louise Orr (q.v.); married to Jerry Ingram (q.v.)

RESIDENCE: Ilfeld, NM

EDUCATION: IAIA, 1963; post graduate work

OCCUPATION: Secretary, tourist guide, teacher, jeweler, textile designer, craftswoman, and painter

PUBLISHED: Snodgrass (1968); biographical publications

EXHIBITS: ACS/ENP; AIAFM; CCHM; HM/G; IAIA; NACLA; RE; SWAIA; TAAII; WWM; Dallas (TX) Indian Market; IAIA Gallery, Santa Fe, NM; Okmulgee (OK) Art Show; Okmulgee (OK) Powwow; Okmulgee (OK) Library; Pecos (NM) Arts and Crafts Show; Santo Domingo Pueblo (NM) Arts and Crafts Show, 1992

AWARDS: ACS/EMP ('91); HM/G ('73, 1st); SWAIA

IN THE MIDDLE OF MANY TRACKS (see Anko)

INN, M. RIDING (see Riding Inn, M.)

INNUKJUAKJU *Inuit (Eskimo)*

A.K.A. Innukjuakjuk; Inukjurakju; Innukjuakju Pudlat

Born 1913 on South Baffin Island, NWT, Canada; died 1972; wife of Pudlo Pudlat (q.v.)

RESIDENCE: Lived in Cape Dorset, NWT, Canada

OCCUPATION: Graphic artist

MEDIA: Black pencil

PUBLISHED: Houston (1967); Goetz, et al. (1977); Jackson and Nasby (1987)

PUBLIC COLLECTIONS: C/AC/MS

EXHIBITS: C/CID, C/TIP

INNUKJUAKJUK (see Innukjuakju)

INNUKJUAKJU

Innukjuakju was one of the main contributors to the early Cape Dorset prints. When a resemblance to her husband's work was noticed, he explained that although they often looked at each other's work they rarely worked together and very seldom made suggestions to each other.

Jackson and Nasby 1987

INSHTATHEUMBA (see Tibbles, Susette La Flesche)

INUKJURAKJU (see Innukjuakju)

IROMAGAJA (see Rain In The Face)

IRON CLOUD, DELBERT *Hunkpapa Sioux*

A.K.A. Del Iron Cloud

Born 17 July 1949 in Wakpala, SD, on the Standing Rock Indian Reservation; son of Saraphine Many Horses and Thomas Iron Cloud; P/GF: Jasper Iron Cloud

RESIDENCE: Security, CO

MILITARY: U.S. Air Force

EDUCATION: Wakpala (SD) High School, 1968; A.A., IAIA, 1969-1970; AAA

OCCUPATION: U.S. Air Force illustrator, commercial artist, and painter

MEDIA: Oil, acrylic, watercolor, pencil, pen and ink, pastel, mixed-media, and prints

COMMISSIONS: *Murals:* Denver International Airport, International Arrivals Terminal, 1993

PUBLIC COLLECTIONS: HCC

EXHIBITS: CPS; DAM; LSS; RC; RE; TIAF; TM/NE'WTF; throughout Europe

AWARDS: RC ('80, 1st; '90, Diederich Award; '92, 1st)

IRON TAIL *Oglala Sioux*

Sinte Maza, Iron Tail

A.K.A. Plenty Scalps

Born ca. 1850; died 29 May 1916 near Fort Wayne, IN, of pneumonia

RESIDENCE: Once lived in Pine Ridge, SD

PUBLISHED: Snodgrass (1968); Dockstader (1977)

PUBLIC COLLECTIONS: MAI

HONORS: Succeeded Sitting Bull as chief

IRON TAIL

An outstanding warrior in the early days of fighting against both Indian and White enemies, Iron Tail was a respected leader by the time Buffalo Bill Cody came onto the prairies. They became friends and, in 1889, he went to Europe with the Wild West Show where he was lionized by French and English society. Iron Tail was one of three models used by James Earle Fraser in 1916, when he designed the "Indian head nickel."

Dockstader 1977

Iron Tail participated in the Battle of the Little Big Horn, during which time he was known as Plenty Scalps.

IRQUMIA, JUANISIALU (see Juanisialuk)

ISA (see Esa, Marjorie)

ISAAC, EUGENE *Kwakwaka'wakw (Kwakiutl)*

RESIDENCE: Canada

OCCUPATION: Printmaker

PUBLIC COLLECTIONS: HCC

EXHIBITS: AUG, HCC, NSU/SD, SDSMT

ISAAC, JACK *Navajo*

Born 16 Nov 1943; son of Mable and Joe Isaac

RESIDENCE: Tuba City, AZ

EDUCATION: Riverside, 1962; OSU/O, 1962

OCCUPATION: Artist

MEDIA: Acrylic, watercolor, pencil, pen and ink, mixed-media, and prints

PUBLISHED: *Arizona Highways* (Dec 1975)

PUBLIC COLLECTIONS: *Arizona Highways* Gallery of Western Art

EXHIBITS: FNAA, ITIC, NWASA

ISHII, SAKAHAFTEWA *Hopi*

EDUCATION: IAIA

PUBLIC COLLECTIONS: IAIA

EXHIBITS: AC/SD, IAIA

ISHULUTAQ, ELEESEEPEE (see Ishulutaq, Elisapee)

ISHULUTAQ, ELISAPEE *Inuit (Eskimo)*

A.K.A. Eleeseepee Ishulutaq
Born 1925 in Kanirterjuak, NWT, Canada; GF: Netsiapik
RESIDENCE: Igaluit, NWT, Canada
OCCUPATION: Graphic artist
MEDIA: Black felt tip pen, pencil and prints
PUBLISHED: Blodgett (n.d.); Collinson (1978); McMasters, et al. (1993)
PUBLIC COLLECTIONS: C/U of AB
EXHIBITS: C/CG, C/ISS, C/TIP

ISHULUTAQ, ELIZABETH *Inuit (Eskimo)*

Born 1950
RESIDENCE: Pangnirtung, NWT, Canada
OCCUPATION: Graphic artist
MEDIA: Pencil and prints
PUBLISHED: Blodgett (n.d.)
EXHIBITS: C/AG/WP

ITCHEZ HA BIYE (see Hawk, Jonny)

ITKAMINYAUKE *Sioux*

PUBLISHED: Snodgrass (1968)
PUBLIC COLLECTIONS: MPM (pictographic style on paper)

ITOOLOOKUTNA (see Ittulukatnak, Martha)

ITTUAK'NAAQ (see Ittulukatnak, Martha)

ITTULUKA'NAAQ (see Ittulukatnak, Martha)

ITTULUKATNAK, MARTHA *Inuit (Eskimo)*

A.K.A. Etoolookutna; Itoolookutna; Ittuluka'naaq; Ittuaka'naaq
Born 1912 at Kazan River, NWT, Canada; died 1981
RESIDENCE: Lived at Baker Lake, NWT, Canada
OCCUPATION: Graphic artist
MEDIA: Pencil and prints
PUBLISHED: Goetz, et al. (1977); Woodhouse, ed. (1980); Latocki, ed. (1983); Jackson and Nasby (1987)
PUBLIC COLLECTIONS: C/AC/MS
EXHIBITS: C/AG/WP, C/BLPD, C/CID, C/TIP

IVALUARDJUK (see Evaluardjuk, Henry)

IYO DJDI (see RedHawk, Jim)

IYOLA *Inuit (Eskimo)*

A.K.A. Iyola Kingwatsiak
Born 1933
RESIDENCE: Cape Dorset, NWT, Canada
OCCUPATION: Hunter, graphic artist, and printer
PUBLISHED: Houston (1967; 1976); Larmour (1967); Goetz, et al. (1977). *The Beaver* (spring 1975)
PUBLIC COLLECTIONS: C/NGCA; C/TDB; Museum of Modern Art, New York, NY
EXHIBITS: C/CD, C/EACTDB, C/TIP

ELISAPEE ISHULUTAQ

Ishulutaq started drawing and carving in 1970 when her family moved to Pangnirtung. Her drawings have concentrated on the human figure and the way of life at Pangnirtung, on Baffin Island. She said, "I like to draw Inuit from the old days, pictures of people doing things, not just people but people in action; adults, children. . . . I also draw the things I have seen and lived, what I have experienced in my life."

McMasters, et al. 1993

MARTHA ITTULUKATNAK

Ittulukatnak was nearly sixty when she began to draw, and her career lasted for seven years. She was known for her simple outline images and isolated, repetitive images of human figures and Arctic animals.

Jackson and Nasby 1987

IYOLA

Iyola is both an artist and a printmaker. Among his people he is known for his great physical strength as well as for being steady and patient and always in good humor. He has been one of the mainstays of the Cape Dorset print shop from its inception, and one of the first to do copper-line engraving.

Houston 1967

Jack, August *Squamish*
EXHIBITS: C/RBCM

Jackson, Anita Sue (see Caldwell Jackson, Anita Sue)

Jackson, Edna Davis *Tlingit*
Born 1950 in Petersburg, AK
RESIDENCE: Kake, AK
EDUCATION: B.F.A., U of AK, 1970; OSU/OR, 1980; M.F.A., U of WA, 1983
OCCUPATION: Teacher and artist
MEDIA: Mixed-media
PUBLISHED: Cochran, et al. (1985); Banks (1986); Longfish, et al. (1986). *The Indian Trader* (Aug 1989); *Journal of Alaska Native Arts* (Mar/Apr 1985); *Art Week* (28 Nov 1987); *American Indian Art* (winter, 1987)
PUBLIC COLLECTIONS: ASM/AK; HM; Anchorage (AK) Performing Arts Center; Seattle (WA) Arts Commission-Portable Works Collection
EXHIBITS: AICA/SF; AICH; HM; MFA/AH; NDN; OSU/OR; PAM; SCG; SDMM; SM; U of WA; WSCS; WWM; Museum of History and Industry, Seattle, WA; Mission Cultural Center Gallery, San Francisco, CA
SOLO EXHIBITS: IACH; SCG; Maude Kerns Art Center, Eugene, OR, 1988; Ollantay Center for the Arts, New York, 1988
HONORS: *Scholarships and Fellowships:* U of WA, State Room Scholarship, 1968-1970; Sealaska Heritage Foundation Graduate Fellowship, 1981-1983; Institute of Alaska Native Arts, Anchorage, AK, Chevron Fellowship, 1985. Other: Alaska State Council on the Arts, Anchorage, AK, Native Apprenticeship Grant, 1985

Edna Davis Jackson

Jackson has said of her work, "I am more comfortable using a needle and thread than I am with a paintbrush or drawing pencil. My mother was my first teacher; although when she was teaching me various skills, I'm sure she never considered them 'art lessons' and I never considered the work I was doing 'art.' Those early lessons in sewing, darning, and recycling yarn and fabric are very evident in my art work today."

Younger, et al. 1985

Jackson, Nathan *Tlingit*
Born 1938 near Haines, AK
RESIDENCE: Ketchikan, AK
EDUCATION: IAIA, 1962-1964
OCCUPATION: Art instructor; independent artist since 1967
PUBLISHED: Snodgrass (1968); Gerber and Bruggmann (1989)
PUBLIC COLLECTIONS: SM
EXHIBITS: SAIEAIP, SI, SN, World's Fair, New York, NY, 1964
AWARDS: SN ('67)

Jackson, Robert *Tsimshian*
Born 1948 at Port Edward, BC, Canada
RESIDENCE: Prince Rupert, BC, Canada
EDUCATION: C/KSNCIA, 1973
OCCUPATION: Store owner, carver, jeweler, and graphic artist
PUBLISHED: Steltzer (1976); Macnair, Hoover, and Neary, eds. (1980)
PUBLIC COLLECTIONS: C/CMC, C/INAC
EXHIBITS: C/CIIA, C/RBCM, C/ROM, C/TL

Jackson, Ronald Toahani *Navajo*
Toahani, Near Water
A.K.A. Ron Jackson
Born 1 Apr 1958 at Fort Defiance, AZ; son of Eloise and Jack Jackson; P/GF: Phillip Jackson; M/GP: Flora and John Watchman
RESIDENCE: Tempe, AZ
EDUCATION: Window Rock (AZ) High School, 1976; Albuquerque (NM) Technical Vocational Institute, drafting, 1980; A.A., Mesa (AZ) Community

DETAIL: Ruth Blalock Jones, *Shawnees Playing Dice,* 1978. Philbrook Museum of Art, Tulsa, Oklahoma

College, 1982; B.F.A., ASU, 1987

OCCUPATION: Sculptor and painter

MEDIA: Acrylic, watercolor, pencil, pastel, clay, and prints

PUBLIC COLLECTIONS: HM

EXHIBITS: ACAI, ACS/PG, AICA/SF, CMIC, HM/G, ITIC, MNA, NTF, RE, SJBIM, SNAICF, SWAIA, TWF

AWARDS: ACAI ('93); CMIC ('88, 1st, Best Craftsman); ITIC ('86; '87, 1st, Best in Category; '89; '91; '94, 3-1st); MNA ('87; '88); NTF ('87, 1st; '88, 1st; '89; '90, 1st); RE ('94); SJBIM ('89, 1st); SNAICF ('87; '91); SWAIA ('94, 1st)

HONORS: ACS/PG, poster artist, 1991

JACOB, MURV *Cherokee*

Born 27 Jan 1945; son of Maxine and Murv Jacob; P/GP: Grace Smallwood and Max Jacob; M/GP: Dorothy Carter and Lawrence Brooks

RESIDENCE: Tahlequah, OK

EDUCATION: Studied under Cecil Dick (q.v.)

OCCUPATION: Ceramist and painter

MEDIA: Oil, acrylic, pen and ink, pencil, mixed-media, and clay

PUBLISHED: *The Muskogee Phoenix* (20 Apr 1990); *The Tulsa World* (31 Mar 1993); *Oklahoma Today* (Nov 1994/Jan 1995)

BOOKS ILLUSTRATED: Cover art and/or text illustration for more than 28 books, including: Weisman (1993)

COMMISSIONS: Territorial Book Fair, Tulsa, OK, poster, 1993

PUBLIC COLLECTIONS: HM, FCTM, TTSP

EXHIBITS: CHASC, CNM, FCTM, HM, LIAS, MCI, TIAF, TTSP

SOLO EXHIBITS: CNM, FCTM, MAAIC

AWARDS: CHASC ('93, 1st); CNM ('82; '87, 1st; '88, Grand Award; '90, 1st; '92; '93; '94, 1st); FCTM ('86; '87, IH; '89, IH; '90, 1st; '91, IH; '92; '93; '94, Best of Show); MCI

HONORS: FCTM, Art Under the Oaks, featured artist

MURV JACOB

Jacob's paintings depict Southeast and Cherokee Indian legends and culture, and often give anthropomorphic characteristics to animals.

JACOBS, ALEX A. *Mohawk*

Born 2 Feb 1953 in Hogansburg, NY

RESIDENCE: Roosevelt, NY

EDUCATION: A.F.A., IAIA; B.F.A., KCAI/MO

OCCUPATION: Editor of *Akwesasne News*, poet, and painter

MEDIA: Felt tip markers

PUBLISHED: Ward, ed. (1990); Hill (1992)

COMMISSIONS: *Murals:* IAIA, mural design, 1976-1977

EXHIBITS: AIAI, AKM, IAIA, OLO, RCAS

JACOBS, ARNOLD *Iroquois*

Nah-Gwa-Say

Born 13 Sept 1942 on the Six Nations Reserve, ON, Canada

RESIDENCE: Ohsweken, ON, Canada

EDUCATION: Central Technical School, Toronto, ON, 1942; special art courses

OCCUPATION: Graphic designer and artist

MEDIA: Oil, acrylic, and prints

PUBLISHED: Johannsen and Ferguson, eds. (1983), cover; Ballantine and Ballantine (1993)

BOOKS ILLUSTRATED: Johannsen and Ferguson, eds. (1983), cover

PUBLIC COLLECTIONS: C/INAC; C/CIIA; C/CMC; C/WICEC; SMII; ISAI;

MNA/CL; NACLA; City Hall of Brantford, ON; Iroquois Studies Association, Ithaca, NY; Yager Museum, Oneonta, NY

EXHIBITS: AM; C/AG/TB; C/NCCT; C/WICEC; CNM; NACLA; NU/BC; TRP; Education Center of the Toronto (ON) Board of Education

AWARDS: CNM ('88, 1st)

HONORS: AANNAAC, painting used to promote *Iroquois Arts,* 1980; NACLA, Executive Board

JACOBS, ELWOOD *Cherokee*

RESIDENCE: Sanborn, NY

EXHIBITS: LIAS

JACOBS, FRANCIS E., JR. *Oglala Sioux*

EXHIBITS: RC

AWARDS: RC ('78)

JAKE, ALBIN ROY *Pawnee*

Ahsey Sututut, War Horse

Born 22 June 1922 in Skedee, Pawnee County, OK; died July 1960; brother of John Jake

MILITARY: U.S. Marine Corps, WWII

EDUCATION: BC; graduated Haskell; B.A.E., NSU, 1951; M.F.A., U of OK; studied under Dick West (q.v.) while at BC

OCCUPATION: Teacher, artist-illustrator; full-time artist after 1957

MEDIA: Oil and watercolor

PUBLISHED: LaFarge (1956; 1960); Pierson and Davidson (1960); Dunn (1968); Snodgrass (1968); Brody (1971); Mahey, et al. (1980); Broder (1981). *World Book Encyclopedia* (1960)

COMMISSIONS: *Murals:* NSU; Tinker Air Force Base, conference room [with Bunny Randall (q.v.) and LeRoy McAllister]

PUBLIC COLLECTIONS: HSM/OK, PAC

EXHIBITS: DAM, HSM/OK, JGS, MNM, PAC, PAC/T

SOLO EXHIBITS: PAC

ALBIN ROY JAKE

"In 1957, the artist wrote Philbrook Art Center; 'My modernistic oil paintings are innovations of age-old designs and patterns. The broken color designs bordering some of my paintings are to me representative of the geometric designs, patterns and hide paintings of the Indians of the Great Plains area, a glimpse into and out of something that is by-gone.'"

Snodgrass 1968

JAMASIE *Inuit (Eskimo)*

A.K.A. Jamasie Teevee

Born 1910 near Lake Harbour, NWT, Canada; died 1985

RESIDENCE: Lived at Cape Dorset, NWT, Canada

OCCUPATION: Hunter, fisherman, carver, and graphic artist

MEDIA: Colored felt tip pen, colored pencil, graphite pencil, and prints

PUBLISHED: Larmour (1967); Goetz, et al. (1977); Blodgett (1978a); Collinson (1978); Routledge (1979); Jackson and Nasby (1987). *The Beaver* (spring 1975)

PUBLIC COLLECTIONS: C/TDB, C/U of AB, C/WBEC, DAM

EXHIBITS: C/AG/IGEA, C/AG/WP, C/CID, C/CG, C/EACTDB, C/IA7, C/TIP

JAMASIE

Jamasie was a quiet and patient man who started drawing in the 1960s with the encouragement of James Houston. His drawings were often of a single type of Arctic animal done in a serial arrangement.

Jackson and Nasby 1987

JAMES, ALLEN *Kwakwaka'wakw (Kwakiutl)*

Birth date unknown; died ca 1981

RESIDENCE: Lived in Canada

OCCUPATION: Artist

MEDIA: Watercolor, pen and ink, pencil, and felt pen

PUBLIC COLLECTIONS: C/CRM, C/GM, C/RBCM, DAM

ALLEN JAMES

James painted in a semi-abstract style.

JAMES, DALTON *Hopi*

Born 27 May 1923 in Kykotsmovi, AZ

DALTON JAMES

The artist painted for a very brief period, probably while he was in school.

Seymour 1988

MILITARY: U.S. Army
EDUCATION: Hopi (AZ) High School; Santa Fe; Sherman
OCCUPATION: Carpenter, BIA facility manager, rancher, and painter
PUBLISHED: Seymour (1988)
PUBLIC COLLECTIONS: IACB/DC
EXHIBITS: MNA, WRTD

JAMES, PETER RAY *Navajo*

Born 26 Dec 1963 in NM
RESIDENCE: Prewitt, NM
EDUCATION: Thoreau (NM) High School, 1981; IAIA, 1982-1984; B.F.A., U of NM, 1989
OCCUPATION: Lecturer, ceramist, and painter
MEDIA: Oil, acrylic, pastel, sand, and clay
PUBLISHED: Way, ed. (1988); Jacka and Jacka (1994). *Mountain Living* (May 1986); *The Arizona Republic* (21 June 1986); *The Indian Trader* (July 1986); *The Gallup Independent* (17 May 1988); *The New Mexican* (17 Aug 1989); *Arizona Highway* (Nov 1992); biographical publications
COMMISSIONS: *Murals:* Baca Chapter House, Prewitt, NM. *Other:* Save The Children Organization, ceramics, 1988
PUBLIC COLLECTIONS: IAIA, MNA, U of NM; Genre Art Publishing, Burbank, CA
EXHIBITS: AC/SD, CNM, HM/G, IAIA, ITIC, MNA, NARF, NMSC, NMSF, OIO, RC, SWAIA, U of NM
SOLO EXHIBITS: MNA
AWARDS: ITIC ('86, 1st); MNA ('87, 1st; '88, 1st, Best of Division); NMSF; OIO; RC; Poster Award, Phoenix, AZ, 1987
HONORS: *Scholarships:* RC, Thunderbird Foundation Scholarship, 1984; Monserrat Honor Scholarship, 1984; Helmer G. Olson Memorial Scholarship, 1987-1988. *Other:* IAIA, Outstanding Student, 1984; National Dean's List, 1984; FNAA, poster artist, 1986; Outstanding Young Men of America Award, 1987; U of NM, Dean's List, 1987

PETER RAY JAMES

A painter for ten years, James is best known for his paintings of village scenes and Navajo ceremonial figures. In addition, since 1988, he has been creating ceramic masks of the Navajo yé ii bicheii.

Arizona Highways, *Nov 1992*

JAMES, SAMMY *Navajo*

PUBLISHED: Snodgrass (1968)
PUBLIC COLLECTIONS: MAI

JAMES, TOMMY *Navajo*

PUBLIC COLLECTIONS: MNA

JANVIER, ALEX *Ojibwa*

A.K.A. Alexandre Simeon Janvier
Born 1935 in Legoff, AB, Canada, on the Cold Lake Reserve
RESIDENCE: Cold Lake Reserve, AB, Canada
EDUCATION: St. Thomas College High School, North Battleford, SK; graduated C/ACA, 1960
OCCUPATION: Teacher, rancher, Canadian government cultural advisor, and painter
MEDIA: Oil, acrylic, watercolor, ink, pastel, and pencil
PUBLISHED: Dickason (1972); Fry (1972); Best (1978); McMasters, et al. (1993). *Arts Canada* (Feb/Mar 1972; Feb/Mar 1975); *Native People* (2 Nov 1973); *Artwest* (Mar/Apr 1976), cover; *The Native Perspective* (Vol. 2, no. 9, 1977); *Heritage* (Sept/Oct 1977); *Indian News* (Sept 1980); *The Calgary Herald* (11 Dec 1980); *Masterkey* (winter 1984); *Windspeaker* (12 Dec 1986)

ALEX JANVIER

Although his early work was more realistic, Janvier is best known for his semi-abstract, swirling designs. His designs are an effective means of expressing his belief in the power of nature and its relationship to his people.

COMMISSIONS: *Murals:* Expo '67, Indian Pavilion, Montréal, PQ; Ermineskin Kindergarten, Hobbema, AB; Sherwood Medical Clinic Building, Sherwood Park, AB; Sawridge Motor Hotel, Slave Lake, AB; Explorer Hotel, Yellowknife, NWT; Onion Lake (SK) Elementary School; County of Strathcona Building, Sherwood Park, AB; Muttart Conservatory, Edmonton, AB

PUBLIC COLLECTIONS: C/AAF; C/ACC; C/AG/TB; C/AG/WP; C/AIAC; C/CCAB; C/CMC; C/ESSOC; C/GM; C/INAC; C/MCC; C/MFA/M; C/SCC; C/TDB; C/U of L; British Petroleum Collection; BANAC Husky Oil; Interprovincial Pipe Line; Canadian Utilities; Petro Canada Collection; Edmonton (AB) Public School Board

EXHIBITS: C/ACCCNA; C/AG/TB; C/AG/WP; C/CIARH; C/CMC; C/GM; C/LTAT; C/NAC; C/OWAO; C/ROM; C/TC; C/TGVA; C/TU; C/WICEC; HM; SDMM; All-Alberta Show, Edmonton, AB, spring 1964; Holland Festival, Amsterdam, Holland, 1985; Native Business Summit, Toronto, ON; Canadian Consulate, Los Angeles, CA, 1987; galleries in Alberta and Ontario

SOLO EXHIBITS: Partial listing of more than 19 includes: C/CMC; C/INAC; C/ROM; Gallery Stenhus, Linköping, Sweden; galleries in Alberta and Ontario

HONORS: International Vatican Exhibition, Rome, Italy, Canadian representative

JAQUA, JOE *Mission*

Born 1938 in Pasadena, CA

RESIDENCE: Forest Knolls, CA

MILITARY: U.S. Marine Corps

EDUCATION: San Gabriel (CA) Mission High School; Pasadena (CA) City College; SFSC

PUBLISHED: *Arizona Arts and Lifestyle* (autumn 1981); *The Scottsdale Daily Progress* (27 Nov 1981)

PUBLIC COLLECTIONS: HCC

EXHIBITS: CNM; HCC; HM; HM/G; NWASA; RC; SN; Minneapolis (MN) Museum; Springfield (UT) Fine Art Show

AWARDS: HM/G ('72; '73, 1st; '75, 1st; '80, 1st); NWASA (1st); RC ('78); SN ('75, Special Award)

JARAMILLO, EDWARD GILBERT *Isleta*

EDUCATION: Santa Fe, ca. 1959

PUBLISHED: Snodgrass (1968)

EXHIBITS: MNM

JARAMILLIO, JOSEPH LOUIS *Isleta*

A.K.A. Joe Jaramillio

EDUCATION: St. Catherine's

MEDIA: Tempera and colored pencil

PUBLISHED: Snodgrass (1968); Tanner (1973)

PUBLIC COLLECTIONS: MNM

EXHIBITS: ASM

JAW *Hunkpapa/Sans Arcs Sioux*

Cehu'pa; *Oki'cize Tawa*, His Battle

Born 1850; death date unknown; son of a Hunkpapa mother and Sans Arcs father

PUBLISHED: Snodgrass (1968). *Bulletin 61,* BAE (1918); *Bulletin 173,* BAE (1960), pictographic style

JAW

"The artist was named Cehu'pa by his White brother-in-law; his childhood name was Mázaho Waste (Loud Sounding Metal), and at the age of 17 he was given the name of Oki'cize Tawa."

Snodgrass 1968

JAY, TOM *Hopi*

EDUCATION: Santa Fe, ca. 1938

PUBLISHED: Snodgrass (1968)
EXHIBITS: AIW

JEFFERSON, BENNIE *Sauk and Fox*
Born 1913
EDUCATION: Chilocco
PUBLISHED: Snodgrass (1968)
EXHIBITS: AIEC

JEFFERSON, MARLIN *Maricopa*
Birth date unknown; born on the Pima Reservation, AZ
RESIDENCE: Santa Fe, NM
EDUCATION: Casa Grande (AZ) High School; IAIA High School, 1978
PUBLISHED: *The Indian Trader* (July 1978)

JEMISON, DICK *Seneca*
A.K.A. Richard Jemison
Born 22 Sept 1942
EDUCATION: B.A., U of NC, 1967; Student's Art League, Woodstock, NY, 1969; M.F.A., U of GA, 1972
OCCUPATION: Artist
PUBLISHED: *Artspace* (summer 1983); *Art in America* (July 1984); *The Santa Fean* (June/July 1984)
PUBLIC COLLECTIONS: BMA; U of AL; Anderson Brothers Mfg. Co., Rockford, IL; AT&T, Denver, CO; American Television Communications, Denver, CO; Blount, Inc., Montgomery, AL; Denver (CO) National Bank; Exeter Drilling Northern, Inc.; Vulcan Materials, Birmingham, AL
EXHIBITS: AA; SWAIA; Ackland Museum Show, Chapel Hill, NC, 1967; Mint Museum, Charlotte, NC, 1979; St. John's College, Santa Fe, NM, 1981; Woodstock (NY) Group Show, 1969; see also Awards
SOLO EXHIBITS: BMA; Samford University, Birmingham, AL, 1978; U of AL, 1976
AWARDS: AA; Greater Birmingham (AL) Arts Alliance Show, 1977

JEMISON, G. PETER *Seneca*
A.K.A. Gerald Ansley Jemison
Born 18 Jan 1945 in Silver Creek, NY; son of Margaret and Ansley Jemison; P/GP: Carrie and Woodrow Jemison; M/GP: Minnie and William Wilson
RESIDENCE: Victor, NY
EDUCATION: Silver Creek (NY) Central High School, 1962; University of Siena, Siena, Italy, 1964; B.S., SUNY/B, NY, 1967
OCCUPATION: Display artist, exhibit curator, educator, gallery director, historic site manager, and painter
MEDIA: Oil, acrylic, pencil, egg tempera, and prints
PUBLISHED: Highwater (1980); Katz (1980); Amerson, ed. (1981); Anonymous (1982); Wade, ed. (1986); Hill (1988); Ward, ed. (1990); Archuleta and Strickland (1991); Roberts, ed. (1992); Abbott (1994). *The Conservationist* (Jan/Feb 1976); *Art In America* (summer 1972); *Native Art West* (July 1980); *Soho News* (20 Aug 1980); *Village Voice* (22 Oct 1980); *Indian Truth* (Feb 1983); *The New York Times* (Nov 30, 1984); *New York Magazine* (20 June 1983; 11 June 1990); *The New Mexican* (26 Aug 1983); *The Buffalo Evening News* (16 Oct 1983); *The New York Daily News* (Nov 1983); *The Village Voice* (27 Dec 1983); *The Sacramento Bee* (19 Feb 1984); *Long Island Newsday* (July 18, 1984; Apr 30, 1986); *The Los Angeles Times* (1985); *The Santa Fe Reporter* (Aug 21, 1985); *The Scottsdale Daily Progress* (18 Oct 1985); *The Arizona Republic* (2 Nov 1985); *American Indian Art* (spring

G. PETER JEMISON

"Over the last fifteen years, my work has been concerned with the natural world — animals, birds, fish and trees and the need for them to have a place to live, protected from the destruction of man. If we lose our influence from the animal's (sic) world, we lose a vital part of ourselves."

program, Olean (NY) Public Library Exhibition, 1991

In the early 1980s, Jemison's paintings were done on paper bags (he called them "Indian bags") that he constructed of handmade rag paper. He followed that series with paintings done on handmade paper, using such diverse media as acrylic, animal fur, egg tempera, and oil. Demonstrating his concern for the natural world, the subject of these abstract paintings are most often plants and animals done in bright, vivid colors.

1986); *CEPA Quarterly* (fall 1986); *Native Vision* (Vol. 4, no. 3, 1987); *The Ithaca Times* (4-10 June 1987); *Guardian* (16 Dec 1987); *Artscribe International* (1988); *Northeast Indian Quarterly* (winter 1989); *Crosswinds* (Aug 1991)

BOOKS ILLUSTRATED: Grinde (1976); Kenny (1982; 1983), covers

PUBLIC COLLECTIONS: HM, IACB, SMII, MPI

EXHIBITS: AC/Y; AICA; AICH; AM; BM/B; BRMA; C/WICEC; CNGM; CSU/OK; CTC; CWAM; HM; MAI; MNM; MM/NJ; NACLA; NU/BC; OLO; OSU/G; PAC; PDN; RCAS; RFBAG; QM; SCG; SFFA; SM; SV; TFAG; TRP; WAATAP; Annotecca Siena, Italy; University of Buffalo, Buffalo, NY; St. Bonaventure (NY) University, 1975; The Federal Reserve Bank, Arts Gallery, Kansas City, MO, 1987; galleries in MO, NM, NY, PA, and Washington, D.C.

SOLO EXHIBITS: MPI; SCG; Olean (NY) Public Library, 1991

HONORS: IAIA, President of the Council of Regents

JEMISON, GERALD ANSLEY (see Jemison, G. Peter)

JEMISON, RICHARD (see Jemison, Dick)

JENKINS, CALVIN *Hopi*

PUBLIC COLLECTIONS: MNA

JENKINS, CONNIE *Cherokee*

Born 20 Sept 55 in Tahlequah, OK; daughter of Emma Sanders and Winfred Watkins; P/GP: Minnie and Nelson Watkins; M/GP: Mary and Joe Sanders

RESIDENCE: Pawnee Grove, OK

EDUCATION: Locust Grove (OK) High School, 1973

OCCUPATION: Mother, sculptor, and painter

MEDIA: Acrylic, gouache, pencil, pen and ink, clay, wood, and prints

EXHIBITS: CNM; FCTM; IAF; K; LIAS/M; LC; RE; TIAF; TWF; Anderson County Museum, SC; Willard Stone Show, Locust Grove, OK

AWARDS: CNM ('93); FCTM ('87; '89; '92); K; LC; RC ('92); RE ('92); TIAF

HONORS: TIAF, logo design, 1988

CONNIE JENKINS

Jenkins was raised in Locust Grove in the heart of Oklahoma Cherokee country. Her paintings are done in both contemporary and traditional (flat) styles. When asked why she is an artist, she replied, "I've been blessed with a talent that I do not understand; it's simple and comfortable, doing each piece and having an understanding of what to do next, this is not of me, but of a Higher Power . . . this gift to create, for this I am thankful."

p.c. 1993

JENKINS, NATHAN *Hopi*

PUBLISHED: Snodgrass (1968)

EXHIBITS: HM (while a student, ca. 1951)

JIM, BEN *Navajo*

RESIDENCE: Farmington, NM

EDUCATION: IAIA, and courses at several junior colleges

OCCUPATION: Sculptor and painter

MEDIA: Oil, watercolor, steel, and prints

EXHIBITS: ACS/MV, ITIC, MNA, NNTF, RE; see also Awards

AWARDS: ACS/MV ('88, Artist Achievement Award); ITIC ('89, 1st); MNA (HM); NNTF ('88 & '89, Navajo Tribal Chairman's Choice Award); San Juan County Fair, Farmington, NM ('89, Best of Show)

JIM, FRANK *Navajo*

Born 17 Sept 19?8 in Keams Canyon, AZ

PUBLISHED: Snodgrass (1968)

EXHIBITS: Flagstaff, AZ

JIM, WILSON *Navajo*

Born 1952, near Jeddito Trading Post, AZ

EDUCATION: Santa Fe; 7th grade, Albuquerque, ca. 1964

OCCUPATION: Silversmith and painter; best known as a jeweler

EXHIBITS: NMSF
AWARDS: NMSF ('64)

JOACHIM, KATY (see Joachim, Lola Kathryn)

JOACHIM, LOLA KATHRYN *Cherokee*

Gedi, Katy; *Gad-Hi-Ya,* Can Be In Two Places At Once
A.K.A. Katy Joachim
Born 7 Sept 1938 in Ardmore, OK; daughter of Grossie Rena and E. C. Joachim; P/GP: Lola Pearl Newsum and Peter Herman Joachim; M/GP: Mary Etta Tully and Tom Dorsett
RESIDENCE: Gore, OK
EDUCATION: Walters (OK) High School, 1956; B.S., OSU, 1960; M.S. U of OK, 1981
OCCUPATION: Interior designer, jewelry designer, and painter
MEDIA: Oil, watercolor, pencil, and pen and ink
PUBLIC COLLECTIONS: Grace United Methodist Church, Oklahoma City, OK; Matthews Architectural Firm, Oklahoma City, OK
EXHIBITS: Galleries in Oklahoma

LOLA KATHRYN JOACHIM

Due to serious health problems, Joachim has not painted since 1988, but she hopes to be able to do some work in the future.

artist, p.c. 1992

JOANASSIE *Inuit (Eskimo)*

A.K.A. *Oomayoualook*
Born 8 Apr 1934
RESIDENCE: Cape Dorset, NWT, Canada
OCCUPATION: Graphic artist
PUBLISHED: *Artscanada* (Vol. 28, no. 6, 1971-1972)
EXHIBITS: C/AG/O

JOANISIALU (see Juanisialuk)

JOBIE BEAR (see Byrnes, James Michael)

JOE, EUGENE *Navajo*

Baatsoslani, Many Feathers
A.K.A. Signature: Baatsoslani
Born 1950 in Shiprock, NM
RESIDENCE: Shiprock, NM
OCCUPATION: Sandpainter and painter
MEDIA: Watercolor and colored sand
PUBLISHED: Samuels (1982). *Artists of the Rockies* (winter 1975)
EXHIBITS: DAM; ITIC; NMSF; TAAII; Phoenix (AZ) Indian Arts and Crafts Show; San Antonio (TX) Arts and Crafts Show, 1974; galleries in CA, CO, TX, UT, and WY
AWARDS: ITIC ('78, 1st; '94, 1st); NMSF ('74, Best of Show)

JOE, FRANK LEE *Navajo*

MEDIA: Tempera
PUBLISHED: Tanner (1973)
EXHIBITS: Arizona State Fair; throughout the Southwest

JOE, JAMES B. *Navajo*

Born 15 June 1953 in Shiprock, NM; son of Emma Joe Light and Dan Jim; M/GP: Belle Joe and Big Joe
RESIDENCE: Shiprock, NM
EDUCATION: Shiprock (NM) High School, 1974; U of NM
OCCUPATION: Artist

JAMES B. JOE

Joe has said, "A Navajo artist is inspired by his reservation roots, his study of great art, and a cross-cultural mission." His most recent works, which are dramatic and abstract, show the influence of such painters as Fritz Scholder (q.v.) and Robert Rauschenberg. His earlier works were more realistic and used fine detailing and rigid construction. Joe's best known subjects are the female form and large faces.

artist, p.c. 1992

MEDIA: Oil, acrylic, pencil, pen and ink, pastel, sand, mixed-media, and prints
PUBLISHED: *Art-Talk* (Mar 1984); *The New York Times* (18 Mar 1990)
COMMISSIONS: *Murals:* Roseborough Gallery, Farmington, NM; Pedal Sports, Farmington, NM
PUBLIC COLLECTIONS: MAI; NTM; Mountain Bell Corporate Collection; Pepsi Cola Corporate Collection; San Juan College Foundation, Farmington, NM
EXHIBITS: HM; ITIC; LIAS; NTM; PAC; SFSUFC; U of KS; Farmington (NM) Civic Center; galleries in Farmington and Taos, NM, and New York, NY
AWARDS: ITIC ('86, 1st)

ORELAND C. JOE SR.

Joe was encouraged to use his artistic talent while in high school. His English teacher, Mary L. Peterson, an artist herself, was especially encouraging. After graduation he worked as an illustrator for the school district. In 1981, Ms. Peterson gave him some small alabaster pieces and he discovered that he had a talent for stone carving. From this point he concentrated on sculpture; however, he has expressed a desire to do more painting. Whatever media he uses, Joe's work expresses his Indian heritage. He has described his style as, "... somewhere between realism and abstraction held in unity by an underlying mystical philosophy."

Southwest Art, *Jan 1988*

JOE, ORELAND C., SR. *Navajo/Ute*

Whirlwind Eagle
Born 1958
RESIDENCE: Kirkland, NM
OCCUPATION: Illustrator, hoop dancer, sculptor, and painter
PUBLISHED: *Southwest Art* (Jan 1988)
COMMISSIONS: *Murals:* Kirkland (NM) High School
EXHIBITS: AICA; ABQM; CFD; HM/M; ITIC; SWAIA; Great American West Show, Tucson, AZ
AWARDS: ACIA ('92, Silver Medal); HM/M (1st); ITIC ('86, Best in Class, Best in Category); SWAIA
HONORS: NCHF, National Academy of Western Art, guest artist, 1992; Cowboy Artists of America, member, 1993

JOE, RAY *Navajo/Zia*

Born 23 Nov 1945 at Fort Wingate, NM; son of Mary Houston and Tom Joe; P/GF: Black Joe (Man With Big Whiskers); M/GP: Doan and Bah James Houston
RESIDENCE: Lupton, AZ
EDUCATION: Gallup (NM) High School, 1964
PUBLISHED: Snodgrass (1968)
PUBLIC COLLECTIONS: Paramount Restaurant, Gallup, NM; Manuelito Hall, Gallup (NM) High School
EXHIBITS: ITIC, NACG, NMSF, PAC; see also Awards
AWARDS: NACG (student exhibit); Gallup (NM) Indian Community Center, six awards

RAY JOE

"Listed as an outstanding art student by Duane O. Berg, Gallup art instructor, he received his first award in the Gallup Lions' Club Rodeo Poster contest while in the 4th grade."

Snodgrass 1968

JOHN, ANGELO MARVIN *Navajo*

Born 5 Feb 1946 in Flagstaff, AZ; son of Charlie John
RESIDENCE: Flagstaff, AZ
MILITARY: U.S. Air Force (believed to be the first American Indian pilot)
EDUCATION: IAIA; ASU, 1970
MEDIA: Casein
PUBLISHED: Snodgrass (1968); Tanner (1973)
COMMISSIONS: *Murals:* Cedar Point Great Hall, Mackinac Island, MI
PUBLIC COLLECTIONS: BIA, HM, IAIA, WWM
EXHIBITS: AC/SD, ASF, HM, LGAM, MFA/O, PAC, RM, SN, YAIA
AWARDS: ASF ('65, 1st); SN
HONORS: Fifth Annual Navajo Youth Conference, delegate, Shiprock, NM, 1965; IAIA, Student Body President, 1965

JOHN, DAVID *Navajo*

A.K.A. David K. John
Born 29 Mar 1963

RESIDENCE: Gallup, NM
EDUCATION: Richfield (UT) High School; IAIA, 1986; BYU
OCCUPATION: Sculptor, ceramist, and painter
MEDIA: Oil, acrylic, watercolor, pencil, mixed-media, and clay
PUBLISHED: Jacka and Jacka (1994)
EXHIBITS: IAIA, ITIC, MNA, NTM, RC, SWAIA
AWARDS: ITIC ('93, 1st; '94, 2-1st); MNA ('88, 2-1st); RC ('88, Woodard Award)

JOHN, JOHNNY *Shawnee*
PUBLISHED: Snodgrass (1968); Fawcett and Callander (1982)
PUBLIC COLLECTIONS: MAI
EXHIBITS: HM, MAI

JOHNIEBO (see Johnniebo)

JOHNNIEBO *Inuit (Eskimo)*
A.K.A. Johniebo
Born 1923; died 1972; Husband of Kenojuak (q.v.)
RESIDENCE: Lived in Cape Dorset, NWT, Canada
OCCUPATION: Hunter, trapper, fisherman, whaler, construction worker, and graphic artist
MEDIA: Black pencil and prints
PUBLISHED: Goetz, et al. (1977). *North* (May/June 1970); *Canadian Forum* (Jan 1973); *The Beaver* (spring 1975)
PUBLIC COLLECTIONS: C/TDB, DAM
EXHIBITS: C/EACTDB, C/TIP, DAM

JOHNS, DAVID *Navajo*
Born 13 Nov 1948 in Winslow, AZ
RESIDENCE: Winslow, AZ
EDUCATION: Winslow (AZ) High School, 1968; B.A., U of N AZ, 1982
OCCUPATION: Artist
MEDIA: Oil, acrylic, pencil, pastel, and prints
PUBLISHED: Snodgrass (1968); Medina (1980); Jacka and Jacka (1991; 1994). *Art-talk* (Oct 1983; Aug/Sept 1985; Dec 1993); *Arizona Highways* (May 1986; June 1992); *Southwest Art* (Feb 1987; Mar 1991); *The Phoenix Gazette* (21 June 1988; 20 Aug 1988)
COMMISSIONS: *Murals:* Case Construction Company, Phoenix, AZ, 1989
PUBLIC COLLECTIONS: HCC, MAI
EXHIBITS: FSMCIAF; HCC; HPTU; ITIC; MCC/CA; MNA; NTF; RC; SCG; SDMM; SWAIA; U of N AZ; U of WV; WTF; WWM; Autumn Indian Days, Sedona, AZ; Finnish Film Institute, Helsinki, Finland; galleries in AZ, NM, and WA
AWARDS: ITIC ('85; '86; '88, 1st; '89, 1st; '91, 1st; '92, 1st); MNA (1984, Best of Show, '87, 2-1st); NTF ('88); RC ('72; '79; '82, 1st)
HONORS: Lovena Ohl Trust Fund Foundation, scholarship, 1980; NTF, poster artist, 1986; U of N AZ, Distinguished Alumnus Award, 1990

JOHNS, JOE L. *Seminole*
RESIDENCE: Okeechobee, FL
EDUCATION: IAIA, ca. 1965
PUBLISHED: Snodgrass (1968). *The New Mexican* (9 Aug 1981)
EXHIBITS: YAIA

DAVID JOHNS

Although Johns works in other media, pastel is his primary medium. His style is a blend of contemporary techniques, traditional subject matter, and abstract symbols. Well known for his sensitive portraits, Johns also produces dramatic abstracts using tribal design elements.

Johns most challenging commission to date was the mural, Under The Dome, which he completed on September 15, 1989, a year and a half after he commenced. The mural is located in a dome 50 feet above the floor in Case Construction Company's sixth floor conference room at Concord Place in Phoenix, AZ. The painting covers 1,600 square feet and was reached by climbing five flights of stairs to a wooden platform. It was his intention that the mural should honor all Native Americans, therefore, he included portraits of many historically important tribal leaders. Johns said, "If any person knows beauty, he knows love and will have spiritual thoughts about nature. It all comes together. I wanted to honor my people with this mural. I wanted everything combined to be so spiritual that when you walk into the room, you feel as though you are going into one of the big cathedrals."

Southwest Art, *Mar 1991*

JOHNSON, ALFRED *Cherokee*
Eya
EDUCATION: BC
PUBLISHED: Snodgrass (1968); Brody (1971)
PUBLIC COLLECTIONS: PAC
EXHIBITS: PAC, PAC/T
AWARDS: PAC

JOHNSON, BOBBY *Navajo*
Born 1959
RESIDENCE: Farmington, NM
EDUCATION: Navajo Methodist School, Farmington, NM
PUBLISHED: Schiffer (1991). *The Indian Trader* (Sept 1987)
EXHIBITS: ITIC; in Oklahoma and Arizona
AWARDS: ITIC ('85, 1st; '86, 2-1st; '87, 4-1st, Elkus Award; '88, 2-1st).

BOBBY JOHNSON

Although he began to draw as a small child, it wasn't until Johnson was 16 and attending the Navajo Methodist School that he began to take art work seriously. Johnson is best known for his paintings of pottery, although he also does portraits as well as scenes of people and animals in the desert.

The Indian Trader, *Sept 1987*

JOHNSON, EDWARD *Navajo*
EXHIBITS: CNM
AWARDS: CNM ('84, Newcomer Award)

JOHNSON, ERNEST *(?)*
RESIDENCE: Santa Fe, NM
EXHIBITS: TCIM, RC
SOLO EXHIBITS: TCIM ('92, 1st)

JOHNSON, GARRISON *White Mountain Apache*
Gahn
Born 1933
EDUCATION: Whiteriver (AZ) High School
OCCUPATION: Painter
MEDIA: Watercolor, pastel, and pen and ink
PUBLISHED: Tanner (1973)
EXHIBITS: HM/G

GARRISON JOHNSON

The artist taught himself to paint in the traditional Southwest style with Apache ceremonies and activities as his favorite subject matter. His paintings were first exhibited in the late 1960s.

Tanner 1973

JOHNSON, LISA *Chickasaw/Choctaw*
EXHIBITS: CNM

JOHNSON, RAYMOND *Navajo*
Ne-Chah-He
MEDIA: Watercolor
PUBLISHED: Tanner (1973); Highwater (1978b)
BOOKS ILLUSTRATED: Beck, Walters, and Francisco, eds. (1990)
PUBLIC COLLECTIONS: MNA, MRFM, NCC
EXHIBITS: SN

JOHNSON, ROY *Blackfeet*
Born 26 May 1944 in Browning, MT; son of Frank S. Johnson
MILITARY: U.S. Army
EDUCATION: Valier (MT) High School, 1963
OCCUPATION: Ranch laborer, rancher, and painter
MEDIA: Oil, watercolor, pen and ink, and pencil
PUBLISHED: Ray, ed. (1972)
EXHIBITS: CIA; MPI; throughout the area

JOHNSON, TRACY *Tuscarora*

Ahosta

Born 16 Aug 1940; son of Norma and Tracy Johnson

RESIDENCE: Lewiston, NY

OCCUPATION: Teacher, carver, beadworker, and painter

MEDIA: Acrylic, mixed-media, deerskin, leather, bone, horn, stone, quills, feathers, horsehair, fur, beads, and ironwood

PUBLISHED: Johannsen and Ferguson, eds. (1983)

PUBLIC COLLECTIONS: C/ROM, DAM, HM, MAI, SI

EXHIBITS: ACS/EM; C/CMC ; Cornell; RCAS; Binghamton (NY) Arts Arena Invitational

JOJOLA, E. *Isleta*

PUBLISHED: Snodgrass (1968).

PUBLIC COLLECTIONS: MAI

JOJOLA, VERNON *Laguna/Isleta*

EXHIBITS: AIAFM

JOJOLA-SÁNCHEZ, DEBORAH ANN *Isleta/Jémez*

Born 20 Feb 1962 in Albuquerque, NM; daughter of Reyes Fragua and José Raymond Jojola; P/GP: Marie Anzara and John Jojola; M/GP: Juanita Sabaquie and Anastacio Fragua

RESIDENCE: Isleta Pueblo, NM

EDUCATION: Río Grande High School, Albuquerque, NM, 1980; A.A., IAIA, 1982

OCCUPATION: Wife, mother, and artist

MEDIA: Oil, acrylic, clay, and prints

PUBLISHED: Foss (1982); Lamb (1990). *New Mexico Magazine* (Apr 1991)

PUBLIC COLLECTIONS: IAIA; Technical Vocational Institute, Albuquerque, NM

EXHIBITS: ACS/TOWA; AIAFM; IPCC; NMSF; RC; SJBIM; SWAIA; Isleta Pueblo (NM) Art Exhibition, 1982-1983; New Mexico Registry of the Arts, 1991

SOLO EXHIBITS: IAIA; YMCA, Albuquerque, NM, 1983; Art in the Park, Albuquerque, NM, 1984

AWARDS: CIM ('86, 1st); NMSF (1982-1992, 1st; '90, 1st); IPCC ('91, 1st); SJBIM ('86, 1st); SWAIA ('90, 1st; '91)

HONORS: Honored by Mayor of Albuquerque, NM, 1982; National Art Honor Society, 1979; Institute of Texas, filmed interview

DEBORAH ANN JOJOLA-SÁNCHEZ

Jojola-Sánchez seeks to preserve her culture through her art. She intends to teach and inspire the youth of her Pueblo with their creative heritage.

artist, p.c. 1992

JONES, LAURA ASAH *Kiowa/Comanche*

RESIDENCE: Oklahoma City, OK

PUBLISHED: Snodgrass (1968)

EXHIBITS: PAC

JONES, LEO *Navajo*

EXHIBITS: PAC

AWARDS: PAC ('69, HM)

JONES, RUBY TUESDAY *Cherokee*

Born 5 July 1951 in New Brunswick, NJ; daughter of Christy and Pete Jones; P/GP: Oma Redick and John Jones

RESIDENCE: New Brunswick, NJ

EDUCATION: Franklin High School, Somerset, NJ, 1969; Fashion Institute of Technology, 1971; Rutgers, New Brunswick, NJ, 1977-1979

OCCUPATION: Real estate agent, designer, music writer and producer, and artist

MEDIA: Oil, watercolor, pen and ink, fabric, and stained glass
EXHIBITS: AICH; KCPA; SI; Carrier Foundation Benefit Art Show, NJ; Summit Art Center, NJ; galleries in NJ, NY, and Washington, D.C.

JONES, RUTHE BLALOCK *Delaware/Shawnee/Peoria*

RUTHE BLALOCK JONES

The artist states that the themes or subject matter in her work are generally drawn from personal experience, either first-hand or interpreting stories and events related by family and tribal elders. She is, therefore, carrying on an oral tradition in two-dimensional form. Jones received early encouragement and training from Charles Banks Wilson, nationally acclaimed artist from Oklahoma.

artist, p.c. 1991

Chu-Lun-Dit

Born 8 June 1939 in Claremore, OK; daughter of Lucy Parks and Joe Blalock
RESIDENCE: Okmulgee, OK
EDUCATION: BC High School; A.A., BC, 1970; B.F.A., U of Tulsa, 1972; U of Tulsa, 1972-1974; U of OK, 1985; M.S., NSU, 1989
OCCUPATION: Educator, Bacone College art department director, and painter
MEDIA: Oil, acrylic, watercolor, pen and ink, crayon, pencil, and prints
PUBLISHED: Snodgrass (1968); Brody (1971); Humphrey and King (1980); Gully, ed. (1994). *Christian Science Monitor* (1967); *The Arizona Republic* (Aug 6, 1967); *Nimrod* (Vol. 16, 1972); *Tulsa University Magazine* (1973), cover; *Arizona Republic* (1974); *The Tulsa Tribune* (Dec 23, 1976); *Chronicles of Oklahoma* (spring 1980); brochure, SPIM (1981); *Oklahoma Today* (spring 1985); *The Hill Rag* (28 Sept 1984), cover; *National Geographic Travel* (1986); *Adult Quarterly*, Southern Baptist Convention (Dec 1989); *The Muskogee Phoenix* (16 Sept 1990; 23 Nov 1991); *The Broken Arrow Scout* (15 Jan 1992); *Twin Territories* (Year of the Indian Edition 1992); *The Sunday Oklahoman* (10 Apr 1994)
BOOKS ILLUSTRATED: Wise (1978), Williams and Meredith (1980). *American Indian Exposition* (1991), cover
PUBLIC COLLECTIONS: BC; CAI/KC; FCTM; HM; MAI; NSU; PAC; SPIM; U of Tulsa; USDI; Public School System, Okmulgee, OK, Performing Arts Center Collection, Tulsa, OK; Murrow Indian Children's Home, Muskogee, OK
EXHIBITS: Partial listing of more than ninety includes: AAID; AAUW; AIE; BC/McG; BEAIAC; CAI/KC; CIAI; CNM; DE; FAIEAIP; FCTM; FNAIC; GM; HM; IAF; ITIC; KCPA; LAIS; MMO; MNH/AN; NACLA; NPTA; OIAC; OSC; OU/MA; PAC; PBOIA; PM; RE; SFFA; SI; SN; SPIM; SWAIA; TIAF; WWM; Fogg Art Museum, Harvard University, Cambridge, MA; Sugar Creek Country Club, Houston, TX; regional shows and markets, and galleries in AZ, NM, OK, OR, TX, and WY; see also Awards
SOLO EXHIBITS: Partial listing of 15 includes: HM, BC, SPIM
AWARDS: AAUW; AIE; BEAIAC ('67, Special Award); CNM ('88, 1st); CAI/KC ('79); CIAI ('75); FCTM ('67; '68; '71); HM/G ('78; '79); LIAS ('90, MA); OIAC ('93, Grand Prize); PAC ('69; '71, 1st;'73, Graphics Award; '74, Graphics Award; '78, 1st); PBOIA ('70); RE ('87; '90, 1st; '93); SN ('67); SWAIA ('91, 1st; '94, Crumbo Award); Okmulgee County Annual Art Exhibit, Okmulgee, OK; Ponca Indian Fair
HONORS: Governor's Advisory Committee on the Status of Women, Oklahoma City, OK, certificate; U of Tulsa, grant, 1973-1974; Smithsonian Institution, exhibit poster, 1982; OU/MA, poster, 1984; E.P.I.C. Fellowship, 1989; American Indian Art, 9th International Symposium on Polyaesthetic Culture, Castle Mittersill, Salzburg, Austria, exhibitor and speaker, September, 1990; Oklahoma State Capitol Building, East Gallery, Oklahoma City, OK, Year of the Indian Exhibit, one of eight Indian artists exhibited, 1992; *Biographical Directory of Native American Painters*, Editorial Board; Oklahoma Governor's Arts Awards, Arts and Education Award, 1993

JOOGII (see De Groat, Jay)

JORDAN, JAMES *Choctaw*

EXHIBITS: FCTM
AWARDS: FCTM ('88, IH; '89)

JOSEPH, ALFRED *Carrier*

Born 1927 in Hagwilget, BC, Canada

RESIDENCE: Canada

EDUCATION: C/KSNCIA, 1967

PUBLIC COLLECTIONS: C/RBCM, C/INAC

EXHIBITS: C/CMC, C/ROM, C/TL

JOSEPH, FLOYD *Salish*

RESIDENCE: Canada

PUBLISHED: Hall, Blackman, and Rickard (1981)

PUBLIC COLLECTIONS: HCC

EXHIBITS: AUG, BHSU, HCC, HPTU, NSU/SD, SDSMT, WTF.

JOSHONGEVA *Hopi*

PUBLISHED: Snodgrass (1968). *The Arizona Republic* (28 June 1987)

COMMISSIONS: *Murals:* Mesa Verde National Park, Mesa Verde, CO

PUBLIC COLLECTIONS: CAM/OH, MV

JOSHUA, EDMOND, JR. *Creek/Seminole*

Born 2 Apr 1936; son of Dorothy Tiger and Edmond Joshua; brother of Lee Roy Joshua (q.v.)

RESIDENCE: Okmulgee, OK

EDUCATION: Through 10th grade

OCCUPATION: Sculptor and painter

MEDIA: Oil, acrylic, watercolor, pencil, pen and ink, and stone

PUBLIC COLLECTIONS: HCC

EXHIBITS: AAID; CNM; FCTM; HCC; PAC; RC; SN; Pawnee Bill's Art Show, Pawnee, OK

AWARDS: FCTM ('67; '68; '70, 1st; '71; '72; '80, IH)

EDMOND JOSHUA JR.

Joshua is a self-taught artist. A first cousin of Jerome Tiger (q.v.), his mother and Tiger's father were sister and brother.

artist, p.c. 1990

JOSHUA, LEE ROY *Creek/Seminole*

A.K.A. Lee Joshua

RESIDENCE: Okmulgee, OK

Born 1937 in Holdenville, OK; son of Dorothy Tiger and Edmond Joshua; brother of Edmond Joshua Jr. (q.v.); cousin of Jerome Tiger (q.v.)

EDUCATION: Indian Schools.

MEDIA: Watercolor, tempera, and prints.

PUBLISHED: *The Tulsa World* (10 May 1982)

PUBLIC COLLECTIONS: HCC.

EXHIBITS: AAID, CCHM, CNM, FAIE, FCTM, HCC, HM/G, HSM/OK, ITIC, OAC, NMSF, PAC, SN, SNM; Oklahoma Diamond Jubilee Celebration, Arrowhead Lodge, OK; St. Gregory University Museum, Shawnee, OK; see also Awards

AWARDS: FCTM ('67; '68; '69; '70; '75, 1st, IH; '76, IH, '79, 1st, IH), HM/G ('75), SN ('76); Labor Day Art Show, Henryetta, OK ('71; '72'; '77, 1st); The Barking Water Art Show, Wewoka, OK ('73; '75, 1st; '76, 1st)

HONORS: Oklahoma State Capitol, Governor's Gallery, Oklahoma City, OK, Artist of the Month

LEE ROY JOSHUA

In 1967, when Jerome Tiger died, his mother expressed the wish that someone in the family would continue the work he had started, recording the Creek/Seminole culture. This inspired Joshua to become serious about his own art work and pursue a career as a painter.

artist brochure

JOSTWI (see Beckman, Mary Thompson)

JUANASIALUK (see Juanisialuk)

JUANICO, BRENDA *Acoma*

EXHIBITS: HM/G

AWARDS: HM/G ('70)

JUANISIALU (see Juanisialuk)

JUANISIALUK *Inuit (Eskimo)*

A.K.A. *Joanisialu; Juanasialuk; Juanisialu; Juanisialu Irqumia*

Born 1917; died 1977

RESIDENCE: Lived in Povungnituk, PQ, Canada

PUBLISHED: Larmour (1967); Goetz, et al. (1977); Myers, ed. (1980); McMasters, et al. (1993). *Arts West* (Vol. 3, no. 5, 1978)

PUBLIC COLLECTIONS: C/TDB, DAM

EXHIBITS: C/AG/WP, C/EACTDB, C/TIP, C/TMBI

JUDGE, RAYMOND *Navajo*

A.K.A. Raymond J. Judge

Born 26 Mar 1945 in Lower Greasewood, near Ganado, AZ; son of Rose, weaver, and Slim Judge, council leader and medicine man

RESIDENCE: Flagstaff, AZ

EDUCATION: Phoenix, 1964

OCCUPATION: Surveyor, scaleman, hot plant inspector, transportation construction technician, and painter

MEDIA: Watercolor, tempera, acrylic, watercolor, gouache, pencil, pen and ink, pastel, and prints

PUBLISHED: *Art of the West* (Mar/Apr 1992)

EXHIBITS: CAM/OH; FNAA; HM/G; MNA; NTF; SWAIA; WMNAAF; Apache Junction (AZ) Art Show; Lake Powell Art Show, Page, AZ

AWARDS: MNA, NTF, SWAIA

HONORS: WMNAAF, poster artist, 1992

JUMBO, GILBERT *Navajo*

A.K.A. Gilberto Jumbo

Born 26 Jan 1958 in Ganado, AZ, on the Navajo Reservation; son of Rosanda Begay and David Jumbo; P/GP: Mary Billie and Kador Jumbo; M/GP: Descheene Nez Begay and Ason Chee Begay; cousin of Justin Tso (q.v.)

RESIDENCE: Chinle, AZ

EDUCATION: Chinle (AZ) High School, 1979; Phoenix (AZ) Institute of Technology, 1991; IAIA

OCCUPATION: Construction worker and painter

MEDIA: Watercolor

PUBLISHED: *The Indian Trader* (Dec 1994)

BOOKS ILLUSTRATED: Navajo Tribe, Rough Rock (AZ) Elementary School, eight books

COMMISSIONS: *Murals:* Chinle (AZ) Elementary School, Many Farms (AZ) High School, Tuba City (AZ) High School

EXHIBITS: ACAI; GPWAS; ITIC; NTF; SWAIA; TWF; Death Valley (CA) 49er's Western Art Show; galleries in AZ, FL, MN, and WI

AWARDS: GPWAS (1st); ITIC ('91; '92, 1st; '93, 2-1st, Best in Category; '94); NTF (1st); SWAIA ('92, 1st)

GILBERT JUMBO

Jumbo's love of horses led to his career as a painter. As a child he drew horses in the dirt, on abandoned cars, on cardboard or anything else he could find using a stick, a stone, or a bit of charcoal from the fire.

artist, p.c. 1992

JUMPING BEAR (see Grass, John)

JUMPING BUFFALO(see Spotted Tail)

JUMPING ROCK (see Cooper, Darran G.)

Kaa Am (see Carlo, Margaret E.)

Kabance, Joseph *Potawatomi*

Born 1945 in Horton, KS

RESIDENCE: Albany, NY

EDUCATION: St. Paul's High School, Marty, SD, 1951-1963; IAIA, 1963-1964; Fort Lewis College, Durango, CO, 1964-1965; B.A., U of Wichita, 1970

OCCUPATION: Systems analyst, ceramist, and painter

MEDIA: Oil and mixed-media

PUBLISHED: Mahey, et al. (1980)

PUBLIC COLLECTIONS: MIM, PAC

EXHIBITS: CSPIP, PAC; see also Awards

SOLO EXHIBITS: SPIM

AWARDS: PAC ('72, Grand Award; '73); South Dakota State Fair ('61-'63, 1st)

Kabotie, Fred *Hopi*

Nakayoma, Day After Day; *Tawawiiseoma,* Trailing Sun

Born 20 Feb 1900 in Shungopovi, Second Mesa, AZ; died 28 Feb 1986

RESIDENCE: Lived at Shungopovi, Second Mesa, AZ

EDUCATION: Santa Fe; Santa Fe (NM) High School, 1924; summer sessions, Alfred

OCCUPATION: Teacher, painter, author, lecturer, craftsman, Hopi Silvercraft Guild founder and manager, IACB field specialist, United States Good-Will Ambassador, and painter

MEDIA: Oil, acrylic, watercolor, tempera, and pen and ink

PUBLISHED: Sloan and LaFarge (1931); Underhill (1944); LaFarge (1956; 1960); Dockstader (1962; 1973); Dunn (1968); Snodgrass (1968); Brody (1971; 1992); Tanner (1973); Monthan and Monthan (1975); Warner (1975; 1979); Highwater (1976); Belknap (1977); Stuart and Ashton (1977); Mahey, et al. (1980); Broder (1981); King (1981); Fawcett and Callander (1982); Hoffman, et al. (1984); Golder (1985); Wade, ed.(1986); Jacka and Jacka (1988); Seymour (1988); Williams, ed. (1990); Archuleta and Strickland (1991). *International Studio* (Mar 1922); *Travel* (1931); *Introduction to American Indian Art* (1931); *The American Magazine of Art* (Aug 1932); *Cincinnati Art Museum, Bulletin* (Jan 1938); *Arizona Highways* (July 1951; Apr 1976); *Compton's Pictured Encyclopaedia* (1957); *News Notes* (Dec 1961); *Paintings by American Indians,* CPLH (1962); *Arts Focus* (Aug 1981); *Southwest Art* (June 1983; Nov 1984); *American Indian Art* (spring 1984); *Native Peoples* (fall 1991); biographical publications

BOOKS ILLUSTRATED: DeHuff (1927; 1929; 1932); Kennard (1948); Underhill (1948); Kabotie (1949)

COMMISSIONS: *Murals:* Grand Canyon National Park, Desert View Tower, AZ; Peabody Museum, Harvard University, Cambridge (full-size reproductions of the Awátovi murals), 1930s. *Paintings:* The School of American Research and the Archaeological Society of New Mexico, American Indian Dance paintings, 1920-1926; MAI, Hopi life and customs, 1928-1929

PUBLIC COLLECTIONS: AC/A; AF; BIA; CAM/OH; CAS; CGA; CGFA; CGPS; CMA; DAM; DCC; FAC/CS; GM; HH; HM; IACB/DC; MAI; MKMcNAI; MMA; MNA; MNA/KHC; MNH/CI; MNM; MNM/SAR; MRFM; NPS; OU/MA; PAC; SAR; TM; WOM; Society of Fine Arts, Palm Beach, FL

EXHIBITS: ACC, AIW, DAM, EITA, FAC/CS, IK, ITIC, MAI, MFA/A, MFA/D, MFA/O, MKMcNAI, MMA, MNA, MNM, NGA, OMA, OU/ET, PAC, PAC/T, PM, SFFA, SV, TM, WRTD, WWM

SOLO EXHIBITS: MNA

Fred Kabotie

"In 1906, Kabotie's family, seeking to escape the efforts of the Government to force them to abandon their customs, joined other people of old Oraibi and established Hotevilla. Eventually they were forced to return to Oraibi and Shungopovi, where, in 1913, the children were placed in schools for the first time. Later, as a disciplinary measure, Kabotie was sent to Santa Fe Indian School. There he was encouraged by Mr. and Mrs. DeHuff to develop his artistic talents. Since 1920, his work and his name have usually appeared wherever Indian art is mentioned. His work as an educator prevented him from painting extensively since 1959."

Snodgrass 1968

Kabotie spent his life helping his people. Although a full-time teacher, in 1949 he helped establish the Hopi Silvercraft Guild. In addition to teaching silver design to the guild members, he was the guild's secretary/treasurer and manager. Kabotie was also instrumental in the establishment of the Hopi Cultural Center, Inc. and was its first president.

DETAIL: George Kishketon, *Study for a Mural,* 1941. Philbrook Museum of Art, Tulsa, Oklahoma

AWARDS: ASF; ITIC (Grand Award); MNM; PAC (Grand Award)

HONORS: Partial listing includes: Guggenheim Foundation Fellowship, 1945-1946; Indian Council Fire of Chicago, Indian Achievement Medal, 1949; French Government, Palmes d'Académiques, 1954; IACB, Certificate of Appreciation, 1958; United States Good-Will Envoy to India, 1960

MICHAEL KABOTIE

*"Of his son, Fred Kabotie said: 'Michael learned to paint by watching me work in my studio from the time he was a little boy. He had no formal art training other than my work and guidance. In the beginning of his development, Michael was mainly interested in subjects of a humorous nature, but of late he has concerned himself with more serious subjects (*Arizona Highways, *Aug 1966).'"*

Snodgrass 1968

Michael Kabotie is one of three artists who organized the "Artist Hopid" (q.v.). He is a member of the Snow/Water Clan.

KABOTIE, MICHAEL *Hopi*

Lomawywesa, Walking in Harmony

Born 1942 at Keams Canyon, AZ; son of Alice and Fred Kabotie (q.v.)

RESIDENCE: Flagstaff, AZ

EDUCATION: Hopi; U of AZ, "Southwest Indian Art Project," scholarship, summer 1960; U of AZ, ca. 1964-1966

OCCUPATION: Artist

MEDIA: Acrylic

PUBLISHED: Snodgrass (1968); Brody (1971); Tanner (1968; 1973); Broder (1978; 1981); New (1979); Highwater (1980); Hoffman, et al. (1984); Kabotie (1987); Jacka and Jacka (1988); Seymour (1988); Archuleta and Strickland (1991); Abbott (1994). *Arizona Highways* (Aug 1966)

COMMISSIONS: *Murals:* Hopi Cultural Center Museum, Second Mesa, AZ

PUBLIC COLLECTIONS: AC/RM, CGPS, HCC, DAM, HM, IACB/DC, IAIA, MAI, MNA, MRFM, WWM

EXHIBITS: AC/T; CGPS; FAC/CS; FSMCIAF; HCC; HCCM; HM; HM/G; IK; ITIC; EM; LGAM; MCC/CA; NACLA; OWE; PAC; PAIC; PBS; PM; SDMM; SFFA; SN; SPIM; SV; WCCA; WRTD; WWM; Riverside Community College; Hillsborough County Museum, Tampa, FL; Arizona State Capitol, Phoenix, AZ

AWARDS: HM/G ('69; '70 2-1st, Valley Bank Award); ITIC ('68, 1st, Judges Discretion Award; '70; '87); PAC ('69; '70)

KACHA HONAWAH (see White Bear)

KACHINA TOWN (see Sánchez, Ramos)

FRANCIS KAGIGE

"The artist's first work, executed on cardboard from old shoeboxes and on the backs of looseleaf notebooks, depicted Indian symbols in stylized designs. The artist attended school through the 4th grade and has never had formal art training. He first began to paint in 1962."

Snodgrass 1968

Kagige was provided with painting materials and encouraged to express himself by Solvis Westman, who had seen his work and recognized his potential. Westman also arranged for Kagige's first one-man show which was held in Toronto in 1963.

Southcott 1984

KAGIGE, FRANCIS *Ojibwa*

Born 1929 on Manitoulin Island, ON, Canada, on the Wikwemikong Reserve

EDUCATION: Through 4th grade

OCCUPATION: Road construction worker and painter

MEDIA: Acrylic and gouache

PUBLISHED: Snodgrass (1968); Gooderham, ed. (1969); Dickason (1972); Cinader (1976; 1987); Southcott (1984); Menitove and Danford, eds. (1989); Podedworny (1989). *Native Perspective* (Vol. 3, no. 2, 1978)

BOOKS ILLUSTRATED: Gooderham, ed. (1967; 1979); Johnston (1970)

COMMISSIONS: *Murals:* Indians of Canada Pavilion, Expo '67, Montréal, PQ; Wikewemikong School, Manitoulin Island, ON. *Other:* Film animation for *Pinoccio,* by Ruth Johnston, Toronto, ON, 1979

PUBLIC COLLECTIONS: C/AG/TB, C/CMC, C/INAC, C/MCC, C/ROM, IANA

EXHIBITS: C/AG/TB; C/ROM; C/WCAA; C/WICEC; NYWF; Galerie des Schlosses Klein-Mectenlach, Fueberg, Switzerland; Gallery Prist Noi, Vienna, Austria; International Institute of Metropolitan Toronto, ON; Toronto (ON) Central Library; Japanese Cultural Centre, Toronto, ON; University of Windsor (ON) Art Gallery

KAGYOON, WILLIAM *Inuit (Eskimo)*

RESIDENCE: Holman Island, NWT, Canada

OCCUPATION: Graphic artist

PUBLISHED: Woodhouse, ed. (1980); Napran (1984)

PUBLIC COLLECTIONS: C/TDB
EXHIBITS: C/AG/WP, C/EACTDB, C/VRS

KA HAS BA (see DuBois, Betty Jean Nilchee)

KAHGEGAGAHBOWAH *Ojibwa*

A.K.A. Chief Kahgegagahbowah
PUBLISHED: Hamilton (1950); Snodgrass (1968)

KAHIONHES (see Fadden, John)

KAHIRPEYA (see Runs Over)

KAHN, CHESTER *Navajo*

Tso Yazzie, Big Little
Born 24 Feb 1936 in Pine Springs, AZ
EDUCATION: Shiprock, 1947-1948; Stewart, 1948-1953; U of AZ, "Southwest Indian Art Project," scholarship, summers 1960, 1961; additional summer and night school courses
OCCUPATION: Coordinator and teacher's aide, sign and billboard painter, fabric designer, silversmith, and painter
PUBLISHED: Willoya and Brown (1962); Snodgrass (1968); Tanner (1973)
COMMISSIONS: *Murals:* Gallup (NM) Indian Community Center
PUBLIC COLLECTIONS: ASM; Randee Motel, Sedona, AZ; Window Rock (AZ) Lodge
EXHIBITS: AIAE/WSU, ASF, ITIC, MNA, MNM, NTF, PAC; see also Awards
SOLO EXHIBITS: Nevada State Library, Carson City; Washoe County Library and Tower Theater, Reno, NV; Gallup (NM) Public Library
AWARDS: AIAE/WSU; ASF; ITIC; NTF; PAC; Coconino County Fair, Flagstaff, AZ; Nevada Artists' Association Exhibit, Reno, NV

CHESTER KAHN

"Kahn recalls doing drawings on cardboard and on canyon walls with great joy while herding sheep when he was about seven."

Snodgrass 1968

KAHN, FRANKLIN *Navajo*

Born 25 May 1934 at Pine Springs, AZ
RESIDENCE: Flagstaff, AZ
EDUCATION: Stewart
OCCUPATION: Painter in the late 1950s and 1960s
MEDIA: Tempera and casein
PUBLISHED: Tanner (1973)
PUBLIC COLLECTIONS: CGPS
EXHIBITS: CGPS, LGAM, PM, SN
AWARDS: SN ('62)

KAHSAHYULI (see Seton, Thomas)

KAILUKIAK, JOHN *Eskimo*

Amgalgak
Born 1951
RESIDENCE: Toksok Bay, AK
EDUCATION: IAIA
OCCUPATION: Sculptor, ivory carver, printmaker, and painter.
MEDIA: Oil, acrylic, pencil, mixed-media, ivory, wood, and prints
PUBLISHED: Hill (1992). *The Anchorage Daily News* (1988); *The New Mexican* (1981); *Tundra Times* (1984)
PUBLIC COLLECTIONS: IAIA
EXHIBITS: HM/G; IAIA; MFA/AH; U of AK/F; Institute of Alaska Native Arts

KAI SA (see Sandy, Percy Tsisete)

KAKAROOK, GUY *Eskimo*

Born ca. 1860 in Atnuk on Cape Darby, AK; believed to have died in the early 1900s in Nome, AK

RESIDENCE: Lived in Alaska

EDUCATION: Never attended school

OCCUPATION: Guide, interpreter, deckhand, ivory engraver, and painter

MEDIA: Watercolor, crayon, and ivory

PUBLISHED: Snodgrass (1968); Ray (1969)

PUBLIC COLLECTIONS: SI, U of CA/LMA

EXHIBITS: SI, SJM

KAKAWIN (see Amon, Patrick)

KAKAYGEESICK, ROBERT, JR. *Ojibwa*

Kakaygeesick, Everlasting Sky; *She-Sheep,* Duck

Born 24 Dec 1948 in Warroad, MN; son of Florence and Robert KakayGeesick Sr.; M/GM Rose Cobiness; nephew of Ed Cobiness (q.v.)

RESIDENCE: Calgary, AB

EDUCATION: Warroad (MN) High School, 1967; Milwaukee (WI) Institute of Technology, 1968-1969; Minneapolis (MN) Vocational Technical School, 1969-1970

OCCUPATION: Laborer, draftsman, traditional dancer, lecturer, art teacher, and painter

MEDIA: Oil, acrylic, watercolor, pen and ink, pencil, colored pencil, charcoal, and prints

PUBLISHED: *Journal of Fresh Water* (fall 1979); *The Daily Journal*, International Falls, MN (May 1980); *The Minneapolis Star and Tribune* (Aug 1985); *The Indian Trader* (Aug 1985); *The Pioneer Winter Showcase*, Bemidji, MN (Mar 1986); *American Indian Art* (spring 1990)

PUBLIC COLLECTIONS: HCC

EXHIBITS: HCC; HN; galleries in MN, NY, and Canada; see also Awards

SOLO EXHIBITS: SIM

AWARDS: Invitational Indian Art Show, Rancocas, NJ (1986, Best of Show)

ROBERT KAKAYGEESICK JR.

At the age of twelve, Robert KaKayGeesick sold his first painting to the local baker. The greatest influence in his life was his great-grandfather, KaKayGeesick who was a shaman, and who lived to be over one hundred years old. He impressed his great-grandson with his ability to achieve a balance with all aspects of the natural world, and hence Robert's paintings combine elements of realism and mysticism. They often incorporate a circle as a symbol of the perfect cyclical balance of nature.

artist, p.c. 1990

KAKEGAMIC, GOYCE *Cree*

Born 1948 on Sandy Lake Reserve, ON, Canada; brother of Joshim Kakegamic (q.v.); brother-in-law of Norval Morrisseau (q.v.)

RESIDENCE: Sandy Lake, ON, Canada

EDUCATION: Attended high school at Dryden Lake; Federation College, Thunder Bay, ON; C/U of WON

OCCUPATION: Miner, guidance counselor, and painter

MEDIA: Acrylic and prints

PUBLISHED: Menitove, ed. (1968b); Highwater (1980)

PUBLIC COLLECTIONS: C/AG/TB; C/INAC; C/CMC; C/MCC; C/MI; HCC; Central Marketing Services, Ottawa, ON; Reed Paper Group Canada Ltd.

EXHIBITS: C/AG/TB, C/CNAC, C/ROM, HCC

SOLO/SPECIAL EXHIBITS: Aggregation Gallery, Toronto, ON (dual show), 1974

KAKEGAMIC, JOSHIM *Cree*

A.K.A. Josh Kakegamic

Born 1952 on Sandy Lake Reserve, ON, Canada; brother of Goyce Kakegamic (q.v) and brother-in-law of Norval Morrisseau (q.v)

RESIDENCE: Sandy Lake, ON, Canada
EDUCATION: Studied under Norval Morrisseau and Carl Ray (qq.v.)
OCCUPATION: Artist
MEDIA: Acrylic and prints
PUBLISHED: Warner (1975; 1979); Menitove, ed. (1968b); Highwater (1980); Southcott (1984); Podedworny (1989); Menitove and Danford, eds. (1989).
PUBLIC COLLECTIONS: C/AC/TB; C/CC; C/CC/NB; C/CEG; C/CMC; C/CMS; C/MCC; C/MI; C/ROM; C/U of T; C/WICEC; Central Marketing Services, Ottawa, ON; Hospital for Sick Children, Toronto, ON
EXHIBITS: C/AG/O; C/AG/TB; C/CNAC; C/MCC; C/NCCT; C/ROM; C/U of T; C/WCAA; C/WICEC; Aggregation Gallery Toronto, ON; Shayne Gallery, Montréal, PQ; Oakville Centennial Gallery, Oakville, ON; shows in Red Lake and Ontario since 1969
HONORS: INAC, awards, 1972, 1974; The Canadian Department of Tourism, award, 1973

JOSHIM KAKEGAMIC

In 1973, Joshim and Henry Kakegamic started the Triple K Co-operative at Red Lake. Their other brother Goyce joined them shortly after it was established. It was created in order to give the artists greater control over the printing of their works and an opportunity for greater exposure to the general public. Influenced by Carl Ray and Norval Morrisseau (qq.v.), Kakegamic paints in the "Algonquin Legend Painting" style. His paintings contain large areas of black, sharp points and angles.

KAKEGAMIC, ROBERT *Cree*

Born 1944 on the Sandy Lake Reserve, ON, Canada
RESIDENCE: Ontario, Canada
OCCUPATION: Trapper, teacher, and painter
MEDIA: Oil, acrylic, pen and ink, pencil, and prints
PUBLISHED: Menitove, ed. (1968b)
PUBLIC COLLECTIONS: C/AG/TB
EXHIBITS: C/AG/TB, C/M
SOLO EXHIBITS: Wah-Sa Gallery, Winnipeg, MB; Eagle Doven Gallery, Edmonton, AB

KAKEGAMIC, ROY *Cree*

Born 1961 on Sandy Lake Reserve, ON, Canada
EDUCATION: Native Studies Diploma, C/TU, 1983; B.A., C/TU, 1988
COMMISSIONS: *Murals:* Muzinihbeegey Group Mural, Sandy Lake Artists, 1989. *Other:* Miinatik Native Artists, Thunder Bay, ON; Nishnawebe-Aski Legal Services Corporation, Thunder Bay, ON; Centre for Northern Studies, Lakehead University, Thunder Bay, ON; Northern Bands Indian Hockey Tournament, Sioux Lookout, ON; Northern Nishnawbe Education Council, Sioux Lookout, ON; Trent University Native Association, Peterborough, ON; Ontario Arts Council, Toronto, ON, 1989; Thunder Bay (ON) Indian Friendship Centre; Ministry of Natural Resources, Nipigon, ON
PUBLIC COLLECTIONS: C/AG/TB; C/INAC; C/TU; Brazilian Embassy, Ottawa, ON; Lakehead University, Thunder Bay, ON; National Association of Friendship Centers, Ottawa, ON; Ottawa (ON) Native Counseling Unit
EXHIBITS: Partial listing of more than forty includes: C/AG/TB; C/M; C/TU; C/WICEC; NACLA; Canada House Gallery, London, England; Canadian Consulate, Frankfurt, Germany; Thomas Fiddler Memorial School, Sandy Lake, ON; Japan and Hong Kong
SOLO EXHIBITS: C/CC; C/TU; Sandy Lake (ON) Primary School
HONORS: *Grants:* Material Assistance Grant, 1990; Native Organizations Project Grant

KAKEPETUM, LLOYD *Cree*

A.K.A. Lloyd Kakekapetum
Born 1958 on Sandy Lake Reserve, ON, Canada
RESIDENCE: Sandy Lake, ON, Canada

OCCUPATION: Painter
MEDIA: Acrylic
PUBLISHED: Menitove, ed. (1986b)
PUBLIC COLLECTIONS: C/AG/TB
EXHIBITS: C/AG/TB; Vancouver, BC; Edmonton, AB; Toronto, ON
SOLO EXHIBITS: Toronto, ON; Montréal, PQ; Winnipeg, MB

KAKEPETUM, MORLEY *Cree*
Born 1936 on Sandy Lake Reserve, ON, Canada
RESIDENCE: Ontario, Canada
OCCUPATION: Painter
MEDIA: Acrylic
PUBLIC COLLECTIONS: C/AG/TB
EXHIBITS: C/AG/TB

MORLEY KAKEPETUM

The subjects for Kakepetum's paintings, to a great extent, come from the legends told to him by the Elders of his band. Although he learned much from Carl Ray (q.v.), Kakepetum is basically a self-taught artist.

Menitove, 1986

KAKHYAUT, MYRA (see Kukiiyaut, Myra)

KALER, DANNY *Creek*
RESIDENCE: Okmulgee, OK
MEDIA: Watercolor
EXHIBITS: CNM, FCTM, PAC
AWARDS: FCTM ('71; '72; '73, 1st; '85, 1st)

KALLESTEWA, WISTON *Zuni*
RESIDENCE: Zuni, NM
PUBLISHED: Snodgrass (1968)
EXHIBITS: MNM, 1965
AWARDS: MNM

KALLOAR (see Kaluraq, Francis)

KALLOOAR (see Kaluraq, Francis)

KALLORAR (see Kaluraq, Francis)

KALURAQ, FRANCIS *Inuit (Eskimo)*
A.K.A. Kallooar; Kalloar; Kallorar
Born 1931 in the Kazan River area, NWT, Canada
RESIDENCE: Baker Lake, NWT, Canada
OCCUPATION: Sculptor, printer, and graphic artist
MEDIA: Pencil, colored pencil, and prints
PUBLISHED: Jackson and Nasby (1987)
PUBLIC COLLECTIONS: C/AC/MS
EXHIBITS: C/CID

FRANCIS KALURAQ

In the early 1970s, after a successful career as a carver, Kaluraq joined the Baker Lake Print Shop as a stone cutter, printer, and printmaker. He also produced a number of drawings in which the dominant images are large and crowd the edges of the drawing paper. By 1983 his eyesight and health were failing and he no longer produced drawings.

Jackson and Nasby 1987

KALVAK, HELEN *Inuit (Eskimo)*
A.K.A. Kalvak; Kralvak; Kalvakadlak
Born 1901 at Tahiryuak Lake, Victoria Island, NWT, Canada; died 1984
RESIDENCE: Lived on Holman Island, NWT, Canada
OCCUPATION: Shaman, wife, mother, and graphic artist
MEDIA: Pencil and prints
PUBLISHED: Larmour (1967); Burland (1973); Goetz, et al. (1977); Blodgett (1978a); Collinson (1978); Woodhouse (1980); Latocki (1982); Napran (1984); Driscoll (1987); Jackson and Nasby (1987); McMasters, et al. (1993); Gully, ed. (1994). *North* (Mar/Apr 1974); *Courier,* UNESCO (Jan 1976)

HELEN KALVAK

One of the original members of Holman's drawing and print-making cooperative, Kalvak started drawing in 1960. She was very prolific and produced more than 3,000 drawings. In the 1970s, she developed Parkinson's disease and was no longer able to draw. In addition to being an artist, Kalvak was a respected shaman in her home community of Holman.

Latocki, 1982

PUBLIC COLLECTIONS: C/CAP, C/CMC, C/HEC, C/TDB, C/U of AB
EXHIBITS: C/AG/W; C/AG/WP; C/CID; C/CMC; C/EACTDB; C/SS; C/VRS; HM; Robertson Galleries, Ottawa, ON
SOLO EXHIBITS: C/CGCQ
HONORS: Royal Canadian Academy of Arts, elected a member, 1975; Order of Canada, 1978

KALVAKADLAK (see Kalvak, Helen)

KAMEL, WARHOOP (see Camel, Kenneth Lloyd)

KAMILITISIT, RICHARD *(?)*

Born 1959 in Moosonee, ON, Canada
RESIDENCE: Canada
OCCUPATION: Printmaker; painter since 1975
MEDIA: Acrylic and prints
PUBLIC COLLECTIONS: C/AG/TB; Onakawana Ltd.; Government of Ontario
EXHIBITS: C/AG/TB; Gallery 100, Erin, ON; Joan Ling Gallery, Toronto, ON
SOLO EXHIBITS: C/TMEC

KANAJU *Inuit (Eskimo)*

A.K.A. Pauloosie Kanaju
Born 28 Apr 1937
RESIDENCE: Povungnituk, PQ, Canada
PUBLISHED: *Arts West* (Vol. 3, no. 5, 1978)

KANANGINA (see Kananginak)

KANANGINAK *Inuit (Eskimo)*

A.K.A. Kanangina; Kananginak Pootoogook
Born 1935 at a hunting camp on West Baffin Island, NWT, Canada; son of Ningeeookoloo and Pootoogook, identified by early Whites as the "Eskimo King of Baffin Island"; P/GF: Inukjuarjuk
RESIDENCE: Cape Dorset, NWT, Canada
OCCUPATION: Hunter, boat owner, politician, entrepreneur, carver, printer, and graphic artist
MEDIA: Felt tip pen, pencil, and stone
PUBLISHED: Houston (1967; 1967a); Larmour (1967); Goetz, et al. (1977); Routledge *(1979);* Jackson and Nasby *(1987). Audubon* (July 1978); *The Beaver* (spring 1975)
PUBLIC COLLECTIONS: C/AC/MS, C/TDB, DAM
EXHIBITS: C/AC/MS; C/AG/WP; C/CD; C/CID; C/EACTDB; C/HNG; C/IA7; C/MAD; C/TIP; C/WBEC; DAM; Musikhuset, Aarhus, Denmark
HONORS: Cape Dorset Community Council, chairman; West Baffin Eskimo Cooperative, president; Royal Canadian Academy of Arts, elected a member, 1980

KANANGINAK

An accomplished carver, Kananginak became one of the earliest printers and printmakers in the late 1950s. He mastered techniques of copper engraving, lithography, stonecutting and silkscreening. Although one of the most expert printers, he has become best known for his portraits of wildlife. His drawing style is naturalistic and he is known for the precision and accuracy of his work.

The youngest son of Pootoogook (q.v.), Kananginak is also a recognized community leader. His prints have been included in the annual print collections since 1959, and more recently he has published editions of his own designs.

KANASAWE, ELEANOR *Ojibwa*

Born 1958
RESIDENCE: Buzwah, Manitoulin Island, ON, Canada
EDUCATION: New School of Art, Toronto, ON; George Brown College, Toronto, ON
OCCUPATION: Painter
PUBLISHED: Southcott (1984)

ELEANOR KANASAWE

Kanasawe studied under Martin Panamick (q.v.). Her greatest inspiration and role model is Daphne Odjig (q.v.). Her style is described as precise, fastidious, and somewhat delicate.

Southcott 1984

KANATAKENIATE (see White, Larry)

KANAWARENTON (see Beauvais, Joseph)

Kaniatobe, Robert W. *Choctaw*
A.K.A. Robert W. Kaniweatobe
RESIDENCE: Albuquerque, NM
EXHIBITS: FCTM

Kaniweatobe, Robert W. (see Kaniatobe, Robert W.)

Kanribeloka (see The Crow)

Kaquitts, Frank *Cree/Stoney*
Sitting Wind
Born 1930 on Hobbema Reserve, AB, Canada
EDUCATION: C/BSFA
HONORS: Head chief of the Bearspaw band

Karonhesake (see Fadden, Elizabeth)

Karoniakesom (see Thomas, Harold Gesso)

Karpik, Pauloosie *Inuit (Eskimo)*
Born 1911; died 1988
RESIDENCE: Lived in Pangnirtung, NWT, Canada
OCCUPATION: Whaler and graphic artist
PUBLISHED: Collinson (1978)
PUBLIC COLLECTIONS: C/U of AB
EXHIBITS: C/CG

Pauloosie Karpik

Many of Karpik's paintings depict his memories of whaling and whaling ships.

Kasee, Cynthia *Cherokee*
Born 3 Jan 1958
RESIDENCE: Cincinnati, OH
EDUCATION: Notre Dame Academy, MT; B.A., Thomas More College, Fort Mitchell, KY; Ph.D., Union University, Cincinnati, OH
EXHIBITS: CNM, SNAICF, RC

Kasero, Joseph J. *Laguna*
MILITARY: U.S. Army
EDUCATION: BC, ca. 1960; Santa Fe, ca. 1961
PUBLISHED: Snodgrass (1968)
EXHIBITS: MNM

Kaskalla, David *Zuni*
EDUCATION: Zuni, ca. 1961
PUBLISHED: Snodgrass (1968)
EXHIBITS: MNM

Kaskaske, David *Otoe/Missouri*
Born 29 July 1953 in Pawnee, OK; son of Adam and Betty Tohee Kaskaske
RESIDENCE: Miami, OK
EDUCATION: A.A., NEO; OSU/O; Southwestern Indian Polytechnic Institute, Albuquerque, NM
OCCUPATION: Full-time artist since 1989
MEDIA: Oil, acrylic, watercolor, and pencil
EXHIBITS: CNM; TWF; American Indian Heritage Center, Inc., Tulsa, OK
AWARDS: CNM ('91; '93; '94, 1st)
HONORS: American Indian Heritage Center, Tulsa, OK, Artist of the Month, 1992

David Kaskaske

Essentially a self-taught artist, Kaskaske paints Plains Indians in a realistic style. His favorite subjects are portraits or warriors on horseback. His paintings are usually sold before he finishes them; therefore, it is difficult for him to amass a sufficient number for exhibits.

Katahke (see Palmer, Woodrow Wilson)

KATEXAC, BERNARD T. *Eskimo*

Born 22 May 1922 on King Island, AK; son of Annie and Simon Katexac

RESIDENCE: Nome, AK

EDUCATION: A.A., U of AK/C, 1967

OCCUPATION: Artist

MEDIA: Oil, watercolor, ivory, wood, and prints

PUBLISHED: Snodgrass (1968); Ray (1969). *Alaskan Journal* (fall 1972); *Alaska Geographic* (Vol. 22, no. 3, 1985)

PUBLIC COLLECTIONS: IACB; Quyanna Care Center, Nome, AK

EXHIBITS: MFA/AH; PAC; Juneau and Nome, AK in public buildings

HONORS: BIA Scholarship (first Eskimo to attend U of AK on a BIA scholarship for native Alaskan artists)

BERNARD T. KATEXAC

"The artist is from an isolated island in the Bering Sea. He branched out from ivory carving to painting in oils and watercolors and has been successful in applying the three-dimensional quality of ivory sculpture to wood."

Snodgrass 1968

Since his retirement in 1992, Katexac has produced a limited amount of art.

artist, p.c. 1990

KATONEY, JEANETTE *Navajo*

A.K.A. Jan Katoney

MEDIA: Oil

PUBLISHED: Jacka and Jacka (1994). *Arizona Highways* (Nov 1992)

HONORS: *Grants:* Lovena Ohl Foundation, development grant, 1993

JEANETTE KATONEY

Inspired by her mother, a weaver, Katoney started painting in 1988.

KA TSIDE *San Juan*

PUBLISHED: Snodgrass (1968)

EXHIBITS: AIEC

KATSIEKODIE, CHARLIE (see Washakie, Charles)

KATSINA (see Goya, Robert)

KAVANAUGH, BRADLEY PAUL *Ojibwa*

EXHIBITS: C/AG/TB, C/LS

KAVAVOA *Inuit (Eskimo)*

A.K.A. Kavavoala; Kavavook; Pudlalik Qatsiya

Born 1942

RESIDENCE: Cape Dorset, NWT, Canada

OCCUPATION: Printmaker and graphic artist

MEDIA: Black pencil

PUBLISHED: Houston (1967); Larmour (1967); Goetz, et al. (1977)

EXHIBITS: C/CD, C/TIP

KAVAVOALA (see Kavova)

KAVAVOOK (see Kavova)

KAVIK, JOHN *Inuit (Eskimo)*

A.K.A. Qavik

Born 1897 at Gjoa Haven, NWT, Canada

RESIDENCE: Chesterfield Inlet, NWT, Canada

OCCUPATION: Sculptor, ceramist, and graphic artist

MEDIA: Colored pencil

PUBLISHED: Jackson and Nasby (1987)

PUBLIC COLLECTIONS: C/AC/MS

EXHIBITS: C/CID, C/AC/MS

JOHN KAVIK

Already an accomplished sculptor, Kavik began to draw in 1979 at the request of Stanley Zazelenchuk, a teacher in Rankin Inlet.

Jackson and Nasby 1987

KAWENNINON (see Thompson, Marita)

KAW'LAHNOHNDAUMAH (see Odle Pah)

KAYARVENA, WALTER *Hopi*

Birth date unknown; born at Shipaulovi, Second Mesa, AZ

PUBLISHED: Snodgrass (1968)

PUBLIC COLLECTIONS: LMA/BC

KAYE, ELROY *Navajo*

A.K.A. Elroy Kay

Born 1 Aug 1954 near Kayenta, AZ

RESIDENCE: Fruitland, NM

EDUCATION: Monument Valley (AZ) High School; IAIA, 1974-1976

OCCUPATION: Artist

MEDIA: Oil, acrylic, watercolor, pastel, pen and ink, and charcoal

PUBLISHED: New (1973)

BOOKS ILLUSTRATED: Illustrated report for Center for Anthropological Studies and Research, Albuquerque, NM

COMMISSIONS: *Murals:* Ned A. Hatathli Museum, Tsaile, AZ, financed by Metropolitan Life Foundation; Navajo Tribe, murals for bookmobile

PUBLIC COLLECTIONS: IAIA, MNA

EXHIBITS: ACS/MV, IAIA, ITIC, MNA, NICCAS, NMSF, NTF, NTM, RC, SN; see also Awards

SOLO/SPECIAL EXHIBITS: NTM (dual show)

AWARDS: ACS/MV; ITIC ('81; '86; '88; '89, 2-1st, Best in Category, Best in Class); MNA; NMSF ('77, 1st; '78); NTF ('79, 1st; '80, '82); SN; Aztec (NM) Festival ('83)

HONORS: Scholastic Award for Achievement in Arts, Phoenix, AZ, 1973; NTF, poster artist, 1983

KAYE, WILMER *Hopi*

OCCUPATION: *Katsina* carver and painter

MEDIA: Watercolor and cottonwood root

PUBLISHED: Snodgrass (1968). *Art-Talk* (Nov 1983); *Arizona Highways* (May 1986); *The Indian Trader* (Oct 1987)

PUBLIC COLLECTIONS: MAI

EXHIBITS: ASM; SNAICF; Autumn Indian Days, Sedona, AZ, 1983; Fiesta de la Tlaquepaque, Sedona, AZ, 1987; Crow Canyon Exhibition, Washington, D.C., 1994

AWARDS: SNAICF (1987)

KAYURYUK, SAMSON *Inuit (Eskimo)*

Born 1927

RESIDENCE: Canada

OCCUPATION: Graphic artist

MEDIA: Pencil and colored pencil

PUBLISHED: Latocki, ed. (1983)

PUBLIC COLLECTIONS: C/AG/WP

EXHIBITS: C/AG/WP

KEAHBONE, ELBERT E. (see Keahbone, Ernie)

KEAHBONE, ERNIE *Kiowa*

To-Gem-Hote, Blue Jay

A.K.A. Elbert E. Keahbone

Born 1933 west of Anadarko, OK, on the Keahbone family farm; son of Mark Keahbone; M/GM: Eva Geikaunmah, the granddaughter of Silverhorn (q.v.), Kiowa artist

RESIDENCE: Anadarko, OK
EDUCATION: St. Patrick's, 1952; OCLA
OCCUPATION: Carpet tufting machine operator and painter
MEDIA: Watercolor
PUBLISHED: Blackboy, et al. (1973); Boyd, et al. (1981). *39th American Indian Exposition* (1980), program cover; *The Anadarko (OK) Daily News, Visitors Guide* (16 May 1992), cover
COMMISSIONS: Oklahoma Indian Arts and Crafts Cooperative, Anadarko, OK, tipi cover, 1973
PUBLIC COLLECTIONS: IACB
EXHIBITS: AIE; CSPIP; GPM; PAC; SPIM; in AZ, MO, NM, OK, and Washington, D.C.
SOLO EXHIBITS: Indian Peace Treaty and Pageant, Medicine Lodge, KS
AWARDS: AIE ('66, 1st; '67; '68; '69; '71; '72; '75)

KEAHBONE, GEORGE CAMPBELL *Kiowa*

Asaute
Born 29 Jan 1916 near Anadarko, OK; son of Frances Fletcher and Mark Keahbone; nephew of Spencer Asah (q.v.)
RESIDENCE: Santa Fe, NM
MILITARY: U.S. Navy, WWII
EDUCATION: BC High School, 1934; Santa Fe, 1936; attended Taos, 1947-1948
MEDIA: Tempera
PUBLISHED: Jacobson and d'Ucel (1950); LaFarge (1956); Dunn (1968); Snodgrass (1968); Brody (1971); Broder (1981). *Magazine Tulsa* (May 1948); *Paintings by American Indians*, CPLH (1962); *The Anadarko (OK) Daily News, Visitors Guide* (16 May 1992), cover
PUBLIC COLLECTIONS: CGPS, GM, IACB/DC, JAM, MAI, MNA/KHC, MNH/A, MNM, MRFM, PAC, U of OK
EXHIBITS: AIE; AIW; CGPS; CPLH; ITIC; JAM; MFA/O; MNM; NGA; OU/ET; OU/MA/T; PAC; PAC/T; SFWF; Harwood Foundation, Taos, NM; Vassar College, Poughkeepsie, NY
AWARDS: AIE, ITIC, MNM, PAC

GEORGE CAMPBELL KEAHBONE

"While at Bacone, Princess Ataloa, the arts and crafts instructor, encouraged him to develop his artistic talent and to the attend Santa Fe Indian School where he could study under Dorothy Dunn."

Snodgrass 1968

As of 1968, Keahbone was still living in the southwest.

KEAHBONE, GORDON *Kiowa/Taos*

Born 1943; son of Tonita Luján and George Campbell Keahbone (qq.v.)
RESIDENCE: Santa Fe, NM
EDUCATION: U of AZ, "Southwest Indian Art Project," scholarship, summer 1960
PUBLISHED: Snodgrass (1968)

KEE (see Gorman, Alfred Kee)

KEE, ANDERSEN *Navajo*

Born 1959 in Ganado, AZ
RESIDENCE: Taos, NM
EDUCATION: Chinle (AZ) High School; A.A., IAIA, 1979; CCAC
OCCUPATION: Silversmith, sculptor, and painter
MEDIA: Oil, stone, and silver
PUBLISHED: Jacka and Jacka (1994). *The Santa Fean* (Apr 1992)
EXHIBITS: IAIA; galleries in New Mexico

ANDERSEN KEE

Kee is best known for his oil portraits of Indian figures against simple backgrounds, although some of his paintings combine portraiture and landscape. His early works were landscapes and story paintings and he occasionally returns to those subjects for a change of pace. Kee is also a skilled silversmith and sculptor.

KEEGO, HANNA (see Kigusiuq, Hannah)

KEEGOASEAT (see Kigusiuq, Hannah)

KEEGOOSEEOT (see Kigusiuq, Hannah)

KEEGOOSEEOT, JANET (see Kigusiuq, Janet)

KEEGOOSEOT (see Kigusiuq, Hannah)

KEEGOOSIUT (see Kigusiuq, Hannah)

KEEJANA, ORESTON *Hopi*

PUBLISHED: Snodgrass (1968)
EXHIBITS: OU/SM

KEELEEMEOMEE *Inuit (Eskimo)*

A.K.A. Keekeeleemeoome Samualie
Born 31 July 1919; died 7 Dec 1983
RESIDENCE: Lived in Canada
PUBLISHED: Collinson (1978). *The Beaver* (spring 1975)
PUBLIC COLLECTIONS: C/U of AB
EXHIBITS: C/CG

KEELER, DONEL *Cree/Creek/Santee Sioux*

RESIDENCE: Omaha, NE
EDUCATION: Central High School, Omaha, NE
EXHIBITS: RC; Rapid City, MT; Brigham City, UT; see also Awards
AWARDS: Church of Jesus Christ of Latter Day Saints Exhibit, Omaha, NE; Brigham City, UT (2-1st)

KEENER, BUDDY *Cherokee*

EXHIBITS: FCTM
AWARDS: FCTM ('77; '81; '84)

KEEP FROM THE WATER (see Wa Wa Chaw)

KEETI AHNII (see Draper, Teddy, Sr.)

KEETI BAHI (see Draper, Teddy, Sr.)

KEETSIE (see Shirley, Charles)

KEETSIE, SHIRLEY (see Shirley, Charles)

KEEVAMA, DAVID *Hopi*

Born 6 Mar 1924 in Shungopovi, Second Mesa, AZ
MILITARY: U.S. Navy, WWII
EDUCATION: Santa Fe
OCCUPATION: Grand Canyon National Park employee; Navajo Army Depot inspector, and painter
MEDIA: Watercolor
PUBLISHED: Snodgrass (1968); Seymour (1988)
PUBLIC COLLECTIONS: IACB/DC; Elkus Collection
EXHIBITS: WRTD

DAVID KEEVAMA

According to the artist, his painting was limited to the time he attended Santa Fe.

Seymour 1988

KEHDOYAH (see Battese, Stanley)

KEIGHLEY, RAY *Cree (?)*

Born 1952
EDUCATION: Calgary (AB) Arts Centre, 1967-1969; C/U of SK, 1983-1988
OCCUPATION: Painter and printmaker
PUBLISHED: *Saskatchewan Indian Magazine* (July/Aug 1988)

BOOKS ILLUSTRATED: Cree Indian Language Program, three readers
COMMISSIONS: *Murals:* Duck Lake, SK. *Paintings:* Indian Cultural Calendar, three paintings; Saskatchewan Department of Agriculture, painting for poster; Saskatchewan Potash Corporation, painting for greeting cards
PUBLIC COLLECTIONS: C/INAC; Saskatchewan Education and Fifth House Publishing; Saskatchewan Indian Language Program; Saskatchewan Arts Board
EXHIBITS: C/U of SK; Francis Morrison Library Gallery
HONORS: Bishop James Mahoney High School, artist-in-residence, 1986

KEITH, C. HOBART *Sioux*
Blue Horse
RESIDENCE: Lived in Pine Ridge, SD
PUBLISHED: Snodgrass (1968)
PUBLIC COLLECTIONS: HCC
EXHIBITS: HCC, PAC

KEITH, SIDNEY JOHN *Hunkpapa Sioux*
Little Chief
Born 14 Oct 1919 in Lantry, SD, on the Cheyenne River Reservation
RESIDENCE: Eagle Butte, SD
MILITARY: U.S. Air Force, WW II
EDUCATION: Cheyenne Agency Boarding School, 1921-1939; Phoenix, 1939-1941
OCCUPATION: Sign painting service owner, illustrator, cartoon artist, designer, Public Health Service employee, author, lecturer, art teacher, and painter
MEDIA: Watercolor and tempera
PUBLISHED: Snodgrass (1968); *Sioux Dictionary* (author); a biographical publication
COMMISSIONS: *Murals:* Eagle Butte, SD; Phoenix (AZ) Indian School
EXHIBITS: RC; Arizona and Wyoming
SOLO EXHIBITS: SIM
HONORS: Minneconjou Culture Society, president, 1970; Sioux Nation Arts Council, Eagle Butte, SD, president, 1971-1975

SIDNEY JOHN KEITH

Keith started painting while in high school in 1937. The Second World War interrupted his artistic development, but he resumed his painting career after completing military service.

brochure, SIM, 1974

Keith's lifetime ambition is to preserve the culture, religion, and art of the Plains Indians.

KELHOYOMA, C. T. *Hopi*
PUBLISHED: Snodgrass (1968)
PUBLIC COLLECTIONS: MAI, MNM

KEMOHA (see Patterson, Pat)

KEMP, RANDY *Yuchi/Choctaw*
EXHIBITS: BC/McG, FCTM, HM/G, NTF
AWARDS: HM/G ('80); NTF

KENO, FRANKIE *Paiute/Shoshoni*
Born 13 Sept 1943 in Fallon, NV
EDUCATION: Las Vegas (NV) Public School, 1961; IAIA, 1962
PUBLISHED: Snodgrass (1968)
EXHIBITS: PAC, SN, YAIA

KENOJUAK *Inuit (Eskimo)*
A.K.A. Full name: Kenojuak Udluriaq Amaro Siaja Ashevak; Kenojouk; Kenoyuak; Kinojvack
Born 3 Oct 1927 at Ikerrasak on Southern Baffin Island, NWT, Canada; daughter of Seelaki and Ushuakjuk; wife of Johnniebo (q.v.); P/GP: Echalook and Alareak; M/GP: Koweesa and Kenojuak; niece of Lucy Qinnuayuak (q.v.)

Kenojuak

In 1957, Kenojuak was the first woman in Cape Dorset to make drawings. Although she is best known as Kenojuak, her work has been signed or signed for her in various ways: early works were identified by the notations Ken, Keno or Kenojuak (also spelled Kenoyouk, Kenouyouk, Kenoyoak); since 1962-1963, they have been signed in syllabics in the lower right corner; after 1970, when surnames were chosen, occasionally she has added Ashevak.

Kenojuak uses a few basic themes and subject matter, i.e., birds, human faces, and animals, although she is best known for her birds. Inuit myths and legends do not appear in her drawings. No attempt is made to depict her subjects realistically; her primary concern is with the over-all appearance of the image, its form and color. It is her desire to "make something beautiful, that's all."

Blodgett 1981

RESIDENCE: Cape Dorset, NWT, Canada

OCCUPATION: Wife, mother, craftsperson, carver, and graphic artist

MEDIA: Acrylic, watercolor, graphite, felt tip pen, colored pencil, crayon, ball point pen, seal skin, beads, and prints

PUBLISHED: Houston (1967; 1967); Larmour (1967); Burland (1973); Goetz, et al. (1977); Routledge (1979); LaBarge (1986); Jackson and Nasby (1987); McMasters, et al. (1993); Leroux, Jackson, and Freeman, eds. (1994). *Artscanada* (Vol. 28, no. 6, 1971-1972); *North* (Jan/Feb 1970; May/June 1970; Mar/Apr 1974); *The Beaver* (spring 1975); *UNESCO Courier* (Jan 1976); *Inuit Art Quarterly* (winter 1994)

BOOKS ILLUSTRATED: Blodgett (1985)

COMMISSIONS: *Murals:* Canadian Pavilion at Expo '70, Osaka, Japan. *Stamps:* Print used for 17-cent stamp in the Canadian Post Office's Inuit stamp series, 1980; Six-cent stamp commemorating the centennial of the Northwest Territories. *Prints:* World Wildlife Fund, print for portfolio, 1977; Commonwealth Games in Edmonton, AB, 1978; C/INAC, print to commemorate the signing of the Inuit Land Claims Agreement-in-Principle, 1990; C/INAC, print to commemorate the signing ceremony for the Tungavik Federation of Nunavut Settlement Agreement, 1993. *Other:* Alcan Aluminum, drawing for use on tray, 1963; Canadian Conference of Catholic Bishops, drawing for Sunday Mass book, 1976; Canadian Arctic Co-operative Federation, emblem for the Northern Images stores, 1978; Theo Waddington, portfolio of 12 lithographs (1979), 6 prints (1980)

PUBLIC COLLECTIONS: C/AC/MS, C/AG/V, C/AG/WP, C/CMC, C/GM, C/MCC, C/MFA/M, C/NGCA, C/ROM, C/TDB, C/U of G, C/WBEC, DAM, NMC

EXHIBITS: Partial listing of more than one hundred: C/AC/AE; C/AC/MS; C/AG/WP; C/AMR; C/CD; C/CDE; C/CID; C/CIIA; C/CMC; C/EACTDB; C/EFA; C/HNG; C/IA7; C/NGCA; C/NLC; C/TIP; DAM; FAM; GM; Brussels, Belgium; Musée d'Ethnographie, Neuchâtel, Switzerland; Robertson Galleries, Ottawa, ON

SOLO/SPECIAL EXHIBITS: C/AG/WGP, C/AG/IGEA; C/NSTC [dual show with husband, Johnniebo (q.v.)], 1974

HONORS: *Honorary degrees:* Queens University, Honorary Doctorate, 1991; University of Toronto, Honorary Doctor of Law, 1992. *Other*: National Film Board film, *Eskimo Artist – Kenojuak*, 1962; Order of Canada Medal of Service, received from the Governor General, 1967; Royal Canadian Academy, elected member, 1974; Companion to the Order of Canada, 1982

Kenojouk (see Kenojuak)

Kent, Ruben *Iowa/Kickapoo/Otoe*

Born 11 Sept 1952

PUBLIC COLLECTIONS: HCC

EXHIBITS: HCC, TM/NE

Kerakahi-to (see Red Horn Elk)

Ke Sha Ona Quat (see Haarala, Lloyd)

Kewa (see Hunt, Wolf Robe)

Kewanwytewa, Riguel *Zia/Hopi*

EDUCATION: Albuquerque, NM, ca. 1962

PUBLISHED: Snodgrass (1968)

EXHIBITS: MNM

Kewanyama, Leroy (see Kewanyouma, Leroy)

KEWANYOUMA, LEROY *Hopi*

So Kuva, Morning Star

A.K.A. Leroy Kewanyama

Born 14 Oct 1922 at Shungopovi, Second Mesa, AZ

RESIDENCE: Second Mesa, AZ

MILITARY: U.S. Navy, WWII

EDUCATION: Shungopovi, AZ

OCCUPATION: Silversmith and painter

MEDIA: Tempera, silver, and gemstone

PUBLISHED: Snodgrass (1968); Tanner (1957; 1968; 1973); Harvey (1970); Golder (1985)

PUBLIC COLLECTIONS: MAI, MNA, MNM, MNA/KHC, NPS

EXHIBITS: ASM, AC/HC, HH, PAC, PM

KEYJUAKJUK, MOSESEE *Inuit (Eskimo)*

A.K.A. Keyuakjuk

Born 1933

RESIDENCE: Pangnirtung, NWT, Canada

OCCUPATION: Graphic artist

MEDIA: Pencil

PUBLISHED: Goetz, et al. (1977)

EXHIBITS: C/TIP

KEYS, L. DANO *Chickasaw*

RESIDENCE: Tulsa, OK

EXHIBITS: FCTM, PAC

AWARDS: FCTM ('70, IH; '71, 1st; '72, 1st, IH; '73, IH; '74, 1st, IH; '75 IH; '76, 1st; '77, 1st, IH; '78, 1st, IH; '79, 1st, IH)

KEYUAKJUK (see Keyjuakjuk, Mosesee)

KGOO YA (see Gutiérrez, José Leandro)

KHUP KHU (see Luján, Tonita)

KIAKSHUK *Inuit (Eskimo)*

A.K.A. Kiaksuk

Born ca. 1886; died 1966

RESIDENCE: Lived at Cape Dorset, NWT, Canada

OCCUPATION: Camp leader, hunter, and graphic artist

MEDIA: Graphite, black pencil, and prints

PUBLISHED: Blodgett (n.d.; 1981); Houston (1967; 1967a); Larmour (1967); Burland (1973); Goetz, et al. (1977); Jordan (1979); LaBarge (1986). *The Beaver* (spring 1975)

PUBLIC COLLECTIONS: C/AC/MS, C/AG/WP, C/GM, C/WBEC, DAM

EXHIBITS: C/AC/MS, C/AG/O, C/AG/WP, C/BLQ, C/CD, C/CID, C/GM, C/LS, C/TIP, C/WBEC, DAM, GM

HONORS: Toronto (ON) International Airport, *Inukshuk*; N.F.B. film, *The Living Stone*, storyteller

KIAKSHUK

Kiakshuk was one of the first in the Cape Dorset area to begin to draw. A prolific artist, he was represented in the Cape Dorset annual collections from 1960 to 1967. He was also a very talented carver. His son, Lukta Qiatsuk, has worked in the Cape Dorset print studio since its beginnings and his daughter, Pannichea, is a graphic artist.

LaBarge 1986

KIAKSUK (see Kiakshuk)

KIAWAK *Inuit (Eskimo)*

Born 1933

RESIDENCE: Cape Dorset, NWT, Canada

OCCUPATION: Graphic artist
MEDIA: Black pencil
PUBLISHED: Houston (1967); Goetz, et al. (1977)
EXHIBITS: C/CD, C/TIP

KICKING BEAR *Oglala Sioux*

Birth date unknown; born in a camp at the Big Bend of the Yellowstone River, 1872. (see Vestal 1932; 1934)
PUBLISHED: Snodgrass (1968)
COLLECTIONS: MAI, SM

KICKING BEAR

"In 1898, the aging veteran of the Battle of the Little Big Horn was asked by Frederic Remington to paint his version of the fight. Kicking Bear complied, and the pictographic account is now at the Southwest Museum."

Snodgrass 1968

KIDD, JACK *Cherokee*

EXHIBITS: CNM, FCTM, RC
AWARDS: FCTM ('77)

KIDD, SAM *Cherokee*

RESIDENCE: Muldrow, OK
MEDIA: Pencil and pastel
EXHIBITS: CNM, FCTM, LIAS
SOLO EXHIBITS: FCTM, 1993
AWARDS: CNM ('90); FCTM ('90; '92; '94)

KIE, ROBERT A. *Laguna*

Born 1948 in Winslow, AZ
RESIDENCE: Laguna, NM
EDUCATION: St. Catherine's ca. 1965
PUBLISHED: Snodgrass (1968)
EXHIBITS: MNM, PAC, SAIEAIP

KIGUSIUQ, HANNAH *Inuit (Eskimo)*

A.K.A. Keegoaseat; Keegooseeot; Keegooseot; Keegoosiut; Hanna Keegooseeut; Keyousikuk
Born 4 July 1931 at Gary Lake, NWT, Canada
RESIDENCE: Baker Lake, NWT, Canada
OCCUPATION: Textile and graphic artist
MEDIA: Black pencil and prints
PUBLISHED: Blodgett (n.d.); Goetz, et al. (1977); Latocki, ed. (1983); Jackson and Nasby (1987). *Artscanada* (Vol. 28, no. 6, 1971-1972)
PUBLIC COLLECTIONS: C/AC/MS, C/AG/WP, C/PWNHC
EXHIBITS: C/AC/MS, C/AG/WP, C/BLPD, C/CID, C/LS, C/SC, C/TIP

KIGUSIUQ, JANET *Inuit (Eskimo)*

A.K.A. J. Kigusiuq; Janet Keegooseeot; Janet Kiqusiuq
Born 1926 at Back River, NWT, Canada; daughter of Oonark (q.v.)
RESIDENCE: Baker Lake, NWT, Canada
OCCUPATION: Textile and graphic artist
MEDIA: Pencil, colored pencil, crayon, and prints
PUBLISHED: Blodgett (1978b); Collinson (1978); Routledge (1979); Latocki, ed. (1982); Jackson and Nasby (1987). *Artscanada* (Vol. 28, no. 6, 1971-1972)
PUBLIC COLLECTIONS: C/AC/MS, C/AG/WP, C/U of AB
EXHIBITS: C/AC/MS, C/AG/O, C/AG/W, C/AG/WP, C/CG, C/CID, C/CIIA, C/IA7, C/NGCA, C/SC, C/SS, IAIA

JANET KIGUSIUQ

Kigusiuq's drawings are characterized by her portrayal of wide-eyed human figures with prominent eyelashes and her increasing use of color.

Jackson and Nasby 1987

Her work is recognized for its precise, expressive line.

KIKEKAH WAHTIANKAH (see Wagoshe, Russell William)

Killebrew, Patric B. *Assiniboin/Sioux/Chippewa*

A.K.A. Pat Killebrew

Born 19 May 1953 in Lewiston, MT; son of Bonnie Killebrew and Clarence Beauchamp; adopted by Clyde Killebrew; P/GP: Virginia Swan and Simon Beauchamp

RESIDENCE: Laurel, MT

EDUCATION: Laurel (MT) High School, 1971; Eastern Montana College, Billings, MT, 1983; Scottsdale (AZ) Artist School

OCCUPATION: Art teacher and artist

MEDIA: Oil, pencil, pen and ink, pastel, and prints

EXHIBITS: AC/Y, BSIM, NPTA, RE, UTAE; galleries in MT, UT, and WY; see also Awards

AWARDS: AC/Y, UTAE ('92, 1st); All-Montana Art Show, Sidney, MT (1st)

Kills Two *Oglala Sioux*

Born 1869 on the northeastern High Plains; died 1927 in Mellette County, SD

RESIDENCE: Lived on the Rosebud Reservation, SD

OCCUPATION: Indian Scout, Indian policeman, and painter

MEDIA: Watercolor on hide and muslin

PUBLISHED: Alexander (1938), cover; Sandoz (1961); Dunn (1968); Russell (1968); Snodgrass (1968); Libhart (1970); Highwater (1978b; 1983); Maurer (1992)

PUBLIC COLLECTIONS: C/GM, IACB, SIM

EXHIBITS: CSP, VP

Kills Two

Kills Two is said to have produced numerous paintings on hide and muslin. The subjects included: warrior pursuits, ceremonial dances, individuals on horseback, reconstructions of calendrical histories.

Libhart 1970

"It is reported that his wife placed a hide painting of a Sioux Winter Count in his coffin."

Snodgrass 1968

Kimball, Yeffe *Osage*

Mikaka Upawixe, Wandering Star

Born 30 Mar 1914 in Mountain Park, OK; died 10 Apr 1978 in Santa Fe, NM; daughter of Martha Clementine and Other Good-Man Smith

RESIDENCE: Lived in New York, NY

EDUCATION: ECSC/OK; U of OK; ASL, 1935-1939; private instruction in France and Italy, summers 1936-1939; studied intermittently with Fernand Léger, 1936-1941

OCCUPATION: Illustrator, textile designer, consultant on Native arts, and painter

PUBLISHED: Highwater (1976; 1980); Snodgrass (1968); New (1979). *Book of Knowledge*, American Indian Section (1957). *Art Digest* (1945-1949); *Art in America* (July/Aug 1972); has authored articles on American Indian art

BOOKS ILLUSTRATED: Keech (1940); Brindze (1951); Leekley (1965); Kimball and Anderson (1965)

COMMISSIONS: *Book of Knowledge* and *World Book of Knowledge,* illustrations (1957-1958)

PUBLIC COLLECTIONS: BAM, BIA, CAM/OH, CAM/MA, DAI, EB, IACB, MFA/B, MM, OSAC, PAC, PAM, SPIM, TWA, WA, WLU

EXHIBITS: Partial listing of more than one hundred includes: AGAA; BM/B; CAM/OH; FAIEAIP; MFA/A; MFA/B; MFA/CI; MHDYMM; MNM; NGA; PAIC; PU; SAIEAIP; SBM; SI; TMA; UG; W; WA; Trinity College, Hartford, CT

SOLO EXHIBITS: Partial listing of more than fifty includes: AC/R; CAM/S; DAI; DAM; DMG; FAG/S ; GG; HAU; HS/M; IDM; JAM; JKA; MNM; PAC; PAM; PAM/C; SBM; TMA; U of NM, YK/T; University of Virginia, Charlottesville, VA

AWARDS: PAC

HONORS: ASL, life member, former vice-president, and Board of Control Vice-President

Yeffe Kimball

*"In 1946, a New York critic, Henry McBride, said of Kimball: 'Georgia O'Keeffe had better watch out. Her rival now appears on the desert horizon (*The Sun, *New York, NY, 1946).' In 1965, Edgar J. Driscoll Jr., remarked: 'She has been involved with the outer reaches of space, fiery comets, and spheres, but in her more recent paintings, using acrylic resin medium and pure pigments, she works in oval shapes with concave and convex surfaces (*The Boston Globe, *MA).'"*

Snodgrass 1968

KINCAIDE, JAIWANA *Cherokee*

RESIDENCE: Oktaha, OK

EXHIBITS: CNM, FCTM

KINDIWA MI TAMSA (see English, Janelle)

KING, BRUCE *Oneida*

Born 2 Nov 1950 in Oneida, WI; son of Alberta King; M/GP: Sarah Elizabeth Baird and Albert King

RESIDENCE: Buffalo, NY

MILITARY: U.S. Army

EDUCATION: A.F.A., IAIA, 1970; U of IL/CCC

OCCUPATION: Actor, construction worker, writer, playwright, and painter

MEDIA: Oil, acrylic, watercolor, pastel, mixed-media, and prints

PUBLIC COLLECTIONS: SMII, MAI

EXHIBITS: C/WICEC; CIM; CNGM; HM; IAIA; SMII; LAG; NACLA; NMSF; PAC; QM; RC; SDMM; Niagara Community College, Sanborn, NY; Seton Hall University, South Orange, NJ, 1985; Galerie Tinteniertel, Darmstadt, Germany, 1985

SOLO EXHIBITS: U of IL, 1988; galleries in New Mexico and New York

KING, HARVEY *Assiniboin*

Born 1955 on the Fort Belknap Indian Reservation, MT

EDUCATION: IAIA; U of MT, 1977-1978; Belknap Community College, Harlem, MT

OCCUPATION: Illustrator, jeweler, writer, storyteller, and painter

EXHIBITS: CIAE/MT; GFNAAS; MPI; NAVAM; Fort Belknap Indian Agency, Harlem, MT

KING, JAMES B. *Navajo*

B'ee'dit'lo, Woolen shirt

Born 8 Aug 1951 in Shiprock, NM; son of Margaret and Jim King; P/GM: Nellie Willie; M/GP: Hettie and Jim Tom

RESIDENCE: Shiprock, NM

EDUCATION: Shiprock (NM) High School, 1971; Salt Lake City (UT) Community College, 1973

OCCUPATION: Soil technician, contract trucker, ironworker/high-rise construction; full-time sculptor and painter since 1978

MEDIA: Oil, acrylic, watercolor, pencil, pastel, stone, and prints

PUBLISHED: Samuels (1982); Jacka and Jacka (1988; 1994). *The Indian Trader* (Sept 1984)

COMMISSIONS: *Murals:* DIA, 1993

PUBLIC COLLECTIONS: ABQM, MV, SI

EXHIBITS: ABQM, ACS/MV, AICA, CIM, ITIC, NMSF, SI, SWAIA

AWARDS: ACS/MV ('94); AICA ('89, Bronze Medal; '91, Gold Medal); CIM (Best of Class); ITIC ('79; '84, Best of Class; '85, 2-1st; '86, 1st, Best in Category; '87, 1st; '88, 2-1st, Elkus Award; '89, 1st; '91, 1st; '94, 1st); NMSF ('79, Best of Show; '82, Best of Show); SWAIA ('84, Best of Class; '85, Best of Miniatures, Best of Class; '86, Best of Class; '87, Best of Miniatures)

KING, PAUL *Choctaw*

RESIDENCE: Tulsa, OK

EDUCATION: B.A., SOSU; OSU/O; OSU

OCCUPATION: Teacher and painter

EXHIBITS: AIE, CC/OK, PAC, TSF
AWARDS: AIE (Best of Show); PAC ('79)

KINGERY, BRENDA *Chickasaw*
RESIDENCE: Oklahoma City, OK
EDUCATION: U of OK
OCCUPATION: Teacher and painter
PUBLISHED: *The Santa Fean* (Aug 1994)
EXHIBITS: IAIA/M

KINGMAN, VIOLET *Sioux*
Wachato, Blue Flower
A.K.A. Violet Wilhemina Rivers Kingman
Born 7 July 1913 at the Cheyenne Agency, SD; daughter of Lizzie LeBeau and William Rivers; P/GP: Felecia Traversie and Joseph Ascard Rivers, III; M/GP: Mary Leudurant Marshall and Henry "Omala" Lebeau
RESIDENCE: Rapid City, SD
EDUCATION: Genoa Indian High School, 1933; Black Hills State College, Spearfish, SD, 1968; BBHC, 1989; LaPlace Ceramic Studio; private art schools and workshops; studied art under Oscar Howe (q.v.)
OCCUPATION: Lunch counter owner, cook, dormitory matron, student counselor, teacher, and artist
MEDIA: Watercolor, pastel, tempera, Grussiane paint, Indian paint, yarn, and clay
PUBLIC COLLECTIONS: SIM; USDI; Black Hills Art Association
EXHIBITS: SIM; Indian Art Show, Old Mother Butler Center, Rapid City, SD; Rapid City (SD) Summer Arts Festival; see also Awards
AWARDS: SIM ('89, *Webs of Realism* Award); Western Plains Ceramic Association ('84, 1st); Black Hills Exposition ('68, 1st); Eagle Butte (SD) Fair ('71, 1st; '72, 1st)
HONORS: Federal Civil Servant Exceptional Service Citation, presented by Senator Mundt, 1969; Improving Supervisory Skills Certificate

VIOLET KINGMAN

Kingman has many well-known relatives. Her great-grandfather, Antoine LeBeau, founded the town of LeBeau, SD. She is also related to Chief Four Bear, who was chief of the Two Kettle (Dohenumpa) Band. Her daughter Arlouine Gay K. Wapato is an Indian rights advocate and her son-in-law, Tim Wapato, is Commissioner of Administration for Native Americans.

artist, p.c. 1992

KINGMEATA (see Etidlooie, Kingmeata)

KINGMEATTAR (see Etidlooie, Kingmeata)

KINGMEEATTA (see Etidlooie, Kingmeata)

KINGWATSIAK, IYOLA (see Iyola)

KINYEONNY BEYEH (see Gorman, Carl Nelson)

KIRK, ERNEST *Navajo*
PUBLISHED: Snodgrass (1968)
COMMISSIONS: *Murals:* ASF Coliseum, 1965 (with four other Navajo artists)

KIRKLAND, ROY *Cherokee*
RESIDENCE: Sand Springs, OK
EXHIBITS: FCTM

KIRKPATRICK, VIRGINIA *Cherokee*
RESIDENCE: Tulsa, OK
EXHIBITS: GPM; TCBA; Tulsa (OK) International Mayfest; Children's Medical Center Art Show, Tulsa OK; Pawhuska (OK) Art Show; Stillwater (OK) Art Show; Chandler (OK) Art Show; Oklahoma Art Workshop Annual Art Competition; regional exhibits

KISHKETON, GEORGE *Kickapoo*

Nama Piaska, Splashing Water

Born 1 Feb 1919 in McLoud, OK; son of Mary Murdock and George Kishketon; GF: a Kickapoo chief

RESIDENCE: Walters, OK

EDUCATION: McLoud (OK) High School; BC, 1939-1941

PUBLISHED: Snodgrass (1968)

COMMISSIONS: *Murals:* BC

PUBLIC COLLECTIONS: GM, PAC

EXHIBITS: PAC; Skirvin Hotel, Oklahoma City, OK, 1941

KIVETORUK (see Moses, Kivetoruk)

KIYA AHNII (see Denetsosie, Hoke)

KIYAA NII (see Denetsosie, Hoke)

KLAH TSO (see Big Lefthanded)

KLEE, EDISON *Navajo*

EDUCATION: IAIA

MEDIA: Oil

EXHIBITS: ITIC

KLUTHE, VICKI RICH *Creek*

RESIDENCE: Bellevue, WA

EXHIBITS: CNM, LIAS

AWARDS: LIAS ('89, MA)

KNIFFIN, GUS *Apache/Shoshoni*

A.K.A. Ralph Kniffin

Born 1947 on the San Carlos Apache Indian Reservation, AZ; son of Sadie Stevens and Spike Kniffin

RESIDENCE: San Carlos, AZ

MILITARY: U.S. Marines, Vietnam

EDUCATION: IAIA; ASU

OCCUPATION: Draftsman, writer, poet, and artist

MEDIA: Oil, pen and ink, Prismacolor, and prints

PUBLISHED: Medina (1981). *The Indian Trader* (July 1978; July 1985); *The Arizona Republic* (29 Apr 1981); *The Scottsdale Daily Progress* (1 Jan 1982); *Southwest Art* (June 1982)

EXHIBITS: AC/HC; HM; HM/G; SN; The Arizona Sanctuary Defense Fund, 1985

AWARDS: HM/G ('74; '75, 1st; '76, 1st, Woodard Award; '77, 1st); SN ('67)

KNIFFIN, RALPH (see Kniffin, Gus)

KNIGHT, L. *Ponca*

PUBLISHED: Snodgrass (1968)

PUBLIC COLLECTIONS: PAC

KNOTT, NORMAN *Ojibwa*

Born 1945 on the Curve Lake Indian Reserve, ON, Canada

RESIDENCE: Curve Lake Indian Reserve, ON, Canada

OCCUPATION: Odd jobs, hunting and fishing guide, construction worker, and painter

GUS KNIFFIN

Kniffin is best known for his pen and ink and colored pencil drawings, which border on the art deco style. He described his work as "designs with things like hawks, owls, eagles, women, and horses integrated into the design." A poet as well as an artist, Kniffin sometimes creates blank verse to complement a drawing.

NORMAN KNOTT

Knott's experiences as a hunting and fishing guide have led him to paint animals, and the legends and myths about them. His most common subjects are the thunderbird, turtle, butterfly, loon, and Canadian goose. His paintings express his love of the outdoors and depict life, which he feels must be preserved. Knott's paintings are identified by an annual "series" sign beside his signature: "Soul" series are his works prior to 1977; "Thunderbird" series, 1977 to 1978; and "Bear Paw" series, 1978.

Southcott 1984

MEDIA: Acrylic

PUBLISHED: Southcott (1984). *Artcrafts* (winter 1976); *The Coburg Daily Star* (14 June 1978); *Peterborough Examiner* (15 Sept 1979); *The Borckville Recorder* (1 Nov 1983); *The Calgary Herald* (22 Aug 1989)

COMMISSIONS: Peterborough (ON) Sports Hall of Fame, logo

PUBLIC COLLECTIONS: C/MCC; C/TU; HCC; Canadian General Electronic, Peterborough (ON) Civic Hospital; Quakers Oats Company, Peterborough, ON; Sir Sanford Fleming College, Peterborough, ON; Victoria and Grey Trust Company

EXHIBITS: C/AG/W; C/NCCT; C/WICEC; NACLA; Buckhorn (ON) Community Centre; Commonwealth Institute, Kensington, London, England, 1982; galleries in Ontario

KNOWS GUN, ELLIS *Crow*

A.K.A. Rabbit Knows Gun

Born 2 Sept 1948 at Crow Agency, MT; son of Mamie Hogan and Paul Knows Gun; P/GP: Knows Gun (Driftwood); M/GP: Helen Goes Ahead and George Hogan Sr.

RESIDENCE: Crow Agency, MT

MILITARY: U.S. Army, Vietnam

EDUCATION: Hardin High School, St. Labré High School, Ashland, MT, 1967; U of MT; A.A., Little Big Horn College, Crow Agency, MT; EMC

OCCUPATION: Crow Tribe Reclamation Director; artist since 1973

MEDIA: Oil, acrylic, watercolor, pencil, pen and ink, pastel, and prints

PUBLIC COLLECTIONS: GSW; MPI; Carbon County Arts Guild, Red Lodge, MT; Western State Art Federation, Santa Fe, NM

EXHIBITS: Partial listing of more than thirty includes: BSIM; EMC; MPI; NPTA; RC; SLM; SUNY/RCC; Carbon County Arts Guild, Red Lodge, MT; Little Big Horn Days, Hardin, MT; Yellowstone County Exhibition, Billings, MT; see also Awards

SOLO EXHIBITS: MPI

AWARDS: BSIM ('91); RC ('74, Woodard Award); Native American Fish and Wildlife Society, Broomfield, CO ('90, 1st); Bronx (NY) Zoo ('91, 1st); Fort Washakie (WY) Tribal Fair ('86, 1st)

HONORS: Merton McCluskey Fund, scholarship, 1990

ELLIS KNOWS GUN

Knows Gun is descended from Chief Long Hair, also know as Red Plume in Temple, and He Who Jumps Over Every One, who was painted by George Catlin in 1834. He is also related to Hector Knows Gun, a professional wrestler in the 1920s, and Harvey Driftwood, who received a Silver Star in World War II.

According to Knows Gun, "As an artist I enjoy using a variety of media to enhance my paintings with strong patriotic and religious elements. Using a myriad of cultural themes in a symbolic manner, I combine my Native American values with European values and merge the contemporary with the historical. As a God-given talent I feel that my art is an instrument, whereby God allows me to enrich people's lives with His love for all people. It is my hope and prayer that my paintings will allow people to draw closer to the Lord (Jesus) as we understand Him. As a born-again Christian, I acknowledge His love and presence in my life."

p.c. 1992

KNOWS GUN, RABBIT (see Knows Gun, Ellis)

KNOXSAH, DAVID *Kickapoo*

Born 5 Oct 1948

RESIDENCE: Kansas City, KS

EDUCATION: Chilocco

EXHIBITS: RC; Leavenworth (KS) Plaza Art Show; Wichita (KS) Art Show

KOBA (see Wild Horse)

KOCHA (see Tiger, Jerome Richard)

KOCHA HONAWU *Hopi*

PUBLISHED: Snodgrass (1968)

PUBLIC COLLECTIONS: DAM

KODASEET, ALFRED CALISAY *Kiowa*

Born 1919

EDUCATION: BC, ca. 1938

PUBLISHED: Snodgrass (1968)
EXHIBITS: AIW, OU/MA/T

KOKETHA (see Murdock, Cecil)

KOLAY, JOSH *Dene Tha'*

A.K.A. Josue Kolay
Birth date unknown; son of Elise and Simon Kolay; P/GP: Gata Nee and Johnny Kolay; M/GP: Marie and Paul Metchooyeah; related to Chief Harry Chonkolay, Dene Tha' chief for over fifty years
RESIDENCE: Chateh, AB, Canada
EDUCATION: St. Joseph's Comprehensive High School, Edmonton, AB, 1974; C/U of C, 1976-1978
OCCUPATION: Publisher of *North American Indian Artisan* and painter
MEDIA: Oil, acrylic, watercolor, pencil, pen and ink, and prints
PUBLIC COLLECTIONS: In most of the forty Indian Bands Reserves in Alberta
EXHIBITS: C/IAC; C/IFNA; C/GNAF; more than forty additional shows and markets in the U.S.; see also Awards
AWARDS: Peace Hills Trust Co. Annual Exhibition, Edmonton, AB

KOOKEEYOUT (see Kukiiyaut, Myra)

KOOKEEYOUT, ANINGNERK (see Kookeeyout, Ruby A.)

KOOKEEYOUT, RUBY A. *Inuit (Eskimo)*

A.K.A. Aningnerk Kookeeyout
RESIDENCE: Baker Lake, NWT
OCCUPATION: Graphic artist
PUBLISHED: *Artscanada* (Vol. 28, no. 6, 1971/72)
EXHIBITS: C/SS

KOOKEYOUT (see Kukiiyaut, Myra)

KOO PEEN (see Atencio, Pat)

KOPELEY *Hopi*

PUBLISHED: Snodgrass (1968)
PUBLIC COLLECTIONS: MNM

KOVINATILLAK (see Kovinatillah)

KOVINATILLIAH *Inuit (Eskimo)*

A.K.A. Kovinatillak
RESIDENCE: Cape Dorset, NWT, Canada
OCCUPATION: Graphic artist
PUBLISHED: Larmour (1967). *Artscanada* (Vol. 28, no. 6, 1971-1972)
PUBLIC COLLECTIONS: C/TDB
EXHIBITS: C/EACTDB

KRALVAK (see Kalvak, Helen)

KUCHA HONAWAH (see White Bear)

KUCHA HONAWUH (see White Bear)

KUDLUARLIK, KAKASILDA *Inuit (Eskimo)*

RESIDENCE: Pangnirtung, NWT, Canada
PUBLISHED: Collinson (1978)
PUBLIC COLLECTIONS: C/U of AB

EXHIBITS: C/CG
HONORS: President of Co-op in 1975

KUGEE (see Supernaw, Kugee)

KUKA, KING *Blackfeet*

See Kooks Ee Nah, Blackwolf

Born 1946 in Browning, MT; son of Grace Pepion and Merrel Kuka; P/GP: Martha Rutherford and Joseph Kuka; M/GP: Mabel Davis and Chester Pipon; Artist is a descendant of Mountain Chief.

RESIDENCE: Great Falls, MT

MILITARY: U.S. Army, Vietnam

EDUCATION: IAIA, 1965-1966; B.F.A., U of MT, 1973; M.A. candidate, MSU

OCCUPATION: Educator, gallery owner, personnel director, writer, poet, sculptor; full-time artist since 1979

MEDIA: Oil, acrylic, watercolor, pencil, pen and ink, pastel, stone, bronze, and prints

PUBLISHED: Snodgrass (1968); Allen (1972); Highwater (1980); Medina (1981); Samuels (1982); Fawcett and Callander (1982); Louis (1989). *The Indian Trader* (Apr 1980); *The Tempe Daily News* (21 Feb 1981); *Art Voices* (Sept/Oct 1981); *Art-Talk* (Feb 1982; Mar 1986; Mar 1988); *Southwest Art* (June 1982); *The Scottsdale Daily Progress* (3 June 1983); *The Eagle* (June/July 1988)

BOOKS ILLUSTRATED: Authored and illustrated the children's story, *Ay See Mu Kow*

COMMISSIONS: Browning (MT) High School, sculpture; National Tekakwitha Conference, three bronze statues; Little Flower Church, Browning, MT, designed twenty stained-glass windows

PUBLIC COLLECTIONS: C/CMC; C/WAG; GM; HCC; HM; IAIA; MAI; MNH/CL; MNH/D; MPI; NACLA; RC; Deutsches Museum, Munich, Germany; Museum of Natural History, San Diego, CA; Vatican Collection, Italy; embassies in Germany and Israel

EXHIBITS: AAID; ACMWA; AICA/SF; C/CS; C/IFNA; CNM; GFNAAS; HCC; HM/G; HNAAE; HPTU; IAIA; ITIC; KCPA; LC; LSS; MAI ; MCC/CA; MPI; MSU; NAVAM; NPTA; PAC; RC; RE; RM; SFFA; SI; SMIC; SN; SNAICF; SWAIA; TM/NE; U of MT; U of WV; USDI; WTF; YAIA; Native American Art Expo., Helena, MT; American Fair, Kumamoto, Japan

SOLO EXHIBITS: MPI; U of MT; Ketterer Art Center, Bozeman, MT; galleries in AZ, CA, CO, MT, NM, WY, and TX

AWARDS: Partial listing of more than forty includes: AAID ('73, 1st); GFNAAS ('87; '89, Jurors' Award of Excellence); HM/G ('69, Motorola Award; '71; '79); ITIC ('79, 1st); LC ('88, 1st); MSU ('69, 1st; '71, 2-1st); NPTA ('88, 1st; '89, 1st, Artist of the Year; '91; '92); RC ('78, 1st; '79; '81, 1st; '82, Begay Award; '83; '84; '85; '86, 1st; '89; '90, '93, 1st); SMIC ('90, Best of Class); SNAICF ('88, 1st)

HONORS: C/CS, "Quick Draw Artist," 1991; Native American Art Expo, Helena, MT, featured artist, 1984; GFNAAS, featured artist, 1984; NPTA, poster artist, 1989

KING KUKA

Kuka's style has changed dramatically over the years. He started out painting realistically in the style of Charlie Russell, but wasn't satisfied and started to experiment. His experiments have evolved into a mystical impressionistic style. According to Kuka, "I like to be free. I want my paintings to be the same. Realism and detail are fine for those who do it, but my temperament is not tolerant of that. People say 'you have so much patience.' I don't have any patience. If I did, I wouldn't be much of an artist."
Art Voices, *Sept/Oct 1981*

KUKIIYAUT, MYRA *Inuit (Eskimo)*

A.K.A. Kookeeyout; Kookeyout; Kukiyaut; Kuukiyaut; Myra Kakhyaut

Born 1929

RESIDENCE: Baker Lake, NWT

OCCUPATION: Graphic artist

MEDIA: Colored pencil, graphite, and prints

PUBLISHED: Goetz, et al. (1977); Blodgett (1978a), Collinson (1978), Latocki

MYRA KUKIIYAUT

Kukiiyaut was born at Baker Lake and returned when her children started school so they would not have to stay in foster homes. She said her first drawings were done in 1967, but she quit because she didn't like them. In 1970, she decided to try again and continued to draw for some time. She also produced prints for about three years. Her drawings are always representational and are of hunting, spirit transformations, birds in flight, and the teachings of the Anglican Church.

(1982); Jackson and Nasby (1987); McMasters, et al. (1993). *Artscanada* (Vol. 30, nos. 5 & 6, 1972-1974)

PUBLIC COLLECTIONS: C/AC/MS, C/AG/WP, C/PWNHC, C/U of AB

EXHIBITS: C/AC/MS, C/AG/O, C/AG/W, C/AG/WP, C/BLPD, C/CID, C/CG, C/TIP, C/SC, C/SS

KUKIYAUT (see Kukiiyaut, Myra)

KUMMOK QUIVVIOKTA (see Wooden Leg)

KUNU (see Kuyu)

KUOFDE (see Sánchez, Ramos)

KUPERU OR KU PE RU (see Suina, Theodore)

KU SE PEEN (see Vigil, Tim)

KUTCA HONAUU (see White Bear)

KUUKIYAUT (see Kukiiyaut, Myra)

KUYU *Inuit (Eskimo)*

A.K.A. Kunu

Born 1923; died 1966

RESIDENCE: Lived in Cape Dorset, NWT, Canada

OCCUPATION: Graphic artist

PUBLISHED: Collinson (1978)

PUBLIC COLLECTIONS: C/TDB, C/U of AB

EXHIBITS: C/CG, C/EACTDB

KUYU

Kuyu was one of the original women artists at Cape Dorset. Her prints, along with those of her husband, Niviaqsi, appeared in the Cape Dorset graphic collections as early as 1959. She was seriously ill with tuberculosis in her later years.

Collison 1978

KWA NE RA TA IENI (see Haarala, Lloyd)

KWAYA TSEECK TCHUSS MIYUH (see Frank, Charlie)

KWYATSEEOK TOHUSS MIYUH (see Frank, Charlie)

KYASH PETRACH (see Byrnes, James Michael)

DETAIL: Calvin Larvie, *Buffalo Dance*, 1942. Philbrook Museum of Art, Tulsa, Oklahoma

LABAN, ANTHONY *Hopi*
PUBLIC COLLECTIONS: MNA

LACAPA, MICHAEL *Apache/Hopi/Tewa*
RESIDENCE: Taylor, AZ
EDUCATION: B.A., ASU; M.A., U of N AZ
OCCUPATION: Museum exhibits installation worker, storyteller, author, illustrator, and painter
PUBLISHED: *The Indian Trader* (Apr 1990)
BOOKS ILLUSTRATED: Ekkehart (1988); Lacapa (1990); Lacapa and Lacapa (1994)
EXHIBITS: FNAA; HM/G; MNA; WMNAAF; High Desert Show, Jerome, AZ, 1986.
SOLO EXHIBITS: Arizona Bank, Sedona, AZ
AWARDS: HM/G ('80, Arizona Bank Award); MNA ('86, 1st; '87, 1st; '89, 1st)
HONORS: WMNAAF, poster artist, 1988, 1989; FNAA poster artist, 1990

LACY, JEAN DODGE *Delaware*
EXHIBITS: CNM

LACY, KATE *Cherokee*
RESIDENCE: Ponca City, OK
EXHIBITS: FCTM
AWARDS: FCTM ('77)

LADD, EDMUND JAMES *Zuni*
Fleetfoot; *Helele*; *Lapilakwa*; *Llapilaokya*
A.K.A. Edmond Ladd
Born 4 Jan 1926 at Fort Yuma, AZ
RESIDENCE: Santa Fe, NM
EDUCATION: Zuni; M.A., U of NM
OCCUPATION: Archaeologist and painter
PUBLISHED: Snodgrass (1968)
PUBLIC COLLECTIONS: BIA, MAI
EXHIBITS: MNM

LADY IN THE SUN (see Morgan, Judith Phyllis)

LAFFERTY, DUANE *Oglala Sioux*
Born 1947 on the Pine Ridge Reservation, SD
RESIDENCE: Kyle, SD
EDUCATION: Oglala Community High School, Pine Ridge, SD, 1964-1965; IAIA, 1966-1968; National College of Business, Rapid City, SD
PUBLISHED: Libhart (1970)
PUBLIC COLLECTIONS: IACB, IAIA
EXHIBITS: CSP, OWE, PAC, RC

LAFFERTY, ROBERT *Sioux*
Born 11 Feb 1960
RESIDENCE: Pine Ridge, SD
EDUCATION: Burns Union High; U of SD
EXHIBITS: RC

LA FLESCHE, SUSETTE (see Tibbles, Susette La Flesche)

LA FONTAINE, GLEN *Cree/Chippewa*

EXHIBITS: ITIC

AWARDS: ITIC ('76)

LAFORD, JOHN *Ojibwa*

Born 1954 on Manitoulin Island, ON, Canada, on the West Bay Indian Reserve

RESIDENCE: Toronto, ON, Canada

EDUCATION: Algonquin College; IAIA; workshops and study under Francis Kagige (q.v.), 1971

PUBLISHED: Southcott (1984). *Canadian Geographic* (Dec 1986/Jan 1987)

COMMISSIONS: *Murals:* Fort St. Joseph Island, ON. *Other:* Pacific Editions Ltd., Victoria, BC, prints

PUBLIC COLLECTIONS: C/CMC; C/MCC; C/ROM; C/U of BC/MA; CMA; HCC; IAIA; INAC; Michigan State Museum; Sa Nostra Bank Collection, Ibiza, Spain

EXHIBITS: C/CMC; C/MCC; C/ROM; C/U of BC/MA; HCC; IAIA; Chateâu de Marly-le-Petit, Fribourg, Switzerland

SOLO/SPECIAL EXHIBITS: Partial listing of more than ten includes: C/LUM; C/TIC; C/ROM; Gallery of British Columbia Arts, BC (dual show)

LA FORTUNE, DOUG *Salish*

Born 1953

RESIDENCE: Canada

PUBLIC COLLECTIONS: HCC

EXHIBITS: BHSU, HCC, SDSMT

LAKE, ROSEMARY *Cree*

PUBLIC COLLECTIONS: CNM

EXHIBITS: CNM

AWARDS: CNM ('94)

LALIO, ERNIE *Zuni*

PUBLISHED: Snodgrass (1968)

PUBLIC COLLECTIONS: MNM (dated 1951)

LALLO (see Asah, Spencer)

LAMARR, ELGIN W. *Wichita*

Born 1918 in Anadarko, OK

RESIDENCE: Anadarko, OK

MILITARY: U.S. Army, WWII

EDUCATION: Chilocco, 1933-1934; Verden (OK) High School, 1934-1938; U of Tulsa, 1945-1949

OCCUPATION: Commercial artist, pattern maker, assistant instructor, ceramist, and painter

MEDIA: Oil, watercolor, and clay

PUBLISHED: Snodgrass (1968)

EXHIBITS: AIE, CSPIP, PAC, RC

AWARDS: AIE (before '68, 2 Grand Awards; '78, Grand Award; '80; '88)

LAMARR, JEAN *Pitt River/Paiute*

Born 24 July 1945 in Susanville, CA

RESIDENCE: Susanville Indian Rancheria, CA

EDUCATION: Lassen High School, Susanville, CA, 1963; Philco-Ford Technical Institute, Santa Clara, CA, 1969-1970; San José City College, CA, 1971-1973; U of C/B, 1976

OCCUPATION: Educator, consultant, Title IV coordinator, Community History Project artist, clothing designer, printmaker, beadworker, founder of the Native American Graphic Workshop, and painter

MEDIA: Acrylic and prints

PUBLISHED: Anonymous (1976); Amerson, ed. (1981); Stewart (1988); Lippard (1990); Archuleta and Strickland (1991); Hill (1992); Roberts, ed. (1992); Gully, ed. (1994). *Indian Voice* (1973); *Time to Creez – Third World Connotations* (1974); *America West* (July 1990); *Native Peoples* (summer 1993); *Native Arts Update* (summer 1994)

COMMISSIONS: *Murals:* Joaquin Memorial Community Center, Susanville Indian Rancheria, CA, 1982; City of San Jose (CA), public art project, 1995

PUBLIC COLLECTIONS: HM, IAIA

EXHIBITS: AICA/SF; CAM/S; CCI; CID; CNGM; CTC; CSU/OK; CSU/S; GS; HCCC; HM; HM/G; HS/NV; IAIA; IFA; KF; MMA; OLO; SFSC; SM; SNMA; SS/CW; SV; SW; TCE; WAATAP; WWM; Berkeley (CA) Art Center; East Berlin, Germany; Museum of Modern Art, New York, NY

SOLO EXHIBITS: MPI; Marin County Civic Center, San Rafael, CA, 1976

AWARDS: CID ('80); HM/G ('80, 1st); IFA ('74, 1st); KF ('79)

HONORS: *Scholarships and Fellowships:* Maple Creek Willies Scholarship, 1973-1976; Brandywine Workshop, Philadelphia, PA, fellowship, 1988

LAME DOG *Teton Sioux*

Shunga Hushti

PUBLISHED: Snodgrass (1968)

PUBLIC COLLECTIONS: SI/OAA

LAME MAN (see Cohoe, William)

LANCASTER, PAUL *Cherokee*

Birth date unknown; born in Parson, TN

RESIDENCE: Nashville, TN

OCCUPATION: Painter

MEDIA: Oil and prints

PUBLIC COLLECTIONS: Vanderbilt University School of Medicine, Nashville, TN

EXHIBITS: Vanderbilt University Medical Center, Nashville, TN

PAUL LANCASTER

Lancaster is a self-taught primitive whose work has been characterized as "childlike." His subject matter often shows fairy tale influence and is filled with his own idealism.

brochure, Dr. Everette James, 1992

LANGNESE, PAMELA *Wasco*

Born 28 Mar 1956 in Portland, OR; daughter of Lupe Juanita García Samuels and Walter A. Langnese Jr.; M/GP: Janette Bruno and Manuel García

RESIDENCE: San Francisco, CA

EDUCATION: Pacific North West College of Art, Portland, OR, 1980-1982; B.F.A., CCAC, 1984

OCCUPATION: Painter

MEDIA: Oil, acrylic, pencil, and pastel

COMMISSIONS: Living Sober Conference, 1987; *National Native American AIDS Prevention – Human Health Organization*, cover, 1989

PUBLIC COLLECTIONS: Warm Springs Tribal Courtroom

EXHIBITS: AICA/SF; CCAC; area and regional shows and markets

HONORS: Confederated Tribes, scholarship, 1980-1984

PAMELA LANGNESE

"Although my work is two-dimensional, it is put together to give as much three dimensional perspective as possible to satisfy my sense of sculpture and to bring the figures into as much life as I possibly can."

p.c. 1990

LANSING, NORMAN *Ute Mountain Ute*

Birth date unknown; born in Towaoc, CO, on the Ute Mountain Ute Reservation

RESIDENCE: Durango, CO

OCCUPATION: Ceramist and painter

MEDIA: Acrylic, pen and ink, mixed-media, and clay

PUBLISHED: *The Indian Trader* (Mar 1987)

EXHIBITS: ACS/MV, AICA, FNAA, ITIC, LIAS, LIAS/M

AWARDS: ITIC ('91; '94, 1st); throughout the Southwest

LAPEÑA, FRANK *Wintu/Nomtipom*

Tauhindeuli

Born 5 Oct 1937 in San Francisco, CA; son of Gladys Towndolly and Henry LaPeña; M/GP: Rose Young and Garfield Towndolly; M/GGU: Grant Towndolly, the last traditionally trained Wintu leader

RESIDENCE: Sacramento, CA

EDUCATION: Yreka (CA) Unified High School, 1956; B.A., CSU/C, 1965; Secondary Credential, SFSC, 1968; M.A., CSU/S, 1978

OCCUPATION: Art professor/director of Native American studies, writer, traditional dancer, photographer, and painter

MEDIA: Oil, acrylic, mixed-media, and prints

PUBLISHED: New (1979); Highwater (1980); Amerson, ed. (1981); Wade and Strickland (1981); Wade, ed. (1986); LaPeña (1987); Stewart (1988); Archuleta and Strickland (1991); Abbott (1994). *Art In America* (July/Aug 1972); *New Horizons* (1976); *Four Winds* (spring 1982); *American Indian Art* (spring 1985); *Phoenix Magazine* (Sept 1989); *American West* (July 1990); *Southwest Art* (Mar 1992); *Native Peoples* (winter 1992; Special Edition 1994).

PUBLIC COLLECTIONS: CAM/S; CSU/S; HM; IACB; NACLA; U of UT; WWM; Mendocino (CA) Art Center; Mills College, Oakland, CA; Museum of Modern Art, New York, NY

EXHIBITS: Partial listing of more than one hundred includes: AC/T; AICA/SF; AICH; BM/B; CAI; CAM/S; CNGM; CTC; EM; HM; NACLA; NARF; NU/BC; OLO; PAC; PAIC; SCG; SDMM; SFAI; SFFA; SV; SW; TRP; WIB; WWM; U of CA/D; U of ID; Linden Museum, Stuttgart, Germany, 1973; Oakland (CA) Museum; San Francisco (CA) Museum of Modern Art; see also Awards

SOLO/SPECIAL EXHIBITS: SPIM; WWM; Redding (CA) Museum and Art Center (dual); Sierra Nevada Museum, Reno, NV, 1988

AWARDS: WWM ('78, Best Painting); Kingsley Show, Sacramento, CA ('61); Northern California Art Show, Chico, CA ('61, 1st;'69); North Valley Art Show, Redding, CA ('69; '79); St. John's Religious Art Festival, Sacramento, CA ('69; '76, Best of Show)

FRANK LAPEÑA

LaPeña considers the teachings of his elders to be his most important education. They helped him to understand the joy and sacredness of life. His multimedia paintings are semi-abstract and relate his perception of reality. He uses many symbols, some personal and others of universal Indian origin.

brochure, WWM, 1988

LAPIER, JENNY *Blackfeet*

Born 11 June 1955 in Browning, MT; daughter of Muriel Boyle and Art LaPier

EDUCATION: G.E.D. 1980; Flathead Valley Community College, Kalispell, MT, 1990-1991

OCCUPATION: Wife, mother, beadworker, and painter

MEDIA: Oil, acrylic, watercolor, pen and ink, fabric, and glass beads

EXHIBITS: AAM; AC/H; AICA/SF; Bigfork (MT) Village Art Center; American Art Market, Browning, MT

SOLO/SPECIAL EXHIBITS: MPI (dual show)

LAPILAKWA (see Ladd, Edmund, J.)

LAPILAOKYA (see Ladd, Edmund, J.)

Lapluma, Louis *Eskimo*

PUBLISHED: Yorba (1990); Fawcett and Callander (1982)

PUBLIC COLLECTIONS: MAI

EXHIBITS: CAS, MAI

Lark, Sylvia *Seneca*

RESIDENCE: Berkeley, CA

EDUCATION: University of Siena, Siena, Italy; B.A., SUNY/B; M.F.A., U of WI

OCCUPATION: Teacher and artist

MEDIA: Oil

PUBLISHED: Amerson, ed. (1981); Jemison (1984). *The Report: Journal of the National Art Education Association's Women's Caucus* (fall 1977); *Arizona Arts and Lifestyles* (autumn 1981); *Art News* (Oct 1983); *Art Forum* (Feb 1984); *Images and Issues* (Mar/Apr 1984); *Phoenix Magazine* (winter 1989)

EXHIBITS: AC/T, CAM/S, CTC, OAM, OSU/G, QM, SFMA, WSCS, WWM

HONORS: Fulbright-Hays Grant, 1977; Women's Caucus for Art, National Board of Directors, 1978-1981

Larsen, Mike *Chickasaw*

Born 27 Oct 1944 in Dallas, TX; son of Ruth Carter Larsen and Manly Lanham; P/GP: Mary and Perry Lanham; M/GP: Lela and Otto Carter

RESIDENCE: Oklahoma City, OK

EDUCATION: Amarillo (TX) High School, 1963; Amarillo (TX) Junior College; University of Houston, TX; ASL; West Texas State University, Canyon, TX

OCCUPATION: Painter and sculptor

MEDIA: Oil, acrylic, pencil, pastel, and prints

PUBLISHED: Ballantine and Ballantine (1993). *Oklahoma Art Gallery* (fall 1981); *Art of the West* (Mar/Apr 1989); *Oklahoma Today* (Dec 1990), cover; *The Tulsa World* (3 Nov 1991); *The Tulsa Tribune* (15 Nov 1991; 18 Nov 1991); *The Broken Arrow Scout* (15 Jan 1992); *Southwest Art* (June 1991), cover

BOOKS ILLUSTRATED: Long (1989)

PUBLIC COLLECTIONS: State of Oklahoma, State Capitol Building, Oklahoma City, OK

EXHIBITS: ACAI, AICA, CIM, CNM, FAIE, FCTM, OAC, OSC, LIAS/M, LC, PAC, RE, SWAIA, TIAF

AWARDS: ACAI ('92); AICA (1991, Silver Medal; '92, IH; '93, Best of Show, IH); CIM ('88, 1st); CNM ('83, 1st; '84, 1st; '87, 1st; '88, 1st); FCTM ('80, 1st, IH); MS ('81, Best of Show; '85, Best of Show; '86, Best of Show); RE ('87, Best of Show; '88, 1st; '89, 1st; '90; '91; '92, 1st); SWAIA ('79; '89, 1st)

HONORS: Pastel Society of America, New York, NY, full membership, 1983; Pentagon, Washington, D.C., painting displayed in the rotunda; Oklahoma State Capitol, Oklahoma City, OK, selected to paint mural of the Four Indian Ballerinas, 1991; Oklahoma State Capitol Building, East Gallery, Oklahoma City, OK, *Year of the Indian Exhibition*, one of eight Indian artists exhibited, 1992

Larson, Jackie *Blackfeet*

A.K.A. Jackie Larson Bread

EXHIBITS: AICA/SF, CNM

Larvie, Calvin *Sioux*

Hehaka Hanska, Tall Elk

Born 6 July 1920 in Wood, SD; died 1969 in Rapid City, SD; M/GF: White Yellow Fox (Brûlé Sioux), medicine man who later became a scout for the U.S. Army; P/GGF: Joe Larvie, homesteader at Hot Springs, SD, with his Sioux wife

Sylvia Lark

Lark says she is concerned with "iconographic and emerging forms — natural and human made . . . [whose] mysterious and universal qualities contrast with the intimacy of their painted surface."

Arizona Arts and Lifestyle *autumn 1981*

Mike Larsen

At a young age, polio affected Larsen's right side and he learned to use his left hand instead. Seeking a career in art, as an adult he took a wide variety of classes but it was not until he was 36 years old that he attended the prestigious Art Students League in New York City. After experimenting with a variety of international styles, Larsen developed his own personal style, an often spiritual image that emphasizes elongated, oversized body parts. He uses bold colors accentuated by black and white.

Calvin Larvie

"Woodrow Wilson Crumbo (q.v.) has said that Larvie was one of the finest artists he had ever had in class. He left school during WWII to take part in the invasion of France. He later received the Bronze Star. After the war he spent most of his time in government hospitals, during which time he did little painting. In 1963, he submitted his first completed painting in 21 years to a show in Bismarck, ND."

Snodgrass 1968

MILITARY: U.S. Army, WWII (disabled)
EDUCATION: BC High School, 1940; U of Wichita, 1965
OCCUPATION: Artist
MEDIA: Oil, watercolor, and pencil
PUBLISHED: Jacobson and d'Ucel (1950); Dunn (1968); Snodgrass (1968); Libhart (1970); Brody (1971); Schmid and Houlihan (1980); King (1981). *The Rapid City Journal* (3 Dec 1987)
COMMISSIONS: IACB, U.S. Federal Pavilion, Golden Gate International Exposition, San Francisco, CA, 1939
PUBLIC COLLECTIONS: DAM, GM, IACB, OU/MA, PAC, SIM
EXHIBITS: AC/A; BNIAS; CPS; FAIEAIP; FNAIC; NAP; NGA; OU/ET; PAC; PAC/T; SIM; Mid-America Arts Alliance Project, 1979
SOLO EXHIBITS: PAC; Rosebud (SD) Arts and Crafts Museum
AWARDS: BNIAS (Statement of Recognition); FNAIC

LARVIE, COLLEEN (see Cutschall, Colleen)

LASAUSEE, BLAKE *Zuni*
MEDIA: Acrylic
EXHIBITS: SWAIA
AWARDS: SWAIA ('77)

LAUGHING BOY (see Blue Eagle, Acee)

LAUGHING BULL (see Flores, William Vann)

LAVADOUR, JAMES *Walla Walla*
Born 1951
RESIDENCE: Adams, OR
OCCUPATION: Artist-in-residence, planning technician, and painter
MEDIA: Oil
PUBLISHED: Longfish, et al. (1986); Archuleta and Strickland (1991). *Native Peoples* (winter 1992)
PUBLIC COLLECTIONS: HM; IACB; WSAC; Pacific Northwest Bell Corporation, Seattle Arts Commission, both Seattle, WA; Washington State Arts Commission
EXHIBITS: HM; MMA/WA; NDN; OGC; PAM; PDN; SCG; SV; TPAS; Expo '86, Vancouver, BC; Tacoma (WA) Art Museum, 1986; U of OR Museum of Art, 1984
SOLO EXHIBITS: CNGM; SCG; CC/WA; U of OR Museum of Art, 1982

LAVAND, JOHN PAUL *(?)*
Born 1962 in Kenora, ON, Canada
RESIDENCE: Canada
MEDIA: Pen and ink
PUBLIC COLLECTIONS: C/AG/TB
EXHIBITS: C/AG/TB; C/WI; Winnipeg, MB

LAVERDURE, ANDREW *Chippewa*
Born 13 Nov 1953 at Williston, ND
RESIDENCE: Aberdeen, SD
EDUCATION: Turtle Mountain Community High School, Belcourt, ND; Northfield (MN) Senior High School, 1971; Carleton College, Northfield, MN, 1971-1972; Hamline University, St. Paul, MN, 1972-1973; Turtle Mountain Community College, Belcourt, ND; B.A., U of ND, 1978
OCCUPATION: Teacher, tutor, counselor, supervisor, accountant, craftsman, and painter

MEDIA: Oil, acrylic, watercolor, tempera, pencil, pen and ink, pastel, and charcoal
SOLO EXHIBITS: SIM
HONORS: North Dakota Indian Education Association and Turtle Mountain Community Middle School, recognition for Outstanding Achievement in Indian Education

LAVERDURE, JULIENNE X. *Chippewa*

Born 17 Sept 1960
EDUCATION: Ojibwa Indian School
EXHIBITS: SIM, RC

LAWASEWA, VICTOR C. *Zuni*

PUBLISHED: Dunn (1968); Snodgrass (1968); Tanner (1973)
PUBLIC COLLECTIONS: HM, IACB/DC, MNA/KHC, MNM, PAC

VICTOR C. LAWASEWA

"The artist was one of the founders of the contemporary Zuni school of art (ca. 1922) and apparently has done little painting since that time. He is known for his formal drawings of altars executed in the late 1920s."

Snodgrass 1968

LAY, JOE *Cherokee/Creek*

RESIDENCE: Wagoner, OK
EXHIBITS: CNM

LAYS NEAR HAIR (see Rowell, Charles Emery)

LEADER (see Burton, Jimalee)

LEADER OF WOMEN (see Huser, Yvonne)

LEANDRO, JOSÉ (see Gutiérrez, José Leandro)

LEAN WOLF *Hidatsa*

Birth date unknown
RESIDENCE: Once lived in the areas of Fort Buford and Fort Berthold, Dakota Territory
PUBLISHED: Snodgrass (1968). *4th Annual Report,* BAE (1882-1883); *10th Annual Report,* BAE (1888-1889)

LEARNED HAND, ROBERT N. *Comanche*

Born 14 May 1939 in Anadarko, OK; son of Alma Alice Hayslip and Benjamin Franklin Learned Hand; P/GP: Teata and Stewart Learned Hand; M/GP: Alma Enda and Fred Jackson Hayslip
RESIDENCE: Broken Arrow, OK
EDUCATION: G.E.D., 1957; University of the Americas, Mexico City, Mexico, 1957-1959; B.A., Ringling School of Art, Sarasota, FL, 1961; M.F.A., ASL, 1963
OCCUPATION: Illustrator, designer, layout artist, art director, free-lance artist, teacher, rodeo contestant, sculptor, and painter
MEDIA: Oil, acrylic, watercolor, bronze, and prints
COMMISSIONS: *Murals:* Security Central National Bank, Wheelersburg, OH, 1978; Bank One, Portsmouth, OH, 1980; Notre Dame High School, Portsmouth, OH, 1982
PUBLIC COLLECTIONS: Ashland Oil Co.; BI; Huntington Museum; Thoroughbred Racing Association; Standard Bred Racing Association
EXHIBITS: BI; CIM; CNM; RE; Exhibit 280, Peking, China, 1981; see also Awards
SOLO EXHIBITS: Partial listing of more than twenty includes: Kentucky Highlands Museum
AWARDS: Exhibit 280 (1st); Kentucky Artists Association Show (Gold Medal)

LEBEAU, MILO R. *Cheyenne River Sioux*

Born 23 Apr 1946
RESIDENCE: Eagle Butte, SD

EDUCATION: Cheyenne-Eagle Butte (SD) High School; Denver (CO) Institute of Technology

PUBLIC COLLECTIONS: SI

EXHIBITS: NPTA; RC; H. V. Johnson Cultural Center Art Show; American Indian College Fund, New York, NY

AWARDS: Seven, inc luding 3 first places

LE COEUR, LEON *Huron*

Born 1924 in Hazel Park, MI; son of Goldie (Little Cloud) Brandimore and Arthur George Le Coeur; P/GM: Le Coeur, daughter of Huron chief, Silent Cloud; M/GGF: Chief Fleeting Cloud of the Alpena and Saginaw territory

RESIDENCE: New York, NY

MILITARY: U.S. Navy, WWII

OCCUPATION: Accounting engineer, playwright, poet, composer, sculptor, and painter

PUBLISHED: Snodgrass (1968)

EXHIBITS: Annual Rush Street Art Fair, Chicago, IL; Lynn Kottler Gallery, Village Art Show, NY

SOLO EXHIBITS: Paula Insel Gallery, NY

HONORS: American Education Association, Artist of the Year; Liberty Amendment of Greater New York, special award; Midwest Outdoor Art Exhibition, served on original Board of Directors

LEON LE COEUR

Le Coeur's French ancestors — the Beauchamps, La Fonds, Brandimores, and Le Coeurs were among the first settlers of Fort Detroit.

"An accident orphaning the artist at the age of seven also caused his loss of speech. Until he reached manhood, he attended numerous orphanages. As a young child, no medium adaptable to artistic creations escaped his imaginative mind. When he was taught to speak again through musical therapy, poetry and music were added to his skills. Although Le Coeur creates through many media, painting seems to be the one art which attracts him most."

Snodgrass 1968

Reviews of Le Coeur's art elicited rave comments. "...not since Picasso has a more definitive style and school of art been seen...."

The Chicago Tribune

"... Le Coeur showed a unique talent and definite style that personalized his talents to the fullest. It is wonderful to find an artist who thinks and not just paints."

The Chicago Daily News

LEE, CHARLES *Navajo*

Hush Ka Yel Ha Yah, Warrior Who Came Out

A.K.A. Charlie Lee; Yel Ha Yah Charlie; Rev. Charles Lee. Signature: Yel-Ha-Yah

Born 14 Apr 1926 near Red Rock, AZ, on the Navajo Reservation

RESIDENCE: Shiprock, NM

EDUCATION: Shiprock (NM) High School; Santa Fe, 1946; Central Bible Institute, Springfield, MO

OCCUPATION: Christian minister, silversmith, and painter

MEDIA: Watercolor

PUBLISHED: Snodgrass (1968); Brody (1971); Tanner (1973); Broder (1981); Samuels (1985). *Arizona Highways* (July 1956); *Southwestern Art* (Vol. 2, no. 1, 1967); *The Arizona Republic* (17 Mar 1968); *New Mexico Magazine* (July 1977)

BOOKS ILLUSTRATED: *Pathway To The Sky*

PUBLIC COLLECTIONS: AF; GM; MAI; MNA; MNM; MRFM; PAC; SI; SM; UPA; Peabody Museum of Salem, Salem, MA

EXHIBITS: ASM, HM, ITIC, LGAM, MNM, MNM/T, NMSF, PAC, PAC/T, SN

AWARDS: ITIC ('68; '69; '76); NMSF ('47, 2-1st); SN ('63)

LEE, CHARLIE (see Lee, Charles)

LEE, DAVID *Navajo*

RESIDENCE: Downers Grove, IL

EXHIBITS: HM/G

LEE, EDWARD (see Natay, Ed)

LEE, FRANK *(?)*

PUBLISHED: Snodgrass ('68)

EXHIBITS: SN

AWARDS: SN ('64)

LEE, J. S. *Navajo*
PUBLISHED: Snodgrass (1968); Brody (1971)
EXHIBITS: PAC, MNM

LEE, JERRY *Navajo*
Born 1944 at Wide Ruins, AZ
RESIDENCE: Gallup, NM
EDUCATION: Studied under Beatien Yazz (q.v.)
MEDIA: Tempera
PUBLISHED: Snodgrass (1968); Brody (1971); Tanner (1973)
PUBLIC COLLECTIONS: HCC, HM, MNA, WWM
EXHIBITS: AIAE/WSU, FAIEAIP, HCC, LGAM, PAC, PM, SN
AWARDS: SN ('64, 1st)

LEE, MICHAEL *Navajo*
EXHIBITS: CNM
AWARDS: CNM ('92)

LEE, NANCY ISABEL *Navajo/Santo Domingo*
Birth date unknown; daughter of Juanita C. and Edward H. Lee
RESIDENCE: Albuquerque, NM
EDUCATION: U of N AZ; U of NM
PUBLISHED: Snodgrass (1968). *The Navajo Times* (11 June 1964)
PUBLIC COLLECTIONS: IACB
EXHIBITS: U of NM
AWARDS: U of NM
HONORS: *Scholarships:* Santo Domingo Pueblo (NM) Educational Club, scholarship to U of NM, 1963; United Pueblo Agency, two-year scholarship

LEE, NELSON *Navajo*
EDUCATION: Fort Sill, 1962
PUBLISHED: Snodgrass (1968). *Arizona Highways* (July 1956)
EXHIBITS: PAC

LEE, PAUL *Navajo*
PUBLISHED: Snodgrass (1968)
PUBLIC COLLECTIONS: PAC

LEE, RUSSELL *Navajo*
Born 6 Nov 1976
EXHIBITS: ACS/ENP, CIM, HM/G, ITIC, SWAIA
AWARDS: ACS/ENP (1st); CIM (1st); ITIC (1st); SWAIA (1st)

LEE, SAMUEL *Cheyenne*
Born 5 Nov 1955
RESIDENCE: Clinton, OK
EDUCATION: Clinton (OK) High School
EXHIBITS: RC

LEEDOM, ROBERT *Sioux*
Born 23 Jan 1936 in Winnebago, NE, on the Winnebago Indian Reservation
RESIDENCE: Lame Deer, MT
MILITARY: U.S. Army
EDUCATION: Winnebago (NE) Public School; Marty (SD) Mission; graduated high school after military service, 1965

CHARLES LEE

Lee studied both art and music at Santa Fe and, at one time, sang in a Santa Fe choir. His work shows the same air of delicacy and calm as that of Harrison Begay's with whom he painted at one time. He is perhaps best known for his paintings of horses.

Samuels 1985

Lee is an ordained minister of the Assemblies of God and a missionery to the Navajo people.

SAMUEL LEE

The artist is partially paralyzed and has learned to paint with his left hand. As Lee is not naturally left-handed, developing the necessary control has been a considerable challenge.

artist, p.c. 1985

OCCUPATION: Deputy town marshall, ranch hand, horse breaker, telephone lineman, welder, carpenter; painter since 1967
PUBLIC COLLECTIONS: CIA; MPI; SIM; SLM
EXHIBITS: throughout western Montana
SOLO EXHIBITS: SIM

LEEKELA, HOWARD *Zuni*
PUBLISHED: Snodgrass (1968)
PUBLIC COLLECTIONS: IACB/DC, MAI, MKMcNAI, MNA/KHC

LEFT HAND *Cheyenne (?)*
Na Mos, Left Hand
Birth date unknown
PUBLISHED: Snodgrass (1968)
PUBLIC COLLECTIONS: HI
EXHIBITS: BPG

LEFT HAND

Possibly the same Left Hand as signed the Fort Wise Treaty in 1861, and was listed as an Arapaho chief at Darlington, OK, ca. 1870.

"The artist was among the 72 Plains Indians taken as prisoners from Fort Sill, OK, to Fort Marion, St. Augustine, FL, in 1875."

Snodgrass 1968

LEFTHANDED, BIG (see Big Lefthanded)

LEFTOWICH, BILL *Chickasaw*
EXHIBITS: AIE, FCTM
AWARDS: AIE ('72)

LEFTWICH, ALFRED *Oglala Sioux*
Born 20 Oct 1966 in Cleveland, OH; son of Elizabeth Rowlan and Alfred Leftwich Sr.; M/GP: Elizabeth and Dikki Little Hawk
RESIDENCE: Pine Ridge, SD
EDUCATION: Pine Ridge (SD) High School, 1985; Haskell, 1989
OCCUPATION: Forestry service, teacher, coach, basketball player; painter since 1990
MEDIA: Oil, watercolor, pencil, and pen and ink
PUBLIC COLLECTIONS: BIA
EXHIBITS: Haskell; RC
AWARDS: Haskell ('87, Most Promising Artist; '89, Most Creative Artist)
HONORS: Haskell, Art Department, Most Prominent Student

LEHOLM, MARY FRANCES PICHETTE *Colville/Iroquois*
Born 17 May 1933 in Inchelium, WA, on the Colville Reservation; daughter of Marguriete Christine MacDonald and Joseph Lawrence Pichette; P/GGGF: Louis Dupuois Pichette, a Frenchman, who led an exploring party to Astoria in 1817
RESIDENCE: Pullman, WA
EDUCATION: Inchelium (WA) High School; Columbia Basin College, Pasco, WA; B.F.A., Washington State University, Pullman, WA, 1966; private art instruction under Warren Wilder and Edgar Desautel
OCCUPATION: Housewife, free-lance commercial artist, and painter
PUBLISHED: Snodgrass (1968)
PUBLIC COLLECTIONS: BIA, IACB
EXHIBITS: BNIAS; FAIEAIP; ITIC; MNM; PAC; SAM; Wenatchee (WA) Apple Blossom Festival; Benton-Franklin County Fair, Kennewick, WA; Central Washington Art Festival, Yakima, WA; Washington Art Association, Spokane, WA
SOLO EXHIBITS: Wenatchee, WA; Walla Walla, WA; Pullman Chamber of Commerce, WA; Pasco, WA; Kennewick, WA; Colville Indian Agency, WA; Lewiston, ID
AWARDS: Local fairs

MARY LEE WEBSTER LEMIEUX

Lemieux paints in a realistic style. Her favorite subjects are Indian people in modern reservation settings.

Johannsen and Ferguson, eds. 1983

LEKEELA (see Leekela, Howard)

LELEKA (see Outie, George)

LEMIEUX, MARY LEE WEBSTER *Oneida*

Born 29 Jan 1946
RESIDENCE: Oneida, WI
EDUCATION: U of WI/G
OCCUPATION: Art consultant and painter
MEDIA: Oil and acrylic
PUBLISHED: Johannsen and Ferguson, eds. (1983)
PUBLIC COLLECTIONS: U of WI/G
EXHIBITS: U of WI/G
AWARDS: U of WI/G

LENO, MARCE *Tesuque*

EDUCATION: Tesuque, ca. 1959; IAIA, 1963
PUBLISHED: Snodgrass (1968)
EXHIBITS: MNM, 1959

LENTE, JOE (see Lente, José Bartolo)

LENTE, JOSÉ BARTOLO *Isleta*

A.K.A. Joe Lente
PUBLISHED: Goldfrank (1962; 1967); Snodgrass (1968); Brody (1971)
PUBLIC COLLECTIONS: MAI, MNM

JOSÉ BARTOLO LENTE

"A note regarding Lente's work in the collection of MNM states the painter was known to 'hang around things he didn't belong to. We used to know he sold paintings. He would come back with money.' This work was executed ca. 1930. The artist is deceased. A quantity of his unsigned work is known to exist, the use of which is restricted."

Snodgrass 1968

LESLIE, ERNEST *Navajo*

PUBLISHED: Snodgrass (1968)
COMMISSIONS: *Murals:* ASF, Coliseum, 1965 (with four other Navajo painters)

LEVAN, KATE *Chickasaw*

A.K.A. Mrs. J. R. Levan
EXHIBITS: FCTM
AWARDS: FCTM ('67)

LEVAN, MRS. J. R. (see Levan, Kate)

LEVINGS, MARTIN *Hidatsa*

Black Cloud; Holy Buffalo
Born 14 Oct 1892; son of Hard Horn, Hidatsa chief and medicine man
RESIDENCE: Mandaree, ND
MILITARY: WWII
OCCUPATION: Rancher and painter
PUBLISHED: Snodgrass (1968)
EXHIBITS: BNIAS

MARTIN LEVINGS

"Upon his return from military service, Levings was given his second tribal name at a special ceremony to honor his war record. He started painting about 1923, 'to while away the long snowbound days of winter.'"

Snodgrass 1968

LEWIS, ERNEST *Navajo*

Born 1950 on the Navajo Reservation; brother of Roger Lewis (q.v.)
EDUCATION: Gallup (NM) Public Schools
MEDIA: Casein
PUBLISHED: Tanner (1973). *American Indian Art* (spring 1985)
PUBLIC COLLECTIONS: HCC, EM
EXHIBITS: HM/G, ITIC, NTF, PAC, SN, U of WV
AWARDS: ITIC ('67; '69); PAC ('70); RC ('71); SN ('68; '69)

JIMMY LEWIS

"Listed as a promising student by Duane O. Berg, his Gallup art instructor, Lewis began painting in 1961. . . ."

Snodgrass 1968

LEWIS, JIMMY *Navajo*

Born 1 Jan 1946 at Fort Defiance, AZ
EDUCATION: Gallup (NM) High School, 1965
PUBLISHED: Snodgrass (1968)
EXHIBITS: NACG (student show)

LEWIS, MEKKO *Creek*

RESIDENCE: Eufala, OK
EXHIBITS: FCTM, ITIC, PAC
AWARDS: ITIC ('70. 1st; '76, Technical Excellence); FCTM ('70; '72; '73); PAC ('72)

LEWIS, ROBERT *Cherokee/Navajo/Apache*

Born 10 Oct 1965 in Claremore, OK; son of Lou Aline Kingfisher and Yazzie Lewis; P/GP: Dorothy and Robert E. Lewis; M/GP: Peggy and Skake Kingfisher
RESIDENCE: Tahlequah, OK
EDUCATION: Salina (OK) High School, 1983; NSU, 1990
OCCUPATION: Museum gallery administrator, and painter
MEDIA: Oil, acrylic, watercolor, pencil, pen and ink, clay, and prints
EXHIBITS: CNM, FCTM, NSU, OIAC
AWARDS: CNM ('94)
SOLO EXHIBITS: Joe Vaughn Library, Tahlequah, OK, 1990; galleries in Oklahoma
AWARDS: NSU ('88; '89, 1st; '90)

LEWIS, ROGER *Navajo*

Born 1 Feb 1948 in Pinedale, NM; brother of Ernest Lewis (q.v.); GF: Jeff King, Navajo scout
RESIDENCE: Church Rock, NM
MILITARY: U.S. Armed Forces, 1969
EDUCATION: Gallup (NM) Public Schools
PUBLISHED: Snodgrass (1968); Tanner (1973)
PUBLIC COLLECTIONS: PAC
EXHIBITS: HM/G; ITIC; NAP; NTF; PAC; RC; SN; Gallup (NM) Public Schools
AWARDS: PAC ('67; '71, 1st); SN ('68)

LEWIS, ROSE *Wampanoag*

Born 14 Nov 1939; daughter of Emerson H. Lewis and Ann Thiebeault
RESIDENCE: Somerville, MA
EDUCATION: North Quincy (MA) High School; Massachusetts College of Art, Boston, MA; New England School of Design
OCCUPATION: Attendant at Harvard University Art Museum and artist
MEDIA: Acrylic, pencil, pen and ink, sand, and birch bark
BOOKS ILLUSTRATED: *The Wampanoags of Mash Pee* by Russell Peters
PUBLIC COLLECTIONS: Boston (MA) Children's Museum
EXHIBITS: AIAI; Boston Children's Museum; Massachusetts College of Art
AWARDS: The Artist Foundation, semi-finalist

LIGHTFOOTED RUNNER (see West, Dick)

LIGHTNER, CYNTHIA TAYLOR *Wampanoag*

EXHIBITS: CNM

LIGHTNING (see Nahsohnhoya, Thomas Dolwiftema)

LIMPING (see Alberty, Dewey)

LINA (see Loreen-Wulf, Audrea)

LINKLATER, ALLAN *Cree*

Born 1963 in Moose Factory, ON, Canada

EDUCATION: C/OCA, 1986-1990

PUBLIC COLLECTIONS: C/INAC; C/MMC; Ministry of Natural Resources, Toronto, ON

EXHIBITS: C/AG/TB; C/FCIA; C/OCA; Indian Friendship Centre, North Bay, ON; Native Arts Conference, Sault Ste. Marie, ON; Rideau Valley Arts Festival, Westpost, ON

HONORS: *Scholarships:* Canadian Native Arts Foundation, 1988, 1989; Moose Factory First Nation, 1990. *Other:* Ontario Youth Award from the Premier of Ontario, 1985

LITTLE, BERNADETTE *Mescalero Apache*

Born 1948 in Mescalero, NM

RESIDENCE: Mescalero, NM

EDUCATION: St. Catherine's, 1965

PUBLISHED: Snodgrass (1968)

PUBLIC COLLECTIONS: MAI

EXHIBITS: PAC, SAIEAIP

LITTLE, DAVID M. *Mescalero Apache/San Juan*

Born 1962 in Albuquerque, NM

EDUCATION: Graduated high school, 1979

OCCUPATION: Artist

MEDIA: Acrylic and watercolor

EXHIBITS: HM/G; Albuquerque (NM) Metro City Contest, 1979; *I Am These People,* CA, 1975; Skagit Valley College, Oak Harbor, WA; see also Awards

SOLO EXHIBITS: MPI, IPCC

AWARDS: Albuquerque (NM) Metro City Contest ('79); Northwest International Art Competition, Bellinghamn, WA ('88)

LITTLE BEAR (see Decker, Vernon Edward)

LITTLE BEAR (see Sett'an)

LITTLE BEAR (see Woodring, Carl)

LITTLE BEAR, BOBBY *Osage*

RESIDENCE: Columbia, MD

SOLO EXHIBITS: OTM

LITTLEBEAR, CHARLES *Plains*

PUBLISHED: Snodgrass (1968)

PUBLIC COLLECTIONS: GM

LITTLE BIG MAN *Sioux*

Tanka Cical Wacasa

PUBLISHED: Snodgrass (1968). *10th Annual Report,* BAE (1888-1889)

PUBLIC COLLECTIONS: SI/OAA (pictorial census drawings prepared under the direction of Red Cloud)

LITTLE BIRD, LARRY (see Bird, Larry)

LITTLE BLUFF (see Tohausen)

LITTLE CHIEF (see Keith, Sidney John)

LITTLE CHIEF (see Standingbear, George Eugene)

LITTLE CHIEF, BARTHELL *Kiowa/Comanche*

Tsen-t'ainte, White Horse

Born 14 Oct 1941 in Lawton, OK; son of Merle Poahway and Tom Little Chief, song composer, master beadworker, and Kiowa headman; P/GP: Ko-ya-kay and John Little Chief; M/GP: Kosepeah and Ben Poahway

RESIDENCE: Anadarko, OK

EDUCATION: Lawton (OK) High School, 1961; Cameron Junior College, Lawton, OK; U of OK

OCCUPATION: Silversmith, sculptor, and painter

MEDIA: Acrylic, watercolor, clay, silver, bronze, and prints

PUBLISHED: Ellison (1972); New (1979); Boyd, et al. (1983). *The Rocky Mountain News* (27 Dec 1988); *The Santa Fean* (Nov 1990); *Association News*, SPIM (June 1992); biographical publications

COMMISSIONS: Leanin' Tree Publishing Co., Boulder, CO, greeting cards

PUBLIC COLLECTIONS: IACB, MM/NJ, SM

EXHIBITS: ACAI, AIE, CAI/KC, CIM, CNM, CSPIP, ITIC, MFA/O, NACLA, PAIC, RE, SN, SPIM, TIAF, TWF, VV

SOLO EXHIBITS: SPIM (2)

AWARDS: ACAI ('93); AIE ('75; '77); CAI/KC; CIM ('90, Best Traditional Painter); CNM ('82, 1st; '91, Grand Award; '92); RE ('89; '93, 1st; '94)

BARTHELL LITTLE CHIEF

Early encouragement for Little Chief's artistic endeavors came from James Auchiah (q.v.), a friend of his parents. Auchiah showed him how to mix colors and gave him a secret ingredient to preserve watercolors. Little Chief paints in both the traditional Indian style and in a contemporary abstract style.

The Rocky Mountain News, *27 Dec 1988*

LITTLE CHIEF, BUDDY *Kiowa*

RESIDENCE: Lawton, OK

PUBLISHED: Snodgrass (1968)

PUBLIC COLLECTIONS: Carnegie (OK) High School

LITTLE CHIEF, DANIEL *Northern Cheyenne*

Wuxpais

Birth date unknown; died 1906; son of Little Chief, Cheyenne chief

OCCUPATION: Warrior and artist

PUBLISHED: Snodgrass (1968)

PUBLIC COLLECTIONS: SI/OAA (30 drawings with notes of explanation from artist, translated by Albert S. Gatschet, 1891)

DANIEL LITTLE CHIEF

"Daniel Little Chief's father was Little Chief, a Northern Cheyenne, who was sent south with his people to the Cheyenne Agency, Darlington, OK, ca. 1878-1879. The government eventually permitted the senior Little Chief to return north to South Dakota, 1880-1881, where he became head chief of the Cheyennes at the Pine Ridge Agency in 1891. Daniel Little Chief executed the pictures now at the Smithsonian Institution during the time his father's band was at Pine Ridge. The artist was said to have killed and wounded many soldiers at the Battle of the Little Big Horn."

Snodgrass 1968

LITTLE CHIEF, WILLIAM *Southern Cheyenne*

Birth date unknown; Artist's wife is William Cohoe's (q.v.) niece by marriage.

MILITARY: U.S. Army, scout at Fort Reno, Indian Territory

PUBLISHED: Snodgrass (1968). *American Indian Art* (winter 1992)

PUBLIC COLLECTIONS: YU/BRBML

EXHIBITS: BPG

WILLIAM LITTLE CHIEF

"The artist was among the 72 Plains Indians taken as prisoners from Fort Sill, OK, to Fort Marion, St. Augustine, FL, in 1875."

Snodgrass 1968

LITTLECHILD, GEORGE JAMES *Plains Cree*

Born 16 Aug 1958 in Edmonton, AB, Canada; son of Racheal Littlechild; GGF: Chief Francis Bull

RESIDENCE: Vancouver, BC, Canada

EDUCATION: Diploma, Red Deer (AB) College; B.F.A., Nova Scotia College of Art and Design, Halifax, 1988; C/BCA, 1988

OCCUPATION: Painter

MEDIA: Oil, acrylic, deer hide, and mixed-media

PUBLISHED: Highwater (1983). *Artichoke 1* (Feb 1990)

PUBLIC COLLECTIONS: C/AAF; C/AG/TB; C/AIAC; C/CMC; C/ESSOC; C/TU; C/U of AB; Alberta Government Telephone Company; Alberta Native Secretariat; Native Business Venture Capital, Edmonton, ON

EXHIBITS: ASMG; C/AC/B; C/AG/E; C/AG/TB; C/AM; C/GM; C/LLYC; C/MAM; C/OWAO; C/RDM; C/TGVA; C/U of R/MT; C/U of T/S; DC; HM; Bryant Building, Halifax, NS; Calgary (AB) City Hall; Edmonton (AB) Convention Centre; Esso Plaza, Calgary, AB; Legislative Pedway Concourse, Edmonton, AB; galleries throughout Canada; see also Awards

SOLO EXHIBITS: C/AG/TB; C/WM; Nova Scotia College of Art and Design, Halifax, 1988; Munich, Germany

AWARDS: C/AM ('86; '88, 1st); Esso Resources Canada Ltd. (Native Art Award)

HONORS: *Scholarships and Grantss:* Alberta Indian Arts and Crafts Society, bursary, 1987, and scholarship, 1988; C/NSCAD, Endowment Fund Scholarship, 1987; Loomis and Toles Material, bursary; C/BCA, scholarship, 1988; Canada Council, project grant, 1989

LITTLE COOK *Yankton Sioux*

MEDIA: Watercolor and pencil

PUBLISHED: Snodgrass (1968)

PUBLIC COLLECTIONS: MAI (watercolor and pencil, 1883)

LITTLE DAUGHTER (see Smart, Clara Mary)

LITTLE DOG (see Parsons, Neil)

LITTLE EAGLE *Brûlé Sioux*

Wambali Ches Challah, Little Eagle

OCCUPATION: Soldier, ca. 1879

PUBLISHED: Newell (1912); Snodgrass (1968)

LITTLE FINGER NAIL *Northern Cheyenne*

Birth date unknown; died Jan 1879, killed while traveling north with Dull Knife and Little Wolf

PUBLISHED: Sandoz (1953); Snodgrass (1968)

PUBLIC COLLECTIONS: MNH/A

LITTLE GREY (see Tsinajinnie, Andrew Van)

LITTLE MUSTACHE'S DAUGHTER (see Cassady, Ann Virginia)

LITTLE NO SHIRT (see Beatien Yazz)

LITTLE ROBE (see Yellow Nose)

LITTLE SHEEP *Navajo*

PUBLISHED: Tanner (1957); Snodgrass (1968); Supplee and Anderson (1971)

LITTLE SKY, DAWN *Cheyenne River Sioux*

Born 1932 in Fort Yates, ND, on the Standing Rock Reservation; daughter of Ethel Brugier and John Gates; P/GGF: Chief Two Bear; M/GGF: Chief War Eagle

RESIDENCE: Kyle, SD

EDUCATION: Haskell, 1949; U of KS

OCCUPATION: Walt Disney Production employee, Disneyland Indian entertainer, actress, and artist

PUBLISHED: Snodgrass (1968)

PUBLIC COLLECTIONS: HCC

EXHIBITS: ITIC, NPTA, PAC, RC

AWARDS: NPTA ('94); RC ('94, 1st, Niederman Award, Woodard Award);

GEORGE JAMES LITTLECHILD

Raised by foster parents, it wasn't until he was in his teens that Littlechild began to seek his Native heritage. He did archival research in Edmonton and at the Glenbow Museum, Calgary, AB. The artist has stated, "...As an artist, I see a mutual strength in the marriage I have with the land, flora, fauna, and the ways of the Native culture. My personal struggle is to maintain my Native identity and heritage while drawing from the best of all other cultures...."

artist brochure

LITTLE SHEEP

"The first name that can be suggested in the annals of southwest Indian painting is Little Sheep. He is credited with the paintings [pictographs] of several horsemen low on the wall in Canyon del Muerto in the early decades of the nineteenth century (Tanner 1957)...."

Snodgrass 1968

DAWN LITTLE SKY

"Little Sky is a painter and actress. With her actor husband and four children she has organized a Sioux dance group, which gives exhibition dances for numerous organizations."

Snodgrass 1968

LITTLE SWAN, THE (see The Swan)

LITTLE THUNDER, MERLIN *Southern Cheyenne*

A.K.A. Signature: A bolt of lightning and clouds

Born 9 Feb 1956; son of Connie and George Little Thunder; GGF: Old Bear

RESIDENCE: Tulsa, OK

EDUCATION: Canton (OK) High School, 1975; SWOSU; BC; EOSC

OCCUPATION: Athlete, musician, factory worker, laborer, assistant museum director; full-time painter since 1981

MEDIA: Oil, acrylic, watercolor, pencil, pastel, and prints

PUBLISHED: Ballantine and Ballantine (1993). *Tulsa Magazine* (June 1985); *Oklahoma Home and Garden* (Dec 1985); *Southwest Art* (May 1987); *The Tulsa Tribune* (20 Mar 1987); *Oklahoma Today* (Dec 1990; June 1992; May/June 1993); *Association News*, SPIM (Oct 1993); *Tulsa World* (21 Jan 1995)

COMMISSIONS: Longhorn World Championship Rodeo, painting on a tipi, 1995

PUBLIC COLLECTIONS: SI; American Indian Heritage Center, Tulsa, OK

EXHIBITS: ACAI, AICA, CIM, CNM, FAIE, ITIC, OCSA, PF, TWF; see also Awards

SOLO EXHIBITS: CNM, SPIM

AWARDS: AICA ('91, Gold Medal); CIM ('88, 1st); CNM ('85, 2-1st; '86, 1st; '88, 1st; '92; '94, 1st); ITIC ('90, 1st; '91, 3-1st, Best in Category, Best in Miniature Painting, Mullarky Award; '92, 1st, Best in Category, Mullarky Award; '94, 1st, Best in Category); OCSA; OHT; Cheyenne-Arapaho Museum, Canton, OK (Best of Show); Great Southern Plains Indian and Western Art Show ('86)

HONORS: IEEPF, Easter egg design, 1988; American Heritage Center, poster artist, 1991

MERLIN LITTLE THUNDER

Known for his detailed miniatures, Little Thunder paints history with a sense of humor. As he paints, the artist creates a story about the painting and the painting represents the story's "punch line." A perfectionist, he constantly seeks to improve his technique and spends many hours in research.

artist, p.c. 1990

The multi-matted framing done by Little Thunder is also distinctive.

LITTLETREE, JASPER *Navajo*

RESIDENCE: Kirtland, NM

EDUCATION: Trade school, Provo, UT

OCCUPATION: Journeyman industrial electrician and painter

MEDIA: Oil, acrylic, and watercolor

EXHIBITS: ACS/MV, TF

AWARDS: ACS/MV ('94)

LIVERMORE, CYNTHIA *Blackfoot/Coast Salish*

Born 21 Oct 1959 in Nanaimo, BC, Canada; daughter of Earl Livermore (q.v.); two uncles are also professional artists

RESIDENCE: Susanville, CA

EDUCATION: Adult Education Program, Hupa Tribal Career Center; College of Redwoods, Hoopa, CA; Lassen College, Susanville, CA

MEDIA: Oil and watercolor

EXHIBITS: AICA/SF; RC; U of CA/D; Indian Day Celebration, Cal-Expo, Sacramento, CA; Eureka Humbolt Cultural Center, Eureka, CA

SOLO EXHIBITS: MPI

LIVERMORE, EARL *Blackfeet*

Born 29 Nov 1932 in Browning, MT

EDUCATION: Edison Technical High School, Seattle, WA; Haskell; U of WA, 1958-1961; Burnley Professional School of Art, Seattle, WA; Academy of Art, San Francisco, CA, 1964

OCCUPATION: Director of American Indian Center and alcoholism treatment program, and painter

EARL LIVERMORE

Livermore's realistic paintings are of life on the reservation: powwows, dancers, encampments, amd traditional themes.

MEDIA: Oil, watercolor, casein, tempera, pen and ink, pencil, and charcoal
PUBLISHED: Ray, ed. (1972)
EXHIBITS: AAID; AICH/SF; CIA; HS/AI; KF; NIFA; USDI; San Francisco (CA) Arts Festival
SOLO EXHIBITS: MPI
AWARDS: Partial listing includes: AAI, ('68; '70)

LIZER, VERA *Navajo*
Born 1942
EDUCATION: U of AZ, "Southwest Indian Art Project," scholarship, summer 1960
PUBLISHED: Snodgrass (1968)

LIZZIE *Inuit (Eskimo)*
RESIDENCE: Cape Dorset, NWT, Canada
PUBLISHED: Houston (1967); Larmour (1967)
PUBLIC COLLECTIONS: C/TDB
EXHIBITS: C/CD, C/EACTDB

LLAPULAOKYA (see Ladd, Edmund J.)

LOBA HEIT (see Taulbee, Dan)

LOCKE, JAMES *Sioux*
PUBLISHED: Snodgrass (1968)
PUBLIC COLLECTIONS: MNM (back of painting is inscribed, "10th grade-1946")

LOCKE, MERLE *Oglala Sioux*
Born 21 Jan 1960 in Pine Ridge, SD; son of Gladys M. Shorthorn and Frank J. Locke; related to Kevin Locke, hoop dancer and flute player
RESIDENCE: Porcupine, SD
EDUCATION: Little Wound High School, Kyle, SD, 1979; OLC, 1994
OCCUPATION: Heavy equipment operator, student, and painter
COMMISSIONS: *Murals:* Museums throughout South Dakota
PUBLIC COLLECTIONS: Oglala Sioux Tribal Office, SD; Oglala Lakota College, Kyle, SD; Oglala Sioux Parks and Recreation Department
EXHIBITS: AIHEC, CHAS/SD, RC; American Indian College, New York, NY; Matths Talent Agency Art Exhibit, Colorado Springs, CO
AWARDS: AIHEC ('92); CHAS/SD ('92, 1st)

LOCKLEAR, GENE *Lumbee*
Born 1949 in North Carolina
RESIDENCE: San Diego, CA
EDUCATION: Graduated high school, 1968
OCCUPATION: Professional baseball player and painter
MEDIA: Oil, acrylic, pencil, and prints
EXHIBITS: MCC/CA, SDMM
HONORS: State of North Carolina, Gene Locklear Day, 31 Jan 1976

GENE LOCKLEAR

Locklear's paintings reflect his life: they are of North Carolina farm life, sports, and Indian lore.

artist, p.c. 1990

LOCO, MOSES *Chiricahua Apache*
Born 17 Feb 1909 near Fort Sill, OK
MEDIA: Oil
PUBLISHED: Snodgrass (1968), Seymour (1993)
PUBLIC COLLECTIONS: MNA
EXHIBITS: County fairs
SOLO EXHIBITS: County fairs

MOSES LOCO

"In 1936, the Oklahoma WPA Art Project noted that 'Loco has unusual talent, but does not keep to primitive or original work. He would do more work but his eyes are weak. . . .'"

Snodgrass 1968

LOC'-PITZ-HE-Á-LISH (see Bear's Arm)

LOFT, MARTIN *Mohawk*

RESIDENCE: Mercier, PQ, Canada
PUBLISHED: *Newsletter*, NASAC/ACEAA (winter 1991)
EXHIBITS: AICH, AC/DS, C/AMO

LOGAN, JIM *Cree/Sioux*

Born 1955 in New Westminster, BC, Canada
RESIDENCE: Canada
EDUCATION: Certificate in Graphic Design, David Thompson University, BC, 1983
OCCUPATION: Graphic designer, missionary, and painter
MEDIA: Oil, acrylic, and prints
PUBLISHED: *Up Here Magazine* (Oct/Nov 1985); *The Canadian Journal of Native Studies* (Vol. 10, no. 1, 1990), cover; *Maclean's Magazine* (4 May 1992); *American Indian Art* (autumn 1992)
PUBLIC COLLECTIONS: C/INAC; Alberta Government Telephone, Edmonton, AB; Northwest Telephone Art Collection, Whitehorse, YT; Sohio Oil, Anchorage, AK; Yukon Indian Development Corporation, Whitehorse, YT; Yukon Territorial Government Collection
EXHIBITS: Partial listing of more than twenty includes: C/I; C/PV; Caribou Regional Juried Exposition, Prince George, BC, 1981; Expo '86, Yukon Pavilion, Vancouver, BC; McBride (BC) 50th Anniversary Jubilee; Peace Hill Trust Art Collection Show, Edmonton, AB; St. John (BC) Public Library; West Kootenay Regional Juried Exposition, Nelson, BC
SOLO EXHIBITS: Partial listing of 13 includes: C/U of C; Camrose (BC) Lutheran College; galleries in AB, AK, BC, and YT
HONORS: Society of Canadian Artists of Native Ancestry, co-chair, 1992

LOGAN, LINEY *Seneca*

RESIDENCE: Washington, D.C.
EDUCATION: IAIA; B.F.A., Rochester S.T.
MEDIA: Acrylic and chalk
PUBLIC COLLECTIONS: SMII
EXHIBITS: AIAI, AICH

CHARLES LOLOMA

Loloma was an innovator as a designer and a leader as a teacher. He single-handedly changed the history of Indian jewelry through his sophisticated and unconventional designs and use of exotic materials (i.e., gold, diamonds, lapis lazuli, etc.). Due to his high powered collection of three airplanes, a Jaguar XK-E and a "Rolls," the "struggling artist" concept did not apply to him in the last quarter of his career.

Snodgrass-King, p.c. 1994

LOISELLE, ALICE *Chippewa*

PUBLISHED: Hill (1992)
PUBLIC COLLECTIONS: IAIA
EXHIBITS: IAIA

LOLOMA, CHARLES *Hopi*

Born 7 Jan 1921 at Hotevilla, AZ; died 9 June 1991; son of Rachel and Rex Loloma; married to Otellie Pasivaya (q.v); divorced 1965
MILITARY: U.S. Army, WWII
EDUCATION: Phoenix, 1940; Alfred; Dale Carnegie Classes, AZ; mural instruction under Olaf Nordmark, Fort Sill
OCCUPATION: Operator of arts and crafts shops, ceramist, teacher, painter, sculptor, silversmith, and jeweler
MEDIA: Watercolor, clay, silver, gold, and gemstone
PUBLISHED: Dunn (1968); Snodgrass (1968); Tanner (1973); Monthan and Monthan (1975); Medina (1981); New (1981); Wade and Strickland (1981); Seymour (1988); Mather (1990). *Arizona Highways* (Jan 1972; Aug 1974; Apr 1979; May 1986); *Artists of the Rockies and the Golden West* (summer 1975); *The*

Quarterly, SWAIA (fall 1977); *American Indian Art* (spring 1984); *Southwest Profile* (Aug/Sept/Oct 1992)

BOOKS ILLUSTRATED: Kennard (1940; 1948)

COMMISSIONS: *Murals:* SFWF, assistant (age 16); Radio Station KOY, Phoenix, AZ; Oraibi High School; Kaimi Lodge, Scottsdale AZ; Phoenix, AZ; Verde Valley School, AZ. *Other:* President Lyndon Johnson, jewelery gifts for the Queen of Denmark and Imelda Marcos

PUBLIC COLLECTIONS: DAM, IACB, IACB/DC, MRFM, WWM

EXHIBITS: AC/SD; ASF; HM; IAIA/M; MCC/CA; MMA; NACLA; NMSF; PAC, SFFA; SWAIA; WRTD; WWM; Museum of Contemporary Crafts, New York, NY; national exhibits sponsored by American Craftsmen Council; in Europe

SOLO EXHIBITS: HM

AWARDS: SN (seven first prizes); state and national competitions

HONORS: Whitney Foundation Fellowship, 1949; First Convocation of American Indian Scholars, Princeton University, arts panelist; Arizona Commission on the Arts and Humanities, member, 1973; American Indian Historical Society, Princeton University, board member; NACLA, board member; Japan, 1974; NEA, artist-in-residence, Japan, 1974; American Indian Center for Living Arts, New York, NY, Board of Directors; American Crafts Council, Fellow

LOLOMA, OTELLIE *Hopi*

A.K.A. Otellie Pasivaya Loloma

Born 1922 in Sipaulovi Village, Second Mesa, AZ; died 30 Jan 1993; married to Charles Loloma (q.v.); divorced 1965

EDUCATION: Oraibi (AZ) High School; Alfred, 1947-1949; U of AZ, 1958-1959; U of N AZ, 1960-1961; CSF/SF, 1962

OCCUPATION: Co-operator of arts and crafts shops, IAIA educator, jeweler, painter, and ceramist

PUBLISHED: Snodgrass (1968); Brody (1971); Monthan and Monthan (1975); New (1981); Younger, et al. (1985). Southwest Profile (Aug/Sept/Oct 1992)

PUBLIC COLLECTIONS: IACB, HM, IAIA/M, MAI, PAC

EXHIBITS: AC/SD; AIATC; AICH; ASF; HM; IAIA; IAIA/M; MAI; NACLA; PAC; SFFA; SN; SWAIA; WSCS; WWM; CAIA, 1968; PU, 1970; Museo de Bellas Artes, Buenos Aires, Argentina; Berlin, Germany

SOLO EXHIBITS: IAIA/M

AWARDS: Partial listing for ceramics includes: ASF ('60, 1st); PAC ('63, 1st); SN ('62, 1st; '65, 1st); SWAIA ('83)

HONORS: Alfred (NY) University, scholarship; National Women's Caucus for Art, Honor Award, 1991

OTELLIE LOLOMA

"Best known for her work in ceramic sculpture, Loloma has recently (ca. 1968) also turned to painting with great success."

Snodgrass 1968

In 1961, she was an instructor for the Southwest Indian Art Project, University of Arizona, and, in 1962, was named to the original staff for the newly created Institute of American Indian Arts.

LOMA, HELENA (see Lomayesva, Helena)

LOMADAMOCVIA (see Polelonema, Otis)

LOMAHAFTEWA, ALONZO *Hopi*

Born 28 Feb 1917 in Shungopovi, Second Mesa, AZ; died 1945 in Italy during WWII; son of Helen and Viets Lomahaftewa

MILITARY: U.S. Army, WWII

EDUCATION: Phoenix; Santa Fe

MEDIA: Watercolor

PUBLISHED: Seymour (1988)

PUBLIC COLLECTIONS: IACB/DC

EXHIBITS: MNA, WRTD

ALONZO LOMAHAFTEWA

In 1945, Lomahaftewa was severely wounded rescuing a fellow soldier in Italy during World War II and died shortly thereafter. He was buried in the American Cemetery and Memorial at Nettuno (Anzio), Italy.

Seymour 1988

LOMAHAFTEWA, DAN VIETS *Hopi/Choctaw*

Born 3 Apr 1951 in Phoenix, AZ; brother of Linda Lomahaftewa (q.v.)

RESIDENCE: Fort Duchesne, UT

EDUCATION: B.F.A., ASU, 1981

OCCUPATION: Artist

MEDIA: Oil, acrylic, pastel, mixed-media, and prints

PUBLISHED: *Sun Advocate* (24 Dec 1989); *Steamboat Magazine* (winter/spring 1990); *The Indian Trader* (May 1993)

COMMISSIONS: NMIA, painting used on Christmas cards; Turner Broadcast System, two paintings used for promotion of American Indian project

PUBLIC COLLECTIONS: HM

EXHIBITS: ACAI; AIAFM; AICH; EM; HM; HM/G; OLO; SMA; MNH/LA; RE; SWAIA; Bottle Hollow Inn Indian Art Show, Fort Duchesne, UT; Springville (UT) Museum of Art; Verde Valley Art Association Gallery, Jerome, AZ; Crow Canyon Exhibition, Washington, D.C., 1994; galleries in AZ, CA, NM, NY, and UT; see also Awards

SOLO/SPECIAL EXHIBITS: AICH (dual show)

AWARDS: ACAI ('93, 1st); ASU ('80; '81, Painting Award); HM/G ('81, Best of Classification, Best of Division); RE ('91); SWAIA ('89, 1st; '90, 1st); Utah Arts Council

HONORS: Utah Visual Arts Fellowship, 1989; AIAFM, poster artist, 1993; SWAIA, poster artist, 1993

DAN VIETS LOMAHAFTEWA

Explaining the inspiration for his art, Lomahaftewa says, "In my work, I use symbolic imagery from many sources: hide paintings, shields, body paint, basket and pottery designs, petroglyphs and pictographs, etc., all of which I have come in contact with during my life either in religious ceremonies, social dances, or on my own direct research.... What I'm trying to create are images of my own interpretation of these symbolic representations of Native Americans."

LOMAHAFTEWA, HARVEY *Hopi*

PUBLIC COLLECTIONS: MNA (4)

LOMAHAFTEWA, LINDA *Hopi/Choctaw*

Born 3 July 1947 in Phoenix, AZ; sister of Dan Lomahaftewa (q.v.)

RESIDENCE: Santa Fe, NM

EDUCATION: IAIA, 1966; B.F.A. SFAI, 1970; M.F.A., SFAI, 1971

OCCUPATION: Educator and painter

MEDIA: Oil, acrylic, and prints

PUBLISHED: Snodgrass (1968); Blue Cloud (1972); New (1974; 1979; 1981); New Horizons (1976); Gonyea, ed. (1980); Highwater (1980); Amerson, ed. (1981); Wade and Strickland (1981); Rubenstein (1982); Broder (1984); Carhart (1984); Younger (1984); Steward (1988); Ward, ed. (1990); Archuleta and Strickland (1991); Abbott (1994). *Art in America* (July/Aug 1972); *News Letter,* Amon Carter Museum (Feb/Mar 1973); *The Indian Trader* (July 1978; Mar 1989); *Art Voices South* (Sept/Aug 1978); *Americas* (Aug 1981); *Turtle Arts* (winter 1981); *Calyx* (spring 1984, cover); *The Scottsdale Progress* (12 Oct 1985); *Artspace* (fall 1985); *American Indian Art* (spring 1986); *America West* (July 1990); *ATLATL* (winter 1990-1991); biographical publications

PUBLIC COLLECTIONS: C/U of L; HM; HS/AI; IAIA; IACB; MRFM; NACLA; WWM; Center of the Arts of Indian America, Washington, D.C.

EXHIBITS: ACAI; AICA/SF; AICH; AIWSAF; ASC/PG; BEAIAC; BM/B; CCDLR; CSF/SF; CTC; FNAA; FSMCIAF; GM; HM; IAIA; MNM; MFA/O; MMA/WA; MNH/LA; MSW; NACLA; ND; NU/BC; OLO; OSU/G; OWE; PAC; PAIC; RE; WIB; SAIEAIP; SFAI; SFFA; SI; SM; SN; SPIM; SV; SW; SWAIA; WSCS; WWM; YAIA; Galería Latinamericana de la Casa de las Américas; see also Awards

AWARDS: ACS/PG ('90); BEAIAC ('67, Graphics Award); IFA ('74, 1st); SN ('70); RE ('91); SN ('70); SWAIA ('83; '87; '88, Hardin award; '89; '90); Center for the Arts of Indian America, Washington, D.C. ('67, 1st, Purchase Award)

HONORS: Brandywine Workshop, Philadelphia, PA, fellowship, 1988; HM/G, poster artist, 1994

LINDA LOMAHAFTEWA

"My imagery comes from being Hopi and remembering shapes and colors from ceremonies and from the landscape. I associate a special power and respect, a sacredness, with these colors and shapes, and this carries over into my work." Images that tend to recur in Lomahaftewa's work are parrots, petroglyphs, mountain lions, shamans, corn maidens, and Hopi symbols such as lightning, clouds and rainbows.

artist, p.c. 1991

Lomahi I' Quil Va A (see Duwyenie, Preston)

Lomakema, Marshall (see Lomakema, Milland, Sr.)

Lomakema, Milland, Sr. *Hopi*

Dawakema, House of the Sun

A.K.A. Marshall Lomakema

Born Aug 1941 at Shungopovi, Second Mesa, AZ, on the Hopi Reservation; son of Jane and Charles Lomakema

RESIDENCE: Second Mesa, AZ

EDUCATION: Academy of Harding College, Searcy, AR, 1957-1959; Academy of Magic Valley Christian College, Delco, ID, 1960; G.E.D., Roswell, NM, 1969; workshops

OCCUPATION: Cultural preservation specialist, revenue officer, legal research assistant, director and manager of the Hopi Arts and Crafts Co-operative, and painter

MEDIA: Acrylic and watercolor

PUBLISHED: Snodgrass (1968); Harvey (1970); Tanner (1973); Broder (1978; 1981); Silberman (1978); New (1979); Highwater (1980); Hoffman, et al. (1984); Wade, ed. (1986). *Wassaja* (20 Sept 1975); *Americas* (Aug 1981); *Southwest Art* (June 1982); *Four Winds* (spring 1982)

COMMISSIONS: *Murals:* HCCM. *Other:* Hopi Project (Byron Harvey III, Collection), 62 paintings, 1964-1965; Hopi Police Department, decal design; City of Winslow (AZ), decal design

PUBLIC COLLECTIONS: AC/RM, CGPS, HCC, HM, EM, MAI, MNA, MRFM, SM, WWM

EXHIBITS: CGPS; DCM; FAC/CS; HCC; HCCM; HM; HM/G; HT; IK; ITIC; MNH/D; NACLA; NTF; OMA; PAC; PAIC; SDMM; SFFA; SPIM; WCCA; WWM; Riverside Community College; Hillsborough County Museum, Tampa, FL; Arizona State Capitol Building, Phoenix, AZ

AWARDS: ASF ('69); HM/G ('69; '75); ITIC ('68; '71); NTF ('69, 1st); PAC ('71; '75); SN

Milland Lomakema Sr.

Lomakema is a member of the Corn/Water Clan and one of the original members of Artist Hopid (q.v.). He has been very active in the support and promotion of Hopi arts and crafts, often to the detriment of his own artistic endeavors.

Lomatewama, Ramson *Hopi*

Born 20 Oct 1953 in Victorville, CA; son of Corrine and Cyrus Lomatewama

RESIDENCE: Flagstaff, AZ

EDUCATION: Flagstaff (AZ) High School, 1971; A.A., Northland Pioneer College, Holbrook, AZ, 1979; B.A., Goddard College, Plainfield, VT, 1981

OCCUPATION: Consultant, lecturer, cultural anthropologist, writer, poet, educator, *katsina* carver, weaver, and artist

MEDIA: Acrylic, watercolor, pastel, cottonwood root, stained glass, yarn, and prints

PUBLISHED: Lomatewama (1983; 1987). *The Scottsdale Daily Progress* (19 Sept 1983); *The Arizona Republic* (23 June 1984; 5 Nov 1986; 8 Jan 1989); *The Phoenix Gazette* (6 Oct 1983; 3 Oct 1986; 30 June 1990); *The Tucson Citizen* (29 July 1985); *The Christian Science Monitor* (2 Dec 1986); *ATLATL* (summer 1989); *Native Peoples* (fall 1992)

EXHIBITS: EM, FNAA, HM, HM/G, MNA, SM, SWAIA, TYAC; Fiesta de la Tlaquepaque, Sedona, AZ; National Handicrafts and Handloom Museum, New Delhi, India

AWARDS: MNA ('88, 1st, HM; '89, 2-1st, Best of Division; '91, 1st); SWAIA ('90, 1st)

HONORS: American Indian Arts Foundation, NY, award for accomplishments in poetry, 1987; Flagstaff Arts Council, Arizona Senator's Arts Award, 1989

Ramson Lomatewama

Lomatewama says, "As an artist, my continual search for a greater appreciation and respect for others can only come through the practice of my own creativity. It is with this in mind that I have chosen both the visual and literary arts to continue my quest for greater awareness."

artist, p.c. 1992

Lomawywesa (see Kabotie, Michael)

LOMAY, LOUIS *(see Lomayesva, Louis)*

LOMAYAKTEWA, NARRON *Hopi*

Born 1946 at Shungopovi, Second Mesa, AZ, on the Hopi Reservation; GF: Mishongnovi, village chief of Shungopovi

EDUCATION: Albuquerque, 1946

OCCUPATION: *Katsina* carver and painter

PUBLISHED: Snodgrass (1968); Harvey (1970); Golder (1985); Tanner (1987). *The Indian Trader* (Sept 1982)

PUBLIC COLLECTIONS: LMA/BC, MAI, MNM

EXHIBITS: HH; ITIC; Hopi Craftsmen Exhibition, Phoenix, AZ, 1959

LOMAYAKTEWA, V. *Hopi*

A.K.A. Art Holmes

Birth date unknown; born at Shungopovi, Second Mesa, AZ, on the Hopi Reservation

PUBLISHED: Snodgrass (1968)

PUBLIC COLLECTIONS: MAI

LOMAYESVA, HELENA *Hopi*

A.K.A. Helena Loma

Birth date unknown; born at Shungopovi, Second Mesa, AZ, on the Hopi Reservation

EDUCATION: Santa Fe, ca. 1937

PUBLISHED: Snodgrass (1968)

PUBLIC COLLECTIONS: MAI

EXHIBITS: AIEC, 1937

LOMAYESVA, LEWIS *(see Lomayesva, Louis)*

LOMAYESVA, LOUIS *Hopi*

A.K.A. Louis Lomay; Coma Pesva; Lewis Lomayesva

Born 1920s

RESIDENCE: Lived in Old Oraibi, AZ

EDUCATION: New Oraibi (AZ) Day School; Albuquerque; Santa Fe

OCCUPATION: House painter, silversmith, shop owner, and painter

MEDIA: Oil, watercolor, and silver

PUBLISHED: Dunn (1968); Snodgrass (1968); Tanner (1973); Seymour (1988); Williams, ed. (1990)

PUBLIC COLLECTIONS: BM/B, IACB/DC, MAI, MKMcNAI, MNA/KHC, MNM, OU/MA, PAC, SM, U of CA/LMA

EXHIBITS: FHMAG, MKMcNAI, MNM, PAC, PAC/T, WRTD

LOMAYESVA, S. A. *Hopi*

PUBLIC COLLECTIONS: MNA

LOMAYESVA, WILLIAM *Hopi/Mission*

A.K.A. Bill Lomayesva

Birth date unknown; born in Arizona

RESIDENCE: Parker, AZ

EDUCATION: IAIA

PUBLISHED: Snodgrass (1968)

EXHIBITS: FAIEAIP, RC, SN

AWARDS: RC, SN

LOUIS LOMAYESVA

"The artist is known for his fine paintings of katsinas. *He has also been both silversmith and house painter. He has often signed his paintings 'Louis Lomay,' as well as an elaborate rendering that appears to be 'Coma Pesva.'"*

Snodgrass 1968

Lomayesva has done very little painting since the 1940s, concentrating instead on his silver work for which he has won many awards.

LONE BEAR

"Lone Bear may have lived in the area of Fort Phil Kearny in the mid-1800s and was possibly a Miniconju Sioux (see Vestal 1932; 1934)."

Snodgrass 1968

MICHAEL LONECHILD

Lonechild's paintings are realistic and his subject matter is the real life of the Plains Cree people after they moved to the reserve. He has said, "I try to tell a story about the way the people used to live on the reserve not so many years ago. I want to do this so everyone can remember how it used to be. They shouldn't forget these things."

Artists of the Rockies and the Golden West, *summer 1978*

LONE DOG

"There were several men named Lone Dog during the 1800s. Chief White Bull listed a Lone Dog as one who fell during the Custer battle at Little Big Horn; however, the artist was in the area of Fort Peck, MT, in 1876.

LOMAYN DO *Taos*
PUBLISHED: Snodgrass (1968)
PUBLIC COLLECTIONS: AF

LONE BEAR *Oglala Sioux*
Birth date unknown
PUBLISHED: Snodgrass (1968)
PUBLIC COLLECTIONS: MAI (ledger drawings)

LONE BULL (see Schildt, Gary Joseph)

LONECHILD, MICHAEL *Plains Cree*
Born 30 Oct 1955 near Carlyle, SK, Canada, on the White Bear Reserve; son of Irene and George Lonechild
EDUCATION: Punnichy (SK) High School; studied under Ernest Luthi
MEDIA: Acrylic
PUBLISHED: *Artists of the Rockies and the Golden West* (summer 1978); *The Indian Trader* (Apr 1979)
PUBLIC COLLECTIONS: HCC
EXHIBITS: C/AG/TB; HCC; RC; galleries throughout Canada
AWARDS: RC ('78, 1st)

LONE DOG *Yankton Sioux*
Shunka Ishnala, Lone Dog; *Chinosa*, A Lone Wanderer
Birth date unknown
PUBLISHED: Jacobson and d'Ucel (1950); Snodgrass (1968). *4th Annual Report*, BAE (1882-1883); *10th Annual Report*, BAE (1888-1889). Susan B. Bettelyoun, the artist's granddaughter, filed an informative manuscript on the Red Lodge (Tishayaote) group at the Nebraska Historical Society
PUBLIC COLLECTIONS: MAI (Winter Count)

LONE HORSE *Oglala Sioux (?)*
Sunka Wonka Wanjila
Birth date unknown
RESIDENCE: From Pine Ridge Agency, SD (see Black Heart)
PUBLISHED: Snodgrass (1968)
PUBLIC COLLECTIONS: MAI

LONESOME POLECAT (see Patterson, Pat)

LONE WANDERER, A (see Lone Dog)

LONE WOLF *Kiowa*
A.K.A. Chief Lone Wolf
Born ca. 1820; died 1879
OCCUPATION: Chief, warrior, and artist
PUBLISHED: Snodgrass (1968); Dockstader (1977)
EXHIBITS: BPG

LONE WOLF (see Schultz, Hart Merriam)

LONEWOLF, GREGORY M. *Santa Clara*
RESIDENCE: Española, NM
EXHIBITS: MCC/CA

(continued) He was the son of Red War Bonnet (Tawapasha), originally from Minnesota. Lone Dog and his father, with a group of immigrant Miniconju, moved into the camp of the Brûlé in the White River area in southern South Dakota, ca. 1810."

Snodgrass 1968

It is not thought that Lone Dog was old enough in 1800 to paint the Winter Count. Either he received the earlier records from a predecessor, or, when older, he gathered the tribal traditions from the elders and worked back (see Cloud Shield).

LONE WOLF

After the death of Satank and the imprisonment of Big Tree and Satanta (q.v.), Lone Wolf became the principal chief of the Kiowa living around Fort Sill. He signed the Little Arkansas Treaty, in 1865 and was one of nine who signed the Treaty of Medicine Lodge of 1867 which placed the Kiowa on a reservation. He took part in the Battle of Adobe Walls, 1874 and surrendered February 26, 1875. Lone Wolf was one of 72 Plains Indians taken as prisoners from Fort Sill, OK, to Fort Marion, St. Augustine, FL, in 1875.

Dockstader 1977

"In 1868, Lone Wolf and Satanta (q.v.) painted a robe which told of their battles with the Utes and Navajos (see Keim 1870, p. 223)."

Snodgrass 1968

LONEWOLF, JOSEPH *Santa Clara*
A.K.A. Joseph Tafoya
Born 1932
RESIDENCE: Española, NM
PUBLIC COLLECTIONS: EM
EXHIBITS: MCC/CA, WWM

LONG, CHARLES VEE *Navajo*
EDUCATION: IAIA, 1962-1963; U of AZ
PUBLISHED: Snodgrass (1968)
COMMISSIONS: *Murals:* ASF (with four other Navajo painters)
HONORS: U of AZ, scholarship

LONGBOAT, GREG *Iroquois*
Born 1965 on the Six Nations Reserve, ON, Canada
RESIDENCE: Canada
EXHIBITS: C/AG/W; C/WICEC; NACLA; Ogwatsih Artisans, St. Catherine's, ON

LONGBOAT, STEVEN *Iroquois*
Born 1955 on the Six Nations Reserve, ON, Canada
RESIDENCE: Canada
EXHIBITS: Partial listing of more than ten includes: C/NCCT; C/WICEC; NACLA

LONGBOAT, HARVEY, JR. *Iroquois*
Born 1963 on the Six Nations Reserve, ON, Canada
RESIDENCE: Canada
EXHIBITS: C/AG/W; C/WICEC; NACLA; Ogwatsih Artisans, St. Catherine's, ON

LONG CAT *Oglala Sioux*
A.K.A. Chief Long Cat
RESIDENCE: At various times he was at White River, Chadron Creek, Spotted Tail Agency (Camp Sheridan), and Pine Ridge Agency, SD
PUBLISHED: Snodgrass (1968)
PUBLIC COLLECTIONS: MAI
HONORS: Dance chief; soldier chief; drum chief; presided at council meetings

LONGFISH, GEORGE *Seneca/Tuscarora*
Born 22 Aug 1942 in Oshweken, ON, Canada
RESIDENCE: Davis, CA
EDUCATION: Tulley High School, Chicago, IL, 1960; B.F.A., CAI, 1970; M.F.A., CAI, 1972
OCCUPATION: Clerk, art teacher, professor, writer, lecturer, curator, and artist
MEDIA: Oil, acrylic, pencil, pen and ink, mixed-media, and prints
PUBLISHED: New (1979); Highwater (1980); Amerson, ed. (1981); Roberts, ed. (1992); Hoffman, et al. (1984); Wade, ed. (1986); Stewart (1988); Gentry, et al. (1990); Archuleta and Strickland (1991); Zurko, ed. (1992); Abbott (1994). *Horizon* (Sept 1980); *Artspace* (summer 1982); *Northeast Indian Quarterly* (fall 1989); *Art News* (Feb 1992); *Southwest Art* (Mar 1992); *American Indian Art* (autumn 1992)
EXHIBITS: Partial listing of more than 150 includes: AC/B; AC/Y; AICA/SF; AICH; C/CMC; C/I; C/NWNG; C/U of L; C/U of R/MG; CIA; CIAE; CSU/S; CTC; CWAM; EM; FWMA; HM; HM/G; HS/OH; IAIA; IK; KCPA; MMA/WA; MM/NJ; MPI; NACLA; NDM; NU/BC; OLO; OSU/G; PAC;

GEORGE LONGFISH

Longfish says of his art, "Since my training was not oriented toward Native art such as the Institute of American Indian Arts or the Southwest area in general, I have approached my painting and drawing in an abstract sense that was in tune with concepts that are either European or American."

Highwater 1980

He is a leading proponent of non-objective painting of American Indian subjects.

PAIC; PAM; QM; SCG; SFFA; SFMA; SM; SN; SS/CW; SV; SW; TFAG; TRP; U of C/D; U of MI; U of ND; U of WA; WHB; Loch Haven Art Center, Orlando, FL, 1984; State Capitol Building, Sacramento, CA, 1975; The Center for Contemporary Arts, Sacramento, CA; The New Museum of Contemporary Art, New York, NY; University of Northern Iowa, Cedar Falls, IA; see also Awards

SOLO EXHIBITS: Partial listing of more than 15 includes: AICA/SF; CAM/S; MPI; WSU/P; U of MT; Second Unitarian Church, Chicago, IL, 1971; Yuba College, Woodland, CA

AWARDS: CIAE ('74, Juror's Grand Award; '77, 1st; '80, 1st); HM/G ('73); October ArtFest, Davis, CA ('81, 1st)

LONGMAN, MARY *Saulteaux*

Born 1964 at Fort Qu'Appelle Valley, SK, Canada

RESIDENCE: Canada

EDUCATION: C/ECC; C/NSCAD; C/CU

OCCUPATION: Sculptor, graphic artist, and painter

PUBLISHED: *Concordia's Thursday Report* (Vol. 15, no. 9, 1990)

PUBLIC COLLECTIONS: C/INAC

EXHIBITS: Partial listing of more than ten includes: C/CU; C/I; C/ECC; C/NSCAD

SOLO EXHIBITS: C/ECC

HONORS: C/ECC, Bursary Award, 1985, 1986; First Citizen's Fund, 1986, 1988; Mungo Martin Award, 1989; Catholic Services Award, 1989; Concordia University Award, Montréal, PQ, 1990

LONG SOLDIER, DANIEL *Oglala Sioux*

Born 1949 at Little Eagle, SD, on the Standing Rock Reservation, SD

RESIDENCE: Lincoln, NE

OCCUPATION: Commercial artist, and painter

MEDIA: Acrylic, watercolor, gouache, pencil, pen and ink, and charcoal

PUBLISHED: *The Indian Trader* (May 1989)

COMMISSIONS: Tipi Press, note cards

PUBLIC COLLECTIONS: CGPS; HCC; Atka Lakota Museum

EXHIBITS: CGPS, HCC, RC

SOLO/SPECIAL EXHIBITS: SIM (dual show)

AWARDS: RC ('87, Erickson Award)

DANIEL LONG SOLDIER

Long Soldier considers his talent to be a gift from God, he says, "Sometimes I think that all I do is clean brushes." Most of his paintings begin with a story and are portrayals of the ways and spiritual life of his people.

brochure, SIM, 1988

LOOKING ELK (see Martínez, Albert)

LOOKS IN THE CLOUDS (see Standing, William)

LOON (see Palmer, Woodrow Wilson)

LOREEN-WULF, AUDREA *Inuvialuit (Eskimo)*

A.K.A. Kowichuk; Audria; Lina

Born 2 Jan 1952 at Stanton, NWT, Canada; daughter of Annie Loreen

RESIDENCE: Burns Lake, BC, Canada

EDUCATION: U of AB

OCCUPATION: Teacher, craft shop manager, radio reporter/announcer, graphic designer, illustrator, graphic artist, and painter

COMMISSIONS: Northwest Telephone, directory cover

EXHIBITS: Expo '86, NWT Pavilion; galleries in British Columbia and Ontario

SOLO EXHIBITS: Arctic Art Gallery, Yellowknife, NWT

LORENTZ, TRUMAN *Wichita/Pawnee*

MEDIA: Watercolor

EXHIBITS: CNM

LORENZO (see Baca, Lorenzo)

LORETTO, LEONARD *Jémez*

EDUCATION: Santa Fe, ca. 1960

PUBLISHED: Snodgrass (1968)

EXHIBITS: AAIE, MNM

LOUIS, JAMES M. *(?)*

PUBLISHED: Snodgrass (1968)

PUBLIC COLLECTIONS: CGA

LOUIS, JULIAN J. *Pueblo*

PUBLISHED: Snodgrass (1968)

PUBLIC COLLECTIONS: MNM

LOUVIER, NANCY RAINS *Cherokee*

Born 3 Jan 1936 in Tulsa, OK; Daughter of Elsie Heft and Roy Rains; P/GP: Nancy Annie Crane and Charles Lafayette Rains; M/GP: Olive Place and John Henry Heft

EXHIBITS: McLain High School, Tulsa, OK, 1964; B.A., U of Tulsa, 1970

OCCUPATION: Teacher; full-time painter since 1971

MEDIA: Oil, acrylic, pencil, and prints

EXHIBITS: FCTM, RE, TIAF

AWARDS: FCTM ('77; '78; '80); TIAF ('95)

LOVATO, AMBROSIO *Santo Domingo*

Born 1934

PUBLISHED: Snodgrass (1968)

PUBLIC COLLECTIONS: MNM

CHARLES FREDRIC LOVATO

Most of Lovato's major paintings were accompanied by poems. At times the poem came first and other times the painting inspired the poem. His abstract paintings were unique and did not evolve from a painting tradition at his Pueblo. He was the only major painter to come from Santo Domingo. Lovato was also one of the most gifted of the artisans creating the heishe necklaces for which Santo Domingo Pueblo is well known. He credited his friend, R.C. Gorman (q.v.), with helping him get his career started.

Monthan and Monthan 1975

LOVATO, CHARLES FREDRIC *Santo Domingo*

A.K.A. Signature: C. F. Lovato

Born 23 May 1937 in Santo Domingo Pueblo, NM; died 1987 at Santo Domingo Pueblo, NM; GM: Monica Silva, potter; adopted at an early age by his grandmother, Monica Silva

RESIDENCE: Lived in Peña Blanca, NM

MILITARY: U.S. Navy

EDUCATION: Santa Fe; studied under José Ray Toledo (q.v.)

OCCUPATION: Poet, jeweler, craftsman; painter after 1967

MEDIA: Acrylic, pen and ink, and casein

PUBLISHED: Dunn (1968); Tanner (1973); Monthan and Monthan (1975); Broder (1981); Medina (1981). *The Indian Trader* (July 1978); *Art Voices South* (Sept/Oct 1979); *Four Winds* (spring 1980)

BOOKS ILLUSTRATED: Lovato (1982)

COMMISSIONS: *Murals:* IPCC

PUBLIC COLLECTIONS: CGPS, HCC, HM, MAI, MNA, MRFM, PAC, IPCC

EXHIBITS: AC/HC; CGPS; HM/G; ITIC; PAC; PM; RC; SN; galleries in CA, NM, NY, OK, and TX

AWARDS: HM/G ('68, Bialac Purchase Award; '69, Avery Award; '71, Avery Award; '77); ITIC ('69, Keney Award; '71; '72, Elkus Award); RC ('71); PAC ('70, 1st; '71; '79); SN ('70); RC ('71)

LOVER OF HOME (see Orr, Howell Sonny)

LOW BLACK BIRD (see Amiotte, Arthur Douglas)

LOWE, TRUMAN *Winnebago*

EDUCATION: M.F.A., U of WI/M, 1973
OCCUPATION: Sculptor and painter
PUBLISHED: Zurko, ed. (1992)
EXHIBITS: AICA/SF, HM, SCG, WHB
SOLO EXHIBITS: EM; U of WI/G, Lawton Gallery, 1991; galleries in Atlanta, GA, and New York, NY

LOWEKA, BILL *Zuni*

PUBLISHED: Snodgrass (1968)
PUBLIC COLLECTIONS: MNM

LOWRY, JUDITH *Maidu*

Born 1948 in Washington, D.C.
RESIDENCE: McKinleyville, CA
EDUCATION: B.A., HSU, 1988; M.F.A., CSU/C, 1992
PUBLISHED: Gully, ed. (1994)
COMMISSIONS: *Murals:* Lassen County Arts Council, Susanville, CA
EXHIBITS: CNGM, HM; Eureka (CA) Cultural Center, 1989; Falkirk Cultural Center, San Rafael, CA, 1992; Lassen County Arts Council Gallery, Susanville, CA, 1993

LUBO, F. BRUCE, SR. *Laguna*

Born 29 Mar 1911 in Laguna Pueblo, NM; son of Anne and Syluas Lubo.
RESIDENCE: Palm Springs, CA
EDUCATION: Riverside (CA) Poly High School, 1930; Riverside (CA) Junior College, 1933; Riverside (CA) City College, 1936
OCCUPATION: Aircraft design engineer, gallery owner; full-time professional artist since 1960
MEDIA: Oil, acrylic, watercolor, pencil, pen and ink, and pastel
PUBLISHED: Samuels (1982)
PUBLIC COLLECTIONS: PM; New Mexico Cultural Center
EXHIBITS: ACS/ENP, AICA, CIM, HM, HM/G, ITIC, NWASA, PM, SN, SWAIA
AWARDS: Partial listing of more than fifty (27-1sts, 2-Best of Shows) includes: SWAIA ('72, 2-1st; '78, 1st)

LUCERO, ALONDO *Jémez*

EDUCATION: Santa Fe, ca. 1955
PUBLISHED: Snodgrass (1968)
PUBLIC COLLECTIONS: MNM
EXHIBITS: ITIC, MNM
AWARDS: MNM, 1958

LUCERO, BEN *Tarahumara/Maya/Kiowa*

Born 1937 in Arizona
EDUCATION: M.A., San Diego (CA) State University
OCCUPATION: Educator and artist
MEDIA: Acrylic
PUBLISHED: *New Horizons* (1976)
EXHIBITS: SM, SW

LUCERO, GUADALUPE *Jémez*

EDUCATION: Santa Fe, ca. 1958
PUBLISHED: Snodgrass (1968)
PUBLIC COLLECTIONS: MNM

LUCERO, LUPITA *Jémez*

Born 1949
EDUCATION: Jémez, ca. 1960-1963; IAIA, 1965-1966
PUBLISHED: Snodgrass (1968)
EXHIBITS: ITIC, MNM, PAC, SN
AWARDS: ITIC, MNM, SN

LUCERO, MARY ROSE *Jémez*

EDUCATION: Jémez, ca. 1963
PUBLISHED: Snodgrass (1968)
EXHIBITS: MNM; SN; Washington, D.C.

LUCERO, NORA ALICE *Jémez*

PUBLISHED: Snodgrass (1968)
PUBLIC COLLECTIONS: MAI

LUCERO, VICTOR *Jémez*

EDUCATION: Jémez, ca. 1962
PUBLISHED: Snodgrass (1968)
EXHIBITS: MNM

LUCERO-GIACCARDO, FELICE *San Felipe*

Born 1946 at San Felipe Pueblo, NM
EDUCATION: St. Catherine's; B.F.A., U of NM, 1979
MEDIA: Oil, acrylic, watercolor, pastel, graphite, and mixed-media
PUBLISHED: Gully, ed. (1994). *American Indian Art* (winter 1987)
PUBLIC COLLECTIONS: HM, MAI; Chase Manhattan Bank
EXHIBITS: CNM; HM; KCPA; MAI; NMSC; SCG; SM; Seattle, WA; Santa Fe, NM; Kansas City, MO
SOLO EXHIBITS: ASU/M

LUCHETTI, ARLENE *Taos*

Born 6 June 1948; daughter of Mary and Carl Schlosser; P/GP: Helen and Elois Schlosser; M/GM: Cecelia A. Concha
RESIDENCE: Taos, NM
EDUCATION: Taos (NM) High School, 1966; College of Marin, Kentfield, CA; IAIA, 1972
OCCUPATION: Gallery sales clerk, sculptor, and painter
MEDIA: Oil, acrylic, pencil, pen and ink, mixed-media, and stone
EXHIBITS: CNM, MRFM, SNAICF
AWARDS: SNAICF ('87)

LUCI *Jémez*

PUBLISHED: Snodgrass (1968)
PUBLIC COLLECTIONS: IACB/DC, MAI

LUCK *Inuit (Eskimo)*

RESIDENCE: Cape Dorset, NWT, Canada
OCCUPATION: Graphic artist

PUBLISHED: *North* (Mar/Apr 1974)

EXHIBITS: Robertson Galleries, Ottawa, ON

LUCY *Inuit (Eskimo)*

A.K.A. Lucy Qinnuayuak; Tickeetoo; Quinnuajuak

Born 1915 at Sugluk, PQ, Canada; died 10 Sept 1982; daughter of Sanaaq; stepdaughter of Takata Meesa

RESIDENCE: Lived in Cape Dorset, NWT, Canada

OCCUPATION: Sculptor, painter, and graphic artist

MEDIA: Acrylic, watercolor, crayon, graphite, colored felt tip pen, and prints

PUBLISHED: Houston (1967; 1967a); Larmour (1967); Goetz, et al. (1977); Blodgett, (1978b; 1983); Routledge (1979); Marsh (1985); Jackson and Nasby (1987); Leroux, Jackson, and Freeman, eds. (1994). *Canada Today* (Apr 1971); *North* (Mar/Apr 1974); *The Beaver* (autumn 1967; spring 1975; winter 1983); *The Toronto Star* (5 June 1976); *The Edmonton Journal* (31 Mar 1980); *The Inuit Art Quarterly* (Vol. 1, no. 2, 1986)

COMMISSIONS: *Posters:* Summer Olympics Poster, 1976. *Other:* UNICEF, greeting card, 1972

PUBLIC COLLECTIONS: C/AC/MS; ACMWA; C/AG/LR; C/AG/M; C/AG/O; C/AG/GV; C/AG/LR; C/AG/O; C/AG/TT; C/AG/U of L; C/AG/WI; C/AG/WP; C/CCAB; C/CGCQ; C/CMC; C/DEA; C/GM; C/ICI; C/LUM; C/NBM; C/NGCA; C/PWNHC; C/RDM; C/ROM; C/TDB; C/U of AB; C/U of NB; C/YU; DAM; HMA; NMC; Macmillan-Bloedel Limited, Vancouver, BC; Tate Gallery, London, England; Teleglobe Canada, Montréal, PQ

EXHIBITS: Partial listing of more than eighty includes: ACMWA; C/AG/E; C/AGO; C/AG/GV; C/AG/O; C/AG/U of L; C/AG/WP; C/AV; C/CB; C/CG; C/CGCQ; C/CID; C/CIIA; C/CMC; C/GAEC; C/GTOW; C/HNG; C/IA7; C/IGV; C/INAC; C/ITP; C/LS; C/MCC; C/MFA/NS; C/NGCA; C/SFG; C/TDB; C/TIP; C/WLA; C/U of AB; C/U of G; MSU; U of MI; Konstframjandet, Stockholm, Sweden, 1967; Alaska Methodist University Galleries, Anchorage, AK; Jerusalem Artists' House Museum, Jerusalem, Israel; University of New Brunswick, Long Gallery, St. John, NB; National Gallery of Modern Art, Rome, Italy; UNESCO, Paris, France; galleries in the U.S. and Canada

SOLO EXHIBITS: Partial listing includes: Montréal, PQ; Toronto, ON; Hastings-On-Hudson, NY; Minneapolis, MN; galleries in Hamilton, ON

HONORS: Design for an Olympic banner was one of four selected, displayed at the Art Gallery of Ontario, Toronto, 1976; United Nations, Habitat Conference, print included in the Habitat Folio, 1976

LUCY

Lucy's father died when she was about four years old and her mother, Sanaaq, emigrated to Baffin Island from Sugluk, Québec, where Sanaaq remarried. One of the best known Inuit artists, Lucy was recognized for her paintings and drawings of birds and womanly pursuits. Her paintings have been described as "busy people doing things." By disregarding the usual practice of outlining a figure she gave her figures the appearance of fur or feathers. Prints made from Lucy's drawings have been included in the Cape Dorset collections since 1961. In 1973, Lucy was introduced to paints by Kate Graham who set up a painting studio for the summer in Cape Dorset. She was equally as talented in that medium.

LUJÁN, ALBERT *Taos*

A.K.A. Alfred Luján

Born 10 July 1922

EDUCATION: Santa Fe; Taos

OCCUPATION: Arts and crafts instructor and advisor, radio station employee, and artist

PUBLISHED: Snodgrass (1968); Golder (1985). *American Indian Art* (spring 1995)

COMMISSIONS: Kiwanis International of Taos, NM, *Things To See And Do*, tourist brochure

PUBLIC COLLECTIONS: BIA, GPM, MAI, SM, WWM

EXHIBITS: ASM; GPM; HH; USDS; Taos (NM) Art Association; Phoenix, AZ; Santa Fe, NM

LUJÁN, ALFRED (see Luján, Albert)

LUJÁN, DENNIS EUGENE *Taos*

Eagle Pipe

Born 9 Jan 1961 in Great Falls, MT; son of Cynthia and David Luján; P/GP: Raysita Romero and Johny Luján; M/GP: Gertrude Darling and August Znader; related to Gilbert Luján (q.v.) and Juan de Jesús Romero

RESIDENCE: Colorado Springs, CO

EDUCATION: G.E.D.; Pike's Peak Community College, Colorado Springs, CO

OCCUPATION: Graphic art business owner, poet, and painter

MEDIA: Acrylic, watercolor, pencil, pen and ink, pastel, and prints

PUBLISHED: *In Step Magazine* (1985), cover

COMMISSIONS: Upstart Performing Ensemble, Colorado Springs, CO, logo and program design, 1993

EXHIBITS: FAC/CS; Business of Art Center, Manitou Springs, CO, 1993; galleries in Colorado; see also Awards

AWARDS: HIT 105 FM, logo contest, La Crosse, WI, ('86); Pike's Peak Community College ('79, 1st)

HONORS: May D & F Department Store, Colorado Springs, CO, Scholastic Art Awards, 1976; Publication Award, for poem, *You and I*, 1988

LUJÁN, GILBERT *Taos*

RESIDENCE: Taos, NM

EDUCATION: Albuquerque, ca. 1960

PUBLISHED: Snodgrass (1968)

EXHIBITS: MNM

AWARDS: MNM

LUJÁN, JAMES *Taos*

Born 1941; brother of Jerry Luján (q.v.)

RESIDENCE: Mesa, AZ

EDUCATION: BC; Santa Fe; U of AZ, "Southwest Indian Art Project," scholarship, summer 1960; B.A., ASU

PUBLISHED: Snodgrass (1968)

PUBLIC COLLECTIONS: IACB

EXHIBITS: MNM, MNM, PAC

LUJÁN, JERALYN *Taos*

EXHIBITS: AIWSAF

LUJÁN, JERRY *Taos*

Born 1945; brother of James Luján (q.v.)

RESIDENCE: Taos, NM

EDUCATION: Central High Catholic School, Taos, NM

PUBLISHED: Snodgrass (1968)

PUBLIC COLLECTIONS: MNM

LUJÁN, LORENZO A. *Taos*

Bilokila, Floating Plumes

Born 1922 in Taos, NM; died 1962; father of Emille Mirabel

RESIDENCE: Lived in Taos Pueblo, NM

EDUCATION: Santa Fe; Taos

PUBLISHED: Snodgrass (1968)

PUBLIC COLLECTIONS: MRFM

EXHIBITS: Harwood Foundation, NM

LUJÁN, MANUEL *Taos*

PUBLISHED: Snodgrass (1968)
PUBLIC COLLECTIONS: MFA/Z

LUJÁN, MARGARET *Taos*

Born ca. 1928
PUBLISHED: Snodgrass (1968)
PUBLIC COLLECTIONS: MAI

LUJÁN, MERINA (see Pop Chalee)

LUJÁN, MIKE *Taos*

PUBLISHED: Snodgrass (1968)
EXHIBITS: FWG

LUJÁN, TONITA *Taos*

Khup Khu
Birth date unknown; wife of George Campbell Keahbone (q.v.)
RESIDENCE: Santa Fe, NM
EDUCATION: Santa Fe
PUBLISHED: Snodgrass (1968)
BOOKS ILLUSTRATED: Clark (1940b)
COMMISSIONS: *Murals:* Santa Fe Indian School (assisted with a frieze)
EXHIBITS: AIEC, AIW, NGA

TONITA LUJÁN

"The artist has painted very little, if at all, since the late 1930s."

Snodgrass 1968

LUJÁN, WAHLEAH *Taos*

RESIDENCE: Taos Pueblo, NM
EDUCATION: St. Catherine's, ca. 1965
PUBLISHED: Snodgrass (1968)
EXHIBITS: PAC, 1965
HONORS: Miss Indian America, 1966

LUKE, WILLIAM *Eskimo (Inuit)*

Born ca. 1927 in White Mountain, AK
RESIDENCE: Seattle, WA
OCCUPATION: Employed by Leonard F. Porter, Inc. (Seattle, WA) ca. 1969
PUBLISHED: Ray (1969)

LUKTA *Inuit (Eskimo)*

A.K.A. Luktak; Lukta Kiakshuk
Born 1928
RESIDENCE: Cape Dorset, NWT, Canada
OCCUPATION: Graphic artist and printmaker
PUBLISHED: Houston (1967; 1967a); Larmour (1967); Goetz, et al. (1977). *The Beaver* (spring 1975)
PUBLIC COLLECTIONS: C/TDB
EXHIBITS: C/CD, C/EACTDB, C/TIP

LAKTAK (see Lukta)

LUMHEE HOLATTEE (see Blue Eagle, Acee)

LUNA, JOHN *Hopi*

PUBLIC COLLECTIONS: MNA

Donald D. Lynch

Using a realistic style, Lynch seeks to express a nostalgia for the past.

Johannsen and Ferguson, eds. 1983

Ly Dam Lilly (see Day, Frank)

Lynch, Donald D. *Cayuga*

Born 13 Feb 1948

RESIDENCE: Ohsweken, ON, Canada

EDUCATION: Cornell, 1966; SUNY/G, 1967-1969

MEDIA: Oil and watercolor

PUBLISHED: Johannsen and Ferguson, eds. (1983)

EXHIBITS: C/WICEC, SUNY/G

Lyons, Oren *Onondaga*

Jo Ag Quis Ho

Born 1930 in Syracuse, NY; M/GM: Jessie Pierce

RESIDENCE: Nedrow, NY

OCCUPATION: Commercial artist, art instructor, art director, author, illustrator, publisher, educator, lecturer, panelist, lacrosse player, consultant, tribal leader, and painter

PUBLISHED: New (1981); Johannsen and Ferguson, eds. (1983). *The Conservationist* (Jan/Feb 1976); *Four Winds* (spring 1982); *The Indian Trader* (spring 1986); *Muskogee Daily Phoenix* (16 Sept 1993); *Native Peoples* (Special Edition 1994; Jan/Feb/Mar 1995)

BOOKS ILLUSTRATED: Sneve (1972; 1974a; 1974b); Anonymous (1974)

COMMISSIONS: Onondaga Savings Bank, series of paintings of Onondaga history; North-South All State Lacrosse Game, program cover, 1975; Franklin Mint, text and design for silver medallions, 1977

EXHIBITS: Partial listing includes: ACS/EM; ACS/H; AICH; AM; C/BJNJ; CAOR; FAIEAIP; INAAT; ITIC; NACLA; NSC; NU/BC; PAC; QM; SU/NY; TRP; WASG; Havana, Cuba

AWARDS: ITIC; Council of Interracial Books for Children, *Little Jimmy Yellow Hawk* (1st-illustrations)

HONORS: Onondaga Council of Chiefs, member; NMAI, The Art and Cultural Achievement Award, 1994

Lyons, Spencer *Mission*

EDUCATION: IAIA

MEDIA: Oil

EXHIBITS: AC/SD

Lyons, Mrs. Tony *Choctaw/Chickasaw*

RESIDENCE: Holdenville, OK

EXHIBITS: FCTM

MAAS, CAROLINE ORR (see Orr, Caroline Louise)

MAAS, MRS. J. A. (see Orr, Caroline Louise)

MACMILLAN, JAMES H. *Zia*

PUBLISHED: Snodgrass (1968)
EXHIBITS: AIEC

MACPHEE, TERESA (see Marshall, Teresa MacPhee)

MAGAWBO (see DesJarlait, Patrick R.)

MAGGINO, WAKA IGNACIO *Zia*

A.K.A. Probably the same person as Ignacio Moquino (q.v)
PUBLISHED: Snodgrass (1968)
PUBLIC COLLECTIONS: OU/MA

MAHO, ROBERT ALLEN *Hopi/Menomini*

Born 2 Oct 1964 in Keams Canyon, AZ; son of Gaynelle Marie Pérez and Lawrence Martin Maho Sr.; P/GM: Patricia Honie; M/GP: Camilo Pérez
RESIDENCE: Stillwater, MN
EDUCATION: Flandreau (SD) Indian School, 1982; Minneapolis (MN) Community College; U of MN; Metro State College, Minneapolis, MN; IAIA
OCCUPATION: Graphic artist and painter
MEDIA: Oil, acrylic, watercolor, pencil, pen and ink, and pastel
EXHIBITS: RC; see also Awards
AWARDS: Flandreau (SD) Indian School ('82, 1st, Best of Show); Wo-O-Be Winnebago Art Show ('82, 1st); Penal Press Competition ('90)

MAHSE NOMPAH (see Red Corn, Raymond Wesley)

MAHSETKY, WENDY AMBER *Comanche/Kickapoo*

Nhma Peta, Our Daughter
Born 8 Jan 1969 in Lawton, OK; daughter of Mary E. Hair and Michael D. Mahsetky; P/GP: Annette and Marcey Mahsetky; M/GP: Lois and Houston Hair
RESIDENCE: Norman, OK
EDUCATION: Yukon (OK) High School, 1987; B.A., CSU/OK; U of OK, 1993
MEDIA: Oil, acrylic, mixed-media, and prints
PUBLIC COLLECTIONS: OU/MA
EXHIBITS: JH, MMO, LIAS, OIAC, OU/MA
AWARDS: OIAC ('95)
HONORS: U of OK, T. G. Mayes Purchase Award, 1992

MAHTHELA (see Spybuck, Ernest)

MAHTOHN AHZSHE (see Standingbear, George Eugene)

MAH TO TOH PA (see Four Bears)

MAHTO WICHA KIZA (see Winters, Ray)

MAIORIELLO, CARRI *Choctaw*

Born 30 Aug 1972
RESIDENCE: Manhattan Beach, CA
EDUCATION: Immaculate Heart High School; Mira Costa (CA) High School
PUBLIC COLLECTIONS: HCC
EXHIBITS: RC, TM/NE

DETAIL: Rafael Medina, *Answered Prayer,* 1965. Philbrook Museum of Art, Tulsa, Oklahoma

MAKING MEDICINE

"The artist was among the 72 Plains Indians taken as prisoners from Fort Sill, OK, to Fort Marion, St. Augustine, FL, in 1875."

Snodgrass 1968

JOE MAKTIMA

Maktima says of his art, "The artistry that surrounds my ancestry, which is Hopi and Laguna Pueblo, is where I draw my creativity from. Researching old designs from pottery and kiva murals, I find the inspiration for my own artistic expressions.... In stating my role as an artist, I feel comfortable in saying that it is the challenge of expressing old ideas in a new way, which most motivates me. Art, being a natural and integral part of my culture, is where my work has its roots. And through the artistic expression of individualism, I hope to convey my personal views of the past, present and future."

p.c. 1990

NONA MALONEY

In addition to her paintings done in the more common media, Maloney creates works of art using "praintage," a combination of printing and painting.

artist, p.c. 1992

MAKING MEDICINE *Cheyenne*

A.K.A. David Pendleton Oakerhater

Born ca. 1843; died 1931

MEDIA: Pencil and crayon

PUBLISHED: Grinnell (1915); De Camp (1960); LaFarge (1960); Dines and Price (1961); Petersen (1968); Dunn (1968); Snodgrass (1968); Irvine, ed. (1974); Wade, ed. (1986); Hill (1992). *The Tulsa World* (2 May 1993); *Native Peoples* (summer 1993); *Southwest Art* (July 1993)

PUBLIC COLLECTIONS: HS/MA, HSL/SA, SI, SI/OAA, YU/BRBML

EXHIBITS: BPG

HONORS: Episcopal Church, cannonized a saint in recognition of his lifelong devotion to the church, 1986

MAKTIMA, JOE *Hopi/Laguna*

A.K.A. Willard Joseph Maktima

Born 15 Mar 1962 in Winslow, AZ; son of Josephine and Willard Maktima; P/GP: Amelia and Guy Maktima; M/GP: Louise and Levantonio Siow

RESIDENCE: Flagstaff, AZ

EDUCATION: Coconino High School, Flagstaff, AZ, 1980; A.F.A., IAIA, 1985

OCCUPATION: Artist

MEDIA: Acrylic, pencil, pastel, and prints

PUBLISHED: Jacka and Jacka (1988); Gentry, et al. (1990). *Akwekon Literary Journal* (Sept 1985); *Art-Talk* (Sept 1985); *The Santa Fe Reporter* (19 Aug 1987); *The Arizona Republic* (2 Oct 1987); *Southwest Art* (May 1991)

PUBLIC COLLECTIONS: IAIA, MNA, MRFM

EXHIBITS: AICH; ACS/ENP; ACA; CIM; EM; FNAA; FSMCFA; HM/G; HU/VA; IAIA, MNA; PSU/NC; SDMM; SNAICF; SWAIA; WMNAAF; WWM; Pembroke (NC) State University

SOLO EXHIBITS: WWM

AWARDS: ACS/ENP ('85, 1st; '87, 2-1st); IAIA ('85, T.C. Cannon Award); MNA ('85, 1st; '86; '87, 1st, Best of Division; '88, 1st; '90, 2-1st); SNAICF ('87, Tony Begay Award; '89, 1st); SWAIA ('85, 1st, Hinds Award; '86, 1st; '90)

HONORS: FNAA, poster artist

MALEGOTKUK, FLORENCE (see Chauncey, Florence Nupok)

MALONEY, NONA *Cherokee*

Born 17 Jan 1914; daughter of Laura Sorenson and Milton Grover McNamar; P/GP: Mary Manley and Commodore C. McNamar; M/GP: Matilda Behnke and Andrew Sorenson

RESIDENCE: Arcadia, CA

EDUCATION: Monrovia (CA) High School, 1954; Otis-Parsons Art School, Los Angeles, CA; graduate school, Claremont (CA)

OCCUPATION: Art Instructor, illustrator, and painter

MEDIA: Acrylic, watercolor, pencil, pen and ink, and pastel

PUBLIC COLLECTIONS: The Carter Center, Atlanta, GA

EXHIBITS: Area exhibits

SOLO EXHIBITS: Otis-Parsons Art School; libraries throughout Southern California

AWARDS: Los Angeles County, *Graphics Club Magazine*, award for cover, 1981; 1st, 2nd, and 3rd places from area competitions

HONORS: Otis-Parsons Art School, scholarship

MALOTTE, JACK *Shoshoni/Washoe*

Born 4 Dec 1953 on Walker River Reservation, NV

RESIDENCE: Reno, NV

EDUCATION: Wooster High School; CCAC, 1971-1974

OCCUPATION: U.S. Forest Service firefighter and wilderness patrolman, paste-up and editorial artist, graphic designer, illustrator; full-time painter since 1975

MEDIA: Acrylic, watercolor, colored pencil, graphic pencil, pastel, pen and ink, and prints

PUBLISHED: Banks (1986); Ward, ed. (1990). *The Indian Trader* (Aug 1981); *Nevada Magazine* (3 Oct 1981); *The Washington Post* (15 Mar 1982); *Mountain Express* (28 Mar 1982); *The Gazette-Journal* (14 Aug 1983); *Native Vision* (May/June 1985; Nov/Dec 1985; Sept/Oct 1986); *Art-Talk* (Aug/Sept 1985; Oct 1987); *The Lakota Times* (16 Oct 1985), cover; *The Arizona Republic* (24 June 1989)

BOOKS ILLUSTRATED: SI, *Handbook of North American Indians*, 1985

COMMISSIONS: *Illustrations:* National Congress of American Indians Annual Convention, program, 1985; Capp Street Foundation, San Francisco, CA, corporate report, 1985; American Indian National Water Conference, Oakland, CA, program, 1985; *The Lakota Times,* 16 Oct 1985, cover. *Other:* Nevada Indian women who have had positive impacts on their communities

PUBLIC COLLECTIONS: HM

EXHIBITS: AIAS; AICA/SF; AICH; CID; CNGM; CNM; HM; IAIA; IIAS; ITIC; KCPA; MR; NWASA; OLO; OSC; PAC; RC; SCA; SI; SNMA; SRJC; SUSC; U of CA/D; U of CA/S; U of NV; D-Q University, Davis, CA; Charleston Heights Art Center, Las Vegas, NV, 1984; Mission Cultural Center Gallery, San Francisco, CA, 1984; Staatliche Kunsthalle, Berlin, Germany, 1983

SOLO EXHIBITS: IAIA; MPI; SNMA; U of CA/D; Northeastern Nevada Museum, Elko, NV

AWARDS: CNM ('82); ITIC ('76, 1st)

HONORS: *Grants:* Nevada State Council on the Arts, Reno, NV, 1982

JACK MALOTTE

The artist's paintings are used to convey his message that mankind will destroy the land, water, and sky if we are not careful. He has strong feelings about the environment which leads him to make statements with his art.

MAMAKEESIK, SAUL (see Mammakeesik, Saul)

MAMMAKEESIK, SAUL *Ojibwa*

A.K.A. Saul Mamakeesik

RESIDENCE: Ontario

EXHIBITS: Throughout the U.S. and Canada

SAUL MAMMAKEESIK

The artist is among those Woodlands Indian painters whose works deal with legends and spiritual topics.

MAMMEDATY *Kiowa*

A.K.A. Elk Creek Lone Wolf (in later years)

PUBLISHED: Snodgrass (1968)

MAMMEDATY

"With Lone Wolf and Tohausen (qq.v.) (Kiowas) and other warriors, the artist fought in a skirmish known as the Lost Valley Fight, in Texas, July 16, 1874. Immediately following this encounter, Lone Wolf 'made a gift of his name to Mammedaty (the preferred family spelling).' He succeeded his uncle, Chief Lone Wolf, in 1879 and remained chief until his death. A calendar executed by Mammedaty is in the possession of his descendant, Justin Poolow (see Momaday, Al)."

Snodgrass 1968

MAMMOKSHOARLUK (see Mumnqshoaluk, Victoria)

MAMMOOKSHOARLUK (see Mumnqshoaluk, Victoria)

MAMNGUQSUALUK, VICTORIA (see Mumngshoaluk, Victoria)

MANA *Apache*

Hayokah

PUBLISHED: Snodgrass (1968)

PUBLIC COLLECTIONS: PM

EXHIBITS: PM

MAN ALONE (see Cochran, George McKee)

MANLEY, CLESTA MARTIN *Cherokee*

Born 23 Nov 1924; daughter of Mack M. Martin; P/GP: Callie Bell and Nathaniel R. Martin; M/GP: Ida and Charles Stinson

RESIDENCE: Pryor, OK

EDUCATION: Graduated high school, 1944; Rogers State College, Claremore, OK; private art instruction

OCCUPATION: Banker, art teacher, and painter

MEDIA: Oil, acrylic, watercolor, pencil, pen and ink, pastel, mixed-media, and prints

PUBLIC COLLECTIONS: Chouteau Museum, Salina, OK; Mayes County Historical Society, Pryor, OK

EXHIBITS: TIAF; RE; Okmulgee (OK) Indian Art Festival; exhibits in northeast Oklahoma

MANN, S. LEE *Cherokee/Blackfeet*

Born 19 Nov 1939

RESIDENCE: McLouth, KS

EDUCATION: Arlington Heights High School, Fort Worth, TX, 1958; B.F.A., U of TX/Arlington, 1972; M.F.A., U of OK; studied Chinese landscape painting at Zhejiang Academy of Fine Art, Hangzhou, People's Republic of China

OCCUPATION: Art professor and painter

EXHIBITS: Partial listing of more than 35 includes: DCLA; KSU; LIAS; OCSA; Art Research Center, Kansas City, MO; Lawrence (KS) Arts Center; Spiva Art Center, Joplin, MO; Sumi-e Society of America, Salmagundi Club, New York, NY; St. Pierre-le-Pucellier, Orléans, France; Women Art II, Wichita, KS; Zhejiang Academy of Fine Art, Hangzhou, People's Republic of China

SOLO EXHIBITS: U of OK; Baker University, Baldwin, KS; Drake University, Des Moines, IA; Northern State College, Aberdeen, SD

AWARDS: LIAS ('90, Best of Show; '91, Best of Show)

HONORS: *Grants:* Ten, including: Kansas Arts Commission/NEA, 1990. *Other:* Oriental Brush Work Society, OCSA, featured artist, 1987

MANN, TYLER *Cherokee*

EXHIBITS: FCTM

MANNING, FERDINAND *Ute*

PUBLISHED: Snodgrass (1968)

PUBLIC COLLECTIONS: HM

MAN THAT WALKS HIGH *Cheyenne*

MILITARY: U.S. Army

PUBLISHED: *American Indian Art* (winter 1992)

PUBLIC COLLECTIONS: SM

MAN THAT WALKS HIGH

Man That Walks High was one of forty Cheyenne men who were recruited to serve as scouts at Fort Supply, Indian Territory, in 1885. Their duties were to police the reservation and to support the military and agency staff in peacekeeping. A drawing by Man That Walks High, which was done in 1884 on a single sheet of paper, is in the Southwest Museum collection.

American Indian Art
winter 1992

MANUEL, LORENZO *San Carlos Apache*

RESIDENCE: Santa Fe, NM

EDUCATION: IAIA, 1978; Atlanta (GA) College of Arts

MEDIA: Oil and acrylic

PUBLISHED: *The Indian Trader* (July 1978)

EXHIBITS: IAIA; in MT and NM

MANUEL, TOBIAS K. *Pima*

RESIDENCE: Sacaton, AZ

OCCUPATION: Teacher, ceramist, and painter

PUBLISHED: *The Tucson Citizen* (5 Feb 1992)

EXHIBITS: ACS/PG; HM/G; Scottsdale (AZ) Native American Tourism Center; Mesa (AZ) Southwest Museum

MANUELITO, MONTE *Navajo*

PUBLISHED: Snodgrass (1968)

EXHIBITS: MNM

AWARDS: MNM

MAN WHO CARRIES THE SWORD *Oglala Sioux*

PUBLISHED: Snodgrass (1968)

PUBLIC COLLECTIONS: MAI

MAN WITH LIGHT COMPLEXION (see Mitchell, George Charlie)

MANYI-TEN *Cherokee/Apache*

Born 3 Oct 1952 in Amarillo, TX; daughter of Ethel Goerke Patty and Ervin Kepple Williamson; P/GP: Willa Kepple Williamson and Macduant LeRoy Williamson; M/GP: Ruth Anna Many and Arnold E. Goerke

RESIDENCE: Berkeley, CA

EDUCATION: Norman (OK) High School, 1971; U of OK, 1974; Antioch University, San Francisco, CA, 1980

OCCUPATION: Individual and family therapist and painter

MEDIA: Acrylic, watercolor, pencil, metallic paper, and prints

EXHIBITS: CIM; CNM; LIAS; SJBIM; Berkeley (CA) Ethnic Arts Show; Stanford Powwow, Palo Alto, CA; throughout northern California; see also Awards

AWARDS: CIM ('85); CNM ('86, 1st; '87, 1st, Grand Award; '88, 1st; '90; '91, 1st; '94); LIAS ('91, MA); SJBIM ('86, 1st; '87, 1st); Colorado Historical Society, Denver, CO

MAPERA MOHE (see Cohoe, William T.)

MA PE WI (see Herrera, Velino Shije)

MARACLE, CLIFFORD *Mohawk*

RESIDENCE: Toronto, ON, Canada

Born 1944 near Deseronto, ON, Canada, on the Tyendinaga Reserve

EDUCATION: George Brown College, 1969; honors degree, C/OCA, 1975; graduate studies, C/OCA, 1979

OCCUPATION: Sculptor and painter

MEDIA: Acrylic and stone

PUBLISHED: *The Intelligencer* (27 Feb 1974); *Glove and Mail* (16 Sept 1976); *The Native Perspective* (Vol. 3, no. 2, 1978); *The Prince Rupert News* (23 Apr 1982); *Canadian Art Magazine* (winter 1985); *The Art Post* (Dec/Jan 1986)

PUBLIC COLLECTIONS: C/INAC, C/MCC, C/WICEC

EXHIBITS: C/AG/TB; C/AG/W; C/CIIA; C/CMC; C/CNAC; C/CS; C/LTAT; C/MCC; C/NCCT; C/ROM; C/TU; C/U of WON; C/WICEC; NACLA; SM; Demeervaart Cultural Centre, Amsterdam, Holland; Memorial University Art Gallery, St. John's, NF; North American Mohawk Exhibition, Syracuse, NY; Seneca College, Toronto, ON

SOLO EXHIBITS: Partial listing includes: C/WICEC; Memorial University Art Gallery, St. John's, NF

HONORS: C/INAC, Cultural Grant, 1975-1976

MARCHAND, VIRGIL T. *Colville*

Spa-poole, Smokey

Born 24 Feb 1951 in Inchelium, WA; son of Barbara and Virgil I. Marchand; P/GP: Mary Camille and Louis Marchand; M/GF: Jesse McClung

RESIDENCE: Omak, WA

EDUCATION: IAIA, 1971

OCCUPATION: Colville Tribe Planner II and artist

COMMISSIONS: *Murals:* Coulee Dam (WA) Elementary School; Colville Tribes Museum, Coulee Dam, WA; Keromeous Elementary School, BC

PUBLIC COLLECTIONS: National Park Service, Harpers Ferry, WV

EXHIBITS: IAIA, UTAE

AWARDS: UTAE ('92, Best of Show)

MARKED MOUNTAIN MAN (see Zuni, Stan J.)

MARLER, NADINE *Cherokee*

RESIDENCE: Tulsa, OK

PUBLISHED: *The Muskogee Phoenix* (17 Oct 1982)

PUBLIC COLLECTIONS: HCC

EXHIBITS: CNM, FCTM, LIAS, PAC, RC

AWARDS: CNM ('81, Reynolds Needlepoint Award; '83; '84)

MARMON, MIRIAM A. *Laguna*

EDUCATION: U of NM, ca. 1936

PUBLISHED: Snodgrass (1968)

PUBLIC COLLECTIONS: MNM

MARSHALL, JAMES *Cheyenne River Sioux*

Sitting Eagle

Born 15 May 1953 at Eagle Butte, SD

RESIDENCE: Dupree, SD

EDUCATION: Cheyenne River High School, Eagle Butte, SD, 1972; workshops, U of ND, 1974, 1977

OCCUPATION: Writer, sculptor and painter

MEDIA: Oil, watercolor, pen and ink, earth pigments, hide, stone, and wood

PUBLIC COLLECTIONS: St. Joseph's; St. Joseph's Lakota Development Council

SOLO EXHIBITS: SIM

AWARDS: CRSFA ('82, 1st; '83)

JAMES MARSHALL

Marshall says that all his work is spiritual and that he tries to convey the spiritual interpretations of Lakota ceremonies. He uses a pointillism technique combined with the traditional Lakota hide painting style

brochure, SIM, 1985

MARSHALL, LAURA *Creek*

RESIDENCE: Muskogee, OK

EXHIBITS: FCTM

AWARDS: FCTM ('71, 1st)

MARSHALL, TERESA MACPHEE *Micmac*

A.K.A. Teresa MacPhee

Born 1962 in Truro, NS, Canada; P/GM: Rachel Marshall, First Chief of Milbrook (band)

RESIDENCE: Halifax, NS, Canada

EDUCATION: Dalhousie University, Halifax, NS; B.F.A., C/NSCAD, 1990

OCCUPATION: Educator, actress, costume designer, lecturer, illustrator, graphic designer, curator, sculptor, exhibit installation worker, and painter

MEDIA: Acrylic, watercolor, stone, multi-media, and prints

PUBLISHED: *Site Sound* (Sept/Oct 1991)

PUBLIC COLLECTIONS: C/MFA/NS; Micmac Family and Children's Services; The Confederacy of Mainland Micmacs; The Micmac Association of Cultural Studies; The Multi-cultural Association of Nova Scotia

EXHIBITS: C/AG/NS; C/LSP; C/MSVU; C/WICEC; La Nationale Galerie, Tunisia, Africa; North Street Cultural Centre, Halifax, NS; St. Francis Xavier University, Atigonish, NS; The Congress Centre, Ottawa, ON; World Trade and Convention Centre, Halifax, NS

SOLO EXHIBITS: C/MSVU; two galleries in Halifax, NS

AWARDS: The Assembly of First Nations, Omer Peters Award, 1989; The Confederacy of Mainland Micmacs, Outstanding Scholastic Achievement Award, 1990

HONORS: *Travel Grants:* Air Canada; Department of Tourism and Culture; The Confederacy of Mainland Micmacs; The Micmac Association of Cultural Studies. *Scholarships:* The Confederacy of Mainland Micmacs, 1989; The Department of Education, 1989; C/NSCAD; Royal Trust, Scholarship Competition Award

MARTIN, BOBBY C. *Cherokee*

RESIDENCE: Tahlequah, OK

OCCUPATION: Artist

MEDIA: Oil, acrylic, and prints

EXHIBITS: CNM, FCTM, OIAC

AWARDS: FCTM ('92; '94); OIAC ('93, 1st; '95, 2-1st, Best of Show)

HONORS: OIAC, scholarship, 1993

MARTIN, JACK (see Martin, Michael James)

MARTIN, JAMES, JR. *Osage*

Night Walker

Born 16 Sept 1927 in Pawhuska, OK; son of Martin Take Away Gun; brother of Mike Martin (q.v.); M/GF: John Logan

MILITARY: WWII

EDUCATION: Graduated Chilocco; Haskell; NEO

PUBLISHED: Snodgrass (1968)

PUBLIC COLLECTIONS: SM

EXHIBITS: PAC; Pawhuska, OK

MARTIN, JOSEPH L. *Laguna*

PUBLIC COLLECTIONS: IACB/DC

MARTIN, MARY LOUISE *Micmac*

Born 22 Mar 1956 in Florida

RESIDENCE: Sackville, NB, Canada

EDUCATION: Maynard (MA) High School, 1974; Arcadia University, Wolfville, NS, 1974-1975; Nova Scotia Teacher's College, 1977-1979, 1987-1989; C/NSCAD, 1984-1985

OCCUPATION: Employee of the Department of Indian and Northern Affairs Canada, poet, writer, and artist

MEDIA: Watercolor, pencil, Prismacolor, pen and ink, and prints

COMMISSIONS: *Publication covers:* St. Thomas University, Fredricton, NS; Dalhousie University, Halifax, NS. *Other:* Country Basket, River John, NS, lithographed note cards with poems

EXHIBITS: AG/NS; galleries in Halifax, Moncton, and Tatamagouche, NS

MARTIN, MICHAEL JAMES *Caddo*

Silvermoon

A.K.A. Mike Martin; Jack Martin

Born 1891 in Binger, OK; died 1969 in Lawton, OK; GM: Choah

MILITARY: WWII

EDUCATION: Carlisle

OCCUPATION: Silent motion picture actor, commercial artist, and painter; worked with William de Forest Brush, New York artist

MEDIA: Oil

PUBLISHED: Snodgrass (1968); Brody (1971); Boyd, et al. (1983). *American Indian Art* (spring 1995)

PUBLIC COLLECTIONS: GM, GPM, HSM/OK

EXHIBITS: CSPIP, GM, GPM, HSM/OK

MICHAEL JAMES MARTIN

Martin was riased by his grandmother, Choah, after his mother's death when he was approximately six years old.

MARTIN, MUNGO *Kwakwaka'wakw (Kwakiutl)*

Chief Nakapenkum; Nakapenkem, Ten Times A Chief

Born 1879 at Fort Rupert, BC, Canada; died 16 Aug 1962, drowned while fishing off the coast of Victoria, BC, Canada; son of Sarah Finlay, the daughter of a Hudson's Bay Company employee and Yanukwalas (Kwuksutinuk), a Kwakwaka'wakw leader; stepfather Charlie James taught him to carve

OCCUPATION: Carver, fisherman, philosopher, Hereditary Chief, and artist

MEDIA: Watercolor, earth pigments in a fish oil base, pencil, and wood

PUBLISHED: Holm (1965; 1983); Dockstader (1977); Hall, Blackman, and Rickard (1981); Stewart (1984); Hawthorne (1988); McMaster, et al. (1993). *Masterkey* (winter 1984)

COMMISSIONS: City of Victoria, BC, 127' 6" high totem pole for Beacon Hill Park, 1956; 100' high totem pole celebrating the centennial of Queen Elizabeth II, 1958

PUBLIC COLLECTIONS: C/RBCM

EXHIBITS: Burke Museum, Seattle, WA

SOLO EXHIBITS: U'mista Cultural Centre, traveling exhibit, 1991

MUNGO MARTIN

As Hereditary Chief, Martin married well and thus inherited mask and ceremonial rights. His wife, Bessy, was the daughter of David Hunt and granddaughter of George Hunt. In addition to his art work, Martin was noted for his work preserving and perpetuating the traditions of his people.

Holm 1983

MARTIN, RAYMOND *Navajo*

PUBLISHED: Snodgrass (1968)

COMMISSIONS: *Murals:* Arizona State Fair Coliseum, 1965 (with four other Navajo painters)

MARTIN, RINGLIN *Apache*

PUBLISHED: Snodgrass (1968)

EXHIBITS: FWG

MARTINDALE, CARLA SCOTT *Choctaw/Chickasaw*

RESIDENCE: Amarillo, TX

OCCUPATION: Painter

MEDIA: Acrylic and mixed-media

PUBLISHED: *The Indian Trader* (Sept 1991)

EXHIBITS: ITIC; Ducks Unlimited National Wildlife Show; Kansas Fish and Game Commission State Shows; Taos (NM) Fall Arts Festival; West-Fest Fine Arts Show, Copper Mountain, CO

AWARDS: ITIC ('91)

HONORS: National Buffalo Association, Artist of the Year, 1982; Western Sportsman's Association, Artist of the Year, 1980, 1981

CARLA SCOTT MARTINDALE

Martindale has been painting for over 17 years. She started out as a wildlife artist but now paints Indian subjects. She has said, "The more I learn of my heritage, the more I feel compelled to express it through a pencil and a brush."

The Indian Trader, *Sept 1991*

MARTINE, BOB *Navajo*

A.K.A. Bob Martínez

EDUCATION: Santa Fe, ca. 1959
PUBLISHED: Snodgrass (1968)
EXHIBITS: MNM, SN
AWARDS: MNM, SN

MARTINE, DAVID BUNN *Shinnecock/Montauk/Chiricahua Apache*

Born 11 June 1960 in Southampton, NY; son of Marjorie Martínez and Thomas Siklos; M/GP: Alice Osceola and Charles Martínez
RESIDENCE: Southampton, NY
EDUCATION: Southampton (NY) High School, 1978; B.F.A., U of OK, 1982; IAIA, 1983; M.Ed., CSU/OK, 1984
OCCUPATION: Teacher, gallery owner, sculptor, and painter
MEDIA: Oil, acrylic, pencil, pen and ink, and pastel
BOOKS ILLUSTRATED: *The Thompson Begonia Guide* (1972); *The Shinnecock Indians: A Culture History* (1984); *Good Ground Remembered* (1984); *The Southeastern Ceremonial Complex* (1989)
COMMISSIONS: *Murals:* Suffolk County Archaeological Association Institute, Hoyt Farm Park, Commack, NY, 1989. *Other:* Fort Sill Apache Tribe, seal design, 1984; Wantaugh Culture Arts Program, 1990
EXHIBITS: MMA/NY; PAM/NY; Huntington (NY) Arts Council; Jamaica Arts Center, Queens, NY; Wantaugh (NY) Public Library, 1989; galleries in New York
SOLO EXHIBITS: LIU/S, 1985

MARTÍNEZ, ADAM *San Ildefonso*

Birth date unknown; possibly the son of María and Julian Martínez (q.v.) and brother of Popovi Da (q.v.)
OCCUPATION: Potter and painter
MEDIA: Watercolor
COLLECTIONS: JAM

MARTÍNEZ, ALBERT *Taos*

Looking Elk
A.K.A. Albert Looking Elk
Born ca. 1888; died 30 Nov 1940; father of Joe (José) R. Martínez (q.v.)
EDUCATION: Santa Fe (no art training)
MEDIA: Oil and watercolor
PUBLISHED: Parsons (1936); Snodgrass (1968); Tanner (1973); Ballantine and Ballantine (1993). *The Taos Valley News* (16 July 1918); *El Palacio* (15 Sept 1923); *The Taoseno* (Vol. 2, no. 6, 1940)
PUBLIC COLLECTIONS: MAI, MNA, MNM, SM, SAR
EXHIBITS: SWAIA
AWARDS: SWAIA ('23, 1st)
HONORS: Governor of Taos Pueblo, NM, 1938

MARTÍNEZ, ANACITA *(?)*

A.K.A. Anecito Martínez
PUBLISHED: Snodgrass (1968)
PUBLIC COLLECTIONS: MRFM

MARTÍNEZ, BENJAMIN *Navajo*

EXHIBITS: SN
AWARDS: SN ('68)

ADAM MARTÍNEZ

The Joslyn Art Museum believes that the paintings in their collection signed Adam Martínez may have been by the son of María and Julian Martínez (q.v.). Martínez is married to Santana Roybal and assists her with her pottery.

ALBERT MARTÍNEZ

"The artist was known to have executed a number of paintings, each of which illustrated a creation myth and carried an explanation written by him. He was a close friend of the famed Taos artist, Oscar Berninghaus. He often worked in oil."

Snodgrass 1968

In addition to being a friend of Berninghaus, Martínez served as a model for him. It is believed that when Martínez decided that he wanted to become a painter, Berninghaus gave him lessons. Best known for his oil paintings of Taos Pueblo, in 1927 Martínez did a series of watercolor paintings of a "creation myth" for Mary Cabot Wheelwright. These paintings are now at the School of American Research, Santa Fe, NM.

Sam E. Watson
Masters Thesis, 1994

Martínez studied with Oscar Berninghaus and painted landscapes and genre scenes in the European manner, which offended many White collectors and curators of the day.

Dockstader, p.c. 1995

MARTÍNEZ, BOB (see Martine, Bob)

MARTÍNEZ, CRESCENCIO *San Ildefonso*

Te E, Home Of The Elk

A.K.A. Signature: Ta'e; Crescencio (Te e) (Martínez)

Born 1879 in New Mexico; died 20 June 1918 in a New Mexico flu epidemic; uncle of Alfonso Roybal (Awa Tsireh) (q.v.); related by marriage to María Martínez, potter

OCCUPATION: Janitor, pottery painter, archaeological laborer, and artist

MEDIA: Watercolor and pencil

PUBLISHED: Dunn (1968); Snodgrass (1968); Brody (1971; 1992); Highwater (1976); Tanner (1973); Monthan and Monthan (1975); Dockstader (1977); Silberman (1978); Hoffman, et al. (1984); Samuels (1985); Wade, ed. (1986); Seymour (1988); Archuleta and Strickland (1991); Tryk (1993). *El Palacio* (Aug 1918); *Travel* (1931); *Art Focus* (Aug 1981); *Southwest Art* (June 1983)

COMMISSIONS: MNM and The School of American Research, Santa Fe, NM, painting series, 1917

PUBLIC COLLECTIONS: GM, MNM, MNM/SAR, MRFM, SAR

EXHIBITS: EITA; FAC/CS; HM; IK; MFA/O; MNH/A; OMA; SV; WWM; Society of Independent Artists, New York, NY, ca. 1918-1919; Corona Mundi International Art Center, New York, NY, 1927, 1936

CRESCENCIO MARTÍNEZ

"Martínez first began to draw before 1910, when Dr. Edgar L. Hewett found him using the ends of cardboard boxes and gave him paper and watercolors. The artist was known to have painted pottery before this time. He is considered to be one of a small group at the Pueblo who began the modern watercolor movement, for he painted extensively after he received Dr. Hewett's gift. His career lasted only two years, but during this period he almost completed a series of paintings for the Museum of New Mexico and The School of American Research depicting all the costumed dances of San Ildefonso's summer and winter ceremonies."

Snodgrass 1968

MARTÍNEZ, CYNTHIA *Luiseño/Mission*

RESIDENCE: Seattle, WA

EXHIBITS: RC

MARTÍNEZ, DAISY *San Ildefonso*

RESIDENCE: San Ildefonso Pueblo, NM

EDUCATION: St. Catherine's, ca. 1964-1965

PUBLISHED: Snodgrass (1968)

EXHIBITS: PAC

AWARDS: PAC, student award, 1965

MARTÍNEZ, DIXON *Navajo*

Birth date unknown; born in Thoreau, NM

RESIDENCE: Bloomfield, NM

OCCUPATION: Pipe fitter, bricklayer, and painter

MEDIA: Oil, acrylic, watercolor, pen and ink, pastel, and pencil

EXHIBITS: ACS/MV, TF; Native American Days, Farmington, NM

MARTÍNEZ, DAVE *Navajo*

RESIDENCE: Prewitt, NM

PUBLISHED: Snodgrass (1968)

EXHIBITS: FAIEAIP

MARTÍNEZ, JERRY *Taos*

Birth date unknown; son of Avelina Luján Martínez

RESIDENCE: Taos Pueblo, NM

EDUCATION: Albuquerque, ca. 1960

PUBLISHED: Snodgrass (1968)

PUBLIC COLLECTIONS: MNM

EXHIBITS: MNM

MARTÍNEZ, JOE R. *Taos*

Paaokela

A.K.A. José Martínez
Birth date unknown; son of Albert Martínez (q.v.)
RESIDENCE: Taos Pueblo, NM
PUBLISHED: Snodgrass (1968)
PUBLIC COLLECTIONS: MNM
EXHIBITS: MNM

MARTÍNEZ, JOHN D. *San Ildefonso*
A.K.A. Juan Martínez
Born 12 Nov, ca. 1917-1920 in Santa Fe, NM; death date unknown; son of María Montoya and Julián Martínez, (q.v.); brother of Popovi Da (q.v.)
MILITARY: U.S. Army, WWII
EDUCATION: Santa Fe (NM) High School, ca. 1940; Georgia Military Academy, ca. 1942; SU, ca. 1946-1948
OCCUPATION: Road engineer, engineering draftsman, and painter
PUBLISHED: Snodgrass (1968)
PUBLIC COLLECTIONS: GM, MRFM, SU
EXHIBITS: AIEC, ASM, HM, U of NM
SOLO EXHIBITS: SU; Atlanta (GA) Museum of Fine Arts; Duke University, Durham, NC

MARTÍNEZ, JOSÉ (see Martínez, Joe R.)

MARTÍNEZ, JOSÉ MIGUEL *San Ildefonso*
Wa Chin Cadi
Birth date unknown; son of Crescencio Martínez, (q.v.); cousin of Julián Martínez (q.v.)
OCCUPATION: Painter
PUBLISHED: Alexander (1932); Snodgrass (1968). *American Magazine of Art* (Aug 1933)
COMMISSIONS: *Murals:* IAIA, 1932; Mesa Verde National Park, CO, 1935
PUBLIC COLLECTIONS: DAM, HM

JOSÉ MIGUEL MARTÍNEZ

By 1950 Martínez was painting infrequently.

MARTÍNEZ, JUAN (see Martínez, John D.)

MARTÍNEZ, JUAN JOSÉ *Picurís*
PUBLISHED: Snodgrass (1968)
PUBLIC COLLECTIONS: SM

MARTÍNEZ, JULIÁN *San Ildefonso*
Pocano, Coming Of The Spirits
Born 1897 in San Ildefonso Pueblo, NM; died 6 Mar 1943 in San Ildefonso Pueblo, NM; husband of María, potter; father of Popovi Da (Tony Martínez) (q.v.)
OCCUPATION: Farmer, laborer, janitor, pottery designer, and artist
MEDIA: Watercolor and ceramic paint
PUBLISHED: Alexander (1932); Jacobson and d'Ucel (1950); Glubok (1964); Dunn (1968); Snodgrass (1968); Brody (1971); Tanner (1973); Highwater (1976); Dockstader (1977); Stuart and Ashton (1977), Silberman (1978); Schmid and Houlihan (1979); Broder (1981); Fawcett and Callander (1982); Hoffman, et al. (1984); Golder (1985); Samuals (1985b); Wade, ed. (1986); Trimble, S. (1987); Seymour (1988); Mather (1990); Williams, ed. (1990), Archuleta and Strickland (1991); Tryk (1993). *American Magazine of Art* (Sept 1928; Aug 1933); *New York Times Magazine* (29 Nov 1931); *Theatre Arts Monthly* (Aug 1933); *Santa Fe Reporter* (15 Aug 1990); biographical publications

JULIÁN MARTÍNEZ

"Julián decorated his wife's famous pottery. Although he had been painting since before 1920 and had ventured into several periods of 'realistic' paintings, his more outstanding works were designs of the type found on María's pottery."

Snodgrass 1968

Although he did some realistic paintings including dancers, Martínez was best known for his symbolic designs and geometric figures.

COMMISSIONS: *Murals:* Partial listing includes: Santa Fe Indian School; Mesa Verde National Park, CO, 1935. *Other:* School of American Research, Santa Fe, NM

PUBLIC COLLECTIONS: ACMWA, AF, ASM, CAM/OH, CGFA, CMA, DAM, DCC, GM, JAM, MAI, MFA/O, MKMcNAI, MNA/KHC, MNH/A, MNM, MRFM, OU/MA, RM, SAR, SM, U of PA/M, WWM

EXHIBITS: ACC; AIEC; ASM; EITA; FWG; HH; HM; IK; JAM; LGAM; MAI; MKMcNAI; NAP; OMA; OTIS; OU/ET; SI; SV; WWM; Corona Mundi International Art Center, New York, NY, 1927; Fair Park Gallery, Dallas, TX, 1928

HONORS: Elected Governor of San Ildefonso Pueblo, NM

MARTÍNEZ, MANUEL *Taos*

Good Rain

Birth date unknown; son of Albert Martínez (q.v.)

OCCUPATION: U.S. Navy and painter

MEDIA: Watercolor

PUBLISHED: Snodgrass (1968)

PUBLIC COLLECTIONS: MNA, MNM

EXHIBITS: AC/HC, PM

MARTÍNEZ, MARIO *Yaqui*

Born 1953 in Phoenix, AZ

RESIDENCE: San Francisco, CA

EDUCATION: B.F.A., ASU, 1979; M.F.A., SFAI, 1985

OCCUPATION: Educator and painter

MEDIA: Mixed-media

PUBLISHED: Ward, ed. (1990); Antoine and Bates (1991); Roberts, ed. (1992); Zurko, ed. (1990); Abbott (1994). *The Phoenix Gazette* (3 Sept 1987); *Phoenix Magazine* (Sept 1989)

EXHIBITS: AC/B; AC/T; ACA; AICA/SF; ASU; CNGM; CWAM; DAM; EMC; FSMCFA; OLO; SFAI; SS/CW; U of CA/D; WHB; Academy of Art, San Francisco, CA; San Francisco Arts Commission Festival, 1988; Berkeley (CA) Art Center, 1989.

SOLO EXHIBITS: CNGM; U of WI, Lawton Gallery

AWARDS: ASU

MARTÍNEZ, MIGUEL *San Ildefonso*

PUBLISHED: Snodgrass (1968)

PUBLIC COLLECTIONS: MFA/A

MARTÍNEZ, PHILIP *San Ildefonso*

PUBLISHED: Snodgrass (1968)

PUBLIC COLLECTIONS: MIA

MARTÍNEZ, POPOVI DA (see Da, Popovi)

MARTÍNEZ, R.M. (see Martínez, Ralph)

MARTÍNEZ, RALPH *Taos*

A.K.A. R. M. Martínez

PUBLISHED: Snodgrass (1968)

PUBLIC COLLECTIONS: MNM

MARTÍNEZ, RAYMOND *San Ildefonso*

Born ca. 1942

EDUCATION: Haskell, ca. 1963

PUBLISHED: Snodgrass (1968)
PUBLIC COLLECTIONS: MNM

MARTÍNEZ, RICARDO (see Martínez, Richard)

MARTÍNEZ, RICHARD *San Ildefonso*
Opa Mu Nu
A.K.A. Ricardo Martínez
Born 1904; died 1987
RESIDENCE: Lived at San Ildefonso Pueblo, NM
MEDIA: Tempera
PUBLISHED: Alexander (1932); Dunn (1968); Snodgrass (1968); Brody (1971); Tanner (1973); Highwater (1973). *American Magazine of Art* (Sept 1928); *American Indian Art* (spring 1985)
COMMISSIONS: *Murals:* Santa Fe Indian School
PUBLIC COLLECTIONS: CAM/OH, CGA, CGPS, CMA, DAM, GM, JAM, MAI, MNA, MNM, MR, MRFM, SM, U of CA/LMA, WOM
EXHIBITS: CGPS, EITA, JAM, LGAM

RICHARD MARTÍNEZ

"As one of the original students at Santa Fe Indian School, the artist assisted in the execution of a mural series in the student dining room in 1936. He painted as early as 1920, and, in 1950, he was still painting mythological and ceremonial subjects. . . ."

Snodgrass 1968

According to collector James Bialac (Tanner 1973) and Snodgrass, Martínez was not painting in the late 1960s or early 1970s.

MARTÍNEZ, SANTANA R. *Tewa/San Ildefonso*
A.K.A. Santana Roybal Martínez
Birth date unknown; daughter of Alfonsita Martínez, potter, and Juan Estebán Roybal; sister of Awa Tsireh and Juan Cruz Roybal (qq.v.); niece of Crescencio Martínez (q.v.); wife of Adam Martínez (q.v.), potter and son of María and Julián Martínez (q.v.)
RESIDENCE: Santa Fe, NM
OCCUPATION: Potter and painter; best known for ceramics
PUBLISHED: Snodgrass (1968); Golder (1985); Trimble, S. (1987); Seymour (1988). *New Mexico Magazine* (Aug 1986); *The Santa Fean* (Dec 1993)
PUBLIC COLLECTIONS: MAI, MKMcNAI
EXHIBITS: HH, HM, IAIA, SWAIA
AWARDS: SWAIA

MARTÍNEZ, TONY (see Da, Popovi)

MASANUMPTEWA, RALPH *Hopi*
MEDIA: Watercolor
PUBLISHED: Seymour (1988)
PUBLIC COLLECTIONS: IACB/DC

MASON, PATRICIA JOAN *Cherokee*
A.K.A. P. J. Mason
Born 9 Jan 1960 in Tahlequah, OK; daughter of Dorothy Gage and Frank Gilliam; P/GP: Sarah Runyon and Lloyd Gilliam; M/GP: Seanna Hays and William Gage
RESIDENCE: Tahlequah, OK
EDUCATION: Fort Gibson (OK) High School, 1978; B.F.A., NSU, 1991
OCCUPATION: Museum gift shop manager, museum art coordinator, and artist
MEDIA: Acrylic and watercolor
EXHIBITS: CNM, FCTM

MASTAKE (see Murry, Daniel M.)

MATCHES, WALTER *Cheyenne*
Chee-Si-Se-Iau, Matches
Born 1857; died 1888

WALTER MATCHES

The artist was imprisoned at Fort Marion, St. Augustine, FL. While there he produced a sketch book that is now in the University of Pennsylvania Museum. After attending Hampton Institute and Carlisle Indian School, Matches returned to Indian Territory in September of 1880 and worked as a carpenter at the Indian Agency.

Arthur Silberman, p.c. 1994

EDUCATION: Hampton; Carlisle
OCCUPATION: Warrior, Indian agency employee, carpenter, and artist
PUBLISHED: *American Indian Art* (winter 1992)
PUBLIC COLLECTIONS: U of PA/M
EXHIBITS: BPG

MATHEWS, DEWAYNE *Cherokee/Chickasaw*
Fishinghawk
EXHIBITS: BB, CNM, FCTM, PAC
AWARDS: FCTM ('90, IH), PAC ('74)

MATHEWS, FADIE MAE *Cherokee*
Born 10 Mar 1909 in TN; daughter of Alyie and Tom Blackwell; M/GGGF: Chief Taw; M/GGF: surnamed Garrett, killed in Georgia before the Cherokee removal
RESIDENCE: Fort Worth, TX
EDUCATION: Ellis and Circle Park Schools, Fort Worth, TX, 1919-1925
PUBLISHED: Snodgrass (1968); Brody (1971)
COMMISSIONS: South Wayside Baptist Church, Fort Worth, TX
PUBLIC COLLECTIONS: Security Life Insurance Collection and Faith Chapel, Fort Worth, TX; New Orleans Treasure House, Arlington, TX
EXHIBITS: Englewood (CA) Art Center; galleries in Texas

MATHEWS, WILLIAM P. (see Red Corn)

MATHLAW, WELCH *Eskimo*
Born 1940 in Mekoryuk, AK
RESIDENCE: Mekoryuk, AK
EDUCATION: Manpower Development and Training Act Retraining Project, Port Chilkoot, AK, 1965-1966
OCCUPATION: Worked with Alaska Indian Arts, Inc., in Port Chilkoot, AK
PUBLISHED: Ray (1969)
EXHIBITS: SAIEAIP

MATO HUNKA *Sioux*
PUBLISHED: Snodgrass (1968)
PUBLIC COLLECTIONS: MPM (pictographic style on paper)

MATO MUNKA (see Murray, Daniel M.)

MATO MYALUTA (see Red Living Bear)

MATO NAJIN (see Standing Bear)

MATO SAPO (see Black Bear)

MATO TOPE (see Four Bears)

MATOUSH, GLENNA *Ojibwa*
Born 1946 on the Rama Reserve, ON, Canada
RESIDENCE: Canada
EDUCATION: Museum of Fine Arts and Design, Montréal, PQ
MEDIA: Watercolor and pen and ink
PUBLISHED: *Windspeaker* (12 Dec 1986)
PUBLIC COLLECTIONS: C/INAC; Basilica del Santo, Padova, Italy; Regional Administration, Val d'Or and Québec
EXHIBITS: C/ACCCNA; C/C; C/NIACC; Cultural Centre, Val d'Or, PQ, 1987; Gala des Grands Prix du Tourisme Québecois, Val d'Or, PQ; Hydro Québec

Exhibition, 1990; International Symposium of Northern Québec, 1987; Social-Cultural Centre, Amos, PQ, 1987; Villleneuve, Tolosane, France, 1987

SOLO EXHIBITS: Amerindian Museum, Pointe Bleue, PQ; Art Gallery Moderna "Benvenuti," Venice, Italy; Centre d'Art Rotary, La Sarre, PQ; Salle Augustin Chenier, Ville-Marie, PQ; Social-Cultural Centre, Amos, PQ

MATO WANTAKPE (see Grass, John)

MATTHEWS, TANIS *Tlingit*

Born 1951 in Skagway, AK

RESIDENCE: Bellingham, WA

EDUCATION: USU, 1979-1980; B.F.A., U of AK/F, 1987; M.F.A., U of AZ, 1993

PUBLISHED: Gully, ed. (1994)

PUBLIC COLLECTIONS: U of AK/F; Washington State Art Commission, Olympia, WA

EXHIBITS: AICA/SF; HM; Institute of Alaska Native Arts, Fairbanks, AK, 1993; Washington State University, Bellingham, WA, 1992

MAULDIN, JANE *Choctaw*

A.K.A. Carol Jane McCarty Mauldin

Born 19 Jan 1936 in Tulsa, OK; daughter of Madelyn Helen Beck and Vernon Clay McCarty; sister of Valjean McCarty Hessing (q.v.); P/GP: Etta Regina Davis and Carl Clay McCarty; M/GP: Sada Lewis and Fred Logan Beck

RESIDENCE: Tulsa, OK

EDUCATION: Central High School, Tulsa, OK, 1954

OCCUPATION: Commercial artist for 24 years; full-time painter after 1974

MEDIA: Oil, acrylic, watercolor, pencil, mixed-media, and prints

PUBLISHED: Snodgrass (1968). *The Indian Trader* (Apr 1982); *Art-Talk* (June/July 1985); *Oklahoma Today* (July/Aug 1985)

PUBLIC COLLECTIONS: BIA, GM, HCC, RC

EXHIBITS: CIM; CNM; FAIEAIP; FCTM; GM; Haskell; HM; HM/G; HPTU; IAF; IS; ITIC; KCPA; LSS; MNH/AN; MPABAS; PAC; RC; RE; SN; SWAIA; TIAF; TM/NE; U of WV; WTF; Council of American Indians Exhibition, Tulsa, OK

SOLO/SPECIAL EXHIBITS: HM (dual show, 1972); SPIM, 1982

AWARDS: CNM ('90); FCTM ('68, Tiger Award; '70; '71; '74, Reynolds Award; '75, 1st; '78; '79, 1st; '81; '84, 1st; '86; '87; '88; '90; '91; '94); HM/G ('78); IS ('92, 1st); PAC ('71; '79); RC ('82, 1st; '83, 1st, Begay Award; '82, '93); SWAIA ('82; '83); TIAF ('94)

JANE MAULDIN

"Upon graduation from high school, the artist married and devoted herself to both family and career for about eight years. In 1963, she again began to paint and enter her work in competitions."

Snodgrass 1968

"I usually paint at night — a habit I developed over the years — when the house is quiet. I have no preconceived idea of where I'm going; using enhancement to bring forth the major structure of the painting." Her paintings often depict women and children, subjects to which she "easily relates."

MAULSON, GERALD *Chippewa/Ottawa*

Bedonni Quid, Slow Cloud

Born 7 Dec 1941 in Haywood, WI

RESIDENCE: Chicago, IL

EDUCATION: Lakeland Union High School, Winocqua, WI, 1955; Santa Fe, 1960-1961

OCCUPATION: Roofer, coil winder, and painter

PUBLISHED: Snodgrass (1968)

PUBLIC COLLECTIONS: BIA, IACB

EXHIBITS: AC/HC, BNIAS, MNM, PAC, USDS

SOLO EXHIBITS: MNM

MA-WHOLO-PEEN (see Roybal, Ralph)

MAXHEBAHO (see Hollowbreast, Donald)

ROBERT MAYOKOK

Mayokok's teenage years were plagued with trauma, fear and loneliness. When he was 15 his mother died tragically and in 1918, almost half of the people of his village, including his father and grandfather, died in a flu epidemic. For a time he drifted,taking a multitude of jobs and traveling.

artist, p.c. 1991

In 1945, he developed tuberculosis and spent two periods of several years each in a hospital in Seward, AK. To overcome loneliness and to avoid depression he was encouraged to write and paint. These activities and his strong Christian faith sustained him. After his release from the hospital,he moved to Anchorage where he sold his first paintings. In addition to his painting he wrote and illustrated several booklets and designed Christmas cards and other paper products.

He said of his paintings, "I don't think my picture[s] are as good as some other artist's work,but they seem to sell better. It's God-given talent that I don't care for myself, but other people like that work because God put something in them so they take to liking my pictures."

Yorba 1991

MAYOKOK, ROBERT *Eskimo*

Born 1903 in Wales, AK; died 1983

RESIDENCE: Lived in Nome, AK

EDUCATION: Educated through 5th grade. He further educated himself using a Sears and Roebuck catalogue as an English dictionary (Yorba 1991).

OCCUPATION: Longshoreman, tin miner, deck hand, interpreter, substitute teacher, store manager, hunter, trapper, author, illustrator, and painter

MEDIA: India ink, marking pencil, cardboard, paper, and animal skin

PUBLISHED: Snodgrass (1968); Ray (1969); Yorba (1991). *The Alaska Journal* (Vol. 6, no. 4, 1972; autumn 1976; autumn 1983)

BOOKS ILLUSTRATED: Mayokok (1951; 1957; 1959; 1960; 1960a; 1965); Casswell (1968); Ray (1969); Silook (1970); Wells (1974); Ticusak (1981)

EXHIBITS: AAIEAE

MAYOREAK *Inuit (Eskimo)*

A.K.A. Mayoreak Ashoona

Born 1946 at Shatureetuk, South Baffin Island, NWT, Canada; daughter of Sheouak Parr, graphic artist; wife of Qaqaq Ashoona, sculptor; daughter-in-law of Pitseolak Ashoona (q.v.)

RESIDENCE: Shatureetuk, South Baffin Island, NWT, Canada

OCCUPATION: Wife, mother, and graphic artist

PUBLISHED: Leroux, Jackson, and Freeman, eds. (1994). *Inuit Art Quarterly* (winter 1994)

PUBLIC COLLECTIONS: C/AG/WP, C/ICI, C/CMC, C/NGCA, C/PWNHC

EXHIBITS: C/AG/AE, C/AG/B, C/AG/WP, C/AG/V, C/CGCQ, FAM

MAYTUBBIE, DOUGLAS *Choctaw*

A.K.A. Melvin Douglas Maytubbie; Doug Maytubbie

Born 15 Aug 1940 in Battiest, OK

RESIDENCE: Midwest City, OK

EDUCATION: Graduated Chilocco, 1959; A.A., EOSC, 1979; B.A., CSU/OK, 1981

OCCUPATION: Maintenance man and painter

MEDIA: Watercolor, tempera, and pencil

PUBLISHED: *Oklahoma Today* (June 1992); *Indian Territories* (Vol. 3, no. 1, 1993)

COMMISSIONS: CSU/OK, painting presented to the President of the University of TX

PUBLIC COLLECTIONS: HCC; CSU/OK; EOSC; Oklahoma Republican Party; Red River Museum, Broken Bow, OK

EXHIBITS: ACS/RSC; BB; CAI/KC; CNM; FCTM; LSS; RC; SPIM; TM/NE; TWF; U of OK; U of WV; in CO, ND, NM, and TX

SOLO EXHIBITS: EOSC Library; Edmond (OK) Public Library; Edmond (OK) Chamber of Commerce

AWARDS: FCTM ('82); RC ('90, Neiderman Award)

HONORS: CSU/OK, Art Department, named Artist of the Month

MAZUHA HOKSHINA (see Howe, Oscar)

MCALISTER, BARBARA *Cherokee*

EXHIBITS: FCTM

AWARDS: FCTM ('67; '71; '72; '75)

MCALLISTER, PAT *Cherokee*

Born 3 Mar 1942 in Many, LA; daughter of Mina Raywinkle and Rupert

McKaskle; P/GP: Nancy Davis and George W. McKaskle; M/GP: Nora Dickerson and Edward Raywinkle

RESIDENCE: Eureka Springs, AR

EDUCATION: Many (LA) High School, 1960; Louisiana State University, Baton Rouge, LA, 1964; studied art in Europe and the Philippines for eleven years

OCCUPATION: Teacher and painter

MEDIA: Oil, watercolor, pastel, and prints

PUBLIC COLLECTIONS: HCC

EXHIBITS: AIAF, AIAFM, CIM, CNM, GPIAE, IACA, IS, ITIC, LIAS, RC, RE, TCIM, TIAF, TM/NE, TWF, WIAME; see also Awards

SOLO EXHIBITS: Adams Mark Hotel, Houston, TX

AWARDS: CIM ('89); CNM ('93); GPIAE; IACA ('94); ITIC ('89); RC ('93, The White Buffalo Award; '94, WKI Award); TIAF ('94); Winter Park, CO ('89, Best of Show)

HONORS: GPIAE, featured artist, 1983

McBRIDE, DEL *Quinault*

RESIDENCE: Nesqually, WA

PUBLISHED: Snodgrass (1968)

EXHIBITS: PAC

McCABE, JOHN KEE *Navajo*

Born 10 Oct 1946 in Ganado, AZ

RESIDENCE: Eagle Mountain, CA

MILITARY: U.S. Air Force, Vietnam

EDUCATION: Parker (AZ) High School; AWC; Arizona School of Art, Phoenix, AZ

MEDIA: Oil, acrylic, watercolor, charcoal, and pen and ink

PUBLIC COLLECTIONS: HCC

EXHIBITS: CNM; HM/G; NICCAS; RC; SDMM; Holy Rosary Mission, Pine Ridge, SD; Indio (CA) Date Festival; Museum of North Orange County, Fullerton, CA; North Yuma County Fair, AZ; Riverside County Museum, Riverside, CA

AWARDS: HM/G ('72; '76, Graphics Award; '79); ITIC ('93, 1st); more than twenty blue ribbons at county and state fairs

McCABE, MICHAEL *Navajo*

Birth date unknown; born at Fort Defiance, AZ

EDUCATION: IAIA

OCCUPATION: Teacher and graphic artist

PUBLIC COLLECTIONS: HM, MPI, USDI, WWM

EXHIBITS: AA, FNAA, FSMCFA, ITIC, NMSC, RC, WWM

SOLO EXHIBITS: MPI, WWM

AWARDS: ITIC ('94, 1st, Best in Category)

McCABE, TONY *Navajo*

PUBLIC COLLECTIONS: MNA

McCALLUM, RAYMOND *Plains Cree*

PUBLISHED: *Masterkey* (winter 1984)

McCARTER, JACK *Cherokee*

Yona, Bear

A.K.A. Signature: Jack McCarter and a bear paw print

MAYOREAK

After living for more than fifteen years in Cape Dorset, Mayoreak and her husband, Qaqaq Ashoona, returned to the traditional Inuit camp life in the late 1970s. Her mother was Sheouak Parr, one of the first women to take up drawing when James Houston initiated the printmaking experiment at Cape Dorset. One of Sheouak's images is still used as a logo for the West Baffin Eskimo Co-operative. Mayoreak began to draw in the early 1960s and her images were first included in the Cape Dorset print collection in 1978. Her work was not included in the 1988 and 1992 print collections because of family responsibilities.

Leroux, Jackson, and Freeman, eds. 1994

PAT McALLISTER

McAllister uses an indirect painting technique that is closely associated with the Flemish style. She paints Indian and western subjects.

artist, p.c. 1990

Born 27 Oct 1960 in Tahlequah, OK; son of Jessie Mae Stover and Louis McCarter; P/GP: OO-Ga-We-Yoo and Joe McCarter; M/GP: Mary Cummens and Willie Stover

RESIDENCE: Tulsa, OK

EDUCATION: Oaks (OK) High School, 1978; Climate Control Institute, 1985-1986

OCCUPATION: Welder, electrician, and painter

MEDIA: Acrylic, watercolor, pencil, pen and ink, and pastel

EXHIBITS: CNM; FCTM; TWF; Indian Summer Festival, Tulsa, OK; see also Awards

AWARDS: Eufala (OK) Art Guild ('92)

HONORS: Indian Health Care Resource Center, poster artist, 1992

McCLEVE, MICHAEL G. *Creek*

Born 1946 in Medford, OR

EDUCATION: Glendale (AZ) Community College

OCCUPATION: Ironworker/high-rise construction, welder, mechanic, foundry worker, and painter

PUBLISHED: Amerson, ed. (1981)

EXHIBITS: BM/B, CTC, HM

McCLOSKEY, BARBARA THOMAS *Cherokee*

EXHIBITS: CNM, FCTM

McCOMBS, PERRY *Creek*

RESIDENCE: Eufala, OK

EXHIBITS: CNM, FCTM, PAC, SN

McCOMBS, SOLOMON *Creek*

Born 17 May 1913 west of Eufaula, OK; died 18 Nov 1980 in Tulsa, OK; son of Ella McIntosh and Rev. James McCombs; P/GU: Rev. William McCombs, a founder of Bacone College for whom McCombs Memorial Art Gallery is named

RESIDENCE: Lived in Tulsa, OK

EDUCATION: Bacone College High School, 1937; BC; Tulsa (OK) Downtown College; studied under Acee Blue Eagle (q.v.) while at BC

OCCUPATION: Thirty years of government service as a designer-illustrator, cartographer, draftsman and envoy; full-time painter after 1973

MEDIA: Casein

PUBLISHED: Jacobson and d'Ucel (1950); Jacobson (1964); Dunn (1968); Snodgrass (1968); Brody (1971); Monthan and Monthan (1975); Silverman (1978); Mahey, et al. (1980); Schmid and Houlihan (1980); Broder (1981); Samuels (1985); Williams, ed. (1990). *Sunday Oklahoman, Orbit Magazine* (26 May 1963); *Smoke Signals,* IACB (autumn 1965); *The Phoenix Gazette* (14 Aug 1974); *Oklahoma Art Gallery* (spring 1980); *The Tulsa World* (22 Feb 1981); *Twin Territories* (Year of the Indian Edition 1992); *Oklahoma Today* (May/June 1994); biographical publications

COMMISSIONS: *Murals:* U.S. Post Office, Marietta, OK; State of Montana. *Other:* U.S. Army, painting of a WWII American Indian recipient of the Congressional Medal of Honor, 1980

PUBLIC COLLECTIONS: BIA, CCHM, DAM, GM, HM, IACB, IACB/DC, JAM, MNM, OSAC, OU/MA, PAC, WWM

EXHIBITS: AAID; AAIE; AAUW; AIEC; AIE/T; AIW; BC; BC/McG; BNIAS; CAI/KC; CGA; CIAI; CNM; DAM; FANAIAE; GM; HM; HM/G; ITIC; JAM; JGS; LGAM; MIF; MKMcNAI; MMA; MNM; MPABAS; NAP; OAC; OMA; OU/ET; PAC; PAC/T; PBOIA; SAIEAIP; SI; SN; USDS; throughout the U.S., Africa, Asia, and Europe

SOLOMON McCOMBS

"An injury in his youth confined the artist to his bed for a considerable time, and it was then that he became interested in art. McCombs exhibited in Philbrook Art Center's Indian Annual every year from its inception in 1946 until it was discontinued in 1979. He represented the Indian through exhibits and lectures abroad, as well as in the U.S."

Snodgrass 1968

SOLO EXHIBITS: Partial listing includes: HM; JAM; PAC; SPIM

AWARDS: AAID ('68, 1st; '70); CAI/KC ('80, 1st); CNM ('72, 1st, Grand Award; '73, 1st; '76, 1st; '77, 1st, Grand Award); FCTM ('67; '70, 1st; '71; '72, Grand Award); FCTM/M ('75; '77, 1st, IH; '79, IH; '80, IH); ITIC; MNM; PAC ('69, Grand Award; '71; '72; '73, 1st; '75, Hunt Award; '76, 1st; '79); PBOIA ('70); SN ('62, 1st; '64, 1st)

HONORS: U.S. Department of State, Goodwill Ambassador to the Far East and Africa, 1954; American Indian and Eskimo Cultural Foundation, Washington, D.C., a founder and president; Society of Federal Artists and Designers, Washington, D.C., member, finance auditor, and treasurer, 1956-1957; FCTM, design selected for seal, 1956; PAC, Waite Phillips' Trophy Award for Outstanding Contributions to Indian Art, 1965; American Indian and Eskimo Cultural Foundation, Shield Award, Washington, D.C., 1968; FCTM, designated a Master Artist, 1975

McCREARY, BILL *Cherokee*

A.K.A. William McCreary

Born 21 Aug 1939 in Anderson, IN; son of Nell Ward and Leroy McCreary; P/GP: Tressie Hittle and William B. McCreary; M/GP: Pauline Wright and Matt Ward

RESIDENCE: Miami, FL

EDUCATION: Anderson (IN) High School, 1957; B.S., University of Miami, FL, 1961; M.A.T., University of South Florida, Tampa, FL, 1973

OCCUPATION: Environmental science teacher and painter; has exhibited since 1989

MEDIA: Watercolor, pen and ink, and Prismacolor

EXHIBITS: CNM; shows in Crystal River, Jensen Beach, and Port Charlotte, FL; see also Awards

AWARDS: Belleview (FL) Fine Arts ('89); Cocoa Beach (FL) Art Show ('92); Country Walk, Miami, FL ('89, 1st; '90, 1st; '91, Best of Show); Deland (FL) Fine Arts Show ('89); Hialeah (FL) Fine Arts ('90)

HONORS: Coconut Grove (FL) Chamber of Commerce, named to the list of Better Artists of Miami, FL, 1991

McCULLEY, BILL *Seminole/Creek*

A.K.A. William McCulley

RESIDENCE: Pryor, OK

EDUCATION: Rogers State College, Claremore, OK

OCCUPATION: Full-time artist since 1990

MEDIA: Oil, acrylic, watercolor, pencil, and pastel

EXHIBITS: FCTM; Zwicau Art Gallery, Zwicau, Germany

McCULLOUGH, MICHAEL C. *Choctaw*

Born 19 Sept 1949 in Pampa, TX; son of Jean Jackson and J. A. McCullough; P/GF: J. A. McCullough; M/GM: Mamie Jackson Reddout

RESIDENCE: Albuquerque, NM

EDUCATION: M.F.A., West Texas State University, Canyon, Texas, 1973

OCCUPATION: Gallery owner, sculptor, and painter

MEDIA: Acrylic, watercolor, bronze, and prints

EXHIBITS: CNM, LIAS, NMSF, RE, TAIAF, TIAF, WIAME; see also Awards

AWARDS: CNM (2-1st); NMSF ('92, Best of Show, Purchase Award, Merit Award); TIAF ('92, Best of Show; '95); Beaver Creek (CO) Arts Council Show ('93, Best of Show); New Mexico Arts and Crafts Show, Albuquerque, NM ('93, Purchase Award); St. George (UT) Festival of the Arts ('94, Purchase Award)

MICHAEL C. McCULLOUGH

An accomplished artist, McCullough is known for his paintings of New Mexico scenes, Pueblo pottery and artifacts, and petroglyphs.

McDANIELS, CRUZ FREDERICK, II *Sioux/Zuni/Kiowa*

Set-Koy-Ke, Kiowa Bear

Born 6 June 1950 in Lawton, OK; son of Maude Mausape and Paul A. McDaniels; P/GF: Cruz Frederick McDaniels; M/GP: Eugenia and Caddo Mausape

RESIDENCE: Anadarko, OK

MILITARY: U.S. Marine Corps, Vietnam

EDUCATION: Anadarko (OK) High School, 1968; B.A., SWOSU, 1978; B.S., M.Ed., SWOSU; studied under George Calvert and Jim Terrell

OCCUPATION: Teacher, art instructor, football and track coach, and painter

MEDIA: Acrylic, watercolor, pen and ink, pencil, pastel, mixed-media, and prints

PUBLISHED: *The Indian Trader* (July 1985), cover

EXHIBITS: AIE; CNM; ITIC; TAIAF; RE; Gallup-McKinley County Art Fair

SOLO EXHIBITS: Gallup (NM) Public Library

AWARDS: AIE ('81; '88, 1st; '89; '92, Best of Show); ITIC ('85)

CRUZ FREDERICK McDANIELS II

McDaniels started to draw while in grade school. One of his earliest memories is of his father comforting him just as the moon set. To honor his father he always includes a moon in his paintings. His favorite colors are red and orange, which he relates to fire and warmth, and blue, which he uses to depict feelings of cold or sadness.

The Indian Trader, *July 1985*

McGOUGH, WANDA SAGER *Cherokee*

RESIDENCE: Grove, OK

MEDIA: Acrylic, volcanic clay, and mixed-media

EXHIBITS: FCTM, LIAS

AWARDS: FCTM ('92, IH Award)

McGUIRE, PAT *Haida*

MEDIA: Watercolor and pen and ink

PUBLISHED: *Masterkey* (winter 1984)

PUBLIC COLLECTIONS: C/RBCM

McINTOSH, ALEX C. (see Blue Eagle, Acee)

McKAMEY, MARY KALAL *Paiute/Navajo/Blackfeet*

Born 27 Aug 1963; daughter of Loe Ann Andrew and David Crutis; P/GM: Miny Crutis; M/GP: Marie Andrew and George Pepion

RESIDENCE: Hermiston, OR

EDUCATION: Hermiston (OR) High School, 1981; IAIA, 1983

OCCUPATION: Beadworker and painter

MEDIA: Oil, acrylic, watercolor, pencil, pen and ink, pastel, beads, and prints

EXHIBITS: ACS/SM; BSIM; CIM; CNM; GFNAAS; ITAE/M; RC; Pendleton (OR) Round-Up; Trade Fair and Exposition, San Francisco, CA; Western Art in Eastern Oregon, Enterprise, OR; Willamette Western Art, Salem, OR; Indian art shows in the Northwest

SOLO EXHIBITS: Western Heritage, Pendleton, OR; First Independent, Vancouver, WA

AWARDS: ACS/SM (1st)

McKENSIE, HUGH *Cree*

Born 31 Mar 1943 on the Bear Island Reserve, Canada

RESIDENCE: Canada

OCCUPATION: Trapper, hunter, hunting and fishing guide, and painter

PUBLISHED: Southcott (1984)

PUBLIC COLLECTIONS: HCC

HONORS: Ontario Society of Artists, membership, 1979

HUGH McKENSIE

McKensie worked with and was a close friend of Benjamin Chee Chee and developed a style very similar to his. For the last two years of Chee Chee's life they shared a studio. After Chee Chee's sudden death in 1977, McKensie returned to Bear Island and didn't paint for a year.

Southcott 1984

McKINNEY, ROGER *Kickapoo*

Sinnagwin

Born 24 Feb 1957 in Kansas City, MO; son of Ruby Mann and Lowell McKinney;

P/GP: Anna and Henry McKinney; M/GP: Nora and Carroll Mann; brother of Barbara Pahponee Elston, ceramist

RESIDENCE: Higley, AZ

EDUCATION: Port Angeles (WA) Senior High, 1975; B.A., GC, 1982; M.F.A., The American University, Washington, D.C., 1986

OCCUPATION: Art instructor, program management, development and design specialist, photographer, educator, and painter

MEDIA: Oil, acrylic, watercolor, pencil, pen and ink, pastel, film, and prints

PUBLIC COLLECTIONS: GC; WG/AU; Kickapoo Nation School, Powhattan, KS

EXHIBITS: GC; HM/G; IAIA; ITIC; LIAS; SWAIA; U of CA/SB; WG/AU; Internal Revenue Service, American Indian Exhibition, Washington, D.C., 1987; galleries in CA, PA, VA, and Washington, D.C.; see also Awards

SOLO EXHIBITS: Haskell

AWARDS: GC ('82, Guitano Capasso Award); ITIC ('89); LIAS ('90, MA, '92, Best of Show); WG/AU ('86, Wolpoff Award); Fairfax County Parks, Burke, Virginia ('84)

HONORS: HM, DeGrazia artist-in-residence, 1990

ROGER MCKINNEY

McKinney says, "My images flow from the recognition of the past as an integral part of my heritage, but also captures the heart and spirit of American Indians today. Mine is a spiritual journey of the soul of America."

artist, p.c. 1992

McLAIN, BRAD *Cherokee*

Born 22 Dec 1941; son of John C. McLain

RESIDENCE: Durant, OK

EDUCATION: Blue (OK) High School, 1959; U of OK, 1968

MEDIA: Oil, watercolor, and prints

EXHIBITS: CNM; FCTM; Best of the West, Plano, TX; see also Awards

AWARDS: FCTM ('87; '88, Grand Award); Owo-Chito Regional, Beavers Bend, OK (Best of Show)

McLAIN, KIM *(?)*

Born 1964 in Oxbow, SK, Canada

RESIDENCE: Edmonton, AB, Canada

EDUCATION: St. Mary's High School, Calgary, AB; C/ACA

OCCUPATION: Silversmith, carver, and painter

MEDIA: Acrylic, copper, silver, wood, cotton fabric, and glass beads

PUBLISHED: Cardinal-Schubert (1992)

PUBLIC COLLECTIONS: C/INAC; C/AIAC; C/PHT; Alberta Native Secretariat

EXHIBITS: Partial listing of more than 15 includes: C/AM; C/MAM; C/PHT; C/TFD; C/TGVA; DC; Amherst, MA; galleries in AB, BC, and ON

AWARDS: C/AM ('84; '85; '86; '87, 1st, scholarship); C/PHT ('84)

McLEAY, DON *Métis*

Born 1940 in North Battleford, SK, Canada

RESIDENCE: Canada

OCCUPATION: Carver, graphic artist, and painter

COMMISSIONS: *Murals:* Board of Education, Cherokee Public School, North York, ON, 1976; Seattle (WA) Indian Centre, 1974. *Other:* Boy Scouts of Canada, Toronto, ON, totem pole, 1979; Landsdowne Park, Ottawa, ON, totem pole, 1989; Meadowvale Public School, Scarborough, ON, totem pole, 1979; Native Centre of Toronto (ON), totem pole, 1979; Thompson Gallery, Toronto, ON, totem pole, 1980

PUBLIC COLLECTIONS: C/CMC; C/INAC; C/ROM; Boy Scouts of Canada, Toronto, ON; City of Ottawa (ON); National Native Women's Association, Ottawa, ON; Museum of Natural History, Cleveland, OH

EXHIBITS: Partial listing of more than 23 includes: C/AFIA; C/McMU; C/MI;

C/NCCT; C/NIACC; C/WICEC; Art Show '83, Fort McMurray, AB, 1983; London, England, 1976; World Assembly of First Nations, Regina, SK, 1982

SOLO EXHIBITS: Galleries in BC, MB, and ON

McMASTER, GERALD R. *Plains Cree*

Born 9 Mar 1953 in North Battleford, SK, Canada

RESIDENCE: Ottawa, ON, Canada

EDUCATION: North Battleford (SK) Comprehensive High School, 1972; A.A., IAIA, 1975; B.F.A., MIA, 1977; C/BSFA, 1986

OCCUPATION: Semi-professional baseball player, educator, museum curator, sculptor, and painter

MEDIA: Acrylic, pencil, pastel, lacquer, wood, and mixed-media

PUBLISHED: Menitove, ed. (1986b). *Tawow* (Vol. 4, no. 3, 1974); *Echo* (Vol. 4, no. 7, 1984); *The Saskatchewan Indian* (July/Aug 1988); *Artscraft* (summer 1990); SAW News (Vol. 3, no. 3, 1990); *Native Peoples* (Special Edition 1994)

BOOKS ILLUSTRATED: McMaster (1981); Children's book illustrations, Saskatchewan Public Libraries, Regina, SK

COMMISSIONS: *Logos:* Saskatchewan Indian Agricultural Program, Regina, SK, 1978; Native Courtworker Services, Regina, SK, 1979; Saskatchewan Indian Federated College, C/U of R, 1980. *Murals:* CKCK-TV, Regina, SK, 1979. *Posters:* Saskatchewan Indian Federated College, C/U of R, recruitment poster, 1980; C/U of R, conference poster, 1978. *Other:* Canyon Records, Scottsdale, AZ, record jacket, 1975; Native American Studies Program, U of MN, letterhead design, 1977; La Loche (SK) Centre for Learning, book, 1981; Parachute Club, Toronto, ON, record jacket, 1988; Canadian Museum of Civilization, Treasures, dedication page, 1988

PUBLIC COLLECTIONS: C/CCAB; C/CMC; C/INAC; C/MCC; C/NAM; C/QU; C/ROM; C/SICC; C/U of R; IAIA; City of Ottawa (ON) Municipal Collection; City of Regina (SK), Municipal Collection; Gettysburg (PA) College Art Gallery; Museum für Völkerkunde, Vienna, Austria; Osler, Hoskins and Harcourt, Ottawa, ON; Peking Chinese Opera, China

EXHIBITS: C/AG/TB; C/INAC; C/ISS; C/MCC; C/UG; C/U of BC/MA; C/U of R/MG; C/WDY; C/WICEC; HM; OSU/G; SNAICF; SPIM; Gettysburg (PA) College Art Gallery, 1990; Eco-Art, Río de Frances, Brazil, 1992

SOLO EXHIBITS: Partial listing of seven includes: C/AG/TB, C/MCC, C/UG, C/U of BC/MA

AWARDS: C/LRCL; C/NFB; SN ('76)

HONORS: La Loche (SK) Centre for Learning book contest, *Bryon and His Balloon*, 1st prize

McMURTRY, ROBERT *Comanche*

Eka Kwasu, Red Shirt

A.K.A. Aquasu; Robbie McMurtry

Born 21 Oct 1950 in San Antonio, TX

RESIDENCE: Morris, OK

EDUCATION: B.A., OCLA, 1973

OCCUPATION: Counselor, instructor, author, playwright, cartoonist, illustrator, lecturer, Indian cultural coordinator, and painter

MEDIA: Acrylic, watercolor, pencil, pen and ink, pastel, and prints

PUBLISHED: King (1981). *Art Voices* (Sept/Oct 1981); *Tulsa* (July 1984); *Intertribal* (July 1990); *Tulsa World* (11 Mar 1994)

BOOKS ILLUSTRATED: *Song of the Moon Pony*, by McMurtry, 1992

PUBLIC COLLECTIONS: CGPS, USDI

ROBERT McMURTRY

McMurtry credits three major influences in his paintings. The first is a childhood fascination with cartoons, especially the fantasy images of artist Frank Frazetta. Another is his father, who was a cowboy much of his life and told wonderful stories which he illustrated for his son. And last but not least, are the stories told him by his part Comanche grandmother. McMurtry says that art not only is fun, but should be, and he would rather do it than anything else.

p.c. 1992

EXHIBITS: AC/A; AIE; CGPS; CNM; HM/G; ITIC; MFA/O; MIF; OIAP; PAC; TIAF; Grand Palais, Paris, France; Mid-America Indian Center, Wichita, KS; galleries in CO, KS, NM, NY, OK, and TX

SOLO EXHIBITS: Schweitzer Gallery, Luxembourg City, Luxembourg, Germany

AWARDS: AIE ('71); CNM ('82); HM/G ('76); ITIC ('78; '85); TIAF ('95)

MCNAMARA, PAULA JANE *Chippewa*

Two Moons

Born 9 Apr 1940; daughter of Mary Jane Marshall; P/GF: Paul Henrichs; M/GP: Elizabeth Belonga and William Marshall

RESIDENCE: Grand Rapids, MI

EDUCATION: Aquinas College, Grand Rapids, MI; A.A., North Central Michigan College, Petoskey, MI, 1980; B.A., Grand Valley State College, Allendale, MI, 1982

OCCUPATION: Designer, photographer, and artist

MEDIA: Pastel and film

PUBLIC COLLECTIONS: Saugatuck (MI) Library

EXHIBITS: AC/VM; BCAM; BG/MI; FSPC; GRAF; MMA/MI; Mt. Clemons All State Annual XIX; see also Awards

AWARDS: AC/VM ('90, 2-Best of Show); BG/MI (Amway Award); FSPC (Purchase Award); Festival of Religious Arts, Grand Rapids, MI (Best of Show); Holland (MI) Friends of Art Fine Art Exhibit (Best of Show)

PAULA JANE MCNAMARA

As she was growing up, McNamara spent summers with her Chippewa maternal grandmother and aunts on Mackinac Island, MI. She says "I am most proud of my American Indian heritage. I believe it gives me insight. I feel if something moves me, it will move others. But it must be honest. I like to turn my realities into something that might be of interest to others." She explains her paintings in this way, "I am telling a story and trying to draw people into the story, to touch them with a common feeling about our environment and our lives in this century and the next."

p.c. 1991

MEDICINE CROW *Crow*

A.K.A. Chief Medicine Crow

Birth date unknown; father of Joe Medicine Crow, anthropologist

PUBLISHED: Jacobson and d'Ucel (1950); Snodgrass (1968); Warner, ed. (1985)

EXHIBITS: AC/Y

MEDICINE CROW

"The artist was known to have visited Washington, D.C.. Upon his return to the reservation, he painted from memory the many animals he had seen in museums there. (see Jacobson and d'Ucel1950)."

Snodgrass 1968

MEDICINE MOUNTAIN (see Gonzales, Louis)

MEDINA, J. D. (see Medina, José D.)

MEDINA, JAMES D. *Zia*

PUBLISHED: Snodgrass (1968)

PUBLIC COLLECTIONS: CGPS, MAI

EXHIBITS: CGPS

MEDINA, JOSÉ D. *Zia*

A.K.A. J. D. Medina

Birth date unknown; born at Zia Pueblo, NM; brother of Rafael Medina (q.v.)

RESIDENCE: Santa Fe, NM

MILITARY: U.S. Marine Corp

EDUCATION: Santa Fe, 1949-1953; IAIA

MEDIA: Oil, acrylic, watercolor, casein, and pen and ink

PUBLISHED: Snodgrass (1968); Brody (1971); Tanner (1973)

COMMISSIONS: *Murals:* IPCC

PUBLIC COLLECTIONS: CGPS, HCC, MAI, MNA

EXHIBITS: CGPS, MNM, PAC, PM, RC, SN

MEDINA, JOSÉ DE LA CRUZ *Zia*

A.K.A. José la Cruz

RESIDENCE: Santa Fe, NM

EDUCATION: Santa Fe

MEDIA: Tempera

PUBLISHED: Snodgrass (1968); Williams, ed. (1990)
PUBLIC COLLECTIONS: HM, MNM.
EXHIBITS: AC/HC, ASM, MKMcNAI, MNM, PAC, PM, SN

MEDINA, JUAN B. *Zia*

EDUCATION: Santa Fe
PUBLISHED: Dunn (1968); Snodgrass (1968); Brody (1971)
PUBLIC COLLECTIONS: MAI, SM
EXHIBITS: AIW, NGA, OU/ET

MEDINA, RAFAEL *Zia*

Teeyacheena
Born 10 Sept 1929 at Zia Pueblo, NM; P/GM: Trinidad Medina, potter
RESIDENCE: Gallup, NM
EDUCATION: Santa Fe; NM; studied under Velino Shije Herrera, José Rey Toledo, and Gerónima Montoya (qq.v.)
OCCUPATION: Artist
MEDIA: Tempera
PUBLISHED: Snodgrass (1968); Tanner (1968, 1973); Highwater (1976); Silberman (1978); Mahey, et al. (1980); Schmid and Houlihan (1980); Broder (1981); Hoffman, et al. (1984); Trimble, S. (1987); Williams, ed. (1990). *Southwest Art* (winter 1977-1978); *Tamaqua* (winter/spring 1991)
PUBLIC COLLECTIONS: AC/RM, ASM, MAI, MNA, MNM, MRFM, PAC
EXHIBITS: AC/HC, AIAE/WSU, ASM, DAM, HM, HM/G, IK, ITIC, JGS, MKMcNAI, MNM, NAP, OMA, PAC, PM, SN
SOLO EXHIBITS: ASM
AWARDS: AIAE/WSU (six); HM/G ('69); ITIC ('70); PAC ('66, Grand Award; '70; '72); SN ('67, 1st; '71, 1st)

RAFAEL MEDINA

"As a young man, 'barely old enough to hold the weight of a single shotgun,' he often hunted. At the same time he studied the appearance of the animals and birds, which he believes has helped him greatly in his art work. While still a young student, he was encouraged and aided by Mary Mitchell."

Snodgrass 1968

His first sale while he was still a student at Albuquerque Indian School was a commission from Mary Mitchell for 50 Christmas dinner place cards.

MEECHES, GARRY J. *Saulteaux/Ojibwa*

Born 1957, in Manitoba, Canada, on the Long Plains Reserve
RESIDENCE: Manitoba, Canada
EDUCATION: Plains Indian Survival School, Minneapolis, MN; Great Grasslands Graphics, Winnipeg, MB
OCCUPATION: Artist
PUBLISHED: *Masterkey* (winter 1984); *Indian Art Magazine* (spring 1990)
COMMISSIONS: National Indian Art Calendar, Montréal, PQ
PUBLIC COLLECTIONS: HCC
EXHIBITS: C/TGVA; C/WICEC; CPS; WTF; throughout western Canada
HONORS: International Powwow, Winnipeg, MB, poster artist, 1983

GARRY J. MEECHES

The artist is known for his nostalgic paintings that look back to traditional Indian culture. They are similar to the Plains art style in the United States.

American Indian Art
spring 1990

MEEKIS, JOHNSON *Cree*

Born 1954 at Red Lake, ON, Canada
RESIDENCE: Sandy Lake, ON, Canada
EDUCATION: Lakehead University; B.A. University of Thunder Bay, ON, 1982; B.Ed., University of Thunder Bay, ON summer 1982
OCCUPATION: Teacher and painter
PUBLISHED: Southcott (1984). *Masterkey* (winter 1984)
EXHIBITS: C/CNAC; galleries in Peterborough, Thunder Bay, Toronto, and Winnipeg, ON, England, and Germany

MEEKO, LUCY *Inuit (Eskimo)*

RESIDENCE: Great Whale River, NWT, Canada

OCCUPATION: Graphic artist
PUBLISHED: *North* (Mar/Apr 1974)
PUBLIC COLLECTIONS: DAM
EXHIBITS: Robertson Galleries, Ottawa, ON

MEE'NAH-TSEE (see White Swan)

MEET ME IN THE NIGHT *Omaha/Sioux*
PUBLISHED: Snodgrass (1968)
MEDIA: Watercolor
PUBLIC COLLECTIONS: MAI (watercolor, 1882)

MELCHIOR, RAY *Cochití*
A.K.A. Reyes Melchoir; Ray Melchor
Born 1924 at Cochití Pueblo, NM
RESIDENCE: Las Cruces, NM
EDUCATION: Santa Fe
PUBLISHED: Snodgrass (1968)
EXHIBITS: AIW; MNM; Old Town, Albuquerque, NM

MELCHIOR, REYES (see Melchior, Ray)

MELCHOR, RAY (see Melchior, Ray)

MELFORD, EARL *(?)*
PUBLISHED: Snodgrass (1968)
EXHIBITS: ITIC
SOLO EXHIBITS: ITIC

MEMEAH, MARLENE (see Riding In Memeah, Marlene)

MENCHEGO, ART *Santa Ana*
A.K.A. Arthur Menchego
Born 10 Feb 1950
RESIDENCE: Santa Ana Pueblo, NM
EDUCATION: High school and three years of college
OCCUPATION: Sculptor and painter
MEDIA: Oil, watercolor, pencil, and stone
PUBLISHED: Tryk (1993)
EXHIBITS: ACS/ENP, AIAFM, CNM, HM/G, ITIC, NMSF, RC, RE, SDCC, SWAIA
AWARDS: ACS/ENP ('82, 1st; '83, 1st; '84, 1st, Best in Painting and Drawing; '85; '88, 2-1st); CIM ('86, '89); CNM ('84, 1st); ITIC ('80, 1st, Best of Class; '81; '82; '83, 1st; '84; '85, 1st; '87); NMSF ('84, 1st; '88, 1st); RE ('88; '89; '94); SWAIA ('82, 1st; '83, 1st; '84; '91).

MEPAA KTE (see Wife Eagle Deer)

MESQUAKIE (see Pushetonequa, Charles)

METOXEN (see York, Doris J.)

METSCHER, TERRI *Potawatomi*
RESIDENCE: Moore, OK
EXHIBITS: CNM, RC
AWARDS: CNM ('87, 1st)

MIKAKA UPAWIXE (see Kimball, Yeffe)

MIKE, JUDY *Winnebago*
Birth date unknown; born in Wisconson
RESIDENCE: Wisconsin
EDUCATION: IAIA
PUBLISHED: Snodgrass (1968)
EXHIBITS: FAIEAIP

MIKKELSEN, LEATRICE *Navajo*
Born 1936 at Klamath Agency, OR
RESIDENCE: Corte Madera, CA
EDUCATION: B.A., Dominican College, San Rafael, CA, 1959; M.A., San Francisco (CA) State University, 1963
OCCUPATION: Teacher, and artist
MEDIA: Oil and pastel
PUBLISHED: Amerson, ed. (1981); Zurko, ed. (1992)
EXHIBITS: AICA/SF; CTC; CWAM; HCCC; NU/BC; OSU/G; SFMA; WHB; Marin Civic Center, San Rafael, CA; Chaw'se Cultural Center, Pine Grove, CA

MIKPICA, ANNI (see Mikpiga, Annie)

MIKPIGA, ANNIE *Inuit (Eskimo)*
A.K.A. Anni Mikpica; Mikpigak; Annie Mikpiqak
Born 1900; died 1984
RESIDENCE: Lived in Povungnituk, PQ, Canada
OCCUPATION: Graphic artist
MEDIA: Pencil and prints
PUBLISHED: Larmour (1967); Goetz, et al. (1977); Myers, ed. (1980). *Arts West* (Vol. 3, no. 5, 1978)
EXHIBITS: C/AG/WP, C/TIP, C/TMBI

MIKPIGAK (see Mikpiga, Annie)

MIKPIQAK, ANNIE (see Mikpiga, Annie)

MILES, DALE *Yavapai*
PUBLIC COLLECTIONS: MNA

MILES, DOUG *Pima/San Carlos Apache*
A.K.A. Douglas Duncan Miles
Born 27 Nov 1963 in Phoenix, AZ; son of David Norman Miles II
RESIDENCE: San Carlos, AZ
EDUCATION: MCC
EXHIBITS: HM/G; ITIC; OT; SWAIA; All-Indian Days, Scottsdale, AZ
AWARDS: HM/G ('92, 1st, Best in Class, Best of Category); ITIC ('91, 1st)

MILFORD, ELMER *Navajo*
PUBLIC COLLECTIONS: MNA

MILLER, DAVID *Potawatomi*
Born 13 June 1936
RESIDENCE: Glendale, CA
EDUCATION: St. Gregory's College, Shawnee, OK; CSU/OK; U of CA/LA; Parsons School of Design, Los Angeles, CA
EXHIBITS: LIAS
AWARDS: LIAS

MILLER, FRANCES *Navajo*

PUBLISHED: Snodgrass (1968)

PUBLIC COLLECTIONS: MNA

EXHIBITS: ITIC

MILLER, GEORGE *Omaha*

Birth date unknown; member of Ictasanda (Thunder) clan

OCCUPATION: Historical informant and artist for BAE ethnologist James Owen Dorsey

PUBLISHED: Snodgrass (1968). *11th Annual Report,* BAE (1889-1890)

PUBLIC COLLECTIONS: SI/OAA (original drawings which appear in the BAE publication)

MILLER, KAY *Comanche/Métis*

Born 1946 in Houston, TX

RESIDENCE: Iowa City, IA

EDUCATION: B.S., University of Houston (TX), 1970; B.F.A., U of TX, 1975; Naropa Institute, Boulder, CO, 1978; M.F.A., U of TX, 1978

OCCUPATION: Artist

PUBLISHED: Younger, et al. (1985); Lippard (1990); Roberts, ed. (1992)

EXHIBITS: CGA; OSU/G; WSCS; WWM; SS/CW; Aspen (CO) Museum of Art; Cleveland (OH) Center for Contemporary Art; Cleveland (OH) State University; Dougherty Arts Center, Austin, TX; The New Museum of Contemporary Art, New York, NY

MILLER, R. GARY *Mohawk*

A.K.A. R. G. Miller; Gary Miller

Born 1950 on the Six Nations Reserve, ON, Canada

RESIDENCE: Toronto, ON, Canada

EDUCATION: Burlington (ON) High School; graduated with honors, C/OCA, 1974; C/U of T

OCCUPATION: Lecturer, graphic artist, and painter

MEDIA: Oil, acrylic, watercolor, pen and ink, and prints

PUBLISHED: Green (1975); Huges and Goller (1981); Johannsen and Ferguson, eds. (1983). *The Toronto Star* (4 Jan 1977; 28 Oct 1978); *The Native Perspective* (Vol. 3, no. 2, 1978); *The Ontario Indian* (Vol. 4, no. 2 1981), cover; *National Native Art Auction Catalog* (1981), cover; *The Sterling News* (5 Oct 1983); *The Intelligencer* (8 Sept 1984)

COMMISSIONS: *Murals:* Iroquois Junior Public School. *Portraits:* National Indian Brotherhood; Pauline Johnson Public School.

PUBLIC COLLECTIONS: C/AG/TB; C/CMC; C/GM; C/INAC; C/OAC; C/RBCM; C/WICEC; Assembly of First Nations, Ottawa, ON; Her Majesty's Royal Collection, England; National Indian Brotherhood, Ottawa, ON; Texaco Collection

EXHIBITS: Partial listing of more than thirty includes: C/AG/TB; C/AG/W; C/McIG; C/NAF; C/NCCT; C/ROM; C/WICEC; RCAS; SM; Education Centre of the Toronto Board of Education, ON, 1976; Holland Festival, Amsterdam, Holland; McDonald Gallery, Government of Ontario, Toronto, 1980

SOLO EXHIBITS: Partial listing includes: Belleville (ON) Public Library and Gallery; galleries in Sault Ste. Marie, Sudbury, and Toronto, ON

HONORS: C/OAC, art grant, 1977-1980

R. GARY MILLER

Miller considers himself a contemporary painter who uses traditional Native designs and themes. His style tends to be realistic although it is occasionally impressionistic.

Johannsen and Ferguson, eds. 1983

MILLER, TED W. *Peoria/Miami*

RESIDENCE: Santa Fe, NM

OCCUPATION: Knifemaker and painter

EXHIBITS: ITIC

AWARDS: ITIC ('90)

MILLER, VEL *Potawatomi*

Born 1936 in Nekoosa, WI; daughter of Celia and Clarence Krause

RESIDENCE: Atascadero, CA

EDUCATION: San Juan High School, Fair Oaks, CA, 1953; Art League of Los Angeles (CA); studied under Joe De Yong

OCCUPATION: Ranch wife, mother, art instructor, sculptor, and painter

MEDIA: Oil, watercolor, and bronze

PUBLISHED: *Artists of the Rockies and the Golden West* (summer 1981); *Southwest Art* (June 1990)

EXHIBITS: SIRU; TMA/AZ; WH; Cheyenne Frontier Days Governor's Invitational (1986); Coors Western Art Exhibit, Denver, CO; Haley Library Show, Midland, TX; Mountain Oyster Club Art Show, Tucson, AZ; Rocky Mountain Rendezvous, Durango, CO (1987); Stamford (TX) Art Foundation Show; Cowboy Classics, Phoenix, AZ

AWARDS: More than forty 1st place and Best of Shows

VEL MILLER

Joe De Yong, Western artist and protege of Charlie Russell was Miller's mentor for 15 years. When he died she inherited some items from his studio. Among these items was an ugly green palette which she uses and loves because it was his.

Southwest Art, *June 1990*

MILLER, WADE *Omaha/Seneca*

Tio-um-baska, White Lightning

A.K.A. Wallace Wade Miller

Born 17 July 1921 in Walthill, NE, on the Omaha Reservation; death date unknown

RESIDENCE: Lived in Macy, NE

EDUCATION: Sisseton (SD) High School, 1940-1941; Omaha (NE) Art School, 1963-1964; B.A., U of NE, 1978

OCCUPATION: Teacher and painter

PUBLIC COLLECTIONS: HCC; Nebraska Historical Society

EXHIBITS: HCC; JAM; RC; U of NE, Lutheran Student Chapel; Library of Congress, Washington, D.C.; Seneca Indian Tribal Office, Miami, OK; Miami (OK) Civic Center

SOLO EXHIBITS: SIM; Unitarian Church, Lincoln, NE

AWARDS: RC ('74)

MINOCH, MILO (see Minock, Milo)

MINOCK, MILO *Eskimo*

A.K.A. Milo Minoch; Milo Minok

RESIDENCE: Pilot Station, AK

MEDIA: Pen and ink, paper, and hide

PUBLISHED: Snodgrass (1968). *Alaska Geographic* (Vol. 12, no. 3, 1985)

PUBLIC COLLECTIONS: HM, SMNAI

EXHIBITS: HM, MFA/AH

MINOK, MILO (see Minock, Milo)

MINTHORN, P.Y. *Cayuse/Nez Percé*

A.K.A. Philip Minthorne

Born 1960 in Pendleton, OR

RESIDENCE: West Richland, WA

EDUCATION: U of CO, 1979; A.F.A., IAIA, 1981; Pacific Northwest College of Art, Portland, OR, 1982
OCCUPATION: Poet and painter
MEDIA: Oil, oil pastel, pen and ink, and prints
PUBLISHED: Minthorn (1981; 1991); Banks (1986); Longfish, et al. (1986); Ward, ed. (1990); Minthorn (1991). *Greenfield Review* (1981; 1983)
PUBLIC COLLECTIONS: WSAC; Inland Empire Bank, Seattle, WA
EXHIBITS: AICA/SF; IAIA/M; MMA/WA; NDN; OLO; PAM; SAM; SAP; SC; SNMA; TPIS; U of CO/B; Williamette University, Salem, OR, 1984; Lewis and Clark State College, Lewiston, ID; Public Space, Seattle, WA

MIRABEL, ERNEST *Tewa/Nambé*

RESIDENCE: Nambé Pueblo, NM
EXHIBITS: AIAFM

MIRABEL, EVA *Taos*

Eah Ha Wa, Green Corn
Born 1920; death date unknown
RESIDENCE: Lived in Taos Pueblo, NM
EDUCATION: Santa Fe; Taos
OCCUPATION: Artist-in-residence, counselor, and artist
MEDIA: Tempera
PUBLISHED: Jacobson and d'Ucel (1950); Dunn (1968); Snodgrass (1968); Brody (1971); Tanner (1973); Broder (1981). *El Palacio* (Aug 1950); *G. I. Gertie,* U.S. Army; *Southwest Art* (June 1983)
COMMISSIONS: *Murals:* Santa Fe Indian School; Veteran's Hospital, Library, Albuquerque, NM
PUBLIC COLLECTIONS: GM, MAI, MNM, MRFM, PAC, UPA, WOM
EXHIBITS: AIEC, AIW, GM, MNM, NGA, PAC
AWARDS: MNM, PAC

EVA MIRABEL

"Mirabel lived at Taos Pueblo with her children and painted infrequently. Her husband's career was in the Navy and the artist served in the Woman's Corps during WW II."

Snodgrass 1968

MIRABEL, LEON *(?)*

PUBLISHED: Snodgrass (1968)
EXHIBITS: ITIC
AWARDS: ITIC

MIRABEL, VICENTE *Taos*

Chiu Tah, Dancing Boy
A.K.A. Chi-u-Tah
Born 1918; died ca. 1946
MILITARY: U.S. Army, WWII; Battle of the Bulge
EDUCATION: Santa Fe
OCCUPATION: Teacher and artist
MEDIA: Watercolor and tempera
PUBLISHED: Jacobson and d'Ucel (1950); Dunn (1968); Snodgrass (1968); Tanner (1973); Seymour (1988). *Arizona Highways* (Aug 1952); *Southwest Airlines Spirit* (Oct 1986); *Scottsdale Daily Progress* (19 Dec 1986); *The Arizona Republic* (26 Dec 1986)
PUBLIC COLLECTIONS: CAMSL, CGPS, IACB/DC, MAI, MFA/O, MNA, U of OK, WOM
EXHIBITS: AIW, CGPS, HM, NGA, WRTD
AWARDS: SFWF Poster Contest (1st)

VICENTE MIRABEL

"The artist's career as a painter was so promising when he entered military service that he was regarded as the most up-and-coming artist from Taos Pueblo."

Snodgrass 1968

MIS TA MOO TO VA (see Blackowl, Archie)

MISTY (see Ortiz, Joseph)

MITCHELL, ANTHONY, JR. *Creek/Seminole*

Born 12 July 1965 in Wetumka, OK; son of Cilla and Tony Mitchell

RESIDENCE: Dustin, OK

EDUCATION: Hartshorne (OK) High School, 1984; private art instruction under Christine Verner

OCCUPATION: Full-time artist

MEDIA: Acrylic, watercolor, pencil, and pen and ink

PUBLIC COLLECTIONS: Haskell; Coo-Y-Yah Museum, Pryor, OK; Hartshorne (OK) Public School Library; Pryor (OK) Public Library; Jones Academy Library, Hartshorne, OK

EXHIBITS: BB; CNM; FCTM; TIAF; TWF; RC; RE; regional shows and markets; see also Awards

AWARDS: FCTM ('91, HM); TIAF ('92; '95); TWF ('92); Eufaula (OK) Art Guild Show; Holdenville (OK) Professional Artist Show (1st); McAlester (OK) Italian Festival (1st); Okmulgee (OK) Indian Market

HONORS: E.S.A. Nu Beta, awarded for the Field of Arts, McAlester, OK; Hartshorne, OK, Bronze and Gold Art pin

MITCHELL, BARBARA GERARD (see Gerard-Mitchell, Barbara)

MITCHELL, FREEMAN *Creek/Seminole*

Loga, Turtle

A.K.A. Signature: LOGA drawn in the shape of a turtle

RESIDENCE: Okay, OK

OCCUPATION: Full-time artist

MEDIA: Acrylic

PUBLIC COLLECTIONS: HCC

EXHIBITS: BC/McG; CNM; FCTM; PAC; RC; WTF; Milwaukee, WI; New York, NY; Princeton, NJ; Denver, CO; in Oklahoma

AWARDS: CNM ('73, Grand Award; '74, Award); FCTM ('77, IH; '78, 1st, IH; '80); RC ('76, Jolly Rancher Americana Award; '77)

MITCHELL, GEORGE CHARLIE *Navajo*

Dineh Ligaai, Man With Light Complexion

Born 2 Mar 1926 in Lukachukai, AZ; son of Charlie Bitsi; GF: Charlie Mitchell, tribal policeman, interpreter, and tribal leader; brother of Stanley Mitchell (q.v.)

RESIDENCE: Tuba City, AZ

MILITARY: U.S. Navy, WWII

EDUCATION: Chilocco, 1949; two-year printer's school; B.A., NSU, 1963

OCCUPATION: Interpreter, counselor, teacher, education specialist, and painter

PUBLISHED: Snodgrass (1968); Brody (1971)

COMMISSIONS: BIA, illustrated textbooks; Chilocco, wrote captions and compiled pictures for educational brochure; Navajo Tribe, greeting card designs

EXHIBITS: FAIEAIP, PAC; Indian fairs

MITCHELL, PETER *Navajo*

EDUCATION: Riverside; Good Shepherd's Mission School, Fort Defiance, AZ; U of AZ, "Southwest Indian Art Project," scholarship, summers 1961, 1962

PUBLISHED: Snodgrass (1968)

MITCHELL, RON *Cherokee*

Tsalagiasiwisti, Fourman

A.K.A. Ronald Gene Mitchell; Ron "Fourman" Mitchell. Signature: Ron Mitchell

Born 25 Dec 1943 in Fort Benning, GA; son of Marie Hensly and George S. Mitchell; P/GP: Maude Foreman and Calvin J. Mitchell

RESIDENCE: Oklahoma City, OK

EDUCATION: Lawton (OK) High School, 1962; Cameron University, Lawton, OK; Art Instruction, Inc

MEDIA: Acrylic, watercolor, pen and ink, and prints

EXHIBITS: AIAF, AIAFM, CIM, CNM, FCTM, IACA, ITIC, RE, TIAF, TWF, WIAME

AWARDS: Partial listing of more than one hundred includes: CNM ('74, 2-1st); FCTM ('74)

RON MITCHELL

Mitchell says, "Dreaming my dreams and thinking of the old ways, I create a painting using a combination of traditional flat style and airbrush techniques (despite red-green color blindness). In a style as modern as today, but drawn from inspirations that link the past, I take the viewer through a 'window' by capturing the essence of a place or time in the Native American's life."

MITCHELL, STANLEY C. *Navajo*

Che Chilly Tsosie, Slim Curly Hair

A.K.A. Signature: Chi Chilly Tsosie, or Chi Chilly Tseiso

Born 1920 in Tsaile, AZ; brother of George Charlie Mitchell (q.v.)

MILITARY: WWII

EDUCATION: Santa Fe

OCCUPATION: Owner and operator of a silversmith shop (Las Vegas, NV) and painter

MEDIA: Oil, watercolor, tempera, silver, and gemstone

PUBLISHED: Jacobson and d'Ucel (1950); Dunn (1968); Tanner (1973); Brody (1971). *Arizona Highways* (July 1956); *The Santa Fean* (Mar 1995)

COMMISSIONS: *Murals:* Fort Wingate (AZ) Vocational High School; West Yellowstone (WY) business establishment

PUBLIC COLLECTIONS: AF, IACB/DC, MNA/KHC, PAC, U of OK

EXHIBITS: AIW, ASF, MNM, PAC

STANLEY C. MITCHELL

"The artist began painting at Santa Fe Indian School and received training as a silversmith. He exhibited his silver work regularly at the Inter-Tribal Indian Ceremonials but was no longer an active painter (in 1968)."

Snodgrass 1968

MITCHELL, TONY, JR. *Creek*

RESIDENCE: McAlester, OK

EXHIBITS: FCTM

MIX, RONALD JOSEPH *Potawatomi*

A.K.A. Ron Mix

Born 20 Mar 1949; son of Mildred Rapp and Lawrence Mix; P/GP: Sarah Quigano and R. C. (John) Mix; M/GP: Nora Alexis and John B. Rapp

RESIDENCE: Dowagiac, MI

EDUCATION: Southwestern Michigan College, Dowagiac, MI, 1988

MEDIA: Oil, acrylic, watercolor, pencil, pen and ink, pastel, and prints

EXHIBITS: Native American Exhibit, Moscow, USSR, 1988; New Initiatives for the Arts (traveling exhibit, 1990); Niles (MI) Show, 1987; Nishnawbe Festival, Petoskey, MI, 1989; Pontiac Creative Arts Conference

HONORS: Fine Arts Scholarship, 1987; Phi Theta Kappa, national honor fraternity, 1987; Howard Yackus Memorial Award, 1988

MOFSIE, LOUIS BILLINGSLY *Hopi/Winnebago*

Weepama Quedaecouka, Green Rainbow; *Mofsie,* Sharp Shooting

Born 3 May 1936 in Brooklyn, NY; son of Alvina Lowery and Morris Mofsie, painter from Second Mesa, AZ; Great aunt: Red Wing St. Cyr, silent screen star

RESIDENCE: Maywood, NJ

EDUCATION: High school, School of Industrial Arts, New York, NY; B.S., SUNY/B,

1958; Pratt Institute, New York, NY; special classes, Museum of Modern Art and Ethical Culture School, New York, NY

OCCUPATION: Art instructor, traditional Indian dance group director, and painter

MEDIA: Acrylic, watercolor, pen and ink, and prints

PUBLISHED: Dunn (1968); Snodgrass (1968)

PUBLIC COLLECTIONS: AICH, Woodard's Art Museum

EXHIBITS: AICH, ITIC, MMA, MNM, PAC

SOLO EXHIBITS: MNM

AWARDS: ITIC, MNM

MOHE (see Cohoe, William T.)

MOHR, BRIAN *Seneca*

Born 19 June 1959

RESIDENCE: Salamanca, NY

EDUCATION: Salamanca (NY) Central High School

OCCUPATION: Tour guide, newsletter editor, traditional dancer and singer, carver, beadworker, and painter

MEDIA: Oil, watercolor, pencil, and glass beads

PUBLISHED: Johannsen and Ferguson, eds. (1983)

EXHIBITS: NYSF; Salamanca (NY) Central High School

AWARDS: NYSF ('77, 1st)

MOLINE, BOB *Comanche*

Born 1938 in Amarillo, TX

RESIDENCE: Fort Worth, TX

OCCUPATION: Horse trainer, saddlemaker; full-time painter and sculptor since 1973

PUBLISHED: Samuels (1982). *Cattleman* (Oct 1981)

BOOKS ILLUSTRATED: Pirtle (1975); *Colt Pistols* (1976)

PUBLIC COLLECTIONS: GM

EXHIBITS: AICA; CFD; CNM; ITIC; NCHF; PAC; SIRU; TRM; WH; WT; Mountain Oyster Club, Tucson, AZ; Texas Cowboy Artists Association Exhibition; Western Heritage Art Fair, Littleton, CO; see also Awards

AWARDS: ITIC ('88, 1st, Best in Category, Best in Class; '90, 1st, Mullarky Award; '91, 1st; '94, 1st); Western Trails Show ('77, Gold Medal)

BOB MOLINE

Moline's father was a horse trader near Amarillo, Texas, and as a boy, the artist helped him train green horses before they were sold. Once he had finished school, an interest in saddlemaking led Moline to take a job with a saddlery in Fort Worth. Since he had always enjoyed sketching, he was soon designing his own patterns for hand tooling the saddles. The success of these designs led him to try painting in his spare time. He says that it took seven years before he did a painting that was "halfway good." His first paintings were sold to customers at the saddle shop. Soon his employer was using Moline's paintings in saddle catalogs and a gallery in Amarillo carried his work. By 1973, his paintings were selling so well he gave up saddle making and became a full-time painter. Moline is one of the founders of the Texas Cowboy Artists Association.

Samuels 1982

MOLLER, MILDRED L. (see Moller, Tommie)

MOLLER, TOMMIE *Cherokee/Choctaw*

A.K.A. Mildred L. Moller. Signature: Tommie Moller

Born 19 Jan 1924 in Arkansas; daughter of Effie Nettie Smith and John Jackson Coleman; P/GP: Eliza Edison and William Argustus Coleman; M/GP: Sarah Elizabeth Akin and Bowen Lockhart Smith

RESIDENCE: Loomis, CA

EDUCATION: Monette (AR) High School, 1941; Memphis (TN) School of Commerce, 1942; Universidad de Guadalajara, Jalisco, Mexico, 1981; B.A., U of CA/S, 1991

OCCUPATION: Sculptor and painter

MEDIA: Oil, acrylic, watercolor, pencil, pen and ink, pastel, bronze, and prints

BOOKS ILLUSTRATED: Four pamphlets

PUBLIC COLLECTIONS: Sierra College, Rocklin, CA; West Valley Community College, Saratoga, CA

TOMMIE MOLLER

Moller states that her intent in art is to portray the peace and contemplation reflective of the inner spirit, embodying the flow of love and serenity rather than depicting negative aspects or making political statements. Since she and her family moved onto a former Maidu Indian campsite in Loomis, CA, her art has been almost exclusively of Native American subjects.

p.c. 1992

EXHIBITS: CNM; Placer County Fair, Roseville, CA; Roseville (CA) Art Center Open Show; see also Awards

AWARDS: CNM ('84, 1st; '90); Feats of Clay, national exhibit, Lincoln, CA ('90); California Arts League, Fair Oaks, CA ('90, 1st); Placer Arts League, Auburn, CA ('89, Best of Show; '90); Sierra College Art Festival, Rocklin, CA ('86, 1st)

MOMADAY, AL *Kiowa*

Haun Toa, War Lance

A.K.A. Alfred Morris Momaday

Born 2 July 1913 in Mountain View, OK; died Nov 1981 in Jémez Springs, NM; son of A-ho and Mammedaty (Standing High); father of N. Scott Momaday (q.v.); GF: George Poolaw, Kiowa medicine man

MILITARY: U.S. Corps of Engineers, War Department, WWII

EDUCATION: BC, 1931-1934; U of NM, 1936-1937; U of CA/LA, 1956; Famous Artists School, Westport, CT, correspondence course

OCCUPATION: Director of arts and crafts, teacher, school principal, and artist

MEDIA: Oil, watercolor, tempera, pastel, charcoal, pen and ink, and prints

PUBLISHED: LaFarge (1956; 1960); Pierson and Davidson (1960); Haskell (1960); Willoya and Brown (1962); Dunn (1968); Snodgrass (1968); Brody (1971); Tanner (1973); Irvine, ed. (1974); Silberman (1978); Schmid and Houlihan (1979); Mahey, et al. (1980); Boyd, et al. (1981); Broder (1981); King (1981); Medina (1981); Trimble, S. (1987) Seymour (1988); Williams, ed. (1990). *Tulsa Magazine* (May 1948); *The Lutheran* (28 May 1958); *Indian Life* (1960); program, Region VI American Camping Association Convention (1965), cover; *The Arizona Republic* (17 Mar 1968); *New Mexico Magazine* (Jan/Feb 1970); *Four Winds* (summer 1980); *The Indian Trader* (Nov 1980); biographical publications

BOOKS ILLUSTRATED: Momaday (1969)

COMMISSIONS: *Murals:* Curtiss Wright, 1957. *Other:* St. Luke's Lutheran Church, Albuquerque, NM, designed eight altar plaques, 1958; designed medal honoring his son, N. Scott Momaday (q.v.), 1975

PUBLIC COLLECTIONS: AC/RM, BIA, CWC, GM, IACB, KM, MAI, MNA, MNM, MRFM, NMSF, PAC, SM, TWS, WM

EXHIBITS: AC/A, AAID, AAIE, AIE, ASF, BG, CSPIP, DAM, FAIEAIP, HM/G, LGAM, MFA/D, NAP, OMA, PAC, PBS, SAIEAIP, SFFA, SN, U of NM, U of OK, USDS

SOLO EXHIBITS: BG, HM, MFA/D, MNA, OTP, PAC, U of OK

AWARDS: AAID (2 Grand Awards); AIE (2 Grand Awards); DAM; HFA (Best in Show); ITIC ('69, Grand Award; '72, Woodard Award); MFA/D; MNM; NMSF (2 Grand Awards); PAC ('71), SN

HONORS: Dallas Exchange Club, Tribe of Teal Wing, Outstanding Southwestern Indian Artist, 1956; Western (NY) Art Association, Ho-ennywe Society, Outstanding Indian Artist Award, 1965; IACB, Certificate of Appreciation, 1967; PAC, Waite Phillips Special Trophy, 1975; Lawrence University, Appleton, WI, Honorary Doctorate

AL MOMADAY

"At Jémez Pueblo, Momaday initiated a program of arts and crafts which brought international recognition to the school. He organized parent groups to discuss problems and programs within the Pueblo, and was a progressive leader in many educational and Indian art activities."

Snodgrass 1968

MOMADAY, NAVARRE SCOTT *Kiowa*

Tsoai-talee, Rock Tree Boy

A.K.A. N. Scott Momaday

Born 27 Feb 1934 in Lawton, OK; son of Natachee Scott and Al Momaday (q.v.)

RESIDENCE: Tucson, AZ

EDUCATION: A.B., U of NM, 1958; A.M., SU, 1960; Ph.D., SU, 1963

OCCUPATION: Educator, poet, author, and artist

MEDIA: Acrylic, watercolor, pen and ink, pastel, and prints

PUBLISHED: Momaday (1965; 1969; 1969; 1973; 1974; 1976; 1977; 1989); Trimble (1973); Cambell, ed. (1993). *Four Winds* (summer 1980); *The Indian Trader* (Nov 1980); *The Arizona Republic* (12 May 1986); *The Tulsa World* (24 Sept 1987); *Native Peoples* (spring 1992; Special Edition 1994); biographical publications

BOOKS ILLUSTRATED: Momaday (1976; 1977; 1989); Andrews (1983); Woodard (1988)

EXHIBITS: BBHC; HM; NACLA; OCSA; OIO; SFFA; U of ND/G; The Wrigley Mansion, Scottsdale, AZ; galleries in AZ, ID, NM, Germany, and Switzerland

AWARDS: OIO ('82, 1st)

HONORS: Guggenheim Fellowship, 1966; Pulitzer Prize for Fiction, 1969; American Indian Exposition, Anadarko, OK, Outstanding Indian of the Year, 1969; The Geographic Society of Chicago Publications Award, 1973; The Western Heritage "Wrangler" Award, 1974; U of NM Alumni Association, Zimmerman Award, 1975; MAI, Trustee, 1978-1983; California Association of Teachers of English, "Author of the Year" Award, 1980; Pulitzer Prize for Fiction, juror, 1981, 1990, Chairman, 1986; Association of Western Literature, Distinguished Service Award and Life Membership; Neustadt Award for International Literature, juror, 1983; PEN, American Center, Executive Board, 1985-1986; New Mexico Endowment for the Humanities Service Award, 1987; Oklahoma Hall of Fame, inducted, 1987; Library of Congress, Distinguished Board of Scholars, member, 1988; National Center for American Indian Enterprise Development, Los Angeles, Jay Silverheels Achievement Award, 1990; SWAIA, poster artist, 1991; ten honorary doctorates

MONETO (see Snake, Steven)

MONIGNOK, GABRIEL *Eskimo*

Birth date unknown; born in Mekoryuk, AK; died 29 Sept 1965 while fishing

RESIDENCE: Lived in Alaska

EDUCATION: Santa Fe

PUBLISHED: Snodgrass (1968)

PUBLIC COLLECTIONS: MAI

EXHIBITS: MNM, PAC

AWARDS: MNM, PAC

MONONGYE, PRESTON *Hopi*

Born 1927 in Los Angeles, CA; died 1991

MILITARY: WWII

EDUCATION: Haskell; Occidental College, Los Angeles, CA

OCCUPATION: Silversmith, potter, sculptor, *katsina* carver, and painter; primarily a silversmith

MEDIA: Acrylic

PUBLISHED: Tanner (1973); Monthan and Monthan (1975)

EXHIBITS: ITIC, SN

AWARDS: ITIC ('70, 1st; '71, 1st)

MONROE, AVIS J. *Oglala Sioux*

Born 13 May 1962 in Pine Ridge, SD, on the Pine Ridge Reservation; daughter of Sharon and Wilson Black Elk (stepfather)

RESIDENCE: Pine Ridge, SD

EDUCATION: Pine Ridge (SD) High School, 1980; A.F.A., IAIA, 1984; CCAC, 1984-1985; U of NM

OCCUPATION: Sculptor and painter

MEDIA: Oil, acrylic, pencil, pastel, charcoal, mixed-media, stone, and prints

PUBLIC COLLECTIONS: HCC
EXHIBITS: IAIA, RC, NPTA, SIM; see also Awards
SOLO/SPECIAL EXHIBITS: SIM (dual show)
AWARDS: RC ('84; '85; '86; '87, Hensler Award); CSF/SF ('88, Dickey Pfaelzer Award)
HONORS: RC, Thunderbird Foundation Scholarship, 1984, 1985, 1987, 1990, 1994

MONTANA, DAVID *Tohono O'odham (Papago)*
Born 1947 in Sells, AZ
RESIDENCE: Sells, AZ
EDUCATION: IAIA, 1965-1966
MEDIA: Oil
PUBLISHED: Snodgrass (1968); Hill (1992). *YAIA Catalog*
PUBLIC COLLECTIONS: IAIA
EXHIBITS: AICH, FAIEAIP, IAIA, OWE, YAIA

MONTGOMERY, GARY *Seminole*
Born 18 Sept 1950 in Seminole, OK; son of Sara Jane Davis and William Clarence Montgomery; M/GP: Liddie Miller and Jesse Tiger; Artist is related to Pete Miller, Seminole medicine man.
RESIDENCE: Shawnee, OK
EDUCATION: Strother (OK) High School, 1968; Murray State College, Tishomingo, OK; ECSC/OK
OCCUPATION: Artist
MEDIA: Oil, acrylic, pencil, pastel, charcoal, and prints
PUBLISHED: *Oklahoma Art Gallery* (spring 1980); *Southwest Art* (June 1982)
PUBLIC COLLECTIONS: BA/AZ, CNM, HM, SI
EXHIBITS: ACAI, AIE, AICA, CIM, CNM, FAIE, FCTM, FCTM/M, HM/G, ITIC, MFA/O, MNH/AN, NMSF, OAC, PAC, RE, SI, SNM, SWAIA
AWARDS: AICA ('79, Gold Medal); CNM ('84, 1st; '85, 1st; '86, Grand Award); FCTM ('82); FCTM/M ('86, Grand Award; '87; '89; '91; '93, Best of Show); ITIC ('87; '94); NMSF (Best of Show); RE ('91, HM); SNM (1st)
HONORS: FCTM, designated a Master Artist, 1983

GARY MONTGOMERY

After a broken arm in high school, Montgomery ended a budding baseball career and changed his focus to art. At first he attempted traditional Indian painting techniques but he found them too limiting. The artist then turned to what has been termed "romantic realism," with representational and naturalistic paintings. Not interested in creating historically correct paintings, he tries to express the spiritual nature of his subject. He says of his art, "I paint the omens, legends and truths of the Native American in an environment of 100-150 years ago."

Southwest Art, *June 1982*

MONTILEAUX, DONALD L. *Oglala Sioux*
Yellowbird
Born 3 Jan 1948 at Pine Ridge, SD, on the Pine Ridge Indian Reservation
RESIDENCE: Rapid City, SD
EDUCATION: Rapid City (SD) High School, 1963-1966; IAIA, 1966-1968; BHSU; U of SD, Indian Art Workshop, 1964, 1965
OCCUPATION: Teacher, lecturer, IACB employee, and painter
MEDIA: Oil, acrylic, pencil, and mixed-media
PUBLISHED: Libhart (1970); Highwater (1980). *The Rapid City Journal* (3 Dec 1989)
PUBLIC COLLECTIONS: HCC, IACB
EXHIBITS: CSP, HCC, HM, NPTA, RC, SIM
SOLO EXHIBITS: SIM
AWARDS: RC ('72; '84, 1st; '85, Niederman Award; '89, Barkley Art Center Award; '92; '93, Niederman Award; '94)

DONALD L. MONTILEAUX

Montileaux is known for his abstract, flat, two-dimensional paintings done in the brilliant colors typical of the Plains Indians. His inspiration comes from his Sioux heritage, especially the early pictographs found on buffalo hides and tipis. He has attributed his style to his friend and fellow artist Herman Red Elk (q.v.).

Montileaux is a member of The Dream Catchers Artists Guild, Ltd. (q.v.).

MONTOUR, DAVE *Delaware/Mohawk*
A.K.A. David A. Montour
Born 4 Sept 1959 in Winner, SD

OCCUPATION: Artist-in-residence, flute player, illustrator, sculptor, jeweler, and painter

MEDIA: Watercolor, pencil, pen and ink, wood, stone, bronze, silver, and gemstone

COMMISSIONS: U.S. Department of Transportation, book covers

EXHIBITS: HM, ITAE

SOLO EXHIBITS: SI

AWARDS: ITAE (1st)

MONTOUR, MARK D. *Mohawk*

Born 19 Nov 1952

RESIDENCE: Caughnawaga, PQ, Canada

EDUCATION: City College of New York, NY, 1973; B.F.A., C/CU, 1977; M.A., C/CU

OCCUPATION: Teacher and painter

MEDIA: Acrylic, mixed-media, wood, feather, and beads

EXHIBITS: Manitou Community College, 1976; Dawson College, 1977; Sir George Williams U., 1974, 1977

MONTOYA, ALFREDO *San Ildefonso*

Wen Tsireh, Pine Tree Bird

Born ca. 1890; died 21 May 1913; brother of Isabelita Montoya (q.v.); brother-in-law of Crescencio Martínez (q.v.)

EDUCATION: San Ildefonso

OCCUPATION: Artist-recorder and painter

MEDIA: Watercolor and pencil

PUBLISHED: Underhill (1944); Dunn (1968); Snodgrass (1968); Tanner (1973); Brody (1992), Tryk (1993). El Palacio (June 1943); *Arizona Highways* (July 1956)

PUBLIC COLLECTIONS: MAI; MNM (gift of the Fred Harveys, ca. 1909); MNM/SAR

EXHIBITS: WWM

ALFREDO MONTOYA

*"During excavations on Pajarito Plateau, ca. 1915, Montoya was unable to work as a digger because of a tubercular condition. Therefore, he became a recorder, drawing replicas of the Pueblo ceremonial life unearthed there. Bertha Dutton said that he was 'perhaps the young man from San Ildefonso who initiated modern Pueblo painting (*El Palacio, *June 1943).'"*

"In 1911, his art instructor, Elizabeth Richards, sent his paintings to Barbara Freire-Marreco in England for display."

Snodgrass 1968

Montoya sold paintings at the School of American Research archaeology field camps at Rito de los Frijoles (now Bandelier National Monument) from about 1909 until his early death in 1913. His paintings are very rare.

Brody 1992

MONTOYA, CHARLES *San Ildefonso*

Oqowamono

PUBLISHED: Snodgrass (1968)

PUBLIC COLLECTIONS: MFA/A

MONTOYA, GERÓNIMA CRUZ *San Juan*

P'otsunu, Shell

A.K.A. Po Tsunu; Signature: Potsunu

Born 22 Sept 1915 at San Juan Pueblo, NM; daughter of Crucita Trujillo, potter, and Pablo Cruz; mother of Robert Montoya (q.v.)

RESIDENCE: Santa Fe, NM

EDUCATION: St. Joseph's; Santa Fe, 1935; U of NM, 1935-1936; Claremont, 1945, 1948; B.S., U. of ABQ, 1958; studied under Dorothy Dunn, Alfredo Martínez (q.v.), Jean Ames, and Kenneth Chapman

OCCUPATION: Educator, art department director, lecturer, and artist

MEDIA: Casein, tempera, gouache, pencil, and prints

PUBLISHED: Jacobson and d'Ucel (1950); Dunn (1968); Snodgrass (1968); Brody (1971); Tanner (1973); Fawcett and Callander (1982); Samuels (1985); Seymour (1988), Tryk (1993); Gully, ed. (1994). *Native Peoples* (Jan/Feb/Mar 1995); biographical publications

PUBLIC COLLECTIONS: AAID, BIA, IACB, IACB/DC, ITIC, MAI, MNM, MHDYMM, MRFM

EXHIBITS: AIW; ASM; BNIAS; HM; HM/G; ITIC; JGS; LGAM; MAI; MHDYMM, MNM; MNM/T; MHDYMM; MRFM; NMSF; PAC; SFFA; SN; USDS; WRTD; Scripps College Arts Gallery, Claremont, CA

SOLO EXHIBITS: MNM; PAC; Amerika Haus, Nuremburg, Germany

AWARDS: AAID; ITIC (six); MNM; MHDYMM (Purchase Award); NMSF; PAC ('62); SAR (Purchase Award); SN

HONORS: Henry Dendahl Award for Outstanding Student, Santa Fe; received honorarium when her student, Ben Quintana (q.v.), won the National Youth Forum's art contest; NMAI, The Art and Cultural Achievement Award, 1994

MONTOYA, GUADALUPE *San Juan*

PUBLISHED: Snodgrass (1968)

PUBLIC COLLECTIONS: DAM

MONTOYA, ISABELITA *San Ildefonso*

Birth date unknown; mother of Gilbert Atencio (q.v.)

RESIDENCE: San Ildefonso Pueblo, NM

EDUCATION: Santa Fe

MEDIA: Pencil and crayon

PUBLISHED: Snodgrass (1968)

MONTOYA, JOE (see Montoya, José L.)

MONTOYA, JOSÉ L. *Isleta*

A.K.A. Joe Montoya

Born 12 Dec 1903 at Isleta Pueblo, NM

RESIDENCE: Albuquerque, NM

EDUCATION: B.F.A., U of NM, 1951

PUBLISHED: Snodgrass (1968)

EXHIBITS: MNM, U of NM

MONTOYA, JUAN B. *San Juan*

PUBLISHED: Snodgrass (1968)

PUBLIC COLLECTIONS: MAI

MONTOYA, MONTY (see Montoya, Sidney, Jr.)

MONTOYA, NED *San Juan*

EDUCATION: Santa Fe, ca. 1958

PUBLISHED: Snodgrass (1968)

PUBLIC COLLECTIONS: MNM

EXHIBITS: MNM

AWARDS: MNM

MONTOYA, NELLIE *San Juan*

PUBLISHED: Snodgrass (1968)

PUBLIC COLLECTIONS: MAI

MONTOYA, PAUL T. *Sandía/San Juan*

OCCUPATION: Artist

EXHIBITS: SWAIA

AWARDS: SWAIA ('78; '89; '90)

MONTOYA, ROBERT B. *Sandía/San Juan*

Soe Khuwa Pin, Fog Mountain

A.K.A. Bob Montoya

GERÓNIMA CRUZ MONTOYA

"This highly respected teacher has devoted the major portion of her career instructing others. Only recently did she find the necessary time for her own painting. 'She does not force their work into any preconceived pattern . . . she allows the student to project his own ideas, simply guides him into a more rounded development of his initial creative impulse. (Dorothy Morang, El Palacio, *May 1940)' . . . Montoya is credited by many Indian artists as being the teacher who gave them most encouragement."*

Snodgrass 1968

According to the artist, "My style of painting is very simple. My subjects are mainly traditional dances, home scenes, and designs. My inspiration also comes from Mimbres figures, pictographs, and petroglyphs. I continually experiment with new forms and styles."

Shutes and Mellick 1979

ISABELITA MONTOYA

"During her school days in Santa Fe, Montoya executed charming pencil and crayon sketches."

Snodgrass 1968

JOSÉ L. MONTOYA

"The artist was known as a still-life painter. In 1950, he was working in Albuquerque, and no longer painting."

Snodgrass 1968

Born 4 Mar 1947 in Santa Fe, NM; son of Gerónima Cruz and Juan A. Montoya (q.v.)

RESIDENCE: Albuquerque, NM

EDUCATION: St. Michael's High School, Santa Fe; B.A., U of NM; M.A., U of OK

OCCUPATION: Architect, BIA employee, jeweler; painter since 1970

PUBLISHED: Tryk (1993). *New Mexico Magazine* (Dec 1980)

BOOKS ILLUSTRATED: Hill (1995)

COMMISSIONS: *Murals:* AC/DS; IPCC

PUBLIC COLLECTIONS: AC/DS, EM

EXHIBITS: ABQM, ACS/ENP, NMSF, IPCC, SWAIA, WWM

SOLO EXHIBITS: SCG

AWARDS: Partial listing includes: ACS/ENP; NMSF; SWAIA ('73, 2-1st, Best of Show; '77, 1st; '78, 1st, Hinds Award; '86, 1st; '89)

HONORS: Ford Foundation Fellowship, 1970

MONTOYA, SIDNEY, JR. *San Juan/Navajo*

SIDNEY MONTOYA JR.

Monyoya's last known profession was as a photo engraver. By 1967 he was no longer painting.

Thun Povi, Sun Flower

A.K.A. Monty Montoya

Born 4 Sept 1928

RESIDENCE: Chamita, NM

EDUCATION: Albuquerque; B.A., U of NM; graduate work toward M.A., Drury College, Springfield, MO

PUBLISHED: Snodgrass (1968)

PUBLIC COLLECTIONS: MNA, MNM

EXHIBITS: MNA, MNM, NMSF, PAC

MONTOYA, TOMMY *San Juan*

TOMMY MONTOYA

The work of Tommy Montoya is a blending of old and new. It is both traditional and abstract. The subject matter is centuries old, but the techniques and materials usd are contemporary. He does both figurative studies of dancers and purely abstract studies of color and form; both are full of movement.

Southwest Profile, *Jan/Feb 1986*

Ts'ay Ta

A.K.A. Thomas Edward Montoya; Signature: early, Tommy Montoya; later, Ts'ay Ta

Birth date unknown; born in San Juan Pueblo, NM; son of Carmelita and Luis Montoya

RESIDENCE: San Juan Pueblo, NM

EDUCATION: Albuquerque, 1963; A.F.A, IAIA, 1965; B.F.A., CCAC,1971; M.F.A., U of CA/B, 1973

OCCUPATION: Free-lance artist and designer, layout artist and sign painter, graphic designer, photographer, technical illustrator, poet, and painter

MEDIA: Oil, watercolor, oil pastel, pencil, and charcoal

PUBLISHED: YAIA (1965); Snodgrass (1968); Jacka and Jacka (1988). *Journal of the American Medical Association* (21 Mar 1966); *Southwest Art* (June 1983); *Southwest Profile* (Jan/Feb 1986)

BOOKS ILLUSTRATED: *The Traditional Bread of the Pueblo Indians*

COMMISSIONS: *Murals:* IPCC

PUBLIC COLLECTIONS: BIA

EXHIBITS: ITIC; HM/G; MNM; NACLA; NMSF; SWAIA; YAIA; The Foreign Correspondent's Club Gallery, Tokyo, Japan

AWARDS: ACS/ENP ('77, 2-1st); ITIC ('91, 1st); HM/G ('77, 1st, Avery Award; '78, 1st); MNM; NMSF ('75, 1st; '78; '79, 1st); SPIM ('79, 1st); SWAIA ('76, 1st, Hinds Award; '79, 2-1st)

MOONE, GARY *Navajo*

Born ca. 1960

RESIDENCE: Teec Nos Pos, AZ

EDUCATION: IAIA
MEDIA: Oil, acrylic, pencil, pen and ink, and pastel
PUBLISHED: *The Indian Trader* (July 1984)
EXHIBITS: IAIA; ITIC; NNTF; NTF; Durango (CO) Area Arts Council Competition
SOLO/SPECIAL EXHIBITS: NTM (dual show)
AWARDS: ITIC; NNTF; NTF ('83, Best of Class)

MOORE, GARY L. *Navajo*

RESIDENCE: Teec Nos Pos, AZ
EXHIBITS: ITIC
AWARDS: ITIC ('85; '86, 1st)

MOORE, GEORGIANNA *Chippewa*

PUBLISHED: Snodgrass (1968)
EXHIBITS: PAC, USDS

MOORE, MONROE *Cherokee*

EXHIBITS: FCTM
AWARDS: FCTM ('74)

MOORE, REX *Santee Sioux*

Born 30 July 1926 at Warwick, ND, on the Fort Totten Reservation
RESIDENCE: Fort Totten, ND
MILITARY: U.S. Army, 1943-1963
EDUCATION: Fort Totten (ND) High School, 1943; George Washington University, Washington, D.C., 1954-1956; Monterey (CA) School of Languages, 1956-1958; American University, Beirut, Lebanon, 1958
OCCUPATION: Advisor, interpreter, translator, taxidermist, gallery owner, materials manager, and painter
EXHIBITS: Expo '74, World's Fair, Spokane, WA
SOLO EXHIBITS: SIM

MOOTZKA, WALDO *Hopi*

Mootska, Point of Yucca
A.K.A. Walter Mootska
Born 1910 at New Oraibi, AZ; died 1940 in an automobile accident in Phoenix, AZ; son of Tom Mootzka
RESIDENCE: Lived in Santa Fe, NM
EDUCATION: Albuquerque; Santa Fe
OCCUPATION: Illustrator, painter, and silversmith
MEDIA: Watercolor
PUBLISHED: Nelson (1937); Dunn (1968); Snodgrass (1968); Brody (1971); Tanner (1968; 1973); Dockstader (1977); Silberman (1978); Broder (1981); Fawcett and Callander (1982); Hoffman, et al. (1984); Wade, ed. (1986); Seymour (1988); Archuleta and Strickland (1991). *Theatre Arts Monthly* (Aug 1933); *The Arizona Republic* (12 Dec 1965; 17 Mar 1968); *Tamaqua* (winter/spring 1991); *Southwest Art* (June 1983; Mar 1992)
BOOKS ILLUSTRATED: *Rhythm for Rain* by John Louw Nelson
PUBLIC COLLECTIONS: AF, BA/AZ, BM/B, GM, IACB/DC, MAI, MKMcNAI, MNA/KHC, MRFM, PAC, SM, U of OK, WOM, WWM
EXHIBITS: AIEC, ASM, HM, IK, LGAM, NAP, NGA, OMA, PAC, PAC/T, SV, WRTD, WWM

WALDO MOOTZKA

"Mootzka had no formal art training. He often observed Fred Kabotie (q.v.) painting at Oraibi Day School, and it may have been there that he learned the technique of watercolor painting. Later, in Santa Fe, he was sponsored by Frank Patania, who taught him silversmithing. At the time of his death, Mootzka was devoting almost all his artistic talents to silverwork."

Snodgrass 1968

According to Dockstader (1977), Mootzka was especially noted for his representations of tribal ceremonies and mythological scenes. Using a full palette, he demonstrated a great feeling for color. Also notable was his attention to fine detail. Mootzka experimented with a variety of styles and some of his work suggests a European influence due to a three-dimensional effect achieved through modeling with colors.

Stephen Mopope

"Mopope's grandfather was a Spanish captive, kidnaped by the Kiowas from a wagon train crossing the prairie and reared by Chief Many Bears. On the Kiowa side he was a descendant of Appiatan, a noted Kiowa warrior. His granduncles were Silverhorn (Haungooah) (q.v.) and Hakok. They found him drawing designs in the sand and decided to teach him how to paint on tanned skins in the old Kiowa way. Mopope's childhood education by his grandmother was in the Kiowa tradition. He is one of the original Five Kiowas (q.v.) and was primarily a painter and dancer most of his life."

Snodgrass 1968

Mopope, Stephen *Kiowa*

Qued Koi, Painted Robe

Born 27 Aug 1898 near Red Stone Baptist Mission on the Kiowa Reservation, Indian Territory; died 3 Feb 1974 at Fort Cobb, OK; M/GF: Appiatan, Kiowa warrior

RESIDENCE: Lived in Fort Cobb, OK

EDUCATION: St. Patrick's, 1916; non-credit instruction at U of OK, 1926-1929

OCCUPATION: Dancer, flute player, farmer, and painter

MEDIA: Watercolor, tempera, and prints

PUBLISHED: Jacobson (1929, 1964); Jacobson and d'Ucel (1950); LaFarge (1956); Dunn (1968); Snodgrass (1968); Brody (1971); Warner (1975); Highwater (1976); Dockstader (1977); Silberman (1978); Broder (1981); Boyd, et al. (1981; 1983); King (1981); Fawcett and Callander (1982); Hoffman, et al. (1984); Samuels (1985); Wade, ed. (1986); Archuleta and Strickland (1991). *American Indian Exposition Program* (1946; 1948), cover; *The Cherokee Nation News* (21 Nov 1975); *Southwest Art* (winter 1977-1978); *The Indian Trader* (July 1978); *Tamaqwa* (winter/spring 1991); *The Anadarko Daily News, Visitor Guide* (1991-1992; 1992-1993); *American Indian Art* (spring 1995); biographical publications

COMMISSIONS: *Murals:* FSM; HSM/OK; NSU; St. Patrick's; U of OK; USDI; Federal Building, Muskogee, OK; First National Bank of Anadarko, OK; Muskogee (OK) Junior College; NEO; U.S. Navy Hospital, Carville, LA; U.S. Post Office, Anadarko, OK

PUBLIC COLLECTIONS: ACM; BA/AZ; CMA; DCC; GM; HM; HSM/OK; IACB; IACB/DC; MAI; MKMcNAI; MNA/KHC; MNM; MRFM; OAC; OSAC; OSAF/GC; OU/L; OU/MA; OU/SM; PAC; SM; SPIM; SPL; VV; WOM; WWM; Peabody Museum of Salem, MA

EXHIBITS: AC/A; AIEC; AIW; ASM; CSPIP; EITA; HM; HSM/OK; IK; JH; LGAM; MPABAS; NACLA; NAP; OMA; OU/ET; OU/MA/T; PAC; PAC/T; SI; SMA/TX; SPIM; SV; First International Art Exposition, Prague, Czechoslovakia, 1928; Kermac Mural Design Exhibit, 1965

SOLO EXHIBITS: AIE, JH, SPIM

HONORS: National Folk Festival Conference, Chicago, IL, speaker, May 1957; IACB, Certificate of Appreciation, 1966

Moqui *Hopi*

Wickahtewah

PUBLISHED: Snodgrass (1968)

PUBLIC COLLECTIONS: MNM

Ignacio Moquino

"The artist left school after his father's death to care for his family. While working part-time as a shoemaker, he began his art career by designing and painting pictures of various tribal costumes. He later turned his interests to silversmithing."

Snodgrass 1968

Moquino, Ignacio *Zia*

Waki Yeni Dewa

Signature: Waka Yeni Dewa

Born 7 May 1917 at Zia Pueblo, NM; died ca. 1982

RESIDENCE: Lived at San Juan Pueblo, NM

MILITARY: U.S. Army, WWII

EDUCATION: Santa Fe; two years graduate work in art under Dorothy Dunn and Gerónima Montoya (q.v.)

OCCUPATION: Teacher, silversmith, and artist

MEDIA: Watercolor, tempera, silver, and gemstone

PUBLISHED: Jacobson and d'Ucel (1950); Dunn (1968); Snodgrass (1968); Tanner (1973); Golder (1985); Seymour (1988)

COMMISSIONS: *Murals:* SFWF [with Charles Loloma and Joe Duran (qq.v.)]

PUBLIC COLLECTIONS: DAM, HM, IACB/DC, MAI, MNA/KHC, MNM, MRFM, U of OK, USDI

EXHIBITS: AIW, HH, HM, ITIC, JGS, LGAM, MNM, OU/ET, PAC, SFWF, WRTD

AWARDS: ITIC

MOQUINO, JUANITO *Zia*

RESIDENCE: Zia Pueblo, NM

PUBLISHED: Snodgrass (1968)

PUBLIC COLLECTIONS: MNM

MOQUINO, TORIBIO *Zia*

PUBLISHED: Snodgrass (1968)

PUBLIC COLLECTIONS: MNM

MORAN, ROSE AZURE *Chippewa/Cree*

Che-Nogie

A.K.A. Signature: Includes a painted rose

Born 10 Apr 1933 at Belcourt, ND

EDUCATION: Turtle Mountain Ojibwa Indian Elementary School; studied under Del Lyonais.

OCCUPATION: Homemaker, arts and crafts teacher, and painter

EXHIBITS: MPI

SOLO EXHIBITS: MPI

MOREZ, MARY *Navajo*

Born 16 Jan 1946 in Tuba City, AZ, in the Navajo Nation; daughter of Marene and Alex Morez

RESIDENCE: Phoenix, AZ

EDUCATION: Phoenix; U of AZ; RVSA, 1962; Maricopa Technical College, Phoenix, AZ; U of AZ, "Southwest Indian Art Project," scholarhip, summer 1960

OCCUPATION: Illustrator, fashion designer, engineer draftsman, museum curator, graphic artist, and painter

MEDIA: Oil, acrylic, charcoal, conte crayon, ink wash, pen and ink, and mixed-media

PUBLISHED: Snodgrass (1968); Katz (1970; 1977; 1980); Iacopi, ed. (1972); Tanner (1973); Hoffman, et al. (1984); Archuleta and Strickland (1991); Jacka and Jacka (1994). *American Indian Crafts and Culture* (May 1972); *Art In America* (July/Aug 1972); *The Arizona Republic* (17 Sept 1972; 22 Nov 1974); *The American Way* (serialized); *The Phoenix Gazette* (27 May 1978); *Indian Arizona* (June 1978); *Native Arts/West* (Dec 1980); *Phoenix Magazine* (1981); *Four Winds* (spring 1982); *Plateau* (Vol. 54, no. 1, 1982); *The Navajo Times* (28 Sept 1983); *Phoenix Home and Garden* (1988); *The Flinn Foundation* (No. 2, 1991); biographical publications

BOOKS ILLUSTRATED: *Navajo Times*; *The New Mexico Review and Legislative Journal*

COMMISSIONS: Phoenix Indian Center, Native American Film Festival, Sept 1989; U.S. Department of Health, Education and Welfare, illustrations for health care pamphlets; Canyon Records, jackets

PUBLIC COLLECTIONS: BM/B; HCC; HM; MNA; WWM; Institut für Englische Philologie der Universität Wurburg, Germany

EXHIBITS: AAID, BM/B, CIAE, CIAI, CPS, FNAA, HM, HM/G, HPTU, IK, ITIC, MCC/CA, NACLA, NAP, RC, SDMM, SN, SV

SOLO EXHIBITS: HM; NTM; WWM; Museum of Navajo Ceremonial Art, Santa Fe, NM; Verde Valley Artists Association, Jerome, AZ; Newport Harbor Art Museum, Balboa, CA

MARY MOREZ

After the death of her parents, Morez was raised by her grandparents on the Navajo Reservation in Northern Arizona until she was sent to the Phoenix Indian School. In Phoenix she was adopted by a non-Indian couple and thus came to live in that world. Her Navajo heritage has remained very important to her and she has learned of it not only from her grandparents but by extensive study.

As a child, Morez suffered from polio which required corrective surgery. Later, as an adult she developed additional problems with the disease which led to a period of 15 years in which she painted very little. In the early 1990s she once again became an active painter. In addition to her art, she spends a great deal of her time and energy helping others at the Phoenix Indian Hospital. The artist has said of her life, "When I grow old I want to know I've left something behind. Not as an artist but as a human being who loves and cares and tends and helps other human beings. To do that is to walk in beauty."

p.c. 1992

AWARDS: AAID ('68; '71, 1st); HM/G ('70; '71, 1st); ITIC ('75, 1st; '79; '82); RC ('69, 2-1st, Best of Show; '71, 1st; '89, Woodard Award)

HONORS: Ray Vogue School of Arts, Chicago, IL, scholarship; Phoenix (AZ) Indian Center, Board of Directors; Phoenix (AZ) Civic Plaza Indian Cultural Center Committee, appointed by Mayor; Phoenix (AZ) Indian Medical Center, Outstanding Volunteer; Phoenix Indian School Hall of Fame, inducted; Camelback High School, Phoenix, AZ, recognized for contributions to Indian education; invited by Governor Bruce Babbitt to participate in symposia and shows as a part of "Arizona Women's Partnerships," 1985

MORGAN, JUDITH PHYLLIS *Tsimshian*

Simclosh, Lady In The Sun

A.K.A. Mrs. Willis O. Fitzpatrick; Judith Phyllis Morgan-Fitzpatrick

Born 27 Apr 1930 at Kitwanga, BC, Canada; M/GF: Chief of the Eagle clan and consultant to the tribe

RESIDENCE: Kitwanga, BC, Canada

EDUCATION: Kitwanga (BC) Day School; Alberni Indian Residential School, BC; Cottey Junior College, Nevada, MO; Elementary Teaching Certificate; studied art under G.N. Sinclair

OCCUPATION: Housewife and artist

PUBLISHED: Snodgrass (1968); *European Review of Native American Studies* (Vol. 5, no. 1, 1991)

PUBLIC COLLECTIONS: C/GM; C/U of BC; British Columbia Provincial Archives; Provincial Government, Victoria, BC

EXHIBITS: C/ACSV; C/AG/V; C/GM; C/MNBC; C/NNEC; C/RBCM; C/U of BC; PAM; Community Bank Exhibition; Kitanmax Centennial Museum, 1987; 'Ksan Gallery, Hazelton, BC; National Art Gallery, Toronto, ON; represented in a cross-country tour from Vancouver, BC, to Toronto, ON; exhibited throughout Canada, 1940s; throughout the U.S.; see also Awards

AWARDS: C/ACSV ('48); Pacific National Exhibition ('47, 1st); Victoria, BC, poster contests (2-1st)

JUDITH PHYLLIS MORGAN

Both of the artist's parents were hereditary chiefs. Her father was Chief of the Wolf clan whose family originated in Kitsegukla and moved to Kitwanga to be closer to their property rights. Her mother was a member of the Grouse clan whose family originated in Kitwanga on the Skeena River. Her brother, Raymond, carved the totem crests which still stand at Kitwanga.

"Morgan has been painting since about 1953. She concentrates on depicting the Northwest Coast and her family tribe in non-traditional Indian style."

Snodgrass 1968

MORGAN, ROBERT *Mescalero Apache*

RESIDENCE: Mescalero, NM

PUBLISHED: Snodgrass (1968)

EXHIBITS: MNM, SN

AWARDS: SN ('67)

MORGAN, ROGER *Navajo*

RESIDENCE: Florence, AZ

EXHIBITS: LIAS

MORGAN, VANESSA *Kiowa/Pima*

Paukeigope

A.K.A. Vanessa Paukeigope Morgan

Born 5 Oct 1952 in Tempe, AZ; GF: Stephen Mopope (q.v.)

RESIDENCE: Anadarko, OK

OCCUPATION: Painter

EXHIBITS: BPG, LIAS

AWARDS: LIAS ('92, MA)

MORGAN-FITZPATRICK, JUDITH P. (see Morgan, Judith Phyllis)

MORNING DOVE (see Seth, Leroy L.)

MORNING STAR (see Humetewa, James Russell, Jr.)

MORNING STAR (see Kewanyouma, Leroy)

MORNING STAR (see Toledo, José Rey)

MORRIS, RUTH ELLA *Navajo*

Born 1944

RESIDENCE: Window Rock, AZ

EDUCATION: U of AZ, "Southwest Indian Art Project," scholarship, summer 1960

PUBLISHED: Snodgrass (1968)

MORRISON, EDDIE *Cherokee*

Born 29 Sept 1946; son of Margaret Brackett Morrison Hummingbird; M/GP: Jane A. Batt and Mige Brackett

RESIDENCE: Caldwell, KS

EDUCATION: Tahlequah (OK) High School, 1964; NSU, 1969

OCCUPATION: Sculptor and painter

MEDIA: Acrylic, pencil, wood, stone, and prints

PUBLIC COLLECTIONS: HCC

EXHIBITS: AICA; CAI/KC; CHMG; CNM; FCTM; HCC; PAC; SNAICF; TM/NE; Plaza Art Show, Kansas City, MO; Smoky Hill Museum, Salina, KS, 1990

MORRISON, GEORGE *Chippewa*

Wah-Wah-Teh-Go-Na-Ga-Bo, Standing in the Northern Light

Born 30 Sept 1919 in Chippewa City, MN; son of Barbara Mesaba and George Morrison; P/GP: Mary Caribou and James Morrison; M/GP: Mary and John Mesaba

RESIDENCE: Grand Portage, MN

EDUCATION: Grand Marais (MN) High School, 1938; MCAD, 1943; ASL, 1943-1946; University of Aix-Marseille, Aix-en-Provence, France, 1952-1953

OCCUPATION: Educator, sculptor, and painter

MEDIA: Acrylic, tempera, pen and ink, mixed-media, and wood

PUBLISHED: Snodgrass (1968); Kostich (1977); New (1979); Highwater (1980); Katz (1980); Amerson, ed. (1981); Hoffman, et al. (1984); Wade, ed. (1986); Ward, ed. (1990); Archuleta and Strickland (1991); Zurko, ed. (1992). *Art In America* (July/Aug 1972)

COMMISSIONS: *Murals*: Day Break Star Indian Cultural Center, Seattle, WA. *Other:* MRNAC, emblematic exterior design

PUBLIC COLLECTIONS: Partial listing of more than forty includes: AC/W; ACMWA; AH; AHM; AK; BMJ; CAI; CAM/M; CCH; CCHS; CNGM; CU/WM; DAI; DFNB; GO; IAIA; IACB; IBM; JAM; LJMA; LS; MFA/V; MIA; MWPI; MSIC; NMAS; NYU; PMA; PMA/MN; PNIC; PSU; SCI; SC; TM; U of MM/D; W; WAC; Bezalel National Art Museum, Jerusalem, Israel

EXHIBITS: Partial listing of more than two hundred includes: BEAIAC; BM/B; CAM/OH; CGA; CTC; CWAM; DAM; FIE; HM; IK; LACM; MAI; MHDYMM; MIA; MSU; MSW; NU/BC; OAE; OLO; OSU/G; OWE; PAC; PAIC; SFFA; SV; TI; TRP; U of C/D; W; WASG; WHB; Detroit (MI) Institute of Arts; Museum of Rhode Island School of Design, Providence, RI; Toledo (OH) Museum of Art; see also Awards

SOLO EXHIBITS: Partial listing of thirty includes: ACMWA; BSU; CNGM; CU/WM; DAI; HM; MIA; TM; U of MN; U of ND; Minnesota Museum of Art, St. Paul, MN, 1990; Walker Art Center, Minneapolis, MN, 1973

AWARDS: AC/W (Purchase Prize); BEAIAC ('67, 1st); FIE ('68, Grand Award); Arrowhead Exhibition, Duluth, MN (1st); Critic's Show, New York, NY, 1946; Rhode Island Arts Festival, Providence, RI ('65, 1st)

GEORGE MORRISON

"Morrison has distinguished himself and his tribe by establishing what is probably the most outstanding record of any Indian painter in the fine arts field."

Snodgrass 1968

After traditional training in the visual arts in the late 1930s and early 1940s, Morrison became well established as an Abstract Expressionist, and for years was better known outside Native American art circles than within. After retiring from the University of Minnesota as a full professor of art, he added complex three dimensional art to his works that incorporate weathered wood and other found materials, continuing his abstract approach.

HONORS: *Scholarships:* Women's Club Scholarship to Minneapolis Art Institute, 1942; Consolidated Chippewa Agency, scholarship grants, 1941-1942; Fulbright Scholarship to France, 1952-1953; Vanderlip Traveling Scholarship, 1943; Bernay's Scholarship, 1953; John Hay Whitney Fellowship, 1953-1954. *Other:* Lucy Gilbert Award, 1941; MCAD, Honorary Master of Fine Arts, 1969; Rhode Island School of Design, Providence, RI, Honorary Doctorate of Fine Arts, 1991

MORRISSEAU, NORVAL *Ojibwa*

Copper Thunderbird

Born 14 Mar 1931 near Beardmore, ON, Canada, on the Sand Point Reserve

RESIDENCE: Jasper, AB, Canada

OCCUPATION: Professional artist since 1959

MEDIA: Oil, acrylic, pen and ink, pastel crayon, and prints

PUBLISHED: Dickason (1972); Sinclair and Pollock (1979); Highwater (1980, 1983); McLuhan and Hill (1984); Southcott (1984); Menitove, ed. (1986b); Podedworny (1986); Cardinal-Shubert (1992); McMasters, et al. (1993). *The Toronto Daily Star, Weekend Magazine* (12 June 1962); *The Toronto Daily Star* (13 Sept 1962; 3 Nov 1962; 28 Aug 1975; 29 Aug 1977; Sept 1977; 9 Feb 1984); *The London Free Press* (29 Sept 1962); *The Toronto Telegram* (22 Sept 1962); *Time Magazine* (28 Sept 1962; 25 Aug 1975); *Artscanada* (Jan/Feb 1963) *Western Producer* (7 Mar 1963); *Canadian Art* (Jan/Feb 1963; Nov/Dec 1964); *The Winnipeg Free Press* (4 Dec 1964; 4 Dec 1965); *The Toronto Globe and Mail* (27 Jan 1965; 29 May 1972; 4 Nov 1972; 25 Nov 1972; 23 Dec 1972; 19 Aug 1975; 9 July 1981); *Tawow* (spring 1970; Vol. 4, no. 4, 1974); *Art Magazine* (summer 1974; summer 1976; Nov/Dec 1979); *American Indian Art* (summer 1978; autumn 1982); *Native Perspective* (Vol. 3, no. 2, 1978); *Maclean's Magazine* (22 Jan 1979; Mar 1984); *Indian News* (Sept 1980); *Americas* (Aug 1981); *The Ottawa Citizen* (10 July 1982; 17 Mar 1984; 28 Oct 1991); *Artwest* (May 1983); *Masterkey* (winter 1984); *Windspeaker* (12 Dec 1986); *The Calgary Herald* (25 Feb 1987); *The Indian Trader* (Aug 1987); *Artpost* (Vol 5, no.5, 1987; fall 1991); *The Vancouver Sun* (9 Dec 1989); *The Toronto Sun* (25 Mar 1990)

BOOKS ILLUSTRATED: Dewdney, ed. (1965); Schwartz (1969)

PUBLIC COLLECTIONS: Partial listing of more than fifty includes: C/AG/H; C/AG/O; C/AG/TB; C/AG/WI; C/CCAB; C/CMC; C/GM; C/INAC; C/MCC; C/MFA/M; C/MQ; C/ROM; C/SFG; C/U of T; HCC; RCAS; Canadian Imperial Bank of Commerce Collection; Citicorp of Canada Ltd., Toronto, ON; City of Toronto, ON; Confederation Centre Art Gallery and Museum; Crown Life Insurance, Toronto, ON; Davies, Ward, and Beck, Toronto, ON; Montréal Trust Company Collection; Noreen Energy Resources Ltd.; Proctor and Gamble, Toronto, ON; Province of Manitoba, Winnipeg, MB; Seneca College, Toronto, ON; The Constellation Hotel, Toronto, ON; *The Toronto (ON) Star*

EXHIBITS: Partial listing of more than seventy includes: C/AC/AE; C/AG/O; C/AG/TB; C/AG/V; C/CIARH; C/CIIA; C/CMC; C/CNAC; C/GM; C/INAC; C/LTAT; C/MCC; C/McIG; C/NCCT; C/ROM; C/TC; C/TFD; C/TU; C/U of R/MG; C/TMEC; C/U of T; C/WCAA; C/WICEC; HPTU; HS/OH; CTC; IAIA; NACLA; PAC; RCAS; SM; Bergens Kunsfoeing, Bergen, Norway; Burlington (ON) Public Library; Canada House, London, England; Expo '67, Montréal, PQ, 1967; University of Kitchener, ON; University of Waterloo (ON) Art Gallery, 1965, 1973

SOLO EXHIBITS: Partial listing of more than thirty includes: C/AG/TB; C/U of T; NACLA; Scarborough (ON) Public Library; galleries throughout Canada

HONORS: Royal Canadian Academy of Art, membership, 1970; The Order of Canada, 1978; McMaster University, Montréal, PQ, Honorary Doctorate of Laws Degree, 1980

NORVAL MORRISSEAU

Morriseau is considered one of Canada's principal Native painters. He never studied art formally and, until he was confined to a tuberculosis sanitorium in Fort William, did very little painting. His paintings are an effort to illustrate stories that have been passed down to him by his grandfather, who had learned them from his grandfather. Morrisseau's personal style and artistic achievement have generated a "school" of artists called the Algonquin Legend Painters (also known as the Woodland Indian School of Art).

MORSE, BARBARA WAHLELL WARE *Osage/Cherokee*

Born 2 Jan 1922 in Claremore, OK; daughter of Kathryn Edmondson and Elija Ware

RESIDENCE: Tulsa, OK

EDUCATION: Monte Casino, Tulsa, OK, 1939; U of AR; U of Tulsa

OCCUPATION: Shop owner, real estate broker, and painter

MEDIA: Oil, acrylic, and pastel

EXHIBITS: Sells paintings but does not enter competitive exhibits

MOSE, ALLEN *Navajo*

Born 19 Feb 1957 at Keams Canyon, AZ, on the Navajo Reservation

RESIDENCE: Colorado Springs, CO

EDUCATION: Many Farms (AZ) High School; Pike's Peak Community College, Colorado Springs, CO

OCCUPATION: Construction worker, jeweler, and painter

MEDIA: Oil, acrylic, watercolor, charcoal, pastel, pencil, pen and ink, and prints

PUBLISHED: *The Indian Trader* (Aug 1984); *Art-Talk* (Mar 1986)

COMMISSIONS: *Murals:* DIA, 1993

EXHIBITS: ACS/ENP; ACS/PG; CIM; CNM; FAC/CS; FNAA; HM/G; IACA; ITIC; LIAS; MNA; MNM; NTM; RC; SMIC; SNAICF; SWAIA; U of KS; Ute Indian Museum, Montrose, CO; galleries in AZ, CA, CO, IN, NJ, NY, and PA

SOLO/SPECIAL EXHIBITS: NTM (dual show)

AWARDS: ACS/ENP ('89); CIM ('83, 1st; '85, 1st, Best of Division; '86, 1st, Best of Show Theme); ITIC ('86; '88); LIAS ('90, MA); MNA ('85, 1st; '86; '87); SMIC ('86, 1st; '88, 1st); SNAICF ('88); SWAIA ('87; '89; '90, 1st)

ALLEN MOSES

Moses is best known for his pastel portraits of Native American people with rug or pottery design backgrounds. He has said, "I'm a people person. I like people and enjoy just watching them whenever I can — certain faces interest me, even if I don't know the person. I always like to go beyond their face in my paintings or try to get to know them. It doesn't always come easy, but it's a challenge that I enjoy."

artist brochure

MOSES, JAMES KIVETORUK *Eskimo*

Kivetoruk, Bark Dye

A.K.A. Kivetoruk Moses

Born 10 Feb 1903 near Cape Espenberg, AK; died 1982; son of Kivoluk, who, with his partner Charlie Browers, established whaling stations along the Arctic coast using Eskimo crews and skin boats; brother-in-law of George Ahgupuk (q.v.)

RESIDENCE: Lived in Nome, AK

EDUCATION: Through 3rd grade, Shishmaref, AK

OCCUPATION: Deerherder, trapper, hunter, fisherman, store clerk, office manager, ivory engraver; full-time painter after 1954

MEDIA: Watercolor, India ink, and colored pencils

PUBLISHED: Snodgrass (1968); Ray (1969); Fitzhugh and Kaplan (1982); Wade, ed. (1986), Archuleta and Strickland (1991); Yorba (1991). *American Heritage* (June 1975); *The Alaska Journal* (fall 1971; spring 1972; spring 1978); *Alaska Geographic* (Vol. 12, no. 3, 1985); *Artifacts* (June 1991); *Southwest Art* (1992)

BOOKS ILLUSRATED: Fitzhugh and Kaplan (1982)

PUBLIC COLLECTIONS: ASM/AK, CAS, IACB, MFA/AH

EXHIBITS: BNIAS, FNAIC, MFA/AH, MNM, PAC, SAIEAIP, SV, USDS

AWARDS: BNIAS, FNAIC, MNM, PAC

JAMES KIVETORUK MOSES

Moses' parents died when he was very young and he was adopted by his uncle who was a hunter and trapper. An injury in an airplane accident in 1954 led to his career as a painter. His paintings are largely of actual historical events or his interpretations of folk tales, and are known for their primitive style and attention to detail. He often accompanied his paintings with a handwritten story. Due to poor health Moses no longer painted in 1978.

Yorba 1990

MOSES, KIVETORUK (see Moses, James Kivetoruk)

MOUNTAIN BOW, MANUEL *Picurís*

EDUCATION: IAIA

OCCUPATION: Jeweler and painter

MEDIA: Oil, acrylic, pastel, pencil, pen and ink, silver, and gemstone

EXHIBITS: ACS/ENP; FNAA; IAIA; IPCC; ITIC; SWAIA; Inter-Tribal Center, Dallas, TX; Picurís Pueblo (NM) Museum; Río Grande Pueblo (NM) Museum
AWARDS: ACS/ENP, IAIA, SWAIA

MOUNTAIN COUGAR (see Shipshee, Louis)

MOUNTAIN OF THE SACRED WIND (see Atencio, Gilbert Benjamin)

MOUNTAIN ROCK (see Atencio, Pat)

MOUSE, KISSIE L. *Seminole/Creek*

A.K.A. Kissie Haney Mouse

Born 21 Sept 1954 in Talihina, OK; daughter of Tilda Bender and Rev. Samuel H. Haney; P/GP: Winey and Rev. Willy Haney; M/GP: Kissie and Joseph Bender; related to Enoch Kelly Haney (q.v.) and Woodrow Haney, flute maker

RESIDENCE: Yukon, OK
EDUCATION: Bowlegs (OK) High School, 1973
OCCUPATION: U.S. Postal Service employee and painter
MEDIA: Watercolor, pencil, and pen and ink
EXHIBITS: AIAF; BB; CIM; IS; ITAE; LIAS; RE; Chickasaw Festival, Tishomingo, OK; Dallas (TX) Indian Market; Mayfest, Tulsa, OK

MOUSE, VINCENT *Cherokee*

RESIDENCE: Spavinaw, OK
MEDIA: Oil
EXHIBITS: RC
HONORS: RC, Thunderbird Foundation Scholarship, 1993

MOUSSEAU, ROY *Saulteaux*

RESIDENCE: Hope, BC, Canada
EDUCATION: Portland (ME) School of Art
PUBLIC COLLECTIONS: HCC
EXHIBITS: CPS, HCC, RC; see also Awards
AWARDS: Vancouver (BC) Art Show (1st)

MOVING WHIRLWIND (see Whirlwind)

MOWATT, KEN *Tsimshian*

A.K.A. Kenneth Mowatt

Born 1944 in Kitanmax, BC, Canada

RESIDENCE: Hazelton, BC, Canada
EDUCATION: C/KSNCIA
OCCUPATION: Sculptor, silversmith, graphic artist, and painter
MEDIA: Oil, silver, and wood
PUBLISHED: Stewart (1979); Hall, Blackman, and Rickard (1981); Gerber and Bruggmann (1989). *Canadian Indian Artscraft* (Vol.1, no. 1, 1974); *TAWOW* (Vol. 4, 1975)
BOOKS ILLUSRATED: C/KSNCIA, 1977
PUBLIC COLLECTIONS: C/CMC, C/GM, C/INAC, C/RBCM, C/SFG
EXHIBITS: C/GM, C/CMC, C/KSNCIA, C/CIIA, C/LTAT, C/ROM, C/TL

MUMMOOKSHOAR (see Mumnqshoaluk, Victoria)

MUMNQSHOALUK, VICTORIA *Inuit (Eskimo)*

A.K.A. Mammookshoarluk; Mamnguqsualuk; Mammokshoarluk; Mummookshoarluk; Tulrealik

Born 1930 in the Garry Lake area, NWT, Canada; daughter of Jessie Oonark
RESIDENCE: Baker Lake, NWT, Canada
OCCUPATION: Seamstress, carver, and graphic artist
MEDIA: Black pencil, colored pencil, stone, and prints
PUBLISHED: Goetz, et al. (1977); Blodgett (1978b); Woodhouse (1980); Lotocki, ed. (1982; 1983); Jackson and Nasby (1987). *North* (Mar/Apr 1974)
PUBLIC COLLECTIONS: C/AC/MS, C/AG/WP
EXHIBITS: C/AG/W; C/AG/WP; C/BLPD; C/CID; C/TIP; Robertson Galleries, Ottawa, ON

MUN DE MA (see Honahnie, Anthony E.)

MUNGITA (see Mungitok)

MUNGITOK *Inuit (Eskimo)*
A.K.A. Mungita
RESIDENCE: Cape Dorset, NWT, Canada
OCCUPATION: Graphic artist
MEDIA: Pencil and prints
PUBLISHED: Hudson (1967; 1967a); Larmour (1967)
PUBLIC COLLECTIONS: C/TDB, DAM
EXHIBITS: C/CD, C/EACTDB

MURDOCK, CECIL *Kickapoo*
Koketha, Turning Bear (or Running Bear)
Born 13 Oct 1913 in McLoud, OK; died 14 Dec 1954 in McLoud, OK
MILITARY: Air Force, WWII
EDUCATION: Chilocco; Friends University, Wichita, KS, 1932-1933; U of Wichita, KS; U of OK; studied mural techniques with Olaf Nordmark at the Indian Art Center, Fort Sill, OK, 1938
OCCUPATION: Demonstrated mural techniques at the Palmer House, Chicago, IL, 1940-1941
PUBLISHED: Jacobson and d'Ucel (1950); Dunn (1968); Snodgrass (1968); Brody (1971); Boyd, et al. (1981)
COMMISSIONS: *Murals:* WPA project, Lawton, OK, and Anadarko, OK, two years; U of OK; Ohio State University, Columbus, OH
PUBLIC COLLECTIONS: GM, IACB/DC, MNA/KHC, OU/MA, PAC, SM
EXHIBITS: AIW; CSPIP; HM; PAC; PAC/T; SPIM; Chicago, IL; Washington, D.C.; Oklahoma City, OK; Lawton, OK; New York World's Fair, 1939-1940
AWARDS: PAC

CECIL MURDOCK

"The artist lived with his grandmother until he was 16, and 'she developed and nourished my learning and the love of being an Indian. . . .' In 1946, Murdock wrote Philbrook Art Center that his accomplishments in art were 'greatly due to Oscar B. Jacobson's guidance and encouragement.' His military service resulted in a 20 percent disability, and he consequently painted less frequently after the war."

Snodgrass 1968

MURPHY, WILLIAM *Navajo*
PUBLISHED: Jacka and Jacka (1994)
EXHIBITS: ITIC
AWARDS: ('93, 1st, Best of Category)

MURRAY, ALICE HEARRELL *Chickasaw/Choctaw*
PUBLISHED: Snodgrass (1968)
PUBLIC COLLECTIONS: HSM/OK

MURRAY, DANIEL M. *Iowa/Otoe*
Nhuschingyay, No Heart; *Masteke,* The Fox; *Mato Munka,* Medicine Bear
Born 28 May 1934 in Perkins, OK; son of Martha McGlasin and Franklin Murray; P/GP: Emily and Charles Murray; M/GP: Elsie and Daniel McGlasin; Artist is a descendant of Chief White Cloud.

DANIEL M. MURRAY

"In 1968 the artist had just begun to exhibit his three-dimensional oil paintings. It was his ambition to expose the honors and the downfalls committed upon his people, to paint Indians of Oklahoma as well as the state's heritage and present daily life."

Snodgrass 1968

No records have been found that indicate Murray continued to paint after 1968.

RESIDENCE: Cushing, OK

MILITARY: U.S. Marine Corps, disabled in Korea

EDUCATION: Perkins (OK) High School; OSU/O; two years college in Los Angeles, CA

OCCUPATION: Free-lance landscape artist, sculptor, and painter

MEDIA: Oil, acrylic, watercolor, pencil, pen and ink, pastel, mixed-media, and stone

PUBLISHED: Snodgrass (1968). *Sunday Oklahoman, Orbit Magazine* (2 Feb 1964)

PUBLIC COLLECTIONS: GWS

EXHIBITS: Partial listing includes: PAC; Temple Emanuel, Dallas, TX; Cayuga County Community College, Auburn, NY; Pawnee Bill's, Pawnee, OK

MURRAY, SAUNDRA *Cherokee*

RESIDENCE: Bella Vista, AR

EDUCATION: Studied art under Jerry Ellis, Carthage, MO; John Fitzgibbon

MEDIA: Pen and ink

COMMISSIONS: *Logos:* Bella Vista, AR, logos for local businesses

EXHIBITS: IS; see also Awards

AWARDS: Parsons (KS) Art Show

MUSGRAVE, CHRISTINE *Osage*

A.K.A. Chris Musgrave

Born 19 Feb 1959; daughter of Charlene and Ted Potter; M/GP: Ruth Jane and Charles Callahan

RESIDENCE: Baldwin, KS

EDUCATION: Graduated high school, 1977

OCCUPATION: Painter

MEDIA: Acrylic, oil pastel, pen and ink, mixed-media, and prints

COMMISSIONS: Kansas Artist's Post Card series, 1989

PUBLIC COLLECTIONS: CGPS

EXHIBITS: CGPS; LIAS; National Works on Paper, Minot, ND; see also Awards

SOLO EXHIBITS: In Kansas

AWARDS: LIAS ('91, MA; '92, MA; '93, Best of Show); Aesthetics '90, McPherson, KS; Smokey Hill Show, Hays, KS; Verdigris Valley Exhibit, Independence, KS

MUSICALLY INCLINED (see Ingram, Veronica Marie)

MUS TRUWI (see Toledo, José Rey)

MUZINIHBEEGEY

Muzinihbeegey is a Native art organization on the Sandy Lake Reserve, Ontario. The main objective of this organization is to encourage and promote public interest in, and support for, the Native art movement in northwestern Ontario, with special emphasis on Sandy Lake. Muzinihbeegey's first group project was a large mural that was painted in the late spring of 1989 for presentation to Walter Sunahara of the Ontario Arts Council. Ringo Fiddler, Rocky Fiddler, Goyce Kagegamic, Joshim Kakegamic, Robert Kakegamic, Roy Kakegamic, Lloyd Kakekapetum (qq.v.), and Bart Meekis are members of this organization.

Na-Ai-Che (see Naiche)

Nagawbo (see Des Jarlait, Patrick Robert)

Naha, Archie A. *Hopi*

Birth date unknown; uncle of Raymond Naha (q.v.)

PUBLISHED: Snodgrass (1968)

EXHIBITS: ASM, HM

Naha, Raymond *Hopi*

A.K.A. Ray Naha

Born 5 Dec 1933 at Polacca, First Mesa, AZ; died 1975; son of Raymond Naha; GM: Lucy Nahee

MILITARY: U.S. Army

EDUCATION: Phoenix; Inter-Mt.; studied under Fred Kabotie (q.v.), high school

OCCUPATION: *Katsina* carver and painter

MEDIA: Acrylic, casein, pen and ink, and cottonwood root

PUBLISHED: Dunn (1968); Snodgrass (1968); Brody (1971); Tanner (1973); Warner (1975; 1979); Highwater (1976); Silberman (1978); Hoffman, et al. (1984); Williams, ed. (1990). *The Arizona Republic* (12 Dec 1965); *Arizona Highways* (Aug 1966)

PUBLIC COLLECTIONS: AC/HC, AF, ASM, BA/AZ, BIA, EM, HCC, HM, IACB, MAI, MKMcNAI, MNA/KHC, MRFM, OMA, SM, WOM

EXHIBITS: AC/HC, AIAE/WSU, ASM, FAIEAIP, FHMAG, HM, HM/G, IK, ITIC, LGAM, MKMcNAI, MNM, OMA, PAC, PM, SAIEAIP, SN, USDS

AWARDS: AIAE/WSU; ITIC ('68, 1st; '70, 1st); MNM; PAC ('62; '69, 1st; '70; '72); SN ('67, Grand Award; '70)

Nah-Gwa-Say (see Jacobs, Arnold)

Nahohai, Randy *Zuni*

EDUCATION: IAIA

MEDIA: Acrylic

EXHIBITS: AC/SD

Nahsohnhoya, Thomas Dolwiftema *Hopi*

Dolwiftema, Lightning

A.K.A. Thomas Dolwiftema Nahsonhoya; Thomas Dolwiftema Nasonhoya

Born 15 Oct 1929 at Sichomovi, First Mesa, AZ

RESIDENCE: Polacca, AZ

EDUCATION: Hopi

PUBLISHED: Snodgrass (1968)

EXHIBITS: PAC

Naiche *Chiricahua Apache*

Na-Ai-Che, Meddlesome; A Mischief-maker

A.K.A. Chief Naiche; Nachee

Born ca. 1857; died 1921 in Mescalero, NM, of influenza; son of Cochise, hereditary Apache chief; M/GF: Mangas Coloradas (Dasoda-hae), war chief and leader of the Mimbreño Apache band

OCCUPATION: Raiding party leader, chief of the Chiricahua, and painter

MEDIA: Oil, vegetable dye, ink and pencil on hides

PUBLISHED: LaFarge (1956); Snodgrass (1968); Dockstader (1977); Silberman (1978); Deupree (1979); Seymour (1993). *American Heritage* (Oct 1956); *Masterkey* (Jan/Feb 1956)

Naiche

"In the spring of 1885, as prisoners of the Government, Naiche and Geronimo escaped near the White Mountain Reservation in Arizona and began a campaign of resistance against White settlement. In September, 1886, he surrendered, and was taken to Fort Pickens, FL. In May, 1888, he was transferred to Vermont, Va., where he worked for the Government until October, 1894 (see Barett 1906).

Naiche was Chief of the Apaches at Fort Sill, OK, in 1899, and was well-known as an artist. He lived to an old age at Mescalero (see Sonnichsen 1958)."

Snodgrass 1968

DETAIL: Gerald Nailor, *Navajo Woman on Horseback*, 1940. Philbrook Museum of Art, Tulsa, Oklahoma

PUBLIC COLLECTIONS: FSM, HSM/OK, MAI, SI/MNH
EXHIBITS: HSM/OK, OMA

NAILOR, GERALD *Navajo*

Toh Yah, Walking By The River

Born 21 Jan 1917 in Pinedale, NM; died 13 Aug 1952; son of Mary Arviso and Thomas Touchin

RESIDENCE: Lived in San Lorenzo, Picurís, NM

MILITARY: WW II

EDUCATION: Graduated Albuquerque; Santa Fe; U of OK; special instruction under Dorothy Dunn, Kenneth Chapman, and Olaf Nordmark

OCCUPATION: Rancher, illustrator, designer, and painter

MEDIA: Oil, watercolor, tempera, and fresco

PUBLISHED: Jacobson and d'Ucel (1950); Dunn (1968); Snodgrass (1968); Brody (1971); Tanner (1968; 1973); Highwater (1976); Dockstader (1977); Silberman (1978); Broder (1981); King (1981); Hoffman, et al. (1984); Samuels (1985); Wade, ed. (1986); Seymour (1988); Jacka and Jacka (1994). *Arizona Highways* (Feb 1950; July 1956); *El Palacio* (Sept 1952); *Masterkey* (Vol. 26, 1952); *Compton's Pictured Encyclopedia* (1957); *Indian Life* (1960); *American Scene* (Vol. 6, no. 3); *Southwestern Art* (Vol. 2, no. 1, 1967); *Plateau* (Vol. 54, no. 1, 1982); *Southwest Art* (June 1983); *American Indian Art* (spring 1985; spring 1995); *The Phoenix Gazette* (9 Dec1987); *Southwest Profile* (Feb 1988); *Tamaqua* (winter/spring 1991)

BOOKS ILLUSTRATED: Enochs (1940)

COMMISSIONS: *Murals:* USDI, 1942; Mesa Verde National Park Post Office, Mesa Verde, CO; Navajo Tribal Council House, Window Rock, AZ, 1942

PUBLIC COLLECTIONS: BIA, CMA, GM, IACB/DC, MAI, MNA, MNM, MRFM, PAC, SM, U of OK, WOM

EXHIBITS: AC/A, AIEC, AIW, ASM, DAM, HM, IK, ITIC, LGAM, MAI, MFA/O, MMA, MNM, NAP, NGA, OMA, OU/ET, PAC, PAC/T, PM, SM, WRTD, WWM

GERALD NAILOR

"In 1937, Nailor shared a studio in Santa Fe with Allan Houser (q.v.). His paintings were exhibited in the home of Mrs. Hall Adams from 1943 to 1952. At the time of his death, he was living with his family at Picurís Pueblo, NM."

Snodgrass 1968

Tragically, Nailor was only 35 years old when died from injuries received in an attempt to help a woman whose husband was brutally beating her.

NAILOR, JERRY *Picurís*

Birth date unknown; possibly the son of Gerald Nailor (q.v.)

EDUCATION: Santa Fe, 1958

PUBLISHED: Snodgrass (1968)

EXHIBITS: MNM

NAKAIDINAE, ARTHUR M. *Navajo*

RESIDENCE: Window Rock, AZ

MILITARY: U.S. Marine Corps, Vietnam

EDUCATION: Rocky Mountain School of Art, Denver, CO; Arapahoe Community College, Littleton, CO

OCCUPATION: Power plant worker, jeweler, and painter

MEDIA: Acrylic, watercolor, pen and ink, silver, and gemstone

COMMISSIONS: *Murals:* Arapahoe Community College, Education Opportunity Center, Littleton, CO, 1977

PUBLIC COLLECTIONS: HCC

EXHIBITS: HCC, HM/G, RC, SWAIA

AWARDS: HM/G ('80); SWAIA ('76, 1st, Hinds Award)

NAKAPENKEM (see Martin, Mungo)

NAKAYOMA (see Kabotie, Fred)

NAKOWHOADONIULZI (see Bushyhead, Allan)

NAMA PIASKA (see Kishketon, George)

NAMINGHA, DAN *Hopi*

A.K.A. Daniel Namingha

Born 1950 in Keams Canyon, AZ, on the Hopi Indian Reservation; son of Dextra Nampeyo, potter; GGM: Rachel Nampeyo, potter

RESIDENCE: Santa Fe, NM

MILITARY: U.S. Marine Corps

EDUCATION: Keams Canyon (AZ) High School; U of KS, summer arts program, 1967; A.F.A, IAIA, 1968; AAA

OCCUPATION: Musician, lecturer, lithographer, sculptor, and painter

MEDIA: Oil, acrylic, pencil, pastel, mixed-media, wood, bronze, and prints

PUBLISHED: Green (1978); New (1979; 1980; 1981); Highwater (1980); Amerson, ed. (1981); Medina (1981); Wade and Strickland (1981); Page and Page (1982); Samuels (1982); Hoffman, et al. (1984); Wade, ed. (1986); Jacka and Jacka (1988); Hill (1992). *Southwest Art* (Apr 1973; June 1981; Jan 1989); *Arizona Highways (*Aug 1976; Feb 1983); *The Los Angeles Times* (Nov 1977); *The San Francisco Examiner and Chronicle* (19 Dec 1978); *The Santa Fean* (May 1980; Oct 1984; Aug 1989; June 1992); *American Artist* (Sept 1979); *Southwest Profile* (May 1984; Aug/Oct 1992); *The Santa Fe Reporter* (14 Aug 1984); *American Indian Art* (spring 1985); *Air and Space* (June/July 1986); *The Indian Trader* (Feb 1987; Mar 1989); *Art-Talk* (Nov 1988; Jan 1995); *New Mexico Magazine* (May 1988); *The Washington Post* (14 Sept 1989); *The Christian Science Monitor* (4 Mar 1991); *The* (Aug 1994); *Indian Artist* (spring 1995); biographical publications

COMMISSIONS: *Murals:* Sky Harbor International Airport, Phoenix, AZ

PUBLIC COLLECTIONS: BA/AZ; CAS; HM; IACB; IAIA; MAI; MAM; MM/NJ; MRFM; MNA; MNM; NACLA; Arthur Anderson Corporate Collection; City of Phoenix (AZ), Sky Harbor International Airport; City of Scottsdale (AZ) Fine Arts Collection; Delhem Museum, Berlin, West Germany; Gallery of East Slovakia, Kosice, Czechoslovakia; Hallmark Collection and Archives, Kansas City, MO; Intrawest Financial Corporate Collection, Denver, CO; Mountain Bell Collection, Denver, CO; Museum of American Indian Arts and Culture, Chicago, IL; National Aeronautical and Space Administration, Washington, D.C.; Palm Beach (FL) Polo and Country Club; Phoenix (AZ) Baptist Hospital; St. Joseph's Hospital, Phoenix, AZ; The Arizona Bank Collection, Phoenix, AZ; The British Royal Collection of Princess Anne, England; The Naprstkov Museum, Prague, Czechoslovakia; Wasatch Academy, Mt. Pleasant, UT

EXHIBITS: ABQM; AC/K; AC/SD; CAS; CSU/S; HM; HM/G; CAS; FNAA; IAIA/M; IK; MAI; MCC/CA; MFA/O; MNA; NACLA; NMSC; NSM; NU/BC; PAC; PAIC; PBS; SFFA; SI; SN; TRP; U of KS; U of NE; USIS; WWM; Kennedy Space Center Art Gallery; Muckenthaler Cultural Center, Fullerton, CA, 1974; Museum of American Art, New Britain, CT, 1978; NASA, 1977, 1978; Sangre de Cristo Arts and Conference Center, Pueblo, CO

SOLO EXHIBITS: Partial listing of more than 16 includes: FAM/MA; HM; MNA; USIS; National Academy of Sciences, Washington, D.C.; Orange Coast College, Costa Mesa, CA, 1977; Sonoma County Library, Santa Rosa, CA, 1978; California Academy of Science, 1979; Palm Springs (CA) Desert Museum, 1991; The Arizona Bank, Phoenix, AZ, 1980

AWARDS: HM/G ('75); PAC ('72)

HONORS: NASA, selected to do art work, 1987; FNAA, poster artist; The Harvard Foundation, Harvard University, special award in recognition of outstanding contribution to American Art, Native American culture, and inter-cultural relations, 1994; *Indian Artist* magazine, recognition for efforts and achievement in promoting Indian art and culture, 1995

DAN NAMINGHA

Initially a realistic painter, Namingha began to paint in a more abstract way after 1972, when he returned from the U.S. Marine Corps. He credits Otellie Loloma, (q.v.) with having encouraged him to extend his ideas and to experiment. In addition to Hopi landscapes, Namingha's subjects are: Pueblos, dancers, katsina *spirits, pottery designs, and, occasionally, things he sees as he travels. Using only eight or nine colors and white, he constantly experiments with a variety of techniques and styles.*

Southwest Art, *June 1981*

NAMINGHA, GIFFORD *Hopi*
Birth date unknown
RESIDENCE: From Hoteville, AZ
PUBLISHED: Snodgrass (1968)
PUBLIC COLLECTIONS: MAI (painting executed ca. age 15)

NAMOKI, DAN *Hopi*
PUBLIC COLLECTIONS: BA/AZ, WWM

NA MOS (see Left Hand)

NANATSIDE (see García, Carlos)

NANNEHI TOLESE SIAM (see Burrus, S.S.)

NANOGAK, AGNES *Inuit (Eskimo)*
A.K.A. Nanogak; Nanoqak
Born 1925
RESIDENCE: Holman Island, NWT, Canada
OCCUPATION: Graphic artist
MEDIA: Black pencil and colored felt tip pen
PUBLISHED: Goetz, et al. (1977); Blodgett (1978a); Collinson (1978); Routledge (1979); Woodhouse, ed. (1980); Napran (1980); Latocki (1982); McMasters, et al. (1993). *The Kitchner-Waterloo Record* (5 Oct 1974)
BOOKS ILLUSTRATED: Metayer, ed. (1972)
PUBLIC COLLECTIONS: C/CAP, C/HEC, C/TDB, C/U of AB, DAM
EXHIBITS: C/AG/W, C/AG/WP, C/CG, C/EACTDB, C/IA7, C/SS, C/EIP, C/VRS
SOLO EXHIBITS: Inukshuk Galleries, Waterloo, ON, 1974

AGNES NANOGAK

Nanogak's paintings recount a wide variety of folk tales. Her work reflects shamanism, magic, and other ritualistic material.

The Kitchener-Waterloo Record, 5 *Oct 1974*

NAPACHIE (see Nawpachee)

NAPARTUK, HENRY *Inuit (Eskimo)*
Born 15 Feb 1932; died 15 Nov 1985
RESIDENCE: Lived at Great Whale River, NWT, Canada
PUBLISHED: North (Mar/Apr 1974)
EXHIBITS: Robertson Galleries, Ottawa, ON

NAPE SICA HOKSILA (see Claymore, Thomas William)

NAPI (see Billedeaux, Donald)

NAPOLEON, ROBERT *Zuni*
PUBLIC COLLECTIONS: IACB/DC, MNA
EXHIBITS: MNA

NARANJO, ADOLPH *Santa Clara (?)*
Ogowee, Road Runner
Born 1916 at Santa Clara Pueblo, NM
EDUCATION: Santa Fe
PUBLISHED: Jacobson and d'Ucel (1950); Snodgrass (1968)
EXHIBITS: AIW

NARANJO, BLARDO *Santo Domingo*
PUBLISHED: Snodgrass (1968)
PUBLIC COLLECTIONS: SM

NARANJO, BEN *Santa Clara*
PUBLISHED: Snodgrass (1968)

PUBLIC COLLECTIONS: MFA/A

NARANJO, JOSÉ DOLORES *Santa Clara*

Ce Komo Pyn

A.K.A. Signature: Ce-Komo-Pyn

RESIDENCE: Santa Clara Pueblo, Española, NM

PUBLISHED: Dunn (1968); Snodgrass (1968); Samuels (1985)

PUBLIC COLLECTIONS: CMA

EXHIBITS: NGA

NARANJO, LOUIS *Santa Clara*

EDUCATION: Santa Fe, 1937

PUBLISHED: Snodgrass (1968)

PUBLIC COLLECTIONS: CGPS

EXHIBITS: AIEC, CGPS

NARANJO, MICHELLE TSOSIE *Santa Clara/Navajo/Laguna/Mission*

Born 11 July 1959 in Albuquerque, NM; daughter of Carol and Paul Tsosie

RESIDENCE: Española, NM

EDUCATION: Window Rock (AZ) High School, 1977; CSF/SF; *Up With People*, 1976

OCCUPATION: Fashion designer, model, gallery owner, museum sales associate, and painter

MEDIA: Acrylic, watercolor, pencil, pastel, pen and ink, mixed-media, gold leaf, and metallic paint

PUBLISHED: *The Indian Trader* (July 1978; Aug 1983; Aug 1989); *Art-Talk* (Oct 1986); *The Santa Fe Reporter* (16 Aug 1989)

PUBLIC COLLECTIONS: HM; Sandia Gallery, Basel, Switzerland

EXHIBITS: ACS/ENP; CNM; CSF/SF; FNAA; HM, HM/G; ITIC; MNA; NMSF; SDMM; TAAII; RC; WSCS; WWM; SWAIA; Sundance, Provo, UT

AWARDS: Partial listing of more than twenty 1st and 2nd places includes: ACS/ENP; ITIC ('79, 1st); ITIC; MNA ('89, Best of Division); NMSF ('77, 1st); SWAIA ('78, 1st; '81, Hinds Award); TAAII

HONORS: Miss Arizona Teen Pageant, 1st runner-up, 1975; WWM, Board of Trustees

MICHELLE TSOSIE NARANJO

"I wish to express my life as it is, a Native American woman living in today's world, to relay a message of beauty, spirit, motherhood, womanhood, and traditionalism in a very contemporary lifestyle."

p.c. 1984

NARANJO, VICTOR *Santa Clara*

PUBLISHED: Snodgrass (1968)

PUBLIC COLLECTIONS: MNM

NARCOMEY, JACKSON *Creek/Seminole*

Crazy Horse

A.K.A. Jackson Leon Narcomey

Born 25 Jan 1942 in Tahlequah, OK; son of Frances and Rev. Raymond Narcomey

RESIDENCE: Tulsa, OK

MILITARY: U.S. Air Force

EDUCATION: Sequoyah

OCCUPATION: Full-time sculptor and painter after 1968

MEDIA: Watercolor, pencil, and stone

PUBLIC COLLECTIONS: HCC

EXHIBITS: AAID; ACS/SC; CNM; FCTM; ITIC; OIAC; PAC; RC; RE; TWF; WTF; Charles Allis Art Library, Milwaukee, WI; St. Charles (IL) Arts and Craft Show

SOLO/SPECIAL EXHIBITS: CCHM (dual show)

AWARDS: AAID ('76, 1st, Grand Prize); CNM ('75, 1st); FCTM ('70, IH; '86, 1st); ITIC ('70); RC ('78)

NARCOMEY, LUTHER *Creek*

Born 2 Dec 1946 in Holdenville, OK

RESIDENCE: Holdenville, OK

EDUCATION: Holdenville (OK) High School, 1965; IAIA; A.A., Haskell, 1976; U of KS

OCCUPATION: Painter

MEDIA: Oil and acrylic

PUBLISHED: *Native Arts/West* (Apr 1981)

PUBLIC COLLECTIONS: Haskell

EXHIBITS: CCHM; CNM; OIAC; TIAF; George Nigh Rehabilitation Center, Okmulgee, OK; galleries in KS, MN, and OK

SOLO EXHIBITS: SPIM

AWARDS: OIAC ('95, 1st)

NARDA (see Caton, Narda)

NASEYOWMA, GILBERT *Hopi*

PUBLIC COLLECTIONS: MNA

EXHIBITS: MNA

NASH, DANIEL *San Carlos Apache*

Birth date unknown; brother of Wesley Nash (q.v.)

RESIDENCE: Garland, TX

EDUCATION: Mescalero (AZ) High School

MEDIA: Watercolor

PUBLISHED: Seymour (1993)

PUBLIC COLLECTIONS: MAI, MNM, SAR

NASH, JOEL *Hopi*

PUBLISHED: Snodgrass (1968)

EXHIBITS: FWG, HM

NASH, WESLEY *San Carlos Apache*

Born 22 Sept 1926 at San Carlos, AZ

RESIDENCE: Chinle, AZ

MILITARY: U.S. Navy, U.S. Army Paratroopers, WWII

EDUCATION: Santa Fe, 1948; BC, 1952-1953; USU, 1959-1960

MEDIA: Tempera

PUBLISHED: Dunn (1968); Snodgrass (1968); Brody (1971); Tanner (1973); Seymour (1988)

PUBLIC COLLECTIONS: HCC, MRFM

EXHIBITS: AAID; HCC; HM; HM/G; MNM; NGA; PAC; SN; tribal fairs

AWARDS: AAID ('68); PAC ('71); tribal fairs

WESLEY NASH

"Nash recalls an interest in art as early as the 3rd grade. In 1942, Wilma Ferguson, now Mrs. James Watson, encouraged the artist to enter Santa Fe Indian School, where he remembers especially the help received from Vicente Mirabel, Gerónima Cruz Montoya (qq.v.) and a Miss Kerwin."

Snodgrass 1968

NASHBOO, WILLIAM *Zuni*

EDUCATION: Albuquerque, 1963

PUBLISHED: Snodgrass (1968)

EXHIBITS: MNM

NASHOBA (see Pettigrew, Jack)

NASONHOYA, THOMAS DOLWIFTEMA (see Nahsohnhoya, Thomas Dolwiftema)

NATACHU, CHRIS *Zuni*

RESIDENCE: Zuni, NM
PUBLISHED: Schiffer (1991)
EXHIBITS: CNM, ITIC, LIAS, NMA
AWARDS: CNM ('90, 1st; '91, 1st; '92, 1st; '93, 1st; '94); ITIC ('88, 1st, Best in Category; '89, 1st; '90, 1st, Best Miniature Painting; '91; '93, 1st; '94); LIAS ('93, MA); MNA ('88, Best of Division)

CHRIS NATACHU

Natachu is known for his very detailed miniature paintings of Pueblo Indian subjects.

NATACHU, FRED *Zuni*

RESIDENCE: Zuni, NM
OCCUPATION: Jeweler and painter
MEDIA: Tempera, silver, and gemstone
PUBLISHED: Snodgrass (1968)
EXHIBITS: ITIC, MNM

NATATCHES, JAMES J. *Navajo/Mohawk*

RESIDENCE: Chinle, AZ
EDUCATION: Santa Fe, 1960-1961; Rock Point Mission School, Chinle, AZ; U of AZ, "Southwest Indian Art Project," scholarship, summers 1961, 1962
PUBLISHED: Snodgrass (1968)
EXHIBITS: MNM, PAC

NATAY, EDWARD LEE *Navajo*

Nat Tay Yelth Le Galth, Walking Leader
A.K.A. Ed Natay
Born 15 Dec 1915; died 15 Jan 1967 in Phoenix, AZ; father was a medicine man and Indian scout; mother was a weaver
OCCUPATION: Instructor, ironworker, journeyman welder, recording artist, radio announcer, promoter for a railroad company and movie studios, and painter
MEDIA: Watercolor
PUBLISHED: Snodgrass (1968); Tanner (1957; 1973). *Arizona Highways* (July 1956)
EXHIBITS: ASF, ASM, CAA, CU, HM, ITIC, PAC, SN
AWARDS: CAA ('56, 1st, Bronze Medal of Honor)

EDWARD LEE NATAY

Natay was a well-known radio announcer in Flagstaff, Arizona, where he also sang at powwows. In addition to occasional paintings, he created designs which were made into wrought iron objects.

Dockstader, p.c. 1994

NATCHEZ, STAN *Shoshoni/Paiute*

Born 14 Nov 1954 near Bishop, CA, on the Shoshoni-Paiute Reservation
EDUCATION: Bachelor of Science
OCCUPATION: Teacher, dancer, lecturer, community worker, and painter
PUBLISHED: *The Navajo Times* (1 Mar 1984)
EXHIBITS: ITIC
AWARDS: ITIC ('91, 1st)

NAT TAY YELTH LE GALTH (see Natay, Ed)

NA-TON-SA-KA (see Walters, Harry)

NAUJA (see Nauya, Pierre)

NAUMOFF *Eskimo*

PUBLISHED: Snodgrass (1968). *10th Annual Report,* BAE (1888-1889)

NAUMOFF

"The drawing illustrated in the BAE 10th Annual Report *was made in 1882. The 'designs were traced upon a strip of wood, which was then stuck upon the roof of the house belonging to the draftsman (*10th Annual Report, *BAE, 1888-1889).'"*

Snodgrass 1968

NAUPOCHEE (see Nawpachee)

Pierre Nauya

Nauya started to paint using some old boards, house paint, and a cut down canoe paintbrush. Robert Williamson, anthropologist at Rankin Inlet, encouraged him and provided him with oils, brushes, and canvas. Nauya was stricken with polio in 1949, but recovered and was once again able to hunt, trap, fish, and, in his spare time, paint. He frequently divided his paintings into wide horizontal strips with the scene progressing from the top of the page to the bottom. This gave the viewer the feeling of the Arctic landscape stretching on forever.

The Beaver, *autumn 1967*

Simon Peter Nava

Nava says, "I never had any formal training in art. Only through the gift of God can I paint these expressions . . . I don't know how to categorize my work since many of my pieces are spiritually inspired. Again, I'd like to thank my Creator for this opportunity and hope the viewers enjoy my work. I have the never-ending urge of rightfully hanging on to my cultural heritage. It's all that I am."

Naurja (see Nauya, Pierre)

Nauya, Pierre *Inuit (Eskimo)*

A.K.A. Nauja; Naurja; Nauyark

Born 1914; died 1977

RESIDENCE: Lived at Rankin Inlet, NWT, Canada

OCCUPATION: Hunter, trapper, fisherman, sculptor, and painter

MEDIA: Oil, house paint, stone, and plywood

PUBLISHED: Blodgett (n.d.); Blodgett (1978b). *The Beaver* (autumn 1967); *The WAG Magazine* (Feb/Mar 1986), cover; *Inuit Art* (spring 1988)

PUBLIC COLLECTIONS: C/AG/O, C/AG/WP

EXHIBITS: C/AG/WP, C/LS, C/MCC, C/U of R/MG

SOLO EXHIBITS: C/MCC

Nauyark (see Nauya, Pierre)

Nava, Julia *Lipán Apache*

RESIDENCE: Falfurrias, TX

EXHIBITS: AIAFM, SDCC, WWM

Nava, Simon Peter *Comanche/Apache*

A.K.A. Signature: S. P. Nava-Ha

Born 4 Feb 1944 in Garden City, KS; son of Julita R. and Simon V. Nava

RESIDENCE: San Pedro, CA

EDUCATION: San Pedro (CA) High School, 1962

OCCUPATION: Full-time painter since 1974

MEDIA: Oil, acrylic, watercolor, pencil, and prints

EXHIBITS: AIWR; CSU/LB; SM; SMIC; Antelope Valley Indian Museum, CA

SOLO EXHIBITS: Caballo Museum, NM, 1981; Arco Plaza, Los Angeles, CA, 1983

AWARDS: Partial listing includes: AIWR ('83, Best of Show); SMIC ('85, Best of Show)

HONORS: AIWR, featured artist, 1992

Nava-Ha, S.P. (see Nava, Simon Peter)

Naviaqsi (see Niviaksiak)

Nawpachee *Inuit (Eskimo)*

A.K.A. Nepachee; Napachie; Naupochee; Napatchie Pootoogook; Napachie Pootoogook

Born 1938; daughter of Pitseolak Ashoona (q.v.); wife of Eegyudluk (Eegyvudluk Pootoogook), sculptor and printmaker

RESIDENCE: Cape Dorset, NWT, Canada

OCCUPATION: Graphic artist, sculptor, and painter

MEDIA: Acrylic, pencil, stone, and prints

PUBLISHED: Houston (1967); Collinson (1978); Leroux, Jackson, and Freeman, eds. (1994)

PUBLIC COLLECTIONS: C/AG/GV, C/CMC, C/GM, C/NGCA, C/ROM, C/U of AB, C/U of BC/MA

EXHIBITS: C/AG/WP; C/CD; C/CG; C/AV; C/EACTDB; C/SFG; C/WBEC; C/WM; U of MO; Raven Gallery; National Gallery of Modern Art, Rome, Italy, 1981; Thenon, France; Liege, Belgium

Nawtlunsi Galagina (see Craker, Richard Joseph)

Nazia (see Blackmore, Bill)

NE-CHAH-HE (see Johnson, Raymond)

NEE ZOH GA BOE EKWAY (see Blue, Karen Savage)

NEHAKIJE (see Vincenti, Steven)

NELSON, BENNIE JAMES (see Yellowman)

NELSON, BENJAMIN JACOB *Taos/Navajo/Kiowa*

Born 6 Sept 1972 in Albuquerque, NM; son of Diana Lynne Tsoodle and Bennie "Yellowman" Nelson (q.v.); P/GP: Virginia Henderson and Tom Dinéttsoii Nelson; M/GP: Frances Lou Goombi and Wendell D. Tsoodle

RESIDENCE: Albuquerque, NM

EDUCATION: Cleveland Middle School, Albuquerque, NM

OCCUPATION: Student and painter

MEDIA: Watercolor and pen and ink

PUBLIC COLLECTIONS: WWM

EXHIBITS: ACS/PG; AIAFM; NMSF, RE; SWAIA; San Geronimo, Toas, NM

AWARDS: AIAFM ('93 1st, Young Emerging Artist Award); NMSF ('93, 1st, Purchase Award); SWAIA ('93; '94, 1st, Best of Division, Suazo-Hinds Award)

NE NUPA WANICA (see No Two Horns, Joseph)

NEPACHEE (see Nawpachee)

NEPHEW, RICHARD *Seneca*

Born 7 May 1957

RESIDENCE: Versailles, NY

OCCUPATION: Craftsman and painter

MEDIA: Acrylic, pencil, pen and ink, bone, antler, feather, and porcupine quills

PUBLISHED: Johannsen and Ferguson, eds. (1983)

COMMISSIONS: Johnson-O'Malley Program, illustrations for pre-school coloring book, 1978

EXHIBITS: NYSF; see also Awards

AWARDS: NYSF ('78, 1st); Indian Fall Festival, Cattaraugus, NY ('77, 1st; '78, 1st)

NEQUATEWA, EDMOND (see Nequatewa, Edward)

NEQUATEWA, EDWARD *Hopi*

A.K.A. Eddie Nequatewa; Edmond Nequatewa

RESIDENCE: Hotevilla, AZ

OCCUPATION: Carver and painter

PUBLISHED: Dunn (1968); Snodgrass (1968)

PUBLIC COLLECTIONS: HM, OU/MA, SM

EXHIBITS: AIW, OU/ET

NESSELROTTE, WILLIAM L. *Cherokee*

Born 11 Feb 1943; son of Agnes L. Umbenhauer and William C. Nesselrotte; P/GP: Willa Stanley and Clarence F. Nesselrotte; M/GP: Estallin Mark and Harry Lee Umbenhauer

RESIDENCE: Jerome, AZ

EDUCATION: Northeastern High School, 1961; two years, Wittenberg University, Springfield, OH

OCCUPATION: Frame shop and gallery owner, and painter

MEDIA: Acrylic, pencil, and mixed-media

EXHIBITS: Verde Valley (AZ) Art Association Shows; see also Awards

AWARDS: Jerome (AZ) Art Show

NETAOSHE (see Orr, Howell McCurly)

NETOSTIMI (see Schildt, Gary Joseph)

NAVAMOKEWESA (see Saufkie, Morgan)

NEVAQUAYA, JOYCE LEE TATE (see Nevaquaya, Doc Tate)

NEVAQUAYA, DOC TATE *Comanche*

A.K.A. Joyce Lee Tate Nevaquaya; Doc Tate
Born 1932 in Apache, OK

RESIDENCE: Apache, OK

EDUCATION: Fort Sill, 1951; Haskell, 1951-1952

OCCUPATION: Teacher, Methodist lay minister, lecturer, historian, dancer, composer, singer, flutist, and painter

MEDIA: Oil, acrylic, watercolor, tempera, and prints

PUBLISHED: Ellison (1972); Highwater (1976); Silberman (1978); New (1981); Price (1981); Boyd, et al. (1983); Coe (1986). *Oklahoma County Medical Society Bulletin* (Feb 1969), cover; *Key Magazine* (12-18 Aug 1972), cover; American Indian Exposition, Anadarko, OK (1972), program cover; *American Indian Crafts and Culture* (Feb 1973), cover; All-Indian Arts and Crafts Show, St. Charles, IL (1973), program cover; *Southwest Art* (Dec 1974; Jan 1976; Apr 1990); *Wassaja* (20 Sept 1975); *The Indian Trader* (Sept 1975; Sept 1980; Nov 1986; July 1990; Mar 1991); *The Tulsa Tribune* (14 June 1987); *Art-Talk* (Apr/May 1990); *The New York Times* (4 Dec 1990); *Oklahoma Today* (Dec 1990; Apr 1990); *The Anadarko Daily News Visitors Guide* (1991-1992), cover; *Association News*, SPIM (June 1992); *The Storyteller* (winter 1993); biographical publications

COMMISSIONS: Comanche Tribe, designed and executed a buffalo hide painting for presentation for the Fort Sill Centennial; SI, designed and executed a Comanche shield to honor the Tomb of the Unknown Soldier during the National Folk Festival; SPIM, created and decorated a full-size Comanche tipi; Oklahoma Diamond Jubilee Commission, design for two coins, 1982

PUBLIC COLLECTIONS: GM, WOM

EXHIBITS: ACS/RSC; AIE; CNM; FAIE; HM; ITIC; OAC; MAI; MFA/O; NACLA; NMSF; NTF; OAC; OMA; PAC; RC; RE; VV; SCG; SI; SN; SPIM; SIAF; U of OK; WWM; Indianapolis (IN) Museum of Art; Southern Methodist University, Dallas, TX; throughout the region; see also Awards

SOLO EXHIBITS: HSM/OK, SPIM

AWARDS: ACS/RSC; AIE ('58, 1st; '69, Grand Award; '70, 1st, Grand Award; '71, 1st; '72, 1st; '75, 2-1st, Grand Award); CNM ('81, Painting Award; '82); ITIC ('79; '85; '86, 1st; '88; '90, 2-1st; '91, 1st; '92, 1st, Best in Category; '94, 1st); PAC ('71); SN ('75); Oklahoma City (OK) Trades Fair (1971, 1st); All American Indian Art Show, St. Charles, IL (Grand Award); Southwestern Indian Arts Festival, Albuquerque, NM ('73, Grand Award)

HONORS: Governor of Oklahoma, appointed Director of Indian Art, first Inaugural Art Show; Southwestern State College, Weatherford, OK, Outstanding Indian Artists Award, 1969; City of Weatherford, OK, gold key to the City, 1969; Oscar Rose Junior College, Midwest City, OK, Indian Of The Year, 1975; International Theater Conference's first American visit, selected to present an Indian Cultural program, 1975; Kennedy Center for the Performing Arts, Washington, D.C., Night of the First American, flute performance, 1982; Apache Oklahoma Chamber of Commerce, Diamond Jubilee Heritage Week, Outstanding Citizen, 1982; NEA, fellowship, 1986; American Indian Support Society, Washington, D.C., reception held in his honor at the Capitol Building, 5 Sept 1986; Comanche Tribe, proclaimed second Friday in October *Joyce "Doc" Tate Nevaquaya Day*, 1986; Oklahomans for Indian Opportunity, LaDonna Harris

DOC TATE NEVAQUAYA

A physician by the name of Dr. Joyce delivered the artist, and Nevaquaya's family honored the doctor by using Joyce for their son's first name. Perhaps because of his relationship to this doctor he was nicknamed Doc. When orphaned at the age of 13, Nevaquaya went to live with his grandparents, thus strengthening ties to his Comanche heritage. In addition to his painting, he is a very talented flute maker and performer.

Award, 10 Oct 1986; listed by Ralph Oliver as one of the "best investments in Indian art for 1987"; named a Living Legend, 1990; Carnegie Hall, New York, NY, flute performance, 1990; Red Earth, Inc., Advisory Board, 1994; AICA, Artist of the West Award, 1994; more than 25 television appearances including: "On the Road With Charles Kuralt," "Good Morning America," and television appearances in England

NEVAQUAYA, FRANK *Comanche*

Born 14 Nov 1942; son of Margaret Tarsee and Malcolm Nevaquaya; P/GP: Victoria and Lean Nevaquaya

RESIDENCE: Lawton, OK

EDUCATION: Fort Sill, 1961; BC; NSU; B.A., Cameron University, Lawton, OK, 1975; M.A. CSU/OK, 1976

OCCUPATION: Art instructor and artist

MEDIA: Acrylic, watercolor, pencil, pen and ink, Prismacolor, and prints

EXHIBITS: AIE, RE

AWARDS: AIE ('75, 1st; '76, Grand Award; '78, 1st; '79; '80, 1st; '81; '83; '87, 1st; '88, 1st; '92)

NEVAQUAYA, JOE DALE *Yuchi/Comanche*

Birth date unknown; nephew of Doc Tate Nevaquaya (q.v.)

RESIDENCE: Bristow, OK

EDUCATION: IAIA

OCCUPATION: Poet, performance artist, artist-in-residence, and painter

PUBLISHED: *Tamaqua* (winter/spring 1991)

EXHIBITS: TIAF

AWARDS: TIAF ('92, Best of Division)

NEW, EULALIA *Cherokee/Choctaw*

Born 10 Oct 1910

RESIDENCE: Odessa, TX

EDUCATION: B.S.; graduate credits

OCCUPATION: Teacher and painter

EXHIBITS: CNM; Library Club, Menard, TX, 1986

AWARDS: CNM ('88, 1st)

NEW BEAR *Hidatsa (?)*

Above

MEDIA: Watercolor and pen and ink

PUBLISHED: Maurer (1992). *American Indian Art* (spring 1993)

PUBLIC COLLECTIONS: Eastern Montana College Library, Billings, MT

EXHIBITS: MIA; JAM; VP; St. Louis (MO) Art Museum

NEW BEAR

Drawings by New Bear, ca. 1883, were collected by Charles H. Barstow, a BIA clerk on the Crow Reservation in Montana.

American Indian Art *spring 1993*

NEWINI *Zuni*

A.K.A. Newmi

PUBLISHED: Snodgrass (1968)

PUBLIC COLLECTIONS: MNM

NEWINI

"It has been reported that the artist was painting in 1927."

Snodgrass 1968

NEWMAN, JEN *Cherokee*

RESIDENCE: Huntsville, AR

EXHIBITS: CNM, FCTM

NEWMI (see Newini)

NEWTON, RANZY ALISON *Kiowa*
Chief Charging Skunk
Born 21 Apr 1894 in Weatherford, TX; raised in Altus and Olustee, OK
RESIDENCE: Stockton, CA
MILITARY: U.S. Army, WWII
PUBLISHED: Snodgrass (1968)
EXHIBITS: PAC; Spring Hill (AL) College

NEZ, BRIAN *Hopi/Navajo*
EDUCATION: IAIA
MEDIA: Mixed-media
EXHIBITS: AC/SD

NEZ, D.M. *Navajo*
PUBLISHED: Snodgrass (1968)
PUBLIC COLLECTIONS: MAI

NEZ, DOROTHY *Paiute/Navajo*
EXHIBITS: PAC

NEZ, FORD *Navajo*
PUBLISHED: Snodgrass (1968)
PUBLIC COLLECTIONS: MNM

NEZ, GUY B., JR. *Navajo*
Born 26 Dec 1946 White Cone, AZ on the Navajo Indian Reservation
RESIDENCE: Indian Wells, AZ
EDUCATION: Holbrook (AZ) High School; IAIA; Los Angeles (CA) Trade Technical College
OCCUPATION: Jeweler, potter, sculptor, and painter
MEDIA: Oil, watercolor, pencil, pen and ink, silver, gemstone, and prints
PUBLISHED: Tanner (1973)
PUBLIC COLLECTIONS: BA/AZ, EM, HCC, MNA
EXHIBITS: CPS, HM/G, ITIC, MNA, NMSF, PAC, RC, SN, SWAIA, U of WV, WTF
AWARDS: HM/G ('70, 1st); ITIC ('70; '71; '94, 1st); NMSF ('73); PAC ('68, 1st; '70); RC ('71); SN ('70)

NEZ, REDWING T. *Navajo*
Born 24 Feb 1960 in Winslow, AZ; son of Josephine, silversmith, and Homer Nez
RESIDENCE: Tuba City, AZ
EDUCATION: Page (AZ) High School; three years, U of N AZ
OCCUPATION: Tuba City School District Cultural Department employee, tutor, actor, painter, and free-lance artist
MEDIA: Oil, acrylic, watercolor, and mixed-media
PUBLISHED: Jacka and Jacka (1988; 1994). *Art-Talk* (Mar 1991); *Southwest Art* (Nov 1994)
PUBLIC COLLECTIONS: GM
EXHIBITS: CIM, HM, HM/G, ITIC, MNA, NTF, SDCC, SIRU, SWAIA, RE
AWARDS: HM/G ('74, 1st); ITIC ('88, 1st); MNA ('85; '86; '87, 1st, Best of Show; '88, 1st); NTF (1st); SWAIA (1st)

NEZ, VIRGIL J. *Navajo*
PUBLISHED: Jacka and Jacka (1994)
EXHIBITS: MNA
AWARDS: MNA ('92, 1st, Best of Division)

NHUSCHINGYAY (see Murray, Daniel M.)

NHMA PETA (see Mahsetky, Wendy Amber)

NICHOLAS, DANIEL D. *Oneida/Cree*

Born 7 Apr 1949 in Detroit, MI; son of Little Pigeon and Grey Owl, Oneida chief

RESIDENCE: Streetsboro, OH

MILITARY: U.S. Army

EDUCATION: Sheridan High School, Somerset, OH; B.F.A., U of OH, 1971; studied under Grey Owl, Little Pigeon, Charles Dietz, and George Chalmers

OCCUPATION: Artist

MEDIA: Acrylic, gouache, and pen and ink

PUBLISHED: *American Indian Crafts and Culture* (Apr 1973), cover

PUBLIC COLLECTIONS: AC/Z, BIA, C/ROM, HM, USDI

EXHIBITS: AC/Z; AIE; C/ROM; GPM; PAC; throughout Ohio

SOLO EXHIBITS: U of OH; American Indian National Bank, Washington, D.C.

AWARDS: AIE ('73, 1st); PAC ('72, 1st; '78; '79)

HONORS: Army ROTC Scholarship, 1968

NICHOLS, KATIE *Miwok*

Born 5 Dec 1905 in Merced, CA

EDUCATION: Karl Thorpe Art School; Polytechnic High School, Riverside, CA; Adult Evening College, Sacramento, CA

PUBLISHED: Snodgrass (1968)

EXHIBITS: CSF; Northern California Art Fair, Sacramento, CA

NICHOLS, MILTON *Hopi*

PUBLISHED: Snodgrass (1968)

EXHIBITS: HM (student) 1951

NICHOLS, SARA LETHA PHILLIPS *Cherokee*

A.K.A. S. Letha Nichols

Born 10 Mar 1914 in Broken Arrow, OK; daughter of Florence Genette Holland and Elmer Lee Phillips; P/GP: Sarah and Henry Phillips; M/GP: Sarah and William Holland

RESIDENCE: Broken Arrow, OK

EDUCATION: Broken Arrow (OK) High School, 1931; NSU; U of Tulsa; OSU; workshops under Frederick Taubes, Robert Higgs, and Daniel Greene

OCCUPATION: Teacher, speaker, and painter

MEDIA: Oil, acrylic, watercolor, pencil, and pastel

COMMISSIONS: *Logos:* Broken Arrow (OK) Schools, 1930; Broken Arrow (OK) Historical Society. *Murals:* First National Bank of Broken Arrow, OK. *Portraits:* Partial listing from seven states includes: First National Bank, Broken Arrow, OK, F. S. Hurd; Nimitz Elementary School, Tulsa, OK, Admiral Chester W. Nimitz; Martin East Regional Library, Tulsa, OK, Alle Beth Martin; Auburn (AL) Polytechnical School, dormitory, Kate Conway Broun Fulghum

PUBLIC COLLECTIONS: National Daughters of the American Revolution Museum

EXHIBITS: CNM; NLAPW; PAC; Holland Hall School Invitational, Tulsa, OK; see also Awards

AWARDS: NLAPW; Mutual of New York Art Exhibition (Grand Prize)

HONORS: National League of Pen Women, Oklahoma State Art Chairman; Broken Arrow (OK) Historical Society, founding member; City of Broken Arrow, OK, Honorary Vice-Mayor, 1989

NICK *Cheyenne*
Beeh-Eese
A.K.A. Big Nose
Birth date unknown; died 1879
EDUCATION: Haskell, 1978
PUBLISHED: Snodgrass (1968)
PUBLIC COLLECTIONS: BPG, YU/BRBML

NICK

"The artist was among the 72 Plains Indians taken as prisoners from Fort Sill, OK, to Fort Marion, St. Augustine, FL, in 1875."

Snodgrass 1968

NICOTEEMOSIE, NOWYOOK (see Nowyook, T.)

NIELSON, LEO *Cree*
A.K.A. Signature: Sweetpea
Born ca. 1968
RESIDENCE: Winnipeg, MB, Canada
MEDIA: Acrylic
PUBLISHED: *American Indian Art* (spring 1990)
PUBLIC COLLECTIONS: HCC
EXHIBITS: CPS, HCC, WTF

LEO NIELSON

Nielson was a protégé of Garry Meeches (q.v.). His work also shows the influence of Benjamin Chee Chee and Clemence Wescoupe (qq.v.). Best known for his paintings of birds and animals, Nielson produces many of his paintings by combining stencils and sponge work. A brush is then used to add his distinctive sweeping lines.

According to John Warner, the artist's work often exhibits touches of humor and irony.

American Indian Art *spring 1990*

NIETO, BALARDO *Santo Domingo*
Birth date unknown; died World War II
PUBLISHED: Snodgrass (1968)
PUBLIC COLLECTIONS: MNM, MRFM, SM

NIETO, HARRY *Zuni*
PUBLISHED: Snodgrass (1968)
PUBLIC COLLECTIONS: U of CA/LMA

NIGH, CHARLES WILLARD *Cherokee*
Born 9 Aug 1950 in Wagoner, OK; son of Joseph C. Nigh; P/GF: G.W. Nigh; M/GF: Charley Fox Taylor
RESIDENCE: Muskogee, OK
MILITARY: U.S. Marine Corps, Vietnam
EDUCATION: G.E.D., Okay (OK) High School; BC; NSU
OCCUPATION: Emergency medical technician and painter
MEDIA: Oil and pencil
PUBLISHED: *Playboy Magazine* (1971)
EXHIBITS: CNM, NSU

CHARLES WILLARD NIGH

Nigh was a combat artist in Vietnam, 1970-1972. He considers himself to be a modern abstract expressionist and a design colorist who does "free life" drawings.

artist, p.c. 1992

NIGHT RIDER (see Pepion, Dan, Jr.)

NIGHT WALKER (see Martin, James, Jr.)

NIITSITAIPOYI (see Standing Alone, Henry)

NILCHEE, BETTY JEAN (see Dubois, Betty Jean Nilchee)

NINGEWANCE, DON *Ojibwa*
Born 1948 at Lac Seul, ON, Canada
RESIDENCE: Canada
OCCUPATION: Painter
MEDIA: Acrylic
PUBLISHED: Menitove, ed. (1986b)
PUBLIC COLLECTIONS: C/AG/TB; C/INAC; Government of Alberta; Government of Ontario
EXHIBITS: C/AG/TB; Winnipeg, MB; Calgary, AB; and Victoria, BC

NISHIMOTO, KIM CORNELIUS *Oneida*

RESIDENCE: De Pere, WI

EXHIBITS: LIAS

NITOH MAHKWI (see Schultz, Hart Merriam)

NIVIAKSIAK *Inuit (Eskimo)*

A.K.A. Niviaksie; Naviaqsi; Niviaqsi; Signature: drawings, Niviaksie; prints, Niviaksiak

Born 1891; died 1959

RESIDENCE: Lived in Cape Dorset, NWT, Canada

OCCUPATION: Graphic artist

MEDIA: Stone and pencil

PUBLISHED: Houston (1967); Larmour (1967); Goetz, et al. (1977).

EXHIBITS: C/TIP

NIVIAKSIAK

Niviaksiak was among the first group of artists from Cape Dorset to begin drawing. His prints were included in the first two print catalogs. Niviaksiak died in 1959 of injuries incurred in an attack by a bear. His two sons, Keatshuk and Pitseolak are printmakers. Pitseolak was also a carver.

Larmour 1967

NIVIAKSIE (see Niviaksiak)

NIX, BILL (see Red Corn)

NOAH, WILLIAM *Inuit (Eskimo)*

A.K.A. Noah

Born 1944 at Back River, NWT, Canada

RESIDENCE: Baker Lake, NWT, Canada

OCCUPATION: Sculptor, graphic artist, and printmaker

MEDIA: Colored pencil, crayon, stone, and prints

PUBLISHED: Blodgett (n.d.; 1978a); Goetz, et al. (1977); Routledge (1979); Latocki, ed. (1983); Jackson and Nasby (1987). *Artscanada* (Vol. 30, nos. 5 & 6, 1973-1974)

PUBLIC COLLECTIONS: C/AG/WP

EXHIBITS: C/AC/MS, C/AG/O, C/AG/WP, C/BLPD, C/CID, C/CMC, C/IA7, C/LS, C/SS, C/TIP

HONORS: Northwest Territories Legislature, Yellowknife, elected a representative

NOBLE, KAREN LYNN (see Tripp, Karen Noble)

NO BRAID *Sioux*

A.K.A. Chief No Braid

PUBLISHED: Snodgrass (1968)

PUBLIC COLLECTIONS: MPM (pictographic style on paper)

NOCKKOIST (see Bear's Heart, James)

NOEL, MAXINE *Santee/Oglala Sioux*

Ioyan Mani, Walk Beyond

A.K.A. Signature: Ioyan Mani

Born 1946 in Miniota, MB, Canada

OCCUPATION: Legal secretary and painter

PUBLISHED: *The Globe and Mail* (10 Mar 1980); *Ontario Indian* (Vol. 3, no. 4, 1980); *Dimensions* (Mar/Apr, 1981); *The Leader-Post* (15 Mar 1982); *The Edmonton Journal* (15 Oct 1983; 19 Oct 1985); *Sweetgrass* (May/June 1984); *The Brantford Expositor* (12 May 1984); *Windspeaker* (12 Dec 1986); *American Indian Art* (spring 1990)

PUBLIC COLLECTIONS: Lyndhurst Hospital, Toronto, ON

EXHIBITS: Partial listing of more than 35 includes: C/ACCCNA; C/AG/W; C/BWF; C/NB; C/NCCT; C/NNEC; C/WICEC; SM; Rideau Valley Art Festival, ON

MAXINE NOEL

Noel is best known for her fluid depictions of Native American women.

American Indian Art *spring 1990*

NOFCHISSEY, ALBERTA *Navajo*

RESIDENCE: Clifton, OK

EDUCATION: IAIA, ca. 1954

MEDIA: Oil and mixed-media

PUBLISHED: Snodgrass (1968); New and Young (1976). *Native American Arts 2* (1968)

EXHIBITS: FAIEAIP, IAIA, YAIA

NO HEART (see Murray, Daniel M.)

NO HEART (see Tinzoni)

NO HEART *Sioux*

Cante Wani Ca

RESIDENCE: Standing Rock Reservation, SD

OCCUPATION: Medicine man

PUBLISHED: Snodgrass (1968); Irvine, ed. (1974)

PUBLIC COLLECTIONS: HS/ND, SI

NOHNICAS (see Cohoe, William)

NOMKAHPA (see Two Strikes)

NOM-PA-AP'A (see Two Strikes)

NOOGOOSHOWEETOK (see Enooesweetok)

NOPAH, TRAVIS L. *Mohave*

Born 2 July 1948 in Parker, AZ; died 15 Feb 1988 in an automobile accident

RESIDENCE: Lived in Parker, AZ

MILITARY: U.S. Army, 1977-1979

EDUCATION: Parker (AZ) High School, 1967; U of AZ, "Southwest Indian Art Project," scholarship, summer 1963; Brooks School of Fine Arts, Santa Barbara, CA, 1974; Santa Barbara (CA) Art Institute, 1975

OCCUPATION: Director of Neighborhood Youth Corps, commercial artist, and painter

MEDIA: Oil, pencil, pen and ink, and pastel

PUBLISHED: *The Indian Trader* (May 1988)

COMMISSIONS: Parker (AZ) United School District, painting for La Pera Elementary School

PUBLIC COLLECTIONS: HCC

EXHIBITS: AAID; HCC; HM/G; ITIC; NICCAS; RC; WTF; Northern Yuma County (AZ) Fair; Santa Barbara (CA) Art Festival

AWARDS: RC ('82; '83, 1st; '84)

HONORS: Colorado River Indian Tribes, education grant

TRAVIS L. NOPAH

Nopah's art work was concerned with the life and traditions of the Mohave people. He said, "The message I try to convey is about my people, the Mohave, to other tribes who have little or no knowledge of us. This I do through my art."

p.c. 1984

NO-PA-WALLA (see Pahsetopah, Mike)

NORDWALL, RAYMOND C. *Pawnee/Cherokee/Chippewa*

Born 24 Sept 1965 in Muskogee, OK; son of Eva and Al Nordwall, ceremonial pipe maker; P/GP: Rose and Tony Nordwall; M/GP: Ahiewake and Arthur Fields; GGF: Roam Chief, Pawnee religious chief; nephew of Adam Fortunate Eagle, sculptor

RESIDENCE: Santa Fe, NM

EDUCATION: Muskogee (OK) High School, 1983; OSU; BC; A.A, IAIA, 1987; studied under Johnny Tiger Jr. (q.v.) and Frank Howell

OCCUPATION: Gallery salesman and painter

RAYMOND C. NORDWALL

Nordwall credits Johnny Tiger Jr. (q.v), under whom he studied for seven years, with getting him started as an artist. He says, "I never would have started

MEDIA: Acrylic, watercolor, and prints

PUBLISHED: *Art of the West* (July/Aug 1990; July/Aug 1993); *Shaman's Drum* (spring 1992); *Art-Talk* (Feb 1995)

EXHIBITS: CNM, FCTM, RC, RE, SWAIA, WWM; see also Awards

SOLO EXHIBITS: IAIA/M

AWARDS: CNM ('93, 1st); FCTM ('80; '90, Best of Show); RE ('93; '93); SWAIA ('87, 1st; '88; '89, 1st; '90; '91); Grand Lake Art Show, Eufala, OK ('85, Best in Show); Oklahoma Indian Art Festival, Oklahoma City, OK ('84)

HONORS: RC, Thunderbird Foundation Scholarships, 1986, 1987

NORMAN, DARREL LEE *Blackfeet*

Ee-Nees-Too-Wahsee, Buffalo Body

Born 20 Jan 1942 in Browning, MT

MILITARY: U.S. Navy

EDUCATION: Blanchet High School, 1956-1958; Ballard High School, Seattle, WA, 1960; U of WA, 1960-1961; Sales Training Incorporated; A.F.A., North Seattle (WA) Community College, 1980

OCCUPATION: Antique salesman, furniture restorer, insurance salesman, traditional dancer and singer, craftsman, sculptor, and painter

MEDIA: Paint, hide, and mixed-media

PUBLIC COLLECTIONS: MPI

EXHIBITS: AICA/SF; MPI; SCG; North Seattle (WA) Community College

SOLO EXHIBITS: MPI, SCG

NORRIS, JERRY W. *Iowa*

A.K.A. Dotman

Born 16 Nov 1950

RESIDENCE: Independence, MO

EDUCATION: Truman High School

EXHIBITS: LIAS; *Art Happening*, St. Louis, MO; Countryside, Omaha, NE; Plaza Art Fair, Kansas City, MO; Smokey Hills River Festival, Salina, KS; Kansas City and St. Louis, MO, area

AWARDS: Listing of more than 25 (ten 1st places and two Best of Shows) includes: LIAS ('90, MA)

NORTH, JOSEPHINE MOTLOW *Seminole*

Born 24 Dec 1952 in Fort Lauderdale, FL; daughter of Mary Buster, Seminole patchwork artist, and Jack H. Motlow; P/GP: Jane and John Motlow; M/GP: Susie and Johnny Buster

RESIDENCE: Hollywood, FL

EDUCATION: Hollywood (FL) Hills High School, 1971; IAIA, 1973; Fort Lauderdale (FL) Art Institute, 1979

OCCUPATION: Public relations and promotion, social services caseworker, educator, and painter

MEDIA: Oil, acrylic, watercolor, pencil, and pen and ink

PUBLISHED: *Boca Raton Magazine* (1982); *The Fort Lauderdale News* (Mar 1984); *Cultural Quarterly* (fall 1991)

COMMISSIONS: U.S. Department of Housing and Urban Development, Seminole Tribal Housing Authority, Hollywood, FL, proposal series illustrations, 1992; Broward Community College, Fort Lauderdale, FL, Commemoration of Native America, posters and handbills, 1992

EXHIBITS: AICA/SF, IAIA, KCPA, RC, SAF, STF

AWARDS: IAIA ('72); STF ('85, 1st)

RAYMOND C. NORDWALL

(continued) painting if it hadn't been for him."

Nordwall's earliest paintings were "traditional" as exemplified by the Bacone College and Santa Fe "Studio" styles. He now depicts traditional Native American subjects in a bold and contemporary manner. His originals, acrylic paintings on large canvases, portray action and emotion in vivid color. Nordwall does careful research to insure historical accuracy.

JOSEPHINE MOTLOW NORTH

North uses her art to achieve three goals: 1) to demonstrate her traditional concepts and the influence of traditional art; 2) to show the results of her experiences with other Indian cultures as well as with non-Indian cultures; and 3) to ultimately produce a message which provokes the viewer to new levels of thought and feeling. Whenever possible, she attempts to break out of the American Indian art stereotype and produce something different.

artist, p.c. 1992

NORTHCUTT, HARRELL *Chickasaw*
EDUCATION: BC, ca. 1951
PUBLISHED: Snodgrass (1968)
EXHIBITS: DAM, PAC

NORTON, BILLY *Navajo*
EXHIBITS: DAM

NORTON, JERRY R. *Eskimo*
Born 20 July 1942 in Kivalena, AK
RESIDENCE: Kivalena, AK
EDUCATION: IAIA, 1963-1966
MEDIA: Watercolor
PUBLISHED: Snodgrass (1968); Ray (1969); Yorba (1991)
PUBLIC COLLECTIONS: BIA, CAS, IACB, MNM
EXHIBITS: MNM, PAC, SFSUFC, USDS
AWARDS: MNM

NO SENSE (see Red Corn, Jim)

NOSIE, MONTIE *Apache*
PUBLISHED: Snodgrass (1968)
PUBLIC COLLECTIONS: MAI

NOTAH, NED *Navajo*
EDUCATION: Santa Fe, ca. 1936-1938
PUBLISHED: Dunn (1968); Snodgrass (1968). *Arizona Highways* (July 1956)
EXHIBITS: AIW, NGA

NOT-TOO-IN IS-CAW-NEE-MA (see Owens, Gary W., Sr.)

NO TWO HORNS, JOSEPH *Hunkpapa Sioux*
He Nupa Wanica
A.K.A. White Butterfly
Born 1852; died 28 Sept 1942; son of Woman In Sight and Red Hail
RESIDENCE: Lived in Cannon Ball, ND
OCCUPATION: Warrior, horse raider, keeper of Winter Count, craftsman, carver, and painter
MEDIA: Pencil, ink, watercolor, leather, cloth, and wood
PUBLISHED: Murphy (1927); Snodgrass (1968); Maurer (1992). *American Indian Art* (Vol. 3, no. 2, 1984; summer 1993)
PUBLIC COLLECTIONS: DAM; HS/ND (43 paintings depicting Indian battles); Bonanzaville USA, West Fargo, ND; Mandan Indian Shriners, El Zagel Temple, Fargo, ND; Science Museum of Minnesota, St. Paul, MN
EXHIBITS: VP

JOSEPH NO TWO HORNS

As a warrior, No Two Horns participated in approximately 40 battles including the Battle at the Little Big Horn in 1876. Shortly after that battle he joined Sitting Bull in his flight to Canada, but later returned to live at the Standing Rock Agency in North Dakota. In spite of having lost the use of his right hand as a young man, No Two Horns became a prolific artist who produced carvings, weaponry, and paintings on hide, cloth, and paper. The majority of his work created between 1890 and 1920 was made for sale. His paintings were done in a pictographic style and largely depicted battles in which he had participated.

American Indian Art
summer 1993

NOVA, A. M. *Hopi*
RESIDENCE: From Shungopovi, Second Mesa, AZ
PUBLISHED: Snodgrass (1968)
PUBLIC COLLECTIONS: MAI

NOVAKEEL, TOMMY *Inuit (Eskimo)*
A.K.A. Tommy Nuvaqirq
Born 1911; died 1982
RESIDENCE: Lived in Pangnirtung, NWT, Canada

OCCUPATION: Graphic artist
MEDIA: Colored and black pencil
PUBLISHED: Goetz, et al. (1977); Collinson (1978); Routledge (1979); McMasters, et al. (1993)
PUBLIC COLLECTIONS: C/PECL, C/U of AB, DAM
EXHIBITS: C/CG, C/IA7, C/TIP

NOWJUK (see Nowyook, T.)

NOWYOOK, T. *Inuit (Eskimo)*
A.K.A. Nowjuk; Nowyook Nicoteemosie
Born 1902
RESIDENCE: Pangnirtung, NWT, Canada
OCCUPATION: Graphic artist
MEDIA: Pencil
PUBLICATIONS: Goetz, et al. (1977)
PUBLIC COLLECTIONS: DAM
EXHIBITS: C/TIP

NOYES, PHYLLIS *Colville*
Born 1947 in Omak, WA
EDUCATION: IAIA, 1965-1966
PUBLISHED: Snodgrass (1968)
EXHIBITS: IAIA, SAIEAIP, YAIA

NUKOA (see White Deer, Gary)

NUMKENA, DENNIS C. *Hopi*
Born 1941 at Upper Moenkopi, AZ; son of Lewis Numkena Sr., Moenkopi village leader; brother of Lewis Numkena Jr. (q.v.)
RESIDENCE: Phoenix, AZ
EDUCATION: Scottsdale (AZ) High School; ASU
OCCUPATION: Computer programmer, architect, theatrical designer, writer; painter since 1974
MEDIA: Oil, polymer, and prints
PUBLISHED: Tanner (1973); Jacka and Jacka (1988). *The Scottsdale Daily Progress* (7 Nov 1980; 12 Mar 1982); *Arizona Living* (1 Feb 1981; Vol. 13, no. 1, 1982); *The Phoenix Gazette* (15 Apr 1982; 2 June 1988); *Art-Talk* (Mar 1983; Oct 1985); *Arizona Arts and Travel* (Mar/Apr 1983); *The Arizona Daily Sun* (4 Sept 1987); *Native Peoples* (fall 1987); *Southwest Profile* (May/June 1989); *The Indian Trader* (Dec 1992); *New American Art* (Vol. 3, 1989; Vol. 4, 1990)
COMMISSIONS: *Murals:* Nature's Window, Scottsdale, AZ; San Carlos Apache Cultural Center, AZ; Sedona (AZ) Spirit Theater; St. Bridget's Parish Center, Mesa, AZ; Overhead murals and papal stage for Pope John Paul II's visit, 1987; Pyramid Lake Museum, NV; Yavapai Apache Cultural Center. *Other:* ASU, *The Magic Flute*, costumes and sets, 1977; ASU, *The Cunning Little Vixen*, costumes and sets, 1984; Phoenix Symphony Orchestra, 1985; Anasazi Resort, Phoenix, AZ, 300 paintings
PUBLIC COLLECTIONS: MNA
EXHIBITS: HM, HM/G, SN
AWARDS: HM/G ('69, Motorola Award); SN ('70)
HONORS: American Institute of Architects, scholarship

TOMMY NOVAKEEL

Novakeel's drawings show great detail and are largely of whaling and related activities.

Collinson 1978

T. NOWYOOK

Nowyook, in addition to being an artist, is the leader of one of the few remaining Inuit groups that continue to live in camps in the Canadian Arctic.

Goetz, et al. 1977

NUMKENA, JANEELE TALAYUMPTEWA *Hopi*

EXHIBITS: HT, ITIC, SWAIA

AWARDS: ITIC ('91)

NUMKENA, LEWIS, JR. *Hopi*

A.K.A. Lewis Numkena Junior. Signature: Lewis Numkena Junior; Lewis N. Junior

Born 24 July 1927 in Moenkopi, AZ; son of Lewis Numkena, Moenkopi village leader; brother of Dennis C. Numkena (q.v.)

RESIDENCE: Tuba City, AZ

EDUCATION: Santa Fe

MEDIA: Shiva and casein

PUBLISHED: Snodgrass (1968); Tanner (1973). *Arizona Highways* (Feb 1950); *Art-Talk* (Apr/May 1988)

PUBLIC COLLECTIONS: MNA

EXHIBITS: MNA; MNM; PAC; Tulsa, OK

AWARDS: MNA, PAC

NUÑEZ, BENITA CALACHAW (see Wa Wa Chaw)

NUNGUSUITUQ (see Enooesweetok)

NUPOK OR NUPOK, FLORENCE (see Chauncey, Florence)

NUTCHUCK *Inuit (Eskimo)*

PUBLISHED: Snodgrass (1968)

BOOKS ILLUSTRATED: *Back to the Smoky Sea*, by Nutchuck; *Son of the Smoky Sea*, by Nutchuk

NUVAQIRIQ, TOMMY (see Novakeel, Tommy)

NUVAYOUMA, ARLO *Hopi*

Nuvayouma, Snow Carry

Born 6 Sept 1923 at Shungopovi, Second Mesa, AZ

EDUCATION: Second Mesa, AZ

OCCUPATION: Arizona Country Club (Phoenix, AZ) employee, and artist

PUBLISHED: Snodgrass (1968); Harvey (1970); Tanner (1973); Golder (1985)

BOOKS ILLUSTRATED: Harvey (1968)

COMMISSIONS: Thirty-three paintings illustrating Hopi village life (now in the MAI/HF collections), 1964-1965

PUBLIC COLLECTIONS: MAI

EXHIBITS: ASM, HH

NUVAYOUMA, MELVIN *Hopi*

PUBLIC COLLECTIONS: WWM

NV TSI (see Smith, Janet Lamon)

OAKERHATER, DAVID PENDLETON (see Making Medicine)

OAKIE, DAVID *Eskimo*

Born 1933 in Teller, AK

RESIDENCE: Shishmaref, AK

EDUCATION: DCTP, 1964-1965

MEDIA: Pen and ink and prints

PUBLISHED: Ray (1969)

OAU NAH JUSAH (see Smoky, Lois)

O'BOY YAHN (see Connywerdy, Kevin)

OCTUCK, JOHN *Eskimo*

PUBLISHED: Snodgrass (1968); Fawcett and Callander (1982)

PUBLIC COLLECTIONS: MAI (with the note: "Point Hope, Alaska, 1905")

EXHIBITS: NAP

ODJIG, DAPHNE *Ojibwa*

Odjig, Kingfisher

A.K.A. Daphne Odjig Beavon

Born 1919 on Manitoulin Island, ON, Canada, on the Wikwemikong Indian Reserve; GGF: Assikinak, Great Partridge

RESIDENCE: Anglemont, BC, Canada

OCCUPATION: Gallery owner, author, illustrator, art instructor, and artist

MEDIA: Oil, acrylic, watercolor, pen and ink, pastel, mixed-media, and prints

PUBLISHED: Dickason (1972); Southcott (1984); McLuhan and Vanderburgh (1985); Menitove and Danford, ed. (1989); Cardinal-Schubert (1992); Odjig, Vanderburgh, and Southcott (1992); McMasters, et al. (1993). *The Brandon Sun* (13 Nov 1968); *The Winnipeg Free Press* (22 Feb 1969; 30 Oct 1971); *The Winnipeg Tribune* (14 Dec 1971); *Arts Canada* (autumn 1971); *The Edmonton Journal* (7 May 1977); *Artswest* (Vol. 2, no. 2, 1977); *Native Perspective* (Vol. 2, no. 3, 1978; Vol. 3, no. 1, 1978); *The Ottawa Journal* (25 Nov 1978); *Toronto Life* (June 1979); *The Vancouver Sun* (24 Oct 1979); *The Ottawa Citizen* (15 Mar 1980); *Native Arts/West* (Jan 1981); *Masterkey* (winter 1984); *American Indian Art* (Vol. 10, no. 2, 1985; autumn 1990); *Financial Post* (27 Apr 1985); *The Manitoulin Recorder* (19 June 1985); *The Globe and Mail* (13 Dec 1985); *Equinox* (Vol. 28, 1986); *Windspeaker* (12 Dec 1986); *C Magazine* (fall 1991)

BOOKS ILLUSTRATED: Schwarz (1974); Nulegak and Metayer (1966); Ginn and Co., Toronto, ON, ten Nanabush Indian legend children's books , 1971

COMMISSIONS: *Murals:* Pequis Indian School, Hodgson, MB, 1971; C/MMMN, Centennial Commission, 1972; National Museums of Canada, 1978. *Paintings:* C/LUM, 1984; C/ROM, 1973; Expo '70, Osaka, Japan; Glenview Corporation, Ottawa, ON. *Other:* El Al Airlines, Israel, posters, 1975

PUBLIC COLLECTIONS: C/AG/TB; C/AG/TT; C/AG/WP; C/BU; C/CCAB; C/CGCQ; C/CIMS; C/CMC; C/GM; C/INAC; C/LUM; C/MCC; C/MMMN; C/OCF; C/ROM; C/U of T; C/WICEC; HCC; Ameco Canadian Petroleum Ltd., Calgary, AB; El Al Airlines, Israel; Energy Mines and Resources Collection; Glenview Corporate Collection, Ottawa, ON; Government of Israel, Jerusalem, Israel; Government of Manitoba, Winnipeg, MB; Government of Newfoundland, St. John's, NF; Government of Ontario, Sudbury, ON; Imperial Oil Collection, Toronto, ON; Manitoba Centennial Centre Corporate Collection, Winnipeg, MB; Manitoba Indian Brotherhood; Nova Corporate Collection, Calgary, AB; PetroCanada Collection, Calgary, AB; Pontiac School, Wikwemikong, ON; Prince Edward Island Museum, Charlottetown; Peguis High School, MB;

DAPHNE ODJIG

Odjig's earliest works were done in a realistic style and were portraits or genre paintings of everyday life on the reserve. In 1967, she began to develop her distinctive style and experimented with collages. With no formal training in art, Odjig taught herself through traveling and studying art in museums and art galleries in Canada and Europe. She admires the work of Pablo Picasso and his influence can be seen in many of her paintings.

Native Arts/West, *Jan 1981*

DETAIL: Gerald Osborne, *Pawnee Indian Hand Game*, ca. 1950. Philbrook Museum of Art, Tulsa, Oklahoma

Princess Margaret Hospital, Toronto, ON; Readers Digest, Montréal, PQ; Sir Wilfred Laurier University, Waterloo, ON; Toronto (ON) Hospital for Sick Children

EXHIBITS: Partial listing of more than fifty includes: C/AC/AE; C/ACCCNA; C/AG/O; C/AG/TB; C/AG/WP; C/CGCQ; C/CIARH; C/CIIA; C/CNAC; C/GM; C/LTAT; C/LUM; C/NB; C/ROM; C/TC; C/TFD; C/TIIS; C/TU; C/U of MB; C/U of R/MG; C/U of T; C/WCAA; C/WICEC; NACLA; OMA; SM; Columbus Centre, Toronto, ON; Etobicoke Civic Center, ON, 1976; Expo '70, Osaka, Japan; Gallery Anthropos, London, England, 1973; Holland Festival, Amsterdam, Holland, 1985; *Images for a Canadian Heritage*, Vancouver, BC; Minot (ND) State University, 1970; Osaka World's Fair, Osaka, Japan; Smotra Folk Festival, Yugoslavia

SOLO EXHIBITS: Partial listing of more than thirty includes: C/AB/TB; C/AG/WP; C/BU; C/CGCQ; International Peace Gardens, Manitoba/North Dakota, 1970; Lakehead Art Centre, Port Arthur, ON, 1967; Minot (ND) State University, 1970; Smotra Folklore Festival, Yugoslavia, 1971

HONORS: British Columbia Federation of Artists, member; Arts grant for Somotra Folklore Festival, Yugoslavia, tour and exhibition, 1971. Swedish Brucebo Foundation Scholarship, 1973; Manitoba Arts Council Bursary Award; Canadian Silver Jubilee Medal, 1977; Wikwemikong Reserve, presented with an eagle feather in recognition of her accomplishments; Laurentian University, Sudbury, ON, Honorary Doctor of Letters, 1982; C/U of T, Honorary Doctor of Law, 1985; Office of the Order of Canada, 1986; Royal Canadian Academy of Arts, 1989

ODLE PAH

"The artist executed a calendar history of the Kiowas, drawn with colored crayons in a ledger book. She began ca. 1885, and continued until her death in 1934."

Snodgrass 1968

ODLE PAH *Kiowa (?)*

Kawlahnohndaumah, Footprints Of A Buffalo

Birth date unknown; died 1934

PUBLISHED: Snodgrass (1968)

PUBLIC COLLECTIONS: FSM

OEWOTOH (see Buffalo Meat)

OF THE DAWN (see Smoky, Lois)

O-GE-ID (see Herrera, Diego)

OGOWEE (see Naranjo, Adolph)

OHEITOINT, CHARLIE (see Ohet Toint)

OHET TOINT

"The artist was among the 72 Plains Indians taken as prisoners from Fort Sill, OK, to Fort Marion, St. Augustine, FL, in 1875."

Snodgrass 1968

OHET TOINT *Kiowa (?)*

A.K.A. Charlie Oheitoint; Charles Chet-toint; Charlie Buffalo; Ohittoint

Birth date unknown; died 1934

OCCUPATION: Warrior, teacher, school recruiter, clerk, carpenter, policeman, farmer, stockman, and painter

PUBLISHED: Snodgrass (1968); Fawcett and Callander (1982)

PUBLIC COLLECTIONS: SI (model shields and tipis); YU/BRBML (listed as Charles Chet-toint)

EXHIBITS: BPG

OHITTOINT(see Ohet Toint)

MONA OHOVELUK

Ohoveluk is a woman artist who seems to be challenged and inspired by the puzzle of solving difficult compositional problems.

Collinson 1978

OHOVELUK, MONA *Inuit (Eskimo)*

A.K.A. Ohoueluk

Born 1935

RESIDENCE: Holman Island, NWT, Canada

OCCUPATION: Graphic artist

PUBLISHED: Collinson (1978)

PUBLIC COLLECTIONS: C/U of AB, DAM
EXHIBITS: C/CG, C/SS

OH'ZAN (see Pretty Hawk)

O'JOHN, CALVIN *Ute*
EDUCATION: IAIA, 1965-1966
PUBLISHED: Snodgrass (1968)
EXHIBITS: IAIA, YAIA

OKI'CIZE TAWA (see Jaw)

OKIE, JOHN WILLIAM *Eskimo*
A.K.A. Jack Okie
OCCUPATION: Carver and painter
MEDIA: Watercolor and pen and ink
PUBLISHED: Snodgrass (1968)
EXHIBITS: PAC

OKIEIZE TAWA (see Jaw)

OKLAGA, FRANÇOISE *Inuit (Eskimo)*
Born 1924 at Coral Harbor, NWT, Canada
RESIDENCE: Baker Lake, NWT, Canada
OCCUPATION: Seamstress and graphic artist
MEDIA: Pencil, colored pencil, hide, fabric, embroidery floss, and thread
PUBLISHED: Jackson and Nasby (1987)
PUBLIC COLLECTIONS: C/AC/MS
EXHIBITS: C/CID

OKPEALUK, JAMES *Eskimo*
Born 1932 on Little Diomede Island, AK
RESIDENCE: Teller, AK
EDUCATION: DCTP, 1964-1965
PUBLISHED: Ray (1969)

OKUMA, SANDRA *Luiseño/Shoshoni/Bannock*
Petitsingvey, Killdeer
Born 26 Aug 1945 in Fallbrook, CA; daughter of Lavna L. and Robert C. Nelson; P/GP: Myrtle Blodgette and William Nelson; M/GP: Anne and Edward Edmo, writer and storyteller
RESIDENCE: Pauma Valley, CA
EDUCATION: Benjamin Franklin High School, Los Angeles, CA, 1963; Los Angeles (CA) Trade Technical College, 1970
OCCUPATION: Graphic designer and painter
MEDIA: Watercolor and gouache
PUBLISHED: *Southwest Art* (Dec 1994)
EXHIBITS: CNM; LIAS; RC; Women Artists of the West, Visalia, CA; see also Awards
AWARDS: LIAS (2-MA; '91, MA; '94, Best of Show); RC (Erickson Award; '93, Tony Begay Award, Diederich Award; '94, Begay Award); Shoshoni Bannock Festival, Fort Hall, ID (2-1st, Spectator's Choice)

OKU-MA-TSA (see Baca, Henry)

OKUWASTA (see Baca, Henry)

JOHN WILLIAM OKIE

"The following comment appears in a letter to Philbrook Art Center from Wilbur Wright Walluk (q.v.), written August 22, 1946: '. . . he draws art pictures once in a great while. As matter of fact, he always have other works to do. He especially does ivory carving. He likes ivory business during the war, but now the ivory conditions are change after the war is over. The price of ivory is low down since the war is over. He probably give up his ivory business and start painting. Jack Okie is a very good Eskimo artist. His works use to be better than Ahgupuk (q.v.) and my works. My dear mama is Jack's cousin. Mama use to tell me that Jack sure like to draw pictures when he was a kid. He sure can draw pictures with a pen and ink and watercolor. He probably knows how to work with oils too.'"

Snodgrass 1968

FRANÇOISE OKLAGA

Oklaga colors her drawings boldly and gives them texture by placing her drawing paper over corrugated cardboard.

Jackson and Nasby 1987

OLANNA, MELVIN *Eskimo*

Azittauna

Born 5 May 1941 at Ikpik Village on the Bering Strait; died 3 Sept 1991

RESIDENCE: Lived in Shishmaref, AK

EDUCATION: IAIA, 1963-1965; Indian Arts and Crafts Board Demonstration-Workshop, Sitka, AK, 1967-1968; U of AK/C; studied under Allan Houser and Ron Senungetuk (qq.v.)

OCCUPATION: Sculptor and graphic artist

MEDIA: Pencil, stone, bronze, silver, and prints

PUBLISHED: Ray (1969). *Alaskan Journal* (fall 1971; fall 1972); *Alaska Geographic* (Vol. 12, no. 3, 1985)

PUBLIC COLLECTIONS: ACMWA; IACB; MFA/AH; SFNB/WA; U of AK/F; Bell Telephone, Seattle, WA; Ranier Bank, Seattle, WA; Whatcom County Museum, Bellingham, WA

EXHIBITS: MFA/AH, U of AK/F; see also Awards

AWARDS: MFA/AH (1975); Alaska Association for the Arts ('80)

OLAYOU (see Ulayu)

OLD BUFFALO *Sioux*

Tatankehanni; *Tatanka Yotanka*; *Tatanká Ehan'ni*

A.K.A. Old Bull

Born 1845; death date unknown

PUBLISHED: Snodgrass (1968); Maurer (1992). *Bulletin 61*, BAE (1918), pictographic style

PUBLIC COLLECTIONS: Mandan Indian Shriners, El Zagel Temple, Fargo, ND

EXHIBITS: VP

OLD BUFFALO

"In 1913, the artist, with Swift Dog (q.v.), went to McLaughlin, SD, to confer with Frances Densmore."

Snodgrass 1968

OLD BULL (see Old Buffalo)

OLD BULL, MOSES *Hunkpapa Sioux*

Born 1851; died 1935; adopted nephew of Sitting Bull (q.v.).

RESIDENCE: Lived on the Standing Rock Reservation, SD

OCCUPATION: Warrior, Indian agency policeman, historical informant, and painter

MEDIA: Watercolor, pencil, colored pencil, and crayon

PUBLISHED: Vestal (1932; 1934a; 1934b); Snodgrass (1968). *American Indian Art* (summer 1992; summer 1994)

PUBLIC COLLECTIONS: OU/L; Iowa State Department of History and Archives, Des Moines, IA (a calendar, dated 1812-1879, marked "Bullhead, SD"; also a pictographic listing catalogued as "the dead and wounded since coming to Standing Rock Reservation, 1831-1833.")

MOSES OLD BULL

A friend and an aide to Sitting Bull, Old Bull joined him in many raids and battles. He accompanied Sitting Bull in 1876 when he went into exile in Canada, and returned to the reservation with him when he surrendered in 1881. From 1928 to 1932, Walter Stanley Campbell (pen name, Stanley Vestal) corresponded and visited with Old Bull and recorded his memories of Sitting Bull. Sometime during this period, Old Bull completed a series of seventeen autobiographical drawings that were commissioned by Campbell.

American Indian Art *summer 1994*

OLD DOG *Sioux*

PUBLISHED: Snodgrass (1968)

PUBLIC COLLECTIONS: HS/ND (a muslin drawing labeled "a party of Hidatsa Indians with Sioux in 1856")

OLD HOSTIN CLAW (see Big Lefthanded)

OLD JOE (see Talirunili, Joe)

O'LEARY, DIANE *Comanche*

Opeche-Nah-Se

Born 27 Dec 1939 in Waco, TX; daughter of Mary Otipoby and John Robert McNiel

RESIDENCE: Scottsdale, AZ

EDUCATION: High school, Fort Worth, TX; BC; B.A., Texas Christian University, Fort Worth, TX; M.A., SU; M.A., Harvard University; studied with Eric Gibberd and Georgia O'Keeffe

OCCUPATION: Laboratory technician, nurse, sculptor, and painter

MEDIA: Oil, tempera, casein, pencil, pen and ink, and prints

PUBLISHED: Broder (1981); Samuels (1982). *Arizona Highways* (Sept 1972); *American Indian Crafts and Culture* (Mar 1973); *The Scottsdale Daily Progress* (10 Mar 1975); *The Indian Trader* (July 1978)

PUBLIC COLLECTIONS: BC; BM; DAM; GM/NY; HM; MAI; MIM; MRFM; PAC; PM; SU; U of KS; U of OK; U of TX; WWM; Guggenheim Museum

EXHIBITS: BM/B, HM, HM/G, MKMcNAI, MNA, SFFA, SN, PBS, RC; Baylor University, Strecker Museum, Waco, TX

SOLO EXHIBITS: HM

AWARDS: HM/G ('74)

OLNEY, NATHAN HALE, III *Yakama/Hupa*

Born 30 Jan 1937 in Wapato, WA; son of Alice Pratt and Nathan Hale Olney Jr.; P/GGGF: Capt. Nathan H. Olney, Indian Agent at Dallas, OR, 1855, who married a Washoe girl

RESIDENCE: Wapato, WA

MILITARY: U.S. Army, 1960-1962; battle group artist

EDUCATION: Wapato (WA) High School, 1955; WSC, 1956-1959; University of Wurzburg, Germany, ca. 1960-1962

OCCUPATION: BIA employee and painter

PUBLISHED: Snodgrass (1968); Brody (1971)

EXHIBITS: AAID; AC/HC; HM/G; FNAIC; ITIC; SN; Central Washington and Western Washington Fairs; La Grande (OR) Arts and Crafts Festival; Southern Command Art Show, Schweinfurt, Germany; Anacortes (WA) Arts and Crafts Show; Yakima (WA) Junior College, Larsen Gallery; Ohio Art Congress Exhibition

SOLO EXHIBITS: Yakima (WA) Library; Kamiath-Trinity High School, Hoopa, CA; Seattle (WA) Indian Center; Federal Building, Portland, OR

AWARDS: AAID ('70; '73, 1st); HM/G ('71); SN ('67, 1st)

O'MAHK-PITAWA (see Parsons, Neil)

OMUKA-NISTA-PAYH'PEE (see Tailfeathers, Gerald)

ONE BULL *Hunkpapa Sioux*

OCCUPATION: Warrior and painter

MEDIA: Pigment and muslin

PUBLISHED: Maurer (1992)

PUBLIC COLLECTIONS: SIM; Mandan Indian Shriners, El Zagel Temple, Fargo, ND

EXHIBITS: VP

ONLY DAUGHTER, THE (see Pahdopony, Juanita)

OOMAYOUALOOK (see Joanassie)

OONARK, JESSIE *Inuit (Eskimo)*

A.K.A. Una Oonark; Una; Oonark; Taviniq; S. Toolooklook

Born 1906 in the Back River area, NWT, Canada; died 1985 in Churchill, MB, Canada

RESIDENCE: Lived at Baker Lake, NWT, Canada

ONE BULL

A warrior of Sitting Bull's band, One Bull participated in the Battle of the Little Big Horn on June 26, 1876.

Maurer 1992

JESSIE OONARK

Jessie Oonark is generally regarded as Baker Lake's most famous artist. The widowed mother of eight children, her first drawings appeared in the 1960 Cape Dorset annual print catalog. Under the name Una, her prints were the first from outside the Cape Dorset area to be seen in Southern Canada. Her drawings typically included a formal arrangement involving human figures. She often used the human face, presented frontally or in profile, or both together. She was also known for her wall hangings.

OCCUPATION: Wife, mother, designer, seamstress, graphic artist, and printmaker
MEDIA: Colored and graphite pencil, crayon, pen and ink, colored felt tip pen, embroidery floss, thread, fabric, and prints
PUBLISHED: Blodgett (n.d.; 1978a; 1978b; 1981); Larmour (1967); Goetz, et al. (1977); Collinson (1978), Routledge (1979); Myers, ed. (1980); Woodhouse, ed. (1980); Latocki, ed. (1983); Jackson and Nasby (1987); McMasters, et al. (1993). *Artscanada* (Vol. 30, nos. 5 & 6, 1973-1974); *North* (Mar/Apr 1974); *Inuit Art Quarterly* (winter 1994)
PUBLIC COLLECTIONS: C/AC/MS, C/AG/WP, C/SC, C/U of AB, DAM
EXHIBITS: C/AG/WP, C/CD, C/CG, C/CID, C/IA7, C/LS, C/SS, C/TIP, C/TMBI, FAM
SOLO/SPECIAL EXHIBITS: C/OP (dual show)
HONORS: Royal Canadian Academy of Arts, member

OONARK, UNA (see Oonark, Jessie)

OON NAH SUSAH (see Gritts, Franklin)

OOSAHWEE, HARRY J. *Cherokee*
Born 10 Dec 1949
RESIDENCE: Tahlequah, OK
EDUCATION: Hulbert (OK) High School; BC; NSU
EXHIBITS: CNM, FCTM, RC
AWARDS: FCTM ('82, IH; '87; '90); RC ('84, Niederman Award)
HONORS: Western Oklahoma Bacone Alumni Association, commendation

HARRY J. OOSAHWEE

The artist has stated that his goal is, "To promote the true culture and heritage of the American Indian in its purest form through my paintings." His art depicts, "the everyday life of the Cherokee people, his spirit, his legends, his lore and his history through the use of symbolism and the traditional method of Indian painting."

OO SKA SES DEE (see Smith, Kevin Warren)

OOSUAK *Inuit (Eskimo)*
A.K.A. Barnabus Oosuaq
Born 1940
RESIDENCE: Baker Lake, NWT, Canada
PUBLISHED: Collinson (1978)
PUBLIC COLLECTIONS: C/U of AB
EXHIBITS: C/CG

OOSUAQ, BARNABUS (see Oosuak)

OOTENNA, GEORGE *Eskimo*
Born 1877 in Wales, AK
RESIDENCE: Wales, AK
EDUCATION: Cape Prince of Wales School
PUBLISHED: Ray (1969)
BOOKS ILLUSTRATED: *The Eskimo Bulletin* (Vol. 3, July 1897)

OOTSKUYVA (see Qotskuyva, R.)

OPA MU NU (see Martínez, Richard)

OPECHE-NAH-SE (see O'Leary, Diane)

OQOWAMONO (see Montoya, Charles)

OQUA OWIN (see Sánchez, Ramos)

OQUA PI (see Oqwa Pi)

OQUWA (see Roybal, José D.)

OQWA PI *San Ildefonso*

Oqwa Pi, Red Cloud

A.K.A. Abel Sánchez; Oqua Pi

Born 1 Aug 1899 at San Ildefonso Pueblo, NM; died 21 Mar 1971 at the Los Alamos (NM) Medical Center

RESIDENCE: Lived in Santa Fe, NM

EDUCATION: Santa Fe

OCCUPATION: Farmer, served his pueblo in secular and spiritual capacities, muralist, and painter

MEDIA: Watercolor

PUBLISHED: Sloan and LaFarge (1931); Spinden (1931); Alexander (1932); Jacobson and d'Ucel (1950); Dunn (1968); Snodgrass (1968); Brody (1971; 1992); Tanner (1968; 1973); Warner (1975); Dockstader (1977); Stuart and Ashton (1977); Schmid and Houlihan (1980); Broder (1981); Fawcett and Callander (1985); Golder (1985); Samuels (1985); Seymour (1988); Williams, ed. (1990). *International Studio* (Feb 1930); *New York Times* (29 Nov 1931); *American Magazine of Art* (Aug 1933); *Encyclopaedia Britannica* (1954); *The Quarterly,* SWAIA (summer 1971)

COMMISSIONS: *Murals:* Santa Fe Indian School

PUBLIC COLLECTIONS: AF, BM/B, CAM/OH, CGFA, CIS, CMA, DAC, DAM, JAM, MAI, MKMcNAI, MNA/KHC, MNH/A, MNM, MRFM, PAC, SAR, SM, RM

EXHIBITS: AIEC; AIW; ASM; CGA; CAM/OH; EITA; HH; ITIC; JAM; MKMcNAI; MMA; MNM; NAP; NGA; NJSM; PAC; PM; SU; WWM; Yale U; Milwaukee (WI) Art Institute; Philadelphia (PA) Art Alliance Exhibition of Contemporary Pueblo Indian Art

AWARDS: ITIC, MNM

HONORS: Elected Governor of San Ildefonso, NM, six times; unique posthumous recognition from All-Indian Pueblo Council and 19 Pueblo governors

OQWA PI

"I, Oqwa Pi, have been painting since the early 1920s. As I found that painting was the best among my talents, I decided to do my best to win me fame as an Indian artist. . . . as an artist, I have raised a big, healthy family for my painting brought in good income . . . "

artist
letter to Philbrook Art Center

"When Oqwa Pi died, the All-Indian Pueblo Council and the governors of nineteen New Mexico Pueblos signed a resolution of sorrow and presented it to his widow, Nepomucena Sánchez."

Snodgrass 1968

ORDUÑO, ROBERT *Gabrielino*

Born 5 Sept 1933 in Ventura, CA; son of Mary and Octovio Orduño; P/GP: Grandmother Duarte and Beningno Orduño; M/GM: Lorenza Estrada

RESIDENCE: Santa Fe, NM

MILITARY: U.S. Navy

EDUCATION: San Fernando (CA) High School, 1952; Los Angeles (CA) Trade Technical College, 1952-1954; Los Angeles (CA) Valley College; LAACS, 1959-1964

OCCUPATION: Musician, art director, designer, advertising illustrator, editorial artist, teacher, sculptor, and painter

MEDIA: Oil, acrylic, watercolor, bronze, and prints

PUBLISHED: *The Great Falls Tribune* (26 June 1984; Aug 1984; 17 Mar 1985; 18 Jan 1987); *Southwest Art* (June 1990; Nov 1990; Jan 1991; July 1991; Jan 1992); *The New Mexican* (16 Nov 1990); *International Fine Art Collector* (Feb 1992); biographical publications

COMMISSIONS: *Murals:* Great Falls (MT) Municipal Airport, 1983

PUBLIC COLLECTIONS: BBHC, HCC

EXHIBITS: AICA; BBHC; CIM; C/U of L; CIAE/MT; CIM; CMRM; CPS; GFNAAS; HCC; RC; Great Falls (MT) Civic Center, 1987; Montana Indian Nations Art Rendezvous, Helena, MT, 1987; galleries in CA, ID, MT, SD, and WA; see also Awards

AWARDS: BBHC; CIM; GFNAAS ('86, Artist Choice Award; '89, MA); RC ('85, 1st, Begay Award; '86, 1st; '87); Montana Great Ad Awards ('77, Best of Category; '78, Best of Category)

ROBERT ORDUÑO

Orduño's work shows the influences of both Impressionism and Expressionism. He is known for his dynamic use of color and his paintings of Native American legends and dancers.

Southwest Art, *June 1990*

HONORS: Art Director's Club, Los Angeles, CA, scholarship, 1952; GFNAAS, featured artist, 1985

ORIOLE (see Herrera, Velino Shije)

ORR, CAROLINE LOUISE *Colville/Wenatchee*

CAROLINE LOUISE ORR

"Orr has been actively engaged in painting her people, in non-traditional Indian style, since 1956. She has completed two collections of Indian portraits and has taken courses in anthropology to further her knowledge of Indian cultures."

Snodgrass 1968

A.K.A. Caroline Orr Maas; Mrs. J. A. Maas

Born 21 Aug 1943 in Republic, WA; daughter of Caroline Nelson and Samuel A. Orr; sister of Veronica Ingram (q.v.); M/GGGF: Long Alec, Colville chief, U.S. Marshall, and pony express rider; Artist is a descendant of Moses, famous Wenatchee chief.

RESIDENCE: Seattle, WA

EDUCATION: Public Schools in Omak, WA; B.A., U of WA, 1965; C/U of MB, 1970; U of MT, 1971-1972; studied under Edith Nelson, Ernest Norling, and Sakino, Japanese woodcut artist

OCCUPATION: Museum staff artist, rancher, and painter

PUBLISHED: Snodgrass (1968). *The Omark Chronicle* (1964); *Spokesman Review* (Western Edition 1961); *Wenatchee World* (1952); *An Okanogan Drying Vension*, Okanogan Vocational publication booklet (1961)

PUBLIC COLLECTIONS: BIA; BIA/P; CBC; CM/C; FOM; GCD; HCC; HM; IACB; OL; OPS; PNIC; RC; WHCO; Fort Okanogan Historical Museum, Brewster, WA; Gonzaga University, Spokane, WA; Vatican Library, Rome, Italy

EXHIBITS: AAID; BEAIAC; CIAI; FAIEAIP; HCC; IFA; ITIC; KG; HCC; HM/G; MNM; NIFA; PAC; PNIC; SAM; U of CO; Winnipeg (MB) Centennial Center; Osaka, Japan.

SOLO EXHIBITS: Partial listing of 26 includes: HM; The Carey Museum, Cashmere, WA; Gonzaga University, Spokane, WA; Fort Okanogan Museum, Brewster, WA; The Indian Center, Seattle, WA

AWARDS: AAID ('69; '70, 1st); HM/G ('70, Avery Award; '71, 1st; '83, Graphics Award; '78); U of WA (Arts Award); Human Education Poster Contest, Stanford, CA

HONORS: *Scholarships:* Colville Confederated Tribes, 1961-1965; U of WA, 1961-1962; *Other:* United States Department of Labor, Washington, D.C., Career Planning for Minority Groups, delegate, 1962

ORR, HOWELL MCCURLY *Chickasaw/Cherokee*

HOWELL MCCURLY ORR

"The artist is particularly interested in the work of Mexican muralists and in the technique of batik painting, in which he was trained at Instituto San Miguel de Allende."

Snodgrass 1968

Orr says, "My art is American Indian, expressionistic style, influenced by Dick West (q.v.), George Calvert, Rufino Tamayo, and the Mexican masters."

Ihunter, Lover of Home; *Netaoshe*, Young Bear

A.K.A. Sonny Orr

Born 20 May 1929 in Washington, OK; son of Annie Burns and N. F. Orr; P/GF: John A. Orr; M/GF: C. A. Burns; M/GGF: Hatak Shauee, last chief of the Chickasaw Nation

RESIDENCE: Phoenix, AZ

MILITARY: U.S. Ski Patrol, Korean War

EDUCATION: Chilocco; BC; B.A., NSU; graduate study, U of Tulsa; M.A., Instituto de San Miguel de Allende, Guanajuato, Mexico

OCCUPATION: Educator, craftsman, and painter

MEDIA: Oil, acrylic, watercolor, pencil, pen and ink, pastel, wax, dye, cotton fabric, and prints

PUBLISHED: Snodgrass (1968); Brody (1971). Biographical publications

COMMISSIONS: Pickens Inter-Tribal Powwow, Madill, OK, program cover, 1956

PUBLIC COLLECTIONS: BIA, PAC

EXHIBITS: AIE; CNM; FANAIAE; HM; HM/G; IACB; ITIC; MNM; PAC; SAIEAIP; SN; USDS; Cuarto Exposición Anual de San Miguel de Allende, Guanajuato, Mexico; American-Mexican Cultural Center; Bellas Artes National,

Mexico; Instituto de San Miguel de Allende, Guanajuato, Mexico; state and national shows

SOLO EXHIBITS: Las Vegas (NV) Art League, 1965

AWARDS: AIE; CNM ('87, 1st); ITIC; MNM; PAC ('70); SN ('68, 1st)

HONORS: National American Folk Festival, Oklahoma City, OK, Indian tribal dance coordinator, 1957

ORR, SONNY (see Orr, Howell McCurly)

ORR, VERONICA (see Ingram, Veronica Marie)

ORTIZ, JOSEPH *San Juan*

So Whay, Misty

Born 21 Mar 1939 in Santa Fe, NM; son of Esther Martínez

RESIDENCE: San Juan Pueblo, NM

EDUCATION: Santa Fe, 1952-1958; BC, 1960; U of AZ, "Southwest Indian Art Project," scholarship

PUBLISHED: Snodgrass (1968)

EXHIBITS: BC, ITIC, MNM, NMSF, PAC, U of N AZ

AWARDS: ITIC, MNM, NMSF, U of N AZ

HONORS: Mrs. J. A. Armstrong, Berkely, CA, scholarship to Bacone College

JOSEPH ORTIZ

"Ortiz believes that Dick West (q.v.) at Bacone College, Mr. and Mrs. James E. Watson (formerly of Santa Fe Indian School), and Mrs. J. A. Armstrong encouraged him most in his art career. He wishes to continue in the field of education and teach art education and biology."

Snodgrass 1968

ORTIZ, LOUIS *Cochití*

Birth date unknown; died ca. 1943

PUBLISHED: Snodgrass (1968)

PUBLIC COLLECTIONS: MNM

ORTIZ, MARK ANTHONY *Taos*

Born 10 Apr 1955 at Taos Pueblo, NM; P/GP: Julia and Joseph Ortiz; Artist was raised by his paternal grandparents.

RESIDENCE: Ranchos de Taos, NM

EDUCATION: Albuquerque; Southwestern Indian Polytechnic Institute, Albuquerque, NM; private study with Lee Whitehorse and Robert Davidson (q.v.)

OCCUPATION: Jewelry designer, sculptor, and painter

MEDIA: Acrylic, pencil, pen and ink, silver, gemstone, stone, and prints

PUBLISHED: *Tempo* (18 Oct 1990)

EXHIBITS: CIM; ITIC; MRFM; SWAIA; galleries in CO, NM, and NY

SOLO EXHIBITS: MRFM

AWARDS: ITIC ('90, 1st)

MARK ANTHONY ORTIZ

Ortiz has worked since 1980 to develop his own unique style without the aid of masking tape or an airbrush and would like to be known as a perfectionist. He traces his interest in art to his grandparents who encouraged him and even partitioned off part of their home for him to use as a studio. He has said that one of the most important things that he did for himself and his art was to quit drinking in 1984. "It's been a long road, God's been good to me. And, I'm going to try to help my people in the best way I can."

Tempo, *MRFM, Oct 1990*

OSAPANA (see Whiteman, James Ridgley)

OSBORNE, FLOYD *Shoshoni*

Born 1947 in Fort Washakie, WY

EDUCATION: Chilocco

OCCUPATION: Traditional dancer, housing program director, and painter

MEDIA: Oil, watercolor, tempera, pen and ink, and pencil

PUBLISHED: Ray, ed. (1972)

EXHIBITS: CIA; local exhibits

OSBORNE, GERALD *Pawnee*

Birth date unknown; died ca. 1964

PUBLISHED: Snodgrass (1968)

PUBLIC COLLECTIONS: PAC

EXHIBITS: PAC
AWARDS: PAC

OSBORNE, GORDON *Quechan*
EDUCATION: IAIA
PUBLISHED: *Native American Arts 2* (1968)

OSBURN-BIGFEATHER, JOANNA L. *Cherokee*
Born 1952 in Felixstone, England
RESIDENCE: Santa Cruz, CA
EDUCATION: A.A., IAIA, 1987; B.A., U of CA/SC, 1990; SUNY/A
PUBLIC COLLECTIONS: HM, IAIA, SI
EXHIBITS: AICA/SF; CNM; HM/G; IAIA; LIAS; MR; RBP; RC; U of CA/SC; U of NM; Claremont (CA) College
AWARDS: LIAS ('93, MA)
HONORS: U of CA/SC, Irwin Scholarship

OSCEOLA, HENEHAYO *Seminole*
Born 19 Feb 1958; son of Peggy Jim and John McKinley Osceola; P/GP: Alice Willie and William McKinley Osceola; M/GP: Annie and Willie Jim Tiger
RESIDENCE: Ochopee, FL
OCCUPATION: Chickee builder, carpenter, and artist
EXHIBITS: See Awards
AWARDS: Calle Ocho/Open House, Miami, FL ('80, 1st); Miccosukee Arts Festival, Ochopee, FL
HONORS: Everglades Miccosukee Executive Council, councilman; Unconquered Miccosukee Tribe of the Seminole Nation, Religious Leader/Bundle Carrier

OSCEOLA, MARY GAY *Seminole*
Born 16 Mar 1939
RESIDENCE: Hollywood, FL
EDUCATION: Santa Fe, 1960-1961; IAIA, 1961-1965; A.A., Broward Community College, Fort Lauderdale, FL
PUBLISHED: Snodgrass (1968)
PUBLIC COLLECTIONS: BIA
EXHIBITS: CNM, FCTM, MNM, PAC, RC, STF
AWARDS: FCTM ('67; '71; '72); MNM ('63); STF (1st)

OSHUITOQ, ANIRNIK *Inuit (Eskimo)*
A.K.A. Annick; Annee; Anernik; Arnirnik; Anerga; Anerngna
Born 1902 aboard the ship, *Arctic*, on Lake Harbour; died 1983
RESIDENCE: Lived in Cape Dorset, NWT, Canada
OCCUPATION: Seamstress and graphic artist
MEDIA: Pencil, colored pencil, crayon, felt tip marker, fabric, thread, embroidery floss, and animal skin
PUBLISHED: Jackson and Nasby (1987)
PUBLIC COLLECTIONS: C/WBEC
EXHIBITS: C/CID

ANIRNIK OSHUITOQ

Oshuitoq was about 60 years old when she began to draw. She used simple forms and frequently drew birds or bird-like shapes.

Jackson and Nasby 1987

OSTI, JANE HITCHCOCK *Osage*
RESIDENCE: Tahlequah, OK
OCCUPATION: Ceramist and painter
EXHIBITS: ACAI; CNM; IS; RE; Powwow of Champions, Tulsa, OK

OTAH, TERRANCE *Hopi*
PUBLIC COLLECTIONS: MNA

OTELALEYA *Cochití*
PUBLISHED: Snodgrass (1968)
PUBLIC COLLECTIONS: AIEC, MNA

OTHOLE, HERRIN *Zuni*
RESIDENCE: Zuni, NM
EXHIBITS: CNM, ITIC, HM/G
AWARDS: ITIC ('79; '84; '85; '87)

OTIPOBY, CLYDE LELAND, SR. *Comanche*
Otipoby
Born 31 Jan 1940 in Clinton, OK; son of Eva Lee King and Leonard Otipoby; P/GP: Peddy and Bob Otipoby; M/GF: Ruben King
RESIDENCE: Newkirk, OK
MILITARY: U.S. Air Force
EDUCATION: Newkirk (OK) High School, 1958; Arkansas City (KS) Junior College; OSU, 1968
OCCUPATION: Illustrator, visual arts teacher, ceramist, sculptor, and painter
MEDIA: Acrylic, watercolor, pencil, and clay
EXHIBITS: AIE; CSPIP; PAC; SPIM; Gilcrease Museum Rendezvous, Tulsa, OK; arts and crafts shows
AWARDS: AIE ('67; '69; '70; '71, 1st); PAC ('73, 1st); area arts and crafts shows

OTTEN, JOHN *Cherokee*
Born 23 Oct 1944
RESIDENCE: Tahlequah, OK
EDUCATION: Cascia Hall, Tulsa, OK; Bishop Kelley High School, Tulsa, OK; OSU; NSU
OCCUPATION: Social worker and painter
EXHIBITS: CNM, FCTM, RC; see also Awards
AWARDS: Harvest of Talent, Tahlequah, OK

OTTO, STEVE *Ottawa/Chippewa*
A.K.A. Steven Ott
RESIDENCE: Petoskey, MI
EDUCATION: Petoskey (MI) High School; North Central Michigan College, Petoskey, MI
EXHIBITS: Anishinabe Aki Museum; Ann Arbor (MI) Powwow; Nishawbe Festival, Petoskey, MI; see also Awards
SOLO EXHIBITS: Genesee Indian Center
AWARDS: Elm Point Portside Arts Fair (Award of Merit)
HONORS: Ann Arbor (MI) Powwow, poster artist, 1987

OTTOCHIE, TIMOTHY *Inuit (Eskimo)*
Born 1904; died 1982
RESIDENCE: Lived in Cape Dorset, NWT, Canada
OCCUPATION: Sculptor and graphic artist
PUBLISHED: Collinson (1978)
PUBLIC COLLECTIONS: C/U of AB
EXHIBITS: C/AC/MS, C/AG/WP, C/CG

Lawrence Outah

"The artist is reportedly from Oraibi, AZ. While in the 10th grade at Santa Fe Indian School in 1948, he was cited for 'outstanding ability in art.'"

Snodgrass 1968

Outah, Lawrence *Hopi*

Born ca. 1932

EDUCATION: Santa Fe; Haskell

PUBLISHED: Dunn (1968); Snodgrass (1968); Brody (1971); Tanner (1973)

PUBLIC COLLECTIONS: GM, MAI, MNA, MNM

EXHIBITS: MNM, MFA/O, PAC

Outie, George *Hopi*

Leleka, Snake

Born 16 Nov 1926 in Winslow, AZ

RESIDENCE: Tuba City, AZ

MILITARY: U.S. Air Corps, WWII

EDUCATION: BC, 1949

PUBLISHED: Snodgrass (1968)

PUBLIC COLLECTIONS: HM, MAI, PAC

EXHIBITS: PAC, PAC/T

AWARDS: PAC

Owen, Narcissa Chisholm *Cherokee*

MEDIA: Oil

PUBLISHED: Snodgrass (1968)

PUBLIC COLLECTIONS: GM, HSM/OK

Gary W. Owens Sr.

Gary Owens' paternal grandfather was Jackson Looking who was an elder brother of Sitting Bull and was at the Battle of the Little Big Horn in 1876. His great grandfather was the Cree chief, Broken Arm, who signed the treaty of 1851, at Laramie, Wyoming, with Governor Stevens. Using the colors common to the Plains culture, the artist paints in a unique abstract style that he developed through the study of the art of Picasso and other early 20th century artists.

artist, p.c. 1992

Owens, Gary W., Sr. *Piegan/Assiniboin/Crow/Blood*

Not-Too-In-Is-Caw-Nee-Ma, Petrified Buffalo Medicine Indian Boy; *Waa-Nee-A-Too*, Winter

Born 1 Jan 1934 on Chicken Hill, near Oswego, MT; son of Susan Ground and James Charles Owens; P/GP: Mary Wounded by White Man and Charles Wilkens; P/GP: Mary Gaurdipee and John Ground "Chief Eagle Calf"

RESIDENCE: Mesa, AZ

EDUCATION: Bremerton (WA) High School, 1952; BYU; USU

OCCUPATION: State employment service employee, custodian, and painter

MEDIA: Oil, acrylic, watercolor, pencil, and pastel

PUBLISHED: Ray, ed. (1972)

EXHIBITS: CIA, HM/G, SN

AWARDS: HM/G ('69, 1st, Motorola Award)

Owipo (see Tracy, Edmond L.)

Owl Eagle (see Eagle Feather, Elijah)

Owu Tewa (see Chávez, Manuel "Bob")

Oxendine, Lloyd *Lumbee*

RESIDENCE: Arlington, VA

EDUCATION: M.F.A., Columbia University, New York, NY

OCCUPATION: Sculptor and painter

MEDIA: Mixed-media

PUBLISHED: *Art In America* (Sept/Aug 1972)

EXHIBITS: AICH, BM/B, MIA

HONORS: New York Council on the Arts, grant

OXFORD, EVA MAE *Cherokee*

Hard Head (or Get Mad Easy)

Born 16 Jan 1941 at Locust Grove, OK; Daughter of Hester Walkins and William Peoples; GGF: Charley Huges Wasa, medicine man

RESIDENCE: Hulbert, OK

EDUCATION: Locust Grove (OK) High School, 1958

OCCUPATION: Welder and painter

MEDIA: Oil, acrylic, and pencil

EXHIBITS: CNM, FCTM, LIAS, MCI; area shows

OYEBI (see Geionety, George)

OYE GI (see Herrera, Senofre)

OYÉGI PIN (see Padilla, Michael)

OYSLA (see García, Ernest P.)

OZISTALIS (see Speck, Henry)

Paaokela (see Martínez, Joe R.)

Pablito, Thomas *Zuni*

a.k.a. Tomás Pablito

published: Snodgrass (1968)

public collections: MAI

Packer *Arapaho or Cheyenne*

Sto Ko Wo; Nunnetiyuh

a.k.a. Backer

Born 1851; died 1893

occupation: Warrior, policeman, laborer, and landowner

published: Snodgrass (1968)

public collections: HI/ML

exhibits: BPG

Packer

"The artist was among the 72 Plains Indians taken as prisoners from Fort Sill, OK, to Fort Marion, St. Augustine, FL, in 1875."

Snodgrass 1968

Packer returned to Indian Territory (now Oklahoma) in 1878.

Paddlety, David Leroy *Kiowa/Crow/Arapaho/Cheyenne*

Born 3 June 1923 in Anadarko, OK. son of Magdalene Padoti and David Paddlety; P/GP: Pahquoye and Paddlety; M/GP: K'yah-Tye-Ah-Kaumah and Keintaddle; GGF: Daun-Pie

residence: Anadarko, OK

education: BC High School, 1947; BC; B.A., Oklahoma Baptist University, 1992

occupation: BIA employee and painter

media: Oil, acrylic, watercolor, pencil, and silver

exhibits: AIE; BC/McG; Wind River Valley Art Exposition, Lander, WY; Lander Valley Art Guild Shows

awards: AIE ('67, 1st; '69; '72; '73, 1st)

Paddock, Hugh *Navajo*

published: Snodgrass (1968)

public collections: MAI

Padilla, Fernando, Jr. *Navajo/San Felipe*

Born 29 July 1958 in Los Angeles, CA; son of Marie Setalla and Fernando Padilla; P/GP: Rosita Marie and José L. Padilla; M/GP: Modesta Clark and William Dixon Sr.

residence: Oklahoma City, OK

education: Río Grande High School, Albuquerque, NM, 1976; Nazarene Bible College, Colorado Springs, CO; Southern Nazarene University

occupation: Truck driver; full-time sculptor and painter since 1987

media: Acrylic, watercolor, pencil, pen and ink, pastel, alabaster, and prints

published: Ballantine and Ballantine (1993). *The Tulsa World* (27 June 1993; 6 Nov 1994; 12 Feb 1995); *The Storyteller* (winter 1993)

commissions: *Murals:* DIA, 1993

public collections: CAI/KC, IPCC

exhibits: ACAI, ACS/RSC, AIAF, BAM, BB, CAI/KC, CHAS, CNM, FAIE, IAF, IS, ITIC, LC, OCSA, RC, RE, SWAIA, TIAF; see also Awards

solo exhibits: CAI/KC; Bethany (OK) Nazarene College

awards: ACS/RSC ('85), CAI/KC ('86), CHAS (Grand Prize), CNM ('85, Newcomers Award; '86, 1st; '89, 1st); ITIC ('87, 2-1st; '88; '90, 1st; '91, 1st; '92); LC ('88; '90, Grand Prize); RE ('89, 1st; '92; '93; '94); TIAF ('91); Oklahoma Indian Youth Art Festival, Oklahoma City, OK ('81, Best of Show)

honors: TIAF, featured artist, 1995

Fernando Padilla Jr.

Padilla began to draw before he entered kindergarten, but until he was injured in an accident that forced him from commercial truck driving, he didn't work at it seriously. His paintings are done in the traditional Pueblo style and are either realistic or stylized.

artist, p.c. 1992

detail: Paul Pahsetopah, *Our People Lived Here*, 1967. Philbrook Museum of Art, Tulsa, Oklahoma

Padilla, Joe *Isleta*

Born ca. 1900 at Isleta Pueblo, NM; died ca. 1930s

EDUCATION: Albuquerque

OCCUPATION: Carpenter and painter

MEDIA: Tempera

PUBLISHED: Seymour (1988)

PUBLIC COLLECTIONS: IACB/BC

EXHIBITS: WRTD

Joe Padilla

Padilla apparently painted very little, mostly small paintings of one or two Indian dancers. He died of heart failure when he was about thirty-five.

Seymour 1988

Padilla, Michael *Santa Clara*

EDUCATION: Albuquerque, 1961-1962

PUBLISHED: Snodgrass (1968)

PUBLIC COLLECTIONS: CAS, MRFM

EXHIBITS: MNM

AWARDS: MNM

Padilla, Michael *San Juan*

Oyégi Pín, Frost Mountain

Born 12 May 1960

RESIDENCE: Albuquerque, NM

MILITARY: U.S. Air Force

EDUCATION: A.A., IAIA, 1979; Southwest Polytechnic Institute, Albuquerque, NM; U of NM

OCCUPATION: Dancer and painter

MEDIA: Watercolor

PUBLISHED: *Art-Talk* (Aug/Sept 1987)

PUBLIC COLLECTIONS: HM, MRFM

EXHIBITS: ACS/ENP, CIM, HM/G, MRFM; see also Awards

AWARDS: ACS/ENP; Regional Fine Arts Competition, Barksdale Air Force Base, LA ('84; '85)

Padlo (see Pudlo)

Padloo (see Pudlo)

Pahdopony, Juanita *Comanche*

Pahn Nah Vet Tah, The Only Daughter

A.K.A. Nita Pahdoponey

Born 18 Jan 1947 in Portland, OR; daughter of Marjorie and Sam Pahdopony; P/GP: Mary and John Pahdopony; M/GP: Ida and Sam Tahmahkera; Artist is a descendant of Quanah Parker.

RESIDENCE: Lawton, OK

EDUCATION: Lawton (OK) High School, 1965; SWOSU, 1970; M.Ed., U of OK, 1990

OCCUPATION: Educator, poet, and artist

MEDIA: Oil, acrylic, pastel, and mixed-media

PUBLISHED: University of Virginia, Deptartment of English, Native American publication, 1994; U of AZ, poetry publication, 1995

PUBLIC COLLECTIONS: GPM; Comanche Tribe, Lawton, OK

EXHIBITS: CNM, DAM

HONORS: McMahon Arts and Humanities Grant, 1994

Pah-Pu-Son-Tse (see Gray, Gina)

Pahsetopah (see Pahsetopah, Paul)

Loren Louis Pahsetopah

"The artist's interest in drawing and painting began when he was about seven years old. Participation in pow-wows has aided him in depicting tribal costuming."

Snodgrass 1968

Pahsetopah, Loren Louis *Osage/Cherokee*

Shapa Nazhi, Stands Brown (a buffalo)

Born 10 Sept 1934 in Pawhuska, OK; son of Lorraine and Chris Pahsetopah; P/GF: Great Hunter Pahsetopah; brother of Paul Pahsetopah (q.v.)

RESIDENCE: Pawhuska, OK

EDUCATION: Pawhuska (OK) High School, 1952; Chilocco

OCCUPATION: Painting contractor, interior decorator, and painter

MEDIA: Tempera and gouache

PUBLISHED: Snodgrass (1968); Mahey, et al. (1980)

PUBLIC COLLECTIONS: GM, IACB, PAC

EXHIBITS: ASM, CNM, CSPIP, FAIE, GM, HM, ITIC, MNM, MIF, MPABAS, PAC, SFFA, SN, USDS; see also Awards

AWARDS: PAC ('68, 1st; '74, Painting Award, '76, Grand Prize; '79); Oklahoma School Student's Competition, 1949

Pahsetopah, Mike *Osage/Yuchi/Creek*

No-Pa-Walla, Fear Inspiring

A.K.A. Michael Peyton Pahsetopah

Born 16 Jan 1958 in Tulsa, OK; son of Jean and Paul Pahestopah (q.v.); P/GP: Lorraine and Chris Pahsetopah; M/GP: Mary and Leonard Bevenue; nephew of Loren Pahsetopah (q.v.)

RESIDENCE: Sapulpa, OK

EDUCATION: Kellyville (OK) High School, 1976

OCCUPATION: Indian dancer, dance instructor and dance troupe leader, lecturer, actor, model, and painter

MEDIA: Acrylic, watercolor, and pencil

EXHIBITS: FCTM; PAC; Creek Nation Art Show, Okmulgee, OK

AWARDS: FCTM ('77, IH)

Paul Pahsetopah

"At the age of 14, the artist showed an interest in painting and drawing. He had already made his first dance costume. It was not until Acee Blue Eagle (q.v.) encouraged him to paint in the 1950s, that he worked seriously in art."

Snodgrass 1968

Pahsetopah considers himself to be a guardian of tradition. He is especially knowledgeable about Indian songs, costumes, dance canes, and beaded gourds.

Pahsetopah, Paul *Osage/Cherokee*

Pahsetopah, Four Hills

Born 10 Sept 1932 in Pawhuska, OK; son of Lorraine and Chris Pahsetopah; father of Mike Pahsetopah (q.v.); brother of Loren Louis Pahsetopah; P/GP: Veva and Paul (P. Y.) Pahsetopah; M/GF: Wahti-An-Kah (Osage Leader) Chief John Oberly

RESIDENCE: Sapulpa, OK

MILITARY: U.S. Army, Korea

EDUCATION: Pawhuska (OK) High School; Chilocco

OCCUPATION: Singer, dancer, flutist, craftsman, historian, and artist

MEDIA: Watercolor, casein, pencil, and prints

PUBLISHED: Snodgrass (1968); Bell Telephone Co., pamphlet; Oklahoma school textbooks

COMMISSIONS: Powwow program covers; Indian music album covers

PUBLIC COLLECTIONS: BIA, EM, GM, PAC

EXHIBITS: BIA; CSPIP; FAIE; FCTM; HM; MNM; MFA/O; MIF; OHT; PAC; SFFA; SN; Governor's Art Show, Oklahoma City, OK

AWARDS: FCTM ('73; '78, IH; '80); PAC ('69; '70; '71; '72, 1st; '73, Painting Award)

Pai-Doung-U-Day (see Cannon, T.C.)

Paisano, Michael N. *Navajo/Laguna*

Born 5 Nov 1964 at Fort Defiance, AZ; son of Rhoda R. Nelson and James F. Paisano; P/GP: Dade R. Dawes and Alfred Paisano; M/GP: Effie and Ned Nelson; G/uncle: Teofilo Tafoya (q.v.)

RESIDENCE: Oakland, CA
EDUCATION: John C. Fremont Senior High, 1992; IAIA; California College of Arts and Crafts, 1987
OCCUPATION: Shipping and receiving clerk and painter
MEDIA: Oil, watercolor, pencil, and pastel
PUBLIC COLLECTIONS: IAIA
EXHIBITS: ACS/ENP; CNM; American Indian Film Institute Art Show; Stanford (CA) Powwow

PAISLEY, LARRY GRANT *Blackfeet*

Born 9 Aug 1942 in Browning, MT
EDUCATION: Cut Bank (MT) High School, 1959; Northern Montana College, Havre, MT, 1959-1960; B.S., Western Montana College, Dillon, MT, 1964; MSU, 1965-1966; D.V.M., WSU/P, 1970; M.S., U of MN, 1972
OCCUPATION: Veterinarian, educator, and painter
MEDIA: Oil, charcoal, and bone
EXHIBITS: Veterinarian's Art Exhibit, Pullman, WA; see also Awards
SOLO EXHIBITS: MPI
AWARDS: Palouse Empire Fair, Colfax, WA ('75, 1st; '76, 1st; '77, 1st; '78, 1st; '79, 1st; '80, Best of Show)

PAI-TU-MU (see Thompson, Robert)

PAJOMA, PENI *Tesuque*

PUBLISHED: Snodgrass (1968)
PUBLIC COLLECTIONS: MNM

PALADIN, DAVID CHETHLAHE *Navajo*

Chethlahe, Little Turtle Who Cries in the Night
Born 1926 at Canyon de Chelly, AZ; died 19 Dec 1984 in Albuquerque, NM
RESIDENCE: Lived in Albuquerque, NM
MILITARY: U.S. Army, WW II, prisoner of war 2½ years
EDUCATION: Santa Fe; City College, San Mateo, CA; California School of Fine Arts, Oakland, CA; CAI; studied with Marc Chagall and Mark Tobey
OCCUPATION: Sailor, window designer, broadcaster, teacher, writer, Unitarian minister, lecturer, sculptor, jeweler, and painter
MEDIA: Oil, acrylic, watercolor, sand, clay, bonding substances, glycerin, pigment, mixed-media, and prints
PUBLISHED: Snodgrass (1968); Tanner (1968); Brody (1971); New and Young (1976), cover; Houlihan and Schmid (1979); Medina (1981); Chase (1982); Paladin (1992). *The Arizona Republic* (17 Mar 1968); *Arkansas Teacher* (Dec 1970); *The Prescott Courier* (10 Aug 1974; 19 Dec 1975); *Ford Times* (Aug 1976), cover; *Outdoor Arizona* (Mar 1977); *Southwest Art* (Apr 1977); *American Indian Art* (spring 1977); *Arizona Arts and Lifestyles* (spring 1980); *The Santa Fean* (July 1981), cover; *Art Voices* (Sept/Oct 1981); *Plateau* (Vol. 54, no. 1, 1982); *The Albuquerque Journal* (18 Oct 1983); *Art-Talk* (Mar 1984; Mar 1985); *The Indian Trader* (Feb 1985); biographical publications
COMMISSIONS: *Murals:* Howard Johnson's, Southfield, MI, 1968; La Casa Vieja Restaurant, Tempe, AZ, 1971; Quinta El Santuario, Prescott, AZ, 1981. *Posters:* Scottsdale (AZ) Arts Festival VI, 1975; Germaine Monteil Cosmetics; Studio Southwest, Scottsdale, AZ four posters, 1983. *Other:* UNICEF, Christmas card designs, 1970; City of Phoenix, AZ, four tapestries, 1972; Foundation for Blind Children, Christmas card designs, 1975; Cannon River Mills, fabric designs, 1977; New Mexico Easter Seals, Christmas card designs, 1978; Iliff School of Theology, catalog covers, 1981, 1983

LARRY GRANT PAISLEY

In addition to paintings on canvas, Paisley paints Indian portraits and wildlife scenes on sun-bleached shoulder blades taken from rangeland bone piles found in western Montana. His preference for painting portraits of Indians and western characters reflects his early fascination with the work of Charles Russell.

brochure, MPI, 1982

PENI PAJOMA

"Paintings by the artist are said to be dated as early as 1920."

Snodgrass 1968

DAVID CHETHLAHE PALADIN

Paladin gave credit to the influence of Mark Tobey, Morris Graves, and Marc Chagall for influencing him to abandon his early traditional style of painting and embark on a more contemporary style. While still a student, Paladin met Marc Chagall at an exhibition of the artist's works at the Chicago Art Institute. Chagall encouraged him to use his Navajo heritage but not to illustrate anything, instead he should listen to the story, dream it, and paint it. The influence of Mark Tobey and Morris Graves, whom he met in Portland, Oregon, led him to experiment with texture, mixing clay, sand, and mud, and adding them to his paintings. In the early 1950s, while experimenting with other styles, he did some paintings in the Santa Fe Studio style, "just to survive."

Arizona Arts and Lifestyle
spring 1980

PUBLIC COLLECTIONS: ABQM; AC/RM; Carnegie; CBMM; HCC; HM; MFA/B; MFA/CI; MMA/MN; MNM; MRFM; NTM; PAM; SU; WWM; UNICEF; USDI; USDS; Detroit (MI) Institute of Fine Arts; Phoenix (AZ) Civic Center Concert Hall; San Francisco Palace of the Legion of Honor; United Nations; West Texas Museum, Lubbock, TX; William Penn Memorial Museum, Harrisburg, PA; Scottsdale, AZ; Phoenix, AZ; Albuquerque, NM; Harrisburg, PA; State of PA; corporate collections in the U.S. and abroad

EXHIBITS: Partial listing of 46 includes: ABQM; ACMWA; AICA; ASM; FNAA; HM; ISU; LGAM; MCC/CA; NAP; NTM; OWE; PAC; IPCC; SDMM; SN; U of N AZ; WWM; Charles Bowers Memorial Museum, Santa Ana, CA; Yavapai College, Prescott, AZ; Prescott (AZ) Fine Arts Association

SOLO EXHIBITS: HM; MFA/CI; Pittsburgh Educational Institute, 1969; William Penn Memorial Museum, Harrisburg, PA, 1969; Center for American Indian Arts, New York, NY, 1975

AWARDS: AICA ('78, Gold Medal); SN ('67, 1st, Special Award, experimental; '68, Jacobson Award; '70, *Phoenix Gazette* Award; '71)

HONORS: *Newsweek*, cited as the nation's "leading Navajo modern artist," 1975; Carnegie Medal for Achievement in the Arts; Cambridge University, Distinguished Service to the Arts and Education Commendation, 1970; International Biographical Center, London, England, Distinguished Service in Education and the Arts, 1976, and Distinguished Achievement Award, 1976; Italian Academy of Art, Gold Medal, 1981; *Santa Fean Magazine,* Artist of the Year, 1981

Pale Moon, Princess (see Huser, Yvonne)

Palmanteer, Theodore (see Palmenteer, Theodore)

Palmanteer, Theodore *Colville/Nez Percé*

A.K.A. Theodore Palmenteer

Born 28 June 1943

RESIDENCE: Nespelem, WA

MILITARY: U.S. Army, Vietnam, 1967-1969, wounded

EDUCATION: IAIA, 1962-1963; B.A., Central Washington University, Ellensburg, WA, 1973

OCCUPATION: Teacher and painter

MEDIA: Acrylic plastic, hide, and mixed-media

PUBLISHED: Snodgrass (1968). *Southwestern Art* (Vol. 2, no. 1, 1967); *YAIA Catalog*

EXHIBITS: IAIA, MNM, OGC, SFFA, YAIA

SOLO EXHIBITS: MPI

Palmer, Dixon *Kiowa/Choctaw*

Tsain-Sah-Hay, Blue Hail

Born 20 Sept 20 in Anadarko, OK

RESIDENCE: Anadarko, OK

MILITARY: U.S. Army, WWII

EDUCATION: St. Patrick's, 1938

OCCUPATION: Guide and assistant manager at Indian City U.S.A. (Anadarko, OK), employee of Riverside Indian School, dancer, craftsman, artist

PUBLISHED: Snodgrass (1968); Blackboy, et al. (1973); Maurer (1992)

COMMISSIONS: Oklahoma Indian Arts and Crafts, Anadarko, OK, Kiowa tipi, 1973; MIA, tipi

EXHIBITS: PAC, SPIM, VP

SOLO EXHIBITS: SPIM

PALMER, IGNATIUS *Mescalero Apache*

Born 1921 at Mescalero, NM

RESIDENCE: Mescalero, NM

MILITARY: U.S. Army Air Corps, WWII

EDUCATION: Santa Fe

OCCUPATION: Construction worker and painter

MEDIA: Casein

PUBLISHED: Snodgrass (1968); Brody (1971); Tanner (1973); Highwater (1976); Fawcett and Callander (1982); Seymour (1988; 1993). *The Indian Trader* (Mar 1988)

BOOKS ILLUSTRATED: Bent-Mescalero (NM) Elementary School, Apache stories for bilingual classes

COMMISSIONS: *Murals:* Bent-Mescalero (NM) Elementary School; Maisel's Indian Trading Post, Albuquerque, NM, 1939. *Other:* Mescalero Apache Tribe, NM

PUBLIC COLLECTIONS: IACB/DC, LMA/BC, MAI, MNM, UPA, WOM, WWM

EXHIBITS: HM, MNM, MAI, NMSF, PAC, SN, WRTD

AWARDS: NMSF, SN

PALMER, WOODROW WILSON *Miami/Peoria*

Katahke, Loon

Born 1 Dec 1916 in Miami, OK; son of Ada Moore, second chief of the Peoria tribe, 1930-1951, and Harvey T. Palmer (Spotted Loon), Miami Chief, 1910-1963

RESIDENCE: Colorado Springs, CO

MILITARY: U.S. Navy, WWII, Korean War

EDUCATION: Seneca, 1931; Haskell, 1932-1933; graduated Sherman, 1934; studied mural painting under Harold Ashodian, landscape painting under Elton Furlong, and anatomy under Karnig Nalbandian, Providence, RI

OCCUPATION: Newspaper columnist, proofreader, and painter

PUBLISHED: Snodgrass (1968)

COMMISSIONS: *Murals:* Club El Rio, Providence, RI; Baby Grande Lounge, Providence, RI; Celebrity Club, Providence, RI; Jimmy's Place, Providence, RI; Louis Monterio, private residence, Providence, RI

PUBLIC COLLECTIONS: GM

EXHIBITS: BNIAS; ITIC; MNM; PAC; SN; Contemporary Artists of Rhode Island; Providence (RI) Art Club; Boston (MA) Arts Festival

WOODROW WILSON PALMER

Palmer's paternal grandfather was Chief T. F. Richardville, who named the town of Miami, OK, and secured land from the government for the purpose of founding Bacone College. His maternal grandfather, Senator James K. Moore, was a charter member of Oklahoma's Legislature in 1907. His great grandfather was Peshewa (or Richardville), nephew of Little Turtle, who defeated General Washington, and General St. Clair.

"Palmer is the inventor of 'dualism,' a modern painting style using Indian motifs. Its fundamental stages are a careful underpainting with wax and an overlay of the initial composition with a major theme. The final step is the engraving or scoring of the overlay, causing a release of the 'inner light' and an orchestration of color over the entire work. For the most part the palette consists of the primary colors and black."

Snodgrass 1968

PANAMICK, MARTIN *Ojibwa*

Born 1956 on Manitoulin Island, ON, Canada, on the West Bay Reserve; died June 1977

EDUCATION: Manitou Arts Foundation, summer 1972

OCCUPATION: Painter

MEDIA: Acrylic

PUBLISHED: Southcott (1984)

COMMISSIONS: Ojibwa Cultural Foundation, logo

PUBLIC COLLECTIONS: C/ROM

EXHIBITS: C/AG/TB, C/CNAC, C/ROM

MARTIN PANAMICK

At one time Panamick was the official artist of the Ojibwa Cultural Foundation at West Bay. His designs were used in educational materials and for various commercial products. He was killed early in his career in a motorcycle/school bus accident.

Southcott 1984

PANANA, GERALD *Jémez*

EDUCATION: Jémez

PUBLISHED: Snodgrass (1968)

EXHIBITS: MNM

AWARDS: MNM

PANANA, SOPHIE *Jémez*
Born 1945
EDUCATION: Jémez
PUBLISHED: Snodgrass (1968)
PUBLIC COLLECTIONS: MNM
EXHIBITS: PAC

PANANA, VERONICA *Jémez*
Born 1945
PUBLISHED: Snodgrass (1968)
EXHIBITS: MNM, PAC

PANINGAJAK, TIVI (see Paningina, Tva)

PANINGINA, TIVA *Inuit (Eskimo)*
A.K.A. Tiva Paningina; Tivi Paningajak
Born 1917
RESIDENCE: Canada
PUBLISHED: North (Mar/Apr 1974)
EXHIBITS: C/AG/WP; Robertson Galleries, Ottawa, ON

PAN YO PIN (see Vigil, Thomas)

PA O KELO *Pueblo*
PUBLISHED: Snodgrass (1968)
PUBLIC COLLECTIONS: AF

PAPERK, JOSIE *Inuit (Eskimo)*
A.K.A. Josie Papialuk; Josie Papi
Born 1918
RESIDENCE: Povungnituk, PQ, Canada
OCCUPATION: Graphic artist
MEDIA: Pen and ink, crayon, and prints
PUBLISHED: Larmour (1967); Goetz, et al. (1977); Myers, ed. (1980); McMasters, et al. (1993). *Arts West* (Vol. 3, no. 5, 1978)
PUBLIC COLLECTIONS: C/TDB
EXHIBITS: C/AG/WP, C/CIIA, C/EACTDB, C/TIP, C/TMBI, C/U of R/MG

JOSIE PAPERK

Known for his humor and whimsy, Paperk's drawings are frequently of his favorite subjects, tattooed faces, wavy lines, and birds.

Goetz, et al. 1977

Intangible elements (speech, footprints, wind and motion patterns) were often included in his paintings through the use of color, vibrating lines, etc.

PAPI, JOSIE (see Paperk, Josie)

PAPIALUK, JOSIE (see Paperk, Josie)

PAPPIO, BUDDY *Kiowa*
EXHIBITS: AIE
AWARDS: AIE ('76; '78, 1st; '79, 1st)

PARACLITA, SISTER MARY *Shoshoni/Bannock*
Butterfly
A.K.A. Eula Cosgrove
Born 1904 on the Fort Hall Reservation, ID
EDUCATION: St. Mary of the Wasatch, Salt Lake City, UT; St. Mary's, IN; Holy Names, Oakland, CA; B.F.A., U of UT
OCCUPATION: Holy orders, art teacher, beadworker, and painter
MEDIA: Oil, watercolor, tempera, pen and ink, pastel, pencil, charcoal, and beads
PUBLISHED: Ray, ed. (1972)
EXHIBITS: CIA; throughout California and Utah
AWARDS: Multiple

PARA DAS, RENA (see Paradis, Rena)

PARADIS, RENA *Navajo*

A.K.A. Rena Para Das
RESIDENCE: Tucson, AZ
Born 1945
EDUCATION: Roosevelt High School, Seattle, WA, 1961
OCCUPATION: Co-owner of Las Canastas Shop, ceramist, and painter
PUBLISHED: Snodgrass (1968). *The Navajo Times* (2 Jan 1964)

PARKS *Delaware (?)*

MEDIA: Pencil and crayon
PUBLISHED: Snodgrass (1968)
PUBLIC COLLECTIONS: U of PA/M (pencil and crayon drawings of the Bear Feast, 1930)

PARR *Inuit (Eskimo)*

Born 1893 in a remote campsite on the southern shore of Baffin Island, NWT, Canada; died 3 Nov 1969; husband of Eleeshushe (q.v.)
RESIDENCE: Lived in Cape Dorset, NWT, Canada
OCCUPATION: Hunter, fisherman, and graphic artist
MEDIA: Graphite pencil and prints
PUBLISHED: Houston (1967a); Larmour (1967); Burland (1973); Blodgett (1978b); LaBarge (1986); Jackson and Nasby (1987). *Artscanada* (Vol. 28, no. 6, 1971-1972); *The Beaver* (spring 1975); *Courier*, UNESCO (Jan 1976)
PUBLIC COLLECTIONS: C/AC/MS; C/CMC; C/INAC; C/TDB; C/WBEC; DAM; Inuit Gallery, Toronto, ON
EXHIBITS: C/AC/MS, C/AG/WP, C/CD, C/CID, C/EACTDB, C/GM, C/NGCA, C/TIP, GM

PARR, ELEESHUSHE (see Eleeshushe)

PARR, QUIVIANATULIAK *Inuit (Eskimo)*

A.K.A. Kovinatilliak; Kovinatilliah
Born 1930; son of Eleeshushe (q.v.) and Parr (q.v.)
RESIDENCE: Cape Dorset, NWT, Canada
OCCUPATION: Graphic artist
PUBLISHED: Larmour (1967). *Artscanada* (Vol. 28, no. 6, 1971-1972)
PUBLIC COLLECTIONS: C/TDB
EXHIBITS: C/EACTDB, C/WBEC

PARSONS, NEIL *Blackfeet*

O'mahk-pitawa, Tall Eagle
A.K.A. Little Dog
Born 2 Mar 1938 in Browning, MT; son of Florence DeGuire and Henry Parsons; GGGGF: Chief Tall Eagle
RESIDENCE: Browning, MT
EDUCATION: Browning (MT) High School, 1956; B.A., MSU, 1961; M.A., MSU, 1964
OCCUPATION: Art director, consultant, educator, and painter
MEDIA: Oil, acrylic, pencil, pastel, mixed-media, and prints
PUBLISHED: Snodgrass (1968); Brody (1971); Ray, ed. (1972); New (1976; 1979; 1981); Highwater (1980); Amerson, ed. (1981); Bivens (1983); Hoffman, et al. (1984); Longfish, et al. (1986); Roberts, ed. (1992). *Art In America* (July/Aug

RENA PARADIS

"The artist has received no formal art education other than a one-year high school art class. She particularly enjoys painting children in non-traditional Indian style because 'they don't hide their feelings. . . .'"

Snodgrass 1968

PARR

As a young man, Parr suffered frostbite that caused the partial amputation of one foot and incapacitated him for the hunt. He was sixty-eight years old when he began to draw in 1961, shortly before he moved to Cape Dorset. He developed pneumonia in 1962 and spent a year in a hospital in Brandon, Manitoba. In spite of this, Parr produced more than 2,000 drawings before he died in 1969. According to LaBarge (1986), "For Parr, the act of drawing was an emotive affirmation of the Inuit world." Parr's drawings are known for their rough direct style similar to ancient pictographs. To him only the story told by his drawings was important, not the technique.

NEIL PARSONS

Parsons has been quoted as saying of his singular painting style, ". . . The idea of abstract Indian painting took form as a result of a change in attitude. Earlier, it had seemed that in order to succeed in painting it would be necessary for me to overcome the compulsions of my
(continued)

1972); *Arizona Arts and Lifestyle* (autumn 1981); *Artspace* (Dec 1981); *Native Arts/West* (Apr 1981); *American Indian Art* (spring 1986); *Phoenix Magazine* (Sept 1989)

COMMISSIONS: MPI, four-part abstract composition, 1964

PUBLIC COLLECTIONS: AC/SL, BIA, HM, IAIA, IACB, MMA/WA, NDN, PAIC

EXHIBITS: AC/T; AICH; ASPS; BBHC; BM/B; CCAC/MT; CIA; CIAE/MT; CTC; DAM; DAM/I; EIAF; HM; HM/G; HSM/MT; IK; IPSE; KCPA; MNM; MAI; MMA/WA; NACLA; NAVAM; NDN; NU/BC; OLO; OSU/G; OU/MA; OWE; PAIC; PAM; RC; SAIEAIP; SAM; SCG; SFFA; SI; SN; SS/CW,;U of WA/HAG; USDI; international festivals in Berlin, Germany, and Tokyo, Japan; see also Awards

SOLO EXHIBITS: AC/RM; AC/Y; CCAC/MT; MPI; Lewiston (MT) Art Center; Paris-Gibson Square, Great Falls, MT

AWARDS: HM/G; Inter-Mountain Printmaker's Exhibit, Salt Lake City, UT

HONORS: NAA, featured artist, 1985

PATKOTAK, PAUL *Eskimo*

Born 24 Nov 1892 in Snowhouse, Alaska, on the Utukok River; death date unknown

RESIDENCE: Lived in Wainwright, AK

OCCUPATION: Village marshal, carver, and graphic artist

MEDIA: Oil, watercolor, ink, sealskin, and ivory

PUBLISHED: Snodgrass (1968)

EXHIBITS: PAC; Alaska Native Service Office, Juneau, AK; Wainwright (AK) Day School

PATTERSON, GEORGE W. PATRICK (see Patterson, Pat)

PATTERSON, PAT *Apache/Seneca*

Kemoha, Lonesome Polecat

A.K.A. George W. Patrick Patterson

Born 29 Dec 1914 in Centralia, IL

RESIDENCE: Bartlesville, OK

EDUCATION: B.F.A., U of OK, 1940

OCCUPATION: Museum director and painter

PUBLISHED: Ke Motta (1952); Snodgrass (1968)

COMMISSIONS: *Murals:* St. John's Church, Bartlesville, OK. *Other:* more than five hundred portraits

PATTERSON, ROSEMARY *Seneca*

Born 4 Dec 1952

RESIDENCE: Salamanca, NY

OCCUPATION: Sculptor, jeweler, beadworker, teacher, and painter

MEDIA: Oil, acrylic, watercolor, tempera, charcoal, pencil, sterling silver, turquoise, petrified wood, soapstone, and beads

PUBLISHED: Johannsen and Ferguson, eds. (1983)

EXHIBITS: ECFE; Indian Fall Festival, Cattaraugus, NY

PATTON, KENNETH (see Patton, Wade)

PATTON, WADE *Oglala Sioux*

A.K.A. Kenneth Wade Patton

Born 23 Jan 1966 on the Pine Ridge Reservation, SD

RESIDENCE: Rapid City, SD

EDUCATION: Central High School, Rapid City, SD; B.F.A., BHSU, 1991

NEIL PARSONS

(continued) Indian background, and try to lose my identity with that tradition in the overwhelming atmosphere of a big, modern city. However, I gradually realized that the forces of a motivating atmosphere like the city, and those of an individual's background are two different things; and that I might be able to express myself through the use of traditional Indian cultural ideas in an intellectualized contemporary manner."

Amerson, ed. 1981

As an educator, Parsons is highly praised by his colleagues for his ability to encourage and inspire his students.

PAUL PATKOTAK

"Patkotak is a self-taught artist. In 1958, he said, 'I do not draw anymore. My eyes are getting dull.' At one time in his career his work sold well at Point Barrow, Alaska."

Snodgrass 1968

According to Snodgrass-King, in 1948, when it was time to receive art work for the Philbrook Art Center's Indian Annual, Patkotak's paintings were the first to arrive. She was very impressed, this being his first time to enter and, in spite of living in an isolated area far removed from Tulsa, Oklahoma, his paintings arrived not only on time but early.

Snodgrass-King, p.c. 1994

OCCUPATION: Commercial artist and painter
MEDIA: Oil, acrylic, watercolor, graphite, and prints
PUBLIC COLLECTIONS: HCC
EXHIBITS: BHSU, LSS, RC
SOLO EXHIBITS: SIM
AWARDS: BHSU ('88, 1st, Viewer's Choice); RC ('91; '94, Barkley Art Center Award)
HONORS: *Scholarships:* Crazy Horse Memorial Foundation; BHSU, Fine Arts Scholarship; RC, Thunderbird Foundation Scholarships, 1990, 1991

PAUKEI (see Paukei, George)

PAUKEI, GEORGE *Kiowa*
Paukei, Gifts (or Donations)
Born 1918 in Anadarko, OK
EDUCATION: Mountain View (OK) Public School
OCCUPATION: Electrician and painter
PUBLISHED: Snodgrass (1968)
PUBLIC COLLECTIONS: ACM
EXHIBITS: AIE, PAC
AWARDS: AIE

PAUL, LAWRENCE B. *Coast Salish/Okanagan/Cowichan*
Yuxweluptun
A.K.A. Lawrence Paul Yuxweluptun
Born 1957 in Kamloops, BC, Canada
RESIDENCE: Vancouver, BC, Canada
EDUCATION: Graduated with honors, Emily Carr College of Art and Design, Vancouver, BC, 1983
MEDIA: Acrylic
PUBLISHED: Hoffman (1988); Gerber and Katz (1989); Douglas, ed.(1991). *The Vancouver Sun* (21 Mar 1985); *America West Airlines Magazine* (Oct 1987); *The Seattle Post-Intelligencer* (Apr 1989); *Western News* (19 July 1989); *Newsletter,* NASAC/ACEAA (winter 1991); *American Indian Art* (autumn 1992)
COMMISSIONS: Arts Umbrella Auction, banner, 1985; Arts Umbrella Auction, fan, 1986
PUBLIC COLLECTIONS: C/INAC; PAC; Staatliche Museum; Preussischer Kulturbesitz, Berlin, West Germany; Museum für Völkerkunde, Berlin, Germany.
EXHIBITS: C/AG/V; C/CMC; C/I; C/INAC; C/NMC; C/RSMC; HM; SAM; SCG; WNAA; British Columbia Festival of Arts, Prince George, BC; Downtown Eastside Festival, Vancouver, BC, 1986; Warehouse Show, Vancouver, BC, 1984
SOLO EXHIBITS: National Native Indian Artists' Symposium; two in Vancouver, BC
HONORS: First Citizen's Fund, Victoria, BC, 1983

PAUL, LEONARD *Micmac*
Born 1953 in Halifax, NS, Canada
RESIDENCE: Wolfville, NS, Canada
EDUCATION: B.F.A., Arcadia University; C/NSCAD, 1975
OCCUPATION: Painter
MEDIA: Oil, acrylic, watercolor, pencil, pastel, and prints
PUBLISHED: *The Halifax Mail Star* (15 Mar 1978); *The Halifax Chronicle Herald* (18 Nov 1983); *The Daily News* (15 Mar 1985)

PAT PATTERSON

"Patterson's father was a 'frustrated artist' who rebelled at long hours of practice and ran away to join a circus as a balloonjumper and wirewalker. Pat was born on the old Sells-Floto Circus circuit enroute to an Illinois engagement. Pat's father decided his son would be the artist he had not been and proceeded to expose him to every teacher available."

Snodgrass 1968

WADE PATTON

Patton gives credit to the "pop art" movement for his inspiration. His work is Indian only in the sense that he uses Native American imagery.

brochure, SIM, 1992

LAWRENCE B. PAUL

Much of Paul's work concerns Native social issues. His paintings are commonly done on a large scale in vivid colors.

LEONARD PAUL

Paul says that art moves in stages, and the current stage is directly affected by those that came before. In Canada the previous stage was an experimental stage where major changes occurred. The current stage allows the individual artist the freedom to experiment with a wide variety of styles until he finds his own. Paul has chosen a realistic style for himself.

Art Amerindian '81, *Oct 1981 (Review by Rob Belfry)*

PUBLIC COLLECTIONS: C/AG/MSVU; C/INAC; C/NSAB; Boswick Brokers; Dofasco Steel Co.; Norcen Energy Resources, Co. Ltd.

EXHIBITS: C/AG/MSVU; C/CIIA; C/NAC; C/NWNG; C/WICEC; Arts Atlantic, 1977; galleries in Nova Scotia

SOLO EXHIBITS: C/AG/MSVU; C/AG/NS; C/MFA/NS; galleries in Halifax and Wolfville, NS

PAUL, MICHAEL M. *Colville*

Swoo-Whee-Ya, Red Ant

Born 23 June 1936 in Inchelium, WA

MILITARY: U.S. Army, 1958-1960

EDUCATION: Coulee Dam (WA) High School, 1957; Wenatchee (WA) Valley Junior College, 1960-1961; Academy of Art College, San Francisco, CA, 1964-1966; Gonzaga University, Spokane, WA, 1970-1971

OCCUPATION: Aircraft worker, lumber company sawyer, journeyman painter, teacher, drum and dance instructor, Indian curriculum developer, author, sculptor, and painter

MEDIA: Acrylic, mixed-media, and stone

BOOKS ILLUSTRATED: Spokane (WA) school system, textbooks

COMMISSIONS: *Murals:* Spokane (WA) school system, three murals, 1976; American Indian Community Center, Spokane, WA, 1976

EXHIBITS: IFA

SOLO EXHIBITS: MPI

AWARDS: IFA ('68, Grand Award; '69, Grand Award; '70, Grand Award)

HONORS: Ford Foundation Fellowship Award, 1969-1970

PAUL, TIM *Kwakwaka'wakw (Kwakiutl)*

Born 1950 in Zaballos, Vancouver Island, BC, Canada

EDUCATION: Apprenticed to John Livingston, Gene Brabant (q.v.), and Richard Hunt (q.v.)

OCCUPATION: Lumberjack, museum artist, carver, graphic artist, and painter

MEDIA: Wood, paint, and prints

PUBLISHED: Stewart (1979); Macnair, Hoover, and Neary (1980); Gerber and Bruggmann (1989). *Sound Heritage* (Vol. 7, no. 2, 1978)

PUBLIC COLLECTIONS: C/INAC, C/RBCM, HCC

EXHIBITS: AUG, BHSU, C/TL, HCC, NSU/SD, SDSMT, WTF

PAULL, PERCY *Coast Salish*

MEDIA: Acrylic

PUBLIC COLLECTIONS: C/RBCM

PAUNICHIAK *Inuit (Eskimo)*

Born 1920; died 1968

RESIDENCE: Lived in Cape Dorset, NWT, Canada

PUBLISHED: Blodgett (n.d.)

PUBLIC COLLECTIONS: C/TDB

EXHIBITS: C/AG/WP, C/EACTDB, C/LS

PAUTA *Inuit (Eskimo)*

Born 1916

RESIDENCE: Cape Dorset, NWT, Canada

OCCUPATION: Sculptor and graphic artist

MEDIA: Felt tip pen

PUBLISHED: Houston (1967a); Larmour (1967); Goetz, et al. (1977); Collinson (1978). *The Beaver* (spring 1975)
PUBLIC COLLECTIONS: C/TDB, C/U of AB
EXHIBITS: C/CD; C/CG; C/EACTDB; C/TIP; Sculpture of the Inuit, international tour

PAYTIAMO, JAMES P. *Acoma*
Flaming Arrow
EDUCATION: Haskell
OCCUPATION: Instructor, entertainer, author, illustrator, and painter
PUBLISHED: Paytiamo (1932); Snodgrass (1968)

JAMES P. PAYTIAMO

"The author-illustrator has recorded many of the Pueblo folk tales for Columbia University, later published in the American Folk Lore Journal. He is a well-known entertainer who has traveled with his own Pueblo company under the Swarthmore Chautauqua."

Snodgrass 1968

PAYTON, TRESA LYNN *Cherokee*
RESIDENCE: Tulsa, OK
EDUCATION: Tulsa (OK) Christian Academy
EXHIBITS: AAID, FCTM, PAC, RC
AWARDS: FCTM

PAZ (see Dittbenner, Carol)

PAZ, CAROL (see Dittbenner, Carol)

PEARCE, JESSIE *Mohawk*
Born 1948
EDUCATION: Cayuga Technical Commercial High School, 1962-1966; C/OCA, 1968-1972
OCCUPATION: Arts and crafts instructor, draftswoman, color coordinator for architect, craftswoman, and painter
MEDIA: Acrylic, macramé yarn, leather, and reed
PUBLISHED: Johannsen and Ferguson (1983)

JESSIE PEARCE

Painting in acrylics, Pearce has developed a style reminiscent of Andrew Wyeth's. She is also an accomplished crafts person and enjoys teaching and encouraging others to develop their talents.

Johannsen and Ferguson 1983

PEBEAHSY, CHARLES *Comanche/Wichita*
RESIDENCE: Norman, OK
OCCUPATION: Sculptor and painter
MEDIA: Acrylic and clay
EXHIBITS: AIE, HM/G
AWARDS: AIE ('80, 1st; '81, 1st)

PECOS, JOSÉ D. *Cochití*
PUBLISHED: Snodgrass (1968)
EXHIBITS: AIEC

PEEN TSEH (see Trujillo, Manuel)

PEINA, DAN *Zuni*
PUBLISHED: Snodgrass (1968)
EXHIBITS: FWG

PEÑA, AMADO MAURILIO, JR. *Yaqui*
Born 1 Oct 1943 ; son of María and Amado Peña; P/GP: Guadalupe and Eduardo Peña; M/GF: Matias Arambula
RESIDENCE: Austin, TX
MILITARY: U.S. Army, National Guard of Texas
EDUCATION: Martin High School, Laredo, TX, 1961; Laredo (TX) Junior College; B.A., TAIU, 1965; M.A., TAIU, 1971
OCCUPATION: Teacher and artist

Amado Maurilio Peña Jr.

Many of Peña's early works were concerned with the Chicano political movements. His more recent paintings contain Mexican and American Indian motifs. The re-occurrence of a modeled, angular face makes his work instantly identifiable. In recent years, his faces are usually facing the viewers left. He uses these profiled figures as a means of simplifying and communicating the individual's essence or story to the public. Peña has explained that the source of his profiled figures is the mestizo, the blending of Indian and Mexican.

Southwest Art, *Aug 1990*

MEDIA: Acrylic, pencil, pen and ink, mixed-media, and prints

PUBLISHED: Anderson (1981); Samuels (1982). *Southwest Art* (Nov 1979; Aug 1990); *Four Winds* (1980); *The Arizona Republic* (7 Jan 1983; 6 Dec 1984); *Art-Talk* (June/July, 1983; Oct, 1983; Nov, 1983; Dec, 1983; Mar 1984; Aug/Sept 1986; Mar, 1987; Oct, 1987; June/July 1989); *The Scottsdale Progress* (23 Jan 1983); *The Santa Fe Reporter* (15 Aug 1984; 19 Aug 1987); *Art Gallery* (Apr/May 1985); *The Phoenix Gazette* (13 Mar 1987; 21 May 1988); *The Santa Fean* (Oct 1987); *The Indian Trader* (May 1988; June 1990); *Scottsdale Magazine* (spring 1991); *The Dallas Morning News* (24 Oct 1993); biographical publications

COMMISSIONS: *Paintings:* TAIU, 1988; U of TX Nursing School, 1988. *Posters:* LGAM, 1988; Austin (TX) Community College, 1988; Goldwater's Department Stores, 1988

PUBLIC COLLECTIONS: SI

EXHIBITS: ABQM; ACAI; AIAF; CIM; LACM; LGAM; MCC/CA; MFA/EP; NCHF; SFFA; SI; SWAIA; TMA/AZ; WWM; Dine'Bi'Keyah Museum, Page, AZ; galleries throughout the U.S.; see also Awards

SOLO EXHIBITS: Partial listing of more than one hundred includes: MFA/S; MNAC; NM HIGHLANDS U; SCA; TAIU; WSU/P; Americana Museum, El Paso, TX; Nuevo Santander Museum, Loredo, TX

AWARDS: LGAM, ('82, Citation Award); Mead Paper, Austin, TX ('82, Award of Merit); Printing Industries of America, Inc. ('83, Graphic Arts Award)

HONORS: City of Austin (TX), Distinguished Service Award, 1976; American Bicentennial in Austin (TX) Committee, Distinguished Service Award, 1976; Corpus Christi (TX) Foundation Award, 1979; Maricopa Foundation For Community Colleges, Phoenix, AZ, Appreciation Award, 1983; Laredo (TX) Chamber of Commerce Recognition Award, 1983; Caminos, Los Angeles, CA, Hispanic of the Year Award (nominee); Austin (TX) Independent School District, Hispanic Heritage Award, 1983; City of Austin (TX) Recognition of Contributions and Proclamation, 1983; Dieciseis de Septiembre Sobresaliente Award, Laredo, TX, 1985; Guadalupe Cultural Art Center, San Antonio, TX, Award for Outstanding Contributions, 1985; City of Austin (TX), Amado M. Peña Day, 1985; City of Laredo (TX), Amado M. Peña Day; Tejano Achievement Award, San Antonio, TX; Austin (TX) Walk of Fame, name added, 1994

PEÑA, BEN *Cochití*

PUBLIC COLLECTIONS: MNA

José Encarnación Peña

"... Peña was painting in the early 1920s and was still active in 1968."

Snodgrass 1968

Jeanne Snodgrass-King described Peña's work as somewhat primitive in appearance with the faces and especially the noses out of proportion to the rest of the figure. When he painted multiple figures they were "carbon copies" of one another.

p.c. 1993

PEÑA, CHRISTINO *San Ildefonso*

Soqueen

Born 24 Nov 1942(?) at San Ildefonso Pueblo, NM; son of José Encarnación Peña (q.v.)

RESIDENCE: Santa Fe, NM

EDUCATION: Pojoaque (NM) School, ca. 1957; U of AZ, "Southwest Indian Art Project," scholarship, summers 1960, 1961 (textiles major)

MEDIA: Watercolor

PUBLISHED: Dunn (1968); Snodgrass (1968); Brody (1971)

PUBLIC COLLECTIONS: HM

PEÑA, JOSÉ ENCARNACIÓN *San Ildefonso*

Soukwawe, Frost on the Mountain

A.K.A. Enky; So Kwa A Weh. Signatures: Soqween; Soqueen

Born 25 Mar 1902 at San Ildefonso Pueblo, NM; died 19 Oct 1979 at Cochití Pueblo, NM; nephew of María Martínez, potter

EDUCATION: Santa Fe

MEDIA: Watercolor

PUBLISHED: Alexander (1932); Dunn (1968); Snodgrass (1968); Brody (1971); Tanner (1973); Schmid and Houlihan (1979); King (1981). *Pueblo Horizons* (Dec 1979)

COMMISSIONS: *Murals:* IPCC

PUBLIC COLLECTIONS: CGFA, CMA, DAM, MAI, MFA/H, MNA, MNM, MRFM, RAM, SM

EXHIBITS: ASM, DAM, JGS, MNM, NAP, PAC, SWAIA

AWARDS: MNM ('57, "Best example of original use of traditional material"); SWAIA ('78)

PEÑA, TONITA *San Ildefonso*

Quah Ah, White Coral Beads; *Qua H Ah*

A.K.A. Tonita Vigil Peña; Tonita Chávez; Tonita Herrera; Tonita A. Peña; Tonita P. Arquero; Tonita Peña A.; baptized, María Antonia Peña

Born 10 May 1893 at San Ildefonso Pueblo, NM; died 1 May 1949; daughter of Natividad Peña and Ascención Vigil; niece of Florention Montoya; After her mother's death when she was twelve years old, the artist was raised by her aunt, Martina Vigil of Cochití.

EDUCATION: San Ildefonso; St. Catherine's

OCCUPATION: Housewife, art instructor, and painter

MEDIA: Watercolor, tempera, and pencil

PUBLISHED: Sloan and LaFarge (1931); Underhill (1944); Jacobson and d'Ucel (1950); LaFarge (1960); Dunn (1968); Snodgrass (1968); Brody (1971; 1992); Tanner (1973); Monthan and Monthan (1975); Highwater (1976); Dockstader (1977); Silberman (1978); Schmid and Houlihan (1979); Broder (1981); Fawcett and Callander (1982); Hoffman, et al. (1984); Samuels (1985); Wade (1986); Seymour (1988); Gray (1990); Archuleta and Strickland (1991); Gully, ed. (1994). *The Christian Science Monitor* (20 May 1933); *The Arizona Republic* (17 Mar 1968); *The Indian Trader* (Oct 1990)

COMMISSIONS: *Murals:* James W. Young's Rancho La Cañada, ca. 1933; Society of Independent Artists, 1933; Chicago World's Fair; Santa Fe Indian School

PUBLIC COLLECTIONS: AC/RM, AF, BA/AZ, CAM/OH, CAMSL, CGA, CGFA, CGPS, CIS, CMA, DAM, DCC, GM, HM, MAI, MKMcNAI, MNA/KHC, MNH/A, MNH/CI, MNM/SAR, MRFM, MV, OU/MA, PAC, SAR, SM, U of CA/LMA, U of PA/M

EXHIBITS: AC/HC; AIEC; AIW; ASM; ASU/M; CGPS; EITA; HM; IK; ITIC; MFA/O; MNM; MV; NGA; NMSF; OMA; OU/ET; PAC; PM; SV; SWAIA; WWM; Whitney

AWARDS: EITA ('31, Best in the Show)

HONORS: One of the artists who made copies of the Pajarito murals on the Parajito Plateau north of Santa Fe, NM, preparatory to the restoration work; Exposition of Indian Tribal Arts, painting included, 1931

PENATAC, JOHN *Eskimo*

Born 1940 on King Island, AK

RESIDENCE: College, AK

EDUCATION: IAIA, 1963-1965; DCTP, 1964-65; Indian Arts and Crafts Board Demonstration-Workshop, Sitka, AK, 1967-1968; U of AK/C

PUBLISHED: Ray (1969)

PENINGINA, TIVA (see Paningina, Tva)

TONITA PEÑA

"Peña began painting when she was seven years old. Surrounded by artistic relatives, such as Martina Vigil the potter, it is not surprising that by the age of 21, she was selling and exhibiting widely. She was the only woman painter in her generation and was one of the original group who participated in the contemporary watercolor movement. Oscar B. Jacobson referred to her as the 'grand old lady of Pueblo art.' Peña often said that she preferred to paint children and animals. In 1934, Oren Arnold stated in the Los Angeles Times, *'The canvases of Miss Peña and her associates [Awa Tsireh, Fred Kabotie, and Oqwa Pi (qq.v.)] depict figures which are not unlike the figures of Greek vase painters.'"*

Snodgrass 1968

Peña signed her paintings in a variety of ways. At first her paintings were unsigned, then she signed "Tonita" to which she later added Quah Ah. For a time she used variations of her married names. Her later works were signed "Tonita Peña — Quah Ah" or "Tonita Peña Cochití Pueblo."

Brody 1992

The artist is the mother of Joe Herrera (q.v.), who is also well known because of his work as a teacher and for his innovative paintings.

ROBERT PENN

Penn has said of his art, "As a Native American living in modern society I have a dual role as artist and interpreter, and have attempted with my paintings to use contemporary forms to express cultural themes. As an artist it is my goal to expand and explore new ways of expressing the duality of my world through my art, translating into modern methods and materials, and propagating cultural arts by making them less separate and mysterious to the non-Indian audience. Abstraction of symbols and themes can re-interpret and integrate the modern world as seen from an Indian viewpoint without strict adherence to traditional art forms, and can transcend both worlds to become contemporary modern art as well as a cultural statement. This is what I hope to accomplish through my paintings."

artist brochure 1991

Penn is a member of the Dream Catchers Artists Guild, Ltd. (q.v.).

PENN, ROBERT *Brûlé Sioux/Omaha*

Wicanhpi, Star

Born 3 May 1946 in Omaha, NE; son of Cornelia Stead and Arthur Penn

RESIDENCE: Vermillion, SD

EDUCATION: St. Francis Mission High School, SD, 1966; B.F.A., U of SD, 1972; studied with Oscar Howe (q.v.) at U of SD

OCCUPATION: Illustrator, musician, art teacher; full-time painter since 1986

MEDIA: Oil, acrylic, pen and ink, and prints

PUBLISHED: Milton, ed. (1969); Libhart (1970); Maurer (1992). *South Dakota Review* (1969); *The Indian Trader* (Apr 1976); *Minnesota Monthly* (Mar 1990); *South Dakota Magazine* (July 1991); *The Bulletin* (Aug 1992)

COMMISSIONS: *Murals:* W. H. Over Museum, Vermillion, SD, 1972; Rosebud Hospital, 1989; U of SD, Lakota Dining Hall (also four round paintings), 1989; DIA, 1993

PUBLIC COLLECTIONS: AC/OH; CU/NE; HCC; IACB; MIA; SI; SIM; SJIS; U of SD; Rosebud (SD) Hospital; St. Joseph's Indian School, Chamberlain, SD

EXHIBITS: AICA/SF; CIM; CPS; HCC; LAC; NPTA; SI; SIM; SN; U of SD; VP; Dream Catchers Artists Guild, Ltd. exhibits

SOLO EXHIBITS: AC/OH; AICA/SF; AUG; CU/NE; FAC/D; SIM; U of ND; U of SD; Concordia College, St. Paul, MN, 1971; Macalester College, St. Paul, MN, 1971; Sioux Falls (SD) College, 1969; South Dakota State University, 1971; Yankton (SD) College, 1972

AWARDS: CIM ('86, Best of Category); NPTA

HONORS: South Dakota Governor's Award for Distinction in Creative Achievement in the Arts, 1992

PENNIER, GEORGE *Salish*

Born 20 Mar 1957 in Mission City, BC, Canada; cousin of Willis Peters, carver

RESIDENCE: Canada

EDUCATION: Studied under Tony Hunt (q.v.), 1980; worked with Floyd Joseph (q.v.); apprenticed under Beau Dick (q.v.) and Francis Horne

OCCUPATION: Carver and graphic artist

PUBLIC COLLECTIONS: HCC

EXHIBITS: BHSU, HCC

PENROD, MICHAEL *Apache*

RESIDENCE: Fort Apache, AZ

EDUCATION: ASU; U of AZ, "Southwest Indian Art Project," scholarship, summer 1962; Rochester, scholarship, 1962-1964

PUBLISHED: Snodgrass (1968)

PENTEWA, RICHARD SITKO *Hopi*

Sitsgoma, Pumpkin Flower

A.K.A. Richard S. Pentewa; Dick Pentewa

Born 12 Apr 1927 at New Oraibi, AZ; son of a *katsina* carver

RESIDENCE: Oraibi, AZ

EDUCATION: Hopi; OSU, 1957

PUBLISHED: Snodgrass (1968); Brody (1971); Tanner (1973); Broder (1981)

PUBLIC COLLECTIONS: GM, HM, MNA

EXHIBITS: ASF, ASM, ITIC, MNA, PAC

AWARDS: ASF, MAN

PENTEWA, RICHARD S. (see Pentewa, Dick R.)

PEN YO PIN (see Vigil, Thomas)

PEOPLE FROM THE GREEN VALLEY (see Sakyesva, Harry)

PEPHYRS, STEVEN G. *Assiniboin*

Birth date unknown; born in Seattle, WA

RESIDENCE: Seattle, WA

EDUCATION: G.E.D., 1982; U of WA

EXHIBITS: RC

PEPION, DAN, JR. *Blackfeet/Sioux*

Night Rider

Born 14 June 1947 in Browning, MT; son of Mary Gobert and Webb Pepion (q.v.), artists; P/GF: Webb Pepion; M/GP: Josephine Ball and Irvin Gobert

RESIDENCE: Valier, MT

MILITARY: U.S. Army, 1966-1969, Vietnam

EDUCATION: IAIA High School, 1965; IAIA, 1976-1978; Blackfeet Community Free School, Browning, MT, 1975; studied under Neil Parsons (q.v.)

OCCUPATION: Rancher, art instructor, surveyor, and painter

MEDIA: Oil, acrylic, watercolor, pencil, pen and ink, pastel, and prints

PUBLISHED: Snodgrass (1968); Ray, ed. (1972)

COMMISSIONS: Blackfeet Tribal Council, oil painting devoted to cultural documentation, 1979

PUBLIC COLLECTIONS: IAIA, IACB

EXHIBITS: CIA, IAIA, MPI, YAIA

SOLO/SPECIAL EXHIBITS: MPI (dual show)

PEPION, ERNEST *Blackfeet*

A.K.A. Ernie Pepion

Born 11 May 1943 in Browning, MT, on the Blackfeet Indian Reservation

RESIDENCE: Bozeman, MT

MILITARY: Vietnam, 1965-1967

EDUCATION: Valier (MT) High School, 1961; B.F.A, MSU, 1984; M.F.A., MSU, 1989

OCCUPATION: Carpenter, rancher, and painter

MEDIA: Oil, acrylic, watercolor, tempera, pastel, pencil, pen and ink, and charcoal

PUBLISHED: Ward, ed. (1990); Gentry, et al. (1990); Lippard (1990); Roberts, ed. (1992); Zurko, ed. (1992)

EXHIBITS: AC/Y; CWAM; CWY; EM; GFNAAS; MMA/MT; MR; MSU; NAAS; OLO; RC; SS/CW; U of ID/PG; WHB; Orlando (FL) Museum, 1988; Sweet Pea Festival Art Show, Bozeman, MT; The Couch House at the Rocks, Sydney, Australia, 1992; galleries in Montana; see also Awards

SOLO EXHIBITS: MMA/MT, MPI

AWARDS: MSU ('84); Sister Kenny Institute, Minneapolis, MN ('82, 1st, Most Promising Artist; '84, 1st, Best of Show)

HONORS: Montana Council for the Arts Fellowship

ERNEST PEPION

An auto accident in 1971 damaged Pepion's spine and left him a quadriplegic. While undergoing rehabilitation at the Veteran's Administration Rehabilitation Center in Long Beach, CA, he was taught the art of mixing colors by a veteran in an iron lung. With the aid of a brace and his teeth he mixed his own colors and took up painting. His subject matter is basically western and Native American and often is devoted to scenes of the Blackfeet Reservation.

brochure, MPI, 1989

PEPION, HOWARD *Blackfeet*

Born 1938 in Browning, MT, on the Blackfeet Indian Reservation; nephew of Victor Pepion (q.v.)

RESIDENCE: Browning, MT

MILITARY: U.S. Air Force

EDUCATION: Browning (MT) High School; Northern Montana College, Havre, MT, 1956; American School of Commercial Art, Dallas, TX, 1958-1960

HOWARD PEPION

Pepion paints realistic scenes of traditional Blackfeet activities.

Ray, ed. 1972

OCCUPATION: Commercial artist, sign painter, house painter, free-lance artist, museum employee, and painter

MEDIA: Oil, watercolor, tempera, casein, pen and ink, wash, pencil, charcoal, and prints

PUBLISHED: Ray, ed. (1972); Blackboy, et al. (1973)

COMMISSIONS: Oklahoma Indian Arts and Crafts Cooperative, Anadarko, OK, tipi, 1973

EXHIBITS: CIA, SPIM

PEPION, LEVI HENRY *Blackfeet*

Born 28 Oct 1948 in Browning, MT, on the Blackfeet Indian Reservation; son of Mildred UnderBear and Willard Pepion Sr.

RESIDENCE: Browning, MT

MILITARY: U.S. Army, Vietnam

EDUCATION: Browning (MT) High School; G.E.D., 1966; IAIA, 1972-1974; Blackfeet Community College, Browning, MT

OCCUPATION: Employee of the BIA Forestry Department, U.S. Park Service , and Indian Health Service Hospital, and painter

MEDIA: Oil, watercolor, pencil, pen and ink, and charcoal

EXHIBITS: IAIA; MPI; RC; art shows in northwestern Montana

SOLO/SPECIAL EXHIBITS: MPI (dual show)

HONORS: IAIA, Dean's List, fall 1974

LEVI HENRY PEPION

Pepion's paintings are realistic and largely consist of landscapes and portraits. He prefers to paint narrative style works which tell stories.

brochure, MPI, 1985

PEPION, VICTOR *Blackfeet*

Double Shields

Born 10 Mar 1907 at Birch Creek, MT, on the Blackfeet Indian Reservation; died 4 Mar 1956 at Cut Bank, MT; son of Julia and John Pepion; nephew of Lone Wolf, descendant of the last hereditary chief of the Blackfeet

MILITARY: U.S. Marine Corps, U.S. Air Corps; WW II

EDUCATION: LACAI, 1939-1940; Army Art School, Shrivenham, England, 1945; U of OK, 1945; U of NM, 1946-1947; B.F.A, U of SD, 1948; M.A., NM Highlands U, 1949; private instruction under Winold Reiss and Olaf Nordmark

OCCUPATION: Art instructor, sculptor, and painter

MEDIA: Tempera, casein, watercolor, pen and ink, pencil, pastel, charcoal, secco, plaster, and terra cotta

PUBLISHED: Jacobson and d'Ucel (1950); Dunn (1968); Snodgrass (1968); Brody (1971); Ray, ed. (1972); Broder (1981)

BOOKS ILLUSTRATED: Blackboy, et al. (1973)

COMMISSIONS: *Murals:* MPI, 1941; Oglala Boarding School; Pine Ridge (SD) Indian Agency; Fort Sill Indian School; NM Highlands U. *Other:* MPI, diorama

PUBLIC COLLECTIONS: MPI, OU/MA, PAC

EXHIBITS: CIA, MPI, OU/MA, PAC

SOLO EXHIBITS: MPI

AWARDS: PAC ('56, 1st)

VICTOR PEPION

"Pepion painted in a style which bordered on the primitive. His untimely death in a house fire cut short a colorful career."

Snodgrass 1968

The first Blackfeet Indian artist to achieve a high degree of success, and one of the first Northern Plains artists to return and teach other Indian students his skills.

catalog, CIA, 1971

PEPION, WEBB *Blackfeet*

Sleeps In The Thunder

Born 29 Mar 1919 near Robare, MT, on the Blackfeet Indian Reservation; son of Julia Boy Chief and John B. Pepion; P/GP: Little Snake Women and Poliet Pepion

RESIDENCE: Valier, MT

MILITARY: WWII

EDUCATION: Blackfeet Indian Reservation, public schools; Riverside, CA, public schools

WEBB PEPION

Pepion's work is based on the cultural traditions of the Blackfeet Indians of the 19th century. A talented musician and painter, he is best known for his wood sculptures. The artist's father, John B. Pepion, was a close friend of Charles M. Russell and acted as his interpreter when Russell first was in Montana.

brochure, MPI, 1977

OCCUPATION: Rancher, musician, actor, sculptor, and painter
MEDIA: Oil, pencil, pen and ink, and wood
EXHIBITS: CMRM; art shows in Montana
SOLO EXHIBITS: MPI

PERA, RALPH *(?)*
PUBLISHED: Hill (1992)
PUBLIC COLLECTIONS: IAIA
EXHIBITS: IAIA

PEREZ, LARRY *Cochití*
Born ca. 1929; brother-in-law of Bob Chávez (q.v.)
EDUCATION: Santa Fe, ca. mid-1940s
PUBLISHED: Seymour (1988)
PUBLIC COLLECTIONS: IACB/DC
EXHIBITS: WRTD

LARRY PEREZ

It is likely that Perez only painted while he was at Santa Fe Indian School in the mid-1940s.

Seymour 1968

PERRY, ANGELA LEE *Choctaw/Osage*
RESIDENCE: Santa Fe, NM
MEDIA: Watercolor
PUBLISHED: Snodgrass (1968)
EXHIBITS: PAC, SN
AWARDS: SN

PERSHALL, TOM E. *Cherokee*
A.K.A. Thomas E. Pershall
EXHIBITS: PAC
AWARDS: PAC

PESATA, MELVIN AARON *Apache*
EDUCATION: IAIA
MEDIA: Pastel
EXHIBITS: AC/SD

PESHLAKAI, PETER *Navajo*
PUBLIC COLLECTIONS: MNA

PESVA, COMA (see Lomayesva, Louis)

PETE *Shoshoni*
PUBLISHED: Snodgrass (1968). *4th Annual Report,* BAE (1882-1883)

PETE

"The chief's personal exploits are recorded in the BAE 4th Annual Report. *He is known to have visited Washington, D.C., in 1880."*

Snodgrass 1968

PETERS, DONALD B. *Saulteaux*
Born 13 Feb 1960 in St. Boniface, MB, Canada
RESIDENCE: Burnaby, BC, Canada
OCCUPATION: Artist
MEDIA: Acrylic and prints
PUBLIC COLLECTIONS: HCC
EXHIBITS: CPS; HCC; RC; WTF; Canadian Native Arts and Crafts, Calgary, AB; Expo '88, Brisbane, Australia

PETERS, JOHNSTON *Pima*
PUBLISHED: Snodgrass (1968)
PUBLIC COLLECTIONS: SM

KEVIN PETERS

Peters says of his art, "I don't want to copy the old pieces. I'm a Nez Percé living in the twentieth century and I want my pieces to show that."
Minthorn 1991

PETERS, KEVIN *Nez Percé*

Born 6 Jan 1957 in Lewiston, ID
RESIDENCE: Lewiston, ID
EDUCATION: Lewiston (ID) High School, 1975; A.F.A., IAIA, 1977; CCAC; Lewis and Clark State College, Lewiston, ID
OCCUPATION: Tribal liaison, park ranger, craftsman, sculptor, and painter
MEDIA: Oil, acrylic, watercolor, pencil, pen and ink, charcoal, mixed-media, bronze, and wood
PUBLISHED: Minthorn (1991), dust jacket
COMMISSIONS: Yakama Nation Cultural Center, pen and ink drawing for opening of Yakama Nation Museum, Toppenish, WA
EXHIBITS: IAIA, NWASA, SAP; see also Awards
SOLO EXHIBITS: MPI
AWARDS: Armory, Pendleton, OR ('79); Idaho State Industrial Creative Art, Boise, ID ('75)

PADDY PETERS

Peters is a member of the Triple K Co-operative (q.v.) and has exhibited extensively with them.

PETERS, PADDY *Ojibwa*

Born 1956 on Pikangikum Reserve, ON, Canada
RESIDENCE: Pikangikum, ON, Canada
MEDIA: Acrylics and prints
PUBLISHED: Menitove, ed. (1986b)
PUBLIC COLLECTIONS: C/AG/TB, HCC
EXHIBITS: C/AG/TB, C/ROM, HCC, RC

PETERS, RON *Ojibwa*

Born 1957 in Fort Frances, ON, Canada
RESIDENCE: Canada
OCCUPATION: Graphic artist and painter
MEDIA: Acrylic, watercolor, egg tempera, charcoal, chalk, and prints
PUBLISHED: Menitove, ed. (1986b)
BOOKS ILLUSTRATED: Book compiled by a group of ethnologists on the Micmac Indians
COMMISSIONS: Chief Dan George Memorial Foundation, Vancouver, BC, painting; Vancouver (BC) Indian Centre Society, logo.
PUBLIC COLLECTIONS: C/AG/TB
EXHIBITS: C/AG/TB; Indian Art Exhibit, Marseilles, France, 1982; see also Awards
AWARDS: Indian Arts and Crafts Exhibit, British Columbia Trade Show ('82, 1st; '83, 1st)

SANDRA TURNER PETERS

Peters says that her greatest talent and gift is in the reproduction of "Historical Native Art." Most of her work is done in the traditional Indian art form, which is a flat two-dimensional style.
p.c. 1991

PETERS, SANDRA TURNER *Creek/Cherokee*

Yellow Eyes
Born 4 Nov 1944; daughter of Fannie Mae Cook and Reuben R. Turner; P/GP: Ella Blundell and C. J. Turner III; M/GP: Dolly Yonder and Thomas Sebastian Cook
RESIDENCE: Sparks, OK
EDUCATION: Eufaula (OK) High School, 1962; A.A. & B.A., NSU, 1967
OCCUPATION: Counselor and painter
MEDIA: Pencil, clay, and prints
PUBLISHED: Biographical publications
PUBLIC COLLECTIONS: CNM; FCTM; City of Watauga (TX) Community Complex; State National Bank, Eufaula, OK

EXHIBITS: BC; CNM; FCTM; LIAS,;U of AZ; Harding University, Searcy, AR
AWARDS: CNM ('83, Tiger Award; '85, 1st); FCTM ('74; '79, 1st, Needlepoint Guild Award; '82; '83; '87, 1st; '88; '89, IH)

PETERS, VELMA O. *Sioux*
PUBLIC COLLECTIONS: DAM

PETE THREE LEGS *Sioux*
PUBLISHED: Snodgrass (1968)
PUBLIC COLLECTIONS: MAI (colored pencil drawing, "*Sioux Grass Dance*, 1889, Fort Bennett, SD")

PETITSINGVEY (see Okuma, Sandra)

PETTIGREW, JACKSON D. *Chickasaw*
Nashoba
A.K.A. Jack D. Pettigrew
Born 2 July 1942 in Ada, OK
RESIDENCE: Ada, OK
EDUCATION: ECSC/OK
OCCUPATION: Gallery owner and artist
EXHIBITS: ACS/RSC; AIE; CNM; FCTM; RC; Central Oklahoma Association Arts and Crafts Show; see also Awards
AWARDS: FCTM ('85, 1st); Magic Brush Art Show ('85, 1st); SOCCA Spring Show ('85)

PEZI (see Grass, John)

PHILLIP, DAN *Zuni*
PUBLIC COLLECTIONS: IACB/DC, MNA

PHILLIPS, DWIGHT E. *Choctaw*
RESIDENCE: Crestline, CA
OCCUPATION: Commercial art instructor and painter
PUBLISHED: Dunn (1968); Snodgrass (1968); Brody (1971)
PUBLIC COLLECTIONS: PAC
EXHIBITS: DAM, PAC

PHILLIPS, OLIVER *Sioux*
PUBLISHED: Snodgrass (1968)
PUBLIC COLLECTIONS: PAC

PHILLIPS, RITA *Mohawk*
Wita
Born 27 May 1929
RESIDENCE: Caughnawaga, PQ, Canada
EDUCATION: Manitou Community College
OCCUPATION: Educator, Mohawk language resource person, illustrator, craftswoman, and painter
MEDIA: Watercolor, pastel, charcoal, beads, fabric, and apples
BOOKS ILLUSTRATED: Deering and Harries (1976); Horne, et al. (1976)

PIAN WE LE NE (see Archuleta, Manuel)

PIAPOT, ALGIE *Chippewa/Plains Cree/Assiniboin/Blackfeet*
Bird Chief

Born 22 May 1943 on the Rocky Boy Indian Reservation; son of Bessie and John Piapot; P/GP: Mary and George Piapot; M/GP: Dog Woman and Art Raining Bird

RESIDENCE: Box Elder, MT

EDUCATION: Havre (MT) High School; G.E.D., 1967; U of MT; Stone Child College, 1989

OCCUPATION: Teacher, sculptor, and painter

MEDIA: Acrylic, watercolor, and stone

EXHIBITS: BSIM; CIM; GFNAAS; TCIM; RC; Havre (MT) Art Association Show; see also Awards

SOLO EXHIBITS: MPI

AWARDS: American Indian Higher Education Art Show (1st)

PIKITCHWANO (see Eteeyan, Warren Hardy)

PIKONGANNA, ALOYSIUS *Eskimo*

Born 1940 on King Island, AK

RESIDENCE: College, AK

EDUCATION: DCTP, 1964-1965

PUBLISHED: Ray (1969)

PILLI, DONNA *Navajo*

PUBLISHED: Snodgrass (1968)

PUBLIC COLLECTIONS: U of CA/LMA

PIN, PAGNA *Tesuque*

PUBLISHED: Snodgrass (1968)

PUBLIC COLLECTIONS: ASM

PINAYO PIN (see Vigil, Thomas)

PINCION, PETER *Zuni*

PUBLISHED: Snodgrass (1968)

PUBLIC COLLECTIONS: MAI, MRFM

PINE TREE BIRD (see Montoya, Alfredo)

PINGLETON, STEPHANIE R. *Creek*

Born 19 Aug 1961 in Tulsa, OK; daughter of Ann Hawkins and Johnnie Whittaker

RESIDENCE: McAlester, OK

EDUCATION: Morris (OK) High School, 1979; EOSC, 1986

OCCUPATION: Auto and small engine mechanic and artist

MEDIA: Pencil and pastel

EXHIBITS: CNM; GM; PAC; fairs throughout Oklahoma

HONORS: MIA, Certificate of Merit

PIÑO, BARBARA *San Ildefonso*

Born 1947 in Santa Fe, NM

RESIDENCE: Santa Fe, NM

EDUCATION: St. Catherine's, ca. 1965

PUBLISHED: Snodgrass (1968)

EXHIBITS: MNM, PAC, SAIEAIP

PIÑO, JUAN ISIDRO *Tesuque*

A.K.A. Juan Ysidro Piño; Juan The Elder

Birth date unknown; died ca. 1953

JUAN ISIDRO PIÑO

"In 1950, the artist was employed at Los Alamos, NM, by which time he was no longer working in art. He was an accomplished, self-taught artist in the medium of woodblock prints."

Snodgrass 1968

OCCUPATION: Graphic artist
MEDIA: Woodblock prints
PUBLISHED: Dunn (1968); Snodgrass (1968); Tanner (1973)
PUBLIC COLLECTIONS: DAM, MNM, SM, U of CA/LMA
EXHIBITS: DAM

PIÑO, KATHY *San Ildefonso*
RESIDENCE: San Ildefonso Pueblo, NM
EDUCATION: St. Catherine's, ca. 1965
PUBLISHED: Snodgrass (1968)
EXHIBITS: PAC

PIÑO, LORENZO *Tesuque*
EDUCATION: Albuquerque, 1960-1961
PUBLISHED: Snodgrass (1968)
EXHIBITS: MNM
AWARDS: MNM

PINO, PAUL D. *Laguna/Acoma*
RESIDENCE: New Laguna, NM
PUBLIC COLLECTIONS: MRFM
EXHIBITS: HM/G
AWARDS: HM/G ('70, '76)

PINTO, DENNIS PAUL *Navajo*
EDUCATION: Santa Fe, 1959; Albuquerque, 1950-1963
PUBLISHED: Snodgrass (1968)
PUBLIC COLLECTIONS: HCC, MAI
EXHIBITS: ITIC, HCC, MNM
AWARDS: MNM

PINTO, EMILY *Zuni*
PUBLISHED: Snodgrass (1968)
PUBLIC COLLECTIONS: MAI

PIOCHE, DENNIS *Navajo*
Birth date unknown; born near Huérfano Peak in northwestern New Mexico
RESIDENCE: Aztec, NM
MILITARY: U.S. Navy
OCCUPATION: Folk art carver and painter
MEDIA: Watercolor, wood, and prints
EXHIBITS: ACS/MV ('93)

PIQTOUKUN, DAVID *Inuit (Eskimo)*
A.K.A. Ruben Piqtoukun; David Ruben Piqtoukun
Born 10 May 1950 at Paulatuk, NWT, Canada, in a settlement on the western Arctic Ocean
RESIDENCE: Toronto, ON, Canada
EDUCATION: Residential schools in the north
OCCUPATION: Sculptor, graphic artist, and painter
PUBLISHED: Routledge (1979); Wight (1989). *Monday Magazine* (July 1975); *Canadian Antiques and Art Review* (Apr 1981); *Arts and Culture of the North* (fall 1981); *About Arts and Crafts* (Vol. 5, no. 3, 1982); *Inuktitut* (Jan 1983); *Native Press* (24 July 1987); *News/North* (July/Sept 1987); *Inuit Art Quarterly* (fall 1987);

DAVID PIQTOUKUN

Piqtoukun wrote in 1980, "Our legends and mythologies have been passed on through songs and stories for a long time but recently, our traditional lifestyle has been influenced greatly by the Western Culture. Despite this sudden integration of opposing lifestyles, we will continue to exist through our art forms and there will always be a variety of media through which to share our Inuit thoughts and feelings."

Up Here (Oct/Nov 1987); *Intercom* (Dec 1988); *The Winnipeg Free Press* (2 Jan 1988)

COMMISSIONS: UNESCO, painting, 1988; Telefilm Canada, sculpture

PUBLIC COLLECTIONS: C/AG/O; C/AG/WP; C/CMC; C/ICI; C/MCC; C/PWNHC; C/U of BC/MA; Staatliche Museum für Völkerkunde, Münich, West Germany

EXHIBITS: Partial listing of more than 24 includes: C/AG/IGEA; C/AG/V; C/AG/WP; C/AV; C/CMC; C/DKA; C/GNAF; C/IA7; C/IGV; C/MA; C/PWNHC; HM

SOLO EXHIBITS: Expo 1986, Northwest Territories Pavilion, Vancouver, BC, 1986; Family Hall, Inuvik, NWT, 1983; Gallery of British Columbia Arts, Vancouver, BC

HONORS: *Grants:* Canada Council Exploration Grant, 1982. *Other:* Canadian Eskimo Arts Council, 1980; UNESCO, Canadian Committee for the World Decade of Cultural Development; visiting artist in the Dominican Republic, the Ivory Coast, and Mexico

PIQTOUKUN, RUBEN (see Piqtoukun, David)

PITALOOSIE *Inuit (Eskimo)*

A.K.A. Pitaloosee; Pitalouisa; Pitaloosie Saila

Born 11 July 1942 in Cape Dorset, NWT, Canada; stepdaughter of Mary Pudlat; P/GM: Quppa; niece of Pudlo Pudlat (q.v.), Osoochiak Pudlat, and Kigmeata Etidlooie (q.v.); second-cousin of Peter Pitseolak (q.v.)

PUBLISHED: Leroux, Jackson, and Freeman, eds. (1994). *Inuit Art Quarterly* (winter 1994)

PUBLIC COLLECTIONS: C/AG/LR, C/AG/M, C/AG/O, C/AG/WP, C/CGCQ, C/CMC, C/GM, C/MCC, C/McMU, C/MFA/M, C/NAM, C/NGCA, C/SFG, C/U of C

EXHIBITS: C/AMR; C/AV; C/ISS; C/GTOW; C/TIP; FAM; St. Avold, France, 1989-1990

HONORS: Canadian Post Office, print used on 12-cent stamp, 1971; UNICEF, print used on greeting card, 1983

PITALOOSIE

Pitaloosie spent seven years in hospitals in southern Canada recovering from spinal injuries that resulted from a fall when she was seven or eight years old. She returned to her parents' camp at Keatuk in 1957, when she was fifteen. Her return led to many difficult adjustments, for example, she had learned to speak English and French but had forgotten her own language (Inuktitut). In the early 1960s Pitaloosie decided to learn to draw and developed her own distinctive style. She is known for her drawings of women, birds, and mythical figures. A very prolific graphic artist, she considers her images a means of preserving her culture.

Leroux, Jackson, and Freeman, eds. 1994

PITALOUISA (see Pitaloosie)

PITSEOLAK *Inuit (Eskimo)*

Pitseolak, Sea Pigeon

A.K.A. Pitsolak; Pitseolak Ashoona

Born ca. 1904 on Nottingham Island in the Hudson Strait, NWT, Canada; died 1973; daughter of Timungiak and Ottockie, hunter

RESIDENCE: Lived in Pangnirtung, Cape Dorset, NWT, Canada

OCCUPATION: Wife, mother, seamstress, author, and graphic artist

MEDIA: Watercolor, colored marker, pencil, crayon, colored felt tip pen, and prints

PUBLISHED: Goetz and Schrager (n.d.); Houston (1967; 1967a); Larmour (1967), Eber (1971); Goetz, et al. (1977); Blodgett (1978a); Collinson (1978); Routledge (1979); Woodhouse, ed. (1980); Johnson and Nasby (1984); LaBarge (1986); McMasters, et al. (1993); Leroux, Jackson, and Freeman, eds. (1994). *Artscanada* (Vol. 28, no. 6, 1971-1972); *North* (Mar/Apr 1974); *The Beaver* (spring 1975; autumn 1976); *North/Nord* (Vol. 29, no. 3, 1982); *Art and Culture of the North* (Vol. 6, no. 3, 1983)

BOOKS ILLUSTRATED: Pitseolak (1977); Pitseolak and Eber (1972; 1975)

PUBLIC COLLECTIONS: C/AC/MS, C/AG/LR, C/AMR, C/AG/O, C/AG/V, C/CMC, C/GM, C/LUM, C/MCC, C/NGCA, C/PWNHC, C/ROM, C/SFG, C/TDB, C/U of AB, C/U of L, C/U of NB, C/WBEC, DAM, HMA

EXHIBITS: C/AC/AE; C/AC/MS; C/AG/O; C/AG/WP; C/CD; C/CG; C/CID;

PITSEOLAK

Pitseolak was the matriarch of a large talented family of carvers and printmakers. She grew up in a family that was very skillful at making things and her father was especially artistic. She has been associated with the Cooperative at Cape Dorset since its inception. Her first painting was done in 1939 for John Buchan, son of Canada's Governor General, who worked at the trading post in Cape Dorset. Pitseolak was the most prolific artist in Cape Dorset and her work was included in

C/ISS; C/CMC; C/EACTDB; C/GTOW; C/HNG; C/IA7; C/MAD; C/NGCA; C/SS; C/TIP; ACMWA; GM; Studio 44, Brussels, Belgium; Robertson Galleries, Ottawa, ON

SOLO EXHIBITS: C/P, SI

HONORS: The Royal Canadian Academy of the Arts, 1974; Canada Council Senior Arts Grant, 1975; The Order of Canada, 1977

PITSEOLAK, PETER *Inuit (Eskimo)*

Born 2 Sept 1902 on Nottingham Island, NWT, Canada; died 1973 in Cape Dorset, NWT, Canada; cousin of Nungusuituq (q.v.), early pencil artist

RESIDENCE: Lived in Cape Dorset, NWT, Canada

OCCUPATION: Camp leader, hunter, fisherman, photographer, author, sculptor, graphic artist, and painter

MEDIA: Watercolor, pencil, colored pencil, felt tip marker, film, stone, and prints

PUBLISHED: Burland (1973); Blodgett (1978a); Bellman (1980), Jackson and Nasby (1987). *The Beaver* (spring 1975)

BOOKS ILLUSTRATED: Pitseolak and Eber (1975)

PUBLIC COLLECTIONS: C/AC/MS

EXHIBITS: C/AC/MS, C/AG/WP, C/CID

PITSIUAK, LIPA (see Pitsiulak, Lypa)

PITSIULAK, LYPA *Inuit (Eskimo)*

A.K.A. Lipa Pitsiulak; Lipa Pitsiuak; Lypa; Laban; Pitsulack

Born 1943 in Iglootalik in Cumberland Sound, NWT, Canada

RESIDENCE: Pangnirtung, NWT, Canada

OCCUPATION: Sculptor and graphic artist

MEDIA: Black pencil, colored felt tip pen, stone, and prints

PUBLISHED: Goetz, et al. (1977); Collinson (1978); Routledge (1979); Jackson and Nasby (1987); McMasters, et al. (1993)

PUBLIC COLLECTIONS: C/INAC, C/U of AB, DAM

EXHIBITS: C/AG/TB, C/CID, C/CT, C/IA7, C/TIP

PITSOLAK (see Pitseolak)

PITSULACK (see Pitsiulak, Lypa)

PLATERO, BILLY *Navajo*

EDUCATION: Santa Fe

EXHIBITS: PM

PLATERO, LEO R. *Navajo*

Born 19 Jan 1944 in Crownpoint, NM; son of Bessie Chávez and Sam Platero; P/GP: Betty Chaco and Krip Platero; M/GP: Andres Chávez; Artist is related to Manuelito, Navajo headman during the 1860s.

RESIDENCE: Montezuma Creek, UT

MILITARY: U.S. Air Force ROTC at BYU, 1963-1964

EDUCATION: Gallup (NM) High School; BYU; U of NM, 1974; U of UT

OCCUPATION: Art teacher, author, sports writer, lecturer, salesman, silversmith, photographer, and painter

MEDIA: Oil, acrylic, watercolor, pencil, pastel, silver, gemstone, film, and prints

PUBLIC COLLECTIONS: Inter-Mt.

EXHIBITS: HM/G; ITIC; Utah State Fair; Centennial Exhibition, Monticello, UT, 1988; see also Awards

SOLO EXHIBITS: Brigham City, UT, 1972

PITSEOLAK

(continued)twenty annual print collections. Her book, Pictures Out of My Life, *was the first book to appear in an English/Inuktituk edition. Pitseolak once said of her drawings, "I am going to keep doing them until they tell me to stop. If no one tells me to stop, I shall make them as long as I am well. If I can, I'll make them even after I am dead."*

Goetz and Schrager, n.d.

PETER PITSEOLAK

Peter Pitseolak first painted in the late 1930s when Lord Tweedsmuir gave him a set of watercolors. His prints appeared in the annual collection catalogs from 1970 to 1975. Pitseolak also became a photographer and, starting in 1942, documented the vanishing way of life of Inuit of the Cape Dorset area.

LYPA PITSIULAK

Pitsiulak's drawings have been inspired by the Inuit oral traditions depicted in songs and stories (Jackson and Nasby 1987). He said, "I usually try to relate my drawings to the history, the life of our ancestors." In 1985, he took up etching and continues to carve and draw.

McMasters, et al. 1993

AWARDS: Blanding (UT) Centennial Exhibition (1st); Monticello (UT) School District Art Show (1st); New Mexico State Fair

HONORS: Navajo Tribal Band, member, traveled to the Rose Bowl, Pasadena, CA and Presidential Inauguration, 1972; translator for The Church of Jesus Christ of Latter Day Saints World Central Conference, Salt Lake City, UT

PLATERO, LORENZO *Navajo*

EDUCATION: Albuquerque, 1959

PUBLISHED: Snodgrass (1968)

EXHIBITS: MNM

PLATERO, RAYMOND *Navajo*

EDUCATION: Santa Fe, 1960

PUBLISHED: Snodgrass (1968)

EXHIBITS: MNM

AWARDS: MNM

PLATERO, TOM *Navajo*

EDUCATION: Albuquerque, 1958-1959

PUBLISHED: Snodgrass (1968)

EXHIBITS: MNM

PLENTY CHIEF, WALTER, SR. *Arikara*

RESIDENCE: New Town, ND

PUBLISHED: Snodgrass (1968)

EXHIBITS: BNIAS

PLENTY COUPS *Crow*

A.K.A. Chief Plenty Coups

PUBLISHED: Jacobson and d'Ucel (1950); Snodgrass (1968); Warner (1985)

EXHIBITS: AC/Y

PLENTY COUPS

"The artist was captured by the Crow Indians when a baby. He grew to manhood with the Crows and became wealthy. For him, painting was a practical tool — he owned a grocery store but, because he could not compute effectively, he kept books by drawing the names of buyers and purchases made. (see Jacobson and d'Ucel 1950)."

Snodgrass 1968

PLENTY SCALPS (see Iron Tail)

POCANO (see Martínez, Julián)

POINT, SUSAN A. *Coast Salish*

A.K.A. Susan Sparrow

Born 1952

RESIDENCE: Vancouver, BC, Canada

OCCUPATION: Artist

MEDIA: Acrylic, silver, gold, and prints

PUBLISHED: Gerber and Bruggmann (1989); Gerber and Katz (1989); McMasters, et al. (1993)

COMMISSIONS: Thirty-three for various charities, schools, municipalities, and Native organizations

PUBLIC COLLECTIONS: C/INAC, C/RB

EXHIBITS: Partial listing of more than thirty includes: C/AG/GV; C/AG/LR; C/AG/NS; C/AG/TB; C/ANIWS; C/CCPC; C/CGCQ; C/DM; C/FVU; C/ISS; C/RSMC; C/U of BC/MA; AC/SWA; HM; SCG; TBMM; Sandia Gallery, Basel, Switzerland; Völkerkunde Museum der Universität Zürich, Switzerland

SOLO EXHIBITS: C/CMC, C/FVU, C/U of BC/MA; Galerie für Indianerkunst Nordamerikas, Basel, Switzerland; Steilacoom Tribal Museum, Steilacoom, WA

POITRAS, JANE ASH *Plains Cree*

Born 11 Oct 1951 in Fort Chipewyan, AB, Canada

RESIDENCE: Edmonton, AB, Canada

EDUCATION: B.S., C/U of AB, 1977; B.F.A., C/U of AB, 1983; M.F.A., Columbia University, New York, 1985

OCCUPATION: Industrial microbiologist, educator, printmaker, and painter

MEDIA: Oil, mixed-media, and prints

PUBLISHED: Cardinal-Schubert (1992). *The Edmonton Journal* (17 July 1984; 28 July 1984; 17 Aug 1985; 13 Aug 1986); *Visual Arts Newsletter* (Aug 1984); *AMMSA* (27 Sept 1985; 11 Oct 1985); *Windspeaker* (12 Dec 1986); *Art Post* (spring 1989); *Now Magazine* (Aug 1989); *Matriart* (Vol. 2, no. 1, 1991); *C Magazine* (fall 1991); *Artscrafts* (winter 1991); *The North Shore News* (4 Sept 1991); *American Indian Art* (autumn 1992); *The Santa Fean* (Aug 1994)

COMMISSIONS: Fort Chipewyan (AB) Bicentennial, 1988

PUBLIC COLLECTIONS: C/AIAC; C/AG/TB; C/AG/WP; C/CCAB; C/CMC; C/INAC; C/LUM; C/MCC; C/PHT; C/WICEC; C/U of AB; C/YU; Alberta Art Foundation, Edmonton; Attorney-General, Alberta; Columbia University, New York, NY; House of Commons, Ottawa, ON; Interprovincial Pipe Line; Native Services Unit, Government of Alberta, Edmonton; Peguis Indian Band, Winnipeg, MB; University of Alberta Hospital, Edmonton

EXHIBITS: Partial listing of more than fifty includes: AIAI/M; AICH; BM/B; C/AC/AE; C/ACA; C/ACCCNA; C/AG/E; C/AG/TB; C/AG/WP; C/AG/V; C/AM; C/C; C/CMC; C/I; C/ISS; C/LUM; C/NB; C/NGCA; C/PM; C/TFD; C/U of AB; C/WICEC; C/YU; HM; SCG; SM; U of CA/LA; WASG; Cabo Frio International Print Biennial, Brazil, 1985; Metropolitan Museum of Fine Art, Tokyo, Japan; Museo de Art Contemporáneo Ibiza, Spain, 1984

SOLO EXHIBITS: Partial listing of more than 14 includes: C/AG/E; C/AG/TB; C/CCC; C/CMC; C/PM; C/U of BC/MA

AWARDS: Graphex Purchase Award

HONORS: *Scholarships and Grants:* Alberta Culture Study Grant; Helen R. Elser Scholarship; Indian and Northern Affairs Bursary; Lady Rodney Scholarship; Northern Alberta Development Council Bursary; Syncrude Canada Scholarship; Emerging Native Artists of Alberta Scholarship, 1984

POLAN YI KATON *Kiowa/Apache*

Polan Yi Katon, Rabbit Shoulder

PUBLISHED: Snodgrass (1968)

POLAN YI KATON

"The artist is known to have executed and maintained a calendar which was said to have been buried with him."

Snodgrass 1968

POLELONEMA, OTIS *Hopi*

Lomadamosiva, Springtime; *Polelonema*, Making Ball

Born 2 Feb 1902 at Shungopovi, Second Mesa, AZ; died 1981; son of Quiuysio and Tawamenewa

RESIDENCE: Lived at Shungopovi, Second Mesa, AZ

EDUCATION: Santa Fe, 1914-1920; Santa Fe (NM) High School

OCCUPATION: Farmer, poet, composer of ritual songs, weaver, and painter

MEDIA: Oil and watercolor

PUBLISHED: Sloan and LaFarge (1931); Spinden (1931); Jacobson and d'Ucel (1950); Dunn (1968); Snodgrass (1968); Brody (1971; 1992); Tanner (1968; 1973); Monthan and Monthan (1975); Highwater (1976; 1978); Silberman (1978); Fawcett and Callander (1982); Hoffman, et al. (1984); Samuels (1985); Seymour (1988); Williams, ed. (1990); Golder (1985); Archuleta and Strickland (1991); Tryk (1993). *The American Magazine of Art* (Aug 1932); *Magazine Tulsa* (May 1948); *The Arizona Republic* (17 Mar 1968; 17 Sept 1972; 4 Dec 1986); *Arizona Highways* (Aug 1976); *Arts Focus* (Aug 1981); *The Scottsdale Progress* (24 Oct 1986); *The Phoenix Gazette* (25 Oct 1986)

BOOKS ILLUSTRATED: De Huff (1922)

OTIS POLELONEMA

"The artist believed his experience at Santa Fe Indian School and his contact with Mrs. Willis DeHuff encouraged him the most in the art field. He had painted since 1917 and was active for a time in the WPA Art Project."

Snodgrass 1968

PUBLIC COLLECTIONS: AF, CGFA, DAM, GM, IACB, IACB/DC, MAI, MKMcNAI, MNA/KHC, MNM, MRFM, OU/MA, PAC, SM, SMNAI, WOM

EXHIBITS: ACC, AF, ASF, ASM, DAM, EITA, FAC/CS, HH, FHMAG, HM, HM/G, IK, ITIC, JGS, LGAM, MAI, MFA/D, MFA/O, MKMcNAI, MNM, MRFM, NAP, OMA, OU/ET, PAC, PAC/T, PM, SAIEAIP, SFWF, SI, SN, SV, SWAIA, WRTD, WWM

AWARDS: DAM ('54, Evans Memorial Award); HM/G ('69, 1st; '76); ITIC ('70); MNA; MNM; PAC; SN ('70, Buehler Award); SWAIA

POLELONEMA, TYLER *Hopi*

Duvayestewa, Praying For All

Born 24 Jan 1940 at Shungopovi, Second Mesa, AZ; son of Jessie Salaftoche and Otis Polelonema (q.v.)

RESIDENCE: Fort Leonard Wood, MO

EDUCATION: Oraibi (AZ) High School; Stewart

OCCUPATION: Kitchen assistant and artist

MEDIA: Acrylic and watercolor

PUBLISHED: Snodgrass (1968); Tanner (1973)

PUBLIC COLLECTIONS: CGPS; WWM; Hopi Arts and Crafts Guild Shop, Second Mesa, AZ

EXHIBITS: ASM; CGPS; HM/G; SAIEAIP; Reno, NV, 1962; area shows in Phoenix, AZ

AWARDS: Reno, NV (three awards); Stewart (NV) Indian School (Awards Day pin)

POLEY, ORIN *Hopi*

Born 1942 in Bacabi, AZ

EDUCATION: U of N AZ

OCCUPATION: Sculptor and painter

EXHIBITS: HM/G; MNA; NACLA; SWAIA; Bullock's Exposition, Santa Monica, CA

E. D. POLEYESTEWA

"The artist was active in the late 1930s and early 1940s."

Snodgrass 1968

POLEYESTEWA, E. D. *Hopi*

A.K.A. Edward Poleyestewa

PUBLISHED: Snodgrass (1968). The Amerind Foundation, Dragoon, AZ, gallery guide

PUBLIC COLLECTIONS: MNA

EXHIBITS: AF

POLEYESTEWA, EDWARD (see Poleyestewa, E.D.)

WILLIAM POLLOCK

"Pollock was given his non-Indian name at the Agency school. At Haskell Institute, he was an outstanding student, played in the band, and painted pictures on the wagons used by the Indians. At the age of 22, he received a government land allotment, and about six years later, just before his death by pneumonia, he signed a contract to join Buffalo Bill's Wild West Show."

Snodgrass 1968

POLLOCK, WILLIAM *Pawnee*

Tayloowayahwho

Born 1870; died Mar 1899 in Pawnee, OK

MILITARY: Spanish-American War (see Roosevelt 1899)

EDUCATION: Pawnee (OK) Agency School; Haskell

OCCUPATION: Pawnee (OK) Agency Office employee and painter

PUBLISHED: Snodgrass (1968)

EXHIBITS: SI

HONORS: Veterans of Foreign Wars, Pawnee Post, named for him

PONCA, CARL *Osage*

Po'n-ge Wah-ti-an-kah

Born 1938 in the Osage Nation in OK

RESIDENCE: Pawhuska, OK

EDUCATION: U of OK; B.F.A., KCAI/MO; CCAC; SI; Sul Ross University, Alpine, TX; National Museum of Anthropology, Mexico City, Mexico

OCCUPATION: Educator, museum director, and artist

EXHIBITS: NACLA; Osage Museum, Pawhuska, OK

Pon-Cee-Cee (see Roye, Paladine H.)

Poneoma, Bert *Hopi*

MEDIA: Tempera

PUBLISHED: Seymour (1988)

PUBLIC COLLECTIONS: IACB/DC; MRFM; SM (? signed W. Poneoma, 1934)

Po'n-ga Wah-ti-an-kah (see Ponca, Carl)

Pooacha-Eli, Ermalinda *Zuni*

Born 19 May 1962; daughter of Delphine Yatsayte and Amos Pooacha; P/GP: Leolepa and Dominic Pooacha; M/GP: Josephine and Guy Yatsayte

RESIDENCE: Zuni, NM

EDUCATION: Fort Sill, 1980

OCCUPATION: Painter

MEDIA: Acrylic and textile paint

EXHIBITS: HM, MNA; see also Awards

AWARDS: HM (Best of Show); MNA; Chilocco Indian School Art Show (1st, Best of Show)

Pooano (see Martínez, Julían)

Poodry, C. Earl *Sauk-Fox/Seneca*

Quenipea, Fish In Water

Born 1915 in Akron, NY; GF: last chief of the Senecas

EDUCATION: Haskell; BC

PUBLISHED: Jacobson and d'Ucel (1950); Snodgrass (1968); Brody (1971)

PUBLIC COLLECTIONS: PAC

EXHIBITS: PAC, U of OK

C. Earl Poodry

"Poodry lived in eastern Oklahoma during his childhood. He is known for his paintings and his woodcarvings and cartoons."

Snodgrass 1968

Pookertnak (see Pukingnak, Nancy)

Pookootna (see Pukingnak, Nancy)

Poolaw, Thomas *Kiowa/Delaware*

A.K.A. Thomas Lee Poolaw

Born 24 Feb 1959 at Fort Sill, OK; son of Martha Kauley and Captain Robert W. Poolaw Sr.; P/GP: Winnie, Delaware tribal elder, and Horace Poolaw, Kiowa photographer

RESIDENCE: Norman, OK

EDUCATION: Camp Lejeune (NC) School, 1973-1975; El Camino High School, Oceanside, CA, 1977; B.F.A., U of OK, 1992

OCCUPATION: Museum curator of exhibits and painter

MEDIA: Acrylic and mixed-media

PUBLIC COLLECTIONS: SPIM, OU/MA, PNAS

EXHIBITS: AIE, DAM, JH, LIAS, MMO, OIO, PNAS, OU/MA; see also Awards

SOLO EXHIBITS: SPIM

AWARDS: AIE ('78); PNAS (Grand Award); LIAS ('94); OU/MA ('79, Grand Award; '80, T. G. May Purchase Award); All-Indian Art Show ('88, Best In Show); CANA Invitational Exhibition, Norman, OK; Potawatomi National Indian Art Exhibit, Shawnee, OK ('80, Grand Award)

Thomas Poolaw

"Known in the past for his colorful compositions dealing more directly in style and technique with traditional Native American painting, Poolaw is now searching for a very modern interpretation of old and new visions. Currently he seems to be focusing on the calligraphic effect of pictograph style images rendered in subdued blacks, grays, and whites."

Carol Whitney, Director Jacobson Foundation, 1994

POOLER, RUSSELL *Miami/Ottawa*

RESIDENCE: Yuma, AZ

EXHIBITS: HM/G, SN

AWARDS: HM/G, SN

POOLHECO, SIDNEY *Tewa/Hopi*

Born 25 May 1941

EDUCATION: Graduated high school

PUBLISHED: Snodgrass (1968)

EXHIBITS: ITIC, PAC

POORBOY, WILLIAM G. *Cherokee*

RESIDENCE: Hindsville, AR

EXHIBITS: FCTM

POOTAGOK (see Pootoogook)

POOTAGOOK (see Pootoogook)

POOTOGOOK (see Pootoogook)

POOTOOGOOK *Inuit (Eskimo)*

A.K.A. Pootagok; Pootagook; Pootogook; Putoogoo; Kanaginak Pootoogook

Born 1887; died 1959

RESIDENCE: Lived in Cape Dorset, NWT, Canada

OCCUPATION: Graphic artist

MEDIA: Pencil

PUBLISHED: Houston (1967); Goetz, et al. (1977); McMasters, et al. (1993). *The Beaver* (spring 1975)

PUBLIC COLLECTIONS: C/NGCA

EXHIBITS: C/TIP

POOTOOGOOK, KANANGINAK (see Kananginak)

POOTOOGOOK, NAPACHIE (see Nawpachee)

POOTOOGOOK, NAPATCHIE (see Nawpachee)

POP CHALEE *Taos*

Pop Chalee, Blue Flower

A.K.A. Merina Luján; Merina Luján Hopkins

Born 20 Mar 1906 in Castle Gate, Utah; died 11 Dec 1993 in Santa Fe, NM; daughter of Merea Margherete Luenberger, of East Indian descent (a.k.a. Myrtle Ellen Green) and Joseph Cruz Luján; aunt of Pop Wea (Lo Ree Tanner)

RESIDENCE: Lived in Santa Fe, NM

EDUCATION: Santa Fe, 1937; two years training in art instruction; worked and studied with Harrison Begay, Allan Houser, Gerald Nailor and Quincy Tahoma (qq.v.) at "The Studio"

OCCUPATION: Textile designer, designer, entertainer, art instructor, lecturer, radio personality, singer, and painter

MEDIA: Watercolor, tempera, and casein

PUBLISHED: Jacobson and d'Ucel (1950); Tanner (1957; 1968); Carlson, et al. (1964); Snodgrass (1968); Dunn (1968); Brody (1971); Silberman (1978); Broder (1981); Hoffman, et al. (1984); Samuels (1985); Seymour (1988); Archuleta and Strickland (1991); Tryk (1993); Gully, ed. (1994). *School Arts Magazine* (1936); *Arizona Highways* (Feb 1950); *The Arizona Republic* (22 Feb 1970); *Night Of The First Americans* (1982), cover; *Southwest Art* (June 1983);

POOTOOGOOK

Pootoogook was a leader among the Kingnaimuit of southern Baffin Island. A respected and enterprising man, he believed in the skills of man's hand, organization, and hard work.

Houston 1967

Due to poor health in the late 1950s, he moved to Cape Dorset and it was there that he began to draw. His drawing was used for the first print made at Cape Dorset which was included in the 1959 collection. His prints were also included in the 1961 collection catalog.

POP CHALEE

"Pop Chalee long ago developed a unique style of painting which combines Oriental and Amerindian motifs. She has traveled extensively, exhibiting and selling her work. In November, 1936, School Arts Magazine published one of her many articles."

Snodgrass 1968

Accused of painting in the "Bambi style," Pop Chalee explained that it was the other way around — Disney Studios painted in her style. At one time Walt Disney visited Santa Fe and unsuccessfully tried to recruit Indian painters to work in his studio. Before returning to California he purchased one of her forest scenes. It was her belief that one of her deer was the inspiration for Bambi.

Seymour 1988

The Indian Trader (Mar 1988); *The Santa Fean* (Aug 1989); *Santa Fe New Mexican* (16 Feb 1990; Oct 1990); *New Mexico Magazine* (Aug 1990; Dec 1990); *The Albuquerque Journal* (Oct 1990); *Native Peoples* (fall 1991); *Southwest Profiles* (winter 1991-92)

BOOKS ILLUSTRATED: Keech (1940)

COMMISSIONS: *Murals:* Albuquerque (NM) International Airport Terminal Building, ten murals; Roswell, NM, and Santa Fe, NM, air terminals; Maisel's Trading Post, Albuquerque, NM; Santa Fe Railroad (now moved to WWM); Marshall Field's Department Store, Chicago, IL; Hinkle's, Santa Fe, NM, two murals, 1943 (now stored at IAIA and U of NM); Arkansas Valley Bank (now United Bank of Pueblo, CO), five murals, 1952; Santa Fe Railway Ticket Office, Santa Fe, NM, early 1950s; New Mexico State Capitol Building, Santa Fe, NM, 1992; Grand Hotel, Mackinac Island, MI; Rainbow Man Shop, Santa Fe, NM; The General Holmes House, La Cienega, CA; McCormick Ranch, AZ; and in private residences. *Other:* State of New Mexico, Governor's collection at the Round House, painting

PUBLIC COLLECTIONS: Partial listing includes: AC/RM; CMA; DAM; EM; GM; HM; IACB/DC; IAIA/M; MNM; MNA/KHC; MMA; MRFM; RMC/AZ; SAR; SM; SU; U of NM; Albuquerque (NM) International Airport Art Collection; Pueblo (CO) Community College; Stanford Fine Arts Museum, Stanford, CA

EXHIBITS: Partial listing of hundreds includes: ABQM; AIEC; ASM; CAI; CMA; IK; AIW; FWG; HM; ITIC; LACM; LGAM; MKMcNAI; MNM; MMA; NGA; OMA; RMC/AZ; SAIEAIP; SFFA; SM; SV; USDI; WIB; WRTD; Elliot O'Hara School, Biddleford, ME; Academy of Sciences, San Francisco, CA; Museum of Natural History, Albuquerque, NM, 1992

SOLO/SPECIAL EXHIBITS: HM (dual show)

AWARDS: ITIC (Grand Award)

HONORS: State of New Mexico, Governor's Award for Excellence and Achievement in the Arts, 1990; Democratic Party of New Mexico, Women of Distinction Award, 1992

POPOV (SEE DA, POPOVI)

POPOVI DA (see Da, Popovi)

POP WEA *Taos*

A.K.A. Lori Tanner; Lo Ree Tanner

Birth date unknown; died 1966; niece of Pop Chalee (q.v.)

PUBLISHED: Snodgrass (1968); Tanner (1973)

EXHIBITS: ITIC, SN

AWARDS: SN ('65, 1st)

POP WEA

Pop Wea's paintings were frequently of nontraditional subjects and done in a nontraditional style. According to Tanner (1973), she occasionally combined traditional and symbolic motifs.

PO QUI (see Tafoya, Teofilo)

POQUIN TAH (see Trujillo, Ascensión)

PORTER, BOB *Pima*

Born 1938

RESIDENCE: Phoenix, AZ

EDUCATION: U of AZ, "Southwest Indian Art Project," scholarship, summer 1960

PUBLISHED: Snodgrass (1968)

PORTER, BRIAN *Oneida*

Born 11 Feb 1961

RESIDENCE: Ohsweken, ON

OCCUPATION: Sculptor and painter

BRIAN PORTER

Most of Porter's paintings are commentaries on events of today and are done in a surrealistic style.

Johannsen and Ferguson, eds. 1983

MEDIA: Oil, acrylic, pencil, cast lead, and plaster
PUBLISHED: Johannsen and Furguson, eds. (1983)
EXHIBITS: C/WICEC; Six Nations Fall Fair

PORTER, FRANK *Chippewa*
RESIDENCE: Nett Lake, MN
EXHIBITS: RC

POSEYESVA, RAYMOND JOHN *Hopi*
MEDIA: Tempera
PUBLISHED: Snodgrass (1968); Tanner (1973); Seymour (1988)
PUBLIC COLLECTIONS: AF, IACB/DC, MAI, MNA, MNM, SM, WWM

RAYMOND JOHN POSEYESVA

"The artist is well-known for his paintings of katsinas. *Originally from Shungopovi, AZ, he lived in Winslow, AZ, at one time."*

Snodgrass 1968

POSTOAK, TRACY *Choctaw/Seminole*
RESIDENCE: Tulsa, OK
MEDIA: Oil and acrylic
EXHIBITS: CNM, FCTM
AWARDS: CNM ('89); FCTM ('91)

P'OTSUNU (see Montoya, Gerónima Cruz)

PO TSUNU (see Montoya, Gerónima Cruz)

POURIER, LESTER *Oglala Sioux*
A.K.A. Les Pourier
RESIDENCE: Porcupine, SD
EXHIBITS: RC, TM/NE

POVE PEEN (see Durän, Joe Evan)

POWELL, CHARLES *Kiowa*
RESIDENCE: Lawton, OK
EXHIBITS: AIE
AWARDS: AIE ('78)

POWERS, GENNI *Cherokee*
Born 18 Oct 1939
RESIDENCE: Muskogee, OK
EDUCATION: Porum (OK) High School; Connors State College, Warner, OK; BC
OCCUPATION: Sculptor and painter
MEDIA: Acrylic, tempera, bronze, and wood
EXHIBITS: CNM, BC/McG, FCTM, HM/G, ITIC, PAC, RC
SOLO EXHIBITS: FCTM
AWARDS: CNM; FCTM ('76, IH)

POWLESS, BEVERLY *Mohawk*
Born 14 Sept 1937
RESIDENCE: Nedrow, NY
EDUCATION: Famous Artists Correspondence Course
OCCUPATION: Secretary, seamstress, beadworker, jeweler, and painter
MEDIA: Oil, pastel, pencil, pen and ink, cloth, velour, wool, beads, silver, and shell
PUBLISHED: Johannson and Ferguson, eds. (1983). *The Herald Journal* (4 Apr 1970)
EXHIBITS: ACS/EM, CAOR, INAAT; Kodak Building, Rochester, NY; Lafayette (NY) Public Library
HONORS: Board Member AANNAAC

BEVERLY POWLESS

Powless has received recognition for her portraits and political cartoons. She also paints designs on T-shirts.

Johannson and Ferguson, eds. 1983

POWLESS, BILL P. *Mohawk*

Born 11 Jan 1952; son of Naomi Powless (q.v.)

RESIDENCE: Wilsonville, ON, Canada

EDUCATION: Six Nations Art Council, 1964, 1965; Mohawk College, Brantford, ON, 1974

OCCUPATION: Graphic designer and artist

MEDIA: Pen and ink

PUBLISHED: Johannsen and Ferguson, eds. (1983)

BOOKS ILLUSTRATED: A book by Alma Green

COMMISSIONS: Six Nations Council House, portrait of Frank Montour

PUBLIC COLLECTIONS: SMII

EXHIBITS: C/NAF; C/NFC; C/SNFF; C/WICEC; AM; NACLA; Education Centre of the Toronto Board of Education, ON, 1976

BILL P. POWLESS

Powless intends that his realistic paintings express his opinions on contemporary Native issues. He feels his best work is done on paintings with which he can identify personally. He has been sketching since he was three.

Johannsen and Ferguson, eds. 1983

POWLESS, NAOMI *Mohawk*

Born 16 Apr 1922; mother of Bill Powless (q.v.)

RESIDENCE: Wilsonville, ON, Canada

EDUCATION: Six Nations Council House, 1968; C/GAG, 1974

MEDIA: Acrylic

PUBLISHED: Johannsen and Ferguson, eds. (1983)

EXHIBITS: C/SNFF, C/WICEC

POWLESS, SANDRA MARIE *Seneca*

Born 13 Oct 1940 in Ohsweken, ON, Canada; daughter of Rose Gibson and Walter Bomberry; P/GP: Leana and William Bomberry; M/GP: Elizabeth and Simeon Gibson

RESIDENCE: Ohsweken, ON, Canada

EDUCATION: Caledonia High School

OCCUPATION: Textile designer and painter

MEDIA: Oil, acrylic, watercolor, pen and ink, and acrylic on hide

PUBLISHED: Johannsen and Ferguson, ed. (1983)

COMMISSIONS: Two paintings for a book of Woodland legends

EXHIBITS: AM, C/SNFF, C/WICEC; see also Awards

AWARDS: C/SNFF ('77, 1st; '78, 1st); Simcoe Fair ('78)

PO YE GE *San Ildefonso*

RESIDENCE: San Ildefonso Pueblo, NM

MEDIA: Watercolor

PUBLISHED: Evans and Evans (1931); Snodgrass (1968); Tanner (1973)

PUBLIC COLLECTIONS: MNM

PO YE GE

According to Tanner (1973), Po Ye Ge did one ambitious job and then dropped out of sight. This job was the illustrations for the book, American Indian Dance Steps, *by May and Bessie Evans (1931). Other than this, very little information is available about the artist and his work.*

PRAIRIE FLOWER (see Darling, Marcell J.)

PRATT, CHARLES *Arapaho/Sioux/Cheyenne*

Hawk

A.K.A. Charlie Pratt; Joseph Horselip (signature used on early paintings)

Born 8 Nov 1937 at Concho, OK; brother of Harvey Pratt (q.v.)

EDUCATION: El Reno (OK) High School, 1955

OCCUPATION: Auto body repair, dancer, sculptor, and painter

MEDIA: Tempera, watercolor, wood, fiberglass, metal, gemstone, and bronze

PUBLISHED: *Oklahoma Art Gallery* (spring 1980)

PUBLIC COLLECTIONS: HCC, SGC/OK

CHARLES PRATT

Although he began his career as a painter, he is now best known for his sculptures.

EXHIBITS: AICA, CAI/KC, CNM, HCC, HM, HPTU, IACA, ITIC, FAIE, OCSA, PAC, SDMM, SM, SN, SWAIA, TAAII, RC; see also Awards

SOLO EXHIBITS: SPIM

AWARDS: AICA ('79, Gold Medal); CAI/KC ('80, 1st, Best of Show); CNM ('80, Grand Award); HM; PAC (' 75, Grand Award); IACA ('93); SN; SWAIA ('73, 1st, SWAIA Award; '74, 1st, SWAIA Award); TAAII ('77); Red Ridge Museum, Oklahoma City, OK ('72, 1st)

PRATT, HARVEY *Cheyenne/Arapaho/Sioux*

Going To Be A Chief

A.K.A. Harvey Phillip Pratt

Born 13 Apr 1941 in El Reno, OK; son of Ann Guerrier and Oscar Pratt; P/GF: Nobel Pratt; M/GF: William Guerrier; brother of Charles Pratt (q.v.)

RESIDENCE: Oklahoma City, OK

MILITARY: U.S. Marine Corps, Vietnam

EDUCATION: St. Patrick's, 1962; A.A. in Police Science, 1971

OCCUPATION: Assistant Director of the Oklahoma State Bureau of Investigation, forensic consultant, sculptor, and painter

MEDIA: Oil, acrylic, watercolor, pencil, pen and ink, pastel, wood, clay, bronze, and prints

BOOKS ILLUSTRATED: Oklahoma public schools, history book

PUBLIC COLLECTIONS: SI

EXHIBITS: AIE, CNM, ITIC, LC, RC, RE

AWARDS: CNM ('80, Grand Award); ITIC ('94); RE ('94, 1st)

HONORS: Southern Cheyenne Tribe, "Southern Cheyenne of the Year," 1985; Oklahoma State Bureau of Investigation, two Distinguished Service Medals

HARVEY PRATT

Pratt found his artistic talent to be a valuable asset in his position as an investigator with the Oklahoma State Bureau of Investigation. He used it in forensic composite drawing, skull reconstruction, and photo retouching. Retired and serving as a special consultant in forensic art for the Bureau, Pratt is now a full-time artist and currently painting Plains warriors in action, especially in winter scenes.

artist, p.c. 1993

PREACHER, WILLIE *Shoshoni/Bannock*

Born 28 Sept 1952 in Blackfoot, ID, on the Fort Hall Indian Reservation

RESIDENCE: Blackfoot, ID

EDUCATION: Blackfoot (ID) High School, 1970; U of ID; Idaho State University, Pocatello, ID

OCCUPATION: Training specialist and painter

MEDIA: Oil, watercolor, pencil, pen and ink, and rawhide.

EXHIBITS: ACS/SM; CNM; RC; Cultural Center, Pocatello, ID; Idaho State Fair, Blackfoot, ID; see also Awards

SOLO/SPECIAL EXHIBITS: MPI, 1977; 1993 (dual show)

AWARDS: ACS/SM; Shoshoni-Bannock Indian Festival, Fort Hall, ID

WILLIE PREACHER

Preacher was involved in establishing the Shoshoni-Bannock Fine Arts Council and has served as its chairman. The main purpose for the council is to provide a source of exposure for the tribal artists of the Fort Hall Indian Reservation. His paintings are of the traditional life (prior to 1800) in the various areas in Idaho that were significant to the Indians of the Fort Hall Reservation area.

brochure, MPI, May 1993

PRENDERGAST, MIKE *Cherokee*

RESIDENCE: Nashville, TN

EXHIBITS: CNM

PRESTON, BERT *Hopi*

Tenakhongva

A.K.A. Tenak

Born 6 Dec 1930 in Hotevilla, AZ; son of Lloyd Tenakhongva from Old Oraibi, AZ

RESIDENCE: Tuba City, AZ

EDUCATION: BC

OCCUPATION: School teacher and painter

PUBLISHED: Snodgrass (1968); Brody (1971); Tanner (1973)

PUBLIC COLLECTIONS: KM, PAC

EXHIBITS: HM/G, LGAM, MNA, PAC, PAC/T, RC, SN; see also Awards
AWARDS: HM/G ('75; '76); PAC; Muskogee (OK) State Fair

PRESTON, DANIEL *Tohono O'odham (Papago)*
PUBLISHED: Snodgrass (1968)
PUBLIC COLLECTIONS: SM

PRETENDSEAGLE, THOMAS D. *Sioux/Omaha/Bannock*
Born 22 Feb 1951; son of Mary A. Pretendseagle and Nelson B. Levering
RESIDENCE: Winnebago, NE
EDUCATION: Winnebago (NE) High School, 1970; A.A., Nebraska Indian Community College, 1987
OCCUPATION: Printer, layout designer, and painter
MEDIA: Oil and acrylic
EXHIBITS: Local art shows
AWARDS: Blue ribbons and cash awards in local art shows

PRETTY HAWK *Yankton Sioux*
Oh' Zan
A.K.A. Chief Pretty Hawk
MEDIA: Pigment and hide
PUBLISHED: Alexander (1938); Snodgrass (1968); Maurer (1992)
PUBLIC COLLECTIONS: PM
EXHIBITS: VP

PRETTY HAWK

"Pretty Hawk's work at the Peabody Museum, executed about 1864, had been used at one time as an inner hanging in a lodge."

Snodgrass 1968

PRIBBLE, COREY LYN *Kickapoo/Potawatomi*
Wahwasuk
EXHIBITS: CNM, LIAS

PRINGLE, WILMA JANE REED *Choctaw/Chickasaw*
Born 1928 in Wilberton, OK; daughter of Ida Black and George W. Reed
RESIDENCE: Malibu, CA
EDUCATION: Haskell; St. Joseph's Academy, Dallas, TX, 1948; Los Angeles (CA) City College; studied sculpture under Jon Raymond, Topanga, CA, 1966
OCCUPATION: Temporary secretarial services and artist
EXHIBITS: FAIEAIP, FANAIAE, ITIC, MCA, MNM, PAC, SAIEAIP, WAA
SOLO EXHIBITS: Dallas Osteopathic Hospital, ca. 1962
AWARDS: PAC, SN

PRINTUP, ANDY *Seneca*
A.K.A. Andrew Printup
Born 17 Jan 1964
RESIDENCE: Basom, NY
EDUCATION: Tonawanda Cultural Education Building, art classes
OCCUPATION: Jeweler and painter
MEDIA: Oil, acrylic, pen and ink, pencil, charcoal, and prints
PUBLISHED: Johannsen and Ferguson, eds. (1983)
PUBLIC COLLECTIONS: SMII, NYSF

PRINTUP, ERWIN, JR. *Cayuga*
Born 1956 in Niagara Falls, NY
RESIDENCE: Lewiston, NY
EXHIBITS: C/AG/W, C/NCCT, C/WICEC, ITAE/M, NACLA

PRINTUP, JOEL *Tuscarora/Cayuga*

Born 14 Jan 1960

RESIDENCE: Sanborn, NY

OCCUPATION: Carver, ceramist, and graphic artist

MEDIA: Pencil, charcoal, stone, and prints

PUBLISHED: Johannsen and Ferguson, eds. (1983)

COMMISSIONS: New York Iroquois Conference, program booklet, 1977

EXHIBITS: NYSF; HM; New York State Iroquois Conference

PRINTUP, WAYNE *Cayuga*

Born 14 Feb 1952

RESIDENCE: Sanborn, NY

EDUCATION: Buffalo (NY) State Teacher's College

OCCUPATION: Roofer, jeweler, ceramist, and painter

MEDIA: Acrylic, pencil, pen and ink, charcoal, silver, turquoise, gemstone, shell, and clay

PUBLISHED: Johannsen and Ferguson, eds. (1983)

COMMISSIONS: *Portraits*: Niagara (NY) Wheatfield School, superintendent; Niagara County (NY) Community College, president. *Other:* Brochure covers for local lacrosse and wrestling events

EXHIBITS: NYSF; New York State Iroquois Conference; see also Awards

AWARDS: NYSF ('77, Museum Award); Maid of the Mist Festival, Niagara Falls, NY; New York State Iroquois Conference ('71, 1st)

PROCTOR, THOMAS *Cherokee*

EXHIBITS: CNM

PROCTOR, TIANA *Cherokee*

Birth date unknown; P/GF: Ezekiel Proctor, Senator of the Cherokee Nation

RESIDENCE: Watts, OK

EDUCATION: Watts (OK) High School

MEDIA: Oil and acrylic

PUBLIC COLLECTIONS: BIA, HCC

EXHIBITS: CIM, CNM, FCTM, HCC, LIAS, OIAC, RC, TIAF, TM/NE

AWARDS: CNM ('93)

PUCUNUBBI (see Collins, Adele)

PUDLAT (see Pudlo)

PUDLAT, INNUKJUAKJU (see Innukjuakju)

PUDLAT, PUDLO (see Pudlo)

PUDLO *Inuit (Eskimo)*

A.K.A. Padlo; Padloo; Pudlat; Pudlo Pudlat

Born 1916 at camp Kamadjuak near Cape Dorset, NWT, Canada

RESIDENCE: Cape Dorset, NWT, Canada

OCCUPATION: Hunter, fisherman, sculptor, and graphic artist

MEDIA: Acrylic, black pencil, colored pencil, colored felt tip pen, crayon, and prints

PUBLISHED: Blodgett (n.d.; 1978a; 1983); Houston (1967; 1967a); Larmour (1967); Swinton (1972); Ritchie (1974); Roch, ed. (1974); Goetz, et al. (1977); Collinson (1978); Routledge (1979; 1990); Woodhouse (1980); Marsh, ed. (1985); LaBarge (1986); Jackson and Nasby (1987); McMasters, et al. (1993).

PUDLO

Pudlo spent his childhood in traditional camps on Baffin, Coates, and Southampton Islands. He began to draw and carve in the late 1950s when he moved to Cape Dorset with his third wife, Innukjuakuk. An injury to his right arm made carving difficult and he soon

Artscanda (Vol. 28, no. 6, 1971-1972); *The London Evening Free Press* (Nov 1972); *The Toronto Star* (17 Feb 1978); *The Edmonton Journal* (4 July 1978; 31 Oct 1978); *The Oakville Banner* (15 Nov 1978); *About Arts and Crafts* (winter 1978); *Intercom* (Vol. 21, no. 6, 1979); *The Winnipeg Free Press* (9 May 1981); *The Beaver* (autumn 1984); *Arts Manitoba* (summer, 1985); *Inuit Art Quarterly* (Vol. 1, no. 2, 1986; Vol. 1, no. 3, 1986; summer 1987); *The Globe Mail* (9 Feb 1988); *The Ottawa Citizen* (13 Jan 1989); *Inuit Art World* (Vol. 5, 1990-1991)

COMMISSIONS: United Nations Habitat Conference, 1976; Indian and Northern Affairs Canada; The Queen Elizabeth Hotel, Montréal, PQ, 1978; Canadian Guild of Crafts, Montréal, PQ, 1979

PUBLIC COLLECTIONS: Partial listing includes: ACMWA; C/AC/AE; C/AC/MS; C/AG/GV; C/AG/H; C/AG/IGEA; C/AG/LR; C/AG/M; C/AG/O; C/AG/U of L; C/AG/V; C/AG/WI; C/AG/WP; C/CAP; C/CCAB; C/CGCQ; C/CMC; C/GM; C/INAC; C/LUM; C/NGCA; C/PWNHC; C/ROM; C/SFG; C/TCC; C/TDB; C/U of AB; C/U of NB; C/WBEC; C/YU; Mount Allison University, Sackville, NB; Northern Michigan College, Traverse City, MI; Province of British Columbia, Victoria, BC

EXHIBITS: Partial listing of more than one hundred includes: ACMWA; C/AC/AE; C/AC/MS; C/AG/E; C/AG/O; C/AG/U of L; C/AG/WP; C/AV; C/CD; C/CG; C/CGCQ; C/CID; C/CIIA; C/EACTDB; C/EFA; C/GAEC; C/GM; C/IA7; C/IGV; C/LS; C/LUM; C/MCC; C/MBAM; C/NGCA; C/SFG; C/SS; C/TIP; C/U of AB; C/U of G; U of R/MG; C/WBEC; C/WLA; C/YU; EG; GM; MMA/MN; SUNY/B; U of MI; U of MT; Art Association of Newport, RI, 1968; Jerusalem Artists' House Museum, Jerusalem, Israel, 1978; Museum of Science and History, Fort Worth, TX, 1984-1985; National Library of Canada, 1985-1986; St. Mary's University Gallery, Halifax, NS, 1977

SOLO EXHIBITS: Partial listing of 16 includes: C/AG/CC; C/AG/IGEA; C/CGCQ; C/INAC; C/PP; C/UG; Inuit Galerie, Mannheim, Germany

HONORS: Canadian Postal Service, print reproduced on postage stamp, 1978; UNICEF, design chosen for greeting card

PUDLO

(continued) turned to drawing. His drawings reflect the changes that were occurring around him. His fascination with new technology led him to include airplanes, helicopters, motorboats, and snowmobiles in his work. He says of his drawing, "I have been drawing a long time now. I only draw what I think, but sometimes I think the pencil has a brain too."

"Pudlo has been one of the most consistent and reflective of the Cape Dorset artists... Narrative and documentation have never interested Pudlo. He has been preoccupied with the abstract possibilities of forms, and with objects as spiritual symbols."

LaBarge, 1986

Pudlo was greatly honored by arrangements that were made so he could be present at exhibits of his work in Toronto, 1976; Ottawa, 1988; and Mannheim, Germany, 1989.

PUENTE, RAYMOND *Navajo*

Born 31 Dec 1952 at Fort Defiance, AZ

RESIDENCE: Sanders, AZ

MEDIA: Acrylic and pencil

EXHIBITS: ITIC; NTF; Navajo County Fair, Holbrook, AZ; see also Awards

AWARDS: ITIC ('90, 1st); NTF ('90, 1st); Utah State Fair

PUERTO, LEONARD *Apache*

RESIDENCE: Dulce, NM

PUBLISHED: Snodgrass (1968)

EXHIBITS: MNM (student division)

PUGLAS, FRANK *Kwakwaka'wakw (Kwakiutl)*

MEDIA: Watercolor and pen and ink

PUBLIC COLLECTIONS: C/RBCM

PUKINGNAAQ (see Pukingnak, Nancy)

PUKINGNAK, NANCY *Inuit (Eskimo)*

A.K.A. Nancy Pukingrnak Aupaluktuk; Pookertnak; Pookootna; Pukingnaaq; Pukingnerk

Born 1940; daughter of Oonark and Qablunaaq; GM: Naataq

RESIDENCE: Baker Lake, NWT, Canada

OCCUPATION: Seamstress, carver, and graphic artist

NANCY PUKINGNAK

Pukingnak's family moved to Baker Lake in 1958 after her father died. She was married the same year and is now the mother of seven children. When she was in her early 1930s she began to carve and draw to help with the family finances.

Latocki 1982

MEDIA: Graphite pencil, colored pencil, crayon, stone, thread, skin, and prints
PUBLISHED: Blodgett (n.d.); Routledge (1979); Latocki (1982); Jackson and Nasby (1987)
PUBLIC COLLECTIONS: C/AC/MS
EXHIBITS: C/AC/MS, C/AG/W, C/AG/WP, C/CID, C/IA7, C/LS

PUKINGNERK (see Pukingnak, Nancy)

PULLING ROOTS (see Houser, Allan)

PUMPKIN FLOWER (see Pentewa, Dick R.)

PUSH, CHARLIE (see Pushetonequa, Charles)

PUSHETONEQUA, CHARLES *Sauk-Fox*

Pushetonequa; *Wawabano Sata,* Dawn Walker; *Mesquakie,* Red Earth People
A.K.A. Charlie Push
Born 1915 in Tama, IA; died 25 Aug 1987
RESIDENCE: Lived in Tama, IA
MILITARY: U.S. Air Force, WWII
EDUCATION: Haskell; Santa Fe
PUBLISHED: Snodgrass (1968); Brody (1971); Broder (1981)
PUBLIC COLLECTIONS: DAM, HS/MC, PAC
EXHIBITS: ADIA; PAC; Hawaiian Islands; Association on American Indian Affairs, Inc., New York, NY, 1963
AWARDS: ADIA ('67)

CHARLES PUSHETONEQUA

"The artist lived on the Tama Indian Settlement. His paintings depicted the life and environment of the Sauk-Fox tribe and were reproduced and widely distributed by the Tama Indian Crafts organization."

Snodgrass 1968

PUTOOGOO (see Pootoogook)

PU YO PIN (see Vigil, Thomas)

QARLIKSAQ, HAROLD *Inuit (Eskimo)*

A.K.A. Qarliksaq

Born 1928 at Garry Lake, NWT, Canada; died 1980

RESIDENCE: Lived at Baker Lake, NWT, Canada

OCCUPATION: Trapper, hunter, and graphic artist

MEDIA: Graphite pencil and prints

PUBLISHED: Blodgett (1978a; 1978b); Collinson (1978); Routledge (1979); Jackson and Nasby (1987)

PUBLIC COLLECTIONS: C/AC/MS, C/AG/WP, C/U of AB

EXHIBITS: C/AC/MS, C/AG/WP, C/BLPD, C/CG, C/CID, C/IA7

QATSIYA, PUDLALIK (see Kavovoa)

QAULLUARYUK, RUTH *Inuit (Eskimo)*

A.K.A. Koaluaayuk; Qauluaryuk

Born 1932

RESIDENCE: Baker Lake, NWT, Canada

OCCUPATION: Graphic artist

MEDIA: Black pencil, colored pencil, and prints

PUBLISHED: Goetz, et al. (1977); Latocki, ed. (1983)

PUBLIC COLLECTIONS: C/AG/WP

EXHIBITS: C/AG/WP, C/TIP

QINNUAYUAK, LUCY (see Lucy)

QMALUK, LEAH *Inuit (Eskimo)*

A.K.A. Leah Qumaluk

Born 17 Apr 1934

RESIDENCE: Povungnituk, PQ, Canada

OCCUPATION: Graphic artist

PUBLISHED: Routledge (1979); Meyers, ed. (1980). *North* (Mar/Apr 1974); *Arts West* (Vol. 3, no. 5, 1978)

PUBLIC COLLECTIONS: DAM

EXHIBITS: C/AG/WP; C/IA7; C/TMBI; Robertson Galleries, Ottawa, ON

QOTSKUYVA, ROBERT *Hopi*

Quotskuyva

A.K.A. Robert Quotskuyva; Ootskuyva; Quatskuyva

Born 12 Aug 1911

RESIDENCE: Kykotsmovi, AZ

EDUCATION: Albuquerque

OCCUPATION: Weaver, *katsina* carver, and painter

MEDIA: Tempera, watercolor, and cottonwood root

PUBLISHED: Snodgrass (1968); Seymour (1988)

PUBLIC COLLECTIONS: AF; IACB/DC; MAI (signed "Robert"); MNA; SMNAI (signed "Ootskuyva"); U of CA/LMA (signed "Quatskuyva")

EXHIBITS: WRTD

QUAH AH (see Peña, Tonita)

QUAMAHONGNEWA, HASTINGS *Hopi*

PUBLIC COLLECTIONS: MNA

HAROLD QARLIKSAQ

Qarliksaq, who began to draw in 1970, is considered one of the most inventive artists from Baker Lake. His design concepts were totally original. An extreme delicacy of line made them impossible to translate accurately into a print.

Jackson and Nasby 1987

ROBERT QOTSKUYVA

Qotskuyva thinks he stopped painting when he was in his twenties. At that time he switched to the more traditional art forms of weaving and katsina *carving.*

Seymour 1988

DETAIL: Ben Quintana, *Deer Dance*, 1943. Philbrook Museum of Art, Tulsa, Oklahoma

QUAMAHONGNEWA, REDFORD *Hopi*

RESIDENCE: Oraibi, AZ
PUBLISHED: Snodgrass (1968)
PUBLIC COLLECTIONS: MAI

QUAMEOMAH (see Havier, Michael)

QUANANAAPIK (see Quananapik)

QUANANAPIK *Inuit (Eskimo)*

A.K.A. Kuananaapi; Quananaapik
Born 1938
RESIDENCE: Povungnituk, PQ, Canada
OCCUPATION: Graphic artist
MEDIA: Pencil
PUBLISHED: Goetz, et al. (1977); Myers, ed. (1980). *Arts West* (Vol. 3, no. 5, 1978)
PUBLIC COLLECTIONS: DAM
EXHIBITS: C/TIP, C/TMBI

QUANDELACY, WILMER *Zuni*

RESIDENCE: Zuni, NM
PUBLISHED: Snodgrass (1968)
EXHIBITS: MNM

QUANNIE, EMERSON HORACE (see Quannie, Emerson T.)

QUANNIE, EMERSON T. *Hopi*

A.K.A. Emerson Horace Quannie
Born Mar 1916 in Kykotsmovi, AZ; died 1948; son of Jenny and Horace Quannie
EDUCATION: Albuquerque, 1932
OCCUPATION: Trading post bookkeeper and painter
PUBLISHED: Snodgrass (1968); Seymour (1988); Williams, ed. (1990)
COMMISSIONS: *Murals:* Albuquerque (NM) movie theater
PUBLIC COLLECTIONS: IACB/DC, MKMcNAI, MNA
EXHIBITS: MKMcNAI, WRTD

EMERSON T. QUANNIE

After leaving Albuquerque Indian School, Quannie did very little painting. His wife knew of only one that was done after their marriage in 1939.

Seymour 1988

QUANNIE, LORENZO H. *Hopi*

A.K.A. Quannig
Birth date unknown
RESIDENCE: Believed to be from Oraibi, AZ
PUBLISHED: Snodgrass (1968)
PUBLIC COLLECTIONS: MAI; MNA/KHC (signed "Quannie"); MNM (signed "Quannie, 1934, Oraibi"); SM (23, one signed "Quannig")

QUANNIE, MERRILL *Acoma/Hopi*

Dyaakudruwi, Yellow Butterfly
Born 26 Sept 1965 in Belmont, AZ; son of Mary L. Martínez and Merrill H. Quannie; P/GP: Jenny and Horace Quannie; M/GP: Santana and José Martínez; nephew of Lorenzo H. Quannie (q.v.)
RESIDENCE: Albuquerque, NM
EDUCATION: Coconino High School, Flagstaff, AZ; U of AZ; U of ABQ; Albuquerque (NM) Technical-Vocational Institute, 1984
OCCUPATION: Land conveyance examiner; full-time artist after 1988
MEDIA: Acrylic, watercolor, gouache, pen and ink, pastel, mixed-media, and prints

MERRILL QUANNIE

Quannie's works combine Pueblo mythology, Mimbres art and archaeology with Gestalt and Jungian psychology. His intricate geometric designs are done in vibrant colorful inks. Each work of art incorporates the mythological character Kokopelli, the flute player.

artist, p.c. 1992

PUBLISHED: Tryk (1993). *The Albuquerque Tribune* (30 Aug 1990)

COMMISSIONS: *Posters: Take Five Magazine*, 1988; Indian Child Welfare Act Conference, 1992; The Nature Company, catalogue; Wrubel Gallery, Berkeley, CA, featured artist, 1991; State Bar of New Mexico, Annual State Conference, 1991; U.S. Department of Education, Office of Indian Education, 1992. *Other:* Albuquerque (NM) Convention and Visitors Bureau, public bus panels, 1991

PUBLIC COLLECTIONS: MRFM; IPCC; Museum of Indian Arts and Culture, Santa Fe, NM

EXHIBITS: NMFA; NMSF; SWAIA; Albuquerque Festival of Arts; see also Awards

AWARDS: NMFA ('90, MA, Purchase Award); NMSF ('90; '92) SWAIA ('89; '90; '91, 1st)

HONORS: Bien Mur Indian Market, poster artist; Weatherhead Scholarship, U of AZ; Democratic Party of New Mexico, Albuquerque, Business Leader Award, artist, 1991

QUANNIG (see Quannie, Lorenzo H.)

QUATSKUYVA, R. (see Qotskuyva, R.)

QUAYESVA (see Honewytewa, Louis Calvin F.)

QUED (see Archuleta, Betty Keener)

QUED KOI (see Mopope, Stephen)

QUENIPEA (see Poodray, C. Earl)

QUETAQUE, JEFFERSON YATOK (see Quetoque, Jefferson)

QUETONE (see Quoetone, Jimmy)

QUETONE, DAISY *Comanche/Kiowa*

RESIDENCE: Lawton, OK

EXHIBITS: AIE

AWARDS: AIE ('83; '85, 1st; '86, 1st)

QUETOQUE, JEFFERSON *Zuñi*

A.K.A. Jefferson Yatok Quetaque

PUBLISHED: Dunn (1968); Snodgrass (1968)

PUBLIC COLLECTIONS: MNM

EXHIBITS: MNM; NGA (a "Quetoque" exhibited), 1953

QUETOQUE, LEO *Zuñi*

PUBLISHED: Snodgrass (1968)

PUBLIC COLLECTIONS: MNM

EXHIBITS: NGA (a "Quetoque" exhibited), 1953

QUEYESVA (see Honewytewa, Louis Calvin, Jr.)

QUICK THUNDER *Sioux*

PUBLISHED: Snodgrass (1968)

PUBLIC COLLECTIONS: MPM (pictographic style on paper)

QUIN CHA KE CHA *Ute*

PUBLISHED: Snodgrass (1968)

PUBLIC COLLECTIONS: MNM

QUINNUAJUAK (see Lucy)

Ben Quintana

"Quintana did not paint after 1942. He died in 1944 at 21 years of age in military action during WWII. For bravery and heroism under fire he was posthumously awarded the Silver Star."

Snodgrass 1968

Quintana, Ben *Cochití*

Ha A Tee

Born ca. 1923 at Cochití Pueblo, NM; died 9 Nov 1944 at Leyte, Philippines, during WWII

MILITARY: WWII

EDUCATION: Santa Fe; art instruction under Tonita Peña and Gerónima Montoya (qq.v.)

OCCUPATION: Painter

MEDIA: Watercolor and tempera

PUBLISHED: Jacobson and d'Ucel (1950); Dunn (1968); Snodgrass (1968); Brody (1971); Tanner (1973); Highwater (1976); Dockstader (1977); Silberman (1978); Fawcett and Callander (1982); Samuels (1985); Seymour (1988). *Arizona Highways* (Aug 1952); *The American Scene* (Vol. 6, no. 3); *The Indian Trader* (Mar 1988)

COMMISSIONS: *Murals:* Cochití (NM) Day School; Santa Fe; Maisel's Indian Trading Post, Albuquerque, NM, 1939

PUBLIC COLLECTIONS: GM, IACB/DC, MAI, MNA/KHC, MRFM, OU/MA, PAC, UPA, SM, WWM

EXHIBITS: AIW, ASM, FWG, HM, MFA/O, MAI, NGA, OMA, OU/ET, PAC, PAC/T, WRTD

AWARDS: New Mexico State Coronado Quadricentennial Celebration('40, 1st - awarded when a teenager); *American Magazine* poster contest ($1,000 prize - competed against 50,000 entries)

HONORS: National Youth Forum Art Contest (1st-student, Santa Fe)

Joe A. Quintana

According to Tanner 1973, Quintana did little or no painting after he left school.

Quintana, Joe A. *Cochití*

Birth date unknown; born at Cochití Pueblo, NM

RESIDENCE: Cochití Pueblo, NM

PUBLISHED: Snodgrass (1968); Tanner (1973); Samuels (1985)

PUBLIC COLLECTIONS: MNA/KHC

EXHIBITS: AIW; *American Magazine* Contest

Quintana, Johnnie *Cochití*

EDUCATION: Santa Fe, ca. 1958

PUBLISHED: Snodgrass (1968)

EXHIBITS: MNM

Quintana, Marcelino *Cochití*

PUBLISHED: Snodgrass (1968)

PUBLIC COLLECTIONS: MNM

Quintana, Trinidad *Cochití*

Born ca. 1916

PUBLISHED: Snodgrass (1968)

PUBLIC COLLECTIONS: MNM

Qui Tone (see Quoetone, Jimmy)

Quiver, Dan *Sioux*

RESIDENCE: Wanblee, SD

PUBLISHED: Snodgrass (1968)

PUBLIC COLLECTIONS: MAI

QUIVER, ROBERT A. *Sioux*

Wagacho, Cottonwood Tree
Born 18 Feb 1936 in Hisle, SD
RESIDENCE: Pine Ridge and Wanblee, SD
MILITARY: U.S. Navy, WWII
EDUCATION: Oglala Community High School, Pine Ridge, SD
PUBLISHED: Snodgrass (1968)
EXHIBITS: Shows and markets in South Dakota

QUIYAVEMA (see Sunrise, Riley)

QUMALUK, LEAH (see Qmaluk, Leah)

QUOETONE, JIMMY *Kiowa*

A.K.A. Qui Tone; Quetone
Birth date unknown; died ca. 1955 in Oklahoma; GF: Anzahte (Kicking Bird), Kiowa participant in the Cut Throat Massacre; brother of Tah Bone Mah (Iseeo), Kiowa scout and member of the U.S. Cavalry
PUBLISHED: Snodgrass (1968)

JIMMY QUOETONE

Quoetone took a calendar from Haw Vahte's grave before it was covered and kept it up to date with the aid of Charles Emery Rowell (q.v.), a relative.

Snodgrass 1968

This calendar is now known as the Haw Vahte calendar.

QUOTSKUYVA, ROBERT (see Qotskuyva, Robert)

QUOYAVEMA (see Sunrise, Riley)

QUOYAVEMA, RILEY (see Sunrise, Riley)

QUSSAY YAH *Comanche*

PUBLISHED: Snodgrass (1968)
PUBLIC COLLECTIONS: FSM (colored crayon on paper, ca. 1930)

Bill Rabbit

As a child, Rabbit was strongly influenced by stories told to him by the Cherokee elders. Many of his earlier paintings are very detailed depictions of the common everyday life of the early Cherokee settlers in Oklahoma. Rabbit's style has changed periodically, from the realistic to the ethereal. He paints as he feels, not as the public thinks (although he has achieved considerable commercial success with Ralph Oliver listing his paintings as "one of the best investments for 1987"). According to the artist, "I came to the realization early on that if you have the courage to do the best you can and the courage to put it in front of the public and if you can learn to accept rejection, then you can do whatever you want to do."

p.c. 1991

DETAIL: Alfonso Roybal (Awa Tsireh), *Koshare Rainbow Dance*, ca. 1947. Philbrook Museum of Art, Tulsa, Oklahoma

RABBIT, BILL *Cherokee*

A.K.A. William E. Rabbit

Born 1946 in Casper, WY; son of Doris and Swimmer Rabbit; father of Traci Rabbit (q.v.)

RESIDENCE: Pryor, OK

MILITARY: U.S. Army, Vietnam

OCCUPATION: Salesman, deputy sheriff, welder, shop and gallery owner, jeweler, and artist

PUBLISHED: Jones (1988); Hogan (1990), book jacket. *Oklahoma Art Gallery* (spring, 1980); *Art Gallery* (July/Aug 1982); *Oklahoma Today* (Dec 1990); *U.S. Art* (Nov 1991); *The Broken Arrow Scout* (15 Jan 1992); *Art of the West* (July/Aug 1992); *The Muskogee Daily Phoenix* (4 Oct 1993); *The Tulsa World* (12 Feb 1994)

PUBLIC COLLECTIONS: CNM, FCTM, HCC, ITIC, NACLA, SN, TTSP

EXHIBITS: ABQM; CNM; FCTM; HCC; IACA; IEEPF; ITIC; KCPA; LSS; MNH/AN; NACLA; OAC; OIAP; OSC; PF; RC; RE; SI; SIRU; TIAF; TTSP; U of WV; galleries throughout the U.S.

SOLO EXHIBITS: CNM, 1987

AWARDS: CNM ('79, Class II Award, '82; '83, 1st, Tiger Award; '86, 1st; '87, 1st); FCTM ('81, 1st; '82; '84, Grand Award); FCTM/M ('86, IH; '90; '93); ITIC ('82, 3-1st, Best in Class, Momaday Award; '85; '87, 1st; '90); RE ('81; '86, Powers Award)

HONORS: ITIC, poster artist, 1984; FCTM, designated a Master Artist, 1986; TF, poster artist, 1988; AICA, Artist of the Year and poster artist, 1989; Oklahoma State Capitol, *Year of the Indian* exhibition, one of eight Indian artists exhibited, 1992; IEEPF, Easter egg design (twice); TIAF, featured artist, 1994

RABBIT, TRACI *Cherokee*

A.K.A. Traci Rochelle Rabbit

Born 29 Oct 1969 in Claremore, OK; daughter of Karen Jones and Bill Rabbit (q.v.); P/GP: Doris and Swimmer Rabbit; M/GP: Ruby and Bill Jones

RESIDENCE: Pryor, OK

EDUCATION: Pryor (OK) High School, 1987; B.A., NSU, 1993

OCCUPATION: Artist

MEDIA: Acrylic

PUBLIC COLLECTIONS: Sallisaw (OK) Health Center; Cherokee Nation, Tahlequah, OK

EXHIBITS: CNM, FCTM, ITIC; see also Awards

AWARDS: CNM ('90; '92); FCTM; Northeast Area Artists Association Show (1st); ITIC ('94)

RABBIT SHOULDER (see Polan Yi Katon)

RABENA, GLEN *Yakama*

RESIDENCE: Canada

PUBLISHED: Hall, Blackman, and Rickard, eds. (1981)

EXHIBITS: C/WICEC

RACINE, ALBERT BATISTE *Blackfeet*

Apowmuckcon, Running Weasel

Born 19 Apr 1907 in Browning, MT; died 1984

RESIDENCE: Lived in Browning, MT

MILITARY: U.S. Army, WWII, 1942-1945

EDUCATION: Browning (MT) High School, 1928; Haskell, 1921-1922; studied under Winold Reiss, Edward Everett Hale Jr., Adrian Voisin, Carl Hurtig Sr., and John L. Clark

OCCUPATION: Commercial sign painter, wood carver, and painter

PUBLISHED: Snodgrass (1968); Ewers (1986)

COMMISSIONS: Browning (MT) Methodist Church

PUBLIC COLLECTIONS: HCC; MPI; Methodist Mission, Browning, MT

EXHIBITS: BNIAS; HCC; MPI; PAM; Fairmont Hotel, San Francisco, CA; Glacier National Park Hotel, MT; Great Falls and Helena, MT

ALBERT BATISTE RACINE

"The artist began painting in 1926, but in 1936 he turned to sculpture. During WWII he did no art work. In 1956, he began sculpting again and did very little painting. He has carved gavels for Presidents John F. Kennedy and Lyndon B. Johnson, and for Senator Robert Kennedy and Governor Edmund G. Brown [California]."

Snodgrass 1968

RACKLEFF, ED *Cherokee*

A.K.A. Edwin Neal Rackleff

Born 20 Nov 1961 in Tahlequah, OK; son of Agnes Youngbird and Barkie Rackleff; P/GP: Nancy Tail and Johnny Rackleff; M/GP: Ahniwake Foreman and Bill Youngbird

RESIDENCE: Claremore, OK

EDUCATION: Sequoyah High School, Tahlequah, OK, 1977-1980; BC, 1983-1984; Rogers State College, Claremore, OK, 1992-1993

OCCUPATION: Silversmith and painter

MEDIA: Oil, acrylic, watercolor, pencil, and pen and ink

PUBLISHED: Biographical publications

EXHIBITS: CHASC, CNM, FCTM, LIAS, RE, TWF, U of KS; see also Awards

AWARDS: FCTM ('78, Best of Show; '86, IH; '87; '89); Cherokee National Holiday Art Show ('87)

RAFAEL, DONALD *Navajo*

EDUCATION: Albuquerque, 1962-1963

PUBLISHED: Snodgrass (1968)

EXHIBITS: MNM

RAGEE, EGEVADLUQ (see Eegyvudluk)

RAINBOW AROUND THE SUN (see Lomakema, Milland, Sr.)

RAINBOW COUGAR (see Edwards, Ken)

RAIN GOD (see Roybal, José D.)

RAIN GOD TOWN (see Sánchez, Ramos)

RAIN IN THE FACE *Hunkpapa Sioux*

Iromagaja

A.K.A. Chief Rain In The Face

Born ca. 1825 "near the forks of the Cheyenne River"; died 14 Sept 1904 at Standing Rock Agency, ND

MEDIA: Crayon and graphite

PUBLISHED: Snodgrass (1968); Fawcett and Callander (1972); Dockstader (1977); Maurer (1992)

PUBLIC COLLECTIONS: GM, MAI

EXHIBITS: GM, MAI, VP

RAIN IN THE FACE

"Rain In The Face was in the Battle of the Little Big Horn in 1876. Work by the artist in the MAI is dated Standing Rock, Dakota Territory, 1885."

Snodgrass 1968

RAMOS, JEAN D. *Yurok/Wintun/Chilula*

A.K.A. Signature: Jeanie Ramos

Born 24 Nov 1944 in Eureka, CA; daughter of Winifred Marshall and Amos Cooper; P/GP: Nellie Billie and Yarnell Cooper; M/GP: Stella Brett and Fredrick Cripe

RESIDENCE: Brentwood, CA

EDUCATION: Brentwood (NY) High School and Morehead City (NC) High School, 1963; CSU/H; Los Medanos College, Pittsburg, CA

OCCUPATION: Full-time artist

MEDIA: Oil, acrylic, pen and ink, pastel, porcelain overglaze, and mixed-media

PUBLIC COLLECTIONS: HTM/CA; Cocopa Tribal Office

EXHIBITS: CNGM; HM; HTM/CA; Native American Art Exhibit, Governor's Office, Sacramento, CA; see also Awards

AWARDS: HM (Judge's Choice); CID (Frank Day Award, Damon Hailstone Award)

HONORS: Hopi documentary film, *Where the Trails Return*, featured her painting, *Natinook*

RANDALL, BUNNIE *Creek*

Wiyo

Born 1923; death date unknown

EDUCATION: OSU/O

OCCUPATION: Instructor at the Tinker Air Force Base Graphics Office (Oklahoma City, OK) and painter

PUBLISHED: Snodgrass (1968)

COMMISSIONS: *Murals:* Tinker Air Force Base, Oklahoma City, OK [with Albin Roy Jake (q.v.) and LeRoy McAllister]

PUBLIC COLLECTIONS: PAC

EXHIBITS: MNM, PAC

RANDALL, CATHERINE *Sioux*

Born 1 Apr 1956 in Denver, CO

EDUCATION: Los Altos (CA) High School, 1970-1974; U of CA/SB, 1974-1976; B.A., BHSU, 1979

OCCUPATION: Upward Bound (BHSU) teacher, counselor, and instructor, and painter

MEDIA: Oil, acrylic, pencil, pen and ink, and prints

PUBLIC COLLECTIONS: HCC

EXHIBITS: BHSU, HCC, RC

SOLO EXHIBITS: SIM

HONORS: South Dakota Indian Education Association, Pierre, SD, scholarship

RANI, BIST *Zuni*

PUBLISHED: Snodgrass (1968)

PUBLIC COLLECTIONS: U of PA/M

RATTEY, HARVEY L. *Assiniboin*

PUBLIC COLLECTIONS: HCC

EXHIBITS: HCC, TM/NE

RATTLING THUNDER, TRACI LEVAY *Chippewa/Yankton Sioux*

Born 25 Mar 1968 in San Diego, CA; daughter of Bonita Gereszek and Donald LeVay; P/GP: Isabelle and Peter LeVay; M/GP: Alice and Richard Gereszek

RESIDENCE: Poplar, MT

EDUCATION: Poplar (MT) High School, 1986; correspondence courses, MIA

OCCUPATION: Housekeeper and artist

MEDIA: Acrylic, pencil, and pen and ink

COMMISSIONS: *Murals:* Poplar (MT) High School. *Other*: Montana communities and Indian agencies, four jacket designs

PUBLIC COLLECTIONS: HCC

EXHIBITS: HCC; IAIA; LSS; RC; WTF; Poplar (MT) Centennial Celebration Art

Show, 1992; Roosevelt County Fair, Culbertson, MT; Visual Individualists United Open Show, New York, NY

AWARDS: IAIA ('86, 1st); RC ('91, Begay Award, Aplan Award; '92, Erickson Award; '93, Erickson Award)

HONORS: RC, Thunderbird Foundation Scholarship, 1991

RAVE, AUSTIN JERALD *Sioux/Winnebago*

Wawe Hakta, Cares For His People

Born 5 Aug 1946 on the Cheyenne River Reservation, SD

RESIDENCE: Eagle Butte, SD

EDUCATION: Cheyenne-Eagle Butte (SD) High School, 1964; A.A.,IAIA, 1966; SFAI, 1966

OCCUPATION: Architectural draftsman, designer, and painter

MEDIA: Oil and acrylic

PUBLISHED: Snodgrass (1968); Libhart (1970); Highwater (1976). *Smoke Signals*, IACB (autumn 1965)

PUBLIC COLLECTIONS: IACB, IAIA, SIM

EXHIBITS: CSP, IAIA, SAIEAIP, YAIA, RC, SN

AWARDS: SN ('66, Governor's Trophy)

RAW HIDE RATTLE (see Washakie)

RAY, CARL *Cree*

Tall Straight Poplar

Born 18 July 1943 on the Sandy Lake Reserve, ON, Canada; died Sept 1978 at Sandy Lake, ON, Canada

RESIDENCE: Lived on the Sandy Lake Reserve, ON, Canada

EDUCATION: Residential School, McIntosh, ON

OCCUPATION: Trapper, hunter, logger, miner, writer, editor, teacher, printmaker, and painter

MEDIA: Acrylic, pen and ink, and prints

PUBLISHED: Highwater (1980); Southcott (1984); Menitove, ed. (1986b); Menitove and Danford (1989); Podedworny (1989); McMasters, et al. (1993). *The Indian Trader* (July 1978); *Masterkey* (winter 1984)

BOOKS ILLUSTRATED: Ray and Stevens (1971)

COMMISSIONS: *Murals:* Indians of Canada Pavilion, Expo '67; Sandy Lake (ON) Friendship Centre. *Other:* Sandy Lake School Teachers, portrait of the Sandy Lake School principal

PUBLIC COLLECTIONS: C/AG/WP; C/AG/TB; C/CMC; C/GOAC; C/INAC; C/MCC; C/ROM; C/U of T; Fort Frances (ON) Public Library; Manitoba Centennial Corporation, Winnipeg, MB; Peat, Marwick, Mitchell and Company, Toronto, ON; Queen's Park, Toronto, ON; Red Lake (ON) Fellowship Centre; Sioux Lookout (ON) Fellowship and Communications Centre; Sioux Lookout (ON) Public Library

EXHIBITS: C/AG/TB; C/BU; C/CC; C/CIARH; C/CNAC; C/MCC; C/ROM; C/TU; C/U of T; C/WCAA; C/WICEC; U of MN; Fort Frances (ON) Public Library, 1971; Minnesota State College, International Falls, MN, 1971; Northern Ontario Art Tour, 1972

SOLO EXHIBITS: Partial listing of twelve includes: C/BU; C/CC; U of MN; Fort Frances (ON) Public Library, 1972; Indian-Métis Friendship Centre, Winnipeg, MB, 1969; Terryberry Library, Hamilton, ON, 1973

HONORS: *Grants:* INAC, 1969; Canada Council, 1969; Department of National Health and Welfare, Indian Affairs Branch, Cultural Development Grant, 1971, 1973

CARL RAY

Ray was one of the earliest adherents of the Woodlands School of Art. He painted in both a realistic style and the Algonquin Legend Painting style. Ray started painting the tribal legends as a young man. Because the elders did not approve, he quit and sought other employment. Working as a gold miner, he developed tuberculosis and while in the hospital, he began to paint again. Recovered, he returned to his village to discover that the attitude toward painting had changed. One of Ray's reasons for painting was to save the legends and culture of his people by depicting the sacred stories told to him by his grandfather, a holy man among the Cree of Sandy Lake.

RAY, RICHARD (see Whitman, Richard Ray)

RAYMOND, CHARLENE TETERS (see Teters, Charlene)

RAYNOR, LENNEY FRANKLIN *Cherokee*

RESIDENCE: Fort Gibson, OK

EDUCATION: Fort Gibson (OK) High School; BC

PUBLIC COLLECTIONS: HCC

EXHIBITS: CNM, HCC, FCTM, HM/G, RC

AWARDS: CNM ('73, 1st; '74, 1st); FCTM ('71, 1st; '74, IH, Grand Award; '78); RC ('77)

HONORS: Fort Gibson (OK) High School, Salutatorian; BC, Salutatorian, 1973; BC, Phi Theta Kappa

REAL BIRD, KEN *Crow*

A.K.A. Kenneth Real Bird

Born ca. 1953 in Garryowen, MT

EDUCATION: IAIA, 1983-1984

OCCUPATION: Jeweler, rodeo contestant, and painter

MEDIA: Watercolor, pencil, silver, and gemstone

EXHIBITS: CIAE/MT; GFNAAS; NAVAM; NMSF; Governor's Award Winners Invitational Art Show, Albuquerque, NM; OS Ranch Art Show, Post Falls, TX

AWARDS: NMSF ('83, Best in Category)

REASON, JAMIE *Cherokee*

Tawodi

EXHIBITS: CNM

REASOR, MAGGIE *Cherokee*

Born 20 Dec 1939 in El Paso, TX; daughter of Iris Vera Evans and Morgan Curtis Looney; P/GP: Badie Mae (Lahaya) Shannon and Ormand Edgar Looney; M/GP: Helena Amanda Mousner and Sidney Pardue Evans

RESIDENCE: Port Aransas, TX

EDUCATION: Corpus Christi (TX) High School; St. Mary's University, San Antonio, TX; San Antonio (TX) Art Institute

OCCUPATION: Poet and artist

MEDIA: Pastel, mixed-media, and prints

EXHIBITS: CNM; FCTM; ACCC; 20th Annual International Art Show, Brownsville, TX, ('91); Dote Foundation Exhibit, San Antonio, TX, 1989

SOLO EXHIBITS: Corpus Christi (TX) Main Library (1990)

AWARDS: ACCC ('89; '90; '90, 1st, Membership Show)

HONORS: *Artist-in-Residence:* Art Center of Corpus Christi (TX), 1990. *Other:* Art Patron Reception and Show, Lubbock, TX, held in her honor, 1989

RECTOR, JOE A. *Cherokee*

Birth date unknown; born in Muskogee, OK

RESIDENCE: Muskogee, OK

EDUCATION: Central High School, Muskogee, OK; Muskogee (OK) Junior College; B.A., NSU; OSU

OCCUPATION: Gallery owner and painter

PUBLISHED: *Home Services Directory* (spring/summer 1993), cover

EXHIBITS: FCTM

AWARDS: FCTM ('74, IH)

Red Bear, Martin E. *Oglala Sioux*

Born 12 Oct 1947 at Rosebud, SD, on the Rosebud Indian Reservation

RESIDENCE: Rushville, NE

MILITARY: U.S. Army, 1969-1971

EDUCATION: Oglala Community High School, SD; A.F.A., IAIA, 1973; B.A., CSF/SF; M.A., U of NM

OCCUPATION: Museum employee, printer's assistant, teacher, art professor, dancer, and painter

MEDIA: Acrylic

PUBLISHED: Maurer (1992). *Arts and Activities* (Oct 1981; June 1984); *The Indian Trader* (Feb 1985); *Argus Leader* (23 Sept 1988); *American Indian Art* (spring 1993)

BOOKS ILLUSTRATED: Steinmetz (1984)

COMMISSIONS: *Posters:* National Indian Child Welfare Training Conference, Oklahoma City, OK, 1986; Oglala Lakota College, Continuing Education Department, Kyle, SD, 1986; American Indian Higher Education Consortium, Oglala Lakota College, SD, 1986

PUBLIC COLLECTIONS: CSF/SF, HCC; IAIA/M; MAI; SIM; Oglala Lakota College Collection, Kyle, SD; St. Joseph's Indian School, Chamberlain, SD

EXHIBITS: AIAE; AIE; CNM; HCC; HM; HSAS; IAIA; JAM; MAI; NAAE; NARF; NMSF; NPTA; OLC; PAC; PBS; RC; SNAICF; SWAIA; TM/NE; U of NM; VP; WTF; St. Louis (MO) Art Museum

SOLO EXHIBITS: SIM

AWARDS: AIAE (Best of Show); AIE ('74), NMSF ('79; '81; '82); NPTA ('91; '92, 1st); HSAS; OLC ('86, 1st); RC ('75, 1st; '81, Woodard Award; '89, Decker Award; '90, WKI Award; '91, Niederman Award, Woodard Award; '92, Woodard Award); SNAICF; SWAIA ('83, 1st)

HONORS: NPTA, poster artist, 1988

Red Bird (see Hill, Joan)

Red Bird *Cheyenne*

A.K.A. Chief Red Bird

PUBLISHED: Dunn (1968); Snodgrass (1968)

PUBLIC COLLECTIONS: SPIM

Red Bird

The Southern Plains Indian Museum collection contains a skin painting reputed to depict the war exploits of Chief Red Bird, which apparently was primarily painted by him, although several other hands may have been involved in the work. It is dated somewhere between 1865 and 1880.

Snodgrass 1968

Redbird, Robert, Sr. *Kiowa*

Born 22 July 1939 in Lawton, OK; GF: Monroe Tsatoke (q.v.); father of Robert Redbird Jr. (q.v.)

RESIDENCE: Phoenix, AZ; Formerly of Anadarko, OK

EDUCATION: Oak Cliff High School; OSU/O, 1962

OCCUPATION: Welder, mechanic, auto-body painter and repairman, commercial artist, Pentecostal minister, gospel singer, lecturer, and painter

MEDIA: Oil, acrylic, watercolor, gouache, pencil, pastel, pen and ink, and prints

PUBLISHED: Snodgrass (1968); Ellison (1972); Boyd, et al. (1981; 1983). *American Indian Crafts and Culture* (Dec 1972); *The Indian Trader* (Sept 1979; May 1987; Oct 1987; May 1988); *Art-Talk* (Dec 1982; Mar 1983; Mar 1986; Apr/May 1986; Jan 1991; Apr/May 1991); *The Anadarko Daily News* (16-17 Aug 1986); *The Phoenix Gazette Magazine* (13 Apr 1987); *Scottsdale Magazine* (winter 1987-1988); *Southwest Art* (Oct 1990)

COMMISSIONS: Anadarko (OK) High School, painting and sculpture; U.S. Open Polo Game, Palm Springs, CA, poster

PUBLIC COLLECTIONS: BAM; DAM; HCC; HM; SI; USDI; Anadarko (OK) High School Auditorium

Robert Redbird Sr.

Although Redbird is an urban Indian, raised in Dallas, Texas, he uses stories from his grandfather and the tribal elders to preserve and communicate the Kiowa culture and way of life. He was eight years old when he was inspired to paint by his grandfather, one of the Five Kiowa (q.v.) and a farmer in Kiowa, OK. In 1987, Ralph Oliver listed Redbird's paintings as "one of the best investments in Indian art."

EXHIBITS: AIE; CIM; CSPIP; HCC; HM; HM/G; ITIC; MIF; OAC; PBS; RC; SDCC; SN; SPIM; VV; Concho (OK) Centennial; Oklahoma Indian Trade Fair; galleries in AZ, CA, NM, OK, and Europe

SOLO EXHIBITS: OAC

AWARDS: AIE ('72, Grand Award; '73, 1st; '74, 1st; '79; '82); ITIC ('85, 1st; '88; '89, 1st; '90, 1st; '91, 1st); CIM; SDCC ('86, 1st); RC ('76); Concho (OK) Centennial ('72, 1st)

REDBIRD, ROBERT, JR. *Kiowa*

Emhee

Born 23 Aug 1964 in Anadarko, OK; son of Robert Redbird Sr. (q.v.)

RESIDENCE: Anadarko, OK

EDUCATION: Anadarko (OK) High School

EXHIBITS: HM/G; and galleries in AZ, NM, and OK

REDBONE, LARRY *Kiowa/Apache*

A.K.A. Larry Tse Lee

Born 8 June 1955

RESIDENCE: Anadarko, OK

EDUCATION: Fort Cobb (OK) High School; IAIA

COMMISSIONS: Area newspapers and visitor's guides, illustrations

EXHIBITS: AIE

AWARDS: AIE ('74; '77, Grand Award; '78, 1st, '80)

HONORS: AIE, program cover artist, 1978

RED BUFFALO (see Romero, Frankie)

RED BULL, ELMER *Sioux*

RESIDENCE: Eagle Butte, SD

PUBLISHED: Snodgrass (1968)

EXHIBITS: BNIAS

REDCLAY, BEN *Mescalero Apache*

Born 1944

RESIDENCE: Topanga, CA

EDUCATION: Burges High School, CA; U of TX

OCCUPATION: Art instructor, editor, and painter

EXHIBITS: ITIC; SDMM; SNAICF; RC; U of CA/LA; see also Awards

AWARDS: ITIC ('87); SNAICF ('87, Best of Division); Los Angeles (CA) Open Competition ('73)

RED CLOUD (see Oqwa Pi)

RED CLOUD (see Silva, Marcus)

RED CLOUD *Northern Cheyenne*

A.K.A. Chief Red Cloud

Born winter of 1821-1822, between the Dakota Black Hills and the Missouri River, Dakota Territory; died ca. 1906

MEDIA: Pigment and muslin

PUBLISHED: Dunn (1968); Snodgrass (1968); Brody (1971); Maurer (1992)

PUBLIC COLLECTIONS: MAI, MNH/F

EXHIBITS: VP

RED CLOUD

"Paintings on an MAI buffalo robe, dated 1871, represent a fight with the Shoshoni."

Snodgrass 1968

RED CORN *Osage*

Hadacütse

A.K.A. Bill Nix; William P. Mathews
Birth date unknown; adopted by William P. Mathews
PUBLISHED: Snodgrass (1968). *4th Annual Report,* BAE (1882-1883)

RED CORN, JIM *Osage*

Walanke, No Sense; *Ha-Pah-Shu-Tse*
A.K.A. Jim Lacy Redcorn; James Redcorn
Born 9 May 1938 in Pawhuska, OK; died 27 June 1994; P/GP: Bertha Hudson and Raymond Red Corn; nephew of Raymond Wesley Red Corn (q.v.)
RESIDENCE: Pawhuska, OK
EDUCATION: Pawhuska (OK) High School, 1956; U of OK, 1958-1961; U of AZ, "Southwest Indian Art Project," scholarship, summers 1961, 1962; B.A., NSU, 1965
OCCUPATION: Teacher, textile designer, and painter
MEDIA: Oil, textile, silkscreen, and watercolor
PUBLISHED: Snodgrass (1968). *The Tulsa Tribune* (25 Aug 1962); *American Indian Art* (spring 1985); *Pawhuska Daily Journal-Capital* (14 June 1985); *Ponca City News* (14 June 1985)
BOOKS ILLUSTRATED: Brown (1962); *Cherokee Bilingual Story Book,* published by Carnegie Cross-Cultural Project, Tahlequah, OK, 1966
PUBLIC COLLECTIONS: ASM, HM, IACB, MNA, OTM, OU/L, PAC
EXHIBITS: AIE; ITIC; PAC; SN; U of AZ; U of OK; Association of Interior Decorators and Designers, 1962, Chicago, IL; Pacific Art Conference, Seattle, WA, 1961; State University of Iowa, Iowa City, IA
SOLO EXHIBITS: HM; SPIM; The Fort, Denver, CO
AWARDS: AIE ('67; '78); HM/G ('63); ITIC ('64); PAC ('68; '69)
HONORS: *Scholarships:* U of OK; U of AZ; NSU; *Other:* Association of Interior Decorators and Designers, International Award for Design, 1962; Oklahoma Arts and Humanities Council, Oklahoma City, OK, artist-in-residence

JIM RED CORN

The artist started painting when he was five years old and sold his first painting when he was thirteen. He terms his style "realistic Western."

RED CORN, RAYMOND WESLEY *Osage*

Mahse Nompah, Straight Reed; *Ha-Pah-Shu-Tse*
A.K.A. Rev. Raymond Wesley Red Corn
Born 22 Aug 1911 in Pawhuska, OK; son of Bertha Hudson and Raymond Red Corn; P/GF: Wahinglainkah (Red Corn); uncle of Jim Lacy Redcorn (q.v.)
RESIDENCE: Pawhuska, OK
EDUCATION: Through 11th grade, Pawhuska (OK) High School; Baptist Bible Institute, New Orleans, LA, 1934; Chillicothe (MO) Business College, 1934
OCCUPATION: General contractor, Baptist minister, and painter
PUBLISHED: Snodgrass (1968)
PUBLIC COLLECTIONS: Osage Indian Agency, Pawhuska, OK
EXHIBITS: PAC; Osage Museum, Pawhuska, OK; county fairs
HONORS: First person of Osage descent ordained a Baptist minister

RAYMOND WESLEY RED CORN

"The artist specializes in portraits and has done many through the years as gifts."

Snodgrass 1968

RED CRANE *Blackfeet*

PUBLISHED: Grinnell (1896); Snodgrass (1968)
PUBLIC COLLECTIONS: MAI (illustrations of the artist's coups; drawn on the lining of a hide lodge, collected by George B. Grinnell, 1889)

RED DOG *Sioux*

PUBLISHED: Snodgrass (1968)
EXHIBITS: SI/OAA (record of the artist's exploits drawn in a sketch book)

RED EARTH PEOPLE (see Pushetonequa, Charles)

Red Elk, Herman *Yanktonai Sioux*

Hegaka Wambdi, Eagle Elk

A.K.A. Hehaka Wambdi

Born 27 Mar 1918 in Poplar, MT, on the Fort Peck Reservation; died 1986; son of Maggie Iron Cloud and Herman Red Elk Sr.; P/GF: Joseph Red Elk (Hehaka Duta), participant in the Battle of the Little Big Horn

RESIDENCE: Poplar, MT

MILITARY: U.S. Army, WWII

EDUCATION: Salem Indian School, Chemawa, OR, 1935-1939; studied drawing as occupational therapy, Sioux Sanitorium, Rapid City, SD, 1961-1962; workshops, U of SD, where he studied under Oscar Howe (q.v.), 1964

OCCUPATION: Army Corps of Engineers employee, electrician, general contractor, museum aide, commercial artist, teacher, and painter

MEDIA: Oil, acrylic, casein, earth pigment, and hide

PUBLISHED: Snodgrass (1968); Libhart (1970); Brody (1971); Blackboy, et al. (1973); Schmid and Houlihan (1979); Maurer (1992). *The Indian Trader* (Apr 1976); *Smithsonian* (Nov 1992)

COMMISSIONS: Oklahoma Indian Arts and Crafts Cooperative, Anadarko, OK, tipi, 1973

PUBLIC COLLECTIONS: HCC, IACB

EXHIBITS: ADIC, BBHC, BHIAE, CPS, HCC, HM/G, MIA, NAP, PAC, SAIEAIP, SIM, SN, SPIM, VP; throughout AZ, OK, SD, and Washington, D.C.

SOLO EXHIBITS: SIM

AWARDS: ADIC ('67); BHIAE

Herman Red Elk

Red Elk was responsible for the marked revival of hide painting among the Sioux, starting in the 1960s.

Dockstader p.c. 1995

Red Feather (see Colbert, Frank Overton)

Red Fish *Oglala Sioux*

Hogan Luta, Red Fish

A.K.A. Chief Red Fish

Birth date unknown; born at Fort Laramie, WY

MEDIA: Pencil and colored pencil

PUBLISHED: Snodgrass (1968)

PUBLIC COLLECTIONS: HS/ND; MAI (Winter Count)

Red Fish

"[Red Fish was] prominent ca. 1840, but lost prestige following a defeat at the hands of the Crows in 1841. He lived at Cannon Ball, ND, and was an old man in 1880, at Standing Rock Agency. Met with Father De Smet at Fort Pierre in 1841."

Snodgrass 1968

Redfox, Mark *Arikara/Sioux*

Born 1955 at Minot, ND

RESIDENCE: Missoula, MT

EDUCATION: IAIA, 1975

OCCUPATION: Art instructor, designer, illustrator, photographer, and painter

MEDIA: Acrylic, watercolor, pen and ink and film

PUBLISHED: *The Missoulian* (1984)

EXHIBITS: NAVAM; Alfred Whiteman Native American Artists Group Show, Missoula, MT; Orchard Homes Women's Club Art Show, Missoula, MT

Red Hail *Sioux*

PUBLISHED: Snodgrass (1968)

PUBLIC COLLECTIONS: MPM (pictographic style on paper)

Red Hawk *Sioux*

Cetan Luta

MEDIA: Pencil, crayon, colored pencil, and pen and ink

PUBLISHED: Snodgrass (1968); Maurer (1977). *Sioux Indian Drawings*, Milwaukee Public Museum (1961)

PUBLIC COLLECTIONS: CGPS, MPM, WWM
EXHIBITS: CGPS, VP

RED HAWK, JIM *Creek*
Iyo Djdi, Red Hawk
Born 31 Dec 1949
RESIDENCE: Fairplay, CO
EDUCATION: Sunray High School, 1968
OCCUPATION: Sculptor and painter
MEDIA: Oil, acrylic, clay, and prints
EXHIBITS: CIM; FCTM; TIAF; TWF; RE; WIAME; Denver (CO) Indian Rendezvous and Trade Fair
AWARDS: FCTM, TIAF

RED HORN BULL BUFFALO *Oglala Sioux*
Tantaha Heluta
RESIDENCE: From Pine Ridge Agency, SD (see Black Heart)
PUBLISHED: Snodgrass (1968)
PUBLIC COLLECTIONS: MAI (bull buffalo with red horn)

RED HORN ELK *Oglala Sioux*
Kerakahi-to
RESIDENCE: From Pine Ridge Agency, SD (see Black Heart)
PUBLISHED: Snodgrass (1968)
PUBLIC COLLECTIONS: MAI (green elk with red antlers)

RED HORSE *Miniconjou Sioux*
A.K.A. Chief Red Horse
MEDIA: Colored and graphite pencil
PUBLISHED: Dunn (1968); Snodgrass (1968), Russell (1968); Maurer (1992). *10th Annual Report,* BAE (1888-1889)
PUBLIC COLLECTIONS: GM, SI/OAA (series of sign language accounts and drawings of the Battle of the Little Big Horn)
EXHIBITS: VP
HONORS: Miniconjou Tribal Council, member; Cheyenne River Agency, chosen to act as a buffalo scout, ca. 1882

RED LIVING BEAR *Sioux*
Mato Myaluta
PUBLISHED: Snodgrass (1968)
PUBLIC COLLECTIONS: MPM (pictographic style on paper)

RED MOON (see Sandy, Percy Tsisete)

RED OWL, RICHARD *Oglala Sioux*
A.K.A. Rich Red Owl
Born 14 Aug 1940 on the Pine Ridge (SD) Indian Reservation
RESIDENCE: Kyle, SD
MEDIA: Acrylic
PUBLIC COLLECTIONS: HCC
EXHIBITS: AIAFM, CPS, HCC, NPTA, RC, WTF
AWARDS: NPTA ('91, 1st, '93; '94); RC ('74; '77; '92, White Buffalo Award; '94, Oscar Howe Award)

RED HORN BULL BUFFALO

"Wounded in the Battle of the Little Big Horn, 1876."

Snodgrass 1968

RED HORSE

"[Red Horse] was on the Yellowstone, below the mouth of the Little Big Horn River, WY, 1865; on the Tongue River, MT, 1876; and went to Cheyenne River Agency, SD. He surrendered his camp in 1877. (see Hyde 1961)"

Snodgrass 1968

In 1881, Charles E. McChesney, M.D., Acting Assistant Surgeon, persuaded Red Horse, who had participated in the Battle of the Little Big Horn, to make some pictorial accounts of the action. Red Horse executed forty-two large drawings which McChesney sent to Colonel Garrick Mallery who included them in his study of the picture writing of the American Indian, published by the Bureau of American Ethnology in its 10th Annual Report.

Maurer 1992

RICHARD RED OWL

Although he is largely self-taught, the artist credits Oscar Howe (q.v.) with being an early influence on his work. Red Owl was one of the organizers of The Dream Catchers Artists Guild, Ltd. (q.v.) Family obligations prevent Red Owl from competing nationally, but he exhibits extensively in local shows.

artist, p.c. 1991

RED ROBIN *Zuni (?)*

Born ca. 1918; death date unknown

OCCUPATION: Textile designer and painter

PUBLISHED: Snodgrass (1968); Brody (1971)

PUBLIC COLLECTIONS: HS/CO; DAM; GM; MNM; MRFM; Denver (CO) Public Library

EXHIBITS: PAC

AWARDS: PAC

RED ROBIN

"The artist is known to have resided in Taos and Santa Fe, NM, Denver, CO, and New York City, his last known residence, where he was engaged as a textile designer. Although claiming relationship with many tribes, his actual tribal origin is unknown."

Snodgrass 1968

A Red Robin was living in the Santa Fe area in 1992.

RED STAR, CONNIE *Crow*

EDUCATION: IAIA

MEDIA: Acrylic

PUBLISHED: *Native American Arts 2* (1968)

EXHIBITS: PAC

RED STAR, KEVIN *Crow*

Running Rabbit

Born 9 Oct 1943 on the Crow Reservation; son of Amy, craftswoman, and Wallace Red Star Sr.

RESIDENCE: Red Lodge, MT

EDUCATION: IAIA, 1962-1965; SFAI, 1965-1966; MSU, 1968-1969; EMC, 1971-1972

OCCUPATION: Rodeo contestant, janitor, musician, teacher, gallery owner; professional artist since 1965

MEDIA: Oil, acrylic, watercolor, pen and ink, pencil, charcoal, crayon, mixed-media, and prints

PUBLISHED: Snodgrass (1968); Ray, ed. (1972); Blackboy, et al. (1973); Silberman (1976); Highwater (1980); Medina (1981); Samuels (1982); Hoffman, et al. (1984); Coe (1986); Wade (1986); Hill (1992). *Native American Art 2* (1968); *Arizona Highways* (Jan 1972), *Southwest Art* (Feb 1976; Apr 1980; July 1990); *Americas* (Aug 1981); *The Indian Trader* (June 1981; Oct 1983); *MIA News Letter* (Dec 1984), cover; *The Santa Fean* (Aug 1989); *U.S. Art* (Nov 1991); *Southwest Profile* (Aug/Sept/Oct 1992)

COMMISSIONS: Oklahoma Indian Art and Crafts Cooperative, Anadarko, OK, created and painted a tipi, 1973

PUBLIC COLLECTIONS: DAM, EM, HCC, HM, IAIA, IACB, MAI, MPI, MRFM, SDMM, SM, WWM

EXHIBITS: Partial listing of more than fifty includes: AAID; AC/K; AC/SD; BBHC; CIA; CPS; FAIEAIP; HM; HM/G; HPTU; IAIA; IAIA/M; IK; KCPA; MAI; MCC/CA; MNM; MFA/O; MNH/D; NACLA; NU/BC; OMA; OWE; PBS; PSDM; RM; SDMM; SFFA; SI; SN; SU; SWAIA; TRP; USDI; WTF; WWM; YAIA; Pierre Cardin Exhibit, Paris, France; Edinburgh, Scotland; London, England; Berlin and Munich, Germany; Tokyo, Japan; and Peking, China

SOLO/SPECIAL EXHIBITS: Partial listing of more than twenty includes: MPI; HM (dual show)

AWARDS: AAID ('68); HM/G ('64; '71); MNM ('67, Special Award); SN ('65, 1st, Governor's Choice, Baker Award; '69, 1st)

HONORS: San Francisco Art Institute, scholarship; IAIA, first artist trained at IAIA to be invited to serve as an artist-in-residence, 1976

KEVIN RED STAR

For inspiration, Red Star often uses old Crow photographs and tape recordings of tales told by Crow elders. His vivid contemporary compositions done in rich textures are imaginative interpretations of traditional Native American subjects. He has described himself as a romanticist and says that he tries to capture the era of the late 1880s when the Crow way of life started to change. His style of Crow male portraiture is distinctive.

RED TURTLE (see Harrison, Louise)

Reid, Bill *Haida*

Born 1920 in Victoria, BC, Canada

RESIDENCE: Vancouver, BC, Canada

EDUCATION: Victoria (BC) schools; Ryerson Technical Institute of Jewelry, Toronto, ON, 1948; apprenticed at Platinum Art Company, Toronto, ON

OCCUPATION: Broadcaster, writer, teacher, carver, jeweler, graphic artist, and painter

MEDIA: Pen and ink, pencil, paint, wood, argillite, bronze, silver, gold, ivory, and prints

PUBLISHED: Holm and Reid (1975); Stewart (1979; 1984); Macnair, Hoover, and Neary (1980); Hall, Blackman, and Rickard (1981), Wade and Strickland (1981); Reid (1984); Duffek (1986); Shadbolt (1987); Reid and Bringhurst (1988); Mather (1990); Bringhurst (1991); Cardinal-Schubert (1992); McMasters, et al. (1993). *Indian News* (Sept 1980); *Masterkey* (winter 1984); *The Indian Trader* (Mar 1987); *The Wall Street Journal* (5 Dec 1991)

COMMISSIONS: *Sculptures:* C/U of BC/MA, yellow cedar sculpture, 1980; Canadian Chancery, Washington, D.C., bronze sculpture. *Other:* Expo '86, Vancouver, BC, designed and constructed a cedar canoe, 1986

EXHIBITS: C/AG/V; C/TC; C/TFD; C/TL; C/U of BC/MA; PAC; Musée de l'Homme, Paris, France, 1989; The Nippon Club, 1986

SOLO EXHIBITS: C/AG/V; U of WA; Children of the Raven Gallery, Vancouver, BC

HONORS: Canada Council Study Fellowship, 1968

Bill Reid

A multi-talented artist, Bill Reid is one of the most important of the senior artists on the Northwest Coast. He is well known for his work in wood, paper, argillite, silver, and gold.

Restoule, Tim *Ojibwa*

Born 1960 on Dokis Reserve, ON, Canada

EDUCATION: Manitoulin Island Art Program, ON

EXHIBITS: C/WICEC; Anishnawbe Mee-kum, Manitoulin Island, ON; Cambrian College, Sudbury, ON

RI (see Riding In Mameah, Marlene)

Richardson, Arnold *Cherokee/Tuscarora*

RESIDENCE: Hollister, NC

EXHIBITS: CNM, HM/G

AWARDS: HM/G ('77, Wynne Award)

Rickard, Jolene *Tuscarora*

RESIDENCE: New York, NY

EXHIBITS: AICH, CSU/OK, OLO

Riddles, Leonard *Comanche*

Black Moon

Born 28 June 1919 in Walters, OK; son of a white man and a Comanche woman; M/GGF: Pahkuuh (Dried Robe), Comanche medicine man; foster son of Mrs. W.A. Williams

RESIDENCE: Walters, OK

MILITARY: U.S. Army, WWII, 1941-1945

EDUCATION: Fort Sill, Valedictorian, 1941; mural instruction under Olaf Nordmark

OCCUPATION: Rancher, carpenter, teacher, muralist, and painter; active in farm programs and Indian affairs

MEDIA: Acrylic, watercolor, tempera, and gouache

PUBLISHED: Jacobson and d'Ucel (1950); Snodgrass (1968); Brody (1971);

Leonard Riddles

"Riddles states his major desire is to depict the Comanche people authentically and extensively. 'My own set requirement is that my paintings meet the approval of my elder relatives and friends.'"

Snodgrass 1968

Blackboy, et al. (1973); Silberman (1978); New (1981); Samuels (1985). Museum News (June 1962); *The Sunday Oklahoman, Orbit Magazine* (31 Mar 1963); *The Arizona Republic* (23 Nov1965); *American Indian Crafts and Culture* (Sept 1973), covers; biographical publications

BOOKS ILLUSTRATED: Cotton County Historical Society, book cover, 1979

COMMISSIONS: *Murals:* Walters (OK) Depot, commissioned by Cotton County Art Council, 1990; Fort Sill (OK) Indian School; Riverside Indian School, Anadarko, OK. *Others:* Comanche Little Pony War Society Dance Group, emblem; Oklahoma Indian Arts and Crafts Cooperative, Anadarko, OK, hide paintings, 1968, and tipi, 1973; Oklahoma Numismatic Association, coin designs, 1988, 1989

PUBLIC COLLECTIONS: BIA; HCC; IACB; PAC; SPIM; U of OK; Lyman Allyn Museum, New London, CT

EXHIBITS: AAIE; AIE; AIW; BNAIS; CNM; CSPIP; FAIEAIP; FANAIAE; HCC; HM; ITIC; NACLA; OIO; OMA; OU/MA/T; PAC; RC; RE; SN; SPIM; USDS,;WTF; Lyman Allyn Museum, New London, CT; Lawton (OK) Chamber of Commerce, OK; see also Awards

SOLO EXHIBITS: SPIM (two)

AWARDS: AIE ('58, 1st, Grand Award; '61, 1st; '64, Grand Award); BNIAS ('63), ITIC ('63), OIO ('82, 1st), MNM (Curtin Award), PAC ('62, 1st, '69, 1st; '72); SN; Waurika (OK) Arts Festival ('88, 1st; '89, 1st; '90, 1st)

HONORS: IACB, special award for contributions to American Indian art, 1976; painting presented to Pierre Messmer, Prime Minister of France under Charles de Gaulle, 1989

RIDGELY, EUGENE, JR. *Northern Arapaho*

RESIDENCE: Riverton, WY

EDUCATION: Lander Valley (WY) High School; U of WY

OCCUPATION: Teacher and artist

EXHIBITS: NPTA, RC

AWARDS: NPTA ('92)

RIDING IN MAMEAH, MARLENE *Pawnee*

Ska-Dodah-Dah-Sak

A.K.A. M. Riding Inn; Marlene Mary Supernaw; Marlene Mameah; Signature: RI (Riding In)

Born 3 Mar 1933 in Council Valley, OK; daughter of Ethel Wilson and Frank Riding In; P/GP: Virginia Walking Bear and William Riding In; M/GP: Lena Otter and Samuel Wilson

RESIDENCE: Pawnee, OK

EDUCATION: Chilocco, 1949; BC

OCCUPATION: Editor, housewife, painter; full-time silversmith since 1975

MEDIA: Tempera

PUBLISHED: Dunn (1968); Snodgrass (1968); Brody (1971)

PUBLIC COLLECTIONS: PAC

EXHIBITS: AIE; BNIAS; ITAE; ITIC; MNM; MNM/T; PAC; PAC/T; RE; SI; WWM; shows jewelry at regional Indian markets and powwows

AWARDS: AIE (Grand Award, 1963); ITAE; MNM; PAC

MARLENE RIDING IN MAMEAH

"The artist began painting ca. 1949 and credits Dick West (q.v.) as having most encouraged her."

Snodgrass 1968

She painted until 1964, when she started working as a silversmith. She says she soon was selling more jewelry than paintings. Since 1965, she has concentrated on her silver work and no longer paints.

artist, p.c. 1993

RIDING INN, M. (see Riding In Mameah, Marlene)

RIDOURT, LUCILE *San Ildefonso*

PUBLISHED: Snodgrass (1968)

PUBLIC COLLECTIONS: MNM

RILEY, SHARON TATE *Cherokee*
RESIDENCE: Neosho, MO
EXHIBITS: CNM, LIAS

RILEY, VICTOR *Laguna*
EDUCATION: Santa Fe, ca. 1958
PUBLISHED: Snodgrass (1968)
EXHIBITS: MNM
AWARDS: MNM

RILLINGS, MICHAEL *Ottawa/Sioux*
RESIDENCE: Fort Thompson, SD
EXHIBITS: RC
HONORS: RC, Thunderbird Foundation Scholarship, 1992

RINGO, GOOD *(?)*
PUBLISHED: Snodgrass (1968)
PUBLIC COLLECTIONS: MRFM

RIPLEY, DAVID J. *Arikara/Blackfeet*
Born 12 Sept 1947 in Emmet, ND
RESIDENCE: Emmet, ND
EDUCATION: Emmet (ND) High School, ca. 1963
PUBLISHED: Snodgrass (1968)
EXHIBITS: BNIAS; North Dakota State Fair, Minot, ND

RITCHIE, LESA *Cherokee*
EXHIBITS: CNM

RIVET, RICHARD JAMES *Métis*
Born 1949 in Aklavik, NWT, Canada
EDUCATION: B.A., U of AB, 1972; B.F.A., U of V, 1980; C/BSFA, 1981; M.F.A., U of SK, 1985
OCCUPATION: Educator and painter
PUBLISHED: *The Chronicle Herald, Halifax,* NS (1 May 1990; 7 June 1990); *Maclean's Magazine* (4 May 1992)
PUBLIC COLLECTIONS: C/CMC, C/INAC, C/MAM, C/U of SK
EXHIBITS: Partial listing includes: C/CMC; C/GNAF; C/I; C/MAM; C/U of SK; Roy Thompson Hall, Toronto, ON; The Amouries Building Show, Victoria, BC, 1980; The Saskatchewan Open '86, Saskatoon, SK 1986
SOLO EXHIBITS: C/AG/TB, C/WICEC
AWARDS: Victoria (BC) Arts Council Award, 1979; Government of Newfoundland Arts and Letters Competition Award, 1988
HONORS: *Scholarships and Grants:* C/BCA, 1980; The Vancouver Foundation Bursary Award, 1980; The Mungo Martin Student Grant, 1983-1984; Northwest Territories Government Supplementary Grants, 1983-1986; British Columbia Cultural Fund, grant, 1984-1985; Saskatchewan Art Board, grant, 1986; Canadian Native Arts Foundation, grant

ROAD RUNNER *(see Naranjo, Adolph)*

ROAN, ELVAN *Navajo*
RESIDENCE: Navajo, NM
EDUCATION: Inter-Mt.
MEDIA: Oil, pencil, and pastel

ELVAN ROAN

The artist is best known for his oil portraits of Navajo people.

PUBLISHED: Snodgrass (1968). *The Indian Trader* (July 1984)
PUBLIC COLLECTIONS: HCC
EXHIBITS: HCC, ITIC, MNM, NMSF, NTF, NTM
SOLO/SPECIAL EXHIBITS: NTM (dual show)

ROAN EAGLE *Oglala Sioux*

MEDIA: Watercolor, pencil, and pen and ink
PUBLISHED: Maurer (1992)
PUBLIC COLLECTIONS: MIA
EXHIBITS: VP

ROANHORSE, RALPH *Navajo*

A.K.A. Bilidaalbahe
MILITARY: WWII
EDUCATION: Albuquerque; Otis ca. 1928-1931
OCCUPATION: Sign painter, carpentry assistant, mail carrier on the Indian reservation; horse wrangler, cowboy, hogan builder, and painter
PUBLISHED: Snodgrass (1968)
PUBLIC COLLECTIONS: MNA
EXHIBITS: FWG

RALPH ROANHORSE

"The priests at St. Michael's Indian Mission taught the artist to read, write, and speak English. It was at Albuquerque Indian School that he had his first opportunity to draw and paint (see Roanhorse 1931)."

Snodgrass 1968

ROARING THUNDER (see Warrior, Antowine)

ROBERSON, GLORIA ERVIN *Choctaw*

EXHIBITS: CNM, FCTM
AWARDS: FCTM ('80, IH; '82)

ROBERTS, DOLONA *Cherokee*

Born 1936 in Santa Fe, NM
RESIDENCE: Santa Fe, NM
EDUCATION: Santa Fe (NM) High School; Colorado College, Colorado Springs, CO; B.A., U of NM
OCCUPATION: Sculptor, ceramist and painter
MEDIA: Oil, acrylic, watercolor, pastel, clay, bronze, and prints
PUBLISHED: Jacka and Jacka (1988). *Southwest Art* (Nov 1984); *The Indian Trader* (July 1986); *Art of the West* (July/Aug 1989)
BOOKS ILLUSTRATED: Gallenkamp (1961)
COMMISSIONS: Goldwater's Department Stores, promotional poster for Gallery of the Southwest
PUBLIC COLLECTIONS: HM; University of Arizona Foundation, Tucson, AZ; Arizona State University Law School, Tempe, AZ; University of Nevada, Las Vegas, NV; McNay Art Institute, San Antonio, TX
EXHIBITS: IEEPF; MCC/CA; SDMM; in Germany, Switzerland, France, Canada, and throughout the U.S. *Traveling exhibits:* Southern Arts Federation; Pensacola (FL) Museum of Art; Discovery Center, Fort Lauderdale, FL; Polk Public Museum, Lakeland, FL; Museum and Art Center, Sylacauga, AL; Arts and Science Museum, Statesville, NC
SOLO EXHIBITS: Galeria Nichido, Paris, France; Galerie Calumet, Heidleberg, Germany
HONORS: *The Santa Fean,* Artist of the Year, 1981; SWAIA, poster artist, 1985

DOLONA ROBERTS

Roberts has painted many subjects, from African masks to landscapes, but she is best known for her paintings of the backs of Indian men and women. The artist says, "At heart, I will always be an abstract expressionist. Colors and shapes are preferable to composition. The paint or the medium becomes the important vehicle and not the subject."

p.c. 1992

ROBERTS, FRANK *Mohawk*

Young Deer
A.K.A. F. Roberts
Birth date unknown

RESIDENCE: Originally from Caughnawaga, PQ, Canada; at one time resided in Brooklyn, NY

PUBLISHED: Snodgrass (1968)

PUBLIC COLLECTIONS: MAI

ROBERTSON, DAVID *Kwakwaka'wakw (Kwakiutl)*

RESIDENCE: British Columbia, Canada

MEDIA: Paint on masonite

PUBLIC COLLECTIONS: C/RBCM

ROBINSON, JOHN *Haida*

Bear

Birth date unknown; possibly born in British Columbia, Canada

PUBLISHED: Snodgrass (1968)

PUBLIC COLLECTIONS: MAI (pencil drawings of Haida designs, "Skidegate, 1892")

ROBINSON, MICHAEL *Cree*

Born 27 Mar 1948 near Tameness, ON, Canada

RESIDENCE: Keen, ON, Canada

EDUCATION: Adam Scott Collegiate and Vocational Institute, Peterborough, ON; Sheridan College School of Design, 1969-1971; studied under Andy Bolici, Mark Pieser, Paul Machnik, Walter Sunahara, and George Raab

OCCUPATION: Ontario Ministry of Natural Resources employee, ceramist, glassblower, draughtsman, silversmith, writer, poet, printmaker, and painter

MEDIA: Pen and ink, glass, silver, clay, and prints

PUBLISHED: Southcott (1984); Menitove, ed.(1985); Podedworny (1985); Cinader (1987); Menitove and Danford (1989). *The Native Perspective* (Vol. 3, no. 2, 1978)

BOOKS ILLUSTRATED: Robinson (1987; 1991; 1992)

COMMISSIONS: Ontario Place, 1973; Ontario Institute for Studies in Education, book illustrations, 1985

PUBLIC COLLECTIONS: C/ACC; C/CCAB; C/CMC; C/GM; C/IOC; C/MCC; C/POC; C/ROM; C/SCC; C/WLU; MNH/D; Chevron Oil Corporation, Calgary, AB; Northern Telecom, London, ON; Teleglobe Canada, Montréal, PQ; Bank of America Canada, Toronto, ON; Grindleys Bank of England Canada, Toronto, ON; Manufacturers' Hanover Canada, Toronto, ON; Manufacturers' Life Insurance, Toronto, ON; New York Life, Toronto, ON; Toronto (ON) Dominion Bank, Xerox Research Canada, Toronto, ON

EXHIBITS: Partial listing of more than 26 includes: C/AG/LR; C/AG/TB; C/AG/TT; C/AG/V; C/AG/W; C/CGCQ; C/CIIA; C/CMC; C/CNAC; C/MCC; C/NCCT; C/ROM; C/WCAA; C/WICEC; C/WLU; IAIA; LACM; Marsil Museum, Québec, PQ; Museum of Modern Art, Rijekia, Yugoslavia, 1970; Native Cultural Center, Ann Arbour, MI; North Bay (ON) Arts Centre; O'Keefe Centre, Toronto, ON; Ontario Crafts Council; Ontario Science Centre, Toronto, 1972; see also Awards

SOLO EXHIBITS: C/AG/TB; C/OCF; galleries throughout Ontario

AWARDS: C/CGCQ ('72, Glass Award); C/ROM (1970, Paola Award; '71, Best Craft Award); Ceramics '72 ('72, Glass Award)

HONORS: *Grants:* Ontario Arts Council, 1972; C/CCAB, Exploration Grant, 1985

MICHAEL ROBINSON

According to the artist, drawing has always been a way for him to work out problems, a means of escape. He draws about the Indian and the earth and hopes that his paintings will contribute to the renewal of Native spiritual values. Fish are a major symbol for Robinson and he often uses them in his paintings.

Southcott 1984

ROBINSON, ROSE *Hopi*

PUBLISHED: Snodgrass (1968)

EXHIBITS: USDS, 1963

ROBLES, RONALD A. *Yakama/Yaqui*
EXHIBITS: SFFA, SI ('83)

ROBSON *Haida*
PUBLISHED: Snodgrass (1968)
PUBLIC COLLECTIONS: MAI

ROCK, HOWARD *Eskimo*
Weyahok
Born 1911 at Point Hope AK; died 1976; son of Keshorna (Emma) and Weyahok (Sam) Rock; GF: Kakairnok
RESIDENCE: Lived in Point Hope, AK
MILITARY: U.S. Army, WWII
EDUCATION: White Mountain Boarding School; U of WA, 1938-1940; apprenticeship with an Oregon artist
OCCUPATION: Editor, Native activist and leader, ivory engraver, and painter
MEDIA: Oil and ivory
PUBLISHED: Ray (1968; 1969). *The Tundra Times* (28 Nov 1973); *Alaskan Journal* (winter 1974); *Alaska's Native People* (Vol. 6, no. 3, 1979)
EXHIBITS: MFA/AH

HOWARD ROCK

Rock was adopted by an aunt and uncle as a child. He became one of the best-known commercial ivory engravers and worked for Dell W. Thomas, Inc. and James L. Houston Manufacturing Co., in Seattle, WA, in the 1940s. In 1961, Rock returned to his native village and became involved in village activities. He helped found The Tundra Times, a statewide newspaper for Native peoples to inform them of government and AEC (sic) activities. Rock's work resulted in passage of the Native Claims Act in 1971.

ROCKY MOUNTAIN (see Vigil, Tim)

ROGERS, LEE *Cherokee/Sioux*
Born 27 Feb 1939
RESIDENCE: Russellville, AR
EDUCATION: B.A., Arkansas Tech University, Russellville, AR
EXHIBITS: CNM, LIAS
AWARDS: CNM ('90); LIAS ('90, MA)

ROGERS, WILL PAUL *Cherokee*
Born 28 Dec 1927 at Fort Gibson, OK; son of Charlotte and Lewis Rogers
RESIDENCE: Fort Gibson, OK
EDUCATION: BC
MEDIA: Watercolor
PUBLISHED: Snodgrass (1968)
PUBLIC COLLECTIONS: FCTM, GM, PAC
EXHIBITS: NSU; OSU; PAC; Oklahoma State Fair, Muskogee, OK
AWARDS: PAC (1947)

WILL PAUL ROGERS

"Acee Blue Eagle (q.v.) once said, 'Rogers is a young genius who has the right to call himself an artist.' He paints infrequently."

Snodgrass 1968

ROMAN NOSE *Miniconjou Sioux*
Woohkinih
A.K.A. Crow Nose; Chief Roman Nose
Birth date unknown; half brother of Chief Red Cloud (Sioux)
OCCUPATION: Warrior and artist
PUBLISHED: Snodgrass (1968)
PUBLIC COLLECTIONS: SI/OAA (sketch book of drawings taken from the artist at the time of his capture in 1866)

ROMAN NOSE

Roman Nose was involved in the hostilities on the Powder River and near Whitestone Agency, SD, ca. 1869-1873

ROMAN NOSE, HENRY CARUTHERS *Southern Cheyenne*
Who Whinny; Wo-Ke-Nos
Born 30 June 1865; died 13 June 1917 in Oklahoma; son of Day Woman and Shot in Nose, a.k.a. Naked Turkey; GF: Limber Nose; GM: Big Crow Woman
MILITARY: U.S. Army, scout at Fort Reno, Indian Territory

HENRY CARUTHERS ROMAN NOSE

"Roman Nose was one of 72 Plains Indians taken as prisoners from Fort Sill, OK to Fort Marion, St. Augustine, FL, in 1875. After being released from prison and attending schools in the East, the artist returned to Darlington Agency in 1881. He had adopted the 'White man's ways,' had a good knowledge of English, and was a

EDUCATION: Equivalent of 3rd grade, Fort Marion, FL; Hampton, 1878; Carlisle, ca. 1879; 4½-month "refresher" course in tinsmithing, Carlisle, 1883
OCCUPATION: Sawmill hand, scout, policeman, herder, tinsmith, and artist
MEDIA: Watercolor, pencil, colored pencil, tin, and crayon
PUBLISHED: Snodgrass (1966). *American Indian Art* (winter, 1992); *Native Peoples* (summer 1993)
PUBLIC COLLECTIONS: MAI, YU/BRBML
EXHIBITS: BPG
HONORS: Roman Nose State Park and Roman Nose Canyon, OK, are named for him.

ROMERO, CIPRIANA *Cochití*

RESIDENCE: Cochití Pueblo, NM
EDUCATION: Santa Fe
PUBLISHED: Snodgrass (1968)

ROMERO, DOROTHEA *Tlingit*

Born 19 Aug 1942 in Petersburg, AK
RESIDENCE: Seattle, WA
OCCUPATION: Full-time artist since 1983
MEDIA: Oil, hand made paper, and mixed-media
PUBLISHED: Younger, et al. (1985)
EXHIBITS: ESC; MPI; PDN; SCG; WSCS; WWM; Washington State Capitol Museum, Olympia, WA, 1985
SOLO EXHIBITS: MPI

ROMERO, FRANKIE *Taos*

Red Buffalo
Birth date unknown; died ca. 1982
RESIDENCE: Lived in Taos, NM
EDUCATION: Postgraduate, IAIA, 1963
PUBLISHED: Snodgrass 1968
PUBLIC COLLECTIONS: BIA
EXHIBITS: MNM, YAIA

ROMERO, MATEO *Cochití*

Born 1967
RESIDENCE: Santa Fe, NM
EDUCATION: Dartmouth College, Hanover, NH
PUBLISHED: *USA Weekend; Gallup Independent* (9-11 Aug 1991); *Southwest Art* (Sept 1993); *Art-Talk* (Feb 1995)
EXHIBITS: DAM; SWAIA; WWM; Crow Canyon Exhibition, Washington, D.C., 1994
SOLO EXHIBITS: WWM

ROMERO, MICHAEL *Santa Clara/Taos*

A.K.A. Mike Romero
Born 1950
RESIDENCE: Santa Fe, NM
EDUCATION: IAIA, 1964-1973
OCCUPATION: Sculptor, graphic artist, and painter
MEDIA: Oil, acrylic, pencil, stone, wood, and prints
PUBLISHED: New (1974). *Taos News* (9 Jan 1975; 16 Jan 1975)

HENRY CARUTHERS ROMAN NOSE

(continued) trained tinsmith. He took his name, Henry Caruthers, from a good friend and patron, as did many Indians away at school. Adverse circumstances prevented his working steadily as a tinsmith, and eventually he reverted almost completely to 'Indian ways.' He was made a chief, ca. 1898. He executed his paintings and sketches while a prisoner at Fort Marion, St. Augustine, FL, in 1875, and apparently did not paint after leaving prison."

Snodgrass 1968

Roman Nose, William Cohoe (q.v.) and ten other Cheyennes went to Washington in 1899 as a delegation to see the President and to express their dissatisfaction with government treatment (see Petersen 1968).

DOROTHEA ROMERO

Romero has said, "Through my art I am hoping that I can show the beauty of my homeland, the Northwest weather and landscape. I try to capture the forces of nature, their changing moods, color and movement of the sky, winds and sleet, of the ocean storms. . . . "

brochure, MPI, 1986

FRANKIE ROMERO

"The artist received postgraduate instruction at the Institute of American Indian Arts, where he majored in painting. He also studied exhibition arts and assisted with the installation of displays in the school art gallery."

Snodgrass 1968

PUBLIC COLLECTIONS: IAIA, HCC

EXHIBITS: ACMWA; HCC; HM; IAIA; ITIC; MFA/O; MNM; NACLA; ND; PAC; SFFA; SIM; SN; SWAIA; WWM; White Buckskin Art Center, Taos, NM

AWARDS: ITIC ('76); SWAIA ('75, 2-1st)

ROMERO, RICHARD *Tewa*

Born 1949 in Española, NM

RESIDENCE: Alcade, NM

EDUCATION: St. Catherine's, 1965

PUBLISHED: Snodgrass (1968)

PUBLIC COLLECTIONS: BIA

EXHIBITS: MNM, PAC, SAIEAIP

ROMERO, SANTIAGO *Cochití*

PUBLISHED: Snodgrass (1968)

EXHIBITS: AIEC

ROPE, VINE *Cheyenne*

PUBLISHED: Snodgrass (1968)

PUBLIC COLLECTIONS: MAI

ROREX, JEANNE WALKER *Cherokee*

Born 6 May 1951 in Checotah, OK; daughter of Allie Stone and L. E. "Buster" Walker; niece of Willard Stone (q.v.), sculptor; P/GP: Jessie Llalman and John Walker; M/GP: Lydia Blanche Hedrick and George Maloy Stone

RESIDENCE: Oktaha, OK

EDUCATION: Oktaha (OK) High School, 1969; A.A., BC, 1980; B.S., NSU

OCCUPATION: Commercial artist and painter

MEDIA: Oil, acrylic, watercolor, pencil, pen and ink, and prints

PUBLISHED: *Southwest Art* (Jan 1989); *Twin Territories* (Vol. 3, no. 3, 1993)

PUBLIC COLLECTIONS: TTSP

EXHIBITS: BC/McG, CHAS, CNM, FCTM, IACA, ITIC, LIAS, LC, OIAP, RC, RE, SPIM, TIAF, TTSP

SOLO EXHIBITS: CNM; Illinois College Art Gallery, Jacksonville, IL, 1993

AWARDS: CHAS ('90, 1st); CNM ('83; '85, 1st; '86, 1st; '87, 1st; '90, 1st; '92, 1st); FCTM ('83; '84; '86, 1st; '87; '89, 1st; '90; '93); ITIC ('89, 1st); LC ('89, 1st; '90, 1st); TIAF ('92, 1st; '94)

HONORS: Oktaha (OK) High School, Valedictorian, 1969; BC, Salutatorian, 1980

ROSE, WENDY *Miwok/Hopi*

Born 7 May 1948 in Oakland, CA

EDUCATION: El Cerrito (CA) High School, 1963-1964; Contra Costa Junior College, San Pablo, CA, 1967-1974; M.A., U of CA/B, 1978

OCCUPATION: Educator, poet, and painter

MEDIA: Watercolor and pen and ink

BOOKS ILLUSTRATED: Cox (1976); Niatum (1974); Niatum, ed.(1975); Rose (1973; 1976; 1977; 1978; 1979; 1980); Salisbury (1979); Windt (1980)

COMMISSIONS: Logos for various California Indian organizations; Graphics for various magazines

EXHIBITS: SI; group shows throughout AZ, CA, KS, MS, NV, and NJ

SOLO EXHIBITS: MPI

HONORS: Pulitzer Prize in Poetry, Nominee, 1980

ROSS, JACK *Cheyenne*

Born 17 Apr 1949 at Mobridge, SD

RESIDENCE: Dickinson, ND

EDUCATION: B.A., Dickinson (ND) State College, 1971

OCCUPATION: Professional painter

MEDIA: Oil

PUBLISHED: *North Dakota Horizons* (spring 1982)

EXHIBITS: Annual Contemporary International Art Exhibition, Chico, CA; International Peace Garden Contemporary Art Invitational, 1968

SOLO EXHIBITS: SIM

HONORS: *Scholarships and Fellowships:* Kappa Pi Honorary International Art Fraternity, scholarship. *Other:* American Association of University Professors Award, 1971

ROSSO, LARRY *Carrier*

Sisokolas

Born 21 Aug 1944 at Burne Lake, BC, Canada

OCCUPATION: Silkscreen business owner and manager, teacher, carver, and graphic artist

PUBLISHED: Hall, Blackman, and Rickard (1981)

EXHIBITS: Pacific National Exhibition; Vancouver (BC) Sea Festival

ROULLIER, FREDERICK *Flathead*

BOOKS ILLUSTRATED: Pinchette (1974)

EXHIBITS: MPI

ROWELL, CHARLES EMERY *Kiowa*

A.K.A. Charles Emerson Rowell; C. E. Rowell

Born 3 Apr 1909 north of Old Meers, OK; M/GU: Jimmy Quoetone (q.v.)

RESIDENCE: Lawton, OK

MILITARY: U.S. Army, WWII

OCCUPATION: Stone mason, carpenter, laborer; full-time artist since 1968

MEDIA: Oil and watercolor

PUBLISHED: Snodgrass (1968); Boyd, et al. (1981; 1983)

PUBLIC COLLECTIONS: ACM, GM

EXHIBITS: AIE; HM; PAC; regional fairs and sidewalk shows

AWARDS: AIE ('72, 1st)

CHARLES EMERY ROWELL

"Rowell's mother was a member of the Sun Boy family. His father was a prominent physician, rancher, farmer, and political leader, who came to Oklahoma in 1897, and built the 'little red store' on Medicine Creek. . . . Since about 1944, the artist has been painting prolifically, executing in 1964 alone, 59 watercolors and 27 oils. He assisted Jimmy Quoetone (q.v.) in recording Haw Vahte's (q.v.) calendar. He has continued the entries alone since Quoetone's death, and has recently completed a copy of the Anko Calendar."

Snodgrass 1968

ROWELL, SKIP *Cherokee*

Born 1 Aug 1943 in Durant, OK; son of Cleda Bennight and O.D. Rowell; P/GP: Noke and Jack Rowell; M/GP: Mattie and W.B. Bennight

RESIDENCE: Haywood, OK

MILITARY: U.S. Army, Vietnam

EDUCATION: Atoka (OK) High School, 1961; OSU/O, 1962-1963

OCCUPATION: Saddlemaker, scrimshaw artist, and painter

MEDIA: Oil, watercolor, pastel, pen and ink, ivory, bone, horn, and prints

EXHIBITS: ACAI, CIM, CNM, FCTM, LIAS, TIAF, TIMSS

AWARDS: ACAI (Best of Category); CIM; CNM ('90); FCTM ('86; '87; '88; '91; '92; '94, 1st); TIAF (3-1st)

HONORS: TIAF, poster artist, 1988

ROWLAND, CHRIS *Northern Cheyenne/Sioux*

Born ca. 1966 at Crow Agency, MT; nephew of Nellie Means, artist

RESIDENCE: Lame Deer, MT

EDUCATION: Colstrip (MT) High School, 1983; Dull Knife Memorial College, Lame Deer, MT

MEDIA: Oil

PUBLISHED: *Southwest Art* (Mar 1995)

EXHIBITS: NAVAM; Dull Knife Memorial College, Lame Deer, MT; Rosebud County Art Show, Forsyth, MT

ROWLODGE, ARTHUR, SR. *Arapaho*

Born 1915 in Geary, OK

RESIDENCE: Geary, OK

EXHIBITS: SPIM

ROYBAL, ALFONSO (see Awa Tsireh)

ROYBAL, BERNICE *San Ildefonso*

PUBLIC COLLECTIONS: PAC

EXHIBITS: PAC

ROYBAL, GARY ALAN *San Ildefonso*

Born 11 Sept 1973; son of Marie Tenorio and Gary Steven Roybal (q.v.); P/GP: Julia and José D. Roybal (q.v.); P/GGF: Juan Cruz Roybal (q.v.); P/GGU: Awa Tsireh (q.v.)

RESIDENCE: Santa Fe, NM

EDUCATION: St. Catherine's, 1990

MEDIA: Acrylic, watercolor, and prints

PUBLIC COLLECTIONS: IAIA

EXHIBITS: IAIA, SWAIA

AWARDS: SWAIA ('92, 1st; '93, 1st)

ROYBAL, GARY STEVEN *San Ildefonso*

Born 17 June 1951; son of Julia Dasheno and José D. Roybal (q.v.); father of Gary Alan Roybal; P/GP: Tonita and Juan Cruz Roybal (q.v.); P/GU: Awa Tsireh

RESIDENCE: Santa Fe, NM

EDUCATION: St. Catherine's, 1970; IAIA, 1982

OCCUPATION: Museum curator and painter

MEDIA: Watercolor

EXHIBITS: AHM/CO

ROYBAL, JOSÉ D. *San Ildefonso*

JOSÉ D. ROYBAL

"The artist's day school teacher, Helen Culley, was the first to encourage him to paint in 1930. He began to paint more seriously ca. 1955."

Snodgrass 1968

Oquwa, Rain God

A.K.A. J. D. Roybal; Dissy Roybal; Disiderio Roybal

Born 7 Nov 1922 at San Ildefonso Pueblo, NM; died 28 June 1978; son of Tonita and Juan Cruz Roybal (q.v.); father of Gary Steven Roybal (q.v.); nephew of Awa Tsireh (q.v.)

MILITARY: U.S. Army, 100% disability discharge

EDUCATION: St. Catherine's, 1942; Santa Fe (NM) Business College, 1959-1960

OCCUPATION: Potter and painter

MEDIA: Watercolor and clay

PUBLISHED: Snodgrass (1968); Brody (1971); Tanner (1973); Highwater (1976); Silberman (1978); Schmid and Houlihan (1979); Broder (1981); Hoffman, et al.

(1984). *The Arizona Republic* (17 Mar 1968); *SFR Voices* (summer 1982)

PUBLIC COLLECTIONS: BA/AZ, HCC, MAI, MNA, MNM, MRFM, SM

EXHIBITS: ASM, HM, HM/G, IK, LGAM, MNM, NAP, OMA, SN, SWAIA, PAC

AWARDS: HM/G ('69, HM); ITIC ('72, Elkus Award); SN ('71); SWAIA ('42; '72, 1st; '73; '74, 1st; '76, Best of Paintings)

HONORS: San Ildefonso Pueblo, NM, council member

ROYBAL, JUAN CRUZ *San Ildefonso*

Birth date unknown; father of José D. Roybal (q.v.); brother of Awa Tsireh (q.v.)

PUBLISHED: Snodgrass (1968)

PUBLIC COLLECTIONS: MNM

ROYBAL, LOUIS *(?)*

PUBLISHED: Alexander (1932); Snodgrass (1968)

ROYBAL, RALPH *San Ildefonso*

Ma-Wholo-Peen

Born 15 Nov 1916 in San Ildefonso Pueblo, NM

EDUCATION: Santa Fe; St. Louis (MO) University

MEDIA: Oil and watercolor

PUBLISHED: Tanner (1973)

EXHIBITS: HM/G, SN

AWARDS: SN ('66)

ROYBAL, SEFERINO *San Ildefonso*

PUBLISHED: Snodgrass (1968)

PUBLIC COLLECTIONS: MNM

ROYE, BURGESS *Ponca*

Birth date unknown; born in Pawnee, OK

RESIDENCE: Grand Junction, CO

EDUCATION: High school

OCCUPATION: Poet and artist

MEDIA: Watercolor, tempera, pencil, and prints

PUBLISHED: *The Phoenix Gazette* (11 June 1986)

PUBLIC COLLECTIONS: Phillips University, Enid, OK; Kennedy Gallery, Washington, D.C.

EXHIBITS: CIM, OAC, OIAP, PAC

AWARDS: PAC ('79)

ROYE, PALADINE H. *Ponca*

Pon-Cee-Cee, Watch Out For This One

RESIDENCE: Austin, TX

EDUCATION: Graduated high school

OCCUPATION: Full-time painter since 1979

MEDIA: Acrylic, watercolor, gouache, and prints

PUBLISHED: Medina (1981). *The Indian Trader* (Sept 1982); *Southwest Art* (July 1989)

PUBLIC COLLECTIONS: GM

EXHIBITS: AIAFM; CIM; CNM; HM/G; ITIC; PAC; RE; SMIC; TCIM; TIAF; Pasadena (CA) Indian and Western Show

AWARDS: AIAFM; CIM ('86, Best of Show; '88, Best Graphic); CNM ('93); HM/G ('79); ITIC; RE ('88, 1st); TCIM ('91)

BURGESS ROYE

Roye says "You seek within yourself to give back to life, however you express your thoughts. You come to understand your limits, that what you give away you keep. I am practicing to be known as an artist, as I am practicing to be a father, a husband, a friend. One thing for sure is I don't know — but when I die, you will." Chris Kiana, in an artist's brochure, said of Roye, "I would like to define Burgess Roye's style of art as 'combined complex simplicity.' He has been developing this unique style of abstract art for 20 years and now feels comfortable enough with himself to do series work, the first being the Black Robe [series]. . . . Roye includes prose with his paintings, this helps the art critic understand why Burgess painted what he did."

artist, p.c. 1990

ROYSE, MARVIN *Cherokee*

RESIDENCE: Muskogee, OK

EXHIBITS: CNM, FCTM

RULEAUX, DONALD D. *Oglala Sioux*

DONALD D. RULEAUX

Ruleaux is one of the original organizers of The Dream Catchers Artists Guild, Ltd. (q.v.).

Born 9 June 1931 in Martin, SD; son of Helen Kendall and Herbert Ruleaux; P/GP: Leta Livermont and Nicholas Ruleaux; M/GP: Isabella Frank and Ernest Kendall

RESIDENCE: Spearfish, SD

EDUCATION: Gordon (NE) High School, 1950; B.F.A., Chadron (NE) State College, 1959; George Washington University, Washington, D.C., 1967; M.A., ASU, 1968

OCCUPATION: Cartographer, package designer, free-lance commercial artist, teacher, ceramist, and painter

MEDIA: Oil, watercolor, polymer, pencil, silverpoint, pen and ink, clay, and prints

COMMISSIONS: *Murals:* Kelly's Motor Inn, Spearfish, SD

PUBLIC COLLECTIONS: BIA; HCC; SIM; DeRance Corporation, Milwaukee, WI; Kelly's Motor Inn, Spearfish, SD

EXHIBITS: Partial listing of more than fifty includes: AICH; ASU; BBHC; BHAA; BHSU; CNM; CPS; FAC/D; GWWAS; HCC; HPTU; HSAS; LSS; NARF; NPTA; RC; SIM; TM/NE; U of NE; U of WV; WTF; Gordon (NE) Centennial Celebration; North Platte Valley (NE) Artist Guild; see also Awards

SOLO EXHIBITS: MCCC; Chadron (NE) State College

AWARDS: BBHC; BHAA ('61-'65, 2-1st, 4-Best of Category); HSAS; NPTA ('91; '92, 2-1st; '93; '94); RC ('72, 1st; '74; '75, 2-1st; '77; '79; '80, 1st; '81; '86, Erickson Award, Woodard Award; '90; '91; '92, Diederich Award, Powers Award; '93, 2-1st, Diederich Award; '94, 2-1st, Diederich Award); Dakota Artist Guild, Rapid City, SD ('66, 1st)

HONORS: *Fellowships and Grants:* National Institute of Art; George Washington University, Washington, D.C.; National Gallery of Art, Washington, D.C.; South Dakota Arts Council, 1979. *Other:* Lead (SD) Chamber of Commerce Board of Directors, William F. Cody Award, nominee, 1979

RUNNELS, VIC *Oglala Sioux*

VIC RUNNELS

Runnels was one of the original organizers of The Dream Catchers Artists Guild, Ltd. (q.v.) and exhibited extensively in exhibitions they organized.

A.K.A. Victor Runnels

RESIDENCE: Hill City, SD

OCCUPATION: Teacher and painter

PUBLIC COLLECTIONS: HCC

EXHIBITS: HCC, LAC, NPTA, RC, SIM, U of WV, WTF

AWARDS: NPTA ('91, '93); RC ('77; '78, 1st; '81, 2-1st, Begay Award; '83)

RUNNER, O. B. *Sioux*

PUBLISHED: Snodgrass (1968)

PUBLIC COLLECTIONS: MAI

RUNNING ANTELOPE *Hunkpapa Sioux*

RUNNING ANTELOPE

"The chief was at Grand River, Dakota Territory, in 1873. His exploits as a warrior are recorded as early as 1853."

Snodgrass 1968

OCCUPATION: Warrior and painter

PUBLISHED: Hamilton (1950); Snodgrass (1968). *4th Annual Report,* BAE (1882-1883); *10th Annual Report,* BAE (1888-1889)

RUNNING DEAR *Sioux*

PUBLISHED: Snodgrass (1968)

PUBLIC COLLECTIONS: MPM (pictographic style on paper)

RUNNING WEASEL(see Racine, Albert Batiste)

RUNNING WOLF (see Davis, Jessie Edwin, II)

RUNNING WOLF, GALE, SR. *Blackfeet*

Born 27 Oct 1950; son of Annie and George Running Wolf

RESIDENCE: Billings, MT

EDUCATION: Flandreau Indian School (High School), 1968

OCCUPATION: Carpenter and full-time artist

MEDIA: Oil, acrylic, watercolor, pencil, and gouache

PUBLISHED: Ray, ed. (1972). *The Indian Trader* (May 1989)

COMMISSIONS: Custer Battlefield Trading Post, logo design and posters; Custer Battlefield National Monument Board of Directors, painting; St. Labré Museum, Ashland, MT, portrait of Chief Rain-In-The Face; Native American Herbal Tea, Inc., Aberdeen, SD, art work

PUBLIC COLLECTIONS: HCC; MPI; SIM; Arlee (MT) Clinic; Browning (MT) Hospital

EXHIBITS: C/CS; CIA; CIM; CMRM; CNM; BBHC; HCC; ITIC; MPI; GFNAAS; NAVAM; NPTA; RC; SNAICF; TM/NE; Montana Indian Art Rendezvous, 1987; U.S. Senate Building, Washington, D.C., 1984; Kiwanis-Plainsman Western Art Extravaganza, Clearwater, FL, 1985

SOLO/SPECIAL EXHIBITS: SIM (dual show)

AWARDS: CNM ('86, Newcomer Award); BBHC ('87); GFNAAS ('87; '88, Artist's Choice; '89, Peoples Choice); NPTA ('88); RC ('87; '89, WKI Award; '90; '91, WKI Award; '92, WKI Award, Begay Award; '93; '94)

HONORS: Native American Art Association, Great Falls, MT, Award of Appreciation

GALE RUNNING WOLF SR.

The loss of Running Wolf's job as a carpenter became an opportunity to concentrate on his painting. Because of his natural talent and his great enthusiasm he was successful. He is a self-taught artist with no formal training whose paintings reflect his Plains Indian heritage.

brochure, SIM, 1988

RUNS OVER *Oglala (?) Sioux*

Kahirpeya

Birth date unknown

RESIDENCE: From Pine Ridge Agency, SD (see Black Heart)

PUBLISHED: Snodgrass (1968)

PUBLIC COLLECTIONS: MAI

RUNSTHROUGH, DOUGLAS *Sioux/Assiniboin*

Born 3 Sept 1951 at Poplar, MT, on the Fort Peck Reservation

RESIDENCE: Frazer, MT

MILITARY: U.S. Army, 1971-1972

EDUCATION: Frazer (MT) High School; Eastern Montana College, Billings, MT, 1971

OCCUPATION: Commercial artist and painter

MEDIA: Oil, acrylic, watercolor, pen and ink, and pastel

COMMISSIONS: College of Great Falls (MT), painting for pamphlets

SOLO EXHIBITS: SIM

AWARDS: Tribal Education Department, design competition cash prizes, 1976

DOUGLAS RUNSTHROUGH

Runsthrough says that he has been painting and drawing since he was in elementary school. He paints the life of the Plains Indian warriors, a life that is long gone but an important part of his heritage. He takes pride in, and is very knowledgeable about his tribe's history.

brochure, SIM, 1978

RUSSELL, BURT *Cherokee*

Born 24 Dec 1943; son of Lizzie Grits and Bill Russell; P/GF: Jack Russell M/GP: Maggie and Bird Grits

RESIDENCE: Tahlequah, OK

EDUCATION: Tahlequah (OK) High School, 1963; IAIA, 1965

OCCUPATION: Photographer and painter

MEDIA: Oil, pencil, pastel, and film

EXHIBITS: CNM; Fort Smith (AR) Art Center

BURT RUSSELL

The majority of Russell's work is of female nudes in a natural, outdoor, setting. According to the artist, "The theme has been a visual representation of our beginnings and environmental connection with nature. The female nude figure is used as a symbol of 'a bearer of life' for the future."

p.c. 1990

Russell, Cindy *Osage/Kaw*

Born 19 June 1940; daughter of Cynthia Lassert Grapes; M/GP: Cora and Frank Lassert

RESIDENCE: Kaw City, OK

EDUCATION: Ponca City (OK) High School, 1958

OCCUPATION: Wife, mother, clerical worker, and painter

MEDIA: Oil, watercolor, and pen and ink

EXHIBITS: TIAF; local and area exhibits

Russell, Harvey, Jr. *Cheyenne*

Bear Shield

Born 1946 in El Reno, OK; son of a Cheyenne chief

RESIDENCE: Canton, OK

EDUCATION: IAIA

PUBLIC COLLECTIONS: IAIA

EXHIBITS: IAIA, SPIM; galleries in NM, OK, and TX

Harvey Russell Jr.

The artist, who is a Cheyenne headman, a member of the Bowstring Society, and a priest in the Cheyenne Sun Dance, paints using his strong cultural background as an inspiration. He frequently uses symbols from the Native American Church and Cheyenne ceremonies.

artist, p.c. 1990

Russell, James, Jr. (see Humetewa, James Russell, Jr.)

Rutledge, Jacque *Cherokee*

Born 7 Oct 1928; daughter of Dorothy Lily Mae Peveteau Clower and Marshall W. Richardson; P/GP: Mary Susan Welty Shields and George Washington Richardson; M/GP: Jewel Manning and Era Tray Peveteau Clower

RESIDENCE: Talihina, OK

EDUCATION: Shawnee (OK) High School, 1947; B.S., HSU, 1963; M.S., NSU, 1982; M.B.S., SOSU, 1985

OCCUPATION: School principal, public health coordinator, art teacher, sculptor, and painter

MEDIA: Acrylic, watercolor, pencil, pen and ink, pastel, and stone

PUBLIC COLLECTIONS: SI; Eastern Oklahoma State University, Durant, OK

EXHIBITS: CNM; FCTM; KCPA; OSC; SI; Fort Smith (AR) Art Center; Le Centre d'Art, Paris, France; Talihina (OK) Art Show; local art shows

SOLO EXHIBITS: CNM

AWARDS: CNM ('78, 1st)

Rutledge-Gates, Catherine Ann *Choctaw/Cherokee*

A.K.A. Cathy Rutledge; Signature: C. A. Rutledge; Cathy Rutledge Gates

Born 8 Jan 1937 in Charleston, MS

RESIDENCE: Albuquerque, NM

EDUCATION: Charleston (MS) High School, 1954; Drury College, Springfield, MO; Missouri University, Columbia, MO, 1954-1958

OCCUPATION: Art teacher and painter

MEDIA: Oil, watercolor, conté, pencil, charcoal, pastel, mixed-media, and prints

PUBLISHED: *Oklahoma Art Gallery* (winter 1980); *The Muskogee Phoenix* (17 Oct 1982); *Southwest Art* (June 1983)

COMMISSIONS: Democratic Commission of Cedar Rapids, IA, portrait of Joan Mondale, wife of Walter Mondale

EXHIBITS: CMRM, CNM, FCTM, FCTM/M, ITIC, KCPA, OAC, SI

SOLO EXHIBITS: SPIM

AWARDS: CNM ('82, 1st, Grand Prize; '83, 1st); FCTM ('80, 1st, Grand Award, IH; '81, 1st, Grand Award, IH; '82, 1st, Needlepoint Guild Award); FCTM/M ('83, 1st, IH; '84; '85); ITIC ('81)

HONORS: FCTM, designated a Master Artist, 1983

Catherine Ann Rutledge-Gates

Rutledge-Gates paints in the photo-realism style. Although she works from photographs she has explained that she does not simply copy them. They are used for a reference when she needs to know how a garment hangs or a shawl drapes on a figure.

brochure, SPIM, 1982

SAAKA (see White Bear, Alton)

SACOMAN, BEVERLY JOSÉ *Mescalero Apache/Navajo*

Born 4 Dec 1946; daughter of Byrdian Sombrero and John José; P/GP: Ella and Ben José; M/GP: Katerina and Solon Sombrero

RESIDENCE: Santa Fe, NM

EDUCATION: G.E.D.; Sitka (AK) Community College, 1977-1984

OCCUPATION: Homemaker and artist

MEDIA: Oil, watercolor, pencil, pen and ink, pastel, and prints

PUBLIC COLLECTIONS: HCC

EXHIBITS: AC/BC; HCC; LSS; MFA/AH; MIC; RC; B.A.C.A. All-Alaska Art Show; Alaska State Fair; Minot (ND) National Art Competition; juried exhibits in Alaska

SOLO EXHIBITS: U of ND

AWARDS: Partial listing includes: RC ('87, Powers Award; '90, Powers Award; '94, Powers Award)

BEVERLY JOSÉ SACOMAN

Sacoman says "My pictures usually depict people from my background. They are in me somehow and their faces appear on my canvases. My work is in homage to my relatives and ancestors."

p.c. 1990

SAGE, OSCAR *Eskimo*

Born 1924 in Kivalina, AK

RESIDENCE: Kivalina, AK

EDUCATION: DCTP, 1964-1965

PUBLISHED: Ray (1969)

SAGER-MCGOUGH, WANDA *Cherokee*

RESIDENCE: Grove, OK

EDUCATION: U of Tulsa; studied with Charles Banks Wilson, Alexandre Hogue, and Greg Kreutz

OCCUPATION: Art teacher, sculptor, and painter

MEDIA: Oil, polyform, leather, and fiber

EXHIBITS: BB; FCTM; LIAS; Bartlesville (OK) Art Association; Springfield (MO) Art Museum; galleries in Siloam Springs, AR, and Grove, OK

AWARDS: FCTM ('92, Heritage Award)

SAGGASHI, FRED *Cree*

Born 1950 in Pikangikum, ON, Canada

RESIDENCE: Pikangikum Reserve, ON, Canada

MEDIA: Acrylics, watercolor, and ink

PUBLISHED: Menitove, ed. (1986b)

PUBLIC COLLECTIONS: C/AG/TB

EXHIBITS: C/AG/TB; C/WICEC; exhibits in New York, NY, and London, England

SOLO EXHIBITS: C/TU

FRED SAGGASHI

Saggashi paints only in black and white, although he uses a variety of media.

Menitove, ed. 1986b

SAGGIASSIE *Inuit (Eskimo)*

Born 1924 in Canada

RESIDENCE: Cape Dorset, NWT, Canada

OCCUPATION: Graphic artist

MEDIA: Black pencil and prints

PUBLISHED: Houston (1967a); Goetz, et al. (1977)

EXHIBITS: C/CD, C/TIP

SAHMIE, RANDY *Hopi*

PUBLISHED: Hill (1992)

PUBLIC COLLECTIONS: IAIA

EXHIBITS: IAIA

DETAIL: Virginia Stroud, *The Give Away People*, 1977. Philbrook Museum of Art, Tulsa, Oklahoma

Sah Quo Dle Quoie (see Turkey, Moses)

Sah Wa (see Vigil, Rufina)

Saila, Pitaloosie(see Pitaloosie)

Sainnawap, Noah *(?)*

Born 1954 in Pickle Crow, ON, Canada
RESIDENCE: Canada
PUBLISHED: Menitove, ed. (1986b)
PUBLIC COLLECTIONS: C/AG/TB, C/MCC, C/ROM; in Regina, SK, and Vancouver, BC
EXHIBITS: C/AG/TB, C/ROM
SOLO/SPECIAL EXHIBITS: C/CC (dual show)

Noah Sainnawap

Early in his career, Sainnawap's paintings reflected the influence of the Algonquin Legend Painting School of Art, however, his more recent works are less narrative and more abstract.

Menitove, ed. 1986b

Sain-Tah-Oodie (see Harjo, Sharron Ahtone)

St. Martin, James *Paiute*

A.K.A. Jim St. Martin
Born 10 June 1945 in Burns, OR
RESIDENCE: Burns, OR
EDUCATION: Woodrow Wilson High School, Portland, OR, 1960-1962; A.A., IAIA, 1964; PSU/OR, 1964-1965; B.F.A., SFAI, 1972; SFSC; M.S., PSU/OR, 1977
OCCUPATION: Community art coordinator, teacher, writer, CETA director, management consultant, photographer, jeweler, craftsman, and painter
MEDIA: Oil, pen and ink, silver, turquoise, leather, feathers, and beads
PUBLISHED: *Art in America* (July/Aug 1972)
COMMISSIONS: KPIX Television, San Francisco, illustrated documentary, 1974
BOOKS ILLUSTRATED: Northwest Regional Labs, traditional stories of the Burns (OR) Paiute, 1978-1980
EXHIBITS: BM/B, IAIA, OAM
SOLO EXHIBITS: MPI

James St. Martin

St. Martin says, "I am a product of changing times. My art neither reflects tradition as it once was nor is it completely contemporary.... My art is concerned with the transition of time and people, not with what was or what will be...."

brochure, MPI, 1981

St. Pierre, Roger *Chippewa (?)*

PUBLISHED: Snodgrass (1968)
PUBLIC COLLECTIONS: HS/ND (pictographic style painting on canvas of a buffalo hunt)

Roger St. Pierre

The North Dakota Historical Society files indicate that St. Pierre was possibly a member of the Turtle Mountain Band of the Chippewa of North Dakota.

Snodgrass 1968

Sakeva, Al *Tewa/Hopi*

A.K.A. Alfonso Sakeva
Born 20 Jan 1952 in Winslow, AZ
EDUCATION: Ganado (AZ) High School; IAIA, 1969-1971
PUBLISHED: Tanner (1973)
COMMISSIONS: *Murals:* IAIA, 1969-1971 (with several other students)
EXHIBITS: HM/G, ITIC, MFA/O, RC, SN
AWARDS: HM/G ('70, 1st); ITIC ('70, '71, 1st, MA); RC ('71)

Sakhomenewa (see Albert, Robert Stephen)

Sakyesva (see Sakyesva, Harry)

Sakyesva, Harry *Hopi*

Sakyesva, People From The Green Valley
Born 1921 in Hotevilla, AZ
RESIDENCE: Phoenix, AZ
EDUCATION: Hopi

Harry Sakyesva

"The artist is known not only as a painter, but also as a maker of katsina *dolls and as a silversmith. He has had no formal art training."*

Snodgrass 1968

OCCUPATION: Carver and painter
MEDIA: Wood and watercolor
PUBLISHED: Snodgrass (1968); Brody (1971); Tanner (1973)
PUBLIC COLLECTIONS: MNA/KHC; MNM (name spelled "Sakyewa"; possibly the same artist); PAC
EXHIBITS: MNM, MFA/O, PAC

SAKYEWA, HENRY *Hopi*
PUBLISHED: Snodgrass (1968)
PUBLIC COLLECTIONS: MNM

SALAS, DIEGO *Zia*
Born 1948
EDUCATION: Santa Fe
MEDIA: Watercolor
PUBLISHED: Snodgrass (1968); Seymour (1988)
PUBLIC COLLECTIONS: IACB, IACB/DC, MNM, MNA/KHC, MRFM, SM
EXHIBITS: FWG, MNM, MNA

SALAS, FERMÍN *Mescalero Apache/Yaqui*
Born 30 Nov 1957 in Fresno, CA
EDUCATION: U of NM, CSU/S, CCAC
OCCUPATION: Artist
MEDIA: Acrylic
PUBLISHED: *American West Airlines Magazine* (Oct 1987)
PUBLIC COLLECTIONS: HM
EXHIBITS: Partial listing of more than thirty includes: CID; CSU/S; HM; SRJC; U of N AZ/G; U of NM; Haggin Museum, Stockton, CA, 1977; Museo de las Américas, Madrid, Spain; Point Reyes (CA) Visitor Center; Stockton (CA) Library, 1977; Universidad Internacional Menéndez Pelayo, Madrid, Spain
SOLO EXHIBITS: CCAC

SALO WHU (see Humetewa, James Russell, Jr.)

SALT, FREDDIE *Navajo*
Born 14 Dec 1940
RESIDENCE: Tonalea, AZ
EDUCATION: Santa Fe, 1960-1961
PUBLISHED: Snodgrass (1968)
EXHIBITS: MNM, PAC

SALTER, JOHN R. *Abenaki*
Born 16 Apr 1898 in Cambridge, MA; died 9 Apr 1978; father of Richard M. Salter
MILITARY: Military service, WWII
EDUCATION: B.F.A., CIA, 1932; M.A., U of IA, 1940; M.F.A. (with honors), U of IA, 1954
OCCUPATION: Teacher, designer, illustrator, ceramist, sculptor, and painter
MEDIA: Oil, acrylic, watercolor, stone, wood, clay, and prints
PUBLISHED: *The Arizona Republic* (18 Dec 1955; 19 May 1973; 24 Aug 1973); *The Arizona Daily Sun* (14 Feb 1968; 20 Feb 1970; 2 Apr 1971; 27 Aug 1979); biographical publications
COMMISSIONS: *Murals:* St. Pius Church, Flagstaff, AZ, 1969. *Other:* Church of the Epiphany, Flagstaff, AZ, paintings and sculpture, 1959; Our Lady of Guadalupe Church, Flagstaff, AZ, woodblock print

HENRY SAKYEWA

"It is possible that Henry Sakyewa and Harry Sakyesva (q.v.) are the same man, for both last names are apparently variations of the phonetic spelling of Sakyestewa (meaning, literally, the People From The Green Valley)."

Snodgrass 1968

EXHIBITS: CIA; HM; JAM; OAM; PAM/AZ; RC; TMA/AZ; U of N AZ; WAM; Allied Artists, National Academy of Design, 1966; Arizona Artists Traveling Exhibition; Arizona Watercolor Association, 1966; Elgin Academy, IL; Federation of Rocky Mountain States Exhibition, 1971; Prairie Watercolor Society

SOLO EXHIBITS: AC/SD; U of KS; U of N AZ; Topeka (KS) Art Center; Tubac (AZ) Art Association, 1976; Wichita (KS) Art Association; and Jerome, AZ, and Yuma, AZ

SALTER, RICHARD M. *Abenaki/Penobscot/Micmac*

Born 7 May 1940 at Iowa City, IA; son of John Salter Sr. (q.v.)

RESIDENCE: Lake Geneva, WI

EDUCATION: Flagstaff (AZ) High School, 1958; B.A., U of N AZ; M.F.A., Instituto San Miguel Allende, Guanajuato, Mexico

OCCUPATION: Art teacher, photographer, and painter

MEDIA: Acrylic, pencil, pen and ink, film, and mixed-media

PUBLISHED: Hill (1983). *The Rockford Register-Star* (24 May 1970; 31 Mar 1974; 31 Mar 1978); *The Arizona Sun* (24 Mar 1970; 11 Mar 1972; 22 Sept 1975); *Regional News* (23 Nov 1978); *The Taos News* (4 Jan 1979); biographical publications

COMMISSIONS: Orput and Orput, Rockford, IL; U.S. Borax Co., Boron, CA

PUBLIC COLLECTIONS: HCC; U of N AZ; USDI; Big Foot High School, Walworth, WI; Lake Geneva (WI) Public Library; Phoenix Indian School; Pioneer Savings and Loan, Racine, WI, and Walworth, WI; Western Illinois University, Macomb, IL; Wisconsin Civil Liberties Union, Milwaukee, WI

EXHIBITS: C/WICEC; CNM; HM/G; HPTU; KCPA; NACLA; RC; SI; U of N AZ/G; Beloit (WI) College, 1973; Burpee Art Museum, Rockford, IL; Rock Valley College, Rockford, IL, 1974; Springville (UT) Annual, 1975

SOLO EXHIBITS: Partial listing of more than 17 includes: MIM; SIM; U of WI/G; Delavan Art Museum, WI; Mitchell Museum, IL; Ozaukee Art Center, Cedarburg, WI; Rock Valley College Gallery, Rockford, IL; colleges and universities throughout Illinois and Wisconsin

AWARDS: HM/G ('76, 1st; '78, 1st; 79, 1st, Best of Mixed-media; '80); RC ('76, 1st; '77; '78; '80, 1st; '81, 1st)

RICHARD M. SALTER

Salter lived most of his early life in Flagstaff, Arizona, where his father was head of the art department of Northern Arizona University. Because of a close friendship with members of the Laguna Pueblo, the artist and his family became adopted members of the Pueblo. Salter's paintings are predominantly abstracts, often incorporating objects from everyday Indian life, historical and contemporary.

SALVADOR, MARÍA LILLY *Acoma*

A.K.A. María "Lilly" Torivio Salvador; María Salvador

Born 6 Apr 1944 at Acoma Pueblo, NM; daughter of Frances Torivio

RESIDENCE: Acoma Pueblo, NM

EDUCATION: Grants (NM) High School, 1963; NMSU

OCCUPATION: Potter, silversmith, textile artist, and painter

MEDIA: Acrylic, clay, and silver

PUBLISHED: *US News and World Report* (July 1991)

PUBLIC COLLECTIONS: HM, MFA/B

EXHIBITS: AC/ENP, CIM, HM/G, ITIC, MFA/B, MNH/LA, SDMM, SWAIA

AWARDS: CIM ('92, 1st); HM/G ('91); SWAIA ('91, 1st)

SALVADOR, MARÍA TORIVIO (see Salvador, María Lilly)

SALWAY, ORVILLE *Oglala Sioux*

Paha Ska

A.K.A. Signature: Paha Ska

Born 23 Oct 1924 at Pine Ridge, SD

RESIDENCE: Keystone, SD

EDUCATION: Oglala Community High School, Pine Ridge, SD; studied with Pedro Salazar in Mexico and Hobart Keith (q.v.) in Pine Ridge, SD

OCCUPATION: Construction and oil field worker, and painter

MEDIA: Oil, canvas, and velvet

PUBLIC COLLECTIONS: SIM

EXHIBITS: RC, SI, U of SD

SOLO EXHIBITS: SIM

AWARDS: RC ('74, 1st)

SAMPSON, WILL *Creek*

Samsogee, Owl Man

A.K.A. William S. Sampson Jr.

Born 27 Sept 1933; died 3 June 1987; son of Mable Lewis Hill and Wiley Sampson; P/GGF: George McKinley Hill, Creek Chief

MILITARY: U.S. Navy

EDUCATION: Preston (OK) High School; Haskell; OSU/O; Los Angeles (CA) Art Center School, 1950-1951

OCCUPATION: Oil field worker, rodeo contestant, actor, sculptor, and painter

PUBLISHED: Snodgrass (1968); Brody (1971). *The Anadarko Daily News* (14 Aug 1978); *The Tulsa Tribune* (16 Nov 1983; 12 Apr 1984; 4 Apr 1987; 8 June 1987); *The Arizona Republic* (24 Apr 1987)

COMMISSIONS: *Murals:* CCHM; Wagon Wheel Restaurant, Kansas City, MO; International Petroleum Exposition, Tulsa, OK

PUBLIC COLLECTIONS: CCHM; PAC; Ramsey Winch, Tulsa, OK

EXHIBITS: FCTM; MFA/D; PAC; USDI; Fort Gibson (OK) Traders Show; Okmulgee (OK) Art Guild; Muskogee (OK) State Fair; McAlester (OK) Union Stock Yards

SOLO/SPECIAL EXHIBITS: PAC (dual show); Muskogee (OK) Country Club

HONORS: American Indian Exposition Association, Anadarko, OK, Outstanding Indian of the Year, 1978; The Tulsa (OK) Indian Theater Association, Tulsa (OK) Indian Arts Festival, dedicated to his memory, 1988

WILL SAMPSON

Although Sampson drew and painted wherever he went, he never wanted to be a full-time painter as there were too many other things to do. According to the artist he sold his first painting, which was done with a match stick and laundry blueing on white butcher paper, when he was three years old. As an actor, Will Sampson is probably best known for his performance in the Oscar-winning movie, One Flew Over the Cuckoo's Nest.

The Tulsa Tribune
12 *Apr 1984*

SAMUALIE, KEEKEELEEMEOOME (see Keeleemeomee)

SAMUEL *Sioux*

PUBLISHED: Snodgrass (1968)

PUBLIC COLLECTIONS: MAI (ledger sheet)

SAMUEL, TONY *Tesuque*

EDUCATION: Santa Fe, ca. 1958

PUBLISHED: Snodgrass (1968)

EXHIBITS: MNM

SÁNCHEZ, ABEL (see Oqwa Pi)

SÁNCHEZ, ARSENIO *Pueblo*

PUBLISHED: Snodgrass (1968)

PUBLIC COLLECTIONS: RM

SÁNCHEZ, GUADALUPITO *Pueblo (Tewa)*

PUBLISHED: Snodgrass (1968)

EXHIBITS: FWG

SÁNCHEZ, HUBERT PATRICK *Zuni*

A.K.A. Patrick Sánchez

Born 30 Nov 1960

RESIDENCE: Zuni Pueblo, NM
EDUCATION: Zuni (NM) High School, 1980; two years of college
OCCUPATION: Laborer and painter
EXHIBITS: ITIC, MNA, NMSF
AWARDS: ITIC ('89); MNA (3-1st, Best of Division); NMSF (1st)

SÁNCHEZ, JOSEPH MARCUS *Taos*

Born 24 Feb 1948
RESIDENCE: Scottsdale, AZ
MILITARY: U.S. Marine Corps
EDUCATION: Alchessay High School, Whiteriver, AZ, 1966
OCCUPATION: Museum and gallery employee, musician, sculptor, and painter
MEDIA: Oil and prints
PUBLISHED: *The Phoenix Gazette* (14 Apr 1982); *The Arizona Republic* (2 May 1982; 20 July 1983)
COMMISSIONS: *Murals:* ASU, College of Business. *Other:* Canadian Music Industry Awards, 1974; Winnipeg Centennial Commission, 1974
PUBLIC COLLECTIONS: C/INAC; HM; CHIN Radio International; Northern Supply Corp, Winnipeg, MB
EXHIBITS: C/ROM; C/U of W; C/WICEC; FNAA; Arizona Chicano Art Show, Phoenix, 1978; Arizona State Capitol, Phoenix, 1979; First National Bank, Minneapolis, MN; Scottsdale (AZ) Community College, 1979; Scottsdale (AZ) Public Library, 1978; University of Hermosillo, Mexico, 1981

SÁNCHEZ, LAURA *Tewa*

Born 1951 in Santa Fe, NM
EDUCATION: St. Catherine's, 1965
PUBLISHED: Snodgrass (1968)
PUBLIC COLLECTIONS: MRFM
EXHIBITS: PAC, SAIEAIP

SÁNCHEZ, RAMOS *San Ildefonso*

Oqwa Owin, Katsina Town (or Rain God Town); *Kuofde*
Born 17 Mar 1926 at San Ildefonso Pueblo, NM; son of Oqwa Pi (Abel Sánchez) (q.v.)
MILITARY: U.S. Navy, WWII
EDUCATION: Santa Fe; Pasadena (CA) Junior College, 1944
OCCUPATION: Apprentice carpenter, bulldozer operator, and painter
MEDIA: Watercolor
PUBLISHED: Snodgrass (1968)
PUBLIC COLLECTIONS: MAI, MNA, OU/MA, SM, U of PA/M, WWM
EXHIBITS: ITIC; OU/ET; Philadelphia (PA) Art Alliance Exhibition of Contemporary Pueblo Indian Art, 1961
HONORS: San Ildefonso Pueblo, NM , assisted in establishing the present Pueblo government, 1957; San Ildefonso Pueblo, NM, Lieutenant Governor (1962), council member, and sheriff; Pojoaque (NM) Valley School Board, Vice-chairman, 1964

RAMOS SÁNCHEZ

"The artist achieved his desire to see the world outside the Pueblo culture when an opportunity to complete school in Pasadena was provided by Mr. and Mrs. Harry James."

Snodgrass 1968

SAND BURR (see Brave, Franklin P.)

SAND GENERATION (see Talahytewa, Gibson)

SANDERVILLE, RICHARD *Blackfeet*

A.K.A. Chief Bull

Born ca. 1864; died Feb 1951; son of Isodore Sandoval Jr.; raised by a Quaker family
RESIDENCE: Raised in Browning, MT
EDUCATION: Carlisle, 1890-1893
OCCUPATION: Farmer, government interpreter, assistant director of a woodcraft school, and painter
PUBLISHED: Snodgrass (1968)
PUBLIC COLLECTIONS: SI/OAA

SANDOVAL, BENNY *San Felipe*
EDUCATION: Albuquerque, ca. 1960
PUBLISHED: Snodgrass (1968)
EXHIBITS: MNM
AWARDS: MNM

SANDOVAL, CARMEN *Navajo/Cheyenne*
Born 24 Nov 1961 in California; daughter of Lorena and Joe Sandoval
RESIDENCE: Leavenworth, KS
MILITARY: U.S. Marine Corps
EDUCATION: Fort Wingate (NM) High School, 1980; Río Salado Community College, Phoenix, AZ, 1987
OCCUPATION: Traditional dancer, welder, and painter
MEDIA: Acrylic, watercolor, pencil, pastel, and prints
PUBLIC COLLECTIONS: HCC; Shannon County Gas, Pine Ridge, SD
EXHIBITS: HCC; RC; U of WV; TM/NE; Phoenix (AZ) Art Show, 1986
AWARDS: RC ('89; '92); awards while in junior and senior high school

SANDOVAL, RONALD *Navajo*
Born 4 June 1947 at Crownpoint, NM
RESIDENCE: Gallup, NM
EDUCATION: Gallup (NM) Public Schools
PUBLISHED: Snodgrass (1968)
EXHIBITS: NACG
AWARDS: NACG

SANDOVAL, TONY *Navajo*
RESIDENCE: Santa Fe, NM
EDUCATION: IAIA, ca. 1965
PUBLISHED: Snodgrass (1968), Schiffer (1991)
EXHIBITS: IAIA, YAIA

SANDS, RICKY LEE *Creek*
MEDIA: Oil
EXHIBITS: RC
AWARDS: RC ('93, WKI Award)

SANDY, PERCY TSISETE *Zuni*
Kai Sa, Red Moon
A.K.A. Tsisete. Signature: Percy Sandy; Kai-Sa; Percy Sandy Tsisete
Born 1918 at Zuni Pueblo, NM; died 15 May 1974 in Taos, NM
RESIDENCE: Lived in Taos, NM
EDUCATION: Albuquerque, 1940; Santa Fe; Sherman
OCCUPATION: Farmer, illustrator, muralist, and painter

RICHARD SANDERVILLE

Sanderville was the grandson of Isodore Sandoval Sr., who traveled from Spain to join the American Fur Co. at Old Fort Union. Isadore married a Blackfeet woman and became an interpreter for Prince Maximilian, 1833. Sanderville wrote an entire genealogy of the families of the Blackfeet tribe and assisted General Hugh L. Scott for one year in recording Indian sign language.

Snodgrass 1968

PERCY TSISETE SANDY

"It was at Zuni Day School that the artist was told to paint, and he found he enjoyed it. However, he was 18 when his formal art instruction began at Albuquerque. 'As an Indian artist, I hope to be instrumental in artistically and authentically depicting the customs of my people. This, I hope, will be my small contribution to a great race,' said the artist in 1940. In 1959, he was severely injured in an accident. . . . "

Snodgrass 1968

His paintings of religious subjects caused his ostracism from Zuni Pueblo, and he was forced to move to Taos, where he lived for the rest of his life.

Dockstader, p.c. 1995

MEDIA: Oil, watercolor, charcoal, and chalk

PUBLISHED: Tanner (1957; 1973); Snodgrass (1968); Brody (1971); Schmid and Houlihan (1979); Broder (1981); King (1981); Golder (1985); Samuels (1985)

BOOKS PUBLISHED: Clark (1945)

COMMISSIONS: *Murals:* La Fonda Hotel, Santa Fe, NM; Black Rock (NM) School; Black Rock (NM) Hospital

PUBLIC COLLECTIONS: AF, BIA, CGPS, GM, HCC, HM, IACB, IACB/DC, KM, MAI, MNA/KHC, MNM, MRFM, OU/MA, PAC, RM, SMNAI, UPA, WOM

EXHIBITS: AC/A; ASM; CGPS; HCC; HH; HM; HPTU; ITIC; JGS; LGAM; MNM; NAP; NMSF; PAC; PAC/T; SN; USDS; galleries in California and New Mexico

SA PA (see Abeyta, Emiliano)

SAPIEL SELMO *Passamaquoddy*

A.K.A. Chief Sapiel Selmo

PUBLISHED: Snodgrass (1968). *10th Annual Report,* BAE (1888-1889)

SAPIEL SELMO

"In 1887 Sapiel Selmo lived at Pleasant Point, Maine. He was the son of Selmo Soctomah (corruption of St. Thomas), who commanded 600 Passamaquoddy Indians in the Revolutionary War. When a young man, Sapiel and his father had a temporary camp at Machias Lake, Maine."

Snodgrass 1968

SAPP, ALLEN *Plains Cree*

Sapoestaken, Arrow Going Through

Born 1929 on Red Pheasant Reserve, SK, Canada; M/GM: Maggie Soonias, who raised him; Artist is a direct descendant of Chief Red Pheasant.

RESIDENCE: North Battleford, SK, Canada

OCCUPATION: Wood cutter, hobby shop clerk, and painter

MEDIA: Oil and acrylic

PUBLISHED: MacEwan (1971); Dickason (1972); Warner (1979); Highwater (1980); Cardinal-Schubert (1992); McMasters, et al. (1993). *TAWOW* (Vol. 1, no. 3, 1969); *The Native People* (19 Oct 1973); *The Beaver* (winter 1973); *American Indian Art* (Vol. 2, no. 1, 1974); *The Edmonton Journal* (30 Nov 1974); *The Vancouver Sun* (4 Nov 1977); *Native Perspective* (Vol. 3, no. 2, 1978); *The Indian Trader* (Apr 1979); *Southwest Art* (Vol. 4, no. 7, 1979); *The Calgary Herald* (6 Oct 1979); *The Star Phoenix* (20 Oct 1979); *Native Arts/West* (Nov 1980); *Masterkey* (winter 1984); *Windspeaker* (12 Dec 1986); *C Magazine* (fall 1991)

COMMISSIONS: UNICEF, paintings used for Christmas cards

PUBLIC COLLECTIONS: C/ACC; C/AG/M; C/CMC; C/GCC; C/GM; C/INAC; C/MCC; C/POC; C/RBC; Alberta Gas Trunk Line; Adeco Drilling; Congress Resources; Hudson's Bay Oil and Gas; PetroCan, Calgary, AB; Royal Trust; Jones, Black, and Company

EXHIBITS: Partial listing of more than eighty includes: C/AG/MU; C/AG/TB; C/CIARH; C/CIIA; C/IAC; C/LTAT; C/MJAM; C/ROM; C/TC; C/TFD; C/U of SK; C/U of R/MG; PAC; SM; Teacher's College, Saskatoon, SK, 1968; New Brunswick Museum, St. John, NB, 1970; galleries throughout the U.S., Canada, and England

SOLO EXHIBITS: Hammer Galleries, New York, NY, 1976

HONORS: Canada Council Arts Bursary, 1969; Royal Canadian Academy of Arts, inducted, 1975; MacEwan (1971), chapter dedicated to Sapp; Saskatchewan Award of Merit, 1985; Officer of the Order of Canada, 1987

ALLEN SAPP

Sapp's early life was difficult and plagued by illness which started with a childhood attack of meningitis. In addition, his mother and four brothers and sisters died of tuberculosis. Because of his poor health, he did not attend school and never learned to read and write. He speaks English with great difficulty.

With the patronage of Dr. A. B. Goner and instruction from Professor Winona Mulcaster, Sapp developed his own distinctive style. He paints his people and their way of life on the reserves as it was in the 1930s and 1940s, not an idealized ancient past. He is recognized as one of the founders of the narrative realistic school of Canadian art. Sapp says of his art, "I can't write a story or tell one in the Whiteman's language so I tell what I want to say with my paintings . . . I put it down so it doesn't get lost and people will be able to see and remember."

Warner 1979

SARYERWINNIE, HOUSTON *Comanche*

Born 17 Sept 1929 in Apache, OK

RESIDENCE: Russell, KS

MILITARY: U.S. Navy, Korea

EDUCATION: Riverside; extension course in art, KSU, 1960

OCCUPATION: House painter, interior decorator, and artist

PUBLISHED: Snodgrass (1968)

PUBLIC COLLECTIONS: IACB/DC; Museum of Cottonwood Falls, KS
EXHIBITS: AIE, MNM, LIAS, PAC
AWARDS: AIE

SATANTA *Kiowa*

Satanta, White Bear
A.K.A. Gúaton-bain, Big Ribs (childhood name); Set T'ainte; Chief Satanta
Born ca. 1830; died 11 Oct 1878, committed suicide while in prison at Huntsville, TX; father of Tsalaute
OCCUPATION: Chief, warrior, and artist
PUBLISHED: Snodgrass (1968); Dockstader (1977)
HONORS: Kiowa War chief; signed the Little Arkansas Treaty, 1865

SATSEWA, PAUL *Laguna*

EDUCATION: Albuquerque, 1938
PUBLISHED: Snodgrass (1968)

SAUFKIE, MORGAN *Hopi*

Nevamokewesa, Snow Carry
Born 20 Aug 1926 at Shungopovi, Second Mesa, AZ
EDUCATION: Hopi, ca. 1951-1952
PUBLISHED: Snodgrass (1968)
PUBLIC COLLECTIONS: LMA/BC
EXHIBITS: PAC
AWARDS: PAC

SAUL, C. TERRY *Choctaw/Chickasaw*

Tabaksi, Ember of Fire (or Coal)
A.K.A. Chief Terry Saul; Chief T. Saul
Born 2 Apr 1921 in Sardis, OK; died 24 May 1976; son of Nona Anderson and John B. Saul
RESIDENCE: Lived in Bartlesville, OK
MILITARY: U.S. Army, WWII
EDUCATION: BC High School; BC, 1940; B.F.A., U of OK, 1948; M.F.A., U of OK, 1949; ASL, 1951-1952; studied under Woody Crumbo and Acee Blue Eagle (qq.v.) while at BC
OCCUPATION: Studio owner, illustrator, commercial artist, educator, and artist
MEDIA: Oil on gesso, tempera, and casein
PUBLISHED: Jacobson and d'Ucel (1950); Carlson (1964); Dunn (1968); Snodgrass (1968); Brody (1971); Highwater (1976); Schmid and Houlihan (1979); Mahey, et al. (1980); Broder (1981); Archuleta and Strickland (1991). *Art Digest* (Aug 1947); *Tulsa Magazine* (May 1948); *The American Indian,* AIA. (spring 1952); *The Washington Post* (Mar 1963); *The Sunday Oklahoman, Orbit Magazine* (10 Mar 1963; 2 June 1963); 13th Annual Tulsa Powwow (Aug 1964) program cover; *Philnews* (Sept 1964); *The Arizona Republic* (13 June 1965; 5 Feb 1967); *Indians of Oklahoma,* BIA (1966); *American Illustrated,* USDS (No. 33)
BOOKS PUBLISHED: Gregory and Strickland (1972)
COMMISSIONS: *Murals:* Union National Bank, Bartlesville, OK. *Other:* Maloney (1955), dust jacket
PUBLIC COLLECTIONS: BIA; CNM; DAM; FCTM; GM; HCC; HM; IACB; MNM; NMLHM; OU/MA; OU/SM; PAC; RMC/AZ; College High School, Bartlesville, OK; First National Bank, Dewey, OK; Fort Sill Indian Hospital, Lawton, OK; Masonic Temple, Bartlesville, OK; Union National Bank,

HOUSTON SARYERWINNIE

"The artist began painting about 1953, encouraged by Susie Peters and Tennyson Eckiwauda (q.v.). Since leaving the reservation, about 1958, he has been active in Indian lore as a dance instructor and councilman for the Boy Scouts in Russell, Kansas."

Snodgrass 1968

SATANTA

In addition to being a fearless warrior, Satanta was known as an eloquent and persuasive speaker. He was one of the major Kiowa leaders to sign the Medicine Lodge Treaty of 1867.

Dockstader 1977

After his speech at the signing of the Medicine Lodge Treaty, Satanta became known as the "Orator of the Plains." "In 1868, he and Lone Wolf (q.v.) painted a robe which told of their battles with the Utes and Navajos."

Snodgrass 1968

PAUL SATSEWA

"While a student at the Albuquerque Indian School, the artist was chosen to execute a sketch based on Coronado's first night in the Zuni village. This sketch was used for publicity purposes by the Coronado Quadricentennial Commission of New Mexico."

Snodgrass 1968

Bartlesville, OK; in Denmark, Austria, The Netherlands, Germany, and Afghanistan

EXHIBITS: Partial listing of more than forty includes: AAID; AAIEAE; AIE; BNIAS; DAM; FANAIAE; FCTM; FNAIC; GM; HM; HM/G; ITIC; LGAM; MHDYMM; MNM; MNM/T; MPABAS; NAP; NJSM; PAC; PAC/T; RC; RMC/AZ; SI; SN; SPIM; SV; USDI; U of OK; USDS; VV; WPA; Addison Museum, Andover, MA; Rappahannock Library, Washington, VA; Southwest Artists Biennial, Santa Fe, NM: Syracuse (NY) Museum of Fine Arts; see also Awards

SOLO EXHIBITS: FCTM; HM; NMLHM; PAC; U of OK; Art Center, Bartlesville, OK

AWARDS: AAID ('58, 1st; '65 '70, 1st); AIE ('63, 1st); BNIAS; DAM; FCTM ('67; '68, 1st, IH; '69, 1st, Grand Award, IH; '70, 1st, IH; '71, IH); FNAIC; GM ('58, Purchase Award); ITIC ('57-'64, 5-1st); MNM ('61, Glaman Award; '62, SAR Award; '63, SWAIA Award); PAC ('48-'65, 5-1st, 2-Purchase Awards; '69; '70; '71; '73, 1st; '74, 1st); SN ('63, 1st; '68); UTAE ('64); American Indian Exposition, Charlotte, NC ('65, 1st)

HONORS: Art Student's League, New York, NY, life member; PAC, Waite Phillips Trophy, 1970; FCTM, designated a Master Artist, 1974

C. Saul Terry

"About 1961, Saul began to perfect an oil-on-gesso technique using dentist tools to etch away the oil over painting to form the picture. . . . In May, 1963, Saul said, 'Each painting should be a departure from the one before. You've got to keep improving and growing. An artist cannot afford to become stagnant.'"

Snodgrass 1968

The artist's given name was Chief, it was not a title. Saul was the director of the Art Department at Bacone College, Bacone, OK, from 1970 to 1975. Among his many honors were awards from FCTM, where in 1976 the annual art competition was dedicated to his memory.

Sau Peen (see Aguilar, José Vincente)

Saupitty, Timothy L. *Comanche*

Saupitty, Many People Came

Born 28 May 1961 in San Jose, CA; descendant of Comanche war chiefs White Wolf and Moway; P/GU: Larry Saupitty (q.v.)

RESIDENCE: Lawton, OK

EDUCATION: Fort Sill

EXHIBITS: AIE; CNM; PAC; RE; St. Gregory's Museum Art Show, Shawnee, OK; see also Awards

AWARDS: AIE ('78, Grand Award; '82, 1st, Grand Award; '85, 1st); Anadarko (OK) Fair (1st)

Saupity, Larry *Comanche*

Born 1924 in Oklahoma; death date unknown

MILITARY: U.S. Army, WWII code talker

EDUCATION: U of OK

PUBLISHED: Snodgrass (1968)

Larry Saupity

"The artist had been drawing and painting since childhood. War injuries received at St. Lô, France, forced him to withdraw from the School of Art at the University of Oklahoma, where he had enrolled after WWII."

Snodgrass 1968

Savage-Blue, Karen *Chippewa*

Nee Zho Ga Boe Ekway, Double Standing Woman

Born 29 Jan 1958 in Duluth, MN; daughter of Beverly and Richard Savage; P/GP: Katherine and Lyzime Savage; M/GF: Zacher

RESIDENCE: Cloquet, MN

EDUCATION: Duluth (MN) Central High School, 1976; IAIA, 1980; University of Minnesota, Duluth, MN, 1992

OCCUPATION: Student, sculptor, and painter

MEDIA: Oil, acrylic, watercolor, pencil, and pastel

BOOKS ILLUSTRATED: Educational workbooks

COMMISSIONS: *Murals:* Fond du Lac Indian Reservation, MN, tribal chamber

PUBLIC COLLECTIONS: Mi No Aya Win Human Services Center

EXHIBITS: AC/D; OAE; TM; RC; WGAI; Johnson Heritage Center, Grand Marais, MN

AWARDS: OAE ('88; '89; '90; '91, 1st); TM ('91, 1st, Tommy Award)

SAVES LIFE, GEORGE *Sioux*

PUBLISHED: Snodgrass (1968)

PUBLIC COLLECTIONS: SIM (hide painting depicting 1880-1920)

SA WA PIN (see Aguilar, Alfred)

SAW WHU (see Humetewa, James Russell, Jr.)

SCARANO, PATRICIA *(?)*

RESIDENCE: Port Angeles, WA

EDUCATION: U of WA; studied under Leslie B. DeMille, David Barkley, and John Pogony

OCCUPATION: Wife, mother, art instructor, and painter

MEDIA: Oil

PUBLISHED: *Desert* (Sept 1976)

EXHIBITS: CMRM; GWWAS; NWASA; Pacific Northwest Indian Center Show; Western and Wildlife Bicentennial Art Exhibit; galleries in California

PATRICIA SCARANO

Scarano started painting in 1970. Her grandmother was one-half Indian giving her a heritage which she believes contributes to her sensitivity to Indian subjects.

Desert, *Sept 1976*

SCHILDT, GARY JOSEPH *Blackfeet*

Netostimi, Lone Bull

Born 5 June 1938 in Helena, MT; son of Marie Schildt Williamson and Donald Billadeaux; P/GP: Winifred and Greely Billadeaux; M/GP: Cecelia and Andrew Schildt; Artist was adopted by his maternal grandparents at age ten.

RESIDENCE: Florence, AZ

EDUCATION: Browning (MT) High School, 1958; U of MT; San Francisco (CA) Art College; A.A., San Francisco (CA) City College, 1962; San Francisco (CA) Academy of Fine Arts

OCCUPATION: Free-lance artist, sculptor, and painter

MEDIA: Oil, watercolor, charcoal, pen and ink, pencil, pastel, conté, bronze, and prints

PUBLISHED: Snodgrass (1968); Ray (1972); Broder (1981); Samuels (1982). *Art West* (winter 1977); *Flathead Valley Outdoor Journal* (winter 1981); *Southwest Art* (Feb 1988)

COMMISSIONS: Montana Historical Society Museum, Helena, MT, three paintings, 1988; Sculpture of Senator Lee Matcalfe for Montana State Capitol Building

PUBLIC COLLECTIONS: CMRM, SI, HSM/MT

EXHIBITS: ADIA; CIA; CMRM; GFNAAS; HSM/MT; MNAC; MPI; MR; NWR; SN; National Sculpture Society Exhibition, NY, 1980; Plein Air Painter's Art Show, Santa Catalina, CA, 1969; Annual Governor's Salute to the Arts, Helena, MT, 1977; galleries in California and Montana; see also Awards

SOLO EXHIBITS: CMRM (four); MPI; HSM/MT (two)

AWARDS: ADIA ('67); MNAC ('76, Best of Show); NWR ('81; '83); SN ('69, 1st); Beaux Arts Ball and Art Auction ('68, 3-1st); Blackfoot Art Auction, Lincoln, MT ('81-'83, 1st)

HONORS: San Francisco (CA) Academy of Fine Arts, scholarship; Havre (MT) Art Show, guest artist, 1988; C. N. Russell Museum Auction, Great Falls, MT, selected to sculpt guests of honor, 1986-1988; National Arts for the Parks, one of top 100 artists

GARY JOSEPH SCHILDT

Schildt's earliest paintings were of historic subjects, but he soon became interested in depicting life on the reservation and other contemporary themes. Frequently using the very old and the very young as subjects, Schildt says he prefers them because, "they are free of pretense, they are only themselves." In his art he tries to analyze Plains Indian life and make it understandable to everyone. His paintings and sculptures show the influence of traditional Western style artists, especially Charles Russell.

SCHINAGI (see Yellow Blanket)

SCHOLDER, FRITZ WILLIAM *Luiseño*

Born 6 Oct 1937 in Breckenridge, MN; son of Ella Mae Haney and Fritz William Scholder IV

Fritz William Scholder

Fritz Scholder is considered first and foremost a colorist. When listing the important elements of a painting, he says that color comes first, second is a strong image and third is subject matter. Asked if he is an Indian painter, Scholder replied, "... I don't consider myself an Indian painter. I am often called an 'Indian artist' and I am on the official government rolls, but still I am not simply an Indian painter. Although I am extremely proud of being one quarter Luiseño Indian from Southern California, one cannot be any more or less than what he is."

Highwater 1980

Perhaps Scholder is best described by other Indian artists. Clifford Beck (q.v.) credits him with "destroying barriers to Indian artists' freedom of expression." Earl Biss (q.v.) is quoted as saying, "I wish to emulate Fritz in his dedication to art and in singleminded determination to leave his image of society and his understanding of modern culture to future artists and historians.... I look at Fritz and realize he is a true artist — a great innovator and colorist."

Southwestern Art
winter 1977-1978

RESIDENCE: Scottsdale, AZ

EDUCATION: Ashland High School, 1956; A.A., Sacramento (CA) State College, 1958; B.A., Sacramento (CA) State University, 1960; M.F.A., U of AZ, 1964; U of AZ, "Southwest Indian Art Project," scholarship, summers 1961; 1962

OCCUPATION: Educator and artist

MEDIA: Oil, acrylic, watercolor, and prints

PUBLISHED: Snodgrass (1968); Brody (1971); Breeskin (1972); Monthan, ed. (1972); Tanner (1973); Monthan and Monthan (1975); Silberman (1978); Highwater (1976; 1978b; 1983; 1980); New (1979); Taylor, et al. (1982); Hoffman, et al. (1984); Samuels (1982; 1985); Wade, ed. (1986); Archuleta and Strickland (1991); Campbell, ed. (1993); Ballantine and Ballantine (1993). *New Mexico Magazine* (May/June 1971); *Nimrod* (spring/summer 1972); *American Indian Art* (spring 1976); *The Arizona Republic* (17 Sept 1972; 16 Mar 1992); *The Indian Trader* (July 1978; July 1981); *Americas* (Aug 1981); *Artspace* (summer 1983); *Arizona Alumnus* (spring 1986); *Southwest Profile* (Feb 1987); *The Phoenix Gazette* (1 Apr 1989); *Phoenix Home and Garden* (Mar 1988; Mar 1990); *American West* (July 1990); *Southwest Art* (May, 1980; Nov 1984; Mar 1992); *Native Peoples* (winter 1992); *The Tulsa World* (27 Sept 1992; 25 Sept 1992); *The* (Aug 1994); biographical publications

PUBLIC COLLECTIONS: BAM; BIA; BM/B; CAI; CAM/OH; CAM/S; C/AG/O; CGA; CMA; DAM; EM; EM/NY, FAC/CS; FAM/MA; FIA; FWAC; HM; IACB; IAIA; JAM; MFA/B; MFA/D; MFA/EP; MFA/H; MM/NJ; MRFM; MSW; U of NM/AM; WSU; WWM; Albright-Knox Art Gallery, NY; Bibliothéque National, Paris, France; Brooks Memorial Art Gallery, Memphis, TN; Centre Cultural Américain, Paris, France; Princeton University Art Museum, NJ

EXHIBITS: AAID; AC/K; ASM; BBHC; BEAIAC; BI; BM; BM/B; C/GM;] CGA; CIAI; CPLH; DAM; DG; FAC/CS; FAIEAIP; FAM/MA; FIA; FWAC; GAWHM; HCC; HG; HM; HM/SV; HNSM; IAIA/M; IK; IMA; JAM; MCC/CA; MFA/AH; MFA/EP; MFA/H; MFA/O; MFA/D; MIA; MKMcNAI; MNM; NAP; NACLA; OMA; OWE; PAC; PAIC; PM; SAIEAIP; SAM; SCA; SI,; SN; U of AZ; U of KS; U of ND; U of TX; USDI; W; WIB;] WSU; WWM; Edinburgh Art Festival, Scotland; Berlin Festival, West Germany; Museo de Bellas Artes, Buenos Aires, Argentina; Biblioteca National, Santiago, Chile; American Embassy, Bucharest, Rumania; Amerika Haus, Berlin, West Germany; Museum of Modern Art, Skopje, Yugoslavia; American Embassy, London, England; Museo la Tertulia, Calí, Colombia; Linden Museum, Stuttgart, West Germany; Museum of Contemporary Crafts, NY; Institute of Contemporary Art, Boston, MA; National Museum of Modern Art, Tokyo, Japan; National Museum of Modern Art, Kyoto, Japan; Ausstellungszentrum am Fernsehtrum, Germany; Museum of Chinese History, Beijing, China; Shanghai Museum of Fine Art; Grand Palais, Paris, France; The Hermitage, Leningrad, Russia; Himeji City Museum of Art, Japan; see also Awards

SOLO EXHIBITS: Partial listing of more than 42 includes: AC/RM; AC/Y; ASM; ASU/M; CAM/S; CSF/SF; HM; SM; TMA/AZ; U of NM/AM; WWM

AWARDS: AAID ('68); BEAIAC ('67, Grand Award); MFA/H; MNM; SN ('68, Kinkner Award; Grand Prize); 10th Southwest Painter's Annual (Festival Award); Tucson (AZ) Art Center; California Spring Festival, Sacramento, CA ('61, 1st); Ford Foundation Purchase Award (1962); West Virginia Centennial ('63, 1st); Intergrafiks, Berlin, Germany ('80, International Prize in Lithography)

HONORS: *Guest artist:* Oklahoma Summer Arts Institute; University of Southern California at Idyllwild; Vermont Studio School; Santa Fe (NM) Art Institute; The Dakota Centennial Arts Congress, Aberdeen, SD; Black Hills State College, Spearfish, SD; American University, Washington, D.C., guest artist. *Honorary degrees:* Ripon (WI) College; University of Arizona, Tucson, AZ; Concordia College, Moorhead, MN; The College of Santa Fe, NM. *Other:* John Hay Whitney Opportunity Fellowship, 1962-1963. Dartmouth College, artist-in-residence, 1973; State of North Dakota, Governor's Award in the Arts; State of New Mexico, Governor's Award in the Visual Arts; Arizona State University, Tempe, AZ, Distinguished Achievement Award; American Academy of Achievement, Golden Plate Award; American Academy of Arts and Letters, appointment; Sociétaire, Salon d'Automne, Paris, France, appointment; Phoenix (AZ) Indian Center, Annual Benefit Dinner, Guest of Honor, 1992

SCHOPPERT, JAMES ROBERT *Tlingit*

A.K.A. Jim Schoppert; R. James Schoppert

Born 1947 in Juneau, Alaska; died 2 Sept 1992 in Ojai, CA

RESIDENCE: Lived in Ojai, CA

EDUCATION: Juneau-Douglas (AK) High School; Anchorage (AK) Community College, 1975; B.F.A., U of AK, 1978; M.F.A., U of WA, 1981; Instituto de San Miguel Allende, Guanajuato, Mexico

OCCUPATION: Carpenter, artist-in-residence, teacher, consultant, lecturer, poet, sculptor, and painter

MEDIA: Acrylic, stone, wood, ivory, metal, and mixed-media

PUBLISHED: Banks (1986); Longfish, et al. (1986); Wade, ed. (1986)

COMMISSIONS: Sheraton Anchorage (AK) Hotel; Kenai (AK) Community College; Skagit Valley College, Mt. Vernon, WA; Alaska Mutual Bank, Bellevue, AK; Anchorage (AK) Museum of History and Arts; Sullivan Sports Arena, Anchorage, AK, sculpture

PUBLIC COLLECTIONS: BNR; CIRI; HM; MFA/AH; NM; U of AK; WSAC; Calista Corporation, Anchorage, AK; City of Seattle, WA; Commonwealth Corporation, Anchorage, AK; The First National Bank of Alaska, Juneau, AK; Rainier Bank Collection, WA; Washington State Arts Commission

EXHIBITS: Partial listing of more than thirty includes: AC/Y; AICA/SF; ASM/AK; CNGM;] HM; IANA; MMA/WA; NDN; PAC; SCG; SFFA; TPAS; U of AK/M; WIB; WNAA; North Central Washington Museum, Wenatchee, WA; Bellevue (WA) Art Museum; Willamette University, Salem, OR; see also Awards

SOLO EXHIBITS: ASM/AH; galleries in Alaska and Washington

AWARDS: IANA; Anchorage (AK) Community College; Skagit Valley College, Mt. Vernon, WA

HONORS: NACLA, Outstanding Native American Poet, 1985; Institute Of Alaska Native Arts, Board of Trustees

JAMES ROBERT SCHOPPERT

Schoppert explained his unique approach to art in this way, "The exquisite work of our ancestors teaches us to create work suited for the day in which we live. By taking the old, breathing new life into it, and developing a new creation, the spirit of our people lives."

gallery brochure

Schoppert's art is based on traditional Tlingit forms but incorporates his own ideas and shows the influence of other Alaskan or Native American cultures.

SCHULTZ, HART MERRIAM *Blackfeet*

Nitoh Mahkwi, Lone Wolf

Born 18 Feb 1882 at Birch Creek, MT, on the Blackfeet Reservation; died 9 Feb 1970 in Tucson, AZ; son of Natahki or Mutsiawotan Ahki (Fine Shield Woman) and James Willard Schultz, author

RESIDENCE: Lived in Tucson, AZ

EDUCATION: Portland (OR) Public Schools; Los Angeles (CA) Art Students League, 1910; CAI, 1914-1915; studied under Thomas Moran

OCCUPATION: Cowboy, horse trainer, commercial artist, sculptor, and painter

MEDIA: Oil, watercolor, and bronze

PUBLISHED: Snodgrass (1968); Ray (1972); Dockstader (1977); Samuels (1985). *The Indian Trader* (Jan 1985); *Southwest Art* (Dec 1990)

COMMISSIONS: *Murals:* Church of Jesus Christ of Latter Day Saints, Eager, AZ

HART MERRIAM SCHULTZ

"Until he left the reservation in 1904, the artist, a range rider, often amused his fellow cowboys with his sketches. Although he had painted since 1893, Schultz recalled especially the encouragement of the noted art critic and editor of The Los Angeles Times, *Harry Carr, and that of Thomas Moran. He often sketched 'for his father's books' and continued to sign his paintings and sculpture with a line drawing of a wolf's face. His work has been compared with that of Remington and Russell."*

Snodgrass 1968

Schultz's father, James Willard Schultz, was the author of many books with Indian subjects. In *(continued)*

HART MERRIAM SCHULTZ

(continued) 1918, he dedicated his book, Bird Woman, to his son Lone Wolf. In the dedication he says of his son, "Born near the close of the buffalo days he was, and ever since with his baby hands he began to model statuettes of horses and buffalo and deer with clay from the riverbanks, his one object has been the world of art."

Samuels 1985

PUBLIC COLLECTIONS: AF, BA/AZ, GM, MNA, MPI, SFRR, SM, U of NE
EXHIBITS: ASM; CIA; MPI; galleries in New York, NY; first major show was in Los Angeles, CA, 1916
SOLO EXHIBITS: MPI

SCOTT, CHESTER *Creek*

RESIDENCE: Eufala, OK
EXHIBITS: FCTM
AWARDS: FCTM ('69, IH; '72, IH; '77, Needlepoint Guild Award; '79, IH; '80, 1st; '81, 1st, IH; '83)

SCOTT, DUARD *(?)*

PUBLISHED: Snodgrass (1968)
PUBLIC COLLECTIONS: SM
EXHIBITS: PAC

SCOTT, JOE, JR. *Cherokee*

EXHIBITS: CNM

SCOTT, JOHNSON LEE (see Jonny Hawk)

SCOTT, KENNETH *Creek*

EXHIBITS: CNM

SCOTT, MARCUS B. *Creek*

A.K.A. Marc Scott
RESIDENCE: Oklahoma City, OK
MEDIA: Oil
EXHIBITS: CNM; FCTM; Dupont Plaza Hotel, Washington, D.C.
AWARDS: FCTM ('85, 1st; '87, 1st)

SCOTT, RITA F. *Choctaw*

Born 16 July 1954 in Marietta, OK; daughter of Lavene Brokeshoulder and Frank J. Johnson
RESIDENCE: Ada, OK
EDUCATION: Marietta (OK) High School, 1970; B.A., ECSC/OK, 1975; M.Ed., ECSC/OK, 1978; U of OK
OCCUPATION: Planner/developer for Chickasaw Nation, art teacher, art consultant, workshop speaker, and painter
MEDIA: Acrylic
PUBLISHED: *The Ada Evening News* (24 Sept 1987; 30 June 1989)
BOOKS PUBLISHED: Van Horn (1989)
COMMISSIONS: *Illustrations:* Lucille Herrera, four workbooks to be used in private schools, 1987. *Logos:* Leachco, Inc., Ada, OK; Bob's Bar-B-Que, Ada, OK; Ada (OK) Veterinarian Clinic
EXHIBITS: CNM; ECSC/OK; FCTM; KCPA; U of OK; Battered Women Association Art Show, Ada, OK; Chickasaw Nation Benefit Art Auction, 1992; see also Awards
AWARDS: CNM ('94); FCTM ('82; '83; '85; '90; '91); Artist of the Arbuckles Art Show, Sulphur, OK (1st); Madill (OK) Spring Art Show; Seminole (OK) Spring Art Show (1st); Waurika (OK) Art Show (1st)
HONORS: Quartz Mountain Institute, Altus, OK, scholarship

SEABOURN, BERT *Cherokee*

A.K.A. Bert D. Seabourn

Born 9 July 1931 in Red Barn, TX; son of F. Leeper Thompson and James A. Seabourn

RESIDENCE: Oklahoma City, OK

MILITARY: U.S. Navy, Korea

EDUCATION: Purcell (OK) High School, 1950; OCU, 1962; U of OK, 1976; Famous Artists Correspondence Art School

OCCUPATION: Commercial artist and draftsman, free-lance artist, publicity and advertising director, journalist, sculptor; full-time painter after 1978

MEDIA: Oil, acrylic, watercolor, pen and ink, and prints

PUBLISHED: Snodgrass (1968); Brody (1971); Highwater (1976); Silberman (1978); Frontain (1979); New (1979); Medina (1981); Samuels (1982). *The Arizona Republic* (22 Nov 1974); *The Indian Trader* (Nov 1975; June 1980; Mar 1990); *Oklahoma Art Gallery* (spring 1980); *Southwest Art* (June 1981); *Art Voices* (Sept/Oct 1980, cover; Sept/Oct 1981); *Santa Fe Profile* (Aug 1982); *The Santa Fean* (Aug 1984); *The Anadarko Daily News* (22 Aug 1990); *Twin Territories* (Year of the Indian Edition 1991); *Muskogee Daily Phoenix* (4 Oct 1993); biographical publications

BOOKS PUBLISHED: Conley (1991), cover; Owens (1992), cover

PUBLIC COLLECTIONS: Partial listing includes: BA/AZ; BIA; CAI/KC; FCTM; HCC; HM; IACB; ITIC; OAC; OSAC; PNIC; Fidelity Bank, Oklahoma City, OK; IBM, Tucson, AZ; Kerr-McGee Corporation, Oklahoma City, OK; Lianhe Bao Limited, Singapore; Liberty National Bank and Trust Company, Oklahoma City, OK; McClain County Historical Society, Purcell, OK; National Palace Museum, Taipei, Taiwan; Oklahoma Gas and Electric, Oklahoma City, OK; Southwestern Bell Telephone, Oklahoma City, OK; The Vatican Museum of Modern Religious Art, Vatican City, Italy

EXHIBITS: AAID; AC/HC; AC/K; CNM; FAIE; FCTM; FCTM/M; HCC; HM; IACA; IEEPF; ITIC; MFA/O; MNH/AN; MNH/D; NACLA; OAC; OAGA; OMA; OSC; PAC; PAIC; PM; RC; RE; SI; SN; SPIM; SWAIA; WWM; Oklahoma Biennial Art Show, Oklahoma City, OK, 1969; Overseas Export Fair, Berlin, Germany, 1975; see also Awards

SOLO/SPECIAL EXHIBITS: Partial listing of more than forty includes: FCTM; HM; SPIM (dual show)

AWARDS: Partial listing of more than one hundred includes: AAID ('68); CNM ('84, 1st; '85, 1st; '86, 1st); ITIC ('70, 1st; '79; '89, 1st; '93); FCTM ('68; '70; '71; '72; '73, 1st, Grand Award); FCTM/M ('79; '80; '82; '83; '84, 1st; '85; '86, 1st; '87, 1st; '88, Best of Show; '91, 1st; '93, 1st; '94, Spirit of Oklahoma Award); HM/G ('74, 2-1st, Swazo Award); OAC ('64, Purchase Award); OAGA ('66, Best of Show; '69, 1st, Purchase Award); PAC ('72, '75, 1st; '79); RC ('74, Best of Show; '75); RE; SN ('68, '70; '74, 1st; '75, 1st); SWAIA ('72, 1st; '75, 1st; '76); Best of the West, Plano, TX ('90, Best Graphic); Oklahoma Watercolor Association ('75, 1st); Penn Square Art Show and Festival of the Arts, Oklahoma City, OK, ('60)

HONORS: FCTM, designated a Master Artist, 1976; Sixth Annual Oklahoma Governor's Art Award, 1982; RE, poster artist, 1987; ITIC, poster artist, 1989; named a "Living Legend" by Ralph Oliver, 1990

BERT SEABOURN

From as early as the 1st grade, Seabourn wanted to be an artist. He sold his first cartoon to King Features Syndicate when he was in the 8th grade. When he was in high school, he and a friend would "hop a freight" or hitchhike to Oklahoma City from Purcell to visit the Oklahoma Museum of Art. Seabourn joined the Navy during the Korean War, and although he lacked an art background, they put him to work as an illustrator. This was the beginning of his career as an artist. As he worked as a commercial artist/draftsman he began to explore his Indian heritage and incorporate it in his art.

Seabourn is best known for his paintings of an old, wise Indian man's face combined with birds or animals. He says that the face does not represent one tribe but is, instead, a composite face representing the medicine men, the keepers of the culture of all Indian tribes. The artist has said that he is trying to show feelings and compassion through his paintings for a way of life which once was, but will never be again.

p.c. 1991

SEABOURN, CONNIE *Cherokee*

A.K.A. Connie Seabourn Regan

Born 20 Sept 1951 in Purcell, OK; daughter of Bonnie Jo Tompkins and Bert Seabourn (q.v.)

RESIDENCE: Oklahoma City, OK

EDUCATION: Western Heights High School, Oklahoma City, OK, 1969; OCU; CSU/OK; B.F.A., U of OK, 1980

CONNIE SEABOURN

Connie Seabourn is the daughter of Bert Seabourn, which she considers both an advantage and a disadvantage. She learned a lot from her father, but has had to struggle for her own recognition. The artist is best known for her delicate watercolors and bold, bright serigraphs. They demonstrate her interest in strong, rounded, monumental shapes and her favorite themes; family unity, a mother's love, and living in peace with the earth.

p.c. 1990

OCCUPATION: Commercial artist; full-time artist after 1980

MEDIA: Acrylic, watercolor, pastel, and prints

PUBLISHED: Ragan (1986); Jones (1988); Campbell, ed. (1993). *Art Gallery* (winter 1980); *The Sunday Oklahoman* (26 July 1981); *Oklahoma 81 Magazine* (Nov 1981); *The Indian Trader* (Oct 1982); *Carefree Enterprize* (Aug 1983); *Artspeak* (1 Oct 1983); *The Daily Oklahoman* (5 Aug 1983); *Art-Talk* (Nov 1983); *Oklahoma Art Gallery* (winter 1990), cover; biographical publications

COMMISSIONS: Leanin' Tree Publishing Co., Boulder, CO, paintings for note cards and Christmas cards; Oklahoma Mental Health Association, painting for note cards, 1980

PUBLIC COLLECTIONS: Partial listing of more than twenty includes: CHMG; GM; HCC; HM; MIA; OSAC; SPIM; His Excellency Nubuo Matsunaga, Japan; Iowa State University Memorial Union, Ames, IA; Maybee-Gerrer Museum, Shawnee, OK; McClain County Historical Museum, Purcell, OK; Oklahoma Memorial Hospital, Oklahoma City, OK; Presbyterian Hospital, Oklahoma City, OK; Southwestern Bell Telephone Company; University Heights YWCA, Oklahoma City, OK; Verde Valley School, Sedona, AZ; Xerox International Headquarters

EXHIBITS: CNM; CNAIA; FA; FCTM; HCC; HM; HM/G; HPTU; IACA; IEEPF; ITIC; KCPA; MIA, MNH/AN; OAC; OCSA; OMA; OSC; SDCC; SDMM; SI; SPIM; RE; RSC; SI; Fred Jones Memorial Museum, Norman, OK; Grover Cleveland Art Institute, Oklahoma City, OK; Kenesaw College Art Gallery, Marietta, GA; galleries throughout the U.S.

SOLO/SPECIAL EXHIBITS: SPIM (dual show); Grover Cleveland Art Institute, Oklahoma City, OK; YWCA, Oklahoma City, OK

AWARDS: FCTM ('92); CNM ('85, 1st; '93); HM/G ('90, 1st); ITIC ('84; '90); RE ('87, 1st, Grand Award); RSC ('82, 1st; '83, 1st)

SEAMUC (see Holm, Adrian L.)

SEARCHING (see Weckeah)

SEAT, RON *Cherokee*

EXHIBITS: CNM

SEBASTIAN, ROBERT *Carrier/Tsimshian*

RESIDENCE: Prince George, BC, Canada

EDUCATION: GSNCIA; apprenticed to his brother, Ron Sebastian (q.v.)

OCCUPATION: Traditional dancer, carver, jeweler, and graphic artist

PUBLISHED: Stewart (1979)

COMMISSIONS: Kansas City, MO, totem pole

PUBLIC COLLECTIONS: HCC

EXHIBITS: AC/NC, AUG, BHSU, CPS, HCC, HPTU, NSU/SD, SDSMT, U of SD, U of WV, WTF

SEBASTIAN, RON *Carrier/Tsimshian*

Born 1945 in Prince Rupert, BC,Canada, on the fishpacker that took his mother to the hospital; brother of Robert Sebastian (q.v.)

EDUCATION: GSNCIA, 1971-1973

OCCUPATION: Carver, jeweler, and graphic artist

PUBLISHED: Steltzer (1977); Stewart (1979). *Indian News* (Vol. 19, no. 4, 1978)

COMMISSIONS: *Murals:* Indian and Northern Affairs of Canada, Hull, PQ

PUBLIC COLLECTIONS: C/INAC, C/RBCM

EXHIBITS: C/CMC, C/VCM

SECATERO, JOHN *Navajo*

A.K.A. Johnny Secatero

Born in the late 1940's

MEDIA: Watercolor

PUBLISHED: Tanner (1973)

PUBLIC COLLECTIONS: EM, MNA, WWM

EXHIBITS: ASM; HM; ITIC; PAC; PM; SN; The Art Center, Hastings (NE) College, 1973

AWARDS: ITIC ('66; '69; '71, 1st; '72, 2-1st, Woodard Award; '79, 1st; '85; '86, 1st; '87; '88, 1st, Best in Category; '91; '92, 1st; '94); SN ('67)

SECATERO, MCCOY *Navajo*

EDUCATION: Albuquerque, 1958

PUBLISHED: Snodgrass (1968)

EXHIBITS: MNM

SECODY, MODESTA *Navajo*

PUBLIC COLLECTIONS: MNA

SECODY, RUSSELL *Hopi*

PUBLIC COLLECTIONS: MNA

SECONDINE, DONALD HENRY, JR. *Delaware/Cherokee*

Ay-Hah-Pee-Kwes, He Plays The Flute Repeatedly

Born 27 Jan 1952 in Nowata, OK; son of Sarah J. Smith and Donald H. Secondine; P/GP: May and Henry Anderson Secondine; M/GP: Virginia E. and Jim Smith

RESIDENCE: Wichita, KS

EDUCATION: Sequoyah High School, Tahlequah, OK; A.A., Haskell, 1973; B.F.A., U of KS, 1976; studied under Loren Pahsetopah, Riley White, and Dick West (qq.v.)

OCCUPATION: Art instructor, consultant, museum curator, lecturer, researcher, silversmith, flutemaker; full-time artist since 1992

MEDIA: Oil, watercolor, pencil, pen and ink, pastel, silver, wood, and prints

PUBLISHED: Ellison (1972). *The Kansas City Star, Sunday Magazine* (1972), article and cover; *Kansas Magazine* (spring 1981); *The Phoenix Gazette* (11 Apr 1987)

COMMISSIONS: *Murals:* Haskell Indian Junior College, Lawrence, KS; Ottawa (KS) University, 1971. *Other:* SPIM, painting

PUBLIC COLLECTIONS: HCC

EXHIBITS: ACS/FR, CIAE, CNM, CSPIP, FCTM, HCC, ITIC, HSM/KS, LIAS, PAC, RC, SPIM, TM/NE

AWARDS: ACS/FR ('81, 1st); CIAE ('73, Purchase Award); ITIC ('70); PAC ('71); RC ('91, White Buffalo Award); U of OR (Purchase Award)

HONORS: University of Kansas, Lawrence, KS, scholarship; Haskell Indian Junior College, Helen Hoover Award, 1975; Oklahoma's Folklife Festival, featured artist, 1991; Natchitoches Folklife Festival, featured artist, 1991

DONALD HENRY SECONDINE JR.

The artist's goal is to preserve Native history and culture. He wants people to experience life in the old days through his art work. Secondine says he is attempting to express a love of nature and to project a sense of responsibility to Mother Earth. He tries to show American history from the Indian point of view and he hopes that people who are not Indian will understand "we are people who hurt, laugh, love, and have an undying reverence for this land and for life."

p.c. 1992

SE-DAH-NI (see Crews, Faren Sanders)

SEECODY, MARK *Navajo*

PUBLIC COLLECTIONS: MNA

SEEGANNA, PETER *Eskimo*

Born 1938 at King Island, AK

RESIDENCE: King Island, AK

OCCUPATION: Demonstration aide, arts and crafts assistant, sculptor, ivory carver, and graphic artist

MEDIA: Wood, stone, ivory, and prints

PUBLISHED: Ray (1969). *The Alaskan Journal* (fall 1972)

EXHIBITS: BEAIAC; U of AK/M (1982)

AWARDS: BEAIAC ('67, 1st)

SEE KOOKS ED NAH (see Kuka, King)

SEEKYESVA *Hopi*

Birth date unknown; The artist was living and painting in 1930.

PUBLISHED: Snodgrass (1968)

PUBLIC COLLECTIONS: MAI

SEE RU (see Herrera, Joe Hilario)

SEKAHO (see Shelton, Peter H., Jr.)

SEMPLE, JANE (see Umsted, Jane Semple)

SENUNGETUK, JOSEPH ENGASONGWOK *Eskimo*

A.K.A. Inusuyauq Sinuyituq

Born 29 Mar 1940 in Wales, AK; son of Helen and Willie Senungetuk; brother of Ronald Senungetuk (q.v.); P/GP: Sanigug and Pavikialug; M/GP: Atgag and Anayugug

RESIDENCE: Anchorage, AK

MILITARY: U.S. Army, Korea, 1963-1965

EDUCATION: Nome (AK) High School, 1959; U of AK, 1959-1961; B.F.A., SFAI, 1970

OCCUPATION: Hardware store manager, artist-in-residence, educational program director and instructor, cultural coordinator, curator, writer, editor, lecturer, teacher, sculptor and painter

MEDIA: Acrylic, watercolor, pencil, pen and ink, stone, wood, and prints

PUBLISHED: Steinbright (1968); Ray (1969), cover; *Senungetuk* (1972). *Journal of Ethnic Studies* (book reviews); *Alaskan Journal* (fall 1972); *Journal of the American Medical Association* (29 Apr 1974), cover; *American Indian Art* (winter 1978), cover; *Alaska Geographic* (Vol. 12, no. 3, 1985)

COMMISSIONS: *Illustrations: Anchorage Daily News*; Alaska State Commission for Human Rights; Alaska Anthropological Association, illustrations and poster design. *Murals:* U of AK; Chugiak (AK) High School; Anvil Mountain Correctional Center, Nome, AK; Anchorage (AK) International Airport

PUBLIC COLLECTIONS: ASM/AK; CIRI; MFA/AH; MNH/F; U of AK/A; U of AK/F; CIRI, Inc.; Hunter Elementary School, Fairbanks, AK; Governor's Mansion, Juneau, AK; Seatac Airport, Seattle, WA; Seattle (WA) City Lights Collection; Whatcom Museum, Bellingham, AK

EXHIBITS: ACE; AICA/SF; ASM/AK; BEAIAC; FIE; HS/AI; IACB; IANA; MFA/AH; MMA/NY; NM; SI; galleries in Anchorage, AK, and Seattle, WA; see also Awards

SOLO EXHIBITS: HS/AI; Visual Arts Center of Alaska, Anchorage, AK

AWARDS: FIE ('68); IACB ('60, 1st); MNH/F (Excellence award, poster design); IANA ('80, Juror's Award); MFA/AH ('77, 1st); Alaska Centennial Arts Exhibit ('67)

SENUNGETUK, RONALD *Eskimo*

Born 1933 in Wales, AK; brother of Joseph Senungetuk (q.v.)

RESIDENCE: College, AK

EDUCATION: B.F.A., Rochester S.T., 1953-1954, 1957-1960; Statens Handverks og-Kunstindustriskole, Oslo, Norway, 1960-1961

OCCUPATION: Educator and artist

PUBLISHED: Ray (1969)

HONORS: Fulbright Scholarship, 1960-1961

SEOWTEWA, ALEX *Zuni*

Born 29 Apr 1933; son of Charlie Chuyate (q.v.), Zuni historian and painter; father of Gerald and Kenneth Seowtewa (qq.v.); M/GF: Na-Seowdewa, Zuni high priest of the north and head of the Zuni theocratic government

RESIDENCE: Zuni Pueblo, NM

MILITARY: Korea

EDUCATION: St. Anthony's, 1952; 1 year, St. Joseph's

OCCUPATION: Bus driver, lecturer, cultural practitioner, and artist

MEDIA: Oil, acrylic, watercolor, pencil, pen and ink, and pastel

PUBLISHED: *Yah Weh* (May 1976); *New Mexico Magazine* (June 1977); *Sunset Magazine* (Mar 1983); *National Geographic* (Nov 1987); *Zuni History* (Sec. II, p. 28, 1991); Zuni Mission Mural Project (1991), brochure; *Native Peoples* (winter 1992)

COMMISSIONS: *Murals:* Our Lady of Guadalupe Mission, Zuni, NM, a series of 30 Zuni Kokko (*katsinas*) supported by a grant from the NEA and the New Mexico State Legislature

HONORS: University of St. Joseph, scholarship; New Mexico Cultural Affairs, New Mexico Preservation Heritage Award; NEA, two-year grant, 1989-1991; New Mexico Governor's Award for Excellence in the Arts, 1991; Soviet Union's Fine Artists Union Award, 1991

ALEX SEOWTEWA

In the late 1960s, Seowtewa conceived the idea of painting murals on the walls of the Our Lady of Guadalupe Mission and approached Fr. Niles Kraft, O.F.M., the pastor of St. Anthony's, with the idea. Seowtewa was inspired by his father who had painted a series of small murals on the walls of the church and rectory of St. Anthony's in the 1930s. In 1970, the lifelong project was approved. By 1983, he and his two sons, Gerald and Kenneth (qq.v.), had completed 24 figures of various katsinas *and other religious leaders. The project has been done with the approval and guidance of Zuni religious elders. Seowtewa and his wife Odelle Panteah raised ten children.*

SEOWTEWA, GERALD *Zuni*

Birth date unknown; son of Odelle Panteah and Alex Seowtewa (q.v.); P/GF: Charlie Chuyate (q.v.)

COMMISSIONS: *Murals:* Our Lady of Guadalupe Mission, Zuni, NM (assisted his father)

SEOWTEWA, KENNETH *Zuni*

Birth date unknown; son of Odelle Panteah and Alex Seowtewa (q.v.); P/GF: Charlie Chuyate (q.v.)

OCCUPATION: Teacher and artist

COMMISSIONS: *Murals:* Our Lady of Guadalupe Mission, Zuni, N (assisted his father)

SEQUAPTEWA, EDWIN *Hopi*

PUBLIC COLLECTIONS: MNA

SERVILICAN, RICHARD *Washoe*

Born 9 Oct 1932 in Carson City, NV

RESIDENCE: Minden, NV

MILITARY: U.S. Navy

EDUCATION: Ganado (AZ) Mission High School, 1950; B.A., St. Joseph's, 1960

OCCUPATION: Teacher and painter

MEDIA: Pen and ink

PUBLISHED: Snodgrass (1968). *Native Vision* (Sept/Oct 1986)

EXHIBITS: CSF; MNM; NMSF; St. Joseph's; National Indian Education Conference, Reno, NV, 1986

AWARDS: MNM, 1965; ribbons from state fair competitions

LEROY L. SETH

Seth's works depict contemporary reservation life, ranging from traditional dancers to personal interpretations of the problems that Native Americans today must deal with. He says he strives for a "feeling of movement, both subtle and strong." The artist considers his work to be modern realism, not abstract or geometric but a combination of the two.

Minthorn 1991

SETH, LEROY L. *Nez Percé*

Mourning Dove

Born 23 Dec 1936 in Lewiston, ID; son of Sally Seth and Roy White; P/GP: Deliah and Charles White; M/GP: Elsie and Martin Seth.

RESIDENCE: Lapwai, ID

MILITARY: U.S. Army

EDUCATION: Lapwai (ID) High School, 1956; Lewis and Clark State College, Lewiston, ID; B.A., Eastern Washington State University, Cheney, WA, 1961; M.A., U of MT, 1972

OCCUPATION: Art teacher, community health educator, photographer, and artist

MEDIA: Oil, acrylic, watercolor, tempera, gouache, pencil, pen and ink, pastel, charcoal, and film

PUBLISHED: Ray (1972); Minthorn (1991)

COMMISSIONS: Nez Percé Tribe, illustrations for tribal publications

PUBLIC COLLECTIONS: MPI

EXHIBITS: CIA, MPI, SAP; New York, NY

HONORS: Nez Percé Tribal Council, 1968

SET-KOY-KE (see McDaniels, Cruz, II)

SETON, THOMAS *Eskimo*

Kahsahyuli

RESIDENCE: Hooper Bay, AK

PUBLISHED: Snodgrass (1968)

EXHIBITS: MNM

AWARDS: MNM

SET T'AINTE (see Satanta)

SETT'AN

"Sett'an's calendar was inspired by, but not copied from, the Tohausen (q.v.) Calendar."

Snodgrass 1968

SETT'AN *Kiowa*

Sett'an, Little Bear

Born summer 1833

PUBLISHED: Mayhall (1962); Snodgrass (1968). *17th Annual Report*, BAI (a calendar recording tribal history, 1833-1892)

JACKIE SEVIER

Sevier's works are based on realism and high-lighted with abstract flourishes. Her subjects are her life, her heritage, her family, her exposure to the rodeo world (her husband is a PRCA saddle bronc rider), and her love of nature.

p.c. 1990

SEVIER, JACKIE *Northern Arapaho*

A.K.A. Jackie K. Sevier

Born 30 July 1953 in Riverton, WY; daughter of Esther Chamberlin and Bruce Allen; P/GP: Loretta and Ethan Allan; M/GP: Esther and Jesse Chamberlin

RESIDENCE: Seneca, NE

EDUCATION: Natrona County High School, Casper, WY, 1971; Casper (WY) College

OCCUPATION: Artist

MEDIA: Pastel, embossed paper, mixed-media, and prints

COMMISSIONS: National Campaign of the National Museum of the American Indian, Washington, D.C., note cards

EXHIBITS: ACAI; BBHC; CIM; DAM; GFNAAS; ITIC; LAIS; LC; LSS; NPTA; RC; RE; SIM; SM/NE; SWAIA; TCIM; TIAF; TWF; Crazy Horse Monument, Custer, SD; World Exposition, Shizuoka, Japan; Wyoming Native American Showcase, Casper, WY

AWARDS: ACAI ('92; '93); CIM; ITIC ('94, 1st); LIAS ('92, MA); NPTA ('91; '93, 1st); RC('85, Aplan Award; '89; '91, 1st, Diederich Award; '92, 1st; '94, Erickson Award); RE ('90); SWAIA ('93, 1st); TCIM ('91; '92); TIAF ('94, 1st; '95)

SHAPA NAZHI (see Pahsetopah, Loren Louis)

SHARP SHOOTING (see Mofsie, Louis Billingsly)

SHAVE HEAD *Cheyenne or Arapaho*

Chenenaete, Shave Head; *Ouksteu*

A.K.A. John Wicks

PUBLISHED: Snodgrass (1968)

PUBLIC COLLECTIONS: YU/BRBML

EXHIBITS: BPG

SHAVE HEAD

"An Arapaho named Shave Head signed the Fort Wise Treaty in 1861. The artist was among the 72 Plains Indians taken as prisoners from Fort Sill, OK, to Fort Marion, St. Augustine, FL, in 1875."

Snodgrass 1968

After leaving Fort Marian, Shave Head studied to be an Episcopal missionary and returned to Indian Territory in 1880.

SHEBOLA, DIXON *Zuni*

RESIDENCE: Lived at Zuni Pueblo, NM

EDUCATION: Santa Fe, 1955; Albuquerque, 1956

PUBLISHED: Snodgrass (1968)

COMMISSIONS: *Murals:* Barelos Community Center [with Charles Vicenti and James Michael Byrnes (qq.v.)]

PUBLIC COLLECTIONS: HM, MNM, PAC, SMNAI

EXHIBITS: ITIC, NMSF

AWARDS: ITIC (1964)

SHEBOLA, PHILBERT *Zuni*

PUBLISHED: Snodgrass (1968)

EXHIBITS: AIAE/WSU

SHEBOLA, SULLIVAN *Zuni*

PUBLISHED: Snodgrass (1968); Brody (1971); Tanner (1973)

PUBLIC COLLECTIONS: MAI, MNA

EXHIBITS: PAC, SN

AWARDS: SN ('64, '67)

SHELL (see Montoya, Gerónima Cruz)

SHELLING CORN (see Humetewa, James Russell, Jr.)

SHELTON, HENRY *Hopi*

A.K.A. H. Shelton

Born 1929 at Oraibi, AZ; son of Lillie Seumptewa and Peter Shelton Sr.; brother of Peter Shelton Jr. (q.v.)

RESIDENCE: Flagstaff, AZ

OCCUPATION: *Katsina* carver and painter; best known for his carving

MEDIA: Cottonwood root and tempera

PUBLISHED: Snodgrass (1968); Tanner (1976, 1987); Wright (1977); Bromberg (1986); Seymour (1988). *American Indian Art* (spring 1984); *Arizona Living* (Apr 19, 1974); *The Indian Trader* (Sept 1982); *The Navajo-Hopi Observer* (10 June 1992)

PUBLIC COLLECTIONS: MAI, MNA, SI

EXHIBITS: ASM; HM/G; ITIC; PAC; SNAICF; SWAIA; Native American Arts Festival, Litchfield Park, AZ; annual Indian art shows in AZ, CA, CO, FL, KS, MO, NM, OH, OR, and TX

AWARDS: Partial listing of more than 14 Grand Awards includes: HM/G (Grand Award); ITIC (Grand Award); SWAIA (Grand Award)

HONORS: Named an Arizona Living Treasure, 1992

HENRY SHELTON

"As an artist I feel that I have contributed to the Hopi people and have kept the Hopi culture, religion, and language from dying out."

artist, p.c. 1992

PETER SHELTON JR.

According to his son, Peter H. Shelton III (q.v.), in 1992 the artist was doing very little, if any, painting.

SHELTON, PETER, JR. *Hopi*

Sekaho, Yellow Arrow

A.K.A. Peter Henry Shelton Jr.

Born ca. 1920s in Kykotsmovi, AZ; son of Lillie Seumptewa and Peter Shelton Sr.; brother of Henry Shelton (q.v.)

RESIDENCE: Kykotsmovi, AZ

EDUCATION: Hopi High School; Santa Fe, four years; studied under Fred Kabotie (q.v.)

OCCUPATION: Free-lance artist, jewelry designer, and painter

PUBLISHED: Dunn (1968); Snodgrass (1968); Tanner (1968; 1973); Brody (1971); Seymour (1988). *Modern American Indian Painting,* MPI (June-Sept 1963), cover; *Petroleum Today* (winter 1965); Region VI American Camping Association Convention, Norman, OK (17-20 Feb 1965), program

PUBLIC COLLECTIONS: GM, IACB/DC, LMA/BC, MAI, MNM, PAC

EXHIBITS: GM, HM/G, ITIC, MNA, MNM, NMSF, PAC, PAC/T, PBS, SWAIA, WRTD

AWARDS: HM/G; ITIC (Denman Award); NMSF; SWAIA

SHELTON, PETER H., III *Hopi*

Birth date unknown; son of Peter Shelton Jr. (q.v.)

RESIDENCE: Flagstaff, AZ

PUBLIC COLLECTIONS: MNA

EXHIBITS: HM/G

AWARDS: HM/G ('91)

SHENDO, JOE RAY *Jémez*

Born 1948

EDUCATION: Jémez, ca. 1962

PUBLISHED: Snodgrass (1968)

EXHIBITS: MNM, PAC

AWARDS: MNM

SHEOUAK

A talented artist, who died in her mid-thirties, Sheouak was married to a seal hunter. Her prints were included in the 1960 and 1961 Cape Dorset collections.

SHEOUAK *Inuit*

A.K.A. Sheowak

Born 1928; died 1961

RESIDENCE: Lived in Cape Dorset, NWT, Canada

OCCUPATION: Wife, mother, and graphic artist

MEDIA: Black pencil and prints

PUBLISHED: Houston (1967; 1967a); Goetz, et al. (1977)

EXHIBITS: C/CD, C/TIP

SHEOWAK (see Sheouak)

SHE-WHO-CATCHES-THE-RAINBOW (see Amylee)

SHEYKA, P. *Zuni (?)*

PUBLISHED: Snodgrass (1968)

EXHIBITS: SN

AWARDS: SN

SHIJE, MARCUS *Zia*

PUBLISHED: Snodgrass (1968)

PUBLIC COLLECTIONS: MNM, MRFM

SHILLING, ARTHUR *Ojibwa*

Born 1941 near Orillia, ON,Canada, on the Rama Reserve; died 1986 on the Rama Reserve

RESIDENCE: Lived on the Rama Reserve, ON, Canada

EDUCATION: Mohawk Institute Residential School, Brantford, ON; Royal College of Art; C/U of T; Ontario College of Art, Toronto, ON

OCCUPATION: Textile designer, draughtsman, and painter

MEDIA: Oil, acrylic, watercolor, pencil, and pastel

PUBLISHED: Dickason (1972); Menitove, ed. (1986); McMasters, et al. (1993). *The Globe and Mail* (1 Feb 1964; 1 Feb 1966; 15 Sept 1976; 16 Dec 1976; 27 June 1986); *The Orillia Packet and Times* (29 Nov 1965); *TAWOW* (Vol. 2, no. 2, 1970; Vol. 7, no. 1, 1980); *Native Perspective* (Vol. 1, no. 4, 1976; Vol. 3, no. 2, 1978); *The Toronto Sun* (8 July 1979; 31 May 1982; 19 Nov 1982); *Arts West* (Vol. 6, no. 9, 1981; Vol. 7, no. 1, 1981-1982); *The Spectator* (31 Oct 1981); *The Muskoka Sun* (Vol. 12, no. 5, 1982; Vol. 13, no. 9, 1983); *The Kitchener-Waterloo Record* (26 Nov 1983); *Masterkey* (winter 1984)

BOOKS PUBLISHED: Stone (1984), Shilling (1986)

PUBLIC COLLECTIONS: C/CMC; C/INAC; C/IOC; C/MCC; C/ROM; C/WLU; C/WICEC; Allandale Recreation Centre, Barrie, ON; Dofasco Inc., Hamilton, ON; St. Michael's Hospital, Toronto, ON

EXHIBITS: C/AG/TB; C/CIARH; C/CIIA; C/CMC; C/CNAC; C/LTAT; C/MCC; C/ROM; C/TU; C/WICEC; Bellview (ON) Public Library; In The Spirit of Sharing Festival, West Bay, ON; Indian Hall of Fame, Toronto, ON; Museum für Völkerkunde, Hamburg, Germany; Museum of São Paulo, Brazil

SOLO EXHIBITS: Partial listing of more than 25 includes: C/AG/TB; C/AG/TT; Orillia (ON) Public Library; galleries throughout Canada

AWARDS: Canadian Indian Christmas Card Design, ('67, 1st)

HONORS: Globe and Mail Art Fund Award for Aspiring Young Artists, 1962; Department of Indian and Northern Affairs Canada, scholarship, 1964; Centennial Medal, 1967

ARTHUR SHILLING

"A gifted portraitist, the artist's view that 'color is everything' is reflected in his impressionistic use of light and color. His paintings done in the late 1970s were more 'expressionistic' due to their concern with the subject's 'inner being.'"

Menitove, ed. 1986b

SHINAGI (see Yellow Blanket)

SHIPROCK (see Cohoe, Grey)

SHIPSHEE, LOUIS *Potawatomi*

Shipshee, Mountain Cougar

Born ca. 1900 on the Potawatomi Reservation, Oklahoma; died ca. 1975; son of Shipshee, U.S. Deputy Marshal; M/GF: Lucian, U.S. Army scout; M/GGF: French explorer in the Great Lakes area

RESIDENCE: Lived in Topeka, KS

MILITARY: WW I

EDUCATION: Neadreau, OK (where he learned to speak English); Haskell; Chilocco

OCCUPATION: Industrial crafts instructor, interior decorator and instructor, textbook author, house painter, free-lance artist, and painter

MEDIA: Oil and acrylic

PUBLISHED: Snodgrass (1968); Brody (1971). *American Indian Crafts and Culture* (Jan 1974)

PUBLIC COLLECTIONS: HCC, SMNAI

EXHIBITS: AAID; AIE; HCC; ITIC; Lawton, OK

AWARDS: AAID, AIE, ITIC

LOUIS SHIPSHEE

"Shipshee was a free-lance artist who traveled extensively throughout the Southwest painting in various media, often on velvet or buckskin. He did landscape paintings and woodcarvings but preferred portrait work."

Snodgrass 1968

SHIRLEY, ALBERT (see Shirley, Burt)

SHIRLEY, BURT *Navajo*

A.K.A. Albert Shirley

Born 7 June 1955

RESIDENCE: Church Rock, NM

EDUCATION: U of NM

OCCUPATION: New Mexico State Legislator and painter

MEDIA: Oil, acrylic, pen and ink, and prints

PUBLIC COLLECTIONS: BA/AZ

EXHIBITS: ITIC; CIM; NTF; RC; U of NM; New Mexico Governor's Gallery, Indian Fine Arts Exhibit

AWARDS: CIM ('88); ITIC ('88)

HONORS: U of NM, Indian Fine Arts Exhibit, poster artist

SHIRLEY, CHARLES KEETSIE *Navajo*

Keetsie, Small One

A.K.A. Keetsie; Shirley Keetsie

Born Mar 1909 near Aspen Water Springs, AZ, on the Navajo Reservation; died 25 Nov 1971; father of Nelson Dodge Shirley (q.v.)

EDUCATION: Haskell; Albuquerque, 1929; University of Denver, CO; trained as a draftsman at Fort Defiance, AZ

OCCUPATION: Auto mechanic, truck driver, Bureau of Land Management draftsman, and painter

MEDIA: Oil, tempera, pencil, and pen and ink

PUBLISHED: Underhill (1954); Tanner (1957; 1973); Snodgrass (1968); Brody (1971). *The Desert Magazine* (Jan 1948); *Arizona Highways* (Feb 1950; July 1956)

COMMISSIONS: *Murals:* Arizona Title and Trust Company, Tucson, AZ, 1947. *Other:* Brochure designs for various organizations; Bucking horse logo for a potato chip company

PUBLIC COLLECTIONS: DAM, MNA

CHARLES KEETSIE SHIRLEY

The artist's son remembers that his father's paintings of horses were very popular in the eastern United States and numerous articles about his work appeared in newspapers.

Nelson Shirley, p.c. 1993

SHIRLEY, NELSON DODGE *Navajo*

Hashkay-ha-nah

Born 21 Oct 1938 at Fort Defiance, AZ; son of Charles Keetsie Shirley (q.v.)

MILITARY: U.S. Navy

EDUCATION: Graduated high school; I.T.C. Technical College of San Francisco, CA; Maricopa Technical College, Phoenix, AZ

OCCUPATION: Designer, illustrator, draftsman, and painter

MEDIA: Watercolor, gouache, pencil, charcoal, and pastel

COMMISSIONS: Franklin Mint, Philadelphia, PA, medallion design

PUBLIC COLLECTIONS: BIA; Arizona Bank, Phoenix, AZ; Thunderbird Bank, Phoenix, AZ

EXHIBITS: HM; HM/G; HS/AI; KF; PAC; SDMM; SN; Civic Center Plaza, San Francisco, CA; Civic Plaza, Phoenix, AZ; Southern Pacific Railroad Art Show

AWARDS: Listing of juried student exhibits includes certificates and a Gold Medallion Key from the National Geographic Society and National Scholastic Exhibits.

SHIRLEY, VINCENT *Navajo*

RESIDENCE: Chinle, AZ

COMMISSIONS: *Murals:* Ned A. Hatathli Museum, Tsaile, AZ (financed by a grant from Metropolitan Life Foundation), 1985

SHIRLEY, WALTER *Navajo*

EDUCATION: BC, 1951; NSU
PUBLISHED: Snodgrass (1968). *Arizona Highways* (July 1956)
PUBLIC COLLECTIONS: MNA
EXHIBITS: PAC
AWARDS: PAC

SHOBAH WOONHON (see Toledo, José Ray)

SHOEMAKE, BARBARA (see Zotigh, Barbara)

SHOEMAKER, BEN *Quapaw/Shawnee/Cherokee*

A.K.A. Ben Adair Shoemaker
Born 1945
RESIDENCE: Locust Grove, OK
MILITARY: U.S. Army, Vietnam
EDUCATION: Central High School, Tulsa, OK; U of Tulsa; TJC
OCCUPATION: Full-time artist since 1978
MEDIA: Acrylic, watercolor, gouache, and prints
PUBLISHED: *The Tulsa World* (7 May 1983); *The Tulsa Tribune* (17 Mar 1987); *Muskogee Daily Phoenix* (4 Oct 1993)
PUBLIC COLLECTIONS: FCTM, GM, HCC, RSC
EXHIBITS: ACS/RSC; CNM; HCC; NM; FCTM; HSM/OK; KCPA; OAC; OIAP; OSC; RC; SI; SN; SWAIA; TIAF; U of WV; WTF; J. M. Davis Museum, Claremore, OK; NSU Indian Symposium, Tahlequah, OK
AWARDS: ACS/RSC ('83, 1st); CNM; FCTM ('81; '82, 2-1st; '83, 1st; '84, 2-1st, IH; '85, IH); FCTM/M ('86, 1st; '87; '88; '90, 1st, IH; '91; '92, IH; '94, IH); RC ('87)
HONORS: FCTM, designated a Master Artist, 1986; TIAF, poster artist, 1987

SHONTO, WILSON (see Begay, Shonto)

SHOOK, TONYA HOLMES *Cherokee*

Born 28 Nov 1935; daughter of Dorothy Dowell and C. E. Holmes; P/GP: Beulah and C.W. Holmes; M/GP: Roe and Elmer Dowell
RESIDENCE: Hastings, OK
OCCUPATION: Cartoon artist, gallery owner, author, and painter
MEDIA: Oil and prints
PUBLISHED: Shook (1986)
EXHIBITS: CNM; OSU; U of NM: Cherokee Strip Museum, Perry, OK; Fall Fest, Duncan, OK; Lawton (OK) Junior Service Show; Sheppard Air Force Base, Wichita Falls, TX; State Capitol of Texas, Austin, TX; see also Awards
AWARDS: Oklahoma State Fair, Oklahoma City, OK ('86, 1st)

SHORT BULL *Brûlé Sioux*

Tatanka Ptecela
A.K.A. Chief Short Bull
Born ca. 1847 in the Niobrara River country of Nebraska; died 1935; grandfather of Norman Shortbull (q.v.)
RESIDENCE: Lived on Pine Ridge Reservation, SD
OCCUPATION: Warrior, medicine man, prophet, performer, cultural informant, and artist
MEDIA: Watercolor, pencil, pen and ink, and crayon
PUBLISHED: Dunn (1968); Snodgrass (1968); Dockstader (1977); Maurer

BEN SHOEMAKER

Shoemaker grew up in Osage county close to the Gilcrease Museum. By drawing for his son and taking him to visit the Gilcrease Museum, his father encouraged the boy's interest in art. Another major influence on the artist was Alexandre Hogue, head of the University of Tulsa's Art Department, who saw Shoemaker's art work at Central High School and encouraged him go to college. According to the artist, "Our lives are a composite of our past, so from my thoughts I paint these pictures with more than first meets the eye. I may take a person with a feather in his hair. On closer examination, the feather also is a person or bird, just hanging there. Most of my paintings are in my mind. Seldom do I look at things to try to copy them. . . . I get a kick out of thinking things up."

Mildred D. Ladner 1984

SHORT BULL

Short Bull was known by the Lakota as a holy man and a warrior of proven bravery. He participated in the Battle of the Little Bighorn and became a leader in the messianic "Ghost Dance" movement. When the movement was crushed by the Wounded Knee massacre, Short Bull led a group of the Lakota into the Badlands. Captured by General Nelson A. Miles at Pine Ridge, he and eighteen other (continued)

(1992). *Bulletin 30,* BAE (1907); *American Indian Art* (summer 1992); *European Review of Native American Studies* (Vol. 4, no. 1, 1990)

COMMISSIONS: MNH/A, two 2½ x 5' paintings of Sun Dance scenes, 1918

PUBLIC COLLECTIONS: IACB; MNH/A; SI; SIM; Eugene Buechel Lakota Museum, St. Francis, SD; Hamburgisches Museum für Völkerkunde, Hamburg, Germany; Museum für Völkerkunde, Leipzig, Germany

EXHIBITS: VP

SHORT BULL

(continued) prisoners were sent to Fort Sheridan, IL. They were released to William F. (Buffalo Bill) Cody and traveled with his "Wild West Show" in the United States and Europe. When this phase of his life ended, he returned to the Pine Ridge area where he provided historical information for several individuals seeking to record the vanishing tribal ways. Many drawings and several notebooks of his art work have survived, some of which are in the Indian Arts and Crafts Board collection and in Leipzig and Hamburg (Germany) museums.

American Indian Art
summer 1992

SHORT BULL, ARTHUR *Oglala Sioux*

RESIDENCE: Mondamin, IA

EXHIBITS: RC

SHORTBULL, NORMAN *Sioux*

Born 11 Mar 1918 in Wanblee, SD; P/GF: Short Bull (q.v.)

MILITARY: U.S. Army

EDUCATION: Art school, Denver, CO

OCCUPATION: House painter, art instructor, and painter

PUBLISHED: Snodgrass (1968)

PUBLIC COLLECTIONS: St. Francis Museum, SD; Mother Butler Center, SD

EXHIBITS: BNIAS; regional exhibits in South Dakota and Colorado

AWARDS: Exhibits in Rapid City and Igloo, SD, and Denver, CO

NORMAN SHORTBULL

"The artist has been painting since 1951 and prefers portrait work. He was strongly encouraged in his career by Angelo Di Bennedetto and Phil Steele."

Snodgrass 1968

SHORTY, H. ROY *Navajo*

PUBLIC COLLECTIONS: MNA, WWM

SHORTY, LAVINA *Navajo*

EXHIBITS: HM/G, PAC

AWARDS: HM/G ('70, 1st)

SHOWS THE FEATHER *Sioux*

PUBLISHED: Snodgrass (1968)

PUBLIC COLLECTIONS: MPM (pictographic style on paper)

SHUNKA ISHNALA (see Lone Dog)

SHUNKA SAPA (see Black Horse)

SHUPELA, DOUGLAS *Hopi*

Born 22 Aug 1932 on First Mesa, AZ

RESIDENCE: Polacca, AZ

EDUCATION: Hopi

OCCUPATION: *The Arizona Sun* employee (1961), and painter

PUBLISHED: Snodgrass (1968)

PUBLIC COLLECTIONS: PAC

EXHIBITS: PAC

DOUGLAS SHUPELA

"As a child Shupela often painted the decorative motifs on his mother's pottery."

Snodgrass 1968

SHURLEY, LAURA G. *Navajo*

Born 15 Sept 1961 in Winslow, AZ; daughter of Margaret and Walter Shurley, artist and silversmith

RESIDENCE: Winslow, AZ

EDUCATION: Winslow (AZ) High School; Grand Canyon College, Phoenix, AZ; B.A., U of AZ, 1984; Otis-Parsons School of Design, Los Angeles, CA

OCCUPATION: Craftswoman, seamstress, fashion designer, teacher, and painter

MEDIA: Oil, acrylic, and prints

COMMISSIONS: *Murals:* DIA, 1993

EXHIBITS: ACS/PG, CIM, FNAA, HM/G, ITIC, MNA, SNAICF, SWAIA, U of AZ, WIEAS, WWM

SOLO EXHIBITS: WWM

AWARDS: ITIC ('76; '86, 1st, Watson Award; '88, 1st, Best in Category); MNA; SNAICF ('89, Best of Class); WIEAS

SIKCHIDA OR SIK CHIDA (see Yellow Feather)

SILAS, WARREN *Hopi*

MEDIA: Tempera

PUBLISHED: Seymour (1968)

PUBLIC COLLECTIONS: IACB/DC

EXHIBITS: WRTD

SILVA, ANTHONY *Laguna*

Born 1947 in Albuquerque, NM

RESIDENCE: Old Laguna, NM

EDUCATION: St. Catherine's, ca. 1965

PUBLISHED: Snodgrass (1968)

EXHIBITS: MNM; PAC; SAIEAIP ('65)

SILVA, DENNIS M. *Santa Clara*

RESIDENCE: Española, NM

EDUCATION: NM Highlands U

OCCUPATION: Bookkeeper and painter

MEDIA: Watercolor

COMMISSIONS: *Murals:* IPCC

EXHIBITS: CNM, HM/G, NMSF, SNAICF

AWARDS: HM/G ('71, 1st, Outstanding Student; '75, 1st)

SILVA, EUGENE *Santa Clara*

PUBLIC COLLECTIONS: MNA, MRFM

SILVA, MARCUS *Santa Clara*

Red Cloud

A.K.A. Mark Silva

Born 1921

RESIDENCE: Española, NM

EDUCATION: Santa Fe

PUBLISHED: Snodgrass (1968); Brody (1971); Tanner (1973)

EXHIBITS: CNM, FAIEAIP, MNM, HM/G, SN

SOLO EXHIBITS: MNM

AWARDS: HM/G ('71)

SILVER, MARK *(?)*

Born 1946 in Battle Creek, MI

EXHIBITS: C/AG/W; C/NAC; C/ROM; C/WICEC; MAI; TRP; Great Western Indian Arts and Crafts, Los Angeles, CA

SILVERHORN, GEORGE *Kiowa*

Boy Hero

A.K.A. Dutch Silverhorn

Born 1911 in Caddo County, OK; died 1969 in Lawton, OK; son of James Silverhorn (Haungooah) (q.v.)

RESIDENCE: Lived in Anadarko, OK
EDUCATION: Fort Sill; Riverside, ca. 1917-1925
OCCUPATION: Metalsmith, carver, and painter
MEDIA: Tempera
PUBLISHED: Snodgrass (1968); Ellison (1969). *The Daily Oklahoman, Orbit Magazine* (23 July 1967); *House Beautiful* (June 1969); *Smoke Signals* (spring 1967)
PUBLIC COLLECTIONS: GM; MRFM; SI; SPIM; Museum of the Great Plains, Lawton, OK
EXHIBITS: CSPIP; PAC; SPIM; in Scottsdale, AZ, Gallup, NM, and Washington, D.C., 1964

JAMES SILVERHORN

"Silverhorn was one of a delegation of Kiowas taken to the Congress of the United States. While in Washington, he sketched what he saw. His work usually portrays religious ceremonies and tribal myths."

Snodgrass 1968

According to Maurer (1992), Silverhorn "was perhaps the most prolific and versatile Plains artist of all times." His pictographic style was "characterized by light and airy figures and attention to detail." In addition to the traditional subjects of warfare, hunting, and courtship, Silverhorn depicted myths, ceremonies, and every day life.

Silverhorn learned to paint from his brother, Ohet Toint, who, in turn, had learned to paint while a prisoner at Fort Marion, St. Augustine, FL. Using part of an old Army target record book, the artist kept a diary from August 24, 1891 to November 23, 1894. Ca. 1918, Silverhorn, Ohet Toint and other Kiowa elders collaborated to create a full-size version of his family's "Tipi of Battle Pictures." Silverhorn stopped painting ca. 1918-1919.

SILVERHORN, JAMES *Kiowa*

Haungooah

A.K.A. Haungoonpau; Haungooah; Hogoon; Hawgone; Silver Horns; Silverhorn
Born 1861; died ca. 1941; uncle of Stephen Mopope (q.v.); Artist is a descendant of Tohausen.
RESIDENCE: Lived in Oklahoma
OCCUPATION: Participated in the last Kiowa outbreak, 1874; medicine man and guard to a "grandmother medicine pouch"; soldier under General Hugh L. Scott, 1889-1894; graphic artist, silversmith, and featherworker
MEDIA: Graphite, crayon, colored pencil, pen and ink, pigment, muslin, hide, German silver, and feather
PUBLISHED: Alexander (1938); Mayhall (1962); Snodgrass (1968); Highwater (1976); Maurer (1977; 1992); Silberman (1978); Boyd, et al. (1981); Wade, ed. (1986); Williams, ed. (1990). *Smoke Signals* (spring 1967); *Smithsonian* (Nov 1992); *American Indian Art* (summer 1985; spring 1993); *American Indian Art* (spring 1995)
PUBLIC COLLECTIONS: CC; GPM; MKMcNAI; MNH/A; MNH/F; NL; PAC; SI/OAA; Fort Sill (OK) Museum
EXHIBITS: HSM/OK; JAM; MIA; MKMcNAI; OMA; SPIM; VP; National Museum of Natural History, Washington, D.C., 1994; St. Louis (MO) Art Museum

SILVER HORNS (see Silverhorn)

SILVERMOON (see Martin, Michael James)

SILVERSMITH, MARK *Navajo*

Birth date unknown; born near Manuelito, NM
RESIDENCE: Farmington, NM
EDUCATION: Wingate (NM) High School; B.A., SWOSU
OCCUPATION: Teacher; full-time painter after 1982
MEDIA: Acrylic, watercolor, pastel, pencil, Prismacolor, stone, and prints
PUBLISHED: Jacka and Jacka (1994). *The Indian Trader* (Nov 1985); *The Phoenix Gazette* (11 Dec 1986); *Art-Talk* (Mar 1987); *The Gallup (NM) Independent* (Aug 1988); *Cross Currents* (15 July 1994), cover; *New Mexico Area Guide*, Farmington, NM (1994), cover
COMMISSIONS: Rocky Mountain Quality Conferences, paintings for awards; American Endangered Species Foundation, promotional card
PUBLIC COLLECTIONS: SWOSU; Harley-Davidson; Hewlett-Packard; Southwest Bank, Gallup, NM
EXHIBITS: ACAI; ASC/PG; CNM; HM/G; ITIC; SDCC; SWAIA; TF; galleries in AZ, CA, CO, IL, NM, TX, UT, and Europe

MARK SILVERSMITH

A full-blood Navajo, Silversmith thinks of himself as a Southwest artist rather than an Indian artist, although he paints Indian subjects. His paintings depict not only his own Navajo

AWARDS: ITIC ('85, 2-1st; '86, 1st; '87, 1st; '88, 1st; 89', 3-1st, Woodard Award, Mullarky Award; '90); SWAIA ('90; '91, 2-1st, Best of Division)
HONORS: AICA, Artist of the Year, 1986; ITIC, poster artist, 1988

SILVERTHORNE, RUTH *Salish/Chippewa/Kickapoo/Oneida/Mohawk*
Born 20 Mar 1952; daughter of Edna Mae Masquat and Woodrow W. Silverthorne
RESIDENCE: Mt. Vernon, WA
EDUCATION: Roan High School, 1970; B.A., U of MT, 1978; M.A.Ed., MSU, 1980
OCCUPATION: Artist
MEDIA: Oil, watercolor, pencil, and prints
EXHIBITS: AICH; galleries in New York and Washington, D.C.

SIMBOLA, IRENE *Picurís*
Born 25 Aug 1942
RESIDENCE: Peñasco, NM
EDUCATION: IAIA, 1962-1963
OCCUPATION: Ceramist and painter
PUBLISHED: Snodgrass (1968)
EXHIBITS: PAC

SIMCLOSH (see Morgan, Judith Phillis)

SIMEON, DAVID *Sarcee*
Walking Eagle
RESIDENCE: Canada
PUBLIC COLLECTIONS: C/GM

SIMILY, MAXINE WAHELLA *Cherokee*
Wahella
Birth date unknown; daughter of Roxie Belle King and Charley Johnson; P/GP: Cora P. Layne and C. Johnson; M/GP: Sarah Cox and Will King
RESIDENCE: Hemet, CA
EDUCATION: High School, 1983; U of OK, 1938-1939
OCCUPATION: Singer, co-owner of Indian art promotion business, housewife, and painter
MEDIA: Oil, acrylic, watercolor, and pen and ink
PUBLISHED: *The Indian Trader* (July 1978)
EXHIBITS: ASF; CNM; HM/G; LIAS; PAC; state and county fairs in AZ, CA, CO, and MO
AWARDS: CMN ('88, 1st; '81; '94); area fairs

SIMLA, MARLENE R. *Yakama/Puyallup/Siletz/Kanaka*
Born 1 Jan 1939; daughter of Catherine A. Andrews and James Jay Spencer Jr.; P/GF: James Jay Spencer Sr.; M/GF: Frank Andrews
RESIDENCE: Toppenish, WA
EDUCATION: Toppenish (WA) Senior High School, 1957; IAIA, 1963; Fort Lewis College, Durango, CO, 1967; Heritage College, Toppenish, WA
OCCUPATION: Indian child welfare worker and painter
MEDIA: Oil, acrylic, and watercolor
EXHIBITS: ACS/SM, IAIA; see also Awards
AWARDS: ACS/SM; Granger Cherry (WA) Festival; Yakima County (WA) State Fair

MARK SILVERSMITH

(continued) traditions but the traditions of many other tribal groups. Silversmith says, "My main motivation is not just my family and art, but being a Christian as well. Without it, I don't know what I would have done."

The Gallup Independent
Aug 1988

SIMMS, NORMAN *Navajo*

RESIDENCE: Fruitland, NM

EXHIBITS: ACS/MV

AWARDS: ACS/MV ('93; '94, 1st)

SIMON, JAMES *Ojibwa*

Born 1954 on Manitoulin Island, ON, Canada, on the Wikwemikong Reserve

RESIDENCE: Wikwemikong, ON, Canada

EDUCATION: Manitoulin (ON) Secondary School; Laurentian University, Sudbury, ON

OCCUPATION: Carpenter, art teacher, and painter

PUBLISHED: Southcott (1984)

COMMISSIONS: Illustrated classroom material for an Ojibwa language primary school

EXHIBITS: C/CNAC; Rome, Italy; Milan, Italy

SIMON, LUKE *Micmac*

Born 30 May 1953; brother of Roger Simon (q.v.)

RESIDENCE: Big Cove, NB, Canada

EDUCATION: Graphic Design Technician Certificate, George Brown College of Applied Arts and Technology, Toronto, ON; A.F.A., IAIA, 1983; B.F.A., CSF/SF, 1985

OCCUPATION: Commercial artist, radio broadcaster, art instructor, storyteller, sculptor, and painter

MEDIA: Acrylic

PUBLISHED: Hill (1992). *Arizona Highways* (May 1986)

COMMISSIONS: *Murals:* C/IACB, Toronto Regional Office, 1976; Big Cove (NB) Federal School, 1977; Miramichi Hospital, Newcastle, NB

PUBLIC COLLECTIONS: IAIA

EXHIBITS: ACS/ENP; C/I; CSF/SF; IAIA; NACLA; NARF; SCG; SFFA; SWAIA; galleries in New Mexico and Canada; see also Awards

AWARDS: CSF/SF ('85); SWAIA ('83, 1st); March of Dimes Benefit Gala, Santa Fe, NM ('83, Grand Prize)

HONORS: IAIA, T. C. Cannon Memorial Award, 1983; IAIA, Outstanding Student Award and The National Dean's List, 1982, 1983

SIMON, ROGER *Micmac*

Born 1954 in Big Cove, NB, Canada; brother of Luke Simon (q.v.)

RESIDENCE: Big Cove, NB, Canada

EDUCATION: George Brown College, Toronto, ON, 1974-1977; New Brunswick Crafts School, Fredericton, NB, 1983

COMMISSIONS: *Murals:* Big Cove (NB) Band Office; C/IACB, Toronto, ON; Micmac/Maliceet Institute, Fredericton, NB; Miramichi Hospital, Newcastle, NB; St. Mary's (NB) Band Office

PUBLIC COLLECTIONS: C/INAC

EXHIBITS: Partial listing of more than 24 includes: C/AC/D; C/CCAB; C/CIIA; C/LNFC; C/U of SK; RC; Dalhousie University, Halifax, NS; Harriet Tubman House Gallery, Boston, MA; Kougibogouc National Park, NB; Monsignor Boyd Centre, Fredericton, NB; St. Thomas University, Fredericton, NB; University of Moncton, NB

SIMON, WILMA *Ojibwa*

OCCUPATION: Graphic artist

MEDIA: Prints
EXHIBITS: C/ROM, HM/G
AWARDS: HM/G ('70)

SINE, DAVID W. *Apache*

Born 13 Aug 1921 at Camp Verde on the Yavapai-Apache Reservation, AZ
RESIDENCE: Camp Verde, AZ
MILITARY: U.S. Army, WWII
EDUCATION: Phoenix; business school
OCCUPATION: BIA employee, sculptor and painter
MEDIA: Oil, watercolor, pencil, pastel, charcoal, mixed-media, stone, and clay
PUBLISHED: Snodgrass (1968); Seymour (1988)
COMMISSIONS: *Murals:* Tohono O'odham Church on the Tohono O'odham Reservation, AZ; Tohono O'odham (Papago) Agency office, Sells, AZ
PUBLIC COLLECTIONS: IACB/DC
EXHIBITS: AC/SD, FWG, HM, HM/G, ITIC, SN, WRTD
AWARDS: ITIC ('52, 1st)
HONORS: U.S. Army, designed emblem for Arizona Bushmasters, WWII; named an Arizona Indian Living Treasure, 1989

DAVID W. SINE

Sine worked for the Bureau of Indian Affairs for thirty years and considers himself to be a weekend artist. He has painted since a 7th or 8th grade teacher encouraged him to use his talent. The general focus of Sine's art work is the traditional ways of the Apache. He says, "This is what I want to paint, the past and present of my people, the dances, the gathering of fruit and nuts, and whatever I saw my people doing during my time."

Seymour 1988

SINE, DUKE WASAAJA *Yavapai/Apache*

Wasaaja, Come Follow Me (or Come In My Direction)
Born 1955 in San Carlos, AZ; son of David W. Sine (q.v.)
RESIDENCE: Sells, AZ
EDUCATION: IAIA, 1973
OCCUPATION: Carpenter, laborer, firefighter, and artist
MEDIA: Acrylic, watercolor, pen and ink, pastel, Prismacolor, and mixed-media
PUBLISHED: *American West Airlines Magazine* (Oct 1987)
PUBLIC COLLECTIONS: IAIA
EXHIBITS: ACS/PG, FHMAG, HM, ITIC, MNA, OT, SWAIA
HONORS: SWAIA, poster artist, 1987

DUKE WASAAJA SINE

The artist is the son of an artist, and has two brothers who are also artists. He says that they all painted together on weekends and it was his father who inspired them with a desire to strive for excellence in all that they do. Of his work he says, "I see my art as a means of reaching for something higher within myself. Everything I paint comes from my heart and the center of my being. Art has become a religious experience for me. I believe I am helping to protect what the Creator has given to us as a people by accurately portraying our legends and ceremonies in my art."

Kate Thorne 1987

SINGER, BEVERLY R. *Santa Clara/Navajo*

Born 12 Dec 1954 at Santa Clara Pueblo, NM; daughter of Bert and James Singer; P/GP: Florence Naranjo and Lawrence Singer; M/GP: Rosita Velarde and Herman Paul Tsosie; G/aunt: Pablita Velarde (q.v.)
RESIDENCE: New York, NY
EDUCATION: Española (NM) High School and Phillips Exeter Academy, NH, 1971; IAIA; B.A., College of Santa Fe, NM, 1975; M.A., U of CH, 1977; IAIA, 1984
OCCUPATION: Educator, video producer, Native rights advocate, and painter
MEDIA: Oil, acrylic, watercolor, pastel, and prints
PUBLISHED: Zurko, ed. (1992). *Ikon Magazine for the Arts* (May 1992)
PUBLIC COLLECTIONS: IAIA; For Our Children's Sake Foundation, NY; Episcopal Church Center, NY; Multi-Media, Inc., Rockefeller Center, NY
EXHIBITS: AICA/SF; AICH; IAIA; CWAM; WWM; Queens College Museum, NY; Center of Contemporary Art of Seattle, WA; galleries in CT, MA, NY, and WA
HONORS: United Nations School, New York Foundation for the Arts, artist-in-residence; Bob Blackburn Studio of Printmaking, New York, NY, fellowship

Ed Singer

Singer is known for his paintings of traditional Indians (most often a single figure) with contemporary props. The Timex watch or the folding aluminum chair is a symbol of the Indian's struggle to hang on to the past and live in the present. He has said that he doesn't intend to paint a story, but instead he is seeking an abrupt confrontation between the viewer and the painting.

Art Voices South
Sept/Oct 1979

Stanley Devereaux Sinnett

The artist says of his career, "Being an illustrator and story-teller and loving to draw people and animals, all combined to lead me into the Western genre with my fine art."

p.c. 1992

Sinte

"The Cronau album consists of 112 individual original drawings by American Indians, commissioned and collected by an illustrator for a German periodical, Rudolf Cronau, at Standing Rock Agency, Pine Ridge Agency, Fort Randall, etc., 1880-1883. In 1886, a number of these artists, including Sinte, were taken on a tour of Europe by Cronau, who was especially impressed by Sinte's uncanny ability to draw from memory. Among this artist's 19 drawings was an original map, of which Cronau said: 'This map [was] made by Sinte in my presence from memory without the Indian having seen a

Singer, Ed *Navajo*

A.K.A. Edward Singer

Born 17 June 1951 in Tuba City, AZ; son of Isabelle Jensen and Harry Singer; P/GP: Fannie Singer and Hatathlie Tsosie; M/GP: Hanna and Luke Jensen

RESIDENCE: Cameron, AZ

EDUCATION: Brigham City (UT) High School, 1970; U of UT; Southern Utah State College, Cedar City, Utah, 1972; SFAI, 1973; U of N AZ

OCCUPATION: Rodeo contestant, teacher; full-time painter since 1977

MEDIA: Oil, acrylic, watercolor, pencil, pen and ink, pastel, and prints

PUBLISHED: Samuels (1982). *Artspace* (summer 1978); *Santa Fe Profile* (June 1979); *Southwest Art* (Apr 1980; June 1981); *Art Voices South* (Sept/Oct 1980); *The Phoenix Gazette* (22 Jan 1983); *The Indian Trader* (Aug 1984)

BOOKS PUBLISHED: Beck, Walters, and Francisco (1990)

PUBLIC COLLECTIONS: GM; HCC; HM; MAI; MRFM; PAC; Jesuit University, Dallas, TX; United Bank, Denver, Co

EXHIBITS: FSMCIAF; HCC; HM; HM/G; HPTU; IPCC; MAI; MPDC; NACLA; NTM; PAC; RC; SFFA; WWM; Salon d'Automne, Paris, France, 1981

SOLO/SPECIAL EXHIBITS: NTM (dual show)

AWARDS: HM/G ('77, 2-1st); RC ('77, 1st; '78, 1st, Woodard Award); MPDC ('78, 1st); PAC ('78, Best of Drawing and Best of Lithography); RC ('77, 1st)

Singer, James *Navajo/Santa Clara*

Born 1937

RESIDENCE: Española, NM

EDUCATION: U of AZ, "Southwest Indian Art Project," scholarship, summer 1960

PUBLISHED: Snodgrass (1968)

Sings About Everything (see Blackrider, Radford)

Sinnagwin (see McKinney, Roger)

Sinnett, Stanley Devereaux *Blackfeet*

Born 1 May 1925 in Conrad, MT; son of Iva Devereaux and Walter Sinnett; M/GP: Lenor LaBreche and Henry Devereaux; Artist was raised by his maternal grandparents.

RESIDENCE: Downey, CA

MILITARY: U.S. Air Force, WWII

EDUCATION: Cut Bank (MT) High School, 1942; B.F.A., Chouinard Art Institute, Los Angeles, CA, 1970; M.A., CSU/F, 1973

OCCUPATION: Auto mechanic, free-lance illustrator, teacher, and artist

MEDIA: Oil, acrylic, watercolor, pencil, pen and ink, pastel, and clay

PUBLISHED: Samuels (1982)

PUBLIC COLLECTIONS: MPI

EXHIBITS: TIAF; Brea (CA) Cultural Center; Cattlemen's Western Art Show, CA; Ceres Western Art Show; Death Valley (CA) Art Show; Downey (CA) Museum of Art; Syntex Corporation Exhibition, Palo Alto, CA; Estes Park (CO) Art Show

SOLO EXHIBITS: MPI; Downey (CA) Museum of Art; Lancaster Museum of Art, CA; Whittier (CA) Art Association Gallery; galleries in California

AWARDS: Regional art competitions

HONORS: Included in Noel Goldblatt's *People of the Century* collection

Sinte *Sioux*

PUBLISHED: Snodgrass (1968)

PUBLIC COLLECTIONS: MNH/A (Cronau album)

SINTE GALESKA (see Spotted Tail)

SINTE GLESKA (see Spotted Tail)

SINTE MAZE (see Iron Tail)

SINUYITUQ, INUSUYAUQ (see Senugetuk, Joseph Engasongwok)

SIOUI, PIERRE *Huron*

Born 2 Sept 1950 in Montréal, PQ, Canada
RESIDENCE: St. Marc-sur-le-Riche, PQ, Canada
EDUCATION: Centre de Conception Graphique
OCCUPATION: Framer, farmer, graphic artist, and painter
MEDIA: Mixed-media and prints
PUBLISHED: McMasters, et al. (1993)
PUBLIC COLLECTIONS: C/IAC; ALCAN Company of Canada, Montréal, PQ; La Société Immobilière du Québec, Montréal, PQ; Seneca Communication, Montréal, PQ
EXHIBITS: C/AG/TB; C/INAC; C/NACF; C/WICEC; HM; Columbia University, New York, NY
HONORS: Ministère des Affaires Culturelles du Québec, bursary, 1985-1986

SIS-BE-GOOT (see Wood, Glen)

SIS-HU-LK (see Batiste, Francis)

SISNEROS, MARIE *Santa Clara*

EDUCATION: Haskell
PUBLISHED: Snodgrass (1968)
EXHIBITS: PAC

SISOKOLAS (see Rosso, Larry)

SITSGOMA (see Pentewa, Dick R.)

SITTING BEAR (see Whiteman, Alfred, Jr.)

SITTING BUFFALO BULL (see Sitting Bull)

SITTING BULL *Hunkpapa Sioux*

Tatanka Iyotanka, Sitting Buffalo Bull; *Tatanka Yotanka*; *Hunkesni,* Slow (childhood name)
A.K.A. Chief Sitting Bull
Born ca. 1834, near old Fort George or at Grand River, SD; died 15 Dec 1890; son of subchief Jumping Bull; nephew of chiefs Four Horns and Hunting His Lodge
EDUCATION: Received art instruction from Rudolf Cronau
OCCUPATION: Hunter, warrior, chief, medicine man, and Indian politician
MEDIA: Watercolor, pencil, pen and ink, crayon, and muslin
PUBLISHED: Dunn Jr. (1886); Kelly (1926); Vestal (1932); Sterling (1938); Smith (1948); Schmitt and Brown (1948); LaFarge (1956; 1960); Ewers (1965); Dunn (1968); Snodgrass (1968); Dockstader (1977); Maurer (1992). *Harpers Weekly* (1876); *The World Book Encyclopedia* (1975); *American Heritage* (June 1964); *American Indian Art* (spring 1993)
PUBLIC COLLECTIONS: MAI; MIA; JAM; SI/OAA; SM; St. Louis (MO) Art Museum
EXHIBITS: VP
HONORS: Became chief, ca. 1868

SINTE

(continued) cartographic representation in our concept. This sheet shows a tremendous testimony for the orthographic development of the man's mind.' Other artists represented in the album are The Crow, Fast Deer, Yellow Blanket, and Black Horse (qq.v)."

SITTING BULL

"In 1870, a series of autobiographical drawings by Sitting Bull, admittedly stolen, were sold by a group of Yankton Sioux to an army officer at Fort Buford, MT, for $1.50. The pictures were outlined in ink and shaded with colored chalk and colored pencils. In the corner of each was a buffalo bull on his haunches, the artist's 'totem' [name glyph] or signature. This book of drawings, later sent to the Army Medical Museum Library, Washington, D.C., is now known as the Kimball Pictographic Record."

"While on a four-month tour with Buffalo Bill's Wild West Show, Sitting Bull sold autographs for one dollar."

Snodgrass 1968

Sitting Bull was a medicine man and a spiritual leader of the Sioux. He performed a Sun Dance before the Battle of the Little Big Horn and the resulting vision indicated victory. In 1881, under a promise of amnesty, he surrendered at Fort Buford and was sent to a reservation. In 1882, he did a series of 22 drawings that have come to be known as the Smith Record.

SITTING CROW *Teton Sioux*

PUBLISHED: Snodgrass (1968)

PUBLIC COLLECTIONS: MAI (pencil and color sketch, ca. 1880); MPM (pictographic style on paper)

SITTING EAGLE (see Honewytewa, Louis Calvin, Jr.)

SITTING EAGLE (see Marshall, James)

SITTING EAGLE *Miniconjou Sioux*

A.K.A. Harry Hand

RESIDENCE: Sitting Eagle was once at Pine Ridge, Dakota Territory, and was on the Rosebud River, Dakota Territory, in 1867 (see Black Heart).

PUBLISHED: Snodgrass (1968)

PUBLIC COLLECTIONS: MAI (autograph sketch)

SITTING EAGLE

"Sitting Eagle's brother-in-law, Steamboat, began a Miniconjou calendar and taught Sitting Eagle to interpret it. When Steamboat died, Sitting Eagle took possession of this record."

Snodgrass 1968

SITTING HAWK *Sioux*

Cetaniyatake (?)

PUBLISHED: Snodgrass (1968)

PUBLIC COLLECTIONS: MPM (pictographic style on paper)

SITTING WIND (see Kaquitts, Frank)

SIVURAQ, THOMAS *Inuit (Eskimo)*

Born 1941

RESIDENCE: Baker Lake, NWT, Canada

OCCUPATION: Sculptor, graphic artist, and printer

PUBLISHED: Collinson (1978)

PUBLIC COLLECTIONS: C/U of AB

EXHIBITS: C/AG/O, C/AG/WP, C/CG

SKA-KODAH-DAH-SAK (see Riding In Memeah, Marlene)

SKEETER, RAMONA *Creek*

EXHIBITS: PAC

AWARDS: PAC ('78)

SKY PAINTER (see Turner, Lowell Kevin)

SLEEPS IN THE THUNDER (see Pepion, Webb)

SLICK, DUANE *Sac-Fox/Winnebago*

Born 1961 in Waterloo, IA

RESIDENCE: Cedar Falls, IA

EDUCATION: SUNY/P, 1983; West Chester (PA) University, 1984; Skowhegan School of Painting and Sculpture, 1986; B.F.A., University of Northern Iowa, Cedar Falls, 1986; M.F.A., U of CA/D, 1990

OCCUPATION: IAIA painting instructor and painter

MEDIA: Oil, acrylic, charcoal, and mixed-media

PUBLISHED: Ward, ed. (1990); Roberts, ed. (1992). *The Santa Fean* (Aug 1994)

EXHIBITS: CNGM; CWAM; HM; OLO; SS/CW; WHB; Charles H. McNieder Museum, Mason City, IA; galleries in Illinois and Massachusetts

SOLO EXHIBITS: Fine Arts Work Center, Provincetown, MA, 1991; Cedar Falls (IA) City Hall

HONORS: *Fellowships:* Vermont Studio School, Johnson, VT, 1989; Fine Arts Work Center, Provinceton, MA, 1991, 1992

SLIM CURLEY HAIR (see Mitchell, Stanley C.)

SLIM NAVAJO (see Denetsosie, Hoke)

SLOAN, JOHN *Navajo*

PUBLIC COLLECTIONS: MNA

SLOW CLOUD (see Maulson, Gerald)

SLOWTALKER, THOMAS *Navajo*

PUBLIC COLLECTIONS: MNA

SMALL, IVAN J., SR. *Northern Cheyenne*

Born 28 Apr 1920; son of Josephine Rondeau and Thomas L. Small; GGF: Chief High Wolf (High Hump Back Wolf), who signed the Peace Treaty of 1825

RESIDENCE: Lodge Grass, MT

MILITARY: 101st Airborne, WW II

OCCUPATION: Rodeo contestant, rodeo stock contractor, rancher, and artist

MEDIA: Watercolor and pen and ink

EXHIBITS: AIAFM, ITAE/M, MPI, RC

SOLO/SPECIAL EXHIBITS: MPI (dual show)

AWARDS: AIAFM (Best of Show)

SMALLCANYON, EVELYN *Navajo (?)*

EDUCATION: Richfield (UT) High School, ca. 1964

PUBLISHED: Snodgrass (1968)

EXHIBITS: NACG

AWARDS: NACG

SMART, CLARA MARY *Eskimo*

Buniyuk, Little Daughter

Born 16 Jan 1941 at Hooper Bay, AK; daughter of Irene Bunyan and Knute Smart Sr.

RESIDENCE: Denver, CO

EDUCATION: Hooper Bay (AK) School, 1958; St. Mary's High School, 1959; Mt. Edgecumbe High School, ca. 1961-1962; IAIA

PUBLISHED: Snodgrass (1968)

PUBLIC COLLECTIONS: IAIA

EXHIBITS: IAIA, MNM

CLARA MARY SMART

"Smart has been painting since 1962 and has been encouraged by her instructors to continue. She also writes poetry, another potential career."

Snodgrass 1968

SMILER, ISA (see Smiller, Isa)

SMILLER, ISA *Inuit (Eskimo)*

A.K.A. Isa Smiler

Born 1921; died 1986

RESIDENCE: Lived in Inukjuak, PQ, Canada

OCCUPATION: Carver and painter

MEDIA: Watercolor and soapstone

PUBLISHED: *The Beaver* (autumn 1967)

SMITH, BRAD *Cherokee*

RESIDENCE: Muskogee, OK

EDUCATION: Muskogee (OK) High School, 1993

PUBLISHED: *Cherokee Advocate* (Aug 1993)

AWARDS: Cherokee National Holiday Logo Contest ('92, 1st); Oklahoma Indian Education Art Competition (1st)

HONORS: Oklahoma Indian Education, Dick West Scholarship, 1993

SMITH, CAROL ANN *Chippewa*

Born 5 Nov 1952

RESIDENCE: Minneapolis, MN

EDUCATION: Waller High School, Chicago, IL; Johnson High School, St. Paul, MN; MCAD; U of OK; BSU; Minneapolis (MN) Technical Institute

OCCUPATION: Artist

MEDIA: Oil and charcoal

EXHIBITS: CAI; MIC; OAE; PMA/MN; RC; TI; U of MN/B; Landmark Center, St. Paul, MN; see also Awards

AWARDS: CAI; OAE (1st); RC ('91, Powers Award); Augsburg College, Minneapolis, MN

HONORS: WARM Mentor-Protegee, scholarship, 1984-1985

SMITH, EDISON *Navajo*

EXHIBITS: PAC

SOLO EXHIBITS: WWM

SMITH, ERNEST *Seneca*

Gaon Yah, From The Middle Of The Sky

Born 1907, on the Tonawanda Reservation, NY; died 26 Feb 1975 near Akron, NY; son of Pete Smith; brother of Kidd Smith (q.v.), carver, and Rose Spring, beadwork artist

EDUCATION: Buffalo (NY) Public Schools

OCCUPATION: Illustrator and cultural consultant for author William N. Fenton, sculptor, and painter

MEDIA: Oil, watercolor, pen and ink, wood, and prints

PUBLISHED: LaFarge (1960); Underhill (1965); Snodgrass (1968); Brody (1971); Irvine, ed. (1974); Highwater (1978b); Fawcett and Callander (1982); Archuleta and Strickland (1991); McMasters, et al. (1993). *Bulletin 156*, BAE (1953); *The Conservationist* (Jan/Feb 1976); Calendar, Canadian Indian Marketing Service and RAMAS (1977); *The Indian Trader* (July 1978)

BOOKS PUBLISHED: Books by William N. Fenton and Jeanette Collamer

COMMISSIONS: RMAS, 1935-1941

PUBLIC COLLECTIONS: IACB, SMII, RMAS, SI

EXHIBITS: HM; MAI; RMAS; SV; Albany (NY) Unitarian Society; Everson Museum, Syracuse, NY; First Unitarian Society, Schenectady, NY; Siena College, Londonville, NY

SOLO EXHIBITS: SIM ('75); RMAS (2 shows)

HONORS: Iroquois Conference, first recipient of the Iroquois of the Year Award, 1972

ERNEST SMITH

"The Rochester Democrat and Chronicle *(21 August 1950) reviewed the artist's show at RMAS as follows: '... he has been painting since he was 10... titles of his paintings indicate the wide range of daily life covered by legends and fairy tales of the Senecas... much of his work was produced under the Federal Indian Art Project.'"*

Snodgrass 1968

SMITH, GIBSON R. *Apache/Navajo/Yuma*

RESIDENCE: McNary, AZ

EDUCATION: U of AZ, "Southwest Indian Art Project," scholarship, summers 1961, 1962

PUBLISHED: Snodgrass (1968)

SMITH, JACK (see Dawangyumptewa, David)

SMITH, JANET LAMON *Cherokee*

Nv Tsi (Nancy), One Who Walks About As In Spirit

Born 14 May 1943 in Tahlequah, OK; daughter of Alta Lucille Watt and John Lingan Lamon; P/GP: Mattie E. Clingan and William A. (Cap) Lamon; M/GP: Maude Campbell and Jona S. Watt

RESIDENCE: Broken Arrow, OK

EDUCATION: Okay (OK) High School; B.A., NSU, 1985; M.S., Emporia (KS) State University, 1989; BC, studied under Dick West and Ruthe Blalock Jones (qq.v.)

OCCUPATION: Telephone operator, art teacher, art therapist, counselor, and artist

MEDIA: Oil, acrylic, watercolor, and prints

PUBLISHED: *Twin Territories* (Vol. 3, no.1, 1993)

PUBLIC COLLECTIONS: BC; TTSP; Southwestern Bell Telephone Co., Tulsa, OK; Okay (OK) High School; Pillsbury Corporation, St. Louis, MO

EXHIBITS: BC/McG; CAI/KC; CIM; CNM; FCTM; HM; ITIC; LIAS; MAAIC; MCI; NSU; OSC; RC; RE; TIAF; TTSP; Pamanuke Indian Festival; Babylon, NY; All-Indian Days, Scottsdale, AZ

AWARDS: BC ('83, People's Choice Award); FCTM ('85, IH); NSU ('85, 2-1st)

SMITH, JAUNE QUICK-TO-SEE *Salish/Cree/Shoshoni*

Insightful Awareness

Born 1940 on the Flathead Reservation, MT

RESIDENCE: Corrales, NM

EDUCATION: B.A., Framingham (MA) State College, 1976; M.A., U of NM, 1980

OCCUPATION: Farm hand, waitress, librarian, veterinarian assistant, teacher, critic, lecturer, curator, and painter

MEDIA: Oil, acrylic, pastel, pencil, pen and ink, mixed-media, and prints

PUBLISHED: Highwater (1980; 1983); Amerson, ed. (1981); Hoffman, et al. (1984); Broder (1985); Declue (1985); Wade, ed. (1986); Jacka and Jacka (1988); Archuleta and Strickland (1991); Maurer (1992); Campbell, ed. (1993); Abbott (1994). *SOHO Weekly News* (Nov 1979); *Artspace* (fall 1979; summer 1980); *Art In America* (Mar 1980; Jan 1991; Oct 1991); *Southwest Art* (Apr 1981); *Portfolio* (July 1982); *Art News* (Oct 1983); *Artlines* (Aug 1983), cover; *New York Magazine* (20 June 1983); *People Magazine* (14 Mar 1983); *Arts Magazine* (summer 1984; Jan 1986; Jan 1987); *The Arizona Republic* (24 Feb 1989); *The Albuquerque Journal* (21 June 1985; 26 Aug 1990; 7 June 1992); *New York Daily News* (9 June 1985); *America West* (July 1990); *Santa Fe Reporter* (Aug/Sept 1990); *C Magazine* (summer 1991); *Native People* (winter 1992); *The Indian Trader* (Dec 1992); *Art and Antiques* (Jan 1993)

PUBLIC COLLECTIONS: Partial listing includes: ABQM; AC/RM; BIA; C/U of R; DAM; HM; ISU/B; MIA; MNM; NCGM; NDM; NM; OU/MA; SFCC; SM; SPIM; U of CA/D; WSAC; American Medical Association, Chicago, IL; AT&T Corporate Art Collection; Atlantic Richfield, Los Angeles, CA; Birmingham (AL) Museum of Art; Eastern New Mexico State University; Flathead Indian Reservation, Pablo, MT; Framingham (MA) State College Art Museum; Mount Holyoke Art Museum, South Hadley, NY; Phillips Collection, Washington, D.C.; Phillips Petroleum, NY; Prudential Insurance Company of America; Stamford (CT) Museum; Steinberg Museum, St. Louis, MO; The Museum of Mankind, Vienna, Austria

EXHIBITS: Partial listing of more than one hundred includes: ABQM; AC/K; AC/RM; AC/Y; AICA/SF; AICH; BBHC; BM/B; BRMA; C/ACA; C/BCA; C/U of R/MG; C/BCA; CCDLR; CGA; CTC; CWAM; FSMCIAF; FWMA; HM; HS/OK; IK; KCPA; MIA; MM/NJ; MMA; MMA/WA; MSW; NACLA; NU/BC; OSU/G; PAC; PAM; SFFA; SFMA; SI; SPIM; SUNY/O; SUNY/PT; SV; SWSE; TMA/AZ; TPAS; U of NE; U of NM/MM; VP; WIB; WSCS; WWM; Aldrich Museum of Contemporary Art, Ridgefield, CT; Aspen (CO) Center for the Arts; Fort Wayne (IN) Museum of Art; Galleria d'Arte l'Argentario, Trento, Italy; Massachusetts College of Art, Boston, MA; Museo de Arte Contemporáneo de Monterrey, Mexico; Ohio State University, Columbus, OH; Palo Alto (CA) Cultural Center; San Diego (CA) State University Art

JAUNE QUICK-TO-SEE SMITH

The list of Smith's accomplishments and activities in support of Native American art is extensive. She serves on numerous Indian art-related boards, curates a long list of exhibits, frequently serves as a juror in art competitions, lectures in universities throughout the United States, and serves as a trustee for several important Indian art organizations. In addition, she has founded, and is the curator of exhibits for the Indian artist co-operatives, Coup Marks Coop and Grey Canyon Artists. In addition to all these activities, Smith continues to be at the forefront of contemporary Native American art and produces abstract works of art that express the vital concerns of the Native American community.

Gallery; Scottish Arts Council, Edinburgh, Scotland; Stamford (CT) Museum and Nature Center; Tampa (FL) Museum of Art; Cuenca (Ecuador) International Biennial of Painting, 1994

SOLO EXHIBITS: Partial listing of more than 34 includes: AC/Y; MMA/MT; MSU; NDM; U of CA/LB; U of MO; Lawrence (KS) Art Center; North Dakota Arts Council and NEA touring exhibit; University of Pittsburgh, PA; Washington State Arts Commission Tour; galleries in AZ, ND, NM, NY, and Italy

HONORS: The Academy of Arts and Letters, NY, Purchase Award; Western States Art Foundation, Fellowship Award, 1988; Washington University, St. Louis, MO, Honorary Professor, Beaumont Chair, 1989; The Association of American Cultures Arts Service Award, 1990; MCAD, Honorary Doctorate, 1992

SMITH, JERRY *Inuit (Eskimo)*

RESIDENCE: Canada

OCCUPATION: Graphic artist

PUBLISHED: Hall, Blackman, and Rickard (1981)

SMITH, JOHN A. *Creek*

EXHIBITS: FCTM

AWARDS: FCTM ('81; '82, IH; '84; '85, IH)

SMITH, JOHNNY *Eskimo*

Donvirak

RESIDENCE: Hopper Bay, AK

PUBLISHED: Snodgrass (1968)

EXHIBITS: MNM

AWARDS: MNM

SMITH, KEVIN WARREN *Cherokee*

Oo Ska Ses Dee

Born 7 Dec 1958

RESIDENCE: Tulsa, OK

EDUCATION: Jenks (OK) High School, 1977; B.A., NSU, 1991; ASL, summer 1990; Certificate of Art, BC, 1991

OCCUPATION: Lecturer, art instructor, Native American art and culture consultant, museum curator of education, and artist

MEDIA: Oil, acrylic, watercolor, gouache, pencil, pen and ink, mixed-media, and prints

PUBLISHED: *Muskogee Phoenix* (24 May 1992); *Publisher's Weekly* (16 Nov 1992)

BOOKS PUBLISHED: Turner Publishing, Atlanta, GA; VIP Publishing, Springdale, AR

COMMISSIONS: *Murals:* BC, administration building

PUBLIC COLLECTIONS: BC; HCC; W. W. Hastings Indian Hospital, Tahlequah,OK; U of OK Health Sciences Center, Oklahoma City, OK

EXHIBITS: AICH; BC; CNM; FCTM; HCC; LGAM; LIAS; NSU; PAC; RC; TM/NE; TWF; Phi Theta Kappa National Convention Art Show, Chicago, IL; Center For Tribal Studies, Tahlequah, OK, 1992; University of Maryland, College Park, MD, 1992; NSU Quincentenary Exhibition, 1992; Amnesty International Native American Art Exhibition, Tulsa, OK, 1993; see also Awards

AWARDS: BC ('89, Best of Show; '90); FCTM ('92, Cecil Dick Award); RC ('89); Willard Stone Memorial Art Show, Locust Grove, OK ('88); BC, President's Christmas Card Contest, ('88, 1st); Central Baptist Theological Seminary Logo Design Competition, Kansas City, KS (1st); American Red Cross Indian Art Exhibition, Tulsa, OK ('92)

HONORS: *Scholarships:* Forrest Gresham Memorial Art Scholarship, Muskogee, OK; RC, Thunderbird Foundation Scholarship, 1989-1992; BC, Irene Horton Indian Art Scholarship, 1990. *Other:* BC, Division of Humanities Award, 1989

SMITH, KIDD *Seneca*

Birth date unknown; brother of Ernest Smith (q.v.)

PUBLIC COLLECTIONS: RMAS

SMITH, O. J. *Omaha*

Happy Faces

RESIDENCE: Harrison, AR

EXHIBITS: CNM; see also Awards

AWARDS: CNM ('88, 1st); Oklahoma Wildlife Festival, Tulsa, OK ('85, 1st); Mayfair Festival, Norman, OK (1st); Missouri Spring Festival of Art, St. Louis, MO (Award of Excellence); World Leather Painting Competition, Fort Worth, TX (1st)

SMITH, PATRONELLA *Quechan*

RESIDENCE: Winterhaven, CA

EDUCATION: Santa Fe, 1960-1961; IAIA, 1962-1963; U of AZ, "Southwest Indian Art Project," scholarship

PUBLISHED: Snodgrass (1968)

EXHIBITS: MNM

SMOKY, LOIS *Kiowa*

Bougetah (and *Bougeta, Boudetah*), Of The Dawn

A.K.A. Bougetah Smoky; Louise Smoky. Signature: Lois Smokey; Lois Smoky; Bou-Ge-Tah Smoky

Born 1907 near Anadarko, OK; died 1 Feb 1981; daughter of Enoch Smoky; Great nephew of Chief Appiatan (Kiowa)

RESIDENCE: Lived in Virden, OK

EDUCATION: Oklahoma Indian schools; non-credit instruction, U of OK, 1927

OCCUPATION: Painter, wife, and mother

PUBLISHED: Jacobson (1929); Jacobson and d'Ucel (1950); Blue Eagle (1959); Dunn (1968); Snodgrass (1968); Highwater (1976); Broder (1981); Williams, ed. (1990); Archuleta and Strickland (1991)

PUBLIC COLLECTIONS: GM, MAI, MKMcNAI, MRFM, PAC

EXHIBITS: AIE/T, GM, HM, MKMcNAI, NAP, OU/MA/T, SV; throughout the U.S. with the Five Kiowa exhibits

HONORS: IACB, Certificate of Appreciation, 1966

LOIS SMOKY

"Smoky was one of the Five Kiowas (q.v.) who received special art training at the University of Oklahoma. It has long been customary among the Plains Indians that women not draw or paint in a representational style. Because of this feeling, Smoky fought some resentment on the part of the Kiowa group at the University. Although her family, renowned as warriors, became well-known as craftsmen, Smoky's art career was brief. She married and devoted herself fulltime to her husband and family."

Snodgrass 1968

Smoky was at the University of Oklahoma for a short time; when she dropped out of class, her place was taken by James Auchiah, who therefore became one of the Five Kiowas. She is all-too-often overlooked when the "Five Kiowa artists" are mentioned; she had talent that was never allowed to blossom. There were actually six artists involved in the experiment.

Dockstader, p.c. 1994

SMOKY, LOUISE (see Smoky, Lois)

SNAKE (see Outie, George)

SNAKE, STEVEN *Shawnee*

Moneto, Divine Wind

A.K.A. Steven Ray Snake

Born 31 Mar 1966 in Norman, OK; son of Jennie and Amos Snake; P/GP: Nellie McCoy and Luther Snake-man; M/GP: Lizzie Ellis and Thomas Bullfrog Mohawk; Artist is a direct descendant of Tecumseh.

RESIDENCE: Cushing, OK

EDUCATION: Cushing (OK) High School, 1980-1984; B.A., OSU, 1992

OCCUPATION: Actor and artist

MEDIA: Oil, watercolor, pencil, pen and ink, and pastel

EXHIBITS: BB; CIM; area exhibits; see also Awards
AWARDS: CIM ('87); American Indian Perspective Show, Norman, OK ('88, 1st)

SN'KS (see Gibson, Gordon Philip, Jr.)

SNOW (see Suina, Theodore)

SNOW, CAROL *Seneca*

Birth date unknown; born on the Allegany Indian Reservation, NY; descendant of Hiakatoo, Seneca chief
RESIDENCE: Taos, NM
EDUCATION: Salamanca (NY) High School, 1960; B.S., Zoology, Syracuse University; M.S., U of WY, 1968
OCCUPATION: Full-time artist since 1973
MEDIA: Acrylic, pen and ink, and prints
PUBLISIIED: *The Indian Trader* (Dec 1993); *Newsletter,* IACA (Nov/Dec 1993)
BOOKS ILLUSTRATED: BIA, publications on rare and endangered species
COMMISSIONS: Wintercount, New Castle, CO, paintings
PUBLIC COLLECTIONS: HCC
EXHIBITS: ACAI, HCC, IACA, RC
AWARDS: ACAI ('93, Best of Class); IACA ('93, Best of Category); RC ('82, 1st; '87, 1st)
HONORS: IACA, Artist of the Year, 1994

CAROL SNOW

According to Snow, "I think more than anything what I hope happens with my paintings is some measure of success in communicating to human beings that we really are connected to everything — that it is a great truth and not just some catchy phrase. What we do to the Earth and all her residents we truly are doing to ourselves as well." The artist is best known for her nature paintings, especially of animals.
The Indian Trader, *Dec 1993*

SNOW CARRY (see Nuvayouma, Arlo)

SNOW CARRY (see Saufkie, Morgan)

SNOWMAN (see Yellow Owl, Anthony)

SNYDER, JIM *Mohawk*

RESIDENCE: Canada
PUBLISHED: *Newsletter,* NASAC/ACEAA (winter 1991)
EXHIBITS: C/AMO

SNYDER, KIM *Shoshoni*

Born 5 June 1942 at Fort Washakie, WY, on the Wind River Indian Reservation
MILITARY: Wyoming National Guard
EDUCATION: Dubois (WY) High School, 1960; U of WY; Casper (WY) College, 1966-1967; A.A., CWC/WY, 1970; B.A., Idaho State University, Pocatello, ID, 1974
PUBLIC COLLECTIONS: CWC/WY
EXHIBITS: CWC/WY; U of ID; Columbia Basin College, Pasco, WA; Dubois (WY) Public Library; Dubois (WY) Medical Clinic; Wind River Valley National Art Exhibit, Lander, WY; area exhibits
SOLO EXHIBITS: MPI

KIM SNYDER

Using a blend of abstraction and realism, Snyder paints Indian myths and legends.

brochure, MPI, 1975

SOARING EAGLE *Cheyenne*

Ume-Ha-Tse
Born 1854; died 1887
EDUCATION: Hampton, 1979
OCCUPATION: Warrior, policeman, and graphic artist
PUBLISHED: Snodgrass (1968)
PUBLIC COLLECTIONS: YU/BRBML
EXHIBITS: BPG

SOARING EAGLE

"The artist was among the 72 Plains Indians taken as prisoners from Fort Sill, OK, to Fort Marion, St. Augustine, FL, in 1875."

Snodgrass 1968

After attending Hampton, Soaring Eagle returned to Indian Territory in 1879.

SOATIKEE, CAROL A. *Apache/Pima*

RESIDENCE: Anadarko, OK
Born 1942 in Phoenix, AZ
EDUCATION: Lawton (OK) High School; Cameron University, Lawton, OK, 1960-1962; B.A., CSU/OK, 1965
OCCUPATION: Teacher and painter
MEDIA: Oil, acrylic, tempera, mixed-media, and pen and ink
PUBLISHED: Irvine, ed. (1974)
PUBLIC COLLECTIONS: SPIM, USDI
EXHIBITS: CNM, CSPIP, HM/G, PAC, SPIM
SOLO EXHIBITS: SPIM
AWARDS: HM/G ('74, 1st); PAC ('76)
HONORS: Kappa Pi Honorary Art Fraternity, membership

SOE KHUWA PIN (see Montoya, Robert B)

SO HAH NEY (see Wilkinson, Douglas)

SO KUVA (see Kewanyouma, Leroy)

SO KWA A WEH (see Peña, José Encarnación)

SOLOMON, FLOYD *Laguna/Zuni*

A.K.A. Floyd R. Solomon
Born 1952 in Albuquerque, NM
EDUCATION: U of NM, 1976-1982; IAIA, 1989-1991
PUBLISHED: Roberts, ed. (1992)
EXHIBITS: NMSF; SS/CW; SWAIA; Invitational Show, Sheraton Hotel, Santa Fe, NM, 1985; White House Conference on Indian Education, Washington, D.C., 1984
AWARDS: NMSF ('83; '84; '85; '87, 1st)
HONORS: New Mexico State Fair Commission, The Best of New Mexico Award, 1984; White House Conference on Indian Education, poster artist, 1992

SON OF MILK (see Begay, Apie)

SON OF THE STAR (see White Bear, Alton)

SON OF THE TOWERING HOUSE PEOPLE (see Gorman, Carl Nelson)

SOONAGROOK, WILLIAM, SR. *Eskimo*

Born 1934 in Nome, AK
RESIDENCE: Gambell, AK, on St. Lawrence Island
EDUCATION: DCTP, 1964-1965
PUBLISHED: Ray (1969)

SOO WOEA (see Humetewa, James Russell, Jr.)

SOQUEEN (see Peña, Christino)

SOQUEEN (see Peña, José Encarnación)

SOQWEEN (see Peña, José Encarnación)

SOROSEELUTU *Inuit (Eskimo)*

A.K.A. Soroseelutu Ashoona; Sorosilutoo; Sorosilutu
Born 1941
RESIDENCE: Cape Dorset, NWT, Canada
OCCUPATION: Graphic artist

MEDIA: Pencil, colored felt tip pen, and prints

PUBLISHED: Goetz, et al. (1977); Collinson (1978); Routledge (1979); Woodhouse (1980). *The Beaver* (spring 1975)

PUBLIC COLLECTIONS: C/WBEC, C/U of AB, DAM

EXHIBITS: C/AG/WP, C/CG, C/IA7, C/SS, C/TIP

SOROSILUTOO (see Soroseelutu)

SOROSILUTU (see Soroseelutu)

SOUKWAWE (see Peña, José Encarnación)

SOULIGNY, ALICE L. *Cherokee/Delaware*

Born 16 July 1931 in Ponca City, OK

RESIDENCE: Ponca City, OK

EDUCATION: Ponca City (OK) High School, 1949; studied under Gene Daugherty and Edgar A. Whitney

OCCUPATION: Painter since 1977

MEDIA: Oil, acrylic, and watercolor

PUBLISHED: *The Indian Trader* (July 1978); *Western Horseman* (Mar 1978); *The Cherokee Advocate* (Apr 1979); *Oklahoma Art Gallery* (summer 1981)

EXHIBITS: AIE; CNM; GM; HM/G; NCHF; OMA; Renaissance West Arts Fair, Denver, CO; galleries in CO, KS, NM, OK, TX, and Washington, D.C.; see also Awards

SOLO EXHIBITS: SPIM

AWARDS: AIE ('77); American Indian Market, Pueblo, CO; area exhibits

HONORS: Colorado State Fair, guest artist, 1977; Sundance Ranch, Provo, UT, guest artist, 1977

ALICE L. SOULIGNY

Souligny paints portraits of Indian people, illustrations of old legends, and re-creations of events from historic and contemporary Native American culture.

brochure, SPIM, 1979

SO WHAY (see Ortiz, Joseph)

SOWLE, WARREN ADLOOAT *Eskimo*

A.K.A. Adlooat; Warren Adlooat

Born ca. 1870s

RESIDENCE: Alaska

PUBLISHED: Ray (1969), back cover. *The Eskimo Bulletin* (Vol. 4, 1898; Vol. 8, 1902)

PUBLIC COLLECTIONS: U of AK

SOZA, BILLY WAR SOLDIER *Cahuilla/Apache*

A.K.A. Billy Soza; War Soldier

Born 1949 in Santa Ana, CA

EDUCATION: Hemet (CA) High School; IAIA High School, 1964-1968; IAIA, 1969

MEDIA: Oil

PUBLISHED: Highwater (1976; 1980); New (1974; 1979); Amerson, ed. (1981). *Native American Arts 2* (1968); *Art News* (Feb 1992)

PUBLIC COLLECTIONS: IAIA

EXHIBITS: AC/T, AICH, CTC, FSM/CFA, FSMCIAF, IAIA, ND, OWE, PAIC

BILLY WAR SOLDIER SOZA

War Soldier was very involved in the Indian activism movement in the 1970s and served eleven months in various federal penal institutions for his activities. His work reflects his concern with contemporary Indian problems.

Highwater 1980

SPA-POOLE (see Marchand, Virgil T.)

SPARROW, SUSAN (see Point, Susan A.)

SPECK, HENRY *Kwakwaka'wakw (Kwakiutl)*

Ozistalis

A.K.A. Chief Henry Speck; The Greatest

Born 12 Aug 1908 on Turnour Island, BC, Canada; died 27 May 1971

EDUCATION: Through 4th grade, Alert Bay, BC, Canada

OCCUPATION: Carver, painter, and printmaker

MEDIA: Watercolor, pen and ink, and wood

PUBLISHED: Snodgrass (1968); Hall, Blackman, and Rickard (1981); Hoffman, et al. (1984); Hawthorne (1988); McMasters, et al. (1993). *Kwakiutl Art By Chief Henry Speck*, New Design Gallery, Vancouver, BC (1964); *Masterkey* (winter 1984)

PUBLIC COLLECTIONS: C/GM, C/RBCM, SM

EXHIBITS: C/GM; C/RBCM; IK; PAC; SM; New Design Gallery, Vancouver, BC

SOLO EXHIBITS: New Design Gallery, Vancouver, BC, 1964

HONORS: Chief of the Tlawitsis (Powerful People), a Kwakwaka'wakw (Kwakiutl) group on Turnour Island, BC

HENRY SPECK

"'My art talent was handed down to me from my mother's father. I just grew up with it. When I was a little boy I used to copy everything from mail order catalogues,' said Speck in 1963. . . . His art forms are seldom used in traditional ceremonies but he recorded them honestly and prolifically."

Snodgrass 1968

SPECK, MARSHALL *Kwakwaka'wakw (Kwakiutl)*

MEDIA: Watercolor and pen and ink

PUBLIC COLLECTIONS: C/GM, C/RBCM

SPECK, TOMMY *Kwakwaka'wakw (Kwakiutl)*

MEDIA: Watercolor and pen and ink

PUBLIC COLLECTIONS: C/GM, C/RBCM

SPECKLED ROCK, PAUL J. *Santa Clara*

RESIDENCE: Española, NM

OCCUPATION: Sculptor and painter

PUBLIC COLLECTIONS: HCC

EXHIBITS: HCC, HM/G, MRFM, RC, WWM

SPENCER, JERI *Yakama*

EDUCATION: BC

PUBLISHED: Snodgrass (1968)

EXHIBITS: DAM, PAC

SPENCER, MARLENE R. *(?)*

PUBLISHED: Snodgrass (1968)

EXHIBITS: MNM

SPENCER, RANDY *Navajo*

EXHIBITS: CNM, ITIC

AWARDS: CNM ('90; '93); ITIC ('89; '94, 1st)

SPICER, THOMAS W. *Seneca/Cayuga*

EXHIBITS: CNM

SPLASHING WATER (see Kishketon, George)

SPOTTED EAGLE BOY, B. J. *Omaha*

EDUCATION: U of NE; U of CO

EXHIBITS: CNM

AWARDS: CNM ('87, 1st)

SPOTTED ELK, LEO *Sioux*

RESIDENCE: St. Francis, SD

PUBLISHED: Snodgrass (1968)

PUBLIC COLLECTIONS: SMNAI

EXHIBITS: PAC

SPOTTED HORSE (see Biss, Earl, Jr.)

SPOTTED HORSE *Oglala (?) Sioux*

Sunkklesha

RESIDENCE: from Pine Ridge Agency, SD (see Black Heart)

PUBLISHED: Snodgrass (1968)

PUBLIC COLLECTIONS: MAI

SPOTTED TAIL *Brûlé Sioux*

Sinte Gleska, Spotted Tail

A.K.A. Jumping Buffalo (in his youth); *Sinte Galeska; Zintalah Galeshka*

Born ca. 1823 along the White River; died 5 Aug 1881 at the Rosebud Agency, Dakota Territory, where he was shot and killed by Crow Dog; son of Walks With The Pipe and Cunka (Tangled Hair)

PUBLISHED: Snodgrass (1968); Dockstader (1977)

PUBLIC COLLECTIONS: MAI (personal exploits of several warriors, painted on elkskin)

HONORS: Selected to be head chief; signed Treaty at Fort Laramie, 29 Apr 1868

SPOTTED TAIL

Although not a hereditary chief, because of his integrity and ability, Spotted Tail was selected to be head chief and later was appointed chief of all the Sioux at Rosebud and Spotted Tail Agencies.

Dockstader 1977

SPRINGTIME (see Polelonema, Otis)

SPYBUCK, ERNEST *Shawnee*

Mahthela

Born 1883 near Tecumseh, IT, on the Potawatomi-Shawnee Reservation; died 1949 at his home west of Shawnee, OK; son of Peahchepeahso and John Spybuck.

EDUCATION: Shawnee (OK) Boarding School; Sacred Heart Mission, south-central Oklahoma

OCCUPATION: Farmer, historical informant, and painter

MEDIA: Oil, watercolor, pencil, and pen and ink

PUBLISHED: Harrington (1921); LaFarge (1956; 1960); Gilstrap (1960); Underhill (1965); Snodgrass (1968); Brody (1971); Irvine, ed. (1974); Dockstader (1977); Silberman (1978); Highwater (1978b); Fawcett and Callander (1982); Callander and Slivka (1984); Archuleta and Strickland (1991). *Indians At Work* (1938)

COMMISSIONS: Murals

PUBLIC COLLECTIONS: CCHM, GM, HM, HSM, OK, MAI, OMA, OSAF/GC

EXHIBITS: AIEC, HM, HSM/OK, MAI, OMA, SV

ERNEST SPYBUCK

"Spybuck never studied art, but painted from the age of six. Harriet Patrick Gilstrap, his teacher at Shawnee, mentioned him in her memoirs and said that when he was eight, he did nothing but draw and paint pictures recounting events in his life. In 1937, it was noted that he had never been out of the county of his birth. He is buried in the family burial ground near his home."

Snodgrass 1968

M. R. Harrington, anthropologist and collector who commissioned twenty-seven paintings, is credited with encouraging Spybuck and bringing his talent to its full expression. Spybuck is known for his somewhat primitive, realistic paintings of Shawnee life eighty years ago. He developed his own style and perspective.

Callander and Slivka 1984

His nephew, Thurman Spybuck, a Tulsa, OK, police officer, was killed in the line of duty.

SQUINT EYES *Cheyenne*

Tichkematse

A.K.A. John Squint Eyes; Tich-ke-matse

Born 1857; died 1932

MILITARY: U.S. Army

EDUCATION: Hampton

OCCUPATION: Warrior, Smithsonian Institution employee, scout, policeman, landowner, farmer, and painter

MEDIA: Watercolor and pen and ink

PUBLISHED: Dunn (1968); Snodgrass (1968). *American Indian Art* (winter 1992)

PUBLIC COLLECTIONS: Hampton, SI/OAA, YU/BRBML

EXHIBITS: BPG

SQUIRE, MIKE *Creek/Seminole*

EXHIBITS: CNM

STACY, RICHARD D. *Creek*

Birth date unknown, in Okmulgee, OK

RESIDENCE: Okmulgee, OK

EDUCATION: Okmulgee (OK) High School; UT, Austin, TX

OCCUPATION: Student in 1976

EXHIBITS: PAC

AWARDS: PAC ('76)

STALKIA, JANE *Interior Salish*

MEDIA: Watercolor and gouache

PUBLIC COLLECTIONS: C/RBCM

STANDING, WILLIAM *Assiniboin*

Fire Bear; Looks In The Clouds

Born 27 July 1904 near Oswego, MT; died 27 June 1951 on Fort Belknap (MT) Indian Reservation in an automobile accident; son of Stephen Standing (Standing Rattle); M/uncle: Lance, Sioux medicine lodge painter

EDUCATION: Wolf Point (MT) Presbyterian Mission; Haskell, 1920-1924

OCCUPATION: Artist

MEDIA: Oil, watercolor, pen and ink, and pencil

PUBLISHED: Snodgrass (1968); Brody (1971); Ray (1972)

BOOKS PUBLISHED: First Boy (1942); Kennedy (1961)

COMMISSIONS: Montana Federal Art Program, illustrations, 1930s

PUBLIC COLLECTIONS: CGPS

EXHIBITS: CIA; MPI; Washington (DC) Art Club; Colonial Exposition, Paris, France, 1931; WPA Art Center, Great Falls, MT; galleries in CO, ID, and OK

SOLO EXHIBITS: HSM/MT

STANDING ALONE (see Dick, Cecil)

STANDING ALONE, HENRY *Blackfoot*

Niitsitaipoyi

Born 1935 in Cardston, AB, Canada

RESIDENCE: Glenwood, AB, Canada

OCCUPATION: Artist

MEDIA: Pen and ink, wash, and mixed-media

PUBLISHED: Cardinal-Schubert (1992)

COMMISSIONS: Magazine covers and book illustrations

PUBLIC COLLECTIONS: Frank and Associates, Calgary, AB; International Canadian Embassies

EXHIBITS: C/IFNA; C/TFD; C/TGVA; Universiade Convention Centre, Edmonton, AB

STANDING BEAR (see Byrnes, James Michael)

STANDING BEAR (see Standingbear, George Eugene)

STANDING BEAR *Miniconjou Sioux*

Mato Najin

Born Dec 1868; died 1933

MEDIA: Graphite pencil and colored pencils

PUBLISHED: Standing Bear (1928); Neihardt (1932); Hamilton (1950); Snodgrass (1968); Maurer (1992)

PUBLIC COLLECTIONS: DAM (tipi, signed Standing Bear), MNH/A (?), MPM; St.

SQUINT EYES

"The artist was among the 72 Plains Indians taken as prisoners from Fort Sill, OK, to Fort Marion, St. Augustine, FL, in 1875."

Snodgrass 1968

After attending Hampton Institute, Squint Eyes worked for the Smithsonian Institution for whom, after learning taxidermy, he collected birds on the Cheyenne reservation. He later enlisted in the U.S. Army at Fort Supply as a scout.

WILLIAM STANDING

"Through his paternal lineage, the artist's direct ancestor is Iron Arrow Point, Chief of the Stone Band during the Revolutionary War, and whose son, In-the-Light (Azan Zan Na) was the first Assiniboin ambassador from Fort Union to visit the capitol, 1831-1832. '... In the White man's custom I am William Standing after the first name of my father. My father called me Looks In The Clouds. My own choice of names is Fire Bear: this was my grandmother's name ... it makes no difference to me. If people want me to sign a name on pictures in White man's way and buy more pictures, that is alright. But I'd rather be Fire Bear ... I like to do what is called an independent artist and draw and paint what I see.' After completing high school, the artist traveled extensively throughout the U.S. exhibiting his oils, watercolors, and sketches. He returned to the reservation where he married and remained until his death."

Snodgrass 1968

Joseph (MO) Museum; Foundation for the Preservation of American Indian Art and Cultures, Inc., Chicago, IL

EXHIBITS: VP

STANDINGBEAR, EUGENE GEORGE *Oglala Sioux*

Born 7 Mar 1905 in Pine Ridge, SD; died 11 July 1980 in Greeley, CO; father of George Eugene Standingbear (q.v.)

OCCUPATION: Draftsman, dancer, musician, actor, and artist

MEDIA: Oil, watercolor, charcoal, pencil, and colored sand

STANDINGBEAR, GEORGE EUGENE *Osage/Sioux*

Zshingka Heka, Little Chief (Osage name); *Mahtohn Ahzshe,* Standing Bear (Sioux name)

Born 31 Oct 1929 in Pawhuska, OK; died 16 June 1974; son of Mary Nora Lookout and Eugene George Standingbear (q.v.); M/GP: Julia Ann Mongre and Fred Lookout, last hereditary chief of the Osage; P/GGM: the sister of American Horse; P/GGF: Standing Bear (Mahtohn Ahzshe); M/GGGF: Nathaniel Pryor, member of the Lewis and Clark Expedition and the person for whom the city of Pryor, OK, is named

RESIDENCE: Lived in Tulsa, OK

EDUCATION: Pawhuska (OK) High School, 1947; B.A., U of Tulsa, 1952; graduate work, U of Tulsa

OCCUPATION: Technical editor, illustrator and analyst; fencing and art instructor; painter

PUBLISHED: Snodgrass (1968); Brody (1971)

COMMISSIONS: *Murals:* Catholic Information Center, Tulsa, OK. *Other:* Tulsa (OK) Charity Horse Show, posters and publicity brochure, 1964

EXHIBITS: PAC; University of Tulsa, OK; see also Awards

SOLO EXHIBITS: Benedictine Heights College, Tulsa, OK

AWARDS: Tulsa Fine Arts Festival ('64, Grand Award)

HONORS: Tulsa Philharmonic Cinderella Ball, art director

STANDING BUFFALO *Ponca*

Totay Gonai, Standing Buffalo

PUBLISHED: Snodgrass (1968). *Bulletin 195,* BAE (1965), copy of a drawing, by a young warrior, showing a battle between the Ponca and the Sioux

STANDING CHIEF, ROBERT *Cree*

RESIDENCE: Belcourt, ND

PUBLISHED: Snodgrass (1968)

EXHIBITS: BNIAS

STANDING DEER (see Blue Spruce)

STANDING LEAF *(?)*

PUBLISHED: Snodgrass (1968)

PUBLIC COLLECTIONS: DAC

STANDING RAINBOW (see Preston, Bert)

STANDING SOLDIER, ANDREW *Oglala Sioux*

Born Feb 1917 near Hisle, SD, on the Pine Ridge Reservation; died 12 Mar 1967 in Omaha, NE; son of Julia Fast Wolf and Elk Standing Soldier

RESIDENCE: Lived on the Pine Ridge Reservation, SD

EDUCATION: Oglala Community High School, Pine Ridge, SD; studied mural technique and fresco application with Olaf Nordmark, 1937

STANDING BEAR

"A leader among the Sioux and an ancestor of Arthur Douglas Amiotte (q.v.), Standing Bear was well known as an illustrator and storyteller."

Snodgrass 1968

EUGENE GEORGE STANDINGBEAR

The actor/artist performed in such television series as Chishom II *with Robert Preston, and* Grizzly Adams *with Dan Haggerty. Standing Bear was a self-taught painter who developed a unique method in which he affixed colored sands to paper and drawing boards.*

GEORGE EUGENE STANDINGBEAR

The artist was given his Osage name by Chief Bacon Rind (Osage) when he became an official member of the Bear Clan.

Snodgrass 1968

OCCUPATION: Commercial sign painter, muralist, illustrator, and artist

MEDIA: Oil, watercolor, tempera, gouache, casein, and pen and ink

PUBLISHED: Clark (1954); Snodgrass (1968); Libhart (1970); Wade, ed. (1986); Day and Simon, et al. (1990). *Compton's Pictured Encyclopedia* (Vol. 7, 1957); *The Rapid City Journal* (3 Dec 1990)

BOOKS PUBLISHED: Clark (n.d.; 1940c; 1942a; 1942b; 1943b; 1944; 1947)

COMMISSIONS: *Murals:* American Horse Day School, Allen, SD; BIA School, Standing Rock, ND; Oglala Community High School, auditorium, Pine Ridge Reservation, SD; Standing Rock Reservation, Fort Yates, ND; U.S. Post Offices, Blackfoot, ID, and Valentine, NE

PUBLIC COLLECTIONS: BIA/SD, CGPS, HCC, IACB, SIM, SM

EXHIBITS: CPS, HCC, SIM

SOLO EXHIBITS: HCC, U of NC/OM

AWARDS: SFWF

Andrew Standing Soldier

Standing Soldier was the youngest of eight children and grew up on a ranch on the Pine Ridge Reservation helping his father and older family members with the ranch work. He painted subjects that he knew well: the Indian family, cowboys, and ranchers of his time. He did not participate in art shows because very few existed at that time for Western or Indian artists and he wasn't interested in winning awards. He painted not for himself but for the pleasure of others.

Day and Simon, et al. 1990

Standridge, WA (see Greene, Wanda Annette)

Stands Brown (see Pahsetopah, Loren Louis)

Starr, Diane *Cherokee*

A.K.A. Diane Star Gibson

Born 19 May 1939

RESIDENCE: Witter, AR

EXHIBITS: CNM; FCTM; RC; John Brown University Art Show, Siloam Springs, AR; Southeast Art Show, El Dorado, AR

AWARDS: FCTM ('76, 1st)

Starr, Neil *Chippewa*

RESIDENCE: Milwaukee, WI

EXHIBITS: ITAE/M

Starr, Terry *Creek*

EXHIBITS: FCTM

AWARDS: FCTM ('77, 1st; '78, 1st)

Starr, Terry *Tsimshian*

RESIDENCE: Victoria, BC, Canada

EXHIBITS: C/INV

Steinsiek, Tommy *Creek/Cherokee*

A.K.A. Mrs. Carl Steinsiek

Born 26 Mar 1953

RESIDENCE: Okmulgee, OK

EDUCATION: Morris (OK) High School; EOSC; Tulsa (OK) Business College

OCCUPATION: Commercial artist, art teacher, illustrator, museum curator, pet boutique and art gallery owner, and painter

PUBLISHED: *The Muskogee Phoenix* (17 Oct 1982); *Intertribal* (Sept 1990); *The Tulsa World* (24 Apr 1994)

COMMISSIONS: *Illustrations:* American Diabetes Association, brochure; *The Folklore of the Muscogee (Creek) People* (educational video), film illustrations. *Logos:* Creek Nation Head Start Program; Oklahoma Indian Council on Aging

EXHIBITS: BC; CNM; FCTM; IS; RC; Checotah (OK) Art Guild Show; Henryetta (OK) Art Guild Show

AWARDS: BC ('78); FCTM ('80; '81, IH; '82; '84, IH; '85; '86, IH; '87; '88, IH)

Tommy Steinsiek

"I always want to portray a warm and loving bond in my people subjects and show the love of God in His careful creation of wildlife."

artist, p.c. 1990

STEPHENS, DAVID *Cherokee*

RESIDENCE: Tahlequah, OK
EDUCATION: BC
OCCUPATION: Painter
PUBLISHED: *Tulsa World* (12 July 1983)
EXHIBITS: CNM, FCTM, MPABAS, OIAP, PAC
AWARDS: FCTM ('72, IH; '73; '75, Needlepoint Guild Award; '82)

DAVID STEPHENS

Stephens credits his wife and his father-in-law, William C. Glory, the last full blood Cherokee chief of the Keetoowah Society, with being the greatest influences on his art. They taught him about the way things used to be. He paints in the traditional flat style and depicts the ancient Cherokee way of life.

Tulsa World, *12 July 1993*

STEPHENS, VERNON *Tsimshian*

Born 1949
RESIDENCE: Hazelton, BC, Canada
OCCUPATION: Teacher, carver, graphic artist, and painter
PUBLISHED: Stewart (1979); Macnair, Hoover, and Neary (1980); Hall, Blackman, and Rickard (1981)
BOOKS PUBLISHED: Kitanmax School (1977)
EXHIBITS: C/TL

VERNON STEPHENS

A talented carver, Stephens prefers painting and working on murals. Using a unique approach, Stephens adapts traditional elements of two-dimensional design to produce non-traditional, realistic silhouettes of animal and human figures. He was the first of the 'Ksan-trained artists to do so, and his influence is seen in the work of other artists from this area.

Hall, Blackman, and Rickard 1981

STERNE, MABLE *Zuni*

PUBLISHED: Snodgrass (1968)
PUBLIC COLLECTIONS: MNM

STERRITT, ART *Tsimshian*

A.K.A. Arthur Sterrit
Born 1945 in Hazelton, BC, Canada
RESIDENCE: Canada
OCCUPATION: Carver, jeweler, and graphic artist
PUBLISHED: Steltzen (1976); Stewart (1979). *The Native Perspective* (Vol. 3, no. 2, 1978)
PUBLIC COLLECTIONS: C/INAC
EXHIBITS: C/CMC, C/INAC, C/VCM

STEVENS, ABRAHAM *Ojibwa*

MEDIA: Pen and ink
EXHIBITS: C/ROM

STEVENS, JIM *Apache*

A.K.A. Sun Cloud
Born 1937 in Globe, AZ, near the San Carlos Reservation; died 7 Dec 1991
RESIDENCE: Lived in Coolidge, AZ
EDUCATION: St. John's; IAIA
OCCUPATION: Farmer and painter
PUBLISHED: Snodgrass (1968). *Arizona Highways* (Oct 1963)
COMMISSIONS: *Murals:* Twenty murals in six Arizona missions
PUBLIC COLLECTIONS: HM, IAIA
EXHIBITS: IAIA

JIM STEVENS

"While in the 5th grade, the artist executed a painting, the face of a crowned and bleeding Christ, which is preserved at St. Peter's Mission in Bapchule Brophy Preparatory College, Phoenix, AZ. To finance his education, the artist maintained various jobs, and had little time to paint . . . "

Snodgrass 1968

STEVENS, LEROY *Navajo*

RESIDENCE: Crystal, AZ
PUBLISHED: Snodgrass (1968)
PUBLIC COLLECTIONS: BIA, IACB, SMNAI
EXHIBITS: USDS

STEWART, ALBERT *Navajo*

EDUCATION: Fort Sill

PUBLISHED: Snodgrass (1968). *Arizona Highways* (July 1956)
EXHIBITS: PAC

STEWART, BRENDA BURNHAM *Iroquois*

RESIDENCE: Aurora, IL
EDUCATION: B.A., BYU, 1980; M.Ed., BYU, 1986; Northern Illinois University, DeKalb, IL
OCCUPATION: Museum researcher and interpreter, teacher, and painter
PUBLISHED: Biographical publications
COMMISSIONS: José Solis, Fox Valley, IL, historical portrait
EXHIBITS: RC; Rocky Mountain Print Show, 1983; Salt Lake City (UT) Art Center, Annual Statewide Exhibition, 1981
SOLO EXHIBITS: Blackberry Historical Farm and Museum, Aurora, IL
AWARDS: RC ('80, 1st)
HONORS: American Indian Scholarships, Albuquerque, NM, 1982-1984; State of Illinois, Illinois Consortium Educational Opportunity Grant, 1989

STEWART, FRANKLIN *Navajo*

PUBLIC COLLECTIONS: MNA

STEWART, KATHRYN *Crow/Blackfeet*

Carries The Colors
A.K.A. Kathie Stewart
Born 25 June 1951 in Livermore, CA; daughter of Minnie Cobell and Grover Stewart; sister of Susan Stewart (q.v.); P/GP: Kate Yarlott and David Stewart; M/GP: Verna White and John Cobell
EDUCATION: Joel E. Ferris High School, Spokane, WA, 1969; EMC; U of NV, 1970-1972; B.A., Mills College, Oakland, CA, 1974; M.A., U of MT, 1984
OCCUPATION: Teacher, resource specialist, educational advisor, administrative coordinator, and artist
MEDIA: Oil, crayon, and colored pencil
PUBLISHED: Anonymous (1976); Roberts, ed. (1992). *Phoenix Magazine* (Sept 1989)
EXHIBITS: AC/T; AICA/SF; CNGM; FSMCFA; HCCC; KCPA; MMA/MT; NAVAM; OLO; SCG; SM; SNMA; SS/CW; SW; U of NV; Beall Park Art Center, Bozeman, MT; Bismarck (ND) Museum of Art; Cambridge (MA) Multi-cultural Arts Center; Dallas (TX) Summer Arts Festival; Marin County Civic Center, San Rafael, CA; Oakland (CA) Art Festival; San Rafael, CA; Petrified Forest Museum, AZ, 1977; Tempe (AZ) Art Center; galleries in Montana and Washington
SOLO/SPECIAL EXHIBITS: MPI (dual show)

STEWART, PAT *Cherokee*

RESIDENCE: Springdale, AR
MEDIA: Oil, pen and ink, bronze, clay, and prints
EXHIBITS: CNM, LIAS/M, RC, RE
AWARDS: CNM ('91)

STEWART, PATRICIA J. GILLIAM *Cherokee*

OCCUPATION: Painter and sculptor
MEDIA: Pen and ink and clay
EXHIBITS: CNM, FCTM
AWARDS: FCTM ('94)

STEWART, RICHARD *Paiute*

Born 1944 in Bishop, CA

PUBLISHED: Snodgrass (1968)

EXHIBITS: SAIEAIP, MNM

STEWART, SUSAN *Crow/Blackfeet*

Esh-Ba'-E-Loua-It-Chay, Her Colors Are Good

Born 22 May 1953 in Livermore, CA; daughter of Minnie Cobell and Grover Stewart; sister of Kathryn Stewart (q.v.); P/GP: Kate Yarlott and David Stewart; M/GP: Verna White and John Cobell

RESIDENCE: Bozeman, MT

EDUCATION: Proctor Hug High School, Reno, NV, 1971; CCAC, 1974; B.A., U of MT, 1981

OCCUPATION: Teacher, clothing store manager, and painter

MEDIA: Oil, acrylic, pastel, and prints

PUBLISHED: Anonymous (1976); Stewart (1988); Roberts, ed. (1992); Abbott (1994). *The Indian Trader* (Feb 1978); *Phoenix Magazine* (Sept 1989)

PUBLIC COLLECTIONS: MPI, NDM

EXHIBITS: AC/T; AC/Y; AICA/SF; AICH; CCAC; CCDLR; CNGM; FSMCFA; HCCC; KCPA; MPI; MR; NAVAM; NDM; OLO; RCGM; SCG; SFMA; SI; SM; SNMA; SS/CW; SW; TMINR; U of MT; U of WI; WW; Beall Park Art Center, Bozeman, MT; Custer County Art Center, Miles City, MT; Marin County Civic Center, San Rafael, CA, 1975; Petrified Forest Museum, AZ, 1977; Touchstone Art Center, Spokane, WA, 1984; galleries in MA, MT, and WA

SOLO/SPECIAL EXHIBITS: AICA/SF, MPI (dual show)

HONORS: *Scholarships and Fellowships:* Max C. Fleishmann Foundation; Crow Tribal Council. *Other:* Phi Kappa Phi Honor Society; ATLATL, Second Circle Regional Board Of Directors; Montana Indian Arts and Cultural Association Board of Directors, president

STIMONE (see Herrera, Justino)

STO KO WO (see Packer)

STONE, GERALD *Seminole/Cherokee*

RESIDENCE: California

MEDIA: Oil, acrylic, and watercolor

PUBLIC COLLECTIONS: GM

EXHIBITS: CNM, FCTM, PAC, RE, SN

AWARDS: FCTM ('86, IH; '87); RE ('87, 1st); SN ('67)

STONE, JOAN *Cherokee*

EXHIBITS: FCTM, PAC

AWARDS: FCTM ('67; '78, Needlepoint Guild Award)

STONE, LELANI *Cherokee*

A.K.A. Lelani Faye Stone

Born 11 Aug 1947; daughter of Carol Lee Johnson and C. A. Fuller; P/GP: Faye Flora Hargrove and Clyde Roy Fuller; M/GP: Fern Ester Daisey Edwards and Henry Lee Johnson; daughter-in-law of Willard Stone (q.v.)

RESIDENCE: Locust Grove, OK

EDUCATION: Pryor (OK) High School, 1965; Northeast Area Vocational College, Pryor, OK, 1973; El Paso (TX) Community College, 1981; studied under Carol Fuller

OCCUPATION: Nurse and painter

MEDIA: Acrylic, watercolor, pencil, pen and ink, pastel, and prints
EXHIBITS: CNM, FCTM, RC, TIAF; see also Awards
AWARDS: Eastern Trails Art Association Exhibition ('88)

STONE, WILLARD *Cherokee*

Ne-ah-yah, Rock

Born 29 Feb 1916 in Oktaha, OK; died 5 Mar 1985; son of Lyda Blanche Headrick and George Stone

RESIDENCE: Lived in Locust Grove, OK

EDUCATION: Oktaha (OK) public schools; BC; studied drawing under Acee Blue Eagle and Woody Crumbo (qq.v.)

OCCUPATION: Sharecropper, odd jobs, ornamental iron pattern maker, aircraft dye maker; full-time sculptor after 1962

MEDIA: Pencil, colored pencil, pen and ink, wood, and bronze

PUBLISHED: *Oklahoma Art Gallery* (fall 1980); *Southwest Art* (Oct 1991)

BOOKS PUBLISHED: Gregory and Strickland (1969)

COMMISSIONS: *Sculptures:* Will Rogers Memorial Commission, 1964; National Hall of Fame for Famous American Indians, Anadarko, OK, 1964; Oklahoma Historical Society, 1965; National Cowboy Hall of Fame, 1966. *Other:* FCTM, Grand Award medallion, 1967

PUBLIC COLLECTIONS: CNM, FCTM, GM, NCHF, SI, USDI

EXHIBITS: CNM, FCTM, GM, SI

SOLO EXHIBITS: GM, SPIM

AWARDS: FCTM ('67, 1st, Grand Award; '68, 1st, Grand Award, IH; '69, 1st; '70, 1st; '72, 1st); FCTM/M ('74, Grand Award, IH; '75, Grand Award, Jerome Tiger Award; '78, Grand Award; '79, 1st; '80, 1st)

HONORS: Gilcrease Art Museum, artist-in-residence, 1948-1951; IACB, Certificate of Appreciation, 1966; Council of American Indians, Tulsa, OK, Outstanding Indian Award, 1969; Oklahoma Hall of Fame, 1970; PAC, Waite Phillips Award, 1971; Bacone College, honorary degree, ca. 1972; FCTM, designated a Master Artist, 1973; Oklahoma Christian College, Oklahoma City, OK, American Citizenship Center, Distinguished American Citizen, 1974; People of Locust Grove (OK), Citizen of the Year, 1976; Oklahoma Christian College, Oklahoma City, OK, Doctor of Humanities Degree, 1976

WILLARD STONE

Although known principally as a sculptor, Stone usually produced pencil drawings of his proposed sculpture, prior to beginning work in wood or clay. He also produced a few drawings for friends, but the loss of portions of his right thumb and two fingers as a young teenager limited his development as a painter. It was only later that his talent for sculpting was discovered and encouraged, principally by Thomas Gilcrease, the well-known Tulsa oil man. His first national sculpture award was in 1938, when he won second place in a contest sponsored by Proctor and Gamble for a carving done using a bar of Ivory soap.

Stone's drawings and sculptures are frequently elongated and graceful, often depicting children and woodland animals. His art has a serene, almost spiritual, character.

STONECHILD, DALE *Plains Cree*

Born 1964 in File Hills, SK, Canada

RESIDENCE: Calgary, AB, Canada

MEDIA: Acrylic, watercolor, and pencil

PUBLISHED: Cardinal-Schubert (1992)

PUBLIC COLLECTIONS: C/GM

EXHIBITS: C/PAT; C/TFD; C/TGVA; throughout Canada

AWARDS: C/PAT ('88)

STONE MAN *Sioux*

Born ca. 1864

RESIDENCE: From the Fort Yates, ND area

PUBLISHED: Snodgrass (1968)

PUBLIC COLLECTIONS: HS/ND (pictographic painting, 1917)

STOPS, RICKY DAWN *Crow*

Born ca. 1963

OCCUPATION: House painter and artist

MEDIA: Oil, acrylic, and watercolor
EXHIBITS: NAVAM; High School Art Show, Bozeman, MT; St. Labré Indian School, Ashland, MT

STORE, EDMUND *Navajo*
PUBLIC COLLECTIONS: MNA

STRAIGHT REED (see Red Corn, Raymond Wesley)

STRAIT, DOROTHY MAY *Cherokee*
Doekwote Hana
A.K.A. Dorothy May Hannah Strait
Born 6 Sept 1935 in Phoenix, AZ; daughter of Charley Benjamin Hannah; P/GP: Margret Annvine Kincade and Willamin Penn Hannah; M/GP: Milida Lavona Honngley and Archie Yella Donowho
RESIDENCE: Apache Junction, AZ
EDUCATION: Mesa (AZ) High School, 1957; Scottsdale (AZ) Community College
OCCUPATION: Artist
MEDIA: Oil, acrylic, watercolor, pastel, and prints
PUBLISHED: Campbell, ed. (1993). *Art-Talk* (Mar 1986)
PUBLIC COLLECTIONS: SI; Washington County Museum of Fine Arts, Hagerstown, MD
EXHIBITS: ACS/PG; CIM; CNM; FCTM; HM; HM/G; ITIC; KCPA; OT; SI/MNH; RC; RE; WMNAAF; Washington County Museum of Fine Arts, Hagerstown, MD
AWARDS: CNM ('84); FCTM ('90); HM/G ('79; '81, 1st); ITIC ('88, 1st; '89; '90; '91, 1st; '92, 1st); RC ('85, 1st)
HONORS: ITIC, poster artist, 1988

MOSES STRANGER HORSE

During World War I, Stranger Horse was stationed in Paris, France. After the war, he stayed in Paris to study oil painting. When he returned to the United States, he traveled extensively throughout the western United States. During his travels he gave public demonstrations of his technical dexterity as an artist. He was the first Sioux artist to learn and master the European style of painting. His paintings were highly romanticized, sweeping vistas of western mountain ranges which included, in a secondary way, views of Sioux Indian life.

Libhart 1970

STRANGER HORSE, MOSES *Brûlé Sioux*
A.K.A. Signature: Sundown
Born 1890 near Wood, SD, on the Rosebud Reservation; died 1941 on the Rosebud Reservation
MILITARY: U.S. Army, WWI
EDUCATION: Carlisle Indian School, PA, ca. 1911; studied oil painting in Paris, France, after WWI
MEDIA: Oil, colored pencil, and pencil
PUBLISHED: Libhart (1970). *The Rapid City Journal* (3 Dec 1989)
PUBLIC COLLECTIONS: IACB
EXHIBITS: CSP; SIM; World's Fair, New York, NY, 1939; rodeos and fairs

STRATUS CLOUD (see Moquino, Ignacio)

DYANNE STRONGBOW

A native of Austin, Strongbow's earliest paintings were of the Texas landscape. In 1972, she started painting Native American subjects. She is known for her use of negative space, which, she explains, she uses to prevent the painting from becoming too cluttered with detail. She portrays the present and past as well as the sometimes forgotten lifestyles of many tribes. She does composites and overlapping subjects, and uses subtle washes.

Art of the West, *July/Aug 1990*

STRONGBOW, DYANNE *Choctaw*
A.K.A. Dyanne Weber Strongbow
Born 22 Jan 1951 in Austin, TX
RESIDENCE: Albuquerque, NM
EDUCATION: B.A., Southwestern Texas State U., San Marcos, TX
OCCUPATION: Commercial artist and painter
MEDIA: Watercolor
PUBLISHED: *New Mexican* (18 Aug 1983); *The Rapid City Journal* (3 Dec 1989); *Art of the West* (July/Aug 1990)
PUBLIC COLLECTIONS: ABQM, HCC
EXHIBITS: CNM; FCTM; HCC; PBS; RC; SWAIA; New Mexico Art League/Saga Show, 1981; New Mexico Watercolor Society Show, 1980

AWARDS: ABQM (Purchase Award); FCTM ('80; '82; '83, 1st; '85)

HONORS: SWAIA, poster artist, 1983

STROUD, VIRGINIA A. *Cherokee/Creek*

Born 13 Mar 1951 in Madera, CA; adopted daughter of Evelyn Tahome and Jacob Ahtone, Kiowa Tribal Chairman, 1978-1980

RESIDENCE: Durango, CO

EDUCATION: Muskogee (OK) High School, 1968; BC, 1968-1970; U of OK; studied under Dick West (q.v.) and Ahmed Moghbel

OCCUPATION: Teacher, lecturer, consultant, and artist

MEDIA: Tempera, gouache, and prints

PUBLISHED: Wade and Strickland (1981); Hoffman, et al. (1984); Jacka and Jacka (1988); Jones (1988). *Nimrod* (spring/summer 1972); *Oklahoma Today* (spring 1971; Dec 1990); *Art Voices South* (Apr 1979); *Four Winds* (spring 1979; winter 1980; spring 1982); *The Scottsdale Daily Progress* (27 Nov 1981); *Southwest Art* (June 1983; Aug 1993); *The Indian Trader* (Apr 1990); *The Columns* (fall 1993)

PUBLIC COLLECTIONS: GM, MRFM, PAC

EXHIBITS: ABQM; AIE; FCTM; GM; HM/G; HNSM; IK; ITIC; MIF; OAC; OIAP; PAC; SDMM; SFFA; SPIM; SWAIA; OU/MA; PAC; WIB; WWM; galleries in AZ, CO, OK, and TX

SOLO EXHIBITS: CNM (two), SPIM

AWARDS: AIE ('73; '75; '76); FCTM ('72, IH; '77; '84, 1st); GM; HM/G ('78, 1st; '79, 1st); ITIC ('86; '87; '90; '91, 2-1st; '94); PAC ('70, 1st; '75, Painting Award; '78; '79, 2-1st; Best in Category); PAC ('70, 1st; '75, 1st; '79, 1st); SWAIA ('91, 1st, Best of Division)

HONORS: Miss Cherokee Tribal Princess, 1969; Miss National Congress of American Indians, 1970; World Congress of the Boy Scouts of America, "Youth of the Year," 1970; Miss Indian America XVII, 1971; FCTM, designated a Master Artist, 1986; AICA, Artist of the Year, 1982; Ralph Oliver, designated her paintings "one of the best investments in Indian Art," 1987; AICA, Board of Directors

VIRGINIA A. STROUD

Stroud's mother died when she was eleven and she went to live with her sister in Muskogee, OK. With her sister's encouragement she began to study the heritage of all Indian tribes, especially her own. An additional inspiration was Dick West (q.v.) who, impressed with her artistic ability, made the young girl his assistant. She sold her first painting by the time she was thirteen. Using a modification of the pictographic style of the 19th Century ledger drawings, Stroud paints to show that the historical Indian culture still survives in contemporary society. Considering herself a "visual orator" she says, "I want people to look back at my work just like today we look back at the ledger drawings to see how it was then. I'm working 100 years after those people and saying this is how we still do it . . . we still have our traditions."

Southwest Art, *Aug 1993*

The Cherokee National Museum, Tahlequah, OK, honored Stroud with a retrospective exhibition, 1993. At that time she announced that it would be her last show. She said that in the future she was going to concentrate on writing and illustrating children's books about Native Americans.

The Columns, *fall 1993*

STUMBLINGBEAR, ELTON *Kiowa-Apache*

Born 1937 in Lawton, OK; son of Gertrude Chalepah

EDUCATION: Anadarko (OK) High School, 1958

OCCUPATION: Indian City U.S.A. (Anadarko, OK) announcer and tour guide, carver, silversmith, and painter

MEDIA: Paint, silver, gemstone, stone, and hide

PUBLISHED: Blackboy, et al. (1973)

EXHIBITS: SPIM

STUMP, SARAIN *Shoshoni/Cree/Flathead*

Born 1943, Manitoulin Island, West Bay, ON, Canada; died 1974

RESIDENCE: Lived in Saskatoon, SK, Canada

OCCUPATION: Poet, illustrator, and painter

MEDIA: Acrylic and pen and ink

PUBLISHED: Dickason (1972); Ferguson (1973); Irvine, ed. (1974); McMasters, et al. (1993). *Artscanada* (Vol. 30, nos. 5 & 6, 1972-1973)

BOOKS PUBLISHED: Stump (1970)

PUBLIC COLLECTIONS: C/INAC

EXHIBITS: C/CIARH; C/ROM; Mount St. Vincent University Exhibit, Halifax, NS

SOLO EXHIBITS: C/GM

STURR, JONATHAN *(?)*

PUBLISHED: Snodgrass (1968)
EXHIBITS: ITIC (juvenile class)
AWARDS: ITIC

SUA PEEN (Aguilar, José Vicente)

SUATHOJAME, CLIFF *Hudálapai*

EDUCATION: IAIA
MEDIA: Acrylic
EXHIBITS: AC/SD

SUAZO, DAVID GARY *Taos*

Evening Snow Comes
Born 17 Aug 1965 in Taos, NM; son of Reycita M. and David Suazo
RESIDENCE: Taos, NM
EDUCATION: East High School, Denver, CO, 1983; A.A., IAIA, 1987
OCCUPATION: Full-time painter since 1987
MEDIA: Oil, acrylic, watercolor, pencil, pen and ink, pastel, and prints
EXHIBITS: ACS/ENP; HM; IAIA/M; ITIC; MRFM; RC; SWAIA; National Western Stock Show, Denver, CO
AWARDS: ACS/ENP ('90, 1st; '91); ITIC ('89); MRFM ('88, Best in Category)

DAVID GARY SUAZO

"As a full-blood Taos Indian, I draw much of my inspiration from the experience of Indian life and the values of Taos Pueblo. The colors of the landscape, the architectural beauty of the Pueblo, the horno (the Pueblo cooking oven) all symbolize the simplicity and quietness of Pueblo life. My objective is to express the true peacefulness in my art. And to look back in the past, before modernization was introduced to Pueblo life. . . ."

artist, p.c. 1992

SUCTWA QUINKUM (see Ingram, Veronica Marie)

SUETOPKA, ELLIOT *Hopi*

EDUCATION: In 1951 Suetopka was enrolled in 8th grade.
PUBLISHED: Snodgrass (1968)
PUBLIC COLLECTIONS: MNM

SUHONVA (see Honahniein, Ramson R.)

SUINA, HERMAN *Cochití*

EDUCATION: Santa Fe
PUBLISHED: Snodgrass (1968)
EXHIBITS: MNM

SUINA, THEODORE *Cochití*

Ku Pe Ru
Born 18 Feb 1918 at Cochití Pueblo, NM
RESIDENCE: Cochití Pueblo, NM
EDUCATION: Santa Fe, 1942; Hill and Canyon School of the Arts, Santa Fe, NM, 1950; B.S., St. Joseph's, 1953
OCCUPATION: Draftsman and painter
MEDIA: Tempera and Shiva
PUBLISHED: Jacobson and d'Ucel (1950); Dunn (1968); Snodgrass (1968); Tanner (1973); Broder (1981); Seymour (1988); Williams, ed. (1982)
COMMISSIONS: *Murals:* Maisel's Indian Trading Post, Albuquerque, NM, 1939
PUBLIC COLLECTIONS: DAM, GM, IACB, IACB/DC, MAI, MKMcNAI, MNA/KHC, MNM, MRFM, OU/MA, PAC, UPA, WOM, WWM
EXHIBITS: AAID; DAM; FAIEAIP; HM/G; ITIC; JGS; LGAM; MNM; NMSF; OU/ET; PAC; PAC/T; SFWF; SN; U of NM; USDS; WRTD; Civic Center, San Francisco, CA; Southern Illinois University, Carbondale, IL; see also Awards
AWARDS: AAID ('68, 1st); DAM; ITIC; MNM; NMSF; PAC; SN; Terry National Art Exhibition, Miami, FL, 1952

THEODORE SUINA

"While recovering from a broken neck, a result of a boyhood accident, the artist began to paint seriously. His teachers, Mary Mitchell at the Day School and Geronima Montoya (q.v.) at the Santa Fe Indian School, encouraged him to continue. . . ."

Snodgrass 1968

HONORS: Governor of Cochití Pueblo, NM

SULLIVAN, DOROTHY ANN *Cherokee*

Born 8 Jan 1939; P/GM: Elizabeth Tidwell; M/GF: Eddie Barker

RESIDENCE: Bethany, OK

EDUCATION: Horace Mann High School, Ada, OK, 1957; ECSC/OK, 1966

OCCUPATION: Teacher, commercial artist, sculptor, and painter

MEDIA: Oil, acrylic, watercolor, Prismacolor, pen and ink, pastel, mixed-media, sandstone, clay, and prints

PUBLISHED: *The Sunday Oklahoman* (1 Mar 1992); *The Columns* (fall 1993)

COMMISSIONS: CNM, thirteen paintings for a calendar, 1993

EXHIBITS: CHASC; CNM; FCTM; K; OIAC; PIPM; RE; TIAF; TWF; U of OK; Stillwater (OK) Art Guild Spring Art Show; see also Awards

AWARDS: CHASC ('93); CNM ('88, 1st; '90; '91, '92; '94, Best of Show); FCTM ('88; '89, IH); K ('91, 1st); Oklahoma University Heritage Art Contest, Norman, OK ('91); Chisholm Trail Art Show, Yukon, OK ('88, 1st; '89; '90; '91); see also Awards

HONORS: CNM, Trail of Tears Art Show, poster artist, 1994

SUMA (see Aguilar, José Vincente)

SUMATZKUKU, EDGAR *Hopi*

RESIDENCE: Tuba City, AZ

PUBLIC COLLECTIONS: HCC, MNA

EXHIBITS: HCC, ITIC, WTF

AWARDS: ITIC ('87; '88; '89)

SUMATZKUKU, N. *Hopi*

PUBLIC COLLECTIONS: MNA, WOM

SUMMER MOUNTAIN (see Vigil, Thomas)

SUN CLOUD (see Stevens, Jim)

SUNDANCE (see Geshick, Joe)

SUNDOWN (see Stranger Horse, Moses)

SUNDUST (see Dewey, Wilson)

SUN FLOWER (see Montoya, Sidney, Jr.)

SUNGA HUSHTI (see Lame Dog)

SUNKA LU-ZAHAN (see Swift Dog)

SUNKA WONKA WANJILA (see Lone Horse)

SUNKKLESHA (see Spotted Horse)

SUN RISE (see Sunrise, Riley)

SUNRISE (see Byrnes, James Michael)

SUNRISE, RILEY *Hopi*

Quoyavema; Quiyavema

A.K.A. Riley Quoyavema; Sun Rise

Birth date unknown; born in Anadarko, OK

RESIDENCE: Second Mesa, AZ

EDUCATION: St. Patrick's

OCCUPATION: Actor and painter

RILEY SUNRISE

"While in the 3rd grade at Anadarko, the artist submitted a series of Hopi symbols in a statewide newspaper contest and received second award. Adopted by a Kiowa family, his work seems to reflect the influence of Kiowa painting."

Snodgrass 1968

PUBLISHED: Dunn (1968); Snodgrass (1968); Brody (1971); Tanner (1973); Stuart and Ashton (1977); Fawcett and Callander (1982); Williams, ed. (1990)
BOOKS PUBLISHED: Nelson (1937)
COMMISSIONS: *Paintings:* MAI, 1930s; SM
PUBLIC COLLECTIONS: CIS, DAM, GM, MAI, MKMcNAI, SM
EXHIBITS: GM, MAI, MKMcNAI, SM

SUNS TRAIL IN THE SKY (see Dawavendewa, Cedric)

SUOTWA QUINKUT (see Ingram, Veronica Marie)

SUPERNAW, KUGEE *Osage*

Kugee, Second Son; *Ga Ne Sheka*, Little Thunder
A.K.A. William J. Supernaw III
Born 29 Apr 1939 in Skiatook, OK; son of Pearl Irene and William J. Supernaw Jr.; P/GP: Maude and William J. Supernaw Sr.
RESIDENCE: Skiatook, OK
EDUCATION: Skiatook (OK) High School, 1957
OCCUPATION: Store owner, silversmith, and painter
MEDIA: Acrylic, alkyd, silver, and German silver
EXHIBITS: AIAFM; CNM; IS; ITAE; LIAS; OIAC; TIAF; TWF; RE; American Indian Market, Arlington, TX; Annual Campus Art Show, Pawhuska, OK; Native America 1992, Hollywood, FL; Seminole Festival, Hollywood, FL; see also Awards
AWARDS: IS ('93); ITAE ('93), LIAS ('93), TIAF ('91, Best of Division; '93), TWF ('92); RE ('92); Oklahoma Indian Art Competition, Tulsa, OK ('93)

KUGEE SUPERNAW

Supernaw became a full-time artist in 1991. It is his desire to depict the history of the Osage and Quapaw, especially subjects that have never been painted before. His desire for accuracy has led him to do extensive research.

p.c. 1992

SUPERNAW, MARLENE MARY (see Riding In Mameah, Marlene)

SUPERNAW, WILLIAM J., III (see Supernaw, Kugee)

SUSUNKEWA, MANFRED *Hopi*

Susunkewa, Beautiful
Born 10 Oct 1940 at Second Mesa, AZ
MILITARY: ROTC, U of AZ
EDUCATION: Stewart, 1959; Haskell, 1959-1961; Santa Fe; IAIA, 1964; U of AZ, "Southwest Indian Art Project," scholarship, summers 1961, 1963; U of AZ; California art schools
OCCUPATION: Commercial artist, *katsina* carver, fabric artist, weaver, ceramist, sculptor, and painter
PUBLISHED: Snodgrass (1968); New (1973); Tanner (1973). *Arizona Highways* (May 1975)
PUBLIC COLLECTIONS: BIA, HM, IAIA, MNA
EXHIBITS: ASF, FIE, HM, HM/G, IAIA, IACB, MNA, PAC, SN, SWAIA, WWM
AWARDS: FIE; HM/G ('70, Woodard Award; '72); MNA; SN; SWAIA ('74, 1st)

MANFRED SUSUNKEWA

"The artist was employed and encouraged in an art career by Charles Loloma (q.v.) and Lloyd New at their respective shops in Scottsdale, AZ."

Snodgrass 1968

SU TA (see Atencio, Tony)

SVARNY, GERTRUDE *Aleut*

EXHIBITS: CNM

SWALLOW, MARVIN *Sioux*

RESIDENCE: Manderson, SD
EXHIBITS: RC

SWAN, THE *Miniconjou Sioux*

A.K.A. The Little Swan; The Swanor

THE SWAN

"The Swan, a chief, kept a calendar record on a dressed skin of an antelope or deer, claiming it had been maintained in his family for 70 years. The calendar was called 'History of the Miniconjou Dakotas,' and represented the events of 1800-1871."

Snodgrass 1968

Birth date unknown

RESIDENCE: Resided at the Cheyenne River Agency, Dakota Territory, in 1872, where he recorded his calendar for Mallery.

PUBLISHED: Snodgrass (1968). *4th Annual Report*, BAE (1882-1883)

PUBLIC COLLECTIONS: SI/OAA

SWANOR, THE (see The Swan)

SWAZO, JOSÉ PATRICO (see Hinds, Patrick Swazo)

SWAZO, JUAN G. *Tesuque*

Birth date unknown; died sometime before 1968

PUBLIC COLLECTIONS: WWM

EXHIBITS: AIEC, AIW

SWEET FRUIT (see Zotigh, Barbara Tallamonts)

SWEETPEA (see Nielson, Leo)

SWEET POTATO (see Anderson, Jimmy)

SWEEZY, CARL *Arapaho*

Wattan, Black

A.K.A. Waatina

Born ca. 1879 on the old Cheyenne-Arapaho Reservation, near Darlington, OK; died 28 May 1953, in Lawton, OK; son of Hinan Ba Seth (Big Man); Sweezy's mother died when he was very young.

EDUCATION: Mennonite Mission Schools, Darlington, OK, and Halstead, KS; Carlisle; Chilocco

OCCUPATION: Indian policeman, farmer, dairyman, historical informant and recorder for anthropologist, teacher, professional baseball player; painter after 1920

MEDIA: Oil, watercolor, and enamel

PUBLISHED: Jacobson and d'Ucel (1950); Brody (1971); Snodgrass (1968); Highwater (1976); Dockstader (1977); Silberman (1978); Broder (1981); King (1981); Hoffman, et al. (1984); Wade, ed. (1986); Archuleta and Strickland (1991). *Annual Report*, Oklahoma State Hospital Department (July 1951), frontispiece

BOOKS PUBLISHED: Sweezy (1966)

PUBLIC COLLECTIONS: CMNH, GM, HM, HSM/OK, IACB/DC, MAI, OU/L, OU/MA, OU/SM, PAC, SI, SM

EXHIBITS: AIE; AIW; GM; HM; HSM/OK; IK; ITIC; MKMcNAI; MPI; OMA; OU/MA/T; PAC; PAC/T; SV; Louis and Clark Exposition, Portland, OR (work lent by SI); U of OK, Anthropology Department

SWIFT DOG *Hunkpapa Sioux*

Sunka Lu-zahan; Ta-Sunka-Duza (possibly a different Swift Dog)

Born 1845; died 1925 on the Standing Rock Reservation, SD; son of Running Fearlessly (Kagi Sni Inyanka), a Hunkpapa chief, who received a medal from the U.S. Government while in Washington, D.C. Swift Dog was a member of the Bad Bow Band (Sitting Bull's people).

OCCUPATION: Warrior, cultural informant, and painter

MEDIA: Watercolor, crayon, pen and ink, pigment, and muslin

PUBLISHED: Praus (1961); Snodgrass (1968); Maurer (1992). *Bulletin 61*, BAE (1918); *Bulletin 173*, BAE (1960), a pictographic Winter Count representing the years 1797-1798 through 1911-1912; *American Indian Art* (summer 1994)

CARL SWEEZY

"The artist's older brother, while at the Mennonite school in Halstead, KS, took the name of Fieldie Sweezy (Sweezy being the name of the railway agent there). The other children of the family were given the same surname, and Wattan became Carl Sweezy. At 14, the artist returned from school to the reservation with a baseball, a hat, a catcher's mitt, and a box of newly-acquired watercolor paints, which a White woman at the agency had taught him to use. His most prolific period came during and after he worked for anthropologist James Mooney. To the end of his life he continued to paint in what he called 'the Mooney way.' His oils and watercolors, often unsigned, are excellent ethnographic examples."

Snodgrass 1968

SWIFT DOG

Swift Dog, a member of Sitting Bull's band and the White Horse Riders warrior society, fought in the Battle of the Little Big Horn. Following the battle, he joined Sitting Bull in exile in Canada, and in 1881, when Sitting Bull surrendered, Swift Dog returned with him to the Standing Rock Reservation in South Dakota. In the early 1900s, Swift Dog served as a cultural informant and did drawings for Frances Densmore, Smithsonian Institution ethnomusicologist. Late in his life, possibly as a source of income, he produced winter counts, miniature tipis, ledger drawings, and an autobiographical muslin.

American Indian Art
summer 1994

PUBLIC COLLECTIONS: HS/ND (attributed); Cranbrook Institute of Science, Bloomfield Hills, MI

EXHIBITS: VP, WWM

Swoo-Whee-Ya (see Paul, Michael M.)

Syliboy, Alan *Micmac*

Born 1952 in Truro, NS, Canada, on the Millbrook Reserve; GM: Rachael Marshall, first female chief of the Millbrook Band

RESIDENCE: Truro, NS, Canada

EDUCATION: C/NSCAD, 1975-1976; studied under Shirley Bear (q.v.)

OCCUPATION: Teacher, owner of a Native art marketing company, and painter

MEDIA: Oil, acrylic, pencil, pastel, and prints

PUBLISHED: *The Chronicle-Herald* (Canada) (3 Sept 1992)

COMMISSIONS: *Murals:* Millbrook (NS) Gymnasium, 1988; Multicultural Festival, Dartmouth, NS, 1991. *Other:* Public Service Commission of Canada, calendar design.

PUBLIC COLLECTIONS: C/NAC; Dartmouth (NS) Heritage Museum, 1992; Mount Allison University, Sackville, NB; Nova Scotia Teachers College, Truro, NS,

EXHIBITS: Partial listing of more than ten includes: C/ARIA; C/MG; Fraser Memorial Gallery, Tatamagouche, NS, Canada, 1989; Mount Allison University, Sackville, NB; galleries in Nova Scotia

SOLO EXHIBITS: Nova Scotia Teachers College, Truro, NS, 1990; galleries in Nova Scotia

Alan Syliboy

Much of Syliboy's work is inspired by the Kejimkujik petroglyphs. He uses them because they belong to his people and haven't been influenced by European art. He doesn't copy them but instead incorporates them in his own images. They are contemplative images of quest, faith, and renewal.

The Chronicle-Herald
3 Sept 1992

TABAKSI (see Saul, C. Terry)

TAFOYA, CAMILIO *Santa Clara*

A.K.A. Sunflower Tafoya

PUBLISHED: Snodgrass (1968)

PUBLIC COLLECTIONS: MFA/A

EXHIBITS: WWM

TAFOYA, FRANCIS G. *Santa Clara*

Born 1947 in Santa Fe, NM

RESIDENCE: Española, NM

EDUCATION: St. Catherine's, 1965; A.A., IAIA; NM Highlands U

OCCUPATION: Teacher, educational planner, and painter

MEDIA: Acrylic, watercolor, pen and ink, pencil, and prints

PUBLISHED: Snodgrass 1968

COMMISSIONS: *Murals:* IPCC; Neighborhood Facility Council Chambers, Santa Clara Pueblo, NM

PUBLIC COLLECTIONS: IAIA

EXHIBITS: ACS/ENP; CNM; HM/G; IAIA; NMSF; PAC; SAIEAIP; SIAF; SN; SWAIA; Original American Indian and Western Relic Show, Long Beach, CA

AWARDS: ACS/ENP; SIAF; SN; SWAIA ('71, 2-1st; '73)

TAFOYA, JOE (see Baca, Henry)

TAFOYA, JOSEPH (see Lonewolf, Joseph)

TAFOYA, MARY AGNES *Santa Clara*

RESIDENCE: Española, NM

PUBLISHED: Snodgrass (1968)

PUBLIC COLLECTIONS: SM

TAFOYA, ROSITA *Santa Clara*

PUBLISHED: Snodgrass (1968)

PUBLIC COLLECTIONS: MNM, OU/MA

EXHIBITS: AIW

TAFOYA, TEOFILO *Santa Clara*

Po Qui

A.K.A. Teo Tafoya

Born 15 May 1915 at Santa Clara Pueblo, NM; son of Severa and Cleto Tafoya

RESIDENCE: Albuquerque, NM

EDUCATION: Santa Fe, 1933-1936; B.A., U of NM, 1941

OCCUPATION: Teacher and artist

MEDIA: Watercolor, tempera, pencil, and pen and ink

PUBLISHED: Dunn (1968); Snodgrass (1968); Brody (1971); Tanner (1973); Monthan and Monthan (1975); Seymour (1988); Williams, ed. (1990). *Southwest Art* (June 1983)

COMMISSIONS: *Murals:* Santa Fe (NM) Indian School; Santa Clara (NM) Day School; Julius Rosenwald Building, Chicago, IL; Maxwell Public School

PUBLIC COLLECTIONS: IACB/DC, MAI, MKMcNAI, MRFM

EXHIBITS: ASM, HM, ITIC, MFA/O, MKMcNAI, MMA, MNM, NMSF, SWAIA, U of NM, WRTD

AWARDS: ITIC, NMSF, SWAIA

FRANCES G. TAFOYA

Tafoya started painting when he was a 6th grade student.

TEOFILO TAFOYA

Teaching and painting serve the same purposes in Tafoya's life. They are a means of preserving his culture and its art. His subject matter is Indian life and ceremonies.

Seymour 1988

DETAIL: Merle Thunderhawk, *Painted Warrior No. 4*, ca. 1970. Philbrook Museum of Art, Tulsa, Oklahoma

TAGOONA, ARMAND *Inuit (Eskimo)*

A.K.A. Tagungrnaaq

Born 1926 in Repulse Bay, NWT, Canada; died 12/91

RESIDENCE: Lived at Baker Lake, NWT, Canada

OCCUPATION: Hunter, tractor driver, mechanic, missionary, Anglican priest, Royal Canadian Mounted Police, and artist

MEDIA: Oil, watercolor, gouache, crayon, colored pencil, felt tip pen, and prints

PUBLISHED: Blodgett (n.a.); Routledge (1979); Latocki, ed.(1983). *North* (Mar/Apr 1974); *Arts Manitoba* (fall 1984); *Northwest Explorer* (Vol. 6, no. 3, 1987)

BOOKS ILLUSTRATED: Tagoona (1975)

COMMISSIONS: C/CCAB, C/AG/WP, C/CMC

PUBLIC COLLECTIONS: C/CMC

EXHIBITS: C/AG/WP; C/CMC; C/IA7; C/LS; Jerusalem Artists' House Museum, Jerusalem, Israel, 1978; The Upstairs Gallery, Winnipeg, MB

SOLO EXHIBITS: Robertson Galleries, Ottawa, ON

HONORS: Ordained a deacon in the Anglican Church; the first Inuit minister in the history of the Anglican Church, 1959; ordained to the priesthood, 1960

TAGUNGRNAAQ (see Tagoona, Armand)

TAHALYTEWA, STACY (see Talahytewa, Stacy)

TAHCAWIN *Sioux*

Tahcawin, Fawn

A.K.A. Tahcawin Rosebud Josephine Marie Louise de Cinq-Mars

Born 10 Jan 1929 in New York, NY; daughter of Rosebud Yellow Robe, lecturer on Sioux history and customs, and Arthur Edmond de Cinq-Mars, actor and theatrical director

EDUCATION: Bayside High School, NY, 1947; Naum Los School of Art, NY, 1947-1948; Brooklyn (NY) Museum Art School, 1948-1949; ASL, 1949-1951; studied photography under Maurice Lehv and ethnic dance under La Meri

OCCUPATION: Recreation director, style colorist, receptionist, dancer, photographer, and painter

PUBLISHED: Snodgrass (1968)

PUBLIC COLLECTIONS: MAI, PAC

EXHIBITS: MFA/A, PAC

AWARDS: PAC

HONORS: New York World's Fair, chosen to represent the "First Americans" in the dedication ceremony of the American Common, 1939

TAHO, MARK *Hopi*

PUBLISHED: Snodgrass (1968)

EXHIBITS: FWG

TAHO, WILBERT *Hopi*

Birth date unknown

RESIDENCE: from Oraibi, AZ

PUBLISHED: Snodgrass (1968)

EXHIBITS: FWG, PAC

TAHOMA, QUINCY *Navajo*

Tahoma, Water Edge

Born 1920 near Tuba City, AZ; died Nov 1956 in Santa Fe, NM

MILITARY: U.S. Army, Code Talker, WWII

QUINCY TAHOMA

"While at Santa Fe Indian School, the artist developed his unique painting style. He was active in sports and set a district track record in 1940. After WWII, he established himself as a full-time artist and shared his studios in the Southwest with artists who are now well

EDUCATION: Albuquerque, 1936-1940; post graduate work at Santa Fe
OCCUPATION: Briefly employed in Hollywood movie studios, painter
MEDIA: Watercolor, casein, and tempera
PUBLISHED: Jacobson and d'Ucel (1950); LaFarge (1957); Tanner (1957; 1968; 1973); Dockstader (1962; 1977); Carlson, et al. (1964); Dunn (1968); Snodgrass (1968); Brody (1971); Monthan and Monthan (1975); Highwater (1976); Silberman (1978); Mahey, et al. (1980); Broder (1981); Fawcett and Callander (1982); Hoffman, et al. (1984); Samuels (1985); Wade, ed. (1986); Seymour (1988); Williams, ed. (1990); Archuleta and Strickland (1991); Jacka and Jacka (1994). *El Palacio* (June 1938; Nov1953); *Encyclopaedia Britannica Junior* (1964); *Arizona Highways* (Feb 1950; July 1956); *Indian Ceremonial Magazine*, ITIC (1957); *Southwestern Art* (Vol. 2, no.1, 1967); *The Arizona Republic* (17 Mar 1968; 24 Sept 1977); *Plateau* (Vol. 54, no.1, 1982); *Southwest Art* (June 1983); *Art-Talk* (Apr/May 1988); *Tamaqua* (winter/spring 1991)
COMMISSIONS: *Murals:* Santa Fe. *Posters:* MFA/NM, *Man Becomes an Artist*, Laboratory of Anthropology Exhibit
PUBLIC COLLECTIONS: AF; GM; HM; KM; MAI; MNM; MNA/KHC; MRFM; PAC; RMC/AZ; SM; U of CA/B; U of CA/LMA; U of OK; UPA; WOM; WWM; Encyclopaedia Britannica
EXHIBITS: AIW; ASM; FWG; HM; IK; JGS; LGAM; MAI; MFA/MN; MKMcNAI; NAP/MAI; OMA; IMA; PAC; PAC/T; RMC/AZ; SFWF; SV; U of NM; Foundation of Western Art, Los Angeles, CA, 1941
AWARDS: ITIC, NMSF, PAC; two Grand Awards

QUINCY TAHOMA

(continued) established. Clara Lee Tanner rightly said he was '. . . one of the most dynamic, imaginative, and gifted of Southwest artists.' During most of his life, he experienced misfortune, and died at the age of 35."

Snodgrass 1968

Tahoma painted a wide variety of subject matter but was perhaps best known for his dynamic action filled paintings. He also painted pictures full of humor. His signature included a vignette, a miniature scene which depicted what happened after the action in the painting.

TAIL FEATHERS (see Tailfeathers, Gerald.)

TAILFEATHERS, BOB *Blackfeet*

RESIDENCE: Browning, MT
EDUCATION: Browning (MT) High School; B.S., U of MT
OCCUPATION: Sculptor and painter
MEDIA: Acrylic
COMMISSIONS: *Posters:* Kyi-Yo-Youth Conference, MT; Montana Upward Bound
EXHIBITS: GFNAAS
HONORS: Montana Arts Council, Governor's Award, 1982

TAILFEATHERS, GERALD *Blood (Blackfoot)*

Omuka-nista-payh'pee, Big Walking Away; *Eets-pahp-awag-uh'ka*, Walking On Top
A.K.A. Gerald Tail Feathers; Tail Feathers. Signatures: Gerald T. Fethers; Gerald Feathers; Gerald T. Feathers; Gerald Tailfeathers; Tailfeathers
Born 14 Feb 1925 near Standoff, AB, Canada; died 1975 of a heart attack; son of Fred Tailfeathers, farmer, rancher, and minor chief of the Blood tribe; nephew of Percy Two Gun, artist
RESIDENCE: Lived in Calgary, AB, Canada
EDUCATION: St. Paul's Anglican Residential School, AB, 1932-1942; St. Mary's Lake Summer School, Glacier Park, MT, 1935-1937, studied under Carl Linck, and Winold Reiss; C/BSFA, 1941, studied under W. J. Phillips, H. G. Glyde, and Charles Comfort; Provincial Institute of Technology and Art, Calgary, AB, 1944
OCCUPATION: Draftsman, commercial artist, sculptor, and painter
MEDIA: Oil, watercolor, pen and ink, charcoal, chalk, pastel, and clay
PUBLISHED: Snodgrass (1968); Irvine, ed. (1974); Dempsey (1978); Stebbins (1981); Cardinal-Schubert (1992); McMasters, et al. (1993). *The Lethbridge Herald* (22 Apr 1959; 13 Jan 1960; 23 Nov 1966; 11 June 1968; 24 Oct 1968; 4 June 1969; 21 Jan 1970; 28 Jan 1970; 19 Oct 1970; 27 Oct 1970; 15 Apr 1971; 21 Apr 1971; 3 Nov 1971; 3 Dec 1971; 25 Sept 1972; 15 Feb 1973); *La Presse* (9 Jan

GERALD TAILFEATHERS

Tailfeathers was one of the earliest and most successful easel painters of the Canadian Plains region. His paintings, done in the Charles Russell "Western Romantic" style, show a nostalgic view of the Blood Indians, who are depicted as they were in the 1800s, before acculturation. Although his earliest works were done in watercolor, tempera, charcoal, and pastel, he later worked in oil.

1960); *The Delta Times* (14 Jan 1960); *Western Week* (26 Jan 1966); *The Western Producer* (1 Sept 1966); *The Calgary Herald* (9 Nov 1967; 14 Apr 1970; 8 Oct 1970; 26 Oct 1970; 27 Oct 1970; 8 Oct 1971); *The Calgary Albertan* (29 June 1967); *The Indian News* (Feb 1968); *The Whitehorse Star* (20 Nov 1969); *The Star Weekly* (27 Nov 1971); *American Indian Crafts and Culture* (Jan 1973); *The Native Perspective* (Vol. 3, no. 2, 1978); *The Edmonton Journal* (22 Apr 1981); *Masterkey* (winter 1984)

BOOKS ILLUSTRATED: Ewers (1966)

COMMISSIONS: Expo '67, Indian Pavilion, large painting; Indian Association of Alberta, logo; Calgary (AB) Stampede, painting for presentation to Prime Minister John G. Diefenbaker; Glenbow Museum, Calgary, AB, series of pen and ink sketches of Indian medicinal herbs and, in 1960, 18 paintings of Plains Indian life; Department of Indian Affairs and Northern Development, 1967; Calgary (AB) Stampede, trophy sculptures, 1971; Canadian Post Office, Ottawa, ON, painting used for postage stamp, 1972

PUBLIC COLLECTIONS: C/INAC, C/CMC, C/GM

EXHIBITS: C/AG/CC; C/AG/SA; C/AG/TB; C/CIARH; C/CIIA; C/CS; C/GM; C/TC; C/TFD; C/U of C; OAIS; All-Indian Show, San Francisco, CA, 1968; Calumet Indian Club Exhibition, Calgary, AB; Chautauqua House, San Francisco, CA; Exposition '67; Medicine Hat Museum, 1969; Whitehorse (YT) Public Library, 1969

SOLO EXHIBITS: C/GM, Lethbridge (AB) Public Library, 1938; galleries in Calgary and Lethbridge, AB

HONORS: *Scholarships:* C/BSFA; Anglican Church. *Other:* Became a minor chief of the tribe, 1930; Band Council, member, 1964; C/U of L, Honorary Doctorate, 1973; Alberta Achievement Award

TAILFEATHERS, LAWRENCE *Blackfeet*

Born 26 Jan 1941 in Browning, MT

RESIDENCE: Browning, MT

OCCUPATION: Craftsman, sculptor, and painter

MEDIA: Acrylic, watercolor, pen and ink, and polyform

EXHIBITS: GFNAAS

TAIT, NORMAN *Tsimshian*

Born 20 May 1941 at Kincolith, BC, Canada

RESIDENCE: Vancouver, BC, Canada

OCCUPATION: Carver, silversmith, and graphic artist

MEDIA: Pen and ink, wood, horn, ivory, silver, gold, and prints

PUBLISHED: Stewart (1979); Hall, Blackman, and Rickard (1981)

EXHIBITS: C/IGV

TAKADO, JERRY *Jémez*

MEDIA: Watercolor

EXHIBITS: SWAIA

AWARDS: SWAIA ('72, 1st)

TAKALA, JASON *Hopi*

RESIDENCE: Second Mesa, AZ

PUBLIC COLLECTIONS: WWM

EXHIBITS: LIAS

AWARDS: LIAS ('93, MA)

TAKILNOK, RICHARD DAVIS *Eskimo*

Born 25 Feb 1927 on Nunivak Island, Mekoryuk, AK

MILITARY: Alaska National Guard, two years
PUBLISHED: Snodgrass (1968)
PUBLIC COLLECTIONS: MHDYMM
EXHIBITS: MHDYMM, PAC
AWARDS: MHDYMM

TAKOTOKASI (see Warrior, Antowine)

TAKZI *Apache*

Born ca. 1862
RESIDENCE: Lived in the area of Anadarko, IT (now Oklahoma), 1884
PUBLISHED: Snodgrass (1968)
PUBLIC COLLECTIONS: SI/OAA

TALAHAFTEWA, ROY *Hopi*

RESIDENCE: Phoenix, AZ
EXHIBITS: HM/G, SM

TALAHYTEWA, GIBSON *Hopi*

Dewayesva, Sand Generation
Born 10 Mar 1934 in Moenkopi, AZ
RESIDENCE: Tuba City, AZ
EDUCATION: Santa Fe, ca. 1954
MEDIA: Gouache
PUBLISHED: Dunn (1968); Snodgrass (1968)
PUBLIC COLLECTIONS: MNM, MNA
EXHIBITS: AAID, MNM, NGA
AWARDS: MNM

TALAHYTEWA, STACY *Hopi*

A.K.A. Stacy Tahalytewa
PUBLISHED: Snodgrass (1968) (spelled "Tahalytewa")
PUBLIC COLLECTIONS: MNA
EXHIBITS: FWG

TALASHOMA, LOWELL *Hopi*

Birth date unknown; son of Rose and Wilburt Talashoma
RESIDENCE: Shipaulovi, AZ
EDUCATION: Tuba City (AZ) High School, 1969
OCCUPATION: *Katsina* carver, sculptor, and painter

TALASWAIMA, TERRANCE, JR. *Hopi*

Honvantewa, Bear Making Tracks
A.K.A. Terrance Honvantewa; Terry Talaswazma. Signature: Two turkey Feathers plus Honvantewa
Born 6 Nov 1939 in Shipaulovi, AZ; died Jan 1988; son of Lucille and Lloyd Talaswaima
RESIDENCE: Lived on Second Mesa, AZ
EDUCATION: Hopi HS, AZ; Catalina High School, Tucson, AZ, 1958; U of AZ, 1966-1973; U of N AZ; U of AZ, "Southwest Indian Art Project," scholarship, summer 1960
OCCUPATION: Museum director, composer, lecturer, storyteller, *katsina* carver, and painter
MEDIA: Acrylic and watercolor
PUBLISHED: Snodgrass (1968); Tanner (1973); Broder (1978; 1981); New (1981);

TERRANCE TALASWAIMA JR.

Talaswaima was a founding member of Artist Hopid (q.v.). He considered his art to be an extension of his involvement in traditional Hopi activities. "What I am trying to do with my art right now . . . my first responsibility . . . is to teach people the values of Hopi traditions. I'm into documenting every aspect of Hopi life." He did not attempt to depict it realistically but to express the spiritual essence of it.

Seymour (1988). *The Arizona Republic* (30 Mar 1974; 4 Mar 1983); *Forum* (June 1978); *Southwest Art* (June 1982)

COMMISSIONS: *Murals:* U of N AZ, College of Business, 1975; HCCM, 1975

PUBLIC COLLECTIONS: AC/RM, CGPS, HCC, IACB/DC, LMA/BC, MNA, MRFM, U of N AZ

EXHIBITS: ASF; CGPS; DCM; FAC/CS; HCC; HCCM; HM; HM/G; ITIC; MAAIC; MNA; NACLA; NICCAS; NMSF; NTF; PAC; SFFA; SPIM; U of CA/LMA; WCCA; WRTD; WWM; Arizona State Capitol Building, Phoenix, AZ; Texas A & M, College Station, TX

AWARDS: ASF (1st); HM/G ('75, '76); ITIC ('76); MNA; NTF (1st); PAC ('75)

TALASWAZMA, TERRY (see Talaswaima, Terry)

TALAYUMPTEWA, JENEELE (see Numkena, Jeneele Talayumptewa)

TALBERT, CARL D. *Cherokee*

RESIDENCE: Tulsa, OK

EXHIBITS: CNM

TALIRUNILI, JOE *Inuit (Eskimo)*

A.K.A. Old Joe; Joe; Joe T; Joe Talirunilik; Putugu Joe Talirunili; Joe Talisunili

Born Jan 1899 at Neahungnuk, PQ, Canada; died 11 Sept 1976; cousin of Davidialuk (q.v.)

RESIDENCE: Lived in Povungnituk, PQ, Canada

OCCUPATION: Trapper, fisherman, hunter, guide, lay preacher, carver, and graphic artist; His first drawings were done in 1961.

MEDIA: Pencil, stone, and prints.

PUBLISHED: Larmour (1967); Goetz, et al. (1977); Myers (1977); Routledge (1979); Myers, ed. (1980); Jackson and Nasby (1987); McMasters, et al. (1993). *UNESCO Currier* (Jan 1976), *Arts West* (V. 3, no. 5, 1978)

PUBLIC COLLECTIONS: C/TDB, DAM

EXHIBITS: C/AG/IGEA, C/CID, C/EACTDB, C/IA7, C/TIP, C/TMBI; Canadiana Galleries, Edmonton, AB, 1978

JOE TALIRUNILI

Talirunili's right arm was injured in a shooting accident when he was a boy and it never completely healed. In spite of this he led a full life, in his later years becoming a successful graphic artist and carver. Talirunili was primarily a historian; he chronicled life as he knew and lived it at the turn of the century. A favorite subject for his drawings and carvings was a "migration" disaster that he had survived as a child. Although not technically skilled his work was unique and original.

TALIRUNILI, PUTUGU (see Talirunili, Joe)

TALIRUNILIK, JOE (see Talirunili, Joe)

TALIWOOD, RICHARD *Navajo*

Born 1942 at Fort Defiance, AZ

EDUCATION: Phoenix; U of AZ, "Southwest Indian Art Project," scholarship, summer 1960; RVSA

MEDIA: Watercolor, tempera, and sand

PUBLISHED: Brody (1971); Tanner (1973)

PUBLIC COLLECTIONS: HCC, HM, MNA

EXHIBITS: AIAE/WSU, HCC, HM/G, ITIC, PAC, SN

AWARDS: HM/G ('71, 1st); ITIC ('71; '79; '85; '86, 1st; '91; '94); SN ('64; '65, Elkins Award)

TALLAMONTS (see Zotigh, Barbara)

TALLAS, LOREN *Hopi*

PUBLIC COLLECTIONS: MNA

TALLAS, TERRANCE *Hopi*

Birth date unknown; born at Shungopovi, Second Mesa, AZ

PUBLISHED: Snodgrass (1968)

PUBLIC COLLECTIONS: MNM

TALL BEAR, JOHN *Cheyenne*

Born 9 Nov 1948 in Clinton, OK; son of Mary Block and Paul Tall Bear; P/GP: Florence Black Wolf and Wacomb Tall Bear; M/GP: John Block

RESIDENCE: Rio Rancho, NM

MILITARY: U.S. Marine Corps, 1967-1969

EDUCATION: IAIA; Santa Fe (NM) High School, 1967; B.U.S., U of ABQ, 1981; M.P.A., U of NM, 1990

OCCUPATION: Tribal government employee, and painter

MEDIA: Oil, acrylic, watercolor, and prints

EXHIBITS: ACS/ENP; ITIC; SWAIA; TIAF; RE; Albuquerque (NM) Indian Market

TALL ELK (see Larvie, Calvin)

TALLER, HERMAN *Hopi*

Born ca. 1939

PUBLISHED: Snodgrass (1968)

PUBLIC COLLECTIONS: MNM

TALL STRAIGHT POPLAR (see Ray, Carl)

TALL WOMAN FROM PEACH SPRINGS (see Whitethorne-Benally, Elizabeth)

TANCAN HANSKA (see Eder, Earl)

TANEQUOALE, CARLTON *Kiowa*

EXHIBITS: AIE

AWARDS: AIE ('82, 1st; '86; '87)

TANKA CICAL WACASA (see Little Big Man)

TANNER, LO REE (see Pop Wea)

TANNER, LORI (see Pop Wea)

TANNER, THOMAS *Chippewa*

Born 5 Nov 1946 in Great Falls, MT

OCCUPATION: Powwow dancer, teacher, and painter

EXHIBITS: Boise (ID) State University, 1979; penal complexes at: Lincoln, NE, 1972; Soledad, CA, 1973; Woodland, CA, 1975

SOLO EXHIBITS: MPI

THOMAS TANNER

In spite of incarceration by the Idaho State Department of Corrections in the 1970s, Tanner has always maintained and worked on developing his artistic ability. Whenever possible he studies books and publications devoted to art. He is an active member of the North American Indian League (an organization of inmates of Indian descent) and of the Cloistered Artist Guild of the United States.

brochure, MPI, 1980

TANTAHA HELUTA (see Red Horn Bull Buffalo)

TANUGA SHINGA (see White, Clarence A.)

TARTSAH, JIM *Kiowa (?)*

Tar Tsah

RESIDENCE: Anadarko, OK

PUBLISHED: Snodgrass (1968)

PUBLIC COLLECTIONS: PAC, SM

TASUMKE WITKA *Sioux*

PUBLISHED: Snodgrass (1968)

PUBLIC COLLECTIONS: MPM (pictographic style on paper)

TA-SUNKA-DUZA (see Swift Dog)

TATANKA CANTE SICE (see Bad Heart Buffalo, Amos)

TATANKÁ EHAN'NI (see Old Buffalo)

TATANKA IYOTANKA (see Sitting Bull)

TATANKA PETECELA (see Short Bull)

TATANKA YOTANKA (see Sitting Bull)

TATANKEHANNI (see Old Buffalo)

TATE, BARBARA *Cherokee*

A.K.A. Barb Tate
RESIDENCE: Vinita, OK
MEDIA: Oil, watercolor, and pencil
EXHIBITS: CNM, FCTM, HM/G, PAC
AWARDS: FCTM ('74); PAC ('74)

TATE, DOC (see Nevaquaya, Doc Tate)

TATEYUSKANSKAN, GABRIELLE WYNDE *Sisseton Sioux*

Born 28 Oct 1955
EDUCATION: A.A., IAIA, 1974; Fort Lewis College, Durango, CO, 1979-1980; Boston (MA) Museum of Fine Arts School; St. Catherine's College, St. Paul, MN, 1986-1987
PUBLIC COLLECTIONS: HCC
EXHIBITS: HCC, MFA/B, NPTA, RC, WTF
AWARDS: NPTA ('91)
HONORS: IAIA, Achievement Award; St. Catherine's College, St. Paul, MN, Art Award; Minneapolis (MN) Public Schools, artist-in-residence, 1987

TATSII, MEENJIP *Shawnee*

RESIDENCE: Dayton, OH
PUBLIC COLLECTIONS: HCC
EXHIBITS: CNM, PAC, RC
AWARDS: PAC ('77; '78)

TATYA, WINNIE (see Tyya, Winnie)

TAUHINDAULI (see La Peña, Frank)

TAULBEE, DAN *Comanche*

Loba Heit, Wolf Alone
A.K.A. Daniel J. Taulbee
Born 7 Apr 1924 in St. Ignatius, MT, on the Flathead Reservation; died Mar 1987
RESIDENCE: Lived in Butte, MT
MILITARY: U.S. Army, WWII
EDUCATION: Polson (MT) High School, 1942
OCCUPATION: Ranch hand, rancher, miner, gallery owner, sculptor, and painter
MEDIA: Oil, watercolor, pen and ink, metal, and stone
PUBLISHED: Snodgrass (1968); Ray, ed. (1972); Ballantine and Ballantine (1993)
PUBLIC COLLECTIONS: HCC, IACB, MAI
EXHIBITS: BNIAS; CIA; CSPIP; FAIEAIP; HCC; HM; MPI; PAC; SI; U of ID; U of MT; Deer Lodge (MT) Bank and Trust; Great Falls (MT) National Bank; National Academy of Fine Arts, New York, NY; Peabody Museum, Salem, MA; Williston (ND) National Bank; see also Awards
SOLO/SPECIAL EXHIBITS: HM; MPI; PAC (dual show); Farnsworth Museum, Rockland, ME; Peabody Museum, Salem, MA; Statesville (NC) Museum
AWARDS: Burr Gallery, NY, 1959

DAN TAULBEE

"In 1963 Taulbee said, 'I am a breed. I paint what I see and what I hear from the old people of many tribes. I'm usually known as a "Montana Historical Indian Artist" — strictly a realist.'"

Snodgrass 1968

TAVINIQ (see Oonark, Jessie)

TAVITI (see Davidialuk)

TAWAKWAPTEWA *Hopi*

Tawakwaptiwa, Sun Shining Down

A.K.A. Tawakwaptiwa; Tawaquaptewa; Tewaquaptewa; Chief Tawakwaptewa; Wilson Tawakwaptewa; Wilson Tewaquapetewa

Born ca. 1882 at Oraibi, Third Mesa, AZ; died 1960; son of Cheuka

EDUCATION: Riverside, 1906-1910

OCCUPATION: *Katsina* carver and painter; best known as a carver

PUBLISHED: Snodgrass (1968); Tanner (1973); Dockstader (1954; 1977)

PUBLIC COLLECTIONS: DAM, HM

HONORS: Village Chief, Oraib, AZ

TAWAKWAPTIWA (see Tawakwaptewa)

TAWAQUAPTEWA (see Tawakwaptewa)

TAWAWIISEOMA (see Kabotie, Fred)

TAWODI (see Reason, Jamie)

TAYLOOWAYAHWHO (see Pollock, William)

TAYLOR, ELLEN MARY *Cayuse/Umatilla*

MEDIA: Pastel and pen and ink

EXHIBITS: MMA/WA, SWAIA

TAYLOR, ROBERT LEE *Blackfeet/Cherokee*

Born 30 Jan 1951 in Tulsa, OK; son of Mary Jane Hughes and Norman Ray Taylor; P/GP: Daisy Henry and Otis Ray Taylor; M/GP: Emma Thorpe and Virgil Hughes

RESIDENCE: Broken Arrow, OK

MILITARY: U.S. Navy, Vietnam

EDUCATION: Will Rogers High School, Tulsa, OK, 1969; Central Missouri State University, Warrensburg, MO

OCCUPATION: Artist

MEDIA: Acrylic, watercolor, pen and ink, and prints

PUBLISHED: *Oklahoma Today* (June 1992; May/June 1994)

PUBLIC COLLECTIONS: TTSP; corporate collections

EXHIBITS: CNM; FCTM; ITIC; LAICAF; RE; SI; Jane Goodall Foundation Exhibits, Dallas, TX, 1990, and Hollywood, CA, 1991; International Art Festival, New York, NY, 1990; see also Awards

AWARDS: CNM ('84, 1st, Tiger Award; '85, 1st; '87, 1st; '90; '91, Tiger Award; '92); FCTM ('87; '88; '92, 1st); ITIC ('82); TTSP; Eastern Trails Art Show, Vinita, OK ('79-'83, Premium Awards); Special Olympics Art Exhibit ('79, Premium Award)

TAYLOR, URSHEL *Ute/Pima*

Owl Ear

Born 31 May 1937 in Phoenix, AZ; son of Susan and Claude Taylor; P/GF: William Taylor

RESIDENCE: Tucson, AZ

MILITARY: U. S. Marine Corps, Vietnam, 1956-1963

OCCUPATION: Director of cultural arts program, gallery owner, sculptor, and painter

TAWAKWAPTEWA

According to Tanner (1973), the Denver Art Museum's collection contains a painting by Tawaquaptewa that is probably one of the earliest Hopi paintings. Its provenance indicates it was done in the early 1900s. In 1901, at the death of his uncle, Lolóloma, from smallpox, Tawaquaptewa became the leader of Oraibi.

Dockstader 1977

He played a major role in the 1906 village split between the Hostile and Conservative factions.

ROBERT LEE TAYLOR

The artist works primarily with acrylics on untempered hardboard or canvas that has been gessoed and/or sanded for the desired texture. Taylor says he has been strongly influenced by Paul Pletka, Karl Bodmer, Bruegel, Oscar Howe (q.v.), and the surrealistic and symbolistic movements. He uses distortion, such as small heads and enlarged bodies and hands, as symbols. For example, the enlarged hand is a symbol of its importance in elevating the human species above all other species.

artist, p.c. 1990

URSHEL TAYLOR

Taylor is known for his landscape paintings and carvings of bear fetishes and dance figures. In addition to his artistic endeavors he writes colomns for US Art *magazine and is director for the Tucson Indian Center's* All Native American Women Art Show.

MEDIA: Oil, acrylic, watercolor, pastel, hardwood, and prints
EXHIBITS: IACA, RE, SDMM, SWAIA; see also Awards
SOLO EXHIBITS: MPI
AWARDS: SWAIA ('84, 1st; '85, 1st; '86, 1st; '87, 1st; '88, 1st; '89, 1st); Pasadena Western Art Show ('85, 1st, Best of Show); Utah Peach Days, Bingham City, UT ('86, 1st, People's Choice; '87)

TAYLOR, VIRGINIA *Cherokee*
Born 15 Sept 1922 in Los Angeles, CA
RESIDENCE: Albany, OR
EDUCATION: High school; Los Angeles (CA) Art Center School; Chouinard Art Institute; University of Southern California; U of AZ
OCCUPATION: Commercial artist, medical and scientific illustrator, university publications staff artist, university art faculty, graphic art service owner, sculptor, and painter
MEDIA: Acrylic, watercolor, pastel, pen and ink, stone and prints
PUBLISHED: Snodgrass (1968). *The West* (Feb 1966); *The Phoenix Gazette* (14 Sept 1974); biographical publications
PUBLIC COLLECTIONS: PAC
EXHIBITS: CNM; FCTM; HM; PAC; shows and markets throughout Oregon
AWARDS: PAC ('74, 1st)

TE E (see Martínez, Crescencio)

TEEVEE, JAMASIE (see Jamasie)

TEEYACHEENA (see Medina, Rafael)

TEGA, CHARLES *Eskimo*
Born 10 Apr 1942 in Tanacross, AK
RESIDENCE: Fairbanks, AK
EDUCATION: Mt. Edgecumbe (AK) High School; IAIA
PUBLISHED: Snodgrass (1968)
EXHIBITS: FAIEAIP; IAIA; MNM; Mt. Edgecumbe, AK; New York, NY

TEKARONHANEKA (see White, Andrew)

TELARIOLIN (see Vincent, Zacharie)

TELESE, GILBERT *Zuni*
PUBLISHED: Snodgrass (1968)
PUBLIC COLLECTIONS: MNM

TENAK (see Preston, Bert)

TENAKHONGVA (see Preston, Bert)

TENNYSON, TERRY *Cherokee*
RESIDENCE: Tulsa, OK
MEDIA: Dye and feather
COMMISSIONS: Oklahoma Air National Guard, painted feather, 1993
PUBLISHED: *The Tulsa World* (13 Jan 1994)

TERAPIN, WAYNE *Cherokee*
Born 19 July 1934 in Stilwell, OK
RESIDENCE: Stilwell, OK
MILITARY: U.S. Army
EDUCATION: Stilwell (OK) High School; A.A., BC

OCCUPATION: Commercial artist, advertising manager, and painter
EXHIBITS: FCTM; Fort Gibson (OK) Arts and Crafts Show; Joplin (MO) Exhibition
SOLO EXHIBITS: FCTM
AWARDS: FCTM ('70)

TERASAZ, MARIAN *Comanche*
Aukemah
Born 1916
RESIDENCE: Oklahoma
EDUCATION: BC, ca. 1938
PUBLISHED: Jacobson and d'Ucel (1950); Snodgrass (1968)
PUBLIC COLLECTIONS: MAI
EXHIBITS: AIW

MARIAN TERASAZ

"In 1950, the artist had a family and was no longer painting."
Snodgrass 1968

TERRAZAS, HELEN HARDIN (see Hardin, Helen)

TETERS, CHARLENE *Spokane*
A.K.A. Char Teters; Charlene Teters Raymond
Born 25 Apr 1952 in Spokane, WA
RESIDENCE: Santa Fe, NM
EDUCATION: Shadle Park High School, 1970; Fort Wright College, Spokane, WA, 1974-1975; A.A., IAIA, 1986; B.F.A., CSF/SF, 1988; studied under Delbert Gish, Sergei Bongart, Paul Milosevich, and Sylvia Sleigh
OCCUPATION: Teacher, writer, illustrator, film actress, technical advisor, and painter
MEDIA: Oil
PUBLISHED: Hill (1992). Biographical publications
COMMISSIONS: Spokane (WA) Art in Public Places; Kateri Tekawitha National Conference, Spokane, WA, pen and ink drawing of Kateri Tekawitha
PUBLIC COLLECTIONS: HCC, IAIA, SIM
EXHIBITS: ACS/SM; AIAS; CNM; CPS; HCC; HM; HM/G; IAIA; IPCC; ITIC; MNAC; NCC; NIFA; NWASA; OIO; PSU/NC; RC; SIM; SWAIA; Cheney Cowles Museum, Spokane, WA; Seattle (WA) American Indian Art Show, 1980-1982; see also Awards
SOLO EXHIBITS: IAIA/M
AWARDS: ASC/SM ('81, 1st); AIAS ('81, 1st); MNAC ('81, 1st); RC ('82, Woodard Award; '85, Powers Award; '86); La Junta (CO) Fine Arts League National Show ('81, Purchase Award); Spokane (WA) Art in Public Places, Purchase Award, 1982
HONORS: *Scholarships:* RC, Thunderbird Foundation, 1985, 1986, 1987, 1989. *Other:* College Board Talent Roster 1985-1986; National Dean's List, 1985-1986

TEWAHIARITA (see Arquette, Mary Francis)

TEWAQUAPTEWA (see Tawakwaptewa)

THAYHAIYA (see Darby, Raymond Lee)

THEROUX, CAROL *Cherokee*
RESIDENCE: Bellflower, CA
EDUCATION: John C. Fremont High School, Los Angeles, CA, 1948; Cerritos College, Norwalk, CA, 1976
OCCUPATION: Teacher and artist
MEDIA: Oil, acrylic, watercolor, pencil, pen and ink, pastel, clay, and prints
PUBLISHED: Goldblot (1983); Krantz (1990); Samuels (1982). *Art of the West* (Nov/Dec 1987; July/Aug 1990); *Southwest Art* (Apr 1983)

CAROL THEROUX

Theroux's pastels are recognized for their realistic characterization of Indian children and young women, often participants at powwow celebrations. She uses artifacts and objects from her own collection in her paintings.

PUBLIC COLLECTIONS: Los Angeles (CA) County Museum; Prescott (AZ) Chamber of Commerce

EXHIBITS: ABQM; CAWA; CIM; CMRM; CNM; GFNAAS; TIAF; Ceres (CA) Western Art Show; Classic-American Western Art Show, Beverly Hills, CA; Panorama of Traditional Art, Paramount, CA; see also Awards

AWARDS: Los Angeles (CA) County Museum (1st)

HONORS: Ceres (CA) Western Art Show, poster artist, 1993

They Have Gone Back (see Gritts, Franklin)

They Have Returned (see Gritts, Franklin)

Thomas, Christopher *Laguna/Pima*

RESIDENCE: Santa Fe, NM

PUBLIC COLLECTIONS: HCC

EXHIBITS: CPS, HCC, HM/G, WTF

Thomas, Clifford *Tlingit*

A.K.A. Cliff Thomas

RESIDENCE: Haines, AK

EDUCATION: Santa Fe

PUBLISHED: Snodgrass (1968)

EXHIBITS: IANA, MNM

AWARDS: IANA

Thomas, Edson *Onondaga*

Birth date unknown; born in New York, NY; son of George Thomas, chief of the Onondaga Iroquois

PUBLISHED: Snodgrass (1968)

PUBLIC COLLECTIONS: MAI

Thomas, Elias G. *Onondaga*

A.K.A. Eli Thomas

Born 11 May 1955; son of Vera Moses and Elias Thomas; P/GP: Eliza and Elias Thomas; M/GF: William Moses

RESIDENCE: Cazenovia, NY

EDUCATION: LaFayette Central Schools, 1974; SUNY/PT; SUNY/B

OCCUPATION: Art demonstrator and lecturer in central New York State public schools, and painter

MEDIA: Acrylic, watercolor, pencil, pen and ink, and prints

PUBLIC COLLECTIONS: New York State Museum, Albany, NY

EXHIBITS: Partial listing of more than thirty includes: NYSF, RE; see also Awards

AWARDS: NYSF (1st); Native Festival, Haddam, CT (1st); Rancocas (NJ) Reservation Festival; North Syracuse Art Show, Cicero, NY (1st)

Elias G. Thomas

Thomas started drawing when he was five and learned to paint with acrylics in high school. Using personal and cultural symbolism he has developed a technique he calls "Landscape Imagery." He explains, "My art reflects a relationship with the environment developed from the Onondaga traditional culture."

p.c. 1990

Thomas, Evans S. *Eskimo*

PUBLISHED: Snodgrass (1968)

EXHIBITS: PAC

Thomas, Gregory M. *Onondaga*

Born 10 Sept 1957

RESIDENCE: Nedrow, NY

EDUCATION: Lafayette Central School; Alfred (NY) Agricultural and Technical College

OCCUPATION: Teacher, technical illustrator, and painter

MEDIA: Pen and ink

COMMISSIONS: *Murals:* Onondaga Indian School. *Other:* American Indian Society Calendar, 1979, 1980

EXHIBITS: NYSF; see also Awards

AWARDS: Lafayette Central School

THOMAS, HAROLD GESSO *Mohawk*

Karoniakesom

Born 28 Oct 1952; son of Gorgia Point Thomas and Frank Standing Arrow Thomas

RESIDENCE: Hogansburg, NY

EDUCATION: Three semesters, St. Lawrence University, Cornwall, ON

OCCUPATION: Artist

MEDIA: Oil, acrylic, watercolor, pen and ink, scratch board, enamel, and mixed-media

COMMISSIONS: *Murals:* St. Regis Tribal Building, 1978; Montréal Friendship Centre, 1981; C/NAITC, 1984. *Other:* Akwesasne Notes Calendar, 1978, 1985; Akwesasne Notes, poster, 1985; Native Directory, cover page, 1987; Alcohol and Drug Abuse, billboard designs, 1988; Bears Den, billboard designs, 1985-1988

PUBLIC COLLECTIONS: C/CMC

EXHIBITS: Partial listing of more than forty throughout New York and Canada includes: U of NH; SUNY/P; C/NAITC; International Art Festival, Congress Center, Montréal, PQ, 1985; International Art Show, Vancouver, BC, 1986

HONORS: John White Eagle Memorial Powwow, NH, poster artist, 1986

THOMAS, JOHN BIGTREE *Mohawk*

Born 5 Aug 1958; son of Georgia and Frank Thomas

RESIDENCE: Hogansburg, NY

OCCUPATION: Traditional singer and dancer, carver, and painter

MEDIA: Acrylic, tempera, pen and ink, pencil, charcoal, and wood

PUBLISHED: Johannsen and Ferguson, eds. (1983)

BOOKS ILLUSTRATED: Salmon River Central School, Bilingual/Bicultural Program, illustrated language books

COMMISSIONS: *Murals:* Akwesasne Library and Cultural Center. *Other:* Akwesasne Notes and Calendars, paintings; North American Indian Traveling College, Cornwall, ON, poster

PUBLIC COLLECTIONS: C/WICEC; St. Regis Bank, PQ

EXHIBITS: PAC; Katerie Hall Art and Craft Exhibit, 1978

THOMAS, KENNETH *Paiute*

EDUCATION: Santa Fe, 1960-1961

PUBLISHED: Snodgrass (1968)

EXHIBITS: MNM, PAC

AWARDS: MNM

THOMAS, LEE EDISON *Iroquois*

Born ca. 1920; died ca. 1971

RESIDENCE: Lived in Onondaga, NY

MILITARY: U.S. Army, WWII

OCCUPATION: Commercial artist, musician, and painter

MEDIA: Watercolor, charcoal, pen and ink, and pencil

PUBLISHED: Johannsen and Ferguson, eds. (1983)

PUBLIC COLLECTIONS: SMII, MAI

EXHIBITS: ACS/EM, CAOR

LEE EDISON THOMAS

The artist was best known for his paintings that depicted the traditional Iroquois culture. His work was an important influence on other artists at Onondaga. Thomas was also a talented musician.

Johannsen and Ferguson, eds. 1983

THOMAS, ROY *Ojibwa*

Gahgahgeh, Crow

A.K.A. Roy Harvey Thomas. Signature: originally, the Cree syllabics 6699; later he added a small drawing of a crow.

Born 29 Dec 1949 in Longlac, ON, Canada

EDUCATION: St. Joseph's Boarding School, Thunder Bay, ON, 1965-1966; Geraldton High School

OCCUPATION: Railroad worker, truck driver, guide, and painter

MEDIA: Acrylic, watercolor, and prints

PUBLISHED: McLuhan and Hill (1984); Southcott (1984); Menitove, ed. (1986b); Menitove and Danford, eds. (1989); Podedworny (1989). *Native Perspective* (Vol. 3, no. 2, 1983); *The Indian Trader* (July 1978)

PUBLIC COLLECTIONS: C/AB/TB; C/INAC; C/CMC; C/MCC; C/MMMN; C/ROM; HCC; Imperial Oil; Inuit Gallery, Mannheim, Germany; National Museum of Ethnology, Osaka, Japan

EXHIBITS: AC/NC; C/AG/O; C/AG/OV; C/AG/TB; C/CNAC; C/INAC; C/MCC; C/MMMN; C/NCCT; C/ROM, C/U of T; C/WCAA; C/WICEC; HCC; HPTU; SM; U of SD; WTF; Kinder Des Nanabush, Hamburg, Germany

SOLO EXHIBITS: Partial listing of more than twelve includes: C/CC/TB; Mary J. Black Library, Thunder Bay, ON

ROY THOMAS

A few years after his parents were killed in 1963 in a car accident, Thomas dropped out of school and started to travel. He worked at a variety of jobs as he hitchhiked and jumped trains throughout Ontario and the United States. As he traveled, he painted in Salvation Army hostels and even during the three and a half years he spent in jail. He is self-taught and says there have been no outside influences on his art. His major themes are his love of nature, and Ojibwa legends and family life.

artist brochure

THOMAS, SUSAN DIANE *Cherokee/Creek*

Born 3 June 1950 in Oklahoma City, OK; daughter of Lela Carpenter and John Allsup; P/GP: Effie Lowe and Charles Spurgeon Allsup; M/GP: Linnie and Walter Hall

RESIDENCE: Delaware, OK

EDUCATION: Delaware (OK) High School, 1968; B.F.A. OSU, 1971; M.S., U of OK, 1985

OCCUPATION: Art instructor and artist

MEDIA: Watercolor, pen and ink, and prints

EXHIBITS: CNM; IS; Wildlife Show, Tulsa (OK) Zoo

AWARDS: IS

THOMAS, TONA *Hunkpapa Sioux*

Birth date unknown; born at Fort Yates, ND, on the Standing Rock Reservation

EDUCATION: Darby (MT) High School; B.F.A., BYU, 1989

OCCUPATION: Teacher and painter

PUBLISHED: *The Indian Trader* (Vol. 21, no. 5, 1990)

COMMISSIONS: *Murals:* Darby (MT) High School

EXHIBITS: Area exhibits

SOLO EXHIBITS: SIM

THOMAS, YVONNE *Lummi*

RESIDENCE: Santa Fe, NM

EDUCATION: Burlington-Edison High School; A.F.A., IAIA, 1981; B.A., Evergreen State College, Olympia, WA, 1984

PUBLISHED: *The Indian Trader* (July 1978)

EXHIBITS: RC

THOMAS-DIXON, MARY *Seminole/Creek*

PUBLIC COLLECTIONS: AIE

AWARDS: AIE ('74; '76)

THOMASON, BOB *Cherokee*

Born 23 July 1944 in Whittier, CA; son of Ada Mineo and Earvin Thomason

RESIDENCE: Broken Arrow, OK

MILITARY: U.S. Air Force, Vietnam

EDUCATION: U of Tulsa; Famous Artists School, Westport, CT; Cowboy Artists of America Museum, Kerrville, TX; studied under Gary Carter, Robert Pummill, Frank McCarthy, and Harvey Johnson

OCCUPATION: Air traffic controller; full-time painter since 1981

MEDIA: Oil, acrylic, watercolor, pencil, clay, bronze, and prints

PUBLISHED: *Art Gallery* (Sept/Oct 1983; Dec/Jan 1983-1984); *The Broken Arrow Ledger* (25 Jan 985); *The Daily Oklahoman* (Nov 1987); *The Broken Arrow Marketplace* (28 Mar 1990); *The Broken Arrow Scout* (Mar 1990; 9 Aug 1992; 20 Oct 1993); *The Grand Lake Waterfront* (23 July 1992); *The Tulsa Tribune* (26 Aug 1992); *The Woodward News* (1 May 1993)

COMMISSIONS: U of Tulsa, brochure illustrations

PUBLIC COLLECTIONS: Broken Arrow (OK) Public Library

EXHIBITS: FAIE; LGAM; OHT; Fort Concho Benefit, San Angelo, TX, 1987; April Art Fest '83, Bartlesville, OK; Art Institute for the Permian Basin, Odessa, TX, 1987; Bristow (OK) Historical Society Art Show, 1991; Color of Hope Benefit Art Show, Muskogee, OK; Fall Festival of the Arts, Elk City, OK; Happy Canyon Western Art Invitational, Pendleton, OR; Original Western Art Show, Rapid City, SD, 1983; galleries in Oklahoma and Texas; see also Awards

SOLO EXHIBITS: PIPM; Affiliated Bank of Sapulpa (OK), 1983; Oklahoma Governor's Mansion, Oklahoma City, OK, 1988

AWARDS: Annual Fall Fine Art Show, Oklahoma City, OK, 1982

BOB THOMASON

Thomason admits that he sometimes paints the world as he would like to see it, not as it is. He describes himself as a storyteller with paint and brush and says, "I prefer not to paint conclusions but, rather, anticipations and to leave room for people to use their imaginations as they view my work.... Let them participate in the painting."

p.c. 1993

THOMPSON, ALEX *Navajo*

EDUCATION: Ganado (AZ) Public School, ca. 1964

PUBLISHED: Snodgrass (1968)

EXHIBITS: NACG

AWARDS: NACG

THOMPSON, ART *Nuu-Chah-Nulth (Nootka)*

Born 1948 in Whyac, BC, Canada

RESIDENCE: Victoria, BC, Canada

EDUCATION: Cameron College, Victoria, BC; studied under Ron Hamilton and Joe David (qq.v.)

OCCUPATION: Logger, tribal band manager, carver, silversmith, painter, and printmaker

MEDIA: Acrylic, pastel, wood, silver, and prints

PUBLISHED: Stewart (1979); Macnair, Hoover, and Neary (1980); Hall, Blackman, and Rickard (1981); McMasters, et al. (1993). *Windspeaker* (12 Dec 1986); *The Province* (26 Oct 989); *Maclean's Magazine* (13 Nov 1989)

PUBLIC COLLECTIONS: C/INAC, HCC, WSAC

EXHIBITS: AC/NC, AUG, C/ACCCNA, C/RBCM, BHSU, HCC, HPTU, NSU/SD, SDSMT, TPAS, U of SD, U of WV, WTF

THOMPSON, BETTY *Cherokee*

RESIDENCE: Tahlequah, OK

Birth date unknown; wife of E. G. Thompson (q.v.)

EDUCATION: Chilocco; B.S., NSU; U of Tulsa; U of OK; M.A., NSU; OSU

OCCUPATION: Teacher, real estate broker, gallery owner, and painter

EXHIBITS: Area exhibits

Thompson, E. G. *Cherokee*

Birth date unknown; husband of Betty Thompson (q.v.)

RESIDENCE: Tahlequah, OK

EDUCATION: Pryor (OK) High School; B.A., NSU; U of Tulsa; M.A., NSU; OSU

OCCUPATION: Teacher, illustrator, author, lecturer, Indian art gallery owner, and painter

PUBLISHED: *The Indian Trader* (12 articles; 11 articles authored by artist, 1978-1979); *Oklahoma Art Gallery* (spring 1980)

PUBLIC COLLECTIONS: FCTM; Victor Federal Savings and Loan, Pryor, OK

EXHIBITS: PAC; Fort Robinson (NE) Western Art Show; area exhibits

Thompson, Marita *Mohawk*

Kawenninon

Born 26 Feb 1956

RESIDENCE: Hogansburg, NY

EDUCATION: General Vanier Secondary School

OCCUPATION: Teacher, basketmaker, craftswoman, and painter

MEDIA: Oil, acrylic, pencil, pen and ink, pastel, and charcoal

PUBLISHED: Johannsen and Ferguson, eds. (1983)

EXHIBITS: Throughout New York and Florida

Thompson, Ray *Apache*

EXHIBITS: HM/G

AWARDS: HM/G ('75, Best of Apache Award)

Thompson, Robert *Laguna*

Pai-tu-mu

PUBLISHED: Snodgrass (1968)

PUBLIC COLLECTIONS: SM

EXHIBITS: AIW

Thompson, Roger *Seneca*

RESIDENCE: Gowanda, NY

MEDIA: Prismacolor

PUBLIC COLLECTIONS: SMII

Thompson, Thomas *Laguna*

PUBLISHED: Snodgrass (1968)

EXHIBITS: AIEC, AIW

Thornton, Clinton Evan *Cherokee*

Born 7 Apr 1941 in Rose, OK; son of C. R. Thornton

RESIDENCE: Jay, OK

EDUCATION: Salina (OK) High School; NEO, 1958-1959; B.A., NSU, 1962

PUBLISHED: Snodgrass (1968)

PUBLIC COLLECTIONS: BIA, IACB

EXHIBITS: PAC; Springfield (MO) Art Center; see also Awards

AWARDS: Muskogee (OK) Annual Art Show

Three Stars, Elton A. *Oglala Sioux*

RESIDENCE: Sioux Falls, SD

OCCUPATION: Sculptor and painter

MEDIA: Oil, acrylic, and watercolor

COMMISSIONS: *Murals:* DIA, 1993

EXHIBITS: ITAE/M ('91)

THUNDER CLOUD *Southern Cheyenne*

A.K.A. Richard A. Davis

PUBLISHED: Dorsey (1905)

THUNDERHAWK, MERLE *Brûlé Sioux*

Born 11 Apr 1950

RESIDENCE: Dallas, TX

EDUCATION: N. R. Crozier Technical High School, Dallas, TX; El Centro Junior College, Dallas, TX; IAIA

MEDIA: Oil

PUBLISHED: Mahey, et al. (1980); Hill (1992)

PUBLIC COLLECTIONS: IAIA, PAC

EXHIBITS: IAIA, PAC, RC, SN

AWARDS: IAIA; PAC ('70, Grand Award); RC ('85, Pepion Family Award); SN

THUNDERMAKER (see Waresback, Charles)

THUN POVI (see Montoya, Sidney, Jr.)

THU-YINE-HOOTSUU (see Hood, Larry)

THYMA (see Adams, Elliot)

TIA NA (see Toledo, José Rey)

TIASAH (see Watt, Gailey)

TIBBLES, SUSETTE LA FLESCHE *Omaha*

Inshtatheumba, Bright Eyes

A.K.A. Yosette

Born 1854 in Bellevue, NE, on the Omaha Reservation; died 1903 in Lincoln, NE; daughter of Mary Gale (Hinnuaganun, The One Woman) and Joseph La Flesche (Ishtamaza), the last Omaha chief

EDUCATION: Omaha Presbyterian Mission School; Elizabeth (NJ) Institute for Young Ladies

OCCUPATION: Teacher, illustrator, interpreter, and painter

PUBLISHED: Dockstader (1977); Samuels (1985). Biographical publications

TICHKEMATSE (see Squint Eyes)

TICKEETOO (see Lucy)

TIGER, CHRIS (see Tiger, Jerome Christopher)

TIGER, DANA *Creek/Seminole/Cherokee*

A.K.A. Dana Irene Tiger

Born 9 Dec 1961; daughter of Peggy Richmond and Jerome Richard Tiger (q.v.); sister of Jerome Christopher and Lisa Tiger (qq.v.); P/GP: Loucinda and John Tiger; M/GM: Ella Richmond; P/uncle: Johnny Tiger Jr. (q.v.)

RESIDENCE: Tahlequah, OK

EDUCATION: Muskogee (OK) High School, OK, 1980; OSU; studied under Johnny Tiger, Jr (q.v.)

OCCUPATION: Lecturer; full-time artist since 1985

MEDIA: Acrylic, watercolor, and pencil

PUBLISHED: *Twin Territories* (Vol. 3, no. 1, 1993), cover; *The Tulsa World* (3 Dec 1993; 6 Feb 1995)

PUBLIC COLLECTIONS: GM

THUNDER CLOUD

Along with Hubble Big Horse (q.v.), Bear Wings (Charles Murphy), and William Fletcher, Thunder Cloud created drawings of shields, painted tipis, warrior victories, or other aspects of Cheyenne life for James Mooney, ethnologist, 1901-1902.

Peter J. Powell, p.c. 1993

SUSETTE LA FLESCHE TIBBLES

Tibbles became very involved in Indian affairs and, with her newspaper publisher husband, toured the United States and England to lecture on Indian rights and White wrongs. She and her husband appeared before Congressional committees in an effort to see that Indian needs received a fair hearing. They also lectured and wrote extensively.

Dockstader 1977

DANA TIGER

The artist was only five years old when her well-known father, Jerome Tiger, died. She says that she studied his art as a means of getting to know him. With tutoring and encouragement from her uncle, Johnny Tiger Jr. (q.v.), she became a full-time painter in 1985. Her paintings portray the dignity, strength, and determination of contemporary Indian women.

p.c. 1990

EXHIBITS: CIM; CNM; FCTM; HM/G; IS; ITAE/M; NARF; PAC; SDCC; TAIAF; TIAF; TWF; Ya-Ta-Hay Festival, New London, CT; United National Indian Tribal Youth Art Show, Washington, D.C.

AWARDS: CNM ('88, 1st; '89); FCTM ('76, 1st-student; '78, Best of Show; '80, Best of Show; '87); HM/G ('78, Judge's Choice-student); TIAF ('88, 1st; '89, Featured Artist)

HONORS: The International Association of Chiefs of Police Convention, Tulsa, OK, print presented to selected individuals; *Native American Rights Fund Magazine*, first woman featured as cover artist; TWF, featured artist, 1993

TIGER, DONNA J. *Seminole*

Born 29 May 1957

RESIDENCE: Tulsa, OK

EDUCATION: Holdenville (OK) High School; BC; ECSC/OK; Connors State College, Warner, OK

OCCUPATION: Craftswoman and painter

EXHIBITS: BC; CNM; ECSC/OK; FCTM; IS; RC; TIAF; Jefferson Tour Art Festival, Muskogee, OK; National Women's Association Conference, Washington, D.C.; Willard Stone Memorial Art Show, Locust Grove, OK

AWARDS: BC, ECSC/OK

HONORS: Bacone College, Irene Horton Indian Art Scholarship

JEROME CHRISTOPHER TIGER

Chris Tiger died at age 23 from a gunshot wound to the head after a night spent partying with several acquaintances. Ironically, Jerome Tiger, his father, also died as the result of a gunshot wound to the head when Chris was only two weeks old.

TIGER, JEROME CHRISTOPHER *Creek/Seminole/Cherokee*

A.K.A. Chris Tiger

Born Aug 1967; died 9 May 1991 in Muskogee, OK; son of Peggy Richmond and Jerome Richard Tiger (q.v.); brother of Dana and Lisa Tiger (qq.v.); P/uncle: Johnny Tiger Jr. (q.v.)

RESIDENCE: Lived in Muskogee, OK

PUBLISHED: *The Muskogee Daily Phoenix* (11 May 1990); *The Tulsa World* (11 May 1990; 25 Feb 1991; 28 Feb 1991)

EXHIBITS: CNM, FCTM, PAC, TIAF; see also Awards

AWARDS: FCTM ('80, 1st; '85, Arrington Award); PAC ('75, Student Award); Indian Student Art, Region One Show ('84, 1st)

JEROME RICHARD TIGER

"The artist first began to paint 'Indian style' in 1962, and submitted his initial works to the Philbrook Indian Annual that year. Much credit for Tiger's recognition must be given Nettie Wheeler of Muskogee, OK, who worked tirelessly in his behalf throughout the country."

Snodgrass 1968

While curator of Indian Art at Philbrook Art Center, Jeanne Snodgrass invited Tiger to have his first major exhibition at the museum. When almost all of the paintings in the exhibition sold on the opening night Snodgrass asked Tiger to

TIGER, JEROME RICHARD *Creek/Seminole*

Kocha

Born 8 July 1941 in Tahlequah, OK; died 13 Aug 1967; son of Loucinda Lewis and Rev. John M. Tiger; father of Dana, Lisa, and Jerome Christopher Tiger (qq.v.); brother of Johnny Tiger Jr. (q.v.); M/GF: Rev. Coleman C. Lewis

RESIDENCE: Lived in Muskogee, OK

MILITARY: U.S. Navy Reserve

EDUCATION: Eufaula (OK) High School, 1961; Cleveland (OH) Engineering Institute, 1963-1964

OCCUPATION: Laborer, prizefighter, sculptor, and painter

MEDIA: Oil, watercolor, tempera, casein, pencil, and pen and ink

PUBLISHED: Snodgrass (1968); Brody (1971); Warner (1975, 1979); Highwater (1976; 1978b); Dockstader (1973; 1977); Silberman (1978); Mahey, et al. (1980); Tiger and Babcock (1980); Broder (1981); King (1981); Fawcett and Callander (1982); Hoffman, et al. (1984); Wade, ed. (1986); Williams, ed. (1990); Archuleta and Strickland (1991); Ballantine and Ballantine (1993). *Checker Links* (Jan/Feb 1965); *The Arizona Republic* (17 Mar 1968); *Oklahoma Today* (summer 1971; Dec 1990; June 1992); *Native Arts West* (Mar 1981); *The Indian Trader* (June 1981); *Southwest Art* (Dec 1986; 1992); *Tamaqua* (winter/spring 1991); *Native* (winter/spring 1991); *Native Peoples* (fall 1991)

BOOKS ILLUSTRATED: Foreman (1989), cover

COMMISSIONS: *Murals:* Calhoun's Department Store, Muskogee, OK

PUBLIC COLLECTIONS: BIA; FCTM; GM; MAI; MNM; PAC; USDI; WOM; Muskogee (OK) Public Library

EXHIBITS: AAID; AC/A; ASM; FAIEAIP; GM; HM; HSM/OK; IK; ITIC; MKMcNAI; MNM; MPABAS; NAP; OAC; OMA; PAC; SN; SV; Marymount College, Tarrytown, NY; Presbyterian Convention, Ridgecrest, NJ; see also Awards

SOLO EXHIBITS: CNM; FCTM; PAC; Muskogee (OK) Public Library; Central National Bank, Enid, OK; Fort Smith (AR) Art Center

AWARDS: AAID ('65, Grand Award); ITIC; MNM; PAC; SN; National Exhibition of American Indian Art, Oakland, CA ('66, 1st)

TIGER, JOHNNY, JR. *Creek/Seminole*

Born 13 Feb 1940 in Tahlequah, OK; son of Loucinda Lewis and Rev. John M. Tiger; brother of Jerome Tiger (q.v.) M/GF: Rev. Coleman C. Lewis

RESIDENCE: Muskogee, OK

EDUCATION: BC, 1959-1960

OCCUPATION: Automotive body shop employee, teacher, commercial artist, gallery owner; full-time painter and sculptor since ca. 1971

MEDIA: Oil, acrylic, watercolor, charcoal, pencil, and bronze

PUBLISHED: Highwater (1976). *Southwest Art* (Dec 1974; Mar 1975; Aug 1988); *The Indian Trader* (July 1978; Feb 1992); *Oklahoma Art Gallery* (spring 1980); *The Sunday Oklahoman* (22 Dec 1991); *The Muskogee Daily Phoenix* (26 Sept 1982; 4 Oct 1993); *The Tulsa World* (3 Dec 1993)

PUBLIC COLLECTIONS: FCTM, GM, CNM

EXHIBITS: BC/McG; CNM; FCTM; HM/G; ITAE; ITAE/M; ITIC; MPABAS; OIAP; OSC; PAC; SDCC; TIAF; TWF; SN; WIAME; Fort Smith (AR) Art Center; Highgate Literary Institute, London, England; Okmulgee (OK) Art Guild Show; Russian Cultural Museum, Togliate, Russia; Seminole Nation Art Show, Wewoka, OK; galleries in AZ, FL, OK, TN, and Washington, D.C.; see also Awards

SOLO EXHIBITS: FCTM

AWARDS: CNM ('74, 1st; '92; '94); FCTM ('67, 1st; '68, 1st, IH; '70, Tiger Award, IH; '71; '72, Tiger Award; '75; '77, 1st, Tiger Award; '78, 1st, Grand Award, IH; '80); FCTM/M ('83, Traditional Award; '84, Traditional Award; '87; '91; '92, 2-1st; '93, IH; '94, Best of Show); ITIC ('72; '76; '87); PAC ('70; '72; '74; '75; '78); TIAF; WIAME ('94); Creek Nation Art Show ('89, 1st, Best of Show); Oklahoma Indian Heritage Art Show (1st)

HONORS: Oklahoma State Capitol Building, Oklahoma City, Artist of the Month, Jan 1978; FCTM, designated a Master Artist, 1982; ITAE, poster artist, 1991; TWF, featured artist, 1993

TIGER, JON *Creek*

A.K.A. Johnathan Mark Tiger

Born 17 June 1954 in Talihina, OK; son of Harriett and Yahola Tiger; P/GP: Katie and Miller Tiger; M/GP: Susie Cosar and Bennie Buckskin Scott; cousin of Jerome Tiger and Johnny Tiger Jr. (qq.v.)

RESIDENCE: Eufaula, OK

EDUCATION: Sequoyah High School, Tahlequah, OK, 1973; IAIA 1973-1974; OSU/O; University of Science and Arts, Chickasha, OK

OCCUPATION: Elder Nutrition employee, graphic artist, and painter

MEDIA: Acrylic, watercolor, pencil, pen and ink, and pastel

COMMISSIONS: Native Language Institute, logo

PUBLIC COLLECTIONS: FCTM; HCC; Claremore (OK) Indian Hospital

JEROME RICHARD TIGER

(continued) produce more paintings to replace those sold. Before the close of the exhibition, Tiger had replaced the paintings twice.

Snodgrass-King, p.c. 1994

Tiger was a high school dropout, a street and ringfighter, and a laborer but, most of all, an artist. At twenty-six years of age he died of an apparently unintentional, self-inflicted gun shot wound to the head. He left behind a unique view of his Indian heritage and a remarkable legacy of beauty.

JOHNNY TIGER JR.

Tiger is best known for his detailed paintings of Plains Indian dancers and warriors. He has also won awards for his sculptures.

JON TIGER

"Many of the themes and subjects I choose are of the legendary, spiritual or everyday life of the first people. Reading Indian history, listening to elders and being aware of current events are just a part of depicting the true Indian. Research is a must if one wants to portray the Indian accurately."

artist, p.c. 1990

EXHIBITS: AIAFM, AIIM, CCH/OK, CNM, FCTM, HCC, LIAS, OIAC, OIO, PNAS, RC, TIAF, TM/NE, WIAME; see also Awards

SOLO EXHIBITS: FCTM

AWARDS: CNM ('88, 1st; '89, 1st; '90; '94); FCTM ('73, 1st, Best in Show-student; '76. IH; '77; '79); OIO ('88); RC ('90, 1st); Eufaula (OK) Art Guild ('88; '89); Potawatomi Art Show, Shawnee, OK ('80); Tulsa (OK) Indian Art Fair ('71)

TIGER, LISA *Creek/Seminole/Cherokee*

A.K.A. Lisa Lou Ella Tiger

Born 2 Mar 1965; daughter of Peggy Richmond and Jerome Richard Tiger (q.v.); sister of Dana and Jerome Christopher Tiger (qq.v.); P/uncle: Johnny Tiger Jr. (q.v.)

RESIDENCE: Muskogee, OK

PUBLISHED: *The Muskogee Sunday Phoenix*(22 Feb 1981)

EXHIBITS: FCTM, PAV, TWF

AWARDS: FCTM ('78, 1st, Brown Heritage Award; '80, Brown Heritage Award); PAC ('76, 1st)

HONORS: TWF, featured artist, 1993

TIGER, STEPHEN *Seminole*

RESIDENCE: Hialeah Gardens, FL

OCCUPATION: Painter

EXHIBITS: SFFA, WIB

TIKITO *Inuit (Eskimo)*

A.K.A. Tikitok

Born 1908

RESIDENCE: Cape Dorset, NWT, Canada

OCCUPATION: Graphic artist

MEDIA: Black pencil

PUBLISHED: Houston (1967a); Goetz, et al. (1977)

EXHIBITS: C/CD, C/TIP

TIKITOK (see Tikito)

TIKTAAL, IRENE (see Avaalaqiaq, Irene)

TIMECHE, BRUCE *Hopi*

Born 9 Nov 1923 at Shungopovi, Second Mesa, AZ; died Apr 1987; son of Myra Joshua and Porter Timeche

RESIDENCE: Lived in Phoenix, AZ

EDUCATION: Phoenix; Kachina School of Art, Phoenix, AZ, 1955-1958; Phoenix College; B.F.A., ASU, 1975

OCCUPATION: Sales clerk, barber, teacher, *katsina* carver, and painter

MEDIA: Oil, acrylic, watercolor, pen and ink, pencil, and cottonwood root

PUBLISHED: Dunn (1968); Snodgrass (1968); Brody (1971); Tanner (1973); Seymour (1968)

COMMISSIONS: *Murals:* First National Bank, Phoenix, AZ (assistant); Desert Hills Motel, Phoenix, AZ (assistant)

PUBLIC COLLECTIONS: BA/AZ; IACB; IACB/DC; LMA/BC; MAI; MNA; SMNAI; Bank of America (formerly The Arizona Bank)

EXHIBITS: ASF; FAIEAIP; HM; HM/G; ITIC; MNA; MNM; PAC; SN; WRTD; Maricopa County Fair, Mesa, AZ; Grand Canyon National Park, Visitor's Center, AZ; Artist-in-Particular, Phoenix, AZ; Waldorf-Astoria Scholarship Fund Exhibition, New York, NY

BRUCE TIMECHE

"Through Mrs. C. V. Whitney, the artist received a scholarship making formal art training possible for 30 months. He was a portrait artist, a carver of excellent katsinas, *and was equally adept in the execution of Hopi ethnographic paintings. He began painting about 1955."*

Snodgrass 1968

AWARDS: ITIC; HM/G ('64; '72, '77, 1st); MNM; PAC; SN
HONORS: Mrs. Cornelius Vanderbilt Whitney, scholarship, 1955

TIMECHE, HAROLD *Hopi*
Born 23 June 1924; died 7 Mar 1948
EDUCATION: Phoenix, 1938-1941; studied under Fred Kabotie (q,.v.), 1941-1943
PUBLISHED: Snodgrass (1968); Tanner (1973)
EXHIBITS: ASF

HAROLD TIMECHE

"For many years the artist's father was employed at Hopi House in Grand Canyon. A frail boy most of his life, Timeche was in several tuberculosis sanitariums before he returned to his home in Shungopovi, AZ. It was during this time that he did most of his paintings. Shortly after completing a painting for Philbrook's Indian Annual in 1948, the artist contracted flu and died."

Snodgrass 1968

TIMMONS, DAN B. *Cherokee*
Birth date unknown; born in Norman, OK
RESIDENCE: Norman, OK
EDUCATION: B.F.A., U of OK, 1976
OCCUPATION: Engraver, illustrator, and painter
MEDIA: Watercolor
EXHIBITS: CIAI, CNM, FCTM
AWARDS: FCTM ('78)

TIMMONS, DAVID R. *Cherokee*
RESIDENCE: Tahlequah, OK
EXHIBITS: FCTM, PAC
AWARDS: FCTM ('75, IH); PAC ('75, 1st)

TINNING, JOANN *Cherokee*
EXHIBITS: CNM

TINZONI *Shoshoni*
A.K.A. No Heart
PUBLISHED: Snodgrass (1968). *Bulletin 61,* BAE (1918)
PUBLIC COLLECTIONS: DAM

TINZONI

"The artist was painting in the area of the Shoshoni Reservation, WY, in 1885."

Snodgrass 1968

TI OOKEAH BAHZE (see Fireshaker, Franklin)

TIO-UM-BASKA (see Miller, Wade)

TITLA, PHILLIP *San Carlos Apache*
Born 17 Sept 1948 in Miami, AZ
RESIDENCE: San Carlos, AZ
OCCUPATION: Sculptor and painter
MEDIA: Watercolor, pen and ink, and stone
EXHIBITS: HM/Gl SDCC ('86)

TOAHANI (see Jackson, Ronald Toahani)

TOAHTY, ZACHARY *Kiowa/Otoe*
EDUCATION: IAIA, 1965-1966
EXHIBITS: YAIA

TOBÁÁHE (see Gene, Jack Tobááhe)

TO-BO-HAWN-THA (see Cabaniss, Donnie)

TODACHEENIE, BARRY *Navajo*
EDUCATION: U of OK, 1965
OCCUPATION: Commercial artist and painter
PUBLISHED: Snodgrass (1968)
PUBLIC COLLECTIONS: MNA
HONORS: Navajo Tribal Scholarship

BARRY TODACHEENIE

"The artist prefers to execute landscapes and portraits in oils. He believes he has inherited his art ability from his mother, a fine weaver living near Leupp, AZ."

Snodgrass 1968

TO'DACHINE (see Hadley, Wade)

TODACHINE, GILBERT *Navajo*

Born 28 May 1953 in Ganado, AZ

RESIDENCE: Fort Defiance, AZ

EDUCATION: Monument Valley (AZ) High School; American Indian Bible College

MEDIA: Oil, acrylic, watercolor, pencil, and charcoal

EXHIBITS: ITIC, NICCAS, NTF, RC; see also Awards

SOLO EXHIBITS: NTM

AWARDS: ITIC ('83); NICCAS; NTF ('81, 1st, Best of Show; '82, 2-1st; '83, 3-1st, Best in Class); Gallup (NM) Area Arts Council Art Show

GILBERT TODACHINE

Todachine paints realistic pictures of the Navajo Reservation and its people. He says that he especially likes to do portraits of the children and elders, and strives to catch their different expressions.

TODDY, CALVIN *Navajo*

Born 1955; son of Jimmy Toddy Sr. (Beatien Yazz) (q.v.); brother of Frances, Irving, and Marvin Toddy (qq.v.)

RESIDENCE: Chinle, AZ

OCCUPATION: Silversmith and painter

MEDIA: Oil, acrylic, watercolor, silver, and gemstone

PUBLISHED: Median (1981); Jacka and Jacka (1994). *The Indian Trader* (Sept 1985); *The Navajo Times* (6 Oct 1988)

PUBLIC COLLECTIONS: HCC, MNA

EXHIBITS: HCC, ITIC, MNA, NTF

AWARDS: ITIC ('85, 3-1st; '86, 1st; '87, 1st; '88, 2-1st; '89, 1st; '90, 1st; '91, 1st; '92, 4-1st, Best in Category, Best in Class; '94, 2-1st); NTF ('88, 1st)

HONORS: ITIC, poster artist, 1995

TODDY, FRANCES *Navajo*

Born 7 Feb 1969; daughter of Virginia Goodluck and Jimmy Toddy Sr. (Beatien Yazz) (q.v.); sister of Calvin, Irving, and Marvin Toddy (qq.v.); P/GP: Desbah and Joe Toddy; M/GP: Desbah and Frank Goodluck

RESIDENCE: Chambers, AZ

EDUCATION: Valley High School, 1987

OCCUPATION: Artist

MEDIA: Oil and acrylic

EXHIBITS: CNM, ITIC

AWARDS: ITIC ('90; '91)

FRANCES TODDY

The artist says, "I have painted since I was ten, however, I didn't sell any paintings. Gradually, when I was in middle school and high school I started entering exhibitions. I also did illustrations for various projects in high school. After high school I apprenticed under two of my older brothers, Marvin and Irving (qq.v). . . . My father is Beatien Yazz (q.v.), and I learned the basic way to develop form on a canvas from him. . . . I hope I can establish myself in my own right and talent. I also hope to attend art school in the very near future, as my father and brother did."

p.c. 1991

TODDY, IRVING *Navajo*

Born 4 Feb 1951; son of Elizabeth Roanhorse and Jimmy Toddy Sr. (Beatien Yazz) (q.v.); brother of Calvin, Frances, and Marvin Toddy (qq.v.)

RESIDENCE: Window Rock, AZ

EDUCATION: Inter-Mt; B.A., USU

OCCUPATION: Photographer, illustrator, tribal administrator, and painter

MEDIA: Oil, acrylic, watercolor, pencil, pen and ink, conté, charcoal, and film

PUBLISHED: Tanner (1973). *The Gallup New Mexico Independent* (10 Aug 1977); *The Indian Trader* (May 1977; Sept 1985)

PUBLIC COLLECTIONS: HCC, MNA

EXHIBITS: CNM, CPS, HCC, HM/G, ITIC, MNA, MNH/D, NMSF, NU/BC, PAC, RC, SN, SWAIA, WTF

AWARDS: HM/G ('79, 1st; '80); ITIC ('76, 1st; '79, 1st; '82, 1st; '85, 3-1st; '86, 1st; '87; '88; '89, 1st; '90, 1st; '91, 1st); PAC; RC ('75; '77; '79, 1st; '80, 1st, Woodard Award); SN; SWAIA ('86, Hinds Award; '89)

TODDY, JIMMY (see Beatien Yazz)

TODDY, MARVIN *Navajo*

Born 1954; son of Jimmy Toddy Sr. (Beatien Yazz) (q.v.); brother of Calvin, Frances, and Irving Toddy (qq.v.)

RESIDENCE: Window Rock, AZ

EDUCATION: Winslow (AZ) High School

MEDIA: Oil, watercolor, and pencil

PUBLISHED: Tanner (1973); Medina (1981); Samuels (1982); Jacka and Jacka (1994). *Arizona Living* (1 Mar 1982); *The Indian Trader* (Oct 1982; Sept 1985); *The Arizona Republic* (13 Aug 1983)

PUBLIC COLLECTIONS: HCC, MNA

EXHIBITS: HCC, HM/G, ITIC, MNA, NMSF, PAC, RC, SN, SWAIA, TAAII

AWARDS: HM/G ('70); ITIC ('68; '69, 1st; '71, 2-1st; '72, 2-1st; '76, 2-1st; '79, 2-1st; '82, 4-1st; '83, Best of Class; '85, 1st; '86, 1st; '89, 2-1st; '90, 2-1st, Elkus Award; '91, 1st; '94); RC ('77; '92, 1st); PAC ('70); SN ('68, Woodard Award)

TODEA, ROCKY *Navajo*

PUBLISHED: Snodgrass (1968); *7th Annual Report,* BAE (1885-1886)

COMMISSIONS: *Murals:* The Navajo Nation Museum, Window Rock, AZ

PUBLIC COLLECTIONS: SI/OAA

TO-GEM-HOTE (see Keahbone, Ernie)

TOHANNI KU SNI (see Broken Rope, Godfrey)

TOHASAN (see Tohausen)

TOHAUSEN *Kiowa*

Tohausen, Top Of The Mountain, Little Mountain (or Little Bluff)

A.K.A. Tohasan; Tohosa; T'ow-haw-san; Dohasan; Doha; Dohate; Aanote

Born ca. 1805; died ca. 1866 in Oklahoma; son of Chief Old Tohausen (the spelling preferred by his descendants)

PUBLISHED: Snodgrass (1968); Dockstader (1977); Boyd, et al. (1981)

TOHDACHEENY, BERNIE *Navajo*

Born 1958 in Shiprock, AZ; son of Woody Tohdacheeny

RESIDENCE: Kayenta, AZ

MILITARY: U.S. Marine Corps

EDUCATION: New Mexico Military Institute High School, Roswell, NM, 1978; college, 1980

OCCUPATION: Sculptor and painter

MEDIA: Oil, acrylic, watercolor, pencil, pen and ink, pastel, sand, stone, wood, clay, and metal

EXHIBITS: ITIC; NNTF; TF; Flamingo Gardens Folklife Festival, Miami, FL; see also Awards

AWARDS: ITIC ('85, 1st; '86, 1st); NNTF ('85, 1st, Best of Show; '86, 1st); Southern California Art Festival ('87, 1st, Governor's Award)

TOHOSA (see Tohausen)

TOHTSONIE, ANDY *Navajo*

PUBLIC COLLECTIONS: MNA

TOH YAH (see Nailor, Gerald)

IRVING TODDY

Toddy's favorite subject matter is the Navajo people and their environment, done in a realistic style. He believes that "the essence of an exceptional painting is a good drawing" and he feels it is his drawing ability that has helped him develop his unique style. A great admirer of Andrew Wyeth's work, Toddy considers him a major influence on his own style.

artist brochure 1992

MARVIN TODDY

Toddy describes his work as "detailed and realistic." His scenes are always complex and the longer you study them the more you see. Although the artist says he has no favorite subject, he especially enjoys painting children, animals, and older Navajo people.

The Indian Trader, *Sept 1985*

TOHAUSEN

"Tohousen was the fourth (and last) Kiowa tribal chief from 1833 until his death. He was prominent at the Medicine Lodge treaty signing. The chief was known to have made a Kiowa calendar on heavy manila wrapping paper using colored pencils. After his death, his nephew and namesake kept the calendar. Drawings by Silverhorn (Haungooah) (q.v.) of Tohausen's Winter Count are in the collection of the Marion Koogler McNay Art Institute."

Snodgrass 1968

TOINTIGH, JACKIE D., JR. *Kiowa/Apache*

Black Horse

Born 11 Nov 1948

RESIDENCE: Anadarko, OK

EDUCATION: Apache (OK) High School: Oklahoma University of Science and Art, Chickasha, OK; U of OK

OCCUPATION: Sculptor; full-time painter since 1974

MEDIA: Acrylic, watercolor, and stone

EXHIBITS: AIE, NTF, RE

AWARDS: AIE ('77, 1st; '78; '79, 1st; '81, 1st, Grand Award; '82; '83, 1st; '85, 1st; '86, 1st); NTF (Grand Award)

TOLEDO, JEROME *Kiowa*

EDUCATION: Santa Fe

PUBLISHED: Snodgrass (1968)

EXHIBITS: MNM

TOLEDO, JERRY *Navajo*

MEDIA: Watercolor and mixed-media

EXHIBITS: SWAIA

AWARDS: SWAIA ('73; 75, 1st; 76, 1st)

TOLEDO, JOE R. *Jémez*

RESIDENCE: Ignacio, CO

EDUCATION: B.A., Southwestern College, Winfield, KS; M.F.A., University of Northern Colorado, Greeley, CO

OCCUPATION: Teacher and artist

MEDIA: Watercolor and prints

EXHIBITS: ACAI, RE, TWF, UTAE

AWARDS: RE ('92, 1st; '94, 1st); UTAE ('92)

TOLEDO, JOSÉ REY *Jémez*

Shobah Woonhon, Morning Star; *Tia Na*, Northeast Place (used by his father's people); *Aluh Hochi*, Lightning; *Mus Truwi*, "a little mountain creature with great power" (literal translation)

Born 28 June 1915 at Jémez Pueblo, NM; died 1 Apr 1994; son of Refugia Moquino, potter, and José Ortiz Toledo; father was chief of the Jémez Arrow Society (a warrior lodge) and the first Jémez Indian to own a modern general store.

RESIDENCE: Lived in Jémez Pueblo, NM

EDUCATION: Albuquerque, 1935; Santa Fe; B.A., U of NM, 1951; M.A., U of NM, 1955; M.P.H., U of CA/B, 1972

OCCUPATION: Art instructor, education health specialist, administrator of Indian health programs, actor, educator, lecturer, muralist, and painter

MEDIA: Watercolor

PUBLISHED: Jacobson and d'Ucel (1950); Dunn (1968); Snodgrass (1968); Milton, ed. (1969); Brody (1971); Tanner (1958; 1968; 1973); Highwater (1976); Silberman (1978); Mahey, et al. (1980); Broder (1981); King (1981); Hoffman, et al. (1984); Golden (1985); Samuels (1985); Seymour (1988); Scarberry-García (1994). *Arizona Highways* (Feb 1950); "Pine Tree Ceremonial Dance," postal card of the last authentic Pine Tree Ceremonial Dance performed by the Jémez Indians painted at the dance and printed by OU/MA; *New Mexico Sun Trails* (Vol. 7, no.1, 1953); *Southwest Art* (June 1983)

BOOKS ILLUSTRATED: Reed (1979)

JOSÉ REY TOLEDO

"In his youth, the artist's observations of his cousin, Velino Shije Herrera (q.v.) painting, stimulated his interest in art. His career became well established. In 1965, after several years of little painting activity, the artist said, 'I have not lost hope to again paint seriously.'"

Snodgrass 1968

In a 1984 letter to Snodgrass, Herrera said that he was once again painting on "almost a daily basis." Herrera has been referred to as a "graphic historian" because of his recordings of the social and religious ceremonies of the Pueblo people.

COMMISSIONS: *Murals:* IPCC

PUBLIC COLLECTIONS: CGPS; GM; HM; IACB/DC; ITIC; MAI; MNA; MNM; MRFM; OU/MA; OU/SM; PAC; SAR; SDMM; SI; SM; U of NM/AM; WOM; Fred Jones Jr. Museum of Art, Norman, OK; Muskogee (OK) Public Library

EXHIBITS: AC/A, AIE, AIEC, ASM, CGPS, DAM, HH, HM, HM/G, IK, ITIC, MNM, NGA, NMSF, OMA, OU/ET, PAC, PAC/T, IPCC, SFFA, SFWF, SM, U of NM, WRTD

SOLO EXHIBITS: IPCC; Museum of Indian Arts and Culture, Santa Fe, NM, 1994

AWARDS: HM/G; ITIC; MNM; NMSF; PAC ('47, 1st); SM

TOLEDO, STEVEN J. *Jémez*

MEDIA: Watercolor

EXHIBITS: RC, TWF

AWARDS: RC ('93, Aplan Award, Woodard Award)

HONORS: RC, Thunderbird Foundation Scholarship, 1993, 1994

TO-LE-NE (see Durán, Roland)

T'OLIKT, GEORGE PEOPEO *Nez Percé*

Born 1800s; died 1935

MEDIA: Pencil and crayon

PUBLISHED: Minthorn (1991)

EXHIBITS: SAP

GEORGE PEOPEO T'OLIKT

Recording the truth of Nez Percé history and culture forms the core of Peopeo T'olikt's works, both his visual accounts of events during the 1877 War and his personal life, as well as his narratives of Nez Percé history transcribed by Sam Lott in 1935. These depictions of events witnessed in his life are complete with the detail and insight only personal involvement provides.

Minthorn 1991

TOMAHAWK, A.E. (see Edaakie, Anthony P.)

TOMOSSEE, T. *Hopi*

PUBLISHED: Dunn (1968); Snodgrass (1968); Fawcett and Callander (1982)

PUBLIC COLLECTIONS: MAI

EXHIBITS: MAI, NAP/MAI

TOMMY, TONY J. *Eskimo*

RESIDENCE: Newtok, AK

EDUCATION: Mt. Edgecumbe (AK) High School; Alaska Methodist University, Anchorage, AK

OCCUPATION: Field counselor, school aide, and painter

EXHIBITS: RC

TONEPAHOTE, BILLY *Kiowa*

RESIDENCE: Anadarko, OK

PUBLISHED: Snodgrass (1968)

EXHIBITS: PAC

TO'OAN *Kiowa*

RESIDENCE: Lived in the area of Fort Sill, OK, ca. 1886

OCCUPATION: Warrior and artist.

MEDIA: Crayon and lined paper (ledger)

PUBLISHED: Snodgrass (1968); Irvine, ed. (1974)

PUBLIC COLLECTIONS: MAI

TOODLOOK (see Tuu'luq, Marion)

TOOKOOME, SIMON *Inuit (Eskimo)*

A.K.A. Tookoome

Born 1934 near Gjoa Haven, NWT, Canada

RESIDENCE: Baker Lake, NWT, Canada

SIMON TOOKOOME

Multiple images of faces are common in Tookoome's work.

OCCUPATION: Hunter, traditional dancer, storyteller, sculptor, and graphic artist
MEDIA: Pencil, colored pencil, and prints
PUBLISHED: Goetz, et al. (1977); Jackson and Nasby (1987); Blodgett (1978a; 1978b); Routledge (1979); Latocki, ed. (1983); McMasters, et al. (1993). *Artscanada* (Vol. 28, no. 6, 1971-1972; Vol. 30, nos. 5 & 6, 1973-1974), *North* (Mar/Apr 1974)
COMMISSIONS: C/AG/WP, C/SC
PUBLIC COLLECTIONS: C/AC/MS
EXHIBITS: C/AC/MS; C/AG/O; C/AG/WP; C/CID; C/IA7; C/MAD; C/SS; C/TIP; Robertson Galleries, Ottawa, ON; Print and Drawing Council of Canada, Toronto, ON, 1976

TOOLOOKLOOK, S. (see Oonark, Jessie)

TOP OF THE MOUNTAIN (see Tohausen)

T'O POVE (see Atencio, Lorencita)

TOPPAH, HERMAN *Kiowa*

Al Qua Kou, Yellow Hair
Born 17 Aug 1923 in Carnegie, OK
RESIDENCE: Carnegie, OK
EDUCATION: St. Patrick's; Riverside; Chilocco; mural instruction under Olaf Nordmark; studied under James Auchiah, Spencer Asah, Leonard Riddles, Archie Blackowl, and Cecil Murdock (qq.v.)
MEDIA: Watercolor and casein
PUBLISHED: Jacobson and d'Ucel (1950); Snodgrass (1968); Brody (1971); Irvine, ed. (1974); King (1981)
PUBLIC COLLECTIONS: PAC; SPIM; USDI; Carnegie (OK) High School
EXHIBITS: AC/A; AIE; BNIAS; CSPIP; FANAIAE; ITIC; PAC; National Motorola Art Shows; in NC, ND, NM, and OK; see also Awards
AWARDS: AIE ('82); ITIC; PAC ('63); Regional Motorola Art Show

TORA QUA TAY (see Franks, Rhonda)

TORIVIO, LOLITA A. *Acoma*

EDUCATION: Santa Fe
MEDIA: Tempera
PUBLISHED: Dunn (1968); Snodgrass (1968)
EXHIBITS: AIEC, NGA

TOSA, LAWRENCE *Jémez*

Born 1947
EDUCATION: Jémez
PUBLISHED: Snodgrass (1968)
EXHIBITS: AAIE, MNM
AWARDS: MNM

TOSA, MARY *Jémez*

EDUCATION: Jémez, ca. 1959
PUBLISHED: Snodgrass (1968)
EXHIBITS: MNM

TOSA, PAUL *Zia*

PUBLISHED: Snodgrass (1968)
EXHIBITS: AAIEAE

TOSA, TONY *Jémez*

Born 1947

EDUCATION: Jémez

PUBLISHED: Snodgrass (1968)

EXHIBITS: AAIE, MNM

TOSCANO, DEE *Cherokee*

RESIDENCE: Wheatridge, CO

MEDIA: Oil, watercolor, and pastel

PUBLISHED: Samuels (1982). *Southwest Art* (Nov 1974); *Artists of the Rockies and the Golden West* (spring 1979); biographical publications

EXHIBITS: Local and regional art shows; see also Awards

AWARDS: Allied Artists of America, New York, NY ('77, Fitzgerald Award); Catherine Lorillard Wolfe Art Club, Inc., New York, NY ('77, Gold Medal; '78, Bronze Medal); Mainstreams 1977, OH ('77, 2-Awards of Distinction); Pastel Society of America ('77, Flora Guffuni Award)

TOSHEWANA, ROBERT LEO *Zuni*

EDUCATION: Santa Fe, ca. 1960

PUBLISHED: Snodgrass (1968)

EXHIBITS: 1961-1962: MNM, PAC

AWARDS: MNM ('62)

TOSQUE (see Williams, David Emmett)

TOTAY GONAI (see Standing Buffalo)

TOUCHETTE, CHARLEEN *Blackfeet*

RESIDENCE: Santa Fe, NM

MEDIA: Acrylic

PUBLISHED: Younger, et al. (1985). *Weekly/Willamette Week* (Aug 1983); *Calyx* (spring 1984)

EXHIBITS: FSMCIAF, WSCS, WWM

CHARLEEN TOUCHETTE

Touchette says that she paints images that are positive and life affirming and which create a feeling of peace and harmony. She paints about her life as a woman, daughter, sister, and mother.

Younger, et al. 1985

TOUCHIN, JASON *Navajo*

Born 11 Feb 1969

RESIDENCE: Window Rock, AZ

EDUCATION: St. Michael's (AZ) High School, 1986; ASU

OCCUPATION: Architecture student at ASU and painter

MEDIA: Acrylic

EXHIBITS: HM/G, ITIC, NTF

AWARDS: NTF

TOUGH SOLDIER *Sioux*

Zuyaterila

PUBLISHED: Snodgrass (1968)

PUBLIC COLLECTIONS: MPM (pictograph on paper)

TOUNKEUH *Kiowa*

Tounkeuh, Good Talk

A.K.A. Toun Keuh

Born 1855; died 1882

EDUCATION: Hampton; Carlisle

PUBLISHED: Snodgrass (1968)

PUBLIC COLLECTIONS: YU/BRBML

EXHIBITS: BPG

TOUNKEUH

"The artist was among the 72 Plains Indians taken as prisoner from Fort Sill, OK, to Fort Marion, St. Augustine, FL, in 1875."

Snodgrass 1968

After attending Hampton and Carlisle Indian Schools, Tounkeuh returned to Indian Territory in 1880.

T'ow-haw-san (see Tohausen)

Townsend, Roger *San Felipe*
EDUCATION: Albuquerque, ca. 1959
PUBLISHED: Snodgrass (1968)
EXHIBITS: MNM

Townsend, Roy C. *San Felipe*
EDUCATION: Santa Fe, ca. 1958
MEDIA: Watercolor
PUBLISHED: Snodgrass (1968)
PUBLIC COLLECTIONS: HM
EXHIBITS: MNM

Toya, Johnny *Jémez*
PUBLISHED: Snodgrass (1968)
PUBLIC COLLECTIONS: MAI (1956 painting)

Toya, José María *Jémez*
PUBLISHED: Snodgrass (1968)
PUBLIC COLLECTIONS: MAI

Toya, Mary Isabel *Jémez*
PUBLISHED: Snodgrass (1968)
PUBLIC COLLECTIONS: MNM (acquired when the artist was eleven years old)

Toya, Maxine R. Gachupín (see Gachupín, Maxine)

Toya, Patricia (see Toya, Patricio)

Toya, Patricio *Jémez*
PUBLISHED: Snodgrass (1968)
PUBLIC COLLECTIONS: CGA, MNM
EXHIBITS: ACC, EITA

Toya, Pete *Jémez*
Born 1945 in Jémez Pueblo, NM
EDUCATION: Jémez
PUBLISHED: Snodgrass (1968)
PUBLIC COLLECTIONS: MNA
EXHIBITS: MNM, PAC
AWARDS: MNM

Toya, Rosie *Jémez*
Born 1947 in Jémez Pueblo, NM
EDUCATION: Jémez
PUBLISHED: Snodgrass (1968)
EXHIBITS: AAIE, MNM

Tracey, Edmond L. (see Tracy, Edmond L.)

Tracey, Raymond *Navajo*
RESIDENCE: La Crescenta, CA
PUBLISHED: *The Indian Trader* (July 1986)

Tracy, E. *Pueblo*
PUBLISHED: Snodgrass (1968)
PUBLIC COLLECTIONS: RM

TRACY, EDMOND L. *Navajo*

Owipo

A.K.A. Edmond L. Tracey

OCCUPATION: Painter

MEDIA: Watercolor

PUBLISHED: Dunn (1968); Snodgrass (1968); Brody (1971). *Arizona Highways* (July 1956)

PUBLIC COLLECTIONS: DAM, HM, RM, WWM

EXHIBITS: DAM, HM, WWM

TRACY, JO ELLIS *Cherokee*

RESIDENCE: Pasadena, CA

PUBLISHED: Snodgrass (1968)

EXHIBITS: PAC

TRADER BOY (see Howe, Oscar)

TRAILING SUN (see Kabotie, Fred)

TREAS, BYRON L. *Apache (?)*

PUBLISHED: Snodgrass (1968)

PUBLIC COLLECTIONS: AF

TREAS, RUDOLPH *Mescalero Apache*

Birth date unknown; died 1969

EDUCATION: Santa Fe; U of AZ

MEDIA: Watercolor

PUBLISHED: Dunn (1968); Snodgrass (1968); Brody (1971); Tanner (1973); Seymour (1993)

PUBLIC COLLECTIONS: AF, MAI, MNA, MRFM, PAC, SAR

EXHIBITS: AIAE/WSU, HM, LGAM, MNM, PAC, SAR, SI, SN

AWARDS: MNM, PAC, SAR, SN

RUDOLPH TREAS

Tanner (1973) characterized Treas' work as predominantly flat colors with an occasional suggestion of modeling, flat portrayals of figures against a blank ground, and an occasional bit of ground line. In his later work the background became more elaborate with more realistic figures and action. According to Seymour (1993) Treas exhibited his work from the late 1940s to the early 1960s.

TREE, ROBERT *Navajo*

RESIDENCE: Kayenta, AZ

PUBLIC COLLECTIONS: HCC

EXHIBITS: CNM, HCC, RC

AWARDS: RC ('84, Woodard Award; '89, Niederman Award)

TREON, MARGUERITE MICHELSON *Cherokee*

Born 14 Apr 1922 in Independence, MO; daughter of Lockey Ellis and Alexander Michelson; P/GM: Minnie Michelson; M/GP: Elizabeth Mantooth and George Washington Ellis

RESIDENCE: Las Cruces, NM

EDUCATION: Westport High School, Kansas City, MO, 1939; B.F.A., NMSU, 1980; M.A., NMSU, 1982; KCAI/MO; Otis/Parsons Art Institute, Los Angeles, CA; ASL

OCCUPATION: Educator and painter

MEDIA: Oil, acrylic, watercolor, pencil, pen and ink, pastel, and prints

PUBLIC COLLECTIONS: NMSU

EXHIBITS: AC/Z; BM/B; KCPA; NMSU; The Amarillo (TX) Competition; Art Center, Los Alamos, NM; Branigan Cultural Center, Las Cruces, NM; The Bridge Center for Contemporary Art, El Paso, TX; New Jersey State Art Show; Stifel Arts Center, Wheeling, WV; Somerset Art Association, Far Hills, NJ; Summit (NJ) Art Center; galleries in AZ, MA, NM, NYC, and Washington, D.C.; see also Awards

AWARDS: Hunterdon Art Center, Clinton, NJ ('76, Watercolor Award)
HONORS: Otis/Parson Art Institute, Los Angeles, CA; KCAI/MO

TRIMBLE, CHARLES *Oglala Sioux*

Chun Sha Sha, Red Willow
Born 1935 at Wanblee, SD, on the Pine Ridge Reservation
RESIDENCE: Omaha, NE
EDUCATION: Holy Rosary Mission, Pine Ridge, SD; Cameron University, Lawton, OK; U of SD; U of CO
OCCUPATION: Illustrator, schedules analyst, and painter
PUBLISHED: Libhart (1970). *The Indian Trader* (Apr 1976)
PUBLIC COLLECTIONS: IACB
EXHIBITS: AAID; CSP; Indian Art Exhibit, La Grande, OR; throughout the western U.S.

TRIPLE K CO-OPERATIVE

LOCATION: Red Lake, ON, Canada

The Triple K Co-operative was set up in the fall of 1973 by brothers, Josh (q.v.) and Henry Kakegamic. For over a year, Josh had been concerned about artistic control over the printing of his works and the cost of contract printing. He and Henry created the organization, at first producing unlimited reproductions on cloth and paper, mostly from work done by Josh and his other brother, Goyce. Soon they decided to begin printing original limited-edition prints only, with the artist involved at every stage. In addition to the Kakegamic brothers, Norval Morrisseau, Barry and Paddy Peters, and Saul Williams (qq.v.) have all had prints produced by the co-operative. In 1978, in order to have more time to paint, Goyce sold his share in the press to his brother Howard. The Co-operative closed in 1983 when Henry retired.

BRIAN D. TRIPP

Tripp's art work reflects the tribal values to which he is committed: balance, order, and respect. He is a traditional dancer and singer and he often gives his works titles that reflect these activities. He has said, "Just as the people before me explained their world, I try to understand and bring purpose to mine. My art is a personal reflection of that time and that reality."

catalog, CAM/S, 1985

TRIPP, BRIAN D. *Karok*

Born 1945 in Eureka, CA
RESIDENCE: Eureka, CA
MILITARY: U.S. Army, 1967-1969
EDUCATION: Del Norte County High School, Crescent City, CA; HSU, 1970-1976
OCCUPATION: Educator, cultural consultant, designer, public information officer, graphic art consultant, and artist
MEDIA: Watercolor, pen and ink, colored pencil, Prismacolor, felt tip pen, and mixed-media
PUBLISHED: Anonymous (1976); Amerson, ed. (1981); New (1981). *Native Vision* (July/Aug 1986)
PUBLIC COLLECTIONS: WSAC
EXHIBITS: AICA/SF; CAM/S; CNGM; CSU/S; CTC; HCCC; HM; HSU; NACLA; NU/BC; OSU/G; SM; SRJC; SW; TPAS; U of NV; California State Capitol Building, Sacramento, CA; Carnegie Cultural Center, Oxnard, CA; Edinboro (PA) State College; Hupa Tribal Museum, Hoopa, CA; The Alternati Center for International Arts, New York, NY, 1977

KAREN NOBLE TRIPP

Tripp's realistic paintings are often of ceremonial dances and dance costumes. Her themes also include cosmic mythology and tribal legends. In addition to realism, she explores abstraction and integrated geometric patternings.

catalog, CAM/S, 1985

TRIPP, KAREN NOBLE *Chimariko/Hupa/Karok*

A.K.A. Karen Lynn Noble
Born 5 Aug 1955 in Arcata, CA
RESIDENCE: Arcata, CA
EDUCATION: HSU
OCCUPATION: Jeweler and painter

MEDIA: Oil, watercolor, silver, gemstones, and prints
PUBLISHED: New (1981). *The Indian Trader* (Aug 1989)
EXHIBITS: AICA/SF; CAM/S; CID; CSF; HCCC; HSU; NACLA; NU/BC; PSDM; SDMM; SRJC; U of CA/D; WSCS; Indian Health Benefit Show, Sacramento, CA; Vacaville (CA) Museum, 1986-1987
SOLO/SPECIAL EXHIBITS: CNGM (dual show)

TRUDEAU, RANDY *Ojibwa*
Born 1954 in Buzwah, Manitoulin Island, ON, Canada, on the Wikwemikong Reserve
RESIDENCE: Toronto, ON, Canada
EDUCATION: Graduated Manitoulin Secondary School, ON; Laurentian University, Sudbury, ON, Summer Arts Program
OCCUPATION: Teacher, sculptor, and painter
PUBLISHED: Southcott (1984)
COMMISSIONS: Wikwemikong Recreational and Cultural Centre, paintings on beams (with James Simon)
EXHIBITS: C/CNAC

TRUJILLO, ANDREW *Cochití*
Ca Wate Wa
A.K.A. J. Andrew Trujillo; Andy Trujillo
RESIDENCE: Peña Blanca, NM
EDUCATION: Santa Fe
MEDIA: Watercolor
PUBLISHED: Snodgrass (1968)
PUBLIC COLLECTIONS: HM, MAI

TRUJILLO, ASCENSIÓN *San Juan*
Poquin Tahn
Born 23 May 1933 at San Juan Pueblo, NM; died ca. 1959
EDUCATION: Santa Fe, 1953; U of NM
MEDIA: Watercolor and tempera
PUBLISHED: Snodgrass (1968)
PUBLIC COLLECTIONS: HCC, HM
EXHIBITS: FWG, HCC, MNM, MRFM, PAC
AWARDS: MNM, PAC

TRUJILLO, DEBRA *Tewa*
EXHIBITS: HM/G
AWARDS: HM/G ('91, Best of Class, Best of Division)

TRUJILLO, GREGORY *Cochití*
EDUCATION: Santa Fe, ca. 1958
PUBLISHED: Snodgrass (1968)
PUBLIC COLLECTIONS: HM
EXHIBITS: MNA

TRUJILLO, JENNIE *Taos*
RESIDENCE: Second Mesa, AZ
EDUCATION: IAIA
PUBLISHED: Snodgrass (1968)
EXHIBITS: FAIEAIP

TRUJILLO, MANUEL *San Juan*

Peen Tseh, White Mountain

Born 21 Dec 1927 at San Juan Pueblo, NM

RESIDENCE: San Juan Pueblo, NM

MILITARY: U.S. Army, WWII

EDUCATION: Santa Fe, 1947

PUBLISHED: Snodgrass (1968); Tanner (1973)

PUBLIC COLLECTIONS: MNM, MRFM

EXHIBITS: FWG, ITIC, JGS, MNM, PAC

AWARDS: PAC

TS'A (see Montoya, Tommy)

TSABETSAYE, ROGER J. *Zuni*

ROGER J. TSABETSAYE

"The artist started painting in 1957 and has made exceptional progress in his chosen field of arts and crafts. His contemporary designs in silver are outstanding. He hopes to continue his education and become permanently connected with art education."

Snodgrass 1968

Tsabetsaye, Eagle's Tail

Born 29 Oct 1941 at Zuni Pueblo, NM; GF: Henry Gaspar, Governor of Zuni Pueblo in the 1930s

EDUCATION: Albuquerque, 1957-1960; U of AZ, "Southwest Indian Art Project," scholarship, summer 1961; IAIA, 1962; Rochester S. T.

OCCUPATION: Teacher, silversmith, ceramist, and painter

MEDIA: Oil, casein, clay, gemstones, and silver

PUBLISHED: Dunn (1968); Snodgrass (1968); Brody (1971); Tanner (1973); Axford (1980). *Native American Art 2* (1968)

COMMISSIONS: President Lyndon B. Johnson, silver necklace for presentation to Señora Orlich, wife of the President of Costa Rica

PUBLIC COLLECTIONS: ASM, BIA, IACB, MNA, MNM, PAC

EXHIBITS: ASM, IACB, HM, ITIC, LGAM, MNM, NMSF, PAC, SN, TIAF, USDI, YAIA

AWARDS: ITIC, MNM, PAC, SN

HONORS: Rochester (NY) School of Technology, scholarship; Albuquerque (NM) Indian School, Arts and Crafts Department Certificate of Merit and Student Service Certificate; IAIA, Outstanding Student, 1963

TSADELTAH *Kiowa*

TSADELTAH

"The artist was among the 72 Plains Indians taken as prisoners from Fort Sill, OK, to Fort Marion, St. Augustine, FL, in 1875."

Snodgrass 1968

Tsadeltah, White Goose (or White Swan)

Born 1855; died 1879 of tuberculosis

EDUCATION: Hampton

OCCUPATION: Warrior, farm worker, and painter

PUBLISHED: Snodgrass (1968)

PUBLIC COLLECTIONS: HI

EXHIBITS: BPG

TSAIN-SAH-HAY (see Palmer Dixon)

TSAIT KOPE TA *Kiowa*

TSAIT KOPE TA

"The artist was among the 72 Plains Indians taken as prisoners from Fort Sill, OK, to Fort Marion, St. Augustine, FL, in 1875."

Snodgrass 1968

Tsaitkopeta returned to Indian Territory in 1882.

Tsaitkopeta, Bear Mountain

Born 1852; died 1910 of tuberculosis

MILITARY: U.S. Army

EDUCATION: Terrytown, NY, 1878

OCCUPATION: Warrior, woodcuter, government school employee, scout, policeman, and painter

PUBLISHED: Snodgrass (1968)

PUBLIC COLLECTIONS: HS/MA

EXHIBITS: BPG

Tsalagiasiwisti (see Mitchell, Ron)

Tsa Sah Wee Eh (see Hardin, Helen)

Tsate Kongia (see Bosin, Blackbear)

Tsatlukada *Zuni*

PUBLIC COLLECTIONS: MNA

Tsatoke, Gene E. *Kiowa*

EXHIBITS: AIE

AWARDS: AIE ('74, Grand Award; '77)

Tsatoke, Lee, Jr. *Kiowa*

Birth date unknown; son of Donna Jean Mopope and Lee Monette Tsatoke (q.v.)

MEDIA: Tempera

PUBLISHED: Boyd, et al. (1983)

EXHIBITS: AIE

AWARDS: AIE ('69, 1st; '78; '80)

Tsatoke, Lee Monette *Kiowa*

Tsa To Kee, Hunting Horse

A.K.A. Lee Monett Tsa Toke

Born 21 Mar 1929 at Gotebo, OK; died ca. 1986; son of Martha Koomsa (or Koomsataddle) and Monroe Tsatoke, (q.v.); P/GF: Tsa To Kee (Hunting Horse), Kiowa scout for General Custer; M/GF: Bob Koomstaddle (or Koomsa)

RESIDENCE: Lived in Anadarko, OK

EDUCATION: Riverside, 1948

OCCUPATION: Indian City U.S.A. (Anadarko, OK) guide and free-lance artist

MEDIA: Tempera and prints

PUBLISHED: Dunn (1968); Snodgrass (1968); Brody (1981); King (1981). *American Indian Tradition* (No. 52, 1963), cover

PUBLIC COLLECTIONS: BIA; IACB; IACB/DC; LAG; MAI; MRFM; HSM/OK; PAC; SPIM; Carnegie (OK) High School

EXHIBITS: AAIE; AC/A; AIE; BNIAS; ITIC; LGAM; MNM; HSM/OK; PAC; PAC/T; SPIM; Public Library, St. Louis, MO; see also Awards

SOLO EXHIBITS: PAC; Conners State College, Warner, OK

AWARDS: ITIC; PAC; Kirkwood (MO) Sidewalk Show

Lee Monette Tsatoke

"The artist inherited his interest and talent in art from his famous father; however, he did not become actively engaged in art as a career until 1943. He credits his teachers at Riverside — Acee Blue Eagle (q.v.), Ruth Cox, and Susie Peters (the government worker who did much to encourage his father) — as having encouraged him most through the years."

Snodgrass 1968

Tsatoke is descended from two famous Kiowa chiefs, Satank and Satanta.

Tsatoke, Monroe *Kiowa*

Tsa To Kee, Hunting Horse

A.K.A. Monroe Tsa Toke

Born 29 Sept 1904 near Saddle Mountain, OK; died 3 Feb 1937 of tuberculosis; son of Tsa To Kee, Kiowa scout for General Custer; father of Lee Monette Tsatoke (q.v.); Grandmother was a white captive

RESIDENCE: Lived in Red Rock, OK

EDUCATION: BC; non-credit art classes, U of OK

OCCUPATION: Farmer, singer, fancy war dancer, and painter

MEDIA: Tempera

PUBLISHED: Jacobson (1929; 1964); Jacobson and d'Ucel (1950); Tsatoke (1957); LaFarge (1960); Dunn (1968); Snodgrass (1968); Brody (1971); Highwater (1976; 1983); Dockstader (1977); Silberman (1978); Boyd, et al. (1981; 1983); King (1981); Fawcett and Callander (1982); Hoffman, et al. (1984); Samuels (1985); Williams, ed. (1990); Archuleta and Strickland (1991). *Smoke Signals,* IACB (No. 42, 1964); *American Indian Art and Antiques* (Jan/Feb 1972); *American Indian Art* (spring 1995); a biographical publication

Monroe Tsatoke

"Tsatoke was one of the Five Kiowas (q.v.). It was recorded in 1936 that 'he could always draw pictures, but never took any art lessons until Susie Peters organized a Fine Arts Club of Indian boys and girls who showed talent in drawing and painting, beadwork, and other native work. Mrs. Willie Baze Lane also gave them lessons and encouragement.' He worked hard at his art, responding with all his spirit to the sympathy and encouragement of his teachers at Anadarko and later at the University of Oklahoma.

(continued)

COMMISSIONS: *Murals:* HSM/OK; OU/A; St. Patrick's Mission School, Anadarko, OK; Federal Building, Anadarko, OK

PUBLIC COLLECTIONS: ACM, CMA, GM, GPM, HM, IACB, IACB/DC, JAM, MAI, MKMcNAI, MNA/KHC, MNM, MRFM, HSM/OK, OU/MA, OU/SM, PAC, SPL, WOM

EXHIBITS: AC/A; AIE; AIE/T; CSPIP; GPM; HM; HSM/OK; IK; JAM; MAI; MKMcNAI; NAP; NAP/MAI; NGA; OMA; OU/ET; OU/MA; OU/MA/T; PAC; PAC/T; SPIM; SFWF; SMA/TX; SV; United Nations Conference, San Francisco, CA, 1945

AWARDS: AIE ('60, 1st); ITIC ('54, 1st)

HONORS: University of Oklahoma Press adopted his painting as a colophon

MONROE TSATOKE

(continued) He took great delight in his work, painting the things he knew first-hand. While seriously ill with tuberculosis, the artist joined the Peyote faith, becoming a member of the Native American Church, and began the series of paintings which expressed his religious experiences (published after his death). Music was also important to him; he loved to sing and, for many years, was chief singer at Kiowa dances."

Snodgrass 1968

TSATOKE, MONROE A. *Kiowa*

Birth date unknown; P/GF: Monroe Tsatoke (q.v.); nephew of Lee Monette Tsatoke (q.v.)

EDUCATION: Carnegie (OK) High School; SWOSU

PUBLISHED: *The Stillwater News Press* (3 Apr 1981)

EXHIBITS: AIE; Oklahoma State University Indian Heritage Days, Stillwater, OK

AWARDS: AIE ('70; '74; '77, 1st)

MONROE A. TSATOKE

Tsatoke credits Parker Boyiddle (q.v.) with exerting a major influence on his career. The artist sometimes uses old family photographs for reference when painting.

TSA TO KEE (see Tsatoke, Lee Monette)

TSA TO KEE (see Tsatoke, Monroe)

TS'AY TA (see Montoya, Tommy)

TSE KO YATE (see Big Bow, Woody)

TSEN T'AINTE (see White Horse)

TSE TSAN (see Velarde, Pablita)

TSE YE MU (see Virgil, Romando)

TSIHNAHJINNIE (see Tsinajinnie, Andrew Van)

TSINA *Navajo*

PUBLISHED: Snodgrass (1968)

PUBLIC COLLECTIONS: MAI

TSINAJINNIE, ANDREW VAN *Navajo*

Yazzie Bahe, Little Grey

A.K.A. Andy Tsinahjinnie

Born 16 Feb 1916 at Rough Rock, AZ; son of Anson Nez Tsinhnahjinnie

RESIDENCE: Phoenix, AZ

MILITARY: U.S. Army, WWII

EDUCATION: Santa Fe, 1932-1936; Oakland, 1950

OCCUPATION: Full-time artist after WWII

MEDIA: Oil, acrylic, watercolor, tempera, pencil, pen and ink, pastel, and wood

PUBLISHED: Jacobson and d'Ucel (1950); LaFarge (1956; 1960); Pierson and Davidson (1960); Bahti (1965); Dunn (1968); Snodgrass (1968); Brody (1971); Tanner (1968, 1973); Highwater (1976); Silberman (1978); Mahey, et al. (1980); Broder (1981); King (1981); Chase (1982); Fawcett and Callander (1982); Hoffman, et al. (1984); Samuels (1985); Wade, ed (1986); Jacka and Jacka (1988); Seymour (1988); Williams, ed. (1991); Archuleta and Strickland (1991); Schaffer (1991). *Arizona Highways* (Feb 1950; July 1956; Dec 1958); *The Tie-In* (1st Quarter 1960), cover; *Southwestern Art* (Vol. 1, no. 1, 1967); *Southwest Art* (June 1983); *The Indian Trader* (Mar 1990; Aug 1991)

BOOKS ILLUSTRATED: Clark (1940a; 1960); Thompson (1948); Morgan (1949);

ANDREW VAN TSINAJINNIE

"At about the age of five, 'Andy' learned there were such things as pencils and asked his mother to buy one when she went to the trading post for supplies. He then drew on wrapping paper and the backs of labels from cans. Until that time, the youngster had used 'stone-on-stone' to produce charming drawings. He has been a serious painter since about 1940, and is well known for his 'color periods' — blue, pink, etc. As an outlet for

Schevill (1956); Wyman (1966); Carlson and Witherspoon (1968); Hoffman (1974a); Lynch (1987)

COMMISSIONS: *Murals:* Fort Sill; NTM; Phoenix; Harris Department Stores, Riverside, CA; Navajo Sanitorium, Winslow, AZ; Westward Ho Hotel, Phoenix, AZ; Valley Ho Hotel, Scottsdale, AZ

PUBLIC COLLECTIONS: AF, BA/AZ, BIA, CGA, CGPS, CMA, GM, HCC, HM, IACB, IACB/DC, LMA/BC, MAI, MNM, MKMcNAI, MNA, MNCA, MNH/A, MRFM, OU/MA, OU/SM, PAC, RMC/AZ, SMNAI, WWM

EXHIBITS: AC/A, AC/HC, AIAE/WSU, AIEC, ASM, CGPS, FAIEAIP, HM, HM/G, IK, ITIC, MAI, MKMcNAI, MNA, MNM, NAP/MAI, OMA, OU/ET, PAC, PAC/T, PM, RMC/AZ, SFFA, SN, SNAICF, SV, USDS, WRTD, WTF, WWM

AWARDS: HM/G ('78); ITIC; MNM; PAC; SN; SNAICF ('87); *American Magazine*; national competition, 1930s; Grand Awards in Indian art competitions before 1968

HONORS: French Textile Award; National Design Award, Chicago, IL; Paul Coze Award, France; French Government, Palmes d'Académiques, 1954; Navajo Nation Fair, parade marshall, 1990; named a "Living Legend" by Ralph Oliver, 1990; Arizona Indian Living Treasure Award, 1991

ANDREW VAN TSINAJINNIE

(continued) his other creative interests, he is a member of the Navajo Salt River Band, Scottsdale, AZ, and the Navajo Tribal Band, Window Rock, AZ."

Snodgrass 1968

Tsinajinnie's art production has recently slowed due to problems with his eyesight.

TSISETE, PERCY SANDY (see Sandy, Percy Tsisete)

TSI-SGA-TSI DA-LO-NI DI-GADO-LI (see Dillard, Wanda Marcel)

TSO, JOHN *Navajo*

Birth date unknown; son of Mrs. Ason Gladys Tso, Oraibi, AZ

EDUCATION: Holbrook (AZ) High School, 1964; EAJC

PUBLISHED: Snodgrass (1968)

EXHIBITS: EAJC, Student Center

HONORS: EAJC, art award, 1965

TSO, JUSTIN *Navajo*

Born 22 Nov 1948 in Canyon de Chelly, AZ

RESIDENCE: Chinle, AZ

MILITARY: U.S. Army, 1969-1971

EDUCATION: Gallup (NM) High School; I.T.C., San Francisco, CA; U of N AZ; U of UT; A.A., Northland Pioneer College, Holbrook, AZ

OCCUPATION: Electronics repairman, horseback tour operator and guide, and painter

MEDIA: Oil, watercolor, and casein

PUBLISHED: *Plateau* (Vol. 54, no. 1, 1982); *Southwest Art* (May/June 1993)

EXHIBITS: AICA; SIRU; SWAIA; Transamerica Title Co., Chehalis, WA

AWARDS: AICA ('92, Silver Medal; '93, Bronze Medal)

JUSTIN TSO

Tso is a traditional painter who enjoys painting the Navajo reservation landscape, the proud Navajo people and, most of all, his beloved horses. Although he readily admits that he was influenced by the early traditional painters, especially Robert Chee (q.v.), he has developed his own distinctive style. He uses curved and free-flowing lines with great success.

Plateau, *Vol. 54, no.1, 1982*

TSOAI-TALEE (see Momaday, N. Scott)

TSOODLE, DARWIN CABANISS *Kiowa/Kiowa-Apache*

Dav-Law-T'aine, Reaching For The Stars

Born 17 Jan 1963 in Kaufman, TX; son of Angeline Tsoodle and Donnie Cabaniss

RESIDENCE: Crow Agency, MT

EDUCATION: Anadarko (OK) High School; CIA/CO; IAIA

OCCUPATION: Artist

MEDIA: Acrylic and gouache

EXHIBITS: BSIM; IAIA; Carbon County Arts Guild Exhibition, Red Lodge, MT

AWARDS: Christmas Seal Contest (1st); area exhibits

HONORS: Appointed Ambassador of Goodwill

DARWIN CABANISS TSOODLE

Tsoodle feels strongly that traditional art is the mainstay of Indian art and should be respected as a true art form. He thinks it has been grossly overlooked.

p.c. 1992

TSOODLE, JAMES *Kiowa*

Born 6 Nov 1968
RESIDENCE: Albuquerque, NM
EDUCATION: High school
MEDIA: Pastel, pencil, and pen and ink
PUBLISHED: Snodgrass (1968)
PUBLIC COLLECTIONS: MNA
EXHIBITS: ACS/ENP, AIEC, HM/G, ITIC, NMSF, SWAIA
AWARDS: NMSF

TSOODLE, TIM *Kiowa/Taos*

A.K.A. Timothy Tsoodle
Born 1 June 1958
RESIDENCE: Albuquerque, NM
EDUCATION: High school
OCCUPATION: Municipal firefighter and painter
MEDIA: Acrylic, watercolor, and pen and ink
EXHIBITS: ACS/ENP, HM/G, ITIC, NMSF
AWARDS: ACS/ENP; NMSF ('86, 1st)

TSOSIE, CHE CHILLY (see Mitchell, Stanley C.)

TSOSIE, DANNY RANDEAU *Navajo*

Born 20 Oct 1951 in Snowflake, AZ; son of Pauline Goldtooth and Tom Tsosie; brother of Dennison Tsosie (q.v.); P/GP: Esther and James Tsosie; M/GP: Irene and James Goldtooth
RESIDENCE: Taylor, AZ
EDUCATION: Snowflake (AZ) High School, 1972; Northland Pioneer College, Holbrook, AZ
OCCUPATION: Kerr-McGee Corp. employee, sculptor, and painter
MEDIA: Oil, Prismacolor, pen and ink, pastel, pencil, metal, and mixed-media
PUBLISHED: Jacka and Jacka (1988). *The Indian Trader* (May 1989); *Inter-Tribal America* (Aug 1991)
EXHIBITS: FNAA; HM/G; ITIC; MNA; NICCAS; NMSF; NTF; NTM; RC; SNAICF; TAAII; WIEAS; Washington, D.C.
AWARDS: ITIC ('76, 1st; '79; '87, 1st; '89; '90, 1st, Best In Category; '91, 1st, Elkus Award; '92, 1st); RC ('76); NTF; SNAICF ('87, 1st)
HONORS: ITIC, poster artist, 1991; FNAA, poster artist

DANNY RANDEAU TSOSIE

Tsosie credits his grandmother, a Navajo rug weaver, with being the person who influenced him the most, teaching him to live in the Navajo way. He learned drawing from his father and uncle when he was a child.

The Indian Trader, *May 1989*

TSOSIE, DENNISON *Navajo*

Born 3 Nov 1949; son of Pauline Goldtooth and Tom Tsosie; brother of Danny Randeau Tsosie (q.v.); P/GP: Esther and James Tsosie; M/GP: Irene and James Goldtooth
RESIDENCE: Overgaard, AZ
EDUCATION: Snowflake (AZ) High School, 1970; Safford (AZ) Community College, 2 years
OCCUPATION: Silversmith, sculptor, and painter
MEDIA: Oil, acrylic, watercolor, pen and ink, scratchboard, sand, silver, turquoise, clay, and wood
PUBLISHED: *The Indian Trader* (Mar 1987)
PUBLIC COLLECTIONS: CNM; NTM; Tate Ford Dealership, Holbrook, AZ
EXHIBITS: CNM, NTF, NTM; see also Awards

DENNISON TSOSIE

Dennison Tsosie has developed his own unique painting technique. He first applies several layers of sand on a board then, using an air brush, he creates works of art based on his Navajo heritage. Tsosie is also a silversmith, a craft he learned from his grandfather from whom he inherited handmade silversmithing tools.

The Indian Trader, *Mar 1987*

AWARDS: CNM ('86); NTF (several 1st); Grand National Las Vegas (NV) Indian Show ('87, 1st)

TSOSIE, GEORGE *Navajo*

PUBLISHED: Snodgrass (1968)

PUBLIC COLLECTIONS: MNA

EXHIBITS: ITIC

AWARDS: ITIC

TSOSIE, NELSON *Navajo*

Born 1 July 1961 in Shiprock, NM; son of Lucy and Ben Tsosie Sr.; M/GM: Frances Manuelito

RESIDENCE: Santa Fe, NM

EDUCATION: Window Rock (AZ) High School, 1979; A.A., Yavapai Community College, Prescott, AZ, 1981; U of AZ, 1981-1982

OCCUPATION: Full-time painter and sculptor

MEDIA: Oil, pencil, pastel, and prints

PUBLISHED: Jacka and Jacka (1994). *New Mexico Magazine* (May 1987), The *Navajo Times* (May 1989; Sept 1989; Aug 1989); *The New Mexican, Indian Market Magazine* (Aug 1989); *Pasatiempo Magazine* (Dec 1990); *Southwest Art* (Nov 1994)

PUBLIC COLLECTIONS: NTM

EXHIBITS: AICA; AC/DS; IACA; ITIC; NMSC; NMSF; NTF; RE; SIRU; SWAIA; TAIAF; Artists of Taos (NM), 1987; Goodwill Games Art Exhibit, Seattle, WA; Round-Up on the Pecos, Carlsbad, NM

SOLO EXHIBITS: NTM; King Plow Art Center, Atlanta, GA

AWARDS: IACA ('93, 1st); ITIC ('86; '94, 1st-place awards for sculpture); NTF ('88, 2-1st); RE ('91)

NELSON TSOSIE

Nelson Tsosie is well known for his pastel portraits and figure studies of contemporary and traditional Navajo people set against their native landscape. He has also won many awards for his sculptures.

p.c. 1991

TSOSIE, PAUL *Navajo*

PUBLISHED: Snodgrass (1968)

PUBLIC COLLECTIONS: MRFM, SM

TSOSIE, PAULA K. *Santa Clara/Navajo*

PUBLIC COLLECTIONS: MRFM

EXHIBITS: SWAIA

AWARDS: SWAIA ('77, 1st)

TSO YAZZIE (see Kahn, Chester)

TSR TSX (see Tartsah, Jim)

TUBBY, H. CARL *Choctaw*

A.K.A. Hildreth Carl Tubby

RESIDENCE: Philadelphia, MS

EDUCATION: Pearl River Indian School; IAIA

MEDIA: Acrylic

PUBLISHED: Hill (1992)

PUBLIC COLLECTIONS: IAIA

EXHIBITS: IAIA, RC, SNAICF

TUCSON, LOREN *Zuni*

RESIDENCE: Zuni Pueblo, NM

PUBLISHED: Snodgrass (1968)

EXHIBITS: MNM

TUDLIK

Although a talented graphic artist, Tudlik was best known for his carvings of owls.

TUDLIK *Inuit (Eskimo)*

Born ca. 1890; died 1962

RESIDENCE: Lived in Cape Dorset, NWT, Canada

OCCUPATION: Carver and graphic artist

MEDIA: Pencil, stone, and prints

PUBLISHED: Houston (1967; 1967a); Larmour (1967); Goetz, et al.(1977). *The Beaver* (spring 1975)

EXHIBITS: C/CD, C/TIP

TUDLUQ (see Tuu'luq, Marion)

TUKALA, ISAH AJAGUTAINA *Inuit (Eskimo)*

A.K.A. Ajagutaina

Born 1905; died 1977

RESIDENCE: Lived in Povungnituk, PQ, Canada

PUBLISHED: *Arts West* (Vol. 3, no.5, 1978)

EXHIBITS: C/AG/WP

CHA TULLIS

Using ordinary house paint, Tullis paints murals with American Indian themes on commercial buildings in Hominy, Oklahoma. To date (1994) he has completed 28 and plans to do at least 38 more. He says that once he completes them he will start all over again.

TULLIS, CHA *Blackfeet*

Cha'Tullis

A.K.A. Charles D. Tullis

Born 8 May 1957 in Carthage, MO; son of Shirley Baugh and Jim Tullis; P/GP: Mary Frances McDaniel and James D. Tullis; M/GP: Bessie White and Homer M. Baugh Sr.

RESIDENCE: Hominy, OK

EDUCATION: Hominy (OK) High School, 1975; Paris (TX) Junior College, 1976

OCCUPATION: Jewelry store owner, clothing designer, and painter

MEDIA: Oil, acrylic, pencil, and pen and ink

PUBLISHED: *Country Treasure Gazette* (Apr 1991); *The Tulsa World* (2 May 1991; 5 Jan 1992); *Modern Maturity* (Oct/Nov 1992); *The Oklahoma City Times* (May 9, 1993); *Southern Living* (Oct 1994)

COMMISSIONS: *Murals:* Carthage, MO; Hominy, OK, 1994

EXHIBITS: IS; Lady's Apparel Mart, Dallas, TX; Tulsa (OK) Powwow; Cherokee Heritage Powwow, Tahlequah, OK; Pawhuska (OK) French Exchange Show

HONORS: Oklahoma State Arts Council, Outstanding "Young Talent" Award, 1974, 1975; Oklahoma Department of Commerce, selected to exhibit his clothing line at the Lady's Apparel Mart, Dallas, TX, 1991

TULLIS, CHARLES D. (see Tullis, Cha)

TULLMA (see C.D.T.)

TULLUQ (see Tuu'luq, Marion)

TULMA (see C.D.T.)

TULURIALIK, RUTH ANAQTUUSI (see Annaqtuusi, Ruth)

TUMEQUAH, PENWAH *Laguna/Kickapoo*

Birth date unknown; born in Albuquerque, NM

RESIDENCE: Phoenix, AZ

MEDIA: Oil, acrylic, watercolor, and pastel

EXHIBITS: HM/G

TUMIRA *Inuit (Eskimo)*

Born 1943

RESIDENCE: Cape Dorset, NWT, Canada

OCCUPATION: Graphic artist
MEDIA: Black pencil
PUBLISHED: Houston (1967); Goetz, et al. (1977)
COMMISSIONS: C/TDB
EXHIBITS: C/EACTDB, C/TIP

TUNE (see Two Hatchet, Spencer Lee, Jr.)

TURKEY, MOSES *Kiowa*

Sah Quo Dle Quoie
PUBLISHED: Snodgrass (1968)
PUBLIC COLLECTIONS: ACM
EXHIBITS: PAC
AWARDS: PAC

TURNER, LOWELL KEVIN *Choctaw/Seminole*

Sky Painter
Born 1 Oct 1958 in St. Louis, MO; son of Irene and Lowell Turner; P/GP: Alma and Lowell Turner; M/GP: Nora and Johnny Derrick
RESIDENCE: De Soto, MO
EDUCATION: G.E.D.
OCCUPATION: Sign painter and designer, full-time artist
MEDIA: Oil and acrylic
PUBLISHED: *Popular Archaeology* (17 Apr 1989)
PUBLIC COLLECTIONS: American Museum, Bath, England; Karl May Museum, Radebuel, Germany
EXHIBITS: IACB; *Sons of the American Revolution Exhibit,* St. Louis, MO

TURNER, ROSEMARY *Chickasaw*

RESIDENCE: Rodeo, NM
EXHIBITS: FCTM, HM/G, ITIC, SN
AWARDS: FCTM ('67, Tiger Award); ITIC ('70)

TURNING BEAR (see Murdock, Cecil)

TURNING BEAR *Brûlé Sioux*

A.K.A. Chief Turning Bear
Birth date unknown
RESIDENCE: Turning Bear was with Sitting Bull's camp on the Yellowstone in 1870 (see Grass, John).
MEDIA: Watercolor, pencil, and crayon
PUBLISHED: Dunn (1968); Snodgrass (1968)
PUBLIC COLLECTIONS: MNH/A; private collection, a colored drawing executed for Capt. Leonard Hay, Ninth Infantry

TURNING BEAR

"The artist was a prisoner at Fort Omaha, NE, awaiting trial for murder in October, 1880; he later stood trial and was released (see Hyde 1961; 1956)."

Snodgrass 1968

TUSH-WIK (see Colfax, LeRoy)

TUTTLE, FRANK *Maidu/Yurok/Wailaki*

Born 1957 in Oroville, CA
RESIDENCE: Ukiah, CA
EDUCATION: Ukiah (CA) High School; B.A., HSU, 1981
OCCUPATION: Teacher, consultant, graphic artist, development coordinator, and painter
MEDIA: Oil, pencil, and pen and ink
PUBLISHED: Abbott (1994)

FRANK TUTTLE

The artist's abstract works reflect his heritage and are often inspired by the forms, textures and colors of Native American ceremonial objects.

catalog, Crocker Art Museum, 1985

BOOKS ILLUSTRATED: Indian Historian Press, children's books
PUBLIC COLLECTIONS: CAM/S
EXHIBITS: CAM/S, CNGM, CSU/S, HM, HSU, NACLA, SRJC
SOLO EXHIBITS: Mendocino County Museum, Willits, CA, 1983

TUTTLE, SONNY *Oglala Sioux*

RESIDENCE: Lander, WY
EXHIBITS: RC
AWARDS: RC ('86 and '87, Neiderman Awards)

TUU'LUQ, MARION *Inuit (Eskimo)*

A.K.A. Tudluq; Tulluq; Tuu'luuq; Toodlook; Anguhadluq
Born 1910 in the Back River area north of Baker Lake, NWT, Canada; wife of Luke Anguhadluq (q.v.)
RESIDENCE: Baker Lake, NWT, Canada
OCCUPATION: Seamstress, beadworker, and graphic artist
MEDIA: Pencil, colored pencil, animal skin, beads, and prints
PUBLISHED: Vallee (1967); Blodgett (1976; 1978a); Goetz, et al. (1977); Latocki, ed. (1983); Jackson and Nasby (1987)
PUBLIC COLLECTIONS: C/AC/MS, C/AG/WP, C/CS
EXHIBITS: C/AG/WP, C/CID, C/TIP

TUU'LUUQ (see Tuu'luq, Marion)

TUVAHOEMA, KYRATE *Hopi*

A.K.A. Kyrat Tuvahoema
Born 1914 in Old Oraibi, AZ; died 1 Jan 1942 of tuberculosis
EDUCATION: Albuquerque; Santa Fe, 1933-1935
PUBLISHED: Snodgrass (1968); Tanner (1968); Seymour (1988). *Search Magazine* (Sept 1965)
PUBLIC COLLECTIONS: CGPS, EM, GM, IACB/DC, MAI, MNA
EXHIBITS: AF, ASM, CGPS, HM, WRTD

KYRATE TUVAHOEMA

"The artist's paintings were few; he contracted tuberculosis shortly after leaving school and spent much of his remaining life in sanatoriums in Arizona."

Snodgrass 1968

Most of Tuvahoema's paintings were done in the late 1930s.

TWAISE *Hopi*

PUBLIC COLLECTIONS: MNA

TWAIT (see General, David M.)

TWAKUKU *Hopi*

PUBLISHED: Snodgrass (1968)
PUBLIC COLLECTIONS: AF

TWO-ARROWS, TOM *Onandaga*

Ga Hes Ka; De-Ga-Ya-Wela-Ge
A.K.A. Tom Dorsey
Born 2 Feb 1920 on the Onondaga Reservation, NY; son of Mary and Ira Dorsey
RESIDENCE: Albany, NY
MILITARY: U.S. Army, WWII
EDUCATION: High school, 1942
OCCUPATION: Illustrator, decorator, designer, dancer, display specialist, lecturer, teacher, museum curator, and painter
MEDIA: Acrylic and watercolor
PUBLISHED: Dunn (1968); Snodgrass (1968); Brody (1971); Warner (1975; 1978); Broder (1981); Kushner (1989); Ballantine and Ballantine (1993). *Masks and Men*, MNH/A (1946), catalog; *The Conservationist* (Jan/Feb 1976)

TOM TWO ARROWS

Recognized as an authority on Indian legends and designs, Two-Arrows used traditional Woodlands designs and symbols in his paintings, jewelry, and textiles. In 1992, he was living in Albany, NY, and hunting and fishing and not doing much painting.

p.c. 1992

BOOKS ILLUSTRATED: Two-Arrows (1989); Army booklets

COMMISSIONS: *Murals:* Post Library, Seymore Johnson Air Field; Albany (NY) State Teachers College (skin murals, hung in assembly room). *Other:* Textron, Inc, textile designs; Arzberg Porcelain, dinnerware designs

PUBLIC COLLECTIONS: AIHA, GM, JAM, MAI, MAM, MNH/A, PAC

EXHIBITS: AFA; DAM; JAM; JGS; MAI; MAM; NGA; PAC; PAC/T; U of MN/TC; Indian Art in Industry of India, Calcutta; New York State Museum, 1975; The Helderberg Workshop, Albany, NY, 1980; The Free School, Albany, NY; The Plaza, Albany, NY, 1991

SOLO EXHIBITS: AFA, CPLH, MAM

AWARDS: DAM, PAC

HONORS: Carnegie Scholastic Award

TWO BULLS, ANDREA *Oglala Sioux*

RESIDENCE: Hermosa, SD

MEDIA: Oil, acrylic, and watercolor

PUBLISHED: Day and Simon, et al. (1991)

PUBLIC COLLECTIONS: HCC

EXHIBITS: HCC, RC, TM/NE

AWARDS: RC ('93, 1st; '94, 1st)

TWO BULLS, EDWARD E. JR. *Oglala Sioux*

Hinhan Wicahca, Old Owl

Born 24 Jan 37 at Red Shirt Table, SD, on the Pine Ridge reservation

RESIDENCE: Hermosa, SD

EDUCATION: Seventh Day Adventist Mission School, Red Shirt, SD; Oglala Community School, Pine Ridge, SD

OCCUPATION: Rancher, art teacher, acting director of the Lakota Village Youth Home (Hermosa, SD), sculptor, and painter

MEDIA: Acrylic

PUBLISHED: Libhart (1970); Day and Simon, et al. (1991). *The Indian Trader* (July 1978)

COMMISSIONS: *Murals:* Santee Sioux Tribe, Neighborhood Facilities Building, Niobrara, NE, (four murals) 1974

PUBLIC COLLECTIONS: HCC, IACB

EXHIBITS: CNM; CPS; HCC; LAC; RC; SIM; SI; TM/NE; U of WV; WTF; Colorado State Fair, Pueblo, CO, 1976; Colter Bay Visitor's Center, Grand Teton National Park, WY, 1977; Wyoming State Fair, 1977

EDWARD E. TWO BULLS JR.

Two Bulls is a self-taught artist from an artistic family, however, it was only after an accident left him unable to walk that he began to concentrate on his art. He often portrays traditional themes reflective of popular perceptions of Plains Indians. Other paintings explore the rich cultural heritage of his people.

calendar, Tipi Press, 1990

TWO BULLS, LOREN *Oglala Sioux*

MEDIA: Acrylic

PUBLISHED: Day and Simon, et al. (1991)

EXHIBITS: HCC

TWO BULLS, LORRI *Oglala Sioux*

RESIDENCE: Rapid City, SD

MEDIA: Oil and graphics

PUBLIC COLLECTIONS: HCC

EXHIBITS: HCC, RC

TWO BULLS, MARTY GRANT *Oglala Sioux*

Born 3 Jan 1962 at Rapid City, SD

RESIDENCE: South Dakota

EDUCATION: Central High School, Rapid City, SD; CIA/C
MEDIA: Acrylic, watercolor, and pen and ink
PUBLISHED: Day and Simon, et al. (1991)
EXHIBITS: HCC
SOLO EXHIBITS: SIM

TWO BULLS, MATT *Oglala Sioux*
A.K.A. Matthew Two Bulls
MEDIA: Acrylic
PUBLISHED: Day and Simon, et al. (1991)
PUBLIC COLLECTIONS: HCC
EXHIBITS: HCC
HONORS: NPTA and South Dakotans for the Arts, South Dakota Living Indian Treasure Award, 1993

TWO BULLS, ROBERT *Oglala Sioux*
A.K.A. Rev. Robert Two Bulls
RESIDENCE: Rapid City, SD
MEDIA: Mixed-media
EXHIBITS: RC
AWARDS: RC ('93, Barkley Art Center Award)

TWO BULLS, SAM, JR. *Oglala Sioux*
A.K.A. Sam Two Bulls
Born 3 Jan 1964
EDUCATION: Haskell; IAIA
MEDIA: Acrylic, oil, and mixed-media
PUBLISHED: Day and Simon, et al. (1991)
PUBLIC COLLECTIONS: HCC
EXHIBITS: HCC, HPTU, IAIA, LSS, RC, TM/NE, U of WV, WTF
AWARDS: RC ('92, Diederich Award; '93, Rostkowski Award)
HONORS: *Scholarship:* RC, Thunderbird Foundation, 1992, 1993; Haskell, Dick West Fine Arts Scholarship, 1986

TWO EAGLE, VIOLET *Sioux*
RESIDENCE: Parmelee, SD
PUBLISHED: Snodgrass (1968)
EXHIBITS: BNIAS

TWO EAGLES, D. BRET *Oglala Sioux/Cheyenne*
Born 23 Feb 1945 in Crawford, NE
RESIDENCE: Denver, CO
MILITARY: U.S. Army
EDUCATION: Colorado Mountain College, Glenwood Springs, CO; Los Angeles (CA) Valley College
OCCUPATION: Private investigator, disc jockey, fireman, actor, co-owner of publishing company, and painter
PUBLISHED: *The Indian Trader* (Feb 1982); *The Denver Post, Empire Magazine* (16 May 1982)
EXHIBITS: See Awards
SOLO EXHIBITS: SIM
AWARDS: Glenwood Springs (CO) Art Guild Show ('80)

TWO-HATCHET, SPENCER LEE, JR. *Kiowa*

Tune (Kiowa nickname)

Born 6 Aug 1943 in Lawton, OK; son of Peggy Lois Payahsote and Spencer Two-Hatchet; GGM: niece of Hunting Horse and descendant of Mokeen (Mexican captive who played a prominent role in Kiowa history)

RESIDENCE: Carnegie, OK

EDUCATION: IAIA, 1965

EXHIBITS: AIE, FAIEAIP, ITIC, PAC, SN

AWARDS: SN

SPENCER LEE TWO-HATCHET JR.

"Susie Peters purchased the artist's first painting, encouraging him, as did Mr. and Mrs. Hardy of the Hardy Gallery, to continue to paint."

Snodgrass 1968

TWOHY, JULIUS *Ute*

RESIDENCE: Whiterocks, UT

EXHIBITS: ADIA

AWARDS: ADIA ('67)

TWOITSIE, HANSEN *Hopi*

RESIDENCE: Polacca, AZ

EDUCATION: Santa Fe

MEDIA: Watercolor

PUBLISHED: Dunn (1968); Snodgrass (1968); Tanner (1968)

PUBLIC COLLECTIONS: MNA, MNM/DD

EXHIBITS: NGA

TWOK (see Ahgupuk, George Aden)

TWO MOONS (see McNamara, Paula Jane)

TWO STRIKE (see Two Strikes)

TWO STRIKES *Oglala Sioux*

Nomkahpa, Knocks Two Off

A.K.A. Two Strike; Nom-pa-ap'a

Born 1832 near the Republican River in southern Nebraska; died 1915 on the Pine Ridge Reservation, SD

OCCUPATION: Warrior and war leader

PUBLISHED: Snodgrass (1968); Dockstader (1977). *4th Annual Report*, BAE (1882-1883)

TWO STRIKES

"The artist's 'Partisan' drawing is reproduced in the BAE, 4th Annual Report. *This is a drawing illustrating the man's authority, or leadership of a war party, by an elevated pipe or war club."*

Snodgrass 1968

Two Strikes received his name "Knocks Two Off" from an occasion when he dispatched two enemy Ute warriors from their horses by blows from his war club.

Dockstader 1977

TYNDALL, CALVIN *Sioux or Omaha*

Umpah, Elk

PUBLISHED: Dunn (1968); Snodgrass (1968)

PUBLIC COLLECTIONS: IACB/DC

EXHIBITS: MFA/H

SOLO EXHIBITS: JAM

TYYA, WINNIE *Inuit (Eskimo)*

A.K.A. Winnie Tatya

Born 1931

RESIDENCE: Baker Lake, NWT, Canada

OCCUPATION: Graphic artist and wall hanging maker

PUBLISHED: Collinson (1978)

PUBLIC COLLECTIONS: C/U of AB

EXHIBITS: C/CG

U Do Dalona Gei (see Goshorn, Shan)

Ulaya (see Ulayu)

Ulayu *Inuit (Eskimo)*

A.K.A. Olayou; Ulaya
Born 1904
RESIDENCE: Cape Dorset, NWT, Canada
OCCUPATION: Graphic artist
MEDIA: Pencil, colored pencil, and prints
PUBLISHED: Houston (1967; 1967a); Goetz, et al. (1977); Woodhouse, ed. (1980). *The Beaver* (spring 1975)
PUBLIC COLLECTIONS: C/TDB
EXHIBITS: C/AG/WP, C/CD, C/EACTDB, C/TIP

Umpah (see Tyndall, Calvin)

Umpan Hanska (see Larvie, Calvin)

Umstead, Jane *Choctaw*

A.K.A. Jane Semple Umsted
RESIDENCE: Durant, OK
EXHIBITS: CNM, FCTM
AWARDS: FCTM ('87, IH; '88, 1st)

Una (see Oonark, Jessie)

Unaaq *Inuit (Eskimo)*

RESIDENCE: Baker Lake, NWT, Canada
OCCUPATION: Graphic artist
MEDIA: Pencil, felt pen, pen and ink, and prints
PUBLISHED: *North* (Nov/Dec 1968)

Unaaq

Unaaq's drawings were first noticed by Andrew MacPherson, biologist with the Canadian Wildlife Service. He provided her with materials and found a market for her work. Her work was included in the 1960 Cape Dorset print catalog.

Underwood, Lela Mitchell *Chickasaw*

EXHIBITS: FCTM
AWARDS: FCTM ('80; '81; '83, IH)

Underwood, Ted *Chickasaw*

RESIDENCE: Bristow, OK
EXHIBITS: FCTM
AWARDS: FCTM ('77;'78; '80; '82; '83, IH)

Upright Post (see Chauncey, Florence Nupok)

Uqayuittuq (see Uqayuittuq, Mark)

Uqayuittuq, Mark *Inuit (Eskimo)*

A.K.A. Uqayuittuq
Born 1925
RESIDENCE: Baker Lake, NWT, Canada
OCCUPATION: Graphic artist
MEDIA: Pencil, colored pencil, and prints
PUBLISHED: Blodgett (1978a); Latocki, ed. (1983)
PUBLIC COLLECTIONS: C/AG/WP, C/SC
EXHIBITS: C/AG/WP, C/SS

DETAIL: Artist unknown, *Horse Dance*, 1932. Philbrook Museum of Art, Tulsa, Oklahoma

UQUALLA, MAGGIE *Havasupai*
PUBLIC COLLECTIONS: MNA

USED AS A SHIELD (see Grass, John)

USES KNIFE, MATTHEW R. *Sioux*
Born 1954
RESIDENCE: Eagle Butte, SD
EDUCATION: AAA
OCCUPATION: Museum director and artist
PUBLISHED: *The Indian Trader* (Mar 1992)

USSA HUD'IT (see HorseChief, Sam)

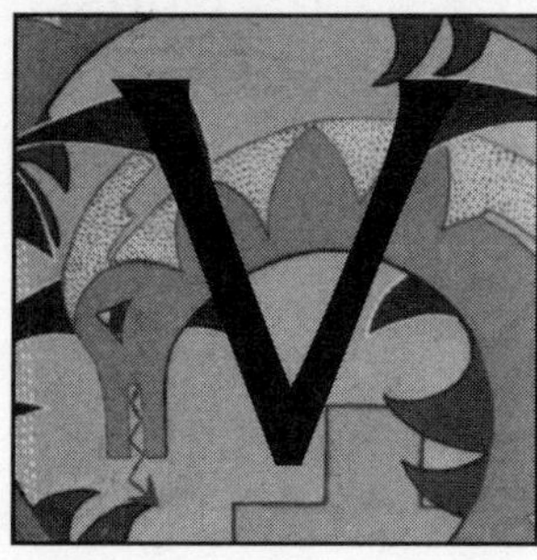

VACIT, GARY *Zuni*

RESIDENCE: Zuni Pueblo, NM
PUBLISHED: Snodgrass (1968)
PUBLIC COLLECTIONS: MNM

VALDEZ, LOUIS *Tohono O'odham (Papago)*

MILITARY: U.S. Armed Forces, WWII
MEDIA: Pastel and pen and ink
PUBLISHED: Tanner (1973)
PUBLIC COLLECTIONS: MNA
EXHIBITS: MNA; PM; Sells (AZ) Fair

LOUIS VALDEZ

Wounded in the Second World War, Valdez became interested in painting while recovering in a hospital in England. He was best known for his pastel portraits, although he also did some desert scenes in the European manner. As far as is known, his career only lasted a short time.

Tanner 1973

VALENCIA, ANNA LOU *(?)*

RESIDENCE: Santa Fe, NM
EDUCATION: St. Catherine's, 1965
PUBLISHED: Snodgrass (1968)
EXHIBITS: PAC

VALLO, PEDRO *Acoma*

PUBLISHED: Snodgrass (1968)
PUBLIC COLLECTIONS: MNM

VANATTA, SHIRLEY *Seneca*

Born 29 Oct 1922; died 12 May 1975
EDUCATION: BC
OCCUPATION: Newspaper editor, public relations, illustrator, and painter
MEDIA: Oil, watercolor, pastel, and pen and ink
PUBLISHED: Johannsen and Ferguson, eds. (1983). Biographical publications
PUBLIC COLLECTIONS: Haley Community Building
EXHIBITS: INAAT
HONORS: New York State, Indian of The Year Award, 1972

SHIRLEY VANATTA

After attending Bacone College, Vanatta worked for several years as an illustrator in Tulsa, OK. She returned to Allegany, NY, in 1967 and became very involved in working for the Seneca Nation. She especially enjoyed painting wild flowers and doing portraits of well-known Allegany elders.

Johannsen and Ferguson, eds. 1983

VAN DEMAN, JIM *Delaware*

OCCUPATION: Commercial artist; full-time painter since 1990
MEDIA: Acrylic
EXHIBITS: RE

VANN, CHARLES LEO *Cherokee*

Fish
Born 19 Apr 1933 in Claremore, OK; son of A. Vann; P/GF: Frank Vann; M/GP: Nellie and George Twist
RESIDENCE: Pryor, OK
OCCUPATION: Musician, sign painter, farmer, sculptor, and painter
MEDIA: Oil, acrylic, watercolor, pencil, pen and ink, wood, and clay
PUBLISHED: Campbell, ed. (1993)
COMMISSIONS: *Murals:* Cherokee Nation Complex, Tahlequah, OK. *Other:* Cherokee Nation Department of Education, Tahlequah, OK, cover of language text; City of Pryor (OK), flag design
EXHIBITS: CNM, PAC
HONORS: Proclaimed Custodian of Cherokee Heritage by Wilma Mankiller, principal chief of the Western Cherokee

VANN, DONALD *Cherokee*

Gwen-Na Da-Ga-Do-Ga, Child In The Night – Stands Up

DETAIL: Pablita Velarde, *Dance of the Aveye and Thunderbird*, 1955. Philbrook Museum of Art, Tulsa, Oklahoma

Born 22 Oct 1948; son of Mary Duck and Arch Vann; P/GF: White Vann; M/GP: Jennie and Joe Mitchell Duck

RESIDENCE: Austin, TX

MILITARY: U.S. Army, Vietnam, 1968-1971

EDUCATION: Stilwell (OK) High School

OCCUPATION: Painter

PUBLIC COLLECTIONS: MNA, PAC, WOM

EXHIBITS: ACAI, CNM, FAIE, ITAE, ITIC, OAC, PAC, RC, RE, TAIAF, TCIM, TIAF, SI

AWARDS: CNM ('90, Grand Award); FCTM ('67, 1st; '70, 1st, Grand Award, IH; '71, 1st, IH; '72, 1st; '73; '76, Grand Award; '77, 1st); ITAE ('91, 1st, Best of Class, People's Choice); ITIC ('70; 1st, '72; '76, 1st, Best Miniature); PAC ('68); RE ('91; '93, 1st); TCIM ('91; '92, 1st); TIAF ('92, 1st)

VARNELL, BILLY *Cherokee*

WiLi, William

A.K.A. William Eugene Varnell; Wili Varnell; William Varnell

Born 18 June 1957 in Tulsa, OK; son of Mina Alberta Eliz and Gene Varnell; P/GP: Opal and Vin Earl Varnell; M/GP: Sarah Elizabeth and Albert Gordon; Artist is a descendant of Chief John Bowles (Dawali).

RESIDENCE: Mannford, OK

EDUCATION: Mannford (OK) High School

OCCUPATION: Auction business and painter

MEDIA: Acrylic, watercolor, pencil, pen and ink, and prints

PUBLISHED: *Minority Directory of Oklahoma Artists*

EXHIBITS: CNM; FCTM; Art Under The Oaks, Muskogee, OK

AWARDS: CNM ('86)

VAUGHN, NINA *Cherokee*

A.K.A. Nina Higdon Vaughn

RESIDENCE: Las Cruces, NM

EXHIBITS: HM/G, PAC

VELARDE, NEITO *Santo Domingo*

PUBLISHED: Snodgrass (1968)

PUBLIC COLLECTIONS: UPA

VELARDE, PABLITA *Santa Clara*

Tse Tsan, Golden Dawn

Born 19 Sept 1918 at Santa Clara Pueblo, NM; daughter of Marianita Chavarria and Herman Velarde; mother of Helen Hardin (q.v.)

RESIDENCE: Albuquerque, NM

EDUCATION: Santa Fe, 1936

OCCUPATION: Teacher, lecturer, author, illustrator, and painter

MEDIA: Oil, watercolor, casein, colored sand, and mixed-media

PUBLISHED: Jacobson and d'Ucel (1950); LaFarge (1956; 1960); De Cala (1967); Dunn (1968); Snodgrass (1968); Brody (1971); Tanner (1973); Highwater (1976); New and Young (1976); Silberman (1978); Schmid and Houlihan (1979); Mahey, et al. (1980); Broder (1981); Hoffman, et al. (1984); Samuels (1985); Wade, ed. (1986); Babcock and Paresi (1988); Seymour (1988); Gray (1990); Williams, ed. (1990); Archuleta and Strickland (1991); Gully, ed. (1994). *El Palacio* (Nov 1952); *National Geographic* (Mar 1955); *Women Speaking* (Apr 1959); *New Mexico* (1960); *The Arizona Republic* (2 Mar 1963; 20 Nov 1966; 17 Mar 1968); *Indian Life,* ITIC (Aug 1961); *American Artist* (Apr 1965); *Carte Blanche Magazine* (Dec

DONALD VANN

Vann says, "Through my images I hope people will be inspired to learn more about the customs and values of America's native people. Our traditions teach many things that can help all people. In today's fast-paced world, it is too easy to get cut off from one's heritage and lose sight of the things that are truly important. If I can make people see with their heart instead of their eyes, then my art has spoken. Then I have succeeded."

p.c. 1994

BILLY VARNELL

The self-described struggling young artist admits that so far he has gained small recognition and fame. However, he feels that with much work and some luck in the future he will be more successful. He recognizes that it is very difficult to be a successful artist.

artist, p.c. 1992

PABLITA VELARDE

"Tonita Peña (q.v.), the 'mother' of Pueblo painting, introduced Velarde to the world of art. There was a period in childhood when an eye disease caused a loss of sight. Upon regaining her eyesight she explained, 'temporary darkness made me want to see everything. . . . I have trained myself to remember, to the smallest detail, everything I see. . . .' In 1938, Velarde benefited greatly from a four-month tour of the U.S.,

(continued)

1972); *The Denver Post* (25 May 1973); *Southwest Art* (winter 1977-1978; May 1978; June 1983); *American Indian Art* (spring 1978); *The Indian Trader* (Sept 1982; Mar 1988); *Pueblo Horizons* (June 1982); *The Santa Fean* (Aug 1989); *South Dakota Museum News* (spring 1991); biographical publications

BOOKS ILLUSTRATED: Velarde (1960); Seton, J. (1962)

COMMISSIONS: *Murals:* MFA/NM; IPCC; Bandalier National Monument, NM; Western Skies Hotel, Albuquerque, NM; Santa Clara Day School; First National Bank, Los Alamos, NM; Maisel's Indian Trading Post, Albuquerque, NM, 1939. *Other:* Bandalier National Monument Museum, ethnological watercolors

PUBLIC COLLECTIONS: AC/RM; AF; BIA; DAM; GM; HCC; HM; IACB; IACB/DC; JAM; KM; LMA/BC; MAI; MHDYMM; MNM; OU/MA; PAC; SDMM; SMNAI; UPA; U of CA/B; State of New Mexico

EXHIBITS: AAID; ABQM; AC/A; AIAE/WSU; AIWSAF; ASM; CCP; CNM; DAM; GM; HCC; HM; HM/G; IK; ITIC; JAM; JGS; LGAM; MCC/CA; MFA/O; MHDYMM; MKMcNAI; MNA; MNH/D; MNM; MRFM; NAP; NMSF; OMA; OU/ET; OU/MA; OWE; PAC; PAC/T; PM; SFFA; SM; SN; SNAICF; SV; SWAIA; USDS; U of CA/B; U of OK; WIB; WRTD; WWM; Bandalier National Monument Museum, NM

SOLO EXHIBITS: MNM; PAC; WWM; Desert Museum, Palm Springs, CA, 1966; Enchanted Mesa, Albuquerque, NM

AWARDS: Partial listing of 1st-place and Grand Awards includes: AAID ('68); CAM; CNM ('87, 1st); ITIC ('68; '72; '82; '86, 1st); MNM; NMSF; PAC; SN ('64, Grand Award; '70); SNAICF; SWAIA ('71, 1st; '73, 1st; '74, 1st; '75, 1st; '77; '84, 1st; '86; '89, 2-1st, Hardin Award; '90, 1st, Hardin Award)

HONORS: French Government, Palmes d`Académiques, 1954; 20th Century Art Club, St. Louis, MO, special recognition, 1955; *Old Father, The Story Teller*, written and illustrated by Velarde, voted one of the Best Western Books of 1961; PAC, Waite Phillips Trophy, 1968; New Mexico Governor's Award for Outstanding Achievement in the Arts, 1977

PABLITA VELARDE

(continued) accompanied by Ernest Thompson Seton, the famous naturalist and lecturer, and his wife. During the tour, she exhibited her paintings, selling several. Upon returning to New Mexico, she built her first studio at the Pueblo and began her painting career. Dorothy Dunn, in speaking of the artist's work, said that her 'style evokes the poise and gentle strength of a Pueblo woman.'"

"In 1956, Velarde began her unique earth paintings, made from various colored rocks that she grinds to powder on a metate, mixes with water and glue for a plastic effect, and applies to Masonite. In 1964, the artist expressed herself in the following way: 'I have not gone to the new trend nor do I wish to do so in the near future. I cannot contribute thoughts of value without appreciating and understanding the past.' She feels there is still very much beauty and dignity to draw upon from the past, and that even if she were to 'catch-up' with the present, she would never have enough time to paint the beauty she sees in yesterday."

Snodgrass 1968

VELINO SHIJE (see Herrera, Velino Shije)

VENEGO, FLORENZO *Apache*

PUBLISHED: Snodgrass (1968)

PUBLIC COLLECTIONS: MNM

VENTERS, OLIF A. *Cherokee*

Born 5 June 1950; son of Elizabeth A. Greene and George Lee Venters; P/GP: Lecinda and Wash Venters; M/GP: Bessy Turner and Thomas Webster Greene, II

RESIDENCE: Vinita, OK

EDUCATION: Vinita (OK) High School, 1968; CSU/N, 1976

OCCUPATION: Artist

MEDIA: Oil, watercolor, pencil, pastel, and pen and ink

PUBLISHED: Biographical publication

PUBLIC COLLECTIONS: Temple B'Nai Emunah of Tulsa, OK; Temple Beth Am, Los Angeles, CA

EXHIBITS: LIAS; Custer County Art Center; Dresden, Germany

VERSCH, ESTHER MARIE *Yaqui*

Birth date unknown; daughter of Juana Hernández and Claro Santellanes; P/GP: Luna Paula Contreras and Martiniano Santellanes; M/GP: Guadalupe Martínez and Sabino Hernández

RESIDENCE: Altadena, CA

EDUCATION: White Pine High School, Ely, NV; East Los Angeles (CA) College, 1964; Pasadena (CA) City College

MEDIA: Oil, acrylic, watercolor, pencil, and prints
PUBLISHED: *Moccasin Tracks* (Nov 1985); *North Light* (June 1986)
PUBLIC COLLECTIONS: Johnson Humrick House, Coshocton, OH
EXHIBITS: AIWR; CNM; LIAS; RC; Cowgirl Hall of Fame, Hereford, TX; Los Angeles Arboretum, Arcadia, CA; Las Vegas (NV) Art Museum; Museum of Science and Industry, Los Angeles, CA; see also Awards
AWARDS: AIWR (Best of Show); Death Valley Open Show (1st); San Gabriel (CA) Fine Arts (Gold Medal); Trail West Show, Las Vegas, NV (1st)

VICENTI, CARL A. *Jicarilla Apache*

Born 8 Jan 1930 in Dulce, NM
RESIDENCE: Alexander, VA
EDUCATION: Albuquerque (NM) High School; Haskell; BYU; USU; B.A., U of UT; National University of Mexico, Mexico City
OCCUPATION: Art instructor, illustrator, and artist
MEDIA: Oil, acrylic, watercolor, pencil, pen and ink, and pastel
PUBLISHED: Dunn (1968); Snodgrass (1968); Brody (1971); Tanner (1973); Williams, ed. (1990)
PUBLIC COLLECTIONS: BIA, HCC
EXHIBITS: ASM, ITIC, MKMcNAI, MNM, PAC, SN, WTF
AWARDS: PAC ('64, 1st); HM/G ('68, 1st); ITIC ('69, 1st, Special Award; '71); SN ('68, '70)

CARL A. VICENTI

Vicenti paints in many different styles, everything from traditional to European realism to abstract. His colors vary from somber to jewel-like.

Tanner 1973

VICENTI, CHARLES *Zuni*

EDUCATION: Albuquerque, ca 1959
PUBLISHED: Snodgrass (1968); Fawcett and Callander (1982)
COMMISSIONS: *Murals:* Barelas Community Center (with other artists)
PUBLIC COLLECTIONS: MAI
EXHIBITS: MAI

VICENTI, JUDITH A. *Jicarilla Apache*

A.K.A. Judith A. Ladd Vicenti
Born 2 Feb 1952; daughter of Melvin Ladd Vicenti Sr.
RESIDENCE: Dulce, NM
EDUCATION: IAIA High School, 1971; A.F.A, IAIA, 1972-1974; CSF/SF
OCCUPATION: Receptionist, ceramist, and painter
MEDIA: Acrylic, watercolor, pencil, pen and ink, and clay
PUBLIC COLLECTIONS: IAIA
EXHIBITS: HM/G, IAIA, MNH/D, RC, SN, SWAIA
SOLO EXHIBITS: IAIA, WWM
AWARDS: HM/G ('75); SWAIA ('80)
HONORS: IAIA, Noni Ecceles Harrison Ceramics Award, 1974

VICENTI, STEVEN *Jicarilla Apache*

Nehakije
A.K.A. Stephen Vicenti
Born 1917 in Dulce, NM; died 1948 at Santa Fe, NM
EDUCATION: Santa Fe
MEDIA: Tempera
PUBLISHED: Dunn (1968); Snodgrass (1968); Tanner (1957; 1973); Seymour (1988). *El Palacio* (Mar 1952)
PUBLIC COLLECTIONS: CGFA, IACB/DC
EXHIBITS: AGAA; AIW; MNM; NGA; SUAG; first exhibited in Santa Fe, NM, 1934

STEVEN VICENTI

"Clara Lee Tanner (1957) refers to the artist as the 'first modern painter of the Apache tribe.'"

Snodgrass 1968

VICKERS, ARTHUR FREEMAN *Tsimshian*

Born 1947 in Vancouver, BC, Canada

RESIDENCE: Vancouver Island, BC, Canada

OCCUPATION: Building contractor, teacher; painter since the early 1980s

VICKERS, ROY HENRY *Tsimshian*

Big Fireweed

Born 1946 in Greenville, BC, Canada

RESIDENCE: Tofino, BC, Canada

EDUCATION: Oak Bay Senior Secondary School, 1965; C/KSNCIA, 1974

OCCUPATION: Lecturer, actor, carver, graphic artist, and painter

MEDIA: Acrylic, wood, and prints

PUBLISHED: Stewart (1979); Hall, Blackman, and Rickard (1981); Gerber and Bruggmann (1989); McMasters, et al. (1993)

COMMISSIONS: National Museum of Japan, Osaka, 1976, 1977; Day Break Art Center, Seattle WA, carved and painted panel, 1978; Eagle Down Gallery, Edmonton, AB, three Commonwealth Games Limited Edition Prints, 1978; Northwest Cultural Society, Vancouver, BC, design, 1978

PUBLIC COLLECTIONS: C/CMC; C/CIMS; C/INAC; C/KA; C/KFC; C/McMBC; C/RBCM; C/U of BC/MA; National Museums of Japan, Osaka.

EXHIBITS: C/CIARH; SDSMT; Tokyo, Japan

SOLO EXHIBITS: C/U of BC/MA

ROY HENRY VICKERS

In 1965, while still in high school, Vickers designed and printed his first silk screen editions which were sold at the school art fair. He was thus the first of the contemporary Northwest Coast artists to produce silk screen prints. The artist's paintings and prints often reflect his deep religious feelings and commitment to Christianity. In his desire to spread Christ's message, he has, at times, had a design printed in unlimited numbers and made them available at low cost.

Hall, Blackman, and Rickard, eds. 1981

VIENNEAU, LAURENCE *Blackfeet*

A.K.A. Laurence E. Vienneau Jr.

Born 1 June 1954 in Boston, MA

RESIDENCE: Nantucket, MA

EDUCATION: B.F.A, SMU/MA, 1977; M.F.A., Southern Illinois University, Carbondale, IL, 1981

OCCUPATION: Teacher and artist

PUBLISHED: Burrows (1973); Linsley (1976). *The Torch* (25 Feb 1977)

PUBLIC COLLECTIONS: Nantucket (MA) Historic Association

EXHIBITS: RC; SIU/M; SMU/MA; Bicentennial Art Center and Museum, Paris, IL; Hunterdon Art Center, Clinton, NJ; Lincoln Trail College, Robinson, IL; Mitchell Museum, Mt. Vernon, IL; Murray (KY) State University; Paint and Clay Club Exhibition; Paducah (KY) Art Guild; Rend Lake College, Ina, IL; Western Illinois University, Macomb, IL; see also Awards

SOLO EXHIBITS: SIU/M

AWARDS: International Marine Art Show, Mystic, CT ('80)

HONORS: Esther Conant Memorial Prize, 1981

VIGIL, ALBERT *San Ildefonso*

Birth date unknown; son of Romando Vigil (q.v.)

RESIDENCE: Santa Fe, NM

MEDIA: Tempera

PUBLISHED: Snodgrass (1968); Tanner (1973); Seymour (1988)

PUBLIC COLLECTIONS: GM, MAI, MNA/KHC, WWM

EXHIBITS: SWAIA, WWM

AWARDS: GM, MAI, MNA/KHC, SWAIA

VIGIL, ALFRED *Jémez*

A.K.A. Alfredo Vigil

EDUCATION: Jémez

PUBLISHED: Snodgrass (1968)
PUBLIC COLLECTIONS: MRFM
EXHIBITS: MNM

VIGIL, ANDREA *Jémez*
EDUCATION: Jémez
PUBLISHED: Snodgrass (1968)
EXHIBITS: MNM
AWARDS: MNM

VIGIL, CALVIN *Jicarilla Apache/Kiowa*
Born 19 June 1924 in Dulce, NM
RESIDENCE: Dulce, NM
MILITARY: U.S. Navy, WWII
EDUCATION: Santa Fe, 1946-1947
OCCUPATION: Farmer, rancher, and artist
PUBLISHED: Dunn (1968); Snodgrass (1968); Brody (1971)
PUBLIC COLLECTIONS: DAM, PAC
EXHIBITS: DAM, ITIC, MNM, PAC

VIGIL, FELIX R. *Jicarilla Apache/Jémez*
RESIDENCE: Jémez Pueblo, NM
EDUCATION: Maryland Institute College of Art, Baltimore, MD, 1980
OCCUPATION: Educator and painter
MEDIA: Oil
EXHIBITS: ASC/ENP, CNM, EM, IAIA, NMSF, SNAICF, SWAIA, WWM
SOLO EXHIBITS: Jicarilla Tribal Council; Council of Energy Resources, Tribes Corporation Building; Pennsylvania State Great Valley Library, Malvern, PA
AWARDS: NMSF, SNAICF, SWAIA

VIGIL, FRANK PAUL *Jicarilla Apache*
Born 24 Sept 1922; died 1979
RESIDENCE: Lived in Dulce, NM
MILITARY: U.S. Army, 1943-1946
EDUCATION: Santa Fe
PUBLISHED: Snodgrass (1968); Tanner (1973)
PUBLIC COLLECTIONS: BIA, DAM, MNA, MRFM, SM, SMNAI
EXHIBITS: AAIE, ASM, HM, ITIC, MHDYMM, NMSF, PAC, SN, USDS
AWARDS: MHDYMM, PAC

VIGIL, JO *Tesuque*
A.K.A. Jo Gabriel Vigil
EDUCATION: Santa Fe
PUBLISHED: Snodgrass (1968)
PUBLIC COLLECTIONS: ASM, OU/MA, U of CA/LMA
EXHIBITS: AIW, OU/ET

VIGIL, JOSÉ EUTIMIO (see Vigil, Utimio)

VIGIL, JUANITA *Tesuque*
EDUCATION: Tesuque, ca. 1959
PUBLISHED: Snodgrass (1968)
EXHIBITS: MNM

Vigil, Lucy *Tesuque*

EDUCATION: Tesuque, ca. 1959
PUBLISHED: Snodgrass (1968)
EXHIBITS: MNM

Vigil, Marco *Zuni*

PUBLISHED: Snodgrass (1968)
PUBLIC COLLECTIONS: MAI

Vigil, Nossman *Apache*

Born 13 Mar 1926 on Jicarilla Apache Reservation, NM
RESIDENCE: Dulce, NM
OCCUPATION: Senior Citizen's Program employee and artist
EXHIBITS: SWAIA
HONORS: Recognition award for Jicarilla Apache Tribal Seal design used during Centennial Celebration, 1987

Vigil, Pete *Tesuque*

Born 16 July 1919
A.K.A. Peter Vigil
EDUCATION: Santa Fe
OCCUPATION: Technician, painter, silversmith, and woodcarver
MEDIA: Tempera, silver, and wood
PUBLISHED: Snodgrass (1968); Seymour (1988)
PUBLIC COLLECTIONS: GM, IACB/DC, OU/SM, U of CA/LMA
EXHIBITS: AIEC, AIW, LGAM, PAC

Vigil, Priscilla *Jémez*

Born 1958 in New Mexico
EDUCATION: Jémez
PUBLISHED: Snodgrass (1968)
EXHIBITS: AAIE

Vigil, Ralph *Jémez*

PUBLISHED: Snodgrass (1968)
PUBLIC COLLECTIONS: MNM

Vigil, Ramon *Tesuque*

EDUCATION: Tesuque, ca. 1959
PUBLISHED: Snodgrass (1968)
EXHIBITS: MNM

Vigil, Romando *San Ildefonso*

Tse Ye Mu, Falling In Water
Born 23 Jan 1902; died 1978; father of Albert Vigil (q.v.); cousin of Tonita Peña (q.v.)
EDUCATION: Santa Fe
OCCUPATION: Walt Disney Studios employee and painter
PUBLISHED: Alexander (1932); Dunn (1968); Snodgrass (1968); Brody (1971); Tanner (1957; 1968; 1973); Silberman (1978); Schmid and Houlihan (1979); Fawcett and Callander (1982); Hoffman, et al. (1984); Wade, ed.(1986); Seymour (1988); Williams, ed. (1990); Archuleta and Strickland (1991). *American Magazine of Art* (Aug 1933); *Tamaqua* (winter/spring 1991)
COMMISSIONS: *Murals:* Santa Fe; The Corcoran Gallery of Art; EITA, 1933 (with Velino Shije Herrera and Oqwa Pi); La Fonda Hotel, Santa Fe, NM; Mesa Verde

ROMANDO VIGIL

"The artist was painting as early as 1920 at the Pueblo. In 1950, he was apparently in California. His style was that of the San Ildefonso school of painting. Some of his work could be found for sale in New Mexico galleries in 1952."

Snodgrass 1968

(CO) National Park, Chapin Mesa Archaeological Museum

PUBLIC COLLECTIONS: AF, BA/AZ, CGPS, CMA, DAM, GM, IACB/DC, JAM, MAI, MIM, MNA/KHC, MNH/A, MNM, MRFM, MV, OU/MA, PAC, RM, U of PA/M, WOM

EXHIBITS: ACC, AIEC, ASM, CGPS, DAM, EITA, HM, IK, LGAM, MKMcNAI, MNM, NAP, OMA, OU/ET, SV, WRTD; see also Awards

VIGIL, RUFINA *Tesuque*

Sah Wa

EDUCATION: Santa Fe

OCCUPATION: Draftswoman and painter

MEDIA: Tempera

PUBLISHED: Dunn (1968); Snodgrass (1968); Seymour (1988)

PUBLIC COLLECTIONS: IACB/DC, MNM, OU/MA

EXHIBITS: NGA, OU/ET

RUFINA VIGIL

"Vigil painted and exhibited in Santa Fe and in Chicago. She received training under Dorothy Dunn. In 1950, however, it was reported that she had stopped painting 'long ago.'"

Snodgrass 1968

VIGIL, THOMAS *Tesuque*

Pan Yo Pin, Summer Mountain

A.K.A. Tomás Vigil; Pen Yo Pin; Pu Yo Pin

Born ca. 1889 at Tesuque Pueblo, NM; died 1960

RESIDENCE: Lived in Santa Fe, NM

EDUCATION: St. Catherine's, 1904-1907

PUBLISHED: Jacobson and d'Ucel (1950); Dunn (1968); Snodgrass (1968); Brody (1971); Tanner (1973); Seymour (1988). *Art-Talk* (Mar 1986)

PUBLIC COLLECTIONS: ASM, CAM/OH, CGFA, CMA, DAM, GM, IACB/DC, MAI, MNA, MNH/A, MNM, MRFM, NMAA, RM, SM, U of OK, U of PA/M, WOM, WWM

EXHIBITS: ACC, ASM, EITA, HM, SI, SI/T

THOMAS VIGIL

"The artist was painting at the Pueblo as early as 1920. In 1950, he occasionally painted on special orders only."

Snodgrass 1968

VIGIL, TIM *Tesuque*

Kusé Peen

Birth date unknown; died 1972; son of Thomas Vigil (q.v.)

OCCUPATION: Employee at Los Alamos, NM, and artist

MEDIA: Watercolor

PUBLISHED: Snodgrass (1968); Tanner (1973); Silberman (1978)

EXHIBITS: HM, OMA, PAC, SN, SWAIA

AWARDS: SWAIA ('71, 1st)

VIGIL, TOM *Jémez*

Born 1945

RESIDENCE: Santa Fe, NM

EDUCATION: Jémez, ca. 1957

PUBLISHED: Snodgrass (1968)

EXHIBITS: AIE, PAC

AWARDS: AIE

VIGIL, TOMÁS (see Vigil, Thomas)

VIGIL, ULTIMIO (see Vigil, Utimio)

VIGIL, UTIMO *Tesuque*

A.K.A. Jose Eutimio Vigil (?); Ultimio Vigil

PUBLISHED: Snodgrass (1968)

PUBLIC COLLECTIONS: MRFM; SM; U of CA/LMA (listed as "Utimio")

EXHIBITS: AIEC (listed as "Ultimio")

Veloy Vigil

Growing up in a farming and ranch environment, but finding that work unfulfilling, Vigil turned to art, a profession that has well rewarded him. Trained as a commercial artist, he was influenced by other artists in the work place who were discovering abstract expressionism. Joining design and color with landscapes and figures and using themes from his Indian and Hispanic heritage, Vigil developed his perspective of modern painting. In this he was influenced by the work of Fritz Scholder (q.v.). In turn, Vigil has encouraged a new generation of artists to explore beyond the traditional realistic depiction of Indian painting.

VIGIL, VELOY *Tesuque*

A.K.A. Veloy Joseph Vigil

Born 1931 in Denver, CO

MILITARY: U.S. Marine Corps

EDUCATION: CIA/CO; Denver (CO) Art Academy

OCCUPATION: Ranch hand, rodeo contestant, dairy farmer, commercial artist, illustrator, art director, and painter

MEDIA: Oil, acrylic, watercolor, pastel, mixed-media, and prints

PUBLISHED: Samuels (1982). *Artists of the Rockies* (spring 1976); *Southwest Art* (Jan 1977; Nov 1983; Apr 1986); *The Santa Fean* (Sept 1983; June 1994); *Arizona Arts and Travel* (Jan/Feb 1984); *Art-Talk* (Feb 1984; June/July 1986; Nov 1986; Dec 1987; Feb 1988; Aug/Sept 1994); *The Santa Fe Reporter* (14 Aug 1984); *Southwest Profile* (July 1985); *The Indian Trader* (Nov 1986; May 1988); *The Scottsdale Progress* (26 Apr 1990); biographical publications

PUBLIC COLLECTIONS: HM, PAM, U of AZ, U of OK; Cleveland (OH) Art Association

EXHIBITS: DAM; FAC/CS; HM/G; LBMA; LGAM; MCC/CA; MFA/VA; OAC; SI; SWAIA; American Watercolor Society; Mount St. Mary's College, Los Angeles, CA; National Academy of Design, New York, NY; Palo Verdes (CA) Art Museum

AWARDS: FAC/CS; HM/G ('76, 2-1st, Avery award; '77, 2-1st); LBMA; LGAM; Mississippi Art Association, Jackson, MS; Springfield (MO) Art Museum

HONORS: New Mexico Arts and Crafts Fair, Albuquerque, NM, poster artist, 1994

VIGIL-GRAY, DARREN *Jicarilla Apache/Kiowa*

Born 29 July 1959 in Dulce, NM

RESIDENCE: Santa Fe, NM

EDUCATION: IAIA, 1975-1977; CSF/SF, 1978-1979; U of NM, 1985-1986; studied serigraphy with Kate Karasin

OCCUPATION: Musician and artist

MEDIA: Oil, acrylic, watercolor, and prints

PUBLISHED: New (1981); Gentry (1990); Hill (1992). *American Indian Art* (summer 1981); *Four Winds* (spring/summer 1981); *Horizon* (Apr 1981); *Portfolio Magazine* (July/Aug 1981); *The Santa Fe Reporter* (14 Aug 1986); *Southwest Profile* (Aug 1988); *The Santa Fean* (Aug 1989); *The New Mexican* (17 Aug 1990); *Art-Talk* (Aug/Sept 1991)

COMMISSIONS: *Saturday Night Live*, art backdrop, 1988

PUBLIC COLLECTIONS: BBHC; C/U of R/MG; DAM; HM; IACB; IAIA; MAI; MRFM; PAC; SI; WWM; Museum of Mankind, Vienna, Austria; The Bruce Museum, Greenwich, CT; The Stamford (CT) Museum

EXHIBITS: AA; BBHC; EM; HM; HMA; IAIA; LG; MAI; MFA/AH; MFA/O; MMA/MT; NACLA; NMSC; OSU/G; OWE; SCG; SFFA; SI; SMIC; SU; SWAIA; WIB; WWM; Armand Hammer United World College, 1982; Quinnipiac College, New Haven, CT, 1984; Lincoln Center, Avery Fisher Hall, New York, NY; Mendocino County Museum of Art, Willita, CA, 1984; Musée de l'Homme, Paris, France, 1983; Museum of Mankind, Vienna, Austria; Scripps College, Lang Museum, Claremont, CA, 1984; Seton Hall University, West Orange, NJ, 1984; Taos (NM) Spring Arts Celebration; Vassar College, Poughkeepsie, NY

AWARDS: SMIC, SWAIA

HONORS: Southwest Ballet Company, poster award, 1975

VILLA, TED *Apache/Zapotec*

A.K.A. Theodore B. Villa

Born 28 Sept 1936 in Santa Barbara, CA

RESIDENCE: Santa Barbara, CA

EDUCATION: B.F.A., U of CA/SB; M.F.A., U of CA/SB

OCCUPATION: Art gallery director, high school and college teacher, lecturer, and artist

MEDIA: Watercolor

PUBLISHED: *Artspace* (spring 1984); *Native Vision* (Nov/Dec 1985); *Southwest Art* (Feb 1986); *Art-Talk* (Mar 1987); *Phoenix Magazine* (Sept 1989)

COMMISSIONS: Desert Mountain Properties, Phoenix, AZ

PUBLIC COLLECTIONS: AT&T, San Francisco, CA; ARCO, Tulsa, OK; Berkus Group, Santa Barbara, CA; Interwest Partners, Menlo Park, CA; Root Corporation, Daytona Beach, FL; Sequoia Capitol Management, Menlo Park, CA; Total Petroleum, Denver, CO; U.S. West, Denver, CO; Wm. Feldman and Associates, Los Angeles, CA

EXHIBITS: AC/T; ACA; AICA/SF; CSF; CSU/LA; HM; FAC/CS; HM; IAIA/M; FSMCIAF; LACM; LBMA; MIA; MRFM; MSU; OSU/G; PDN; SBM; SCG; National Watercolor Society, 1976; Newport Harbor Museum of Art, Newport Beach, CA; Occidental College, Eagle Rock, CA; Purdue University Art Gallery; Santa Barbara (CA) Art Association

SOLO EXHIBITS: FAC/CS; IAIA/M; MRFM; SCG; SBM; U of CA/SB; Santa Barbara (CA) Art Association, 1974; Sun Valley (CA) Center for the Arts and Humanities

VINCENT, ZACHARIE *Huron*

Telariolin

Born 1812; died 1886

RESIDENCE: Lived in Lorette, PQ, Canada

EDUCATION: Studied portraiture under Antoine Plamondon

MEDIA: Oil and charcoal

PUBLISHED: Harper (1970; 1977); Wade, ed. (1986); McMasters, et al. (1993). *Recherches Amérindiennes au Québec* (Vol. 11, no. 4, 1981); *European Review of Native American Studies* (Vol. 5, no. 1, 1991)

PUBLIC COLLECTIONS: Partial listing includes: C/MQ; Château de Ramezay, Montréal, PQ

EXHIBITS: C/MBAM, C/NGCA

ZACHARIE VINCENT

Vincent had some formal training in art as evidenced by the European style of his self portraits which have survived. He also did drawings of the everyday life of a Huron village.

Wade, ed., 1986

VINYARD, KEVIN *Choctaw*

RESIDENCE: Apache, OK

EXHIBITS: AIE

AWARDS: AIE ('89, 1st; '90; '92, 1st)

VIVERS, HALLEE *Cherokee*

RESIDENCE: Paola, KS

EXHIBITS: LIAS ('91)

VOCU, BILLY *Oglala Lakota*

A.K.A. William Vocu

RESIDENCE: Pine Ridge, SD

EXHIBITS: RC

VOCU, JOHN *Oglala Sioux*

RESIDENCE: Pine Ridge, SD

EXHIBITS: RC

Waa-Nee-A-Too (see Owens, Gary W., Sr.)

Waano-Gano, Joseph *Cherokee*

A.K.A. Joseph T. N. Waano-Gano

Born 3 Mar 1906 in Salt Lake City, UT; died 1982; son of Rena May Lash-Heart and James Noonan; godmother was Ah Wahn U, Seneca

RESIDENCE: Lived in North Hollywood, CA

MILITARY: U.S. Air Force, WWII

EDUCATION: Los Angeles (CA) Metropolitan High School, 1922; Von Schneidau School of Art, 1924-1928; extension courses, U of CA/LA; studied under Hanson Puthuff and Theodore N. Lukits

OCCUPATION: Decor designer, actor, dancer, director, outdoor display artist, commercial artist, textile designer, writer, lecturer, sculptor, and painter

MEDIA: Watercolor, tempera, pastel, charcoal, clay, and sandstone

PUBLISHED: Snodgrass (1968); Brody (1971). *California Stylist* (Sept 1946); *Western Art Review* (Oct 1951); biographical publications

COMMISSIONS: *Murals:* Community Chest, Los Angeles, CA; Sherman Institute, Riverside, CA; Los Angeles (CA) General Hospital; Los Angeles (CA) Public Library (assisted Dean Cornwell). *Paintings: Green Virgin of Mexico*, used to raise funds for Mexican education, 1948. *Other:* Indian Council Fire Achievement Annual Award, medal design, 1933; *California Authentics, Santa Fe Trail Series* (14 Sept 1946), cover; *The Amerindian*, masthead design; fabric and fashion design brochure; fabric designs

PUBLIC COLLECTIONS: Gardenia (CA) Public Schools

EXHIBITS: AICA, AAA/T, CAC, CCP, CIAI, CSF, FAIEAIP, FCTM, FMC, GTA, ITIC, LAIC, LBAG, LH, MAF, MAG, MFA/D, MNM, PAC, SAIEAIP, SM, SN

SOLO EXHIBITS: Partial listing of more than 118 includes: BA, BHH, CBMM, CFS, CG, CI, CIFS, DSG, GPL, HB, LACC, LACM, LBAG, MSAC, SFNB, SGAG, SM, TAC, UC, UWC, WCH, WFS; galleries in California and New York

AWARDS: Partial listing of more than one hundred includes: AICA ('78, Bronze Medal); FMC; GTA; HBBA; ITIC; KCF; LACF; LAIC; LBAG; MAF; PAC; SN; worldwide competition, First Award for Outstanding Textile Design, *Katsina Masks*

HONORS: Biltmore Annual, Hermosa Beach, CA, Best Picture to Live With Award, 1952; CCP Hall of Fame, Indian Section; California International Flower Show Art Exhibition, chairman, 1958; Honor Roll of the Greatest Living American Indians, 1933

Joseph Waano-Gano

"As far back as he could remember, from the time he could hold a pencil or brush, Waano-Gano drew or painted. Many of his early creative works were in the medium of clay. His studies were given assistance and guidance by anthropologists Arthur Woodward, Frederick W. Hodge, and M. R. Harrington. As the result of a car accident in 1961, the artist had to force his fingers and wrists to 'work.'"

Snodgrass 1968

Waatina (see Sweezy, Carl)

Wabliska (see White Eagle)

Wachato (see Kingman, Violet)

Wachetaker, Woogee (see Wachetaker, George Smith)

Wa Chin Cadi (see Martínez, José Miguel)

Wade, Bobby *Choctaw*

Born 22 Feb 1940 in Broken Bow, OK

RESIDENCE: Broken Bow, OK

EDUCATION: Broken Bow (OK) High School; BC

PUBLISHED: Snodgrass (1968); Brody (1971)

PUBLIC COLLECTIONS: BIA/M

EXHIBITS: PAC; see also Awards

AWARDS: McCurtain County Fair, Idabel, OK

DETAIL: Dick West, *The Wedding of Art and Science*, n.d. Philbrook Museum of Art, Tulsa, Oklahoma

WADHAMS, LLOYD *Kwakwaka'wakw (Kwakiutl)*

RESIDENCE: Coquitlam, BC, Canada

MEDIA: Watercolor and pencil

PUBLIC COLLECTIONS: C/RBCM, DAM, HCC

EXHIBITS: BHSU, HCC, SDSMT

WADOW, ISIDORE *Algonquin*

A.K.A. Isadore Wadow

EXHIBITS: C/AG/TB

WAGACHO (see Quiver, Robert A.)

WAGOSHE, RUSSELL WILLIAM *Osage*

Kikekah Wahtiankah, Chief of Humor

Born 6 Sept 1911 on Salt Creek, Osage County, OK; died 1974; son of Agnes Bigheart and John Wagoshe; P/GF: Whip Hitter (Wagoshe), Osage chief in 1869, received his name after killing 13 soldiers with a whip.

EDUCATION: Graduated, Osage Boarding School, Pawhuska, OK

MEDIA: Watercolor

PUBLISHED: Snodgrass (1968)

PUBLIC COLLECTIONS: HSM/OK

EXHIBITS: HSM/OK

RUSSELL WILLIAM WAGOSHE

"The artist began painting when he was a small boy. 'One teacher got tired of punishing me so she had me draw pictures on the blackboard.' He painted only what he knew about the Osages and signed his paintings with a sketch of a horizontal feather. . . ."

Snodgrass 1968

WAHACANKA YA (see Grass, John)

WAHA CANKA YAPI (see Grass, John)

WAHAHRAKA, ROMONA BURGESS *(?)*

A.K.A. Romona Burgess Wahahrockah

RESIDENCE: Apache, OK

EXHIBITS: AIE, CNM

AWARDS: AIE ('86, 1st; '88; '89, 1st)

WAHAHROCKAH, ROMONA BURGESS (see Wahahraka, Romona Burgess)

WAHCA SKA (see Bies, Janet)

WAHELLA (see Simily, Maxine)

WAHNEE, B. J. (see Wahnee, Blanche)

WAHNEE, BLANCHE *Kiowa/Comanche*

A.K.A. B. J. Wahnee; Blanche J. Wahnee

Born 8 Mar 1946 in Anadarko, OK

RESIDENCE: Lawrence, KS

EDUCATION: Anadarko (OK) High School, 1964; B.A., SWOSU, 1970; M.A., Columbia University, NY, 1972; studied under Dick West (q.v.) and Max Silverhorn Jr.

OCCUPATION: Counselor, educator, curator, set designer, metalsmith, and painter

EXHIBITS: AIE; SPIM; PAC; U of WY; in Kansas and the Kansas City, MO, area

SOLO EXHIBITS: SPIM

AWARDS: AIE ('70, 1st; '74; '76; '77)

WAHNEE, CARRIE *Comanche*

A.K.A. Water Bird

RESIDENCE: Laguna, NM

EXHIBITS: AIE, PAC

AWARDS: AIE ('74; '75; '77)

WAH PEEN (see Atencio, Gilbert Benjamin)

WAH-WAH-TEH-GO-NA-GA-BO (see Morrison, George)

WAHWASUK (see Pribble, Corey Lyn)

WAITING UP (see Arkeketa, Benjamin)

WA KA *Zia*

A.K.A. Wa Kai
PUBLISHED: Dunn (1968); Snodgrass (1968)
PUBLIC COLLECTIONS: JAM
EXHIBITS: FWG

WA KAI (see Wa Ka)

WAKAN'-JE-PE-WEIN-GAH (see Houseman-Whitehawk, Laurie Jay)

WAKI YENI DEWA (see Moquino, Ignacio)

WAKPA (see Brewer, Donald A.)

WALANKE (see Red Corn, Jim)

WALDEN-KOHN, VONNIE *Cherokee*

RESIDENCE: Azle, TX
EXHIBITS: LIAS
AWARDS: LIAS ('89, MA)

WALKABOUT, JOHN *Cherokee*

EXHIBITS: CNM, FCTM
AWARDS: FCTM ('80, 1st; '81; '82, Grand Award; '86, 1st; '89)

WALKER, THOMAS, JR. *WINNEBAGO*

RESIDENCE: Winnebago, NE
PUBLISHED: Snodgrass (1968)
EXHIBITS: PAC

WALKING BY THE RIVER (see Nailor, Gerald)

WALKING EAGLE (see Simeon, David)

WALKING LEADER (see Natay, Ed)

WALKINGSTICK, JOHNNY *Cherokee*

RESIDENCE: Broken Arrow, OK
EXHIBITS: CNM, FCTM

WALKINGSTICK, KAY *Cherokee/Winnebago*

Born 1935 in Syracuse, NY
RESIDENCE: Long Island City, NY
EDUCATION: B.F.A., Beaver College, Glenside, PA; M.F.A., Pratt Institute, Brooklyn, NY
OCCUPATION: Teacher, lecturer, and artist
MEDIA: Oil, acrylic, watercolor, and mixed-media
PUBLISHED: Longfish and Randell (1983); Younger (1985); Shaman (1987); Roberts, ed. (1992); Zurko, ed. (1992); Archuleta and Strickland (1991); Abbott (1994). *The New York Post* (28 Mar 1980); *Artweek* (13 Oct 1980; 2 Nov 1985); *The New York Times* (19 June 1981; 2 Dec 1985); *The Record* (23 Oct 1983); *The Durango Herald* (1 Nov 1984); *American Indian Art* (Jan 1985); *Native Vision* (Sept/Oct 1986); *The Village Voice* (16 May 1989); *The Phoenix Gazette* (23 Sept 1991); *C Magazine* (summer 1991); *Art-Talk* (Oct 1991); *Art News* (Feb 1992)

KAY WALKINGSTICK

WalkingStick says, "My current paintings are diptychs, one portion is abstract, the other is not. They relate thematically, describing the earth from different viewpoints; both parts are simplified and formally arranged. They represent two kinds of memory — one fleeting and the other permanent and non-specific. The paintings are about these two kinds of understanding."

artist, p.c. 1990

COMMISSIONS: Cathedral of the Sacred Heart, Newark, NJ, 1957

PUBLIC COLLECTIONS: Partial listing of more than twenty includes: C/NMC; NM; WSAC; SPIM; Albert Knox Museum, Buffalo, NY; Israel Museum, Jerusalem, Israel; Johnson Museum, Cornell, Ithaca, NY; La Jolla (CA) Museum of Contemporary Art; Metropolitan Museum of Art, New York, NY; Newark (NJ) Museum; San Diego (CA) Museum of Fine Arts

EXHIBITS: AC/Y; AICH; BM/B; C/LSP; CNGM; CWAM; FIA; HM; MM/NJ; MMA/WA; MSU; NM; OLO; OSU/G; SNMA; SPIM; SS/CW; SV; TPAS; U of CA/D; U of OK; WHB; WWM; Aldrich Museum, Ridgefield, CT; Bronx Museum, 1980; Brooklyn Terminal, 1983; Douglass College, New Brunswick, NJ; Hart Senate Office Building, Washington, D.C.; Israel Museum, Jerusalem, Israel, 1982; Jersey City (NJ) Museum, 1992; Rutgers University, New Brunswick, NJ; The New Museum, New York, NY, 1990

SOLO EXHIBITS: HM; MM/NJ; NJSM; U of CA/D; Beaver College, Glenside, PA; Fort Lewis College, Durango, CO; Cornell University, Hartell Gallery, Ithaca, NY, 1994; Hartwick College Gallery, Oneonta, NY, 1991; Hillwood Art Museum, Long Island University, NY, 1991; Jersey City (NJ) Museum, 1992; Ohio State University, Columbus, OH; Soho Center for Visual Arts, New York, NY; Long Island University, Wood Art Museum, Brookville, NY, 1991

HONORS: *Fellowships:* Danforth Foundation, 1973-1975; New Jersey State Council on the Arts, 1981, 1985-1986; NEA, 1983-1984. *Other:* Beaver College, Golden Disk Award, 1978; one of five artists selected by the NEA and the USIS Office of Arts America to represent the United States at the Cairo International Biennial, Cairo, Egypt, Dec 1994-Jan 1995

WALKUS, CHARLES G. *Kwakwaka'wakw (Kwakiutl)*

MEDIA: Watercolor, pen and ink, and ballpoint pen

PUBLIC COLLECTIONS: C/RBCM

WALLACE, ROBERTA A. *Cherokee*

EXHIBITS: CNM, FCTM

AWARDS: FCTM ('90)

WALLACE, WADE MILLER (see Miller, Wade)

WALLUK, WILBUR *Eskimo*

A.K.A. Wilbur Wright Walluk

Born 24 Jan 1928 in Shishmaref, AK; died 1968 in Seattle, WA

EDUCATION: Shishmaref, AK; Mt. Edgecumbe Vocational School, AK

OCCUPATION: Employee of Leonard F. Porter, Inc. (Seattle, WA), reindeer herder, ivory carver, parka maker and cleaner, and graphic artist

PUBLISHED: Snodgrass (1968); Ray (1969)

PUBLIC COLLECTIONS: GM

EXHIBITS: DAM, PAC; see also Awards

AWARDS: PAC; Northwest Alaska Fair, Nome, AK

WALTER, ROY M. *(?)*

PUBLISHED: Snodgrass (1968)

PUBLIC COLLECTIONS: MAI

WALTERS, DANIEL AARON *Navajo/Pawnee/Otoe*

A.K.A. Signature: D. Walters

Born 6 Sept 1968 in Santa Fe, NM; son of Anne Lee McGlaslin and Harry Walters; P/GP: Rosemary and John Walters; M/GP: May and Luther McGlaslin

EDUCATION: Chinle (AZ) High School, 1986; Albuquerque (NM) Technical-Vocational Institute, 1992

WILBUR WALLUK

"The artist's father was a reindeer herder whose native village was Walluk. Nephew of Kivetoruk Moses (q.v.), the artist began painting 'secretly' at the age of six. In 1946, he wrote: 'I find myself a thin man artist and funny face artist — once I win first prize on funny face drawing. Then when I am 14 year old I learned how to paint with oil paints at school. When I am 10 to 13 year old Mrs. Russell Government school teacher of Native help me little on arts. When I am 14 I finally give up art and start my own Ivory Business more than arts. Ivory Business was more fun to me. I was on Ivory Business 3 year. At the year 1944 I broke my back bone and I quit Ivory carving.' The artist was in the hospital one and one-half years and drew pictures which he gave away and sold. In 1951, when he was not in school, he helped 'mama to make fur parkas' and clean and repair them as well. He also painted neckties and made ivory and wood carvings, which he etched and painted with brush and ink."

Snodgrass 1968

DANIEL AARON WALTERS

Walters states, "I am a self-taught artist who started painting in 1991. I illustrate Navajo mythology to show our children my perspective. Since I have been painting I have become even more aware of the importance of the Navajo Culture and the need to preserve it."

p.c. 1994

OCCUPATION: Painter
MEDIA: Acrylic and pen and ink
EXHIBITS: ACS/ENP, ITIC, SWAIA
AWARDS: ITIC ('93; '94, 1st)

WALTERS, HARRY *Navajo*

Na-Ton-Sa-Ka
Born 10 Mar 1943; nephew of Bluehorse, Navajo medicine man
RESIDENCE: Tsaile, AZ
EDUCATION: Aztec (NM) High School; IAIA, 1962-1963; KCAI/MO; CSF/SF; learned sand painting techniques from his uncle, Bluehorse
OCCUPATION: Staff artist, teacher, historian, museum director, and artist
MEDIA: Acrylic, watercolor, tempera, casein, and pen and ink
PUBLISHED: Wyman (1965), Snodgrass (1968); Tanner (1973). *Newsletter,* NCC (June 1984); *The Indian Trader* (Sept 1982; Mar 1989)
BOOKS ILLUSTRATED: Beck, Walters, and Francisco (1990); *Navajo Birth Tales* by Francis Newcomb
PUBLIC COLLECTIONS: MNA, WWM
EXHIBITS: IAIA; ITIC; MNM; MNCA; NCC; NMSF; NTF; NTM; PAC; SN; galleries in New Mexico
AWARDS: ITIC ('70, 1st; '76; '87; '88); MNM; SN ('71)

HARRY WALTERS

Walters intends to portray Navajo life as it is today. His paintings incorporate incidents from Navajo myths and legends into today's world. He says, "I don't try to romanticize the Indian people — too many artists do that." He paints Indians with Stetsons, pickups, and sunglasses. In addition to his realistic works, he has experimented with surrealism and abstract painting.

Newsletter, *NCC, 1 June 1984*

WALTERS, MAXWELL *Navajo*

PUBLIC COLLECTIONS: MNA

WALZ, PETER FRANK *Chippewa/Ottawa*

Born 14 June 1912 on the White Earth Reservation, MN; died 22 Apr 1983
RESIDENCE: Lived in Albuquerque, NM
OCCUPATION: BIA adminstrative employee, and artist
PUBLISHED: Snodgrass (1968)
EXHIBITS: MNM, PAC, SN, USDS
AWARDS: MNM, SN

WAMBALEE CHES CHALLAH (see Little Eagle)

WANBLE ORKO (see Fast Eagle)

WANBLI TA HOCOKA WASTE (see Amiotte, Arthur Douglas)

WANDERING SPIRIT (see Constant, Alvin)

WAPAH NAHYAH (see West, Dick)

WA-PA-WA-GIE (see Fragua, Laura)

WAPOSTANGI (see Good, Baptiste)

WAPUSKA (see Charlette, Ovide)

WAR CLOUD, PAUL (see Grant, Paul Warcloud)

WARD, VICTOR *Tlingit*

Born 22 Sept 1943
RESIDENCE: Juneau, AK
EDUCATION: Santa Fe
PUBLISHED: Snodgrass (1968)
EXHIBITS: MNM, PAC
AWARDS: MNM

WARDEN, CLEAVER *Arapaho*

MILITARY: U.S. Army
EDUCATION: Carlisle
OCCUPATION: Scout, researcher, and painter
PUBLISHED: *American Indian Art* (winter 1992)
PUBLIC COLLECTIONS: MNH/F

CLEAVER WARDEN

Warden was one of fifty Cheyenne and twenty Arapaho men who were recruited to serve as scouts at Fort Reno, Indian Territory, in 1885. Their duties were to police the reservation and to support the military and agency staff in peacekeeping. Warden was later employed as a researcher by George Dorsey of the Field Museum of Natural History when he did extensive fieldwork on the Northern Cheyenne and Southern Arapaho.

American Indian Art
winter 1992

WARE, WOODROW *(?)*

PUBLISHED: Snodgrass (1968)
PUBLIC COLLECTIONS: HSM/OK

WARESBACK, CHARLES *Cherokee/Osage*

Thundermaker
RESIDENCE: Terlton, OK
EXHIBITS: CNM ('91, '92)

WAR HORSE (see Jake, Albin Roy)

WAR LANCE (see Momaday, Al)

WARM DAY, JONATHAN *Taos*

Birth date unknown; son of Eva Mirabal (q.v.)
EDUCATION: U of NM; NCC
OCCUPATION: Painter and sculptor
MEDIA: Acrylic, wood, and stone
SOLO/SPECIAL EXHIBITS: MRFM (dual show)

WARM MOUNTAIN (see Aguilar, José Vincente)

WARNER, BOYD, JR. *Navajo*

Blackhair
Born 26 May 1937 in Tuba City, AZ
RESIDENCE: Phoenix, AZ
OCCUPATION: Decorator, paperhanger; painter since 1960
MEDIA: Oil, acrylic, watercolor, tempera, sand, and mixed-media
PUBLISHED: Tanner (1973). *The Arizona Republic* (Oct 1971); *Arizona Living* (Apr 1975; Oct 1977; July 1978); *The Scottsdale Daily Progress* (Mar 1975); *The Gallup Independent* (Sept 1974); biographical publications
PUBLIC COLLECTIONS: HCC; General Motors Corporation
EXHIBITS: ASF, HCC, HM, ITIC, NMSF, PAC, SN, TAAII, WTF
SOLO EXHIBITS: Canyon de Chelly National Monument, AZ, 1967; Old Town San Diego (CA) State Historical Park, 1969
AWARDS: ASF ('66; '67; '71); HM/G ('71; '75; '77; '79); ITIC ('71, 1st, Elkus Award; '72, 1st; '76); NMSF ('74, 1st; '76, 1st); TAAII ('71; '73)

BOYD WARNER JR.

While most of Warner's work is done in the traditional style and reflects his Navajo heritage, occasionally he works in the European style with almost full perspective. He has also exhibited abstract paintings and rock art studies.

Tanner 1973

WARNER, FRED *(?)*

PUBLISHED: Snodgrass (1968)
PUBLIC COLLECTIONS: MAI

WARNER, GARY *Omaha/Osage*

Born 3 June 1953
RESIDENCE: Midwest City, OK
EDUCATION: Central High School, Midwest City, OK; IAIA; Haskell
PUBLIC COLLECTIONS: HCC
EXHIBITS: HCC, OIO, PAC, RC

WARPA TANKA KUCIYELA (see Amiotte, Arthur Douglas)

WARREN, HARRY *Navajo*

RESIDENCE: Red Mesa, AZ, on the Navajo Reservation

OCCUPATION: Elementary school teacher, silversmith, and painter

BOOKS ILLUSTRATED: Garaway (1986)

WARRIOR, ANTOWINE *Sauk-Fox*

Takotokasi, Roaring Thunder

Born 4 Jan 1941 in Stroud, OK; son of Mae and Andrew Warrior; M/GP: Bessie and Thomas Morris (Mo-gi-We-mi-ko, Bad Thunder); P/GF: Peatwy-Tuck

RESIDENCE: Pepperell, MA

EDUCATION: BC; Penn Valley Junior College, Kansas City, MO; Haskell; U of AZ, "Southwest Indian Art Project," scholarship, summers 1960,1962

OCCUPATION: Traditional Indian dancer, craftsman, sculptor, and painter

MEDIA: Watercolor, stone, beads, and prints

PUBLISHED: Snodgrass (1968); Brody (1971); Mahey, et al.(1980); Medina (1981). *Four Winds* (summer 1980); *The Tulsa World* (21 Aug 1990)

PUBLIC COLLECTIONS: ASM, BIA, GM, PAC

EXHIBITS: AAIE, AICA, AIE, ASM, BC/McG, CIM, CNM, CSU/OK, FAIE, ITIC, KCPA, MNM, OIAP, PAC, RE, SI, SWAIA

SOLO EXHIBITS: PAC; Sac and Fox Nation Public Library, Stroud, OK

AWARDS: AIE; CIM ('86, Best of Show); ITIC; PAC ('78, Wolf Robe Hunt Award; '79, 1st); RE ('93); SWAIA ('82, 1st, Best of Class, Best of Division; '83)

ANTOWINE WARRIOR

The artist's talent developed at a young age. By the age of 17, his work was exhibited at the Philbrook Art Center. Warrior is a traditional painter who credits his grandfather with being his greatest inspiration. With his paintings, he tries to make the history of his people come alive. It is his way of preserving the old ways.

artist brochure 1992

WARRIOR, SAM *Peigan*

Born 1957 at Pincher Creek, AB, Canada

RESIDENCE: Pincher Creek, AB, Canada

EDUCATION: Alberta College of Art, Calgary, 1980-1984; C/U of C, 1984-1988

COMMISSIONS: *Murals:* Lethbridge (AB) Public School Board, District No. 51, Lethbridge, AB, 1990

PUBLIC COLLECTIONS: C/AG/O; C/AIAC; C/ESSOC; C/NGCA; C/PBEAC; C/U of C; Blood Tribe Board of Education, Levern (AB) School

EXHIBITS: ASMG, C/AM, C/CNAA, C/MC, C/NAM, C/PHT, C/SAGM, C/SC, C/U of C/MG, DC

AWARDS: C/SC ('85); C/AM ('86); C/PHT ('86)

HONORS: Everett Soop INM Scholarship, 1981; Esso Native Art Competition, one of five finalists, with acceptance into Esso Emerging Artists Collection, Calgary, 1987; Calgary (AB) Photo Distributors Annual Award

WARRIOR WHO CAME OUT (see Lee, Charles)

WARRIOR WHO WALKED UP TO HIS ENEMY (see Begay, Harrison)

WAR SOLDIER, BILLY (see Soza, Billy War Soldier)

WASAAJA (see Sine, Duke)

WASABA SHINGA (see Woodring, Carl)

WASCONADIE (see Darling, Marcell J.)

WA-SE-BE-WES-SKA-KA (see Daylight, Larry Clayton)

WASECHUN TASHUNKA (see American Horse)

WASHAKIE *Flathead/Shoshoni*

Washakie, Rawhide Rattle

A.K.A. White Haired Chief With Scarred Face; Chief Washakie

WASHAKIE

"The Chief produced numerous 'artistically decorated' elk skins depicting his hunts, buffalo chases, battles, and personal history. It cannot be determined whether some paintings, signed 'Washakie' are by the chief or by his sons (see Charles Washakie and George Washakie), for the styles are

Born 1798 in Montana, into the Flathead tribe; lived with the Flatheads until he was approximately eight years old; died 20 Feb 1900; son of Paseego and a woman thought to have been a Shoshoni (or Umatilla)

MILITARY: U.S. Army, Fourth Infantry

OCCUPATION: Warrior, sub-chief of the Shoshoni, orator, scout, wrangler, and painter

MEDIA: Pigment and hide

PUBLISHED: Alexander (1938), Snodgrass (1968); Dockstader (1977); Del Monte (n.d.); Maurer (1992)

PUBLIC COLLECTIONS: MAI; SDMM; SI/MNH; SM; Newark (NJ) Museum

EXHIBITS: VP

HONORS: Elected chief of the Shoshoni; united several groups of Eastern Shoshoni; received signed commendation from nine thousand Whites, testifying to his kindly aid; old Camp Brown was officially designated Fort Washakie; Washakie National Forest named for him; received gifts and commendations from two presidents; monument erected in his honor, 1905

WASHAKIE, CHARLES *Flathead/Shoshoni/Crow*

Wobaah

A.K.A. Charlie Washakie; Charlie Katsiekodie

Born 1873 near Crow Heart Butte, WY; son of Ahawhy Persie (a Crow captive) and Washakie (q.v.); P/GF: Paseego (Flathead)

PUBLISHED: Alexander (1938); Snodgrass (1968); Maurer (1992)

PUBLIC COLLECTIONS: MAI; Wyoming State Museum, Cheyenne, WY

EXHIBITS: VP

WASHAKIE, GEORGE *Shoshoni*

PUBLISHED: Snodgrass (1968)

PUBLIC COLLECTIONS: MAI

EXHIBITS: CCP

WA SHUN KEH (see Brave, Franklin P.)

WASSEGIJIG, HELEN *Ottawa/Ojibwa*

Born 1951

EDUCATION: Carleton University, Ottawa, ON; C/U of O

OCCUPATION: Graphic artist

MEDIA: Graphite on paper

PUBLISHED: Menitove, ed. (1986b). *Windspeaker* (12 Dec 1986); *Imprint* (Vol. 2, no. 3, 1987)

PUBLIC COLLECTIONS: C/AG/TB, C/INAC, C/CMC

EXHIBITS: C/ACCCNA; C/AG/TB; C/CIIA; C/INAC; C/LUM; C/MCC; C/NB; C/OCA; C/ SIFC; C/U of O; C/WICEC; SM; Canadian Consulate General, Los Angeles, CA; National Winter Showcase of Canadian Indian Arts, Ottawa, ON; Native Art Foundation, Toronto, ON; Native Art Gallery, Lobby of Indian Affairs, Ottawa, ON; see also Awards

SOLO EXHIBITS: C/AG/TB

AWARDS: Festival of Canadian Arts, Ottawa, ON ('83)

WASSILIE, MOSES *Eskimo*

Born 1946 in Nunapitchuk, AK

RESIDENCE: Bethel, AK

EDUCATION: Mt. Edgecumbe, 1966; IAIA, 1966; U of AK/C, 1967

MEDIA: Oil and acrylic

WASHAKIE

(continued) very nearly identical. The name Washakie (and Wussikhe, The Rattler) came to the artist when he killed his first buffalo, making from it a rattle which he always used when riding to war. His second name, White Haired Chief With Scarred Face, was given him when his hair suddenly turned white following the death of his favorite son. (His scarred face was the result of a Blackfoot arrow.) There are 30 official and unofficial ways of spelling Washakie. Many references refer to the Chief as Shoshoni, but he did not join this tribe until ca. 1826-1830."

Snodgrass 1968

CHARLES WASHAKIE

"Because he lived with the tribe, Charles was generally assumed to have been Shoshoni. It is quite possible that many paintings attributed to his father were actually his work, for their styles are similar."

Snodgrass 1968

GEORGE WASHAKIE

"It is probable that George is one of the twelve children of Washakie (q.v.), for the names of all twelve have not been determined."

Snodgrass 1968

MOSES WASSILIE

The artist is known for his portraits and landscapes.

Ray 1969

PUBLISHED: Ray (1969)
SOLO EXHIBITS: Fairbanks, AK, three solo exhibits by 1969

WATCHETAKER, GEORGE SMITH *Comanche*

Watchetaker, Hide Away

A.K.A. Woogee Watchetaker

Born 1 Mar 1916 in Elgin, OK; died 27 May 1993 in Lawton, OK; son of Dana Pikiyou Chibitty (Tahtahdarsy, Small and Pitiful, or Cute) and Walter Hoke Smith Watchetaker; adopted into the Quanah Parker family as a teenager

RESIDENCE: Lived in Elgin, OK

EDUCATION: Mt. Scott (OK) Rural School, 1923-1927; Fort Sill, 1927-1932; Haskell, 1935; studied under Olaf Nordmark

OCCUPATION: Decorator, sign painter, lecturer, Indian dancer, movie actor, rainmaker; full-time painter after 1970

MEDIA: Oil, watercolor, and tempera

PUBLISHED: Snodgrass (1968), New (1981). *Oklahoma Art Gallery* (winter 1980); *The Indian Trader* (Sept 1982); biographical publications

PUBLIC COLLECTIONS: EM; GM; HCC; IACB; FSM; Southwestern Hospital, Lawton, OK; J. J. Young Eye Clinic, Lawton, OK; in Switzerland, England, and France

EXHIBITS: AIE; CNM,;HM/G; ITIC; NACLA; OAC; PAC; RC; SN; Clinton, OK; Wichita Falls, TX; Albuquerque, NM; Colorado State Fair, Pueblo, CO; powwows and markets; see also Awards

AWARDS: AIE ('67, 1st); CNM ('82); HM/G ('74, 1st); ITIC ('82); RC ('77, Begay Award); Southwest Sidewalk Show, Lawton, OK

HONORS: Television and movie appearances; knighted by Queen Elizabeth of England after a command performance; served on the Comanche Business Committee; spiritual leader of the Comanche Tribe; SI, Bicentennial American Folklife Festival, leader of Comanche delegation, 1976

GEORGE SMITH WATCHETAKER

Watchetaker spent many years traveling to dancing competitions. He was National Champion Indian Dancer five times, and World Champion Indian Dancer three times. In addition, he was the only champion dancer to be recognized officially by the Bureau of Indian Affairs, the award being presented by Secretary of the Interior, Stewart Udall. It has been said that he danced the way he painted, with beauty, dignity and the power of the Comanche way.

Oklahoma Art Gallery
winter 1980

Painting in the traditional flat style, Watchetaker recorded the lifestyle of the Comanches, including ceremonies and dances. Nationally known as a rainmaker, Watchetaker was often engaged by cities in times of drought. More often than not, the rains appeared after he performed his special ceremony.

Snodgrass-King, p.c. 1994

WATCHMAN, BRUCE *Navajo*

EXHIBITS: ITIC

AWARDS: ITIC ('86, 1st; '87, 1st)

WATER BIRD (see Wahnee, Carrie)

WATER EDGE (see Tahoma, Quincy)

WATER ELK (see Cohoe, William)

WATERMAN, CARSON R. *Seneca*

Born 22 Dec 1944 on Cattaraugus Indian Reservation, NY

RESIDENCE: Salamanca, NY

EDUCATION: CSA, 1965-1967, 1970; SI, internship program, Apr-May, 1977; NYSM

OCCUPATION: Preparation and design of exhibits, artist-in-residence, illustrator, art instructor, sculptor, and painter

MEDIA: Oil, acrylic, watercolor, gouache, steatite, basswood, and hardwood

PUBLISHED: Johannsen and Ferguson, eds. (1983). *War Against the Seneca, The French Expedition of 1687* (1986), booklet

BOOKS ILLUSTRATED: *Seneca Story Book*, New York State Education Department

COMMISSIONS: *Murals:* Seneca Nation, Howard S. Billings School, Chateauguay, Québec and Seneca Lane, 1975-1976; Marriott Inn, Rochester, NY, 1978; Delevan College Station tile mural for Niagara Frontier Transit Authority, 1984. *Other:* New York State Department of Transportation, Southern Tier Expressway, designed road signs, 1976; Salamanca (NY) Nursing Home, designed mosaic tiles for building exterior, 1976; Salamanca (NY) Housing and Urban Development, Old Age Home, art projects; Seneca Nation, official logo design; New York State Division for Historic Preservation, designed trail signs, 1986; Warren County-Seneca Heritage, sculpture, 1987

PUBLIC COLLECTIONS: SMII; Lyndon B. Johnson Library, Austin, TX

EXHIBITS: AM, ECFE, INAAT, MAI, MDOWP, NU/BC, NYSM, QM, SINM, SMII, TFAG, TSM, U of PA/M, USDS

SOLO EXHIBITS: The Centre Gallery, Fine Arts Center, Olean, NY (1991)

HONORS: AANNAAC, Board of Directors

WATHEN, GLENDA S. *Cherokee/Choctaw*

A.K.A. Glenda Thompson Wathen

Born 22 Oct 1941 in Butler, MO; daughter of Nadine Lamons and Thomas Glen Thompson; P/GP: Florence and Lawrence Thompson; M/GP: Goldie E. Greathouse Lamons and Antoine Drury

RESIDENCE: Towanda, KS

EDUCATION: Kincaid (KS) Rural High School, 1960; Kansas State Teachers College, Emporia, KS, three years

OCCUPATION: Receptionist, accounting department clerk, writer, sculptor, and painter

MEDIA: Oil, acrylic, watercolor, pencil, pen and ink, pastel, stone, clay, and prints

COMMISSIONS: Agricultural Hall of Fame and National Center, Bonner Springs, KS, portrait sculpture

PUBLIC COLLECTIONS: Warren Hall Coutts III Memorial Museum, El Dorado, KS

EXHIBITS: CNM; IS; TIAF; TIMSS; The Agricultural Hall of Fame and National Center, Bonner Spring, KS; National Arts Club, New York, NY; Wild Onion Indian Dinner, Bartlesville, OK; thirty-six exhibits per year throughout Oklahoma and Texas

AWARDS: CNM ('90; '92); IS ('88; '89); TIAF ('91, 1st)

HONORS: IS, painting used on program cover, 1988

GLENDA S. WATHEN

Wathen is a very versatile artist who creates all types of art in a variety of styles and techniques. After extensive research and study she uses her imagination, not photographs, to create her paintings. Although the artist must use a wheelchair because of polio contracted when she was a child, she says it has never made a difference to those who know her, nor has it caused her to miss any activities. In her words, "It has just never been important in any way. I am a professional artist, my art is all that should be considered."

p.c. 1992

WATSON, STEPHEN *Cherokee*

A.K.A. Stefan De Pojoaque

Born 21 Jan 1955; son of Savern Watson Jr.; P/GF: Savern Watson Sr.; M/GP: Josey Jerman and Ivan Banister

RESIDENCE: Albuquerque, NM

EDUCATION: Pojoaque (NM) High School, 1974; Wesleyan University, Middletown, CT, 1977-1979

OCCUPATION: Commercial artist and painter

MEDIA: Oil

PUBLISHED: *Artspace* (winter 1981; winter 1982); *The Albuquerque Journal* (28 Dec 1981; Feb 1985); *The Santa Fe Reporter* (23 Dec 1981); *Artlines* (Oct 1983; Aug 1985; June 1986)

PUBLIC COLLECTIONS: AC/RM; ABQM; MNM; AT&T, Denver, CO; Mountain Bell Telephone, Denver, CO; Public Service Company of Colorado, Denver, CO; Moncor Bank, Albuquerue, NM; Sunwest Bank, Albuquerque, NM; Mountain Bell Telephone, Albuquerque, NM; Cherokee National Hospital, Tahlequah, OK; Pontifica (OH) Catholic College; Honeywell Corporation, Phoenix, AZ

EXHIBITS: ABQM; CSF/SF; MNM; SFFA; Artists of Albuquerque (NM); Horden Museum, Bergen, Norway; Paper Museum, Duren, West Germany; Vezza, Italy; Wakayama Museum of Modern Art, Wakayama, Japan

Gailey Watt

The majority of Watt's paintings were of the traditional way of life or portraits. He preferred to paint elderly people because of the character in their faces.

Johannsen and Ferguson, eds. 1983

Wa Wa Chaw

Wa Wa Chaw was adopted by Dr. Cornelius Duggan and raised and educated by his sister Mary, a wealthy New York woman. She married Manuel Carmonia-Núñez, and was later divorced. Her foster parents encouraged her interest in the study of anatomy and free brush strokes, and Albert P. Ryder taught her to 'tone down' her colors. For a while, she sold liniment in New York City, then found she could sell her paintings in Greenwich Village. She worked with Dr. Carlos Montezuma, became an activist for Indian causes, and lectured widely. Her paintings are often compared with Edvard Munch; she expressed the same quality of heavy shadows and strong lines.

Dockstader p.c. 1994

Teddy Weakee

"The artist was known to have painted in oils in the European perspective, but was painting infrequently by 1950. He was best known as a carver of fetishes."

Snodgrass 1968

He was a popular character in the village in the 1920s,

WATT, GAILEY *Seneca*

Tiasah

Born 18 Oct 1914; death date unknown

RESIDENCE: Lived in Allegany, NY

EDUCATION: Haskell, 1930s

OCCUPATION: Beadworker, graphic artist, silversmith, craftsman, professional sign painter, and painter

MEDIA: Oil, acrylic, watercolor, pen and ink, charcoal, pastel, beads, silver, feathers, and prints

PUBLISHED: Johannsen and Ferguson, eds. (1983)

EXHIBITS: Seneca Iroquois National Museum; area exhibits

WATTAN (see Sweezy, Carl)

WAWABANO SATA (see Pushetonequa, Charles)

WA WA CHAW *Luiseño*

Wawa Calac Chaw, Keep From the Water

A.K.A. Benita Núñez; Princess Wa Wa Chaw; Benita Wa Wa Calachaw Núñez

Born 25 Dec 1888 at Valley Center,CA, on the Rincón reservation; died 12 May 1972 in New York, NY

RESIDENCE: Lived in New York, NY

EDUCATION: Private schools in the eastern U.S.; Sherman; studied under Albert P. Ryder

OCCUPATION: Activist in behalf of Indian and feminist causes, lecturer, entertainer, and painter

MEDIA: Oil

PUBLISHED: Snodgrass (1968); Dockstader (1977); Steiner (1980); Wade, ed. (1986)

PUBLIC COLLECTIONS: MAI, PAC

EXHIBITS: PAC; Greenwich Village Out-Door exhibits, New York, NY; Europe

WAWE HAKTA (see Rave, Austin)

WEAHKEE, TEDDY (see Weakee, Teddy)

WEAHKIE, TEDDY (see Weakee, Teddy)

WEAKEE, TEDDY *Zuni*

Weahkie; Weakie; Wiacke

A.K.A. Teddy Weahkee; Teddy Weahkie

Born 1900 at Zuni Pueblo, NM; died 1965

EDUCATION: Studied at home for nearly 25 years

OCCUPATION: Carver, silversmith, and painter

MEDIA: Oil, stone, silver, and gemstone

PUBLISHED: Snodgrass (1968). *American Magazine of Art* (Aug 1933)

PUBLIC COLLECTIONS: HM, MAI, SMNAI (deerskin paintings)

EXHIBITS: ITIC

AWARDS: ITIC

WEAKIE (see Weakee, Teddy)

WEBSTER, DAVID *(?)*

EDUCATION: Phoenix, 1964

PUBLISHED: Snodgrass (1968)

EXHIBITS: FAIEAIP

Webster, Glen *West Coast*

Born 1961 on Flores Island, BC, Canada; son of Andrew Webster

RESIDENCE: Canada

OCCUPATION: Commercial fisherman and graphic artist

PUBLIC COLLECTIONS: HCC

EXHIBITS: HCC, RC, SDSMT

Webster, Nick, Jr. *Arapaho*

RESIDENCE: Tulsa, OK

EXHIBITS: RC

Weckeah *Comanche*

Weckeah, Searching

A.K.A. Roberta C. Bradley

Born 1920 in Lawton, OK; daughter of Mary Pache Parker and Edward H. Clark; M/GP: Weckeah and Quanah Parker, Comanche Chief; M/GGM: Cynthia Ann Parker, a non-Indian, captured by Comanches at age nine

RESIDENCE: Lawton, OK

EDUCATION: Cameron High School, Lawton, OK

OCCUPATION: Sculptor and painter

MEDIA: Oil, watercolor, pastel, and charcoal

PUBLISHED: Snodgrass (1968); Brody (1971)

PUBLIC COLLECTIONS: FSM, MNM

EXHIBITS: AIE; MNM; PAC; Duncan (OK) Art Show; Ponca Indian Fair, Ponca City, OK

SOLO EXHIBITS: Fort Sill (OK) Post Service Club; Lawton (OK) Chamber of Commerce; Carnegie Library, Lawton, OK

AWARDS: Duncan, OK; Ponca City, OK; Anadarko, OK

Weddle, Star Tehee *Cherokee*

A.K.A. Glenda Starrlene Teehee Weddle

Birth date unknown; daughter of Pearl McKibben and Hoke Tehee; P/GP: Margaret Butler and Charles Tehee; M/GP: Bessie Cox and B. E. McKibben

RESIDENCE: Houston, TX

EDUCATION: Grandfalls-Royalty High School, Grandfalls, TX, 1958; B.A., Trinity University, San Antonio, TX, 1977

OCCUPATION: Artist

MEDIA: Oil, acrylic, watercolor, pencil, pen and ink, pastel, and prints

PUBLISHED: Biographical publications

PUBLIC COLLECTIONS: AHM/CO; HCC; Delancey Foundation, San Francisco, CA

EXHIBITS: AIAF; AIAFM; CIM; CNM; FCTM; HCC; IACA; ITAE; ITIC; LIAS; RE; SWAIA; Southern Methodist University; Trinity University, San Antonio, TX

AWARDS: ITAE ('91); ITIC ('90); SWAIA ('91, 1st)

HONORS: Trinity University, San Antonio, TX, Trustees' Scholarship, One of six finalists for the title, Texas State Artist

Weebothee, Steven Wayne *Zuni*

Born 18 Aug 1970 ; son of Mary Ann and Lee Taft Weebothee; P/GP: Lula and Wilbur Weebothee; M/GP: Antelaya and Harry Cheeku. Related to Lee and Mary Weebothee, silversmiths

RESIDENCE: Zuni, NM

Teddy Weakee

(continued) making fetishes, painting deer hides, and serving as a general interpreter. He acted as a buffer between the Zuni and the outside world.

Dockstader, p.c. 1995

Weckeah

"The artist is best known in art circles as Weckeah. She seldom paints in the flat Indian style but prefers instead to use oil, pastel, watercolor, and charcoal to depict her history-based art work. She is also a sculptor."

Snodgrass 1968

Steven Wayne Weebothee

Weebothee is especially grateful to his neighbor, Alex Seowtewa (q.v.), for the inspiration and advice he has offered over the years.

p.c. 1992

EDUCATION: Zuni (NM) Junior High School
OCCUPATION: Silversmith and painter
MEDIA: Acrylic, watercolor, clay, and silver
PUBLIC COLLECTIONS: HM; First Inter-State Bank of Gallup, NM
EXHIBITS: HM/G; ITIC; MNA; NMSF; Twin Buttes High School, Zuni, NM
AWARDS: HM, ITIC, MNA, NMSF

WEEKS, RUPERT *Shoshoni*
Born 1918; died 1984
RESIDENCE: Lived in Wyoming
MILITARY: WWII
EDUCATION: BIA boarding schools
OCCUPATION: Farmer, writer, and painter
MEDIA: Acrylic
PUBLISHED: Weeks (1981); *Native American Artists,* Cortland (NY) Arts Council (1987), catalog

RUPERT WEEKS

As a young soldier during WWII, Weeks found that the German people were more interested in his Shoshoni culture than were his fellow Americans. After the war he moved back to his Eastern Shoshoni people, where he became a farmer and a painter of wildlife and landscapes. According to Richard Fleck, University of Wyoming professor of English, Weeks' paintings had a "mythical quality few have expressed."

Native American Artists, *1987*

WEEPAMA QUEDAECOUKA (see Mofsie, Louis Billingsly)

WELLS, CHARLES, JR. *Comanche/Caddo*
Born 1 Nov 1953 in El Reno, OK; son of Charles and Angdine Gonzales Wells
RESIDENCE: Anadarko, OK
EDUCATION: Apache (OK) High School, 1971; Oklahoma City (OK) Community College, 1983
OCCUPATION: Graphic artist and painter
MEDIA: Acrylic, oil, and watercolor
EXHIBITS: AIE, CNM, RE
AWARDS: AIE ('77; '88; '89, 1st)

WELSH, MICKY *Mohave*
EXHIBITS: CNM

WEMYTEWA, EDWARD *Zuni*
RESIDENCE: Zuni, NM
EXHIBITS: HM/G
AWARDS: HM/G ('72, 1st)

WEN TSIREH (see Montoya, Alfred)

WESCOUPÉ, CLEMENCE *Saulteaux/Ojibwa*
Born 1951, on the Long Plains Reserve near Portage La Prairie
PUBLISHED: *The Indian Trader* (Nov 1979); *American Indian Art* (spring 1990)
PUBLIC COLLECTIONS: HCC
EXHIBITS: HCC; ITIC; RC; galleries throughout Canada
SOLO EXHIBITS: Galleries throughout Canada
AWARDS: ITIC ('86)

CLEMENCE WESCOUPÉ

Wescoupé first began to paint while incarcerated in a Manitoba penal institution in the early 1970s. He studied the work of Jackson Beardy (q.v.) and learned a lot from his mastery of formline and color. Bob Checkwitch, owner of Great Grasslands Graphics in Winnipeg, encouraged him and produced prints of some of his early work. Wescoupé's use of flowing lines and startling color and space are distinctive.

John Anson Warner
The Indian Trader, *Nov 1979*

WESLEY, TILLIER *Creek*
Born 27 June 1955 in Oklahoma City, OK; son of Mable and Tillier Wesley; P/GP: Polly and John Wesley; M/GP: Ella and Milton Long
RESIDENCE: Weatherford, OK
EDUCATION: Classen High School, Oklahoma City, OK
OCCUPATION: Mechanic, construction worker; full-time painter since 1987
MEDIA: Acrylic and casein
PUBLISHED: *Southwest Profile* (Nov/Dec 1987)

COMMISSIONS: Six Flags Over Texas, paintings, 1990

EXHIBITS: ACAI, AIAFM, ACS/ENP, TAIAF, TWF, RE, WIAME; see also Awards

AWARDS: ACAI ('92); ACS/ENP (5-1st, '88, 1st; '89, 1st, Best Upcoming Contemporary Artist); NMSF (4-1st); TWF ('92; '93); RE ('91, 1st, Grand Award; '93, 1st); WIAME ('94); Helsinki, Finland, 1988

HONORS: AIAFM, featured artist and program cover artist, 1991

WEST, DICK *Cheyenne*

Wapah Nahyah, Lightfooted Runner

A.K.A. W. Richard West; Walter Richard West

Born 8 Sept 1912 near Darlington, OK, on the banks of the North Canadian River; son of Rena Flying Coyote (A.K.A. Emily Black Wolf) and Lightfoot West; father of W. Richard West Jr., Director of The National Museum of the American Indian, Washington, D.C.; M/GP: Big Belly Woman and Thunder Bull

RESIDENCE: Tijera, NM

MILITARY: U.S. Navy, WWII

EDUCATION: Haskell, 1935; one year vocational training, 1936; A.A., BC, 1938; B.F.A., U of OK, 1941; M.F.A., U of OK, 1950; graduate work, U of Redlands; NSU; U of OK; U of Tulsa; studied mural techniques under Olaf Nordmark, 1941-1942

OCCUPATION: Art teacher, lecturer, consultant, art department chairman, sculptor, painter

MEDIA: Oil, watercolor, tempera, gouache, wood, and metal

PUBLISHED: Llewellyn and Hoebel (1941), dust jacket; Jacobson and d'Ucel (1950); Carter (1955); LaFarge (1956; 1960); Pierson and Davidson (1960); Berthrong (1963); Jacobson (1964); Dunn (1968); Snodgrass (1968); Milton, ed. (1969); Brody (1971); Irvine, ed. (1974); Highwater (1976); Silberman (1978); Schmid and Houlihan (1979); Axford (1980); Mahey, et al. (1980); Broder (1981); New (1981); Fawcett and Callander (1982); Wade and Strickland (1982); Hoffman, et al. (1984); Samuels (1985); Ewers (1986); Wade, ed. (1986); Archuleta and Strickland (1991); Maurer (1992); Ballantine and Ballantine (1993). *The Denver Post, Empire Magazine* (Sept 1953; July 1963); *Readers Digest* (Nov 1955); *National Geographic* (Mar 1956); *Oklahoma Today* (summer 1958); *Life International* (16 Mar 1959); *Baptist Leader* (Nov 1961; *Today* (Mar 1963); *Together* (Mar 1963); *The Sunday Oklahoman, Orbit Magazine* (14 Apr 1963); *Saturday Review* (15 June 1963); *Southwestern Art* (Vol. 2, no. 1, 1967); *Kansas* (spring 1971); *Smoke Signals* (spring 1977); *Daughters of the American Revolution Magazine* (Feb 1980); *Oklahoma Art Gallery* (spring 1980); *Nebraskaland Magazine* (Vol. 62, no. 1, 1984); *Southwest Art* (Oct 1989); biographical publications

BOOKS ILLUSTRATED: Bass (1950); Penny (1953); Lyback (1963); Schlesier (1987)

COMMISSIONS: *Murals:* BC, U of OK; U.S. Post Office, Okemah, OK; Boy's Camp, New Hebron, NH; Phoenix Indian School; H. Dub Stewart home, Muskogee, OK. *Other:* AIE, designed official seal; Franklin Mint, Franklin Center, PA, medallion designs (series of 50 on the history of the American Indian), 1974-1975

PUBLIC COLLECTIONS: BC; BIA; DAM; GM; IACB; JAM; KM; MAI; MNA/KHC; NGA; OU/L; OU/MA; PAC; SPIM; SPL; St. Augustine's Center, Chicago, IL; Muskogee Art Guild, OK; Eastern Baptist College, St. David's, PA

EXHIBITS: AIE; AIEC; AIW; ASU/M; BC/McG; CIAI; CNAIA; CNM; CSPIP; DAM; GM; HSM/KS; IK; ITIC; JAM; JGS; JH; KCPA; MHDYMM; MNM; MFA/A; MFA/O; NACLA; NAP; NGA; OAC; OCSA; OIO; OMA; OU/MA/T; PAC; PAC/T; SAIEAIP; SFFA; SI; SV; USDI; USDS; VP; WIB; Kansas State

TILLIER WESLEY

A full-blood Creek artist, Wesley is completely self-taught. In 1976, because his wife was hired to teach at San Felipe Pueblo, the family moved to New Mexico. While looking for a job as a mechanic, he had some spare time and started drawing. He began to paint after receiving a gift of paints from a lady in his church. His first sales came when his wife took some of the paintings to work. He says, "People bought them and I was surprised." With this encouragement he continued to paint, and since the early 1980s the popularity of his work has grown. He is now a full-time painter.

Southwest Profile
Nov/Dec 1987

DICK WEST

"Dick West is an accomplished artist who is never content to stand still by working only in one medium and one style. He is known for his traditional Indian paintings, as well as for his portraits, abstractions, and other European-derived style paintings and sculpture. Upon receiving the Grand Award at Philbrook Art Center in 1955, West wrote: 'I do not profess to have established anything definite in my experimental dabblings, but I do feel that the Indian artist must be allowed freedom to absorb influences outside of his own art forms and see the promise of a new lane of expression that should keep the Indian's art the art form termed (continued)

Dick West

(continued) "native Indian painting," and I give my students every opportunity to execute it.. .. I believe that Indian artists with formal art background will be going more and more in the direction of the European interpretational influences.'"

Snodgrass 1968

West was Director of the Art Department at Bacone College, Bacone, OK, from 1947 to 1970 and a major influence on a generation of Indian artists.

Museum, Topeka, KS; Mulvane Art Center, Topeka, KS; Museum of History and Science, Kansas City, MO; The Kermac Mural Design Competition Exhibit, Oklahoma City and Tulsa, OK

SOLO EXHIBITS: BC; DAM; EOSC; Haskell; HSM/SK; NSU; PAC; SPIM; U of Redlands, CA; Muskogee (OK) Art Guild; Muskogee (OK) Civic Center, 1969; Oshkosh (WI) Museum; Telfair Academy of Arts and Sciences, Savanna, GA

AWARDS: Partial listing of 1st-place and Grand Awards includes: CNM, DAM, PAC; Oklahoma State Fairs

HONORS: *Honorary degrees:* Eastern Baptist College, St. David's, PA, Honorary Doctor of Humane Letters, 1963; Baker University, Baldwin City, KS, Honorary Doctorate of Fine Arts, 1977. *Other:* Haskell Institute, student body president; International Institute of Arts and Sciences, Zurich, Switzerland, Fellow, 1960; IACB, Certificate of Appreciation, 1960; PAC, Waite Phillips Outstanding Indian Artist Trophy, 1964; Muskogee Art Guild, President; Cheyennes of Oklahoma, Outstanding Cheyenne of the Year, 1968; Haskell Alumni Association, Outstanding Alumnus, 1973; Haskell Institute, Most Outstanding Professor, 1976-1977; IACB, commissioner, 1979; BC, Professor Emeritus of Art, 1980; RE, Honored One, 1989; BC, Hall of Fame, inducted, 1984; Jacobson Foundation, Norman, OK, recipient of the first Jacobson Award, 1992

WEYAHOK (see Rock, Howard)

WHEELER, GARY *Navajo*

RESIDENCE: Franklin, OH

PUBLIC COLLECTIONS: HCC

EXHIBITS: HCC, RC

AWARDS: RC ('77, 1st)

WHEELER, PAULINE DOWNING *Cherokee*

Born 11 Jan 1927 in Bartlesville, OK; daughter of Maude Mosley and Steve Downing; P/GP: Callie and Joseph Downing; M/GP: Mosley. Related to Chief Lewis Downing

RESIDENCE: Tulsa, OK

EDUCATION: College High School, Bartlesville, OK; Webster High School, Tulsa, OK

OCCUPATION: Artist

MEDIA: Oil, acrylic, watercolor, and pastel

EXHIBITS: CNM, FCTM, MCI, RC

AWARDS: FCTM ('85)

WHIRLWIND *Southern Cheyenne*

Hevovitastamiutsts, Moving Whirlwind

A.K.A. Chief Whirlwind

Birth date unknown; died 1891

OCCUPATION: Chief, warrior, and artist

PUBLISHED: Snodgrass (1968)

PUBLIC COLLECTIONS: MFA/M

HONORS: Whirlwind Indian Day School and Mission, Blaine County, OK, named for him

Whirlwind

"Old Whirlwind was a chief of the Southern Cheyenne living at Darlington, Indian Territory (now Oklahoma), in 1872. The artist's work in Montgomery [MFA/M] is a set of pencil and crayon sketches, collected by Lt. Samuel Goode Jones at Fort Reno, Indian Territory, 1890 (see Grinnell 1915; 1923)."

Snodgrass 1968

WHIRLWIND EAGLE (see Joe, Orland)

WHIRLWIND HAWK *Sioux*

PUBLISHED: Snodgrass (1968)

PUBLIC COLLECTIONS: MPM (pictograph on paper)

WHITAKER, WILMA *Cherokee/Potawatomi*

MEDIA: Watercolor
EXHIBITS: OIAC
AWARDS: OIAC ('93)

WHITE, ALBERT *Mohawk*

Born 24 Dec 1950 in Binghamton, NY; son of Mary and Albert White; P/GP: Helen Purvis and David White; M/GP: Lois Sorsen and Joe Nagy
RESIDENCE: Binghamton, NY
EDUCATION: Chenango Valley High School, 1968; SFAI, 1968-1970; B.A., MI, 1974; trained with Anne Schuler, 1975-1979
OCCUPATION: Textile designer, muralist, illustrator, and painter
MEDIA: Oil, acrylic, watercolor, gouache, pencil, pastel, and prints
PUBLISHED: Johannsen and Ferguson, ed (1983). *The Indian Trader* (July 1978)
COMMISSIONS: *Where Has the Eagle Gone,* movie illustrations
PUBLIC COLLECTIONS: SMII; Waterman Center, Apalachin, NY
EXHIBITS: OAG, RCAS; Indian markets, festivals, and powwows
HONORS: MI, Merit Scholarship, 1972-1973; MI, graduated with high honors, 1974

WHITE, ANDREW *Mohawk*

Tekaronhaneka
Born 21 Apr 1947
RESIDENCE: Hogansburg, NY
OCCUPATION: Ironworker/high-rise construction, and painter
MEDIA: Oil, pencil, and charcoal
BOOKS ILLUSTRATED: St. Regis Community Center, Québec, language book
COMMISSIONS: *Murals:* Chenail School
PUBLIC COLLECTIONS: ALCC
EXHIBITS: ACS/EM; Buffalo (NY) North American Indian Culture Center

WHITE, CLARENCE A. *Omaha*

Tanuga Shinga, Little Bull
EDUCATION: BC
PUBLISHED: Snodgrass (1968)
EXHIBITS: PAC

WHITE, GARY (see White Deer, Gary)

WHITE, JOHN A. *Cherokee*

Born 9 Jan 1953 in Anadarko, OK; son of Evelyn Kendall and Robert Harold White; P/GP: Stella Ferguson and Harry B. White; M/GP: Clemie O. Strong and Martin L. Kendall
RESIDENCE: Ardmore, OK
MILITARY: Oklahoma/Arkansas National Guard
EDUCATION: Anadarko (OK) High School, 1971
OCCUPATION: Design draftsman and artist
MEDIA: Watercolor and prints
EXHIBITS: AIAF; CIM; PF; RE; Celebration of American Indian Art, Dallas, TX; Arlington (TX) Indian Market
HONORS: First Celebration of American Indian Art, Dallas, TX, featured artist

WHITE, LARRY *Mohawk*

Kanatakeniate
Born 1 July 1945

ANDREW WHITE

White is known for his paintings of Iroquois history, culture, and ceremonies. He also paints portraits, especially of people working in high-rise construction.

Johannsen and Ferguson, eds. 1983

JOHN A. WHITE

White gives credit to God for his talent. According to him, "All of us have talents of one kind or another. True, we are not all artists or sculptors but we all have talents. Your talent may be accounting, business, medicine, construction, or even digging a ditch. Whatever it is, God gave it to you, but he left it to you to develop and to use." His paintings of the Southwest are done in soft colors and give a feeling of quiet strength and spiritual peace.

gallery brochure

LARRY WHITE

Best known for his portraits, White also paints Native American scenes and events.

Johannsen and Ferguson, eds. 1983

SMALL CAPS LABELS:

RESIDENCE: Hogansburg, NY
MILITARY: U.S. Army
EDUCATION: Community colleges in Texas and Nevada
OCCUPATION: U.S. Army and painter
MEDIA: Oil, acrylic, and charcoal
PUBLISHED: Johannsen and Ferguson, eds. (1983)
PUBLIC COLLECTIONS: ALCC; St. Lawrence University, Canton, NY
EXHIBITS: ACS/EM

WHITE, MICHAEL *(?)*

Born 1946 in Algonac, MI
EDUCATION: Center for Creative Studies, Detroit, MI; St. Clair County Community College, Port Huron, MI
PUBLIC COLLECTIONS: Lambton College, Sarnia, ON; Sarnia (ON) Public Gallery
EXHIBITS: C/WICEC; St. Clair Community College, Huron, MI; Foundation of Native Art, Ottawa, ON; St. Clair Summer Fair; Sarnia (ON) Public Art Gallery; Thames Art Centre, Chatham, ON

WHITE, NANCY P. *Chippewa*

Born 29 Dec 1943
RESIDENCE: Spokane, WA
EDUCATION: Woodrow Wilson High School, Portsmouth, VA; B.S.Ed., U of MO; M.L.S., Rutgers University
EXHIBITS: ACS/SM, CMRM, GFNAAS, RC

WHITE, RILEY *Cherokee*

Born 1912 in DeQueen, AR
RESIDENCE: Tahlequah, OK
MILITARY: U.S. Army and U.S. Air Force, WWII
EDUCATION: Chouinard Art Institute, Los Angeles, CA, ca. 1945; B.F.A., OSU, 1950; M.F.A., OSU, 1954; graduate work, U of NM
OCCUPATION: Art instructor and painter
PUBLISHED: Snodgrass (1968)
EXHIBITS: PAC; Western Hills Lodge, Sequoya State Park, OK
SOLO EXHIBITS: Conners State College, Warner, OK; Tahlequah, OK; Stillwater, OK

WHITE, RUTH M. *Sauk-Fox*

Birth date unknown; death date unknown; daughter of Virginia Holmes and Walter Emmitt McKitrick
RESIDENCE: Lived at Alva, OK, and Muskogee, OK
EDUCATION: Gorman (TX) High School, 1927; Hardin-Simmons College, Abilene, TX; CAI; Morris Harvey College, Charleston, WV; School of Arts and Sciences Trenton, NJ; Philadelphia (PA) Fine Arts Academy; Del Mar College, Corpus Christi, TX; Connors; U of OK; USU; NSU; BC; private instruction under Henry Clayton Staples, Elliot O'Hara, and Frederick Taubes
OCCUPATION: College art instructor, lecturer, writer, sculptor, and painter
MEDIA: Oil, watercolor, and stone
PUBLISHED: Snodgrass (1968). Biographical publications
PUBLIC COLLECTIONS: Connors State College, Warner, OK; Fort Gibson (OK) Museum
EXHIBITS: AEOP/T; Connors; GM; MNM; NAWA/T; PAC; RM; SMNAI; SPIM; WM/T; Continental Museum, Corpus Christi, TX; Galveston (TX) Watercolor

RUTH M. WHITE

"The artist demonstrated her original spoon-painting technique throughout the Southwest and South. She completed a series of Oklahoma Indian portraits in oil and lent them to various educational institutions in the area. She believed artists are made, not born, and 'heartily endorsed the study of art as a hobby and for therapeutic value.'"

Snodgrass 1968

Exhibits; National Academy of Design, NY; National Association of Women Artists Exhibition, National Academy of Art, NY; Texas Watercolor Society Exhibit, San Antonio, TX; see also Awards

SOLO EXHIBITS: Partial listing of more than 16 includes: Connors; Amarillo (TX) Senior High School; Galveston (TX) Art League; Professional Artists' League, NY; National Arts Club, NY; Rosenburg Library; galleries in Louisiana and New York, NY

AWARDS: Partial listing of more than two hundred includes: OAC; SN; Allied Artists of West Virginia Exhibition; Muskogee (OK) Annual Art Show (Grand Award); Muskogee and Tulsa State Fairs, OK; Witte Memorial Museum, San Antonio, TX

WHITE BEAR *Arapaho*

Huhnohuhcoah, White Bear (more correctly Albino Bear)

Born 1852; died 1892; son of Ole Son and Chief Old Crow

RESIDENCE: Lived in Indian Territory

MILITARY: U.S. Army, scout at Fort Reno, IT

EDUCATION: Hampton, 1878; Carlisle, 1879

OCCUPATION: Warrior, scout, farmer, stockman, and painter

PUBLISHED: Dunn (1968); Snodgrass (1968). *American Indian Art* (winter 1992)

PUBLIC COLLECTIONS: HI

EXHIBITS: BPG

WHITE BEAR *(Huhnohuhcoah)*

"The artist was among the 72 Plains Indians taken as prisoners from Fort Sill, OK, to Fort Marion, St. Augustine, FL, in 1875."

Snodgrass 1968

After attending Hampton and Carlisle Indian Schools, White Bear returned to Indian Territory in 1880.

WHITE BEAR *Cheyenne*

PUBLISHED: Maurer (1992)

PUBLIC COLLECTIONS: HS/MT

EXHIBITS: VP

WHITE BEAR *Crow (?)*

PUBLISHED: Snodgrass (1968)

PUBLIC COLLECTIONS: GM (crayon drawings on paper, ca. 1921)

WHITE BEAR *Hopi*

Kutca Honauu (or *Kucha Honau),* White Bear

Born 1869; death date unknown

PUBLISHED: Snodgrass (1968); Samuels (1985). *21st Annual Report,* BAE (1899-1900)

PUBLIC COLLECTIONS: MAI, SMNAI (by "a Hopi named White Bear")

WHITE BEAR *(Kutca Honawuh)*

"White Bear was among the first Indian artists of the Southwest. Between 1899 and 1900, the artist, and several other Hopis, were persuaded by Dr. J. Walter Fewkes to make drawings representing the Hopi gods and to explain the symbolism of the dance rituals. The project resulted in the publication, in 1903, of about 180 katsina *drawings on some 50 color plates. The artist was assisted by his uncle, Homovi."*

Snodgrass 1968

WHITE BEAR *Hopi*

Kucha Honawuh (or *Kucha Honau),* White Bear

A.K.A. Oswald Fredericks

Born 5 Feb 1906 in Old Oraibi, AZ; son of Anna Tuvengyamsi and Charles Fredericks Tuwahoyiwma

EDUCATION: Phoenix (AZ) High School; BC; Haskell, 1933-1937

OCCUPATION: Arts and crafts instructor, art teacher, *katsina* carver, lecturer, writer, dance teacher, and painter

PUBLISHED: Waters (1963); Dunn (1968); Snodgrass (1968); Brody (1971); Tanner (1973); Samuels (1985). *Arizona Highways* (July 1959); *The Arizona Republic, Sunday Magazine* (7 June 1964); *Phoenix Magazine* (1975)

COMMISSIONS: *Murals:* YMCA, New Jersey

PUBLIC COLLECTIONS: MAI [original 72 paintings and drawings published in Waters (1963)]; SMNAI (by "a Hopi named White Bear")

EXHIBITS: ASM; FCTM; Tulsa, OK

ALTON WHITE BEAR

White Bear's great grandfather, Son Of The Star, and his grandfather, Red Bear, were scouts under General George A. Custer in the Seventh Cavalry during the Battle Of the Little Big Horn.

p.c. 1992

"The artist has been interested in art most of his life. He first began to paint ca. 1958. During the winter months he feeds cattle and draws pictures."

Snodgrass 1968

WHITE BIRD

"Capt. Richard L. Livermore's quarters at Fort Keogh in 1890 was a log cabin. To make his cabin more presentable, he covered the inside walls with unbleached muslin. During his stay at the Fort, his Indian friends came to visit and painted pictures on it, many of which were by White Bird. Livermore took the paintings with him when he left the Fort, '. . . some are in the possession of his wife in Denver (see Grinnell 1915).'"

Snodgrass 1968

WHITE BEAR, ALTON *Arikara/Mandan*

SaaKa, Son Of The Star

A.K.A. Signature: A. W. Bear – Son Of The Star

Born 27 Mar 1933 in Elbowoods, ND, on the Fort Berthold Reservation; son of Eleanor and Joseph White Bear; P/GF: White Bear; M/GF: Red Bear (a.k.a. Raymond Red Bear when he joined the Seventh Cavalry); GGF: Son of The Star

RESIDENCE: New Town, ND

EDUCATION: Through 11th grade, 1950

OCCUPATION: Truck driver, mechanic, oil pipeline worker, horse trainer, house and sign painter, and artist

MEDIA: Oil, acrylic, watercolor, pencil, and pen and ink

PUBLISHED: Snodgrass (1968)

PUBLIC COLLECTIONS: TTM

EXHIBITS: BBHC, BNIAS, FBCC, LGAM, SI, TTM, UTIC

AWARDS: FBCC ('92, 1st); UTIC ('84)

WHITE BIRD *Cheyenne/Nez Percé*

Born ca. mid-1800s; death date unknown

OCCUPATION: Warrior, scout, and painter

MEDIA: Watercolor, crayon, pencil, and pen and ink

PUBLISHED: Frost (1964); Dunn (1968); Russell (1968); Snodgrass (1968); Broder (1981). *American Indian Art* (autumn 1982)

PUBLIC COLLECTIONS: DAM

EXHIBITS: DAM

HONORS: Second chief of the Nez Percé

WHITE BUFFALO (see Hill, Bobby)

WHITE BUFFALO, HERBERT *Cheyenne*

Born 1917; GF: Kish Hawkins

RESIDENCE: Lived in Concho, OK

PUBLISHED: Snodgrass (1968)

EXHIBITS: AIAE/WSU, AIEC, OU/MA/T

AWARDS: AIAE/WSU

WHITE BUFFALO MAN, FRANK *Hunkpapa Sioux*

Born 1903 in LaPlante, SD, on the Cheyenne River Reservation; grandson of Sitting Bull, Sioux chief and shaman

RESIDENCE: Seattle, WA

EDUCATION: Salem Indian School, Chemewa, OR; BHSU

OCCUPATION: Dancer, performer, actor, art demonstrator, and painter

MEDIA: Oil

PUBLISHED: Libhart (1970)

PUBLIC COLLECTIONS: IACB

EXHIBITS: CPS

WHITE BULL *Teton Sioux*

Pen san hunka

A.K.A. Chief White Bull; Chief Joseph White Bull

Born 1849 in the Black Hills; died July 1947; son of Good Feather Woman and Makes Room, a Miniconjou chief; M/Uncle: Sitting Bull (q.v.)

RESIDENCE: Lived near Cherry Creek on the Cheyenne River Reservation, SD

MEDIA: Pencil, colored pencil, crayon, and pen and ink

PUBLISHED: Vestal (1934b); Russell (1968); Snodgrass (1968); Howard (1968). *Bulletin 173,* BAE (1960); *American Indian Art* (spring 1995)

PUBLIC COLLECTIONS: SI/OAA, U of OK, U of ND

EXHIBITS: U of OK

WHITE BUTTERFLY (see No Two Horns, Joseph)

WHITE CALICO, GLORIA *Blackfeet/Athabascan*

Born 1960 in Browning, MT

EDUCATION: B.F.A., U of WA, 1990; studied under Marvin Oliver, Michael Spafford, Bill Hixson, and Spencer Mosley

MEDIA: Oil, acrylic, watercolor, pen and ink, pencil, and prints

PUBLISHED: *The Raven's Chronicles* (spring 1992), cover

EXHIBITS: AICA/SF; MSULMAE; group exhibits in the Seattle, WA, area

SOLO/SPECIAL EXHIBITS: MPI (dual show)

AWARDS: MSULMAE ('90, 1st)

WHITECLOUD, JOSEPH *Santa Clara*

EXHIBITS: AICA

AWARDS: AICA ('78, Gold and Bronze Medals)

WHITE CORAL BEADS (see Peña, Tonita)

WHITE COW KILLER *Teton Sioux*

PUBLISHED: Snodgrass (1968). *4th Annual Report,* BAE (1882-1883)

WHITE CROW (see Horn, Miles S.)

WHITE DEER, GARY *Choctaw*

Nukoa, Mad (nickname)

A.K.A. Gary White; Gary Whitedeer

Born 17 Dec 1950 in Tulsa, OK; son of Mary Lee and Gilbert White; P/GP: Minnie and Sampson White; M/GP: Orathy and Robert Northcott; related to Issi Tohhi, White Deer

RESIDENCE: Ada, OK

EDUCATION: Carter Seminary, Ardmore, OK; IAIA, 1968-1969; A.A., Haskell, 1973

OCCUPATION: Dance leader, festival organizer, artist-in-residence, lecturer, and painter

MEDIA: Oil, acrylic, watercolor, and prints

PUBLISHED: *Tulsa Indian News* (Nov 1979); *Broken Arrow Scout* (15 Jan 1992); *Indian Territories* (Vol. 3, no. 1, 1993); *Association News,* SPIM (Oct 1993)

COMMISSIONS: *Murals:* Tunica-Biloxi Regional Museum, Marksville, LA, series of murals and a painting. *Other:* Choctaw Nation, logo for Commemorative Trail of Tears Walk, logo

PUBLIC COLLECTIONS: GM; OSU; Choctaw Nation of Oklahoma; American Embassy, Paris, France

EXHIBITS: AICA; AIE; CNM; ECSC/OK; FCTM; GM; OAC; OSC; PAC; TCIM; TIAF; Columbus (GA) Museum; Natchitoches (LA) Folk Festival; Vereinhaus Glokenhof, Zurich, Switzerland; Kingston, Jamaica; The America House, Stuttgart, Germany; see also Awards

SOLO EXHIBITS: SPIM; Vanderbilt University, Nashville, TN

AWARDS: AICA ('78, 1st, Silver, Patrons Award); AIE (4-1st, '88, Best of Show; Best of Division); FCTM ('74, Tiger Award; '75; '79, IH, Grand Award; '81; '89, IH; '90, IH); PAC ('75); TCIM ('91, 1st; '92); TIAF ('92); Choctaw Nation Days Festival (1st)

WHITE BULL

White Bull made a copy of Sitting Bull's pictographic autobiography (No. I). The original, done by Sitting Bull (q.v.), has been lost but, White Bull's copy is in the Smithsonian Institution's Anthropology Archives in Washington, D.C.

C. M. Simon, p.c. 1994

In 1932 Walter Stanley Campbell paid White Bull seventy dollars to draw his life story. He produced more than forty drawings which Campbell used along with field notes to write a biography of White Bull (Vestal, 1934).

American Indian Art *spring 1995*

WHITE COW KILLER

"The artist kept a winter count which represented about the same years as the counts kept by American Horse and Baptiste Good (qq.v.). He was known to have been at Pine Ridge Agency, ca. 1880."

Snodgrass 1968

GARY WHITE DEER

"My earliest and strongest influence in art came from my father, who painted in the flat, lyrical two-dimensional style of classic, traditional Indian painting. His friendship with Apache artist Allan Houser (q.v.) encouraged his painting. Traditional, two-dimensional Indian art was the first kind of painting that I ever remember seeing; watching my father paint gave me an old-time sense of color and design."

artist, p.c. 1992

HONORS: Choctaw Nation, recognition plaque, 1992; Oklahoma State Capitol Building, Oklahoma City, East Gallery, *Year of the Indian Exhibition*, one of eight Indian artists exhibited, 1992; Palm Springs (CA) International Film Festival, featured artist; Cheyenne (WY) Frontier Days, featured artist; listed five times by art critic Ralph J. Olivas as one of the Top Five Indian Artists for Investment Purposes; Kullihoma Reservation, OK, Ceremonial Town Leader; Yellow Hill Hethla Society leader

WHITE DOVE (see Wing, Henry Behan)

WHITE EAGLE *Oglala (?) Sioux*

Wabliska

Birth date unknown; from Pine Ridge Agency, SD (see Black Heart)

PUBLISHED: Snodgrass (1968)

PUBLIC COLLECTIONS: MAI (a white eagle)

WHITE EAGLE

"Chief White Bull reported that a White Eagle was killed in the Battle of the Little Big Horn, June 25, 1876."

Snodgrass 1968

WHITE EAGLE, CHARLES W. *Winnebago*

RESIDENCE: Hyattsville, MD

PUBLISHED: Snodgrass (1968)

EXHIBITS: AAIEAE, USDS

WHITE EAGLE, ROSCOE *Oglala Sioux*

Born 1912 in Fort Kipp, MT; died 6 Feb 1991; GF: White Eagle, veteran of the Battle of the Little Big Horn

RESIDENCE: Lived in Poplar, MT

EDUCATION: Fort Kipp (MT) Public Schools

OCCUPATION: BIA employee and painter

MEDIA: Oil

PUBLISHED: *The Rapid City Journal* (3 Dec 1989)

EXHIBITS: CIA, NAVAM, SIM

ROSCOE WHITE EAGLE

White Eagle was a self-taught artist with a deep concern for the preservation of Plains Indian culture, traditions, and religious beliefs. His paintings were based on the old Sioux way of life.

Ray, ed. 1972

WHITE HAIRED CHIEF WITH SCARRED FACE (see Washakie)

WHITEHEAD, ERNEST *Mescalero Apache*

EDUCATION: IAIA, ca. 1964

PUBLISHED: Dunn (1968); Snodgrass (1968); Tanner (1973)

PUBLIC COLLECTIONS: IAIA

EXHIBITS: ASM, IAIA, FAIEAIP

WHITE HORSE *Kiowa*

Tsen T'ainte, White Horse

Born 1847; died 1892; brother of Chief Big Bow

OCCUPATION: Warrior and artist

MEDIA: Pencil and crayon

PUBLISHED: Snodgrass (1968); Ray (1972); Batkin (1983)

PUBLIC COLLECTIONS: JAM; YU/BRBML (Previously credited to "White Goose," the work is now thought to be by White Horse.)

EXHIBITS: BPG, JAM, MPI

WHITE HORSE

"The Anko calendar records that White Horse killed a Navajo, ca. 1867-1868. He refused to settle on a reservation, 1873; participated in the Battle of Adobe Walls, 1874; and, with other Plains Indians, was sent to prison at Fort Marion, St. Augustine, FL, in 1875 (see Cohoe, William)."

Snodgrass 1968

WHITEHORSE, EMMI *Navajo*

RESIDENCE: Albuquerque, NM

Born 18 Dec 1956 in Crownpoint, NM, on the Navajo Indian Reservation

EDUCATION: Crownpoint (NM) High School, 1971-1973; Page (AZ) High School, 1975; B.A., U of NM, 1980; M.A., U of NM, 1982

OCCUPATION: Teacher, writer, poet, silversmith, sculptor, photographer, graphic artist, and painter

MEDIA: Conté, oil pastel, dye, sand, silver, stone, film, mixed-media, and prints

PUBLISHED: Amerson, ed. (1981); Hoffman, et al. (1984); Younger, et al. (1985); Wade, ed. (1986); Jacka and Jacka (1988; 1994); Stewart (1988); Campbell, ed. (1993); Abbott (1994). *New York Arts Journal* (Jan 1980); *Turtle* (spring-summer 1980); *Artspace* (fall 1980; 1982); *Native Vision* (Nov/Dec 1985; Sept/Oct 1986); *The Santa Fean* (Aug 1989); *America West* (July 1990); *Art-Talk* (Feb 1991); *The Indian Trader* (Dec 1992); *Montezuma Valley Journal* (19 July 1994)

BOOKS ILLUSTRATED: Hobson (1979)

COMMISSIONS: U of NM, Native American Studies Department, brochure illustrations, 1979; Gateway Park Hotel, Phoenix, AZ, painting

PUBLIC COLLECTIONS: BIA/DC; C/NMC; HM; PAC; SFNB/WA; SPIM; U of NM; WWM; IBM Corporation, Phoenix, AZ; Ivan Chermayeff Associates, New York, NY; Lafayette (LA) Women's Hospital; Phelps Dodge Corporation, Phoenix, AZ; Prudential Insurance, Newark, NJ

EXHIBITS: AICA/SF; AICH; CNAA; CTC; DAM; EMC; FSMCIAF; FWMA; HM; IK; IPCC; MSU; OSU/G; PAM; SCG; SDMM; SFFA; SI; SM; SPIM; SWAIA; U of ND; U of NM; U of SD; WIB; WSCS; WWM; Akmak Gallery, West Berlin, Germany, 1984; Galleria del Cavallino, Venice, Italy, 1980; Green County Council on the Arts, Catskill, NY; Philadelphia (PA) Art Alliance Gallery; Silvermine Guild, New Canaan, CT; Sioux Land Heritage Museum, Sioux Falls, SD; Sun Valley (ID) Center for the Arts, 1982; The Bruce Museum, Greenwich, CT, 1985; galleries in CO, CT, NM, NV, NY, TX, and Europe

SOLO EXHIBITS: WWM

HONORS: *Scholarships:* Navajo Tribe, U of NM; Parent Teacher's Association, scholarship to Page (AZ) High School; Bell Scholarship

EMMI WHITEHORSE

One of the original members of the Grey Canyon Artists (q.v.), Whitehorse first exhibited her work with them in 1978 at the Pueblo Cultural Center in Albuquerque, NM. She explains that her art is influenced by her grandmother, a weaver, and by her native surroundings. She says, "I want to make use of the abstractions I remember and use them aesthetically to help me create my work. This way, I'm closer to building that bridge between not only the new and the old — but also between the two cultures in which I live."

gallery news release, 1985

WHITEHORSE, ROLAND N. *Kiowa*

Hanemi Da, Charging Man

Born 6 Apr 1921 in Carnegie, OK; son of Laura and Charlie White Horse; P/GF: Hanemi Da; M/GF: Rainy Mountain Charlie, son of Sky Walker, keeper of the Grandmother Medicine Bundle

RESIDENCE: Elgin, OK

MILITARY: U.S. Army, WWII

EDUCATION: Washita (OK) High School, 1942; BC, 1947-1948: Dallas (TX) Art Institute 1951-1952

OCCUPATION: Illustrator, graphic supervisor, museum exhibits specialist, sculptor, and painter

PUBLISHED: Dunn (1968); Snodgrass (1968); Irvine, ed. (1974); Boyd, et al. (1981; 1983). *Compton's Pictured Encyclopedia* (1951); *The Anadarko Daily News, Visitor's Guide* (1992-1993)

BOOKS ILLUSTRATED: Marriott (1952), Madrano (1955)

COMMISSIONS: NHFFAI, bust of Tohausan (q.v.)

PUBLIC COLLECTIONS: FSM, GM, PAC, WOM

EXHIBITS: AIE; BC/McG; CSPIP; KCPA; PAC; PAC/T; SPIM; Skirvin Tower, Oklahoma City, OK; joint exhibit with Mopope and Blue Eagle (qq.v.); see also Awards

AWARDS: AIE ('69, 1st; '70, 1st); PAC; Oklahoma Indian Trade Fair, Oklahoma City, OK ('70, 1st)

HONORS: AIE, arts and crafts director, 1960-1964; American Indian Artists Association, chairman, 1965

WHITE MAN (see Ahsit)

WHITEMAN (see Ahsit)

ALFRED WHITEMAN JR.

"Two small White boys, lost on the prairie, were adopted by different Arapaho families. One died shortly thereafter, and the surviving boy, who was given the name White Man (Neotha), grew to manhood and married the chief's daughter, Anna Little Raven. White Man was the artist's paternal grandfather."

Snodgrass 1968

WHITEMAN, ALFRED, JR. *Cheyenne/Arapaho*

Sitting Bear

A.K.A. A. Whiteman

Born 28 Aug 1928 in Colony, OK; son of Nellie R. Rouse and Alfred Whiteman Sr.; P/GGF: Chief Little Raven, signer of the Medicine Lodge Treaty, 1867, and recipient of the Congressional Medal of Honor

RESIDENCE: Stillwater, OK

EDUCATION: El Reno (OK) High School, 1948; Naval preparatory schools in Corpus Christi, TX, and Memphis, TN; Naval Air Technical Training Center, Memphis, TN; OSU/O, 1962

OCCUPATION: Jet engine mechanic, designer, outreach worker, Indian studies consultant, and painter

MEDIA: Tempera

PUBLISHED: Snodgrass (1968); Brody (1971); Irvine, ed. (1974). *The Sunday Oklahoman, Orbit Magazine* (2 Aug 1964); *Oklahoma State Alumni Magazine* (Nov 1964); *The Phoenix Gazette* (14 Sept 1974)

PUBLIC COLLECTIONS: USDI; OSU, Student Union, Stillwater, OK

EXHIBITS: BNIAS; CSPIP; FAIEAIP; HM; HM/G; MNM; PAC; OSU; SPIM; U of AR; YWCA, Oklahoma City, OK; St. Andrew's Episcopal Church, Stillwater, OK

SOLO EXHIBITS: OSU; SPIM; First National Bank; National Conference of American Farm Economics Association (OSU), Stillwater, OK

AWARDS: FNAIC; HM/G ('74); MNM; PAC ('74, Grand Award)

WHITEMAN, JAMES RIDGLEY *(?)*

Osapana

Born 15 Jan 1910 in Portales, NM; son of Katherine Great House and Levi Whiteman

RESIDENCE: Buena Park, CA

EDUCATION: U of NM, 1930; studied sculpture under Brice Sewell, portraiture under Neils Hogner, Indian art under Kenneth Chapman, and archaeology under Edgar L. Hewett

OCCUPATION: Commercial artist, lecturer, sculptor, and painter

PUBLISHED: Snodgrass (1968)

EXHIBITS: FAIEAIP, FCTM, ITIC, LAIC, MNM, PAC, USDI

SOLO EXHIBITS: MNM

AWARDS: ITIC, LAIC

HONORS: Creek Nation of Oklahoma, honorary member; Western Kee Too Wah, council member; Spanish Colonial Art of New Mexico, Federal Art Project, hand printing and color plates, ca. 1939

WHITESHIELD, ROBERTA ANN *Cheyenne/Arapaho*

RESIDENCE: San Antonio, TX

PUBLIC COLLECTIONS: PAC

EXHIBITS: AIAFM, HM/G, PAC

AWARDS: HM/G ('71, 1st); PAC ('70, 1st)

WHITESINGER, DON *Navajo*

Born 15 Nov 1952

RESIDENCE: White River, AZ

EDUCATION: High School, Needles, CA; IAIA, 1970-1971; NCC, 1975-1976

OCCUPATION: Art consultant, audio-visual technician, bilingual-bicultural programs, photographer, sculptor, and painter

MEDIA: Oil, acrylic, watercolor, film, stone, and prints
BOOKS ILLUSTRATED: Navajo Tribe, Department of Education
EXHIBITS: ASU; HM; HM/G; IAIA; NCC; RC; WMNAAF; Northeastern Fine Arts Show, Pinetop, AZ
AWARDS: HM/G ('74); NCC ('76); WMNAAF

WHITE SWAN *Crow*

Mee'-nah-tsee
A.K.A. Strikes Enemy
Born ca. 1852; died 11 Aug 1904; brother of Curley (q.v.)
MILITARY: U.S. Army, Seventh Infantry, scout
OCCUPATION: Warrior, scout, and painter
MEDIA: Oil, watercolor, commercial paints, ink, pencil, crayon, muslin, hide, and butcher paper
PUBLISHED: Seton (Vol. 6, 1897); Burbank (1944); Bradley (1991); Maurer (1992). *American Indian Art* (autumn 1982)
PUBLIC COLLECTIONS: CAM/OH; HM; GM; HS/MT; MAI; MPI; OU/L; SI; SM; SMA/IN; Nez Percé National Historical Park, Spalding, ID; Paul Dyke Foundation, Rimrock, AZ; Seton Memorial Museum and Library, Philmont Scout Ranch, Cimarron, NM
EXHIBITS: VP
SOLO EXHIBITS: SMA/IN

WHITE SWAN

White Swan was a scout with Major Marcus Reno's command at the Battle of the Little Big Horn on June 25, 1876. Seriously injured, he and five Crow scouts survived although few others did. Grace G. Seton, wife of Ernest T. Seton, a naturalist who had White Swan do some drawings for him in 1897, described White Swan as having a bullet-shattered right arm and two other semi-paralyzed limbs as a result of the Custer battle. He also suffered from increasing deafness.

Bradley 1991

WHITETHORNE, BAJE, SR. *Navajo*

Baje, Giggling Boy
Born 9 Aug 1950 near Shonto, AZ, on the Navajo Reservation; son of Alice Black and Leonard "Lynn" Whitethorne; brother of Edward Whitethorne and Elizabeth Whitethorne-Benally (qq.v.)
RESIDENCE: Flagstaff, AZ
EDUCATION: Tuba City (AZ) High School; U of N AZ, 1969-1971; Grand Canyon College, Phoenix, AZ, 1971-1972; Boilermaker National Apprenticeship Program, Scranton, PA, 1978
OCCUPATION: Boilermaker, teacher; professional artist since 1981
MEDIA: Oil, acrylic, watercolor, pen and ink, pastel, and prints
PUBLISHED: Jacka and Jacka (1988, 1994). *Plateau* (Vol. 54, no. 1, 1982; Vol. 60, no. 1); *Metro Phoenix* (Apr 1988); *The Santa Fe New Mexican* (8 Aug 1988); *Southwest Art* (Nov 1990); *Fine Art Posters International* (1985)
BOOKS ILLUSTRATED: Browne (1991); Whitethorne (1994)
COMMISSIONS: Santa Fe (NM) Sports Wear, T-shirt designs; Wintercount, Glenwood Springs, CO, greeting card designs
PUBLIC COLLECTIONS: HM, MNA, NTM, VNB
EXHIBITS: ACAI; AICA; ACS/ENP; ACS/PG; AIWR; ASV; CCHM/NV; CNM; FNAA; HM; HM/G; ITIC; MCC/CA; MNA; SFSUFC; SMIC; SWAIA; WWM; Eastern New Mexico University, Portales, NM; see also Awards
SOLO EXHIBITS: MNA
AWARDS: ACAI ('93, Best in Oil Painting); ACS/ENP ('81); AIWR ('89, 1st; '92, 1st, Best of Show); HM/G ('79, 1st; '81, 1st, '87, 1st, Best of Division; '91); ITIC ('88); MNA ('70, 1st; '83, 1st; '87, '89); RE ('91); SMIC ('85, 1st; '87, 1st, Best Craftsman); SNAICF ('87); SWAIA ('83; '84, 1st; '85, 1st; '86; '89; '90; '91, 1st; '92); WNF ('74, 1st); Lake Powell Art Association, Page, AZ ('74, 1st); Sedona (AZ) Art Show ('80); Coconino County Fair, Flagstaff, AZ ('83, 1st); Fiesta de la Tlaquepaque, Sedona, AZ ('89; '90, 1st)

BAJE WHITETHORNE SR.

Whitethorne's paintings are full of motion and color, whether they are landscapes of the Navajo Reservation or of the Navajo people. With his watercolors he catches a fleeting moment of time as the sunset lights up the canyon walls or as a dancer moves with the joy of life. His paintings often are of everyday reservation life with a bit of humor; a luminous landscape will include a hogan with its ubiquitous metal folding chair and water barrel.

HONORS: Museum of Northern Arizona and the Flinn Foundation, A Separate Vision project, one of four Native American artists, 1984; FNAA, poster artist; NCHF, Western Heritage Wrangler Award for Outstanding Juvenile book, 1991

WHITETHORNE, EDWARD *Navajo*

Birth date unknown; son of Alice Black and Leonard "Lynn" Whitethorne; brother of Baje Whitethorne Sr. and Elizabeth Whitethorne-Benally (qq.v.)

RESIDENCE: Tonalea, AZ

EXHIBITS: Eastern New Mexico University, Portales, NM

WHITETHORNE, TROY L. *Navajo*

RESIDENCE: Tuba City, AZ

MEDIA: Pen and ink

EXHIBITS: HM/G

WHITETHORNE-BENALLY, ELIZABETH *Navajo*

Tall Woman From Peach Springs

Born 10 Nov 1959 in Monument Valley, UT; daughter of Alice Black, weaver, and Leonard "Lynn" Whitethorne; Sister of Baje and Edward Whitethorne (qq.v.); M/GM: Lula Yazzie Bitsui, weaver

RESIDENCE: Pinehill, NM

EDUCATION: Tuba City (AZ) High School; Apollo College (dental assistant), Glendale, AZ; Parks College (welding), Albuquerque, NM

OCCUPATION: Dental assistant, welder; full-time painter since 1989

MEDIA: Acrylic, watercolor, gouache, pencil, pen and ink, bone, and prints

PUBLISHED: Jacka and Jacka (1994)

PUBLIC COLLECTIONS: VNB

EXHIBITS: ACS/PG; ACS/ENP; AHM/CO; AIAF; ASU/M; CIM; FNAA; HM/G; IPCC; ITIC; LIAS; MNA; NMSF; NTF; SWAIA; Eastern New Mexico University, Portales, NM, 1989; L'École des Beaux Art de Grenoble, France, 1992; see also Awards

AWARDS: HM/G ('78, Award of Excellence); IPCC ('91); ITIC ('78; '90); LIAS ('89, MA); MNA ('76, '77, '78, '89); NMSF ('88, 1st); SWAIA ('90); College of Ganado ('78, Woodard Memorial Award); Valley National Bank Purchase Award, 1978

HONORS: National Scholastic Art Award, 1976-1978; Tuba City (AZ) High School, Art Student of the Year, 1978; Pinehill (NM) Schools, artist-in-residence, 1992

ELIZABETH WHITETHORNE-BENALLY

Whitethorne-Benally, who was raised on the Navajo Reservation near Shonto, comes from a large, talented family. Her grandmother and mother are weavers and five of her brothers and two of her sisters are also artists. In addition, two of her nephews are just starting careers as painters. Whitethorne-Benally paints Native Americans of all traditions and cultures. In many of her paintings she uses a "shattering technique" in which her figures are overlaid with ink lines. She explains that this shows the subject's individuality as well as her own individuality as an artist.

p.c. 1992

WHITMAN (see Ray, Richard)

WHITMAN, KATHY *Mandan/Hidatsa/Arikara*

Elk Woman

Born 12 Aug 1952 in Bismarck, ND

RESIDENCE: Scottsdale, AZ

EDUCATION: Dickinson (ND) Central High School, 1970; Standing Rock Community College, Fort Yates, ND; SGC; U of SD, 1973-1978

OCCUPATION: Cafe and crafts shop owner, teacher, sculptor, and painter; since 1984, best known for sculpture

MEDIA: Oil and stone

PUBLISHED: Jacka and Jacka (1988). *The Indian Trader* (May 1984)

EXHIBITS: ACS/ENP; CNM; FCTM; HM/G; MAI; SMIC; SNAICF; Western Museum, Medora, ND; galleries in AZ, CA, CO, NY, TX, and WY; see also Awards

SOLO/SPECIAL EXHIBITS: SIM (dual show)

AWARDS: ACS/ENP ('86, 1st; '87, '90, 1st); CNM ('87, 1st); ITIC ('87); NPTA (Best of Fine Arts, Best of Show); Mobridge (SD) Art Show (Judges Choice Award);

United Tribes Educational and Technical Center, Bismarck, ND (Governor's Choice)

WHITMAN, RICHARD RAY *Creek/Pawnee*

A.K.A. Richard Ray

Born 1949 in Claremore, OK; M/GM: Polly Long

RESIDENCE: Gypsy, OK

EDUCATION: Bristow (OK) High School; IAIA; CIA/CA; Oklahoma School of Photography, Oklahoma City, OK

OCCUPATION: Exhibits technician, artist-in-residence, art instructor, actor, performance artist, author, photographer, poet, and painter

PUBLISHED: Highwater (1980). *Tamaqua* (winter/spring 1991)

EXHIBITS: IAIA/M, CC/OK, PAC, TIAF, U of Tulsa/AC

AWARDS: TIAF ('92, 1st)

HONORS: Served as "Artist in the People's Struggle," Wounded Knee, SD, 1973

WHONNOCK, ROBERT *Kwakwaka'wakw (Kwakiutl)*

MEDIA: Watercolor and pencil

PUBLIC COLLECTIONS: C/RBCM

WHO WHINNY (see Roman Nose, Henry Caruthers)

WIACKE (see Weakee, Teddy)

WICAHPE HINHPAYA (see Winters, Carl)

WICAHPI ISNALA (see Dietz, William)

WICANHPI (see Penn, Robert)

WICKAHTEWAH (see Moqui)

WIFE EAGLE DEER *Oglala Sioux*

Mepaa Kte, Wife Eagle Deer

Born ca. 1869; died ca. 1929

PUBLISHED: Jacobson and d'Ucel (1950); Snodgrass (1968)

WIKSOMNEN (see Alexee, Frederick)

WILCOX, ANNA SUE (see Hebert-Wilcox, Anna Sue)

WILDER, LEONARD *Karok/Assiniboin*

PUBLISHED: Snodgrass (1968)

PUBLIC COLLECTIONS: IACB

WILD HOG *Cheyenne*

A.K.A. Chief Wild Hog

PUBLISHED: Snodgrass (1968)

PUBLIC COLLECTIONS: HSM/KS (manuscripts division: notebook of sketches, dated 1879); SI/OAA (copy of a drawing by Wild Hog)

WILD HORSE *Kiowa*

Koba

Born 1848; died 1880 in Oklahoma Territory, of consumptive tuberculosis

EDUCATION: Hampton; Carlisle, 1879; At Carlisle he was a student in the tinshop with Henry Caruthers Roman Nose (q.v.).

PUBLISHED: Snodgrass (1968); Maurer (1992). *17th Annual Report*, BAE (1895-1896)

WIFE EAGLE DEER

"The artist painted skins depicting Sioux dance scenes and battles between the Crow and Sioux (see Jacobson and d'Ucel, 1950)."

Snodgrass 1968

WILD HORSE

"The artist was one of many Plains Indians arrested at Salt Fork, Red River, Indian Territory, February 19, 1875, and imprisoned at Fort Marion, St. Augustine, FL (see Cohoe, William). Wild Horse, primarily a warrior rather than an artist, participated in raids into the Brazos country in 1872, and attacked the Wichita Agency, August 22, 1874."

Snodgrass 1968

PUBLIC COLLECTIONS: HI, HS/MA, SI/OAA, YU/BRBML
EXHIBITS: BPG, VP

WILI (see Varnell, Billy)

WILKERSON, PATTI JO *Blackfeet*

Born 15 Sept 1953 in Cut Bank, MT
EDUCATION: Havre (MT) High School, 1971; Hill County Community Action Program, Havre, MT; U of MT
OCCUPATION: Clerk/typist, secretary, writer, illustrator, and painter
MEDIA: Oil, pen and ink, and charcoal
BOOKS ILLUSTRATED: Blackfeet Heritage Program, Browning, MT, various publications
EXHIBITS: U of MT
SOLO EXHIBITS: MPI

WILKIE, LAURENCE *Chippewa*

Born 29 Sept 1922 in Belcourt, ND; P/GGF: Alexander "Scotch" Wilkie, leader of North Dakota buffalo hunts
RESIDENCE: Belcourt, ND
MILITARY: U.S. Navy
EDUCATION: Walkers Art Center, Minneapolis, MN
OCCUPATION: Tabulator operator and painter
PUBLISHED: Snodgrass (1968)
EXHIBITS: BNIAS (also designed catalog cover)

LAURENCE WILKIE

"Wilkie has always been interested in art, but did not start painting until about 1946. He usually does not exhibit his work, preferring to paint for pleasure and for his friends and family."

Snodgrass 1968

WILKINSON, DOUGLAS *Sioux (?)*

So Hah Ney
PUBLISHED: Snodgrass (1968)
PUBLIC COLLECTIONS: MAI

WILKINSON, G. *Kwakwaka'wakw (Kwakiutl)*

MEDIA: Acrylic
PUBLIC COLLECTIONS: C/RBCM

WILLCUTS, MICHAEL *Cheyenne River Sioux*

RESIDENCE: Rapid City, SD
EXHIBITS: RC
AWARDS: RC ('92, Aplan Award)
HONORS: RC, Thunderbird Foundation Scholarship, 1992

WILLETO, PAUL *Navajo*

RESIDENCE: Tsaile, AZ
EDUCATION: IAIA; B.F.A., U of NM; M.F.A., U of MI
OCCUPATION: Teacher, painter, and sculptor
COMMISSIONS: *Murals:* Ned A. Hatathli Museum, NCC, Tsaile, AZ (funded by a grant from the Metropolitan Life Foundation), 1985
PUBLIC COLLECTIONS: WWM
EXHIBITS: HM/G

PAUL WILLETO

In the beginning, Willeto's painting style was abstract, but it has become more realistic as he has experimented with different types of materials. He says that he considers himself a contemporary Native American artist — which, he explains, means that his perception of art is contemporary in terms of theory and practice.

Navajo Community College Spirit, *Nov 1990*

WILLIAMS, CAROLE J. *Cherokee*

Born 18 June 1954 in Tulsa, OK; daughter of Mora J. Vantrease and Rufus E. Williams Jr.; P/GP: Addie Austin and Rufus E. Williams Sr.; M/GP: Chloe Frene Perry and Elmer B. Vantrease
RESIDENCE: Hulbert, OK

CAROLE J. WILLIAMS

Williams is best known for her miniature paintings of Cherokee magic and myth.

p.c. 1992

EDUCATION: Charles Page High School, Sand Springs, OK, 1972; NSU, 1992

MEDIA: Oil, acrylic, watercolor, pencil, pastel, and prints

EXHIBITS: CNM, FCTM, NSU; Arkansas Women Artists Association; Georgia Miniature Art Society; see also Awards

AWARDS: Cherokee County Fair (1st); *Harvest of Talent* (2-1st); Northeast Oklahoma Area Art Show

WILLIAMS, DANA A. *Potawatomi*

A.K.A. Dana Alan Williams

Born 1953 in Parry Sound, ON, Canada

RESIDENCE: Canada

EDUCATION: Central Technical High School, Toronto, ON, 1969-1972; George Brown College of Applied Arts, Toronto, ON, 1975; Emily Carr College of Art, Vancouver, BC, 1980-1982; McGill University, Montréal, PQ, 1983-1985

OCCUPATION: Sculptor and painter

MEDIA: Acrylic and soapstone

PUBLISHED: *The Native Perspective* (Vol. 3, no. 2, 1978)

PUBLIC COLLECTIONS: C/CMC; C/INAC; Native Friendship Centre of Montréal (PQ) Inc.

EXHIBITS: AICH; C/INAC; C/NB; C/NAC; C/NWNG; C/U of M; C/U of R/MG; C/WICEC; American Studies Institute, Montréal, PQ; Columbia University, Canada House, New York, NY; Emily Carr College of Art, Vancouver, BC; Le Centre Cultural de la Côte des Neiges, Montréal, PQ; Visual Arts Centre, Westmount, PQ

WILLIAMS, DAVID B. *Ojibwa*

RESIDENCE: Winnipeg, MB, Canada

OCCUPATION: Writer, photographer, carver, and painter

PUBLISHED: *American Indian Art* (spring 1990)

PUBLIC COLLECTIONS: C/AG/M, C/ESSOC, C/GCC, C/NGCA, C/SCC

EXHIBITS: Saskatchewan Open; galleries in BC, MB, and SK

DAVID B. WILLIAMS

According to John Warner, "...Williams' art combines vivid colors and fine lines with elements of stark geometry, abstraction and realism. His work often depicts the cycles of nature...." In his paintings Williams frequently includes three red suns that he says represent his three sons, who live with him. When a yellow sun is also included, it is usually depicted at a distance and represents his daughter, who is not with him. He explains, "These are my kids, I paint for them."

American Indian Art
spring 1990

WILLIAMS, DAVID EMMETT *Kiowa/Tonkawa/Apache*

Tosque, Apache Man

Born 20 Aug 1933 in Lawton, OK; died 8 Nov 1985 in Tulsa, OK; son of Jenny and Emmett Williams, singer and leather designer; Artist is a descendant of Satanka (Sitting Bear), Kiowa war chief.

RESIDENCE: Lived in Tahlequah, OK

EDUCATION: Boone Public School, Apache, OK; Fort Sill, 1941-1954; BC, 1960-1962

OCCUPATION: Teacher of Indian culture, factory worker, traditional dancer, singer, and painter

MEDIA: Acrylic, tempera, gouache, pencil, and prints

PUBLISHED: Snodgrass (1968); Mahey, et al. (1980); Boyd, et al. (1981; 1983). *The Indian Trader* (Mar 1982); *Oklahoma Art Gallery* (spring 1982); *The Tulsa Tribune* (22 Oct 1982)

COMMISSIONS: Bacone College, centennial logo, 1980

PUBLIC COLLECTIONS: GM; HM; MAI; PAC; SM; St. Augustine's Center, Chicago, IL; Carnegie (OK) High School

EXHIBITS: AIE; ASM; BC/McG; BNIAS; CNM; CSPIP; FANAIAE; HM; ITIC; LGAM; MFA/O; MPABAS; OIAP; PAC; SPIM; SM; USDI; Stouffer's Manor Gate House, Pittsburgh, PA

SOLO/SPECIAL EXHIBITS: HM; SM; SPIM; Pasadena, CA, 1964 (dual show); Tryons Gallery, London, England

DAVID EMMETT WILLIAMS

"Williams said when he was a boy he first picked up a brush after he saw his elders painting, although he didn't paint seriously until about 1959. The artist estimated he had completed more than 2,000 paintings before losing his eyesight in 1981 due to diabetes. In his last years he underwent almost constant dialysis treatments but continued to sing at powwows when his health permitted."

Snodgrass-King, p.c. 1993

AWARDS: AIE ('70, 1st; '72); CNM ('72, 1st, '74, Grand Award); ITIC ('86); ITIC ('86); PAC ('68; '69; '71; '72; '73, Grand Award; '76, Wolf Robe Hunt Award; '78)

HONORS: Bacone College, Alumni Hall of Fame, 1983

WILLIAMS, FRANCIS *Haida*

RESIDENCE: Canada

PUBLISHED: Hall, Blackman, and Rickard, eds. (1981)

WILLIAMS, GENE *Chickasaw*

EXHIBITS: BB, CNM, FCTM, PAC

AWARDS: FCTM ('75, 1st; '80; '81, 1st, IH; '83, 1st; '84, IH)

WILLIAMS, SAUL *Ojibwa*

Born 20 Apr 1954 at a bush camp on North Caribou Lake, Canada

RESIDENCE: Canada

EDUCATION: Elliot Lake, summer 1971; Schreiber Island Project, 1972

OCCUPATION: Construction worker and painter

MEDIA: Acrylic and prints

PUBLISHED: Cinader (1976); McLuhan and Hill (1984); Southcott (1984); Menitove, ed. (1986b); Menitove and Danford, eds. (1989); Podedworny (1989)

PUBLIC COLLECTIONS: C/AG/TB, C/CMC, C/MCC, C/ROM, C/TU, C/U of T

EXHIBITS: C/AG/O; C/AG/TB; C/CNAC; C/MAF; C/MCC; C/ROM; C/TU; C/U of T; C/WCAA; C/WICEC; C/YU; NACLA; Guelph University; Kinder des Nanabush, Hamburg, West Germany; Mariposa Festival; Oakville Centennial Gallery; Sarnia (ON) Public Library and Art Gallery

SOLO EXHIBITS: Montréal, PQ; Toronto, ON

SAUL WILLIAMS

Williams' paintings and prints represent an individualistic and often humorous interpretation of the many legends of his ancestors. He was an early member of the Red Lake Triple K Cooperative. In 1976 he participated in a month-long workshop on silk-screen printing and then worked on several editions of his own prints.

artist brochure, n.d.

WILLIAMS, SHARON PILCHER *Potawatomi*

PUBLISHED: Snodgrass (1968)

PUBLIC COLLECTIONS: St. Augustine's Center, Chicago, IL

WILLIAMS, THOMPSON *Caddo/Comanche*

RESIDENCE: Gracemont, OK

EXHIBITS: AIE

AWARDS: AIE ('77, 1st; '78; '79, 1st; '86, 1st)

WILLIAMS, WADE *Potawatomi*

Pequaki

PUBLIC COLLECTIONS: PAC

EXHIBITS: PAC

WILSON, B. CLAYTON *Kwakwaka'wakw (Kwakiutl)*

MEDIA: Watercolor and pencil

PUBLIC COLLECTIONS: C/RBCM

WILSON, CHUCK *Creek/Seminole*

A.K.A. Charles Wilson

Born 8 Mar 1941 in Okmulgee, OK; died 19 Jan 1992 in Tulsa, OK; cousin of Will Sampson (q.v.)

RESIDENCE: Lived in Tulsa, OK

EDUCATION: OSU/O

MEDIA: Oil, acrylic, watercolor, pastel, and pen and ink

EXHIBITS: ITIC; PAC; galleries in CO, KS, NM, OK, and TX

AWARDS: ITIC ('85); PAC ('73)

CHUCK WILSON

In the 1980s the artist lived in Atlanta, GA, while maintaining studios in Denver, CO, and Tulsa, OK. Wilson's favorite subject was Western scenery done in the Remington and Russell style. He was also known for his portraits.

artist brochure, 1982

WILSON, CYNTHIA JUDY *Quechan*

Born 22 Sept 1942

RESIDENCE: Winterhaven, CA

EDUCATION: Santa Fe, ca. 1962

PUBLISHED: Snodgrass (1968)

EXHIBITS: PAC

WILSON, DOUGLAS E. *Umatilla/Cayuse/Walla Walla/Nez Percé*

Born 1942 on the Umatilla Reservation, OR

MEDIA: Watercolor and pen and ink

EXHIBITS: SMIC; RE; Fresno (CA) State College Indian Cultural Center; galleries in CA, NE, and NM; see also Awards

SOLO EXHIBITS: IPCC

AWARDS: SMIC ('85, 2-1st); Box Butte Art Society Show, Alliance, NE ('86, Certificate of Excellence)

HONORS: IPCC, artist-in-residence, 1985

WILSON, J. *(?)*

EDUCATION: Albuquerque

PUBLISHED: Snodgrass (1968)

EXHIBITS: ITIC

AWARDS: ITIC

WILSON, JOE *Salish*

RESIDENCE: British Columbia, Canada

PUBLIC COLLECTIONS: HCC

EXHIBITS: HCC, RC

WILSON, JOHN *Navajo*

EDUCATION: Santa Fe, 1960

PUBLISHED: Snodgrass (1968)

EXHIBITS: MNM

WILSON, JOHN SEVEN, III *Nez Percé*

Born 1966 in Clarkston, WA

RESIDENCE: Lapwai, ID

MEDIA: Acrylic, pen and ink, leather, denim, and canvas

PUBLISHED: Minthorn (1991)

EXHIBITS: SAP

WILSON, LUCY *Navajo*

EDUCATION: Albuquerque, 1959

PUBLISHED: Snodgrass (1968)

EXHIBITS: MNM

AWARDS: MNM

WILSON, LYLE *Haisla/Northern Kwakwaka'wakw (Kwakiutl)*

A.K.A. Lyle Giles Wilson

Born 1955 at Butedale, BC, Canada

EDUCATION: C/U of BC, Native Indian Teacher Education Program, 1976; diploma, Emily Carr College of Art and Design, Vancouver, BC, 1986

OCCUPATION: Sculptor and graphic artist

MEDIA: Pencil, colored pencil, silver, wood, and prints

LYLE WILSON

According to Karen Duffek, Wilson's work, "... explores the territory between what is traditional and what is not. Like many Northwest Coast Indian artists, his approach is based on a knowledge of formal conventions developed over past centuries. Yet he shifts and fragments the ancient symbols into statements on art, culture, history, and power...."

Museum Note No. 38
C/U of BC/MA

EXHIBITS: CNM

SOLO EXHIBITS: C/U of BC/MA

WIMMER, MIKE *Cherokee*

EXHIBITS: CNM, FCTM, HM/G

AWARDS: CNM ('78, 1st, Grand Award; '79, 1st; '82); FCTM ('81). Student awards include: FCTM ('76, 1st-student; '77, 1st-student, '78, 1st-student); HM/G ('78, Best of Student Painting, Judge's Choice)

WING, GARY *Cherokee*

• EXHIBITS: CNM

WING, HENRY BEHAN *Ute*

White Dove

Born 14 Feb 1962 in Cortez, CO; son of Jean and Albert Wing; P/GF: Nathan Wing Jr.; M/GP: Ida Miller Collins and Patten Ketchum

RESIDENCE: Towaoc, CO, on the Ute Mountain Ute Reservation

EDUCATION: Montezuma-Cortez High School, Cortez, CO, 1983

OCCUPATION: Rancher and artist

MEDIA: Acrylic, pencil, pen and ink, and pastel

COMMISSIONS: Northern Star Promotions, Christmas card

EXHIBITS: ITIC, NNTF, RC; see also Awards

AWARDS: State of Colorado Regional Exhibition, U of Denver (CO) (Certificate of Merit, 2-Gold Key Awards); Montezuma-Cortez High School Art Show, Cortez, CO (6-1st); Valley National Bank Art Show, Cortez, CO

WINTERS, CARL *Standing Rock Sioux*

Wicahpe Hinhpaya, Shooting Star

Born 9 Jan 1954 in Bismarck, ND

EDUCATION: IAIA High School, 1969-1972; IAIA, 1972-1973

MEDIA: Oil, watercolor, pencil, pen and ink, charcoal, mixed-media, and prints

BOOKS ILLUSTRATED: Reynolds and Brown (1973); *Indian Educational Book,* BIA (1972)

COMMISSIONS: *Murals:* DIA, 1993

PUBLIC COLLECTIONS: HCC, IAIA

EXHIBITS: CNM, HCC, HM/G, SN, RC; see also Awards

SOLO/SPECIAL EXHIBITS: SIM (dual show)

AWARDS: SN ('70, Educational Award); North Dakota Indian Art Exhibit ('64, 1st)

RAY WINTERS

Winters' earliest paintings were done in the traditional Plains ledger drawing style that he learned from his grandfather. Attendance at The Institute of American Arts where he was exposed to a multitude of artistic influences broadened his style. He now combines his old style with abstract geometric symbols in depicting historical tribal themes.

The Denver Post, *27 Feb 1984*

WINTERS, RAY *Hunkpapa Sioux*

Mahto Wicha Kiza, Fighting Bear

A.K.A. Raymond David Winters

Born 22 May 1950 in Fort Yates, ND; GF: Long Bear

RESIDENCE: Rapid City, SD

EDUCATION: IAIA High School, 1968-1969; IAIA, 1969-1973; Medici Institute, Florence, Italy, 1970; CSF/SF, 1978-1980; The Community College of Denver, CO, 1979

OCCUPATION: Assistant art instructor, lecturer, curriculum developer, and painter

MEDIA: Oil, acrylic, mixed-media, earth pigment, beads, buckskin, and wood

PUBLISHED: Dunn (1968); Highwater (1980); Hill (1992). *The Denver Post* (27 Feb 1984); *The Rapid City Journal* (3 Dec 1989)

COMMISSIONS: *Murals:* Community College, Denver, CO. *Paintings:* Sally Sheppard Brewster, New York, NY, 1972; Bev Panger, 1973. *Other:* Antioch University, three traditional tipis, 1979; CSF/SF, Art Department, 1979; South

Dakota State Employment Division, office designs, 1975; Western Arms Corporation, Santa Fe, NM, commemorative design, 1979

PUBLIC COLLECTIONS: HCC, IAIA, SIM

EXHIBITS: BIA; CIAE; HCC; HM/G; IAIA; PAC; RC; Minority Artist Association, Denver, CO; see also Awards

SOLO/SPECIAL EXHIBITS: IAIA/M; SIM (dual show); Fort Smith, AR; Little Rock, AR

AWARDS: RC ('70); Rosebud (SD) Fair Art Show

HONORS: Campbell Foundation, scholarship to study European art museums, summer 1971

WITA (see Phillips, Rita)

WIYO (see Randall, Bunnie)

WOBAAH (see Washakie, Charles)

WOHAW *Kiowa*

Gu Hau De Or; *Wohaw*, Wolf Robe

Born 1855; died 1924

OCCUPATION: Warrior, policeman, scout, and graphic artist

MEDIA: Pencil and colored pencil

PUBLISHED: Boyd, et al. (1983); Maurer (1992)

PUBLIC COLLECTIONS: HS/MO, SI

EXHIBITS: BPG, VP

WOHAW

Wohaw was introduced to drawing while he was a prisoner at Fort Marion, St. Augustine, FL. He was one of the 72 Plains Indians who were incarcerated in 1875 as representatives of their tribes for depredations against White settlers. He returned to Indian Territory in 1878.

WO-KE-NOS (see Roman Nose, Henry Caruthers)

WOLF ALONE (see Taulbee, Dan)

WOLFE, DAVID MICHAEL *Cherokee*

EXHIBITS: CNM, FCTM

AWARDS: FCTM ('90)

WOLFE, EDMOND RICHARD *Creek/Seminole*

Este Songah, Gone Man

Born 29 Sept 1928

RESIDENCE: Wetumka, OK

MILITARY: U.S. Navy, WWII

EDUCATION: BC; Haskell

PUBLISHED: Snodgrass (1968)

EXHIBITS: PAC

WOLFE, MARK *Cherokee*

EXHIBITS: CNM

AWARDS: CNM ('94)

WOLFE, WILLIAM *Cherokee*

EXHIBITS: FCTM, PAC

AWARDS: FCTM ('68; '70)

WOLF FACE *Apache*

MEDIA: Watercolor, colored pencil, pen and ink, and graphite pencil

PUBLISHED: Snodgrass (1968)

PUBLIC COLLECTIONS: HSM/O

EXHIBITS: HSM/O

WOLF FACE

"While a prisoner of war at St. Augustine, FL, in 1879, he executed paintings on writing paper with watercolor and colored pencil (see Cohoe, William)."

Snodgrass 1968

WONGITILLIN, NICK *Eskimo*

Born 1904 in Gambell, St. Lawrence Island, AK

RESIDENCE: Savoonga, St. Lawrence Island, AK

EDUCATION: DCTP, 1964-1965

PUBLISHED: Ray (1969)

WOOD, GLEN *Tsimshian*

Sis-Be-Goot, Strong Man, or A Messenger

Born 1951 in Prince Rupert, BC, Canada; son of Jessie Ellen Smith and George Noble Wood

RESIDENCE: Vancouver, BC, Canada

EDUCATION: Prince Rupert (BN) Senior High; C/KSNCIA, 1974

OCCUPATION: Carver, jeweler, painter, and printmaker

MEDIA: Acrylic, pencil, pen and ink, wood, silver, gold, and prints

COMMISSIONS: Carved totem poles and house fronts in British Columbia, Japan, and Australia

PUBLIC COLLECTIONS: C/NMC, C/U of BC/MA, HCC

EXHIBITS: AIAFM; C/MNBC; CIM; CNM; HCC; MAI; RE; SCG; SDMM; SDSMT; Marin Museum, Novato, CA; Nexus - Art Exposition and Trade Show, Vancouver, BC

SOLO EXHIBITS: MAI

AWARDS: AIAFM ('92, 2-1st, Best of Class); CIM ('88, 2-1st); CNM ('87, 1st; '88, Best of Category)

WOOD, HARVEY *Navajo*

Born 1944

EDUCATION: Inter-Mt.

PUBLISHED: Snodgrass (1968)

EXHIBITS: FAIEAIP

WOOD, NORMAN *Navajo/Cheyenne*

EXHIBITS: HM/G, PAC, SN

AWARDS: HM/G ('73); SN ('69); PAC ('69)

WOOD, RANDY *Seminole*

A.K.A. Randolph Wood

Born Nov 1942 in Wewoka, OK; died Nov 1982 in an automobile accident; brother of Lana Stone and Virginia Harjo; raised with his cousin, Benjamin Harjo Jr. (q.v.)

RESIDENCE: Lived in Shawnee, OK

EDUCATION: Studied art in Montana

PUBLISHED: *The Tulsa World* (19 Nov 1982)

EXHIBITS: CNM; FCTM; galleries in Oklahoma

AWARDS: FCTM ('73, 1st; '74, IH; '80; '82, IH)

WOOD, ROSEMARY *Osage*

EXHIBITS: CNM

AWARDS: CNM ('87, 1st)

WOODEN LEG

As a young man, the artist was a strong and tireless walker. He was said to have "wooden legs which never tire."

Dockstader 1977

WOODEN LEG *Northern Cheyenne*

Kummok Quivviokta, Wooden Leg

A.K.A. Good Walker

Born 1858 in the Black Hills, near the Cheyenne River; died 1940 in Montana; son of Eagle Feather On The Forehead and White Buffalo Shaking Off the Dust

(also called "Many Bullet Wounds")

OCCUPATION: Warrior, U.S. Army scout, Indian court judge, tribal historian, and painter

PUBLISHED: Marquis (1931); Russell (1968); Snodgrass (1968); Dockstader (1977). *Montana* (spring 1963)

PUBLIC COLLECTIONS: Custer Battlefield National Monument, SD

WOODRING, CARL *Osage*

Wasaba Shinga, Little Bear

A.K.A. Carlton Delmar Woodring

Born 6 Dec 1920 in Arkansas City, KS; died 23 June 1985; son of Gladys Fagen and Orville Leo Woodring; cousin of Harry Woodring, Secretary of War under Franklin D. Roosevelt and former Governor of Kansas

RESIDENCE: Lived in Charlotte, NC

MILITARY: U.S. Army Air Corps, Korea and Vietnam

EDUCATION: Pawhuska (OK) High School, 1938; U of Tulsa, 1956-1958; studied under Acee Blue Eagle (q.v.)

OCCUPATION: Electrical engineer, art instructor, dancer, sculptor, and painter

MEDIA: Oil, watercolor, tempera, and bronze

PUBLISHED: Dunn (1968); Snodgrass (1968); Brody (1971); Broder (1981); Williams, ed. (1990). *Oklahoma Today* (Vol. 8, no. 3, 1958); *Art in America* (No. 3, 1961); *The Indian Trader* (Feb 1983)

PUBLIC COLLECTIONS: BIA, CGPS, GM, IACB, MAI, MNM, PAC

EXHIBITS: AAID; AAIE; AIE; CGPS; CNM; ITIC; KCPA; LAIC; MNM; MKMcNAI; OSU/OR; PAC; PAC/T; PSC; SI; SN; SPIM; SWAIA; USDS; WSC; Ponca Indian Fair, Ponca City, OK; Tulsa (OK) Powwow Arts and Crafts Show; Oil Capitol Art Show, Tulsa, OK; Springfest '82, Charlotte, NC; American Indian Art Show, Houston, TX; American Indian Art Show, Flag Pavilion, Seattle, WA; Indian Days of North Carolina, Charlotte, NC; Charlotte-Mecklenburg Department of Education Exhibition; Central Piedmont College, NC; Brussels, Belgium; Paris, France; Mannheim, Germany; and London, England

SOLO/SPECIAL EXHIBITS: GM (dual show); PAC; SPIM; U of NC/CH; U of NC/P; No Man's Land Museum, Weatherford, OK; Schiele Museum, Gastonia, NC; Appalachian State University, Boone, NC; Arts and Science Museum, Statesville, NC; North Carolina Museum of Natural History, Raleigh, NC; Greensboro (NC) Artists League

AWARDS: AIE; ITIC; MNM; PAC; SN ('67, Kinkner Award; '68); two Grand Awards

HONORS: PAC, received more awards in a single year than any artist ever to enter the Annual Exhibition; Tulsa (OK) Powwow Club, president; AIE, arts and crafts director; Schiele Museum, Gastonia, NC, Board of Directors

CARL WOODRING

"Reared in Pawhuska, OK, the artist began painting in 1956, under the tutelage of Acee Blue Eagle (q.v.). Within a year, he was exhibiting throughout the U.S. and Europe and had become a prolific painter. During 1964 and most of 1965 he virtually ceased to paint, but late in 1965 he began again."

Snodgrass 1968

WOODRING, SARAH H. *Cherokee*

Born 3 July 1927 in Taxahaw, SC; daughter of Lillie Moree and Wilson J. Hildreth; wife of Carl Woodring (q.v.); P/GP: Sarah and Hampton Hildreth; M/GP: Emma and Joseph Moree

RESIDENCE: Charlotte, NC

EDUCATION: Pageland (SC) High School, 1944; Kings College, Charlotte, NC, 1945

OCCUPATION: Secretary and painter

MEDIA: Oil, acrylic, and watercolor

EXHIBITS: AIE; CNM; U of NC/C; U of NC/P; Leon Stacks Invitational, Charlotte, NC; Unitarian Church Invitational, Charlotte, NC; Spring Arts Festival, Lancaster, SC; Stumpton Arts Festival, Matthews, NC; American Indian Art Show, Flag Pavilion, Seattle, WA; Cannon Mills Art Exhibition, Kannopolis, NC

Woodward, Clark Ross *Blackfeet*

Born 19 July 1944 in Browning, MT; son of Margaret Thomas and Calvin Woodward; P/GP: Rose and Hi Woodward

RESIDENCE: St. Croix Falls, WI

EDUCATION: Browning (MT) High School, 1962; MCC, 1979; ASU; KCAI/MO

OCCUPATION: Sculptor, jeweler, and painter

MEDIA: Oil, acrylic, pencil, pastel, stone, silver, and gold

PUBLIC COLLECTIONS: MCC

EXHIBITS: MCC; see also Awards

AWARDS: MCC; North American Indian Days, Blackfeet Indian Reservation, Browning, MT

Woodward, Ken *Cherokee*

A.K.A. Kenneth L. Woodward

Born 18 Oct 1933; son of Chrystal Viola Robinson and Forest L. Woodward; P/GP: Minie May Solts and William Garfield Woodward; M/GP: Dorcas Thomas and James Robinson

RESIDENCE: Tulsa, OK

EDUCATION: Capitol Hill High School, Oklahoma City, OK

MEDIA: Acrylic, watercolor, pencil, pen and ink, and scratch board

PUBLIC COLLECTIONS: HCC, TTSP

EXHIBITS: CNM, FCTM, IACA, MCI, RC, RE, RSC, SWAIA, TIAF, TTSP, WTF

SOLO EXHIBITS: Foreman Historical Home, Muskogee, OK, 1992

AWARDS: CNM ('94, 1st); FCTM ('83, IH; '84; '85; '87; '89; '90, IH; '94, Cecil Dick Award); RC ('84; '85); RSC ('84, 1st); TIAF ('90)

Ken Woodward

Woodward gives his Cherokee wife credit for inspiring him to paint Native American subjects.

p.c. 1990

Although, in recent years, his activity has been limited due to emphysema, the artist continues to paint and exhibit. He likes to paint satirical themes of political and cultural events, especially depicting the Indian in Anglo society.

Woody, Elizabeth *Navajo/Wasco/Colville*

Born 1959 in Ganado, AZ

EDUCATION: IAIA, 1980-1983; B.A., ESC, 1991

OCCUPATION: Author, poet, and artist

MEDIA: Pastel

PUBLISHED: Bruchae, ed. (1983); Woody (1988); Roberts, ed. (1992); Harjo, ed. (1993)

EXHIBITS: AICA/SF; MMA/WA; Woman's Art Registry of Minnesota, Minneapolis, MN; Howard University, Washington, D.C.; Oregon State Capitol Building, Salem, OR

AWARDS: Before Columbus Foundation, American Book Award, Berkeley, CA

HONORS: Brandywine Workshop, Philadelphia, PA, fellowship

Woohkinih (see Roman Nose)

Wooten, Walt *Choctaw*

A.K.A. Walter Wooten

RESIDENCE: Santa Fe, NM

EDUCATION: CAI

OCCUPATION: Advertising art director, free-lance artist, and painter

MEDIA: Oil

EXHIBITS: SCG; Bishop Quarters Artists' Co-op, Oak Park, IL; Hyde Park Art Center, Chicago, IL; Union League Club, Chicago, IL

SOLO EXHIBITS: Rush Presbyterian/St. Luke's Hospital, Chicago, IL; Standard Oil Building, Chicago, IL

Wo Peen (see Gonzales, Louis)

WORTHINGTON, LIONEL *Choctaw/Chickasaw*

EXHIBITS: CNM, FCTM

AWARDS: FCTM ('87; '88)

WOUNDED FACE *Mandan*

A.K.A. Chief Wounded Face

PUBLISHED: Snodgrass (1968)

PUBLIC COLLECTIONS: U of PA/M (autobiographical drawings on muslin, presented as a gift, 1891)

WRIGHT, FRANK *Cherokee*

RESIDENCE: Westville, OK

EXHIBITS: CNM

WUTTUNEE, LAUREN *Cree*

Born 1957 in Regina, SK, Canada

RESIDENCE: Edmonton, AB, Canada

EDUCATION: B.F.A., U of C, 1980; Bachelor of Laws, U of BC, 1983; M.F.A., Instituto de San Miguel Allende, Guanajuato, Mexico, 1989

OCCUPATION: Attorney and painter

MEDIA: Colored pencil, conté, pastel, and mixed-media

PUBLIC COLLECTIONS: C/AIAC

EXHIBITS: C/AIAC, C/AM, C/INAC, C/SM, C/U of C/G, HM

AWARDS: C/AM ('87, Award of Distinction; '88; '89, 1st); Mungo Martin Memorial Award, Vancouver, BC

HONORS: *Scholarships and Grants:* Heintz Jordan Memorial Scholarship, Toronto, ON, 1977; Alberta Culture Major Award Grant, Edmonton, AB, 1979; Canada Council, Department of Visual Arts, Ottawa, ON, 1980; Saskatchewan Arts Board Grant, Saskatoon, SK

WUXPAIS (see Little Chief, Daniel)

WYNNE, BRUCE *Spokane (?)*

Born ca. 1944 near Wellpinit, WA, on the Spokane Reservation

RESIDENCE: Mead, WA

EDUCATION: Mead (WA) High School, 1962; IAIA, 1964; museum training program, U of CO, 1968; B.F.A., U of CO, 1975.

OCCUPATION: Museum exhibits designer, exhibits instructor, free-lance artist, sculptor, and painter

PUBLISHED: Snodgrass (1968); New (1981). *Southwest Art* (Nov 1978); *The Scottsdale Daily Progress* (21 Jan 1983); *Art-Talk* (Mar 1984)

PUBLIC COLLECTIONS: BBHC; HCC; HM; PAC; Diamond L. Foundation, Snyder, TX

EXHIBITS: CNM; FAIEAIP; FANAIAE; HCC; SN; SPIM; SWAIA; WWM; *Origin of American Indian Sculpture,* Santa Fe, NM; in Asia and South America; galleries and invitational shows since 1977

AWARDS: HM/G ('75, Committee's Choice); ITIC; PAC; RC ('70); SN; SWAIA

Anthony Yahola

Although incarcerated in an Oklahoma state prison, Yahola continues to paint. The majority of his paintings are representational and reflect his Indian heritage. Some of his more recent paintings are allegorical.

Edward Kennard Yava

After military service in Vietnam, Yava used the G.I. Bill and government disability benefits to start college in 1975 at Arizona Western College. Although he has work experience in several areas, Yava stated that he has always wanted to be an artist. He is an enrolled member of the Colorado River Indian Reservation.

artist, p.c. 1992

Alice Yazzie

Yazzie grew up in the country around Klagetoh, AZ, on the Navajo Reservation, as a member of the Dark Tree Clan and Tangle Clan. Her art work has been used in Navajo language textbooks and on several commercial projects. She maintains a studio in Albuquerque's Old Town.

DETAIL: Yazzie Bahe (Andrew van Tsinajinnie), *Navajo Fire Dance*, n.d. Philbrook Museum of Art, Tulsa, Oklahoma

---

YAHOLA, ANTHONY *Creek*

MEDIA: Acrylic

EXHIBITS: CNM, FCTM

AWARDS: FCTM ('82, 1st)

YAKA (see Moquino, Delfino)

YATES, GEORGE *Nambé*

PUBLISHED: Snodgrass (1968)

PUBLIC COLLECTIONS: MNM (executed in 9th grade, 1955)

YAVA, AARON *Hopi/Tewa/Navajo*

Born 13 May 1946 on the Hopi Reservation, AZ

RESIDENCE: Parker, AZ

EDUCATION: Parker (AZ) High School; NCC; IAIA; AWC; ASU

OCCUPATION: Lecturer, cultural consultant, sculptor, and painter

MEDIA: Oil, acrylic, bone, feather, wood, and pottery shards

PUBLISHED: *New Horizons* (1976). *Sun Tracks*, U of AZ (Vol. 13, no.1, 1976)

BOOKS ILLUSTRATED: Elder (1975); Rosen, ed. (1975); Hobson (1979); Ortiz (1977); Silko (1974); Sullivan (1974); Yava (1975)

EXHIBITS: AWC; HM/G; IFA; NTF; SN; SM; Hozho Center, Sedona, AZ; Sacramento (CA) State Art Gallery; Governor's Indian Art Show, Sacramento, CA; Oakland (CA) Museum Culture Show; La Peña Cultural Center, Berkeley, CA; regionally in Arizona and California; see also Awards

SOLO EXHIBITS: CNGM; U of CA/B; Academy of Sciences, San Francisco, CA; California State University, Hayward, CA; San Leandro (CA) Library; Lafayette (CA) Library; Holbrook (AZ) Library

AWARDS: HM/G ('72, 1st; '73, 1st); NTF ('74, Grand Award); SN ('74); Northern Yuma County Fair, Parker, AZ ('72; '76, 1st); Indian Art Show, Parker, AZ ('76, 1st)

YAVA, EDWARD KENNARD *Hopi/Tewa/Navajo*

Born 30 Apr 1944 at Keams Canyon, AZ

MILITARY: U.S. Army, Vietnam

EDUCATION: Parker (AZ) High School, 1973; AWC; B.A., Grand Canyon College, Phoenix, AZ, 1981; M.F.A. program, ASU

OCCUPATION: Arts council events coordinator, teacher, writer, illustrator, and painter

EXHIBITS: NICCAS

HONORS: Grand Canyon College, Phoenix, AZ, Dean's List and Native American Student Award in Art, 1978

YAZZ, BEATIEN (see Beatien Yazz)

YAZZIE, ALICE *Navajo*

A.K.A. Alice Yazzie-Rastetter

Born 30 May 1954; daughter of Louise C. and Etsitty Yazzie

RESIDENCE: Albuquerque, NM

EDUCATION: Holbrook (AZ) High School, 1974; AAA, 1976

OCCUPATION: Graphic artist, illustrator, and painter

MEDIA: Watercolor, pastel, and prints

PUBLISHED: *The Indian Trader* (Mar 1990; Nov 1990)

COMMISSIONS: Ladies Pro-Bowlers, trophy design, 1989-1990; SAGA, Inc., card designs, 1986

PUBLIC COLLECTIONS: HCC, NMSF

EXHIBITS: AAPSC; ABQM; ATM; CIM; ITIC; MNA; NMSF; NTF; RC; SNAICF; SWAIA; TM/NE; Chicago (IL) Indian Arts and Crafts Show, 1967; Native American Materials Development Center Art Show; New Mexico Art League Show; Saddleback Western and Wildlife Art Show, Santa Ana, CA; see also Awards

SOLO EXHIBITS: WWM

AWARDS: AAPSC ('85 Grand Award, Poster Award); ITIC ('89; '92, 1st; '93, 1st; '94, 1st); MNA; NMSF ('90, Best in Show); NTF ('90, Best of Show); RC ('85, Erickson Award); SNAICF ('89, Woodard Award); SWAIA ('90, 1st); Best Fest '91, Albuquerque, NM ('90, Best of Show); Pastel Society of NM

HONORS: New Mexico State Fair Indian Art Competition, judge, 1987, 1988

YAZZIE BAHE (see Tsinajinnie, Andrew Van)

YAZZIE, CARL *Navajo*

PUBLISHED: Snodgrass (1968)

PUBLIC COLLECTIONS: MNM

YAZZIE, CHARLES *Navajo*

Born 1944; son of Tso Yazzie

RESIDENCE: Winslow, AZ

OCCUPATION: Painter

MEDIA: Tempera

PUBLISHED: Fawcett and Callander (1982)

PUBLIC COLLECTIONS: HCC, MAI

EXHIBITS: AC/HC, LGAM, PM

YAZZIE, DANIEL WILBUR *Navajo*

Bedonie

Birth date unknown; son of Hosteen Yazzie Bedonie

RESIDENCE: Shiprock, NM

EDUCATION: Riverside, 1964

PUBLISHED: Snodgrass (1968)

HONORS: Philomathic Club of Anadarko (OK), scholarship, 1964

YAZZIE, DOUGLAS *Navajo*

Born 12 Aug 1951

RESIDENCE: Chinle, AZ

EDUCATION: High School graduate

OCCUPATION: Painter

MEDIA: All water-base media

EXHIBITS: CIM, ITIC, NTF, SNAICF

AWARDS: ITIC ('89; '90); NTF (1st)

YAZZIE, EDDIE ADAM *Navajo*

PUBLIC COLLECTIONS: MNA

YAZZIE, ELMER *Navajo*

Born 27 Mar 1954

RESIDENCE: Rehoboth, NM

EDUCATION: B.A., Calvin College, Grand Rapids, MI

MEDIA: Watercolor

EXHIBITS: ITIC; NMSF; NTF; Gallup (NM) Arts Center Show

AWARDS: ITIC ('91, 1st)

ALICE YAZZIE

(continued) According to the artist, "I would like my art work to depict my culture and the beauty of my people. Especially in doing Indian children, I want to capture their unique way of doing things that makes them so adorable and irresistible."

p.c. 1990

YAZZIE, EUGENE, JR. *Navajo*

Born 23 May 1946 in Ganado, AZ

RESIDENCE: Flagstaff, AZ

EDUCATION: Sherman; Inter-Mt.; BYU; U of UT

OCCUPATION: Metalwork instructor, silversmith, and painter

MEDIA: Watercolor, silver, and gemstone

EXHIBITS: AICH; Flagstaff and Sedona, AZ; Houston, TX; New York, NY

SOLO/SPECIAL EXHIBITS: SIM (dual show)

YAZZIE, GARY D. *Navajo*

Born 1946 in Phoenix, AZ

RESIDENCE: Grants, NM

EDUCATION: AAA, 1977-1980

OCCUPATION: Jeweler, sculptor, and painter

MEDIA: Oil, watercolor, charcoal, pastel, silver, gemstone, and prints

COMMISSIONS: *Murals:* DIA, 1993

PUBLIC COLLECTIONS: HCC

EXHIBITS: AC/Y, AIPP, CNAA, CNM, HM/G, ITIC, KCPA, MNA, MNH/LA, NTF, OSU/G, PAC, RC, RE, SI, SIRU, SWAIA, TAAII, WTF

AWARDS: CNM; ITIC ('81, Best in Class; '84, Best in Class; '85; '87; '88, 1st; '89; '90; '91, 1st; '94); NTF ('88, 2-1st, Vice Chairman Award); RC ('77); RE ('87); SWAIA ('83, 1st, 3-Best in Class; '86; '89; '90, 1st)

GARY D. YAZZIE

Yazzie became interested in art as a career in 1973, after an automobile accident left him with nerve damage to his right arm. He most often paints in a style that shows the influence of impressionism and contemporary Western art. He occasionally sculpts and makes jewelry.

Art Gallery, *Mar/Apr 1983*

YAZZIE, JAMES WAYNE *Navajo*

Born 1943; died 1969 in a train accident

RESIDENCE: Lived in Sheep Springs, NM

MEDIA: Oil and watercolor

PUBLISHED: Dunn (1968); Snodgrass (1968); Brody (1971); Tanner (1973); Fawcett and Callander (1982); Samuels (1985). Plateau (Vol. 54, no. 1, 1982)

PUBLIC COLLECTIONS: AF, MAI, MNA, MNM, RMC/AZ, WWM

EXHIBITS: AIAE/WSU, FAIEAIP, RMC/AZ, WSU, WWM

JAMES WAYNE YAZZIE

Yazzie's primitive paintings are full of people doing things and depict Navajo events and activities.

Snodgrass 1968

YAZZIE, JERRY *Navajo*

RESIDENCE: Montezuma Creek, UT

PUBLIC COLLECTIONS: HCC

EXHIBITS: HPTU, RC, WTF

AWARDS: RC ('83, Aplan Award; '85; '87, 1st)

HONORS: RC, Thunderbird Foundation Scholarship, 1983, 1990

YAZZIE, JOHNSON *Navajo*

Born 30 Dec 1957; nephew of Clifford Beck (q.v.)

RESIDENCE: Piñon, AZ

EDUCATION: Certificate in Advertising Arts, MTCC, 1981

OCCUPATION: Coal miner, free-lance commercial artist, and painter

MEDIA: Oil and pastel

PUBLISHED: Jacka and Jacka (1994)

COMMISSIONS: *Murals:* Piñon School, AZ

EXHIBITS: FNAA, ITIC, NTF, SWAIA, TAAII, U of N AZ

AWARDS: FNAA ('87, Corporate Purchase Award); ITIC ('88, 1st; '94, 2-1st, Best in Class, Best In Category); NTF ('87); SWAIA ('87); TAAII ('87); U of N AZ ('85)

HONORS: Grand Central Gallery, New York, NY, scholarship, 1988

JOHNSON YAZZIE

Yazzie's English usage was limited before he enrolled at Maricopa (AZ) Technical Community College. Exposure to other students, as well as summer jobs as a coal strip-miner, aided him in learning English. The artist likes to sign his paintings with a simple "Z."

The Phoenix Gazette
20 *Dec 1983*

YAZZIE, KELVIN *Navajo*

Birth date unknown; born at Church Rock, NM
RESIDENCE: Cedar City, UT
EDUCATION: SUSC, 1985
OCCUPATION: Ceramist and painter
EXHIBITS: MVE; SUAC; SUSC; U of UT; Moapa Valley Exhibition, 1987; Southern Utah Artists Invitational, 1986
AWARDS: SUSC ('87, Best in Show)

YAZZIE, LARRY *Navajo*

A.K.A. Larry L. Yazzie
EDUCATION: IAIA
MEDIA: Acrylic
PUBLISHED: Hill (1992)
PUBLIC COLLECTIONS: IAIA
EXHIBITS: IAIA, SWAIA

YAZZIE, MERLIN *Navajo*

Born 22 Mar 1953
RESIDENCE: Ganado, AZ
EDUCATION: Fort Wingate (AZ) High School; NCC; U of NM
OCCUPATION: High school art teacher and painter
MEDIA: Oil and pastel
PUBLISHED: Snodgrass (1968). *The Indian Trader* (Dec 1994)
EXHIBITS: HM, ITIC, NTF; see also Awards
AWARDS: Partial listing includes: ITIC ('86); Greasewood (AZ) Boarding School Art Show ('65, 1st)

MERLIN YAZZIE

The artist has received "various awards" since 5th grade. Although art was a minor in college, he states he is "basically self-taught."

artist, p.c. 1991

YAZZIE, RAYMOND *Navajo*

A.K.A. Ray Yazzie
Born 15 Mar 1953
RESIDENCE: Albuquerque, NM
EDUCATION: SHS, 1972; CSF/SF; IAIA, 1985
MEDIA: Oil, acrylic, watercolor, pencil, pen and ink, mixed-media, and prints
PUBLIC COLLECTIONS: IAIA, MNA
EXHIBITS: IAIA/M
SOLO EXHIBITS: IAIA
HONORS: National Dean's List, 1985; College Board Talent Roster, 1985; Outstanding National Community College Minority Student, 1985

RAYMOND YAZZIE

Before 1990, the artist worked only on commission, but is currently entering competitive art shows.

artist, p.c. 1990

YAZZIE, RICHARD KEE *Navajo*

Hosh-be
Born 1944 at Crownpoint, NM
RESIDENCE: Gallup, NM
EDUCATION: Santa Fe; Albuquerque; IAIA, 1967
MEDIA: Oil, pencil, pen and ink, and prints
PUBLISHED: Snodgrass (1968); Tanner (1973); New and Young (1976)
EXHIBITS: AC/SD, LGAM, MNM, OWE, PAC, SAIEAIP, SN
AWARDS: SN ('68)

RICHARD KEE YAZZIE

"At one time the artist worked at Wisconsin Dells Indian Village where he produced paintings. He later received a three-year scholarship to study in Oakland, CA."

Snodgrass 1968

YAZZIE, RON *Navajo*

EXHIBITS: ITIC
AWARDS: ITIC ('86; '90)

Sybil L. Yazzie

"The artist received international recognition while a student in Santa Fe. Her paintings of 179 Navajos, in full costume, and 59 horses, were exhibited in London and Paris in 1937 and brought the comment that 'it was not naive and childish, but a finished work of art, expert in draftsmanship, intricate in detail, and unerring in color.'"

Snodgrass 1968

Yazzie, Sybil L. *Navajo*

RESIDENCE: Chinle, AZ
EDUCATION: Santa Fe, 1937
MEDIA: Tempera
PUBLISHED: Dunn (1968); Snodgrass (1968). *Arizona Highways* (July 1956)
PUBLIC COLLECTIONS: SM
EXHIBITS: AIW; NGA: London, England; Paris, France

Yazzie, Terry *Navajo*

RESIDENCE: Phoenix, AZ
MEDIA: Oil, watercolor, pen and ink, and pastel
EXHIBITS: HM/G

Yazzie, Tom K. *Navajo*

Born 1942
EDUCATION: U of AZ, "Southwest Indian Art Project," scholarship, summer 1960
PUBLISHED: Snodgrass (1968)
PUBLIC COLLECTIONS: BIA, IACB, SMNAI (woodcarving)
EXHIBITS: PAC, USDS

Yazzie, Tso *Navajo*

RESIDENCE: Flagstaff, AZ
PUBLISHED: Schiffer (1991)

Yazzie, Vivie *Navajo*

PUBLISHED: Snodgrass (1968)
PUBLIC COLLECTIONS: MNA

Yel Ha Yah Charlie (see Lee, Rev. Charles)

Yellow, Don *Standing Rock Sioux*

RESIDENCE: Rapid City, SD
EXHIBITS: RC

Francis J. Yellow

Yellow states that his contribution to "Indian Art" concerns identity and definition. He says that his art comes from the "Peoples" ways and is for them first and foremost. He is a Lakota artist, and has no wish to be known simply as an artist.

artist, p.c. 1994

Known primarily as a sculptor, Yellow's paintings are attracting attention for their contemporary depiction of classic ledger art.

Yellow, Francis J. *Standing River/Lower Brûlé Sioux*

A.K.A. Ikce Wicasa
Born 18 Aug 1954 in Pierre, SD; son of Henrietta and Francis Yellow; P/GP: Elizabeth and James Yellow; M/GP: Laura and Joseph Traversie
RESIDENCE: Bonduel, WI
MILITARY: U.S. Marine Corps, Vietnam
EDUCATION: BHSU, 1985; U of WI/M
MEDIA: Acrylic, watercolor, and prints
COMMISSIONS: *Sculptures:* Comprehensive Health Care Facility, Rosebud, SD; Unci Maka Arts Council, Eagle Butte, SD
PUBLIC COLLECTIONS: GM, IACB, IAIA, MIM, PM
EXHIBITS: EM; GM; IAIA/M; LIAS; NPTA; PM; RC; RE; Chicago (IL) Native American Cultural Center Exhibit; Western Illinois University, Macomb, IL; galleries in CO, IL, NM, and VA
SOLO EXHIBITS: Western Illinois University, Macomb, IL, 1993
AWARDS: BHIAE ('94, 1st, Governor's Award); LIAS ('93, 2-MA; '94); NPTA ('90; '94, 2-1st, Best of Show); RC ('84, 1st); RE ('94, President's Award); Lakota Arts Exhibit, H. V. J. Cultural Center, Cheyenne River Sioux Reservation ('94, 1st)
HONORS: *Scholarships and Fellowships:* Crazy Horse Scholarship, Crazy Horse Mountain, SD, 1983-1984; RC, Thunderbird Foundation Scholarship, 1984, 1986;

U of WI, Advanced Opportunity Fellowship, 1986, 1989. *Other:* LIAS, poster artist, 1994

YELLOW ARROW (see Shelton, Peter H., Jr.)

YELLOWBIRD (see Montileaux, Donald L.)

YELLOW BLANKET *Sioux*

Shinagi, Yellow Blanket

A.K.A. Schinagi

PUBLISHED: Snodgrass (1968)

PUBLIC COLLECTIONS: MNH/A

YELLOW EYES (see Peters, Sandra Turner)

YELLOW FEATHER *Mandan*

Sikchida (or *Sik Chida*)

Born ca. 1833-1834 near Fort Clark, ND

MEDIA: Watercolor and pencil

PUBLISHED: *Catlin, Bodmer, Miller,* Joslyn Art Museum (1963); Snodgrass (1968)

PUBLIC COLLECTIONS: BM, JAM, NNGCC

EXHIBITS: JAM

YELLOW HAIR (see Hood, Rance)

YELLOW HAIR (see Toppah, Herman)

YELLOWHAIR, JEFF *Kiowa*

RESIDENCE: Apache, OK

OCCUPATION: Artist

MEDIA: Acrylic

PUBLISHED: Boyd, et al. (1983). *Oklahoma Today* (Dec 1990)

EXHIBITS: AIE

AWARDS: AIE ('80, 1st; '81, 1st; '85; '86, Grand Award, Overall Best of Show; '86, 1st; '87, 1st)

YELLOWHAIR, ROBERT *Navajo*

Born 8 Aug 1937 in Na-Ah-Tee Canyon, north of Holbrook, AZ

EDUCATION: Carson

MEDIA: Oil and prints

PUBLISHED: *Dandrick's Travel Tips* (summer 1971), cover; *Another Book ... Another Culture,* National Library Week (Apr 1974), cover; *The Indian Trader* (Jan 1986)

PUBLIC COLLECTIONS: HM/G, SDMM

EXHIBITS: AAID, HM/G, NTF, OT, PAC

AWARDS: AAID ('73, Grand Award); HM/G ('71); NTF ('72, 1st, Grand Award; '73, 1st, Grand Award); OT ('72, Grand Award); Albuquerque, NM; Los Angeles, CA

YELLOWHAWK, JAMES MARK *Minniconjou Sioux/Onondaga*

Ce'Tan'Gi

A.K.A. Jim Yellow Hawk; Jim Yellowhawk

Born 5 June 1958 at Rapid City, SD

RESIDENCE: Dayton, OH

EDUCATION: Cheyenne-Eagle Butte (SD) High School, 1977; B.S., Marion (IN) College, 1981

OCCUPATION: Illustrator, layout artist, commercial artist, graphic designer, and painter

YELLOW BLANKET

"One of five artists whose works, commissioned and collected by Rudolf Cronau, 1880-1883, are now referred to as the Cronau Album (see Sinte)."

Snodgrass 1968

YELLOW FEATHER

"Son of a prominent Mandan chief. During their winter's sojourn at Fort Clark, near the Mandan villages, in 1883-1884, Prince Maximilian and Karl Bodmer were visited by a number of Indians who were fascinated by Bodmer's artistic talents. The White artist gave pencils, watercolors, and paper to some of these Indians and encouraged them to make pictures for the Prince's collection. These watercolors are the earliest known examples of paintings executed by Plains Indians in the White man's art medium. In their striving to portray the details of human and horse anatomy, of costume and accessories, these Indian artists produced paintings which are quite unlike the traditional picture-writing of their people. There are nine examples of this new style of painting in Prince Maximilian's collection. Four of them were executed by Yellow Feather, of whom the Prince wrote: 'He came almost every evening, when his favorite employment was drawing, for which he had some talent, though his figures were no better than those drawn by our children. (Catlin, Bodmer, Miller, exhibition catalog).'"

Snodgrass 1968

MEDIA: Oil, acrylic, watercolor, pencil, and prints

PUBLISHED: Zurko, ed. (1992). *The Indian Trader* (Dec 1981); *The Lakota Times* (20 Sept 1988); *The Lancaster Eagle Gazette* (2 Aug 1990)

COMMISSIONS: *Logos:* Women's Christian Society, Lakota Printing and The Cheyenne River Sioux Tribe Higher Education, Eagle Butte, SD. *Other:* Scioto Society, programs for a dramatic presentation onTecumseh; Tipi Press, note cards

PUBLIC COLLECTIONS: HCC

EXHIBITS: AIAF; CWAM; HPTU; ITAE; ITAE; LSS; NACLA; NPTA; NWAS; TAIAF; RC; RE; TM/NE; WHB; WTF; Cheyenne River Art Show and Women's Christian Society Art Show, Eagle Butte, SD; Marion (ID) College; Marion (ID) Mall Art Show; Grand County Art Show, Marion, ID; Cultural Heritage Series Exhibit, Columbus, OH; Native American Craft Show, Flint Ridge State Memorial; National Wesleyan Art Show, St. Louis, MO; Indian Nations Rendezvous and Trade Fair, Denver, CO; see also Awards

SOLO EXHIBITS: SIM

AWARDS: CSF/SD ('82, Outstanding Abstract Art Award); ITAE ('91, 1st); NPTA ('93); TAIAF ('94); RC ('82, 1st; '83; '92, 1st, Niederman Award); RC ('82, 1st; '83; '92, 1st, Neiderman Award); Power Art Show, Denver, CO ('81, Purchase Award)

HONORS: Cultural Heritage Series Exhibit, recognition, 1983; SJIS, poster artist

YELLOW HORSE *Northern Cheyenne*

Birth date unknown; died 1869 (?)

RESIDENCE: Once lived in the area of Bozeman, MT

MILITARY: U.S. Army

MEDIA: Watercolor, pencil, and pen and ink

PUBLISHED: Snodgrass (1968); Maurer (1977; 1992)

BOOKS ILLUSTRATED: Powell (1979)

PUBLIC COLLECTIONS: SI/OAA; Foundation for the Preservation of American Indian Art and Culture, Inc., Chicago, IL

EXHIBITS: VP

YELLOW HORSE

"In 1933, D. S. Warren of Iowa owned drawings by Yellow Horse that were photographed by the Smithsonian Institution. Then, the drawings were at the Iowa Historical Society in Des Moines; their present whereabouts are unknown."

Snodgrass 1968

Peter J. Powell, a recognized authority on many Plains Indian cultures, has identified Yellow Horse as being either Northern Cheyenne or Lakota. Since the 1950s, Powell has worked with some of Yellow Horse's original drawings and he favors the Northern Cheyenne designation.

Powell, p.c. 1993

YELLOW LODGE *Santee/Yankton Sioux*

RESIDENCE: Lived at Cannonball, ND

PUBLISHED: Snodgrass (1968). *Bulletin 173,* BAE (1960)

YELLOW LODGE

"The Yellow Lodge Winter Count, owned by Eugene Burdick of Williston, ND, and placed on indefinite loan with the North Dakota State Historical Museum in 1932, includes the years 1785-1786 to 1930-1931. A copy of this count, complete through 1951-1952, was kept by Teresa Yellow-lodge of Fort Yates, ND (see Bulletin 173, *BAE, 1960)."*

Snodgrass 1968

YELLOWMAN *Navajo*

Dinextsoii, Yellowman

A.K.A. Bennie James Nelson; Bennie J. Yellowman Nelson. Signature: Yellowman

Born 25 Oct 1952 in Ogden, UT; son of Virginia Henderson, weaver, and Tom D. Nelson, Baptist minister; P/GP: Mable Dinextsoii and Dinextsoii Beyeii; M/GP: Mary and William Henderson

RESIDENCE: Albuquerque, NM

EDUCATION: West Mesa High School, Albuquerque, NM, 1970; College of Santa Fe, NM, 1973

OCCUPATION: School bus driver, teacher, music minister; full-time sculptor and painter after 1977

MEDIA: Oil, acrylic, watercolor, pencil, pen and ink, and alabaster

PUBLISHED: *The Santa Fean* (Apr 1988); *Art-Talk* (Jan 1990)

COMMISSIONS: Southern Baptist Sunday School Board and Indian Quarterly Sunday School publications, illustrations

PUBLIC COLLECTIONS: HCC; Sears, Roebuck Co. Collection

EXHIBITS: ACA/ENP; ACS/MV; ACS/PG; AIAFM; CIM; CMN; HM/G; ITIC; NFSF; RC; SMIC; SWAIA; U of WV; WTF; Weems Artfest, Albuquerque, NM;

YELLOWMAN

In explaining his Indian name, Nelson says, "The name Yellowman has been handed down from generation to generation. It comes from a long time ago when the first Yellowman was presented at birth. (continued)

New Mexico Arts and Crafts Fair, Albuquerque; see also Awards

AWARDS: ACS/ENP (1978-92, 3-1st); ACS/MV; HM/G ('79, 1st); ITIC ('84; '85; '87, 1st; '89, 1st); NMSF ('77, 1st, Best of Show; '78, 1st; '79; '80-92, 2-1st, Best of Show); SMIC ('79); SWAIA (1978-1992, 1-1st; '93, 1st); Albuquerque (NM) Inter-Tribal Arts and Crafts Show ('78, 1st)

YELLOW NOSE *Ute*

Hehuwésse

A.K.A. Little Robe; Crow Indian

Born ca. 1850; died 1910

OCCUPATION: Warrior and painter

MEDIA: Watercolor, pen and ink, pencil, and crayon

PUBLISHED: Cohoe (1965); Snodgrass (1968); Maurer (1992)

PUBLIC COLLECTIONS: JAM, MAI, SI/OAA

EXHIBITS: JAM, MAI, NAP, VP, WWM

YELLOW OWL, ANTHONY *Blackfeet*

Snowman

SOLO/SPECIAL EXHIBITS: MPI (dual show), 1993

YELLOW TAIL *Plains*

PUBLISHED: Snodgrass (1968)

PUBLIC COLLECTIONS: SMNAI (buffalo hide painting)

YELLOW WOLF *Comanche*

A.K.A. Chief Yellow Wolf

PUBLISHED: Snodgrass (1968)

PUBLIC COLLECTIONS: RMAS (drawing, ca. 1859, on blue foolscap painted for Col. Lee, ca. 1859)

YENBA *Navajo*

MEDIA: Colored pencil and ink

PUBLISHED: King (1981)

EXHIBITS: AC/A

YEOMANS, DONALD *Haida/Cree*

Born 1958 in Prince Rupert, BC, Canada; son of Frances and Hector Yeomans; nephew of Freda Diesing (q.v.)

RESIDENCE: Canada

EDUCATION: Vancouver (BC) Community College; studied with his aunt, Freda Diesing, 1970-1971, and Robert Davidson (qq.v.)

OCCUPATION: Carver, jeweler, printmaker, and painter

PUBLISHED: Stewart (1979); Macnair, Hoover, and Neary (1980); Hall, Blackman, and Rickard (1981); McMasters, et al. (1993). *Native Voice* (Vol. 13, no. 2, 1984)

COMMISSIONS: Partial listing of twelve includes: British Columbia Sports Medicine Clinic, Vancouver, BC; British Columbia Provincial Department of Education, Vancouver, BC; Federal Business Development Bank, Vancouver, BC; Kam Tuts School, Vancouver, BC; Vancouver (BC) Community College, Langara Campus

PUBLIC COLLECTIONS: C/INAC, C/U of BC/MA

EXHIBITS: C/AG/GV; C/AG/TB; C/GM; C/IGV; C/INAC; C/MNBC; C/NETIA; C/RBCM; C/RSMC; C/TL; C/U of AB; C/U of BC/MA; SM; British Columbia Ministry of Tourism, San Francisco, CA; Douglas College, New Westminister, BC

YELLOWMAN

(continued) Indian people were named according to certain events that happened in their lives. When Yellowman was brought out of the hogan, the morning sun peaked over the horizon, casting a yellow light. The sun illuminated the child, thus giving him the name Yellowman. For many generations the name Yellowman was given and passed on. I received the name Yellowman from my father, Tom Dinextsoii Nelson." Nelson paints many different Indian cultures. He says, "I feel that as an Indian artist, one should not be limited to capturing only one tribe, but have the freedom to portray many cultures with respect and admiration for the beauty of each tribe and for what they contribute to us all as human beings." In addition to being a full-time artist, Nelson is a deacon and Minister of Music in the First Indian Baptist Church of Albuquerque, New Mexico.

artist, p.c. 1992

YELLOW NOSE

"When Yellow Nose was about four, he and his mother were captured on the Río Grande by Cheyennes and Arapahos led by Dive Backwards. His mother escaped, and he was adopted by Spotted Wolf, a Cheyenne chief. He was living near Geary, OK, in 1909. Three hundred and fifty of his ledger drawings were collected, ca. 1880, by John (continued)

YEPA, EMILINA *Jémez*

EDUCATION: Santa Fe, ca. 1932-1937
PUBLISHED: Dunn (1968); Snodgrass (1968)
EXHIBITS: NGA, 1953

YEPA, RITA *Jémez*

Born ca. 1944
EDUCATION: Jémez, ca. 1960
PUBLISHED: Snodgrass (1968)
EXHIBITS: AAIE, AIE, PAC
AWARDS: AIE

YEPA, JIMMIE *Jémez*

A.K.A. Jimmie Yeppa
EDUCATION: Santa Fe, ca. 1958
PUBLISHED: Snodgrass (1968)
EXHIBITS: MNM

YERXA, LEO *Ojibwa*

Born 5 Apr 1947 near Fort Frances, ON, Canada, on the Couchiching Reserve; brother of Wayne Yerxa (q.v.)
RESIDENCE: Fort Francis, ON, Canada
EDUCATION: Assiniboin Indian Residential School, Winnipeg, MB; Algonquin College, Ottawa, ON, 1967-1968; University of Waterloo, Kitchener, ON, 1974-1976
OCCUPATION: Trapper, hunter, guide, poet, photographer, free lance designer, graphic artist, and painter
MEDIA: Oil, acrylic, watercolor, mixed-media, film, and prints
PUBLISHED: McLuhan (1984); Menitove and Danford (1989); Podedworny (1989). *Indian News* (Dec 1968); *TOWOW* (Vol. 2, no. 3, 1970; Vol. 3, no. 2, 1975); *The Fort Frances Times* (Feb 3, 1971); *Imperial Oil Review* (Feb 1975); *The Toronto Globe and Mail* (8 Nov 1975); *The Winchester Press* (2 Jan 1976); *The Ottawa Citizen* (3 Mar 1978); *The Ottawa Review* (9 Mar 1978); *The Native Perspective* (Vol. 2, no. 9, 1978)
BOOKS ILLUSTRATED: Desbarats, ed. (1969)
COMMISSIONS: *Murals:* University of Waterloo, ON; University of Western Ontario, London, ON. *Other:* Series IV Olympic Coins, quill work designs, 1976; Federal Post Office, book on Indian Stamps
PUBLIC COLLECTIONS: C/AG/TB, C/CMC, C/INAC, HCC
EXHIBITS: C/AG/TB, C/CIIA, C/LTAT, C/ROM, C/WICEC, C/WCAA, NACLA
SOLO EXHIBITS: C/AG/TB; galleries in Ontario and Québec

YERXA, WAYNE *Ojibwa*

Born 1945 near Fort Frances, ON, Canada, on the Couchiching Reserve; brother of Leo Yerxa (q.v.)
RESIDENCE: Ontario, Canada, on the Couchiching Reserve
OCCUPATION: Trapper, hunter, guide, firefighter, and painter
MEDIA: Pen and ink
PUBLISHED: *Harrowsmith Magazine* (May 1979)
PUBLIC COLLECTIONS: HCC
EXHIBITS: C/ROM, C/WICEC; in the Fort Frances, ON, area

YONA (see McCarter, Jack)

YELLOW NOSE

(continued) Gregory Bourke and are now in the Museum of the American Indian collection."

Snodgrass 1968

According to Maurer (1992), "Yellow Nose grew up to be 'all Cheyenne' and a noted warrior leader. He was also one of the most extraordinary painters of his time."

YELLOW WOLF

"In the collection of RMAS is an oil portrait of Chief Yellow Wolf by Col. Arthur T. Lee, with the Eighth Infantry in Texas, who befriended Yellow Wolf."

Snodgrass 1968

LEO YERXA

Although his paintings often reflect his Ojibwa heritage, Yerxa is not a Native painter in the traditional sense. The subjects of his paintings do not come from traditional Indian designs or legends. His subjects have ranged from nudes to landscapes that reflect his interest in Oriental painting.

WAYNE YERXA

The artist's work is known for his use of white space and stylized forms in brilliant colors. His paintings reflect the spirit and legends of his people.

gallery brochure

YORK, DORIS J. *Oneida*

Metoxen

Born 14 Aug 1929 in Milwaukee, WI; daughter of Alice Grimm and Thomas Metoxen; M/GP: Augusta and John Grimm

RESIDENCE: San Diego, CA

EDUCATION: Sun Prairie (WI) High School, 1947; Andrews University, Berrien Springs, MI, 1953; U of CA/B; Alexander School of Painting; San Diego (CA) City College

OCCUPATION: Housewife and artist

MEDIA: Oil, acrylic, sand, and prints

PUBLIC COLLECTIONS: HCC

EXHIBITS: CNM; RC; TM/NE; Associated Senior Artist's Exhibitions, San Diego, CA; California Mid-Winter Fair, Imperial, CA; Hillcrest Community Center, San Diego, CA; People's Bank, National City, CA; San Diego (CA) City Hall; San Diego (CA) Art Institute; San Diego (CA) City Library; San Diego (CA) State University; see also Awards

SOLO EXHIBITS: San Pasqual Academy, Escondido, CA; San Diego (CA) Public Library, Paradise Hills Branch

AWARDS: Amateur Artists Association of America Exhibition, Las Vegas, NV ('84, 1st); Senior Women's Art Contest, San Diego, CA ('83, 1st; '84; '85); Small Works XI, San Diego, CA ('86, Juror's Purchase Prize)

YO SUMCE WITKE *Sioux*

PUBLISHED: Snodgrass (1968)

PUBLIC COLLECTIONS: MPM (pictographic style on paper)

YOUNG, CLEATIS *Cherokee*

RESIDENCE: St. David, AZ

EXHIBITS: CNM

YOUNG, MARY CECILIA BRESSER *Choctaw*

Born 14 Apr 1928 in Muskogee, OK; daughter of Lillie Willis and Herman Bresser.

EDUCATION: Muskogee (OK) Central High School, 1946; St. Mary's of Notre Dame, South Bend, IN; BC; studied under Joan Hill, Ruth M. White, Dick West (qq.v.), Roger Lee White, and John Arthur

OCCUPATION: Housewife and painter

PUBLISHED: Snodgrass (1968); Brody (1971)

EXHIBITS: AIE; FCTM; PAC; MNM; SAIEAIP; SN; Muskogee (OK) Annual Art Show; Muskogee (OK) Art Student's Guild; Oklahoma State Fair, Muskogee, OK

AWARDS: FCTM ('67; '68; '69, 1st; '70; '75, IH; '76, 1st, IH)

HONORS: Muskogee (OK) Annual Art Show, chairman, 1960

YOUNG, PHIL *Cherokee*

Born 1947 in Henryetta, OK

RESIDENCE: Oneonta, NY

EDUCATION: B.A., Tyler School of Art, Temple University, Philadelphia, PA, 1969; M. Div., Wesley Theological Seminary, Washington, D.C., 1974; M.F.A., American University, Washington, D.C., 1975

OCCUPATION: Educator, papermaker, and painter

MEDIA: Acrylic, sand, linen, cotton, organic fiber, and mixed-media

PUBLISHED: Ward, ed. (1990); Roberts, ed. (1992); Zurko, ed. (1992)

PUBLIC COLLECTIONS: IBM, San Diego, CA; Key Corporation, Albany, NY;

PHIL YOUNG

Major themes in Young's art work are the desecration and vandalism of the land because of greed and progress.

5th Biennial catalog, *HM, 1992*

Munson-Williams-Proctor Institute, Utica, NY; Planning Research Corporation, McLean, VA

EXHIBITS: Partial listing of more than sixty includes: HM; LGAM; OAC; OLO; OMA; PP; SS/CW; SU/NY; SUNY/O; WHB; Center of Contemporary Arts, Seattle, WA, 1992; Collegiate School, New York, NY, 1983; Hartwick College, Oneonta, NY, 1988; Holter Museum of Art, Helena, MT, 1989; Memphis (TN) State University, 1987; Munson-Williams-Proctor Institute of Art, Utica, NY, 1992; SUNY, Fine Arts Gallery, Oneonta, NY, 1991; see also Awards

SOLO EXHIBITS: SUNY Fine Arts Gallery, Oneonta, NY; Irene Cullis Gallery, Greensboro (NC) College; Upper Catskill Council on the Arts, Oneonta, NY

AWARDS: Berkeley Gallery, Meriden, NH ('84); Greenhill (NC) Gallery ('76); Upper Catskill Council on the Arts, Oneonta, NY ('79, 1st)

HONORS: *Scholarships and Grants:* Temple University, Treen Memorial Scholarship, 1967-1969; The American University, Cokesbury Scholarship, 1974-1975; Hartwick College, grant, 1981-1988. *Other:* Greensboro (NC) College, Teacher of the Year, 1977-1979; Greensboro (NC) College, Student Government Association, Faculty/Staff Award, 1976-1977

YOUNG, PHILLIP *Micmac*

Born 1938 on the Red Band Reserve in NB, Canada

RESIDENCE: Red Bank, NB, Canada

EDUCATION: Vespe George School of Art, Boston, MA; studied silkscreening at New Brunswick Provinceal Centre, Fredericton, NB, and Boston (MA) Museum of Fine Arts, Museum School

OCCUPATION: Painter and printmaker

MEDIA: Oil, acrylic, watercolor, and prints

PUBLISHED: Ward, ed. (1990)

EXHIBITS: AICH; C/CIIA; C/IAJE; C/PDF; CWAM; HMA; MAI; NACLA; NU/BC; OLO; RC; Boston (MA) Children's Museum; Expo '67, Indians of Canada Pavilion; Harvard University, Science Center, Cambridge, MA; see also Awards

AWARDS: Medford (MA) Arts Council Show ('80, 1st)

YOUNG BEAR, LEONARD *Mesquakie*

Born ca. 1930

RESIDENCE: Tama, IA

MEDIA: Charcoal and pastel

PUBLISHED: *Buy Native American* (summer 1986), catalog

PUBLIC COLLECTIONS: WWM

EXHIBITS: ISU; WWM; in IA, IL, and MN; see also Awards

AWARDS: National Dairy Cattle Congress Exhibit, Waterloo, IA

LEONARD YOUNG BEAR

The artist began sketching at age five but did not seriously work at art until he was about 40 years of age. In 1986, it was reported he was teaching his drawing technique to his five children.

Buy Native American *summer 1986*

YOUNG DEER (see Roberts, Frank)

YOUNGFOX, CECIL *Ojibwa/Métis*

Born 1942 in Blind River, ON, Canada; died 1987

RESIDENCE: Lived in Blind River, ON, Canada

EDUCATION: Longera College, Vancouver, BC

MEDIA: Acrylic

PUBLISHED: *The Sudbury Star* (12 June 1980); *The Sault Saint Marie Star* (28 Oct 1980; 10 Jan 1983; 27 May 1983); *Dimensions* (Mar/Apr 1981); *The Edmonton Journal* (21 Nov 1982); *The Native People* (26 Nov 1982)

COMMISSIONS: UNICF, 1982

EXHIBITS: C/NB; C/NCCT; C/WICEC; NACLA; Algoma University College,

Sault Saint Marie, ON; Canadian Embassy, Lisbon, Portugal; galleries in AB, BC, PQ, and ON

HONORS: Native Council of Canada, Ottawa, ON, Aboriginal Order of Canada

YOUNG MAN AFRAID OF HIS HORSES *Sioux*

Born 1830; died 1900 on the Pine Ridge Reservation, SD

RESIDENCE: Lived in the area of Pine Ridge, SD, in 1880

MEDIA: Paint on Buffalo Hide

PUBLISHED: Snodgrass (1968); Dockstader (1977)

PUBLIC COLLECTIONS: MAI

HONORS: Appointed head of the Bear People by Agent McGillicuddy, 1879; installed by White authorities as President of the Pine Ridge Indian Council and taken on trips to Washington, D.C.

YOUNG MAN AFRAID OF HIS HORSES

"The artist, a minor chief, opposed Red Cloud on the sale of Sioux land (see Hyde 1956)."

Snodgrass 1968

Young Man Afraid of His Horses (more correctly, Young Men Fear His Horses) was a strong friend of the Whites, although he worked to help his people and save their land. He and American Horse tried to convince the Sioux that to follow the Ghost Dancers would bring disaster. After the massacre at Wounded Knee Creek, he took a leading role in negotiations which led to somewhat fairer treatment of the Sioux. He attempted to protect the best interests of the Sioux in the only way he felt would succeed.

Dockstader 1977

YOUNGMAN, ALFRED *Chippewa/Plains Cree*

Eagle Chief

A.K.A. Alfred B. Youngman; Alfred B. Young Man

Born 12 Apr 1948 in Browning, MT; son of Lillian K. Daniels and Joe Youngman; P/GM: Patricia Ground Woman; M/GF: Edward Bonshie

RESIDENCE: Lethbridge, AB, Canada

EDUCATION: IAIA, High School, 1966; IAIA, 1966-1968; B.A., Slade School of Fine Arts, University College of London, England, 1972; M.F.A., U of MT, 1974; Northern Montana College, Havre, MT; Rutgers University, New Brunswick, NJ

OCCUPATION: Teacher, folk singer, media specialist, college professor, writer, photographer, and painter

MEDIA: Oil, acrylic, pen and ink, and prints

PUBLISHED: Brody (1971); Ray, ed. (1972); New (1974; 1979); Highwater (1976; 1978b; 1980); Amerson, ed. (1981); Little Bear, Boldt, and Long, eds. (1984); Hill (1992); McMasters, et al. (1993). *Southwest Art* (June 1974; spring 1985); *American Heritage* (Oct 1976), cover; *The Saskatchewan Indian* (May 1977; Feb/Mar 1982, cover); *The Lethbridge Herald* (27-28 Oct 1984); *Parallelogramme* (Apr/May 1988); *Whetstone,* C/U of L (fall 1988); *Art News* (Feb 1992)

COMMISSIONS: Northwest Regional Laboratories, Portland, OR, drawings

PUBLIC COLLECTIONS: C/INAC; C/U of L; IAIA; MPI; MSU; U of CA/LB; Indian Association of Alberta, Edmonton, AB; Northwest Regional Laboratories, Portland, OR; Peigan Band Administration, Brocket, AB; Rocky Boy (MT) Elementary School; Universiade Collection of Native Art, Edmonton, AB

EXHIBITS: ACMWA; AICH; C/NWNG; C/PHT; C/U of L; CIA; CIAE; CTC; IAIA; MFA/O; MFA/S; MNM; MPI; ND; OWE; PAC; PAIC; PDN; SN; SPIM; U of CA/D; U of MT; College of Great Falls, MT; Yakima (WA) Cultural Center; galleries in the U.S. and Canada

SOLO EXHIBITS: MPI; U of MT; University College of London, England, 1971

AWARDS: CIAE ('74, 1st); SN ('68, 1st)

HONORS: *Scholarships and Grants:* Partial listing includes: BIA, University College of London, England, 1968-1972; U of MT, 1972-1974; Rutgers University, Minority Advancement Program, New Brunswick, NJ, 1989; American Indian Graduate Program, Albuquerque, NM, 1990

YOUVELLA, ELVIRA *Hopi*

MEDIA: Watercolor

PUBLISHED: Seymour (1968)

PUBLIC COLLECTIONS: IACB/DC

YOWYTEWA, ARTHUR (see Yoyetewa, Arthur)

YOYETEWA, ARTHUR *Hopi*

A.K.A. Arthur Yowytewa
MEDIA: Tempera
PUBLISHED: Seymour (1968)
PUBLIC COLLECTIONS: IACB/DC

YUTSUWUNA (see Eckiwaudah, Tennyson)

YUXWELUPTUN (see Paul, Lawrence B.)

YUXWELUPTUN, LAWRENCE PAUL (see Paul, Lawrence B.)

YUYAHEOVA, BEVINS *Hopi*

Lomaquaftewa
Born 11 Dec 1938; died Sept 1969 in an accident
RESIDENCE: Lived on Second Mesa, AZ
MEDIA: Watercolor
PUBLISHED: Tanner (1973); Broder (1978)
PUBLIC COLLECTIONS: MNA
EXHIBITS: ASF, HM/G, PAC, SN
AWARDS: ASF ('68, 1st); HM/G ('68); PAC ('69)

BEVINS YUYAHEOVA

Yuyaheova was strongly influenced by Mike Kabotie who started him in painting. His work was abstract, painted in soft colors using Hopi symbolic designs.

Tanner 1973

Z (see Yazzie, Johnson)

ZAHNE, FRED *Navajo*

Born 19 July 1917 in Marty, SD
PUBLIC COLLECTIONS: MNA

ZEPHIER, ADALBERT, SR. *Yankton Sioux*

RESIDENCE: Flandreau, SD
MILITARY: U.S. Army, 1940-1946
EDUCATION: Rapid City (SD) High School, 1932-1934; Art Institute, Minneapolis, MN, 1967; home instruction art course
OCCUPATION: Billboard artist, counselor, art teacher, commercial artist, and full-time artist
MEDIA: Oil, pencil, pen and ink, wood, and prints
BOOKS ILLUSTRATED: Brown (1970)
COMMISSIONS: *Murals:* Gregory, SD. *Other:* billboards in South Dakota
EXHIBITS: AICA; MIC; NSTC/SD; PIE; RC; SI; SIM; SMIC; U of SD; Brookings (SD) Fine Arts Center; Commercial State Bank, Wagner, SD; Prairie Fine Arts Exhibit, Chamberlain, SD; Yankton (SD) College; Pipestone (MN) National Monument; see also Awards
SOLO EXHIBITS: SIM
AWARDS: PIE ('68, 1st); SI ('67, Certificate of Recognition, Exhibitors Award); Brookings (SD) Fine Arts Club ('77, 1st)

ADALBERT ZEPHIER SR.

The artist has been painting since 1959. His work is often a combination of European and Native American painting styles.

artist, p.c. 1990

ZEPHIER, SHERMAN *Yankton Sioux*

Born 13 Mar 1957
RESIDENCE: Russell, MN
EDUCATION: Marty (SD) Indian School; Southwest State University, Marshall, MN; IAIA
EXHIBITS: IAIA; RC; Southwest State University, Marshall, MN; Pipestone (MN) National Monument
HONORS: BYU, National Indian Poster, 1977

ZEPKO ETTEE (see Big Bow)

ZEYOUMA, PHILLIP *Hopi*

EDUCATION: Santa Fe, ca. 1932-1933
MEDIA: Watercolor
PUBLISHED: Dunn (1968); Snodgrass (1968)
PUBLIC COLLECTIONS: DAM, MRFM
EXHIBITS: NGA

ZIEGLER, ALFRED Y. *Brûlé Sioux*

Big Heart
Born 24 May 1918 in Lower Brûlé, SD; son of Laura and Elmer Ziegler
RESIDENCE: Embudo, NM
MILITARY: U.S. Army, WWII
EDUCATION: SJIS; Trade School, Chicago, IL
OCCUPATION: Rancher, rodeo contestant, hunter, trapper, sculptor, and painter
MEDIA: Oil, wood, stone, and bronze
PUBLISHED: *The Indian Trader* (Jan 1980)
PUBLIC COLLECTIONS: SI, SIM, SJIS
EXHIBITS: Partial listing spanning more than sixty years includes: CIM; HM/G; HS/SD; IAIA; RC; SIM; South Dakota State Fair; Native American Indian Art

ALFRED Y. ZIEGLER

Ziegler is a self-taught, multi-media artist who is best known for his bronze sculptures. He is one of a limited number of sculptors who make their own molds and do their own casting.

artist, p.c. 1992

DETAIL: *Pictograph of Zotom*, ca. 1870–1880.

Center, Phoenix, AZ; Native American Center, Minneapolis, MN
SOLO EXHIBITS: SIM
AWARDS: CIM ('86, Best of Show); HM/G ('71, 1st)
HONORS: South Dakota Cowboy and Western Heritage Hall of Fame, inducted, 1981

ZILLIOUX, MIKE MEDICINE HORSE *Pima/Sioux/Cheyenne*

Born 9 Nov 1952
RESIDENCE: Laveen, AZ
EDUCATION: South Mountain High School, Phoenix, AZ, 1970; U of N AZ, 1970-1973; A.A., IAIA, 1975; United States International University, San Diego, CA, 1976
MEDIA: Watercolor
EXHIBITS: IAIA; Rhode Island School of Design (traveling exhibit), 1975; NEA, 1974

ZINTALA GALESHKA (see Spotted Tail)

ZONEKEUH *Kiowa (?)*

Zonekeuh, Teeth
A.K.A. Zone Keuh
Birth date unknown; died 1879 of tuberculosis
EDUCATION: Tarrytown; Hampton
PUBLISHED: Snodgrass (1968)
PUBLIC COLLECTIONS: YU/BRBML
EXHIBITS: BPG

ZONEKEUH

"The artist was among the 72 Plains Indians taken as prisoners from Fort Sill, OK, to Fort Marion, St. Augustine, FL, in 1875."

Snodgrass 1968

ZOTIGH, BARBARA *Kiowa/Arapaho/Isleta*

Tallamonts
A.K.A. Barbara Tallamonts Zotigh; Barbara Zotigh Showmake; Barbara Shoemake
Born 29 Sept 1925 in Detroit, MI; daughter of Carrie Hunt and Carew H. Tallamonts
RESIDENCE: Tulsa, OK
EDUCATION: Haskell, 1942; Haskell Business College, 1943; U of KS; St. Anthony's Hospital School, 1947; U of Tulsa
OCCUPATION: Radiology technician, chief radiation therapist and dosimetrist, and artist
PUBLISHED: Snodgrass (1968)
EXHIBITS: FAIEAIP, PAC, SN
AWARDS: PAC

BARBARA ZITIGH

"The artist has been painting since about 1961. She has been most encouraged by Mrs. Homer Abbott and Tom Manhart."

Snodgrass 1968

ZO TOM (see Zotom, Paul Caryl)

ZOTOM, PAUL CARYL *Kiowa*

Podaladalte, Snake Head
A.K.A. Zo Tom; The Biter or Hole Biter
Born ca. 1853; died 27 Apr 1913 in Oklahoma; son of Sahpooly, "Owl" (Mother) and Keintikead, "White Shield," full-blooded Kiowa
EDUCATION: Hampton; Paris Hill, near Utica, NY
OCCUPATION: Warrior, Episcopal deacon and missionary, and artist
MEDIA: Colored pencil
PUBLISHED: Dunn (1968); Snodgrass (1968); Peterson (1971); Highwater (1976; 1978b; 1986); Dockstader (1977); Silberman (1978); Schmid and Houlihan

PAUL CARYL ZOTOM

"The artist was among the 72 Plains Indians taken as prisoners from Fort Sill, OK, to Fort Marion, St. Augustine, FL, in 1875."

Snodgrass 1968

At Fort Marion, with the encouragement of Captain Pratt, Zotom earned money producing sketchbooks of drawings and painting ceramics and fans. Once released from prison, Zotom spent three years in the east. By 1881 he was baptized Paul Caryl Zotom and became an ordained deacon of the Episcopal church. He then returned to Indian Territory to establish a mission. Zotom's only other recorded art works were done some twenty years later when he painted tipi models for anthropologist James Mooney.

Maurer 1992

(1980); Fawcett and Callander (1982); Batkin (1983); Hoffman, et al. (1984); Sprague, et al. (1986); Maurer (1992). *Native Peoples* (summer 1993)

COMMISSIONS: Omaha Exposition, model tipi coverings, 1898; series of buckskin shield covers

PUBLIC COLLECTIONS: FAC/CS, HI, MAI, YU/BRBML

EXHIBITS: BPG, FAC/CS, HM, IK, NAP, OMA, VP

ZSHINGKA HEKA (see Standingbear, George Eugene)

ZUAZUA, MICHAEL *Mescalero Apache*

RESIDENCE: Mescalero, NM

PUBLISHED: Snodgrass (1968)

EXHIBITS: MNM, SN

AWARDS: SN ('67)

ZUNI, STAN J. *Isleta/San Juan*

Marked Mountain Man

A.K.A. Stanley J. Zuni

Born 1 Nov 1947

RESIDENCE: Los Angeles, CA

EDUCATION: B.S., B.A., Roosevelt University, Chicago, IL, 1972; M.A., U of C/LA, 1982; U of C/LA, 1982-1986

OCCUPATION: Cinematographer, sound and video technician, editor, writer, script writer, media consultant, lecturer, photographer, and painter

MEDIA: Various paint media, gourd, and film

EXHIBITS: CSU/LB, MAI, U of NM

HONORS: U of CA/LA, Dorothy Danforth Compton Fellowship, 1982-1986

ZUYATERILA (see Tough Soldier)

Tribal Index

Cheyenne

Chickasaw

Abbreviations

AA Armory for the Arts, Santa Fe, NM

AAA American Academy of Art, Chicago, IL

AAA/T *Avenue of American Art Tour of United States.* Conducted by Winifred Scott, 1951-1953.

AAE *All-Alaska Juried Exhibition*, Anchorage, AK (annual, 1st - 1964)

AAID *All-American Indian Days.* Sheridan, WY (annual in Aug)

AAIE *American Indian Exposition.* Sponsored by the American Indian Center, Chicago, IL. (annual 1st - 1953)

AAIEAE *American Indian and Eskimo Art Exhibition and Stage Pageant*, second Annual, 1964. Sponsored by the American Indian and Eskimo Cultural Foundation, Washington, D.C.

AAM American Art Market, Blackfeet Cultural Program, Browning, MT (annual, 1st - 1992)

AANNAAC Association for the Advancement of Native North American Arts and Crafts, Warnerville, NY. Publications: *Iroquois Arts: A Directory Of A People And Their Work*, 1983

AAPSC *All-American Pro-Ski Classic.* Ruidoso, NM

AAUW American Association of University Women

AB Art Bank, Alaskan State Council on the Arts, Juneau, AK

ABQM Albuquerque Museum, Albuquerque, NM

AC/A *Native American Painting.* Organized by Amarillo Art Center, Amarillo, TX, 1981-1983. (exhibit, tour)

AC/B Berkeley Art Center, Berkeley, CA

AC/BC Bemidji Community Arts Center, Bemidji, MN

AC/D Duluth Art Center, Duluth, MN

AC/DS Daybreak Star Art Center, Seattle, WA (collection)

AC/H Hockaday Center for the Arts, Kalispell, MT

AC/HC Hastings College Art Center, Hastings, NE

AC/K Kimball Art Center, Park City, UT

AC/NC Nobles City Art Center, Worthington, MN

AC/OH Oscar Howe Art Center, Mitchell, SD

AC/OHC Old Hyde Park Art Center, Tampa, FL

AC/R Rochester Art Center, Rochester, MI

AC/RM Roswell Museum and Art Center, Roswell, NM

AC/S Summit Art Center, Summit, NJ

AC/SA *Salina Art Center Exhibit.* Salina, KS (annual, juried)

AC/SD Sedona Arts Center, Sedona, AZ

AC/SL Salt Lake Art Center, Salt Lake City, UT

AC/SP Spiva Art Center, Joplin, MO (annual, juried)

AC/SW Southwest Art Center, Dallas, TX

AC/SWA Seattle Center for the Arts, Seattle, WA

AC/T Tempe Arts Center, Tempe, AZ

AC/VM Virginia McClune Arts Center, Petoskey, MI

AC/W Walker Art Center, Minneapolis, MN

AC/Y Yellowstone Art Center, Billings, MT

AC/Z Zanesville Art Center, Zanesville, OH

ACA Arizona Commission on the Arts, Phoenix, AZ

ACAI *Aspen/Snowmass Celebration for the American Indian.* Sponsored by the National Museum of the American Indian, Smithsonian Institution, Aspen, CO. (annual, juried, 1st - 1991)

ACC Arts Club of Chicago, Chicago, IL. *Exhibition of American Indian Paintings and Applied Arts*, 1925

ACCC Art Center of Corpus Christi, Corpus Christi, TX (annual, juried, 1st - 1970)

ACCD Art Center, College of Design, Los Angeles, CA

ACE *Alaska Centennial Exhibition.* Anchorage, AK, 1966

ACE/I *Exhibition of Iroquois Arts and Crafts.* University of Pennsylvania Museum, Philadelphia, PA

ACEAA L'Association Canadienne des Eludes d'Art Autochtone, Hull, PQ, Canada

ACM Anadarko City Museum, Anadarko, OK

ACMWA Amon Carter Museum of Art, Fort Worth, TX

ACS/EM *Iroquois Confederacy Arts and Crafts Exhibition.* Everson Museum of Art of Syracuse and Onondaga County, Syracuse, NY, 1972

ACS/ENP *Eight Northern Pueblos Council Arts and Crafts Show.* San Ildefonso Pueblo, Española, NM (annual, 1st - 1974)

ACS/FR *Flint Ridge Indian Arts and Crafts Show.* Flint Ridge, OH

ACS/H *Houdenosaunee Arts and Crafts Show and Buffalo Roast.* Onondaga, NY

ACS/MV *Mesa Verde Indian Arts and Crafts Show.* Mesa Verde, CO. Sponsored by Farmington (NM) Inter-Tribal Indian Organization. (annual, 1st - 1982)

ACS/PG *Pueblo Grande Arts and Crafts Show.* Phoenix, AZ

ACS/RSC *Rose State College Native American Arts and Crafts Show.* Midwest City, OK (annual, 1st - 1980)

ACS/SC *St. Charles Arts and Crafts Show.* St. Charles, IL

ACS/SM *Speelyi-Mi Arts and Crafts Exhibition.* Yakima, WA

ACS/SW *Southwest Arts and Crafts Festival.* Albuquerque, NM (annual, 1st - 1971)

ACS/TOWA *Towa Arts and Crafts Show.* Jémez Pueblo, NM (annual, 1st - 1991)

ADIA *America Discovers Indian Art.* Sponsored by the Office of Economic Opportunity. Exhibited at the Smithsonian Institution, Washington, D.C. (regional competitions - Arizona State University, University of Utah, and University of South Dakota)

AEOP/T *Aquachromatic Exhibit and Original Palette Permanent Collection.* Sponsored by M. Grumbacher, Inc., New York, NY, 1955. (exhibit, tour)

AF Amerind Foundation, Dragoon, AZ

AFA *Two-Arrows Exhibition.* Sponsored by the American Federation of Arts. Paintings from the collection of the AIHA. (exhibit, tour)

AFNA *Alaska Festival of Native Arts.* Anchorage Museum, Anchorage, AK, 1977

AGAA Addison Gallery of American Art, Phillips Academy, Andover, MA

AH Atlantic House, Inc., Provincetown, MA

AHALA *Allan Houser: A Life in Art.* Organized by Museum of New Mexico, Santa Fe, NM, 1992. (exhibit, tour)

AHM High Museum of Art, Atlanta Art Association, Atlanta, GA

AHM/CO Aurora History Museum, Aurora, CO

AHNHG Aiea Heights Naval Hospital Gallery, Honolulu, HI

AI *Abstract Illusionism.* Organized by Museum of Fine Arts, Springfield, MA, and Danforth Museum, Framingham, MA, 1979.

AIAI American Indian Archaeological Institute, Washington, CT

AIAC *American Indian Arts Collection Show.* Oklahoma City, OK, 1981

AIAE *American Indian Art Exhibit.* Sinte Gleska University, Rosebud, SD

AIAE/WSU *American Indian Art Exhibition.* Wayne State University, Detroit, MI (annual, 1st - 1964)

AIAF *American Indian Art Festival.* Sponsored by Westheimer Colony Association, Inc., Houston, TX. (annual)

AIAFM *American Indian Artfestival and Market.* Dallas, TX. Sponsored by American Indian Arts Council of Dallas. (annual in Nov, 1st - 1990)

AIAS *All-Indian Art Show*, Spokane, WA

AIATC *Art of Indian America - Traditional and Contemporary.* Institute of American Indian Arts, Santa Fe, NM (exhibit, tour - U.S., Europe, and South America)

AICA *American Indian and Cowboy Artists National Western Art Exhibition.* Sponsored by San Dimas Festival of Western Arts and American Indian and Cowboy Arts, Inc., San Dimas, CA. (annual, 1st - 1977)

AICA/SF American Indian Contemporary Arts, San Francisco, CA

AICH American Indian Community House, New York, NY

AIE *American Indian Exposition.* Anadarko, OK (annual, 1st - 1932)

AIE/T *First American Indian Exposition.* Tulsa, OK, 1936

AIEC *American Indian Exposition and Congress.* Tulsa, OK, 1937

AIHA Albany Institute of History and Art, Albany, NY

AIHEC American Indian Health Education Conference, Billings, MT (juried art exhibit, 1992)

AII American Indian Institute, Wichita, KS

AIIM *American Indian Images.* Joplin, MO (juried, 1989)

AIPP *Art in Public Places.* Sponsored by New Mexico State Arts Division, Santa Fe, NM, 1986.

AIPSN *American Indian Painting Since 1900.* Sponsored by Kansas Arts Council and Wichita Art Museum, KS, 1992. (exhibit, tour)

AIW *American Indian Week.* Tulsa County Fairgrounds, Tulsa, OK (annual, 1st - 1935; discontinued)

AIWR *American Indian and Western Relic Show.* Pasadena, CA (annual, juried)

AIWSAF *American Indian Woman's Spring Art Festival.* Indian Pueblo Cultural Center, Albuquerque, NM, 1980

AK Abbott Kimball, Inc., New York, NY (collection)

AKM Akwesasne Museum, Hogansburg, NY

Albuquerque Albuquerque Indian School, Albuquerque, NM

ALCC Akwesasne Library and Cultural Center, Akwesasne, Cornwall Island, ON, Canada

Alfred Alfred University, Alfred, NY

AM Arnot Art Museum, Elmira, NY

ANC *Art for a New Century.* Civic Fine Arts Center, Sioux Falls, SD, and South Dakota Art Museum, Brookings, SD, 1989

ANCAIC *Annual National Congress of the American Indian Convention and Exhibition.* Rapid City, SD (annual, 1st - 1944; Albuquerque, NM, 1979)

AOSOS *Akwesasne: Our Strength, Our Spirit.* World Trade Center, New York, NY, 1984

ARC Atlantic Richfield Corporation (collection)

ASF Arizona State Fair, Phoenix, AZ

ASL Art Students League, New York, NY

ASM Arizona State Museum, University of Arizona, Tucson, AZ

ASM/AH Alaska State Museum, Stonington Fine Art Gallery, Anchorage, AK

ASM/AK Alaska State Museum, Juneau, AK

ASMG Augusta Savage Memorial Gallery, University of Massachusetts, Amherst, MA

ASPS *Annual Southwest Print and Drawing Exhibition.* Dallas Museum of Art, Dallas, TX, 1964

ASU Arizona State University, Tempe, AZ

ASU/M Arizona State University Museum, Tempe, AZ

ASV *A Separate Vision.* 1991 (exhibit, tour)

AU/EX *American University Alumni Art Exhibition.* Chevy Chase, MD, 1986

AUG Augustana College, Sioux Falls, SD

AVIM Antelope Valley Indian Museum, Agua Dulce, CA

AW *Art-In-The-Woods.* Corporate Woods, Overland Park, KS, 1989 (juried)

AW/HH *Art Works 1987.* Holland Hall Middle School, Tulsa, OK

AWC Arizona Western College, Yuma, AZ

BA Bank of America, Studio City, CA (collection)

BA/AZ Bank of America, Phoenix, AZ (collection)

BAA Bloomington Normal Art Association, Bloomington, IL

BAC *Boston Art Club Exhibition.* Boston, MA, 1932

BAE Bureau of American Ethnology, Smithsonian Institution, Washington, D.C.

BAE/AR Bureau of American Ethnology, *Annual Report*, Smithsonian Institution, Washington, D.C.

BAE/B Bureau of American Ethnology, *Bulletin*, Smithsonian Institution, Washington, D.C.

BAM Baltimore Museum of Art, Baltimore, MD

BB *Buffalo Bash*. Sponsored by Red Earth, Inc. and the Center of the American Indian, Kirkpatrick Center, Oklahoma City, OK. (annual, 1st - 1989)

BBHC Buffalo Bill Historical Center, Cody, WY. *Buffalo Bill Art Show* (annual, 1st - 1981)

BC Bacone College, Bacone, OK

BC/McG McCombs Gallery, Bacone College, Bacone, OK

BCAM Art Center of Battle Creek, Battle Creek, MI. *Pastel Competition* (annual, 1st - 1987)

BEAIAC *Biennial Exhibition of American Indian Arts and Crafts*. United States Department of the Interior, Washington, D.C., 1967

BECB Buffalo Erie County Bank, NY (collection)

BENEDICTINE Benedictine Heights College, Tulsa, OK

BF Blandin Foundation, Grand Rapids, MN (collection, exhibits)

BG Botts Gallery, Albuquerque, NM

BG/MI Bergsma Gallery, Grand Rapids, MI (two juried exhibits, 1985)

BHAA Black Hills Art Association, Spearfish, SD

BHH Beverly Hills Hotel and Beverly Hilton Hotel, Beverly Hills, CA

BHIAE *Black Hills Indian Art Exposition*. Rapid City, SD

BHSU Black Hills State University, Spearfish, SD

BI Butler Institute of American Art, Youngstown, OH

BIA Bureau of Indian Affairs, United States Department of the Interior, Washington, D.C.

BIA/A Bureau of Indian Affairs, Aberdeen, SD

BIA/B Bureau of Indian Affairs, Billings, MT

BIA/D Bureau of Indian Affairs, Anadarko, OK

BIA/M Bureau of Indian Affairs, Muskogee, OK

BIA/P Bureau of Indian Affairs, Portland, OR

BIA/R Bureau of Indian Affairs, Rosebud, SD

BLACK MT Black Mountain College, near Black Mountain, NC

BLQ *By the Light of the Qulliq*. Smithsonian Institution Traveling Exhibition Service, Washington, D.C., 1979. Art work from the M. F. Feheley Collection. (exhibit, tour)

BM Berne Museum, Berne, Switzerland

BM/B Brooklyn Museum of Art, Brooklyn, NY

BM/CO Belmar Museum, Lakewood, CO

BMA Birmingham Museum of Art, Birmingham, AL

BMJ Bezalel Museum of Jerusalem, Jerusalem, Israel

BNIAS *Bismarck National Indian Art Show*. Sponsored by the Chamber of Commerce and Bismarck Art Association, Bismarck, ND, 1963.

BNR Burlington Northérn Railroad Collection

BPG *Beyond the Prison Gates: The Fort Marion Experience and its Artistic Legacy*. Organized by The National Cowboy Hall of Fame and Western Heritage Center, Oklahoma City, OK, 1993. (exhibit, tour)

BRMA Boca Raton Museum of Art, Boca Raton, FL

BSIM *Big Sky Indian Market*. Billings, MT (annual in Aug)

BSU Bemidji State University, Bemidji, MN

BU Baylor University, Waco, TX

BYU Brigham Young University, Provo, UT

C/AAF Alberta Art Foundation, Government of Alberta, Edmonton, AB, Canada (collection)

C/AC *Art Credo*. Ottawa, ON, Canada (annual, 1st - 1976)

C/AC/AE Agnes Etherington Art Centre, Kingston, ON, Canada

C/AC/B Bowman Arts Centre, Lethbridge, AB, Canada

C/AC/BA Brandon Allied Arts Center, Brandon, MB, Canada

C/AC/D Dalhousie Art Centre, Halifax, NS, Canada

C/AC/M Meewasin Centre, Saskatoon, SK, Canada

C/AC/MS Macdonald Stewart Art Centre, Guelph, ON, Canada

C/AC/P Portage Arts Centre, Portage La Prairie, MB, Canada

C/AC/PA Port Alberni Art Centre, Port Alberni, BC, Canada

C/AC/S Centre Strathearn, Montréal, PQ, Canada

C/ACA Alberta College of Art, Calgary, AB, Canada

C/ACC AMACO Canada Limited, Calgary, AB, Canada (collection)

C/ACCCNA *A Celebration of Contemporary Canadian Native Art*. Organized by Woodland Indian Cultural Educational Centre, Brantford, ON, Canada, 1987. (exhibit, tour - United States)

C/ACSV Arts and Crafts Society of Victoria, Victoria, BC, Canada

C/AFIA *Atlantic Festival of Indian Arts*. Dalhousie Arts Centre, Halifax, NS, Canada

C/AG/B Burnaby Art Gallery, Burnaby, BC, Canada

C/AG/CC Confederation Centre Art Gallery and Museum, Charlottetown, PQ, Canada

C/AG/D Dalhousie Art Gallery, Halifax, NS, Canada

C/AG/E Edmonton Art Gallery, Edmonton, AB, Canada

C/AG/G Glenhurst Art Gallery, Brantford, ON, Canada

C/AG/GV Art Gallery of Greater Victoria, Victoria, BC, Canada

C/AG/H Art Gallery of Hamilton, ON, Canada

C/AG/IGEA Inuit Gallery of Eskimo Art, Toronto, ON, Canada

C/AG/LR London Regional Art Gallery, London, ON, Canada

C/AG/M Mendel Art Gallery, Saskatoon, SK, Canada

C/AG/MSVU Mount St. Vincent University Art Gallery, Halifax, NS, Canada

C/AG/MU Memorial University Art Gallery, St. John, NB, Canada

C/AG/NS Art Gallery of Nova Scotia, Halifax, NS, Canada

C/AG/O Art Gallery of Ontario, Toronto, ON, Canada

C/AG/OV Oakville Centennial Gallery, Oakville, ON, Canada

C/AG/Q Queens Art Gallery, Sackville, NB, Canada

C/AG/S Surrey Art Gallery, Surrey, BC, Canada

C/AG/SA Southern Alberta Art Gallery, Lethbridge, AB, Canada

C/AG/SAW Saw Gallery, Ottawa, ON, Canada

C/AG/SM Art Gallery of Southwestern Manitoba, Brandon, MB, Canada

C/AG/TB Thunder Bay Art Gallery, Thunder Bay, ON, Canada

C/AG/TT Tom Thomson Memorial Art Gallery, Owen Sound, ON, Canada

C/AG/U of L University of Lethbridge Art Gallery, Lethbridge, AB, Canada

C/AG/U of S Gallerie d'Art du Centre Culturel de l'Universite de Sherbrooke, Sherbrooke, PQ, Canada

C/AG/V Vancouver Art Gallery, Vancouver, BC, Canada

C/AG/W Whetung Art Gallery, Curve Lake, ON, Canada

C/AG/WI Art Gallery of Windsor, Windsor, ON, Canada

C/AG/WGP Walter G. Phillips Gallery, Banff, AB, Canada

C/AG/WP Winnipeg Art Gallery, Winnipeg, MB, Canada

C/AGM Alexander Galt Museum, Lethbridge, AB, Canada

C/AGO/U of G Art Gallery of Ontario, University of Guelph, Guelph, ON, Canada

C/AIAC Alberta Indian Arts and Crafts Society, Edmonton, AB, Canada (collection)

C/AM *Asum Mena.* Front Gallery, Edmonton, AB, Canada, 1986 (juried)

C/AMK *Anishnabe Meekum.* First juried show of Manitoulin Painters, 1980. (exhibit, tour of ON, Canada)

C/AMO *Art Mohawk '92.* Strathern Centre, Montréal, PQ, Canada, Jan 1992

C/AMR *Arctic Mirror.* Organized by the Canadian Museum of Civilization, Hull, PQ, 1990.

C/ANIWS *All Native Indian Womens' Show: Images of Canadian Heritage.* Vancouver, Canada, 1986

C/ARIA *Atlantic Region Indian Art Juried Exhibition.* Organized by the Department of Indian and Northern Affairs Canada, Manuge Gallery, Halifax, NS, Canada, 1985. (tour)

C/AV *Arctic Vision: Art of the Canadian Inuit.* Sponsored by the Department of Indian and Northern Affairs Canada and Canadian Arctic Producers, Ottawa, ON, Canada, 1984-1986. (tour)

C/BCA Banff Center for the Arts, Banff, AB, Canada

C/BCC Burlington Cultural Centre, Burlington, ON, Canada

C/BJNJ *Bò Jou, Nee Jee: Profiles of Canadian Indian Art.* National Museum of Man, Ottawa, ON, Canada (exhibit, tour)

C/BLPD *Baker Lake Prints and Drawings.* Circulated by Winnipeg Art Gallery, Winnipeg, MB, Canada, 1973-1974. (exhibit, tour)

C/BSFA Banff School of Fine Arts, Banff, AB, Canada

C/BU Brandon University, Brandon, MB, Canada

C/BWF *Buckhorn Wildlife Festival.* Buckhorn, ON, Canada

C/CA Centre d'Art, Baie St. Paul, PQ, Canada

C/CAP Canadian Arctic Producers Ltd., Ottawa, ON, Canada (collection)

C/CB *Chisel and Brush.* Department of Indian Affairs and Northern Development, Ottawa, ON, Canada, 1985-1985 (exhibit, tour)

C/C *Changers: A Spiritual Renaissance.* Sponsored by National Indian Arts and Crafts Corporation, Ottawa, ON, Canada, 1990. (exhibit, tour)

C/CC Confederation College, Kenora, ON, Canada (collection)

C/CC/NB Cambrian College, North Bay, ON, Canada

C/CC/TB Confederation College, Thunder Bay, ON, Canada

C/CCAB Canada Council Art Bank, Ottawa, ON, Canada

C/CCC Chatham Cultural Centre, Chatham, ON, Canada

C/CCC/CL Crown Canadian Collection, Crown Life Insurance Company, Toronto, ON, Canada (collection)

C/CCCAC Canadian Catholic Conference Art Collection, Ottawa, ON, Canada

C/CCPC Centre Cultural de Pointe Claire, Montréal, PQ, Canada (exhibit, tour)

C/CD *Cape Dorset: A Decade of Eskimo Prints and Recent Sculptures.* Organized by the National Gallery of Canada in cooperation with the Canadian Eskimo Art committee, Ottawa, ON, Canada, 1967. (exhibit, tour)

C/CDE *Cape Dorset Engravings.* Organized by the Department of Indian and Northern Affairs Canada, Ottawa, ON, Canada, 1974. (tour, United States and Canada)

C/CDG *Cape Dorset Graphics Annual Collection.* NWT, Canada

C/CEG Centre d'Exposition de la Gare, L'Annonciation, PQ, Canada

C/CEL *Canadian Eskimo Lithographs: Third Collection.* Presented under the auspices of the Cultural Affairs Division of the Department of External Affairs Canada, Ottawa, ON, 1973. (tour)

C/CG *Commonwealth Games.* Edmonton, AB, Canada, 1978

C/CGCQ Canadian Guild of Crafts Québec, Montréal, PQ, Canada

C/CIARH *Contemporary Indian Art At Rideau Hall.* Department of Indian Affairs and Northern Development, Ottawa, ON, Canada, 1983

C/CID *Contemporary Inuit Drawings.* Macdonald Stewart Art Centre, Guelph, ON, 1987-1989 (tour)

C/CIIA *Contemporary Indian and Inuit Art of Canada.* Organized by Indian and Northern Affairs Canada, for

The United Nations General Assembly Building, New York, NY, 1983-1984. (exhibit, tour)

C/CIMS Canadian Indian Marketing Services, Ottawa, ON, Canada (collection)

C/CM Centennial Museum, Vancouver, BC, Canada

C/CMC Canadian Museum of Civilization, Hull, PQ, Canada. Formerly The National Museum of Man.

C/CNAA *Contemporary Native Art In Alberta.* Manu Exhibition Area, Edmonton, AB, Canada

C/CNAC *Contemporary Native Art of Canada - The Woodland Indians.* Royal Ontario Museum, Toronto, ON, Canada, 1976 (exhibit, tour - London, England and Lohr, Germany)

C/CNS Central Marketing Services, Ottawa, ON, Canada (collection)

C/CR *Contemporary Rituals.* White Water Gallery, North Bay, ON, Canada, 1990 (exhibit, tour)

C/CRM Campbell River Museum, Campbell River, BC, Canada

C/CS *Calgary Stampede.* Calgary, AB, Canada (annual rodeo and market)

C/CU Concordia University, Montréal, PQ, Canada

C/D *Deadlines.* La Gare Exposition Centre, l'Annonciation, PQ, Canada, 1989-1990 (exhibit, tour)

C/DEA Department of External Affairs, Ottawa, ON, Canada (collection)

C/DKA *Die Kunst Aus Der Arktis.* Inuit Galerie, Mannheim, West Germany, 1986 (exhibit, tour)

C/DM Delta Museum and Archives, Ladner, BC, Canada

C/EACTDB *The Eskimo Art Collection of the Toronto-Dominion Bank.* Toronto, ON, Canada (exhibit, tour)

C/ECC Emily Carr Centre, Victoria, BC, Canada

C/EFA *Eskimo Fantastic Art.* Gallery III, School of Art, University of Manitoba, Winnipeg, MB, Canada, 1972

C/EM Eskimo Museum, Churchill, MB, Canada

C/EMA Edmonton Museum of Arts, Edmonton, AB, Canada

C/ESSOC ESSO Emerging Artists Collections, ESSO Resources Canada Limited, Calgary, AB, Canada

C/FC *Festival Culturel.* Organized by Le Centre d'Amilié Autochtone, Montréal, PQ, Canada, 1987-1988.

C/FCIA *Festival of Canadian Indian Arts.* Victoria Island, Ottawa, ON, Canada

C/FVU Fraser Valley College, Abbotsford, BC, Canada. Currently known as Fraser Valley University.

C/GAEC *Graphic Art by Eskimos of Canada.* Cultural Affairs Division, Department of External Affairs, Ottawa, ON, Canada, 1970-1973 (exhibit, tour)

C/GCC Gulf Canada, Ltd. (collection)

C/GM Glenbow Museum, Calgary, AB, Canada

C/GNAF *Great Northern Arts Festival.* Inuvik, NWT, Canada, July 1989

C/GOAC Government of Ontario Art Collection, Sudbury, ON, Canada

C/GTOW *Grasp Tight the Old Ways.* Art Gallery of Ontario, Toronto, ON, Canada, 1983-85 (tour)

C/HBCC Hudson's Bay Company Collection, New York, NY

C/HEC Holman Eskimo Co-operative, Holman, NWT, Canada (collection)

C/HFH *Hunt Family Heritage.* Organized by Canadian Museum of Civilization, Hull, PQ, Canada, 1981. (exhibit, tour)

C/HNG Houston North Gallery, Lunenburg, NS, Canada

C/I *Indigena.* Organized by the Canadian Museum of Civilization in cooperation with the Society of Canadian Artists of Native Ancestry, Ottawa, ON, Canada, 1992-1994. (exhibit, tour)

C/IAA Indian Association of Alberta, Edmonton, AB, Canada

C/IAC Indian Arts Center, Ottawa, ON, Canada (annual, juried)

C/IAF *Indian Art Forms.* McIntosh Gallery, ON, Canada, 1978

C/IAJE *Indian Art Juried Exhibition, Atlantic Region.* Department of Indian and Northern Affairs Canada, Halifax, NS, Canada, 1985

C/IA7 *Inuit Art in the 1970s.* Department of Indian Affairs and Northern Development, Kingston, ON, Canada, 1979-1980 (tour)

C/ICI Inuit Cultural Institute, Arviat, NWT, Canada

C/IFNA *International Festival of Native Arts.* Calgary, AB, Canada (annual, 1st - 1989)

C/IGV Inuit Gallery of Vancouver, Vancouver, BC, Canada

C/INAC Indian and Northern Affairs Canada, Ottawa, ON, Canada. Formerly Department of Indian Affairs and Northern Development.

C/IOC Imperial Oil, Ltd., Toronto, ON, Canada (collection)

C/ISS *In the Shadow of the Sun.* Art Gallery of Nova Scotia, Halifax, NS, Canada, 1990 (exhibit, tour - The Hague, Netherlands, and Germany)

C/KA 'Ksan Association, Hazelton, BC, Canada (collection)

C/KFC Koerner Foundation Collection, Vancouver, BC, Canada

C/KSNCIA Kitanmax School of Northwest Coast Indian Art at 'Ksan, Hazelton, BC, Canada

C/LCC Lethbridge Community College, Lethbridge, AB, Canada

C/LFCNQ La Fédération des Coopératives du Nouveau-Québec, Montréal, PQ, Canada (collection)

C/LLYC *London Life, Young Contemporaries, '87.* London Regional Art Gallery, London, ON, Canada, 1987 (exhibit, tour)

C/LNFC London Native Friendship Centre, London, ON, Canada

C/LPC *Les Points Cardinaux.* Organized by Boréale Multimédia, Centre d'Exposition de la Gare, L'Annonciation, PQ, Canada

C/LRCL La Roche Center for Learning, Canada. *Bryon and His Balloon*, 1981 (juried)

C/LS *Looking South*. Organized and circulated by the Winnipeg Art Gallery, Winnipeg, MB, Canada. (exhibit, tour)

C/LSP *Land, Spirit, Power*. National Museum of Canada, Ottawa, ON, Canada, 1992 (exhibit, tour)

C/LTAT *Links to a Tradition*. Department of Indian Affairs and Northern Development, Ottawa, ON, Canada, 1977 (exhibit, tour - Brazil)

C/LUM Laurentian University Museum and Arts Center, Sudbury, ON, Canada (collection)

C/M *Muzinihbeegey: Recent Paintings by Sandy Lake Artists*. Organized and circulated by Thunder Bay Art Gallery, A National Centre and Centre for Indian Art, Thunder Bay, ON, Canada, 1990.

C/MA *Masters of the Arctic: An Exhibition of Contemporary Inuit Masterworks*. Presented by AMWAY Corporation at the United Nations General Assembly, New York, NY, 1989. (exhibit, tour)

C/MAD Musée des Arts Décoratifs, Montréal, PQ, Canada

C/MAF *Manitou Arts Foundation Exhibition*. Toronto, ON, Canada, 1974

C/MAM Maltwood Art Museum and Gallery, University of Victoria, Victoria, BC, Canada

C/MBAM Musée des Beaux-Arts de Montréal, Montréal, PQ, Canada (collection)

C/MBSL Musée du Bas-Saint-Laurent, Rivière-du-Loup, PQ, Canada

C/MC Multicultural Centre, Red Deer, AB, Canada

C/MCA Museum of Contemporary Art, Ottawa, ON, Canada

C/MCAF *Multi-Cultural Arts Festival*. North York (Willowdale), ON, Canada

C/MCC McMichael Canadian Art Collection, Kleinburg, ON, Canada

C/McIG McIntosh Gallery, London, ON, Canada

C/McMBC McMillan and Bloedel Collection, Vancouver, BC, Canada

C/McMU McMaster University, Hamilton, ON, Canada

C/MDLC Musée de la Civilisation, Québec City, PQ, Canada

C/MFA/M Montréal Museum of Fine Arts, Montréal, PQ, Canada

C/MFA/NS Nova Scotia Museum of Fine Art and Artifacts, Halifax, NS, Canada

C/MG Manuge Gallery, Halifax, NS, Canada

C/MGC Montréal Guild of Crafts, Montréal, PQ, Canada

C/MI Mohawk Institute, Brantford, ON, Canada (collection)

C/MIE *Maritime Indian Exhibit*. Doomsday Gallery, Halifax, NS, Canada

C/MJAM Moose Jaw Art Museum, Moose Jaw, SK, Canada

C/MMMN Manitoba Museum of Man and Nature, Winnipeg, MB, Canada

C/MNBC Museum of Northern British Columbia, Prince Rupert, BC, Canada

C/MNH Canadian Museum of Natural History, Ottawa, ON, Canada

C/MNH/SK Saskatchewan Museum of Natural History, Regina, SK, Canada

C/MQ Musée du Québec, Québec City, PQ, Canada

C/MSVU Mount St. Vincent University, Halifax, NS, Canada

C/N Nova Corporation of Alberta, AB, Canada (collection)

C/NAC National Arts Centre, Ottawa, ON, Canada

C/NACF *Native Art and Craft Festival*. Calixa-Lovallée Cultural Center, Montréal, PQ, Canada

C/NAF *Native Arts Festival*. Niagara-On-The-Lakes, ON, Canada

C/NAITC North American Indian Traveling College, Cornwall, ON, Canada and St. Regis Mohawk Indian Reservation

C/NAM Nickle Art Museum, Calgary, AB, Canada

C/NB *New Beginnings*. Native Business Summit, Metro Toronto Convention Centre, Toronto, ON, Canada

C/NBAB New Brunswick Art Bank, NB, Canada (collection)

C/NBM New Brunswick Museum, Saskatoon, SK, Canada

C/NCC National Conference Centre, Ottawa, ON, Canada

C/NCC/AB Ninastako Culture Centre, Standoff, AB, Canada

C/NCCT Native Canadian Centre of Toronto, Toronto, ON, Canada

C/NETIA *National Exhibition of Traditional Indian Art*. Department of Indian and Northern Affairs Canada, Ottawa, ON, Canada. (annual, juried, 1st - 1985)

C/NFB National Film Board, Canada (juried exhibit, 1983)

C/NFC Nistawoyou Friendship Centre, Annual National Art Show, AB, Canada

C/NGCA National Gallery of Canada, Ottawa, ON, Canada

C/NHFC Native Heritage Foundation of Canada, Regina, SK, Canada

C/NIACC National Indian Arts and Crafts Corporation, Ottawa, ON, Canada

C/NIIPA/G Native Indian/Inuit Photography Association Gallery, Hamilton, ON, Canada

C/NLC National Library of Canada, Ottawa, ON, Canada

C/NLNA *Native Life, Native Art*. Organized by Villagers/Village Aid, Toronto, ON, Canada, 1987. (exhibit, tour - Canada, Africa, Scotland)

C/NMC National Museum of Canada, Ottawa, ON, Canada

C/NNEC Northwestern National Exhibition Centre, Hazelton, BC, Canada

C/NSAB Nova Scotia Art Bank, Halifax, NS, Canada

C/NSCAD Nova Scotia College of Art and Design, Halifax, NS, Canada

C/NSTC Nova Scotia Technical College, School of Architecture Gallery, Halifax, NS, Canada

C/NWNG *New Works By A New Generation*. Norman Mackenzie Art Gallery, University of Regina, Regina, SK, Canada, 1982

C/NWPCAL Native Women's Professional and Creative Arts League, Hamilton, ON, Canada

C/O *Okanata.* A Space, Toronto, ON, Canada, 1991 (exhibit, tour)

C/OCA Ontario College of Arts, Toronto, ON, Canada

C/OCF Ojibwa Cultural Foundation, West Bay, ON, Canada

C/OCF/OT *Ottawa Canoe Festival, National Exhibit of Indian Art.* Ottawa, ON, Canada (annual)

C/OM *Odi' Min.* Museum and Arts Centre, Laurentian University, Sudbury, ON, Canada, 1988 (exhibit, tour)

C/OP *Oonark - Pangnark.* Organized by the National Museum of Man, National Museums of Canada and presented in cooperation with Canadian Arctic Producers Limited, 1970. (exhibit, tour)

C/OS *Out of Saskatchewan.* Vancouver Art Gallery, Vancouver, BC, Canada, 1986 (exhibit, tour)

C/OWAO *Our Worlds Are One.* Organized by Native Awareness Week Society, sponsored by Mobil Oil, Calgary, AB, Canada, 1991.

C/P *Pitseolak.* Prepared and circulated by the Department of Indian and Northern Affairs in cooperation with the West Baffin Eskimo Co-operative, Cape Dorset, NWT, Canada. (exhibit, tour)

C/PBEAC Piegan Board of Education Art Collection, Brocket, AB, Canada

C/PDF *The People of the Dawn Festival.* Eskasoni Indian Reservation, NS, Canada, 1979

C/PECL Pangnirtung Eskimo Co-operative Limited, Pangnirtung, PQ, Canada. (collection)

C/PHT *Peace Hills Trust Show and Competition.* Peace Trust Gallery, Edmonton, AB, Canada (collection)

C/PM Provincial Museum, Edmonton, AB, Canada

C/POC Pancanadian Oil Corporation, Calgary, AB, Canada. (collection)

C/PP *Pudlo Pudat: Thirty Years of Drawing.* Organized by National Gallery of Canada, Ottawa, ON, Canada, 1990-1991. (exhibit, tour)

C/PV *Points of View.* Yukon Territorial Government Building, Whitehorse, YT, Canada, 1984, 1985

C/PWNHC Prince of Wales Northern Heritage Centre, Yellowknife, NWT, Canada (collection)

C/QU Queen's University Art Centre, Kingston, ON, Canada

C/RBC Royal Bank of Canada (collection)

C/RBCM Royal British Columbia Museum, Victoria, BC, Canada. Formerly British Columbia Provincial Museum. (collection)

C/RDM Red Deer and District Museum and Archives, Red Deer, AB, Canada

C/RF Riveredge Foundation, Devonian Group, Calgary, AB, Canada (collection)

C/ROM Royal Ontario Museum, Toronto, ON, Canada

C/RPL Regina Public Library, Regina, SK, Canada

C/RSMC Robson Square Media Centre, Vancouver, BC, Canada

C/S *Stardusters.* Organized by Thunder Bay Art Gallery, Thunder Bay, ON, Canada, 1986-1987. (exhibit, tour)

C/SAB Saskatchewan Arts Board, Regina, SK, Canada (collection)

C/SAGM Sir Alexander Galt Museum, Lethbridge, AB, Canada

C/SC Sanavik Co-operative, Baker Lake, NWT, Canada (collection)

C/SCANA Society of Canadian Artists of Native Ancestry. Founded in 1983.

C/SCC Shell Canada, Ltd., Calgary, AB, Canada (collection)

C/SFG Simon Fraser Gallery, Simon Fraser University, Burnaby, BC, Canada

C/SICC Saskatchewan Indian Cultural Centre, Saskatoon, SK, Canada

C/SIFC Saskatchewan Indian Federated College, Regina, SK, Canada

C/SNAC Six Nations Arts Council. Exhibits in Brantford and Toronto, ON, Canada, 1964-1967.

C/SNFF Six Nations Fall Fair, ON, Canada

C/SS *Shamans and Spirits: Myths and Medical Symbolism In Eskimo Art.* Sponsored by the National Museum of Man and Canadian Arctic Producers, 1982. (exhibit, tour)

C/SV *Sharing Visions* (exhibit, tour - Korea and Japan)

C/TAG Tribal Arts Gallery, Vancouver, BC, Canada

C/TC *Traditions and Change.* Commissioned by the Communications Branch of Indian and Northern Affairs, Canada, 1980. (exhibit, tour)

C/TCC Teleglobe Canada, Montréal, PQ, Canada. (collection)

C/TDB Toronto-Dominion Bank, Toronto, ON, Canada (collection)

C/TFD *Time For Dialogue: Contemporary Artists* (Triangle Gallery of Visual Arts) and *The Collectors* (The New Gallery). Sponsored by Calgary Aboriginal Awareness Society, Calgary, AB, Canada.

C/TGVA Triangle Gallery of Visual Art, Calgary, AB, Canada

C/TI *Travel and Identity.* Norman Mackenzie Art Gallery, University of Regina, Regina, SK, Canada, 1991 (exhibit, tour)

C/TIC Toronto Indian Centre, Toronto, ON, Canada

C/TIIS *The Indian Individualist.* Joint project of the Assiniboia Gallery, the World Assembly of First Nations, and Saskatchewan Indian Federated College, Regina, SK, Canada, 1981.

C/TIP *The Inuit Print.* Organized by the Canadian Department of Indian and Northern Affairs Canada and the Museum of Man, Ottawa, ON, Canada. (exhibit, tour - Canada, United States, and Europe)

C/TL *The Legacy.* Organized by The Royal British Columbia Museum, Vancouver, BC, Canada, 1971-1980. (exhibit, tour)

C/TMBI *Things Made By Inuit.* La Féderation des Coopératives du Nouveau-Québec, Valle Saint-Laurent, PQ, Canada

C/TMEC Timmins Museum Exhibition Centre, South Porcupine, ON, Canada

C/TU Trent University, McKenzie Gallery, Peterborough, ON, Canada

C/U of AB University of Alberta, Edmonton, AB, Canada

C/U of BC University of British Columbia, Vancouver, BC, Canada

C/U of BC/MA University of British Columbia Museum of Anthropology, Vancouver, BC, Canada

C/U of C University of Calgary, Calgary, AB, Canada

C/U of C/G University of Calgary Galleries, Calgary, AB, Canada

C/U of G University of Guelph, Guelph, ON, Canada

C/U of M University of Montréal, Montréal, PQ, Canada

C/U of MB University of Manitoba, Winnipeg, MB, Canada

C/U of NB University of New Brunswick, Fredericton, NB, Canada

C/U of O University of Ottawa, Ottawa, ON, Canada

C/U of R University of Regina, Regina, SK, Canada

C/U of R/MG Norman Mackenzie Art Gallery, University of Regina, Regina, SK, Canada

C/U of SK University of Saskatchewan, Saskatoon, SK, Canada

C/U of T University of Toronto, Toronto, ON, Canada

C/U of T/S University of Toronto, Scarborough Campus, Scarborough, ON, Canada

C/U of V University of Victoria, Victoria, BC, Canada

C/U of W University of Winnipeg, Winnipeg, MB, Canada

C/U of WA University of Waterloo, Waterloo, ON, Canada

C/U of WON University of Western Ontario, London, ON, Canada

C/UG Ufundi Gallery, Ottawa, ON, Canada

C/VCM Vancouver City Museum, Vancouver, BC, Canada. Formerly Vancouver Centennial Museum

C/VRS *Visions of Rare Spirit: 20 Years of Holman Prints.* Port Colborne Library, ON, Canada, 1984

C/VSA Vancouver School of Art, Vancouver, BC, Canada

C/WBEC West Baffin Eskimo Co-operative, Cape Dorset, NWT, Canada (collection)

C/WCAA *Woodlands: Contemporary Art of the Anishnabe.* Thunder Bay Art Gallery, Thunder Bay, ON, Canada, 1989 (exhibit, tour - United States)

C/WDY *Why Do You Call Us Indians...?* Organized by Ufundi Gallery, Ottawa, ON, Canada, 1989. (exhibit, tour - United States)

C/WI *Waabanda-iwewin.* Thunder Bay, ON, Canada (annual, juried, 1st - 1984)

C/WICEC Woodland Indian Cultural Education Center, Brantford, ON, Canada (annual, 1st -1978)

C/WLA *We Lived By Animals.* Department of Indian Affairs and Northern Development in cooperation with the Department of External Affairs, Ottawa, ON, Canada, 1975-1979. (exhibit, tour)

C/WLU Wilfred Laurier University, Waterloo, ON, Canada

C/WM Whyte Museum of the Canadian Rockies, Banff, AB, Canada

C/YU York University, Toronto, ON, Canada

C/ZS *Zone of Silence.* 1985-1987 (exhibit, tour - Canada and Mexico)

CAA Concord Art Association Gallery, Concord, MA

CAA/AZ Cowboy Artists of America, Sedona, AZ. First held in Oklahoma City, OK, and now in Phoenix, AZ. (annual)

CAC California Art Club, Los Angeles, CA

CAC/AZ Central Arizona College, Coolidge, AZ

CAC/NO Contemporary Arts Center, New Orleans, LA

CAI Art Institute of Chicago, Chicago, IL. Formerly Chicago Art Institute.

CAI/KC Center of the American Indian, Kirkpatrick Center Museum Complex, Oklahoma City, OK. Currently Red Earth Indian Center, 1993.

CAIA Center for the Arts of Indian America, Art Gallery of the United States Department of the Interior, Washington, D.C., 1967-1968

CAINS Chicago American Indian Nations Show, Chicago, IL (juried)

CAM/MA Chrysler Art Museum of Provincetown, MA

CAM/OH Cincinnati Art Museum, Cincinnati, OH

CAM/S Crocker Art Museum, Sacramento, CA. Formerly E. B. Crocker Art Gallery.

CAMSL City Art Museum, St. Louis, MO

CANA *Cultural Arts of Native Americans.* Norman, OK, 1979

CAOR *Contemporary Art of the Onondaga Reservation.* Tyler Art Gallery, Oswego, NY

Carlisle Carlisle Indian School, Carlisle, PA

Carson Carson Indian School, Carson, NV

CAS California Academy of Sciences, Anthropology Department, San Francisco, CA. Elkus Collection of American Indian Art and Artifacts

CAWA Classic-American Western Art, Beverly Hills, CA

CBC Colville Tribal Business Council, Nespelem, WA

CBMM Charles W. Bowers Memorial Museum, Santa Ana, CA. Currently known as The Bowers Museum of Cultural Art.

CC Claremont College, Claremont, CA

CC/OK Claremore College, Claremore, OK. Currently known as Rogers State Junior College.

CC/WA Carnegie Center, Walla Walla, WA

CCAC California College of Arts and Crafts, Oakland, CA

CCAC/MT *One Hundred Years of Montana Women Artists.* Custer County Art Center, Miles City, MT (exhibit, tour)

CCDLR Centro Cultural de la Raza, Balboa Park, San Diego, CA

CCH Cook County Hospital, Grand Marais, MN

CCH/OK *Creek Council House Show.* Okmulgee, OK (annual, juried, 1st - 1988)

CCHM Creek Indian Council House and Museum, Okmulgee, OK

CCHM/NV Clark County Heritage Museum, Henderson, NV

CCHS Cook County High School, Grand Marais, MN

CCI *Counter Colon-ialismo.* Organized by Centro Cultural de la Raza, San Diego, CA, 1991. (exhibit, tour)

CCP *Chicago Century of Progress.* Chicago, IL, 1934

CCT Colville Confederated Tribes, Colville Indian Reservation, WA. *Annual Indian Art Show* (annual, 1st - 1978)

CFD *Cheyenne Frontier Days, Governor's Invitational Western Art Show.* Cheyenne, WY (annual)

CFS Central Federal Savings, Santa Monica, CA

CG Campbell Galleries, Los Angeles, CA

CG/AZ College of Ganado, Ganado, AZ

CGA Corcoran Gallery of Art, Washington, D.C.

CGFA Columbus Gallery of Fine Arts, Columbus, OH

CGPS Center for Great Plains Studies, University of Nebraska, Lincoln, NE (exhibit, collection)

CHAS *A Classic Homecoming Art Show.* Guthrie, OK, 1990

CHAS/SD *Crazy Horse Art Show.* Crazy Horse, SD

CHASC *Cherokee History Art Show/Competition.* Cherokee Nation, Tahlequah, OK. Held in conjunction with Cherokee History Research Symposium, Sept 1993.

Chilocco Chilocco Indian School, Chilocco, OK

Chinle Chinle Indian School, Chinle, AZ

CHMG Cherokee Heritage Museum and Gallery, Cherokee, NC

CI Colonial Inn, Los Angeles, CA

CIA *Contemporary Indian Artists –Montana/Wyoming/Idaho.* Museum of the Plains Indian, Browning, MT, 1971

CIA/CA California Institute of the Arts, Valencia, CA

CIA/CO Colorado Institute of Art, Denver, CO

CIAE *Contemporary Indian Art Exhibition.* Central Washington University, Ellensburg, WA (annual, 1st - 1972)

CIAE/MT *Coyote Indian Art Exhibit.* Montana Indian Artist Project, Missoula, MT, 1986

CIAI *Contemporary Indian Art Invitational.* Oregon State University, Corvallis, OR, 1975 (exhibit, tour)

CIC Chicago Indian Center, Chicago, IL, 1973-1975

CID *California Indian Days Art Exhibit, California Exposition.* Sacramento, CA (annual, juried)

CIFS *California International Flower Show.* Los Angeles, CA

CIM *Colorado Indian Market.* Denver, CO (annual)

CIRI Cook Inlet Region, Inc., Anchorage Museum of History, Anchorage, AK (collection)

CIS Cranbrook Institute of Science, Bloomfield Hills, MI

CLW *Catherine Lorillard Wolf Annual.* New York, NY (juried, 1982, 1983)

CM/C Willis Carey Historical Museum, Cashmere, WA. Currently known as Chelan County Historical Museum.

CMA Cleveland Museum of Art, Cleveland, OH

CMAC Cambridge Multicultural Arts Center, Cambridge, MA

CMB Chase Manhattan Bank, New York, NY (collection)

CMRM C. M. Russell Museum, Great Falls, MT. *Native American Indian Art Exhibit* (annual)

CNAA *Contemporary Native American Art.* Organized by Oklahoma State University, Gardiner Gallery, Stillwater, OK. (exhibit, tour - United States and Canada)

CNAIA *Contemporary Native American Indian Arts.* Smithsonian Institution, The Museum of Natural History, Washington, D.C., 1982-1983

CNGM C. N. Gorman Museum, University of California, Davis, CA

CNM Cherokee National Museum, Tahlequah, OK. *Trail of Tears Art Show* (annual, 1st - 1972)

Cochití Cochití Pueblo Indian School, Cochití Pueblo, NM

Concho Concho Indian School, Concho, OK

Connors Connors State College, Warner, OK

Cornell Cornell University, Ithaca, NY

CPLH California Palace of the Legion of Honor, Fine Arts Museums of San Francisco, CA

CPS Creighton Preparatory School, Omaha, NE (exhibit, 1990)

CRSFA *Cheyenne River Sioux Fair and Art Show.* Eagle Butte, SD

CSA Cooper School of Art, Cleveland, OH

CSAW Corcoran School of Art, Washington, D.C.

CSF California State Fair, Sacramento, CA

CSF/SD Central States Fair, Rapid City, SD

CSF/SF College of Santa Fe, Santa Fe, NM

CSP *Contemporary Sioux Painting.* Sioux Indian Museum and Crafts Center, Rapid City, SD, and the South Dakota Arts Council, 1970. (exhibit, tour)

CSPIP *Contemporary Southern Plains Indian Painting.* Sponsored by Southern Plains Indian Museum and the Oklahoma Indian Arts and Crafts Co-operative, Anadarko, OK, 1972. (exhibit, tour)

CSU/C California State University, Chico, CA

CSU/CAR California State University Art Gallery, Carson, CA

CSU/CO Colorado State University, Fort Collins, CO

CSU/F California State University, Fullerton, CA

CSU/H California State University, Hayward, CA

CSU/LA California State University, Los Angeles, CA

CSU/LB California State University, Long Beach, CA

CSU/N California State University, Northridge, CA

CSU/OK Central State University, Edmond, OK. Formerly Central State College.

CSU/S California State University, Sacramento, CA

CSU/T California State University, Turlock, CA

CT2 *Century II: Woman Art II.* Wichita, KS, 1980 (juried)

CTC *Confluences of Tradition and Change: 24 American Indian Artists.* Organized by R. L. Nelson Gallery and C. N. Gorman Museum, Davis, CA, 1981-1992. (exhibit, tour)

CU/NE Creighton University Fine Arts Performing Center, Omaha, NE. *A Celebration of Arts and Tradition*, 1982

CU/WM Cornell University, Andrew Dickson White Museum of Art, Ithaca, NY

CW *Circle of the World.* Academy of Sciences Museum, San Francisco, 1985

CWAM College of Wooster Art Museum, Wooster, OH

CWC Curtiss-Wright Corporation, Dayton, OH

CWC/I Chicago Women's Club, Chicago, IL

CWC/WY Central Wyoming College, Riverton, WY

CWPC C. W. Post College, Brookville, NY. *Riders With No Horses*, 1988 (exhibit)

CWY *Circle Way: Art of Native Americans.* Cambridge Multicultural Arts Center, Cambridge, MA, 1989 (exhibit, tour)

DAC Wilmington Society of the Fine Arts, Delaware Art Center, John Sloan Collection, Wilmington, DE

DAI Dayton Art Institute, Dayton, OH

DAM Denver Art Museum, Denver, CO

DAM/I Denver Art Museum. *Own Your Own Invitational*, 1964

DAR Daughters of the American Revolution, Washington, D.C.

DC Dartmouth College, Hanover, NH

DCC Dartmouth College Collection, Hanover, NH

DCLA Design Center of Los Angeles, CA

DCM Desert Caballeros Museum, Wickenburg, AZ

DCTP Designer-Craftsman Training Project, Indian Arts and Crafts Board, United States Department of the Interior, Nome, AK, 1964-1965

DE *Daughters of the Earth.* Works by eight Native American female artists, 1985. (exhibit, tour)

DFNB De Witt First National Bank, De Witt, IA (collection)

DG Dulin Gallery of Art, Knoxville, TN

DIA Denver International Airport, Denver, CO

DMG Davenport Municipal Art Gallery, IA. Known as Davenport Museum of Art since 1987.

DSG Walt Disney Studio Gallery, Burbank, CA

EAJC Eastern Arizona Junior College, Thatcher, AZ

EB Encyclopaedia Britannica Collection (no longer intact)

ECFE Erie County Fair and Exposition, NY

ECSC/OK East Central State College, Ada, OK

EG *Eskimo Games: Traditional Sport and Play of the Eskimo.* Arts and Learning Services Foundation, Minneapolis, MN, 1980-1981 (exhibit, tour)

EIAF *Edinburgh Art Festival.* Edinburgh, Scotland

EITA *Exposition of Indian Tribal Arts.* Sponsored by The College Art Association, 1931-1933. (exhibit, tour)

EM Eiteljorg Museum, Indianapolis, IN

EM/NY Everson Museum of Art of Syracuse and Onondaga County, Syracuse, NY

EMC Eastern Montana College, Billings, MT (collection)

EOC East Oregon College, Walter Pierce Museum, La Grande, OR

EOSC Eastern Oklahoma State College, Wilberton, OK

ESC Evergreen State College, Olympia, WA

ESPANOLA Española High School, Española, NM

FA *Festival of the Arts.* Oklahoma City, OK (annual)

FAC/CS Colorado Springs Fine Arts Center, Colorado Springs, CO

FAC/D Dahl Fine Arts Center, Rapid City, SD

FAC/ETG Fine Arts Center En Taos Galleries, Taos, NM (annual)

FAG/S Fine Arts Gallery of San Diego, San Diego, CA

FAIE Franco-American Institute Exhibit, Rennes, France, 1992

FAIEAIP *First Annual Invitational Exhibition of American Indian Paintings.* United States Department of the Interior, Washington, D.C., 1964-1965

FAM Charles and Emma Frye Art Museum, Puget Sound Area, Seattle, WA

FAM/MA Fogg Art Museum, Harvard University, Cambridge, MA

FAM/NM Fuller Lodge Art Center, Los Alamos, NM

FANAIAE *First Annual National American Indian Art Exposition.* Charlotte, NC, 1964. Sponsored by the American Indian College Foundation. (annual in Oct)

FANEA First Annual National Exhibition of Art, New York, NY

FBCC Fort Berthold Community College, Fort Berthold Indian Reservation, ND

FCTM Five Civilized Tribes Museum, Muskogee, OK. *Competitive Show* (annual, juried, 1st - 1966)

FCTM/M Five Civilized Tribes Museum, Muskogee, OK. *Masters Show* (annual, juried, 1st - 1976)

FCTM/S Five Civilized Tribes Museum, Muskogee, OK. *Student Show* (annual, juried, 1st - 1970)

FHG Four Horsemen Gallery, Denver, CO. *Bicentennial Century of Western Art*, 1976 (juried)

FHMAG Fulton-Hayden Memorial Art Gallery, The Amerind Foundation, Dragoon, AZ

FIA Flint Institute of Art, Flint, MI

FIE *Fourth Invitational Exhibition.* Center For Arts of Indian America, Washington, D.C., 1968

Flagstaff Flagstaff High School, Flagstaff, AZ

FMBC *Franklin Mint's Bicentennial Competition*, 1975

FMC Friday Morning Club, Los Angeles, CA

FNAA *Festival of Native American Arts.* Cococino Center for the Arts. Sponsored by Museum of Northern Arizona, Flagstaff, AZ.

FNAIC *International Indian Art Show and Handicraft Trade Fair.* Sponsored by the Foundation of North American Indian Culture, Bismarck, ND, 1964.

FOM Fort Okanogan Historical Museum, Brewster, WA

Fort Sill Fort Sill Indian School, Lawton, OK

Fort Wingate Fort Wingate Indian School, Fort Wingate, NM

FPW Fredericks, Pelcyger, and White, Boulder, CO (collection)

FSM United States Army Artillery and Missile Center Museum, Fort Sill, OK

FSMCFA *Four Sacred Mountains: Color, Form, and Abstraction.* Arizona Commission on the Arts, Phoenix, AZ, 1988-1989 (exhibit, tour)

FSMCIAF *Four Sacred Mountains' Contemporary Indian Arts Festival.* Sponsored by Tuba City High School and Navajo Community College, Tuba City, AZ, 1987.

FSPC *Five State Pastel Competition.* Krasl Art Center, St. Joseph, MN

FWAC Fort Worth Art Center, Fort Worth, TX. Currently known as Modern Art Museum of Fort Worth.

FWG Fred Wilson Gallery and Trading Post, Phoenix, AZ

FWMA Fort Wayne Museum of Art, Fort Wayne, IN

GAG Carolina Art Association, Gibbs Art Gallery, Charleston, SC

Gallup Gallup High School, Gallup, NM

GAWHM Gene Autry Western Heritage Museum, Palm Springs, CA

GC Graceland College, Lamoni, IA

GCD Grand Coulee Dam, Spokane, WA

GCIC Gallup Community Indian Center, Gallup, NM

GDC Galleria del Cavallino, Venezia, San Marco, Italy

GFNAAS *Great Falls Native American Art Show.* Great Falls, MT

GG Galerie Geroux, Brussels, Belgium

GM Thomas Gilcrease Institute of American History and Art, Tulsa, OK

GM/NY Solomon R. Guggenheim Museum, New York, NY

GO Gilbert Originals, Chicago, IL

GPIAE *Great Plains Indian Art Exposition.* Omaha, NE (annual, juried)

GPL Glendale Public Library, Glendale, CA

GPM Museum of the Great Plains, Lawton, OK

GPWAS *George Phippen Western Art Show.* Phippen Museum of Western Art, Prescott, AZ (annual, 1st - 1974)

GRAF *Grand Rapids Art Festival.* Grand Rapids, MI

GS *Governor's Show.* State Capitol Building, Sacramento, CA

GSW Grover, Stetson, and Williams, Albuquerque, NM (collection)

GTA *Greek Theatre Annual.* Los Angeles, CA

GWS Gates Western Store, Stillwater, OK (collection)

GWWAS *Governor's Western and Wildlife Art Show, Nebraskaland Days.* North Platte, NE (annual, 1st - 1969)

Hampton Hampton Institute, Hampton, VA

Haskell Haskell Indian Junior College, Lawrence, KS. Formerly United States Haskell Institute. Currently Haskell Indian Nations University.

HAU Hellenic American Union, Athens, Greece (exhibit)

HB Havenstrite Building, Los Angeles, CA (exhibit)

HBBA *Hermosa Beach Biltmore Annual.* Hermosa Beach, CA

HCAI *High Country Art Invitational.* Fort Collins, CO, 1977

HCC Heritage Center Inc. Collection, Red Cloud Indian School, Pine Ridge, SD

HCCC Humboldt County Cultural Centre, Eureka, CA

HCCM Hopi Cultural Center Museum, Second Mesa, AZ

HFA *Hollywood Festival of Arts.* Hollywood, CA

HG Holleman Gallery, Walters Art Center, Holland Hall School, Tulsa, OK

HH *The Hunt and the Harvest.* Arranged by the Gallery Association of New York State. Paintings from the Museum of the American Indian, New York, NY, 1985. (tour)

HI Hampton Institute, College Museum and Huntington Library, Hampton, VA (collection)

Hiler Hiler College, Santa Fe, NM

HILL Hill and Canyon School of Art, Santa Fe, NM

HM Heard Museum, Phoenix, AZ. Formerly Heard Museum of Anthropology and Primitive Art.

HM/G *Heard Museum Guild Indian Fair and Market.* Phoenix, AZ (annual, 1st - 1958)

HM/VA Hermitage Foundation Museum, Norfolk, VA

HMA Haffenreffer Museum of Anthropology, Brown University, Bristol, RI

HMA/WG Hamburg Museum of Anthropology, Hamburg, West Germany

HN *Heart of the North: Five Native Minnesota Artists.* 1984-1985 (exhibit, tour - upper-midwestern United States)

HNAAE *Helena Native American Art Exposition.* Helena, MT (annual, 1st - 1984)

HNSM Heard Natural Science Museum and Wild Life Sanctuary, McKinney, TX

Hopi HS Hopi High School, Oraibi, AZ

Hotevilla Hotevilla Day School, Hotevilla, AZ

HPTU Hampton University, Hampton, VA

HS/AI American Indian Historical Society, San Francisco, CA

HS/M Mattatuck Historical Society, Waterbury, CT

HS/MA Massachusetts Historical Society, Boston, MA

HS/MC Historical Society of Marshall County, Marshalltown, IA

HS/MN Minnesota Historical Society, St. Paul, MN

HS/MO Missouri Historical Society, Pictorial History Department, St. Louis, MO

HS/MT Montana Historical Society, Helena, MT

HS/ND State Historical Society of North Dakota, Bismarck, ND

HS/NV Nevada State Historical Society, Las Vegas, NV

HS/OH Ohio Historical Society, Columbus, OH

HS/PA Historical Society of Pennsylvania, Library, Philadelphia, PA

HS/SD South Dakota Historical Society, Pierre, SD

HS/WI State Historical Society of Wisconsin, Madison, WI

HSAS *Hot Springs Art Show.* Hot Springs, SD

HSL/SA St. Augustine Historical Society Library, St. Augustine, FL

HSM/CO State Historical Society of Colorado, Fort Garland Museum, Fort Garland, CO

HSM/D Historical Society Museum, Denver, CO. *Artists of America Exhibition* (annual, 1st - 1981)

HSM/KS Kansas Museum of History, Kansas State Historical Society, Topeka, KS

HSM/MT Montana Historical Society Museum, Helena, MT

HSM/OK Oklahoma Historical Society Museum, Oklahoma City, OK

HSU Humboldt State University, Arcata, CA

HT Hopi-tu Tsootsvolla, Sedona, AZ (annual, 1st - 1988)

HTM/CA Hupa Tribal Museum, Hoopa, CA

HU/VA Howard University, Alexandria, VA

I *Introductions: Contemporary American Indian Art and Emerging Artists.* Montana State University, Bozeman, MT, 1990 (exhibit, tour)

IACA Indian Arts and Crafts Association, Albuquerque, NM

IACB Indian Arts and Crafts Board, United States Department of the Interior, Washington, D.C.

IACB/DC Indian Arts and Crafts Board, Denman Collection, United States Department of the Interior, Washington, D.C.

IAESS *International Art Exhibition of Sport Subjects.* Held in connection with Los Angeles Olympics, 1922.

IAF *Iowa Art Festival.* Sponsored by the Iowa Tribe, Bah-Kho-Ge Gallery, Coyle, OK. (annual, 1st - 1992)

IAIA Institute of American Indian and Alaska Native Culture and Arts Development, Santa Fe, NM. Formerly the Institute of American Indian Arts. Commonly known as The Institute.

IAIA/M Institute of American Indian Arts Museum, Santa Fe, NM

IANA Institute of Alaska Native Arts, Fairbanks, AK

IBIIB *In Beauty it is Begun.* Native American Children's Art, Metropolitan Museum of Art, New York, NY, and Smithsonian Institution, 1972 (tour)

IBM International Business Machines Corporation, Gallery of Arts and Sciences, New York, NY

ICC Illinois Central College, East Peoria, IL

IDM Isaac Delgado Museum of Art, New Orleans, LA. Currently known as New Orleans Museum of Art.

IEEPF *Invitational Easter Egg Painting Festival.* White House, Washington, D.C.

IFA *Indian Festival of the Arts.* La Grande, OR (juried)

IH Indian Heritage Award, Five Civilized Tribes Museum, Muskogee, OK. *Annual Competitive Show.* Awarded for the painting that best depicts the heritage of one of the Five Civilized Tribes.

II *Indian Images.* University of North Dakota Art Gallery, Grand Forks, ND, 1977 (tour)

IIAS *International Indian Art Show.* D-Q University, Davis, CA, 1982

IK *Indianischer Kunstler.* Organized by Philbrook Museum of Art, Tulsa, OK, 1984-1985. (exhibit, tour - West Germany)

IMA Indianapolis Museum of Art, Indianapolis, IN

INAAT *Iroquois and Native American Art of Today, 1973-1974.* (exhibit, tour)

Inter-Mt. Inter-Mountain Indian School, Brigham City, UT

IPCC Indian Pueblo Cultural Center, Albuquerque, NM. *American Indian Week Arts and Crafts Show.* (annual, 1st - 1988)

IPSE *Intermountain Painting and Sculpture Exhibition.* Salt Lake Art Center, Salt Lake City, UT, 1964

IRS Internal Revenue Service, Washington, D.C. *American Indian Art Exhibition*, 1987

IS *Indian Summer.* Bartlesville, OK (annual, juried)

ISAI Iroquois Studies Association of Ithaca, Ithaca, NY

ISM Illinois State Museum, Springfield, IL

ISU Iowa State University, Ames, IA

ISU/B Iowa State University, Brunnier Gallery, Ames, IA

IT Indian Territory. Currently the state of Oklahoma.

ITAE *Inter-Tribal Arts Experience.* Dayton, OH (annual, juried, 1st - 1990)

ITAE/M *Inter-Tribal Arts Experience Market.* Dayton, OH. Held in conjunction with a juried exhibit. (annual, 1st - 1990)

ITIC *Inter-Tribal Indian Ceremonials.* Gallup, NM. Now held at Church Rock, NM. (annual, 1st - 1920)

ITM *International Trade Mart.* New Orleans, LA

JAHM Jerusalem Artists' House Museum, Jerusalem, Israel

JAM Joslyn Art Museum, Omaha, NE

Jémez Jémez Pueblo Day School, Jémez Pueblo, NM

JGS *An Exhibition of American Indian Painters.* James Graham and Sons, New York, NY, 1955

JH Jacobson House, Jacobson Foundation, Norman, OK

Jicarilla Jicarilla Indian School, Dulce, NM

JKA John F. Kennedy International Airport, New York, NY

JRAM Jasper Rand Art Museum, Westfield, MA

K *Kituwah, American Indian National Arts Exposition.* Asheville, NC

KCAI/MO Kansas City Art Institute, Kansas City, MO

KCF Kern County Fair, Bakersfield, CA

KCPA John F. Kennedy Center for the Performing Arts. *Night of the First Americans*, Washington, D.C.

KF Kaiser Center, Kaiser Foundation, Oakland, CA. *National American Artists Exhibition* (annual, 1st - 1966)

KIAA Kansas Indian Artists Association, Wichita, KS (annual, juried, 1st - 1984)

KM Kiva Museum of the Koshare Indian, Boy Scouts of America, La Junta, CO

KOREA Korean Conflict (1950-1953)

KSC Kansas State College, Pittsburgh, KS

KSF Kansas State Fair, Hutchinson, KS

KSTC Kansas State Teachers College, Emporia, KS

KSU Kansas State University, Manhattan, KS

KTM Kiowa Tribal Museum, Carnegie, OK

KWS/FS Kansas Watercolor Society, Wichita, KS. *Five State Exhibition*

LAAA *Los Angeles American Arts Exhibition.* Los Angeles, CA, 1976

LAACS Los Angeles Art Center School, Los Angeles, CA

LAC *Lakota Arts Continuum: One Hundred Years of the Art of the Oglala's and Their Relatives.* A South Dakota Centennial Exhibit, 1988 (exhibit, tour)

LACAI Los Angeles County Art Institute, Los Angeles, CA

LACC Los Angeles City College, Los Angeles, CA

LACF Los Angeles County Fair, Pomona, CA

LACM Los Angeles County Museum of Art, Los Angeles, CA

LAF *Lubbock Arts Festival.* Main Gallery, Lubbock, TX, 1986

LAG Lowe Art Gallery, Syracuse University, Syracuse, NY

LAIC Los Angeles Indian Center, Los Angeles, CA

LAICAF *Los Angeles International Contemporary Art Fair.* Los Angeles Convention Center, Los Angeles, CA (annual)

LBAG Laguna Beach Art Association Gallery, Laguna Beach, CA

LBMA Laguna Art Museum, Laguna Beach, CA

LC *A Little Classic Native American Indian Art Show.* Guthrie, OK (annual)

LCAA *Lewis and Clark Art Auction.* Cut Bank, MT

LCIAS *Lewis-Clark Invitational Art Show.* Lewis and Clark State College, Lewiston, ID (annual, juried, 1st - 1984)

LG Lang Gallery, Galleries of the Claremont Colleges, Scripps College, Claremont, CA

LGAM Laguna Gloria Art Museum, Austin, TX

LH Lever House, New York, NY

LIAS *Lawrence Indian Arts Show.* University of Kansas, Museum of Anthropology, Lawrence, KS (annual, juried, 1st - 1989)

LIAS/M *Lawrence Indian Arts Market.* Haskell Indian Junior College, Lawrence, KS (annual, 1st - 1989)

LIU/S Long Island University, Southampton College, Southampton, NY

LJMA La Jolla Museum of Art, La Jolla, CA

LM/KC *Living Masters.* Kirkpatrick Center, Oklahoma City, OK, 1979 (juried)

LMA/BC Logan Museum of Anthropology, Beloit, WI

LNBTC Liberty National Bank and Trust Co., Oklahoma City, OK

LOYOLA Loyola University, New Orleans, LA

LPCA Lake Placid Center for the Arts, Lake Placid, NY

LS Litho Studios, Inc., New York, NY (collection)

LSS *Let the Spirit Speak!* Paul VI Institute for the Arts, Washington, D.C., 1993

M/GF Grandfather, Maternal

M/GGF Great-grandfather, Maternal

M/GGGF Great-great-grandfather, Maternal

M/GGM Great-grandmother, Maternal

M/GM Grandmother, Maternal

M/GP Grandparents, Maternal

MA Merit Award. *Lawrence Indian Art Show*, University of Kansas, Museum of Anthropology, Lawrence, KS. Awarded in place of the usual 1st, 2nd, and 3rd-place awards.

MAAIC Mid-America All-Indian Center Museum, Wichita, KS

MAF *Madonna Art Festival.* Los Angeles, CA

MAG Municipal Art Gallery, Los Angeles, CA

MAI Museum of the American Indian, Heye Foundation, New York, NY. Currently the National Museum of the American Indian, Smithsonian Institution, Washington, D.C.

MAM Montclair Art Museum, Montclair, NJ

MBC *Mother Butler Center Art Show.* Rapid City, SD, 1967 (juried)

MCA Museum of Contemporary Art, Dallas, TX. Merged with Dallas Museum of Fine Arts to form the Dallas Museum of Art.

MCAD Minneapolis College of Art and Design, Minneapolis, MN

MCC Mesa Community College, Mesa, AZ

MCC/CA Mathes Cultural Center, Escondido, CA

MCCC McCook Community College, McCook, NE

MCCG Mission Cultural Center Gallery, San Francisco, CA

MCI Museum of the Cherokee Indian, Cherokee, NC

MDOWP *Master Drawings and Other Works On Paper.* New Gallery, Cleveland, OH

MEIF *Mountain Eagle Indian Festival.* Hunter Mountain, Hunter, NY

Mexico C.C. Mexico City College, Mexico City, D.F., Mexico

MFA/A Nelson-Atkins Museum of Art, Kansas City, MO. Formerly the William Rockhill Nelson Gallery of Art.

MFA/AH Anchorage Museum of History and Fine Arts, Anchorage, AK

MFA/B Museum of Fine Arts, Boston, MA

MFA/CI Carnegie Museum of Art, Pittsburgh, PA. Formerly Carnegie Institute.

MFA/D Dallas Museum of Art, Dallas, TX

MFA/EP El Paso Museum of Arts, El Paso, TX

MFA/G Gadsden Museum of Fine Arts, Gadsden, AL

MFA/H Museum of Fine Arts, Houston, TX

MFA/M Montgomery Museum of Fine Arts, Montgomery, AL

MFA/O Owensboro Museum of Fine Arts, Owensboro, KY

MFA/S Scottsdale Fine Arts Center, Scottsdale, AZ

MFA/VA Virginia Museum of Fine Arts, Richmond, VA

MHDYMM M. H. De Young Memorial Museum, Fine Arts Museums of San Francisco, CA. *American Indian Painting Competition* (annual, discontinued)

MI Maryland Institute, College of Art, Baltimore, MD

MIA Minneapolis Institute of Arts, Minneapolis, MN

MIA/MT Montana Institute of the Arts, Billings, MT

MIC Minneapolis Indian Center, Minneapolis, MN

MIF *Mayfest International Festival.* Winston-Salem, NC, 1991

MILLS Mills College, Oakland, CA

MIM Mitchell Indian Museum, Kendall College, Evanston, IL (collection)

MKMcNAI Marion Koogler McNay Art Museum, San Antonio, TX. Formerly Marion Koogler McNay Art Institute.

MLAS *Makhpeya Luta Art Show.* Rapid City, SD, 1965

MM Mattatuck Museum, Mattatuck Historical Society, Waterbury, CT

MM/NJ Morris Museum, Morristown, NJ

MMA Museum of Modern Art, New York, NY

MMA/MI Muskegon Museum of Art, Muskegon, MI (annual, juried, 1st - 1927)

MMA/MN Minnesota Museum of Art, St. Paul, MN

MMA/MT Missoula Museum of the Arts, Missoula, MT

MMA/NY Metropolitan Museum of Art, New York, NY. *In Beauty It Is Begun*, 1974

MMA/WA Maryhill Museum of Art, Goldendale, WA

MMC Mount Mary College, Milwaukee, WI

MMM *Masks, Masques, Maxs.* Arizona Commission on the Arts, Phoenix, AZ, 1988 (exhibit, tour)

MMO *Moving Murals of Oklahoma: Contemporary Native American Painting.* The Jacobson Foundation, Norman, OK, 1994 (exhibit, tour)

MNA Museum of Northern Arizona, Flagstaff, AZ. Separate Hopi, Navajo, and Zuni exhibits. (annual, juried)

MNA/KHC Museum of Northern Arizona, Katherine Harvey Collection, Flagstaff, AZ

MNAA *Modern Native American Abstraction.* Philadelphia Art Alliance, Philadelphia, PA (exhibit, tour)

MNAC *Museum of Native American Cultures Show.* Spokane, WA (annual, 1st - 1972; discontinued)

MNCA Museum of Navajo Ceremonial Art, Santa Fe, NM

MNH/A American Museum of Natural History, New York, NY

MNH/AN Anniston Museum of Natural History, Anniston, AL

MNH/CA Carnegie Museum of Natural History, Pittsburgh, PA

MNH/CI Cincinnati Museum of Natural History, Cincinnati, OH

MNH/CL Cleveland Museum of Natural History, Cleveland, OH

MNH/D Denver Museum of Natural History, Denver, CO

MNH/F Field Museum of Natural History, Chicago, IL. Formerly the Field Columbian Museum.

MNH/KS University of Kansas, Museum of Natural History, Lawrence, KS

MNH/LA Natural History Museum of Los Angeles County, Los Angeles, CA. *American Indian Festival and Market* (annual)

MNM Museum of New Mexico, Santa Fe, NM

MNM/DD Museum of New Mexico, Museum of Fine Arts, Santa Fe, NM. Dorothy Dunn Kramer/Margaretta S. Dietrich Collections

MNM/IAC Museum of New Mexico, Museum of Indian Arts and Culture, Santa Fe, NM

MNM/SAR Museum of New Mexico, School of American Research Collections, Santa Fe, NM

MNM/T Museum of New Mexico. *Fine Arts Gallery Tour of the United States, 1956-1964.* Selections made from the museum's *Contemporary Indian Artists Annual Exhibition.*

MPABAS *Midwest Professional Artists Benefit Art Show*, Tulsa Garden Center, Tulsa, OK. Sponsored by the Violet Club of Tulsa, 4-5 Oct 1980.

MPDC *Midwestern Printmaking and Drawing Competition and Exhibit.* Tulsa, OK (annual, 1st - 1973)

MPI Museum of the Plains Indian, United States Department of the Interior, Indian Arts and Crafts Board Browning, MT

MPM Milwaukee Public Museum, Milwaukee, WI

MPM/CA Monterey Peninsula Museum of Art, Monterey, CA

MR Museum of the Rockies, Browning, MT

MRFM Millicent Rogers Foundation Museum, Taos, NM. Currently the Millicent Rogers Museum.

MRNAC Minneapolis Regional Native Art Center, Minneapolis, MN

MSAC Mount San Antonio College, Walnut, CA

MSF Montana State Fair, Great Falls, MT

MSIC Mutual Service Insurance Co., St. Paul, MN

MSM Maurice Spertus Museum of Judaica, The Peace Museum, Chicago, IL

MSU Montana State University, Bozeman, MT

MSULMAE *Metropolitan Seattle Urban League's Minority Art Exhibit.* Seattle, WA (juried, annual, 1st - 1978)

MSW Museum of the Southwest, Midland, TX

MTCC Maricopa Technical Community College, Phoenix, AZ

MTF *Moving the Fire: The Removal of the Indian Nations to Oklahoma.* State Arts Council of Oklahoma, 1993 (exhibit, tour)

MUSKOGEE Muskogee Junior College, Muskogee, OK

MV Mesa Verde National Park Museum, Mesa Verde, CO. Formerly Chapin Mesa Archaeological Museum.

MWPI Munson-Williams-Proctor Institute, Utica, NY

NAAE *Native American Artists Exhibition.* College of Santa Fe, Don Humphrey Gallery, Santa Fe, NM

NAAS *Native American Art Show.* Helena, MT (annual, 1st - 1983)

NAC National Arts Club, New York, NY. Pastel exhibit (annual, 1st - 1973)

NACG Navajo Arts and Crafts Guild, Window Rock, AZ

NACLA Native American Center for the Living Arts, Niagara Falls, NY

NAF *Nescatunga Arts Festival.* Alva, OK (annual)

NAP *Native American Paintings.* Mid-America Arts Alliance Project. Organized by the Joslyn Art Museum, 1979-1980. (exhibit, tour)

NAP/MAI *Native American Painting: Selections from the Museum of the American Indian.* Organized by the Museum of the American Indian, New York, NY, 1982.

NARF Native American Rights Fund, Inc., Boulder, CO (annual, 1980s)

NASAC/ACEAA Native Art Studies Association of Canada and L' Association Canadienne des Eludes d'Art Autochtone, Hull, PQ, Canada. Publications: *Newsletter*

NAVAM *Native American Visual Arts and Montana*, Custer County Art Center, MT (two-year regional tour)

NAWA National Academy of Western Art, Oklahoma City, OK (annual)

NAWA/T *National Association of Women Artists Tour of The United States and Japan*, 1958-1959

NCC Navajo Community College, Tsaile, AZ

NCHF National Cowboy Hall of Fame and Western Heritage Center, Oklahoma City, OK

ND *New Directions.* Institute of American Indian Art Museum, Santa Fe, NM, 1973-1974 (exhibit, tour)

NDM North Dakota Museum of Art, University of North Dakota, Grand Forks, ND

NDN *New Directions Northwest: Contemporary Native American Art.* Sponsored by Portland Art Museum and Evergreen State College, Olympia, WA, 1987-1988. (exhibit, tour)

NEA National Endowment for the Arts, Washington, D.C.

NEO Northeastern Oklahoma A and M College, Miami, OK

NGA National Gallery of Art, Washington, D.C.

NHFFAI National Hall of Fame for Famous American Indians, Anadarko, OK

NIACF *Northwest Indian Arts and Crafts Festival.* Flag Plaza Pavilion, Seattle, WA (annual, 1st - 1962)

NICCAS *National Indian Child Conference Art Show.* Sponsored by Save The Children Foundation, Phoenix, AZ. (annual, 1st - 1979)

NIFA *Northwest Indian Festival of Art.* Seattle, WA

NJSM New Jersey State Museum, Trenton, NJ. *Contemporary American Indian Paintings*, 1959-1960

NL Newberry Library, Chicago, IL

NLAPW National League of American Pen Women, Oklahoma City, OK (annual, juried)

NM Newark Museum, Newark, NJ

NM Highlands U New Mexico Highlands University, Las Vegas, NM

NMAA National Museum of American Art, Smithsonian Institution, Washington, D.C. Formerly National Collection of American Art.

NMAI National Museum of the American Indian, Smithsonian Institution, Washington, D.C.

NMAS Norfolk Museum of Arts and Sciences, Norfolk, VA

NMC Northwestern Michigan College, Traverse City, MI (collection)

NMFA *New Mexico Festival of the Arts.* Albuquerque, NM

NMLHM No Man's Land Historical Museum, Panhandle State University, Goodwell, OK

NMSC New Mexico State Capitol Building, Governor's Gallery, Santa Fe, NM

NMSF New Mexico State Fair, Albuquerque, NM

NMSU New Mexico State University, Las Cruces, NM

NNACAF *National Native American Cultural Arts Festival.* Baltimore American Indian Center, Baltimore, MD (annual, juried, 1st - 1990)

NNGCC Northern Natural Gas Company of Omaha Collection, Joslyn Art Museum, Omaha, NE

NNTF *Northern Navajo Tribal Fair.* Shiprock, NM (annual in Sept)

NPM Neville Public Museum of Brown County, Green Bay, WI

NPS National Park Service, United States Department of the Interior, Washington, D.C. (collection)

NPTA *Northern Plains Tribal Arts.* Sioux Falls, SD (annual, 1st - 1988)

NSC Newark State College, Union, NJ. *A Gam Wing: An Indian Fall Festival*

NSM Nevada State Museum, Las Vegas, NV

NSTC/SD Northern State Teachers College, Aberdeen, SD. Currently Northern State College.

NSU Northeastern State University, Tahlequah, OK. Formerly Northeastern State Teachers College.

NSU/SD Northern State University, Aberdeen, SD. Formerly Northern State Teachers College.

NTF *Navajo Tribal Fair and Rodeo.* Window Rock, AZ (annual, 1st - 1946)

NTM Navajo Nation Museum, Window Rock, AZ. Formerly Navajo Tribal Museum.

NU/BC Buscaglia-Castelani Art Gallery, Niagara University, Niagara Falls, NY

NWAS *National Wesleyan Art Show.* St. Louis, MO

NWASA *National Western Art Show and Auction.* Ellensburg, WA (annual, 1st - 1972)

NWCA *Northwestern Colorado Art Show.* Steamboat Springs, CO

NWR *Northwest Rendezvous of Art.* Bellingham, WA

NYSF New York State Fair, Syracuse, NY

NYSM New York State Museum, Albany, NY

NYU New York University Art Gallery, NY

NYWF New York World's Fair 964-1965, New York, NY

OAC Oklahoma Art Center Gallery, Oklahoma City, OK. *All-Oklahoma Indian Artists Invitational* (annual, 1967-1982)

OAE *Ojibway Art Exposition.* Bemidji, MN (annual, juried)

OAG Oswego Art Guild, Oswego, NY

OAGA *Oklahoma Art Guild Annual.* Oklahoma City, OK

OAIS *Oakland American Indian Show.* Oakland, CA

OAKLAND Oakland College of Arts and Crafts, Oakland, CA

OAM Oakland Art Museum, Oakland, CA

OAW Oklahoma Arts Workshop, Tulsa, OK (annual, juried, 1st -1984)

OC Oberlin College, Oberlin, OH

OCV *Our Contemporary Visions.* National Indian Educational Association, Reno, NV, 1986

OCLA Oklahoma College of Liberal Arts, Chickasha, OK

OCSA Oklahoma Center for Science and Art, Kirkpatrick Center, Oklahoma City, OK

OCU Oklahoma City University, Oklahoma City, OK

OG *The Other Gods.* Everson Museum of Art of Syracuse and Onondaga County, Syracuse, NY, 1986-1987 (exhibit, tour)

OGC Oregon State Governor's Office, State Capitol Building, Salem, OR

OHT *Oklahoma's Hidden Treasures.* Sponsored by Oklahoma Congressional Delegation and Indian Territory Gallery (Sapulpa, OK), Washington, D.C., 1989.

OIAC Oklahoma Indian Art Competition, American Indian Heritage Center, and Philbrook Museum of Art, Tulsa, OK (annual, 1st - 1993)

OIAP *Oklahoma Indian Art Program.* Sponsored by McDonnell-Douglas Corporation, Tulsa Management Club, Inc. and Gentry Gallery, Tulsa, OK. (invitational exhibit and sale)

OIO Oklahomans for Indian Opportunity, The Galleria, Norman, OK, 1979-1985 (annual exhibit, juried)

OIS Onondaga Indian School, NY

OL Okanogan Library, Okanogan, WA

OLC Oglala Lakota College, Kyle, SD. *Wazi Paha Oyate Festival* (annual)

OLO *Our Land/Our Selves: American Indian Contemporary Artists.* Organized by University Art Gallery, State University of New York, Albany, NY, 1990. (exhibit, tour)

OM W. H. Over Museum, Vermillion, SD

OMA Oklahoma Museum of Art, Oklahoma City, OK

OPM Old Pueblo Museum, Tucson, AZ

OPS Omak Public Schools, Omak, WA

OSAC Oklahoma State Art Collection, Oklahoma City, OK

OSAF/GC Oklahoma Science and Art Foundation, Inc., Gerrer Collection, Oklahoma City, OK

OSC Oklahoma State Capitol, Oklahoma City, OK

OSU Oklahoma State University, Stillwater, OK

OSU/G Gardiner Art Gallery, Oklahoma State University, Stillwater, OK

OSU/O Oklahoma State University, School of Technology, Okmulgee, OK

OSU/OR Oregon State University, Center of Women Studies, Corvallis, OR. *Northwest Women Artists Symposium* (annual, juried)

OSU/TL Oklahoma State University, School of Technology, Library, Okmulgee, OK

OT *O'odham Tash.* Casa Grande, AZ (annual, juried)

OTIS Otis Art Institute, Los Angeles, CA

OTM Osage Tribal Museum, Pawhuska, OK

OTP Old Town Plaza, Albuquerque, NM

OU/A Auditorium, University of Oklahoma, Norman, OK

OU/ET University of Oklahoma European Tours, 1955-1956, 1958-1961

OU/L Library, University of Oklahoma, Norman, OK

OU/MA Museum of Art, University of Oklahoma, Norman, OK. Currently known as the University of Oklahoma Fred Jones Jr. Museum of Art.

OU/MA/T *Plains Indian Paintings.* Organized by Museum of Art, University of Oklahoma, Norman, OK, 1980. (exhibit, tour)

OU/SM Willis Stovall Museum of Science and History, University of Oklahoma, Norman, OK. Currently known as the Oklahoma Museum of Natural History.

OWE *One With the Earth.* Organized by the Institute of American Indian and Alaska Culture and Arts Development, Santa Fe, NM, 1990-1991. (exhibit, tour)

OWM Old West Museum, Cheyenne, WY

OYMWA *One Hundred Years of Montana Women Artists.* Custer County Art Center, Miles City, MT (exhibit, tour)

P/GF Grandfather, paternal

P/GGF Great-grandfather, paternal

P/GGGF Great-great-grandfather, paternal

P/GGM Great-grandmother, paternal

P/GM Grandmother, paternal

P/GP Grandparents, paternal

PAC Philbrook Art Center, Tulsa, OK. Currently Philbrook Museum of Art. *Annual Indian Art Exhibition.* 1946 - 1979 (juried)

PAC/T Philbrook Art Center. *American Indian Paintings From the Permanent Collection*, 1947-1965 (exhibit, tour)

PACC Potawatomi Agency and Cultural Center, Shawnee, OK

PAF *Pendleton Arts Festival.* Pendleton, OR (annual)

PAIC *Pintura Amerindia Contemporánea/E.U.A.* Sponsored by United States Department of State and International Communications Agency, Washington, D.C., 1975-1980. (tour, Chile, Bolivia, Peru, Colombia, and Ecuador)

PAM Portland Art Museum, Portland, OR

PAM/AZ Phoenix Art Museum, Phoenix, AZ

PAM/C Pasadena Art Museum, Pasadena, CA

PAM/NY Parrish Art Museum, Southampton, NY

PAS *Pryor Art Show.* Sponsored by Pryor Arts and Humanities Council, Pryor, OK (annual)

PAS/OR *Pendleton Art Show.* Pendleton, OR

PBOIA *Pawnee Bill Oklahoma Indian Art Exhibit.* Pawnee, OK (annual, 1st - 1969)

PBS *Paint, Bronze, and Stone.* Mitchell Indian Museum, Kendall College, Evanston, IL, 1989

p.c. Personal communication (letter, interview, etc.)

PDN Palais des Nations, Geneva, Switzerland. *No Beads, No Trinkets*, 1984

PF *Prairie Fire Invitational Art Show.* Sponsored by Prairieland, Inc., Wichita, KS. (annual, 1st - 1989)

Phoenix Phoenix Indian School, Phoenix, AZ

Phoenix J.C. Phoenix Junior College, Phoenix, AZ

PIA *Plains Indian Art: Continuity and Change.* National Museum of Natural History, Smithsonian Institution, Washington, D.C., 1987-1990 (exhibit, tour)

PIE *Plains Indian Arts and Crafts Exposition.* Civic Center, Rapid City, SD (annual 1st - 1978)

PIG Pratt Institute Gallery, Brooklyn, NY

PIPM Plains Indians and Pioneers Museum, Woodward, OK

PM Peabody Museum, Harvard University, Cambridge, MA

PMA Philadelphia Museum of Art, Philadelphia, PA

PMA/MN Plains Art Museum, Moorhead, MN

PNAS *Potawatomi National Art Show.* Potawatomi Tribal Complex, Shawnee, OK

PNCA Pacific Northwest College of Art, Wentz Gallery, Portland, OR

PNIC Pacific Northwest Indian Center, Gonzaga University, Spokane, WA (collection)

PP *Paper and Prints.* Gallery Association of New York, NY, 1980-1984 (exhibit, tour)

PPW *Pike's Peak Western Art Show.* Colorado Springs, CO, 1976

PSA *Pastel Society of America Invitational Show.* New York, NY

PSA/T Pastel Society of America, New York, NY, 1985 (exhibit, tour)

PSC Philander Smith College, Little Rock, AR

PSDM Palm Springs Desert Museum, Palm Springs, CA

PSM State Museum of Pennsylvania, Harrisburg, PA

PSMA Pensacola Museum of Art, Pensacola, FL

PSU Pennsylvania State University, Altoona, PA

PSU/NC Pembroke State University, Pembroke, NC

PSU/OR Portland State University, Portland, OR

PU Princeton University, Princeton, NJ

QACM Qualla Arts and Crafts Mutual, Inc., Cherokee, NC

QM Queens Museum, Flushing, NY

RAM Rose Art Museum, Brandeis University, Waltham, MA

RBP *Raptor - Birds of Prey.* Organized by Institute of American Indian and Alaska Native Culture and Arts Development and the Smithsonian Institution, 1986. (exhibit, tour)

RC *Red Cloud Indian Art Show.* The Heritage Center, Red Cloud Indian School, Pine Ridge, SD (annual, 1st - 1969)

RCAS Roberson Center for the Arts and Sciences, Binghamton, NY

RCBC Rapid City Boy's Club, Rapid City, SD (annual, juried, 1980-1982)

RE *Red Earth Festival.* Indian Art Competition, Myriad Plaza, Oklahoma City, OK (annual, juried, 1st - 1987)

RE/M *Red Earth Festival Market.* Myriad Plaza, Oklahoma City, OK (annual, 1st - 1987)

RFBAG Reichar F. Brush Art Gallery, St. Lawrence University, Canton, NY

RI *Reality of Illusion.* Organized by Denver Art Museum, Denver, CO, and the University Art Galleries, University of Southern California, Los Angeles, CA, 1979-1980. (exhibit, tour)

RISD Rhode Island School of Design, Providence, RI

Riverside Riverside Indian School, Anadarko, OK

RM Riverside Museum, New York, NY

RMA Riverside Museum of Art, Riverside, CA

RMAS Rochester Museum of Arts and Sciences, Rochester, NY

RMC Rocky Mountain College, Billings, MT

RMC/AZ Read Mullan Chevrolet Corporate Collection, Phoenix, AZ

Rochester Rochester School of American Craftsmen, Rochester, NY

Rochester S.T. Rochester School of Technology, Rochester, NY. Name changed to Rochester Institute of Technology.

RSC Rose State College, Midwest City, OK. Formerly Oscar Rose State College.

RVSA Ray Vogue School of Art, Chicago, IL

RVW *Rogue Valley Western Art Show.* Medford, OR (annual, juried)

S *Signals.* Hartje Anthropological Museum, Vienna, Austria, 1984-1987 (exhibit, tour - Austria, West Germany, and Switzerland)

SAA Sarasota Art Association, Sarasota, FL. *Spring Open Exhibition* (annual, juried)

SAF *Seminole Arts Festival.* Fort Lauderdale, FL

SAIEAIP *Second Annual Invitational Exhibition of American Indian Paintings.* United States Department of the Interior, Washington, D.C., 1965

SAM Seattle Art Museum, Seattle, WA

SAM/S Springfield Art Museum, Springfield, MO

San Carlos San Carlos Indian Day School, San Carlos, AZ

San Ildefonso San Ildefonso Pueblo Day School, San Ildefonso Pueblo, NM

San Juan San Juan Pueblo Day School, San Juan Pueblo, NM

Santa Clara Santa Clara Pueblo Day School, Santa Clara Pueblo, NM

Santa Cruz HS Santa Cruz High School, Santa Cruz, NM

Santa Fe Santa Fe Indian School, Santa Fe, NM

SAP *Sapatq'ayn: Twentieth Century Nez Percé Artists.* Sponsored by Idaho Humanities Council, Idaho Commission on the Arts, National Park Service, Nez Percé Tribe, and Northwest Interpretive Association, 1991.

SAR School of American Research, Santa Fe, NM

SBCAM San Bernardino County Art Museum, San Bernardino, CA

SBM Santa Barbara Museum of Art, Santa Barbara, CA

SCAC Sioux City Art Center, Sioux City, IA

SC/IL Springfield College, Springfield, IL

SC/MA Smith College Museum of Art, Northampton, MA

SCA Scottsdale Center for the Arts, Scottsdale, AZ

SCG Sacred Circle Gallery of American Indian Art, Seattle, WA

SCI State College of Iowa, Cedar Falls, IA

SCNAC Schingoethe Center for Native American Cultures, Aurora University, Aurora, IL

SDAM South Dakota Art Museum, Brookings, SD

SDCC South Dallas Cultural Center. *New Harmony: American Indian Art Festival,* 1986 (juried)

SDMM San Diego Museum of Man, San Diego, CA

SDSMT New Gallery, South Dakota School of Mines and Technology, Rapid City, SD

Second Mesa Second Mesa Day School, Second Mesa, AZ

Seneca Seneca Indian School, Wyandotte, OK

Sequoyah Sequoyah Indian School, Tahlequah, OK

SFAI San Francisco Art Institute, San Francisco, CA

SFCC Santa Fe Community College, Santa Fe, NM

SFFA *Santa Fe Festival of the Arts.* Santa Fe, NM (annual)

SFMA San Francisco Museum of Art, San Francisco, CA. Currently San Francisco Museum of Modern Art.

SFNB Security First National Bank, Reseda, CA (collection)

SFNB/WA Sea-First National Bank, Seattle, WA (collection)

SFRR Atchison, Topeka and Santa Fe Railroad, Chicago, IL (collection)

SFSC San Francisco State College, San Francisco, CA. Currently San Francisco State University.

SFSUFC San Francisco State University Faculty Club, San Francisco, CA

SFWF San Francisco World's Fair, San Francisco, CA, 1939-1940. Includes *Golden Gate International Exposition,* 1939.

SGAG San Gabriel Artist's Guild, San Gabriel, CA

SGC Sinte Gleska College, Rosebud, SD. Currently Sinte Gleska University.

SGC/OK St. Gregory's College, Shawnee, OK (collection)

Sherman Sherman Institute, Riverside, CA

Shiprock Shiprock Indian Schools, Shiprock, NM

SHM Shepherd Mall, Oklahoma City, OK. *All-Indian Arts and Crafts Exhibit,* 1973

Shungopovi Shungopovi Day School, Shungopovi, AZ

SI Smithsonian Institution, Washington, D.C.

SI/MNH Smithsonian Institution, Museum of Natural History, Washington, D.C.

SI/OAA Smithsonian Institution, Office of Anthropological Archives, Washington, D.C.

SI/T *Paintings from the Collection of the Riverside Museum.* Circulated by the Smithsonian Institution, Washington, D.C., 1964-1966. (exhibit, tour)

SIAA Sioux Indian Artisans Association, Civic Center, Rapid City, SD. *Indian Art Exhibition,* 1983 (juried)

SIAE *Society of Independent Artists Exhibition.* New York, NY, ca. 1918-1919

SIAF *Southwestern Indian Arts Festival.* Albuquerque, NM, 1973

SIAP *Southwest Indian Arts Project.* Sponsored by Rockefeller Foundation, University of Arizona, Tucson, AZ.

SIAS *Scottsdale Invitational Art Show and Sale.* Sponsored by the Scottsdale Sunrise Rotary Club, Scottsdale, AZ. (annual, 1st - 1986)

SILM San Ildefonso Museum, San Ildefonso Pueblo, NM

SIM Sioux Indian Museum and Craft Center, Indian Arts and Crafts Board, United States Department of the Interior, Rapid City, SD

SINM Seneca Iroquois National Museum, Salamanca, NY

SIRU *Southwestern International Round-Up, Tri-Culture Art Show.* El Paso, TX. Held in conjunctionwith the 63rd Southwestern International Livestock Show and Rodeo. (annual, 1st - 1984)

SIU/M Southern Illinois University Museum, Carbondale, IL

SJBIM *San Juan Bautista Indian Market.* San Juan Bautista, CA (annual)

SJCC *San Juan Community College Selects.* San Juan Community College, Farmington, NM, 1985

SJIS St. Joseph's Indian School, Atka Lakota Museum, Chamberlain, SD

SJM Sheldon Jackson Museum, Sitka, AK

SJSC San Jose State College, San Jose, CA

SLM St. Labré Indian Mission Museum, Ashland, MT

SM Southwest Museum, Los Angeles, CA

SM/NE Stuhr Museum of the Prairie Pioneer, Grand Island, NE

SMA Springville Museum of Art, Springville, UT (annual exhibit)

SMA/IN Snite Museum of Art, University of Notre Dame, Notre Dame, IN

SMA/OR Schneider Museum of Art, Southern Oregon College, Ashland, OR

SMA/TX Stark Museum of Art, Orange, TX

SMIC *Santa Monica Indian Ceremonial.* Santa Monica, CA

SMII Schoharie Museum of the Iroquois Indian, Schoharie, NY

SMM Norwich Free Academy, Slater Memorial Museum, Norwich, CT

SMNAI Southeast Museum of the North American Indian, Marathon, FL. The collection is now housed in the Denver Museum of Natural History, Denver, CO.

SMOM Science Museum of Minnesota, St. Paul, MN

SMU/MA Southeastern Massachusetts University, North Dartmouth, MA

SN *Scottsdale National Indian Art Exhibition.* Scottsdale, AZ (annual, 1st - 1962; discontinued 1972)

SNAICF *Scottsdale Native American Indian Cultural Foundation Arts and Crafts Competition.* Scottsdale, AZ (annual, 1st - 1987; discontinued 1991)

SNIM Six Nations Indian Museum, Onchiota, NY

SNM Seminole Nation Museum, Wewoka, OK

SNMA Sierra Nevada Museum of Art, Reno, NV

SOSU Southeastern Oklahoma State University, Durant, OK

SPAC *Sand Painters Art Club Show.* Valentine, NE, 1975 (juried)

SPIM Southern Plains Indian Museum and Craft Center, Indian Arts and Crafts Board, United States Departmentof the Interior, Anadarko, OK

SPL Seminole Public Library, Seminole, OK

SRJC Santa Rosa Junior College, Native American Museum, Santa Rosa, CA

SS/CW *Submuloc Show/Columbus Wohs.* Organized by ATLATL, Phoenix, AZ, 1992. (exhibit, national tour)

SSA Sumi-c Society of America, Charles Summer School Museum and Archives, Washington, D.C.

SSU Sangamon State College, Springfield, IL

St. Catherine's St. Catherine's Indian School, Santa Fe, NM

St. Joseph's St. Joseph's College, Albuquerque, NM

St. Michael's St. Michael's Indian School, St. Michael's, AZ

St. Patrick's St. Patrick's Mission School, Anadarko, OK

Stewart Stewart Indian School, Stewart, NV

STF *Seminole Tribal Festival, Rodeo, and Art Show.* Fort Lauderdale, FL

SU Stanford University, Stanford, CA

SUAC Southern Utah Arts Council, St. George, UT

SUAG Stanford University Art Gallery, Stanford, CA

SU/NY Syracuse University, Syracuse, NY

SUNY/A State University of New York, Albany, NY

SUNY/B State University of New York, Buffalo, NY

SUNY/BH State University of New York, Binghamton, NY

SUNY/F State University of New York, Fredonia, NY

SUNY/FM State University of New York, Farmingdale, NY

SUNY/G State University of New York, Geneseo, NY

SUNY/O State University of New York, Oswego, NY

SUNY/OW State University of New York, Old Westbury, NY

SUNY/P State University of New York, Plattsburg, NY

SUNY/PT State University of New York, Potsdam, NY

SUNY/RCC State University of New York, Rockland Community College, Suffern, NY

SUSC Southern Utah State College, Cedar City, UT

SV *Shared Visions: Native American Painters and Sculptors in the Twentieth Century.* Heard Museum, 1991-1992 (exhibit, tour)

SVA School of Visual Arts, New York, NY

SWAIA Southwestern Association on Indian Affairs, Inc. Known as Southwestern Association for Indian Arts since 1993. Indian market, Santa Fe, NM (annual in Aug, 1st - 1922)

SWAIA/W Southwestern Association on Indian Affairs, Inc. Winter Market, Santa Fe, NM (1st - 1990; discontinued 1992)

SWFA *Southwest Festival of the Arts.* Weatherford, OK

SWOSU Southwestern Oklahoma State University, Weatherford, OK

SWSE *Second Western States Exhibition/The 38th Corcoran Biennial Exhibition of American Painting.* Corcoran Gallery of Art, Washington, D.C., 1983 (exhibit, tour)

TAAII *Tanner's Annual All-Indian Invitational Pottery and Painting Show.* Scottsdale, AZ

TAC Tuesday Afternoon Club, Glendale, CA

TAI Terry Art Institute, Miami, FL

TAIAF *The American Indian Art Festival.* Sponsored by Westheimer Colony Association, Inc., Houston, TX. (annual, juried, 1st - 1991)

TAIU Texas Agricultural and Industrial University, Kingsville, TX

TAMBA Tribal Artists Mutual Benefit Association, Las Vegas, NV

TAOS Taos Valley Art School, Taos, NM

TAS *Tumutla Art Show.* Pendleton, OR

TBMM Thomas Burke Memorial Museum, University of Washington, Seattle, WA

TC *Texas Classic.* Fort Worth, TX (annual, 1st - 1977)

TCAG The Collective Art Gallery, Topeka, KS, 1990. (invitational, juried)

TCBA *Tulsa County Bar Auxiliary Art Show.* Tulsa, OK (annual, invitational)

TCC *T. C. Cannon, Native American - A New View of the West.* Organized by National Cowboy Hall of Fame,

Oklahoma City, OK, 1990. (exhibit, tour)

TCE *Through Coyote's Eyes*. Sierra Nevada Museum of Art, Reno, NV, 1989 (exhibit, tour)

TCIM *Twin Cities Indian Market and Juried Art Show*. Indian Arts of America, St. Paul, MN (annual)

TCM The Citadel Museum, Charleston, SC

TE *The Elders: Passing It On*. Organized by the Origins Program, Minneapolis, MN, 1989. (exhibit, tour)

Tesuque Tesuque Pueblo Day School, Tesuque Pueblo, NM

TF *Totah Festival*. Farmington, NM (annual, juried)

TFA *Tubac Festival of the Arts*. Tubac, AZ

TFAG Tower Fine Arts Gallery, State University of New York, Brockport, NY

TI *Traditions and Innovation: Seven American Artists*. Plains Art Museum, Moorhead, MN, 1988 (exhibit, tour)

TIAF *Tulsa Indian Art Festival*. Tulsa, OK. Name changed to *Tulsa Art Festival and Pow Wow*, 1992. (annual, 1st - 1987)

TIMSS *Texas Indian Market and Southwest Showcase*. Arlington, TX (annual)

TJC Tulsa Junior College, Tulsa, OK

TM Tweed Museum of Art, Duluth, MN

TM/NE Trailside Museum, Crawford, NE

TMA Toledo Museum of Art, Toledo, OH

TMA/AZ Tucson Museum of Art, Tucson, AZ

TMINR *The Mountain Indian Nation's Rendezvous In Helena*. Governor's mansion, Helena, MT, 1987

TPAS The Public Art Space, Washington State Art in Public Places Program, Seattle, WA

TRM Texas Ranger Hall of Fame Museum, Waco, TX

TRP *The Real People*. International Native-American Council of Arts, Casa de las Américas, Havana, Cuba, 1979

TSC Trenton State College, Trenton, NJ

TSF Tulsa State Fair, Tulsa, OK (annual)

TSM Tennessee State Museum, Nashville, TN

TSU Tennessee State University, Nashville, TN

TTM Three Tribe Museum, Fort Berthold Indian Reservation, ND

TTSP Trail of Tears State Park Gallery, Cape Girardeau County, MO (collection)

TWA Trans-World Airways, Inc., New York, N. (collection)

TWF *Tallasi Winter Festival*. Sponsored by Indian Health Care Resource Center, Tulsa, OK, 1992. (annual, juried, 1st - 1992)

TWIA *Tri-West Indian Art Show*. Tucson, AZ, 1978

TWS Teal Wing Scouts, Dallas, TX (collection)

TYAC Yuma Art Center, Yuma, AZ

UC University Club, Los Angeles, CA

UIM Ute Indian Museum, Montrose, CO

UMA Ulrich Museum of Art, Wichita State University, Wichita, KS

UNESCO United Nations Education, Scientific, and Cultural Organization, New York, NY

UNICEF United Nations International Children's Emergency Fund, United Nations, New York, NY

U of ABQ University of Albuquerque, Albuquerque, NM

U of AK/A University of Alaska, Anchorage, AK

U of AK/C University of Alaska Extension Center for Arts and Crafts, College, AK

U of AK/F University of Alaska, Fairbanks, AK

U of AK/M University of Alaska Museum, Fairbanks, AK

U of AL University of Alabama, Birmingham, AL

U of AR/F University of Arkansas, Fayetteville, AR

U of AR/LR University of Arkansas, Little Rock, AR

U of AZ University of Arizona, Tucson, AZ

U of BC University of British Columbia, Vancouver, BC, Canada

U of CA/B University of California, Berkeley, CA

U of CA/D University of California, Davis, CA

U of CA/LA University of California, Los Angeles, CA

U of CA/LMA The Robert Lowie Museum of Anthropology, University of California at Berkeley, CA. Currently The Phoebe Apperson Hearst Museum of Anthropology.

U of CA/R University of California, Riverside, CA

U of CA/S University of California, Sacramento, CA

U of CA/SB University of California, Santa Barbara, CA

U of CA/SC University of California, Santa Cruz, CA

U of CH University of Chicago, Chicago, IL

U of CO/B University of Colorado, Boulder, CO

U of CT University of Connecticut, Storrs, CT

U of FL/G University of Florida, Gainesville, FL

U of GA University of Georgia, Athens, GA

U of ID University of Idaho, Pocatello, ID

U of ID/M University of Idaho, Moscow, ID

U of ID/PG Prichard Gallery, University of Idaho, Moscow, ID

U of IL University of Illinois, Champaign/Urbana, IL

U of IL/CCC University of Illinois, Chicago Circle Campus, Chicago, IL

U of KS University of Kansas, Lawrence, KS

U of KY University of Kentucky, Lexington, KY

U of MEX University of Mexico, Mexico City, D.F., Mexico

U of MI University of Michigan, Ann Arbor, MI

U of MIM/LAG The Joe and Emily Lowe Art Gallery, University of Miami, Coral Gables, FL

U of MN/B Minneapolis Bell Museum, University of Minnesota, Minneapolis, MN

U of MN/D University of Minnesota, Duluth, MN

U of MN/TC University of Minnesota - Twin Cities, Minneapolis, MN

U of MO University of Missouri, Kansas City, KS

U of MT University of Montana, Missoula, MT

U of MT/WRC Women's Resource Center, University of Montana, Missoula, MT

U of N AZ Northern Arizona University, Flagstaff, AZ

U of N AZ/G Northern Arizona University Art Gallery, Flagstaff, AZ

U of NC/C University of North Carolina, Charlotte, NC

U of NC/CH University of North Carolina, Chapel Hill, NC

U of NC/P University of North Carolina, Pembroke, NC

U of ND University of North Dakota, Grand Forks, ND

U of ND/M University of North Dakota Art Museum, Grand Forks, ND

U of NE University of Nebraska, Lincoln, NE

U of NE/AG University of Nebraska Art Galleries, F. M. Hall Bequest, Lincoln, NE (collection)

U of NH University of New Hampshire, Durham, NH

U of NM University of New Mexico, Albuquerque, NM

U of NM/AM University Art Museum, University of New Mexico, Albuquerque, NM

U of NM/MM Maxwell Museum, University of New Mexico, Albuquerque, NM

U of NV University of Nevada, Reno, NV. *Native American Art Show* (annual)

U of NV/LV/M University Museum, University of Nevada, Las Vegas, NV

U of OH University of Ohio, Athens, OH

U of OK University of Oklahoma, Norman, OK

U of OR University of Oregon, Eugene, OR

U of PA/M University of Pennsylvania Museum, Philadelphia, PA

U of Redlands University of Redlands, Redlands, CA

U of SC/S University of South Carolina, Spartanburg, SC

U of SD University of South Dakota, Vermillion, SD

U of SD/OHG Oscar Howe Gallery, University of South Dakota, Vermillion, SD

U of SD/S University of South Dakota, Springfield, SD

U of SF University of San Francisco, San Francisco, CA

U of SF/G University of San Francisco Gallery, San Francisco, CA

U of Tulsa University of Tulsa, Tulsa, OK

U of Tulsa/AC Allen Chapman Activity Center, University of Tulsa, Tulsa, OK

U of TX University of Texas, Austin, TX

U of TX/EP University of Texas, El Paso, TX

U of UT University of Utah, Salt Lake City, UT

U of UT/FAM Utah Fine Arts Museum, University of Utah, Salt Lake City, UT

U of VA/MFA Museum of Fine Arts, University of Virginia, Charlottesville, VA

U of WA University of Washington, Seattle, WA

U of WA/AG University of Washington Art Gallery, Seattle, WA

U of WI/EC University of Wisconsin, Eau Claire, WI

U of WI/G University of Wisconsin, Greenbay, WI. (collection)

U of WI/M University of Wisconsin, Madison, WI

U of Wichita University of Wichita, Wichita, KS

U of WV University of West Virginia, Morgantown, WV

UPA United Pueblo Agency, Albuquerque, NM

USDC United States Department of Commerce, Washington, D.C.

USDI United States Department of the Interior, Washington, D.C.

USDS United States Department of State, Washington, D.C. *Contemporary American Indian Art.* Co-sponsored by USIA Recreation Association, 1963.

USIS United States Information Service, Washington, D.C. Sponsors art exhibits in foreign countries.

USNM/OA United States National Museum, Office of Anthropology, Washington, D.C.

USU Utah State University, Logan, UT

UTAE *United Tribes Art Exposition.* Bismarck, ND (annual, juried)

UTIC United Tribes Indian College, Bismarch, ND

UWC University Women's Club, Los Angeles, CA

VH *Vision of Hope.* Akta Lakota Museum, Chamberlain, SD, 1990-1991 (exhibit, tour)

Vietnam Vietnam Conflict (1957-1975)

VL *Voices From The Land.* University of Tulsa, Tulsa, OK, 1975

VNB Valley National Bank, Walter Reed Bimsom Gallery of Western Art, Phoenix, AZ (collection)

VP *Visions of the People.* The Minneapolis Institute of Arts, Minneapolis, MN, 1992-1993 (exhibit, tour)

VT *Voices of Today: Cultural Expression of Native People of North America.* American Indian Institute, Bozeman, MT, 1986 (exhibit, tour)

VV *Views and Visions: The Symbolic Imagery of the Native American Church.* Southern Plains Indian Museum, Anadarko, OK, 1981

W Whitney Museum of American Art, New York, NY

WA Wadsworth Antheneum, Hartford, CT

WAA Westwood Art Association, West Los Angeles, CA

WAAG Wichita Art Association, Inc., Gallery, Wichita, KS

WAATAP *We Are Always Turning Around On Purpose.* Organized by State University of New York, Old Westbury, NY, 1986-1987. (exhibit, tour)

WAM Wichita Art Museum, Wichita, KS

WASF Washington State Fair, Puyallup, WA

WASG *We Are The Seventh Generation.* Coordinated and circulated by Native American Indian Media Corporation, Knoxville, TN.

WAW *Womanart West,* Grand Junction, CO

WC *Watercolors,* University of North Dakota, Grand Forks, ND, 1979 (exhibit, tour)

WCCA Western Colorado Center for the Arts, Grand Junction, CO

WCH Woman's Club of Hollywood, Hollywood, CA

WFS Wilshire Federal Savings Art Salon, Los Angeles, CA (exhibition)

WG Whirlwind Gallery, Lake Worth, FL

WG/AU Watkins Gallery, The American University, Washington, D.C.

WGAI WARM Gallery Annual Invitational, Minneapolis, MN

WH *Western Heritage Art Show.* Littleton, CO (annual)

WHB *We, The Human Beings.* Organized by the College of Wooster Art Museum, Wooster, OH, 1992. (exhibit, tour)

WHCO Walt Horan Congressional Office, Washington, D.C.

Whitecone White Cone Day School, White Cone, AZ

WIAME Wichita Indian Art Market and Exhibition, Mid-America All-Indian Center and Museum, Wichita, KS (annual, 1st – 1993)

WIB *Walk In Beauty, A National Invitational Native American Art Show.* Sponsored by the Santa Fe Festival of the Arts, Santa Fe, NM, 1981.

WIEAS *Winslow I-40 Exposition Art Show.* Winslow, AZ

WLU Lee Chapel Museum, Washington and Lee University, Lexington, VA

WM *Western Horseman Magazine.* Colorado Springs, CO (collection)

WM/T *Witte Memorial Art Museum Painting Exhibition.* San Antonio, TX (tours – Texas, Louisiana, and Oklahoma)

WMNAAF *White Mountain Native American Art Festival.* Pinetop-Lakeside, AZ (annual, 1st – 1987)

WMWA Whitney Museum of Western Art, Cody, WY

WNAA *What is Native American Art?* Philbrook Museum of Art, Tulsa, OK, 1986-1988 (exhibit, tour)

WNF *Western Navajo Fair.* Tuba City, AZ

WOM Woolaroc Museum, Bartlesville, OK

WPA Works Progress Administration, United States Government, Washington, D.C.

WRM Will Rogers Memorial, Claremore, OK

WRTD *When The Rainbow Touches Down.* Heard Museum, Phoenix, AZ, 1986 (exhibit, tour)

WSAC Washington State Arts Commission, Olympia, WA (collection)

WSC Washington State College, Ellensburg, WA. Currently Central Washington University.

WSCS *Women of Sweetgrass, Cedar, and Sage.* American Indian Community House, New York, NY (exhibit, tour)

WSU Wisconsin State University, Superior, WI

WSU/P Washington State University, Pullman, WA

WT *Western Trails Art Show and Sale.* Littleton, CO, 1977

WTF *Willow Tree Festival.* Old Cowboy Museum, Gorden, NE (annual, 1989-92)

WW *Women's Work: The Montana Women's Centennial Art Survey Exhibition 1889-1989,* 1989 (exhibit, tour)

WWI World War I (1914-1918)

WWII World War II (1939-1945)

WWM Wheelwright Museum of the American Indian, Santa Fe, NM. Formerly The House of Navajo Religion and Museum of Navajo Ceremonial Art

YAIA *Young American Indian Artists,* Riverside Museum, New York, NY, 1965-1966

Yale U Yale University, New Haven, CT

YK/T *Yeffe Kimball: A Retrospective Exhibition.* Philbrook Art Center, Tulsa, OK, 1966-1967 (exhibit, tour)

YMCA Young Men's Christian Association (exhibit)

YU/BRBML Yale University, Beinecke Rare Book and Manuscript Library, New Haven, CT

YWCA Young Woman's Christian Association (exhibit)

ZAM Zanesville Art Center, Zanesville, OH

Zia Zia Pueblo Day School, Zia Pueblo, NM

Zuni Zuni High School, Zuni Pueblo, NM

Bibliography

Anonymous. 1941. Meet Coyote. BC, Canada: Society for the Futherance of British Columbia Tribal Arts and Crafts.

———. 1965. *Young American Indian Artists.* New York: Riverside Museum. (exhibition catalog)

———. 1967. *The Paintings of Frank Day Maidu Indian Artist.* San Francisco: American Indian Historical Society. (exhibition catalog)

———. 1974. *When the Thunder Spoke.* New York: Holiday House.

———. 1976. *New Horizons.* Los Angeles: Southwest Museum. (exhibition catalog)

———. 1982. *Contact II, From the Center: A Folio of Native American Art andPoetry.* Philadelphia: Strawberry Press.

———. 1982a. *National Indian Child Conference Art Show.* Phoenix: Save the Children Foundation. (exhibition catalog)

———. 1984. *Guide to American Law.* St. Paul, MN: West Publishing House.

Abbott, Lawrence. 1994. *I Stand in the Center of the Good.* Lincoln, NE: University of Nebraska Press

Abeita, Louise. 1939. *I am a Pueblo Girl.* New York: William Morrow & Co.

Adams, Ben. 1959. *Alaska: The Big Land.* New York: Hill and Wang.

Adams, Ben and Richard Newlin. 1987. *The Graphic Works.* Albuquerque: Taos Editions Ltd.

Adams, Helen, Robert Hass and Berry Lopez. 1979. *Blaze of Distance.* Portland, OR: Arts Commission and OregonCommittee for the Humanities.

Ahgupuk, George. 1953. *18 Reproductions of Paintings by George Ahgupuk.* Seattle: Deers Press.

Alexander, Hartley Burr. 1916. *North American Mythology.* Vol. 10. Boston: Marshall Jones Company.

———. 1932. *Pueblo Indian Painting.* Nice, France: C. Szwedzicki.

———. 1938. *Sioux Indian Painting.* Nice, France: C. Szwedzicki. 2 vols., portfolio.

Alivatuk, Jamasie, et al. 1976. *Stories from Pantnertung.* Edmonton, AB: Hurtig.

Allen, Terry D., ed. 1972 *The Whispering Wind.* Garden City, NY: Doubleday.

Amerson, L. Price, Jr., ed. 1981. *Confluences of Tradition and Change: 24 American Indian Artists.* Davis, CA: Richard L. Nelson Gallery, University of California. (exhibition catalog)

Amiotte, Arthur. 1988. *One Hundred Years of the Art of the Oglalas and Their Relatives.* Pine Ridge, SD: Red Cloud Indian School, Heritage Center, Inc. (exhibition catalog)

Anderson, Charles J. 1981. *Amado Maurilio Peña Jr.* Albuquerque: Robert Steven Young Publishing Co.

Andrews, Lynn. 1983. *Flight of the Seventh Moon.* San Francisco: Harper and Row.

Anoee, Eric. 1982. *Eskimo Point/Arviat.* Winnipeg, MB: Winnipeg Art Gallery.

Antoine, Janeen, and Sara Bates. 1991. *Portfolio III: In Native American Artists.* San Francisco: American Indian Contemporary Arts.

Archuleta, Margaret and Renard Strickland. 1991. *Shared Visions.* Phoenix: The Heard Museum. (exhibition catalog)

Arnold, Elliott. 1947. *Blood Brother.* New York: Duell, Sloan and Pearce.

Axford, Roger W. 1980. *Native Americans: 23 Indian Biographies.* Indiana, PA: A.G. Halldin Publishing Co.

Babcock, Barbara. 1986. *The Pueblo Storyteller: Development of a Figurative Ceramic.*Tucson, AZ: University of Arizona Press.

———, and Nancy J. Parezo. 1988. *Daughters of the Desert.* Albuquerque: University of New Mexico Press.

Bahnimptewa, Cliff. 1971. *Dancing Kachinas: A Hopi Artist's Documentary.* Phoenix: The Heard Museum.

Bahti, Tom. 1966. *Southwestern Indian Arts and Crafts.* Flagstaff, AZ: KC Publications.

———. 1970. *Southwestern Indian Ceremonials.* Flagstaff, AZ: KC Publications.

Ballantine, Betty and Ian Ballantine. 1993. *The Native Americans: An Illustrated History.* Atlanta, GA: Turner Publishing.

Banks, Kenneth. 1986. *Portfolio: Eleven American Indian Artists.* San Francisco: American Indian Contemporary Indian Arts.

Baron, Robert A. and Donn Byrne. 1994. *Social Psychology.* Needham Hights, MA: Allyn and Bacon, Inc.

Barrett, Stephen M. 1906. *Geronimo's Story of His Life.* New York: Duffield & Co.

Bass, Althea. 1950. *The Thankful People.* Caldwell, ID: Caxton Printers.

Bassman, Theda. 1991. *Hopi Kachina Dolls and their Carvers.* West Chester, PA: Schiffer Publishing.

Bataille, Gretchen M., and Kathleen Mullen Sands. 1984. *American Indian Women: Telling their Lives.* Lincoln, NE: University of Nebraska Press.

Batkin, Jonathan. 1983. *Plains Indian Painting and Drawing of the 19th Century.* Colorado Springs, CO: Colorado Springs Fine Arts Center.

Baylor, Byrd. 1974. *They Put on Masks.* New York: Scribner.

———. 1977. *Yes is Better Than No.* New York: Scribner.

Beck, Peggy V., Anna Lee Walters and Nia Francisco. 1990. *The Sacred Ways of Knowledge.* Flagstaff, AZ: Northland Press.

Beeler, Joe. 1967. *Cowboys and Indians.* Norman, OK: University of Oklahoma Press.

———. 1974. *The Joe Beeler Sketchbook.* Flagstaff, AZ: Northland Press.

Begay, Shonto. 1992. *Ma'ii and Cousin Horned Toad.* New York: Scholastic, Inc.

Belknap, Bill. 1977. *Fred Kabotie: Hopi Indian Artist.* Flagstaff, AZ: Museum of Northern Arizona.

Bellman, David, ed. 1980. *Peter Pitseolak (1902-1973): Inuit Historian of Seekooseelak.* Montréal, PQ: McCord Museum.

Berthrong, Donald J. 1963. *The Southern Cheyennes.* Norman, OK: University of Oklahoma Press.

Best, Alexander. 1978. *Alex Janvier.* Ontario: Department of Ethnology, Royal Ontario Museum. (exhibition catalog)

Birney, Hoffman. 1935. *Ay-Chee, Son of the Desert.* Philadelphia: Penn Publishing Co.

Blackboy, Cecil, et al. 1973. *Painted Tipis by Contemporary Plains Indian Artists.* Anadarko, OK: Oklahoma Indian Arts and Crafts Cooperative.

Bleeker, Sonia. 1963. *Indians.* New York: Golden Press.

Blish, Helen H. 1967. *A Pictographic History of the Oglala Sioux.* Lincoln, NE: University of Nebraska Press.

Blodgett, Jean. n.d. *Looking South.* Winnipeg, MB: Winnipeg Art Gallery.

———. 1976. *Tuu'log/Anguhadluq.* Winnipeg, MB: Winnipeg Art Gallery.

———. 1978a. *The Coming and Going of the Shaman: Eskimo Shamanism and Art.* Winnipeg, MB: Winnipeg Art Gallery. (exhibition catalog)

———. 1978b. *The Zazelenchuk Collection of Eskimo Art.* Winnipeg, MB: Winnipeg Art Gallery. (exhibition catalog)

———. 1981. *Kenojuak.* Toronto, ON: Mintmark Press.

———. 1983. *Grasp Tight the Old Ways: Selections from the Klamer Family Collection of Inuit Art.* Toronto, ON: Art Gallery of Ontario. (exhibition catalog)

———. 1984. *Etidlooie Etidlooie.* London, ON: London Regional Art Gallery.

Blue Cloud, Peter, ed. 1972. *Alcatraz is Not an Island.* Berkeley, CA: Wingbow Press.

Blue Eagle, Acee. 1959. *Oklahoma Indian Painting – Poetry.* Tulsa, OK: Acorn Publishing Company.

Boyd, Maurice. 1981. *Kiowa Voices: Ceremonial Dance, Ritual and Song.* Vol. I. Fort Worth, TX: Texas Christian University Press.

———. 1983. *Kiowa Voices: Myths, Legends, and Folktales.* Vol. II. Fort Worth, TX: Texas Christian University Press.

Bradley, Douglas E. 1991. *White Swan: Crow Indian Warrior and Painter.* Notre Dame, IN: The Snite Museum of Art, University of Notre Dame. (exhibition catalog)

Breeskin, Adelyn D. (Intro.). 1972. *Scholder/Indians.* Flagstaff, AZ: Northland Press.

Brent, Ricks J. and Alexander E. Anthony, Jr., comps. 1993. *Kachinas: Spirit Beings of the Hopi.* Albuquerque: Avanyu.

Brindze, Ruth. 1951. *The Story of the Totem Pole.* New York: Vanguard Press.

Bringhurst, Robert. 1991. *The Black Canoe.* Vancouver, BC: Douglas and McIntyre.

Britton, Phil. 1981. *The Complete Book of Country Swing and Western Dance and a Bit About Cowboys.* New York: Doubleday.

Broder, Patricia Janis. 1978. *Hopi Painting: The World of the Hopis.* New York: E. P. Dutton and Co.

———. 1981. *American Indian Painting and Sculpture.* New York: Abbeville Press.

———. 1984. *The American West: The Modern Vision.* Boston: Little, Brown and Company.

Brody, J. J. 1971. *Indian Painters and White Patrons.* Albuquerque: University of New Mexico Press.

———. 1992. *A Bridge Across Cultures: Pueblo Painters in Santa Fe, 1910-1932.* Santa Fe: Wheelwright Museum of the American Indian.

Brokschmidt, Rolf. 1982. *Maske Und Regenbild.* Berlin, Germany: Galerie Akmak.

Bromberg, Eric. 1986. *Kachina Doll Carving.* West Chester, PA: Schiffer Publishing, Ltd.

Brown, Vinson. 1962. *Warriors of the Rainbow: Strange and Prophetic Dreams of the Indians.* Healdsburg, CA: Naturegraph Publishers.

———. 1971. *Great Upon the Mountain.* Healdsburg, CA: Naturegraph Publishers.

Brown, William Compton. 1961. *The Indian Side of the Story.* Spokane, WA: C. W. Hill Printing Co.

Browne, Vic. 1991. *Monster Slayer.* Flagstaff, AZ: Northland Publishing.

Bruchae, Joseph, ed. 1983. *Songs From This Earth on a Turtle's Back.* Greenfield Center, NY: Greenfield Review Press.

———. 1993. *Flying With the Eagle, Racing the Great Bear.* Bridge Water Books/Troll Associates.

Burbank, E. A. 1944. *Burbank Among the Indians; as Told by Ernest Royce, ed. by Frank Taylor.* Caldwell, ID: Caxton Printers.

Burland, Cottie. 1973. *Eskimo Art.* Toronto, ON: Hamlyn.

Burrows, Fredrika. 1973. *The Yankee Scrimshander.* Taunton, MA: William Sullwold Publishers.

Burton, Jimalee. 1974. *Indian Heritage, Indian Pride.* Norman, OK: University of Oklahoma Press.

Callander, Lee A., and Ruth Slivka. 1984. *Shawnee Home Life: The Paintings of Ernest Spybuck.* New York: Museum of the American Indian.

Campbell, David, ed. 1993. *Native American Art and Folklore.* Greenwich, CT: Brompton Books, Corp.

Campbell, Joseph. 1988. *Historical Atlas of World Mythology: The Way of the Seeded Earth – Vol. 2, Part 2.* New York: Harper & Row.

Cardinal-Schubert, Joane. 1992. *Time for Dialogue*. Calgary, AB: Calgary Aboriginal Awareness Society. (exhibition catalog)

Carhart, Mary. 1984. *Watercolor: See for Yourself*. New York: Grumbacher, Inc.

Carlson, Raymond, et al. 1964. *Read Mullan Gallery of Western Art*. Phoenix: Read Mullan.(exhibition catalog)

Carlson, Vada, and Gary Witherspoon. 1968. *Black Mountain Boy*. Washington, D.C.: Bureau of Indian Affairs.

Carpenter, Edmund. 1968. *The Story of Comock the Eskimo as Told to Robert Flaherty*. New York: Simon and Schuster.

Carter, E. Russell. 1955. *The Gift is Rich*. New York: Friendship Press.

Casler, Leigh. 1994. *The Boy Who Dreamed of an Acorn*. New York: Philomel Books.

Castellon, Rolando. 1978. *Asthetics of Graffiti*. San Francisco: San Francisco Museum of Modern Art.

Castro, Betti White. 1985. *Celebrate the Spirit*. Escondido, CA: Mathes Cultural Center. (exhibition catalog)

Caswell, Helen Rayburn. 1968. *Shadows from the Singing House*. Rutland, VT: C.E. Tuttle Co.

Catlin, George. 1832. *Letters and Notes of the North American Indian*. New York: Wiley & Putnam.

Chase, Katherine. 1982. *Navajo Painting*. Flagstaff, AZ: Museum of Northern Arizona, *Plateau*. Quarterly, Vol. 54, No. 1.

Chee, Robert. 1975. *The Navajo*. Tucson, AZ: Mark Bahti.

Chevalier, Jacques. 1982. *The Stolen Gift*. Toronto, ON: University of Toronto Press.

Cia, Manual. 1991. *The Color Quest*. Albuquerque: Cia Bellas Arts.

Cinader, Bernhard. 1976. *Contemporary Native Art of Canada: The Woodlands*. Toronto, ON: Royal Ontario Museum. (exhibition catalog)

———. 1977. *Contemporary Indian Art - The Trail from Past to Present*. Trent University, Mackenzie Gallery and Native Studies Program. (exhibition catalog)

———. 1987a. *Contemporary Native Art of Canada - The Woodland Indians*. Thunder Bay, ON: Lehto Printers, Ltd. (exhibition catalog)

———. 1987b. *Manitoulin Island: The Third Layer*. Thunder Bay, ON: Thunder Bay Art Gallery. (exhibition catalog)

Clark, Ann Nolan. 1954. *The Hen of Wahpeton*. Washington, D.C.: Department of the Interior, Bureau of Indian Affairs.

———. 1940a. *Who Wants to be a Prairie Dog?* Phoenix: Office of Education, Bureau of Indian Affairs, Phoenix Indian School Press.

———. 1940b. *Little Boy With Three Names*. Washington, D.C.: Office of Education,Bureau of Indian Affairs.

———. 1940c. *The Pine Ridge Porcupine*. Lawrence, KS: Department of the Interior, Bureau of Indian Affairs, Haskell Institute.

———. 1940-42. *Little Herder Series*. Phoenix: Office of Education, Bureau of Indian Affairs, Phoenix Indian School, 4 vols.

———. 1941. *In my Mother's House*. New York: Viking Press.

———. 1942a. *There Still Are Buffalo*. Lawrence, KS: Office of Education, Bureau of Indian Affairs, Haskell Institute.

———. 1942b. *The Slim Butte Raccoon*. Washington, D.C.: Department of the Interior, Bureau of Indian Affairs.

———. 1943a. *About The Grass Mountain Mouse*. Lawrence, KS: Department of the Interior, Bureau of Indian Affairs, Haskell Institute

———. 1943b. *Young Hunter of Picurís*. Washington, D.C.: Office of Education, Bureau of Indian Affairs.

———. 1944. *Bringer of the Mystery Dog*. Washington, D.C.: Office of Education, Bureau of Indian Affairs.

———. 1945. *Sun Journey*. Washington, D.C.: Office of Education, Bureau of Indian Affairs.

———. 1947. *Singing Sioux Cowboy Reader*. Washington, D.C.: Department of the Interior, Bureau of Indian Affairs.

———. 1954. *Blue Canyon Horse*. New York: Viking Press.

———. 1957. *Little Indian Basket Maker*. Los Angeles: Melmont.

———. 1960. *Peetie the Pack Rat and Other Indian Stories*. Caldwell, ID: Caxton.

———. 1962. *The Desert People*. New York: Viking Press.

Clutesi, George C. 1967. *Son of Raven, Son of Deer: Fables of the Tse-Shat People*. Sidney, BC: Grey's Publishing.

———. 1969. *Potlatch*. Sidney, BC: Grey's Publishing.

Cochran, George M. 1976. *Indian Portraits of the Pacific Northwest*. Portland, OR: Binford & Mort.

Cochran, Jo, et al., eds. 1984. *Gathering Ground, New Art and Writing by Northwest Women of Color*. Seattle: Seal Press.

Coe, Ralph T. 1986. *Lost and Found Traditions*. Seattle: University of Washington Press.

Cohen, Caron Lee. 1988. *The Mud Pony, A Traditional Skidi Pawnee Tale*. New York: Scholastic, Inc.

Collinson, Helen. 1978. *Inuit Games and Contests: The Clifford E. Lee Collection of Prints*. Edmonton, AB: University of Alberta.

Conley, Robert J. 1991. *The Witch of Goingsnake and Other Stories*. Norman, OK: University of Oklahoma Press.

Cook, Cynthia Waye. 1993. *From the Center: The Drawings of Luke Anguhadluq*. Toronto: Art Gallery of Ontario. (exhibition catalog)

Cornplanter, Jesse. 1903. *Iroquois Indian Games and Dances*. Chicago: F. Starr.

———. 1938. *Legends of the Longhouse*. Philadelphia: J. B. Lippincot.

Cox, Sue, ed. 1976. *Female Psychology: The Emerging Self*. Science Research Associates.

Culleton, Beatrice. 1989. *Spirit of the White Bison*. Book Pub. Co.

CURTIS, EDWARD S. 1907-30. *The North American Indian.* Cambridge, MA: Harvard University Press. 20 vols.

CURTIS, NATALIE. 1910. *The Indians' Book.* Second Edition, New York: Harper.

CUSICK, DAVID. 1848. *David Cusick's Sketches of Ancient History of the Six Nations.* Lockport, NY: Turner and McCollum.

———. 1961. *Ancient History of the Six Nations.* Lockport, NY: Niagara County Historical Society.

DAWDY, DORIS OSTRANDER. 1968. *Annotated Bibliography of American Indian Painting.* New York: Museum of the American Indian.

DAY, JOHN A., BROTHER C. M. SIMON, ET AL. 1990. *Andrew Standing Soldier.* Vermillion, SD: University Art Galleries, The University of South Dakota. (exhibition catalog).

———. 1991. *Five Families: Art Exhibition.* Vermillion, SD: University of South Dakota. (exhibition catalog)

DE CALA, REGINA ALBARADO. 1967. *Fables of Tewa Indian Dances.* Albuquerque, NM: Clark Industries.

DECAMP, L. SPRAGUE. 1960. *Man and Power.* New York: Golden Press.

DECLUE, CHARLOTTE. 1985. *Without Warning.* New York: Strawberry Press.

DEERING, NORA, AND HELGA HARRIS DELISLE. 1976. *Mohawk, A Teaching Grammar.* Quebéc, PQ: Thunderbird Press.

DEHUFF, ELIZABETH WILLIS. 1922. *Taytay's Tales.* New York: Harcourt Brace & Co.

———. 1924. *Taytay's Memories.* New York: Harcourt Brace & Co.

———. 1926. *Swift Eagle of the Rio Grande.* Chicago: Rand McNally Co.

———. 1930. *Five Little Katchinas.* Boston: Houghton Mifflin.

DEMALLIE, RAYMOND, AND DOUG PARKS, ED. 1987. *Sioux Indian Religion: Tradition and Innovation.* Norman, OK: University of Oklahoma.

DEL MONTE, H. D. N.D. *Life of the Chief Washakie and the Shoshoni Indians.* Lander, WY: Noble Hotel.

DEMPSEY, HUGH A. 1978. *Tailfeathers: Indian Artist.* Calgary, AB: Glenbow-Alberta Institute. Art Series No. 2.

DESBARATS, PETER. 1969. *What They Used To Tell About.* Toronto, ON: McClelland and Stewart.

DESJARLAIT, ROBERT. 1986. *Manidoo-Wiwin Ojibway.* Ma-En-Gun Studio Press.

———. 1989. *O-Do-I-Daym Ojibway: Clans of the Ojibway Coloring Book.* Minneapolis, MN: Indian Women's Resource Center Press.

———. 1990A. *Nimiwin: A History of Ojibway Dance and Dance Regalia.* Coon Rapids, MN: Anoka-Hennepin Indian Education Press.

———. 1990B. *Art History of the Ojibway: Traditional to Contemporary.* Ma-En-Gun Studio Press.

DEUPREE, HARRY L. 1979. *Sharing Our Wealth.* Oklahoma City: Oklahoma Historical Society Museum. (exhibition catalog)

DEWDNEY, SELWYN, ED. 1965. *Legends of my People, the Great Ojibway.* Toronto, ON: Ryerson Press.

DIPESO, CHARLES C. 1987. *Amerind Foundation, Fulton-Hayden Memorial Art Gallery.* Dragoon, AZ: The Foundation. (gallery guide)

DICKASON, OLIVE PATRICIA. 1972. *Indian Arts in Canada.* Ottawa, ON: Department of Indian Affairs and Northern Development.

DINES, GLEN, AND RAYMOND PRICE. 1961. *Dog Soldiers: The Famous Warrior Society of the Cheyenne Indians.*New York: Macmillan.

DOCKSTADER, FREDERICK J. 1954. *The Kachina and the White Man; The Influence of the White Man on the Hopi Indian Kachina Religion.* Bloomfield Hills, MI: Cranbrook Institute of Science.

———. 1962. *Indian Art in America: The Arts and Crafts of the North American Indian.* Greenwich, CT: New York Graphic Society.

———. 1973A. *Indian Art of the Americas.* New York: Museum of the American Indian.

———. 1973B. *Masterworks from the Museum of the American Indian.* New York: Metropolitan Museum of Art.

———. 1977. *Great North American Indians: Profiles in Life and Leadership.* New York: Van Nostrand Reinhold Company.

———, ED. 1982. *Oscar Howe: A Retrospective Exhibition.* Tulsa, OK: Thomas Gilcrease Museum Association and South Dakota Arts Council. (exhibition catalog)

DODGE, RICHARD IRVING. 1882. *Our Wild Indians: Thirty-Three Years' Personal Experience Among the Red Men of the Great West.* Hartford, CT: A. D. Worthington & Co.

DOOLEY, VIRGINIA, ED. 1981. *Nudes and Foods: Gorman Goes Gourmet.* Flagstaff, AZ: Northland Press.

———, ED. 1989. *Nudes and Foods: Volume II.* Taos, NM: Navajo Gallery.

DOOLING, D. M., AND PAUL JORDAN SMITH, EDS. 1989. *I Become Part of It.* New York: Parabola Books.

DORSEY, GEORGE. 1905. *The Cheyenne. I, Ceremonial Organization.* Chicago: Field Museum of Natural History, Publication 99.

DOUGLAS, FREDERIC, AND RENÉ D'HARNONCOURT. 1941. *Indian Art of the United States.* New York: Museum of Modern Art.

DOUGLAS, STAN, ED. 1991. *Vancouver Anthology: The Institutional Politics of Art.* Vancouver, BC: Talonbooks.

DRISCOLL, BERNADETTE. 1982. *Inuit Myths, Legends and Songs.* Winnipeg, MB: Winnipeg Art Gallery.

———. 1987. *Kalvak/Emerak: Memorial Catalog.* Holman, NWT: Holman Eskimo Co-op. (exhibition catalog)

DUFFEK, KAREN. 1986. *Bill Reid: Beyond the Essential Form.* Vancouver, BC: University of British Columbia. (exhibition catalog)

DUNN, DOROTHY. 1968. *American Indian Painting of the Southwest and Plains Areas.* Albuquerque: University of New Mexico Press.

———. 1969. *Plains Indian Sketchbooks of Zo-Tom and Howling Wolf, 1877.* Flagstaff, AZ: Northland Press.

DUNN, JACOB PIATT, JR. 1886. *Massacres of the Mountains.* New York: Harper & Brothers.

DUNN, LOIS. 1993. *Spider Woman.* New York: Scholastic, Inc.

DUTY, MICHAEL, ET AL. 1992. *New Art of the West 3.* Indianapolis, ID: Eiteljorg Museum. (exhibition catalog)

EBER, DOROTHY, ED. 1971. *Pitseolak: Pictures Out of My Life.* Montréal, PQ: Design Collaborative Books.

EKKEHART, MALOTKI. 1988. *The Mouse Couple.* Flagstaff, AZ: Northland Press.

ELDER, GARY, ED. 1975. *The Far Side of the Storm: New Ranges of Western Fiction.* Los Cerrillos, NM: San Marcos Press.

ELLISON, ROSEMARY. 1972. *Contemporary Southern Plains Indian Painting.* Anadarko, OK: Oklahoma Indian Arts and Crafts Cooperative. (exhibition catalog)

———. 1973. *Painted Tipis by Contemporary Plains Indian Artists.* Anadarko, OK: Oklahoma Indian Arts and Crafts Cooperative. (exhibition catalog)

———. 1976. *Contemporary Southern Plains Indian Metalwork.* Anadarko, OK: Oklahoma Indian Arts and Crafts Cooperative. (exhibition catalog)

ENOCHS, J. B. 1940. *Little Man's Family.* Phoenix, AZ: Phoenix Indian School.

EVANS, BESSIE, AND MARY G. EVANS. 1931. *American Indian Dance Steps.* New York: A. S. Barnes & Company,Inc.

EWERS, JOHN CANFIELD. 1939. *Plains Indian Painting.* Stanford, CA: Stanford University Press.

———. 1965. *Artists of the Old West.* New York: Doubleday & Co.

———. 1986. *Plains Indian Sculpture, A Traditional Art from America's Heartland.* Washington, D.C.: Smithsonian Institution.

FAWCETT, DAVID M., AND LEE A. CALLANDER. 1982. *Native American Painting - Selections from the Museum of the American Indian.* New York: Museum of the American Indian.

FENTON, WILLIAM N. 1978. "Jessie Cornplanter, Seneca, 1889-1957." *American Indian Intellectuals.* Proceedings of the American Ethnological Society.

FERGUSON, B. 1973. *Sarain Stump.* Calgary, AB: Glenbow-Alberta Art Gallery. (exhibition catalog)

FINDLEY, ROWA. 1972. *Great American Deserts.* Washington, D.C.: National Geographic Society.

FINK, KENNETH. 1980. *Indian Art from Cave to Gallery.* Claremore, OK: Claremore College. (exhibition catalog)

FIRST BOY. 1942. *Land of Nakoda, A History of the Assiniboine.* State of Montana.

FITZHUGH, WILLIAM W., AND SUSAN A. KAPLAN. 1982. *Inua: Spirit World of the Bering Sea Eskimo.* Washington, D.C.: Smithsonian Institution.

FITZPATRICK, MARY, ET AL. 1982. *Contemporary North American Indian Art.* Washington, D.C.: Smithsonian Institution.

FOREMAN, CAROLYN THOMAS. 1989. *Indian Women Chiefs.* Muskogee, OK: Hoffman Print Co.

FOREMAN, GRANT. 1989. *The Five Civilized Tribes.* Norman, OK: University of Oklahoma Press.

FORTIN, CLAUDETTE. 1988. *Lance Belanger-Paiewonsky Gallery.* Ottawa, ON: Runge Press.

FOSS, PHILLIP, JR. 1982. *Spawning the Medicine River.* Santa Fe: Institute of American Indian Arts Press.

FREEMAN, EDWINA. 1988. *Robert Freeman: Etchings.* Escondido, CA: A & A Litho.

FREEMAN, ROBERT. 1971. *Rubber Arrows for Indians Only.* Oceanside, CA: Robert Freeman.

———. 1981. *War Whoops and All That Jazz.* Oceanside, CA: Robert Freeman.

FRONTAIN, DICK. 1979. *Cherokee Artist: Bert Seabourn.* Oklahoma City: Prairie Hawk Pub.

FROST, LAWRENCE A. 1964. *The Custer Album.* Seattle: Superior Publishing Co.

FRY, JACQUELINE. 1972. *Treaty Numbers 23, 287, 1171: Three Indian Painters on the Prairie.* Winnipeg, MB: Winnipeg Art Gallery. (exhibition catalog)

———, AND BRIAN MARACLE. 1989. *Decelebration.* Ottawa, ON: Runge Press. (exhibition catalog)

GALLENKAMP, CHARLES. 1959. *Maya: The Riddle and Rediscovery of a Lost Civilization.* New York: David McKay Company.

GARAWAY, MARGARET KAHN. 1986. *Ashkii and His Grandfather.* Tucson, AZ: Treasure Chest.

GARDNER, ETHEL. 1990. *Soarings - Flight Enhancements for the Mind.* St. Paul, MN: Cherokee Publications.

GEIST, OTTO WILLIAM, AND FROELICH G. RAINEY. 1936. *Archaeological Excavations at Kukulik.* Washington, D.C.: University of Alaska, Miscellaneous Publication, Vol. 2.

GENTRY, THOMAS, ET AL. 1990. *New Art of the West.* Indianapolis, IN: Eitlejorg Museum. (exhibition catalog)

GERBER, PETER R., AND EANINA KATZ. 1989. *Susan A. Point, Joe David, Lawrence Paul: Native Artists from the Northwest Coast.* Zürich, Switzerland: Ethnological Museum of the University of Zürich.

———, AND MAXIMILIEN BRUGGMANN. 1989. *Indians of the Northwest Coast.* New York: Facts On File, Inc.

GIBBONS, LULU (COMP.). N.D. *Indian Recipes from Cherokee Indians of Eastern Oklahoma.* Muskogee, OK: Hoffman Printing Co.

GILSTRAP, HARRIET PATRICK. 1960. *Memoirs of a Pioneer Teacher.* Oklahoma City: Oklahoma Historical Society.

GLUBOK, SHIRLEY. 1964. *The Art of the North American Indian.* New York: Harper & Row.

GODIN, DEBORAH, AND JOANE CARDINAL-SCHUBERT. 1985. *Joane Cardinal-Schubert: This is my History.* Thunder Bay, ON: Thunder Bay National Exhibition Center and Center for Indian Art.

GOETZ, HELGA, AND REISSA SCHRAGER. N.D. *Pitseolak.* Cape Dorset, NWT: West Baffin Eskimo Cooperative. (exhibition catalog)

———, ET AL. 1977. *The Inuit Print.* Ottawa, ON: National Museum of Man and National Museum of Canada. (exhibition catalog)

Goldblot, Noel. 1983. *People of this Century.*

GOLDER, NINA. 1985. *The Hunt and the Harvest: Pueblo Paintings from the Museum of the American Indian.* Hamilton, NY: Gallery Association of New York State. (exhibition catalog)

GOLDFRANK, ESTHER S. ED. 1962. *Isleta Paintings.* Washington, D.C.: Bureau of American Ethnology. Bulletin 181.

———. 1967. *The Artist of "Isleta Paintings" In Pueblo Society – Smithsonian Contributions to Anthropology,* Vol. 5. Washington, D.C.: Smithsonian Press.

GONYEA, RAMON, ED. 1980. *Spirit of the Earth: An Exhibition of Contemporary Native American Art.* New York: International Native American Council of Arts. (exhibition catalog)

GOODERHAM, KENT, ED. 1969. *I am an Indian.* Toronto, ON: J. M. Dent & Sons, Ltd.

———, ED. 1979. *Adventures of Nanabush: An Anthology of Ojibway Indian Stories.* Doubleday Canada, Ltd.

GORMAN, R. C. 1992. *Radiance of My People.* Albuquerque: Santa Fe Fine Arts, Inc.

GRAMMER, MAURENE. 1991. *The Bear that Turned White and Other Tales.* Flagstaff, AZ: Northland Press.

GRAY, SAMUEL L. 1990. *Tonita Peña.* Albuquerque: Avanyu Publishing, Inc.

GREEN, MARY BETH. 1983. *R. C. Gorman: The Drawings.* Flagstaff, AZ: Northland Press.

GREEN, PAUL, AND ABBE ABBOTT. 1959. *I am Eskimo, Aknik my Name.* Juneau, AK: Alaska Northwest Pub. Co.

GREEN, SANDRA. 1978. *Dan Namingha.* San Diego, CA: California Academy of Science.

GREENBERG, HENRY, AND GEORGIA GREENBERG. 1984. *Carl Gorman's World.* Albuquerque: University of New Mexico Press.

GREENE, ALMA. 1975. *Tales of the Mohawk.* Toronto, ON: J. M. Dent and Sons, Ltd.

GREENFIELD, VAL. 1984. *3rd Annual Wild West Show.* Calgary, AB: Alberta College of Art. (exhibition catalog)

GREGORY, JACK, AND RENNARD STRICKLAND. 1967. *Sam Houston With the Cherokees, 1829-1833.* Austin, TX: University of Texas Press.

———, AND RENNARD STRICKLAND. 1969. *Cherokee Spirit Tales.* Pensacola, FL: Hoffman Printing Co.

———, AND RENNARD STRICKLAND. 1971. *Creek Spirit Tales.* Pensacola, FL: Hoffman Printing Co.

———, AND RENNARD STRICKLAND. 1972. *Choctaw Spirit Tales.* Pensacola, FL: Hoffman Printing Co.

GRIDLEY, MARION E. 1940. *Indians of Yesterday.* Chicago: M. A. Donohue & Co.

———. 1947. *Indians of Today.* Chicago: Miller Publishing Co.

GRINDE, DONALD. 1977. *The Iroquois and the Founding of the American Nation.* San Francisco, CA: Indian Historian Press.

GRINNELL, GEORGE BIRD. 1895. *Story of the Indian.* New York: D. Appleton & Co.

———. 1915. *The Fighting Cheyennes.* New York: Scribner's Sons.

———. 1923. *The Cheyenne Indians.* New Haven, CT: Yale University Press. 2 vols.

GUEDON, MARIE FRANÇOISE, AND ESTRELLITA KARSH. *Shamans and Spirits: Myths and Medical Symbolism in Eskimo Art.* Ottawa, ON: Canadian Arctic Producers, Ltd., and National Museum of Man/National Museum of Canada. (exhibition catalog)

GULLY, ANNE, ED. 1994. *Watchful Eyes: Native American Women Artists.* Phoenix: The Heard Museum. (exhibition catalog)

GUNNERSON, DOLORES A. 1975. *The Jicarilla Apaches: A Study in Survival.* DeKalb, IL: Northern Illinois University Press.

HALL, EDWIN S., JR., MARGARET B. BLACKMAN AND VINCENT RICKARD. 1981. *Northwest Coast Indian Graphics.* Seattle: University of Washington Press.

HAMILTON, CHARLES, ED. 1950. *Cry of the Thunderbird; The American Indian's Own Story.* New York: Macmillan.

HAMM, MARY ALICE AND WILLIAM S. INGLISH. 1960. *A History of the Baird-Scales Family.* Tahlequah, OK: Go-Ye Mission.

HANNUM, ALBERTA. 1945. *Spin a Silver Dollar.* New York: Viking Press.

———. 1958. *Paint the Wind.* New York: Viking Press.

HARJO, JOY, ED. 1993. *Reinventing Ourselves in the Enemy's Language.* Tucson, AZ: University of Arizona Press.

HARPER, J. RUSSELL. 1970. *Early Painters and Engravers in Canada.* Toronto, ON: University of Toronto Press.

———. 1977. *Painting in Canada: A History.* Toronto, ON: University of Toronto Press.

HARRINGTON, MARK RAYMOND. 1921. *Religion and Ceremonies of the Lenape.* New York: Museum of the American Indian.

HARTJE, KATRINA. 1984. *Signale Indianischer Kunstler.* Berlin, Germany: Galerie Akmak.

HARVEY, BYRON, III. 1970. *Hopi L ife in Hopi Painting.* New York: Museum of the American Indian.

HARVEY, BYRON, III. 1970. *Ritual in Pueblo Art.* New York: Museum of the American Indian.

HARVEY, JOY. 1968. *Antelope Boy.* Phoenix, AZ: Arequipa Press.

HASKELL, ARNOLD L. 1960. *The Story of Dance.* London, U.K.: Rathbone Books, Ltd.

HASSRICK, ROYAL B. 1964. *The Sioux: Life and Customs of a Warrior Society.* Norman, OK: University of Oklahoma Press.

HAWTHORNE, AUDREY. 1988. *Kwakiutl Art.* Seattle: University of Washington Press.

Hebard, Grace Raymond. 1930. *Washakie.* Cleveland, OH: Arthur H. Clark.

Hedgpeth, Don. 1983. *Cowboy Artist: The Joe Beeler Story.* Flagstaff, AZ: Northland Press.

Heidenrich, C. Adrian. 1990. *Native American Studies.* New York: McGraw Hill.

Highwater, Jamake. 1975. *Fodor's Indian America: A Cultural and Travel Guide.* New York: David McKay Co., Inc.

———. 1976. *Song from the Earth: American Indian Painting.* Boston: New York Graphic Society.

———. 1977. *Ritual of the Wind: North American Ceremonies and Dances.* New York: Viking Press, Inc.

———. 1978a. *Journey to the Sky.* New York: Thomas Y. Crowell.

———. 1978b. *Many Smokes, Many Moons: An American Indian Chronology.* New York: J. B. Lippincott

———. 1980a. *The Sun He Dies.* New York: Lippincott and Crowell.

———. 1980b. *The Sweet Grass Lives On.* New York: Lippincott and Crowell.

———. 1983. *Arts of the Indian Americas.* New York: Harper & Row.

———. 1984. *Legend Days.* New York: Harper & Row Publishers.

———. 1986. *Native Land: Sagas of the Indian Americas.* Boston: Little, Brown & Company.

Hill, Rick. 1992. *Creativity is our Tradition: Three Decades of Contemporary Indian Art.* Santa Fe: Institute of American Indian and Alaska Native Culture and Arts Development.

Hill, Rick and Tom Hill. 1994. *Creation's Journey: Native American Identity and Belief.* Washington, D.C.: Smithsonian Institution Press.

Hill, Stephen W. 1995. *Kokopelli.* Santa Fe: Kiva Publishing, Inc.

Hill, Tom. 1983. *Indian Art '83.* Brantford, ON: Woodland Indian Cultural Educational Center. (exhibition catalog)

———. 1988. *Indian Art '88.* Brantford, ON: Woodland Indian Cultural Educational Center. (exhibition catalog)

Hobson, Geary, ed. 1979. *The Remembered Earth.* Albuquerque: University of New Mexico Press.

Hodgson, Stuart. 1976. *Stories from Pangnirtung.* Edmonton, AB: Hurtig Publishers.

Hoffman, Gerhard, et al. 1984. *Indianische Kunst im 20 Jahrhundert.* Münich, Germany.

———. 1988. *Zeilgenoosische Kunst der Indianer und Eskimos in Kanada.* Ottawa, ON: Canadian Museum of Civilization.

Hoffman, Virginia. 1974a. *Navajo Biographies, Volume I.* Phoenix, AZ: Navajo Curriculum Press.

———. 1974b. *Lucy Learns To Weave: Gathering Plants.* Chinle, AZ: Rough Rock Press.

Hogan, Linda. 1990. *Mean Spirit.* New York: Maxwell Macmillan International.

Holm, Bill. 1965. *Northwest Coast Indian Art: An Analysis of Form.* Seattle: University of Washington Press.

———, and Bill Reid. 1975. *Indian Art of the Northwest Coast.* Houston: Rice University Institute for the Arts.

———. 1983. *Smoky Top: The Art and Times of Willie Seaweed.* Seattle: University of Washington Press.

Holton, Anne Tennyson. 1964. *Song of the Cherokees.* Privately Published.

Horne, Josephine, et al. 1976. *Kanien' Ke' Ha' Okara'shon 'A: Mohawk Stories.* Albany, NY: New York State Museum, Bulletin 427.

Houle, Robert. 1982. *New Work by a New Generation.* Regina, SK: Norman Mackenzie Art Gallery.

Houlihan, Patrick T. 1981. *One Thousand Years of Southwestern Indian Ceramic Art.* New York: ACA American Indian Arts.

Houston, James. 1967a. *Cape Dorset: A Decade of Eskimo Prints and Recent Sculptures.* Ottawa, ON: National Gallery of Canada.

———. 1967b. *Eskimo Prints.* Barre, MA: Barre Publishing Company, Inc.

Howard, James H., ed. 1968. *The Warrior Who Killed Custer; The Personal Narrative of Chief Joseph White Bull.* Lincoln, NE: University of Nebraska Press.

Hughes, Art and Claudine Goller. 1981. *Native Peoples of the Americas.* Toronto, ON: Van Nostrand, Reinhold.

Hughes, Kenneth. 1979. *The Life and Art of Jackson Beardy.* Winnipeg, MB: Canadian Dimensions Publishers.

Humphrey, Donald, and Jeanne O. Snodgrass King. 1980. *Centennial Touring Art Exhibit.* Muskogee, OK: Bacone College.(exhibition catalog)

Hurst, Tricia (intro.). 1980. *R. C. Gorman: The Posters.* Flagstaff, AZ: Northland Press.

Huseboe, Arthur, ed. 1989. *An Illustrated History of the Arts of South Dakota.* South Dakota Council on the Arts and Humanities.

Hyde, George E. 1937. *Red Cloud's Folk: A History of the Oglala Sioux Indians.* Norman, OK: University of Oklahoma Press.

———. 1956. *A Sioux Chronicle.* Norman, OK: University of Oklahoma Press.

———. 1961. *Spotted Tail's Folk: A History of the Brûlé Sioux.* Norman, OK: University of Oklahoma Press.

Iacopi, Robert L., ed. 1972. *Look to the Mountain Top.* San Jose, CA: Gousha Publications. Indian Children of the Inkameep.

———. 1945. *The Tale of the Nativity.* Victoria, BC: British Columbia Provincial Museum.

Irvine, Keith, ed. 1974. *Encyclopedia of Indians of the Americas.* St. Clair Shores, MI: Scholarly Press, Inc.

Jacka, Lois Essary, and Jerry Jacka. 1988. *Beyond Tradition: Contemporary Indian Art and Its Evolution.* Flagstaff, AZ: Northland Press.

———. 1994. *Enduring Traditions: Art of the Navajo*. Flagstaff, AZ: Northland Press.

———. Jerry Jacka, and David Johns. 1991. *On the Trail of Beauty*. Scottsdale, AZ: Snailspace Publishing.

Jackson, Marion E., and David Pelly. 1986. *The Vital Vision: Drawings by Ruth Annaqtuusi Tulurialik*. Windsor, ON: Art Gallery of Windsor.

———, and Judith M. Nasby. 1987. *Contemporary Inuit Drawings*. Guelph, ON: McDonald Stewart Art Center. (exhibition catalog)

Jacobson, Oscar B. 1929. *Kiowa Indian Art*. Nice, France: C. Szwedzicki.

———, and Jeanne d'Ucel. 1950. *American Indian Painters*. Nice, France: C. Szwedzicki.

———. 1952. *North American Indian Costumes*. Nice, France: C. Szwedzicki.

———. 1964. *Indian Artists from Oklahoma*. Norman, OK: University of Oklahoma Press.

James, Ahlee. 1927. *Tewa Firelight Tales*. New York: Longmans, Green.

Jemison, Peter. 1984. *Common Heritage: Contemporary Iroquois Artists*. New York: Queens Museum. (exhibition catalog)

Johannsen, Christian B., and John P. Ferguson, eds. 1983. *Iroquois Arts: A Directory of a People and their Work*. Warnerville, NY: Association for the Advancement of Native North American Arts and Crafts.

Johnson, W. Fletcher. 1891. *The Red Record of the Sioux; Life of Sitting Bull and History of the Indian War of 1890-1891*. Philadelphia: Edgewood Pub. Co.

Johnston, Basil. 1976. *Ojibway Heritage*. Toronto, ON: McClelland and Stewart, Ltd.

———. 1978. *How the Birds Got their Color*. Toronto, ON: Kids Can Press.

Johnston, Patronella. 1970. *Tales of Nokomis*. Toronto, ON: Charles J. Musson, Ltd.

Jones, Ruthe Blalock. 1988. *Keepers of the Culture: Contemporary Southeastern Indian Artists*. Anniston, AL: Anniston Museum of Natural History. (exhibition catalog)

Jordan, Wendy Alder. 1979. *By the Light of the Qulliq: Eskimo Life in the Canadian Arctic*. Washington, D.C.: Smithsonian Institution Traveling Exhibition Service. (exhibition catalog)

Josephy, Alvin M., Jr., ed. 1961a. *The American Heritage Book of Indians*. New York: American Heritage Publishing Co.

———, ed. 1961b. *The Patriot Chiefs: A Chronicle of American Indian Leadership*. New York: Viking Press.

Judd, Mary Catherine. 1902. *Wigwam Stories Told by American Indians*. Boston: Ginn & Co.

Kabotie, Fred. 1949. *Designs from the Ancient Mimbreños, with a Hopi Interpretation*. San Francisco: Grabhorn Press.

Kabotie, Michael. 1987. *Migration Tears*. Los Angeles: American Indian Studies Center, University of California.

Kappi, Leoni, ed. 1977. *Inuit Legends*. Yellowknife, NWT: Government of the Northwest Territories, Department of Education.

Katz, Jane B., ed. 1977. *I am the Fire of Time: Voices of Native American Women*. New York: E. P. Dutton Co.

———. 1980. *This Song Remembers: Self-Portraits of Native Americans in the Arts*. Boston: Houghton Mifflin Company.

———. 1990. *Art in America, Guide to Artists, Galleries and Museums*. New York: New York Art Review.

Ke Motta. 1952. *Sally of Woolaroc*. Bartlesville, OK: Frank Phillips Foundation, Inc.

Keech, Roy A. 1940. *Pagans Praying*. Clarendon, TX: Clarendon Press.

Keim, Randolph. 1885. *Sheridan's Troopers on the Borders*. Philadelphia: David McKay.

Keithahn, Edward L. 1943. *Igloo Tales*. Lawrence, KS: Haskell Institute.

———. 1974. *Alaskan Igloo Tales*. Juneau, AK: Alaska Northwest Publishing Co.

Kelly, Luther S. 1926. *Yellowstone Kelly: The Memoirs of Luther S. Kelly*. New Haven, CT: Yale University Press.

Kennard, Edward A. 1944. *Field Mouse Goes to War*. Washington, D.C.: Office of Education, Bureau of Indian Affairs.

———. 1948. *Little Hopi Hopihoya*. Washington, D.C.: Office of Education, Bureau of Indian Affairs.

Kennedy, Michael Stephen, ed. 1961. *The Assiniboines: From the Accounts of the Old Ones Told to First Boy (James Larpenteur Long)*. Norman, OK: University of Oklahoma Press.

Kenny, George. 1978. *Indians Don't Cry*. Toronto, ON: Chimo Publishers.

Kenny, Maurice. 1982. *Kneading the Blood*. Philadelphia: Strawberry Press.

———, ed. 1983. *Wounds Beneath the Flesh*. Marvin, SD: Blue Cloud Quarterly Press.

Kershen, Mike. 1993. *Why Buffalo Roam*. Owens Mills, MD: Stemmons House.

Kilman, Theodore. 1984. *Robert Freeman Drawings*. Valley Center, CA: Friendship Printing.

Kimball, Yeffe, and Jean Anderson. 1965. *The Art of American Indian Cooking*. Garden City, NY: Doubleday and Co.

King, Jeanne Snodgrass. 1981. *Native American Painting*. Amarillo, TX: Amarillo Art Center Exhibition. (exhibition catalog)

Kitanmax School of Northwest Coast Indian Art. 1977. *We-Gyet Wanders On: Legends of the Northwest*. Saanechton, BC: Hancock House Publisher, Ltd.

Klein, Bernard and Daniel Icolari. 1967. *Reference Encyclopedia of the American Indian*. New York: B. Klein and Company.

Kostich, Dragos. 1977. *George Morrison: The Story of an American Indian*. Minneapolis, MN: Dillon Press.

Krantz, Les. 1990. *American Artist: Illustrated Survey of Leading Contemporaries.* Chicago: American References Publishing Corporation.

Kushner, Marilyn, et al. 1989. *Three Hundred Years of American Painting.* Montclair, NJ: Montclair Art Museum. (exhibition catalog)

LaBarge, Dorothy. 1986. *From Drawing to Print: Perception and Process in Cape Dorset Art.* Calgary, AB: Glenbow Museum. (exhibition catalog)

Lacapa, Kathleen and Michael Lacapa. 1994. *Less Than Half, More Than Whole.* Flagstaff, AZ: Northland Press.

Lacapa, Michael. 1990. *The Flute Player: An Apache Folktale.* Flagstaff, AZ: Northland Press.

LaFarge, Oliver. 1956. *A Pictorial History of the American Indian.* New York: Crown Publishers.

———. 1960. *The American Indian.* New York: Golden Press.

LaFlesche, Francis. 1900. *The Middle Five: Indian Boys at School.* Boston: Small, Maynard and Co.

Lamb, Daniel. 1990. *Arts of Enchantment.* Albuquerque. (exhibition catalog)

L'Amour, Louis. 1988. *Haunted Mesa.* New York: Bantam Books.

LaPeña, Frank. 1987. *The World is a Gift.* San Francisco: Limestone Press.

Larmour, W. T. 1967. *Inuit: The Art of the Canadian Eskimo.* Ottawa, ON: Indian Affairs and Northern Development.

Larsen, Dinah, and Terry Dickey eds. 1982. *Setting it Free.* Fairbanks, AK: University of Alaska. (exhibition catalog).

Latocki, Barbara, ed. 1982. *Inuit Myths, Legends and Songs.* Winnipeg, MB: Winnipeg Art Gallery. (exhibition catalog)

———, ed. 1983. *Baker Lake Prints and Print Drawings 1970-1976.* Winnipeg, MB: Winnipeg Art Gallery. (exhibition catalog)

Leekley, Thomas B. 1965. *The World of Manabozho: Tales of Chippewa Indians.* New York: Vanguard Press.

Leroux, Odette, Marion E. Jackson, and Minnie Aodla Freeman, eds. 1994. *Inuit Women Artists: Voices from Cape Dorset.* Vancouver, BC: Douglas and McIntyre.

Libhart, Myles. 1970. *Contemporary Sioux Painting.* Rapid City, SD: Tipi Shop, Inc. (exhibition catalog)

Lindsay, Ian, et al. 1977. *Davidialuk 1977.* Québec, PQ: La Fédération des Coöperatives du Nouveau Québec. (exhibition catalog)

Linsley, Lesley. 1976. *Scrimshaw.* New York: Hawthorn Book, Inc.

Lippard, Lucy R. 1990. *Mixed Blessings: New Art in a Multicultural Media.* New York: Pantheon Books.

Little Bear, Leroy, Menno Boldt and J. Anthony Long, eds. 1984. *Pathways to Self-Determination: Canadian Indians and the Canadian State.* Toronto, ON: University of Toronto Press.

Llewellyn, Karl N., and E. Adamson Hoebel. 1941. *The Cheyenne Way.* Norman, OK: University of Oklahoma Press.

Lomatewama, Ramson. 1983. *Silent Winds: Poetry of One Hopi.* Phoenix, AZ: Heard Museum.

Long, Holly Ann. 1989. *Hokoka.*

Longfish, George, and Joan Rondell. 1983. *Contemporary Native American Art: Contradictions in Indian Territory.* Stillwater, OK: Oklahoma State University Press.

———, et al. 1987. *New Directions Northwest.* Olympia, WA: Evergreen State College. (exhibition catalog)

Longley, Cynthia. 1992. *Walk in Beauty: Connie Seabourn.*

Louis, Adrian C. 1989. *Fire Water World.* Albuquerque: West End Press.

Lovato, Charles. 1982. *Life Under the Sun.* Santa Fe: Sunstone Press.

Lyback, Johanna R. M. 1963. *Indian Legends of Eastern America / Indian Legends of the Great West.* Chicago: Lyons and Carnahan, Inc. 2 vols.

Lynch, Regina. 1987. *A History of Navajo Clans.* Cortez, CO: Mesa Verde Press.

Lyons, Oren. 1973. *Dog Story.* New York: Holiday House.

MacEwan, James William Grant. 1971. *Portraits from the Plains.* Toronto, ON: McGraw-Hill Company/Seattle: University of Washington Press.

MacDonald, Colin S. 1975. *A Dictionary of Canadian Artists.* Ottawa, ON: Canadian Paperback Publishing.

Macnair, Peter L., Alan L. Hoover and Kevin Neary. 1980. *The Legacy: Continuing Traditions of Canadian Northwest Coast Art.* Victoria, BC: British Columbia Provincial Museum.

Madrano, Dan M. 1955. *Heap Big Laugh.* Tulsa, OK.

Mahey, John, et al. 1980. *Native American Art at the Philbrook.* Tulsa, OK: R. F. Rogers, Inc. (exhibition catalog)

Mainprize, Garry. 1986. *Stardusters: New Works by Jane Ash Poitras, Pierre Sioui, Joane Cardinal-Schubert, Edward Poitras.* Thunder Bay, ON: Thunder Bay Art Gallery. (exhibition catalog)

Manning, Phyllis A. 1962. *Spirit Rocks and Silver Magic.* Caldwell, ID: Caxton Printers.

Markoosie. 1970. *Harpoon of the Hunter.* Montréal, PQ: McGill-Queens University Press.

Marquis, Thomas B. 1931. *A Warrior Who Fought Custer.* Minneapolis, MN: Midwest Co.

Marriott, Alice. 1948. *Maria, the Potter of San Ildefonso.* Norman: University of Oklahoma Press

———. 1952. *Winter-Telling Stories.* New York: Thomas Y. Crowell.

Marsh, James, ed. 1985. *The Canadian Encyclopedia.* Edmonton, AB: Hurtig Publishers.

Martinson, David. 1977. *The Legend of Nett Lake, Minnesota.* Chippewa Tribe Publication.

MATHER, CHRISTINE. 1990. *Native America: Arts, Traditions and Celebrations.* New York: Clarkson Potter.

MATHEWS, JOHN. 1988. *Sundown.* Norman, OK: University of Oklahoma Press.

MAURER, EVAN M. 1977. *The Native American Heritage: A Survey of Native American Indian Art.* Lincoln, NE: University of Nebraska Press.

———. 1992. *Visions of the People: A Pictorial History of Plains Indian Life.* Minneapolis, MN: Minneapolis Institute of Arts.

MAYES, VERNON O., AND BARBARA BAYLESS LACY. 1989. *Nanise- A Navajo Herbal.* Tsaile, AZ: Navajo Community College Press.

MAYHALL, MILDRED P. 1962. *The Kiowas.* Norman, OK: University of Oklahoma Press.

MAYOKOK, ROBERT. 1951. *Eskimo Life.* Nome, AK: Nome Nugget.

———. 1957. *Eskimo Customs.* Nome, AK: Nome Nugget.

———. 1959. *True Eskimo Stories.* Sitka, AK: Sitka Printing Co.

———. 1960A. *The Alaskan Eskimo.* Anchorage, AK: Instant Printing.

———. 1960B. *Eskimo Stories.* Nome, AK: Nome Nugget.

MCLUHAN, ELIZABETH. 1984A. *Altered Egos: The Multimedia Work of Carl Beam.* Thunder Bay, ON: Thunder Bay National Exhibition Center and Center for Indian Art.

———. 1984B. *Renegade: The Art of Leo Yerxa.* Thunder Bay, ON: Thunder Bay National Exhibition Center and Center for Indian Art.

———, AND TOM HILL. 1984C. *Norval Morrisseau and the Emergence of the Image Makers.* Toronto, ON: Methuen.

———, AND R. M. VANDERBURGH. 1985. *Daphine Odjig: A Retrospective 1946-1985.* Thunder Bay, ON: Thunder Bay National Exhibition Center and Center for Indian Art.(exhibition catalog)

MCMASTER, GERALD R. 1981. *Byron and His Balloon.* La Loche, SK: La Loche Center for Learning.

———, ET AL. 1993. *In the Shadow of the Sun.* Hull, PQ: Canadian Museum of Civilization.

MEDINA, DANNY. 1981. *Arizona Galleries and their Artists.* Phoenix, AZ: Dandrek Co.

MENITOVE, MARCY, ED. 1985. *Michael Robinson: The Spirit and the Smoke.* Thunder Bay, ON: Thunder Bay Art Gallery. (exhibition catalog)

———, ED. 1986A. *Arthur Shilling.* Thunder Bay, ON: Thunder Bay Art Gallery. (exhibition catalog)

———, ED. 1986B. *The Permanent Collection: Thunder Bay Art Gallery.* Thunder Bay, ON: Thunder Bay Art Gallery. (exhibition catalog)

———, ED. 1989A. *The Painter and His Model: Marble Since '85.* Thunder Bay, ON: Thunder Bay Art Gallery. (exhibition catalog)

———, AND JOANNE DANFORD (EDS.). 1989B. *Woodlands: Contemporary Art of the Anishnabe.* Thunder Bay, ON: Thunder Bay Art Gallery. (exhibition catalog)

———, ED. 1990. *George Littlechild.* Thunder Bay, ON: Thunder Bay Art Gallery.(exhibition catalog)

METAYER, MAURICE, ED. 1972. *Tales From the Igloo.* Edmonton, AB: Hurtig Publishers.

MILTON, JOHN R., ED. 1969. *The American Indian Speaks.* Vermillion, SD: Dakota Press.

MINTHORN, P. Y. 1981. *Ceremonious Blue.* Santa Fe: Institute of American Indian Art Press.

———. (INTRO). 1991. *Sapatq'ayn: Twentieth Century Nez Percé Artists.* Seattle: Northwest Interpretive Association and Confluence Press, Inc. (exhibition catalog)

MOFSIE, LOUIS. 1970. *The Hopi Way.* New York: Lippincott.

MOMADAY, N. SCOTT. 1965. *The Complete Poems of Frederick Goddard Tuckerman.* New York: Oxford University Press.

———. 1969A. *House Made of Dawn.* New York: Harper & Row.

———. 1969B. *The Way to Rainy Mountain.* Albuquerque: University of New Mexico Press.

———. 1973. *Colorado: Summer, Fall, Winter, Spring.* Chicago: Rand McNally.

———. 1974. *Angle of Geese and other Poems.* Boston: David R. Godine.

———. 1976. *The Gourd Dancer.* New York: Harper & Row.

———. 1977. *The Names.* New York: Harper & Row.

———. 1989. *The Ancient Child.* New York: Doubleday.

———. 1994. *Circle of Wonder.* Santa Fe: Clear Light Publishers.

MONTHAN, DORIS, ED. 1972. *Scholder: Indians.* Flagstaff, AZ: Northland Press.

———. 1978. *R. C. Gorman: The Lithographs.* Flagstaff, AZ: Northland Press.

———. 1991. *R. C. Gorman: A Retrospective.* Flagstaff, AZ: Northland Press.

MONTHAN, GUY, AND DORIS MONTHAN. 1975. *Art and Indian Individualists.* Flagstaff, AZ: Northland Press.

———, AND DORIS MONTHAN. 1979. *Nacimientos.* Flagstaff, AZ: Northland Press.

MORGAN, JOHN. 1974. *When the Morning Stars Sang Together.* Agincourt, ON: The Book Society of Canada.

MORGAN, WILLIAM. 1968. *Coyote Tales.* Washington, D.C.: Office of Education, Bureau of Indian Affairs.

MORRILL, CLAIRE. 1973. *A Taos Mosaic.* Albuquerque: University of New Mexico Press.

MORRISSEAU, NORVAL. 1965. *Legends of My People, the Great Ojibway.* Toronto, ON: Ryerson Press.

MOYER, JOHN W. 1957. *Famous Indian Chiefs.* Chicago: M. A. Donohue & Co.

MURPHY, D., AND JOHN G. BAXTER. 1985. *New Mexico, the Distant Land.* Northridge, CA: Windsor Publishing.

MURPHY, HENRY. 1927. *The History of Joseph No Two Horns.* Bismarck, ND: State Historical Society of North Dakota.

Myers, Marybelle, ed. 1977. *Joe Talirunili*. Montréal, PQ: La Fédération des Coöperatives du Nouveau Québec.

———., ed. 1980. *Things Made by Inuit*. Ville Saint-Laurent, PQ: La Fédération des Coöperatives du Nouveau Québec. (exhibition catalog)

Napran, Laura, et al. 1984. *Visions of Rare Spirit: 20 Years of Halman Prints*. Ottawa, ON: Canadian Arctic Producers, et al. (exhibition catalog)

Neihardt, John G. 1932. *Black Elk Speaks*. New York: W. Morrow & Co.

Nelson, John Louw. 1937. *Rhythm for Rain*. Boston: Houghton Mifflin.

Nelson, Mary Carroll. 1971. *Pablita Velarde*. Minneapolis, MN: Dillon Press.

New, Lloyd Kiva. 1974. *The Institute of American Indian Arts Alumni Exhibition*. FortWorth, TX: Amon Carter Museum of Western Art. (exhibition catalog)

———, and David C. Young. 1976. *One with the Earth*. Santa Fe: Institute of American Indian Art. (exhibition catalog)

———. 1979. *Pinturas Amerindas Contemporánes/ E.U.A.* Museo del Instituto de Artes Amerindios.

———. 1981. *American Indian Art in the 1980's*. Niagara Falls, NY: Native American Center for the Living Arts. (exhibition catalog)

———, et al. 1985. *Art of the Native American: The Southwest from the Late 19th Century to the Present*. Owensboro, KY: Owensboro Museum of Fine Art. (exhibition catalog)

Newcomb, Francis Johnson. n.d. *Navajo Birth Tales*.

———. 1967. *Navajo Folk Tales*. Albuquerque: University of New Mexico.

Newell, Cicero. 1912. *Indian Stories*. Boston: Silver, Burdett & Co.

Niatum, Duane. 1974. *Taos Pueblo*. Greenfield Center, NY: Greenfield Review Press.

———, ed. 1975. *Carriers of the Dream*. New York: Harper & Row.

Nuligak, and Maurice Metayer. 1966. *I, Nuligak*. Toronto, ON: Peter Martin Associates, Limited.

Nutchuck. n.d. *Back to the Smoky Sea*. New York: Julian Messner.

Nye, Wilber Sturtevant. 1962. *Bad Medicine and Good: Tales of the Kiowas*. Norman, OK: University of Oklahoma Press.

Odjig, Daphne. 1971. *Tales of Nanabush . . . Books of Indian Legends for Children*. Toronto, ON: Ginn and Company. 10 vols.

———. R. M. Vanderburgh, and M. E. Southcott. 1992. *A Paintbrush In My Hand*. Toronto, ON: Natural Heritage/Natural History, Inc.

Ortiz, Simon. 1977. *A Good Journey*. Berkeley, CA: Turtleback Press.

Owens, Louis. 1992. *The Sharpest Sight*. Norman, OK: University of Oklahoma Press.

Page, Jake, and Susanne Page. 1982. *Hopi*. New York: Harry N. Abrams, Inc.

Paladin, Lynda. 1992. *Painting the Dream: The Visionary Art of Navajo Painter David Chethlahe Paladin*. Rochester, VT: Park Street Press.

Panda, Triloki Nath. 1993. *A Zuñi Looks at Frank Hamilton Cushing*. Zuñi Pueblo, NM: Zuñi Arts and Crafts, A:Shiwi A:Wan Museum and Heritage Center.

Parker, Arthur C. 1910. *Iroquois Uses of Maize and Other Food Plants*. Albany, NY: New York State Museum.

———. 1913. *The Code of Handsome Lake, the Seneca Prophet*. Albany, NY: New

Parks, Stephen. 1983. *R. C. Gorman: A Portrait*. Boston: Little, Brown and Company.

Parsons, Elsie Clews, et al. 1936. *General Series in Anthropology 2*. Menasha, WI: George Banta Publishing Company.

Paytiamo, James P. 1932. *Flaming Arrow's People*. New York: Duffield & Green.

Peiper-Piegrof. 1968. *Zeitgenossische Indianesche Kunst*. West Germany.

Penny, Grace Jackson. 1953. *Tales of the Cheyennes*. Boston: Houghton Mifflin.

Pennington, Robert. 1961. *Oscar Howe, Artist of the Sioux*. Sioux Falls, SD: Dakota Territorial Centennial Commission.

Perrone, Bobette, H. Henrietta Stockel and Victoria Krueger. 1990. *Medicine Women, Curanderas, and Women Doctors*. Norman, OK: University of Oklahoma Press.

Peters, Russell. 1987. *The Wampanoags of Mashpee*. Somerville, MA: Media Action.

Peterson, Harold L. 1965. *American Indian Tomahawks*. New York: Museum of the American Indian.

Peterson, Karen Daniels, ed. 1964. *A Cheyenne Sketchbook*. Norman, OK: University of Oklahoma Press.

———. 1968. *Howling Wolf*. Palo Alto, CA: American West Publishing Co.

———. 1971. *Plains Indian Art from Fort Marion*. Norman, OK: University of Oklahoma Press

Peterson, Nancy M. 1984. *People of the Moonshell: A Western River Journal*. Frederick, CO: Renaissance House.

Pinchette, Pierre. 1974. *Coyote Tales of the Mountain Salish*. Pine Ridge, SD: Tipi Shop, Inc.

Pierson, William H., Jr., and Martha Davidson. 1960. *Arts of the United States*. New York: McGraw-Hill.

Pirtle, Caleb. n.d. *Bob Moline: A Cowboy and His Art*. Waxahachie, TX: Buffalo Creek Publishing Company.

———. 1975. *XIT, Being a New and Original Exploration, in Art and Words, into the Life and Times of the American Cowboy*. Birmingham, AL: Oxmoor House.

Pitseolak, Peter, and Dorothy Harley Eber. 1972. *Pitseolak: Pictures Out of my Life*. Seattle: University of Washington Press.

———, and Dorothy Eber. 1975. *People from Our Side.* Edmonton, AB: Hurtig Publishers.

———. 1977. *Peter Pitseolak's Escape from Death.* Toronto, ON: McClelland andStewart, Ltd.

Podedworny, Carol. 1985a. *Debosegai.* Thunder Bay, ON: Thunder Bay Art Gallery. (exhibition catalog)

———. 1985b. *Michael Robinson: The Spirit and the Smoke.* Thunder Bay, ON: Thunder Bay Art Gallery. (exhibition catalog)

———. 1987. *Eight From the Prairies: Part Two.* Thunder Bay, ON: Thunder Bay Art Gallery. (exhibition catalog)

———. 1989. *Woodlands: Contemporary Art of the Anishnabe.* Thunder Bay, ON: Thunder Bay Art Gallery. (exhibition catalog)

Posey, Alexander L. 1969. *Poems of A. L. Posey.* Muskogee, OK: Okmulgee Cultural Foundation, Inc. and Five Civilized Tribes Heritage Foundation.

Powell, Peter J. 1979. *People of the Sacred Mountain.* San Francisco: Harper and Row.

Praus, Alexis. 1962. *The Sioux, 1798-1922: A Dakota Winter Count.* Bloomfield Hills, MI: Cranbrook Institute of Science.

Price, Harriet K. H. 1981. *From Dreams to Reality.* Wichita, KS: Mennonite Press, Inc.

Raabe, Martha. 1942. *The Little Lost Sioux.* Chicago: A. Whitman & Co.

Ragan, John Edgar. 1986. *The Artist as Printmaker: Connie Seabourn Ragan.* Oklahoma City: John Ragan Publications.

Ray, Carl and James Stevens. 1971. *The Sacred Legends of the Sandy Lake Cree.* Toronto, ON: McClelland and Stewart, Ltd.

Ray, Dorothy Jean. 1961. *Artists of the Tundra and the Sea.* Seattle: University ofWashington Press.

———. 1969. *Native American Arts 2: Graphic Arts of the Alaskan Eskimo.* Washington, D.C.: Indian Arts and Crafts Board, U. S. Department of the Interior.

———, ed. 1972. *Contemporary Indian Artists – Montana/Wyoming/Idaho.* Rapid City, SD: Tipi Shop, Inc. (exhibition catalog).

Reid, Bill. 1984. *Islands at the Edge.* Toronto, ON: Douglas and McIntyre.

———, and Robert Bringhurst. 1988. *The Raven Steals the Light.* Vancouver, BC: Douglas and McIntyre.

Ritchie, Carson. 1974. *The Eskimo and his Art.* Toronto, ON: Macmillan Company.

Roberts, Carla, ed. 1992. *The Submuloc Show/ Columbus Wohs.* Phoenix, AZ: Atlatl. (exhibition catalog).

Robinson, Michael. 1987. *The Freedom of Science.* Lakefield, ON: Wopoone Press.

———. 1991. *The Earth and the Dancing Man.* Keene, ON: Martin House Publishing.

———. 1992. *Touching the Serpent's Tail.* Keene, ON: Martin House Publishing.

Roch, Ernst, ed. 1974. *Arts of the Eskimo: Prints.* Toronto, ON: Oxford University Press.

Roosevelt, Theodore. 1899. *The Rough Riders.* New York: Charles Scribner's Sons.

Rose, Wendy. 1973. *Hopi Roadrunner Dancing.* Greenfield Center, NY: Greenfield Review Press.

———. 1976. *Long Division: A Tribal History.* New York: Strawberry Press.

———. 1977. *Academic Squaw: Reports to the World from the Ivory Tower.* Marvin, SD: Blue Cloud Press.

———. 1978. *Poetry of the American Indian: Wendy Rose.* American Visual Communications Bank.

———. 1979. *Builder Kachina: A Home-Going Cycle.* Marvin, SD: Blue Cloud Press.

———. 1980. *Lost Copper.* Banning, CA: Malki Museum Press.

Rosen, Kenneth ed. 1974. *The Man to Send Rain Clouds: Contemporary Stories by Native Americans.* New York: Viking Press.

———, ed. 1975. *Voices of the Rainbow: Contemporary Poetry by American Indians.* New York: Viking Press.

Routledge, Marie. 1979. *Inuit Art in the 1970's.* Kingston, ON: Agnes Etherington ArtCenter. (exhibition catalog)

———. 1990. *Pudlo: Thirty Years of Drawing.* Ottawa, ON: National Gallery of Canada.

Rubenstein, Charlotte Streifer. 1982. *American Indian Artists.* New York: Avon.

———. 1982. *American Women Artists: From Early Indian Times to the Present.* New York: Avon.

Rushmore, Helen, and Wolf Robe Hunt. 1963. *The Dancing Horses of Acoma; and Other Acoma Indian Stories.* Cleveland, OH: World Publishing Co.

Russell, Don. 1968. *Custer's Last; or Battle of Little Big Horn.* Fort Worth, TX: Amon Carter Museum of Western Art. (exhibition catalog)

Salisbury, Ralph. 1979. *Pointing at the Rainbow.* Marvin, SD: Blue Cloud Press.

Samuels, Peggy, and Harold Samuels. 1982. *Contemporary Western Artists.* New York: Bonanza Books.

———, and Harold Samuels. 1985. *Samuels' Encyclopedia of Artists of the American West.* Secaucus, NJ: Castle/Book Sales, Inc.

Sandoz, Mari. 1953. *Cheyenne Autumn.* New York: McGraw-Hill.

———. 1961. *These Were the Sioux.* New York: Hastings House. (reprint 1985.)

Satter, John. 1954. *A Comparison of Three Fertility Figures.* Iowa City, IA: University of Iowa Press.

Scarberry-García, Susan. 1994. *Dancing Spirits: José Rey Toledo, Tewa Artist.* Santa Fe, NM: Museum of New Mexico. (exhibition catalog)

Schaeffer, Claude E. 1963. *Modern American Indian Art.* Browning, MT: Museum of the Plains Indian. (exhibition catalog)

Schevill, Margaret. 1956. *The Pollen Path: A Collection of Navajo Myths Retold.* Stanford,CA: Stanford University Press.

SCHIFFER, NANCY N. 1991A. *Navajo Arts and Crafts*. West Chester, PA: Schiffer Publishing,Ltd.

———. 1991B. *Miniature Arts of the Southwest*. West Chester, PA: Schiffer Publishing, Ltd.

SCHLESIER, KARL H. 1987. *The Wolves of Heaven*. Norman, OK: University of Oklahoma Press.

SCHMID, FREDRICK, AND PATRICK T. HOULIHAN. 1980. *Native American Painting*. Kansas City, MO: Mid-America Arts Alliance. (exhibition catalog)

SCHMITT, MARTIN F., AND DEE BROWN. 1948. *Fighting Indians of the West*. New York: Charles Scribner's Sons.

SCHWARTZ, HERBERT T. 1969. *Windigo and Other Tales of the Ojibway*. Toronto, ON: McCelland and Stewart.

———. 1974. *Tales from a Smokehouse*. Edmonton, AB: Hurtig Publishers.

SCOTT, JAY. 1989. *Changing Woman: The Life and Art of Helen Hardin*. Flagstaff, AZ: Northland Publishing.

SENUNGETUK, JOSEPH E. 1972. *Give or Take a Century: An Eskimo Chronicle*. San Francisco: Indian Historian Press.

SETON, ERNEST THOMPSON. 1897. *Seton Journals; Volume 6: Yellowstone Bears/Crow Indians*. Cimarron Territory of NM: Seton Memorial Museum and Library, Philmont Museum.

SETON, JULIA MOSS. 1962. *American Indian Arts*. New York: Ronald Press.

SEYMOUR, TRYNTJE VAN NESS. 1988. *When the Rainbow Touches Down*. Phoenix, AZ: Heard Museum. (exhibition catalog)

———. 1993. *The Gift of Changing Woman*. New York: Henry Holt and Company.

SHADBOLT, DORIS. 1987. *Bill Reid*. Vancouver, BC: Douglas and McIntyre, Ltd.

SHAMAN, SAMFORD SIVITZ. 1987. *Twenty Contemporary New Jersey Artists*. Montvale, NJ: Peat Marwick Main & Company.

SHILLING, ARTHUR. 1986. *The Ojibway Dream*. Montréal, MB: Tundra Books.

SHOOK, TONYA HOLMES. 1986. *Displaced Cherokee: Come Home, Come Home*. Wichita Falls, TX: Humphrey Printing Co., Inc.

SHUFELDT, ROBERT WILSON. 1886. *A Navajo Artist and his Notions of Mechanical Drawing*. Washington, D.C.: Smithsonian Institution, Annual Report for 1886.

SHUMARD, GEORGE. 1973. *Billy the Kid*. Mesilla, NM: South Western Old Times.

SILBERMAN, ARTHUR. 1978. *100 Years of Native American Art*. Oklahoma City: Oklahoma Museum of Art. (exhibition catalog)

SILKO, LESLIE. 1974. *Laguna Woman*. Greenfield Center, NY: Greenview Review Press.

SILOOK, ROGER. 1970. *In the Beginning*. Anchorage, AK: Anchorage Printing Company.

SINCLAIR, LESTER, AND JACK POLLOCK. 1979. *The Art of Norval Morrisseau*. Toronto, ON: Methuen Publications.

SLOAN, JOHN, AND OLIVER LAFARGE. 1931. *Introduction to American Indian Art*. New York: The Exposition of Indian Tribal Arts, Inc. 2 vols.

SMITH, DECOST. 1943. *Indian Experiences*. Caldwell, ID: Caxton Printers.

SNEVE, VIRGINIA DRIVING HAWK. 1972. *High Elk's Treasure*. New York: Holiday House Publishers.

———. 1973. *Little Jimmy Yellowhawk*. New York: Holiday House Publishers.

———. 1974A. *Betrayed*. New York: Holiday House Publishers.

———. 1974B. *When Thunders Spoke*. Lincoln, NE: University of Nebraska Press.

———. 1975. *Chi Chi Hoo Hoo Bogey Man*. New York: Holiday House Publishers.

SNODGRASS, JEANNE O. 1968. *American Indian Painters: A Biographical Directory*. New York: Museum of the American Indian.

SOLADAY, MILDRED. 1968. *Oscar Howe, Artist Laureate of the Middle Border*. Mitchell, SD: Mitchell Printing Co.

SONNICHSEN, CHARLES LELAND. 1958. *The Mescalero Apaches*. Norman, OK: University of Oklahoma Press.

SOUTHCOTT, MARY E. 1984. *The Sound of the Drum: The Sacred Art of the Anishnabec*. Erin, ON: Boston Mills Press.

SPINDEN, HERBERT JOSEPH, ET AL. 1931. *Introduction to American Indian Art, Part II*. New York: Exposition of Indian Tribal Arts, Inc.

STACEY, JOSEPH. 1976. *The American Indians of Abeita*. Scottsdale, AZ: Rick Tanner Publications.

STANDING BEAR, LUTHER. 1928. *My People, the Sioux*. Boston: Houghton Mifflin. (Reprint 1974.)

STAN, FREDRICK. 1903. *Iroquois Indian Games and Dances Drawn by Jesse Cornplanter, Seneca Indian Boy*. Pamphlet, 15 leaves.

STARR, JEAN. 1988. *Tales from the Cherokee Hills*. Winston-Salem, NC: John Blair Publishing Co.

STEBBINS, JOAN. 1981. *Gerald Tailfeathers: Fifty Years*. Lethbridge, AB: Southern Alberta Art Gallery.

STEINBRIGHT, JAN, ED. 1986. *Alaskamuit '86*. Fairbanks, AK: Institute of Alaska Native Arts.(exhibition catalog)

STEINER, STAN. 1961. *The Last Horse*. New York: Macmillan.

———, ED. 1980. *The Spirit Woman*. San Francisco: Harper and Row.

STEINMETZ, PAUL. 1984. *Meditations with Native Americans, Lakota Spirituality*. Santa Fe: Bear and Company, Inc.

STELTZER, ULLI. 1976. *Indian Artists at Work*. Vancouver, BC: J. J. Douglas.

STEWARD, IVAN. 1980. *My Brother's Keeper*.

STEWART, HILARY. 1979. *Looking at Indian Art of the Northwest Coast*. Seattle: University of Washington Press.

———. 1984. *Cedar*. Vancouver, BC: Douglas and McIntyre.

STEWART, KATHRYN (FORWARD). 1988. *Portfolio II: Eleven American Indian Artists*. San Francisco: American Indian Contemporary Arts.

STIRLING, MATTHEW W., ED. 1938. *Three Pictographic Autobiographies of Sitting Bull.* Washington, D.C.: Smithsonian Press.

———, ED. 1955. *Indians of the Americas.* Washington, D.C.: National Geographic Society.

STONE, COURT. 1984. *We are the Music-Makers.* Wakefield, PQ: Castenchel Editions.

STREET, ELOISE (COMP.). 1963. *Sepass Poems: The Songs of Y-Ail-Mihth.* New York: Vantage Press.

STRICKLAND, RENNARD. 1980. *Indians of Oklahoma.* Norman, OK: University of Oklahoma Press.

———. 1982. *Fire and the Spirits.* Norman, OK: University of Oklahoma Press.

———. 1984. *The Bacone Indian Art Retrospective: A Half Century of Native American Art.* Muskogee, OK: Bacone College. (exhibition catalog)

STUART, JOZEFA, AND ROBERT H. ASHTON JR. 1977. *Images of American Indian Art.* New York: Walker Publishing Co.

STUMP, SARAIN. 1970. *There is My People Sleeping.* Sidney, ON: Gray's Publishing, Ltd.

SULLIVAN, ROB. 1974. *Hands in the Storm.* Whitehorn, CA: Holmangers Press.

SUPPLEE, CHARLES, BARBARA ANDERSON AND DOUGLAS ANDERSON. 1971. *Canyon De Chelly.* Las Vegas, NV: KC Publications.

SUPREE, BURTON. 1977. *Bear's Heart.* Philadelphia: J. B. Lippincott Company.

SWEEZY, CARL. 1966. *The Arapaho Way.* NY: Clarkson Potter.

SWINTON, GEORGE. 1972. *Sculpture of the Eskimo.* Toronto, ON: McClelland and Stewart.

SZABO, JOYCE M. 1983. *Ledger Art in Transition: Late Nineteenth Century Drawing and Painting on the Plains.* Albuquerque: University of New Mexico Press. (Ph.D. dissertation)

———. 1994. *Howling Wolf and the History of Ledger Art.* Albuquerque: University of New Mexico Press.

TAGOONA, ARMAND. 1975. *Shadows.* Ottawa, ON: Oberon Press.

TANNER, CLARA LEE, ED. 1968. *The James T. Bialac Collection of Southwest Indian Paintings.* Tucson, AZ: University of Arizona Press. (exhibition catalog)

———. 1973. *Southwest Indian Painting: A Changing Art.* Tucson, AZ: University of Arizona Press.

———, ED. 1976. *Indian Arts and Crafts.* Phoenix, AZ: Arizona Highways.

———. 1987. *Ray Manley's Hopi Kachinas.* Tucson, AZ: Ray Manley.

TAYLOR, JOSHUA C., ET AL. 1982. *Fritz Scholder.* New York: Rizzoli.

TEIWES, HELGA. 1991. *Kachina Dolls: The Art of Hopi Carvers.* Tucson, AZ: University of Arizona Press.

THOM, IAN M., ED. 1993. *Robert Davidson: Eagle of the Drum.* Seattle: University of Washington Press.

THOMAS, DAVID HURST, ET AL. 1993. *The Native Americans: an Illustrated History.* Atlanta, GA: Turner Publishing, Inc.

THOMPSON, HILDEGARD. 1948. *Navajo Life Series.* Phoenix, AZ: Phoenix Indian School Printing Department.

———. 1949. *Navajo Life Series: Primer.* Washington, D.C.: U.S. Department of the Interior Bureau of Indian Affairs, Education Branch.

THORNTON, RUSSELL. 1990. *The Cherokees: A Population History.* Lincoln, NE: University of Nebraska Press.

TICUSAK (EMILY IVANOF BROWN). 1981. *The Longest Story Ever Told: Qayaq, the Magical Man.* Anchorage, AK: Alaska Pacific University Press.

TIGER, PEGGY, AND MOLLY BABCOCK. 1980. *Life and Art of Jerome Tiger.* Norman, OK: University of Oklahoma Press.

TRIGGER, BRUCE G., ED. 1978. *Handbook of North American Indians: Northeast.* Washington, D.C.: Smithsonian Institution Press. Vol. 15.

TRIMBLE, MARTHA. 1973. *N. Scott Momaday.* Boise, ID: Boise State College.

TRIMBLE, STEPHEN. 1987. *Talking with the Clay: The Art of Pueblo Pottery.* Santa Fe: School of American Research Press.

TRYK, SHEILA. 1993. *Santa Fe Indian Market: Showcase of Native American Art.* Santa Fe: Tierra Publications.

TSATOKE, MONROE. 1957. *The Peyote Ritual: Visions and Descriptions.* San Francisco: Grabhorn Press.

TURNER, ROBYN, ET AL. (EDS.). 1989. *Art Works.* Austin, TX: Holt, Rinehart and Winston.

TWO-ARROWS, TOM. 1989. *Se-Go.* Albany, NY: Margold Silk Screens. (coloring book)

UNDERHILL, RUTH M. 1938. *Singing for Power: The Song Magic of the Papago Indians of Southern Arizona.* Berkeley, CA: University of California Press.

———. 1940. *The Papago Indians of Arizona, and Their Relatives the Pima.* Washington, D.C.: Office of Education, Bureau of Indian Affairs.

———. 1948. *Pueblo Crafts.* Lawrence, KS: Haskell Institute.

———. 1954. *Workaday Life of the Pueblos.* Phoenix, AZ: Phoenix Indian School Print Shop.

———. 1963. *People of the Crimson Evening.* Haskell, KS: Haskell Press.

———. 1965. *Red Man's Religion: Beliefs and Practices of the Indians North of Mexico.* Chicago: University of Chicago Press.

———. 1979. *Rainhouse and Ocean: Speeches for the Papago Year.* Flagstaff, AZ: Museum of Northern Arizona Press.

VALLEE, FRANK G. 1967. *Kabloona and Eskimo in the Central Keewatin.* Ottawa, ON: Northern Coordination and Research Center.

VELARDE, PABLITA. 1960. *Old Father, the Storyteller.* Globe, AZ: Dale Stuart King.

VAN HORN, BRIAN, AND CHRISTINE VAN HORN. 1989. *Lordy Lamb and the Twelve Lisciples.*

VESTAL, STANLEY. 1932. *Sitting Bull, Champion of the Sioux.* Boston: Houghton Mifflin.

———. 1934A. *New Sources of Indian History, 1985-1891.* Norman, OK: University of Oklahoma Press.

———. 1934B. *Warpath: The True Story of the Fighting Sioux Told in a Biography of Chief White Bull.* Boston: Houghton Mifflin.

VOGEL, VIRGIL J. 1990. *American Indian Medicine.* Norman, OK: University of Oklahoma Press.

WADE, EDWIN L., AND RENNARD STRICKLAND. 1981. *Magic Images; Contemporary Native American Indian Art.* Norman, OK: University of Oklahoma Press.

———, ED. 1986. *The Arts of the North American Indian: Native Traditions in Evolution.* New York: Hudson Hills Press.

WAGNER, SALLIE R. AND J. J. BRODY. 1983. *Yazz, Navajo Painter.* Flagstaff, AZ: Northland Press.

WALDMAN, CARL. 1985. *Atlas of the North American Indian.* New York: Facts On File, Inc.

WALLACE, STEPHEN, REGINA LYNCH, AND MARVIN YELLOWHAIR. 1984. *Navajo Art, History and Culture.* Rough Rock, AZ: Rough Rock Demonstration School.

WALLO, WILLIAM, AND JOHN PICKARD. 1990. *T. C. Cannon, Native American – A New View of the West.* Oklahoma City, OK: National Cowboy Hall of Fame. (exhibition catalog)

WALTERS, HARRY, ET AL. 1972. *Navajo Figurines Called Dolls.* Santa Fe: Museum of Navajo Ceremonial Art.

WARD, DEBORAH, ED. 1990. *Our Land/Ourselves: American Indian Contemporary Artist.* Albany, NY: University Art Gallery, State University of New York. (exhibition catalog)

WARNER, CHRISTOPHER, ED. 1985. *Ledger Art of Crow and Gros Ventre Indians 1879-1897.* Billings, MT: Yellowstone Art Center. (exhibition catalog)

WARNER, JOHN ANSON. 1975. *The Life and Art of the North American Indian.* New York: Crescent Books.

———, AND THECLA BRADSHAW. 1979. *A Cree Life: The Art of Allen Sapp.* Vancouver, BC: J. J. Douglas, Ltd./Seattle: University of Washington Press.

WASHBURN, DOROTHY K., AND ROBERT SAYERS (EDS.). 1984. *The Elkus Collection: Southwestern Art.* San Francisco: California Academy of Sciences.

WATERS, FRANK. 1963. *The Book of the Hopi.* New York: Viking Press.

WAY, J. EDSON, ED. 1988. *Institute of American Indian Art: Merging and Emergence.* Santa Fe: Wheelwright Museum of the American Indian. (exhibition catalog)

WEEKS, RUPERT. 1981. *Pachee Goyo.* Laramie, WY: Jelm Mountain Press.

WEISMAN, JOAN. 1993. *The Storyteller.* New York: Rizzoli.

WELLS, JAMES K. 1974. *Ipani Eskimos: A Cycle of Life in Nature.* Anchorage, AK: Alaska Methodist University Press.

WHITETHORNE, BAJE. 1994. *Sunpainters: Eclipse of the Navajo Sun.* Flagstaff, AZ: Northland Publishing.

WIGHT, DARLENE. 1989. *Out of Tradition: Abraham Anghik/David Ruben Piqtoukun: A Retrospective Exhibition.* Winnipeg, MB: Winnipeg Art Gallery. (exhibition catalog)

WILLIAMS, JEAN SHERROD, ED. 1990. *American Indian Artists in the Avery Collection and the McNay Permanent Collection.* San Antonio, TX: Koogler McNay Art Museum. (exhibition catalog)

WILLIAMS, TERRY TEMPEST. 1984. *Pieces of a White Shell: A Journey to Navajo Land.* New York: Scribner.

WILLOYA, WILLIAM, AND VINSON BROWN. 1962. *Warriors of the Rainbow.* Healdsburg, CA: Naturegraph Co.

WINDT, INGRID. 1980. *Her Own Image.* New York: Feminist Press/McGraw-Hill.

WOODWARD, CHARLES. 1988. *Ancestral Voiçe: Conversations with N. Scott Momaday.* Lincoln, NE: University of Nebraska Press.

WOODHOUSE, LAUREN J., ED. 1980. *The Inuit Amautik: I Like my Hood to be Full.* Winnipeg, MB: Winnipeg Art Gallery. (exhibition catalog)

WOODY, ELIZABETH. 1988. *Hand Into Stone: Poems by Elizabeth Woody.* New York: Contact II Publications.

WORCESTER, DONALD E. 1992. *The Apaches: Eagle of the Southwest.* Norman, OK: University of Oklahoma Press.

WRIGHT, BARTON. 1977. *The Complete Guide to Collecting Kachina Dolls.* Flagstaff, AZ: Northland Press.

———. 1983. *Kachinas: A Hopi Artist's Documentary.* Flagstaff, AZ: Northland Press.

———. 1985. *Kachinas of the Zuni.* Flagstaff, AZ: Northland Press.

WRIGHT, JESSIE G., JR., JOHN A. MACKEY AND RENNARD STRICKLAND. 1980. *Native American Art at Philbrook.* Tulsa, OK: Philbrook Art Center.

WYMAN, LELAND C. 1965A. *The Red Antway of the Navajo.* Santa Fe: Museum of Navajo Ceremonial Art.

———. 1965B. *Big Lefthanded, Pioneer Navajo Artist.* Flagstaff, AZ: Museum of Northern Arizona.

———. 1966. *Snake Skin and Hoops.* Flagstaff, AZ: Museum of Northern Arizona.

———. 1967. *The Sacred Mountains of the Navajo – Four Paintings by Harrison Begay.* Flagstaff, AZ: Museum of Northern Arizona.

YAVA, AARON. 1975. *Border Towns of the Navajo Nation.* Whitehorn, CA: Holmangers Press.

YORBA, JONATHAN. 1991. *Drawn from Surroundings: The Elkus Collection of Eskimo Paintings.* San Francisco: A. S. Graphics.

YORK STATE MUSEUM. BULLETIN 163. 1923. *Seneca Myths and Folk-Tales.* Buffalo, NY: Buffalo Historical Society.

YOUNGER, ERIN, ET AL. 1985. *Women of Sweetgrass, Cedar and Sage.* New York: Gallery of the American Indian Community House. (exhibition catalog)

ZEPP, NORMAN. 1985. *Two Worlds.* Regina, SK: Norman MacKenzie Art Gallery.

ZURKO, KATHLEEN MCMANUS, ED. 1992. *We, The Human Beings.* Wooster, OH: College of Wooster Art Museum. (exhibition catalog)